MANAGEMENT CONSULTING

A GUIDE TO THE PROFESSION

In praise of the fourth edition

"When the first edition of *Management consulting* appeared, hardly any books had been published on the subject. Almost immediately, [it] became the standard text in the field... In today's plethora of books on the subject, the fourth edition still stands out, just like the first. As a guide for the novice consultant and reference for the experienced, this book's grasp of the subject matter, breadth of coverage, simplicity of treatment, and accessibility is unsurpassed. Its perspective on the world of consulting is fresh and down-to-earth."

Gerald A. Simon*, CMC, FIMC, Chairman of the Editorial Board,*
C2M Consulting to Management

"The consulting industry is going through profound changes. Practitioners and clients both need to be aware of these changes in order to ensure that client value continues to be delivered. Milan Kubr's book *Management consulting: A guide to the profession* is a great starting point to understanding the state of the industry and how it's evolving."

Wayne Cooper*, Publisher of* Management Consulting International *and*
Consultants News, *and CEO of Kennedy Information*

"*Management consulting: A guide to the profession* is the most comprehensive capture of the body of knowledge of management consulting. The text is the most thorough guide for those who want to develop the competence leading to certification in this profession."

E. Michael Shays*, CMC, FIMC, Executive Director,*
International Council of Management Consulting Institutes, and Chairman,
Institute of Management Consultants, United States

"How fortunate for both the novice and the battle-scarred veteran to now have a new fourth edition of this classic text, which has been an indispensable tool for me over many years. Balancing the professional and the business aspects of management consulting, Milan Kubr and his team of authors have integrated the spectrum of current theories and practices into a pragmatic guide which will become the handbook of our time."

Patrick J. McKenna*, management consultant and co-author of* First among equals:
How to manage a group of professionals

"The Asian Productivity Organization has greatly benefited from the previous editions of *Management consulting* in developing consultants in Asia. The current edition will contribute to further building up the core competence in consulting services with a pragmatic approach to creating the knowledge economy and enhancing business competitiveness."

Yuji Yamada*, Special Adviser to the Secretary-General, Asian Productivity Organization*

INTERNATIONAL LABOUR OFFICE GENEVA

MANAGEMENT CONSULTING

A GUIDE TO THE PROFESSION

Fourth edition

Edited by MILAN KUBR

BOOKWELL
NEW DELHI

The designations employed in ILO publications, which are in conformity with United Nations practice, and the presentation of material therein do not imply the expression of any opinion whatsoever on the part of the International Labour Office concerning the legal status of any country, area or territory or of its authorities, or concerning the delimitation of its frontiers.

The responsibility for opinions expressed in studies and other contributions rests solely with their authors, and publication does not constitute an endorsement by the International labour Office of the opinions expressed in them.

Reference to names of firms and commercial products and processes does not imply their endorsement by the International Labour Office, and any failure to mention a particular firm, commercial product or process is not a sign of disapproval.

ISBN: 81-85040-44-3

First Indian edition published in 2005 by:

BOOKWELL

Sales Office

24/4800, Ansari Road,
Darya Ganj,
New Delhi-110002, India
Ph: 91-11-23268786

Head Office:

2/72, Nirankari Colony,
Delhi-110009, India
Ph: 91-11-27251283
Fax: 91-11-23281315

E-mail: bkwell@nde.vsnl.net.in
bookwell@vsnl.net

CONTENTS

AUTHORS AND ACKNOWLEDGEMENTS

This book is the result of a collective effort and reflects the experience and knowledge of the international consulting profession.

The first three editions (published in 1976, 1986 and 1996) were written by the following co-authors: Michael Bauer, Roland Berger, George Boulden, Chris Brewster, Chris Cooper, George Cox, James Dey, Alan Gladstone, Colin Guthrie, Malcolm Harper, John Heptonstall, Hari Johri, George Kanawaty, James H. Kennedy, Milan Kubr, Frederic Latham, Gordon Lippitt, David H. Maister, Rebecca Morgan, Leonard Nadler, Philip Neck, Klaus North, Joseph Prokopenko, J. Geoffrey Rawlinson, Edgar H. Schein, Edward A. Stone, John Syme, Denis Tindley and John Wallace.

Short contributions (most presented in box form) and other valuable materials and ideas used in the book were provided by Moïse Allal, William J. Altier, Maurice C. Ashill, Daniel Bas, Bengt Bjorklund, Kenneth L. Block, Ole Bovin, Derek Bowland, Joseph J. Brady, Ken Dawson, Gerry Y. Elliot, W. J. C. McEwan, Praxy Fernandes, Stelan Friberg, Takeyuki Furuhashi, S. R. Ganesh, John E. Hartshorne, Ed Hendricks, Michael Henriques, Shozo Hibino, Pierre Hidalgo, Geert Hofstede, Kate Hook, Jean-Marie van Houwe, Osamu Ida, James H. Kennedy, Václav Klaus, Emile Laboureau, Lauri K. Leppanen, Hans Ake Lilja, William J. McGinnis, Eiji Mizutani, Klaus Molenaar, Lewis S. Moore, Alex Morley-Smith, Gerald Nadler, M. S. S. El Namaki, Robert Nelson, Brian O'Rorke, Graham Perkins, Jean-François Poncet, Alan C. Popham, John Roethle, Steven E. Sacks, Emmanuel S. Savas, Karl Scholz, P. W. Shay, E. Michael Shays, Howard L. Shenson, Marko Simoneti, Carl S. Sloane, Sten Söderman, Fritz Steele, Hedley Thomas, Arthur B. Toan, Arthur N. Turner and W. Trevor Utting.

The author team for the fourth edition, which revised the existing text and wrote new chapters, included Chris Brewster, Martin Clemensson, Gerry Finnegan, Alan Gladstone, Jack Hardie, John Heptonstall, Milan Kubr, Radan Kubr, Mike Malmgren, Klaus North, Joseph Prokopenko, Steven Rochlin, Birte Schmitz, Edward A. Stone, and Jim Tanburn.

Short contributions, advice and assistance were received from Michael Beer, Charles Bodwell, Christine Evans-Klock, Robert M. Galford, Gil Gidron,

Charles H. Green, Else Groen, Claude Hoffmann, Osamu Ida, Kennedy Information Inc., Margot Lobbezoo, David H. Maister, Bruce W. Marcus, Patrick J. McKenna, Eiji Mizutani, Edgar H. Schein, Karl Scholz, E. Michael Shays, Gerald A. Simon, Peter Søresen, Arturo Tolentino and Simon White.

Milan Kubr served as team leader and technical editor for all editions of the book. He is also the principal author. Stylistic and language editing was carried out by Pat Butler, and the project was overseen by Rosemary Beattie.

There are many colleagues in consulting firms and their associations, management institutes and business companies, and in the ILO, whose experience, support and constructive suggestions made the publication of this book possible. The ILO extends its sincere thanks to all co-authors and contributors, including those who could not be mentioned by name.

FOREWORD

Management consulting has long been recognized as a useful professional service that helps managers to analyse and solve practical problems faced by their organizations, improve organizational performance, learn from the experience of other managers and organizations, and seize new business opportunities. Hundreds of thousands of private businesses and public organizations throughout the world have used the services of management consultants, separately or in combination with training, project management, information technology consulting, financial advice, legal advice, audit, engineering consulting and other professional services.

The International Labour Organization (ILO) has been active in management and small-business development, and employment promotion since the early 1950s. Management consulting and the promotion of effective consulting practices were quickly identified as powerful tools for the ILO's activities. Through its technical cooperation projects, the ILO has assisted many member States to establish local consulting services for the various sectors of the economy, and to develop management consultants and trainers. At present, the ILO, through many different programmes, is an important user and developer of consulting services.

To respond to a pressing demand for a comprehensive, practically oriented guide to management consulting, three editions of this book were published between 1976 and 1996. The book quickly became a basic reference work and learning text on management consulting, published in 12 different language editions in addition to the English original (Chinese, Czech, French, Hungarian, Indonesian, Italian, Japanese, Korean, Polish, Portuguese, Romanian and Spanish), and used worldwide by thousands of management consultants, educators and clients of consultants. Universities, business schools and management institutes in the United States and other countries have used the book in their management and consulting courses. Many associations and institutes of management consultants have recommended it to their members as essential reference and study material.

However, management consulting is a dynamic and rapidly changing sector of professional services. To be relevant and useful to clients, consultants have to keep abreast of economic and social trends, anticipate changes that may affect their clients' businesses, and offer advice that helps the client to achieve and maintain high performance in an increasingly complex, competitive and difficult environment. The knowledge-based economy is generating growing demand and creating new opportunities for consultants. Management consulting is affected by information and communication technologies, the Internet, globalization, market liberalization, major changes in geopolitics, the advent of regional economic groupings, demographic changes, the progress of education, shifts in consumer taste and behaviour, the changing role of governments and the public sector, and numerous other developments. Consultants need to "reinvent themselves" continuously to be able to advise clients on these increasingly complex and challenging issues.

As a professional service sector, management consulting also interacts closely with other professions. This interaction has many facets, including both cooperation and knowledge transfer in the clients' interest, and fierce competition in national and international markets. The borders between professions are shifting, professional firms merge or split, and new models and techniques of service delivery emerge.

A fundamental reference text on consulting has to reflect all these developments and challenges. Therefore the fourth edition of this guide describes state-of-the-art consulting practices, issues of major concern to consultants and clients alike, current and emerging trends, and approaches likely to enhance the value of the services provided by consultants. All the chapters and appendices of the third edition have been updated. New topics of growing concern to consultants have been added, including e-business consulting, consulting in knowledge management and the use of knowledge management by the consultants themselves, total quality management, corporate governance, the social role and responsibility of business, company transformation and renewal, and the public sector. More attention and space are devoted to key legal aspects of consulting services, such as consultant liability, contracts and intellectual property issues. A consistently international perspective has been maintained: like previous editions, this fourth edition aims to give a true and balanced picture of consulting as it is practised in various parts of the world.

When ILO first decided to develop and publish a guide to professional management consulting in the mid-1970s, the literature on the topic was surprisingly meagre. There were only a few anecdotal pamphlets on the history and activities of consultants, and several conceptual contributions on intervention methods used in consulting, coming from the behavioural science circles. In 2002, a bibliographic search using the terms "consultant" or "management consulting" will produce hundreds of references. Consulting has become a very popular topic and has been covered by many authors from varying perspectives.

The concept of consulting

In this book, management consulting is treated as a *method* for improving management and business practices first of all. This method can be used by an independent private firm, an internal consulting (or similar) unit in a private or public organization, a management development, productivity or small-enterprise development institute, an extension service, or an individual (e.g. a sole consulting practitioner or a university professor). Even a manager can act as a consultant if he or she provides advice to peers or subordinates.

At the same time, however, management consulting has been developing into a *profession*. Thousands of individuals and organizations have consulting as their full-time occupation, and strive for professional standards in the quality of the advice provided, methods of intervention and ethical principles. Individuals who do some consulting without being full-time members of the profession can also comply with the profession's standards and principles, and should be encouraged and helped to do so.

There is no conflict between these two ways of viewing consulting. Indeed, consulting as a method and consulting as a profession constitute two sides of one coin, and a guide such as this has to deal with both sides.

This book describes the consulting approaches and methods applied to various types of management and business problems, organizations and environments. There is an extremely wide range of consulting approaches, techniques, methods, modes and styles. This diversity is one of the exciting features of management consulting. It means that even clients with very particular problems and characters can usually find a consultant who fits their organization and personality. Conversely, consulting also exhibits certain common principles and methods. Some of them are quite fundamental and are used by the vast majority of consultants. For example, every consultant must be able to use interviewing techniques, diagnose the client's problems and purposes, structure and plan the work to be done, enlist the client's collaboration, communicate with the client, share information and knowledge with the client, and present proposals and conclusions orally and in writing.

Thus, to generalize about consulting and recommend a best way of approaching it is difficult and risky at best, and can even be misleading and counterproductive. We have therefore opted for an eclectic approach, trying to provide a comprehensive and balanced picture of the consulting scene, including the different methods, styles, modes or techniques used, and pointing out their advantages and shortcomings. Readers can make their own choice, consistent with the technical, organizational and human context of the given organization.

However, to say that the authors of this book have no bias whatsoever for any approach to consulting would not be correct. We do have a bias, and a strong one, for consulting in which: (i) the consultant shares knowledge and expertise with the client instead of trying to hide and withhold it; (ii) the client participates as closely and intensively as possible in the assignment; and

(iii) both parties spare no effort to make the assignment a valuable learning experience. Many different methods and techniques can apply within this broad concept.

Purpose of the book

The main purpose of this book is to contribute to the upgrading of professional standards and practices in management consulting and to provide information and guidance to individuals and organizations wishing to start or improve consulting activities. The book is an introduction to professional consulting, its nature, methods, organizational principles, behavioural rules, and training and development practices. It also suggests guidelines to consultants for operating in various areas of management. However, it is not intended to replace handbooks and manuals that deal in depth and detail with management functions and techniques: for this the reader should refer to special sources.

In a nutshell, the book is intended for:

- new entrants to the consulting profession;
- independent management consultants and consulting firms;
- consulting departments of productivity, management and small-business development institutes and centres;
- internal management consultants in business companies and governments;
- management teachers, trainers and researchers (who may be part-time consultants, and whose work is closely related to that of consultants);
- students of management and business administration;
- managers, business people and administrators who wish to use consultants more effectively, or to apply some consulting skills and approaches in their own work.

Finally, many principles and techniques described in the book apply to consulting in general; hence consultants operating in areas other than management and business may also find it useful and inspiring.

Terminology

The most common terms used in management consulting in various countries are explained in the text of the book. But the meaning and use of two basic terms warrant a definition at this early point:

- the term *management consultant* is used in the book as a generic term to apply to all those who perform all or some of the typical consulting functions in the field of management, on either a full-time or a part-time basis;
- the term *client* is also used as a generic term to apply to any manager, administrator or organization using the services of management consultants in private businesses, public enterprises, government agencies or elsewhere.

The two terms relate to consultants and clients in general, regardless of their sex or sectoral, ethnic, country or other characteristics. In referring to these groups in the text, it has sometimes been necessary to use the masculine gender for the sake of style, or in quoting other sources; it is however fully appreciated that in practice there are more and more women among business people, managers and consultants.

Unless specified otherwise, the term *consulting firm* applies to any type of organizational unit whose function is to provide consulting services. This term is sometimes used interchangeably with the terms *consulting unit* or *consulting organization*. The term *consulting process* is used as a generic term to describe the range of activities and the consultant–client interaction in solving the client's problems. A particular job done by a consultant for a particular client is normally called a *consulting assignment (project, case, engagement)*.

The authors are aware of the ongoing debates concerning the changing scope and focus of consulting, the increasingly blurred borders and progressing integration between management, business and information technology consulting, the "intrusions" of other professions in management consulting (and vice versa) and other developments. These trends are reviewed. However, we have maintained our preference for calling the object of our writing "*management consulting*" rather than turning to a new, not yet widely accepted and perhaps only temporary denomination.

Plan of the book

The guide is divided into 38 chapters, grouped in 5 parts, followed by 7 appendices.

Part I (Chapters 1–6) presents an overall view of the consulting method and profession. Emphasis is placed on the consultant–client relationship, on the role and intervention methods of management consultants in the process of change, and on the principles of professional ethics.

Part II (Chapters 7–11) is a systematic review of the consulting process, divided into five major phases: entry, diagnosis, action planning, implementation and termination.

Part III (Chapters 12–26) provides an introduction to consulting in various areas of management and in some specific sectors. The areas covered are general management and corporate strategy, information technology, finance, marketing, e-business, operations, human resources, knowledge management, productivity and performance improvement, quality management, company transformation and renewal, and the social role and responsibility of business. The sectors covered include small businesses, informal sector enterprises and the public sector.

Part IV (Chapters 27–35) deals with the management of consulting processes and firms. The main aspects examined are the nature of management in the professions and in consulting, the strategy of consulting firms, marketing of consulting services, costs and fees, assignment management, quality management and assurance, operational and financial control, knowledge management in consulting, and structuring of consulting firms.

Part V (Chapters 36–38) focuses on careers and remuneration in consulting, the training and development of consultants, and future perspectives of the consulting profession.

The appendices provide selected information supplementing the main text, as well as material and guidelines for a deeper study of consulting methods and processes discussed in various parts of the book:

- Appendix 1 is a concise guide addressed to clients and summarizing the main principles of choosing and using consultants.
- Appendix 2 lists international and national organizations in the consulting profession.
- Appendix 3 is a guide to information and learning sources that are particularly useful to consultants, including a number of Internet-based sources.
- Appendix 4 discusses the key points of consulting contracts, including critical legal aspects.
- Appendix 5 is a primer on current trends and issues in intellectual property.
- Appendix 6 suggests how the case method can be used in consultants' training and learning.
- Appendix 7 summarizes the main principles of report-writing.

ABBREVIATIONS AND ACRONYMS

ADR	alternative dispute resolution
AI	artificial intelligence
AMCF	Association of Management Consulting Firms
APO	Asian Productivity Organization
APS	advanced planning system
ASEAN	Association of South-East Asian Nations
ASP	application service provider
BDS	business development services
BPI	business process improvement
BPR	business process re-engineering
CAD	computer-aided design
CAM	computer-aided manufacturing
CEO	chief executive officer
CMC	certified management consultant
COQ	cost of quality
CPM	critical path method
CRM	customer relationship management
CTM	Community Trade Mark
CVA	customer value added
DCF	discounted cash flow
DOE	design of experiments
DPMO	defects per million opportunities
ECB	European Central Bank
ECU	European currency unit
EDI	electronic data interchange

EDP	electronic data processing
EFT	electronic funds transfer
EPOS	electronic point of sale (system)
ERM	exchange rate mechanism
ERP	enterprise resource planning
EU	European Union
FEACO	European Federation of Management Consulting Associations
FIDIC	Fédération Internationale des Ingénieurs Conseils
GDP	gross domestic product
GNP	gross national product
GRI	global reporting initiative
HR	human resources
HRD	human resource development
HRM	human resource management
HTML	hypertext markup language
ICAAN	Internet Corporation for Assigned Names and Numbers
ICF	International Coaching Federation
ICMCI	International Council of Management Consulting Institutes
ICT	information and communications technology
ILO	International Labour Organization
IPO	initial public offering
IRR	internal rate of return
ISO	International Organization for Standardization
IT	information technology
JIT	just in time
KM	knowledge management
LIBOR	London inter-bank offered rate
MAS	management advisory services
MBA	Master of Business Administration
MBO	management by objectives
MEOST	multiple environment overstress test
MNC	multinational corporation
MTN	medium-term note
NAFTA	North American Free Trade Agreement
NGO	nongovernmental organization
NOAC	next operation as customer
NPV	net present value

OD	organization(al) development
OECD	Organisation for Economic Co-operation and Development
OEM	original equipment manufacturer
PDA	personal digital assistant
PDCA	plan–do–check–act
P/E	price/earnings ratio
PERT	programme evaluation and review technique
PIP	productivity improvement programme
PR	public relations
PSA	professional service automation
QA	quality assurance
QC	quality control
QFD	quality function deployment
QM	quality management
QMS	quality management system
R&D	research and development
ROIC	return on invested capital
SAP	Systeme, Anwendungen, Produkte in der Datenverarbeitung (systems, applications and products in data-processing)
SBU	strategic business unit
SEC	Securities and Exchange Commission (United States)
SLA	service-level agreement
SQC	statistical quality control
TEI	total employee involvement
TPM	total productive maintenance
TQM	total quality management
TRM	total responsibility management
UN	United Nations
WACC	weighted average cost of capital
WIPO	World Intellectual Property Organization
WTO	World Trade Organization
XML	extended markup language

PART I

MANAGEMENT CONSULTING IN PERSPECTIVE

NATURE AND PURPOSE OF MANAGEMENT CONSULTING 1

1.1 What is consulting?

There are many definitions of consulting, and of its application to problems and challenges faced by management, i.e. of management consulting. Setting aside stylistic and semantic differences, two basic approaches to consulting emerge.

The first approach takes a broad functional view of consulting. Fritz Steele defines consulting in this way: "… any form of providing help on the content, process, or structure of a task or series of tasks, where the consultant is not actually responsible for doing the task itself but is helping those who are."[1] Peter Block suggests that "You are consulting any time you are trying to change or improve a situation but have no direct control over the implementation… Most people in staff roles in organizations are really consultants even if they don't officially call themselves consultants."[2] These and similar definitions emphasize that consultants are helpers, or enablers, and assume that such help can be provided by people in various positions. Thus, a manager can also act as a consultant if he or she gives advice and help to a fellow manager, or even to subordinates rather than directing and issuing orders to them.

The second approach views consulting as a special professional service and emphasizes a number of characteristics that such a service must possess. According to Larry Greiner and Robert Metzger, "management consulting is an advisory service contracted for and provided to organizations by specially trained and qualified persons who assist, in an objective and independent manner, the client organization to identify management problems, analyze such problems, recommend solutions to these problems, and help, when requested, in the implementation of solutions".[3] Similar more or less detailed definitions are used by other authors and by professional associations and institutes of management consultants. According to the International Council of Management Consulting Institutes (ICMCI), for example, "management consulting is the provision of independent advice and assistance about the process of management to clients with management responsibilities".[4]

We regard the two approaches as complementary rather than conflicting. Management consulting can be viewed either as a *professional service*, or as *a method of providing practical advice and help*. There is no doubt that management consulting has developed into a specific sector of professional activity and should be treated as such. At the same time, it is also a method of assisting organizations and executives to improve management and business practices, as well as individual and organizational performance. The method can be, and is, applied not only by full-time consultants, but also by many other technically competent persons whose main occupation may be teaching, training, research, systems development, project development and evaluation, technical assistance to developing countries, and so on. To be effective, these people need to master consulting tools and skills, and to observe the fundamental behavioural rules of professional consulting.

In our book, we have chosen to address the needs of both these target populations. Although it has been written primarily about and for professional management consultants, the needs of other people who intervene in a consulting capacity, even though they are not full-time consultants, are borne in mind.

We start by reviewing the basic characteristics of management consulting. The key question is: what principles and approaches allow consulting to be a professional service that provides added value to clients?

Adding value by transferring knowledge

Whether practised as a full-time occupation or an ad hoc service, management consulting can be described as *transferring to clients knowledge required for managing and operating businesses and other organizations*. To provide added value to clients, this knowledge must help the clients to be more effective in running and developing their business, public administration agency or other non-profit organization.

Thus the quintessential nature of consulting is to create, transfer, share and apply management and business knowledge. "What is unique to management is that from the very beginning the consultant played a key role in the development of the practice, the knowledge and the profession of management", wrote Peter Drucker.[5] The term knowledge, as used here and in most of the literature on knowledge management, encompasses experience, expertise, skills, know-how and competencies in addition to theoretical knowledge. Thus, knowledge transfer is concerned not only with the knowledge and understanding of facts and realities, but also with approaches, methods and capabilities required for the effective application of knowledge in particular economic, business, institutional, cultural, administrative or organizational environments.

Management consultants can assume their roles in knowledge transfer because they have accumulated, through study and practical experience, considerable knowledge of effective ways of acting in various management situations. They have learned how to discern general trends and understand changes in the environment, identify common causes of problems with a good chance of finding appropriate solutions, and see and seize new opportunities.

Clearly, management consultants cannot acquire such capabilities by theoretical study only, although this continues to be an essential source of new knowledge during their whole career. They learn from the experience of their colleagues and from the consulting firm's accumulated know-how. However, experience and know-how concerning management and business practices come mainly from working with clients. "Every consultant knows that his clients are his teachers and that he lives off their knowledge. The consultant does not know more. But he has seen more."[6] Thus, knowledge transfer is a two-way process: in enhancing their clients' knowledge and capacity to act effectively, the consultants learn from them and enhance their own knowledge and capacity to advise their clients, current and future, more effectively, in new situations and on new issues.

The fields of knowledge embraced by management consulting relate to two critical dimensions of client organizations:

- *The technical dimension*, which concerns the nature of the management or business processes and problems faced by the client and the way in which these problems can be analysed and resolved.
- *The human dimension*, i.e. interpersonal relationships in the client organization, people's feelings about the problem at hand and their interest in improving the current situation, and the interpersonal relationship between the consultant and the client.

For methodological reasons, our guide will often deal separately with these two dimensions. In real life they are not separated: technical and human issues of management and business are always interwoven. In consulting, it is essential to be aware of these two sides of problems in organizations, but mere awareness is not enough. Ideally, the consultant should choose approaches and methods that uncover and help understand both the technical and the human issues involved, and that help the client to act on both of them. In practice, however, many consultants tend to be concerned more with one or the other dimension of client organizations.

It is even possible to discern two types of consulting. The first type is predominantly *technical*. Its protagonists are technicians competent in providing advice on business processes, strategies, structures, systems, technology, resource allocation and utilization, and similar tangible, quantifiable and measurable issues in areas such as production, finance and accounting. The consultants' knowledge backgrounds may be in technology, industrial engineering, computer science, statistics, mathematics, operations research, business economics, accounting, or other areas. Such consultants tend to treat the client's problems as mainly technical and systems problems, e.g. the client needs a better cost control system, better information on customers' requirements and complaints, a stable network of reliable subcontractors, a strategy for the next five years, or a feasibility study for a merger.

Box 1.1 On giving and receiving advice

"Every man, however wise, needs the advice of some sagacious friend in the affairs of life."

Plautus

"To accept good advice is but to increase one's own ability." *Goethe*

"Many receive advice: few profit by it." *Publius Syrus*

"To profit from good advice requires more wisdom than to give it." *John Collins*

"Men give away nothing so liberally as their advice." *La Rochefoucauld*

"Never give advice in a crowd." *Arabian proverb*

"We give advice by the bucket, but take it by the grain." *William Alger*

"Do not have the conceit to offer your advice to people who are far greater than you in every respect."

Rabindranath Tagore

"Harsh counsels have no effect; they are like hammers which are always repulsed by the anvil."

Helvetius

"Good counsellors lack no clients." *Shakespeare*

"Advice is like mushrooms. The wrong kind can prove fatal." *Unknown*

"The greatest trust between man and man is the trust of giving counsel."
Francis Bacon

"Free advice is often overpriced." *Unknown*

Selected by James H. Kennedy.

The second type focuses on *the human side* of organizations. Its roots are in behavioural sciences and its doctrine is that, whatever the client thinks and tells the consultant, there is always a human problem behind any organizational problem, whether technical or financial. If human problems can be understood and resolved in ways that motivate, energize and empower people, and that make individuals and teams more effective in using their knowledge and experience, all other problems will be resolved, or at least their solution will be greatly facilitated.

Organization development (OD) and human resource development (HRD) consultants are typical representatives of this second type. Their share in the whole consulting industry has been relatively small, but their influence has been out of proportion to their numbers. As distinct from the previous group, the behavioural scientists have been active not only in consulting but also in writing extensively about their approaches and experiences. Most of the writing on consulting concepts and methodologies comes from this group.

Advice and assistance

Consulting is essentially an advisory service. This means that, in principle, consultants are not used to run organizations or to take decisions on behalf of the managers. They have no direct authority to decide on or implement changes. Their responsibility is for the quality and integrity of their advice; the clients carry all the responsibilities that accrue from taking it.

Of course, in the practice of consulting there are many variations and degrees of "advice". Not only to give the right advice, but to give it in the right way, to the right people and at the right time – these are the critical skills and art of a consultant. Above all, the consultant's art consists in "getting things done when you are not in charge".[7] The client in turn needs to become skilful in taking and using the consultant's advice and avoiding misunderstanding on who is responsible for what.

In explaining the nature of consulting we also use the term "help" or "assistance". To be useful to the client and help the client to achieve results, the consultant often needs to do more than give "pure" advice, i.e. suggestions and recommendations that the client may choose to accept and apply, or ignore. In current consulting practice there is a general tendency to extend advice over the whole change cycle, i.e. the client uses the consultant's services for as long as necessary while implementing what the consultant has advised. Furthermore, in addition to advising clients, many consultants do other things that are closely related and complementary to their advisory roles, such as training, encouraging and morally supporting the client, negotiating on behalf of the client, or performing certain activities in the client organization together with its staff.

The term "assistance" can also cover services that are not consulting per se, or at best are on the borderline between consulting and other professional and business services. Outsourcing provides a good example. Currently many firms in management and information technology (IT) consulting also provide services, such as information processing, bookkeeping, record-keeping, marketing, selling, distribution, advertising, recruitment, research, and design on a long-term contract basis.

The consultant's independence

Independence is a salient feature of consulting. A consultant must be in a position to make an unbiased assessment of any situation, tell the truth, and recommend frankly and objectively what the client organization needs to do without having any second thoughts on how this might affect the consultant's own interests. This detachment of the consultant has many facets and can be a tricky matter in certain cases.

Technical independence means that the consultant is in a position to formulate a technical opinion and provide advice independently of what the client believes, or wishes to hear.

Financial independence means that the consultant has no financial interest in the course of action taken by the client, e.g. in a decision to invest in another company or to purchase a particular computer system. The desire to get more business from the client in the future must not affect the objectivity of the advice provided in the current assignment.

Administrative independence implies that the consultant is not the client's subordinate and cannot be affected by his or her administrative decisions. While this does not present a problem to autonomous consulting organizations, it may be a rather complex, although not insurmountable, problem in internal consulting (see section 2.6).

Political independence means that neither the client organization's management nor its employees can influence the consultant using political power and connections, political party membership, club membership and similar influences.

Emotional independence means that the consultant preserves personal detachment and objectivity, irrespective of empathy, friendship, mutual trust, emotional affinities and other personal pressures that may exist at the beginning or develop in the course of an assignment.

It could be argued that absolute independence is a fiction and that no professional adviser can claim to be totally independent from his or her client, and from various interests and objectives pursued by the consulting firm. After all, consultants do depend on clients to get recruited, correctly paid for their work, used again for other work and recommended to other clients. Getting a great amount of work from one client tends to create dependence on this client. Income from non-consulting services is very important to some consultants but may weaken independence. Conversely, clients have no legal obligation to use consultants and can choose them freely. They sometimes attach less importance to individual consultants' independence than to their technical competence and personal integrity. These are valid points and consultants cannot ignore them. Yet the beauty and strength of free professions is in independence. Sacrificing independence and objectivity for short-term benefits may be tempting but risky and self-defeating from a longer-term perspective (see also section 6.2).

Consulting as a temporary service

Consulting is a temporary service. Clients turn to consultants for help to be provided over a limited period of time, in areas where they lack technical expertise, or where additional professional support is temporarily required. This may even be in areas where the requisite skills are available in the organization, but managers or staff specialists cannot be released for a major problem or project. Consultants can not only provide the expertise required, and give undivided, 100 per cent attention to the problem at hand, but will leave the organization once the job is completed. Even if the relationship is excellent and extends over a long period, the client always retains the right to discontinue it.

Consulting as a business

A practitioner who does management consulting for a living has to charge a fee for all the work done for clients. Consulting firms are sellers of professional services and clients are buyers. In addition to being professional service organizations, consulting firms are also businesses.

A consulting assignment must therefore be not only a technically justified activity, but also a financially feasible and profitable commercial undertaking according to both the client's and the consultant's criteria. From the client's point of view, the benefits obtained should exceed the costs incurred, including the fee paid to the consultant and other costs to the client such as staff time or the purchase of new computer programs. From the consultant's point of view, consulting must be a profitable activity as measured by normally applied criteria. This will be examined in detail in Part IV.

In certain cases, the fee paid by the client will not cover the full cost of the consulting service received. As we shall see later, consulting may be subsidized as a result of government economic policy or for another reason, which may be economic, commercial, political or social. For instance, an institution may provide consulting in conjunction with training and subsidize it from the income earned from training; a not-for-profit social organization may provide consulting and counselling as a fully or partially subsidized service to potential entrepreneurs in underprivileged social groups or neglected regions.

What should not be required from consulting

There is an abundance of case histories of successful assignments carried out by some of the world's best management consultancies in order to rescue companies facing bankruptcy, or to give new life to ageing firms. They have created a reputation that suggests that some consulting firms can resolve virtually any management difficulty. This is exaggerated. There are situations where nobody can help. And even if help is possible, it would be unrealistic and unfair to expect consultants to work miracles.

Also, the consultant should never be expected to take a problem away from the client, on to his or her own shoulders. A consultant's presence and intervention may provide considerable relief to a troubled client, but they will not liberate the client from inherent managerial responsibility for decisions and their consequences. If – as sometimes occurs – a consultant agrees to run a client's business and make decisions on his or her behalf, he or she stops being a consultant for that activity and period of time.

As mentioned earlier, consulting does not have to be a full-time occupation. If other professional criteria are met, it is not important whether the consultant is primarily (and for most of the time) a business school professor, a researcher, a retired executive or any other sort of worker. Also, if quality and independence are assured, consulting does not have to be an external service.

Our definition

Following this short discussion of the basic characteristics of management consulting, we offer the following definition:

> Management consulting is an independent professional advisory service assisting managers and organizations to achieve organizational purposes and objectives by solving management and business problems, identifying and seizing new opportunities, enhancing learning and implementing changes.

We have chosen a definition that omits certain characteristics that are not common to all consulting, such as "external" service, or service by "specially trained" persons. Conversely, our definition includes the fundamental, or generic, purposes of consulting that are discussed in the next section.

1.2 Why are consultants used? Five generic purposes

A manager may turn to a consultant if he or she perceives a need for help from an independent professional and feels that the consultant will be the right source of this help. But what sort of help are we talking about? What can be the purpose of using a consultant?

Consulting purposes can be looked at from several angles and described in various ways. Let us look first at five broad, or generic, purposes pursued by clients in using consultants, irrespective of the field of intervention and the specific intervention method used (figure 1.1):

- achieving organizational purposes and objectives;
- solving management and business problems;
- identifying and seizing new opportunities;
- enhancing learning;
- implementing changes.

Figure 1.1 Generic consulting purposes

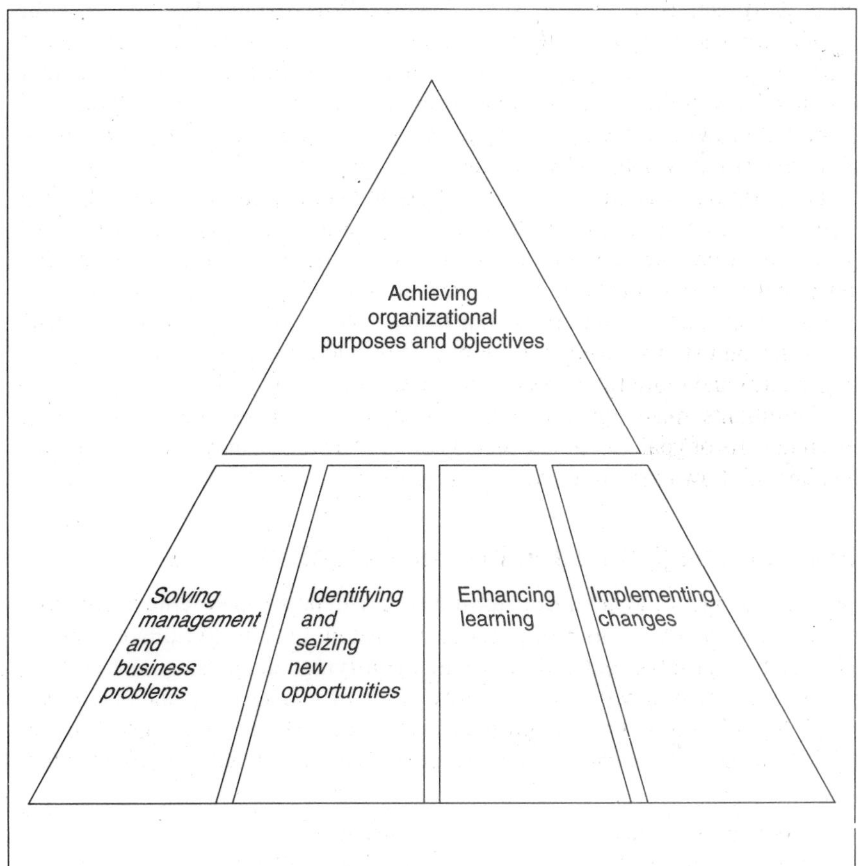

Achieving organizational purposes and objectives

All consulting to management and business tends to pursue a general and overriding purpose of helping clients to achieve their business, social or other goals. These goals may be defined in various ways: sectoral leadership, competitive advantage, customer satisfaction, achieving total quality or productivity, corporate excellence, high performance, profitability, improved business results, effectiveness, growth, etc. Different concepts and terms reflect the thinking and the priorities of both clients and consultants, the current state of the art of management and consulting, and even fashion. Different purposes will be stressed in commercial enterprises, public services and social organizations. The time horizon of a consultancy will differ from case to case. Yet the common denominator remains the same: consulting has to add value to the client organization, and this value should be a tangible and measurable contribution to achieving the client's principal purposes.

This global purpose of management consulting provides a rationale and a sense of direction for all consulting work. What would be the sense of organizational learning or costly and risky restructuring if the client organization could not get closer to its principal goals? What would be the use of successfully solving a few seemingly pressing management problems if "like the mythological hydra that grows two heads for every one cut off, the solutions we develop are often rapidly overwhelmed by a plethora of new problems"?[8]

The purpose of achieving the client organization's goals assumes that the client has defined such goals. In some organizations this is not the case, and management operates without any perspective, goal or sense of mission. The consultant's main contribution may well be in helping the client to develop a vision of the future, set ambitious but realistic goals, develop a strategy, focus on results, and start viewing current problems and opportunities in the light of longer-term and more fundamental organizational goals.

Consultants must appreciate that client organizations may be pursuing different sorts of goals. At times, the objective of a consultancy may be to advise the client on how to maintain the status quo or even how to get out of business.

Solving management and business problems

Helping managers and other decision-makers with problem-solving is probably the most frequently mentioned purpose of consulting. The consultant's task is described as professional assistance in identifying, diagnosing and solving problems concerning various areas and aspects of management and business.

Within a business firm, a "problem" justifying the use of a consultant can result from any of the following (and readers can undoubtedly think of many other causes):

complaining clients
poor business results
unexpected loss
natural disaster
loss of important market
lack of perspective
obsolete control system
wrong investment choice
missed opportunity
reluctance to change
high staff turnover
unrealistic self-image
lack of cash
idle resources
pressure of competition
failure to meet targets
lack of self-confidence
excess of self-confidence
slowness of action
internal conflicts

The reader should be aware of the different uses of the term "problem" and of their practical implications. If "problem" is used to mean only mistake, failure, shortcoming or missed opportunity, the client's and the consultant's perspective will tend to be essentially backward-looking and narrow, and the focus will be on corrective action (with implied criticism and determination of responsibilities).

The term "problem" can also be used as a more general concept to describe a situation where there is a difference or discrepancy between what is actually happening or will be happening and what should be happening. In this definition, a problem is described in relative terms, i.e. as a difference between two situations. In addition, someone has to be concerned about this difference and aim to overcome or reduce it. The problem must "belong" to someone – there must be a "problem owner".

Frequently the current situation of the client organization is compared with a situation that existed in the past. If there has been a deterioration such as falling sales or profits, the problem is defined as a need to restore the original condition. This explains why consultants are sometimes called "troubleshooters", "company doctors" or "business healers".

Alternatively, the current situation may be compared with some standard (benchmark). The problem is then defined as the need to meet or surpass the standard, e.g. a competitor's product quality, range of models offered or after-sales service.

In this sense, even a successful and forward-looking company that has been pursuing and achieving ambitious business objectives may have "problems" – a desire to further enhance its competitive advantage, to become a sector leader, not to miss a new marketing opportunity, to identify a new business partner, to explore an emerging technology, and so on.

In this guide, the term "problem" will be used in this second way – as a generic term describing a client's dissatisfaction with the difference between any comparable (but mainly between existing and desirable) situations in the organization. Thus, some of the problems will be related to past errors and shortcomings that need to be redressed; many others will concern perspectives, opportunities and strategies for improving the business in the future.

A correct definition of the problem to be resolved, and the purpose to be achieved by the consultancy, is critical. Experienced consultants warn against accepting the client's perception of the problem at face value. If the problem has been wrongly defined or misjudged, the consultant will be caught in a trap. He or she will then work on the wrong problem, or the problem and potential benefits from its solution may not justify the consultant's intervention and the costs incurred. To avoid this, most consultants insist on making their own independent assessment of the problem presented to them by the client, and on developing an agreed definition in discussion and collaboration with the client.

The purpose of the consultant's intervention provides a perspective for dealing with particular problems (see box 1.2). It could be argued that "the purpose is to solve the client's problem", but this provides little insight. It has been observed that "effective leaders and problem solvers always placed every problem into a larger context".[9] This implies getting answers to a number of questions about the purposes of the client organization and its key constituents, the focus and the significance of the proposed assignment, and the immediate and ultimate benefits to be obtained by the client if the current problem is resolved. In this way, it will be possible to select the "focus purpose",[10] avoiding purposes that are too narrow, as well as those that are too wide and distant to be tackled by the client at present. However, these wider and longer-term purposes ought to be kept in mind in order

Box 1.2 Define the purpose, not the problem

The way consultants define a problem is critical to the quality of the solution. If they define the problem in terms of its origin or cause, they will tend to focus on who or what is to blame. This is likely to be a fruitless exercise, and can actually get in the way of finding the best solution. It can also discourage staff from taking initiative, in order to avoid being blamed in the future. Rather, management consultants can achieve breakthroughs for their clients by focusing on a series of incrementally larger purposes to be achieved.

Narrow consulting approaches – focusing on the problem, starting with data collection, copying others, taking the first solution that can be made to work, failing to involve others – create problems of their own. These approaches lead to excess costs and time, early obsolescence of solutions, wasted resources and repetition of work in the consulting process.

Breakthrough thinking provides a more effective approach. It is not a step-by-step process but involves seven ways of thinking about problems and their solutions, based on the following principles:

(1) **The uniqueness principle:** Whatever the apparent similarities, each problem is unique and requires an approach based on the particular context.

(2) **The purposes principle:** Focusing on expanding purposes helps strip away non-essential aspects and avoid working on the wrong problem.

(3) **The solution-after-next principle:** Innovation can be stimulated and solutions made more effective by working backwards from an ideal target solution. Having a target solution in the future gives direction to short-term solutions and infuses them with larger purposes.

(4) **The systems principle:** Every problem is part of a larger system of problems, and solving one problem inevitably leads to another. Having a clear framework of the elements and dimensions that comprise a solution ensures its workability and facilitates implementation.

(5) **The limited information collection principle:** Excessive data gathering may create expertise in the problem area, but knowing too much detail may prevent the discovery of some excellent alternative solutions. Always determine the expanded purposes of any proposed information collection before doing it.

(6) **The people design principle:** Those who will implement and use the solution should be intimately and continuously involved in its development by being involved in the first five principles. Also, in designing a solution to be implemented by other people, include only the critical details in order to allow some flexibility during its application.

(7) **The betterment time-line principle:** The only way to preserve the vitality of a solution is to build in and then monitor a programme of continual change to achieve larger purposes and move towards target solutions.

Author: E. Michael Shays. A detailed discussion can be found in D. Nadler and S. Hibino: *Breakthrough thinking: The seven principles of creative problem solving* (Rocklin, CA, Prima Publishing, 1994).

to place the client's problem in a proper time perspective and seek solutions that will not block the path to the future.

Consulting that is confined to corrective measures, aimed at restoring a past situation or attaining a standard already met by other organizations, may produce significant and urgently needed benefits. A crisis may be avoided, negative developments may be arrested and the client's business may survive. Yet merely ensuring a return to a previously existing situation or catching up with competition gives the client no competitive advantage, and little additional competence or strength for coping with new situations and achieving superior performance in the future.

Identifying and seizing new opportunities

Most consultants feel that they can offer much more than simply helping organizations to get out of difficulties. This has been recognized by many business corporations and other organizations that are well managed, successful and ambitious. While they may at times call on a consultant to track back deviations that have taken place, and find and correct the reasons for them, they usually prefer to use consultants for identifying and taking new opportunities. They regard consulting firms as a source of valuable information and ideas that can be turned into a wide range of initiatives, innovations and improvements in any area or function of business: developing new markets and products; assessing and using state-of-the-art technologies; improving quality; becoming more useful to customers; developing and motivating staff; optimizing the use of financial resources; finding new business contacts (and contracts), and so on.

Experience shows that even strong and important corporations have developed many ideas for action and have seized major business opportunities with the help of consultants. Consulting in e-commerce and e-business is a case in point: its purpose has not usually been to solve existing problems, but to help clients to see and take major new opportunities that can be exploited by adopting new approaches to doing business.

Enhancing learning

"The only work that is really worth doing as a consultant is that which educates – which teaches clients and their staff to manage better for themselves", said Lyndon Urwick, one of the main contributors to the development of professional management consulting. In the modern concept of consulting this dimension is omnipresent. Many clients turn to consultants, not only to find a solution to one distinct problem, but also to acquire the consultant's special technical knowledge (e.g. in environmental analysis, business restructuring or quality management) and the methods used in assessing organizations, identifying problems and opportunities, developing improvements and implementing changes (interviewing, diagnosis, communication, persuasion, feedback, evaluation and similar skills).

Consulting assignments become learning assignments. The purpose is to empower the client by bringing new competence into the organization and helping managers and staff to learn from their own and the consultant's experience. It is often stressed that in this way organizations are helped to help themselves and become learning organizations. As already mentioned, this is a two-way exchange, since by helping clients to learn from experience a management consultant enhances his or her own knowledge and competence.

The learning effect of consulting is probably the most important and durable one. The choice of the consulting methods and the degree of the client's involvement can increase or reduce this effect. We shall, therefore, pay considerable attention to these questions in our guide.

Implementing changes

"Change agent" is another label frequently given to consultants. They are proud to be referred to in this way since this is a reflection of another general purpose of consulting: helping client organizations to understand change, live with change and make changes needed to survive and be successful in an environment where continuous change is the only constant. The importance of this consulting purpose has considerably increased in the current period owing to the complexity and pace of environmental changes, the need to keep informed about changes that may affect the organization and to think constantly of possible implications, the speed with which organizations have to adapt, and the increased demands on people's flexibility and ability to cope with change.

1.3 How are consultants used? Ten principal ways

In pursuing the generic purposes outlined in the previous section, consultants can intervene in many different ways. Both clients and consultants can choose among so many alternatives that trying to give an exhaustive and complete picture of these alternatives would be an impossible task. However, most of the consulting assistance to management will be given in one or more of the following ten ways:

- providing information;
- providing specialist resources;
- establishing business contacts and linkages;
- providing expert opinion;
- doing diagnostic work;
- developing action proposals;
- developing systems and methods;
- planning and managing organizational changes;
- training and developing management and staff;
- counselling and coaching.

Providing information

Better, more complete and more relevant information is often the main or only thing that a client needs to make the right decision. It may be information on markets, customers, sector trends, raw materials, suppliers, competitors, potential partners, sources of engineering expertise, government policies and regulations, or other. The consulting firm may have this information in its files, or know where and how to find it. Information gathering and analysis may be the only or the main objective of an assignment. Finally, any consulting assignment will have an information dimension and function. There is no consulting that does not involve working with and providing information.

In providing information, a delicate question of confidentiality may be faced. Consultants have to distinguish between information that can be provided to a client because it is publicly available or has been gathered and developed specifically for that client, and information developed for previous clients or obtained from private sources, which may need to be treated as confidential.

Providing specialist resources

A consultant can be used to supplement the client organization's staff. Usually such consultants will be specialists in areas where the client is looking for short-term expertise, or wants to avoid recruiting a new employee. Some clients, mainly in the public sector, use consultants in this way to bypass restrictive regulations preventing them from recruiting new staff and/or to avoid keeping expensive specialists on the payroll. Other clients may have been forced to cut down their technical departments and find it convenient to recruit short-term specialists from consulting firms.

A special case is "interim management". Recently this way of using consultants has become more widespread and some client firms may "borrow" staff members of consulting firms to occupy a position in their management hierarchy on a temporary basis.

Establishing business contacts and linkages

Many clients turn to consultants in their search for new business contacts, agents, representatives, suppliers, subcontractors, joint-venture and merger partners, companies for acquisition, business and professional networks, sources of funding, additional investors and so forth. The consultant's task may involve identifying one or more suitable candidates (people or organizations), presenting their names to the client, assessing their suitability, recommending a choice, defining and negotiating conditions of an alliance or business deal, and acting as intermediary in implementation. Often these contacts will be in sectors or countries not sufficiently known to the client.

Providing expert opinion

Various activities fall under this heading. The consultant may be approached to provide expert opinion in cases where the client can choose among several alternatives and seeks impartial and independent third-party advice before taking the decision. Consultants may be invited to act as an expert witness (testifying expert) in lawsuits or arbitrations calling for specialized knowledge.

Conversely, expert opinion can be provided in a totally informal way. This is the case when decision-makers use consultants as a sounding-board without asking for a formal report. It should be stressed that any consultancy involving assessment and choice will engage the consultant's expert opinion, in particular if management decisions risk being affected by shortage of information, company myopia, lack of expertise, emotions or vested interests.

Doing diagnostic work

Diagnostic skills and instruments are among the consultant's principal assets. Clients use consultants for a wide range of diagnostic tasks concerning the organization's strengths and weaknesses, positive and negative trends, potential for improvement, barriers to change, competitive position, underutilized resources, technical or human problems requiring management's attention and so on. Diagnostic work may concern the entire business or a part – a department, sector, function, process, product line, information system, organizational structure or other.

Developing action proposals

Effectively completed diagnostic work may be followed by the development of specific action proposals in an area that was diagnosed. The consultant may be asked to do the whole job, share the task with the client or act as an adviser to a client who has chosen to develop new proposals with his or her own resources. Action proposals may involve one or more alternatives. Also, the consultant may be asked to present alternatives with or without recommendations on the course of action to be taken by the client.

Developing systems and methods

A major portion of all consulting services concerns systems and methods in areas such as management information, business planning, operations scheduling and control, business process integration and management, inventory control, client order processing, sales, personnel records, compensation, and social benefits. Traditionally, many consulting firms have developed one or more of these areas as special lines of expertise. The systems may be custom-made or standard. The consultant may take full responsibility for choosing the most appropriate system, establishing its feasibility, adapting it to the client's conditions and putting it into effect in collaboration with the client's staff. Alternatively, clients may play a more active role in developing and adapting the system with the consultant's support. Many organizations prefer to retain the consultant until the system has been "debugged", becomes operational and achieves the promised performance.

In today's consulting, most of the systems provided are computerized, and their development, design and application require a combination of management and information technology consulting. A great amount of new systems development and installation is in the fields of e-commerce and e-business (see Chapter 16).

Planning and managing organizational changes

A fairly common case is that of a client who possesses the technical and managerial expertise to run the organization, but has difficulties and feels insecure when organizational changes are anticipated and cannot be avoided. Often these changes will put a lot of strain on people, since deeply rooted relationships, work habits and individual or group interests will be affected. In such situations, the special expertise sought from a consultant would be in change management – in identifying the need for change, developing a change strategy and plan, choosing and applying the right approaches to encourage change and overcome barriers to change, monitoring the change process, evaluating the progress made and results obtained, and adjusting the approach taken by management at all stages of the change cycle.

Box 1.3 Should consultants justify management decisions?

From time to time consultants may be approached with a request to undertake assignments and submit reports so that a manager can justify a decision by referring to an external consultant's recommendations. In other words, a manager may have determined his or her aims and have reached a personal decision, but wants to be able to say that he or she is putting into effect suggestions made or endorsed by an independent and respected professional adviser.

This can turn out to be another straightforward and correct case of providing expert opinion. It can also be a trap. A consultant who accepts such an assignment may be pulled into the hidden and intricate world of in-company politics. His or her report will have a political role in addition to the technical message it carries. This role may be constructive and useful if a manager is facing strong resistance to changes that are inevitable, and needs to refer to the consultant's authority. It can also happen that a consultant produces a report that will be misused for promoting vested individual or group interests. Independent and impartial assessment of every situation will help the consultant to avoid being used as a scapegoat.

The consultant may provide expertise and advice both on specific methods and techniques that are being changed, and on how to deal with interpersonal relations, conflicts, motivation, team building, and other issues in the organizational and human behaviour field. The weight given to behavioural skills will be greater in assignments where change will put a lot of strain on people, resistance to change can be expected and management feels that its own change management skills are inadequate. In addition to behavioural skills, which are sometimes referred to as "soft" skills, the consultant may also provide help in the "hard" skills area: effective scheduling of change; sequencing; coordination; redefining structures; responsibilities and relationships; reallocating resources; adjusting recording and control systems; preventing gaps and disorder caused by poor monitoring of change operations; ensuring smooth transition from old to new work arrangements, costing the project and measuring the results, etc.

Training and developing management and staff

While learning is a general purpose inherent in all consulting, training and development of managers or staff may be a distinct client service provided separately or in conjunction with and in support of other services.

The client and his or her staff will need to be trained in the new methods and techniques provided by the consultant, so that they become autonomous in using and improving them. There are many ways in which diagnosis, advice, systems development and training can be combined in consulting practice.

Training can be an alternative to the interventions and ways of using consultants described above. Rather than asking a consultant to work on a specific diagnostic, problem-solving or change management assignment, the client may prefer the consultant to prepare and conduct a course or a workshop for managers and/or staff on the subject. For example, instead of requesting the consultant to identify specific productivity improvement measures and present a productivity improvement programme, he or she may be asked to organize a set of workshops on productivity diagnosis and improvement.

Counselling and coaching

Management consultants can render an excellent service to managers and entrepreneurs who need strictly personal feedback and relaxed friendly advice on their leadership style, behaviour, work habits, relations with colleagues, weaknesses that could be damaging to the business (such as the reluctance to make decisions or the failure to seek the advice of collaborators) and personal qualities that need to be well utilized. Personal counselling is necessarily a one-to-one relationship based on trust and respect. It can be informal and should be fully confidential. Coaching, or executive coaching, pursues similar purposes (see section 3.7). Despite its obvious potential, few consultants offer such a service to clients and few clients ask for it.

1.4 The consulting process

An overview

During a typical consulting intervention, the consultant and the client undertake a set of activities required for achieving the desired purposes and changes. These activities are normally known as "the consulting process". This process has a clear beginning (the relationship is established and work starts) and end (the consultant departs). Between these two points the process can be subdivided into several phases, which helps both the consultant and the client to be systematic and methodical, proceeding from phase to phase, and from operation to operation.

Many different ways of subdividing the consulting process, or cycle, into major phases can be found in the literature. Various authors suggest models ranging from three to ten phases.[11] We have chosen a simple five-phase model, comprising entry, diagnosis, action planning, implementation and termination. This model, shown in figure 1.2, will be used consistently in our book. Obviously,

Figure 1.2 Phases of the consulting process

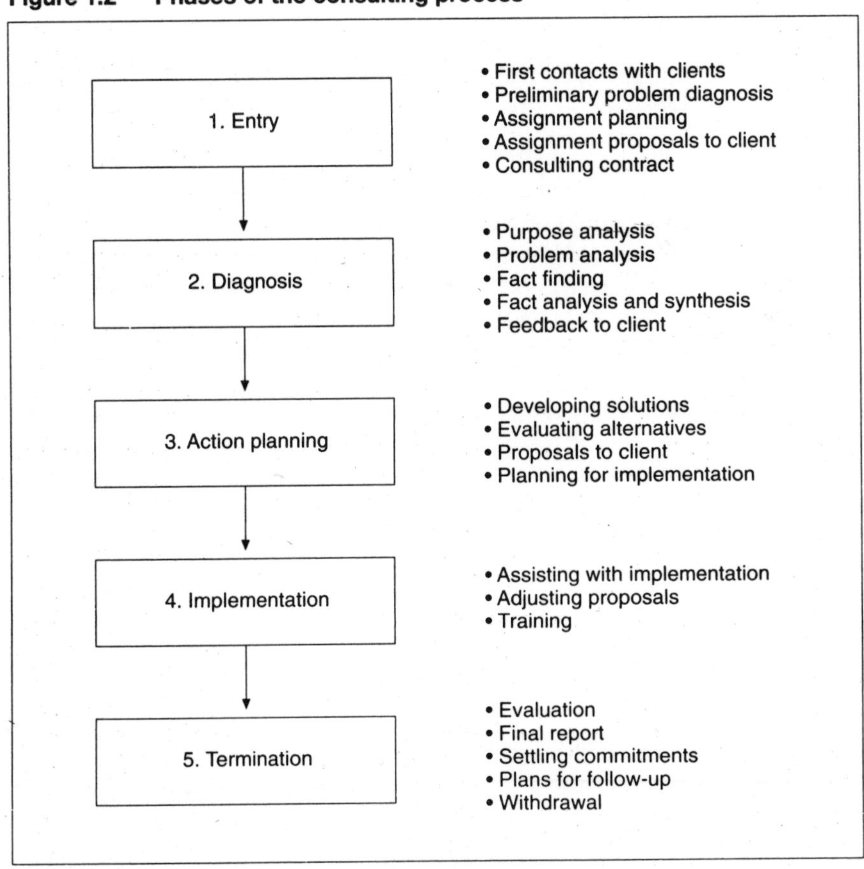

a universal model cannot be applied blindly to all situations, but it provides a good framework for explaining what consultants actually do and for structuring and planning particular assignments and projects.

When applying the model to a concrete situation it is possible to omit one or more phases or let some phases overlap, e.g. implementation may start before action planning is completed, or a detailed diagnosis may not be necessary or can be integrated with the development of proposals. It may be useful to work backwards from a later to an earlier stage. Thus evaluation can serve not only for a final assessment of the results of the assignment and of benefits drawn from change (termination phase) but also for deciding whether to move back and take a different approach.

Every phase can be broken down into several subphases or parallel activities. The whole model has to be applied flexibly and with a great deal of imagination. The consulting process can be viewed as a variant of the change process (Chapter 4), one in which change is planned, managed and implemented with a consultant's help. The reader may have seen various models of planned organizational change and may be interested in comparing them with the model in figure 1.2.

The consulting process will be examined in detail in Chapters 7–11, but at this point it will be helpful to have short descriptions of its five basic phases.

Entry

In the entry phase the consultant starts working with a client. This phase includes their first contacts, discussions on what the client would like to achieve or change in his or her organization and how the consultant might help, the clarification of their respective roles, the preparation of an assignment plan based on preliminary problem analysis, and the negotiation and agreement of a consulting contract.

This is a preparatory and planning phase. It is often emphasized that this phase lays the foundations for everything that will follow, since the subsequent phases will be strongly influenced by the quality of conceptual work done, and by the kind of relationship that the consultant establishes with the client at the very beginning.

In this initial phase, it can also happen that an assignment proposal is not prepared to the client's satisfaction and no contract is agreed, or that several consultants are contacted and invited to present proposals but only one of them is selected for the assignment.

Diagnosis

The second phase is an in-depth diagnosis of the problem to be solved. During this phase the consultant and the client cooperate in identifying the sort of change required, defining in detail the purposes to be achieved by the assignment, and assessing the client's performance, resources, needs and perspectives. Is the fundamental change problem technological, organizational, informational, psychological or other? If it has all these dimensions, which is the crucial one?

What attitudes to change prevail in the organization? Is the need for change appreciated, or will it be necessary to persuade people that they will have to change? The results of the diagnostic phase are synthesized and conclusions drawn on how to orient work on action proposals so that the real problems are resolved and the desired purposes achieved. Some possible solutions may start emerging during this phase.

Fact-finding and fact diagnosis often receive the least attention. Yet decisions on what data to look for, what data to omit, what aspects of the problem to examine in depth and what facts to skip predetermine the relevance and quality of the solutions that will be proposed. Also, by collecting data and talking to people the consultant is already influencing the client system, and people may already start changing as a result of the consultant's presence in the organization. Conversely, fact-finding has to be kept within reasonable limits, determined by the nature and purpose of the consultancy.

Action planning

The third phase aims at finding the solution to the problem. It includes work on one or several alternative solutions, the evaluation of alternatives, the elaboration of a plan for implementing changes and the presentation of proposals to the client for decision. The consultant can choose from a wide range of techniques, in particular if the client actively participates in this phase. Action planning requires imagination and creativity, as well as a rigorous and systematic approach in identifying and exploring feasible alternatives, eliminating proposals that could lead to trivial and unnecessary changes, and deciding what solution will be adopted. A significant dimension of action planning is developing strategy and tactics for implementing changes, in particular for dealing with the human problems that can be anticipated, and for overcoming resistance to, and gaining support for, change.

Implementation

Implementation, the fourth phase of the consulting process, provides an acid test for the relevance and feasibility of the proposals developed by the consultant in collaboration with the client. The changes proposed start turning into reality. Things begin happening, either as planned or differently. Unforeseen new problems and obstacles may arise and false assumptions or planning errors may be uncovered. Resistance to change may be quite different from what was assumed at the diagnostic and planning stages. The original design and action plan may need to be corrected. As it is not possible to foresee exactly and in detail every relationship, event or attitude, and the reality of implementation often differs from the plan, monitoring and managing implementation are very important. This is also why professional consultants prefer to be associated with the implementation of changes that they have helped to identify and plan.

This is an issue over which there has been much misunderstanding. Many consulting assignments end when a report with action proposals is transmitted, i.e. *before* implementation starts. Probably not more than 30 to 50 per cent of consulting assignments include implementation. If the client is fully capable of handling any phase of the change process alone, and is keen to do it, there is no reason why he or she should continue to use a consultant. The consultant may leave as early as after the diagnostic phase.

Unfortunately, the decision to terminate an assignment after the diagnostic or action-planning phase often does not reflect the client's assessment of his or her own capabilities and determination to implement the proposals without any further help from the consultant. Rather it mirrors a widespread conception – or misconception – of consulting according to which consultants do not have to achieve more than getting their reports and proposals accepted by the clients. Some clients choose it because they do not really understand that even an excellent report cannot provide a guarantee that a new scheme will actually work and the promised results will be attained. Other clients may be happy because what they really wanted was a report, not change.

Termination

The fifth and final phase in the consulting process includes several activities. The consultant's performance during the assignment, the approach taken, the changes made and the results achieved have to be evaluated by both the client and the consulting firm. Final reports are presented and discussed. Mutual commitments are settled. If there is an interest in pursuing the collaborative relationship, an agreement on follow-up and future contacts may be negotiated. Once these activities are completed, the consulting assignment or project is terminated by mutual agreement and the consultant withdraws from the client organization.

A consulting assignment

In practice, the five stages of the consulting process are usually structured, organized and implemented through particular and separate consulting assignments (also called engagements, cases, consultancies, projects or client accounts). In a typical assignment, the consultant and the client agree on the scope of the job to be done:

- the purposes (objectives, results) to be achieved;
- the expertise to be provided by the consultant;
- the nature and sequence of tasks to be undertaken by the consultant;
- the client's participation in the assignment;
- the resources required;
- the timetable;
- the price to be paid;
- other conditions as appropriate.

This agreement is confirmed in a consulting contract, which is written in most cases, but can be verbal (section 7.6). The contract will determine the phases of the consulting process that will be covered by the assignment, e.g. the assignment will be completed when an analytical report has been submitted to the client.

Alternatives to separate consulting assignments

An alternative to an assignment covering a distinct task or set of tasks and period of time is a retainer. Under a retainer contract, the client purchases in advance a certain amount of the consultant's time. The nature and purpose of the work to be done are defined in general terms only and will be specified at the beginning of each period covered by the contract. Collaboration extends over a longer period of time, using a cost-effective format. For example, the client may use the consultant's services for two days during the first week of every month to review jointly the general situation of the business, the problems and opportunities that have developed and the key decisions that will have to be taken. Or the agreement may define a more or less regular task for the consultant (e.g. assisting management in preparing board meetings) without specifying in advance the time to be spent.

There are various types of retainer arrangement, but from a technical viewpoint two types tend to prevail:

- *a generalist retainer*, under which the consultant follows global results and trends of the client's business, looking for opportunities for improvement in various areas and feeding the client with new information and ideas;
- *a specialist retainer*, providing the client with a permanent flow of technical information and suggestions in an area where the consulting firm is particularly competent and advanced (e.g. computer systems, quality management, international financial operations, identification of new markets).

Another alternative used in some technical assistance programmes is a framework contract.[12] In this case the consultant is contracted for a certain kind of services over a period of time. Within this framework agreement, specific assignments or missions are requested by the client and agreed upon case by case according to established rules, such as fee rates or consultant profiles, applicable to the whole contract. The negotiation and contracting procedure is thus simplified and accelerated.

There are various other modes of purchasing consultant services for longer periods without defining specific assignments and repeating each time all the phases of a consulting cycle as described above. Consultants may be permanent members of various committees or boards, special advisers to top managers, observers and advisers in management and board meetings, training faculty members and examiners, informal advisers acting as sources of new ideas and sounding-boards, or personal counsellors. Sophisticated clients tend increasingly to use these flexible and often more cost-effective formulas.

1.5 Evolving concepts and scope of management consulting

It is important to be aware of some dilemmas in the nature and purpose of management consulting and to understand how they are reflected in evolving consulting concepts and practices.

Advice or results?

We have shown that consultants are advisers and remain in this position except when they are recruited by clients to become temporary members of staff. Advisers have no authority to make decisions about a client's business and their influence has limits. The assignment may be too short and understaffed to produce tangible results, the client may be unwilling to follow the advice given, staff may not collaborate or their resistance and inertia may be too strong, or the consultant may be unavailable for follow-up and debugging. Even the soundest advice alone cannot provide absolute assurance that there will be tangible, measurable, and sustainable results.

There is therefore a growing tendency to use consultants for more than providing advice. "Advice" tends to be defined more and more loosely and liberally, and consultants are increasingly viewed as assistants, helpers, service providers or even service brokers who work with clients on various issues for as long as necessary to make sure that tangible and measurable results are achieved. Also, consultant remuneration tends to be increasingly related to results, rather than to time spent on providing advice. Clients would be wise not to get bogged down in vaguely defined time-based assignments with unclear consultant responsibilities and uncertain results. In large and expensive projects, which are often focused on management systems and information technology, clients need to have safeguards against escalating costs, low reliability and failure to meet set parameters and promised performances. Consultants may be offered roles and positions likely to increase their impact on results or to give them more authority and responsibility for achieving certain results in client organizations. New ways of remunerating consultants have become widespread, including equity and stock options (see Chapters 30 and 36). In this way the consultant is clearly accepting to be dependent on the wider and longer-term business results and prosperity of the client, sometimes even beyond the scope of improvements that can be attributed to the consultant's intervention.

Management consulting, business consulting, or any consulting?

Traditionally the scope of the services offered by management consultants was confined to functions, subjects and problems regarded as part of management, although the scope of "management" has never been fully and accurately defined. Management consultants were keen to stick to their business and maintain their identity, and most of them were not particularly seeking to broaden their services and explore new territory.

Over recent decades this attitude has changed dramatically, and in several directions, both in management consulting and in other professional services. Management consultants have started to rethink and redefine their business, widening and enhancing their service offerings, merging or establishing alliances with other consultants and professional service firms, and abandoning self-imposed restrictions on the sort of work they are prepared to undertake.

These changes have been triggered by a number of factors, including the growing complexity and sophistication of doing business in national and international environments, market deregulation and liberalization, new opportunities for innovative consulting, growing demand for integrated and "one-stop" professional services, competitive pressure coming from other professions and, above all, the advancement of information technologies and their rapid penetration into management and business processes. In using consulting and other professional services the clients are asking "what will add value to my business", and the service providers must inevitably adopt the same perspective.

In this new environment, some consultants have felt the need to stress that their field of activity is no longer management consulting (narrowly and rigidly defined), but business consulting (a wider concept and service portfolio) or consulting to management, consulting to business or organizational consulting (more open concepts permitting the service portfolio to be easily adjusted as opportunities and demands change).

Consulting coupled with other business?

The information technology giant IBM is often mentioned as a pioneer of a new approach, where management and business consulting is provided by a manufacturer, a software house, an investment bank or another business entity. Traditionally a leading supplier of office and computer hardware, IBM decided in the early 1990s to position itself as a provider of systems and services to clients. This included management consulting alongside IT services. IBM thus became the first large manufacturer and IT service provider with important management consulting services. In 2000, IBM had 50,000 consultants on its payroll and was one of the largest consulting firms in the world. Many other firms in manufacturing, utilities, finance or professional services have adopted a similar strategy and have included integrated management and business consulting (often called management services) in their offer to clients, with considerable success.

The reasons for this success are similar to those mentioned above. Clients that choose these service providers are seeking a complete, integrated and first-hand service in combination with know-how about the latest technology and the sector in general. They may be less concerned about independence and potential conflict of interest, e.g. if a consultant quite naturally suggests software or hardware made by his or her employer, or if a consultant coming from the same industry sector is in some way related to the client's competitors in the sector.

Commoditization

Commoditization is a common trend in professional services and is currently very pronounced in management, business and IT services. Rather than identifying needs, devising a solution and implementing a new and "tailor-made" system for every client, a consulting firm has a range of products that are offered to all clients (or categories of clients). Advice and know-how are turned into a commodity. The client can choose among standard offerings "off the shelf" – diagnostic instruments, change and project management programmes, training and self-development packages, production control systems, enterprise resource planning (ERP) or customer relationship management (CRM) systems, e-business or knowledge management software and so on. These products may be the result of the consultant firm's own research and development and based on its own work experience, or the consultant may have acquired the product from another firm, or be distributing and using it under a licensing agreement.

Commoditization of methods and systems is currently a feature of knowledge management and transfer. It responds to demands from clients, who want to get the best (or at least a good and easily applicable) system, methodology or approach at an affordable price, within reasonable time limits, and with a guarantee of applicability and standard performance. This is what the commoditized professional services aim to provide.

Conversely, the client accepts that the solution will not be unique, may have features that he or she does not need, and will be quite widely used, hence also by competitors. Indeed, most commoditized products cannot provide any distinct competitive advantage. Rather the risk is that a client will be disadvantaged by not following the trend and not buying a product that has become commonly used by his or her competitors.

Professional service providers who have commoditized their knowledge enjoy an enormous business advantage – if the product is in demand and sells well. They can serve large numbers of clients. Clients who would not consider buying a tailor-made solution for their organization may easily become interested in a standard product. Instead of using experienced and highly competent consultants for each assignment, the consulting firm can develop standard procedures for delivering standard products, and hence use more junior and less experienced staff, and cut the price. The spectacular growth of IT and e-business consultancies (discussed in Chapter 2) would not have been possible without considerable service standardization and commoditization.

Outsourcing

Outsourced services are activities that the client previously carried out within its normal structure and resources, but now chooses to contract out to a consultant or another service provider. By branching out into new service areas, management consultants behave in the same way as other professions do – looking for new markets and opportunities and aiming to satisfy their clients' demand for new, innovative and complementary services. The factors that may influence them in deciding to enter other fields of business service are:

- benefit to clients (Will the client appreciate such a service and will the service be really helpful to the client?);
- technical (Do we have the technical capacity and will the new service be synergetic with what we are already doing for the client?);
- legal (Does legalization allow a new service to be combined with the consultant's current service portfolio within the same organization?);
- ethical (Is it appropriate for a management consultant to operate such a service and will no conflict of interest or other ethical problem arise?);
- commercial (Is the new service profitable and a potential source of future income?).

Outsourcing has been transforming the shape of the consulting sector. It has been greatly facilitated and boosted by the new information and telecommunication technologies, which permit software and application service providers to be accessed via the Internet (see Chapters 16 and 22). More and more business and management processes and functions are regarded as suitable for outsourcing, and many developments in IT focus on enlarging the scope and enhancing the efficiency of outsourcing. These developments cover issues such as reliability, confidentiality, speed of data transfer, worldwide access to business information, etc. In addition to the direct provision of outsourced services, new opportunities for consultants are created by the need to select and evaluate systems and providers of outsourcing, identify and modernize processes to be outsourced, assist with organizational and other changes connected with outsourcing, manage and control outsourced services, integrate services outsourced to different providers, etc.

In larger IT and management consulting firms, outsourcing has become the fastest-growing area of service and an indispensable source of stable and long-term income. This reflects the fact that the consulting firm may be better equipped to carry out certain activities, which it can perform more efficiently and economically than the client while keeping up to date with advances in the field. It also reflects new ways of doing business and managing knowledge, in which clients focus on their core business and use intellectual capital and financial resources in areas of their principal strength.

---

[1] F. Steele: *Consulting for organizational change* (Amherst, MA, University of Massachusetts Press, 1975), p. 3.

[2] P. Block: *Flawless consulting: A guide to getting your expertise used* (San Francisco, CA, Jossey-Bass/Pfeiffer, 2nd ed., 2000), pp. xvi and 2.

[3] L. E. Greiner and R. O. Metzger: *Consulting to management* (Englewood Cliffs, NJ, Prentice-Hall, 1983), p. 7.

[4] See www.icmci.org., visited on 19 March 2002.

[5] P. Drucker: "Why management consultants", in *Perspectives* (Boston, MA, The Boston Consulting Group), No. 243, 1981.

[6] Ibid.

[7] See G. M. Bellman: *Getting things done when you are not in charge* (San Francisco, CA, Berrett-Koehler, 1992).

[8] P. Stroh: "Purposeful consulting", in *Organizational Dynamics* (New York, American Management Association), Autumn 1987, pp. 49–67.

[9] G. Nadler and S. Hibino: *Breakthrough thinking: The seven principles of creative problem solving* (Rocklin, CA, Prima Publishing, 1994), p. 128. See also Stroh, op. cit.

[10] Nadler and Hibino, op. cit. p. 149.

[11] Frequently referred to is the Kolb–Frohman model, which includes the following seven phases: scouting, entry, diagnosis, planning, action, evaluation, termination. See D. A. Kolb and A. L. Frohman: "An organization development approach to consulting", in *Sloan Management Review*, Vol. 12, No. 1, Fall 1970.

[12] For example, framework contracts with consultants are used by the European Union in technical assistance programmes.

THE CONSULTING INDUSTRY 2

2.1 A historical perspective

A historical perspective will help us to understand the present scope, strengths and limitations of management consulting. Where does management consulting have its historical roots? How far back can they be traced? What principal events and personalities have given the consulting business its current shape?[1]

Management consulting has its origins in the Industrial Revolution, the advent of the modern factory, and the related institutional and social transformations. Its roots are the same as those of management as a distinct area of human activity and a field of learning. Consulting in or for management becomes possible when the process of generalizing and structuring management experience attains a relatively advanced stage. Methods and principles applicable to various organizations and situations have to be identified and described, and the entrepreneur must be pressed – and motivated – to seek a better way of running and controlling the business. These conditions were not fulfilled until the latter part of the nineteenth century, a period which saw the birth of the "scientific management" movement.

The pioneers of scientific management

There were a number of predecessors of scientific management. One of them was the American manufacturer Charles T. Sampson, who in 1870 reorganized the whole production process in his shoe-making factory in order to be able to staff it with unskilled Chinese workers. One year later, acting in a consulting capacity, Sampson passed on his experience to an owner of a laundry, who accepted the advice and applied the approach previously used by Sampson.

The pioneers of scientific management, including Frederick W. Taylor, Frank and Lillian Gilbreth, Henry L. Gantt and Harrington Emerson, gave a major impetus to the development of consulting. Their technical and methodological approaches to simplifying work processes and raising the productivity of workers and plants were not the same and in certain cases even conflicted with each other. However, they all believed in the application of the scientific method to solving production problems. They believed, too, in the benefit of combining several methods for disseminating their scientific approach and making sure that it would be used by business corporations. They were tireless in lecturing, making studies, writing books and articles, organizing practical demonstrations, and providing advice in every possible way. Later in his life, Taylor chose to become a full-time management and productivity consultant.

These pioneering efforts gave rise to a very important type of management consulting, one which has strongly marked the profession and its image. Consulting as it emerged from the scientific management movement focused mainly on factory and shop-floor productivity and efficiency, rational work organization, time and motion study, elimination of waste and reduction of production costs. This whole area was given the name of "industrial engineering", and is still very important in improving operations. The practitioners, often called "efficiency experts", were admired for their drive and methodical approach and for the improvements they achieved (which were often spectacular). But their interventions were also feared by workers and trade unions because of their often ruthless approach to work intensification.

The controversial early image of the efficiency expert has changed considerably over the years. As new areas of management and new types of problem were tackled and became a normal part of the consulting business, the share of work related to production and work organization decreased. Important changes in the social and labour relations fields tended to limit the use of techniques unacceptable to the workers; negotiation and collaboration became indispensable for handling many assignments affecting employees' interests. The positive side of the efficiency expert's image has been very much preserved: consultants continue to be regarded as able to find new opportunities for saving resources and raising productivity.

Towards a general management approach

The limitations of the industrial engineering and efficiency expert approaches led to a broadened interest in other aspects and dimensions of business organizations, and to the birth of new areas of consulting. One of the first consulting firms of the kind known today was established in Chicago in 1914 by Edwin Booz under the name "Business Research Services".

In the 1920s, Elton Mayo, with his Hawthorne experiment, gave impetus to research and consulting in human relations. Important consulting work in human resource management and motivation was started by Mary Parker Follett. Interest in more effective selling and marketing was fostered by people such as Harold Whitehead, the author of *Principles of salesmanship,* written in 1917. A number of consulting firms were established during the 1920s. These were increasingly able to diagnose business organizations in their totality, treating manufacturing and productivity problems in a wider perspective of sales and business-expansion opportunities.

Consulting in finance, including financing the enterprise and financial control of operations, also started developing rapidly. A number of the new management consultants had a background in accountancy and experience drawn from working with firms of public accountants. One such was James O. McKinsey, a protagonist of the general management and comprehensive diagnostic approach to a business enterprise, who established his own consulting firm in 1925, and today is regarded as one of the founders of the consulting profession.[2]

In the 1920s and 1930s, management consulting was gaining ground, not only in the United States and in Great Britain, but also in France, Germany, and other industrialized countries. Yet its volume and scope remained limited. There were only a few firms, prestigious but rather small, and their services were used mainly by the larger business corporations. The consultant remained unknown to the overwhelming majority of small and medium-sized firms. On the other hand, assignment requests began coming from governments: this was the start of consulting for the public sector.

Consulting for governments, and for the army, played an important role during the Second World War. The United States in particular understood that the war was a major management challenge and that mustering the country's best management expertise was essential to winning on the battlefield. In addition, operations research and other analytical techniques, applied first for military purposes, rapidly found their way into business and public management, adding a new dimension to the services offered by consultants.

The years of growth and prosperity

Post-war reconstruction, the rapid expansion of business coupled with the acceleration of technological change, the emergence of new developing economies and the growing internationalization of the world's industry, commerce and finance, created particularly favourable opportunities and growing demands for management consulting. This was the period in which most consulting organizations that exist today were established and in which the consulting business attained the power and the technical reputation it enjoys at present. For example, PA, the largest consulting firm in the United Kingdom, had only six consultants in 1943, but 370 in 1963, and over 1,300 based in 22 countries in 1984. The total number of full-time management consultants in the United States was assessed at 100,000 at the end of the 1980s, six times the number that existed in the mid-1960s.

Since the 1940s, the expansion of management consulting has been impressive by any standard. Significant qualitative changes have also occurred.

Wider and more diversified service offerings. To meet their clients' needs and to attract clients from new sectors of economic and social activity, management consultants have developed various strategies, creating and offering new special services, specializing in particular sectors or, on the contrary, providing broad comprehensive packages of services.

At the forefront of technical progress. Most management consultants have made it their policy to be associated with the latest developments in management and related fields that can interest their clients, and to offer new sophisticated services before anyone else. The computer business, the use of information technologies in all aspects of management and accounting, and new communication technologies belong to such areas. Consultants do not hesitate to step out of the traditional limits of the management field and deal with plant automation, communication systems, quality control, equipment design, software development, economic studies, environmental protection and the like if these are of interest to clients and can enhance a consultant's competitive edge.

Growing competition in consulting. Competition in management consulting has greatly increased over the past 20 years. In addition to improving service quality and offering new sorts of services, management consultants have become more dynamic and even aggressive in searching for new clients and trying to convince potential clients that they can offer a better service than others. This has brought about many developments in the advertising and marketing of consulting services.

The "Big Eight" come on the scene. A landmark event was the decision of the "Big Eight" public accounting firms to enter management consulting. Considered for several decades as incompatible with professional accounting and auditing, management consulting started being promoted vigorously by the Big Eight in the early 1960s, producing 15–20 per cent of their income initially, and gradually more and more. By the end of the 1980s, the Big Eight had been reduced through mergers to the Big Six. Their management consulting services continued expanding rapidly, generating higher profits than traditional accounting and audit work.[3]

Internationalization. All large and many small consulting firms have sought to internationalize their operations in searching for new markets, adapting to the changes in the international economy, and taking advantage of the new opportunities for consulting in the developing countries and, since the late 1980s, in Central and Eastern Europe. In large consulting firms, foreign operations may contribute 30–70 per cent of income. Many new consulting firms have been established in developing and reforming economies.

Progress in the methodology of consulting. Great efforts have been made to increase the long-term benefits derived by clients from consulting assignments, by diversifying and perfecting the intervention methods applied at all stages of the consulting process. Greater emphasis has been placed on clients' active participation in problem-solving, new and more effective approaches to organizational change, the development of clients' own problem-solving skills, quality management in consulting and the need for clients to learn from every consulting assignment.

Increased client competence in using consultants. Many organizations, private and public, have become experts in using consultants. They have developed their own criteria and methods for selecting consultants, collaborating with them during assignments, monitoring their interventions, learning from their approach and evaluating results. The progress made by the consulting profession would not have been possible without these advances by clients.

Internal consulting. Consulting services provided under various names by internal units within private and public organizations are not a new phenomenon, but their volume and role increased very considerably in the 1970s and 1980s. The internal consultant has become a regular actor on the management consulting stage.

2.2 The current consulting scene

Thanks to the progress outlined in the previous section, and to the numerous challenges faced by businesses worldwide, management consulting has become an important and highly visible professional service sector in terms of size, structure, sophistication, range of services offered, standards applied, results produced and overall influence. Consultants have become acknowledged and often indispensable advisers in major business decisions and transactions. Leading consulting firms are respected and solicited thanks to their broad knowledge base, diversified resources, innovative spirit and capacity to cope with complex and novel situations.

Sector growth

The growth of the consulting sector reflects the high and steady demand for consulting. The estimated value of the world consulting market was US$102 billion in 1999, up 260 per cent from 1992, when the total revenue attained some US$28.3 billion. The 1999 estimate for spending on consulting in Europe was US$33 billion. Average annual growth rates of the world market attained 25 per cent in 1990–94 and 18.9 per cent in 1995–99. At present, the total number of management, business and IT consultants, including e-business consultants, may well be in the range of 650,000–750,000. These figures can only be estimates, because the scope of consulting has not been precisely delimited and data are collected from various sources. Yet the figures give a clear indication of orders of magnitude and trends.

Sector restructuring

Over the past decade, sector restructuring has been significant and impressive. Mergers, acquisitions, new types of alliances and vigorous new business development with the firms' own resources have swept away the division between management and IT consulting, especially in large consulting firms. These firms have become providers of integrated and multidisciplinary services, able to respond to virtually any demand from their client base. While a few years ago it was possible to discern easily distinct types of large consulting firm, such as global multifunctional firms, strategy houses or information technology consultancies, this is no longer possible. It is true that some leading firms have maintained a prevailing technical profile thanks to which they attained their present technical reputation and market position. However, services in general have become more homogenized as many firms have copied competitors when they offer a new consulting product. Emphasis on service integration and complete packages has also made the service offerings of various firms more similar to each other.

The proportion of total consulting business in the hands of the largest firms did not change significantly between 1990 and 1999, when the 20 largest firms held some 50 per cent of the world market. However, the proportion increased in 2000 to nearly 60 per cent as a result of faster growth of large firms, mergers and acquisitions. Concentration among the top firms continued through large-scale operations such as the merger in 1998 of PriceWaterhouse and Coopers & Lybrand, which created the world's fourth largest management and business consultancy (not including the audit and accounting wing of the new firm) with 34,000 employees and annual consulting revenues of US$6.6 billion in 2000. The first position was held by Andersen Consulting (renamed Accenture after the split from Arthur Andersen in 2000) with 62,000 employees and revenues of US$8.9 billion in 2000. The Big Six were reduced to the Big Five. Another major structural change was the acquisition in 2000 of the consulting wing of Ernst & Young by Cap Gemini. Further restructuring, including acquisitions of consulting firms by large non-consulting companies, is plausible, although the negotiations concerning the acquisition of the consulting wing of PricewaterhouseCoopers by Hewlett-Packard in the second half of 2000 were unsuccessful. Other initiatives to merge and create new alliances have had varied outcomes.

Another form of restructuring coming to the fore is the separation of management and business consulting from accounting and audit services in the large firms as a result of evolving perceptions of conflict of interest and other reasons (see section 6.2).

The movement into management and IT consulting markets by large non-consulting firms from the manufacturing, utilities and service sectors – a sporadic occurrence some 6–7 years ago – has turned into a significant trend. Hewlett-Packard employed 6,000 consultants in 1999. In 1992, IBM had 1,500 consultants on its payroll. By 2000, with 50,000 consultants, it had become the world's largest combined IT/management consultancy company measured in terms of annual revenue from consulting (US$10.2 billion). This trend is not confined to computer hardware and software manufacturers. Management and business consulting, often in combination with IT consulting, is offered by airlines, banks, insurance companies, electricity authorities, manufacturing companies, and others. This is the result of several factors: the search for new business opportunities among non-consulting firms; attempts to provide a more complete and better integrated service to customers (including hardware, software, advice and assistance in implementation); and efforts to achieve synergy by integrating key components of the value chain and making full use of firms' special knowledge and business relationships (e.g. in public utilities). It also shows that, at present, financially and technically strong businesses from any sector can add management and business consulting to their service portfolio and that many such developments can be expected in the coming years.

Sector polarization has continued and presents considerable challenges for medium-sized and small firms, which have to search constantly for new strategies to cope with delicate problems of positioning, maintaining identity, finding a niche, surviving and ideally growing in a competitive environment, retaining competent people and convincing clients of their special skills and other advantages. These firms continue to account for an important share of the consulting market especially in Europe (42.3 per cent in 1999).

At the other end of the spectrum, thousands of independent practitioners and small partnerships of 2–5 consultants provide evidence of imagination, adaptability and vitality. In Europe, 82 per cent of consultancy firms are small; these firms delivered only 10 per cent of consulting services in 1999, but the sector concentration and the power of the large consultancies have not driven them out of business, although their conditions of work have changed quite substantially. Once again, the experience of recent years has demonstrated that, in professional services, size is not the only criterion, and that many services can be provided equally well or even better, and under more advantageous terms from the client's point of view, by small operators. Small operators can often win by doing different things from large firms, providing a more personalized service and innovating. Networking and subcontracting have enabled many small operators to participate in large and complex projects, often in cooperation with larger service providers.

E-business consulting

Probably the most significant development that has shaped the consulting industry in recent years has been the emergence and spectacular growth of e-commerce and e-business consulting. Virtually non-existent until the mid-1990s, it has rapidly turned into the most dynamic area of consulting business. By 2000, all the leading management and IT consultancies were also active in e-business consulting, offering software and advisory services for doing and promoting business via the Internet. Many of them have stressed that e-business should not be viewed as a different sector, but as a new dimension of any business and consulting which will soon become a standard and fully integrated component and method of operating.

Equally, a number of new firms have appeared, often providing e-business consulting services in combination with development, marketing and installation of software – the so-called "e-consultancies". At one point a group of them even started calling themselves the "e-five", and statements such as "the new e-stars are set to destroy the old guard"[4] began to appear. Within months, the e-consultancies had thousands of professionals on their payrolls. Many of these consultants came from the larger and more traditional consulting firms, most of which were relatively slow to enter the e-business consulting field.

The spectacular development of "e-consulting" was full of paradoxes. It brought a great deal of innovation, dynamism and entrepreneurship to consulting and its contribution and impact have ensured that "the profession will never be the same again".[5] It has created new opportunities, new business models and new ways of consulting in the era of the Internet and the knowledge economy. It has broken the resistance to change in many long-established companies and paved the way to doing more business through the Internet. It has shaken the self-confidence of large consulting firms, which have realized that any professional service provider can lose its comfortable competitive advantage to dynamic and innovative newcomers if it misses major business trends and opportunities.

Conversely, many providers of e-consulting services, including those regarded as new stars and sector leaders, did not avoid the pitfalls of overselling, pushing clients into hastily prepared and over-ambitious projects, making unrealistic promises to both clients and investors, conceiving and launching "dot.com" businesses with no market and no future, overcharging, recruiting more staff than they were able to train and supervise, and others. In addition, many e-consultancies did not escape financial speculation based on anticipated growth and future earnings supposed to come from the "new economy", rather than on professional reputation, competence and real business results.

This short though spectacular e-consulting euphoria culminated in 2000; by the end of the year, it was over. The share prices of most Internet consultancies dropped by 90 per cent or more, thousands of consultants employed in this sector became redundant, and "what was once a baffling industry, with dozens of firms all promising e-business transformation and transcendental strategic thinking, is now reduced to a rather more digestible shape".[6]

Lessons are still being drawn from this short e-consulting boom.[7] There is no doubt that the Internet has generated unprecedented opportunities for consulting services and that the information and knowledge-based economy will constitute an excellent market for consultants for many years. It is also true that, during the 1999–2000 e-business hype, quite a few consultants put their unrealistic ambitions and short-term financial interests before their professional integrity and their clients' needs and interests.

Accelerated commoditization

High growth rates in consulting could not be maintained over extended periods without increased service standardization and commoditization. To meet existing demand and stimulate further demand, the larger consultancies are increasingly offering more tangible "commodities" – systems, methodologies, application and training packages, learning programmes and materials, etc., as already mentioned in Chapter 1. While commoditization is not a new phenomenon and its elements could be observed in work study and industrial engineering services more than 70 years ago, we are currently witnessing developments of a different scope and impact. Most large consultancies, and even some small ones, are offering sets of more or less standard products, claiming that it is more advantageous to clients to purchase their "brand" product, with or even without adaptation. In many cases these products are the consultants' legally protected intellectual property and have to be treated as such by clients and other users. Some of these products may be unique and distinctly better than competing products. However, most commoditized products tend to differ from each other more in name and presentation, and sometimes in price, than in substance. Consultants who have opted for service commoditization have been relentless in promoting their products' uniqueness and superiority, and have increasingly invested in advertising.

New operating modes

Commoditization, based on tested knowledge and experience, reduces the need to use experienced consultants and modifies the structure of the consulting cycle. For example, the diagnostic phase may be eliminated or reduced to a few questions set out in a standard instrument. There may be no broad survey or the client may be expected to make such a survey himself or herself and then tell the consultant what is to be delivered. This approach has development costs for the consultant (the need to create and maintain standard instruments, systems and packages), but reduces operating costs. As it permits employment of junior and relatively inexperienced consultants under minimum supervision, it is a prerequisite of fast growth rates. It helps to overcome a shortage of highly skilled professional manpower. Clients appreciate the faster and cheaper services, but many are increasingly worried about the absence of experience and a broader outlook in consulting assignments. The exception to this may be projects in new and rapidly evolving fields and technologies, where experience tends to play a less important role.

The scene is set for further developments and structural changes in consulting as well as other professional service sectors. The markets for consulting and other business services are liberal, vibrant and receptive to innovations and structural changes. The knowledge economy and the growing complexity of the business world create new demands and new opportunities for consulting and other professional services.

2.3 Range of services provided

The range of services provided by management consultants mirrors the development of management and business, and of the environmental and other challenges they face. Today's management consultants may be asked to assist with any type of management or business problem in any sort and size of organization, virtually in any sector and part of the world. The same problem may be approached differently by different consultants, hence the service provided will be different. The consultants' service portfolio is extremely wide and diversified, and is evolving fast. Service offerings are changing, partly under the pressure of clients' changing needs, but also as a result of the consulting firms' own research and innovation aiming to anticipate clients' needs and offer new and better services to them. In consulting, service innovation and new ways of service integration are key differentiating factors.

There have been many attempts to describe and classify consulting services. Information and publicity leaflets of consulting firms often give a listing and description of areas of expertise, but in the absence of standard terminology and service description, firms may use identical terms to mean different things. New terminology is often invented to underline uniqueness and novelty. Generally acceptable and easy-to-understand terms and classifications are yet to be developed.

Management functions, processes and systems

Traditionally, management consulting services were structured in accordance with the prevailing structures of management functions and processes. Services were offered in production organization and management, factory management, marketing and sales, distribution, personnel administration and management, training and development, office organization, financial management, general management and organization, and similar fields. This traditional structuring of service offerings has been very much preserved.

Information technology, however, has transformed this area of consulting radically. Currently many consultants assist their clients in implementing IT systems, including assessing needs and feasibility; selecting, developing, adapting, introducing and debugging a system; training staff; and modifying procedures, documentation and work methods accordingly. The general trend has been away from separate systems for each area (production, personnel, etc.) to system coordination and integration, a dominant and promising approach at present.

Specific management problems and challenges

Many consulting services address distinct and separate business problems and challenges, usually cutting across several management functions and processes, reflecting new business opportunities and constraints that require a creative and innovative approach. In these cases the consultant may provide in-depth knowledge, experience and techniques to deal with a particular problem, and help to develop and apply an approach for dealing with the problem effectively in the client' s particular context. Examples are: business expansion to a new territory, technology transfer, licensing agreements, investment project design, structuring and management, adaptation to new environmental legislation, cross-cultural management, starting an e-business or adding an e-business dimension to current business, and exploiting opportunities offered by deregulation and market liberalization.

Approaches to organizational change and performance improvement

Other consultants emphasize that their main strength and usefulness to clients lie not in a detailed knowledge of a specific technical area or system, but in their ability to share with the client their effective work method – for diagnosing and resolving organizational problems, devising action programmes for organizational change and performance improvement, introducing and improving knowledge management systems, and making sure that such programmes and systems are implemented. Their service is defined neither by the area of intervention (e.g. marketing) nor by the problem to be tackled (e.g. high production or distribution costs), but by the consulting approach or method used.

Examples are organizational development, with its wide range of intervention techniques, action learning, team building, business diagnosis, various problem-identification and problem-solving methodologies, creative thinking and innovation techniques, benchmarking, and business process re-engineering. Some of these methods and approaches are highly structured and are applied as complete consulting and training packages, which are often proprietary and protected by copyright. Some are passing fads or new labels for old things. Others are true innovations and their impact on organizational effectiveness and the consulting industry itself can be significant and lasting.

Consulting approaches to organizational change and performance improvement are increasingly offered in combination with special knowledge and skills in areas mentioned in the previous paragraphs.

Business strategy and transformation

At the top of the list of consulting services are those that address the very purpose and future of business. These services are in the areas of corporate strategy, strategic planning and decision-making, business alliances and partnerships, major business restructuring, privatization, mergers and acquisitions, total reorganizations, e-business strategies, divestment, and similar. These are "elite and prestige" consulting services as regards their image, required consultant expertise and style, and level of intervention in client organizations. Their impact on the whole organization can be significant and long-lasting. They are interdisciplinary, multifunctional and conceptual by definition, drawing on other groups of services and combining them as necessary. They are highly knowledge-intensive, require considerable experience and do not lend themselves easily to standardization and commoditization. Except in firms that specialize in this area, their volume in the service portfolio of consultant firms tends to be smaller than that of other service groups.

Human resource consulting services

A range of consulting services falls under the broad denomination "human resources", "human resource management and development", or "human capital". Within this area, a number of different concepts and approaches have been practised by various firms over the years. The services include in particular:

- those related to employee benefits (social insurance, pensions, salaries);
- executive search and personnel recruitment services;
- personnel administration;
- human resource and human capital management and development, including training, and strategies and activities.

Sector-specific services

Some consultants have chosen a sectoral approach: they target all their work at one sector, or have established sectorally specialized divisions. The reasons may be both technical (the need for an intimate knowledge of sector technologies, economics, and business practices and culture) and commercial (many clients' preference for consultants who know their sector). As some practitioners put it: "If you develop a reputation as a sugar-industry consultant, you get sugar-industry clients." This can be quite useful in sectors that traditionally regard themselves as different from other sectors (e.g. the construction or mining industries) and are sceptical about the value of advice coming from outside the sector. In other cases, sectoral specialization may be the pragmatic choice of a consultant who knows one sector particularly well, or who happens to have a number of clients from the same sector.

The shifts in the sectoral focus of consulting reflect the structural changes in the economy. Originally, most consultants worked mainly for industrial and commercial enterprises. Today, consulting for the service sectors tends to be very important; this includes specialized sectoral services in banking, insurance, utilities, telecommunications, transport, community development, central and local government administration, education, health care, voluntary associations, leisure and entertainment.

Sectorally specialized services may encompass any of the areas described earlier, from strategy and company transformation issues to operations and efficiency, and may be provided in combination with services that are not sectorally specialized. Despite some obvious advantages, full sectoral specialization of services may lead to conflict of interest in serving clients who compete with each other within the same sector.

Outsourcing and other emerging lines of service

As mentioned in section 1.5, many consulting firms are now performing outsourced IT, administrative, commercial, financial or other activities for and on behalf of clients. In doing so, the consulting industry is moving towards becoming a wider business-service sector, where consulting remains important, but other services are also offered when this is technically feasible, legally and ethically acceptable, and financially attractive to both the consultant and the client. For example, Accenture describes its 2001 service portfolio under five broad headings: consulting, technology, outsourcing, alliances, and venture capital.

A consulting firm may also offer any other business service that meets the above-mentioned criteria. Such services are not new in the consulting sector. Examples are numerous: technical and managerial training, production and distribution of training packages, collection and distribution of business information, book publishing, psychological testing, opinion polls for market research, consumer preference surveys, advertising, sectoral economic and market studies, management and supervision of investment projects, real estate operations, and so on. Consulting firms have also moved into areas such as choice and transfer of technology, patents and licences, product design and testing, design of control equipment, auctions, venture capital, and others.

2.4 Generalist and specialist services

In consulting, there is a long-standing debate about the pros and cons of generalists and specialists. Some contend that only an all-round generalist is a "real" management consultant; a specialist may be an industrial engineer, a financial analyst, an expert in compensation techniques or an industrial psychologist, but not a management consultant. Others object to this, considering that generalists lack the in-depth knowledge required fully to understand and resolve problems and provide added value in today's business; therefore to be really useful a consultant must be a specialist.

The history and the current profile of the profession indicate that both generalists and specialists have their place in management consulting. The issue is not generalists versus specialists, but how to combine generalist and specialist skills and perspectives to achieve a better total effect.

Specialist work viewed from a generalist perspective

Managing an organization is an interdisciplinary and multifunctional task, and measures taken in one specialist area will affect other areas. Therefore a management consultant should always aim to view specific (and often narrow) problems, requiring the intervention of a specialist, in a wider context. To be a good consultant, the specialist has to be able to look at the problem from the generalist point of view. He or she must be able to apply diagnostic and other methods common to all skilled consultants, and understand organizational relationships. This is one of the main objectives of the theoretical and practical training in a consulting firm.

Cooperation between generalists and specialists

It would be unrealistic to require every consultant to be both a specialist and a generalist, although a few talented and experienced individuals do achieve this. However, in most consulting firms there is some division of work between those who are primarily specialists (and keep up to date in a special area of knowledge and its applications) and those who are generalists (and deal with several areas of management, focusing on their interaction, coordination and integration).

The so-called generalists prepare and coordinate global assignments requiring combined specialist and generalist interventions. They normally take care of preliminary organizational diagnoses, negotiations with clients, assignment planning and coordination, drawing of conclusions from specific observations made by specialists, presentation of final proposals to clients, and so on. Supervisory and managerial functions in consulting are often in the hands of the generalists.

Some assignments are totally or primarily in the general management field and are undertaken by senior generalists. They concern issues such as corporate policy and strategy, leadership, organizational structure, mergers, turnarounds and the like. Most consulting for small businesses is done by generalists, capable of advising the client on the business in its totality. Clients expect the generalist to suggest the participation of a specialist consultant whenever such a need is identified, just as they expect the specialist to refrain from giving advice in areas beyond his or her competence.

The trend towards specialization

In today's management consulting there is a pronounced trend towards specialization, reflecting the growing range and complexity of issues handled by consultants. This trend concerns first of all the service specialization of the consulting firms (of all sizes, including individual practitioners). Increasingly, clients are interested in working with firms that do not present themselves as universal experts in solving business problems, but possess the right specialist knowledge and expertise, e.g. in the industrial sector, functional area or special technique concerned. Many firms have been rethinking their profile to adapt to this trend.

Furthermore, consulting firms have started to modify their internal staff structure, that is, the numbers and the respective roles of the specialists and generalists employed. As clients seek more input from specialists, firms may employ specialists part time, or borrow their services from another firm. However, many of these specialists, outstanding experts in their technical fields, urgently need to broaden their outlook and improve their understanding of the wider issues.

As for all-round generalists, their role in dealing with interdisciplinary and multifunctional problems will remain important. But there are various perspectives and degrees of generalization. Clients are generally less and less interested in consultants who view themselves as universal problem-solvers and claim to be able to handle any situation thanks to their broad experience. Conversely, there is a growing demand for conceptualizers, coordinators and integrators with experience in certain sectors (health, transport) or with particular types of organizational and business problems and situations (mergers and acquisitions, programme coordination, business diagnosis, turnarounds, etc.).

2.5 Main types of consulting organization

The wide range of providers of management consulting reflects the diversity of the clients and markets served, services offered, approaches taken and personalities involved. It also reflects the history of the sector and the growing competition for major clients and contracts. Recently the consulting sector has undergone considerable restructuring and it is still far from being stable. In the literature, firms tend to be grouped and classified by various criteria. In this section, we outline the profiles of the principal groups of actors who shape the current consulting market.

Large multifunctional consulting firms

The market is currently clearly dominated by large multifunctional and multiservice consulting firms, as a result of market growth and concentration over the past 20 years. All the firms in this group have grown thanks both to active business development supported by new staff recruitment and training, and to numerous acquisitions and mergers. A consulting firm employing several hundred professionals can be considered large. There are, however, at least 50 giants in the consulting world with over 1,000 consultants on their staff. In 2000, some 20 firms in this group earned over US$1 billion each.

Most of the giants operate as multifunctional and transnational firms, with offices or affiliated companies in 20 or more countries. Their sheer size and influence permit them to deal with a wide range of clients and most complex management problems; they are sometimes referred to as "full-service consulting firms" able to provide "total service packages". They prefer to serve large and multinational clients, and these clients often prefer to use their services. Many of them also possess certain specialist skills which make them different from each other, e.g. they may be known for sectoral expertise and services, or be particularly strong in management and IT systems, finance, human resources, business restructuring and e-business consulting.

The management advisory services (MAS), first established as divisions of major accounting firms, have grown in recent decades into major multifunctional management consultancies. They loom large within this group and hold the leading position on the consulting market internationally. Today they are the world's largest professional firms not only in accounting and audit, but also specifically in management consulting. They have drawn considerable benefits from their position as leading accounting firms in terms of expertise, image, contacts and assignment opportunities. Previously some of them used to emphasize that they were not keen to undertake just any type of assignment, but only those that "would be expected from a reputable professional accounting firm", above all financial and general management assignments. This was followed by a period of fast expansion in a wide range of consulting and professional service fields, including human resources, organization development, production engineering, total quality management, management information and control systems, and even small business development.

Most recently (2001–2002) these firms have been exposed to growing criticism and pressure of regulatory authorities in the United States and other countries to return to the original model of audit by separating management and other business services from audit services, in order to stop the proliferation of conflicts of interest (see section 6.2).

The concentration of business in the hands of the largest firms is documented by the fact that with one exception (Mercer Consulting Group) the ten largest multifunctional firms are also among the 20 largest operators in the two groups described below (strategy and information technology consultancies).

Strategy and general management consultancies

While most large firms in the groups described above provide consulting in corporate strategy, company organization, business restructuring and other general mangement issues, some firms are particularly focused on this area and position themselves as advisers to management on key issues of strategy (the so-called "strategy houses") and total business development. They have also added e-business strategy to their portfolio. Consultancies with distinct expertise in strategy and general business development include McKinsey, Boston Consulting Group, Bain, Booz-Allen & Hamilton, A.T. Kerney and Roland Berger. These firms typically declare considerably higher earnings per consultant thanks to the higher fees applied to strategy consulting than to now largely standardized and commoditized services in IT and similar systems (for example, in 2000 McKinsey earned US$470,000 per consultant and Bain US$380,000, while Andersen earned US$150,000 and IBM US$204,000).

Information technology and e-business consultancies

A few years ago, there was a separate emerging and dynamic group of firms providing information technology consulting. While pursuing their expansion, most firms in this group have recently undergone more restructuring and transformation than any other consultancies. At present, the listing of the largest IT consulting service providers includes the same names as the lists of multi-functional and integrated management and business consultancies. As information technologies and systems become better integrated, both among themselves and with management functions and processes, consulting services are following this trend. Firms refer to "integrated development models" and to the necessity to adjust IT consulting to the "increasing complexity of clients' businesses". It appears that the future will belong to service providers that can fully and cost-effectively integrate management and IT services, including e-business consulting services.

Employee benefits consultancies

A group of large international consultancies, mainly based in the United States and the United Kingdom, has traditionally specialized in the field of employee benefits, including actuarial services, pension schemes, social insurance and benefits, wage schemes and salary administration, and pension fund management. They also offer consulting in other personnel administration systems and activities. The leaders are Towers Perrin, Watson Wyatt, Mercer Consulting Group, Aon Consulting, and Hewitt Associates. The large multifunctional consultancies and some medium-sized firms are also active in these fields.

Medium-sized generalist and specialist firms

This group embraces a variety of organizations, ranging from a few to 50–100 consultants. Obviously a firm that is small by American standards can be large in a small developing country. Their prevailing technical profiles include:

- general management, strategy and business development consulting for small and medium-sized businesses, often in a limited geographical area;
- consulting in one or a few technical areas, such as personnel, maintenance, quality management, marketing, sales management, technology transfer or environmental auditing and management;
- sectoral specialization, e.g. in urban transport, hospital management, textiles, printing industry, insurance.

Entrepreneurial founders and managers of medium-sized firms have been able to find new niches and maintain their firms' reputation with certain client groups despite the growing power and market share of the large firms. There has been a great deal of restructuring, too. Successful medium-sized firms are viewed as attractive acquisition targets by larger consultancies, especially if they possess specialist expertise sought by a larger service provider or if their acquisition permits entry to new markets. For a medium-sized firm, joining a larger consultancy will often be an attractive solution in a rapidly changing and increasingly competitive consulting market.

Sole practitioners and small partnerships

The existence of thousands of sole consulting practitioners and small partnerships of 2–5 consultants demonstrates that, despite market domination and aggressive marketing by large professional firms, there is plenty of interest in working with independent individuals or small teams and their networks. Small consultancies may be generalists, emphasizing their broad management experience, problem-solving and behavioural skills, or specialists working in a narrow area. Their strength is in a highly personalized and flexible approach, which is more difficult to achieve and apply consistently in a large consulting firm. The services of a senior individual practitioner can also be less expensive, because many of the overhead costs of a large organization are avoided. Before becoming independent consultants, many sole practitioners worked as business executives or employees of large consultancies.

Some clients prefer to entrust a complete assignment to an experienced senior person, one who in a larger firm would probably work as a project leader, supervising the work of several more junior consultants through short visits. Sole practitioners are often connected with other colleagues in informal networks and so can collaborate to undertake large and complex assignments, or can recommend another person for work outside their own area of competence. Most of them consult for small enterprises, but even large companies sometimes turn to sole practitioners and small firms for small assignments, policy advice to senior management and special tasks.

The consulting professors

There are professors, lecturers, trainers and researchers in management who are involved in consulting on a part-time, though fairly regular, basis. Most of them provide ad hoc advice on issues that may be very important from the client's perspective, but that do not require extensive consulting time.

Some full-time consultants do not regard the "consulting professor" as a real management consultant. However, experience has shown that outstanding benefits can be drawn from combining research, teaching and consulting. The consulting professors' main contributions have generally been new perspectives and new ideas, rather than routine organizational and functional consulting. A small group has attained the level of "guru consulting", influencing the thinking of legions of business executives and management consultants alike.

Consulting services of management schools and productivity centres

To promote management consulting and link trainers and teachers of management with the world of practice, a number of business schools, management institutes and productivity centres have established consulting services. In some countries this has been done with technical assistance from international agencies and with the involvement of experienced consultancy firms from other countries. These "institutional" units enjoy some independence in choosing clients and selling services. Some of them employ full-time consultants, while others use the institution's teaching and research personnel to carry out assignments.

A combination of teaching/training and consulting is highly valued by many clients. Often course participants ask their tutors for practical advice and consulting becomes a logical continuation of a relationship that developed it the classroom. A potential problem is harmonization of the various functions of the institution. Individual teachers and trainers who enjoy great autonomy may give priority to their personal clients, from whom they can earn higher income, ahead of assignments negotiated and executed through the institution, and even ahead of classroom teaching. Conversely, it may be impossible to retain competent and ambitious faculty members if they are not given enough freedom and time for consulting.

Non-traditional suppliers of consulting services

A new group of suppliers of management consulting services has emerged in recent years. This group is rather heterogeneous but has one common characteristic: its original and main function is a service other than consulting, but consulting is viewed as a technically useful and financially profitable addition to its products and services. The group includes, among others:

- suppliers and vendors of computer and communication equipment;
- computer software houses;
- commercial and investment banks, brokers, insurance companies and other organizations in the finance sector;
- suppliers of equipment and turnkey projects in energy, transportation, drinking-water, irrigation and other utilities;
- economic, statistical and sectoral research institutes and information centres;
- other organizations that have turned their internal management service groups into external consulting services.

A number of organizations, usually those with a strong mathematical, computer science, operations research or econometrics background, offer special consulting services in areas such as strategic studies, model building, forecasting of consumer demand, systems analysis and design, plant and office automation, and others. Some of them are also referred to as "think-tank" organizations. They may be independent, or associated with a computer firm, a technological university or a research institute. These consulting services tend to be research and/or technology based.

Consulting networks

During the past decade, consulting networks have become important service providers. They exist under various formulas and denominations: long-term partnerships based on formal cooperation agreements operate alongside ad hoc arrangements for single short-term assignments. The obvious advantages of such networks are flexibility, adaptability, potential to augment the marketing and implementation capacity of small service providers, and the opportunities they provide for sharing knowledge and experience. They allow experts who are available for a given project to come together, and permit consultancies to tap expertise outside their existing staff resources, including the expertise of individuals who are not full-time consultants. They also permit individual experts to remain independent while participating in projects that require teams of consultants.

Thanks to their flexibility and ability to muster expertise in various combinations in line with changing client needs, the consulting networks and alliances are particularly suited to the information society and knowledge-based economy. They are therefore likely to become more widespread, and adopt various new formats, in the future.

2.6 Internal consultants

An internal consulting unit is one that is established within an organization – a business corporation, a public utility, a government ministry or department – to provide consulting services to other units of the same organization. Definitions and delimitations are not very precise. These services are given many different names, but the term "management services" prevails. They can be found at different places in the organizational structure. Some of them are consulting services in the full sense of the term – they have a mandate to intervene in an advisory capacity at the request of a senior manager, or a unit manager within the organization. In other cases, consulting is only one of the functions, and the units concerned are also responsible for internal audit, accounting and information systems, records and reporting procedures, organizational circulars, staff development or other similar functions.

The current trend

Internal management consulting services have become common in large businesses; these units are staffed by specialists and generalists, some of whom may have had experience with external management consulting or accounting firms. The same trend can be observed in government administrations. Total numbers of internal consultants are not known, but most probably they are large. After some hesitation, professional bodies of consultants have started recognizing internal consultants. Already in 1976, the Institute of Management Consultants in the United Kingdom agreed that the term independent practice "shall include consultants engaged as in-house consultants who meet the required standards of knowledge, experience and competence and are free at all times to offer objective and independent advice".

The critics

There are many critics of internal consulting. The main criticism comes from some large consulting firms, which contend that internal consulting can be a useful staff function, but does not deserve to be called management consulting. They challenge the internal consultants' independence and objectivity, and criticize their lack of exposure to different situations in various companies. Also, it is said, only a large business firm or government department can really afford a sufficiently large and properly staffed internal unit for consulting work. This criticism is apparently not shared by organizations that continue to build up their own internal consulting services.

Why such an interest?

The rapid growth of internal consulting is a recognition of the power of the consulting approach. Internal units are one way of making consulting more easily accessible and available within an organization.

Further reasons for retaining an internal consultant are quick availability, an intimate knowledge of the organization's internal practices, management style, culture and politics (hence sensitivity and a more rapid orientation in any work situation), and confidentiality. Internal consulting is often thought to be more appropriate for problems that require a deep knowledge of the highly complex internal relations and constraints in large organizations. In governments, they may be given priority for reasons of national security and interest.

The cost factor is not negligible. Because of reduced overheads, travel and other expenses, even a well-paid internal consultant will cost 30–50 per cent less than an external one if the company has enough work for him or her.

Independence and other problems

Independence and objectivity represent a problem in some cases, particularly if the management of the organization and the internal consultants fail to clarify the roles and mutual responsibilities of client and consultant within an organization, if consultants are used for anything that comes into an executive's mind, and if they feel pressured to please top management or their direct client instead of giving an impartial view. An internal consulting service that has low status and no access to top management will not be able to deal with high-level and strategy-related problems, and its recommendations will lack credibility and authority.

Combining internal and external consulting

The use of internal consultants is not a passing fad, but nor will it replace the use of external consultants. The latter will continue to be preferred in situations where internal consultants cannot provide the required knowledge and expertise and meet the criteria of impartiality and confidentiality in dealing with particularly delicate internal issues.

In a growing number of cases, assignments are entrusted to joint teams of external and internal consultants. This is a technically interesting arrangement: it can reduce costs; it helps external consultants to learn quickly about the client organization; it facilitates implementation; and it transfers knowledge to internal consultants.

Many external consultants enjoy this way of working and regard internal consultants as technical partners, not competitors. They have learned not to underestimate or ignore any internal consultant in a client organization. In many situations it is tactically better if proposals are endorsed by an internal unit, or are presented by this unit, than if they represent only an outsider's view. Internal consultants are more and more involved in defining terms of reference for external consultants, establishing short-lists for selecting consultants, making the selection, negotiating the terms of contracts, discussing recommendations, and monitoring implementation. Their use can improve the quality and reduce the costs of implementation quite considerably.

An interesting way of enhancing the competence and credibility of internal consultants is to involve them in external consulting. Consulting is thus added to the product and service portfolio offered to customers and business partners. For example, management services units in several electricity corporations, railways and other public utilities have developed performance improvement, staff training and other programmes that are of interest to public utilities in other sectors or countries. In-company management services units in various sectors have done a great deal of work on project and systems design, technology transfer, consulting and training in developing countries.

From cost centres to profit centres

The traditional way of using internal consultants prevented them from covering their costs from their income. They were treated as cost centres, financed from the company budget as part of the general costs. Their growth was not determined by client demand, or by the consultant's ability to develop and sell better services, but by the company's budgetary process and the consulting unit's ability to negotiate higher budgetary allocations. In this situation, it was difficult to motivate staff to develop and sell more and better services. Conversely, user units did not have to care about the costs of using an internal consultant and many assignments were poorly prepared and managed.

To change this situation, many organizations have started to treat their internal consulting units as profit centres. This is more than a change in budgetary procedures. A profit centre is regarded as a unit that creates value, generates income and contributes to the company's profit. It must be able to sell its services, thus demonstrating that there is demand even if the clients have to pay. Internal clients, however, must have the right to choose. If the internal consulting unit meets their requirements, they buy its services. But they are not forced to do so.

The helping relationship within an organization

Besides the activities of internal consulting units, there are many other opportunities for making effective use of the helping relationship within organizations. Examples are advisory missions of managers and specialists to subsidiaries and plants within a corporation, temporary task forces and project groups, short-term detachments, personal coaching and counselling, ad hoc advice provided by staff departments, and so on. Some of these forms will be described in Chapters 3 and 4 in the discussion of consulting modes and organizational forms and interventions for managing and assisting change. They are often used in connection with a consulting project carried out by an external or internal consulting unit.

Although this sort of helping activity is not normally referred to as consulting, it tends to produce better results if the individuals involved are familiar with the principles and methods of consulting.

2.7 Management consulting and other professions

In previous sections, we have made several references to three trends: first, management consultants have been increasingly moving into new service areas, which may be emerging areas of management consulting, but also areas outside the management consulting field; second, other providers of professional and business services have tended to do more and more management consulting; and third, firms from different professions tend to work together more frequently than in the past. Professions no longer enjoy impenetrable borders and absolute protection against "intruders". They are undergoing profound transformations, which are reshaping individual professions, shifting their borders and changing their status, relationships and methods of work.

Professional service infrastructure of the market economy

To function smoothly, the market economy needs a well-developed, reliable and effective infrastructure of professional services. Management consulting is one of them. The total infrastructure comprises many other services (figure 2.1), all of which serve the same private and public sector client base, including business firms, administrations, social organizations and individuals. They also serve each other.

The structural changes through which business and governments have passed in recent decades have had a major impact on professions providing services to them. The services of lawyers, accountants, investment bankers, management consultants and others are in great demand as the pace of structural changes accelerates and as these changes become radical and complex. Mergers and acquisitions, joint ventures, privatization, structural adjustment, trade liberalization, export development, new forms of cross-border trade and financial operations, major development projects, business alliances, and new laws and agreements regulating business nationally and internationally – all are green pastures for business- and management-related professions.

Most of these business transactions and structural changes do not fall under the jurisdiction of one single profession. They involve legal, financial, accounting, organizational, managerial and other aspects, although one of these aspects

Figure 2.1 Professional service infrastructure

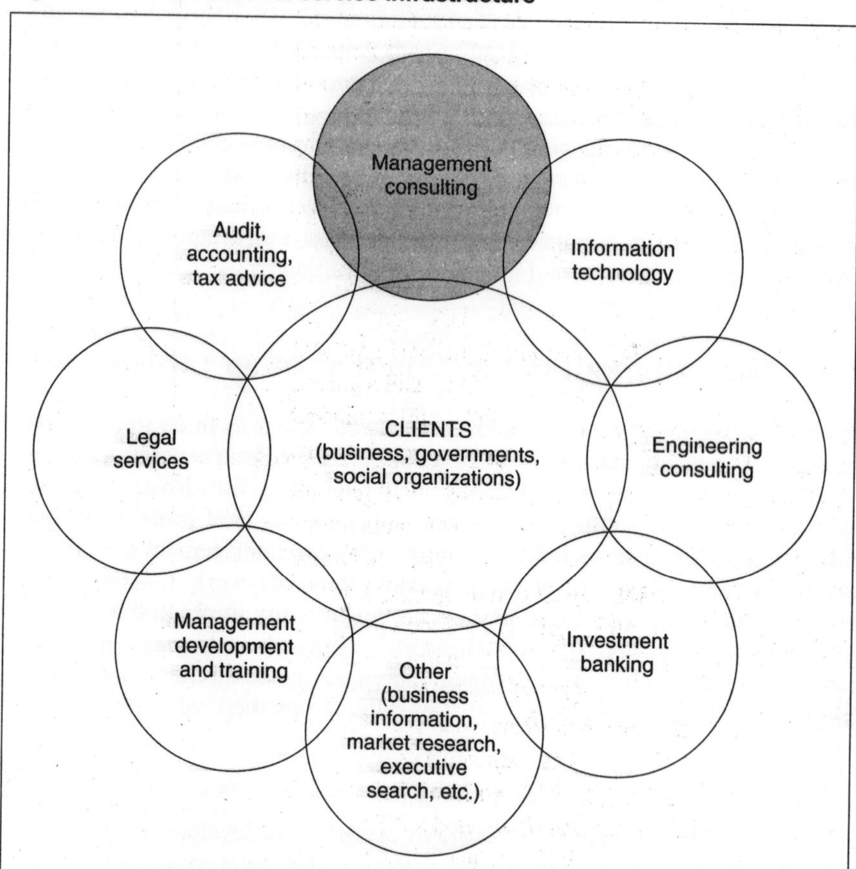

may dominate in a given case. An international perspective and expertise, and a good knowledge of the perspective taken and services offered by other professions, are increasingly required from all professions.

Management consulting has grown and evolved in this context. It has been changing in interaction with other professions, which has included both competition and cooperation. This interdependence is best documented by the spectacular growth of management consulting services of international accounting firms. Within less than 20 years, these firms have been able to become world leaders in consulting in addition to having strengthened their leadership position in accounting and audit.

Competition among professions

Tough competition is one of the main characteristics of the current state of the professions. There is competition both within and among professions. When a new market for professional services starts emerging, firms from several professions may claim that this market is primarily within their province. This has been the case, for example, with privatization, where accounting firms, investment bankers, management consultants and law firms have all been competing for a leadership position and a bigger market share.

If the work to be done requires an interdisciplinary approach – which is more and more the case – a firm in one profession may decide to establish a new service line in an area that falls under another profession from a strictly technical point of view. A management consultant might branch out into tax advice, or a computer firm decide to offer management consulting. The firm thus becomes multi-professional or multidisciplinary. If there are legal or other barriers preventing a combination of certain service lines within one firm, a solution can usually be found by establishing a new sister or affiliated firm for the new service.

In some grey areas competition is straightforward. For example, in many countries, company valuation is not a guarded domain of any profession. Management consultants may have advantages in the field: assessing the potential future earnings of a manufacturing company requires an ability to analyse demand and sectoral trends, the maturity level of the technology used, emerging technologies, raw materials, local and foreign competitors, quality and cost of labour, and the like. Still, accountants and investment bankers also offer valuation services, stressing the accounting and financial market aspects and implications. There are, too, independent experts in property, real estate and company valuation. Thus, several professions compete for the same clients.

Cooperation among professions

Cooperation among different professions is an equally important trend. Clients are not interested in interprofessional skirmishes and jealously guarded borders between professions. They resent corporatist attitudes that put the profession's self-interest before the clients' interests. What they want is a coordinated and even integrated service in which no important aspect of the problem in hand is ignored or treated unprofessionally. If a consulting firm cannot deliver such a service with its own resources, collaboration with other professions can provide a solution.

Management consultants collaborate closely with lawyers on many issues with legal aspects and implications. The initiative often comes from the legal side: legal counsel may feel the need for management or financial advice in dealing with a legal problem, and so turn to a management consulting firm, which may or may not already be on contract to a mutual client. However, the management consultant may also perceive the need for legal advice in a given situation, invite a lawyer to participate in a joint assignment, seek consultation with internal counsel or recommend that the client engage outside legal counsel.

Another area with numerous links to consulting is audit. Statutory audits in the legal sense of the term, that is, checking and certifying accounting records and financial reports, are not consulting. However, they are only a step away. Auditors who express an opinion on the client organization's financial records and reports or recommend an improvement – and this is increasingly required by many clients – act as consultants whether they call themselves consultants or not. Forensic audits (examining the health of an organization's financial management, looking for potential past or future flaws and risks, and identifying responsibilities) are very close to management surveys and audits (Chapters 7 and 12). Auditing often prepares the ground for important consulting projects and can help to promote consulting; this was well perceived by accounting firms when they decided to enter management consulting. Conversely, providing audits, IT and consulting services to the same clients can lead to problems of lack of independence and conflict of interests (see also section 6.2).

Engineering consultants (consulting engineers) constitute a vast and diversified sector providing technical expertise in areas such as civil engineering, the construction industry, architecture, land and quantity surveying, town and country planning, project planning and supervision, mechanical engineering, chemical engineering, patent services, computer science and systems, and so on.

The link between management consulting and consulting in engineering has traditionally been close and the boundaries are in many cases blurred. On the one hand, some engineering consultants also deal with organization and management questions, particularly in areas such as industrial or production engineering and control, quality management, maintenance, feasibility studies, patents and licences, plant design, and project design, implementation and supervision. On the other hand, production management consultants with an engineering background can deal with various production and productivity improvement problems that are of both a managerial and a technological nature. In many contexts the best results will be achieved if management and engineering experts work together on interdisciplinary projects.

Several remarks on the relationships between management consulting and information technology consulting have already been made. Indeed, it is at this interface that the most spectacular and most rapid changes have occurred in recent years – and are likely to continue in the future. Computer software houses and hardware manufacturers first entered management consulting in the area of systems design, development and application, and then widened their interest to embrace general management and strategy consulting, and other areas. Management consultants' strategies have been very similar: they have been adding more and more IT services to their portfolio. On both sides firms have come up with an expanding range of integrated management/systems/IT services, as well as highly specialized services. This has been achieved through numerous mergers and acquisitions, and also through authentic development of new service lines and new competencies.

2.8 Management consulting, training and research

There is a very special relationship between management consulting on the one hand, and management training, development and research on the other. It could even be argued that conceptually they constitute subsectors of the same profession, since they have the same object of study and practical intervention and they tend to pursue the same ultimate purposes. The differences are in the methodology and the immediate purposes.

There are professions where the relationships between practical intervention, education, training and research have been clarified and structured long ago. In medicine, no one would think of the practitioners, the medical schools and the researchers as being from different professions. Management has not yet arrived at that point. It has not been possible to overcome fully the traditional dichotomy between the practically oriented consultant, committed to producing tangible results for the client, and the professor–researcher, writing and teaching about concepts and theories, but less concerned with practical applications.

Consulting and training

There have, however, been signs of real progress in bridging the gap between consulting, and training and development, in the field of management:

- Knowledge transfer and learning are among the main purposes of modern consulting. In choosing working methods and collaborating with the client, the consultant aims to pass on personal know-how and experience. At the same time the consultant learns from the client.
- Consultants often view training (both informal and formal) as their key intervention tool and use it extensively.
- Some consulting firms have established management development and training centres as a special client service, which can be used in conjunction with consulting assignments, or separately.
- Many consultants are part-time teachers or trainers in business schools and other educational and training establishments.
- Conversely, more and more teachers and trainers of management also practise consulting (the "consulting professors" mentioned in section 2.5), drawing from their consulting experience to make training more relevant and practical and encouraging their students to learn consulting approaches and methods.
- In some educational and training establishments, consulting has become an institutional function, organized through special departments and/or projects.
- There are also hybrid firms and institutions, providing combined consulting/training services and stressing the benefits that the client can obtain from their approach.

Consulting and research

Similar comments can be made on the close relationships between management consulting and management research as on consulting and training. Some of the

Box 2.1 Factors differentiating research and consulting

Factor	Research	Consulting
Problem	Mainly fashioned by researcher; more open-ended, especially in exploratory research	Mainly fashioned by client, sometimes on joint basis
Time scale	Usually flexible	Tighter and more rigid
End product	New knowledge and new theories + ? better practice	Better management practice
Ownership of information	Usually publicly available	Often confidential
Decision-making	Focus may change at researcher's discretion subject to plan	Discretion limited to main task only
Academic rigour	Methodology tight	Minimum level appropriate to problem
Evaluation	External, by peers in scientific community, policy-makers	Internal, by company

earlier consultants liked to stress that they were down-to-earth practitioners who had nothing in common with academics and researchers. They saw direct hands-on experience, not research, as the only source of practically usable know-how. This dichotomy, however, reflected a poor theoretical preparation of the consultants and a lack of practical purpose on the side of most academics, rather than an incompatibility between the two approaches.

Despite their differences (see box 2.1), research and consulting have a lot in common and can be very useful to each other.

In dealing with practical management problems, consultants need to know the results of research and draw from them – for example, before recommending an incentive technique it is better to know whether any research has been done into the use of that technique in conditions similar to those experienced by the client. Consulting organizations increasingly encourage their members not only to keep informed about published results of management research, but also to keep in touch with ongoing research projects and leading researchers.

Research, then, can only benefit from close links with consulting. The data collected in client organizations by consultants can serve wider research purposes. Data from a number of organizations can be used for drawing general conclusions on sectoral or other trends, without infringing confidentiality. On becoming aware of this, many consulting firms have also gone into research.

They have their own research programme, undertake contract research, and publish books based on their own research, or they cooperate on research projects with universities and individual researchers. Some consulting firms have gained the reputation of being strongly research based. Business schools and research institutes are increasingly interested in testing and diffusing the results of their research through consulting assignments.

Methodologically, consultants can learn a lot from researchers and vice versa. Action research is an example of research that is on the border with consulting: it aims simultaneously to solve a meaningful practical problem and to yield new knowledge about the social system under study. Action research involves changing what is being investigated; conventional research does not.

---

[1] For a fine account of the history of management consulting see H. J. Klein: *Other people's business: A primer on management consultants* (New York, Mason-Charter, 1977); and P. Tisdall: *Agents of change: The development and practice of management consultancy* (London, Heinemann, 1982).

[2] See W. B. Wolf: *Management and consulting: An introduction to James O. McKinsey* (Ithaca, New York, Cornell University, 1978).

[3] The "Big Eight" included the following international accounting firms: Arthur Andersen; Arthur Young; Coopers and Lybrand; Deloitte Haskins and Sells; Ernst & Whitney; Peat, Marwick, Mitchell; Price Waterhouse; and Touche Ross. In 1989, Ernst & Young was established by merging Ernst and Whitney with Arthur Young. Deloitte Haskins and Sells merged with Touche Ross. Peat, Marwick, Mitchell became KPMG following a 1986 merger with Klynveld Main Goerdeler. The group was thus reduced to the "Big Six".

[4] *Management Consultancy*, Nov. 2000, p. 9.

[5] Ibid., p. 8.

[6] *The Economist*, 9 Dec. 2000, p. 92.

[7] See also *E-business consulting: After the shakeout* (research report by Kennedy Information, 2001), and M. Porter: "Strategy and the Internet" in *Harvard Business Review*, Mar. 2001, pp. 63–78.

THE CONSULTANT–CLIENT RELATIONSHIP 3

The consulting process involves two partners – the consultant and the client. In theory it should be easy to put the consultant's expertise to work on the client's project, since it is fair to assume that both parties will do their best to achieve the same purpose.

The reality is infinitely more complex. The consultant remains external to the organization, someone who is supposed to achieve a valid result in the client organization without being part of its administrative and human system. Even an internal consultant – an organization's employee – is external from the viewpoint of organizational units where he or she is supposed to intervene. Quite independently of its technical relevance and quality, the consultant's advice may or may not be understood and accepted by the client. The consultant can upset people and hurt their feelings in many different ways. Rejection can take many forms. The history of consulting contains thousands of excellent reports that have been buried in managers' desks and never implemented, although they were formally accepted. Many consultants terminate their assignments with feelings of bitterness and frustration. They are absolutely sure that they have provided excellent advice, yet the clients do not follow it. This underlines the critical importance of creating and maintaining *an effective consultant–client relationship*.

Building this relationship is not easy. To achieve success, both consultants and clients need to be aware of the human, cultural and other factors that will affect their relationship, and of the errors to be avoided when working together. They must be prepared to make a special effort to build and maintain a relationship of understanding, collaboration and trust that makes the effective intervention of an independent professional possible. There is no alternative.

3.1 Defining expectations and roles

To begin with, the client and the consultant may look differently at both the expected outcome and the ways of carrying out the assignment. The client may have only a vague idea of how consultants work and may be slightly suspicious – possibly he or she has heard about consultants who try to complicate every issue, require more information than they really need, ask for more time in order to justify longer assignments, and charge exorbitant fees. The client may be approaching the consultant with mixed feelings (see box 3.1). But even if there is no a priori suspicion, and no fear on the client's side, there is a risk of misunderstanding as regards objectives, end results, roles, relationships and other aspects of a consulting assignment.

Box 3.1 What it feels like to be a buyer

(1) I'm feeling **insecure**. I'm not sure I know how to detect which of the finalists is excellent, and which are just good. I've exhausted my abilities to make technical distinctions.

(2) I'm feeling **threatened**. This is my area of responsibility, and even though intellectually I know I need outside expertise, emotionally it's not comfortable to put my affairs in the hands of others.

(3) I'm taking a **personal risk**. By putting my affairs in the hands of someone else, I risk losing control.

(4) I'm **impatient**. I didn't call in someone at the first sign of symptoms (or opportunity). I've been thinking about this for a while.

(5) I'm **worried**. By the very fact of suggesting improvements or changes, these people are going to be implying that I haven't been doing things right up till now. Are these people going to be on my side?

(6) I'm **exposed**. Whoever I hire, I'm going to reveal some proprietary secrets, not all of which are flattering.

(7) I'm feeling **ignorant**, and don't like the feeling. I don't know if I've got a simple problem or a complex one. I'm not sure I can trust them to be honest about that: it's in their interest to convince me it's complex.

(8) I'm **sceptical.** I've been burned before by these kinds of people. You get a lot of promises. How do I know whose promise I should buy?

(9) I'm **concerned** that they either can't or won't take the time to understand what makes my situation special. They'll try to sell me what they've got rather than what I need.

(10) I'm **suspicious.** Will they be those typical professionals who are hard to get hold of, who are patronizing, who leave you out of the loop, who befuddle you with jargon, who don't explain what they're doing or why? In short, will these people deal with me in the way I want to be dealt with?

Source: Adapted from David Maister: *Managing the professional service firm* (New York, The Free Press, 1993). p. 113.

Joint problem definition

First, the reason for which the consultant was brought in needs to be well defined. A manager who wants to call for a consultant's help should not merely recognize a need for such help, but define the problem as he or she sees it, as precisely as possible. In many organizations, top management would not even consider using consultants unless presented with a clear description of the problem and the purpose of the consultancy.

Before accepting the assignment, the consultant must be sure that he or she can subscribe to the client's definition of the problem. Except in the most simple and clear cases, the consultant wants to be able to reach his or her own conclusion as to what the problem is and how difficult its solution might be.

There are many reasons why the consultant's definition of the problem might differ from the client's. Frequently managers are too deeply immersed in a particular situation to be able to assess it objectively, or they may have created the problem themselves. They may perceive the symptoms but not the real issue. They may also prefer the consultant to "discover" certain significant aspects of the problem.

Comparison of the client's and the consultant's definition of the problem lays down the basis of sound working relations and mutual trust for the duration of the assignment. It should be discussed. Both the consultant and the client should be prepared to make changes to their initial definition of the problem and to agree on a joint definition. But this first joint definition should not be considered as final. Once the assignment has started, detailed diagnostic work may uncover new problems and new opportunities, requiring a redefinition of the situation.

Results to be achieved

Secondly, the consultant and the client should clarify what the assignment should achieve and how this achievement will be measured. This may require an exchange of views on how each party regards consulting, how far the consultant should continue working on an agreed task (possibly exceeding the scope of that task), and what his or her responsibility to the client is. As mentioned in section 1.4, there is often a misunderstanding about the consultant's role in implementation. The consultant may be keen to participate in it, but the client may be used to receiving reports with action proposals, and to deciding on implementation only after the consultant has left. If possible, the consultant will often try to be involved in implementation. If cost is what worries the client, the consultant's presence during implementation can be a light one (see also Chapter 10).

The consultant's and the client's roles

Thirdly, it is important to determine how the assignment will be conducted by the two parties:

- What roles will be played by the consultant and what by the client? What will be their mutual commitments?
- Who will do what, when, and how?
- Does the client want to obtain a solution from the consultant, or does he prefer to develop his own solution with the consultant's help?
- Is the client prepared to be intensely involved throughout the assignment?
- Are there specific areas that the consultant should cover without trying to involve the client? And vice versa?

These and similar questions will clarify the client's and the consultant's conception of management consulting and of the roles that the consultant can effectively play. The answers will define the strategy to be followed in order to make the assignment a success by both the client's and the consultant's standards.

During the assignment, many unforeseen events may occur and new facts may be uncovered so that it becomes necessary to review the original definition of expectations and roles. Both the client and the consultant should be alert to this possibility and be flexible enough to adjust their contract and work arrangements. Staff in the client organization may find at some stage that they can easily produce information or action proposals that the consultant was originally supposed to work out, or that the consultant is more useful as a trainer than as a problem-solver. Insisting on keeping to the initial definition of roles, even when conditions change, may be counterproductive.

3.2 The client and the consultant systems

When, how, and between which individuals will the consultant–client relationship be established? The client, in the widest sense of the term, is the organization that employs the services of a consulting firm. There we have an institutional relationship. A professional service firm works for a manufacturing enterprise, an Internet business, or similar. But the term client can also be used in a narrower sense to mean individuals or groups in the client organization who initiate the recruitment of the consultant, discuss the job with him or her, collaborate in the course of the assignment, receive reports and recommend to higher management whether or not to accept them, and so on. Often a number of managers, supervisors, and other staff members will be directly involved in the assignment at its various stages, or will be affected by the conclusions reached.

The situation is similar on the consultant's side. The consultant, in the wider sense of the term, is a service firm, i.e. a legal entity. But the firm employs individuals in various capacities – in management, administration, assignment marketing and planning, supervision, or assignment implementation – who are involved in various ways in negotiating, selling, preparing, managing and executing the assignment. These individuals enter into various relationships with client organizations, their internal units and individual employees.

In the delivery of professional advisory services the consultant–client relationship is always personalized. There will probably be a formal contract between the consulting firm and the organization using its services. However, the service is delivered through direct contact between people acting on behalf of the two organizations. This is fundamental. A productive relationship cannot be guaranteed by any legal contract between organizations; it will depend on the abilities and attitudes of the individuals directly involved, and on the "psychological contract" between them.

In working with client organizations, management consultants may discover highly complex relations. They may face conflicting expectations, hopes and fears, respect and disrespect, confidence and distrust. Information may be readily offered or deliberately concealed or distorted. Consultants refer to the chemistry of "client systems", taking a systems view of the organization and trying to map out the network of relationships in which they are going to operate. This may show that, for the consultant, the client system embraces only one part or aspect of the client organization. Within the client system, the consultant then needs to determine:

- who holds the real power for making decisions related to the assignment (at all stages);
- who has the main interest in the success or failure of the assignment;
- who should be kept informed;
- whose direct collaboration is essential.

Many consultants make the mistake of automatically considering and treating the most senior person as their main client. This can upset the people who know that they will have the main responsibility for implementing the conclusions reached, and that they – not the top manager – will be directly affected and will have to live with the results. On the other hand, it may also be a great mistake to leave out the high-level manager. He or she should be informed and asked for support at an early stage.

During the assignment, the consultant continues to explore the client system and improve his or her understanding of the roles played by various people. He or she does this in order to confirm or modify the original assessment of roles, and also because assignments are dynamic processes and shifts in role can occur at any moment. For example, the appointment of a new manager can change the course of a consulting assignment dramatically.

Some situations may be particularly intricate, e.g. if the consultant does not really understand who the main client is or whom he or she should try to satisfy first of all. This may happen, for example, if top management recruits the consultant, but leaves it solely to a functional department to handle the job, if a consulting assignment is recommended and sponsored by a bank as a precondition of a loan to its client, or if a ministry sends consultants to a public enterprise. In these and similar situations, the consultant needs to clarify whether he or she is supposed to act as an inspector, an auditor, an informant, or a real management consultant. He or she should find out who "owns" the problem and is keen to resolve it – this will be the main client.

Box 3.2 Various categories of clients within a client system

In a complex client system it is useful to think in terms of categories of clients, aiming to understand their various motivations and roles, and how best to work with each category (some clients may belong to two or more categories simultaneously):

(1) **Contact clients:** approach the consultant initially.

(2) **Intermediate clients:** participate in various meetings dealing with fact-finding, assignment planning, reviewing alternatives, and so on.

(3) **Main or primary clients:** "own" a problem for which they need and want help and for which the consultant was brought in. They are likely to be the consultant's principal collaborators.

(4) **Contract clients:** play a key role in the consultant selection procedure and in negotiating and signing a consulting contract.

(5) **Ultimate clients:** their welfare and interests will ultimately be affected by the assignment; they must be considered when the intervention is planned, although they may not be directly involved with the consultant.

(6) **Sponsoring clients:** provide financial resources for the consultancy and may or may not wish to play a role in determining the procedure to follow, choosing the consultant, monitoring execution and approving the proposals to be implemented.

Developed from a typology of clients originally proposed by E. Schein, in *Process consultation,* Vol. II (Reading, MA, Addison-Wesley, 1987), pp. 117–118.

3.3 Critical dimensions of the consultant–client relationship

Different situations and client expectations lead to different definitions of the consultant's roles and methods of intervention. Sections 3.4 and 3.5 will review a number of role models from which to choose. Nevertheless, even if situations, assignment strategies and consultant work methods exhibit considerable differences, all consultants and clients will try to establish and nurture relationships in which they can work together to achieve a common purpose. Three dimensions of these relationships are critical: collaboration, sharing of knowledge, and trust. These dimensions are essential in consulting and could be described as objectives to be pursued in order to make the relationship fully productive and satisfying to both sides.

Collaborative relationship

Without client–consultant collaboration, there is no effective consulting. Yet the need for active collaboration is not automatically perceived by every client and various misconceptions may have to be dispelled. Some clients imagine that by actively collaborating with the consultant they are doing the job themselves, paying the consultant a handsome fee for nothing. The consultant who insists on the client's collaboration may be compared to "the guy who borrows your watch to tell you the time". Often the readiness to collaborate is tested at the fact-finding stage. The client may feel that the consultant should not be given all the data he or she requests and may even instruct staff to withhold information.

The client's reluctance to give the consultant all the information on the state of the business cannot always be interpreted as unwillingness to establish a collaborative relationship. Accounting and financial information, for instance, may be regarded as strictly confidential by the client, and the consultant should only ask for such information if it is strictly necessary.

The modern concept of consulting methodology assumes strong client collaboration for the following main reasons:

(1) There are many things that the consultant cannot do at all, or cannot do properly, if the client is reluctant to collaborate, for example, if the consultant is refused information or cannot exchange ideas with the right people.

(2) Often higher management is unaware of the competence that exists in the organization, and important strengths may be unknown to it. Through collaboration, consultants can help clients to discover and mobilize their own resources. Also, collaboration allows the consultant to refrain from undertaking tasks that the client is able and willing to do, thus saving the consultant's time and reducing the cost of the assignment.

(3) Collaboration is essential if the client is to be fully associated with the definition of the problem and with the results of the assignment. Consultants often emphasize that their client must "own" the problem and its solution. The reason is that people often reject changes proposed or imposed from the outside. By collaborating on a solution the client is more likely to be committed to it and will not put all the responsibility on to the consultant. This commitment will be not only rational, but also emotional. We all know that we tend to have different attitudes towards projects into which we have put long hours of hard work and a lot of energy, and where we have seen solutions emerging from our thinking and debates with other people, and to solutions that we are asked to adopt without ever having been consulted on them.

(4) Most importantly, if there is no collaboration, there can be no transfer of knowledge or learning on either the client's or the consultant's side. Learning does not occur by defining terms of reference, and accepting or rejecting a final report, but by joint work at all stages of an assignment, from problem definition and diagnosis, to implementation and the assessment of results. In a consulting context, learning is embedded in collaboration.

A knowledge-based relationship

The basis of the consultant–client relationship is knowledge transfer, both to client from consultant and to consultant from client. While this appears to be widely recognized, a general statement about knowledge transfer in a consulting contract or on the consultant's web page is not enough. The reality may be totally different if no specific effort is made to transfer and share knowledge when working together.

Both parties have to pursue joint development and transfer of knowledge as one of the key purposes of the collaboration. This requires an understanding of the processes of knowledge creation and transfer, and of their driving and impeding forces, as well as appropriate allocation of time and responsibilities.

For example, a consultant may be hired to install a sophisticated model for financial risk management and show the client how to input data to get answers. However, if the client does not understand and appreciate the underlying theories, principles, criteria, formulas, caveats and limitations of the model, i.e. the model is viewed as a "black box", his or her understanding of risk management may not improve at all. The client may rely on the model in situations where it cannot be applied or may draw wrong conclusions from the data obtained. Conversely, if the consulting firm does not take the trouble to find out how the model is used and works in each client's context, it misses an opportunity to learn from experience and hence to improve its services and develop new services and products.

In *Developing knowledge-based client relationships*,[1] Ross Dawson suggests that professional firms should examine where they stand "on the spectrum between providing black-box services and knowledge transfer". He points out that "clients' perception of the highest value creation will gradually shift towards knowledge elicitation – helping them to develop their own knowledge – as a source of far higher value than black-box services or even communicating existing knowledge". However, there are contexts where clients may be satisfied with acquiring a commoditized consulting product (e.g. a diagnostic instrument) and using it without learning the underlying concepts and theories. Black-box solutions cannot be discarded, but their choice should be explicitly discussed and agreed.

Relationship of trust

Collaboration and knowledge-sharing generate trust. In *The trusted advisor*,[2] David Maister, Charles Green and Robert Galford explain why trust is the most important and critical issue in the consultant–client relationship. Unless the consultant becomes a trusted adviser, the breadth of business issues he or she will be asked to deal with and the depth of the personal relationships he or she will be able to develop with the client will remain limited. This breadth will increase as the personal relationship deepens from (1) a service-offering-based relationship, through (2) a needs-based, and (3) a relationship-based, to (4) a trust-based one. It would not be reasonable to claim and expect the client's full trust at the very beginning of the relationship. Trust must be earned, and this means that the client must be convinced that the consultant merits trust and will not betray it. By trusting an adviser the client obviously takes a personal risk.

Earning the full trust of managers and entrepreneurs is not easy, but it is worth the effort. Indeed, such a relationship can be very rewarding for the consultant.

Once he or she is a client's trusted adviser, the relationship with the client becomes less formal and more open, at times even privileged. The consultant and the client can deal with issues, including delicate personal and confidential business issues, that would not even be mentioned in other circumstances. Less effort is needed to obtain new work and the client is likely to recommend the consultant without hesitation to business contacts. A consultant who demonstrates sincere interest, an understanding of the client's problems and concerns, and flexibility can expect the same from the client. The trusted adviser's status is an important part of the consultant's intellectual capital, and it would be foolish to waste it. Some attributes of trusted advisers are listed in box 3.3.

Box 3.3 Attributes of trusted advisers

Trusted advisers

1. Tend to focus on the client rather than themselves. They have
   - enough self-confidence to listen without prejudging,
   - enough curiosity to inquire without supposing an answer,
   - willingness to see the client as co-equal in a joint journey,
   - enough ego strength to subordinate their own ego.
2. Focus on the client as an individual, not as a person fulfilling a role.
3. Believe that a continued focus on problem definition and resolution is more important than technical and content mastery.
4. Show a strong competitive drive aimed not at competitors, but at constantly finding new ways to be of greater service to the client.
5. Consistently focus on doing the next right thing rather than on aiming for specific outcomes.
6. Are motivated more by an internal drive to do the right thing than by their organization's rewards and dynamics.
7. View methodologies, models, techniques and business processes as means to an end. They are useful if they work and are to be discarded if they don't; the test is effectiveness for *this* client.
8. Believe that success in client relationships is tied to the accumulation of quality experiences. As a result, they seek out (rather than avoid) client contact, and take personal risks with clients rather than avoid them.
9. Believe that both selling and serving are aspects of professionalism. Both are about proving to clients that you are dedicated to helping them with their issues.
10. Believe that there is a distinction between business life and private life, but that both are very personal. They recognize that refined skills in dealing with other people are critical in business and in personal life; the two worlds are often more alike than they are different, and for some, they overlap to an extraordinary extent.

Source: Adapted from D. Maister, C. Green and R. Galford: *The trusted advisor* (New York, The Free Press, 2000), p. 13.

The benefits to the client of a trust-based relationship with a consultant are obvious. In business and management, it is crucial to have colleagues and partners who can be trusted. The considerable risks involved in choosing and employing consultants are thus minimized. Trusted advisers can be involved in difficult and delicate issues and are likely to be easily accessible. Their advice is often available at short notice and will be provided informally if necessary. Conversely, clients know that their trusted advisers will not accept assignments for which they do not feel competent, and will not promise results that cannot be achieved.

3.4 Behavioural roles of the consultant

This section examines the concept of the consultant's behavioural roles (consulting modes), a topic that is very popular in the literature on consulting. It describes, in a condensed form, the most typical and frequent consulting behaviours, how consultants relate to clients, what inputs they make, and in what way and how intensively clients participate. The roles assumed depend on the situation, the client's preferences and expectations, and the consultant's profile.

There is no shortage of descriptions and typologies of consulting roles. We have found it useful to make a distinction between *basic roles*, which include the resource and the process role, and a *further refinement of the role concept*, in which many more roles or sub-roles can be visualized in order to facilitate the understanding of the various intervention modes used in consulting.

Basic roles: the resource role and the process role

In the *resource role* (also referred to as the expert or content role), the consultant helps the client by providing technical expertise and doing something for and on behalf of the client: he or she supplies information, diagnoses the organization, undertakes a feasibility study, designs a new system, trains staff in a new technique, recommends organizational and other changes, comments on a new project envisaged by management, and the like.

Management collaborates with the resource consultant, but this collaboration may be limited to providing information on request, discussing the progress made, accepting or declining proposals, and asking for further advice on implementation. Management does not expect the consultant to deal extensively with the social and behavioural aspects of the change process in the organization, even if the consultant is expected to be aware of these aspects.

In the *process role*, the consultant as an agent of change attempts to help the organization solve its own problems by making it aware of organizational processes, of their likely consequences, and of intervention techniques for stimulating change. Instead of passing on technical knowledge and suggesting solutions, the process consultant is primarily concerned with passing on his or her approach, methods and values so that the client organization itself can

Box 3.4 Why process consultation must be a part of every consultation

The essence of consultation, viewed in its most general sense, is to provide help to a client. Help is often defined in the traditional consultation literature as advice or counsel, generally in response to a question that the client asks. It has become normal to further define such help as a set of recommendations to the client. It is often argued that the consultant's duties are finished when the recommendations have been delivered, and it is up to the client to implement them. If the client does not handle the implementation well, it is the fault of the client. The consultant has collected his or her fee and it is the client's problem from that point on.

What is wrong with this picture?

1. The client may not have adequately formulated the problem and hence the consultant is working on the wrong thing.
2. The consultant may not have sufficient understanding of the personality of the client or the culture of the organization to know whether or not a given set of recommendations is implementable or not.
3. The consultant may not have established a trusting relationship with the client and, therefore, may not be getting the information that would enable him or her to understand the problem in sufficient depth to make workable recommendations.
4. The problem may be of such a nature that the client must solve the problem for him or herself because only the client knows ultimately what will work in his or her organization.
5. The consultation process should train the client in diagnostic and problem-solving skills, not merely provide a solution.

The only way to deal with these five issues is to begin any consultation with "process consultation", in which the primary goal is to establish a helping relationship with the client such that the client and consultant become a team, jointly sharing the diagnostic interventions and responsibility for whatever interventions are implemented.

In this model the client continues to own the problem, but the consultant and client as a team must recognize that figuring out what the problem is, what forces are acting, and what one might do differently is a joint responsibility, not something that the consultant should own. Such joint ownership also forces the client to recognize from the outset that even bringing the consultant into the organization is an intervention and that all so-called "data gathering" activities are themselves major interventions in the organization.

Once the client and consultant have a working relationship in which they trust each other and are working together, it is quite possible to give advice, to confront, to argue, to convince, or whatever else seems appropriate, but the consultation process cannot start out in that mode. Therefore, any consultation must begin with building that helping relationship which is the essence of process consultation.

Author: Edgar H.Schein.

diagnose and remedy its own problems. In various descriptions of process consulting, the organizational behaviour approach comes across loud and clear.

Expressed in simpler terms, while the resource consultant tries to suggest to the client *what* to change, the process consultant suggests mainly *how* to change and helps the client to go through the change process and deal with human and other issues as they are identified and understood. Edgar Schein describes process consultation as "the creation of a relationship with the client that permits the client to perceive, understand and act on the process events that occur in the client's internal and external environment in order to improve the situation as defined by the client".[3] According to Schein, "at the core of this model is the philosophy that the clients must be helped to remain proactive, in the sense of retaining both the diagnostic and remedial initiative because only they own the problems identified, only they know the true complexity of their situation, and only they know what will work for them in the culture in which they live".[4] While any consulting involves some collaboration with the client, the process approach is a collaborative approach par excellence.

Choosing between the basic roles

Some years ago, "pure" resource or expert consulting was quite common. In today's consulting practice, it tends to be used mainly in situations where the client clearly wants to acquire and apply, in one way or another, special technical expertise, and does not want the consultant to become involved in human problems and organizational change. In most situations, the resource and process roles are combined in a complementary and mutually supportive way. This is possible thanks to the increased competence of management consultants: today even technical specialists intervening in a relatively narrow area tend to have some training in the behavioural aspects of organizational change and of consulting, and are keen to help in implementation. On the other hand, the "pure" behavioural scientists, the traditional protagonists of process consulting, have recognized that their ability to help in organizational change would remain limited if they did not improve their understanding of technical, economic, financial and other problems and processes in client organizations. Thus, more and more consultants feel comfortable in both roles.

Nevertheless, there are situations, or phases in assignments, where one or the other approach predominates and is more effective. A consultant may start an assignment in a resource role in order to become acquainted with key data on the client organization and demonstrate to the client that he fully understands what is going on as an expert in the technical field concerned. As time goes on, he may act more and more as a process consultant, involving the client in looking for solutions likely to make effective use of the client's capabilities and to be internalized by the client. He may temporarily switch back to the role of resource consultant to provide missing technical knowledge so that the process of change does not stop.

Conversely, other consultants emphasize that they would start every assignment in the process mode in order to ensure the client's active involvement and develop a fair understanding of the organization's human problems right at the beginning. "It is most necessary early in the encounter because it is the mode most likely to reveal what the client really wants and what kind of helper behaviour will, in fact, be helpful."[5] They would then switch to other roles or models when they feel that this is the right way to proceed.

In choosing a role, the consultant must never forget that it constitutes a "communicating vessel" with the client's role. Both the consultant and the client should feel competent and comfortable in their respective roles and believe that they have made the right choice. No one should try to use a role model that is alien to his or her nature and in which he or she will not be effective. The client may be unaware of the various consulting roles, or may be used to a different consulting style from previous projects. This should be discussed and clarified as early as possible in an assignment.

3.5 Further refinement of the role concept

Reducing the various consulting processes to two basic roles or modes is a simplification that is conceptually useful, but that disregards a number of situational variables. For practical purposes it is instructive to visualize a greater number of consultative roles along a *directive and non-directive continuum*, as suggested by Gordon and Ronald Lippitt and illustrated in figure 3.1. By directive we mean behaviours where the consultant assumes a position of leadership, initiates activity or tells the client what to do. In the non-directive role he or she provides information for the client to use or not. Here again the situational roles are not mutually exclusive and can manifest themselves in many ways in a particular consultant–client relationship. The consultant may find it useful to play two or more compatible roles simultaneously or consecutively, switching from role to role as the relationship evolves. These roles are "spheres of influence" rather than a static continuum of isolated behaviour. Let us examine the different role choices in response to a client's needs.

Advocate

In an advocate role, the consultant endeavours to influence the client. There are two quite different types of advocacy:

- *positional or "contact" advocacy* tries to influence the client to choose particular goods or solutions or to accept particular values;
- *methodological advocacy* tries to influence the client to become active as problem-solver, and to use certain methods of problem-solving, but is careful not to promote any particular solution (which would be positional advocacy).

In this role, the behaviour of the consultant is derived from a "believer" or "valuer" stance on content or a methodological matter.

Figure 3.1 Illustration of the consultant's role on a directive and non-directive continuum

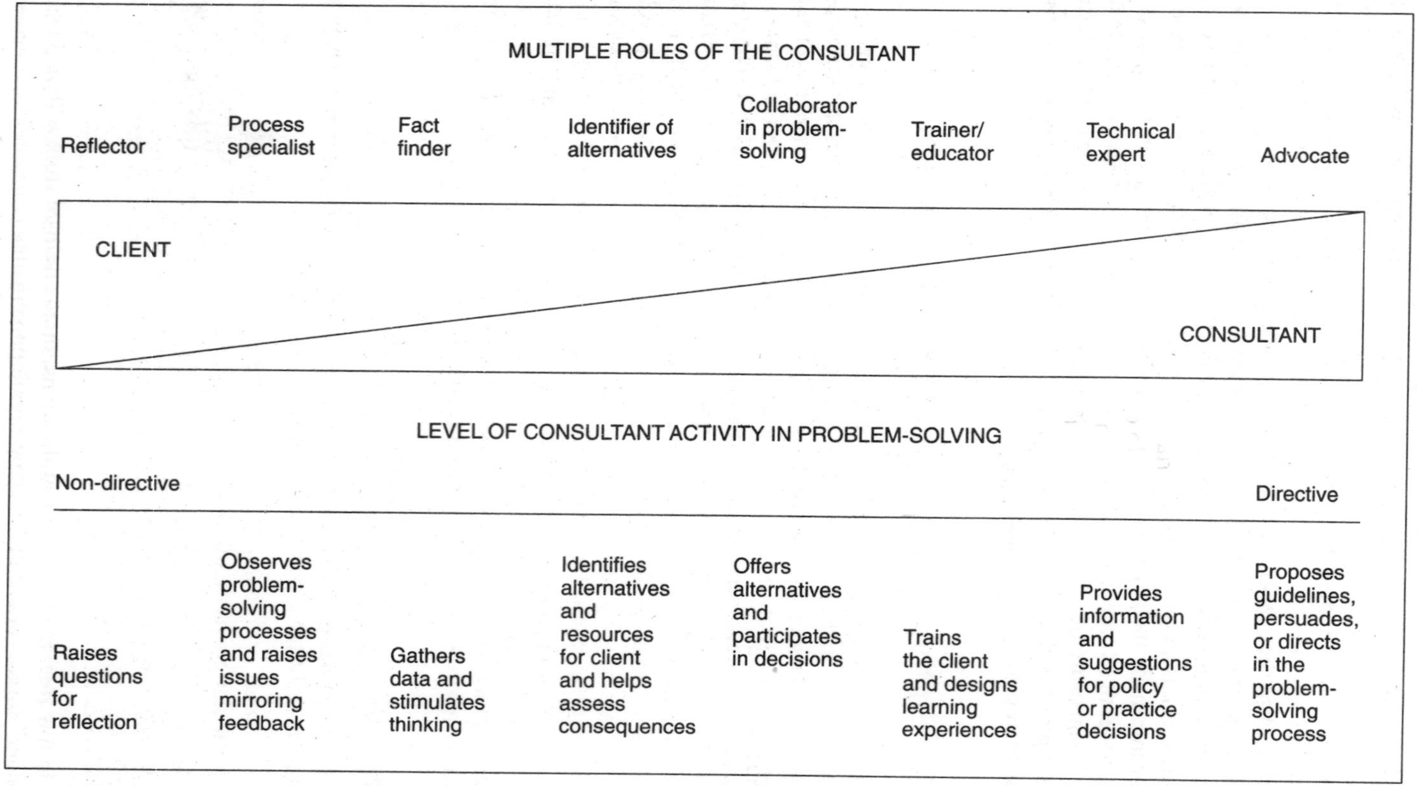

MULTIPLE ROLES OF THE CONSULTANT

Reflector	Process specialist	Fact finder	Identifier of alternatives	Collaborator in problem-solving	Trainer/educator	Technical expert	Advocate

CLIENT

CONSULTANT

LEVEL OF CONSULTANT ACTIVITY IN PROBLEM-SOLVING

Non-directive — Directive

Raises questions for reflection	Observes problem-solving processes and raises issues mirroring feedback	Gathers data and stimulates thinking	Identifies alternatives and resources for client and helps assess consequences	Offers alternatives and participates in decisions	Trains the client and designs learning experiences	Provides information and suggestions for policy or practice decisions	Proposes guidelines, persuades, or directs in the problem-solving process

Source: Adapted from G. Lippitt and R. Lippitt: *The consulting process in action* (La Jolla, CA, University Associates, 1979), p. 31.

Technical expert

One of the roles adopted by any consultant is that of technical specialist or expert. As mentioned above, the traditional role of a consultant is that of an expert who uses special knowledge, skill and professional experience to provide a service to the client. The client is mainly responsible for defining the objectives of the consultation. Thereafter the consultant assumes a directive role until the client is comfortable with the particular approach selected. Later in the relationship the consultant may act as a catalyst in helping to implement the recommendations made. The consultant may be a resource (content) specialist in the client's problem, or a process specialist advising how to cope with a problem and how to implement change. This particular role makes use of the consultant's substantive knowledge.

Trainer and educator

Innovative consultation frequently requires the consultant to carry out periodic or continuous training and education within the client system. In this aspect of the helping relationship, the consultant can suggest the most appropriate learning process, depending upon the situation and the need. The consultant may design learning experiences, or train or teach by imparting information and knowledge directly. This work requires the consultant to possess the skills of a trainer and developer of others' potential.

Collaborator in problem-solving

The helping role assumed by the consultant uses a synergistic (cooperative) approach to complement and collaborate with the client in the perceptual, cognitive and action-taking processes needed to solve the problem. The consultant helps to maintain objectivity while stimulating conceptualization during the formulation of the problem. Additionally, he or she must help to isolate and define the dependent and independent variables that influenced the problem's cause, and will ultimately influence its solution. He or she also assists in weighing alternatives, sorting out salient causal relationships that may affect them, and synthesizing and developing a course of action for an effective resolution. The consultant in this role is involved in decision-making as a peer.

Identifier of alternatives

There are direct costs associated with decision-making. While the value of a decision is dependent upon the attainment of a given set of objectives, in selecting an appropriate solution to a problem the consultant can normally identify several alternatives, along with their attendant risks. The alternatives, together with their economic and other identifiable implications, should be discovered jointly by the client and the consultant. In this helping relationship, the consultant establishes relevant criteria for assessing alternatives and develops cause–effect relationships for each, along with an appropriate set of strategies. In this role, however, the consultant is not a direct participant in decision-making, but a retriever of appropriate alternatives facing the decision-maker.

Fact-finder

Fact-finding is an integral part of any consulting assignment, both for developing a database and for resolving intricate client problems. The consultant's role may even be confined to fact-finding. In this case he or she will assist the client system by choosing the sources of data, using a technique that will get the client more or less involved in gathering and examining data, and presenting data to the client in a way that will show where and why improvements are needed. In this role the consultant functions basically as a researcher.

Process specialist

This is the "pure" process role as described in section 3.4. The consultant focuses chiefly on the interpersonal and intergroup dynamics affecting the process of problem-solving and change. He or she works on developing joint client–consultant diagnostic skills for addressing specific and relevant problems in order to focus on *how* things are done rather than on *what* tasks are performed. Furthermore, the consultant helps the client to integrate interpersonal and group skills and events with task-oriented activities, and to observe the best match of relationships. In this role, an important function of the consultant is to provide feedback.

Reflector

When operating in the mode of a reflector, the consultant stimulates the client to prepare and make decisions by asking reflective questions which may help to clarify, modify or change a given situation. In doing so, the consultant may be an arbitrator, an integrator or an emphatic respondent who experiences jointly with the client those blocks that provided the structure and provoked the situation initially.

3.6 Methods of influencing the client system

Whether the consultant admits it or not, he or she exercises personal influence on the client system in adopting any one of the behavioural roles described in the previous sections. The consultant has to influence people in order to obtain information, gain confidence and respect, overcome passive resistance, enlist collaboration, and get proposals accepted and implemented. This section will therefore review some general methods of exercising personal influence.[6]

Exercising personal influence on the client is not in conflict with a professional approach. The consultant is committed to helping the client to achieve a particular purpose and this may be impossible without influencing certain people. The aim should be to energize and activate the client in the client's own interest, not to manipulate the client in the interest of the consultant. Nevertheless, the consultant must realize that his or her influence on some people may be strong and that exercising this influence engages considerable technical and moral responsibility. This is an important issue of consulting ethics (see also Chapter 6). The consultant will be able gradually to transfer this responsibility to the client by developing the latter's knowledge and problem-solving skills. This will help the client to recognize when and in what sense he or she is being influenced, and reach a judgement on whether there are alternatives.

Various methods are available, and it is difficult to say in advance which one will produce the desired effect. These methods reflect the fact that people's attitudes and decisions have both rational and irrational (emotional) motives, and experience is often the best guide in choosing and combining methods as appropriate. In one case it may be enough to show the client a few meaningful figures and he or she will immediately draw practical conclusions from them. In another case the client may be so impressed by the consultant's personality, which inspires confidence, that he or she will blindly trust the advice received without examining the rationale behind it. Conversely, clumsy and irritating behaviour will make the client suspicious even if the consultant is absolutely right in his or her conclusions.

Demonstrating technical expertise

The consultant should consider whether he or she enters the client organization as a technical expert enjoying prestige or, on the contrary, as someone totally unknown. Demonstration of theoretical knowledge and practical expertise appeals mainly to technically oriented individuals who are themselves experts in the consultant's field. This can be done in informal discussions, such as by passing on information on developments in theory, new techniques and equipment, and successful firms or projects in which the consultant has been personally involved. Technically impressive findings or proposals submitted by the consultant may speak for themselves and influence the client's stance.

Exhibiting professional integrity and sharing knowledge

The consultant's behaviour at work is closely observed by the client, whose attitude can be influenced by the way in which the consultant exhibits commitment, integrity, a methodical approach and efficiency. These qualities can be demonstrated at various stages and aspects of the assignment – in showing self-discipline and perseverance in fact-finding, demonstrating the ability to discover pitfalls about which the consultant was not informed by the client, persisting in looking for a better technique, making rational use of time, handling delicate matters tactfully, and the like. A powerful effect can be achieved if people see that the consultant is sharing knowledge and work methods with them. A sophisticated client quickly recognizes a consultant who is unwilling or unable to share knowledge or is even trying to hide some knowledge (e.g. a decision analysis model) which obviously has an important place in his or her intervention and the advice provided to the client.

Demonstrating empathy with the client

Obtaining the client's confidence is a condition of success in consulting. The client needs to feel that the consultant cares about and enjoys working with him or her, and wants to be as helpful as possible. The consultant's interest in the client's concerns must be genuine and sincere. It must be expressed in deeds, not in flattering words and promises. If the client feels that he or she is regarded and treated as just another income opportunity, the consultant's impact will be considerably weakened even if the proposals made are technically correct.

Using assertive persuasion

This widely applied method uses the force of logical argument to convince other people that what you want them to do is the correct or most effective action to take. As a rule, new ideas or suggestions are put forward together with arguments for and against, as the consultant presents facts or data to support a position. The method is most effective when the consultant is perceived as knowing what he or she is talking about and seen as relatively objective; the consultant should also know enough about the other person's situation to speak to specific needs. However, assertive persuasion tends to be overused in consulting and people often think of it as synonymous with influence.

Developing a common vision

A common vision is a shared picture of where you are headed, what you are trying to accomplish, and why it would be worth while for others to help. Articulating exciting possibilities includes generating images of what the future of the organization could be like if a particular course were followed. In addition, the consultant can influence people by showing enthusiasm for what is to be done and for where that action will take the client. The method tends to be more effective when the consultant must influence a number of people and generate collective commitment to action. It does not work if it is not made clear what people can actually do towards achieving the objective. Common vision tends to be the least utilized mode of influence in consulting.

Using participation and trust

This method implies recognizing and involving others by asking and giving credit for their contributions and ideas, and building on what they propose. This is accompanied by sharing feelings and being open about one's own mistakes, shortcomings and lack of knowledge. The purpose is to develop an atmosphere of collaboration and co-responsibility for achieving a common goal. The other people involved must believe that the consultant's interest in participation and mutual trust is genuine, and that collaboration is the best way to achieve the desired results. Attempts at one-way influence and control should be avoided. Participation is naturally hard to achieve when it is not in the other people's best interest to cooperate. This method is absolutely essential in collaborative consulting styles that emphasize the client's active involvement and "ownership" of the problem, as well as of the solutions representing the final outcome of the assignment.

Using rewards and punishments

Consultants normally do not control the same kinds of rewards and punishments as management in the client organization. Nevertheless, they can influence people by giving or taking away from them something that seems desirable. This could be a public acknowledgement (e.g. in a meeting) of a person's knowledge, achievement or exceptional contribution to the assignment. Enhancing someone's self-esteem is a reward. Omitting to invite someone to a meeting that he or she would probably like to attend, or withholding some information, could be a punishment. Rewards and punishments that do not motivate people, that are out of proportion to the importance of the issue involved, that are chosen arbitrarily, or that create hostile feelings are likely to produce little or an undesirable effect and should be avoided.

Using tensions and anxieties

Although it is not always realized, tensions and anxieties do play a role in consulting. Often, the very presence of the consultant creates tensions because there are speculations about the hidden reasons for his or her presence, and about possible outcomes that could upset the status quo and affect the positions and interests of individuals or groups. The tensions that exist in the organization can be exploited in collecting information to obtain a true picture of the situation. Interdepartmental competition can be used when choosing the unit in which to start applying a new method in order to demonstrate its feasibility to other units.

In generating and strengthening desire for change, it may be useful to explain what would happen to the organization and/or to the individual if the necessary change were sabotaged or delayed, thus creating a state of anxiety. It may be enough to produce data showing that the organization is already or is likely to be in trouble (see also section 4.4).

Here again, a wrongly focused and excessive use of tensions and anxieties will produce negative rather than positive effects. Also, the consultant must be careful not to get entangled in internal power struggles and be perceived as an instrument of one faction.

3.7 Counselling and coaching as tools of consulting

Counselling

Counselling is a method whereby individuals are helped to discover, understand, face and resolve their own personal problems, which may be related to education, health, employment, competence, career, relations with colleagues, family relations and so on. Counselling is often thought of as an intervention that is very different from management and business consulting. Yet there is tremendous potential for using counselling as a tool of consulting, especially in helping individuals or groups to overcome personal difficulties and become more effective as managers and entrepreneurs.

Counselling is necessarily a one-to-one relationship. In the case of small businesses, the person and the business may even be one and the same. A counsellor is consistently concerned in a very personal way with the problems and opportunities facing a particular individual.

The counsellor's aim should be to help his or her personal client rather than the organization, if their interests do not coincide, and it is perfectly possible for the person being counselled to decide to leave the organization or close down the business as the result of an effective counselling process. However, a more frequent and typical result of personal counselling is a client who feels empowered, more self-confident and more independent in pursuing personal objectives and reconciling personal and organizational objectives. It may be not too much of an exaggeration to suggest that the best evidence of an effective counselling relationship is when the client denies that the counsellor has had any role at all in the successful resolution of his or her difficulties.

An effective counsellor is above all a good listener. All too often managers need most of all someone who will listen to them in an understanding way. They may be afraid of the people who are above them in the hierarchy, while those who are below them are afraid of them in their turn. In some organizations, honest admission of confusion and uncertainty is regarded as a sign of incompetence or weakness, and few managers are fortunate enough to have friends outside the organization who have the time or the ability to listen to them. A consultant who has been called in to what appears to be a traditional consulting assignment may find himself or herself in the position of having to be a counsellor to a lonely and distressed person. It is important not to regard time spent in this way as a distraction from the main business: it may well be the most important contribution that an outsider can make.

Good listening in itself is not as simple as it might appear, but there is more to counselling than sympathetic listening. A counsellor is clearly more of a process facilitator than a specialist resource, whose task is to help the client to think through his or her personal situation, difficulties, priorities, and options, and the advantages and disadvantages of each, and then decide to act. Not only should the counsellor not propose solutions to the client, but he or she may not even participate too actively in the process of problem identification. The counsellor should rather help the client to identify his or her own problems, and the solutions to them, by asking questions, listening, and being supportive and encouraging. At the same time he or she must be scrupulously neutral in regard to what the client decides to do, since the objective is to develop the client's ability to perform better in every way, and not merely to advise him or her what to do in a given situation. The fundamental task of the counsellor is to help clients to think things through, to organize their own approach to thinking about their work and perhaps their life in general.

The counsellor must have a genuine desire to put himself or herself out of business by enabling the client to perform effectively without further counselling. Personal development of this sort obviously requires very different skills and, possibly, a different order of responsibility from those normally required of a consultant. A counsellor may need no particular management skills or experience, and such skills can even be a disadvantage, since he or she may be tempted to make technical suggestions to the client rather than letting the client come up with his or her own ideas. The client will be more likely to expect such suggestions and be diffident about putting forward ideas if he or she knows that the counsellor is an expert in the topic at hand.

Because the task is so personal, and so all-embracing, it is easy for counselling sessions to evolve into unstructured conversation. Like any consultancy, counselling almost always involves a series of meetings, and it is important to ensure that the client has a sense of progress from one session to another. One way of doing this is to conclude each session by agreeing on certain tasks that the client, and perhaps the counsellor, will complete before the next session. It is important not to allow assignments of this kind to turn into instructions which take the decision-making away from the client.

Finally, it is all too easy for the client to become dependent on his or her counsellor. This is exactly what must not happen, since the objective is to enable clients to be independent. A good counsellor must "move in" and establish a trusting relationship with the client, so that he or she draws out the client's feelings and all the information that may be relevant, but the counsellor must also learn how to "move out" and leave the client at the end of the process. At the beginning it may seem difficult to create the necessary trust, but in the end breaking away is often even more difficult. An effective counsellor is able to do both.

Coaching

Some professional groups refer to "coaching", by which they mean individualized and non-directive assistance to people to discover and realize their full potential, set and reach better goals, become more self-confident, and overcome various personal problems and barriers to performance and achievement. The basic philosophy of coaching is very close to counselling.

Box 3.5 The ICF on coaching and consulting

The International Coaching Federation defines coaching as a form of consulting. However, coaches do not work on "issues" or tell people what to do. They help clients to understand and enhance their potential, set personal and professional goals, and move ahead in implementing them.

Expertise
Coaches are experts in the coaching process and may not have specific knowledge of a given subject area or industry. Where coaches have expertise in other areas, they may use it to facilitate the coaching process. Coaches do not use this particular expertise to diagnose, direct, or design solutions for the client.

Relationship
Relationship is the foundation of coaching. The coach and client intentionally seek to develop a relationship characterized by a growing and mutual appreciation and respect for each other as individuals. This relationship is not an adjunct to or by-product of the coaching, nor is it based on the client's position or performance.

Use of information
In coaching, information drawn from the client is used by the coach to promote the client's awareness and choice of action. This information is not used to evaluate performance or produce reports for anyone but the person being coached.

Scope
Coaching has the freedom and flexibility to address a wide variety of personal and professional topics. In any given coaching relationship, coach and client alone determine the scope of their work. Coaching is not necessarily restricted to a narrowly defined issue nor is its scope determined in any other way.

Contribution to results
In coaching, any contribution the coach makes to producing the client's desired outcome is through ongoing interaction with the client. The coach's role does not include producing a contracted product or result outside of the coaching sessions.

Ongoing impact
Coaching is designed to provide clients with a greater capacity to produce results and a greater confidence in their ability to do so. Clients should leave coaching with a perception that they will be able to produce similar results in the future without a coach.

Source: International Coaching Federation (www.coachfederation.org), visited on 19 Mar. 2002.

Box 3.5 contains the International Coaching Federation (ICF) definition of the relationship between coaching and consulting. Coaching can be practised in various ways by professional coaches, or by managers, supervisors, human resource specialists, consultants and others who have acquired coaching skills and are willing to act as coaches for their peers and junior colleagues.

Consultants may coach either their clients or their colleagues within the consulting firm. If a partner, team leader or practice leader acts as a coach, he or she will obviously relate the coaching to the work context and focus on helping colleagues to cope with various issues involved, such as stress, work organization, tackling new tasks, dealing with clients, learning, knowledge-sharing and collaboration within the team, professional ethics, harmonizing personal life and professional goals, and others. In any event, the purpose and scope of coaching have to be agreed between the coach and colleagues or clients who wish to be coached.[7]

---

[1] R. Dawson: *Developing knowledge-based client relationships: The future of professional services* (Boston, MA, Butterworth-Heinemann, 2000), pp. 208–209. Thought-provoking reading for consultants.

[2] D. Maister, C. Green and R. Galford: *The trusted advisor* (New York, The Free Press, 2000). Essential reading for consultants! See also I. H. Buchen: "The trusted advisor revealed", in *Consulting to Management*, June 2001, pp. 35–37.

[3] E. Schein: *Process consultation revisited: Building the helping relationship* (Reading, MA, Addison-Wesley, 1999), p. 20.

[4] Ibid., p. 20.

[5] Ibid., p. 21.

[6] The description of assertive persuasion, common vision, participation and trust, and rewards and punishments is adapted from Chapter 8 in F. Steele: *The role of the internal consultant: Effective role shaping for staff positions* (Boston, MA, CBI Publishing, 1982), which refers to a model developed by R. Harrison and D. Berlew. See also T. E. Lambert: *Power of influence: Intensive influencing skills at work (People skills for professionals)* (London, Nicholas Brealey, 1997).

[7] See, for example, an online management and leadership consultancy programme PracticeCoach® (www.practicecoach.com.ai/content/what.html), visited on 19 Mar. 2002.

4 CONSULTING AND CHANGE

Change is the raison d'être of management consulting. If diverse consulting assignments have any common characteristic, it is that they assist in planning and implementing change in client organizations. In Chapter 1, organizational change was mentioned as one of the fundamental and generic purposes of consulting. Organizational change, however, is full of difficulties and pitfalls. In managing change, consultants and clients tend to repeat the same mistakes. Often the very behaviour of those who strive to make changes generates resistance to change and brings the whole process to a standstill. The need for change is recognized, yet there is no change. To avoid this, every management consultant needs to be aware of the complex relationships involved in the change process, and must know how to approach various change situations and help people to cope with change.

This chapter is particularly important for understanding the nature and methods of consulting and of the consultant–client relationship. Throughout the chapter the consultant's point of view and intervention methods will be emphasized. However, they will be reviewed in the wider context of changes occurring in society, in organizations and in individuals, and related to the managers' roles in initiating and managing organizational change. The chapter provides some notions of the theory of organizational change, and also practical guidelines for planning and implementing changes.

4.1 Understanding the nature of change

The concept of change implies that there is a perceptible difference in a situation, a person, a work team, an organization or a relationship, between two successive points in time. How does this difference occur, what are its causes, and what does it mean to a manager or a consultant? To answer these and similar questions, we will first look at the various levels and areas of change, and at the relations between them.

Environmental change

There is nothing new about change: it has always been a feature of the very existence and history of the human race. Without change there is no life, and human efforts to obtain better living conditions imply coping with change. There is a new phenomenon, however: the unprecedented depth, complexity and pace of technological, social and other changes occurring at present. Today's organizations operate in an environment that is continually changing. The ability to adapt to changes in the environment has become a fundamental condition of success and survival in business.

It is not the purpose of this chapter to analyse current development trends or predict future changes in the business and social environment. Other publications are available that attempt to do this from various angles. They show that today the processes of change concern all aspects of human and social life, both nationally and internationally.

In a particular business or other organization, the practical question is what to regard as its external environment. This question is increasingly difficult to answer. Often managers are totally perplexed when they realize that their organization can be affected by forces – economic, social or political – which they would previously never have considered when making business decisions. Competition can come from sectors and countries that in the past were never thought of as potential competitors. New sources of finance and new ways of mobilizing resources for business development and restructuring have required profound changes in corporate financial strategies. New information and communication technologies have permitted many new ways of doing business and running complex organizations that were unthinkable with old technologies. Environmental considerations, increased mobility of people and changing social values have created new constraints and new opportunities for decision–makers responsible for running business firms.

This is where management consultants can step in to render an invaluable service to their clients. Making clients aware of the complexity and dynamics of environmental changes and of new opportunities provided by them, and helping them to react to these changes promptly and effectively, is currently the most important and forward-looking area of management consulting.

Organizational change

Organizations are continually forced to adapt to the environment within which they exist and operate, and to react to new environmental changes, constraints, requirements and opportunities. But more than that, businesses and other organizations also generate changes in their external environment, for example by developing and marketing new products and services that capture a significant part of the market, launching and publicizing products that will change consumer taste, or pioneering new technologies that become dominant and change the shape of whole industrial and service sectors. Thus they modify the business environment, both nationally and internationally.

Change can affect any aspect of an organization. It may involve products and services, technologies, systems, relationships, organizational culture, management techniques and style, strategies pursued, competencies, performances, or any other feature of a business. It can also involve the basic set-up of the organization, including the nature and level of business, legal arrangements, ownership, sources of finance, international operations and impact, diversification, and mergers and alliances with new partners.

Change in people

The human dimension of organizational change is a fundamental one. For it is the behaviour of the people in the organization – its managerial and technical staff, and other workers – that ultimately determines what organizational changes can be made and what real benefits will be drawn from them. Business firms and other organizations are human systems above all. People must understand, and be willing and able to implement, changes that at first glance may appear purely technological or structural, and an exclusive province of higher management, but which will affect the working conditions, interests and satisfaction of many other people.

In coping with organizational change, people have to change, too: they must acquire new knowledge, absorb information, tackle new tasks, upgrade their skills, give up what they would prefer to preserve and, very often, modify their work habits, values and attitudes to the way of doing things in the organization.

It is important to recognize that this requirement relates to everyone in an organization, starting with the most senior manager. Those who want their subordinates and colleagues to change must be prepared to assess and change their own behaviour, work methods and attitudes. This is a golden rule of organizational change.

But how do people change? What internal processes bring about behavioural change? Many attempts have been made to describe the change process by means of models, but none of these descriptions has been fully satisfactory. Different people change in different ways, and every person has particular features that influence his or her willingness and ability to change. The influence of the culture in which a person has grown up and lived is paramount, as will be explained in Chapter 5.

A useful concept of change in people was developed by Kurt Lewin.[1] It is a three-stage sequential model, whose stages are referred to as "unfreezing", "changing" and "refreezing".

Unfreezing postulates a somewhat unsettling situation as it is assumed that a certain amount of anxiety or dissatisfaction is called for – there must be a need to search for new information if learning is to take place. Conditions that enhance the unfreezing process usually include a more than normal amount of tension leading to a noticeable need for change – for example, an absence of sources of information; removal of usual contacts and accustomed routines; and a lowering of self-esteem among people. In some instances, these preconditions for change are present before the consultant arrives on the scene. In other instances, the need for change is not perceived and has to be explained if unfreezing is to occur – for example, by making it clear what will happen if the organization or the person does not change.

Changing, or moving towards change, is the central stage of the model, in which both management and employees start practising new relationships, methods and behaviours. The subprocesses of changing involve two elements:

- *identification*, where the people concerned test out the proposed change, following the external motives presented to them (e.g. by management or a consultant);
- *internalization*, where individuals translate the general objectives and principles of change into specific personal goals and rules; this process may be quite difficult, usually requiring a considerable effort by the person concerned, and a great deal of patience, creativity and imagination on the part of the consultant in assisting the change, to convert the external (general) motives to internal (specific and personal) motives for accepting the change proposed.

Refreezing occurs when the person concerned verifies change through experience. The subprocesses involved require a conducive and supportive environment (e.g. approval by responsible management) and are usually accompanied by a heightening of self-esteem as a result of a sense of achievement derived from accomplishing a task. During the initial phases of the refreezing stage it is recommended that the required behaviour should be continuously reinforced by means of rewards, praise, and so on, to encourage and accelerate the learning process. In the later phases, intermittent or spaced reinforcement will help to prevent extinction of the newly acquired behavioural patterns. Eventually the new behaviour and attitudes are either internalized, or rejected and abandoned.

Change in a particular person takes place at several levels: at the knowledge level (information about change, understanding its rationale), the attitudes level (accepting the need for change and a particular measure of change both rationally and emotionally) and the behavioural level (acting in support of effective implementation of change). Figure 4.1 shows four levels of change: (1) in knowledge, (2) in attitude, (3) in individual behaviour, and (4) in organizational or group behaviour. The relative levels of difficulty and time relationship are also indicated in the diagram. This, however, does not imply that change must always start at the lowest level and proceed to higher levels (see box 4.1).

Change in individuals within an organization is also directly affected by changes in the external environment. This environment is not something that "starts behind the factory gate", but permeates the organization. People "bring the environment with them" and it stays with them when they come to work. Thus, changes occurring in the environment of an organization may facilitate or hamper change in people working within the organization. A frequent problem is that of individuals who are simultaneously exposed to so much change and stress, at work and in their social and family life, that they are not

Figure 4.1 Time span and level of difficulty involved for various levels of change

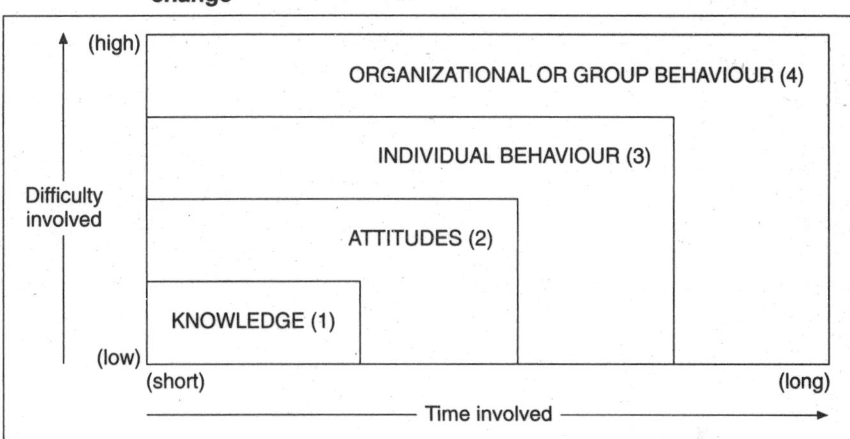

Source: R. Hersey and K. H. Blanchard: *Management of organizational behavior* (Englewood Cliffs, NJ, Prentice-Hall, 1972), p. 100.

Box 4.1 Which change comes first?

The relationship between the various change levels shown in figure 4.1 is an open issue. Some behavioural scientists suggest that the best results will be obtained if the sequence of changing knowledge – attitudes – individual behaviour – group behaviour is fully respected. Others, for either conceptual or practical reasons, do not subscribe to this sequence. Fonviella points out that "trying to change behaviour by changing values and attitudes is unnecessarily indirect ... while attitudes influence behaviour, behaviour influences attitudes".[1] Following a study of several organizational change programmes, Beer, Eisenstat and Spector observe that "most change programmes do not work because they are guided by a theory of change that is fundamentally flawed... The theory that changes in attitudes lead to changes in individual behaviour, and that changes in individual behaviour, repeated by many people, result in organizational change ... puts the change process exactly backward".[2] They conclude that the most effective way to change behaviour is to put people into a new organizational context, which imposes new roles, responsibilities and relationships on them.

[1] W. Fonviella: "Behaviour vs. attitude: Which comes first in organizational change?", in *Management Review* (New York, American Management Association), Aug. 1984, p. 14.

[2] M. Beer, R. A. Eisenstat and B. Spector: "Why change programmes don't produce change", in *Harvard Business Review* (Boston, MA), Nov.–Dec. 1990, p. 159.

able to cope and so break down. On the other hand, many environmental changes, such as an increased penetration of new information and communication technologies into all areas of human life, greatly facilitate the changes that have to be made within particular organizations.

Resistance to change

People are remarkably adaptable, can cope with change and generally accept it as a natural fact of life. Why, then, is change in people so often the bottle-neck of organizational change? Why is "change" such a frightening word for many people?

People resist and try to avoid changes that will leave them worse off in terms of job content, conditions of work, workload, income, relationships, personal power-base, lifestyle and the like. This is understandable. But a great deal of resistance may be met even if the proposed change is neutral, or beneficial to the persons concerned. While there are many reasons for this, psychological and other, the reasons listed in box 4.2 appear to be the most common.

Some of these causes of resistance to change stem from human nature. However, often they are reinforced by life experience, e.g. by negative consequences of past changes. People who have experienced a great deal of unnecessary and frustrating change, such as frequent but useless reorganizations or hectic changes in marketing strategies, or who have been adversely affected by changes presented to them as beneficial, tend to become suspicious about any further changes. This is very important. Causes of trouble are often sought in inherent resistance to change, although they lie elsewhere – for example, in wrong choice of new technology, in failure to explain why change is necessary or in poor coordination of various change interventions. In such cases, resistance to change is only a symptom and the real problem is change management, which is hectic, messy and insensitive to people's concerns and feelings.[2]

There are differences in the character of individuals so far as attitude to change and the ability to cope with change are concerned. In section 4.3 we shall see that some people are natural allies of managers and consultants in preparing and introducing changes in organizations. Unfortunately, but not surprisingly, those who are in greatest need of change often resist it more than anybody else, and require special attention and support. These may be individuals (both workers and managers), groups, organizations, or even whole communities.

Change is not an end in itself

Organizational change is not an end in itself. It is only a means of adjusting to new conditions and sustaining or increasing competitiveness, performance and effectiveness. If an organization can achieve its objectives without disturbing the established product and service lines, practices and relationships, there may be no need for major changes, at least in the short term. Certain changes can be very costly (e.g. if a successful product is phased out and replaced by a new product at the wrong moment). Some managers suffer from chronic "reorganization disease": they feel that to be seen as dynamic, they must periodically reorganize their enterprise or department. Consultants sometimes lack the courage to tell the client that the best solution is to leave things as they are, especially if the work is being done for a client who is obviously eager to make some spectacular changes.

Box 4.2 Reasons for resistance to change

Lack of conviction that change is needed. If people are not properly informed and the purpose of change is not explained to them, they are likely to view the present situation as satisfactory and an effort to change as useless and upsetting.

Dislike of imposed change. In general, people do not like to be treated as passive objects. They resent changes that are imposed on them and about which they cannot express any views.

Dislike of surprises. People do not want to be kept in the dark about any change that is being prepared; organizational changes tend to be resented if they come as a surprise.

Fear of the unknown. Basically, people do not like to live in uncertainty and may prefer an imperfect present to an unknown and uncertain future.

Reluctance to deal with unpopular issues. Managers and other people often try to avoid unpleasant reality and unpopular actions, even if they realize that they will not be able to avoid them for ever.

Fear of inadequacy and failure. Many people worry about their ability to adjust to change, and maintain and improve their performance in a new work situation. Some of them may feel insecure, and doubt their ability to make a special effort to learn new skills and attain new performance levels.

Disturbed practices, habits and relations. Following organizational change, well-established and fully mastered practices and work habits may become obsolete, and familiar relationships may be altered or totally destroyed. This can lead to considerable frustration and unhappiness.

Lack of respect for and trust in the person promoting change. People are suspicious about change proposed by a manager whom they do not trust and respect, or by an external person whose competence and motives are not known or understood.

In a world where technological, social and other changes are occurring at an unprecedented pace and frequency, people and organizations are in need not only of change, but also of relative stability and continuity. Striking the right balance between change and stability, and helping the client to maintain this balance throughout the organization, is one of the vital tasks of the consultant.[3]

4.2 How organizations approach change

Unplanned or planned change?

It is common knowledge that in every organization a great deal of evolutionary, natural change occurs. A typical example is the ageing of equipment and people, which has both problematic aspects (e.g. the need to repair and replace equipment, or to replace managers who have lost their dynamism and drive),

Box 4.3 What is addressed in planning change?

Some typical questions addressed in planning change and choosing strategies of organizational change are:

- What changes are occurring in the environment? What will be their implications for our organization?
- What changes should we foresee in order to achieve our development objectives, improve our performance, increase our share of the market, etc.?
- What undesirable changes will occur in the organization if we do not take timely steps to prevent them?
- What sort of and how much change are we able to manage?
- What sort of and how much change will our people be able to absorb and support? How should we help them to cope with change?
- Should we implement change in stages?
- What will be the relations between various changes that we intend to make? How will they be coordinated?
- Where and how should the change process be initiated?
- How should we manage change? Do we need a consultant? What would be this consultant's role?
- What should be our time horizon and timetable for implementing change?

and positive aspects (technical and managerial competence acquired by years of experience). While most of these changes cannot be kept under full control, it is possible to take preventive measures for avoiding and/or mitigating the negative consequences of evolutionary change.

A great deal of unplanned change is not of an evolutionary nature, but is a fast reaction to a new situation. A manufacturing firm may be compelled by competition to cut its prices, or a strike may force an organization to increase wages. Such changes are *adaptive* or *reactive*. The organization has not planned the change and, quite often, has not foreseen its necessity until very late. The organization makes the change to avoid a crisis, or in order not to lose an unexpected new opportunity that has just emerged.

It is a sign of poor management if the only changes that occur in an organization are inevitable and unplanned changes. Where this happens, it is a demonstration of reluctance or inability to look ahead and prepare the organization to react to future opportunities and constraints. While planning cannot completely eliminate the need for unplanned changes, it helps the organization to prepare itself for changes that can be anticipated, and minimizes the number of situations where hasty (and costly) changes have to be made in an atmosphere of panic.

More than that, the planning of change enables the organization to be proactive and "create the future", e.g. to shape its environment and its own profile and outperform competition by creating new products and services, influencing consumer taste and demand, restructuring the key organizational processes before competition does so, and pushing for changes in the regulatory environment.

The last question in box 4.3 is crucial. Both organizations and individuals can absorb only a limited amount of change over a certain period of time, and this absorptive capacity is different in different countries, organizations and individuals. Conversely, delaying urgent changes can lead to crises and hopeless situations. The pacing of change is therefore one of the main skills needed in planning and implementing change.

Imposed or participative change?

In business practice, a great deal of change is *decided and imposed* on the organization by management. After all, by acting in this way management assumes its basic responsibility. However, change imposed from a position of authority may cause unhappiness and resentment, in particular if the people affected by such changes believe that they should have been consulted, or at least informed well in advance and in a proper way.

If change is initiated from a position of power and imposed upon people, it could be inherently volatile; it could disappear with removal of the power source, or in the absence of appropriate punishments and sanctions. Yet we cannot say that every imposed change is bad. There are emergency situations where discussion is impossible and delaying a decision would be detrimental. There are regulatory and administrative measures that will affect many people, but that are of minor importance and do not justify long discussion and consultation. Imposed change is considered to be more effective when dealing with dependent rather than independent people. In general, the attitude to imposed change is very much influenced by culture, education, access to information, and the existence of alternatives.

A manager should think twice before deciding to impose a change. He or she should do it only if firmly convinced that there is no alternative – if, for example, he or she has been unable to gain the support of the group, yet feels that change is inevitable. Still the manager should always take the trouble to explain the reasons for choosing to impose a change.

People in different national and organizational cultures do not feel the same way about change that is presented to them as an accomplished fact, and imposed on them without prior discussion or consultation. However, *the trend towards participative change* is ever more pronounced in most parts of the world. People want to know what changes are being prepared, and to be able to influence changes that concern them. Managers and administrators are increasingly aware of this fundamental demand and react to it by adopting a more participative approach to change.

A participative change process may be slower and more time-consuming and costly than imposed change, but it is considered to be long lasting. It helps to prevent resistance and generates commitment to change. In addition, participative change helps management to draw on people's experience and creativity, which is difficult to do if change is imposed.

There are *different levels and forms of participation* in the change process, depending on the nature and complexity of the change itself, on the maturity, coherence and motivation of the group, and on the relationship between management and employees (see box 4.4). At the *first level*, the manager or the consultant informs the staff concerned about the need for change and explains the specific measures that are being prepared. At the *second level*, consultation and discussion about change take place in the course of the change process – in identifying the need for change, proposing the specific changes to be made and checking whether people would react negatively to the measures proposed. Suggestions and criticism are solicited and management may reconsider its plan for change on the basis of these. At the *third level*, management seeks the active involvement of the staff in planning and implementing change by inviting them to participate in defining what to change and how to do it, and in putting the agreed changes into effect. This is normally done through workshops, task forces, special committees and projects, staff meetings and other methods reviewed in section 4.5.

In many situations change requires *negotiation*. This takes place when two or more individuals or groups discuss together the changes to be made and the benefits and costs to the parties involved. This may lead to a compromise that neither party considers to be an ideal solution by its own standards. However, the probability of support by those concerned, and hence the probability of implementing the agreement reached, will be much higher.

There are changes that require *negotiation between management and the representatives of employees*, who may be trade union or other representatives. Issues requiring nogotiation may be determined by law, through collective bargaining, or by any other joint agreement, formal or informal. Managers and consultants should be particularly alert to the desirability of a dialogue with employees' representatives, not only in cases explicitly stipulated by laws or formal agreements, but also in preparing any changes that may affect the interests of people in the organization and where employee support may be essential.

Frequent and sincere dialogue with employees and their representatives is the best means for preventing organized large-scale resistance to change, expressed through strikes and similar forms of protest against decisions taken or planned by management. Clearly, resistance to change is not the only reason for strikes. It is, however, a frequent reason, and it can often be traced back to management's failure to consult and inform people, explain why change cannot be avoided, seek alternative solutions, and implement change in ways that minimize hardship to the people concerned.

Finally, in thinking of participative approaches, the perspective is often limited to employee participation, direct or through their representatives. This perspective may prove to be narrow and may miss important inputs. It is useful to think of a wider circle of "stakeholders", i.e. organizations and people having various stakes in the organization in question. Customers are important stakeholders, and learning from them in preparing important changes is essential. Other

Box 4.4 Ten overlapping management styles, from no participation to complete participation

(1) **None:** There is no participation or involvement. People express surprise if the "boss" asks them a problem-solving question. People are paid to "work", not "think". Managers "send down" decisions.

(2) **Persuasive autocracy:** There is some recognition that an effort to "sell" the project or the solution has been considered and will be incorporated "if there is time and money".

(3) **Consultative:** Responsible managers ask people many questions and seek to obtain as many ideas as possible, but establishing criteria, weightings and details are left entirely to managers.

(4) **Reactive control:** The organizations involve others in measuring, comparing and assessing the performance of a satisfactory system. Citizen groups, regulatory boards, peer review, and so on, are means whereby participation is obtained. Policy formulation matters arise only occasionally.

(5) **Bargaining:** More adversarial or at least structured formal involvement is built into normal operations.

(6) **Anticipatory control:** The organization consciously scans the horizon to become aware of possible future occurrences. Groups are allowed to report intelligence that could indicate developments. They can also develop alternatives for responding and "controlling" the future.

(7) **Joint determination:** Although decisions are usually joint, there is a relatively continuous interchange of ideas among those charged with the responsibilities for operating a system and those working in it. Management operates this way because it thinks it is desirable, and workers have no assurance of its continuation. Most other stakeholders may not be included in the participatory effort.

(8) **Supportive collaboration:** Efforts are likely to be more formalized, with some decision responsibilities spelled out (for example, advisory group, citizens' commissions).

(9) **Permanent work groups:** Employees and managers meet regularly (usually during working hours) and seek to solve all types of problems that emerge in any area of concern.

(10) **Complete self-determination:** A joint worker/management board of directors or several joint groups share key decision-making responsibility (budgets, new products, acquisition and divestiture, personnel policies and practices, and so on).

Source: G. Nadler and S. Hibino: *Breakthrough thinking: The seven principles of creative problem solving* (Rocklin, CA, Prima Publishing, 1994), pp. 283–284.

stakeholders include people and authorities in the local community, suppliers of equipment, systems and raw materials, banks and other providers of financial services, and so on. Not only can they provide useful advice, but they are likely to make contributions reflecting the nature and importance of their stakes.

Managing the change process

Change requires *leadership*, and it is natural that this should be provided by the managers who are principally responsible for running the organization. This leadership is necessary even if an important role in the change process is assigned to a consultant and if the approach taken is highly participative. If senior management shows no interest and the handling of particular changes is relegated to lower management or a functional department, this signals to the organization that management has other priorities and does not care much about the changes that are being prepared.

It is, of course, understandable that management must deal both with restructuring, reorganization, launching new products, mergers with other companies and similar major change measures and processes, and with the routine everyday activities of the organization. There may be competition for scarce resources: some key people may be wanted both for preparing a major change and for running current business. A consultant can be used to facilitate the manager's task, but not to manage change on the manager's behalf.

This being said, management has to determine the specific change measures requiring its leadership, and decide on the intensity and style of its direct involvement. The complexity of the changes that are being prepared, and their importance to the organization's future, are key criteria. In a large organization, senior managers cannot be personally involved in all changes, but there are certain changes which they must manage personally, or for which they must find a suitable way, explicit or symbolic, of providing and demonstrating support. Reinforcing messages from the leaders are a key stimulus in a change effort.

The style of leadership should be consistent with the organizational culture, the approach to change that has been chosen, the urgency of the changes to be made and the sophistication of the people involved. Thus, a directive style of leadership will be appropriate for situations of urgency and a relatively unsophisticated and inexperienced audience. In contrast, a low-profile delegating style can be used if responsibility can be given to followers who understand the framework within which the changes need to be planned and put into effect.[4]

The role of innovators and change agents

A change effort requires *a successful start*. Making a correct decision about what to change and assigning responsibilities are not enough. There must be people who have critical and innovative minds, enjoy experimenting, can visualize the future, believe that change is possible, and influence others, not by talking about change, but by demonstrating what can be achieved. These innovators, prime movers, champions or intrapreneurs, as they are sometimes called, may be in managerial jobs, but equally may be design engineers, marketing specialists, project coordinators, experienced workers, supervisors, and others.

Organizations that are keen to change must *encourage innovation, experiments and entrepreneurship*. To management this means not only tolerating departures from routine and tradition, and accepting that this entails some risk, but deliberately employing innovators, giving them some freedom of action, observing their work, and referring to their example in showing what the organization is able to achieve.

Innovative and entrepreneurial individuals and teams often play a prominent role in successful organizational change. They are the organization's principal *change agents*, and it is often in their units that change will start. Some of them will become managers of new units responsible for new product lines or services, coordinators of change projects, or trainers and internal consultants helping other individuals and groups to make the necessary changes.

There are two basic types of change agent: those whose interest is and remains predominantly technical, and who may produce excellent technical ideas without being able to convert them into business opportunities; and those who are mainly entrepreneurs and leaders, and can help to generate and implement changes that require the active involvement of many people, individually or in groups.

A strategy for organizational change may rely entirely on internal capabilities and on managerial and specialist staff members who can play the role of change agents. An alternative is to bring in a change agent from outside as a consultant. This is an important managerial decision affecting the whole approach to the change process. The consultant will not only be contributing technical competence and an alternative viewpoint, but, as we know, will be influencing, by his or her presence and by action taken (or not taken), the behaviour of those concerned in change. The consultant may well influence the behaviour of the very person who has invited him or her. The main factors to consider are:

- the consultant's profile (knowledge, experience and personality: he or she must be acceptable to and respected by people who are being helped to change);
- the mode of consulting to choose in order to assist change (as discussed in Chapter 3, there are various modes; the question is, which mode is likely to generate the desired effects in a particular human system).

Organizational culture supportive of change

It is easier to keep pace with environmental change and generate effective changes from within if change has a prominent place in the organizational culture and if it is not handled as something exceptional, requiring a special campaign and special arrangements in every single case.

High-technology companies in electronics and other fields now operate in an atmosphere of constant change, and people understand that this is a salient characteristic of the sector with which they have to live. The required pace of change in many other fields is not as high. Every organization should define what is the necessary and optimum pace of change in its sector, and try to adopt it as a common value shared by management and staff. This helps to balance change and stability, minimize hectic unplanned changes and avoid change for its own sake.

People should know what preoccupies management and where they should focus efforts to improve individual and group performance, in order to avoid dispersion of resources and help the company where it most needs help. However, every interesting idea should be examined, even if it is not in an area defined as a priority.

To value change and meet the requirements of an organization where the pace of change is high, people must know that it pays to have a positive attitude to change and constantly to look for changes from which the organization can benefit. Innovation and creativity can be stimulated by financial rewards, public recognition, promotions, making the job content more interesting, offering training and self-development opportunities, and so on. Conversely, people must be able to see that it does not pay to be conservative and resist innovation and change.

The values, attitudes and collectively held norms that make up organizational culture (see Chapter 5) develop over a number of years and, once established, they are not easy to change. But it is not impossible to influence and eventually to change them. Therefore if organizational culture constitutes the main obstacle to change, or if it does not stimulate change in an environment that is rapidly changing, managers' and consultants' efforts may need to focus on organizational culture first of all.

4.3 Gaining support for change

One of the principal messages of this chapter is that effective change needs the support of the people involved. This can be a very complex matter. Managers and consultants may feel uncertain about their ability to mobilize support for the change envisaged. If errors are made by management, any existing support may be lost and give way to resistance; to redress the situation may then be a delicate task.

Inviting people to participate actively in a change effort at all its stages is generally a useful method for gaining support and reducing resistance. It helps to create an atmosphere in which people feel they are the "owners" of a change proposal: the idea comes neither from the top, nor from an external person, but from within the group. If things go wrong, the group does not seek a culprit from outside, but takes responsibility, examines the causes and willingly helps in redefining the proposals.

Drawing attention to the need for change

There are numerous methods of drawing the attention of individuals and groups to the need for a change (see section 3.6, where various methods of influencing the client system are discussed). However, two proven methods are of particular interest to consultants.

The most effective manner of arousing immediate attention is by making people *anxious*. In special cases the induction of a state of extreme anxiety is undeniably effective – for example, a building will be cleared very promptly if it is reported that a bomb has been placed in it. However, the continued use of the heightened anxiety approach tends to be self-defeating. Recipients eventually ignore the threats, especially if the alleged events do not occur.

Nevertheless, the induction of a low level of anxiety is an effective attention-arousing device which can be sustained over a long period. A particularly successful combination is to use an anxiety state to draw attention to specific needs (i.e. the unfreezing process described in section 4.1) and to follow up by providing a solution that meets those needs.

The second method is called *the two-step information process*. The underlying idea is that change is effectively introduced and accepted as a result of a multiplier effect in the flow of information.

Research findings suggest that the people most likely to experiment and to be influenced by new approaches possess certain characteristics. These individuals, called "isolates", are inclined to be highly technically oriented; to read widely on their chosen subjects; to attend meetings and conferences frequently; and to travel in order to investigate new schemes. They may be considered by their group to be something akin to "cranks", and are not likely to influence other members of their workgroup directly.

Nevertheless, the activities of these technically oriented isolates are observed by a second type of person who possesses characteristics similar to those of isolates but who generally has less time available to experiment and test new methods in any depth, usually owing to widespread interests in other fields. This second type of person, identified as an "opinion-leader", has considerable influence over the group, and even beyond it. In addition to acknowledged technical expertise, this type of person usually has considerable civic and social standing.

Typically, in the adoption of new procedures, the new scheme is first investigated, along with other possible choices, by the isolate and is eventually chosen over other alternatives because of its technical superiority. The opinion-leader then adopts the new idea once he or she is convinced that the isolate has firmly decided on this new approach. Subsequently an "epidemic" phase erupts as the followers of the opinion-leader also adopt the new approach. Therefore, when introducing change a strong case can usually be made for emphasizing the highly technical aspects of the new approach in order to attract and convince both the isolates and the opinion-leaders who, under normal circumstances, should assist in influencing and convincing the other members of the group.

Getting support for specific proposals

Once the audience's attention has been aroused, and interest created in seeking change, then comes the time to develop a desire for the change proposal. In presenting information to support the selection of a given proposal in preference to alternative schemes, it is often useful to mention some negative aspects of the proposed scheme in addition to the more beneficial ones. Similarly, the positive and negative aspects of existing or alternative schemes should also be presented. This technique of explaining all aspects of the case under review is referred to as an "inoculation" effect; it weakens any objections likely to arise at a later date.

An effective manner of presenting information in support of proposal B, which is intended to displace proposal A, is to employ the following sequence:

(1) present a complete listing of all the positive and beneficial aspects of proposal B;

(2) mention the obvious drawbacks associated with proposal B;

(3) describe a comprehensive listing of the deficiencies of proposal A;

(4) indicate the most pertinent positive features of proposal A.

The manager or the consultant should then draw conclusions as to why proposal B should be chosen by listing the benefits to be accrued (i.e. service provided), the effectiveness of the new proposal (i.e. technical and economic superiority) and, if applicable, instances where such a proposal has already been successfully employed.

Personality composition of the audience

Maintaining control of a gathering or crowd of people is difficult at the best of times. When dealing with individuals or small groups, there are sometimes opportunities to use group members as enhancers of the change process. Individuals who are poised, confident and have a certain amount of self-esteem are often able to influence others who lack these characteristics. In turn, individuals with relatively high self-esteem appear to be more influenced by information containing optimistic rather than pessimistic or negative connotations. The consultant should enlist support for the change process from people with high self-esteem by drawing attention to likely optimistic results. These people are then in a position to support the consultant's proposals to the group.

The informal communication network

Communications on a highly topical issue appear to produce a greater and more rapid change in attitude in an audience when the information is "accidentally overheard", or leaked through informal communication networks than when delivered through formal channels. Rumours, which flourish in the absence of formal communications, are usually confined to informal channels ("the grapevine") and can often be countered by appropriate use of the same network. Even a fundamental piece of information, such as a statement that the future of a particular programme or unit is highly uncertain, may affect people's attitudes more if spread informally than if officially issued by management. Occasionally, both formal and informal channels should be combined to reinforce the message.

Handling objections to change

An essential skill for managing and assisting change is the ability to handle objections. Broadly speaking, objectors can be classified as "sharpeners" or "levellers". *Sharpeners* include those people who ask specific, detailed questions concerning the change process. They tend to be genuine objectors who want to be convinced that the change proposal is justified, and are responsive to logical argument. *Levellers* are those who generalize and broaden the issue under review. They are usually difficult to convince as they are often more interested in the form of their objections than in the content.

Objections and resistance to change can be expressed in many different ways. Non-verbal messages, such as gestures, facial expressions, or repeated attempts to avoid discussing the issue with the manager or the consultant, may be significant and tell more than words. In general, whenever a manager or a consultant senses that people object to the change proposed, he or she should help those concerned to express their doubts or apprehensions. The objections should be analysed: they may point to weaknesses of the proposed scheme, show that not enough information was given to people affected by the change, reflect an aversion to the manager's or the consultant's behaviour, or express fear or resistance that will need to be dealt with.

When the consultant has to handle *specific objections*, it is more useful to repeat the objection, put it in writing if appropriate, break it down into component parts, and treat each component as a separate entity rather than attempt to deal with the problem as a whole. It is recommended to commence with the items on which agreement is most likely to be reached and move later to the items causing most disagreement. The consultant should frequently take the opportunity to recapitulate, and to refer to parts of the original objection on which agreement has already been reached, before continuing with new points. Should a total impasse be reached on an issue, it may be helpful to reword the disagreement in objective terms, since the objector may have used highly emotional words originally.

If a point is reached when the consultant does not have the appropriate information to hand, this should be readily admitted and the objector advised that the information will be obtained and transmitted to him or her at a later date. The consultant should not fail to do this.

4.4 Managing conflict

When objections to change become a matter of intergroup conflict, different problems requiring special treatment may arise. This may happen if a group is to give up its activity or work method to adopt one practised by another group. If a group sees itself as threatened, there will be a closing of the ranks and more cohesive action, and the group will become more tolerant of authoritative rule by its chosen leaders. Hostility to other groups is likely to arise, especially if the situation is perceived as a "win–lose" encounter. Communication will become distorted and difficult, as each group will be prepared to admit only the positive aspects of its own argument and the negative aspects of the "enemy's".

Basic strategies to reduce intergroup conflict (box 4.5) include the establishment of goals upon which both groups can agree in order to restore genuine

Box 4.5 How to manage conflict

In planning and implementing change, interpersonal or intergroup conflict may develop for a number of reasons:

- poor communication;
- disagreement on objectives and results to be pursued;
- disagreement on intervention methods used;
- differences over the pace of change;
- resistance to change;
- fear of losing influence and power;
- competition for resources;
- non-respect of commitments;
- refusal to cooperate;
- personality and culture clashes;
- poor performance and inefficiency.

The principal methods of resolving interpersonal conflict were summarized by Gordon Lippitt in the following terms:

Withdrawal: retreating from an actual or potential conflict situation.

Smoothing: emphasizing areas of agreement and de-emphasizing areas of difference.

Compromising: searching for solutions that bring some degree of satisfaction to the conflicting parties.

Forcing: exerting one's viewpoint at the potential expense of another – often open competition and win–lose situation.

Confrontation: addressing a disagreement directly and in a problem-solving mode – the affected parties work through their disagreement.

As a rule, it is advisable to depersonalize conflict by ensuring that the disputants do not sit in judgement over each other, and to focus the conflict on the basic issue by concentrating disagreement on factual grounds. Withdrawal avoids the issue, but the solution may be only provisional; it may be used as a temporary strategy to buy time or allow the parties to cool off. Forcing uses authority and power and can cause considerable resentment; it may be necessary in extreme cases where agreement obviously cannot be reached amicably. Smoothing may not address the real issue, but permits the change process to continue at least in areas of agreement. Compromising helps to avoid conflict, but tends to yield less than optimum results. Confrontation is generally regarded as most effective, owing to its problem-solving approach involving an objective examination of available alternatives and a search for an agreement on the best alternative. Finally, adopting an attitude of one side winning and the other side losing is like pouring gasoline on the fire of conflict.

Source: Gordon Lippitt: *Organizational renewal* (Englewood Cliffs, NJ, Prentice-Hall, 1982), pp. 151–155.

intergroup communication. It may be useful to identify a common "enemy" – thus setting a superordinate goal. Emphasis should be placed on common needs and goals of different groups. If possible, a reward system which encourages effective communication should be introduced. Groups should take part in numerous activities likely to increase empathy and mutual understanding.

4.5 Structural arrangements and interventions for assisting change

Since the manager bears the main responsibility for managing change in his or her organization or unit, he or she may decide to take charge of a specific change effort personally, involving direct collaborators and other staff members as necessary. In many cases, no special structural arrangements are made, and the manager and the staff work out and implement change proposals while simultaneously handling their other duties.

In the practical life of organizations, however, the use of special *structural arrangements* and *intervention techniques* for handling change may be required for certain specific reasons:

(1) The regular organizational structure may be fully oriented towards current business and could not cope with any additional tasks, for technical reasons or owing to a high workload.

(2) Rigidity, conservatism and resistance to change may be strongly rooted in the existing structure, and it would be unrealistic to expect the structure to generate or manage any substantive change.

(3) In certain cases it is desirable to introduce change in steps, or to test it on a limited scale before making a final decision.

(4) In many cases, management has to look for a suitable formula that is easy to understand and will involve a number of individuals and/or groups in a change effort (possibly including staff from different organizational units), clearly establish a case for change, reveal objections and risks, develop and compare alternative solutions, and mobilize support for the solution that will be chosen.

There is a wide range of structural arrangements and intervention techniques for managing and facilitating the change efforts of individuals, groups and whole organizations. This section will review some commonly used arrangements and techniques which can be applied for various purposes and at various stages of the change process.

Many of the techniques for assisting change are derived from behavioural science, and focus on changes in attitudes, values, and individual or group behaviour. However, in recent decades we have witnessed a shift in the technology of planned change. This technology has moved from an emphasis on team-building, intergroup relations and the like to an emphasis on diagnostic and action-planning processes for coping with the total organization and its environment, designing methods for organizational diagnosis, and implementing comprehensive programmes for business restructuring and transformation (see also Chapter 22). Essentially, there has been a growing understanding of the fact that a one-sided approach, as fostered by some behavioural scientists in the past, has limitations and should give way to a comprehensive view of the organization, embracing all organizational factors and subsystems as well as their interaction with the environment.[5]

The experience of companies that have successfully completed challenging change programmes demonstrates the desirability of combining "soft" techniques for stimulating and assisting change (based essentially on a behavioural science approach and aiming to improve people's attitudes to change and enlist their active participation) with "hard" techniques (aimed at ensuring effective problem identification, needs assessment, sequencing, coordination, resource allocation, quality control, follow-up, and other measures, without which even the best-intended and fully participative change effort can turn into total confusion).

The current panoply of approaches, methods and techniques for assisting organizational change is impressive. Many consultants have specific variants or packages of the "classical" change management and performance improvement approaches and techniques: some of these variants are not described in the literature and are available only to clients as proprietary techniques. In other cases, the technique used is a common one, but is presented under a different name. If a consultant proposes to use a specific and not very well-known technique, the client may wish to ask what is unique in the proposed technique and how it relates to the basic and commonly known techniques. In fact, the consultant should take the initiative and give such an explanation when proposing the method to the client.

This chapter is confined to a short review of selected and fairly well-known techniques. For more detailed study, the reader may wish to refer to specialized sources on change management, project management, organizational development, process consulting, or organizational behaviour and psychology. Change management approaches and techniques are also discussed in other parts of this book, especially in Chapters 3, 8, 9, 10, 20 and 22.

Structural arrangements

Structural arrangements are used to provide a suitable (often temporary) organizational setting for a particular change project or effort, and for use of other change management methods.

Special projects and assignments. This is a very popular form. A person or unit within the existing structure is given an additional special task as a temporary assignment. He or she may be given some additional resources for this purpose if existing resources within the current structure are insufficient.

For mobilizing extra resources and taking decisions that are beyond his or her authority, the project manager or coordinator would, of course, turn to the general manager. This is, in fact, a transitional arrangement between a normal and a special structure.

Temporary groups. Task forces, working parties and other similar temporary groups are frequently used, either at one stage of the change process (e.g. to establish the need for change, gather new ideas, determine priorities or develop alternatives), or for planning and coordinating the whole process. The group should pursue a clearly defined purpose.

Selecting the members of a temporary group is an extremely important step. They should be people who can and want to do something about the problem that is the focus of the change. Often they will come from different organizational units, in particular if change efforts focus on processes that cut across boundaries between units. The group should not be too large and its members must have time to participate in group work. Task forces often fail because they are composed of extremely busy people who give priority to running current business before thinking about future change. They also fail if they are dominated by individuals who use their formal authority to impose their views on the group.

Thanks to modern telecommunication technologies, task forces and other temporary groups can also work effectively in geographically dispersed and multinational organizations. Expensive and exhausting travel can be replaced by email, teleconferencing and other distance communication, reserving face-to-face meetings for situations where it is absolutely necessary.

The group should also have a defined life. One possibility is to use the "sunset calendar" – that is, at a predetermined point the group will cease to exist unless there is a management decision to continue it. This may reduce the possibility of the group slowly disintegrating as more and more members absent themselves from meetings.

The group may use a convener. This could be the consultant or somebody designated by management, after discussion with the consultant. The convener is not necessarily the chairperson of the group, but is the person who gets it moving initially. The group may decide that it does not want a regular chairperson and might rotate the role.

As far as possible, the expected output of the group should be specified. It should bear a direct relationship to the problem and be amenable to review.

Meetings. Meetings or workshops, which are used for many purposes, can also be designed to bring about and manage change. The focus of the meeting, as an intervention in support of change, is to enable various individuals to work on the problem face to face. The form of the meeting must be consistent with the organization's culture: where autocratic management prevails and people know that their views are not likely to be taken into account, a meeting to discuss change will achieve very little.

It is important that the manager or consultant involved should establish the appropriate climate. This may mean that the meeting has to be held on "neutral ground", so that none of the parties has any territorial advantage. The role that the consultant will play during the meeting should be clarified as early as possible. That role, essentially, is as facilitator and process observer. The consultant has the advantage of being external, and his or her comments can prevent the group from falling into the trap of complaining about current difficulties without trying to come up with any practical suggestions for improvement. It is also possible to hold meetings without the consultant. When this is to be done, it is even more important that the relative roles and expectations of all those attending should be made clear prior to the meeting.

Experiments. Experiments are used to test a change process or its results on a limited scale, e.g. in one or two organizational units, or over a short time, say several months. For example, flexible working hours or a new bonus scheme may first be applied on an experimental basis in selected departments.

A true experiment involves pre- and post-test control. Two or more units or groups are used, which have the same or very similar characteristics (this may be difficult to achieve and prove scientifically). Data are collected about both groups. A change is then made in one group (experimental group) but not in the other (control group). Once the change has been made, further observations are made and data collected. The data collected in both groups before and after the change are compared. However, as the famous Hawthorne experiments illustrated, it is possible in a field experiment that some other variable is influencing performance.[6]

Pilot projects. A pilot project may be used to check on a limited scale whether a new scheme – perhaps involving considerable and costly technological, organizational or social change – is feasible, and whether adjustments will be necessary before the scheme is introduced on a larger scale. A great deal of information can be drawn from a properly prepared and properly monitored pilot project, and in this way the risks involved in an important new scheme are minimized.

In drawing conclusions from the evaluation of pilot projects, certain mistakes are commonly made. In order to demonstrate that the proposed change is justified and feasible, both managers and consultants tend to pay special attention to pilot projects (e.g. by assigning the best people to it, intensifying guidance and control, or providing better maintenance services). The pilot project is thus not executed under normal conditions, but under exceptionally favourable ones. Furthermore, it is assumed that the conditions under which a pilot project is undertaken can be replicated for a larger programme. Often this is not possible, for a number of reasons. For example, the organization may be unable to provide support services of the same quality to a large-scale activity. Hence, assessment of a successful pilot project should include an unbiased review of the conditions under which it succeeded.

New organizational units. New units may be established if management has made up its mind to go ahead with a change measure (e.g. to develop and start marketing a new service) and decides that adequate resources and facilities must be fully assigned to it from the outset. As a rule, this would be done if the need for change has been well documented, and the importance of the change envisaged justifies an underutilization of resources which may well occur when the unit is first established.

Christensen and Overdorf[7] emphasize that providing extra resources by establishing or acquiring a new organization may be a powerful instrument for coping with organizational inertia and resistance to change. It is often easier to provide new resources than to change established processes and cultural values. For example, to create new capabilites for accelerating and facilitating change, a consultant might advise management to:

- create new organizational structures in which new processes can be developed;
- establish an independent organization to develop the new processes and values required to solve the new problem;
- acquire another organization whose processes and values closely match the requirements of the new task.

Organization development (OD) techniques

Described below are some examples of techniques originally used by behavioural scientists in organization development (OD) approaches and programmes. As mentioned above, these techniques are now generally applied in combination with other techniques, or within comprehensive change management programmes.

Team-building. This intervention is used frequently. Indeed, there are those who contend that it has been overused and abused. In part, the tendency to use this intervention is rooted in the early days of process consultation. Coming from group dynamics, the T-group approach and the sensitivity movement, it is based on an assumption that the fundamental factor in changing individual and organizational behaviour is to get people working together in groups. While this is important, it is by no means the only, or even the chief, type of intervention that should be considered. As with any other intervention, it should be used based on the diagnosed need.

While there are many variations, the team-building approach essentially focuses on how the team functions, rather than on the content area of the team. Slowly and carefully, the problem or task is introduced into the situation, after work on interpersonal relationships has indicated that the climate is appropriate for moving on.

Team-building is not a one-off activity, although some consultants treat it that way. In many organizations, there is a recurring need to engage in team-building activities.

Confrontation. Within most organizations, there is generally competition for limited resources. There may be times when an organization appears to have access to unlimited resources, but these periods do not usually last long. External influences impose limitations and restrictions. Ignoring internal competition for resources merely forces various organizational members and units to devise ways to defeat other elements of the organization. There is thus a need for some kind of confrontation, where individuals must face each other and take action. It can result either in compromise (win–win), or in a situation where one unit or individual wins points at the expense of the other (win–lose). Confrontation is not necessarily negative – it depends on how individuals deal with it.

Confrontation meetings normally employ a structured approach in which selected staff are exposed to: (1) historical and conceptual ideas about change and organizations; (2) preparation of a list of significant problem areas in their own organization or unit; (3) classification of stated problems into categories; (4) development of plans of action to remedy problems; (5) comparison of the action proposals developed; and (6) planning for implementation.

There are cultures where confrontation is seen as negative, and where it is considered impolite and countercultural to force an individual into decision-making. This does not mean that decisions are not made, but they are not made through confrontation. The level of economic development has little to do with this aspect of cultural behaviour, which can be found in countries such as Japan and Malaysia. The consultant must also determine whether there are some situations in which confrontation is inadvisable or inappropriate.

When a decision needs to be made in a non-confronting culture, the consultant can bring about the needed confrontation as an intervention. He or she must do this very cautiously. One approach is to use a third party – that is, the confronting groups or individuals in the organization do not meet face to face. Instead, the consultant engages in what is sometimes called "shuttle diplomacy". This can work effectively as the entry phase of a confrontation intervention, with the plan that the parties will actually meet at a later phase. In other situations, the entire confrontation may be dealt with indirectly.

Feedback. Feeding back data on individual, group and organizational performance can help to bring about change in individual or group behaviour. It is very important to provide feedback. Research and experience tell us that without feedback, data on behaviour and performance may be meaningless. Particularly when an attitude survey is used, it is important that the participants in the survey receive an analysis of the data that they have provided.

The process of feedback must be handled cautiously, because raw data are frequently misunderstood. Also the analysis may prove critical or damaging to some individuals, and in such a situation the results can be anticipated. Obviously, those individuals will attempt to block any movement towards change.

On a positive note, feedback can be extremely helpful. Many people in an organization do not receive sufficient feedback to enable them to assess their own performance or the performance of the organization as a whole. The consultant should plan carefully, so that there will not be an information overload. Care should be taken with both the process and the content of the feedback.

Coaching and counselling. Commonly used interventions to assist change are coaching and counselling (see also section 3.7). They are often used in process consultation where an individual seeks help in improving his or her own performance or interpersonal relationships. The basic method is for the consultant to observe and review individual performance, listen to the client, provide feedback on problems or behavioural patterns that hinder effectiveness and inhibit change, and help the individual to gain self-confidence, acquire new knowledge and skills and change behaviour as required by the changing nature of the job and the organization.

Training and developing people

Training and development of managers and staff can be a powerful technique for change.

- Management workshops, both external and in-house, can be used to sensitize managers and staff to the need for change, to environmental trends and opportunities, to various options available to their organization and to them as individuals, or to performance and other standards already reached elsewhere. Experience has shown that managers can learn a great deal at workshops where other managers describe and discuss specific experiences with organizational change.
- Training can help people to develop the skills and abilities to cope with change effectively, such as diagnostic and problem-solving techniques, planning, project management and evaluation techniques, or communication and group-work skills.
- Tailor-made and paced training can assist the change process at its various stages by providing missing technical information and skills, thus helping managers and staff to proceed to the next step, and overcoming fear and resistance caused by lack of knowledge or of self-confidence.
- Training of "internal" change agents increases the pool of those on whom management can rely in planning and assisting programmes of organizational change.

Training in support of organizational change can be provided by professional trainers, external or in-house, by management and OD consultants, or by the managers who are in charge of particular change programmes. The participants themselves can make significant inputs, for example by defining their needs in a participative mode, or engaging in action-learning programmes as discussed below. Training can be both formal and informal. The key objective is to facilitate the learning of concepts and skills that are necessary and directly applicable to an ongoing change programme.

In the current context of rapid technological, social and other changes, training and learning are more than useful change techniques: organizations where learning does not enjoy a prominent place find it increasingly difficult to keep track of significant trends in business and its environment, and to maintain the necessary level of competence in their managers and staff.

Action learning. Action learning, pioneered by Reg Revans, is based on the assumption that managers learn best by solving real problems either in their own or in other organizations, and by exchanging relevant experience with other managers. The problems tackled must be meaningful and important to the organization concerned and should involve both technical and human aspects. Emphasis is placed on implementation – that is, on the most difficult part of the change process. Exchange of experience with other managers involved in action learning is organized as a regular part of the programme. If necessary, the participants also receive technical assistance – missing information is supplied or expert advice is given on the approach taken. The ultimate objective is to achieve changes both in individual skills and attitudes, and in organizational practices and performance.

Learning organization. The "learning organization" concept (see section 18.6 for a detailed discussion) aims to link and integrate training and learning with change processes that have a significant impact on company strategy and performance. Emphasis is put on creating favourable conditions and incentives for continuous individual learning and on innovation in training and self-development. To turn individual learning efforts into "organizational learning", various techniques and approaches are used to share and disseminate the results of individual learning, learn in teams, enhance managerial responsibility for training and learning, combine the processes of learning with organizational change processes and use learning to achieve a competitive advantage.

Organizational diagnosis and problem-solving techniques

There is a wide range of such techniques, known under a variety of names. Their main advantage is that they help managers and consultants to apply a systematic and methodical approach, making sure that important factors, relationships or steps are not omitted and symptoms not mistaken for their causes. In a consulting project, the diagnostic phase and the action-planning phase (see Chapters 8 and 9) can also serve as an intervention for making people aware of the need to change, involving them in identifying and analysing problems and opportunities, and developing proposals that meet the organization's needs and objectives.

Campaign-type, action-oriented change programmes

A campaign-type, action-oriented programme is a major organized and planned change effort over a defined period of time to tackle a significant practical problem, mobilizing fairly large teams and often requiring considerable resources. The intervention has to last long enough for bottom-line results to become visible or striking. Feedback on results achieved has to be provided with a view to maintaining interest in the programme and adjusting the approach as appropriate. Also, missing information, skills, equipment and materials have to be made available as necessary. Examples of problems tackled include total business performance, corporate strategy, labour productivity, product and service quality, energy consumption, waste, and accident prevention. As a rule, a great deal is at stake in such programmes and demands on programme management and methodology are high. Several techniques for implementing such programmes are described in Chapter 22 on consulting in company transformation.

Choosing among intervention techniques

Only rarely will one particular technique or approach be appropriate at all stages of a change process. In many situations, managers and consultants have to use a variety of interventions, simultaneously or successively.

A competent consultant will be flexible in choosing intervention and change-assisting techniques, combining several interventions as appropriate and switching to a new technique if the originally chosen technique appears to be ineffective. In some instances, it may even be more effective not to choose a technique at an early stage of the process.[8] Choosing a wrong technique at the outset of the change process can rapidly create a great deal of disenchantment and miss the target; obstinately continuing to use the technique although it is obviously causing more harm than good is a trap to be avoided.

Two criteria are more important than any other in choosing an intervention technique or structural arrangement:

(1) It should ideally be compatible with the organizational culture; if it is not, great care should be taken to explain why the technique had to be chosen and how it will be used; the technique may need to be adapted during its use.

(2) The consultant and the managers responsible for the change programme should feel comfortable with the technique and be able to use it effectively.

It is knowledge and practice of skills in choosing an appropriate approach and employing it in a life situation that set the consultant apart from the theoretician. The techniques may be acquired in part by studying research findings and publications, but, above all, they will be mastered and fine-tuned by experience.

---

[1] An American social psychologist, whose main writings on change date from the 1940s and 1950s. See, e.g., K. Lewin: *Field theory in social science* (New York, Harper, 1951).

[2] See also R. Kegan and L. Laskow Lahey: "The real reason people won't change", in *Harvard Business Review*, Oct. 2001, pp. 85–92.

[3] See also S. Wetlaufer: "The business case against revolution: An interview with Nestlé's Peter Brabeck", in *Harvard Business Review*, Feb. 2001, pp. 113–119.

[4] See also the discussion of situational leadership in P. Hersey and K. Blanchard: *Management of organizational behavior* (Englewood Cliffs, NJ, Prentice-Hall, 1982), Ch. 7.

[5] R. Beckhard and R. T. Harris: *Organizational transition: Managing complex change* (Reading, MA, Addison-Wesley, 1977), p. 5.

[6] The Hawthorne experiments were seminal studies carried out in the 1920s on the effects of illumination and other working conditions on productivity.

[7] See C. M. Christensen and M. Overdorf: "Meeting the challenge of disruptive change", in *Harvard Business Review*, March–April 2000, p. 67.

[8] Beckhard and Harris, op. cit., p. 44.

CONSULTING AND CULTURE 5

In helping clients to plan and implement change, the consultant needs to be aware of the power of culture. Culture is normally defined as a system of collectively shared values, beliefs, traditions and behavioural norms. "Culture is the collective programming of the human mind that distinguishes the members of one human group from those of another group. Culture, in this sense, is a system of collectively held values."[1] Or, in the words of the French mathematician and philosopher Blaise Pascal, "there are truths on this side of the Pyrenees that are falsehoods on the other".

Culture has its roots in the basic conditions of human life, including material conditions, the natural environment, climate, and ways in which people earn their living, and in the historical experience of human communities which includes interaction with other countries and cultures. People develop a culture that helps them to cope with their environment and maintain the cohesion and identity of the community in interacting with other communities. In developing countries, in particular in rural areas, traditional cultures reflect the people's poverty and respect for the forces of nature. Culture tends to be deeply rooted in people's hearts and minds, and cannot be easily changed.

5.1 Understanding and respecting culture

The problem with culture is that although it is omnipresent and its influence on the functioning of organizations and societies is very strong, it is difficult to identify and grasp, since it is nowhere precisely described. It includes taboos – values that people respect, but about which they do not normally talk and sometimes resent talking. Individuals and communities may be unaware of their culture because they have not learned it as a structured subject or a technical skill. Values and beliefs that make up culture evolve over generations, are transmitted from generation to generation, and are normally acquired unconsciously, early in people's lives – in the family, at

Box 5.1 What do we mean by culture?

Culture is composed of many elements, which may be classified in four categories: symbols, heroes, rituals and values.

Symbols are words, objects and gestures that derive their meaning from convention. At the level of national cultures, symbols include the entire area of language. At the level of organizational culture, symbols include abbreviations, slang, modes of address, dress codes and status symbols, all recognized by insiders only.

Heroes are real or imaginary people, dead or alive, who serve as models of behaviour within a culture. Selection processes are often based on hero models of "the ideal employee" or "the ideal manager". Founders of organizations sometimes become mythical heroes later, and incredible deeds may be ascribed to them.

Rituals are collective activities that are technically superfluous but, within a particular culture, socially essential. In organizations they include not only celebrations but also many formal activities defended on apparently rational grounds: meetings, the writing of memos, and planning systems, plus the informal ways in which these activities are performed: who can afford to be late at what meeting, who speaks to whom, and so on.

Values represent the deepest level of culture. They are broad feelings, often unconscious and not open to discussion, about what is good and what is bad, clean or dirty, beautiful or ugly, rational or irrational, normal or abnormal, natural or paradoxical, decent or indecent. These feelings are present in the majority of the members of the culture, or at least in those who occupy pivotal positions.

Author: Geert Hofstede.

school, through religious education, at work and by socializing with other members of the community.

A management consultant faces the same problem. His or her personality and value system have been moulded by the culture in which he or she has grown up, worked and socialized. Yet the consultant may be unaware of it. For as "the last thing that a fish will discover is water", often culture will be the last thing that a management consultant, otherwise an outstanding expert in a particular technical field, will discover.

Being culture-conscious

In management consulting, a concern for culture is as important as a concern for the specific technical problem for which the consultant was brought in. But what can consultants do to be sure that they are culture-conscious and that neither their behaviour nor their suggestions clash with the organizational culture?

To be culture-sensitive, a management consultant does not have to be a sociologist or an anthropologist. Some knowledge of culture can be gained by reading about and discussing cultural issues with other people. Genuine interest in the meaning of culture and in different cultures provides a good background for understanding and correctly interpreting a particular cultural context.

However, this is only the first step. Like any other person, a consultant who has never lived and operated in a culture different from his own will find it difficult to perceive and understand the full meaning and power of another culture, and the role of various factors that may be unknown in his own culture. Only people who have been in contact with a different culture for some time can understand not only that culture but also their own. Social and working contacts with other cultures provide us with a mirror in which we see our own culture.

Being culture-tolerant

Culture is very important to people. Their preference for fundamental cultural values is emotional, not rational. They may even regard certain social norms and traditions as eternal and sacrosanct. In contrast, a management consultant may regard the same norms as anachronistic and irrational. There may be a grain of truth in the consultant's view, since cultures may well include values that, for instance, perpetuate social inequalities or inhibit development. Nevertheless, cultures reflect centuries of society's experience and help people to cope with life. Respect for different cultures and tolerance of their values and beliefs are therefore essential qualities of a good consultant.

In their attitude to other cultures, consultants are inevitably strongly influenced by their own culture. Tolerance towards other cultures, religions and ethnic groups is a cultural characteristic, too: some cultures are highly tolerant of different cultural values, while others are less so. A consultant who has been moulded by a relatively intolerant cultural environment should be particularly cautious when working in other cultures.

5.2 Levels of culture

National culture

The term "national culture" is used to define the values, beliefs, behavioural norms, habits and traditions that characterize human society in a particular country. In an ethnically and linguistically homogeneous country, there may be one national culture, but in many countries there are several distinct cultures. The question is, do these cultures mix with each other, cohabit peacefully and tolerate each other, or do they make coexistence within one country and the functioning of the economy difficult?

Box 5.2 Cultural factors affecting management

The following aspects of national cultures tend to be reflected in management structures and practices:

- the distribution of social roles and the status assigned to them;
- the criteria of success and achievement in economic and social life;
- respect for age and seniority;
- the role of traditional authorities and community leaders;
- democratic versus autocratic traditions;
- individualism versus collectivism;
- spiritual versus material values;
- responsibility and loyalty to family, community and ethnic group;
- socialization and communication patterns;
- the acceptability and the form of feedback, appraisal and criticism;
- religion, its importance in social life and its impact on economic activity;
- attitudes to other cultures, religions, ethnic groups, minorities;
- attitudes to social, technological and other changes;
- the conception of time.

An important cultural phenomenon is the existence of minorities and their relationship to other ethnic groups within society. Often minorities make a special effort to preserve their particular culture in order to protect their identity and ensure survival within an environment where a majority culture dominates and tends to alter or even oppress minority cultures. Certain minorities possess attitudes, skills, historical experience and material means that have helped them to be extremely successful in business. The implications of this are well known in many countries. Thus, while sensitivity to cultural differences is essential in international consulting, a consultant operating within his or her own country also needs to be aware of cultural differences.

Another increasingly important factor is the growing mobility of people between countries and cultures. In many countries the workforce is international and so may be the management team in the client company. People coming from other cultures bring their cultural values and habits with them. They are also influenced by the culture of their country of residence, and the result is an interesting and sometimes peculiar mix.

We would be hard pressed to review here all the factors embraced by the concept of national (or local) culture. It would be even more difficult to point to all the differences between cultures of which a consultant needs to be aware because they may be related to the work assignment. The spectrum of cultural values, norms and rituals can be extremely wide and can concern any aspect of human, economic and social life. Some cultural factors affecting management are listed in box 5.2.

Language plays a prominent role in culture. Cultural concepts are described in words, the meaning of many words is culture-bound and language is a vehicle for the functioning and interaction of cultures. Non-verbal expressions and gestures are also culture-bound and may be very important. Non-verbal communication is more difficult to control consciously than verbal communication and tends therefore to be more trustworthy. Some cultures (e.g. North American) attach more importance to what is said, while in other cultures (e.g. Asian) it is essential to understand non-verbal messages.

National cultures are unique, but they are not totally different and closed systems. There are similarities between cultures for reasons such as common language or religion. Long-term interaction of cultures (e.g. between neighbouring countries or during domination of one country by another) also influences culture. In some developing countries, the social groups most exposed to the culture of the former colonial power (e.g. administrators, intellectuals and the business community) tended to adopt some of its values and behavioural patterns. Thus, strong influences of French culture can be observed in French-speaking Africa, while influences of Dutch culture are still present in Indonesia. Cultural changes occur in many countries under the influence of growing material wealth, better general education, expansion of contacts with different cultures and other factors.

There is a growing interest in exploring the role played by national culture in the economic performance and development of particular countries. For many decades, North American culture has been widely regarded as a major factor in the dynamism, competitiveness and achievement of American businesses. At the present time, managers all over the world are keen to get a deeper insight into Japanese national culture (box 5.3).

Professional culture

Professional culture is one shared by individuals who belong to the same profession, e.g. lawyers, medical doctors, civil engineers or accountants. It is very much related to job content and to the role that the members of the profession play in society. It is influenced by professional education and training and tends to exhibit common characteristics across organizational and national boundaries. One of the objectives of professional associations and societies is to preserve and develop professional culture. Ethical values promoted by professional associations tend to become a part of this culture.

The understanding of professional culture may help a management consultant to establish constructive relations with clients and other professionals in foreign countries. It is useful to be informed about the background of managers and staff in a client organization and know, for example, from which universities they graduated. Some members of a client organization (e.g. accountants, internal consultants, training managers) may share common professional values with the consultant: this may be of particular help in penetrating the problems of local culture.

Box 5.3 Japanese culture and management consulting

Japanese culture, which is a historical growth of indigenous culture with the medieval influence of Chinese culture and the modern influence of Western culture, notably of Western European nations after the Meiji Restoration and American culture after the Second World War, has created a unique approach to management. Two of its key characteristics have strongly influenced business management in Japan.

Group orientation. The values, attitudes and behaviour of managers and workers are oriented towards the interest of the group to which they belong. The basic principle is that the collective interest of the group must be served best. In the Japanese context, the nation and the company are the two groups with which both managers and employees identify most closely.

Long-term orientation. Japanese managers and workers view their work, as well as their life in general, from a long-term perspective and act accordingly. Time is money to them, too, primarily in the sense that the more time is spent on a plan for an activity, the greater the result of its implementation is likely to be. Typically, a Japanese employee makes work decisions in the expectation of a lifetime career with the organization where he or she is employed.

Only those management techniques – be they for decision-making, problem-solving, leadership, motivation, communication, negotiation or change – that match these two characteristics of Japanese culture have been successfully transferred from Western culture. It was these two characteristics that acted as especially strong obstacles to the change that Japanese managers and employees needed to espouse to meet the challenges of the new world order which emerged in the 1990s.

The enormous changes generated by the new economy, characterized by globalization, the telecommunications revolution and deregulation, demand new qualities that have not previously been prominent in Japanese values and practices, specifically flexibility, speed, creativity and individual initiative. This is requiring fundamental cultural change, going far beyond mere cultural adaptation. The development has generated serious problems, collectively called "the lost decade", which could not be addressed by Japanese managers and workers in the traditional way. Going outside their own companies, they are increasingly calling for assistance from consultants, who as outsiders have conventionally been retained primarily for their operational expertise such as production control and sales management. In the current situation, they are being retained to help clients solve critical structural and strategic issues, enabling them to accomplish transformation to the new economy.

A universal challenge for management consultants across Japan now is to facilitate and accelerate the transformation not only technically but also culturally. They must do this by fostering the development of those values, attitudes and behaviour that, while still rooted in the history of the nation, assimilate the relevant elements of the best-practice models of today's world.

Author: Eiji Mizutani.

Organizational culture

Organizations, too, tend to have their specific culture: a mix of values, attitudes, norms, habits, traditions, behaviours and rituals that, in their totality, are unique to the given organization (box 5.4). Some organizations are well aware of their culture and regard it as a powerful strategic tool, used to orient all units and individuals towards common goals, mobilize employee initiative, ensure loyalty and facilitate communication. They aim at creating a culture of their own and making sure that all employees understand it and adhere to it.[2]

Organizational cultures, or micro-cultures, reflect national culture first of all. But they also include other values and norms. Research has provided some insight into the organizational cultures of leading corporations in various countries. It has shown that many companies that have been outstanding performers over a long time exhibit a strong corporate culture. In many multinational corporations, the parent company's culture has considerable bearing on the cultural norms and behaviour of subsidiaries in other countries. This leads to an interesting mix of cultures in the case of foreign subsidiaries, where the influence of local national culture is combined with that of the parent company's culture. The strong personalities of the founders and of certain top managers also influence organizational culture even in very large and complex corporations.

The hidden dimensions of organizational culture tend to surface during company mergers and takeovers, which in many cases fail to produce expected results often because management is unable to harmonize the different cultures.

Many organizations develop a specialized vocabulary and a wide range of symbols and rituals that staff members have to use and respect to avoid being regarded as outsiders by their colleagues.

A management consultant needs to learn about the organizational culture as early as possible in the assignment if he or she does not want to be perceived as a stranger who does not know how things are normally done in the client organization and whose presence is therefore an irritation. But there is another much more important reason for this: the client organization's culture may be one of the causes, or even the principal cause, of the problems for which the consultant was brought in. Even if changes in organizational culture are not explicitly stated among the objectives of the assignment, the consultant may have to deal with them and recommend changes.

Changing organizational culture may be a difficult and painful exercise, especially if it is necessary to change the values of the founders and leaders, and habits and practices that have become collective and have been widely established. Changes in leadership and management styles, and re-education, may be required. However, it has been pointed out that "organizational cultures reside at a more superficial level of programming than the things learned previously in the family and at school".[3] Changing organizational culture is a task of top management, but the consultant's catalytic input can be essential.

Box 5.4 Cultural values and norms in organizations

Within organizations, specific cultural values and behavioural norms may concern, for example:

- **the organization's mission and image** (high technology; superior quality; pride in being a sector leader; dedication to the service ethos; customer satisfaction; innovative spirit; entrepreneurial drive);
- **seniority and authority** (authority inherent in position or person; respect for seniority and authority; seniority as a criterion of authority);
- **the relative importance of different management positions and functions** (authority of personnel department; importance of different vice-presidents' positions; respective roles and authority of operations and marketing);
- **the treatment of people** (concern for people and their needs; equitable treatment or favouritism; privileges; respect for individual rights; training and development opportunities; lifetime careers; fairness in remuneration; how people are motivated);
- **the role of women in management and other jobs** (acceptance of women for positions of authority; jobs either unavailable or reserved for women; respect for women managers; equal treatment; special facilities);
- **selection criteria for managerial and supervisory positions** (seniority versus performance; priority for selection from within; political, ethnic, nationality and other criteria; influence of informal groups);
- **work organization and discipline** (voluntary versus imposed discipline; punctuality; use of time clocks; flexibility in changing roles at work; use of new forms of work organization);
- **management and leadership style** (paternalism; authoritative, consultative or participative style; use of committees and task forces; providing personal example; style flexibility and adaptability);
- **decision-making processes** (who decides; who has to be consulted; individual or collective decision-making; need to reach consensus);
- **circulation and sharing of information** (employees amply or poorly informed; information readily shared or not);
- **communication patterns** (preference for oral or written communication; rigidity or flexibility in using established channels; importance attached to formal aspects; accessibility of higher management; use of meetings; who is invited to which meetings; established behaviour in the conduct of meetings);
- **socialization patterns** (who socializes with whom during and after work; existing barriers and inhibitions; special facilities such as separate dining-rooms or reserved clubs);
- **ways of handling conflict** (desire to avoid conflict and to compromise; preference for informal or formal ways; involvement of higher management); performance evaluation (substantive or formalistic; confidential or public; by whom carried out; how results used);
- **identification with the organization** (manager and staff adherence to company objectives and policies; loyalty and integrity; esprit de corps; enjoying working in the organization).

The consulting firm's culture

The characteristics of organizational cultures are present in consulting firms, as in any other organization. Their cultures encompass values and norms concerning a wide range of issues including consulting methods and practices, commitment to clients, responsibilities and rights of junior and senior consultants, career progression, transfer of know-how to clients, the application of a code of ethics, and many others. Thus, a consulting firm's culture is a unique mix of organizational, professional and national cultural factors. It is essential to be aware of it, in particular if there is any risk of incompatibility and clash with a client's culture.

5.3 Facing culture in consulting assignments

The consultant's behaviour

A great deal of useful guidance is available on how consultants should behave when operating in other cultures. Most of it concerns interpersonal relations and manners. For example, it is good to get advice on:

- how to dress;
- how to deal with people;
- punctuality;
- when and how to start discussing business;
- written and/or oral communication with the client;
- formal and informal interpersonal relations;
- the use of go-betweens;
- display or restraint of emotions;
- what language and terms to use;
- taboos.

Such things are relatively easy to learn and remember. Also, these days it is helpful that more and more clients are becoming tolerant of other cultures. Your client may know that a first contact with an American consultant will be quite different from a contact with a Japanese consultant. However, there is no guarantee that your particular client is "culturally literate" and culture-tolerant. It is therefore wise to find out beforehand how he or she expects a professional adviser to behave.

However important, questions such as whether to use first names and what topics must not be openly discussed represent only the tip of the iceberg in the cross-cultural consultant–client relationship. The less visible and more profound aspects of this relationship concern such issues as power and role distribution, decision-making, confrontation and consensus in problem-solving, use of teamwork, consultation with employees, religious beliefs and practices, and any criteria whereby management will judge the consultant's work and suggestions.

Some consultants feel that they must try to identify themselves with a foreign culture, behaving as the client behaves ("When in Rome do as the Romans do"), and sharing the client's values and beliefs in order to understand his or her environment and render an effective service. This may be impossible, and even undesirable, to achieve. It implies no longer being authentic and genuine, thus abandoning key behavioural characteristics of a professional consultant. Understanding and respecting other people's culture does not imply giving up one's own.

How to explore cultural issues

The consultant has to use all his or her experience and talent to learn about the cultural factors that may be relevant to the assignment. In some cases, direct questions on what values prevail, how things are normally done and what pitfalls to avoid will be perfectly acceptable, in particular if the client is personally aware of the differences between cultures. In other cases, tactful and patient observation of the client's behaviour may produce an answer. A great deal can be learned by mixing with people and observing how they act and socialize, what symbols they use and what rituals they observe.

Discussions of cultural issues should be friendly and informal; formal and structured interviews are not well suited for dealing with culture. Judgement should be suspended until the consultant has learned more. Also, the consultant should try not to be nervous and uneasy in a new situation that appears ambiguous. To detect and overcome cultural barriers, it may be useful to team up with an internal consultant or another member of the client organization who is prepared to help.

A study of the client company's history can be revealing. The roots of present corporate culture may be far back in the past – in the personality of the founder, in past successes or failures, in the growth pattern (e.g. many acquisitions or frequent changes of owners), and the like.

Establishing a climate of trust

We have already emphasized that it is important to establish as early as possible a climate of trust among all the parties in the consultant–client relationship. This can be difficult since in some cultures it is not desirable to trust an outsider. One way of looking at these relations is by comparing high-context and low-context societies.

In a *high-context society*, relationships are based on friendship, family ties and knowing each other well. The context, the total situation, is essential to building relationships. The formation of these relationships happens quite slowly and includes many rituals or rites of passage. This can include eating certain kinds of food, or engaging in various social activities unrelated to work.

In a *low-context society*, the relationship is generally spelled out in a written contract. The client wishes to obtain a precisely defined piece of technical work and may not care much about the total relationship with the consultant. What is not in the contract is not part of the relationship. Of course, there are subtle forms of interaction even in a low-context society. Generally, however, the relationship is built first on the written document; the building of trust follows.

It is possible to develop trust in most cultures, but in some it takes time. This need for time should be recognized and built into the plan of the assignment. Also, the concept of high- and low-context societies is a developing one. The consultant should be careful about applying it to an entire country or an entire people, since there are individual variations.

Criteria of rationality

In working for a client, a management consultant aims to find and recommend solutions that are in the client's interest. To justify the proposed measures to himself and to the client, a consultant applies criteria that are rational by his standards. For example, he may apply economic effectiveness as a criterion and judge various alternatives by their impact on the productivity and financial performance of the organization. He may use cost/benefit analysis and return on investment as the main assessment techniques.

Yet the concept of rationality is culture-bound. Even in Western industrial economies, where the notions of efficiency, competitiveness and profitability have not only an economic but also a strong cultural connotation, economic rationality per se is not always the only or main criterion applied by top management in evaluating alternative decisions. Personal, cultural, social or political preferences may prevail. The desire to maintain the status quo, fear of the unknown, the company owner's social image, or reluctance to make changes affecting collectively shared values, may eventually determine top management's choice even in a European or North American enterprise. In several Asian countries, certain cultural values tend to be applied as criteria of rationality: to preserve harmony, to avoid dismissing employees, to maintain status differences and to respect feelings about ethnic groups may be seen as more rational than to optimize performance in strictly economic and financial terms.

Transferring management practices

Management consultants use their past experience in working with present clients. This involves transferring management practices from one organization or country to another organizational or national environment. Other items could be substituted for "management practices". We could also speak about management techniques, technologies, methods, expertise, systems, concepts, patterns, approaches, and the like, but the question remains the same: to what extent and under what circumstances are management practices transferable?

There are factors whose influence on the choice of management techniques is evident – for example, the nature of the product, the technology used, the technical skills of the employees or the size of the organization. The influence of culture is more subtle and not so easy to perceive, but experience has shown that it tends to be very strong.

Some management techniques are *value laden*. They were developed for use in a particular culture and reflect its value systems and behavioural norms. They concern the human side of organizations: individual and group interests, interpersonal and intergroup relations, motivation and control of human behaviour. The possibility of transferring these techniques has to be carefully examined in each case. A value-laden technique may be difficult or impossible to transfer. Remuneration techniques stimulating individual performance rather than collective solidarity fail in collectivist societies; high wage differentials may not be acceptable in an egalitarian society; organization development methods based on confrontation cannot be used where harmony and conflict avoidance are strongly valued; problem-solving approaches built on democratic values are difficult to apply in a traditionally autocratic culture; matrix organization does not work effectively in cultures where people prefer the unity of command and want to receive orders from one single higher authority. Examples of failures caused by a mechanistic transfer of value-laden techniques are abundant.

Some other techniques were developed in response to organizational characteristics such as the nature and complexity of the production process, or the amount of data to be recorded and analysed; that is to say, they concern the technological, economic and financial side of organizations. Such techniques are relatively *value neutral* and their transfer across cultures is a simpler matter. However, while a technique per se may appear value-neutral, its application creates a new situation that may be value laden. A production control or maintenance scheduling technique required by the technology used may conflict with the workers' beliefs and habits concerning punctuality, work organization and discipline, justified absence from work, accuracy and reliability of records, and the like. Every organization is unique, and the combined effects of national and organizational cultures are key factors of this uniqueness. Thus a seemingly universal and value neutral management technique may have to be modified to fit a different cultural context, or it may even be more appropriate to develop a new technique.

Culture and change

Values and beliefs concerning change have a prominent place in culture. Generally speaking, modernistic and optimistic cultures regard change as healthy; without it, business cannot flourish and society prosper. Cultures dominated by traditionalism value the status quo, stability and reverence for the past. They are suspicious about change and may perceive it as disturbing and subversive even if, in the consultant's professional view, the need for change is self-evident. To realize and appreciate this may be particularly difficult for a consultant who has been used to working with dynamic clients, keen to apply quickly any changes from which the company can derive benefits.

The presence of cultural factors impeding or retarding change does not imply that change is impossible. Even the most conservative individuals and groups are able to reconcile themselves to change if they realize its necessity, in particular if change is imposed by strong external influences, such as the deterioration of material conditions of living. Better information, education, contacts with more dynamic cultures and new technology also affect the traditionalist societies' attitude to change. However, the process of change may be slow and difficult.

When operating in an environment where resistance to change has cultural roots, a consultant will be well advised to bear in mind:

- the sort of change that is acceptable (refraining from proposals that the client will judge to be culturally undesirable or unfeasible);
- the pace of change (deciding whether to plan for a fundamental one-off change, or for gradual changes in a number of small steps; assessing the "acceptance time" needed by clients and their staff to convince themselves about the desirability of proposed changes);
- the client's readiness for change (it is unreasonable to press for change if the client is not ready to face the cultural problems that change may cause);
- the level of management and the particular person (authority) by whom change has to be proposed and promoted in order to be accepted and implemented;
- the persuasion and educational effort needed to convince people that maintaining the status quo is not in their interest.

Consulting in social development

At the present time more and more management consulting is done for social development programmes and projects in sectors such as health, nutrition, basic education, drinking-water supply, sanitation, community development or population control. Many of these programmes are in rural areas of developing countries. There are, too, many programmes of assistance to small entrepreneurs and micro-enterprises in the informal sector (see Chapter 25). Management consultants, including those who have worked in developing countries and are aware of their cultures, are as a rule familiar with the cultural setting encountered in industry and central government administration, but the informal economy, and rural and social development, are likely to be new worlds to them.

In social development, the consultant's clients are not managers operating modern enterprises or well-established administrative structures, but managers, social workers and organizers working with local communities, groups of farmers, or even individual families and persons. The technology used is simple and may not be up to date. The concepts of "professional culture" or "organizational culture" do not apply. In contrast, the power of traditional social culture is very strong. Human behaviour, essentially fatalistic and conservative, is governed by deeply rooted beliefs and prejudices. Cultural characteristics reflect difficult living conditions, poverty and poor education. Passivity, resignation, lack of personal drive, fear of change and uncritical respect for traditional authorities may prevail.

In consulting, knowledge of these factors is essential, but it is not all that is needed. Consultants need to possess cultural and social work skills rather than knowledge of refined management techniques. They need to be patient, to be able to live and operate in imperfect and uncertain situations, to know how to improvise using limited and simple local resources, and to apply a great deal of imagination in proposing solutions that are not to be found in any management handbook. Personal commitment to and empathy with the underprivileged are qualities without which it is hard to succeed.

Consulting to "high-tech" companies

"High-tech" companies in fields such as information technology, the Internet, e-business, telecommunications, microelectronics and biotechnology are at the opposite end of the wide spectrum of environments where consultants

Box 5.5 Characteristics of "high-tech" company cultures

There is a broad spectrum of companies in high-technology sectors. Some cultural patterns tend to predominate in these companies:

- predominance of professional culture over company culture;
- authority vested in innovators and leading researchers;
- little respect for formal authority, hierarchy and seniority;
- tendency to ignore chains of command and break down organizational barriers;
- easy and frequent horizontal communication and knowledge-sharing, easy team-building, spontaneous creation of knowledge-sharing communities;
- hard work and no counting of hours when involved in challenging projects;
- informal interpersonal relations and dress code;
- employees loyal to their profession and to themselves rather than to the organization;
- high mobility of professional employees, more concern for job content than for job security;
- more concern for technical innovation and excellence than for costs and budgets;
- high remuneration regarded as standard.

intervene. Their demand for consulting services is high and they represent a challenging consulting market, not only in Silicon Valley, their cradle, but in many other regions and countries. They exhibit many common cultural characteristics which are derived from the role of knowledge and knowledge workers and the pace of change in these companies, from the professional cultures of their founders and managers, and from the core employee groups who create value. Professional cultures tend to influence strongly whole organizational cultures (see box 5.5). To be accepted and listened to in these companies, consultants have to understand their value systems and find a common language with management and staff.

---

[1] G. Hofstede: "Culture and organizations", in *International Studies of Management and Organization*, No. 4, 1981. See also idem: *Cultures and organizations: Software of the mind* (Maidenhead, Berkshire, McGraw-Hill, 1991). The word "culture", in English and some other languages, is also used when referring to the arts, literature, and so on; obviously, this is not the meaning intended here.

[2] See, e.g., T. E. Deal and A. A. Kennedy: *Corporate cultures: The rites and rituals of corporate life* (Reading, MA, Addison-Wesley, 1982); E.H. Schein: *Organizational culture and leadership* (San Francisco, CA, Jossey-Bass, 2nd ed., 1992); F. Trompenaars and C. Hampden-Turner: *Riding the waves of culture: Understanding cultural diversity in business* (London, Nicholas Brealy, 2nd ed., 1997), and G. Hofstede, op. cit.

[3] G. Hofstede: "Business cultures" in *Courier* (Paris, UNESCO), Vol. 47, No. 4, 1994, pp. 12–16.

PROFESSIONALISM AND ETHICS IN CONSULTING

6

The growth of management consulting has provided ample evidence that at one time almost anyone could call himself or herself a consultant and set up in practice. In its early years and even now, the business attracted the good, the bad and the indifferent. The word "business" is used deliberately: "professions" seldom start as such. Professional awareness and behaviour come when the early juggling with a little knowledge gives way to skilled application of a generally accepted body of knowledge according to accepted standards of integrity. The professions of medicine, the law and the applied sciences all followed this path, and management consulting is proceeding in the same direction.

6.1 Is management consulting a profession?

The criteria normally used to define a profession can be summarized under five headings.

Knowledge and skills

There is a defined body of knowledge proper to the profession, which can be acquired through a system of professional education and training. The necessary level of professional expertise is reached only after a certain number of years of practical experience in addition to completed higher education, preferably under the coaching of senior members of the profession. Furthermore, the practising professional has to keep continuously abreast of developments in theory and practice. The professions tend to have their own criteria and systems for verifying and assessing required knowledge and experience, including examinations on entry, assessment by professional bodies, testing the results of further training, and similar.

The concept of service and social interest

Professionals put their knowledge and experience at the disposal of clients as a service against appropriate remuneration. The real professionals are characterized by the "service ethos": they serve clients' needs and interests, to which they subordinate their own self-interest. Furthermore, they view individual client interests from a wider social perspective, and keep broader social needs and implications in mind when serving individual clients.

Ethical norms

There is a set of recognized ethical norms, shared and applied by the members of the profession. These norms define what is proper and what is improper behaviour in providing a professional service. They demand more than respecting the law: a behaviour that is perfectly legal may not always be ethical judged by the profession's norms.

Community sanction and enforcement

The community in which the profession operates and the clientele recognize the social role, the status, and the ethical and behavioural norms of the profession. There may be explicit recognition (e.g. by means of a legal text governing and protecting professional practice). This may include definitions of educational or other standards required and special examinations to be passed, as well as of behaviours considered as unprofessional and illegal, and of corresponding sanctions.

Self-discipline and self-regulation

While serving clients, members of the profession apply self-discipline in observing the profession's behavioural norms. The profession organizes itself in one or more voluntary membership institutions (associations, institutes, chambers, etc.), thus exercising collective self-regulation over the application of an accepted code of professional conduct and over the development of the profession. An equally important purpose of membership institutions is to defend the collective interests of the profession in dealing with representatives of the clients and the community.

Does consulting meet these criteria?

There has been a long but inconclusive debate on whether management consulting meets the criteria discussed above and deserves to be called a profession. Both scholars and leading consulting practitioners have expressed and emphatically defended diametrically different opinions, which illustrate the current state of management consulting. While consulting exhibits some of the criteria applied to professions, it does not meet others. For example, the scope of consulting has never been clearly defined and the proposed definitions have never gained general acceptance. There are various views and practices regarding required consultant competencies and the conditions of entry into consulting. The borders of consulting and its relationships to other professions are flexible, permeable and mobile and have recently undergone many important changes. Even now, and even in sophisticated business cultures, virtually anyone can call himself or herself a management or business consultant and offer services to business clients without any diploma, certificate, licence, credentials, recommendations or registration. This is the reality of the business and some observers feel that this loose and liberal framework has actually been beneficial to the growth of consulting and has enabled its flexible and fast adaptation to changing environments and client needs.

We can call management consulting an emerging profession, a profession in the making, or an industry with significant professional characteristics and ambitions, provided that we are aware of the gaps that need to be filled and improvements that need to be made. After all, it may not be so important to decide whether consulting is a profession. Consulting has demonstrated that it can exist and prosper without any such decision. More important are the quality and other standards applied by consulting firms and individual consultants, who can demonstrate their professional values and behaviour without waiting for the sector to achieve recognition as a fully fledged profession.

We will comment on these issues in the following sections, showing how the professional level and quality of management consulting can be increased.

6.2 The professional approach

What then are the salient characteristics of a professional approach in management consulting? Some of them can be found, in succinct form, in the codes of ethics or conduct adopted by the membership organizations of management consultants; others are set out in information pamphlets of consulting firms. These are the norms held collectively, i.e. by the members of a consultants' association or of a consulting firm that has formally declared what its ethical rules are. However, in many situations it is not possible to refer to a formal declaration of norms defining professional and ethical behaviour. In such cases the consultant has to be guided by a personal code of professional ethics and behaviour – his or her own conception of what is proper and improper practice, and what is beneficial to the client and the community and what is not.

The consultant is in a position of trust; the client probably believes that certain behavioural norms will be respected without their even being mentioned. Many clients believe that consultants would never use false credentials, and some clients are even unable to evaluate the consultant's technical competence. The consultant may be in a position of technical superiority and possess knowledge and information that the client does not have. The client may then be in a position of weakness, uncertainty, and even distress (box 6.1).

Any consultant who seeks to act in a professional manner must clarify his or her own conception of ethics and the norms to be observed in working for

Box 6.1 The power of the professional adviser

The "technical superiority" of the management consultant, and his or her "power" over clients, are often different from what can be observed in some other professions, e.g. in medicine. There are two main reasons for this. First, if there is a knowledge and experience gap between management consultants and their clients, this gap can be quite small. To many clients, management consulting is not a "black box". Both the consultant and the client may have the same educational background and similar practical experience. The client may be quite well prepared for deciding to use or not to use a consultant and to accept or reject the consultant's advice, and for controlling the consultant's work during an assignment. Clearly, this is not the normal position of a patient who turns to a physician, or of a layperson who seeks legal counsel and in certain situations must retain a lawyer even if he or she would prefer not to. Second, management consulting is not a closed and highly protected profession. In most countries there are no jobs that are reserved to management consultants. The consultant's and the client's roles can even be interchangeable. Someone who is client today can be consultant tomorrow, and vice versa.

There are two typical situations where the consultant's ethics are clearly put to the test: first, if the consultant does enjoy technical superiority because he or she works for an uninformed or technically weak client; and second, if he or she works for a client whose judgement has been impaired by distress and difficulties and who desperately needs help. Such clients may be very vulnerable and easy to manipulate, and the choice of the terms of the consulting contract, the intervention methods and the changes proposed can be very much in the hands of the consultant. Even if a participative consulting method is applied, the client may be subdued, not self-confident and a weak participant.

clients. This applies equally to external and internal consultants, as well as to anyone who intervenes in a consulting capacity.

Technical competence

The consultant's technical competence is the basis of his or her professional approach. Above all, consultants must possess the knowledge and skills needed by particular clients. As a general rule, they must be able and willing to assess critically their own knowledge and skills when considering a new assignment or when reaching a point in a current assignment where different competencies are required. A professional consultant will never misrepresent himself, pretending that he can do a job that is beyond his competence, even if he is short of work and keen to get any assignment. The consultant who wants to tackle a new sort of problem (experience cannot be increased except by trying out something new) will discuss this openly with the client.

The difficulty is that in management and business consulting there is a lack of reliable and objective benchmarks for assessing competence to do a particular job to the client's satisfaction. Consulting associations have attempted to define *a common body of knowledge* of professional consultants, and *the type and minimum duration of experience* which is a condition of association or institute membership or certification (see section 6.4). These, however, are general and rather elementary criteria of admission or certification, which cannot show whether a consultant is competent for a given task. They are not applied to consultants who are not members of associations or who do not seek certification. In addition, the work on developing a generally recognized body of knowledge for the consulting profession is far from being completed. The documents that are available from various consulting associations are useful, but cannot be regarded as normative texts establishing the knowledge base of the profession (see also Chapters 36 and 37 dealing with the careers and development of consultants).

Avoiding conflict of interest

During an assignment and within the limits of a consulting contract, the consultant's competence and time are made available to the client, with the objective of achieving the best possible results in the client's interest. Unfortunately, it is not always obvious what "client's interest" means or what the client really expects from the assignment. There is often a conflict between the client's short-term and long-term interests, or between interests of various groups within a client organization, but the client may not see this until the consultant brings it to his or her attention. In agreeing to serve a client, the consultant must be sure that his or her interests do not conflict with those of the client.

Avoiding a conflict of interest is one of the most delicate and critical issues of professionalism and ethics in consulting. There may be many reasons for this, including the complexity of business ventures and transactions in which consultants become involved as advisers or intermediaries, the multidisciplinary structure of many larger professional firms and the rather liberal interpretation of the meaning of conflict of interest in some cultures and countries.

Box 6.2 lists some situations where conflict of interest may not be obvious at first glance. Conversely, certain instances of conflict of interest are blatant and may be explicitly mentioned in codes of conduct. Thus, consultants may be required to disclose, prior to assignments, all relevant personal, financial and other business interests which could not be inferred from the description of the services offered. In particular this relates to:

- any directorship or controlling interests in any business in competition with the client;
- any financial interest in goods or services recommended or supplied to the client;
- any personal relationship with any individual employed by the client;
- any personal investment in the client organization or in its parent or any subsidiary companies.

Box 6.2 Is there conflict of interest? Test your value system.

- An international consulting firm is an adviser to a government on a privatization project, although it has long-standing work relationships with a potential foreign buyer of the public enterprise to be privatized, and is actually executing, through another branch office and a different team of consultants, an assignment for this potential buyer.
- An auditor suggests that a client should turn to the consulting division of his professional firm with a specific problem that surfaced during the audit, although there may be other consultants who could do the same job better or for a lower fee.
- A consultant keeps an eye on a client's staff and does not miss an opportunity to offer a job to the most talented among the client's people, especially if there is dissatisfaction in the client organization and the consultant can offer a better salary. Another consultant pursues the same objective but waits several months after the end of the contract before approaching any candidate.
- A client does the same in respect of the consultant working for him.
- A consultant is pursuing an assignment step by step, rigorously respecting the work plan defined in the contract, although it is almost certain that she will get nowhere and the proposals will never be implemented.
- A consultant is a leading professional expert in a particular sector – textiles, automotive industry, machine tools, etc. This implies working simultaneously or successively for competing firms, which may or may not know about it. What is the difference between providing the best sector-related expertise to every client, and leaking information from one competitor to another?
- A consultant who has been adviser to a number of public sector companies to be privatized participates in establishing an investment fund, or becomes adviser to an investment fund which takes a financial interest in these companies during the privatization process.

It should be noted that other professions and their public regulators are also concerned about issues of conflict of interest. In the accounting profession, relationships and activities that can impair auditor independence and generate conflict of interest between auditors and their clients have been debated for years. The debate has been difficult and definitive solutions that would be regarded as fully satisfactory by all interested parties have yet to be found (see box 6.3).

The question whether to "empower" a client by sharing expertise, transmitting know-how, and providing training in conjunction with advice, is another complex issue in which conflict of interest may arise. In the previous chapters we have said that a professional consulting approach has a strong learning dimension. To "help clients to learn to help themselves" is a fundamental objective. However, a general declaration of a noble principle is not enough. The consultant must be sure that the assignment is so designed, and the client so involved, that the consultant will pass on to the client knowledge and expertise.

Box 6.3 On audit and consulting

Over the years, professional accounting firms doing statutory audits have been adding new services to their portfolio, notably in consulting, advisory, training, legal, IT, e-business, valuation, actuarial, small business development, mergers and acquisitions, and venture capital. They have become multifunctional or full-service professional firms, offering integrated service packages and advising business clients on a wide range of issues. When the Big Eight entered management consulting in the early 1980s, it was obvious that their audit experience and relationships with audit clients were major assets in their fast progression in consulting. Clients raised no objection. On the contrary, most of them were glad to use consultants from firms that had audited their financial statements and accounts and therefore were already familiar with their problems and possibilities. Cross-selling became an important marketing strategy of accountants and consultants alike, although this was never fully recognized.

However, it also became rapidly obvious that auditor independence was often compromised and overt or covert conflicts of interest became more and more frequent, at times leading to insoluble situations. While auditing accounted for 70 per cent of the total revenues of the largest accounting firms in 1977, it had dropped to 30 per cent in 1999, and consulting and management advisory services went up over the same period from 12 to more than 50 per cent. Cheaper audit services served to promote more lucrative management and financial consulting. Some large firms did not escape escalating internal conflicts, as demonstrated by the splitting of Arthur Andersen into Andersen and Accenture in January 2001, the terms of which were agreed only after a lengthy process of arbitration.

By the end of the 1990s, the Securities and Exchange Commission (SEC) in the United States decided to tighten up the rules governing auditor independence (see www.sec.gov). It identified four key principles by which to measure an auditor's independence: an auditor is **not** independent if he or she (i) has a mutual or conflicting interest with the audit client, (ii) audits his or her own firm's work, (iii) functions as management or employee of the audit client, or (iv) acts as an advocate for the audit client. The new rules list nine types of non-audit services that are deemed inconsistent with an auditor's independence. Most of these services are in the province of consulting. However, auditors are not prevented from providing such services to other clients. It should be noted that in preparing the new rules the SEC had to cope with considerable resistance and lobbying by influential accounting firms. In Europe, principles based on a similar philosophy have been drafted and submitted for consultation within the European Union (see: europa.eu.int/comm/internal_market/en/company/audit).

Despite these undoubtedly useful new principles, the current institutional arrangements concerning the audit function and the relationships of auditors to clients make total auditor independence unrealistic. It has been rightly observed that there will always be some dependence and conflict of interest as long as auditors are selected, appointed, remunerated, extended, fired, recommended to business friends etc. by their clients, and as long as they need to develop and

continued overleaf...

maintain close human links with the client's managers and staff in performing statutory audits. In sum, auditors' judgements are likely to be biased in favour of their own and their client's interests (see M. H. Bazerman, K. P. Morgan and G. F. Loewenstein: "The impossibility of auditor independence", in *Sloan Management Review*, Summer 1997).

A financial scandal of exceptional magnitude and far-reaching consequences, in which auditors were unwilling or unable to reveal management's fraudulent business and reporting practices, had to occur for these and similar warnings to be taken seriously. In December 2001, Enron, the American energy sector giant, filed for bankruptcy. Andersen, its auditor and business consultant, had earned more from Enron in 2000 for non-audit services (US$27 million) than for auditing (US$25 million). It either did not see what was going on at Enron, or preferred to keep silent. Andersen is reported to have shredded documents related to the case.

At the time of writing, it is difficult to predict what regulatory measures authorities in different countries will take, or what lessons the accounting and other professions will draw. It is certain, however, that, as *The Economist* pointed out (9 February 2002), "at the heart of these audit failures lies a set of business relationships that are bedevilled by perverse incentives and conflicts of interest", and "the entire auditing regime needs radical change".

What does all this mean to management consultants? It is in the consultant's interest to follow closely the debates and changes in formal regulations concerning statutory audits and the activities of auditors. Conflicts of interest may arise not only if a firm performs audits and consulting, IT and other projects for the same client, but in many other situations. Management consulting is not a regulated profession and ethical codes tend to refer to conflicts of interest in general and vague terms only. Also, what is seen as conflict of interest in one country or organization may be seen as standard and even effective practice elsewhere. Globalization tends to bring closer together different business values and legal environments, but consultants and consulting firms are, and will continue to be for quite a long time, the main judges and arbitrators in choosing how to handle conflicts of interest. It should be remembered that self-regulation helps to prevent government-imposed regulation.

Consultants who are looking to the future do not see teaching and training clients as a threat. They do not view the future as a simple repetition of the present, which would permit them to continue to do the same things indefinitely. Clients will have new sorts of problems, and a consultant from whom a client has learned useful skills may be called on again. Such a client will also recommend the consultant to business colleagues. Other clients will come, and so on.

Impartiality and objectivity

Clients who turn to professional advisers expect to receive impartial and objective advice. They assume that the consultant will be free of biases, prejudices, preconceived ideas, and prefabricated and prepackaged solutions, which may have worked in other contexts but be inappropriate for the given client. The true professional aims to be as impartial and objective as possible, controlling emotions and not letting prejudices erode the value of advice. In practice, however, absolute impartiality and objectivity are difficult, if not impossible, to attain.

In addition to conflicting interests, other factors may affect impartiality and objectivity. Every consultant is influenced by his or her cultural background and personal value system, which may include political, racial, religious and other beliefs and prejudices. In addition, consultants have their own approaches to problem-solving, change and helping clients who face problems. Some consultants believe strongly in the power of behavioural sciences and process consulting, while others favour a rigorous and systematic approach to problem diagnosis and change management, using highly structured procedures, techniques or models.

The consultant must make every effort to become aware of his or her personal values and biases, as well as of forces and interests within the consulting firm and the client's environment that may affect impartiality and objectivity. An open discussion with the client on these issues may be necessary and helpful. In many cases, objectivity can be increased by reviewing the approach and the solutions envisaged with other members of the consulting firm, who may have faced similar problems with other clients. In an extreme case, a real professional would decline an assignment where he or she cannot be objective.

Internal consultants should be particularly aware of their dependence on their own organization and of the factors that might make them less impartial than an external adviser. They should not be given assignments where they clearly cannot think and behave impartially.

Confidentiality

Confidentiality is another universal principle of work done by independent professionals for their clients. Management consultants should accept neither to disclose any confidential information about clients, nor to make any use of this information to obtain benefits or advantages personally, for their firms, or for other clients. Clients must be sure that they can trust consultants. As a rule, some reference to confidentiality will be made in the consulting contract, but it may be general and could be easily overlooked during the assignment. The client may not specify what information must be treated as confidential and may be unaware of the various risks in working with information (see also Appendices 4 and 5).

In internal consulting, the situation with regard to confidentiality can be complicated. In certain cases consultants have an obligation to (or there is a possibility that they might) disclose information on a client to a common superior (minister, director-general or other official). Under such circumstances, managers regard internal consultants as central management's spies and are reluctant to use them. To counter this, many business corporations have declared confidentiality as a principle that will be scrupulously respected in using internal consultants as well as external ones. A similar approach is increasingly taken within the public sector.

Confidentiality can also be violated unintentionally – by carelessness in handling documentation, naivety in discussing work-related issues in social contexts, or lack of precautions in quoting confidential information in public speeches or articles.

Commissions

Not all commissions are equivalent to bribery. Yet certain commissions are bribery, or can be perceived as such, especially if not disclosed to the client. In any event, commissions are a delicate issue. Codes of ethics do not ignore them, but most codes fail to provide sufficient guidance.

It is of course impossible to give universal guidelines on the acceptability of commissions from the viewpoint of professional ethics. Local business practices and cultures are difficult to ignore. In some countries, commissions and discounts constitute an inevitable means of doing business, including in professional services. In other countries any unreported and untaxed commission is illegal. As a general rule, the client should be informed of commissions or similar favours received, paid or promised by the consultant in connection with the assignment.

Within a professional firm, the issue of commissions may constitute an ethical dilemma. Some consulting firms have lost important contracts only to see that a less able competitor was chosen thanks to greater "flexibility" in offering a commission to a particular decision-maker.

In consultants' circles, the prevailing position on commissions is as follows:

- a commission paid by a consultant to a client or the client's staff in order to obtain an assignment, or to get the consultant's proposals accepted, is unethical;
- a commission accepted by a consultant in order to make certain recommendations, which may concern an issue within the client organization, the selection of a supplier or another issue where the choice proposed by the consultant is likely to affect the client's decision, is also contrary to the code of ethics;
- a commission paid by a consultant to the person or organization that introduced him or her to the client, or acted as an intermediary in a similar way, is acceptable in most cases; such commissions are normal practice in many countries and can even be declared to tax authorities as costs; however, the client should be made aware of the commission and find it acceptable.

Value for money

The fees charged to clients (Chapter 30) raise several ethical questions. Professionals are concerned about the relationship between the benefits drawn by the client and the cost of the assignment. If they feel that the outcome does not justify the cost, or that there will be little or no benefit, they should warn the client before starting the job. Generally speaking, professional ethics require that consultants charge "normal" and "reasonable" fees, judged by the profession's current standards and prevailing practice.

Charging excessive fees to uninformed clients is clearly unprofessional. Undercutting fees and working at a loss in the hope that this will eliminate competition is unprofessional too, in particular if the consultant does this with a new client, knowing that he or she will soon have to readjust the fee to the normal level. Furthermore, certain fee formulas (see Chapter 30) may be regarded as inappropriate or even unethical.

Wider social concerns and the client's ethics

Consulting assignments often involve issues where the client's interest may be in real or potential conflict with wider social interests. Or the consultant may uncover practices that, according to prevailing social norms or in his personal opinion, are socially harmful and undesirable, if not illegal. The consultant may then face an ethical dilemma. He may have an opportunity to seek advice from senior colleagues and advisers, but eventually he must himself resolve such a dilemma, which may be difficult. Codes of consulting ethics provide some guidance for the consultant's behaviour, e.g. on avoiding conflict of interest in working for a client; but they leave it entirely to the consultant to distinguish between ethical and unethical behaviour of the client.

Unfortunately, despite years of research and a proliferation of publications, the concept of managerial and business ethics has remained vague and controversial. True enough, there are extreme situations of clients involved in illegal or fraudulent dealings. A professional consulting firm would withdraw from an assignment where such client behaviour is discovered or suspected. The vast majority of situations are less clear, and recommending a course of action that meets both commercial and ethical criteria may not be easy. As a minimum, the consultant should draw the client's attention to the possibility of conflict between these criteria. As an optimum, the consultant and the client should work towards decisions where business and ethics are not in conflict.

Defining what can be judged as ethical in a given context is in itself difficult. Ethical norms are social, culture-bound norms, and different social groups may hold different views. Consultants are of little help to clients if they take a strictly moralistic stance. They can be more helpful by suggesting how to minimize potentially harmful consequences of business decisions, how to increase the social responsibility of the client's business or how to optimize business decisions in terms of financial and social benefits to the various stakeholders who will be affected (see Chapter 23).

6.3 Professional associations and codes of conduct

Professional associations

In a number of countries management consultants have established voluntary professional associations to represent their common interests (for names and addresses see Appendix 2). These associations have played a leading role in promoting professional standards of consulting and in gaining the confidence of management circles and a good reputation in society.

By and large, associations of management consultants contribute to the strengthening of the industry by:

- developing a common body of knowledge;
- defining minimum qualification criteria for new entrants to the field (education, type and length of experience, references, examinations);
- certifying (accrediting) management consultants;
- developing and promoting a code of professional conduct and practice for their members;
- investigating complaints of violations of the code of conduct and taking disciplinary action;
- examining various aspects of management consulting, organizing an exchange of experience and making recommendations to members on improvements in consulting methods, management of firms, training of consultants and other questions important to the development of the profession;
- organizing training events for consultants;
- providing information on services available from members and helping to identify suitable consultants at the request of potential clients;
- defending their members' common interests in dealing with governments, organizations representing clients and other stakeholders interested in the development of consulting and the use of consulting services.

Membership of a professional association is voluntary, but is governed by several conditions defining the member's profile and commitment to a collectively endorsed moral obligation. Not all consultants are members. There have been cases of large consulting firms that do not subscribe to all conditions of membership, or whose management has taken an elitist approach, feeling that a well-established and strong professional firm can define its own standards and does not need guidance or supervision by a professional association. There are individual consultants, too, who are not members because they do not meet some admission criterion, or do not feel that membership offers them any benefits.

In some countries, there are two types of consultants' organization: associations of firms, and institutes or associations of individual consultants. This reflects different perceptions of what consulting firms need as distinct from individuals employed in these firms or working as sole practitioners. Associations of firms tend to focus on the development of firms and on questions that affect the whole consulting industry, while the institutes are mainly interested in the qualifications and development of individual consultants. This dichotomy is quite common in the English-speaking world, although several attempts have been made to convert the "friendly cohabitation" of these voluntary bodies into more active collaboration and even integration.

Where the two types of membership organization exist, dual and overlapping membership is quite common: a consulting firm may be a member of an association, while some or all of the consultants it employs are individual members of an institute.

On average, about 50 per cent of consultants, practising individually or employed by consulting firms, are members of voluntary professional associations of management and business consultants. This figure includes both individual members and consultants who work for firms that are members of a consulting association. It is a low figure bearing in mind the rapidly changing shape of consulting and the need to strengthen professionalism. Some consultants affirm that they would join a professional association that provided useful services and helped members to find new business opportunities. This, however, may be a vicious circle: without a stronger membership and financial base and without the active involvement of the leading professionals, no voluntary association can fully represent the profession and provide a useful service.

The international scene

At the international level, management consulting lacks a world federation that would organize collaboration among national associations and harmonize national and regional efforts to develop the profession. The leading organizations covering the three principal markets for consulting services (but not the whole world) are AMCF (United States), FEACO (Europe) and ZEN-NOH-REN (Japan).

AMCF (Association of Management Consulting Firms) is the oldest association of firms, established in 1926. Its profile is increasingly international since AMCF's leading members are large multinational consultancies based in the United States; non-American firms can also become members.

FEACO (European Federation of Management Consulting Associations) is a regional federation of national associations of management consulting firms (one per country). Most large firms based in the United States have branch offices or affiliated companies in several European countries and participate in FEACO's work through the national associations. FEACO also works directly with large multinational consultancies through a special committee.

ZEN-NOH-REN is a national association with a wide membership base, including other professional organizations in management and productivity in addition to consulting organizations.

Thus the profiles of these three associations are different. Yet they have started to cooperate on matters of common interest, e.g. by jointly organizing major management consultants' conferences and comparing regional experiences.

Collaboration among national management consulting institutes (with individual membership) has been organized by the ICMCI (International Council of Management Consulting Institutes), established in 1987. The Council has chosen to focus on professional development and quality by promoting consultant certification by individual member institutes (members must be committed to the idea of certification) and its international recognition by the profession and the users' community.

Codes of conduct

Professional associations of management consultants attach great importance to codes of professional conduct (ethics, deontology, professional practice), which they use as basic instruments to establish the profession and protect its integrity, and to inform clients about behavioural rules that should be observed by the consultants. They regard the codes as statements that signify voluntary assumption by members of the obligation of self-discipline which can reach above and beyond the requirements of the law. The full texts of codes of conduct are available from the Web pages of most consulting associations (see the addresses in Appendix 2).

It is, of course, not the code of conduct itself, but its consistent and intelligent application by all members of the association which enhances the professional value and integrity of consulting services. Many codes have a clause that commits consultants to do nothing likely to lower the status of management consulting as a profession. This leaves much to the discretion of the consultants themselves.

This is quite reasonable. A code cannot be excessively detailed and specific, since it needs to be applicable to all members and all situations in which they intervene. Furthermore, a code cannot anticipate new problems and future situations in which consultants may have to weigh what is professional and what is not. As pointed out by Gordon Lippitt, "the process of continually evaluating one's code of ethics and the application of those ethics must continue throughout one's professional life, with the use of trusted colleagues as testers and clarifiers. The acquisition of ethical competence reduces anxiety and increases effectiveness in the situational decision making that is a constant in the consulting process."[1]

Assisting professional development

Consultants' associations can help their members to raise the standards of professional service in many ways. These can include training courses for new consultants, refresher training and workshops for experienced practitioners, conferences aimed at broad exchange of information and experience, research into new consulting approaches and methods, information on useful literature and on what goes on in other professions, reports on new trends in management and business and their implications for consulting, and so on.

As consulting is a young profession, all these activities should have a strong educational dimension, emphasizing professional ethics and behaviour as defined by the association's code, in addition to strengthening technical skills.

6.4 Certification and licensing

Whether and how to apply certification (accreditation) or licensing to management consultants is a notoriously controversial subject, debated not only in consulting firms and associations but also among users. This debate is indicative both of the professional aspirations and the growing sense of social responsibility of consultants, and of the various factors that operate against professionalization.

Certification, it is felt in some quarters, would be a step towards a wide recognition of management consulting as a true profession. Business, governments and the public at large want to have a guarantee that management consultants associated with important decisions in the private and public sectors are proven professionals. Certification should enhance the international position of management consulting and help it to compete with other professions, where certification is a long-established practice. It should put more order into the consulting business and help to separate the wheat from the chaff. Finally, certification should be applied to individuals, not to firms: "No true profession can be based on the qualifying of firms", wrote in 1962 James Sandford Smith, Founding President of the United Kingdom Institute of Management Consultancy.

On the other hand, various objections are raised: that certification cannot guarantee anything more than the application of general and rather elementary criteria of admission to the profession; that it cannot show whether a consultant is actually suitable for a given job; and that, after all, consulting to business is itself a business and a consultant who passes the market test by finding enough clients does not need a paper certifying his or her competence.

Opponents of certification also evoke the difficulties involved in defining the scope of management consulting, the lack of a generally accepted body of knowledge, and the overlap between consulting and other professional sectors. Some larger firms contest the legitimacy of consulting institutes to certify their employees. At best they would agree to the certification of individuals who operate on their own, or to the certification of the firm which in turn would be entitled to certify its own employees.

Developments towards certification

Certification has, in fact, been making modest progress. In some 30 countries, the national management consulting institutes have introduced a voluntary certification procedure; a candidate who meets the criteria becomes a "certified

Box 6.4 International model for consultant certification (CMC)

Requirements	
Experience	Three years in management consulting
Education	Recognized degree or professional qualification or additional five years in management consulting in lieu of a degree
Time spent	1,200 hours per annum in active management consulting during the three qualifying years over the preceding five years and currently active in management consulting
Independence	Owner or employee of a firm in independent practice or internal consultant where currently eligible for admission to the institute
Qualification process	
Examination	Written examination or structured interview to test knowledge of the code of professional conduct and common body of knowledge
Sponsors	Two sponsors who are full Members or Fellows (CMC, FCMC, MIMC, FIMC or equivalent)
References	Written descriptions of five assignments and five client references verified through interview
Designations	
Designation	Professional designation exists
Retention	Member may retain designation even after leaving management consulting as long as he or she remains a member in good standing

Source: ICMCI (see www.icmci.com).

management consultant" (CMC). Alternatively, consultants must meet certain criteria to become full members of the institute; full membership is thus equal to certification.

To promote and standardize certification worldwide, the ICMCI has developed an international model (box 6.4) as a set of minimum requirements to be met by national certification procedures. The aim is to achieve international reciprocity among member institutes, whereby the certification awarded by one member institute would be recognized by other institutes participating in the scheme. To encourage consultancies employing large numbers of consultants to become interested in certification and start applying it to their own employees, the Institute of Management Consultancy in the United Kingdom and some other institutes have introduced the concept of "certified practice". A consulting firm that becomes thus certified can decide who among its staff members qualify for certification. They are then certified without involving external persons in the process.

The advancement of certification has, however, been slow and some controversial questions have yet to be answered. Few clients are aware of the existence and value of certification, which is therefore seldom used as a qualification requirement in selecting consultants. The number of certified consultants has also remained very small. Nevertheless, despite its limited quantitative impact, the CMC initiative has made a significant contribution to the promotion of competence and ethical standards in consulting in many parts of the world and to collaboration of consultants from various countries on these issues of common interest.

Licensing

Certification and similar procedures are voluntary, and fully in the hands of a private membership organization. Licensing or official registration can be made compulsory. This means that, to be authorized to practise, a professional (firm or individual person) must request and obtain an official licence, for which the professional must meet certain criteria. Certification does not have to be a criterion. The licence can be withdrawn in instances of malpractice. Licensing can be done directly by a government authority, or delegated to a semi-official agency or a membership association, which carries it out under government guidance and surveillance.

By and large, management consultants have little experience of licensing; their views on this practice reflect mainly their general attitudes to free competition and to government intervention. Some consultants are strongly opposed to the idea of licensing, which they regard as an unnecessary bureaucracy and infringement of their freedom. They claim that in consulting it is impossible to define any meaningful criteria for licensing except those that concern any business. Others recognize that progression towards professionalism may require some form of flexible and non-bureaucratic licensing, with a key role being played by professional membership organizations enjoying a high reputation and the full confidence, not only of the consultants, but also of clients, government authorities and the general public.

6.5 Legal liability and professional responsibility

Management consultants, as any other professional advisers, are not immune from being held legally responsible in certain cases where their advice or recommendations are deemed to cause pecuniary damage or loss to their clients or, perhaps, others in a relationship with their clients. While such legal liability might be more problematic in the case of engineering or computer consultants, it is not insignificant in the "pure" management consulting area. This section looks briefly into the standards used in various legal systems in determining liability and in assessing the amount of damages awarded, as well as the question of insurance available to consultants to cover such liability, and other means by which consultants may protect themselves.

First, it should be pointed out that, in countries where the courts have easily found liability stemming from professional advice given by consultants, and where clients/plaintiffs have been awarded large amounts of damages, one undesirable effect has sometimes been to induce a certain reticence on the part of consultants to recommend bold, novel and imaginative solutions to their clients' problems. In other words, fear of possible legal action can lead to over-cautiousness and risk avoidance. Even where insurance is available (usually at considerable expense) to mitigate the consultant's actual loss, the mere fact of being deemed responsible for negligence or for contractual breaches, and the repercussions on the consultant's reputation, may be sufficient to dampen his or her enthusiasm and innovativeness in advising clients.

Liability: why and when?

This being said, legal liability will normally, and in principle, flow only from a clear demonstration of malpractice in the form of non-professionalism bordering on or carrying over into the realm of gross negligence or fraud. Although not always respected in practice, the rule should be that an honest error of professional judgement in and of itself should not entail the legal liability of the consultant. As a minimum there should be a demonstration of noncompliance with an accepted standard for the profession and/or deviation from the requirements of the consulting contract.

While this is not often easy to establish, lawsuits are more frequently brought and won (and judgements or settlements are larger) in certain legal systems (many cite the very litigious American system) than in others. Where this is the case, a contributing factor may be the nature of the defendant/consultant, i.e. where a big firm is involved which, in the eyes of a court or jury, can easily pay large amounts in reparation. The same effect may be seen where it is known that the defendant is covered by insurance, and the insurance company itself is seen as having "deep pockets". In both cases the finder of facts, jury or judge, may pay less heed to a thorough search for real fault by the defendant. In fact, in some societies there may be a view that where there has been loss, there must be a legal remedy. In any case there is a general trend towards finding liability more easily, and compensating (sometimes problematical) harm more handsomely, and this warrants consideration and possible defensive action by professional management consultants.[2]

It should be noted that it is normally no defence for the consultant to assert that he or she was merely giving advice or recommendations. The client has the "right" to rely on the expertise proffered by the consultant. The fact that the client was under absolutely no obligation to follow such advice or accept such recommendations counts for little, juridically speaking, if it can be demonstrated that the consultant's action was patently unprofessional and did not meet the standards of the profession. Of course, in order for a plaintiff to prevail, damages or loss directly consequential to following the advice and recommendations of the consultant must be shown as well. In other words, the loss or "injury" must be directly traceable to the negligence (or contractual non-performance) of the consultant.

Another significant aspect of this whole question is the financial situation of the management consultant and, in particular, the single practitioner or the very small firm. If the consultancy is organized as a limited liability company, or even if it has no corporate structure, its assets may not be sufficient to allow the client to recover the loss or damages suffered, or even to make a lawsuit economically worth while. Nevertheless, as noted earlier, it is far from pleasant to be accused of unprofessional conduct in the exercise of a consultancy.

Minimizing liability

One way of minimizing possible legal liability is for consultants to ensure that the terms of reference and specifications of the consultancy are clearly and unambiguously spelled out in the consultancy contract. Ambiguities in this regard often lead to expectations on the part of the client which are not intended by the consultant. Such misunderstandings can in turn lead to allegations of failure by the consultant to adhere to the contract, and to claims and lawsuits. Such a situation should be avoidable if due care is taken in drafting the contract.

Another means of attenuating, if not eliminating, possible liability for the consultant is to negotiate a clause in the consultancy agreement in which such liability is limited to a specified amount. It is quite common to find clauses that specify that the consultant's maximum liability for professional acts of misfeasance or nonfeasance (or breach of the consultancy contract) is to be limited to a specified amount or to the total amount of the fee. Obviously such a clause must be negotiated and mutually agreed, and agreement will depend on the relative bargaining strength of the consultant and the client. The consultant should also keep in mind that there may be national legal restrictions on the possibility and extent of a limitation of liability.

In view of the tendency towards litigation in certain countries, an arbitration clause is sometimes included in the consultancy contract. Such clauses normally stipulate that in case of disagreement over the fulfilment of the obligations of the contract, or in case of other dispute arising under the contract, recourse is to be had to agreed arbitration (a single arbitrator or board of arbitrators) rather than to the courts. The idea is that arbitration of claims by an arbitrator or arbitration board which is knowledgeable and impartial will guarantee that the consultant does not become an innocent victim of the tendency of certain parties to sue at the drop of a hat and for judgements to be out of line with reality. Of course any such clause must be agreed to by the client, who may also take the initiative to include such a clause to better protect his or her interests.

Professional liability insurance

Insurance against professional fault and liability becomes a serious consideration for management consultants who wish to protect themselves from possible economic disaster resulting from the practice of their profession. In some situations the client may insist that the consultant carry appropriate insurance in order to protect the client in case of damage or loss owing to the activities of the consultant. Consultants may insure themselves either generally over a period of time or in respect of a single project. Indeed, the contracting of insurance is current practice for many of the large consultancy firms, and particularly those whose practice can give rise to the possibility of costly claims by clients. However, insurance coverage can be expensive, with rather high "deductibles" (the insured's contribution in meeting losses) and is not available everywhere. Where it is, premiums can amount to a significant percentage of gross billings (as much as 5 per cent or more for consultants who are considered to present higher risks).

Such insurance coverage is not standardized, even in the United States and United Kingdom, where it is probably most common. Thus the policies, in terms of the risks covered, deductible amount, premiums and other aspects, frequently have to be negotiated between the consultant and the insurer. Obviously, the particular nature of typical or specific consultancies performed will figure prominently in the assessment of the risk component. Typically, insurance will cover the consultant if he or she is found to have performed negligently, but not in case of, for example, failure to deliver or fraud. In certain countries, there is a move towards professional associations either arranging for or sponsoring individual or group liability insurance for their members.

Finally, consultants should consider whether their insurance coverage should include personal injury claims of third parties (e.g. employees or clients of the client) who may have claims allegedly resulting from the activities and recommendations of the consultant.

Liability awareness and diverse jurisdictions

Consultants should be aware, at least in a general way, of the possible liability they may be exposed to in undertaking consultancies. This is obviously of greater importance (and more difficult) for consultants who operate internationally and hence are subject to different legislation and jurisprudence depending where the consultancy takes place. In this regard, the consulting contract may specify the governing (applicable) law, in the event of legal claims arising out of the agreement, by reference to a particular country that is related in one way or another to the contractual relationship (e.g. place of conclusion of the contract, domicile of one or the other of the parties, or place where the work is to be performed).

For this and other reasons, consultants may wish to seek competent legal advice, particularly where an assignment may involve more than minimal risks of possible liability. In a number of countries, there is a growing group of lawyers who specialize in legal liability of professionals.

Professional responsibility

The relationship between legal liability and professional responsibility in consulting, generally speaking, is a relationship between law and ethics. Legal liability of professionals is a legal construct, imposed by law. It is applicable only if there are appropriate rules or laws, and an institutional framework able to enforce them. In contrast, professional responsibility can be defined as a set of voluntarily adopted and self-imposed values, norms and constraints, reflecting the professionals' conception of their role in the economy and in society, and their responsibility towards the clients. It is an ethical and cultural concept. Differences in the application of legal liability in various countries are due to different legal systems. Differences in professional responsibility reflect different social and professional cultures.

As discussed earlier, professional responsibility covers a wide range of issues in which a consultant must choose among alternative modes of behaviour. The quality of the consulting service is the best example. In most assignments, the quality of the services provided will depend entirely or predominantly on the consultant's own judgement, which in turn will be guided by his or her sense of responsibility towards the client. Legal liability will be applicable only to a very small number of extreme cases, where service quality has dropped to the level of malpractice and has caused damage to the client.

A strong sense of professional responsibility, and not a cautiously formulated consulting contract, is therefore the best safeguard in avoiding legal liability. Most instances where a professional adviser's legal liability is in question are not due to bad intentions but can be traced to breaches of professional responsibility such as inadequate research and fact-finding, appointment of incompetent staff, hasty and superficial judgement, or failure to inform the client of the risks involved and issues that could not be taken into consideration.

It is the policy of professional consulting associations to define ethical and behavioural norms which express their members' professional responsibility above and beyond the requirements of law. In this way the professional associations guide and educate their members and protect the profession. This protection also includes disciplinary procedures and measures in cases of violation of the codes of conduct. However, in management consulting these disciplinary measures tend to be exceptional and their impact has remained limited. Professional associations can deal with cases of conduct that are contrary to the adopted codes if such cases are brought to their attention. They have no mandate and no resources for acting, on a continuing basis, as inspectors of their members' professional behaviour.

Therefore, in the end it is the consulting firm that must define for itself its perception of professional responsibility and integrity, and instil in every consultant employed by the firm a strong sense of professional responsibility.

[1] G. Lippitt and R. Lippitt: *The consulting process in action* (La Jolla, CA, University Associates, 1978), p. 74.

[2] In some countries a counter-trend has been apparent in recent years. This legislative and practical development is probably a reaction by law-makers and the judiciary to past excesses.

PART II

THE CONSULTING PROCESS

7 ENTRY

Entry is the initial phase in any consulting process and assignment. During entry, the consultant and the client meet, try to learn as much as possible about each other, discuss and define the reason for which the consultant has been brought in, and on this basis agree on the scope of the assignment and the approach to be taken. The results of these first contacts, discussions, examinations and planning exercises are then reflected in the consulting contract, the signature of which can be regarded as the conclusion of this initial phase.

Entry is very much an exercise in matching. The client wants to be sure that he is dealing with the right consultant, and the consultant needs to be convinced that he is the right person, or that his firm is the right consulting organization, to address the problems of this particular client. Such a matching exercise can be difficult technically, but there may be even more difficult psychological problems. True, the client has invited the consultant, or agreed to consider his offer, and did so with some purpose in mind. It may be that he has turned to the consultant with great hopes, or regards him as a last-resort solution in a crisis. Nevertheless, the consultant is a stranger to the client organization. There may be mistrust, uncertainty, anxiety. The consultant has probably been in similar situations before. He knows, however, that his past successes with other clients are by no means a guarantee of repeated success. Furthermore, the client may have decided to talk to several consultants before choosing one for the assignment.

Thus the contacts and activities that constitute the initial phase of the consulting process have to achieve considerably more than the definition of terms of reference and the signature of a contract. The foundations of successful assignments are laid at this very early stage by establishing mutual trust and empathy, agreeing on the "rules of the game", and starting the assignment with shared optimism and a vision of what can be achieved.

The full range of initial contact activities described in this chapter concerns new assignments with new clients. If a consultant returns to a familiar client organization in repeat business, entry will be simplified. Even in such cases, however, a new assignment with a previous client may well involve dealing with different issues and making new relationships between people.

7.1 Initial contacts

The consultant makes the contact

Contacting potential clients without being solicited by them – cold calling – is one of the ways of marketing consulting services (this will be discussed in detail in Chapter 29). A cold call can arouse the interest of the client, who may decide to keep the consultant's name in mind for the future. Only rarely would a cold contact lead immediately to an assignment.

If the consultant contacts a client about whom he has a certain amount of information, and can show that he knows about that client's problems and intentions and has something relevant to offer, the chances are better that such an initiative will produce an assignment. This can also happen if the consultant is introduced by another client for whom he has worked in the past.

A special case is when public authorities or other organizations publicly announce their intention to carry out a consulting project, and invite consultants to manifest their interest or submit proposals. In such a situation, a number of consultants will almost certainly offer their services.

The client makes the contact

In most cases it will be the client who makes the first contact. This implies that he or she is aware of problems and need for independent advice in his or her organization, and has decided to bring in a management consultant. In addition, the client must have a reason for turning to a particular consultant:

- he or she has heard about the consultant's professional reputation;
- a business friend who was satisfied with the consultant's services recommended him or her (very frequent);
- the client found the consultant in a register or directory (less frequent);
- the consultant's publications or interventions at management conferences have impressed the client;
- the client has been contacted by the consultant previously;
- the client is returning to a consultant whose work was fully satisfactory in the past (repeat business can be very important).

In any event, the consultant should find out why the client selected him or her; this will not be difficult.

First meetings

The importance of the consultant's behaviour and performance during the first meetings with the client cannot be overemphasized. In meeting a client to negotiate a specific assignment the consultant is marketing his or her services and it is not certain that a contract will be concluded. The first meeting should therefore be regarded as an opportunity to gain the client's confidence and make a favourable impression.

The consultant should make sure that he or she will meet the decision-maker – the person who is not only technically interested in the assignment but also able to authorize it, and who will make sure that the required resources will be available. If a top executive (managing director or senior administrator) of an important organization agrees to meet the consultant, the consulting firm should send a representative who is at an equally high level.

The question of who should go to the first meeting with the client may present a problem if a consulting organization uses one group of consultants (partners or other seniors) for negotiating assignments, and another group (including both senior and junior staff) for executing them. Some clients know about this pattern of organizing professional services and do not object to it. Many clients, however, do not like it. They emphasize, rightly, that a productive consultant–client relationship starts with the first meetings and preliminary surveys and that it is at this moment that they decide whether they wish to work, not only with the consulting organization, but with the particular people. Also, many resent an approach whereby the best people represent the consulting firm at the beginning in order to impress clients, but execution is in the hands of lower-calibre staff.

Preparing for initial meetings

Initial meetings require thorough preparation by the consultant. Without going into much detail, he or she should collect essential orientation information about the client, the environment, and the characteristic problems of the sector of activity concerned. The client does not want the consultant to come with ready-made solutions, but expects someone who is familiar with the kinds of problems found in his or her company. The consultant should find a subtle way of demonstrating this.

In collecting orientation information, the consultant could start by finding out what products or services the client provides. This information is easily obtained during the very first contact with the client, from a Web site, or by asking for sales literature to be supplied. The nature of the products or services will place the client within a specific sector or trade, and the consultant will need to know its main characteristics and practices. Usually he or she will gather information on:

- commonly used terminology;
- nature and location of markets;
- names and location of main producers;
- types and sources of raw materials;

- weights and measures used in the industry;
- processes and equipment;
- business methods and practices peculiar to the industry;
- laws, rules and customs governing the industry;
- history and growth;
- present economic climate, and main problems and development prospects of the industry.

Trade journals and government publications will provide much of the information, especially on industry sector trends. As regards technology, it is important to find out if the client expects the consultant to know it well or merely show some familiarity with its main characteristics and trends. The consultant also needs some selected information on the position of the client's business before the first meeting. He or she may be able to learn the client's financial position, recent operating results and immediate expectations and problems from published annual reports or returns filed in a public registry or credit service.

Agenda for the first meeting

The first meeting is a form of investigational interview in which each party seeks to learn about the other. The consultant should encourage the client to do most of the talking, to speak about the firm, the difficulties, hopes and expectations. It is as well for the discussion to develop from the general situation to the particular and to focus eventually on the real issue.

In listening and putting questions, the consultant assesses the client's needs in terms of management and business practice, future development prospects, personal concerns, perception of consulting, and readiness to work with consultants assuming different types of role. The consultant decides how best to describe the nature and method of consulting as it applies to the client's context, being careful not to repeat information that is probably already known to the client.

The consultant's key objective at the meeting will be to convince the client that he or she is making the right choice. "Unless their skills are truly unique, professionals never get hired because of their technical capabilities. Excellent capabilities are essential to get you into the final set to be considered, but it is other things that get you hired"[1] (box 7.1).

The individual who invited the consultant into the organization may be the "contact client" and not the "main or primary client" as described in section 3.2, i.e. the person who "owns the problem" and will play the main role in solving it. All too often the consultant is invited in by top management to act as an adviser to somebody lower in the hierarchy. This "client" may not feel the need to work with a consultant, or may even resent being forced to do so by a superior. The consultant may have to spend some time clarifying these relations. Clearly, the client who will work with the consultant should be specifically identified and a rapport should be established between them.

Box 7.1 What a buyer looks for

- In selecting a professional, I am not just buying a service, I am entering into a relationship. Your selling task is to earn my trust and confidence – with an emphasis on the word "earn". How you behave during the interview (or proposal process) will be taken as proxy for how you will deal with me after I retain you.
- The first thing that will catch my attention is your preparation. There is little so off-putting as someone who begins by asking me some basic facts about my company or situation that they could have found out in advance. Preparation is your opportunity to demonstrate initiative.
- Professionals who are over-eager to impress come across as insensitive. I do not want to hear about you and your firm, I want to talk about me and my situation. Show a sympathetic understanding of my role in my company.
- You've got to give a favour to get a favour. There is no better way to win my trust than to be helpful to me right from the beginning.
- Give me an education. Tell me something I did not know. Demonstrate your creativity.
- To avoid coming across as arrogant, patronizing and pompous, turn your assertions into questions. By doing so, you convert possible signs of assertiveness into evidence that you'll respect my opinions and involve me in the thinking process.
- Don't start telling me how you can solve my problems until I have acknowledged that there's a problem or an opportunity here. Convince me that the issue is big enough to bother with.
- If I interrupt you, deal with my question. I want to see how you handle yourself if I ask a question, not how practised you are at your standard spiel.
- Don't try any "closing techniques" on me. If you try to rush me, I'll take it as a sign that you are more interested in making a sale than in helping me.
- The key is empathy – the ability to enter my world and see it through my eyes.

Source: Excerpts from D. Maister: "How clients choose", in *Managing the professional service firm* (New York, The Free Press, 1993).

The client may wish to discuss the proposed work with other clients of the consultant, former or current, and may ask for references at any moment during the entry phase. In giving names, the consultant must respect confidentiality and cite only those clients who have agreed to provide references.

As regards fees, the client may know how consultants charge for their interventions and be aware of the rates applied. If not, the consultant will have to consider at what stage of the entry phase this information should be given to the client. Some clients will ask about standard fees and other costs at the outset; others will wait until the consultant has formulated a proposal and made an offer (see Chapter 30 on consulting fees).

The client may be eager to proceed without any preliminary diagnosis and planning or, on the contrary, may take time to make up his mind, even though he obviously has problems with which the consultant can help. The consultant should take the time and trouble to explain and persuade, keeping mainly to the potential benefits to the client. Pressing for an immediate decision is not a good tactic; it is also not good for the client to get the impression that the consultant badly needs the assignment because he or she does not have enough work.

The consultant should not be insistent if he or she is clearly not on the same wavelength as the client. If the client has firm ideas on how the consultant should proceed, and the consultant does not agree, it is better to drop the assignment. This could be suggested by either the consultant or the client.

Agreement on how to proceed

If the consultant and the client conclude that they are interested in principle in working together, several further questions must be answered. Except in straightforward cases, which are often an extension of past work, it would not be reasonable to start an assignment without some preliminary analysis and work planning. The terms of business must be discussed and agreed. These are the activities that follow the first meeting.

Once the client is ready to agree to a preliminary and short problem diagnosis,[2] the discussion can move on to the arrangements for it, covering:

- scope and purpose of a preliminary diagnosis;
- records and information to be made available;
- who should be seen and when;
- how to introduce the consultant;
- attitudes of staff to the matters to be surveyed;
- when to conclude the preliminary diagnosis and how to present proposals to the client;
- payment for the diagnosis.

If the client has contacted several consultants in order to be able to choose among alternative proposals, he or she should, in principle, tell the consultant about it. In some cases a formal selection procedure may be applied: the consultant's proposals then have to be presented in a predetermined format by a given date. The client will then take some time (say 30–45 days) to compare the proposals received and make a choice.

A preliminary diagnosis or survey that is very short, say one or two days, is not usually charged for. However, if the contract is awarded, the consultant may include in the bill the time spent on this preliminary diagnosis. If, on the other hand, the assignment is complex, and the preliminary diagnosis requires a longer time, the client will usually be asked to pay for it. This helps to avoid two practices that are undesirable:

- the practice of some consultants of using free diagnostic surveys as a marketing tool (since the consultant cannot really work for nothing, another client will then pay for this "free" survey); and
- the practice of some clients of collecting a large amount of information and ideas from several consultants, who are all invited to make the same survey, without paying anything.

Free diagnostic surveys used to be quite common in some countries in the past, but have recently been much less so.

7.2 Preliminary problem diagnosis

The preliminary diagnosis should start from the moment the consultant is in touch with the client. Everything is relevant: who made the initial contact and how; how the consultant is received at the first meeting; what sort of questions the client asks; if there are any undertones in those questions; what the client says about the business and his competitors; if the client is relaxed or tense; and so on. The consultant has to sort out this information and then complete the picture by getting some hard data and looking at the problem from new angles – for example, by talking to people other than those involved in the first meetings.

Scope of the diagnosis

The purpose of the preliminary problem diagnosis is not to propose measures for solving the problem, but to define and plan a consulting assignment or project which will have this effect. The scope of the preliminary diagnosis is limited to a quick gathering and analysis of essential information which, according to the consultant's experience and judgement, is needed to understand the problem correctly, to see it in the wider context of the client organization's activities, achievements, goals, and other existing or potential business and management problems, and realistically to assess opportunities for helping the client.

The scale of this preliminary diagnosis depends very much on the nature of the problem. Very specific and technical issues do not normally require a comprehensive survey of the whole client organization. On the other hand, the consultant must avoid the trap of accepting a client's narrow definition of a problem as technical without looking into the constraints and factors that may impede the solution of that problem, or may show that the problem is much more or much less serious than the client thinks. Therefore even if the problem lies in one functional area only, or concerns the application of some specific techniques, the consultant should always be interested in the more general characteristics of the client organization.

If the consultant is brought in to deal with a general and major problem, such as deteriorating financial results, or inability to maintain the same pace of innovation as competitors, a general and comprehensive diagnosis or management survey of the client organization is essential.

The time allocated to preliminary problem diagnosis is relatively short. As a rule, one to four days would be required. In the case of more complex assignments concerning several aspects of the client's business, five to ten days may be needed. If a more extensive survey is required (e.g. in preparing company turnarounds, major reorganizations, buy-outs or mergers, or for any other reason), this can no longer be considered a preliminary diagnosis, but an in-depth diagnostic survey (see Chapter 12).

Some methodological guidelines

The basic rules, procedures and analytical techniques used in the preliminary problem diagnosis are the same as those of the later diagnosis, as reviewed in detail in Chapter 8. Many consulting firms have developed their own approaches and guidelines for a quick assessment of clients' businesses.

The diagnosis includes the gathering and analysis of information on the client's activities, performance and perspectives. It also includes discussions with selected managers and other key people, and in certain cases also with people outside the client organization. Basically, the consultant is not interested in fine details, but is looking for trends, relationships and proportions. An experienced consultant needs to be observant and can often sense potential problems or opportunities that are not immediately apparent: the way people talk to and about each other, the respect for hierarchical relations, the cleanliness of workshops and offices, the handling of confidential information, the courtesy of the receptionist, and so on.

It is essential to take a dynamic and comprehensive view of the organization, its environment, resources, goals, activities, achievements and perspectives. Dynamism in this context means examining key achievements and events in the life of the organization and probable future trends as reflected in existing plans and assessed by the consultant personally. The client's strengths and weaknesses ought to be viewed in a time perspective – a present strength may be merely short-term, while a weakness, hidden at present, may become a threat to the client's organization in the long term. The consultant should look particularly at future opportunities – indeed, the detailed diagnosis and further work to be proposed to the client should be oriented towards these opportunities above all. This approach is summarized in figure 7.1.

As already mentioned, even if the problem is, or is likely to be, in a single functional area, the consultant should take a comprehensive view of the organization. How comprehensive is a matter of experience and judgement, and no universal recipe can be given. Most management consultants emphasize the need for some sort of wider appraisal of the organization before confirming the existence even of a fairly limited problem, and the feasibility of handling it within certain terms of reference.

It is recommended that the consultant should proceed from the general to the particular: from overall objectives and global performance indicators to the reasons for substandard performance or missed opportunities (or to interesting

Figure 7.1 The consultant's approach to a management survey

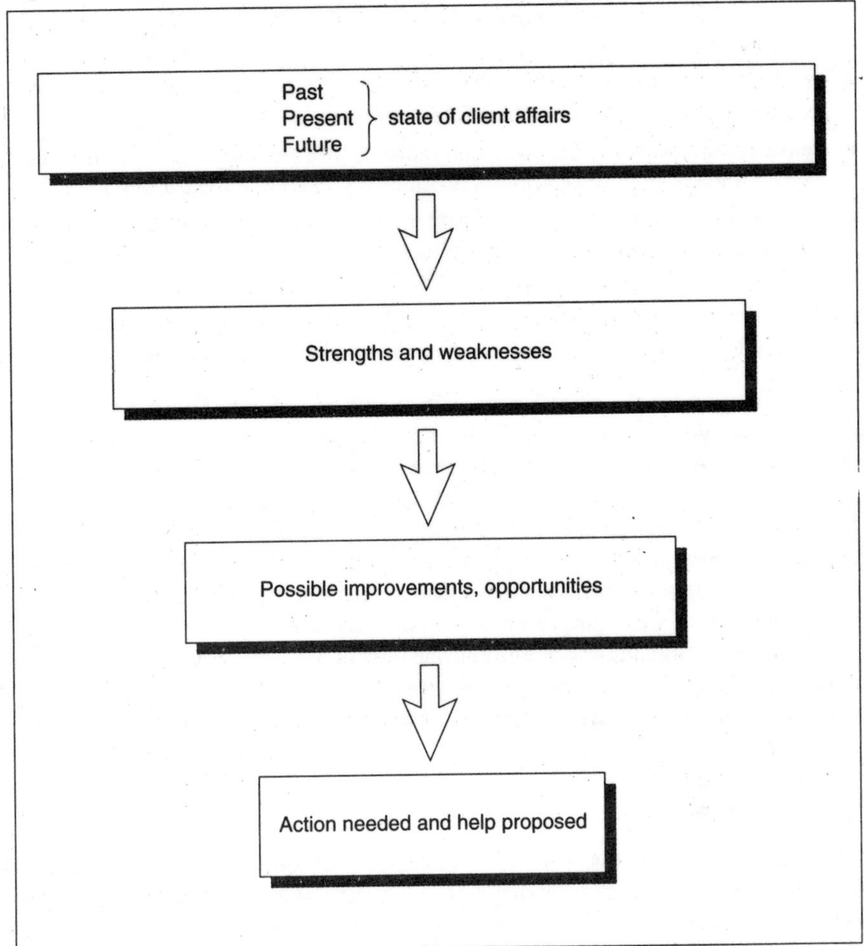

future opportunities), and then to an examination in some detail of selected areas of the organization's activities. An approach that starts the other way round, by examining each management function or process (production, purchasing, marketing, etc.) in turn and hoping for a balanced synthesis at the end, will entail much unnecessary work and might well prove misdirected. The movement from the general to the particular helps the consultant to limit the preliminary diagnostic survey to matters of critical concern, or conversely may indicate that, to stand the best chance of achieving the results expected, the inquiry must take into account every aspect of the enterprise's operation.

Such an approach implies that the consultant's analysis will focus on basic relationships and proportions in the client organization, such as the following:

- relationships and proportions between major processes, functions and activity areas (e.g. allocation of human and financial resources to marketing, research and development, production, administration);
- relationships between main inputs and outputs (e.g. sales related to materials consumed, the wage bill and the total workforce);
- relationships between the principal indicators of performance, effectiveness and efficiency (e.g. productivity, profitability, resource utilization, growth);
- relationships between global performance indicators and main factors affecting their magnitude in a positive or negative way (e.g. influence of the volume of work in progress on working capital and profitability);
- the contribution of the main divisions and product (service) lines to the results (profitability, image, etc.) achieved by the organization as a whole.

The comprehensive, overall approach should be combined with a functional approach as necessary. For example, the precarious financial situation of a company may be caused by problems in any functional area: by badly organized production, by costly or ineffective marketing, by excessive spending on unproductive research, by the shortage or high cost of capital, or something else. As already mentioned, if an assignment is likely to be exclusively or mainly in one technical area, this area will need to be examined in greater depth than other areas, and the examination of the organization as a whole will be limited to what is necessary.

In summary, this approach will tell the consultant if the work envisaged can make a meaningful contribution to the principal objectives of the client organization and what critical relationships and linkages are likely to affect the course of the assignment.

Using comparison

While recognizing that every client organization is unique and has to be treated as such, the consultant needs reference points that can guide him or her in a preliminary quick assessment of strengths, weaknesses, development prospects and desirable improvements. The consultant will find these by making comparisons with:

- past achievements (if the organization's performance has deteriorated and the problem is essentially corrective);
- the client's own objectives, plans and standards (if real performance does not measure up to them);
- other comparable organizations (to assess what has been achieved elsewhere and whether the same thing would be possible in the client organization);
- sectoral standards (available in the consulting firm or from another source).

A comparison of well-selected data with sectoral standards or with data from specific similar organizations is a powerful diagnostic tool. It helps not only in quick orientation, but also in making the client aware of the situation, which may be quite different from what he or she believes.

The comparisons should encompass not only figures, but also qualitative information (e.g. the organizational structure, the corporate culture, the computer applications, or the market-research techniques used). In other words, the consultant should determine what levels of sophistication and performance and what sorts of problems he or she would normally expect to find in an organization of the type of the client enterprise.

Such a consideration is meaningful if the consultant has some method of classifying and comparing organizations (e.g. by sector, product type, size, ownership, market served and the like). For each class there would be a list of various attributes that are characteristic of it. Many well-established consulting firms provide their consultants with such data and guide them by means of manuals and checklists for management surveys and company appraisals. It is in the interest of the new firms to acquire or develop such documentation.[3]

Notwithstanding certain general rules, senior consultants undertaking diagnostic surveys tend to have their personal priorities and specific approaches. Many of them start by looking at important financial data, since these reflect the level and results of the activities of the enterprise in a way that lends itself to synthesis. Others emphasize production: they believe that a simple factory tour is most revealing and tells an experienced observer a great deal about the quality of management. Still others prefer to examine markets, products and services before turning to a financial appraisal and further investigations. These are just different starting-points reflecting personal experience and preferences: eventually the consultant has to study all areas and questions needed for a global diagnosis in order to see the problem in context and perspective.

The client's involvement

The dialogue with the client should be pursued during problem diagnosis. The consultant should find out how the client feels about various aspects of the business: what its goals, objectives and technical and human capabilities are, what its potential is for making changes, and what style of consulting should be applied. The client, on the other hand, gets to know the consultant better and has an opportunity to appreciate his or her way of obtaining information, establishing contacts with people, grasping the overall situation, making judgements and distilling essential facts from the vast amount of data that can be found in any organization.

Sources of information

A successful diagnostic survey is based on the rapid collection of selective information that reveals the type and extent of help that the consultant can give to the client. Diagnostic data tend to be global in nature. The main sources of information for a preliminary diagnostic survey are published material and records (box 7.2), observation and interviewing by the consultant, and contacts outside the client organization.

Box 7.2 Information materials for preliminary surveys

Client's publications (including material published through the Internet):

- annual financial and activity reports;
- financial, statistical, trade and customs returns to government, trade associations and credit organizations;
- economic surveys;
- sales promotion material such as catalogues and advertising brochures;
- press releases, interviews given by management, etc.

Information from other published sources:

- conditions and trends in the client's economic sector, including technological developments;
- information on business firms in the sector;
- industrial outlook studies;
- trade statistics and reports;
- industry norms and key business ratios;
- regulations which the client must observe;
- corporation income tax returns (if published);
- labour–management relations.

Client's internal records and reports:

- information on resources, objectives, plans and performance;
- information on plant, technologies and equipment used;
- reports on financial results and costs of activities, services and products;
- minutes of board and management committee meetings;
- tax returns;
- sales statistics;
- movement of material;
- staff appraisal, etc.

Documentation files of the consulting firm:

- information on the client;
- information on the sector and similar organizations.

Observing activities and interviewing key people are vital to information-gathering. Tours of the client's premises, seeing people in action and hearing their views, worries and suggestions, give direct indications of how the organization works in practice, the pace it sets and the relationships between its workers. These are invaluable insights which records cannot convey; however, extensive interviewing and observation of activities are beyond the possibilities of preliminary surveys.

Contacts with other organizations associated with the client may be made either by the consultant, or by the client personally. During their work, consultants make contact with many organizations apart from those of their clients. These contacts not only assist the current assignment but also establish a relationship which can be used in future work. For example, contacts may be established with trade unions, employers' and trade associations, sectoral research institutions, or management associations.

The consultant should inform the client of the purpose and nature of any contact made. The client may personally contact some outside bodies (e.g. employers' associations), and should know of any consultant contact. Talking to the client's customers is an essential source of information and ideas for management consultants, but contacts with customers should not be made without the client's agreement.

Alternative approaches

The approach described in the previous paragraphs is the traditional consultant's approach: the consultant performs the diagnosis as an expert, using data collection and analytical techniques of his or her choice, with some participation by the client. Moving along the continuum of consulting roles towards the process function, the client and his staff become more active and the consultant focuses on providing effective diagnostic methods instead of personally carrying out the diagnosis.

For example, some consultants use *problem-identification workshops* which can be run as part of a problem- and action-oriented management development programme, or used directly as a technique for identifying problems and opportunities on which the organization will have to act. In this workshop or group approach, the members of the group develop their own lists of problems requiring action, compare and discuss their lists, and agree on a joint list and on priorities. They then work separately on a more detailed definition and analysis of the principal problems from each list, paying attention to relations between various problems. This is followed by other meetings, where individual analyses are compared, a collectively agreed analysis is made and action proposals are developed.

This exercise can be organized in one group, or as a system of groups. The initial groups can be heterogeneous (from various levels and functions of management), thus enabling one organizational process or problem to be examined from several angles. Alternatively, technically homogeneous, functional or departmental groups can first look at one problem from their specific technical angles (financial, organizational, production, staffing, etc.), followed by workshops involving representatives of the different groups, who meet to compare and harmonize their viewpoints and develop a problem definition that is endorsed by all groups. Often it is more effective if groups look at organizational processes rather than at fragmented tasks and units.

Management may decide to involve an external or internal consultant in these group exercises. The consultant's approach may be low-key, reminding the group of the appropriate procedure, of criteria that may have been overlooked, and of methodological errors that might lead to false conclusions.

The use of the group approach is often preceded by a thorough explanation of diagnostic, problem-solving and performance-improvement methods. If appropriate, the consultant may also provide technical information on the problem under discussion (e.g. data from similar organizations for comparison), or help to collect input data on which the groups can work.

Self-diagnosis by individual business owners or managers is another approach which has been used in assisting small firms in various countries. The consultant meets with a group of owners or managers of small firms, provides them with a self-diagnostic instrument adapted to their needs, and explains the method to be used. He or she is then available to review the results of the diagnosis and proposals for action with each individual. Alternatively, the business people may agree to meet again to compare indicators characteristic of their firms, and exchange views on factors explaining differences in performance. They may then decide individually or as a group on the courses of action to follow in each firm. The consultant may be engaged to help them in further group work, or work separately with individual members of the group (see also Chapter 24).

Self-diagnosis can be an individual exercise undertaken by one client firm from the outset. The consultant may supply checklists and methodological tools for the client's use. Or the client may apply his or her own diagnostic approach based on industry experience and practices; the consultant's role is then to check the client's self-diagnosis for completeness and accuracy. The consultant could also help the client to view the business from a wider perspective.

Further approaches are described in section 4.5.

7.3 Terms of reference

Terms of reference (see box 7.3) are the initial statement of the work to be undertaken by a consultant. Some clients, who prefer to do their own problem identification and diagnosis, may prepare terms of reference for the assignment before talking to any consultant. Others may draft the terms of reference after the preliminary problem diagnosis done by a consultant. They may use one consultant specifically for preliminary diagnosis and drafting terms of reference. These terms are then used for initiating a formal selection procedure to designate another consultant who will execute the assignment. The consultant who was employed for drafting the terms of reference may even be excluded from the next phase. Still others may not use any formal terms of reference, but leave the definition of the work to be done to the consulting contract.

The main reasons for these different practices are explained below.

(1) If terms of reference are used:

- the client's policy is to do as much analytical and planning work as possible before considering to use a consultant; often this will be the case with assignments dealing with relatively narrow and well-defined technical issues;
- the client (usually in the public sector) is obliged by existing regulations to draft formal terms of reference, and obtain approval of them, as an initial step in a formal consultant selection procedure.

Box 7.3 Terms of reference – checklist

1. Description of the problem(s) to be solved
2. Objectives and expected results of the assignment (what is to be achieved, final product)
3. Background and supporting information (on client organization, other related projects and consultancies, past efforts to solve problems, etc.)
4. Budget estimate or resource limit
5. Timetable (starting and completion dates, key stages and control dates)
6. Interim and final reporting (dates, form, to whom, etc.)
7. Inputs to be provided by the client (further information and documentation, staff time, secretarial support, transport, etc.)
8. Exclusions from the assignment (what will not be its object)
9. Constraints and other factors likely to affect the project
10. Profile and competencies of eligible consultants (education, experience, working language, etc.)
11. Requested consultant inputs into the project (number of consultants, training inputs, other services)
12. Contact persons and addresses

(2) If terms of reference are not used:

– the client (usually in the private sector) prefers to select a consultant, do the preliminary problem diagnosis, and define the scope of the assignment jointly with him or her. The client then confirms the choice on the basis of a proposal received from the consultant, without using the intermediate stage of drafting terms of reference.

Most management consultants are able to adapt their approach to these various contexts and client preferences. When presented with terms of reference drafted by the client or another consultant, the consultant must be cautious in deciding whether to accept these terms at face value. The terms may describe an assignment that is not feasible.

7.4 Assignment strategy and plan

During the initial contacts with the client and the subsequent preliminary problem diagnosis, the consultant should have collected and evaluated enough information to be able to plan the assignment. This is what the client expects at this stage: he or she will want to receive not only the consultant's findings on the problem to be tackled, but also a proposal describing what the consultant suggests doing and under what terms help is offered.

Right from the first contact with the client the consultant should have been thinking of the approach to take, but the final decision should be made only after he or she has become better acquainted with the situation. For example, the level of cooperation of the client's staff during preliminary problem diagnosis may show what consulting mode will be most appropriate (see Chapter 3), and the quality of the data found during this activity suggests how much time will be needed for detailed fact-finding and analysis.

A fundamental aspect of designing and planning a consulting assignment is the choice of *assignment strategy*. By this we mean the respective roles to be played by the consultant and the client, the consulting mode, the pace of operations, the way (and the time sequence) in which the interventions will be applied and harmonized, and the resources allocated to the assignment.

The *assignment plan*, including the strategy that will be followed, is formally presented to the client as a proposal, as described in section 7.5. Assignment planning and drafting of a proposal are not normally finalized on the client's premises. Unless it has been otherwise agreed, the consultant returns to his or her office with the data collected during preliminary problem diagnosis and works on the proposal, often in collaboration with other senior members of the consulting firm. The consultant should never take more time than the client expects. Momentum can be lost and relations can cool down if the client feels that the matter is not receiving enough attention.

The main elements of assignment planning are given below.

Summary of problem

The conclusions from preliminary problem diagnosis are summarized and the consultant presents a description of the problem. This may include a comparison with the original problem definition made by the client: the consultant may suggest widening or narrowing this definition, or refer to other problems discovered and to possible developments (e.g. the effects of recession, or tensions in labour relations) that may take place during the assignment. As appropriate, the problem will be set in the wider context of the client's objectives, trends and resources.

Objectives to achieve and action to take

The assignment plan then outlines the objectives and the results to be achieved and the kind of technical activities that the assignment will consist of. Whenever possible, the objectives should be presented as performance measures in quantified terms, describing benefits that will accrue to the client if the assignment is successfully completed. Global financial benefits are commented on to ensure that the client understands the implications. For example, savings from a reduced inventory of finished goods would only be achieved when stocks had been run down, and this might require production to be cut back for some time. Benefits in other terms are stated as appropriate, e.g. output would increase (in this case the client would be warned of the need for new orders to keep the factory occupied).

Social and qualitative benefits may be difficult to express in figures, but they should be described as precisely and clearly as possible and carefully explained. Vague notions that lend themselves to many different interpretations should be avoided.

In structuring their outline of assignment strategy and plan, many consultants are guided by the definitions of key concepts and terms that prevail in international technical cooperation and are in use worldwide (box 7.4).

A more detailed discussion of these concepts and terms can be found on the web pages of international agencies, programmes and banks active in technical cooperation.

Box 7.4 Concepts and terms used in international technical cooperation projects

International agencies and banks active in technical cooperation are major users and financial sponsors of consulting services. A number of fairly standardized concepts and terms are used in design and management of projects for these agencies:

- **Beneficiary, target group.** Who will actually benefit from the project. The project beneficiary may be different from the client. There may be different sorts of beneficiaries. A distinction is usually made between direct (immediate) project benefiary or recipient, and intended (ultimate) beneficiaries.
- **Purpose.** What is to be accomplished by the project. It is recommended to clarify purposes and keep them constantly in mind in planning and structuring projects.
- **Result.** Generic term used to stress that projects must be results-oriented and aim at (tangible, measurable) results, not just outline what will be done (activities) and what resources will be applied (inputs).
- **Development objective.** Also called ultimate or longer-term objective. Defines a wider perspective, framework, overall direction and ultimate reason for the project. The project "contributes" to achieving it. There will be other contributions.
- **Objective, or immediate objective.** Defines what is to be achieved by the project at its completion. Shows the change that the project is expected to bring about; objectives cannot be described by listing activities (a frequent error in project design).
- **Output.** Tangible product delivered by the project (training package, technical documentation, number of persons trained to a set standard, reorganization proposal, report etc.).
- **Indicator of achievement.** Measurable and controllable indicator, the achievement of which proves that the project has produced a result and achieved an objective. An indicator cannot be an output of the project.
- **Activity.** A set of actions to produce a project output and meet an objective. As a rule, an activity will be related to one or more objectives. Exceptionally, if an objective cannot be set at the project design stage, an activity can be initiated that will permit an objective to be specified at a later stage.
- **Input.** Any resource (human, material, financial, know-how, software, licence, etc.) to be mobilized for the project by the consultant and the client to achieve project objectives. Expressed in qualitative and quantitative terms as necessary.

Phases of the assignment and timetable

The activities and steps of the assignment have to be programmed in some detail. Basically, the consultant will follow the logic of the consulting process as briefly outlined in section 1.4 and described in detail in Chapters 7–11, but will adjust it to the nature of the assignment and to the client's conditions and preferences. This is essential for work scheduling, but also for several other reasons.

The nature of the consultant's and the client's activities will be changing from phase to phase. Both parties must know exactly what the other party expects at each phase. In particular, the client will want to know whether the assignment is making headway towards its final objectives. To make control possible, the assignment plan will describe the outcome of each phase and define what reports will be submitted to the client at what points during the assignment. A major phase may require an end-of-phase report, but in long and complex assignments short interim reports may be required at the end of each subphase or periodically (monthly, quarterly), for monitoring progress and allowing regular payments to be made to the consultant.

The time dimension of the assignment plan is a key element of strategy. What pace of work should be adopted? The urgency of the client's needs is the main determinant. But there are other considerations, such as:

- the client's and the consultant's technical, manpower and financial capacities;
- the feasible and optimum pace of change (as discussed in Chapters 4 and 5);
- the desirability of a phased approach to implementation (starting in a unit that is prepared for change and willing to cooperate, introducing the new scheme on an experimental basis first, etc.).

Role definition

This is another strategic dimension of assignment planning. The consultant will suggest the style or mode of consulting that he or she considers most appropriate, given the nature of the problem and the motivation and capabilities of the client's staff. A general definition of the mode to be used is not enough; precise arrangements have to be proposed. They should specify:

- what activities will be carried out by the client or by the consultant;
- what data and documents will be prepared by whom;
- what meetings, working parties, project groups and other forms of group work will be used and who will be involved;
- what special training and information activities will be undertaken.

It may be both possible and desirable to foresee a shift in roles during the assignment. For example, intensive training of the client's staff in the subject area covered and in problem-solving and change methodologies, carried out at the beginning, may enable the consultant to suggest reducing his presence and changing his role during subsequent phases.

Lack of precision in defining role expectations for each phase of the assignment can cause much misunderstanding. As already mentioned, this happens frequently in connection with implementation. Is the consultant's objective to design a new scheme and submit it in a report, or to help the client to implement the scheme? Who is responsible for what? Where does the consultant's responsibility end? What does the client actually want? Does he want just a report, or is he really keen to complete a change? In designing an effective assignment these questions must be answered.

Following a detailed role definition, the consultant can determine the resources required for each phase of the assignment. These include resources to be made available:

- by the consultant (consultant time, material, clerical support, special computing, research, legal advice, and other services), including their cost;
- by the client (management and staff time, liaison arrangements, administrative support, office facilities, resources for testing, experimental work, computing, and so on).

Obviously, the client will want to know what resources provided by the consultant he or she will have to pay for. But more than that: the client will participate, too, and the inputs required from his or her organization may be high. The failure to quantify them as precisely as possible may cause considerable difficulties once work has started and the client learns that he is supposed to do something which he has not counted on.

It may be difficult to tell the client at this stage how much implementation will cost: it is the action planning phase (Chapter 9) that will generate precise figures. None the less, a preliminary assessment ought to be made in all assignments that are likely to propose costly changes (e.g. new investment or compensation to staff whose employment will be terminated). The client should have the opportunity to look into these probable financial implications before deciding whether to embark on the assignment.

The costing and pricing of an assignment are discussed in detail in section 30.7.

7.5 Proposal to the client[4]

As a rule, the assignment proposed will be described in a document presented to the client for approval and decision. It may be given different names: survey report, technical proposal, project document, project plan, contract proposal, and the like. Some clients require the consultant to present the proposals in a predetermined format. This facilitates study by the client and evaluation of alternative proposals received from several consultants. Furthermore, the format of the proposal may correspond to the format of the consulting contract to be signed.

A proposal submitted to the client is an important selling document. It is not enough for the consultant to have a clear vision of how to execute the assignment: he or she must be able to describe this vision on paper in a way that will make it clear to other people. This may include individuals who have not met the consultant, and will be forming their opinions solely on the basis of the written proposal.

The proposal should be of high technical quality and business-like in its presentation. Writing "winning" proposals is an art that no consultant can afford to ignore.

Sections of the proposal

In most cases, the proposal to the client will include the following four sections:

- technical aspects;
- staffing;
- consultant background;
- financial and other terms.

The technical aspects section describes the consultant's preliminary assessment of the problem, the purpose to be pursued, the approach to be taken, and the work programme to be followed. These topics were reviewed in sections 7.2 to 7.4.

One caveat has to be entered: the consultant and the client may have a different conception of how detailed and specific this technical section should be. If it is too global, the client may feel that the consultant is not clearly explaining what he or she proposes to do. In contrast, if it is too detailed and specific, the consultant may have gone beyond assignment planning, and have already embarked on executing the assignment without having obtained the client's agreement. This may present no problem if a cooperative relationship has already been established and the consultant is sure to get the assignment. If it is not clear who will be chosen (e.g. if several consultants were invited to submit proposals), this may prove to be a reckless approach: giving away expertise before the assignment has been approved.

The staffing section gives the names and profiles of the consultant company's staff who will be executing the assignment. This includes the senior consultants (partners, project managers) who will be responsible for guiding and supervising the team working at the client's organization. As a rule, the proposal guarantees the availability of particular persons for a limited period of time, say six to eight weeks. If the client delays the response, or decides to postpone the assignment, he knows that he will have to accept other consultants of a comparable profile, or renegotiate the assignment.

The consultant background section describes the experience and competence of the consulting organization as it relates to the needs of the particular client. There may be a general subsection with standard information given to all clients (including a section on ethical standards and professional practice adhered to by the consultant) and a specific subsection referring to similar work done and providing evidence that the consultant will be the right partner to choose. References to former clients should be used only with those clients' prior agreement.

When proposals are evaluated, this section will normally be given less weight than other sections; consultants therefore often tend to underestimate it.

Either they merely include standard documentation on the firm to every proposal, or they provide a great amount of information including irrelevant information on activities and completed projects in the belief that the potential client will be impressed by quantity. Neither of these approaches is likely to strengthen their case.

The financial and other terms section indicates the cost of the services, provisions for cost increases and contingencies, and the schedule and other indications for paying fees and reimbursing expenses, and settling all commitments. If the client applies a selection procedure, the financial section may have to be submitted separately.

If the consultant has a standard description of his or her terms of contract or business, it may be attached to the proposal. Conversely, some clients insist on using their own terms and the consultant may have to comply with these in order to obtain the contract.

Presenting the proposal

Many consultants prefer not just to mail the proposal, but to hand it over to the client in a meeting which starts with a short oral (and visual) introduction of the report's summary. The consultant should be ready to answer questions about the start of the proposed assignment. If the client is keen and ready to begin, there are obvious advantages to doing so while the enthusiasm is there and the contacts established are fresh in people's minds. But an early date may not be easy to meet because of existing commitments.

While the consultant would obviously like to have a decision before the end of the meeting, the client may have good reasons for not wanting to give one. He or she should not be pressed.

If the client wants to read the proposal prior to the oral presentation, or does not want an oral presentation, the consultant should hand the report over without insisting on a meeting. A formal selection procedure may even preclude an oral presentation and require the consultant to present a sealed written proposal by a set date.

The client's reaction

A public-sector client is usually bound by rules which specify a minimum number of tenders and an internal evaluation procedure before a contract is awarded. Private-sector clients may also use a selection procedure based on the evaluation of alternative proposals, in particular for large and complex assignments. In such cases it may be several weeks or months before the client is in a position to decide.

The consultant wants to know the criteria by which he or she will be judged. As a rule, the client will inform the consultant about these criteria in the original invitation to submit a proposal. In most cases, the client will also give the names of the competitors. The consultant should be aware of the relative weight that will be assigned to the various aspects of the proposal in the selection procedure. For example, the World Bank recommends its borrowers to give a weight of 5–10 per cent to the consulting firm's specific experience (background), 20–50 per cent to methodology, 30–60 per cent to key personnel proposed for the assignment, 0–10 per cent to transfer of knowledge and 0–10 per cent to participation of nationals.[5] Thus, even a highly competent consulting firm stands little chance in a selection procedure if it does not propose consultants of the right calibre.

Some clients divide these criteria into subcriteria. However, excessively detailed lists of subcriteria are difficult to justify and use, and can transform a selection exercise from a matter of professional judgement into an exercise in basic arithmetic. Clients should be advised against this approach. This view is shared by the World Bank: "... the number of subcriteria should be kept to the essential. The Bank recommends against the use of exceedingly detailed lists of subcriteria that may render the evaluation a mechanical exercise more than a professional assessment of the proposals."[6]

Negotiating the proposal

The client may be interested in using the consultant's services, but may not be happy with some aspects of the proposal. For example, the client may feel that he or she can play a more active role than foreseen by the consultant and personally undertake various tasks not requiring costly external expertise; or the client may wish to suggest a different timetable. It is normal to review these and similar technical aspects of the proposal and to make changes if the consultant is able to modify his or her approach.

As regards fees, many consultants emphasize that their rates represent a fair charge for a high-quality professional service and hence are not negotiable. A minor provision for the negotiation of fee rates is sometimes made in countries where this is the customary way of doing business (see Chapter 30).

What is not included in the proposal

In parallel with drafting his proposal to the client, the consultant should prepare internal (confidential) notes on the client organization and ideas on the approach to take (box 7.5). These internal briefing notes are particularly important in a large consulting firm if different professionals are used for planning and for executing assignments, and if several units of the same consulting or multiservice professional firm may be in touch with the same client organization on various matters.

7.6 The consulting contract

The entry phase of the consulting process can be regarded as successfully completed if the consultant and the client conclude a contract whereby they agree to work together on an assignment or project.[7]

Contracting practices regarded as normal and advisable depend on each country's legal system and customary ways of doing business. New consultants should

Box 7.5 Confidential information on the client organization

1. Names of managers met and information collected on them.
2. Comments on organizational relationships, management style, and cultural values and norms.
3. Attitudes of various people in the client organization to consultants and likely reactions to the assignment.
4. Best sources of internal information. Sources that cannot be trusted.
5. Additional comments and data on the problem for which the assignment is proposed.
6. Other problems identified, potential problems, or areas of further work not tackled in the proposed assignment and not discussed with the client.
7. Useful background information collected and not used in the proposal to the client.
8. Any other suggestions to the operating team that will execute the assignment.

seek legal advice on the form of contracting authorized by local legislation and preferred by business and government. In addition, they can get advice from the local consultants' association and from professional colleagues. Where alternative forms of contract are admitted, choosing one or more will be a matter of the consulting firm's policy and judgement on what is most appropriate in dealing with particular clients. The form chosen must ensure that mutual commitments will be understood and respected, and misunderstanding avoided on either side.

In some countries the contracting practices in professional services are well defined and enough literature is available. In other countries this is not yet the case. Thus a consultant doing work abroad may have to compromise between what is customary in the home country and what the law and practice in the client's country demand. However, contracting practices in consulting and other professional services are tending to become more and more standardized.

The three main forms of contracting are verbal agreement, a letter of agreement and a written contract. The aspects of consulting assignments that are normally dealt with in a contract are listed in box 7.6. These aspects do not necessarily represent sections of a standard contract since various arrangements are possible (for detailed comments see Appendix 4).

Verbal agreement

A verbal agreement is one given by the client orally either after having reviewed the consultant's written proposal, or even without having reviewed a proposal. Verbal agreement was used extensively in the first decades of management consulting, but now the tendency is to use written contracts. Nevertheless, those who believe strongly in the power of the written word and legal texts might be surprised to find out that even nowadays a lot of consulting is undertaken on the basis of verbal agreements. Verbal agreement may suffice if the following conditions exist:

Box 7.6 What to cover in a contract – checklist

1. Contracting parties (the consultant and the client)
2. Scope of the assignment (as discussed in sections 7.4 and 7.5: objectives, results, description of work, starting date, timetable, volume of work)
3. Work outputs, including reports (documentation and reports to be handed over to the client)
4. Consultant and client inputs (expert and staff time and other inputs)
5. Fees and expenses (fees to be billed, expenses reimbursed to the consultant)
6. Billing and payment procedure
7. Professional responsibilities (consultant's standard of care, avoiding conflict of interest, and other aspects as appropriate – see section 6.2)
8. Representations (by the consultant)
9. Handling of confidential information
10. Protection of intellectual property and copyright in consultant's work product
11. Liability (the consultant's liability for damages caused to the client, limitation of liability – see section 6.5)
12. Use of subcontractors (by the consultant)
13. Termination or revision (when and how to be suggested by either party)
14. Dispute resolution (resolution of disputes in court or through an alternative mechanism such as arbitration)
15. Signatures and dates

- the consultant and the client are well versed in professional practice;
- they trust each other totally;
- they are familiar with each other's terms of business (the client knows the terms applied by the consultant and the consultant knows what to expect from the client, e.g. if the client is able to make an advance payment, or can accept monthly billing, how long it takes to approve a payment, etc.);
- the assignment is not very big or complex (if this is the case, it may be difficult to manage the relationship on both sides without any formal document).

Verbal agreement is used more frequently in repeat business than with new clients. If a verbal agreement is used, the consultant may produce a detailed record of what was agreed, for his or her own benefit and to make sure that other colleagues in the firm are fully and correctly informed. Sending an information copy to the client may be useful.

Letter of agreement

A letter of agreement (other terms used: letter of engagement, of appointment, of confirmation, of intent) is the prevailing way of contracting professional services in many countries. Having received the consultant's proposal (proposal letter), the client sends him or her a letter of agreement, which may confirm that he or she accepts the proposal and the suggested terms, or set out new conditions which modify or supplement the consultant's proposal. In the latter case, the consultant in turn replies as to whether or not he or she accepts these new conditions. Alternatively, all this can be negotiated orally and the final agreement put in a written form.

In some cases, the client may draft the letter describing the work required and the proposed terms of reference, while the consultant gives the written agreement.

In most jurisdictions, a letter of agreement is considered a form of written contract (see below), though it will generally be less formal and detailed than most written contracts.

Written contract

A written consulting contract duly signed by the parties involved may be required for various reasons. It may be imposed by law or by the client's own regulations on the use of external services (this is the case in nearly all public organizations and international agencies, and many private businesses). It is often the best form to choose if the consultant and the client come from different business and legal environments and could misinterpret each other's intentions and attitudes. It is advisable, although not always necessary, for large and complex assignments involving many different people on both the client's and the consultant's side.

It may be the client's practice to use a standard form of contract. Most management consultants are quite flexible and will accept various forms of contract. However, they should not underestimate the need to consult their lawyer if a different form of contract is proposed to them by a client or if they do not fully understand the meaning of certain provisions. Provisions that may look familiar and are sometimes referred to as "boilerplate" may prove particularly onerous for the consultant (e.g. indemnification and dispute resolution clauses; see Appendix 4).

As a rule, the consultant will know in advance that he or she will have to sign a formal contract. He or she should obtain the standard form from the client, show it to a lawyer, and keep it in mind in preparing the proposals for the assignment. In this way, the consultant can formulate the proposals in such a way that they can be directly included in the body of the contract, or attached to it without making any substantial modifications.

A consulting firm should also have its own standard form of contract, to be used with clients who do not have a standard form of their own and expect the consultant to propose one.

Built-in flexibility

The purpose of contracting is to provide a clear orientation for joint work and to protect the interests of both parties. This implies a certain degree of imagination and flexibility.

At any stage of the assignment, the nature and magnitude of the problem may change and other priorities may become more urgent. The consultant's and the client's capabilities and perceptions of what approach will be effective are also evolving. Obviously, a professional consultant will not insist on continuing with a job (as stipulated in a contract) if that job is no longer required and causes unnecessary expense to the client.

Whatever form of contract is used, it should contain provisions specifying how and in which conditions the consultant or the client can withdraw from the contract, or can suggest and make revisions. In some cases it may be better to contract only for one phase of the assignment and delay a decision on the work to follow until further information has been collected and examined.

Psychological contract

In an era in which more and more features of our lives are regulated and constrained by legislation, and formal contracts tend to be more and more common in professional sectors, it is useful to underline that the formal legal side of contracting is *not* the main one. We have explained why a well-drafted formal contract may be required. However, excellent consulting assignments are those where another type of "contract" exists, which is not codified in any document and is not easy to describe: a psychological contract, under which the consultant and the client cooperate in an atmosphere of trust and respect, believing that the approach taken by the other party is the best one to bring the assignment to a successful completion. Such a "contract" cannot be replaced by even the finest legal document.

---

[1] D. Maister: "How clients choose", in *Managing the professional service firm* (New York, The Free Press, 1993), p. 112.

[2] Various terms are used: preliminary problem diagnosis, diagnostic study, management survey, diagnostic survey, consulting survey, diagnostic evaluation, business review, business diagnosis, pilot study, management audit, company appraisal, etc.

[3] Similar classifications, with empirical or recommended performance data, can be obtained from engineering consultants, sectoral research and information centres, suppliers of equipment, centres of interfirm comparison and other sources.

[4] A more detailed discussion of consultant selection, including various procedures, criteria and forms of contract used, can be found in M. Kubr: *How to select and use consultants: A client's guide*, Management Development Series No. 31 (Geneva, ILO, 1993).

[5] World Bank: *Guidelines: Selection and employment of consultants by World Bank borrowers* (see www.worldbank.org/html/opr/consult/contents.html), visited on 19 Mar. 2002.

[6] See www.worldbank.org/html/opr/consult/guidetxt/qcbs.html, visited on 19 Mar. 2002.

[7] See also Kubr, op. cit., Chapters 4 and 6; H. L. Shenson: *The contract and fee-setting guide for consultants and professionals* (New York, Wiley, 1990); and E. Bleach and L. Byars Swindling: *The consultant's legal guide* (San Francisco, CA, Jossey-Bass/Pfeiffer, 1999).

DIAGNOSIS

8

8.1 Conceptual framework of diagnosis

What is diagnosis?

Diagnosis, the second phase of the consulting process, is the first fully operational phase. The purpose of diagnosis is to examine the problem faced and the purposes pursued by the client in detail and in depth, identify the factors and forces that are causing and influencing the problem, and prepare all the information needed to develop a solution to the problem. An equally important aim is to examine the relationships between the problem in question and the global objectives and results achieved by the client organization, and to ascertain the client's potential to make changes and resolve the problem effectively.

The consultant should start the diagnostic work with a clear conceptual framework in mind. To embark on extensive and costly investigations without such a framework could be unproductive. In any organization the consultant will encounter a host of problems varying in importance and nature: technical and human, apparent and hidden, substantial and trivial, real and potential. He or she will hear many opinions as to what the real problems are and what should be done about them. In diagnosing the problem, the consultant will be constantly exposed to the risk of taking a wrong direction, becoming unduly influenced by the views expressed by others, and collecting interesting but unrelated facts while omitting essential information and ignoring some important dimensions of a complex problem, or interesting new opportunities.

Diagnosis is sometimes viewed as equal to collecting, dissecting and analysing vast amounts of data, including a great deal of data that may have no relevance to the purpose of the assignment. This is a misconception. While diagnosis requires data and facts, it is equally true that (a) diagnosis embraces considerably more than data collection and analysis, and (b) effective diagnosis is based on selected data and is consistently focused on the purposes of the project.

In principle, problem diagnosis does not include work on problem solutions. This will be done in the next phase, action planning. Diagnosis may even lead to the conclusion that the problem cannot be resolved, or that the purpose pursued cannot be achieved and the problem is not worth resolving.

In practice, however, it is often difficult or inappropriate to make a strict distinction between the diagnostic and the action planning – and even the implementation – phases of the consulting process. It is not only that diagnosis lays down the basis for the work to follow. Frequently diagnostic work will identify and explore possible solutions. In interviewing people, for example, it may be impracticable and undesirable to confine the discussion to problems and their causes, without touching upon the wider context and possible solutions. Thus, although the phases are considered separately here, they will be combined in practice in a pragmatic way, according to the particular case.

Restating the problem and the purpose

The assignment plan prepared during the entry phase and confirmed by the consulting contract (see sections 7.2 to 7.5) provides guidelines and a basic schedule for diagnosis. It may, however, require revision and adjustment even before the diagnostic work is started. There may be a time-lag of several months between the end of the entry phase and the start of the diagnostic phase, and the client's situation and thinking may have evolved.

Furthermore, many consulting contracts are signed on the basis of general and vague definitions of problem and purpose. When the work starts, the consultant may find that the client actually wants something else or has a different interpretation of the terms used in the contract. One reason may be that the people who start working together on the project are different (on both the client's and the consultant's side) from those who negotiated and signed the contract. Explaining what was intended is not enough since there may be a genuine disagreement over the original definitions.

Thus, it is always useful to review and restate the problem and the purpose of the consultancy when starting the diagnosis. A special meeting with the client may be arranged to this effect. In the vast majority of assignments, some adjustments in the objectives and the timetable are inevitable when the work starts.

The human side of diagnosis

There is another significant phenomenon. As we know, the very fact that a management consultant is present in the organization and starts asking questions puts the change process into motion. There may be an immediate impact on the organization. Many people do not have to be told what to do; it may be enough that someone asks a question that implies that there might be an alternative way of doing a job. Sometimes an employee may be heard to say, "I didn't know they wanted me to do the job that way. Had they spoken to me about it, I would have done it!"

This can have very positive effects. By gradually developing a complete picture of the situation, diagnosis increases awareness of the need to change and indicates more specifically the sorts of change that will be required. If well managed, data collection and analysis can involve the client's staff in the assignment, thus enhancing their sense of ownership of the problem. As a result, at the end of the diagnosis, employees in the client organization will be better prepared to cope with the necessary changes.

There can be a useful learning effect, too. The client and his or her staff should feel not only that they are themselves discovering the truth about their organization or unit and suggesting what to improve, but also that the consultant is sharing his or her diagnostic method with them. The client's problem-solving potential can be considerably improved during diagnosis. If this opportunity is missed, it may be more difficult to solicit people's involvement in developing and implementing action proposals.

Certain negative effects may also occur. Some clients try to keep secret the fact that the organization is using a consultant. It is doubtful whether such a secret can be kept but, even more important, an attempt to do so can cast doubt on the consultant and on the entire process. The informal communication network, or grapevine, in an organization will quickly disseminate the information. In the absence of a formal communication from the client to the system, the informal system will tend to generate negative reports. This will seriously inhibit the ability of the consultant to perform effectively.

Unless the client system is prepared to accept the consultant, the entire relationship can be doomed to failure from the outset. Therefore, if possible, the client should prepare the staff for the consultant beforehand. As clients are not always aware of this need, it may be necessary for the consultant to plan a course of action during the entry phase. Obviously, such action is in itself an intervention in the organization, and must be handled with extreme care (see also section 31.2).

The consultant can use a variety of approaches to dispel fear or misinformation. One way is by being readily available to all those in the organization who would like to meet him or her. Particularly when consulting on human resources and organizational development, the consultant should be generally visible and accessible.

Diagnosis can be a painful exercise in an organization in difficulties. But in any organization, diagnosis may uncover situations and relationships of which the client is not proud, which he or she is unable to handle, and which he or she would have preferred to hide from anybody coming from outside, and even from other colleagues within the company. The consultant, however, may need this sort of insight to be able to do anything useful for the client. Diagnosing delicate situations requires a great deal of tact. An aggressive diagnostic attitude (e.g. if people can infer from the consultant's questions that he or she is looking for errors in their work and is going to criticize them) will invariably generate resistance.

Another type of potentially negative effect is spontaneous change of work methods before a new method has been properly developed, tested and accepted for general use. Such changes may not be real improvements even if they are well intentioned. Energy may be wasted if there is a misunderstanding about the purpose of the project and likely direction of the change effort, and about the sequence of steps in which the consultancy is being carried out. Some people may become disoriented – they change their method of work in good faith, but this is not appreciated by the consultant or by the managers.

These and similar misunderstandings can be prevented by giving frequent *feedback* from diagnostic work. The client and his or her staff need to know how the assignment is progressing, what facts have been established, what solutions are shaping up, and which findings are preliminary – requiring further fact-finding and verification – and which are final, capable of serving as a basis for action. There should be no ambiguity and no suspicion about the type of action that diagnosis is likely to recommend, or about the moment at which action can start.

On the other hand, getting the client's reaction to the feedback given to him or her is feedback to the consultant. The consultant should seek this feedback as much as possible during the whole diagnostic phase.

8.2 Diagnosing purposes and problems

Purposes

In *Breakthrough thinking*, Gerald Nadler and Shozo Hibino explain why focusing on purposes is fundamental to successful problem-solving.[1] They emphasize that defining the purposes of working on a problem ensures that you will apply your efforts in areas where you can have the greatest impact. Instead of starting diagnosis by asking "What's wrong here? What's the matter?", the consultant should ask first "What are we trying to accomplish here? What are we trying to do?" This will help to avoid (a) the conventional urge to start by collecting data and analysing the situation, and (b) working on or being sold a solution to a wrong problem ("moving faster in the wrong direction").

An array of purposes to be achieved by the project should be constructed. In this way the consultant acknowledges that there is a wide range of motivations and results possible in applying change to an existing condition. The problem will be seen in the right perspective if the array of purposes listed is broad enough, and includes small and immediate purposes as well as very broad and far-reaching purposes that are beyond any immediate solution.

It will then be important to identify *the focus purpose*. This will be one that meets all or most of the criteria discussed and chosen by the consultant and the client (such as management's aims, potential financial benefits, cost and capital factors, time limitations, constraints imposed by legislation, future development potential, employment potential, learning opportunities, etc.). Small, limited and trivial purposes that cannot meet these criteria will be eliminated. Excessively broad, distant, risky, costly or unrealistic purposes, as well as those that the stakeholders would not support, will also be eliminated (see example in box 8.1).

Box 8.1 The focus purpose – an example

In one company, the problem as presented to a consultant was a deteriorating quality of several important products, and a growing number and frequency of customer complaints about quality. The discussion of possible purposes of a consulting project defined an array of purposes:

- restoring quality to its previous level and preventing its deterioration;
- preventing customer complaints;
- improving quality management (including better motivation for achieving and maintaining quality);
- increasing customer satisfaction;
- achieving an image of a high-quality producer;
- becoming a sector leader internationally in terms of quality.

The focus purpose chosen was "increasing customer satisfaction". This embraced narrower purposes, such as improving product quality and assuring quality management, but eliminated wider and probably too ambitious purposes, such as international sector leadership in quality. Furthermore, it was agreed that improvements would need to be pursued in after-sales and maintenance services, customer information, behaviour of the sales technicians, product modernization practices, etc. This permitted a diagnosis and the subsequent activities of the consultant and the client to be focused on a clear and realistic purpose.

Problems

It may be useful to recollect what was said about business and management problems in section 1.2. There is a problem if (a) there is a difference between two situations: one real and one potential or desired, and (b) someone is concerned about this difference and wants to reduce it. This difference defines the problem with which the consultant is supposed to deal.

It is not so difficult to find out what is actually happening, i.e. *the actual situation*. In this chapter we will describe a number of fact-finding and analytical techniques that help the consultant to identify and understand the actual situation. To determine what should be happening in the future, i.e. *the ideal or desired situation*, is more complex, but is an essential part of problem diagnosis. For it is only in this way that the problem can be described and analysed, and the consultant's work focused on purposes, future opportunities and improvements.

The client's problem will be identified in terms of the following five principal dimensions or characteristics:

(1) **Substance or identity.** The substance or identity of the problem has to be described (poor performance; shortage of competent staff; lack of ideas on how to invest idle capital; desire to improve after-sales services). There is a need to establish the basis of comparison used and how it is justified. Why do we say that performance is poor? Poor by what standard? The various symptoms of the problem have to be described as well.

(2) **Organizational and physical location.** In which organizational units (divisions, departments, subsidiaries) and physical units (plants, buildings, stores, offices) has the problem been observed? Which other units are or might be affected? How widespread is the problem? Does it affect external relationships?

(3) **Problem ownership.** Which people – managers, staff specialists, other workers – are affected by the existence of the problem and primarily interested in resolving it? Who is likely to make difficulties? Are they aware of the problem? Have they attempted to deal with it?

(4) **Absolute and relative magnitude.** How important is the problem in absolute terms (e.g. amount of working time or money lost, volume of underutilized productive capacity, potential future gains)? How important is it in relative terms (e.g. in comparison with other problems, or with total turnover)? How does it affect the unit where it has been observed, and the people who own the problem? How important is it to the organization as a whole? What will the organization gain if the problem is resolved?

(5) **Time perspective.** Since when has the problem existed? Has it been observed once, or several times, or is it recurrent? How frequently does it appear? What is its tendency: has the problem been stabilized, or is it increasing or decreasing? What forecasts can be made about the future evolution of the problem? Is a future problem anticipated?

Furthermore, diagnosis will aim to establish:

- the causes of the problem;
- other significant relationships;
- the client's potential to solve the problem;
- possible directions of further action.

The causes of the problem

A key task in diagnosis is to identify the forces and factors that are causing the problem. The purpose is to understand the issue, not to point the finger at one or more culprits. The exercise will start with some preliminary knowledge or assumptions about what these causes might be. This will help to establish hypotheses on possible causes. It is useful to form as many hypotheses as possible, without, however, embarking on superficial speculation. Data-gathering and analysis will then focus mainly on the hypothetical causes, aiming to eliminate hypotheses that cannot be justified by the facts, and to add new hypotheses as they emerge. A rigorous scientific approach should be applied. The fact that it is difficult to find data in support of a hypothesis does not mean that the hypothesis should be dropped. Eventually the consultant should be able to identify the real cause or causes among the many factors that are in some way related to the problem (see section 8.4).

Other significant relationships

Any business or management problem is interwoven with other problems; and there are other relationships in addition to that between a problem and its cause or causes. There may be factors that aggravate or alleviate the problem without being its direct cause. They can make the solution of the problem more or less difficult. In solving one problem, new problems may be discovered or created. Quite often a new bottleneck is created by removing an existing one. These relationships and potential problems and risks have to be identified and investigated.

The client's potential to solve the problem

The client's potential has several dimensions. It is necessary to find out whether he or she possesses the material and financial resources and the technical expertise required for solving the problem. If not, the consultancy will have to allow for developing this potential and extending help to the client as necessary. The time perspective is important. What has been the client's experience in solving other problems and making organizational changes of various types and magnitudes? What is the client organization's culture as regards change? How quickly is the client able to act? What will be the likely future development of the client's resources in relation to the problem to be solved? Can he or she mobilize other resources? What attempts have been made to solve the given problem? Have past attempts failed? If so, why?

Considerable attention should be paid to the client's attitudes to the given problem. How do people (at various levels and in various categories) perceive the problem? Are they aware of it and keen to make a change? Are they motivated to make a special effort? Are they prepared to take risks? Have they experienced the problem for so long that they have accommodated themselves to it?

Possible directions of further action

The purpose of diagnosis is preparation for action. Throughout the investigation, information and ideas on how the problem could be resolved and how this would contribute to meeting the client's purposes and improving the business should be collected, recorded and analysed with the same care and determination as data on the nature and causes of the problem. This will provide a link to the next phase, action planning. Action proposals should emerge logically from diagnosis. However, the consultant should keep in mind the pitfalls of making premature changes before the facts have been established and conclusions drawn from diagnosis.

Main steps in diagnosis

The general framework provided above can be used by the consultant to make a detailed plan for diagnostic work, bearing in mind that the scope and

Box 8.2 Issues in problem identification

It is useful to recall briefly some common mistakes made in defining problems, not only by clients but also by some consultants. The way people define problems affects their ability to solve them.

- **Mistaking symptoms for problems.** This is the most common error. Some obvious issues that worry management (e.g. falling sales, shortage of innovative ideas in the research and development department, absenteeism) are looked upon as problems, although they may be only symptoms of more profound difficulties.
- **Preconceived ideas about the causes of problems.** Some managers and consultants feel that, thanks to their experience, they know pretty well what the causes "must" be and that analysing facts cannot reveal anything new.
- **Looking at problems from one technical viewpoint only.** This happens frequently if the diagnosis is made by a manager or a consultant with a strong background and bias in one technical area (e.g. engineering, accounting, behavioural science) and if the interdisciplinary nature of management problems is disregarded.
- **Ignoring how the problem is perceived in various parts of the organization.** For example, the consultant may accept the definition made by top management, without finding out how the problem is seen by the lower management echelons.
- **Wrong appreciation of the urgency of a problem.** Appreciation of the urgency of a problem may be influenced by emotions, resistance to change, incorrect conclusions from diagnosis, and other factors.
- **Unfinished problem diagnosis.** Owing to time and cost constraints or for other reasons, the consultant may be tempted to conclude diagnostic work prematurely. He or she may miss further problems and opportunities that may be directly related to the original issue presented by the client.
- **Failure to clarify the focus purpose.** The purpose is vaguely defined and the consultant wastes time and energy by looking into many issues that will eventually be ignored. He or she works on the wrong problem or on totally unrealistic proposals.

methodology of the exercise will have to be adapted to the nature and complexity of the problem, and the profile and attitude of the client. Diagnosis consists of seeking answers to questions in the areas reviewed above: the purposes pursued; the nature and characteristics of the problem itself; the causes of the problem; other significant relationships; the client's potential to solve the problem; and possible directions of further action. The exercise starts with information obtained through the preliminary problem diagnosis during the entry phase, and with assumptions and hypotheses that the consultant develops at the beginning in collaboration with the client.

In planning the diagnostic phase it is essential to determine the degree and form of the client's involvement in each activity. If the process-consulting mode is chosen, the client will accept the main responsibility for collecting and analysing data, and the consultant will act mainly as a catalyst, making the client aware of the approach taken and drawing attention to questions and facts that should not escape attention. In other instances, however, the consultant will carry out the bulk of the diagnostic work. As a general rule, it is useful to plan for gradually increasing the involvement of the client and his or her staff in the course of the diagnostic phase.

The same approach and sequence of steps may not fit every situation and every consultant. Every client organization is unique and so is every consultant–client relationship. This general rule also applies to the planning of diagnostic work. For example, Jerome Fuchs described his experience in the following terms:

> My personal approach involves techniques which I find most useful. I do not attempt to analyse or compartmentalize data into fact finding, analysis and synthesis, but let it flow as it begins to come in. I let it overlap to a certain extent in each of these stages until a pattern begins to develop. Only then do I begin to weave raw factual material into the analytical phase. When my facts are complete I want them to be so clear that they mirror what the ultimate conclusion of the study will be.[2]

8.3 Defining necessary facts

Facts are the building-blocks of any consulting work. Consultants need a considerable number of facts to get a clear picture of the situation, arrive at a precise definition of the problem and relate their proposals to reality. Facts are also needed if the assignment is trying to develop something new and using a great deal of imagination and creative thinking. Collecting facts may be the most tiring and painful phase of the consultant's work, but there is no alternative.

When diagnosis starts, a certain amount of data will be handed over to the operating consultants by their colleagues who did the preliminary problem diagnosis during the entry phase. The diagnostic phase will go much further, and will define issues and collect facts in considerably greater detail.

The kinds of facts collected will depend on the area in which the assignment takes place, and on the definition of the problem and the assignment objectives. Facts should enable the examination of processes, relations, performances, causes and mutual influences, with special regard to underutilized opportunities and possible improvements. The conceptual framework reviewed in section 8.1 indicates the main areas in which facts are normally collected.

Plan for collecting data

Data collection has to be prepared for by thoroughly defining what facts are wanted. Consultants should continue to apply the principle of selectivity, although at this stage they need more detailed and precise facts than during the preliminary diagnosis. Virtually unlimited amounts of information are available in any organization, but an excessive amount easily becomes unmanageable and cannot be fully utilized in any assignment.

The cost of fact-gathering cannot be ignored, especially if some data are not readily available and special schemes (observations, special record-keeping, numerous interviews) have to be established to obtain them. But the definition of facts needed and their sources should not be too restrictive, since this might exclude some significant information which is often found in unexpected places. At the beginning of the assignment, the consultant may well cast his or her net fairly widely, rejecting some data after preliminary examination, but adding other data, and so on.

In defining the scope of data, the management consultant should keep in mind that the purpose is neither research nor establishing responsibility for past flaws. "The purpose of diagnosis is to mobilize action on a problem – action that will improve the organization's functioning."[3]

The facts to be collected and investigated have to be defined in close collaboration with the client, especially with those members of the client organization who know what records are kept, how reliable they are, and what data will have to be sought from other sources. Collaboration should include the definition of the content of data, degree of detail, time period, extent of coverage, and organization and tabulation criteria.

Content of data

Apparently identical types of data may have a different meaning or content in different organizations. For example, "work in progress" may be defined in a number of different ways: it may or may not include certain items, and its financial value may be determined by various methods. The definition of categories of employees (managers, technicians, supervisors, administrative personnel, production and other workers, etc.) is also subject to many variations. In old firms with established traditions, definition is often complicated by the existence of a specific jargon, which may differ from terminology prevailing in the industry to which they belong. The uniformity of data used in the management of various organizations will be higher in countries where accounting and reporting are subject to government regulations. But even in these cases many differences will be found, especially in the production area.

Degree of detail

The degree of detail required will generally be higher than in preliminary diagnostic surveys. While a general diagnosis may stem from aggregate figures (e.g. total time spent by machines on productive work), change rests upon more detailed data (e.g. machining time for each operation, or time spent on productive work by certain types of machines, or in certain shops). Information may be needed on certain individuals and their attitudes to the problem concerned.

The more detailed the facts, the more time they will take to collect. The consultant may first collect data in broad categories (e.g. total number of days of sick leave taken by all workers). Analysis of these data will suggest more detail for certain categories (e.g. number of days of sick leave taken by each age group during the winter months). Data may thus be gathered in several stages before the consultant has a sufficiently detailed picture of the situation.

Period of time

Defining the period of time is equally important. For example, to design an inventory management system for finished products, the consultant must know the number of products sold. For how many years must he or she calculate the sales and at what intervals? The period of time should be long enough to show a clear pattern of activity, indicate rates of growth or decline, and reveal fluctuations in activity due to seasonal variations or economic cycles.

Periods of time need to be comparable: months have to include the same number of working days and so on. Periods when exceptional events occurred should be excluded for comparison purposes, but recognized and accommodated in the new situation. Periods preceding major changes in operations (e.g. introduction of new products and dropping of old ones) have to be examined separately from periods of normal operation.

If a period close to the start of the assignment is chosen, it needs to be recognized that the mere presence of the consultant may affect the results. In a particular instance, material wastage dropped substantially from the moment the consultant began to ask questions about it and before he actually did anything.

Obviously the choice of the period of time should take account of the availability of past records, and of changes that the client may have introduced in recording procedures.

Coverage

When it comes to coverage, the consultant must decide whether to collect total information (on all products, all employees, whole units and processes), or a selection only. As a rule, information will be collected for the vital few items that account for the bulk of activity in the current period, and for such items as are likely to become vital in the future (prospective new products, etc.). If the productive capacity is clearly limited by one group of machines which have become a bottleneck, the solution of the problems of this group may be a key to the solution of other problems in the department. In other cases, data will be collected for representative samples.

Organization and tabulation of data

Finally, the preparatory work for fact collection should include decisions on organizing and tabulating the data, which should be made in the light of the ultimate use of the data. Typical groupings are:

- for *events* – time, frequency, rate, trends, cause, effect (e.g. number of accidents resulting from specified causes that occurred each day of the week during the past year);
- for *people* – age, sex, nationality, family status, qualifications, occupation, length of service, earnings (e.g. absenteeism by age group);
- for *products and materials* – size, value, technical characteristics, source (e.g. value of materials by type and size in the inventory at the end of the past 12 calendar quarters);
- for *resources, inputs, outputs, processes and procedures* – rates of activity (sales, consumption, production), location, control centre, geographical distribution, use of equipment (e.g. numbers of specified parts produced by selected processes during each of the past 24 months).

Tabulation allows facts to be arranged in digestible form. Descriptions and narratives may be noted separately under selected headings (e.g. responsibilities of each manager). Answers to a questionnaire can be tabulated on a summary questionnaire, i.e. using the same form of questionnaire that is distributed to the respondents. Processes and procedures may be represented by a chain of symbols, such as the activity symbols used by systems analysts or in work study. Shapes are best shown on drawings. Figures are usually set out in tables.[4]

Keeping notes in an orderly way, and organizing files for easy retrieval of information, will help the consultant to keep on course. The meaning of notes should be as clear months after the event as when they were written. No figure should be recorded without being precisely qualified.

8.4 Sources and ways of obtaining facts

Sources of facts

By and large, facts are available to consultants from three sources:

- records;
- events and conditions;
- memories.

Any of these sources may be internal (within the organization), or external (publications, statistical reports, data on customers and competitors, opinions of people outside the organization).

Records are facts stored in forms that are readable or can be transcribed. They include documents (files, reports, publications), computer files, films, microfilms, tapes, drawings, pictures, charts, and so on. Facts are obtained from records by retrieval and study.

Events and conditions are actions and the circumstances surrounding them, and are obtained by observation.

Memories are stored in the minds of people who work in the organization, are associated with it, or simply are able to provide information of use to the consulant (e.g. for comparison). This body of knowledge embraces proven facts, experiences, opinions, beliefs, impressions, prejudices and insights. The mind stores all these data in the form of words, numbers and pictures, which the consultant can reconstruct by means of special reports, questionnaires, interviews, and so on.

Indirect and time-consuming ways of collecting information should be avoided if the same information can be obtained directly and simply. In many cases this means – go and ask people. People at all levels in business firms and other organizations possess an enormous amount of knowledge about their organization, and nearly everybody has some ideas on needed and possible improvements. But they usually do not divulge this information if they are not asked.

Retrieval of recorded data

Records are a prolific source of information, and some records will be examined and studied in any management consulting assignment. Clearly, consultants will give preference to the use of information that is already available in records before looking to other ways of collecting data. There are, however, certain pitfalls to be avoided in using recorded data:

- Many records are not reliable and can give a distorted picture of reality. This is common in such cases as records on machine breakdowns and stoppages, or waste. Materials may be charged to products for which they were not used. Factory plans and layouts are seldom up to date. Organizational and operational manuals may include detailed descriptions of procedures that were abandoned long ago. Mission reports may be incomplete. Computer files may be incomplete and unreliable. If the consultant or the client has doubts, the validity of existing records should be verified before they are used.
- It is common in organizations, both business and government, to find that various departments have different records on the same activities, inputs or outputs. Some departments may be more careful and disciplined than others in record-keeping, and records may differ both in the criteria used and in the magnitude of the recorded data.
- Criteria and values used in recording are modified from time to time and the consultant must find out about all such modifications.

Special recording

Special recording can be arranged if information is not readily available in existing records, or cannot be relied upon. It may be established for a limited period, say a month or two, according to criteria proposed by the consultant. As a rule, the client's employees working in a given area will be asked to record data and pass them to the consultant. For reasons of economy such recording should be kept simple and last no longer than necessary for reliability. Everyone should know at the start how long the period will be, and why special recording has to be introduced.

Observation

Observation is used to obtain information that is not readily recorded. The consultant is present while an event occurs (e.g. while a manager instructs subordinates, or while a production worker performs a task), and sees and hears how the event occurs, so as to be able to suggest an improved practice.

In process consulting, the consultant may observe management and staff meetings, during which it may be possible to identify group processes and behaviours that are related to the problem. Usually, the observation will be of groups, rather than individuals. If, however, the purpose of the consultation is to help an individual improve performance, then the observation can focus essentially on that individual. Alternatively, the consultant may observe patterns of socializing. Where do people gather to talk and exchange information? Who has frequent working or informal contacts with whom? Who is avoiding whom? What pattern emerges from these contacts?

Because most people feel uncomfortable under scrutiny, the consultant must take special care to put employees at their ease before starting to observe their activities. First the consultant should tell them what he or she is going to do. He or she should never start watching employees without warning. The consultant should explain the purpose of the survey and make it clear that it is not critical of particular persons but simply aimed at obtaining reliable information on how certain activities are performed. An exchange of views with those under observation, allowing them to point out the factors that influence the activity or the work relationships and inviting their suggestions for improvement, will probably enlist their cooperation. As far as possible they should behave normally under observation and make no attempt to give a better, worse, faster, or slower performance than usual. If there is any unusual occurrence, the observation should be disregarded and repeated when conditions return to normal.

If procedures, operations and processes are observed, the consultant may choose one of the many methods that have been developed for that purpose and whose description is available in the literature.[5]

If the assignment is dealing primarily with human problems and relations between individuals and groups, the consultant may have to explore the attitudes and behaviour of the client's staff in depth. In other assignments he or she may probe less deeply into these aspects. The consultant should observe the inclinations, preferences and prejudices of people to the extent necessary to understand how these affect the problems he or she is concerned with, and to enlist cooperation. Such observation should continue throughout the assignment. It starts during the introductory meetings when the consultant gains first impressions. These will be verified or modified during later encounters. To a considerable extent the consultant gathers information on attitudes and behaviour as a by-product of interviews to elicit memories, exchange ideas or develop improvements. However, during interviews not directly concerned with personal traits, the consultant would distract both himself and the client by writing down his impressions. He should therefore make mental notes and only afterwards put them in writing and classify them.

By taking personal traits and attitudes into account, the consultant will increase the chances of understanding factors that affect change in the client organization.

Special reports

Individuals or teams in the client organization may be requested to help in the assignment by giving thought to particular aspects of the problem and putting their suggestions in a special report. This should include any supporting information that the author might be able to supply. The method is selective – in cooperation with the client, the consultant should choose employees who are likely to have specific views on the problem in question, who are aware of various pitfalls, and who are a source of good ideas. Anybody in the client organization, however, might offer to prepare a special report on his or her own initiative; this should be welcomed, but treated with some caution.

Questionnaires

In management consulting, questionnaires are useful for obtaining a limited number of straightforward facts from a large number of people (e.g. in a market survey), or from people widely separated from each other (e.g. reasons for equipment failure from users throughout a whole region). They are generally unsatisfactory for gathering all but simple facts.

The questionnaire may be distributed to correspondents with an explanatory note asking them to complete and return it, or canvassers may question people and note their answers on the questionnaire. Either case calls for a full explanation, telling the respondent:

- why he or she is being asked the questions;
- who is asking them;
- what the questioner will do with the replies;
- who else is being asked.

Before drawing up the questionnaire the consultant needs to decide exactly what information is wanted, how it will be used, and how the answers will be summarized and classified. Then precise, simple questions free from ambiguity have to be framed. As far as possible, answers should be "yes" or "no" or numerical. Where longer answers are required, it may be useful to provide a list of possible answers and ask for one to be marked. Questions should be arranged in logical order so that each answer leads to the next.

If there are doubts about the respondents' ability to understand the questions and give clear answers, the questionnaire should be subjected to preliminary tests.

Interviews

In management consulting, interviewing is the most widely used technique of data-gathering, together with the retrieval of recorded data.

One advantage of interviews over questionnaires is that every answer can be tested and elaborated. Questions supplement and support each other, confirming, correcting or contradicting previous replies. They also lead to related facts, often revealing unexpected relationships, influences and constraints. The interview is flexible and adaptable. If one line of questioning fails to produce the required data, another can be tried. This may be suggested by the interviewee's answers.

The consultant needs to be alert and attentive to learn not only from the direct replies but also from the inferences, comments, asides, opinions, anecdotes, attitudes and gestures that accompany them. Non-verbal messages can be very significant.

The consultant should be guided by general rules of effective interviewing, which have been described in various texts.[6] Some more specific experiences and suggestions concerning the use of interviews in management consulting are given below.

What facts. In deciding what facts are needed, the consultant takes account of the knowledge the interviewee is expected to have – for example, a production manager is unlikely to know precisely what terms of credit are extended to customers, while a district sales manager is probably not informed about the planned maintenance of machines. For background information, a general discussion may suffice. On the other hand, information that will help to solve problems or develop improvements needs to be thoroughly examined, probed and understood (e.g. workers' attitudes to simplifying working procedures in order to raise output).

Who should be interviewed. Obviously interviewees should be dealing with the activities under study – for example, for billing procedures, the invoice clerk would be the best source of information. To obtain full cooperation and avoid slighting anyone, however, the consultant should first approach the manager responsible and allow him or her to designate informants. Later the consultant may refer to others to complement or confirm information. During initial interviews he or she can ask who has supporting information.

When to interview. Information gathered from interviews makes more sense if it comes in logical order – for example, if products are known it is easier to follow the operations for manufacturing them. Interviews should therefore follow a sequence so that each builds on information derived from those preceding it. They should be preceded by a careful study of records, so that time-consuming interviews are not used to collect data available in another form. The amount of time an interviewee can make available for the interview and his state of mind cannot be ignored.

Where to meet. Selection of a meeting place should take into account the following:

- proximity to the activity under study;
- the convenience of the interviewee;
- avoidance of noise and interruption.

Generally, people are more relaxed and communicative in their own surroundings. They also have all information to hand there. Only if the interviewee's workplace has serious drawbacks, such as noise, lack of space or frequent interruptions, should the consultant invite him or her to meet elsewhere (perhaps in the consultant's office at the client's premises).

How to proceed. Although the conduct of an interview will vary according to the characters of the interviewee and the consultant, their relationship, and the circumstances under which they meet, the guidelines summarized in box 8.3 usually apply.

In interviewing, the consultant may encounter unexpected resistance. This can be expressed in many different forms: questions are not answered, answers are evasive or too general, doubts are expressed about the usefulness of the exercise and the consultant's approach, and similar (see also section 4.4). If this happens, the consultant should quickly consider whether he or she is provoking resistance by aggressive or tactless questioning, or by asking questions that the informant considers banal or poorly prepared. It may be good tactics to ask the informant directly about his or her feelings concerning the interview: this may unblock the situation. There is, however, not much point in pursuing an interview in which the informant is clearly not cooperating.

Data-gathering meetings

Another possibility in diagnosis is for the consultant to arrange a special meeting, a sort of collective interview, to generate data related to the problem under consideration. During such a meeting, care is needed to ensure that it does not move into discussing possible solutions before sufficient data have been gathered.

Data-gathering should involve all those who are associated with the problem in any way. Sometimes the consultant may suggest including others who are not directly related, but whose presence could be helpful for data-gathering. However, a data-gathering meeting should not be too large; this can inhibit some of those present and prevent the sharing of needed information. It may be preferable to schedule several small meetings in order to offer the more intimate climate essential for gathering data, and to hold separate meetings with people who would not give their views openly in the presence of their superiors or other colleagues (e.g. supervisors may speak more openly in a meeting where the production manager and the personnel manager are not present).

Box 8.3 Principles of effective interviewing

(1) Before the interview

- Prepare questions likely to reveal the required information (the list will merely serve as a guide and a check that the interview covers all the necessary ground, and should not prevent the exploration of related topics).
- Find out about the interviewee's job and personality.
- Inform the interviewee of the purpose of the interview.

(2) During the interview

- Give further detailed explanations to the interviewee at the beginning and request help in solving the problem.
- Start the interview in a relaxed and pleasant atmosphere, making sure that you break the ice at the opening.
- Ask questions likely to lead towards required information, allowing the informant to follow his or her own line of thought so long as it does not stray too far from the subject under review or become too trivial.
- Encourage a spontaneous flow of information by asking further questions, making judicious comments supplementing the interviewee's statements, and showing interest by smiling, nodding, mentioning that information is interesting, new to you, etc.
- Except for such encouraging interjections, don't interrupt. Don't appear critical of the way things are done now since this may antagonize the informant. Don't argue and don't jump in with suggestions for improvements.
- If questions are answered vaguely, pursue them in a pleasant and non-aggressive way until the answers are fully clarified.
- Be alert to non-verbal messages, feelings and impressions.
- Note facts and opinions during the interview (with the respondent's agreement); note impressions and feelings after the interview.
- Before leaving, confirm what you have noted. Thank the informant for help, leaving the way open for further interviews if necessary.

(3) After the interview

- Read over the notes of the interview, list points to be checked and transcribe reliable information in the assignment's classified data record.
- If appropriate, send the interviewee a typed summary for verification.
- Use information from one interview to prepare questions (e.g. for cross-checking) for other interviews.

Surveys of employee attitudes

The attitudes of staff in the client organization play some role in most consulting assignments. The consultant should be alert to attitudes when observing operations and processes, when interviewing people, and in all contacts with the client and the staff. In some assignments, a special survey of employee attitudes may be required. This may be the case in assignments involving changes in employment and working conditions if the consultant needs to establish how people feel about present conditions and how they might react to the change likely to be proposed. As a rule, a survey is more likely to be needed in a large organization than in a small one, especially if it is suspected that different opinions and attitudes exist, but the number of people concerned makes it difficult to judge their relative importance.

The organization and the techniques of attitude surveys are described in specialized publications.[7] A management consultant who is competent in this area may undertake such a survey. Alternatively, the consultant can turn to a specialist in social and behavioural research. The main techniques used are those described above, including observation, interviews and questionnaires. There are also special techniques, as used for instance in sociometric studies or motivational research. Their effective use requires special training, but they would not be needed in most management consulting assignments.

Estimates

When hard data are not available, or are difficult to obtain, the consultant may consider using estimates. Estimates are best made by people directly involved in the activity concerned, who have first-hand knowledge and who, in addition, will more readily accept proposals based on data they themselves have supplied. Wherever possible, estimates should be obtained from more than one source and cross-checked. If there are significant differences, the informants themselves should try to resolve them. If they cannot do so, a test may be applied, observations taken, or special recording installed.

The consultant may accept the client's estimates:

- in respect of facts familiar to the client (e.g. frequent machine operations, or regular patterns of work);
- on aspects of the situation that do not need to be precise (e.g. percentage of total costs represented by administrative overheads, in order to decide whether to control these costs closely);
- to indicate whether further observation would be rewarding (e.g. incidence of machine breakdowns, or of lack of stock of finished products);
- to ascertain whether potential benefits from improvements are worth more accurate measurement (e.g. savings from substitute materials or change of product design);
- where the estimate can be tested (e.g. if estimates of operating times to be used for production planning and control would result in a product cost permitting the client to sell at a reasonable profit).

Before using estimates, the consultant should check their validity against experience. An effective way of doing this is to use a known total volume, quantity, or cost for a recent period or a known capacity. This is compared with the measurement or capacity that results from multiplying the estimate for a single item by the total number of items. For example, the estimated quantity of material required to manufacture a product is multiplied by actual numbers produced during a recent period. This is compared with the quantity of material actually issued from store to production.

Another means of checking estimates is to compare them with data recorded elsewhere. Such a comparison must be made with care and will only be valid if the data being compared relate to identical circumstances. Data for comparison may be found in trade publications, in the files of the consulting organization or from organizations that have collaborated in benchmarking projects.

In addition to checking the validity of estimates, the consultant needs to consider the *degree of error* they entail and decide whether this is tolerable. Where there is a strong probability that the error is within the limits of tolerance, the estimate can be used. If the error is too high, the consultant will have to devise ways of obtaining more precise and reliable data instead of using an estimate.

Estimates often concern data on developments and trends that are independent of the enterprise concerned (e.g. market prices, energy prices, transportation tariffs, exchange rates, interest rates, inflation). Many of these estimates can be obtained from competent specialized sources, such as government agencies, banks, business research institutes, or financial and market analysts. The consultant should choose an external source of estimates with extreme caution, bearing in mind that not all sources are equally reliable. It is useful to know how the estimate was made – is it a "best guess", a common opinion shared by many experts on the topic, or was a forecasting model used? On what concepts was that model built? The consultant should never blindly accept, and provide to the client, estimates on the basis of which the client will have to make important investment and financial decisions. Of course, not all risks can be eliminated, but the use of false information must be avoided.

Cultural issues in gathering data

Sensitivity to cultural factors (see Chapter 5) is very important in data-gathering activities, in which the consultant interacts with many different individuals and groups in the client organization. In this respect the consultant must keep in mind both the country's and the organization's culture (box 8.4). Even the particular microculture in different parts of an organization can influence how an interview is conducted or whether a group can be observed during work. It may be difficult and time-consuming for the consultant to determine the cultural norms of different groups, but it is essential.

8.5 Data analysis

Data cannot be used and converted into meaningful *information* without *analysis*, the purpose of which goes beyond research and appraisal. The ultimate

Box 8.4 Cultural factors in data-gathering – some examples

- In many countries, the interview cannot possibly start until the host (respondent or consultant) has first offered a beverage to the visitor.
- There may be cultural biases that hamper the use of a data-gathering technique. In one country where English was not the first language, a consultant went through the usual steps in preparing a questionnaire to be administered to a large group of people. When the data were reviewed, the unanimity of responses was surprising. As the consultant pursued this with some members of the client system, he discovered that it was the custom in that country for those answering a questionnaire to provide the information that they thought was wanted by those administering the questionnaire. It would have been impolite to do otherwise! The respondents had all determined the kind of answer the consultant would want and had provided it.
- In a Muslim country, a consultant was on an assignment that required data to be gathered from workers, some of whom were female. When the first interview was held, the consultant was surprised to find that the respondent brought along another woman, even though the consultant was herself a woman. Obviously, having another person present during the interview raised a question as to the validity of the data. After several interviews had been conducted, the consultant discussed this with the client. Only then did she learn that in that country (and there are differences among Muslim groups) a woman was not permitted to converse with a stranger, even another female, without an older woman from her own household being present.

aim of the consulting process is to initiate and implement change, and data analysis should help to achieve this.

A correct description of reality, i.e. of conditions and events and their causes, is therefore only one aspect of analysis. The other, more important aspect is to establish what can be done, whether the client has the potential to do it, and what future benefits should be obtained from the envisaged changes.

There is, therefore, no clear-cut distinction between analysis and synthesis. Synthesis, in the sense of building a whole from parts, drawing conclusions and developing action proposals, starts somewhere during data analysis. Thus, data analysis evolves gradually to synthesis. Indeed, analysis and synthesis are two sides of one coin, and consultants apply them simultaneously. A consultant does not have to discover new wholes by combining parts each time he or she undertakes an assignment – theoretical knowledge and practical experience help the consultant to synthesize while analysing.

If the consultant can establish that the problem observed follows a general rule, he or she will apply the deductive method, i.e. assuming that the relationships described by the rule exist in the case being dealt with. The consultant has to avoid the temptation to draw hasty conclusions from superficially analysed facts and allow ideas to become fixed before examining the facts in depth ("This is exactly the same case I have seen many times before!"). Put in other terms, it is not possible to use *deduction* where *induction* applies, and vice versa. In practical consulting work, the two methods are combined and complement each other, as analysis and synthesis do.

Editing the data

Before being analysed as described below, data need to be edited and screened. This includes checking their completeness, verifying the clarity of recording and presentation, eliminating or correcting errors, and making sure that uniform criteria were applied in data-gathering.

As an example, consider the recording of a production operation: if 19 recordings show a duration of between four and five minutes, one recording indicating 12 minutes cannot be used in calculating an average figure. Such an extreme recording can happen in quite different contexts – for example in accounting, where overhead costs may be inaccurately distributed among various products, or where one account may include items that should be in a different account.

Cross-checking helps in some instances: for example, information obtained in an interview can be verified by subsequent interviews. In other cases there is no possibility of cross-checking and the consultant must use experience and judgement, together with advice from the client's staff, to "clean" the data prior to analysing them.

Classification

The classification of data was started before the beginning of fact-finding, when criteria were established for the organization and tabulation of data (section 8.3). Further classification, and adjustments to the classification criteria, are made during and after fact-finding (e.g. the consultant may decide to use a more detailed breakdown of data than originally planned). If facts are recorded in a way that permits multiple classification (e.g. in a computer), the consultant can try several possible classifications before deciding which one is most relevant to the purpose of the assignment.

Both quantified and other information needs to be classified. For example, if complaints about the shortage of training opportunities come only from certain departments, or from people in certain age groups, the classification must reveal this.

The main classification criteria used by consultants are:

- time;
- place (unit);
- responsibility;
- structure;
- influencing factors.

Classification of data by *time* indicates trends, rates of change, and random and periodic fluctuations.

Classification by *place or organizational unit* helps in examining problems associated with various parts of the organization and devising solutions related to the specific conditions of each unit.

Classification by *responsibility for facts and events* is a different matter – in many cases responsibility may lie outside the place (unit) where a fact has been identified. The consultant may need to identify responsible organizational units and/or particular persons in these units.

Classification according to the *structure of entities and processes* is essential and uses a number of criteria. Employees, materials, products, plant and equipment, customers, and so on, can be classified from many different points of view. An important objective in this case is to define how changes in components affect the whole, and to direct action towards those components that have a major influence on total results. For example, the total lead time of a steam turbine may be determined by the machining and assembly time of one component – the rotor. Classification of customer complaints by product or production unit indicates where to focus quality improvement efforts.

Operations in a production process can be classified according to their sequence in time and presented in a table or diagram, or on the plan of the workshop (which makes it possible to indicate the directions and distances of movements of materials). Organizational relations, formal and informal, can be classified by means of charts, diagrams, matrices, and so on.

Classification by *influencing factors* is a preparatory step in functional and causal analysis. For example, machine stoppages may be classified by the factors that cause them: lack of raw material, break in energy supply, absence of worker, delay in scheduling, lack of spare parts, and so on.

In many cases simple classification (by one criterion) will not suffice: *cross-classification* is used, which combines two or more variables (e.g. employees classified by age group, sex, and length of employment with the organization).

Analysing organized data

The data, prepared and organized by classification, are analysed in order to identify relationships, proportions and trends. Depending on the nature of the problem and the purpose of the consulting assignment, a variety of techniques can be used in data analysis. The use of statistical techniques is common (averages, dispersion, frequency distribution, correlation and regression), and various other techniques, including mathematical modelling or graphical techniques, are often used. The reader is referred to the specialized literature for detailed discussion of these.

Statistical and other quantitative analysis is meaningful only where qualitative relations can be identified. For example, an association between two variables can be measured by correlation, but correlation cannot explain the nature and the causes of the relationship.

The main objective of quantitative analysis is to establish whether a specific relationship exists between various factors and events described by the data and, if so, to examine its nature. If possible, the relationship is quantified and defined as a *function* (in the mathematical sense of the term), describing how one or more dependent variables relate to one or more independent variables. The purpose is to discover and define relationships which are substantive and not just accidental. For example, the consultant may find out from data gathered in various firms that the cost of a major overhaul of machine tools is in some relationship to their purchase price. If such a relationship is defined as a function, the consultant can forecast the cost of overhaul and its influence on production costs in other firms using similar equipment.

Using ratios

A common way of expressing and measuring relationships is as ratios. Ratios can be used to test whether inputs to an activity generate commensurate outputs, examine whether resources and commitments are properly balanced, or express the internal structure of a particular factor or resource.

In detailed analytical work, the ratio of global aggregate data may be broken down into analytical ratios. For example, a series of ratios is often used to measure labour productivity:

$$\frac{V}{E} = \frac{V}{DH} \times \frac{DH}{PW} \times \frac{PW}{W} \times \frac{W}{E}$$

where V = value of production,
E = total number of employees,
DH = total direct labour hours,
PW = total number of production workers,
W = total number of manual workers.

There are no limits to the construction of detailed analytical ratios in any business and any functional area of management. Here again, working with a quantitative ratio makes sense if there is some qualitative relationship, and if using a ratio makes the analysis more meaningful by measuring this relationship and comparing it to a standard or another known case.

Causal analysis

Causal analysis (see also box 8.5) aims to discover causal relationships between conditions and events. It provides a key to planning change and improvements. If the causes of certain situations, results or problems are known, they can be examined in depth and action can focus on them.

In most cases, the consultant would start the investigation with one or more hypotheses as to what the cause(s) of a problem may be, based on knowledge and experience. To confirm the possible main causes the consultant needs to have a comprehensive, synthetic view of the total process or system he or she is examining, and of the whole organizational context.

Box 8.5 Difficulties and pitfalls of causal analysis

- **Cause and effect.** Frequently conditions are observed that influence each other and there is a risk of mistaking an effect for a cause. A typical example is the relationship between poor staff morale and low performance of the organization. Is poor staff morale a cause of low business results, or do low results depress the staff and lower morale? If a static view is taken, these conditions influence each other, and there may be a vicious circle; but which condition is the cause of the other?
- **Basic or primary cause.** Suppose that the consultant establishes that falling sales and profits are the cause of low staff morale. What then is the cause of the poor business results? The consultant finds out that it is the loss of an important foreign market. But why was that market lost? It was lost because of a serious mistake in pricing policy. Why was that mistake made? And the exercise goes on... In diagnosing business and management problems, consultants face *chains* of causes and effects. The issue is how deep and how far to go in looking for basic (or primary) causes. Here again, it helps to keep the purpose in mind. The consultant will have to consider one cause as basic, even if it is only "relatively" basic. As a rule, it will be one on which the client will be able to act. The consultant will thus be able to propose solutions that will address fundamental causes, without suggesting the impossible.
- **Multiple causes of one effect.** A problem frequently has two or more causes, although one of the causes may be more important than the others. This is often observed in personnel problems (a manager's behaviour and performance are affected simultaneously by problems encountered in the office and at home), or in organizational problems caused by parallel but independent events (e.g. a change in foreign-exchange rate and retirement of an outstanding marketing manager).
- **Multiple effects of one cause.** The opposite also happens frequently: one condition is found to be the cause of a number of effects. For example, the existence of a political or ethnic clique in an organization can be the cause of numerous personnel, managerial and performance problems.
- **Cause or culprit?** The temptation to designate a person responsible for the existence of a problem may be strong. While this may be inevitable in instances of flagrant mismanagement or personal irresponsibility, in most situations it will make the identification of a real cause more difficult and resistance to change will increase.

Only rarely would a consultant face a situation in which an unusual causal relationship would be discovered. But it may happen; for example, a consultant from an industrialized country working in a developing economy may discover causal relationships between certain cultural factors and the economic performance of an organization which are unknown to him or her from previous studies and work (such as different causes of absenteeism, or ethnic factors affecting the distribution of roles within a factory).

It is always necessary to proceed methodically, examining in detail, on the basis of the information collected, whether a hypothetical cause could really have created the effect observed. Theoretically, it would be possible to remove one hypothetical cause at a time to examine what happens to the effect. For example, in a workshop with poor working conditions workers get tired quickly and every day the output drops considerably after three or four hours of work. If the conditions (e.g. ventilation or lighting) are changed and output does not increase, or only very slightly, the consultant has to look for a different cause. It may be malnutrition. Bad working conditions may aggravate the situation, but are not its main cause.

Unfortunately, to experiment by removing one or more hypothetical causes is not possible, or would be too lengthy and costly, in dealing with management and business problems. In most cases it is the high-quality diagnostic work that has to eliminate some hypothetical causes and establish the real one.

Force-field analysis

One way of looking at relationships and factors affecting change is through force-field analysis, developed by Kurt Lewin (figure 8.1). In this concept, the present state of affairs in an organization is thought of as an equilibrium maintained by two groups of forces working in opposite directions: driving

Figure 8.1 Force-field analysis

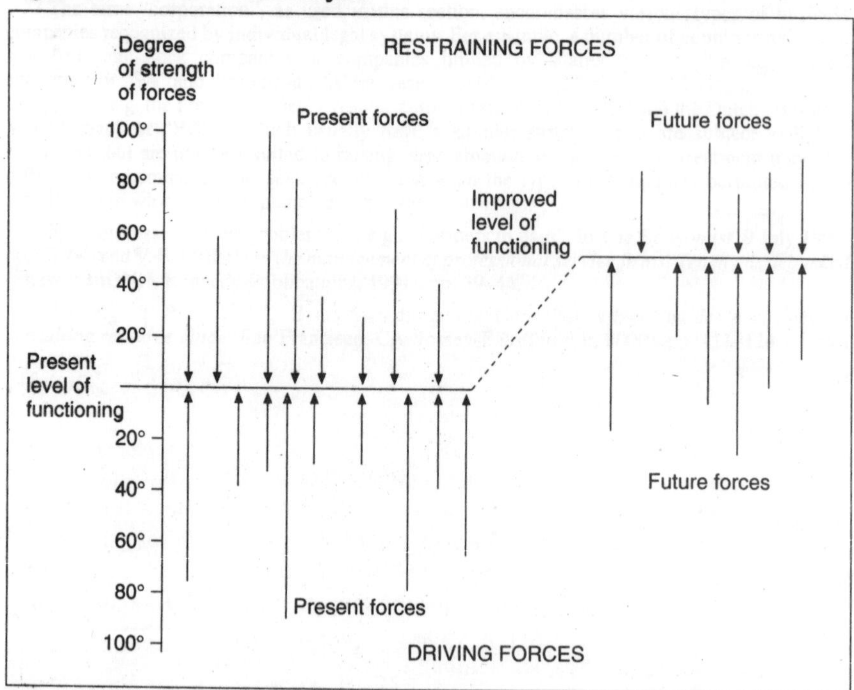

(impelling, helping) forces move towards change, while restraining (impeding, hindering) forces hamper change.

In analytical work, these two sorts of forces have to be identified and the relative strength of each force assessed. Change occurs when imbalance is created between the two groups of forces (e.g. by adding one or more new forces, or increasing or decreasing the strength of an already existing force). Eventually, a new balance between driving and restraining forces is established. And the process continues.

Comparison

Comparison is an essential analytical tool, closely linked to the methodological tools discussed above. The principal alternatives for comparison commonly used in preliminary diagnostic surveys were mentioned in section 7.2. In detailed diagnostic work the same reference points are used, but in addition to global appraisal, comparison is used to examine operating details and develop solutions. The various bases for comparisons made *within* the client organization are represented in figure 8.2. The consultant can compare C with A, C with B, C with D, E with C, and so on.

Of special interest is comparison that helps to establish future standards (of potential achievement) and thus provides guidance for the development of future-

Figure 8.2 Various bases for comparison

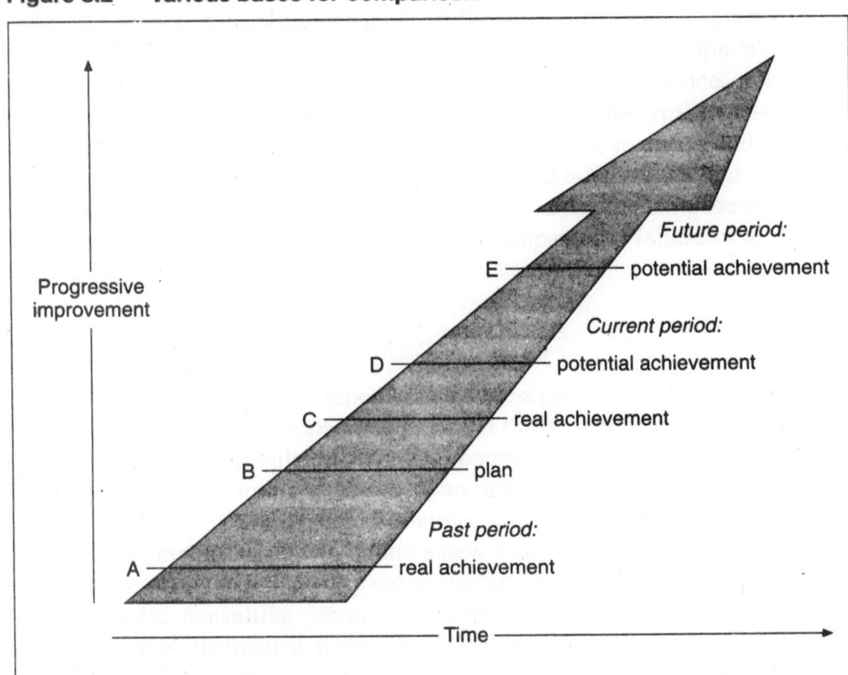

oriented proposals. It is particularly in this connection that comparison turns to examples, models and standards from outside the organization and even outside the sector or country. The consultant should consider whether the diversity of conditions permits such comparison, especially if it is to be used for more than general judgement – namely for specific suggestions to the client as to what he or she should do.

Interfirm comparison is often used to assess global performance indicators against comparable data from other firms, or against sector standards. *Benchmarking* is a more analytical technique, which focuses on specific processes, operations and functions within organizations. It has been used by many firms to identify standards achieved by other organizations collaborating in the same benchmarking project or scheme, compare experiences and conditions, and develop specific proposals for improvements (see also section 20.3).

Analysing the future

Owing to its focus on action and improvements, all consulting work must be essentially oriented to the future. Whether the client is struggling for survival or is a highly profitable company looking for new business opportunities, the key questions will always be: what will be our future opportunities? What shall we do in the future to achieve our purposes? Shall we focus on correcting past errors or shall we take a completely new path?

This future orientation gives a particular slant to data analysis. Consultants have to collect or establish data on a situation that does not yet exist, in addition to collecting data on existing realities. They have to assess these data and recommend desirable courses of action that the client should take.

The future is, of course, related to the past and the present. Many future events and relationships can be predicted. It is therefore essential to analyse trends in data describing the environment and the organization concerned. All consultants are interested in trends, whether the assignment deals with business strategy or with a narrower technical problem such as simplifying or automating production records.

Unfortunately, the most common approach to future-trend analysis is *simple extrapolation*. We tend to think of the future as a mere extension of past trends, because we are unable or unwilling to consider what new developments may alter them radically. In periods of rapid technological, social and other changes – and we are living in one such period – it is normal for past trends not to continue into the future without substantial alterations.

Data on future trends collected from various external sources of information have to be examined cautiously and their reliability assessed. For example, a consultant working for a client enterprise with highly energy-intensive production processes obtains information on new power-generating capacities in construction, on their planned completion dates and on foreseen changes in the price of electricity. He or she should take into account that new power plants can be years behind schedule, that their actual cost is often higher than the original projected cost and that the price of energy will depend on many variables, including the government's tax and regulatory policies. How will this affect the future development structure of costs in a client organization which is a major consumer of electricity? It may be necessary to develop alternative plans and estimate with what probability they are likely to become a reality.

Future developments within the client organization will also be affected by environmental changes. For example, in analysing the time dimension of a product life-cycle it is necessary to consider whether the curve which is usual in a given sector applies, or whether progress in technology imposes the use of a different curve, as has been amply documented by the pace of change in information and communication technologies.

The same applies to ratio analysis. Some ratios may become less important or even meaningless. In retail selling the ratio of sales per employee retained its meaning with the transition from small shops to department stores, supermarkets and self-service stores. However, it is losing its meaning with the advent of automatically controlled sales surfaces if even the cashiers are replaced by electronic control and billing equipment. Ratios such as sales per square metre of selling surface, or sales per $1,000 of invested capital, become more significant. In general, ratios permitting the assessment of total factor productivity are becoming more important than labour productivity ratios.

Synthesis

To a management consultant, analysis and synthesis are two sides of one coin. As data analysis is progressing, the consultant's approach will increasingly involve synthesis – identifying basic relationships, trends and causes, differentiating between fundamental and secondary events and factors, and defining conditions that have to be changed if a whole process or organization is to change. In particular, the consultant operates as a synthesist when looking ahead and helping the client to define an action programme for the organization.

Synthesis is considerably more difficult than pure analysis. Many bulky analytical reports, often based on vast numbers of facts and defining long lists of problems, are difficult to use because they lack synthesis. Key conclusions are not drawn and key measures are not identified. As all the measures proposed cannot be introduced at the same time or with the same vigour, action starts in a haphazard way or is soon abandoned.

Effective synthesis is probably one of the main things that a new management consultant has to learn. Of course, consultants are not the only people who may have problems with synthetic thinking and using the synthetic method effectively. As Alvin Toffler has pointed out:

> Our civilization placed an extremely heavy emphasis on our ability to dismantle problems into their components: it rewarded us less often for the ability to put the pieces back together again. Most people are culturally more skilled as analysts than synthesists. This is one reason why our images of the future (and of ourselves in that future) are so fragmentary, haphazard and wrong... Today we stand on the edge of a new age of synthesis.[8]

Synthesis is the aspect of diagnostic work that provides the link with the next phase of the consulting process – the action-planning phase, which will be discussed in Chapter 9.

8.6 Feedback to the client

We have referred a number of times to the desirability of actively involving the client in data-gathering and other diagnostic operations. The objective is to build a truly collaborative consultant–client relationship at an early stage of the assignment, and to prevent various negative attitudes and reactions on the part of the client. These are difficult to avoid if he or she is poorly informed about what is going on, and if the consultant's findings and conclusions come as a surprise. We have mentioned, too, the need to give feedback to the client during the diagnostic phase.

What is feedback?

Giving feedback provides the client with information that can:

- tell the client something new and meaningful about his or her organization;
- make the client aware of the approach taken by the consultant and the progress made in the investigation;
- increase the client's active contribution to the assignment;
- stimulate the client to help the consultant to stay on the right track, or reorient the investigation if necessary.

Feedback during diagnosis is itself a diagnostic method. Properly selected and presented information will provoke some reaction on the part of the client, and so the consultant should keep firmly in mind what reaction he or she wants to generate:

- Does he need more information on the topic?
- Is she seeking information on a new topic, about which the client was reluctant to speak?
- Should the client criticize the data?
- Does the consultant want to shake up a lethargic client by showing alarming data?

Giving feedback to the client is simultaneously an intervention technique used to stir up change:

- Is this what is wanted?
- Is there enough reliable information to feed back to the client with the intention of stimulating change?

- Is there a risk of causing panic or generating premature changes?
- Should the client be warned against this risk?

When to give feedback

Feedback is more than reporting on the work performed. It should be given at moments when it can serve a specific purpose. One example is to show the client that the data collected so far indicate the existence of some new problem or opportunity, not foreseen in the negotiation and planning of the original assignment; another is when the consultant feels that he or she has enough information to eliminate certain hypotheses formed at the beginning, and wishes to discuss this with the client. A consultant who pursues the strategy of "many small steps" may give feedback each time he or she has enough information to decide on the next step to take.

To whom to give feedback

In principle, feedback should be given to those from whom the consultant expects further help, more information, or action related to the problem. It is often emphasized that if feedback is too restricted (reserved to selected individuals or small groups of senior managers), it is unrealistic to expect other people to be interested in helping the consultant. Some authors regard this as a question of consulting ethics: if people readily provide information and demonstrate their interest in the assignment, they have the right to receive feedback on what has been done with their information. In theory, all people interviewed should thus receive some feedback fairly soon after the interview. In practice there are limits to this. Some information will clearly be confidential and cannot be divulged to a large number of employees. Deciding who should be informed about the consultant's findings, and at what stage, is also a question of consulting tactics. For example, individuals who originally refused to give information to the consultant may change their attitude if they see that the consultant is sharing information with them.

What feedback to give and how

The consultant wants to show that he or she has not been wasting time and has important information to share. But the purpose is not to impress people. The consultant should be selective, sharing information that is meaningful, about which the client is likely to be concerned, to which he will probably react, and which will activate him.

Giving feedback is not telling the client what he or she already knows. This is a general rule, to be consistently observed in reporting and communicating with the client. But when the information collected contains factors that are genuinely new to the client, or shows unsuspected links between effect and cause or hidden strengths and weaknesses, it is wise to give feedback on these issues.

Giving feedback is not evaluating the client. Therefore, the consultant should avoid value judgements; it is the client who should draw such conclusions from the information presented to him or her in an impartial manner. The purpose should always be kept in mind. For example, it is not good tactics to speak only about problems and difficulties encountered by the consultant. Feedback should also point to the client's problem-solving potential, and suggest strong points that might be developed.

Form of feedback

The need for careful preparation of the data and of the form of feedback to be used cannot be overemphasized. Individualized oral feedback to important members of the client organization is very common. Another form is written information (e.g. interim reports or memoranda). Many consultants like to use feedback meetings with various groups in the client organization. These meetings can provide valuable additional information and help the consultant to focus the investigation on key issues. They invariably reveal attitudes to the problem at hand and to the approach taken by the consultant.

Closing the diagnostic phase

The end of the diagnostic phase provides an important opportunity for feedback. Before submitting a diagnostic report, consultants may find it useful to hold one or more feedback meetings to review the main findings; this may help them to identify remaining gaps in the analysis, and also prepare clients for the conclusions that will be formally presented to them.

Even if the assignment is to continue (i.e. if it is clear that there will be a smooth transition from the diagnostic work to action planning and then to implementation), there may be a good case for submitting a progress report at what is ostensibly the end of a predominantly diagnostic stage in an assignment. The period of obtaining and examining facts may have been lengthy, and costly to the client. Many managers may not have been involved very deeply, although they are interested in what the assignment will produce. A good progress report will certainly be welcomed. It should tell the client clearly how the work was focused, whether diagnosis has confirmed the choices made or discovered new problems and opportunities, and how the work on action proposals should be oriented.

There are, then, assignments that will have no further phase, such as management audits and comprehensive diagnostic studies of organizations. In these, the consultant is required to establish and analyse facts, but for some reason the client does not want him to go beyond this point. In such cases the diagnostic report will serve as an end-of-assignment report (see Chapter 11).

If the assignment is to continue, obtaining the client's agreement before embarking on action planning (e.g. on designing a new information system or workshop layout and planning its application) is essential. Consulting contracts often specify in detail what exactly will happen at the end of the diagnostic phase, before it is decided if and how to pursue the assignment.

---

[1] This section is inspired by the discussion of the "purpose principle" in G. Nadler and S. Hibino: *Breakthrough thinking: The seven principles of creative problem solving* (Rocklin, CA, Prima Publishing, 1994).

[2] Jerome H. Fuchs addressing the Society of Professional Management Consultants in New York.

[3] P. Block: *Flawless consulting: A guide to getting your expertise used* (San Francisco, CA, Jossey-Bass/Pfeiffer, 2nd ed., 2000), p. 176.

[4] Many books on business research methods are available on the market. For various methods of representing work processes see G. Kanawaty (ed.): *Introduction to work study* (Geneva, ILO, 4th (revised) ed., 1992). See also S. Nagashima: *100 management charts* (Tokyo, Asian Productivity Organization, 1987).

[5] See, e.g., Kanawaty, op. cit.

[6] See M. Kubr and J. Prokopenko: *Diagnosing management training and development needs: Concepts and techniques*, Management Development Series No. 27 (Geneva, ILO, 1989), or J. Quay: *Diagnostic interviewing for consultants and auditors* (Columbus, OH, Quay Associates, 1986).

[7] See, e.g., T. K. Reeves and D. Harper: *Surveys at work: A practitioner's guide* (London, McGraw-Hill, 1981). Useful recent guidelines on designing workplace surveys are in P. Morell-Samuels: "Getting the truth into workplace surveys", in *Harvard Business Review*, Feb. 2002, pp. 111–118.

[8] A. Toffler: *The third wave* (London, Pan Books, 1981), p. 141.

from business firms. The idea is that talented and dynamic individuals will quickly acquire the necessary practical experience by working in teams with more senior consultants. Executives in business and consulting firms tend to agree that recruiting young consultants without experience is not ideal, but they see no alternative.

The *age at which candidates are recruited* reflects the required education and experience. The lower age limit is usually between 25 and 30 years. In many cases there is also an upper age limit. It may be difficult for a senior manager or specialist, who has reached an interesting position in terms of responsibility and pay, to switch-over to consulting unless he or she is directly offered a senior position with a consulting organization. This happens only in special cases, for example, if senior people have to be recruited from outside to start new lines of consulting or head new divisions.

As a general rule, most consulting firms try to avoid recruiting new staff at senior level. Consulting emphasizes certain work methods and behavioural patterns, and some people would find it difficult to learn and internalize these after a certain age and at a high level of seniority. Also, it is not always easy to adapt to a firm's culture and style. The upper limit for recruitment therefore tends to be between 36 and 40 years. Of course, if an individual decides to open a private consulting practice, he or she can do it at any time. There are retired business executives and government officials who start consulting at the age of 55–60. Some managers who are made redundant turn to consulting, at whatever stage of their career they are, rather than look for another management job in a saturated labour market.

Recruitment sources

There are two main sources of recruitment: business enterprises and universities. But any other source is acceptable, provided it gives the candidate the required experience and skills. Many consulting firms advertise job opportunities in business journals and management periodicals, thus opening their doors to any candidates who meet the criteria.

A third source might be client organizations, although under normal circumstances a consultant should not use this source owing to conflict of interest (see Chapter 6). But there are exceptions. A client may willingly authorize a consultant to offer a job to an employee whose personal qualities would be better utilized in consulting than in the present job.

When recruiting directly from universities and business schools,[2] consulting firms aim to get the best students. They may interview 20 or more candidates for one position. In some countries, consulting careers with leading firms enjoy such a good reputation that the best graduates are interested.

However, consulting firms compete for recruits among themselves, with other professions and with investment banks, IT service providers and other firms, including those in the most dynamic and forward-looking sectors. Therefore the relationship is often reversed: it is not the consulting firm that chooses among

ACTION PLANNING 9

With action planning the consulting process enters its third phase. This phase includes developing possible solutions to the problem diagnosed, choosing among alternative solutions, presenting proposals to the client, and preparing for the implementation of the solution chosen by the client.

The continuity between diagnosis and action planning cannot be overemphasized. The foundations of effective action planning are laid in excellent diagnostic work, i.e. in defining and analysing problems and purposes as well as the factors and forces that stimulate or hamper the change process in the client organization. Diagnosis provides a basic orientation for action-planning efforts.

However, despite this emphasis on continuity and on the need to base action planning on diagnosis, there are significant differences in approach and methodology. The emphasis is no longer on analytical work, but on innovation and creativity. The objective is not to find more data and further explanations for the existence of a problem, but to come up with something new. Obviously, not all solutions to clients' problems will involve totally fresh approaches. Often there will be no need to develop a new solution from scratch because a suitable one already exists somewhere. Yet, even transfer and adaptation require imagination and creativity. Ignoring the uniqueness of the client's condition and mechanically transplanting solutions that have worked in other organizations is one of the worst (though not one of the rarest) consulting flaws.

The client's involvement in action planning should be even more active than in the diagnostic phase. There are several reasons for this:

> Extensive conceptual, design and planning work on possible solutions should only be undertaken if the client is fully familiar and in complete agreement with the approach taken, and will be able to go along with the alternatives that are being pursued. This agreement can best be established by working jointly with people who are in a position to ascertain what the client organization will accept and be able to implement.

- Action planning requires the best talents to be mobilized and all good ideas to be examined; it will be ineffective if the talents within the client organization do not contribute.
- As with diagnosis, the client's personnel can do a great deal of the design and planning work with back-up from the consultant, thus reducing the cost of the project.
- Participation in action planning generates commitment that will be necessary, and put to the test, at the implementation stage.
- Lastly, action planning provides a new range of learning opportunities for the client; these opportunities are even more interesting that those offered by diagnosis, but will definitely be lost if the consultant is left to proceed alone.

Section 4.5 describes various intervention techniques for assisting change. Some of these techniques can be used in working on action proposals in a team with the client and his or her staff.

Time may have become a constraint. In many assignments too much time is spent on collecting and examining facts, and when it comes to the development of proposals there is a general desire to finish the project as soon as possible. The consultant is left with little time to prepare alternatives and rapidly develops only one solution. Even the work on one proposal may have to be concluded short of perfection. This can be avoided by properly scheduling the assignment and making sure that enough time is left for a creative search for the most appropriate solution.

9.1 Searching for possible solutions

The client expects the consultant to recommend the best solution to the problem, or suggest the best way of taking a new opportunity. However, it is seldom possible to point immediately to an obvious best solution. Most business and management problems have more than one solution and in some cases the number of alternative solutions is high, especially if the purposes pursued are complex. The consultant may already be aware of some possible solutions, but unaware of others. Often the complexity and the originality of the situation are such that no clear-cut solution comes to anybody's mind immediately. New situations cannot be dealt with using old approaches, and management consultants operate in a field which is changing extremely rapidly.

The action-planning phase starts therefore with a search for ideas and information on possible solutions to the problem. The objective is to identify all interesting and feasible alternatives and subject them to preliminary evaluation before starting detailed design and planning work on one proposal.

Orienting the search for solutions

The main factor to be considered is the nature of the problem, especially its technical characteristics (functional area, techniques or methods to be changed), complexity (technical, financial, human and other aspects, importance to the client organization, need to respect sectoral technical standards), and degree of newness (whether the consultant and the client are familiar with the problem, whether a completely new solution has to be developed or an established solution can be applied with or without adaptation).

The consultant, in collaboration with the client, will have to decide whether to direct the search towards solutions that may be commercially available (e.g. purchasing a standard software package from an IT firm, or towards a new original solution (developing new software using the client's own resources, or commissioning such work from a specialist software house). It is necessary to decide how far this search should go. Should it be limited to the client organization? Could possible solutions be found in other organizations, sectors, or countries? Is it necessary to screen technical literature? Should a research establishment be involved? Box 9.1 provides a checklist of some questions to consider in deciding how to focus the search for feasible solutions to the problem.

Box 9.1 Checklist of preliminary considerations

(1) What should the new solution achieve?
- what basic purpose?
- what other purposes?
- what level of performance?
- what quality of output?
- what new product, service or activity?
- what behaviour?

(2) How will the new situation differ from the present?
- different products, services or activities?
- different method?
- different system(s)?
- different equipment?
- different location?
- different way of managing?

(3) Are the effects likely to last?
- are the client's business and market changing rapidly?
- is competition likely to come with better solutions?
- is there a possibility that people will revert to present practices?
- should further developments be foreseen?

(4) Where could solutions or ideas be found?
- in the same unit?
- in the same enterprise?
- from business partners or friends?
- in literature?
- in a research institution?
- in the consulting firm?
- from other consultants?

continued overleaf....

- in different sectors?
- anywhere else?

(5) What difficulties may arise?
- technical problems?
- resistance of managers and staff?
- work hazards?
- quality problems?
- over-production?
- shortage of materials?
- customers' reactions?
- shortage of finance?

(6) Who will be affected?
- are employees receptive?
- is management receptive?
- what should be done to prepare them?
- how should they be involved?
- do matching changes have to be made elsewhere?

(7) When is the best time to change?
- at the end of a season?
- during holiday time?
- at the close of a financial period?
- at the beginning of a new calendar year?
- any time?
- as soon as possible?
- in several stages?

Using experience

In devising ways of improving the client's situation, the consultant often draws on experience. He or she considers methods successfully used elsewhere, using knowledge derived from a variety of sources:

- previous assignments and clients;
- the consulting organization's files and documentation;
- colleagues in the consulting organization who have worked in similar situations;
- professional literature (books, periodicals, research reports, etc.);
- producers of equipment and systems software, who may be developing or have developed improvements;
- staff in other departments of the client organization, who may have knowledge of the particular process;
- organizations that are prepared to communicate their experience.

An obvious purpose is to avoid reinventing the wheel. An even more important purpose is to make sure that all available experience is identified and considered, so that the client gets advice that could be qualified as "state of the art", or a solution reflecting the best experience.

This is an acid test for the consultant, who must not cede to the obvious temptation to choose the most comfortable way – suggesting what he or she has done in similar situations with previous clients, or choosing the first solution that comes to mind. For example, a solo practitioner may have completed a thorough diagnosis of the client's problem, but finds that, when it comes to proposing a better system, there is clearly a need for expertise that he does not possess. What will he suggest? Will he go for a second-best solution or admit that another professional should be brought in? The same problem exists in large consultancies, where the partners and other managers do not always appreciate the need to back up the operating consultants with the collective expertise and information sources of the firm.

Creative thinking

In current consulting, there are more and more situations where experience cannot offer any satisfying solution and where both the consulting team and the client organization have to come up with a totally new approach. In this connection, it may be useful to review some principles and methods of creative thinking.

Creative thinking has been defined as *the relating of things or ideas that were previously unrelated.* It combines a rigorous analytical approach with intuition and imagination. The purpose is, of course, to discover or develop something new. Nothing is taken for granted. The history of science and business is full of examples of discovery based on creative thinking, and there is no reason why the consultant cannot approach many practical industrial and management problems using the same method. Creativity can be learned, and is worth learning.

There are five stages in the creative thinking process, and all need to be practised consciously to get the best results:

1. **Preparation:** Obtaining all the known facts; applying analytical thinking as far as possible; defining the problem in different ways, i.e. restating the problem and the purposes pursued.
2. **Effort:** Divergent thinking, to generate multiple ideas, concepts and approaches. This will lead either to possible solutions or to frustration. Frustration is an important feature in the effort stage and in the full creative thinking process. It is usually followed by the production of good ideas.
3. **Incubation:** Leaving the problem in one's subconscious mind while one gets on with other things. This also gives time for inhibitions and emotional blocks to new ideas to weaken, and gives opportunities to pick up additional ideas from what one sees or hears in the meantime.
4. **Insight:** The flash of illumination that gives an answer and leads to possible solutions of the problem.
5. **Evaluation:** Analysing all the ideas obtained in the previous three stages so as to find possible solutions.

Two of the stages – preparation and evaluation – require analytical thinking. The three central stages – effort, incubation and insight – require suspended judgement and free-wheeling. Wild ideas are deliberately fostered, the aim being quantity, not quality. Large numbers of ideas are obtained, new ideas being sparked off by earlier ideas. The key to successful creative thinking is the conscious and deliberate separation of idea-production and idea-evaluation.

Techniques of creative thinking include, among others, the following:[1]

Brainstorming. This is a means of obtaining a large number of ideas from a group of people in a short time. Typically a group of eight to 12 people take a problem and produce ideas in a free-wheeling atmosphere. Judgement is suspended and all ideas, particularly wild ones, are encouraged. In fact the wildest ideas can often be stepping-stones to new and very practical ones. Ideas are displayed on sheets of paper and are produced very quickly; a session may produce over 200 ideas in an hour. Brainstorming is the best known and most widely used of the techniques. Its main disadvantage lies in the fact that all ideas are to be evaluated. Many of them will be foolish or totally irrelevant and have to be discarded to arrive at a few really good ideas. Also, the term "brainstorming" is often misused, to describe any discussion about an existing problem.

Synectics. In this technique, which is similar to brainstorming, a group of about nine people takes a problem. The "client", whose problem it is, explains it, and participants put forward a suggestion for solving it. After a few minutes the client analyses the suggestion, saying what he or she likes about it before touching on the drawbacks. Then new suggestions are put forward and analysed until possible solutions are found.

Attribute listing. This technique lists the main attributes of an idea or object, and examines each one to see how it can be changed. It is normally used on tangible rather than intangible things. For example, a screwdriver has the following attributes: round steel shank; wooden handle; flat wedge end; manual operation; torque by twist. Each attribute is questioned and changes are suggested. Some modern screwdrivers, i.e. with ratchets or a cruciform head instead of the wedge end, are examples of improvement.

Forced relationships. This technique takes objects or ideas and asks the question, "In how many ways can these be combined to give a new object or idea?" For example, a manufacturer of furniture could take the items he makes and see if two or more could be combined to give a new piece of furniture.

Morphological analysis. This technique sets down all the variables in a matrix and tries to combine them in new ways. For example, if a new form of transport is required, the variables could be as shown in box 9.2. Although the matrix does not give all possible alternatives, the various combinations of the variables listed give an impressive number of forms of transport, many of which

Box 9.2 Variables for developing new forms of transport

Travelling in	air, water, space, land surface, underground
Travelling on	wheels, rollers, air cushion, magnetic cushion, skids, moving belt, aerial ropeway
Travel path	reserved, shared with other vehicles
Control	under operator's control, externally controlled
Energy provided by	electricity, petrol, gas, special fuel, atomic power, wind, water
Energy transmitted by	pulling, pushing, ejecting, own engine
Energy transmission	internal: to wheels, propeller (air), propeller (water), caterpillar tracks, ejection external: magnetic, hydraulic, pneumatic, mechanical, via cable, via moving belt, via screw transmission
Position of traveller	sitting, lying, standing, hanging

exist. Many alternatives will be discarded, but some are worth considering and may suggest new, practical, useful and feasible solutions.

Lateral thinking and PO. If a problem is tackled analytically, it is necessary to go into greater and greater depth and detail – this is vertical thinking. Creative thinking involves the examination of all options, including those that appear to be outside the given problem area – that is to say, lateral thinking. Edward de Bono has recommended deferring judgement by prefacing an idea with the letters "PO", which stands for "give the idea a chance, don't kill it too quickly, it may lead to useful ideas".[2]

Checklists. These may be used as pointers to ideas. Lists may be particular to an area (e.g. marketing, design) or general. Osborn's generalized checklist[3] is well known; the main headings are: Put to other uses? Adapt? Modify? Minify? Substitute? Rearrange? Reverse? Combine? Checklists need to be used with care, as they can inhibit creativity by limiting the areas of inquiry.

The six thinking hats. This approach, developed by Edward de Bono, suggests the use of different thought processes for different purposes. Each hat has a different colour and is used as a symbol for a particular way of thinking (*white* – for assessing available and required information; *red* – for feelings and emotions about the issue; *yellow* – for looking at gains and advantages; *black* – for constraints, criticism and risks; *green* – for creativity, new ideas and possibilities; and *blue* – for pulling the whole thinking process together and managing it). Participants in creative thinking sessions are asked to actually wear these hats during the session when they are applying a particular way of thinking.[4]

Breakthrough thinking. This approach, developed by Gerald Nadler and Shozo Hibino, provides "seven principles of creative problem-solving".[5] It does not follow a constant pattern of inquiry, but proposes a general flow of reasoning. Opportunities for a breakthrough must be continually sought in order to increase the probability of one of the three distinct types of breakthrough: (1) the brilliantly creative idea; (2) the solution that produces significantly better results; or (3) bringing to fruition the "good idea", in order to make it real and implement an outstanding system or solution.

The search for new creativity techniques continues. For example, *day-dreaming* has been suggested if long intensive work on a problem does not generate any innovative solution; in such a situation complete relaxation and virtual dreaming may bring about creative insight. The *"group-genius" technique* gathers in one group individuals who normally use different ways of creative thinking, thus forming a team able to combine these techniques.[6] In summary, no matter which technique is used, the following four guidelines apply:

- **Suspend judgement** – Rule out premature criticism of any idea.
- **Free-wheel** – The wilder the ideas the better the results.
- **Quantity** – The more ideas the better.
- **Cross-fertilize** – Combine and improve on the ideas of others.

Barriers to creative thinking

In business and management practice, there is a need to struggle against barriers to creative thinking. Most people are educated and trained to think analytically, and only a few are trained to use their creative ability. Creative thinking is also restricted by:

- self-imposed barriers;
- belief that there is always one right answer;
- conformity or giving the expected answer;
- lack of effort and courage in challenging the obvious;
- evaluating too quickly;
- fear of looking foolish.

Awareness of the barriers to creative thinking, and a conscious effort to break them down in a creative situation, can open a vast area of new ideas or ways of tackling problems. Suspending judgement is a particularly pertinent example of how a better understanding of the creative thinking process can help towards a fuller use of creative abilities in seeking solutions to difficult management problems.

Respect for authority is a major barrier which is difficult to overcome. Even if a person perceived as an authority (a manager, a chief designer, a consultant, a writer, an older person) does not explicitly require conformity and uniformity, and encourages colleagues to look for new ideas, challenging his or her views may be difficult if not impossible in many organizational and national cultures. This is one more reason why managers in both consulting firms and in client organizations should refrain from expressing a preference for one solution if the search for the best solution is to continue.

Success can be a serious barrier to creativity. In a successful company, management can easily become locked into methods and practices that have been its strong points, and may be unwilling to recognize that there can be an even better approach, or that owing to its success the company has stopped working on further improvements.

Excessive individualism and the failure to use teamwork is another serious barrier. If people work in a team examining a complex problem from various angles, a new idea put forward by one team member usually helps other members to widen their outlook, and to come up with other new ideas. Members of a team can not only help but also emulate each other.

The solution-after-next principle

This principle of breakthrough thinking[7] suggests developing alternative solutions that take into consideration future needs. The principle states that the change or system you install now should be based on what the solution might be next time you work on the problem.

This implies anticipating future changes: in the environment, in demand for the client's services or products, in competition and within the client organization itself. An obvious requirement is that, by adopting a new solution, the way is not blocked to further solutions that may become necessary in the future (e.g. by building a production capacity or a database that cannot be expanded). Viewing the problem and the solution from a future perspective helps to arrive at the best possible current solution. It may be useful to visualize an ideal future system. Even if such a system cannot be implemented immediately, certain elements will be usable and the vision of the future will improve the quality of the solution that will be adopted. Box 9.3 gives three checklists as pointers when searching for an ideal solution.

9.2 Developing and evaluating alternatives

Preselecting ideas to be pursued

As mentioned in the previous section, in the search for innovative ideas judgement has to be deferred to avoid blocking the process of creative thinking. There comes a moment, however, when new ideas have to be sorted out, reviewed, discussed and assessed (e.g. very interesting; interesting; trivial; useless; not clear). Since it would be impossible to pursue a large number of ideas, a preselection must be made, e.g. only ideas classed as "very interesting" will be followed up.

Box 9.3 Searching for an ideal solution – three checklists

A. *To inspire group creativity you might:*

(1) Prohibit any criticism when ideas are being generated, allowing a later time for judgement and assessment.
(2) Encourage free-wheeling, however wild the ideas that may emerge.
(3) Involve someone who is not a stakeholder in the project.
(4) Record all ideas so that each receives due consideration.
(5) Pose questions that stimulate or motivate creativity:
 (a) What system or value-added services and outcomes would make us an acknowledged world leader?
 (b) What would the solution be if we faced no constraints?
 (c) What would the ideal system look like if we could achieve all the purposes larger than the one we selected?
 (d) What would the solution look like if we started all over again (clean slate, green field, blank piece of paper)?
(6) Focus discussions on how to make suggested solutions work, rather than on why they won't work. Play the believing game.
(7) In using all of these tools, have fun with humorous activities that stimulate imagination. In generating ideas, humour is a serious matter.

B. *Here are some "red flags" to watch out for on your solution-finding journey*:

- "We can't go beyond our scope."
- "Stay on your own turf."
- "Don't exceed the local budget."
- "Let's get on to the next problem."
- "There's only one correct solution for this problem."
- "That's totally unrealistic."
- "Let's get real here."
- "In our department (group, organization) that's not possible."
- "That's just not done in our industry (profession)."
- "It won't work. Ten per cent of our customers want rhubarb pie."
- "We can't go back to zero."

C. *Always ask yourself these specific questions:*

– Have I generated many solutions-after-next or ideal systems?
– How should we achieve these purposes if we had to start all over again?
– How do I see this purpose and each bigger purpose being accomplished ten years from now?
– What regular occurrences can help us develop the best ideal solution?
– What today is impossible to do but, if we could, would fundamentally change the business?

- Am I seeing the right targets toward which our recommendations should lead?
- Have I looked for a second right answer? A third? A fourth?

Source: Excerpts from Ch. 6 ("The solution-after-next principle"), in G. Nadler and S. Hibino: *Breakthrough thinking: The seven principles of creative problem solving* (Rocklin, CA, Prima Publishing, 1994).

How many ideas should stay on a shortlist and what criteria to use in classifying certain ideas as "very interesting" are questions of judgement. The selection should be made in close collaboration with the client. The client may feel that several ideas could lead to acceptable solutions, but should also realize that parallel work on several solutions will probably increase the length and the cost of the assignment.

Working on alternatives

After the preliminary screening of ideas, the detailed design, systems development and planning work should in theory be started on all alternatives shortlisted. In practice a pragmatic attitude is needed since there may be insufficient resources for working on a number of possibilities simultaneously, and detailed design and planning of several alternatives may be inefficient if only one is to be retained.

A phased approach may help. For example, work may be started on two or three alternatives, but carried only to a pre-project or sketch-plan level. This will make it possible to collect more data, including tentative figures on potential costs and benefits. The pre-projects can then be evaluated with the conclusion that only one will be pursued further or, on the contrary, that the client wishes the design of two or more alternatives to be completed.

Another possibility is to start by developing the idea that received the highest preliminary rating. This alternative may be pursued as long as the facts show that it would provide a satisfying solution. It would be dropped, and work started on a second alternative, only if assessment revealed that the course of action taken was incorrect, or that the cost–benefit was not satisfactory.

It is true that these (and similar) approaches do not give a 100 per cent guarantee that the ideal solution will be found and applied. However, the solutions are being developed in real life, within given time, financial, human and other constraints. The ideal solution may be within the consultant's and the client's reach – but the time or cost required could be prohibitive.

Evaluating alternatives

It is clear that the evaluation of alternatives is not a one-off action to be undertaken at a defined point in time in the assignment. When data are collected and analysed, due regard should be given to the forthcoming evaluation exercises. At the beginning of the assignment, the consultant should define the reference period during which data will be collected for use in comparing new solutions with the existing ones. When action planning has started, a preliminary evaluation may be made in several steps to eliminate ideas and reduce the number of alternatives on which the consultant and the client will do detailed work. A comprehensive evaluation is required when the client finally opts for one particular alternative.

Some comments on the evaluation criteria may be useful. There are some comparatively easy cases, such as the choice between two or three machine tools (of different technical level, productivity, service and maintenance requirements, and price) for the same production operation. The criteria are limited in number and can be quantified, especially if production records are reasonably good. In contrast, there are complex cases, such as a major reorganization in a manufacturing company, an acquisition of another company or a new marketing strategy, which are very "open-ended". There may be several alternatives. Personnel and training measures will be involved, and so on. In these cases some criteria lend themselves to fairly exact calculation of costs and benefits (e.g. the cost of training needed). Others do not (e.g. the greater effectiveness of decision-making following decentralization of authority and responsibility in marketing and product-policy matters, or the improved image of the company following a merger with a well-chosen partner).

In consulting on management and business issues, the following situations prevail:

- alternatives that are ideal by all criteria used are rare, and in most cases there is a need to compare positive and negative consequences of several alternatives;
- the number of criteria is high: certain basic criteria are met by all alternatives and further criteria have to be examined;
- some important criteria (especially environmental, social, cultural and political criteria) are difficult, if not impossible, to quantify;
- the evaluation involves different criteria that are not directly comparable (e.g. financial and political criteria);
- there is a strong subjective element in the evaluation: somebody has to decide how important various criteria are in the given case, and make the evaluation using the "soft" criteria in addition to hard data.

To overcome this last difficulty, and to increase the element of objectivity in subjective evaluations, various attempts have been made to associate numerical values with adjectival scales. The principle is to use a group of experts (from the client organization, the consulting firm or elsewhere) to assign points to particular criteria. The values thus obtained are then used in an evaluation model, e.g. in decision analysis. The scale may be as follows:

Major improvement	=	10
Considerable improvement	=	7
Some improvement	=	4
No change	=	1
Some deterioration	=	–2
Considerable deterioration	=	–5

The *evaluation technique* used will be selected with regard to the nature and complexity of the particular case. It may be a simple break-even analysis, cost–benefit analysis, return on investment analysis, linear programming technique, decision analysis, or some other technique. Broader social and environmental consequences of managerial decisions will, as mentioned, be difficult to quantify and compare with economic and financial costs and benefits. Notwithstanding, the number of techniques that attempt to account for these aspects in evaluation models and schemes is growing.

9.3 Presenting action proposals to the client

When work on action proposals and the evaluation of alternatives has reached an advanced stage, the consultant has to consider the time and form for the presentation to the client. This will depend mainly on the type of project undertaken and the working relationships between the consultant and the client's managerial and specialist staff.

In long and complex assignments, involving strategic issues and costly investment or other measures, the client's staff is usually very much involved and keeps the senior management informed about progress. The consultant submits progress reports and seeks further guidance from the client at several points during the assignment, so the presentation of final proposals does not bring up anything completely new. Essentially, information that the client has had from previous reports and other contacts with the consultant is summarized, confirmed and presented for approval.

In other cases, the reporting which has preceded the presentation of proposals may have been limited. The scope of the assignment may not require reporting and discussions at each step; or, in assignments that will affect some vested interests (e.g. reorganizations), the client does not want to hold many meetings and have information circulated before the solutions have been defined and thoroughly examined by a restricted managerial group. Hence the need for a well-prepared presentation which, in the latter case, may convey completely new information to a number of people.

The presentation

Most consultants prefer to make an oral presentation backed up by written evidence and using audiovisual aids to support the case. The consultant may make an oral presentation, introducing documentation that will be left with the client, to be followed by another meeting once the client has examined the proposal in more detail. Alternatively, the client may prefer to receive the proposal in writing first and arrange a presentation meeting after having read the proposal.

The objective of the presentation is, of course, to obtain the client's acceptance of the recommendations. The degree of persuasion will depend on many factors and must be anticipated, prepared for and built into the presentation. The presentation meeting is held between the consulting team (including the supervisor), the client and those members of the staff chosen to attend. The client's liaison officer and other staff specialists may have an important role to play. Having taken part in the project they will be aware of the key issues and know many details. They can usually be expected to be completely in favour of the recommendations. If they are not, the consultant should be aware of their different views or reservations, and explain to the client why he or she is making the proposals despite some disagreement among the client's staff.

The consultant's presentation should work through a logical series of steps, building up the case for the recommendations in an effective manner, so that the client should have little or no hesitation in accepting them. A presentation should not be made unless the consultant believes that the probability of acceptance is high.

The presentation should not overwhelm decision-makers in the client organization with analytical details, or try to impress them by techniques that are normally the specialist's domain. However, the techniques used in evaluation should be described. A clear picture of all solutions that have been envisaged should be given and the choice proposed by the consultant justified. The consultant must be absolutely honest with the client, especially when explaining:

- the risks involved (the solution has never been used before; some employees will probably be against it; the real investment and/or operating costs may be higher than foreseen);
- the conditions that the client must create and maintain (discipline is needed in recording primary data; maintenance has to be improved; some members of senior management must be transferred);
- the tasks that could not be completed (the search for potential partners could not cover all countries; some evaluation criteria had to be ignored because of lack of data or time);
- the future perspectives (the solution proposed does or does not anticipate future developments such as capacity expansion, automation, transfer to affiliated companies, more stringent environmental protection norms).

Depending on circumstances, acceptance at this point may be in principle only. There may be an agreed intention, but the final decision may be contingent on a detailed study of the written proposals by the client, on consultations with important shareholders or on the recommendations being explained to and accepted by employees' representatives.

Where there have to be further presentations to representatives of trade unions, staff associations or other stakeholder groups, the client takes on the role of persuader and negotiator. Under no circumstances should the consultant take this on alone. He or she should, of course, be ready to back up the client and help to organize whatever explanatory campaign is necessary – and should strongly advise against trying to get everything over at one mass meeting.

Plans for implementation

One section is often missing from action proposals presented to clients: a realistic and feasible plan for the implementation of the proposals. The client receives a static picture, describing the new project or scheme as it should look when implemented. Yet there may be a long way to go to achieve this desired condition, and several different paths may be available. Moreover, the planning of stages and activities to put the new scheme into effect can reveal further problems and needs, allowing the proposal to be further improved before the final version is implemented.

Thus an effective action proposal shows not only *what* to implement but also *how* to do it. A plan for implementation should be included in the proposal. The client and the consultant can agree that this plan will be a global one, leaving the details to a later stage, immediately preceding each step towards implementation.

The decision

It is the client and not the consultant who decides what solution will be chosen and applied. On no account should the client feel that he or she must follow the consultant's choice in order not to upset the whole scheme. A client who feels that a solution was imposed on him or her will not be very active during the implementation phase, and will take the first opportunity to put the blame on the consultant if matters do not work out as expected.

The client's decision on the consultant's proposal is subject to the same influences as any other management decision. The number of important decisions that are determined by emotional rather than rational criteria is surprisingly high. Furthermore, the client's conception of rationality may differ from the consultant's conception, especially if their cultural backgrounds are not the same.

It is essential that the consultant is aware of the *client's personal preferences*, and of *cultural and other factors* affecting decision-making in the client organization. This awareness helps him or her to avoid proposals that will not be accepted, and to recognize again that consulting is much more than presenting technically perfect solutions: it also involves earning confidence and explaining to the client and the staff so that they will accept rational measures as their personal choices.

The decision taken on the consultant's proposals may be the final point of an assignment, if the client wants to undertake the work personally. If the client prefers to involve the consultant in implementation, the decision will act as an introduction to the next step.

[1] See, e.g., J. G. Rawlinson: *Creative thinking and brainstorming* (Farnborough, Hampshire, Gower, 1981), and various publications by Edward de Bono.

[2] E. de Bono: *Lateral thinking: A textbook of creativity* (Harmondsworth, Middlesex, Penguin, 1977).

[3] A. F. Osborn: *Applied imagination* (New York, Charles Scribner & Sons, 1957).

[4] E. de Bono: *Six thinking hats: An essential approach to business management from the creator of lateral thinking* (New York, Bowker, Ingram, 1987).

[5] See G. Nadler and S. Hibino: *Breakthrough thinking: The seven principles of creative problem solving* (Rocklin, CA, Prima Publishing, 1994).

[6] See R. L. Bencin: "How to keep creative juices flowing", in *International Management* (Sutton, Surrey), July 1983.

[7] See Nadler and Hibino, op. cit., Ch. 6.

IMPLEMENTATION 10

Implementation, the fourth phase of the consulting process, is the culmination of the consultant's and the client's joint effort. To implement changes that are real improvements from the client's point of view is the basic purpose of any consulting assignment.

If there is no implementation, the consulting process cannot be regarded as completed. If the client does not accept the consultant's proposals at the end of the action-planning phase, the assignment has been poorly managed by both parties. If the consultant and the client collaborate closely during the diagnostic and action-planning phases, the client cannot really reject proposals that are the product of joint work. If there is any doubt about the focus of the consultant's work during action planning, or about the feasibility of the proposals that are emerging, corrective measures should be taken immediately, without waiting until the proposals have been finalized.

It may happen that the consultant does not find a solution to the client's problem. Maybe the problem as formulated does not have a solution (e.g. the goal set was too ambitious and unrealistic). Such a situation should also have been discovered at an earlier stage and the work on proposals redirected, so that action planning comes up with realistic proposals on how to deal with a redefined problem.

In planning an assignment and negotiating a contract, the client and the consultant should not forget to define what they mean by "implementation" and "results". If the consultant is developing and helping to introduce a customized information system, for example, what operations have to be completed and what parameters have to be achieved before the system can be regarded as fully implemented? What is meant by implementation in an action-learning programme – increased competencies of the participants, approval of the proposals developed in action-learning teams or the completion of all the change measures proposed? What is meant by "learning material" to be delivered by the consultant – a complete package ready for immediate use by the client in internal training programmes, or a detailed outline with guidelines for trainees and trainers, but requiring some further development and adaptation?

It may be difficult to reach agreement on when a very complex project, such as a business restructuring or turnaround, should be regarded as completed. However, the failure to clarify these questions early is a frequent cause of misunderstanding between consultants and their clients.

The general trend in consulting is to involve consultants in implementation, give them responsibility for achieving results and make their remuneration dependent on results. Thus, implementation is increasingly regarded and managed as a crucial element of the consulting process.

10.1 The consultant's role in implementation

Why the consultant should be involved

In Chapter 1 we gave some arguments justifying the consultant's involvement in the implementation phase of an assignment. The issue is important enough to be reviewed once more.

The ultimate responsibility for implementation is with the client. It is the client, not the consultant, who makes all the management decisions and sees to it that they are put into effect. This, of course, is more easily said than done. The more complex the assignment, the higher the probability that implementation will be at least as difficult as diagnosis and action planning. The plan or project presented by the consultant is a model of future conditions and relationships, assuming certain behaviour on the part of the client, as well as particular environmental and other conditions affecting the client organization. The consultant may have made mistakes in developing the model. In addition, many conditions may change after the proposal has been presented and accepted. The consultant's co-responsibility for implementation can help to overcome these difficulties.

The issue of the consultant's participation in implementation should never be underestimated, but should be thoroughly examined and discussed whenever a consulting project is being designed. Both the consultant and the client should give their arguments for and against this participation and consider various alternatives.

The consultant does not have to be involved in implementation:

- if the problem is relatively straightforward and no technical or other difficulties with implementation are anticipated;
- if joint work during the diagnostic and action-planning phases shows that the client has developed a good understanding of the problem and a capability to implement the solutions proposed without further assistance.

The client may be reluctant to involve the consultant for financial reasons. By the end of the action-planning phase the cost of the assignment may already be high and the budget may be exhausted. Or the manager who has to approve the contract may feel that involving the consultant in implementation implies expenditures that can be avoided. Here again a frank discussion can be helpful. The consultant can suggest a more economical design for the assignment in order to free resources that will allow him or her to be involved in implementation.

Finding a suitable arrangement

The failure to involve the consultant in implementation often reflects a lack of imagination and flexibility on either the consultant's or the client's part. Of course the client is concerned about the cost of the assignment, and the more time the project takes, the stronger may be the feeling that the consultants are staying for too long. The following arrangements can keep the consultant involved in implementation without imposing high charges on the client:

- the size of the consulting team present at the client's premises will be gradually reduced during the implementation phase;
- only one consultant will stay during the whole implementation phase, providing advice and bringing in additional expertise from the consulting firm if appropriate;
- the consultant will deal only with the more difficult tasks in implementation, leaving all other work to the client;
- the consultant will visit the client periodically, or at agreed points during implementation, to check progress and provide guidance;
- the consultant will intervene only at the client's special request.

Clearly, not every consulting firm will be able to offer all these options. Larger firms can generally be more flexible. A sole practitioner may well be working with a new client when a former client calls for help in implementation. It may be necessary to warn the new client that the consultant has not fully completed a previous assignment, though he is phasing himself out of it.

The various arrangements described above ought to be given consideration irrespective of the fee formula used (see section 30.4). If a lump-sum or contingency fee is applied, the consultant will make a provision for involvement in implementation when calculating the total fee. The final payment will be due only once implementation is completed and agreed results have been attained.

In addition to defining the end result of the project, the assignment plan and contract should be as precise as possible in defining the roles to be played by both the consultant and the client in the implementation phase. If this is not done, it may be impossible to determine who is responsible if implementation stalls. In the implementation phase the consultant may have to step out of an advisory role in the strict sense of the term to assist the client organization with various tasks involved in making the new system operational.

10.2 Planning and monitoring implementation

A set of proposals for implementation should be part of the action plan presented to the client, as mentioned in section 9.3. Before implementation starts, a detailed work programme should be prepared.

Steps to take

Planning a campaign to introduce a new method or system is an instance of the usefulness of network planning or bar-charting techniques. The day chosen as "implementation day" will be more definite if planned for in this way. The time needed to obtain equipment and to design detailed procedures may be relatively easy to estimate. When there is a major physical move, as required by, say, a new factory or general office layout, a scheduled sequence of individual moves is necessary. When there has to be "business as usual" during the move, the schedule should recognize the need for the minimum of disturbance. Sometimes a short, sharp campaign can take place during an annual shutdown. When it does, all employees should be briefed on what they will find when they return so as to avoid some days of chaos.

Defining new responsibilities and controls

Implementation will create new tasks and relationships, while abolishing old ones. If people's commitment and participation is to be solicited, their contributions must be specified. Such a specification will be particularly helpful for drawing up a training programme and establishing controls for monitoring implementation.

Furthermore, the programme of implementation should define controllable and, if possible, measurable results of individual tasks, operations and steps. This is essential for monitoring.

Pace and lead-time of implementation

Various technical and resource factors will have a bearing on the pace and lead-time of implementation. As a matter of principle, the consultant should aim to schedule implementation in the client's best interest (e.g. to make new production capacity operational as early as possible, or to avoid situations in which the client has to deal with several difficult projects or use old and new information systems simultaneously).

The feasible and desirable pace of change (see Chapter 4) is an important criterion. It may be necessary to gain the commitment and support of a number of individuals, who will constitute a kind of critical mass. Considerable time and effort may be needed to create this critical mass, but once attained its existence will accelerate the whole process. These are important aspects of the strategy of planned change.

In many projects, tests and trials will be needed, or partial and preliminary results will need to be reviewed and commented on by the client. It is a mistake not to allow sufficient time for these activities. A consultant who is behind schedule may feel that the client should provide instant feedback at any moment, but it must be recognized that this is often not feasible.

Built-in flexibility and contingency

The more complex and innovative the assignment, the greater the chance that the work programme will need to be adjusted several times during the implementation phase. Monitoring will show this need. However, adjustments are easier if some flexibility is built in. Completion of the assignment should not be scheduled for the very last moment (i.e. the time when the new scheme or plant must be in operation); some time should be kept in reserve for final adjustments. The same may apply to the allocation of resources and to provision for further help by the consultant during implementation.

Detailing procedures

When a good deal of new methodology is involved, it is usual to prepare a manual for guidance in the procedures to be followed. Virtually all forms of reorganization, irrespective of their functional or interfunctional aspects, and all new systems require instructions on how to operate them. New stationery usually has to be designed. The consultant may do this personally or may adopt part or all of some proprietary system.[1]

Monitoring implementation

When implementation is about to start, the consultant checks that all conditions have been fulfilled and all prerequisites are to hand.

Once the new system starts running, and for some time after, the consultant should be available to answer any queries and to help the client's staff to deal at once with any problem that may arise. This is as much a question of tactics as of technique, since small deficiencies and misunderstandings when a new system is starting up have a tendency to grow and become major difficulties if not dealt with immediately. In this the consultant may have more technical know-how and experience than the client.

It is not uncommon for decision-makers, including the consultant, to experience uncomfortable afterthoughts once a decision has finally been reached and implementation commences. This phenomenon is known as cognitive dissonance. Prior to reaching a decision, the decision-makers usually spend an inordinate amount of time focusing on the benefits of the new scheme and the disadvantages of the present, or alternative, scheme. However, once a decision has been reached, the implementation process commences and the first problems inevitably appear, a good deal of time may be spent on reviewing the advantages of the previous, or displaced, scheme, while comments are voiced on the drawbacks of the new scheme being implemented.

It is readily conceded that it takes considerable talent to examine an existing scheme and, on the basis of investigations and results obtained, devise a new, more effective one. It also takes considerable courage to proceed with the implementation of the new scheme when problems arise in the early stages (as is usually the case). When this happens the consultant would do well to take note of the maxim: "Take time to plan your work, then take time to work your plan."

Jointly with the client, the consultant should make regular and frequent assessments of the progress of implementation. Attention should be paid to the pace of implementation and its broader consequences (e.g. whether the changes in plant layout and organization of the production department are proceeding according to schedule and whether the delivery of any new product will start as promised). Adjustments in the time schedule, the approach taken, or even the original design of the new scheme should be made as appropriate, in an organized manner, avoiding panic decisions.

The consultant's poised behaviour during this phase of the work will affect the attitudes of the client and his or her staff towards implementation. The consultant must be seen as an enthusiastic colleague who feels fully involved and co-responsible, who has a vision of what should be achieved, and who is able to explain the roles and responsibilities of others engaged in the project.

10.3 Training and developing client staff

In Chapters 1 and 2 we showed the logical and natural link between consulting and training. Both have the same ultimate objective – to improve organizational performance and results – and they support each other. In most operating assignments some training and development of client staff is foreseen in the work programme. It may take a variety of forms and its volume will differ from case to case.

Developing the cooperating team

Perhaps the most interesting and efficient, although the least formalized, method of developing client personnel is through knowledge transfer during direct cooperation with the consultant during the assignment. In a small enterprise, the owner–manager may be personally involved. In other organizations, some managers, the liaison officer and other members of the team who are responsible for the project will work jointly with the consultant. A good consultant takes every opportunity not only to use client staff for routine jobs (such as data collection), but increasingly to involve them in the more sophisticated operations, demanding specific skills and experience, and stimulating learning. As this is an excellent learning opportunity, talented people with good development potential should be assigned to this job, and not just those who can be spared from their normal duties for the period of the assignment.

Managers in senior positions will also learn from the assignment if the consultant knows how to communicate with them and if they are keen to find out what the consultant's work methods are. That is why it is more interesting for a senior manager who finds a good consultant to interact with him or her frequently instead of just meeting formally at the beginning and then reading the report at the end of the assignment.

Training for new methods and techniques

A common element in assignments is the training of client staff in specific techniques. This concerns those staff members who are involved in the introduction and use of the technique (e.g. time measurement, statistical quality control, standard costing). A number of people may have to be trained; this may necessitate a precisely defined and scheduled training programme which precedes implementation and may continue during its first stages. A number of approaches are possible, such as:

- on-the-job training by the consultant;
- training of in-company trainers by the consultant;
- training of experimental groups whose members will then train the remaining staff;
- formal in-company training courses (run by the consultant, by special trainers brought in for this purpose, or by the organization's internal trainers);
- participation of selected staff in external training courses;
- appreciation programmes for those who are not directly involved, but should be informed.

Staff development in complex assignments

The more sophisticated and complex the problems tackled by the consultant, the more difficult it is to design and organize related training and development of staff. This is the case, for example, in assignments aimed at major changes, such as extensive reorganizations and restructuring, important changes in product and market strategies, or the establishment of a new plant including the installation of a new management system. In addition to specific training in new techniques which may be needed, there is a case for a collective development effort to bring about substantial changes in management concepts, strategies, communication and styles.

In these situations, training in particular work techniques and systems may have to be supplemented by programmes aimed at behavioural change. These may include seminars, working groups, discussion groups, special project teams, individual project work, exchange of roles, counselling by the consultant and by in-plant trainers, and so on. Some of these intervention techniques were described in Chapter 4.

Another important feature of training provided in connection with consulting is that it generates interest in further training and self-development. Sound management will stimulate and nurture this interest, which may actually be the most lasting contribution of many consulting assignments.

10.4 Some tactical guidelines for introducing changes in work methods

In this section we summarize a few practical guidelines on how to introduce new work methods and help people to master them without major difficulties. Here again, the purpose of the guidelines is not to provide universal recipes for handling any situation, but to alert the consultant to what might happen and suggest in what direction to search for a remedy. The guidelines that follow should be read in conjunction with Chapter 4.

Tactic 1: The best method

It was mentioned in Chapter 4 that the process of change involves (i) identification with the change, and (ii) internalization of the change. Whether these phases occur in sequence or simultaneously is not important. The essential point is that they require commitment, involvement or participation by the person doing the changing. The change must be tested by the individual as he or she moves from the general (identification) to the specific (internalization).

Therefore the people concerned in the change process should be involved as early as possible, so that these two vital elements can be comprehensively covered. However, a strong note of warning is offered as to how participation might be achieved. Apart from attending meetings or brainstorming sessions for specific purposes (such as to build up a data bank of ideas for the creative solution of problems), individuals should not start using their own new methods for performing tasks if the idea is to develop a best method for general use. Studies have shown that where individuals are encouraged to adopt their own approaches and the best method or approved solution is later imposed, those people will exhibit some conformity to the new proposal but will still diverge significantly from the approved method in following their own.

However, where groups are provided with a best method or approved approach in the first instance, individuals will subsequently vary only insignificantly from the set procedures. Diagrammatically, these results are shown in figure 10.1.

In case 1 the end result is that individuals perform in a manner significantly different from the approved method, although not quite as widely different as

Figure 10.1 Comparison of the effects on eventual performance when using individualized versus conformed initial approaches

Case 1: Subsequent behaviour diverges significantly from the conformed approach when individualized approaches are used prior to the introduction of the conformed approach.

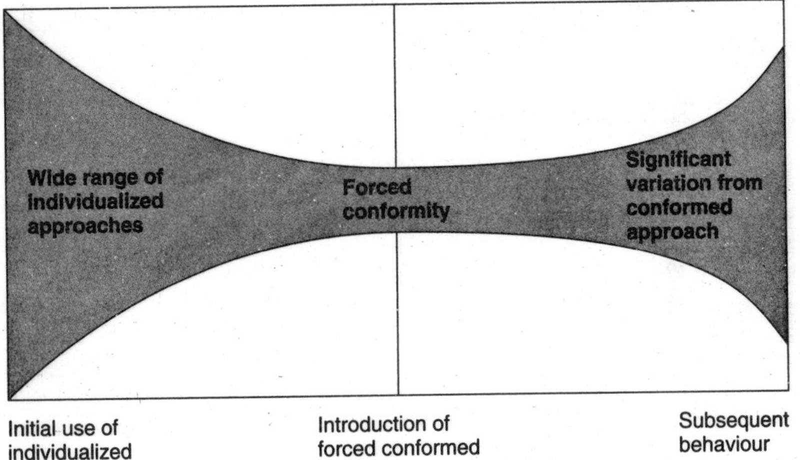

Note: Although subsequent behaviour usually differs significantly from the conformed approach, it is not as widely divergent as the initial individualized approaches.

Case 2: Subsequent behaviour diverges very little from the conformed approach if no opportunity is provided for individual experimentation prior to the introduction of the conformed approach.

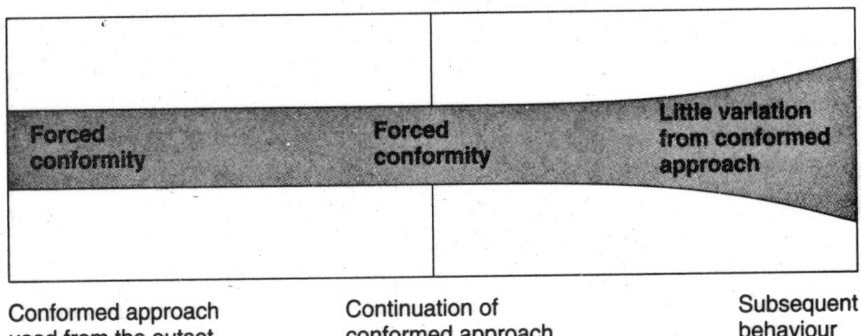

Note: Subsequent behaviour is significantly less divergent from the conformed approach in case 2 than in case 1.

during their initial trials. There is some tendency towards the norm. In case 2 there is much less divergence in subsequent performance from the approved norm because individuals have not had an opportunity to rehearse in any other manner than the approved one.

Thus, where feasible, the consultant should attempt to introduce the approved method as a scheme applying to the whole group where individual differences can be kept to a minimum (often as a result of normal group pressures, coupled with the fact that no opportunity to develop individual ad hoc approaches is provided).

Tactic 2: Spaced practice

Improvement in performance occurs more quickly, in greater depth and lasts for a longer time (i.e. the decay or extinction curve is longer) if new approaches are introduced in relatively short periods, with ample provision for rest periods, than if continuous or massed practice periods are employed.

A generalized improvement in performance noted where the "quick and often" tactic is employed (compared with a continuous practice scheme) is shown in figure 10.2. When a spaced practice approach is used and the results are compared with those of a continuous or massed practice approach for the same period:

Figure 10.2 Comparison of spaced practice with a continuous or massed practice approach in terms of performance

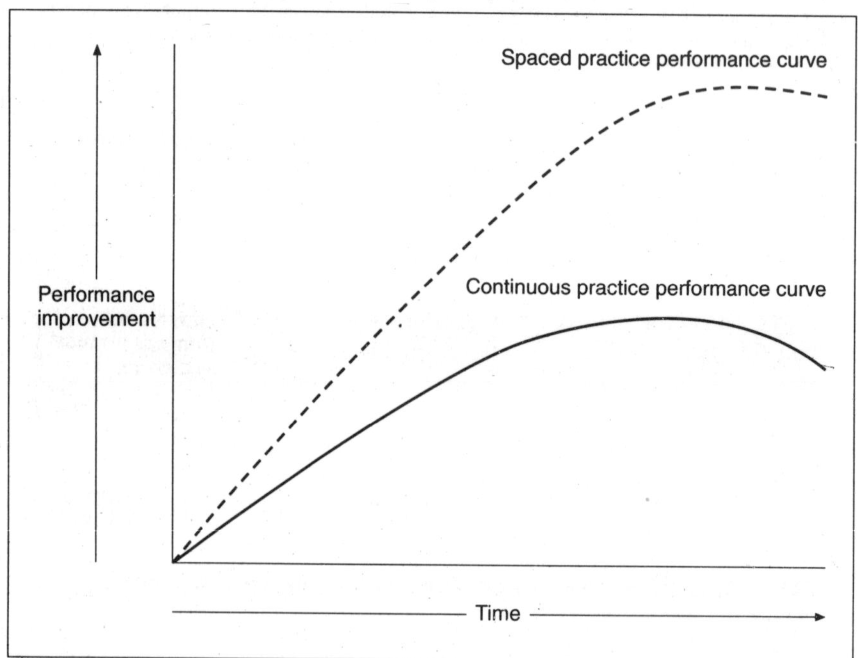

- improvement using spaced practice is quicker, i.e. the performance curve is sharper;
- improvement using spaced practice is greater, i.e. the performance curve is higher;
- improvement lasts longer, i.e. the decay or extinction curve is shallower.

These performance curves will almost invariably be obtained where improvement in skill can be measured as a result of practice or rehearsal. Thus the consultant is well advised to consider introducing change gradually using relatively short practice sessions rather than relying on one great training input.

Tactic 3: Rehearsal

Where skill is involved, results constantly improve with spaced practice, provided, of course, that the correct procedures are followed. As shown in figure 10.2, performance continues to improve with practice until a ceiling or plateau is reached. Continued practice is then required to maintain this level of performance. Constant practice can eventually lead to a condition known as over-learning, in which routine and procedures become virtually automatic reactions.

The consultant must therefore make provision for appropriate training and practice sessions (rehearsals) when introducing new approaches.

Tactic 4: Moving from the known to the unknown

There is considerable evidence that the knowledge of a prior skill can have either a positive or negative transfer effect on the acquisition of a new skill.

As mentioned earlier, the consultant is usually faced at the beginning with the need for an "unfreezing" phase, designed to break down old habits. Surprising as it may seem, to facilitate new learning it is usually more effective to have the learner in an "anxious" rather than a "comfortable" state, because he or she is then more likely actively to seek information to reduce the level of anxiety. In a "comfortable" state, the learner is more likely to select information which will prolong that state, to reinforce old habits rather than seek new approaches.

The consultant can use this attention-rousing device by showing that the "known" procedures are no longer suitable for present purposes. If we move directly to the introduction of new methods without first breaking down established practices, there is a grave risk of negative transfer effects taking place.

When introducing a totally new approach, however, there may be some benefit in building it on an appropriate existing procedure. In short, when introducing change, move from the known to the unknown (new approach).

Tactic 5: Setting demanding but realistic goals

According to S. W. Gellerman, "stretching" is desirable when goals are being established.[2] By this he means that targets should be set a little higher than would normally be expected. D. C. McClelland supports this notion and adds that the goals should be realistic and neither "too easy" nor "impossible", but such that a feeling of achievement can be experienced when they are reached.[3]

There is ample evidence to show that high expectations coupled with genuine confidence in a prestigious person often result in higher performance and productivity. This effect can become cumulative – an individual's improved performance encourages him or her to assume more responsibility and so creates greater opportunities for achievement, growth and development. Conversely, low expectations may lead to low performance and substandard results which, in turn, lead to loss of credibility, distrust and scepticism.

When introducing change, the consultant has to ensure that all those involved readily understand what this means in terms of goals. Goals should be:

- quantitative (able to be measured in numerical terms);
- qualitative (able to be described specifically);
- time-phased (provision of commencement dates and expected duration before final attainment).

It is important to determine correctly the time by which a new goal has to be achieved. Because attitudes and work habits take a long time to form, time must be allowed for replacing them by new ones. Unless there is a perceived dramatic need to institute a change immediately, the process may take longer than originally expected.

Tactic 6: Respecting the absorptive capacity

People differ tremendously in their capacity to absorb new information and their ability to undertake new activities. Many writers have argued that there is a maximum number of "units of information" which an individual can absorb and process at any one time. In this connection G. W. Miller refers to the "magic number seven, plus or minus two" (to allow for variations in individual capacity).[4] By confining information inputs to the lower end of the scale (namely five), the consultant can avoid overtaxing any of the audience, although he may cause some degree of impatience among the most receptive.

The information can first be presented as a whole and then broken down into subunits for more detailed study, or it can be built up gradually by synthesis of the individual parts. The method chosen will depend on the nature of the problem, the composition of the audience and the consultant's personal preference.

During the introductory and concluding phases of an information session, it is as well to provide a summary of the complete presentation. There is support for the idea that the attention of an audience is at its highest level shortly after the commencement of a session and again shortly before its conclusion.

Figure 10.3 Generalized illustration of the high points in attention level of a captive audience

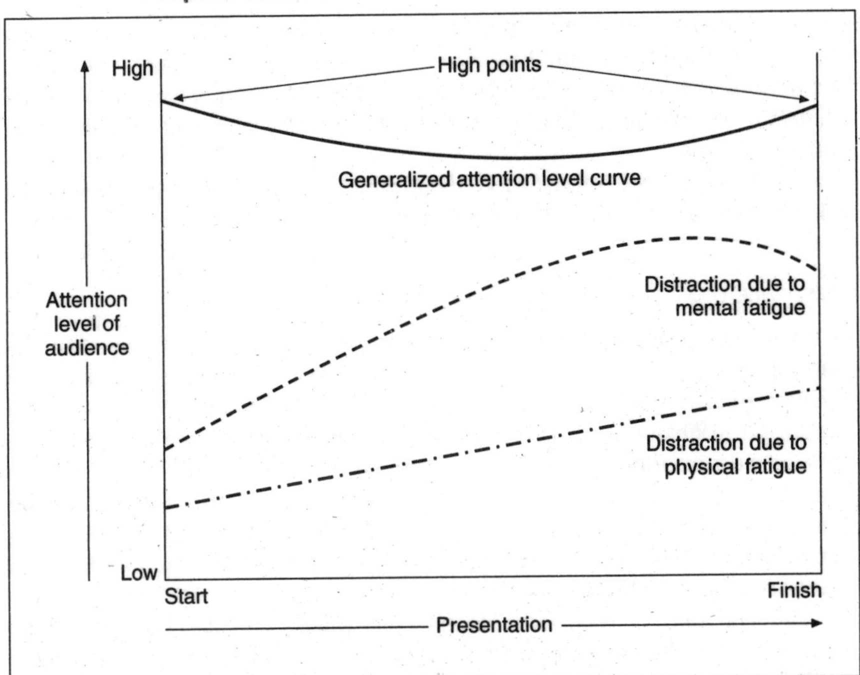

At the outset the exposition probably has a novelty value, which begins to be dissipated as physical and mental fatigue build up. Shortly before the conclusion is reached, however, the level of attention increases again as the audience begins to anticipate the end of this activity and the beginning of a new one. These high points in concentration are illustrated in figure 10.3.

Tactic 7: Providing evidence and feedback

Verbal persuasion is inherently unstable and needs to be supported by hard facts. Actions speak louder than words. The consultant must keep records of all performance improvements as support for the change process. For example, although daily output figures may decrease immediately following a change process, it is possible that errors or accident rates may decrease even more significantly at the same time.

Successful introduction of change requires presentation of appropriate feedback information to permit those undertaking the change process to adjust as necessary. The consultant must make provision for review and reporting sessions, not merely as morale-boosting devices, but as a requisite for control and correction.

10.5 Maintenance and control of the new practice

If a new scheme is to survive and yield more in benefits than it costs, it has to be protected against a number of more or less natural hazards. Standards, systems and procedures are as prone to deterioration through wear and tear and neglect as are machines. Like machines, their performance may eventually be reduced to zero.

Maintenance and control should start while the consultant is still with the client organization, and must continue after his or her departure.

Backsliding

A maintenance and control system has to guard against backsliding, which is liable to occur as long as people remember what they used to do before the change. Backsliding is not always reactionary. If a new method breaks down because of problems with a computer system, equipment, supplies, and so on, work can only continue if people do something else. The most natural thing is to revert to the old practice if that is still possible. While the consultant is well advised never to stop anyone using the old method until it can be completely replaced, he or she should also make sure that after the new method has been proved it is impossible to revert to the old one.

The way this is done will depend, as always, on the function of the assignment and the nature of its problem. A few examples are given below.

Paperwork. When a new documentation procedure is installed, the stock of old forms should be destroyed. One official should be made responsible for maintaining stocks of new forms and signing orders for reprints. The purchasing clerk should not pass on orders for printing signed by any other person.

Filing. When a new filing system becomes operational, old files should be closed and their contents inserted in the new files, moved to archives or destroyed. Provisional and parallel filing outside the new system framework is undesirable.

Operating standards. The maintenance of factory work standards requires vigilance. Working to standards must be made easier than working to non-standards. Any work outside the specification of the product or method should not be feasible using the standard forms and documentation. This is not to say that departures from standard are never allowed, but when they are, they should be made self-evident.

Drawings. In an engineering drawing office it must not be easier to make a new drawing for a part than to find whether an existing part may be used. When a drawing is permanently changed, all old prints should be tracked down and removed. An adequate control system would prevent unauthorized prints being in circulation at any time.

All these measures are, of course, preventive. In their absence, the alternative is often not a cure but a temporary expedient with a strong likelihood of a recurrence of the problem.

Backsliding problems have to be faced in any firm. When General Electric (GE) decided to start applying Internet technology for its commercial operations on a large scale, "the greatest hurdle was not technology but culture. Sales staff, worried that they might be destroying their jobs, had to be offered bonuses for helping customers to use GE websites to order. Managers had to watch carefully for reprobate employees using parallel paths (the telephone, for instance, or a walk to a store) to order supplies or arrange travel. Some offices even closed their mail rooms for all but one day a week (and that only for the incorrigible legal department) to stop employees from using regular post. Others locked their printer rooms except for occasional days when bosses would station themselves at the door and demand from those who came through an explanation for their sad inability to shake old paper habits".[5]

Control procedures

A system of control does not necessarily stop at maintenance in the narrow sense of keeping a scheme in the same state. After a time, any piece of reorganization will begin to suffer from old age, if nothing else. Other changing influences may render it less and less appropriate; the objective for which it was designed may no longer be there. Without a means of control, opportunities to modify and develop in line with changing circumstances may be lost.

It is, however, as easy to overdo control for its own sake as it is to become fascinated by any other technique. The consultant needs only to identify the key points at which significant departures will show up and choose the times at which they are to be checked. It is unnecessary to check everything every day: the criterion is usually how long it would take for anything serious to happen if it were not checked. More frequent checks are needed immediately after a change than later on, when stability at a new level has been reached.

In financial areas, checks are part of budgetary control and made as often as the sensitivity of the situation demands. Labour performance checks may be built into weekly payroll/production analyses. Inventory controls may be in accordance with the main categories of stores.

Business companies accept the annual audit of their books as a matter of course, but may forget that a periodic internal audit of their organization and administrative methods is equally necessary. Apart from those detailed safeguards already mentioned, a periodic audit may be the only way of checking the whole system. Only an audit may reveal whether the total objectives are still being met, or are even still the same. Failure to make such a check allows the passage of time to erode the good work and its benefits.

Staff turnover is a common source of danger. If new staff members are not adequately briefed, they have little option but to act as they think fit. They may pursue surprisingly different objectives and exhibit different work habits. The number of shortcomings that the consultant has met in the client organization may be an indicator of habitual neglect. If the client's basic attitudes to controls does not change, the consultant's work may get no better treatment.

Further improvements

Conversely, it would be unrealistic and totally wrong to assume that the implementation of the consultant's proposals will make the client's business perfect and that for a long time no further changes will be required. Improvements may be suggested by the managers, specialists and workers involved in a new scheme, by customers, by the consultant personally or by other professionals working for the same client. Improvements may become possible and necessary due to developments in information technology and other changes that could not be fully considered in the course of the current assignment. Any such improvements may be suggested and become necessary surprisingly soon, much sooner than the consultant imagined when submitting the new scheme to the client.

There will be improvements that can be easily accepted and introduced during the implementation phase. Other improvements will not fit the scheme that has been chosen, but it will be useful to record them and keep them in mind for the future. Remember the "solution-after-next" principle discussed in Chapter 9. There is no point in aiming to propose and implement definitive and closed solutions to clients' problems when we know only too well that change is the only constant of our times and that better solutions will become both feasible and necessary in the future.

---

[1] In the latter event it has to be remembered that suppliers of such systems have a vested interest in selling stationery and that standard packages may not fit the given situation very well.

[2] S. W. Gellerman: *Management by motivation* (New York, American Management Association, 1969).

[3] D. C. McClelland and D. G. Winter: *Motivating economic achievement* (New York, The Free Press, 1969).

[4] G. W. Miller: "The magic number seven, plus or minus two", in *Psychological Review*, Vol. 63, No. 2, Mar. 1956.

[5] "While Welch waited", in *The Economist*, 19 May 2001, pp. 85–86.

TERMINATION 11

Termination is the fifth and final phase of the consulting process. Every assignment or project has to be brought to an end once its purpose has been achieved and the consultant's help is no longer needed.

It is not enough to execute the assignment in a professional manner. The disengagement also has to be fully professional: its timing and form have to be properly chosen and all commitments settled to the mutual satisfaction of the client and the consultant.

The consultant has primary responsibility for suggesting at what point and in what way he or she would withdraw from the client organization. He or she should bear in mind that the client may feel uncertain about the best moment to terminate the project, in particular if the consultant's presence has clearly contributed to important improvements and the client has become used to seeking advice on important items. The client may feel more secure if the consultant continues to be available to help with any new problems that may arise. This, however, could make the client excessively dependent on the consultant.

Termination applies to two equally important aspects of the consulting process: the job for which the consultant was brought in, and the consultant–client relationship.

First, the consultant's withdrawal means that the job in which he or she has participated:

- has been completed; or
- will be discontinued; or
- will be pursued, but without further help from the consultant.

In deciding to terminate the assignment, the consultant and the client should be clear which of these three applies in their particular case. There should be no ambiguity about this. It is of no benefit to anybody if the consultant is convinced of having done a good job while the client is waiting only for the consultant's departure in order to stop the project. Thus the consultant and the client should jointly establish whether the assignment can be qualified as a success, a failure, or something in between.

Second, the consultant's withdrawal terminates the consultant–client relationship. The atmosphere and the way in which this relationship is discontinued will influence the client's motivation to pursue the project, and his or her attitude to possible future use of the same consulting organization. Here, too, the assignment should not be terminated with uncertain and mixed feelings. Ideally, there should be satisfaction on both sides about the relations that existed during the assignment. The client should be convinced that he has had a good consultant, to whom he would gladly turn again. The consultant should feel that he has been trusted and respected, and that working again for the same client would be another stimulating experience. The relationship has a financial dimension, too: both parties should feel that a proper price was paid for the professional service provided.

Professional consultants attach great importance to the way in which they terminate assignments. The last impressions are very significant, and an excellent performance at the end of an assignment leaves the door open for future work. Repeat business is important to management consultants, and is available only to those whose performance remains flawless until the very end of every assignment.

11.1 Time for withdrawal

To choose the right moment for withdrawal is often difficult, but a wrong decision can spoil a good relationship and jeopardize the success of the project.

Planning for withdrawal

Some assignments may be terminated too early, for example if:

- the consultant's work on the project could not be completed;
- the client overestimated his or her capability to finish the project without having been sufficiently trained for it;
- the client's budget does not permit the job to be finished;
- the consultant is in a hurry to start another assignment.

Instances of assignments that finish later than necessary are also frequent. This may happen if:

- the consultant embarks on a technically difficult project without making sure that the client is properly trained to take it over;
- the job is vaguely defined, and new problems are discovered in the course of the assignment;
- the consultant tries to stay longer than necessary.

To avoid these situations, the question of timely withdrawal should be discussed at the beginning of the consulting process, when the consultant presents the whole assignment cycle to the client. The consulting contract should define when and under what circumstances the assignment will end. As already mentioned, the choices are numerous. The assignment may end after the diagnostic phase, after action planning, at some stage during implementation, or when implementation is completed and agreed results achieved.

It may be difficult at the time of signing the contract to determine the right moment for withdrawal. At such an early stage it is often impossible to foresee how implementation will progress, how deeply the client's staff will be involved, and what new relations and problems will emerge or be discovered during the assignment.

That is why it is recommended that the assignment plan is reviewed at critical points during the assignment; at each review questions should be raised as to how much longer the consultant should stay, and what remains to be done before the assignment can be terminated.

Gradual withdrawal

In many situations, gradual withdrawal may be the best arrangement from both the client's and the consultant's point of view (see section 10.1).

Watching for withdrawal signals

Withdrawal signals, as some consultants call them, show that the client would like to terminate the assignment. They can be very overt, or indirect and hidden. The client may start being less frequently available to meet the consultant, or may indicate in some other way that enough time has been spent on the project. It is essential to be alert to these signals. This does not necessarily mean that the consultant should immediately pack up and leave if he or she has valid professional reasons for pursuing the work, but the point should be discussed frankly with the client.

Never stay longer than necessary!

If the client is convinced that he can proceed alone, the consultant should never insist on staying longer even if he does not share his client's opinion. After all, he who pays the piper calls the tune, and it is the client who is paying the consultant.

Staying longer than necessary is unprofessional and damaging to the consultant's image. Unfortunately, as one practitioner has put it, "some consulting outfits are like a fungus that gets inside the client and keeps finding new areas not in the original agreement and stays on and on, sucking the blood out until someone pulls the plug and says 'enough'. Their advice is superb, but it just gets to be too much."[1]

11.2 Evaluation

Evaluation is a most important part of the termination phase in any consulting process. Without evaluation, it is impossible to assess whether the assignment has met its objectives and whether the results obtained justify the resources used. Neither the client nor the consultant can draw lessons from the assignment if there is no evaluation.

Yet many assignments are never evaluated, or their evaluation is superficial and of marginal interest. This is because of difficulties inherent in the evaluation of change in organizations and human systems. The number of factors affecting such systems is considerable and it may be difficult to isolate factors that change following a consulting intervention. For example, if the purpose of the assignment was to increase output, it cannot be taken for granted that a higher output achieved by the end of the assignment is due only to the intervention of the consultant. It may be that the increase is partly or completely due to other factors. In addition, some changes are difficult to identify, measure, describe and assess.

Evaluation can be the most delicate part of the consultant–client relationship and it may be more comfortable to avoid it, in particular if the client is not happy with the consultant's performance and if it is unlikely that they would collaborate again. Financial reasons also play their role: even the simplest evaluation exercise will cost time and money, and the client may prefer to save this money, since it is not being used to develop something new.

Who should evaluate?

As with the whole consulting process, effective evaluation requires collaboration. Both the client and the consultant need to know whether the assignment has achieved its objectives and can be qualified as a success story.

The client has, of course, certain specific interests and viewpoints. He is evaluating not only the assignment but also the consultant and his performance. If the client is concerned to perform better next time, he will also make a self-evaluation, assessing his own technical and managerial performance in cooperating with the consultant, monitoring the progress of the assignment and making use of the advice received. In the same way, the consultant should evaluate his own and the client's performance.

How much of this will be a joint exercise and what information will be shared is a matter of confidence and judgement. In an assignment that has been a true collaborative effort, evaluation is usually open and constructive. Yet no one can force the client and the consultant to share all the conclusions from their evaluations.

In certain cases, evaluation by an independent third party may be a requirement of the bank or agency that provided funds for the assignment. Independent evaluation may be the best way of preventing conflict and litigation when the client and the consultant cannot agree on the quantity and quality of results achieved and if fee payments are related to results.

Evaluation will focus on two basic aspects of the assignment: the benefits to the client and the consulting process.

Evaluating the benefits to the client

The reasons for evaluating the benefits of the assignment are self-evident. The benefits define the change achieved, a change that must be seen as an improvement, as a new value added to the client's business. Basically, the benefits are evaluated by comparing the situations before and after the assignment. This is only possible if the evaluation was foreseen in designing the assignment, i.e. in defining the results to be achieved and the criteria for measuring and assessing them.

Evaluation will seek answers to the following questions:

- Has the assignment achieved its purpose?
- What specific results and benefits to the client have been achieved?
- What expected results could not be achieved?
- Has the assignment achieved some unexpected and supplementary results?

In typical management consulting assignments there are six kinds of benefit or result:

- new capabilities;
- new systems;
- new relationships;
- new opportunities;
- new behaviour;
- new performance.

New capabilities. These are the new skills acquired by the client: they may be diagnostic and other problem-solving skills, communication skills, change-management skills, or technical or managerial skills in the particular areas affected by the assignment (e.g. new ways of raising finance for the business). New client capabilities in serving customers are particularly important (e.g. ability to deliver new products and services or to meet quality standards in new countries). New capabilities also include qualities such as the client's increased ability to take action, creativity, entrepreneurial spirit, ability to innovate, and sensitivity to environmental issues. In a nutshell, the consultant should have transferred knowledge to the client and the client should have become a more competent and more independent decision-maker.

New systems. Many assignments help to introduce changes in specific systems, such as for information management, marketing, production and quality management, personnel recruitment and appraisal, and preventive maintenance. These systems can be considered as assignment outcomes if they are, or are likely to become, operational.

New relationships. The assignment may have helped to establish new business and other relationships essential to the future of the client's business, such as new strategic alliances, subcontracting arrangements, consortia for implementing construction projects, or agreements on benchmarking.

New opportunities. These may concern various aspects of the client's business. The consultancy may have identified potential new markets, cheaper sources of raw materials, new technologies to be explored, land and buildings to be acquired, and so on.

New behaviour. Changed behaviour is a term applied mainly to interpersonal relations (e.g. between managers and their subordinates, or between cooperating teams from two different departments). However, it also embraces individual behaviour in work situations (e.g. whether or not a worker uses a safety device, how sales personnel treat customers, or whether a general manager stops postponing unpleasant decisions).

New performance. New performance is achieved if changes in the five areas mentioned above produce improvements in economic, financial, social or other indicators used to measure performance. These changes can be observed at individual (workstation), unit (workshop, team, group, plant, department), or organizational (enterprise, agency, ministry) level.

Better performance is an overriding goal and should be used for evaluating outcome and showing benefits whenever possible. Consulting that improves capabilities without aiming at improved performance could be an academic exercise, and a luxury from the financial point of view. It does happen, however, that changed performance cannot be used to assess results (e.g. new capabilities have been developed and opportunities identified, but the client has to postpone the application of measures that will bring about superior performance). Also, under certain circumstances, the client's improved business and managerial capabilities can be regarded as more important and of longer duration than immediate improvements in economic and financial performance.

Short-term and long-term benefits

In some assignments it may be necessary to distinguish and compare the short-term and long-term benefits. Impressive short-term results may ignore the future prospects and needs of the business and may be achieved to the detriment of the client's longer-term interests. Conversely, modest or no short-term results may be justified if the assignment has focused on longer-term benefits. The future prospects of the client's business, and long-term results, should be always kept in mind, even if the assignment has pursued short-term benefits above all.

Evaluating the consulting process

The evaluation of the consulting process is based on the assumption that the effectiveness of the process strongly influences the results of the assignment. This concerns assignments aimed at behavioural changes above all: if new sorts of behaviour and processes are to become established in the client organization (result), the consultant must choose and propose to the client a consulting style and intervention method (process) that can produce the desired outcome. For example, it is unlikely that a real change in the client's problem-solving capabilities will be achieved by the consultant giving a lecture or distributing a technical note on problem-solving and decision-making.

The consultant–client relationship and the intervention method develop during the assignment. Different methods can be used, and the process can be more or less collaborative and participative, and more or less effective. The evaluation should reveal this. The principal dimensions of the consulting process to be evaluated are as follows.

The design of the assignment (the contract). It is useful to begin by examining the start of the relationship. The questions to be raised include the following:

- How and by whom was the need for the consultancy established?
- How was the consultant chosen? What criteria and procedures were used?
- Was the purpose of the consultancy clear? Was it unduly narrow or vague?
- Was the design of the assignment clear, realistic and appropriate with regard to the client's needs and particular conditions?
- Did the original definition of purposes, objectives, results and inputs provide a good framework and guidance for the assignment plan? Were the objectives sufficiently demanding but not impossibly so? Was the definition of expected results clear, detailed and precise?
- Was the consulting style properly defined, discussed and understood? Were people briefed at the outset about their roles and responsibilities?

The quantity and quality of inputs. In addition to assessing the original definition of required inputs in the assignment plan, evaluation should examine the inputs that were provided by the consultant and the client. The main questions are:

- Did the consultant provide a team of the required size, structure and competence?
- Did the client provide the resources (human and other) needed for the assignment?

The consulting mode (style) used. The consultant and the client should assess in retrospect the events that took place and the relationship that existed during the assignment. They may ask in particular:

- What was the nature of the consultant–client relationship? Was there an atmosphere of mutual trust, understanding, respect and support?
- Was the right consulting style used? Was it adapted to the client's capabilities and preferences, and adjusted to the task at hand?
- Was every opportunity taken to increase the client's involvement in the assignment?
- Was proper attention paid to the learning dimension of the assignment? What was done to transfer knowledge and know-how to the client?
- Did the consultant scrupulously observe all ethical and behavioural norms of the profession?

The management of the assignment by the consultant and the client. Gaps and errors in the original assignment plan can be corrected and modifications required by changed conditions can be made if the assignment is aptly managed by both partners. An evaluation should address the following questions:

- Was the necessary flexibility built into the original design of the assignment?
- How did the consulting firm manage and support the assignment? How did it react to complaints and suggestions coming from the client?
- How did the client control and monitor the assignment?
- Did the consultant and the client respect the timetable?
- Was there an interim reporting and evaluation at key points in the assignment? What action was taken on the basis of it?

Evaluation tools

Priority should be given to collecting and examining hard data that permit quantitative assessment. In addition, identifying and examining opinions is important, particularly for evaluating the consultant–client relationship and the consulting style. Classical techniques are used, including interviews, observations, questionnaires and discussions at meetings (see Chapter 8).

A frank discussion between the client and the consultant is essential. Step by step, the discussion should review what happened in the client's and in the consultant's opinion, as well as the causes underlying particular attitudes and behaviours, achievements and errors.

The evaluation should be summarized in a short report, which may be part of the final assignment report, or may be presented separately (e.g. if the evaluation of results takes place several months after the completion of the assignment).

When to evaluate

There is a case for an evaluation as the assignment is coming to an end. Some benefits to the client may already be identifiable and it is possible to evaluate the consulting process in retrospect. The end-of-assignment evaluation is certainly the most important one. But it should not be the only one. Delaying evaluation until the end of implementation may mean that it is too late to suggest any improvements in the assignment, and any suggestions will be of interest only for future assignments. That is why *interim evaluations* should be foreseen at the end of the diagnostic and the action-planning phases. They should be treated as a normal part of the joint control and monitoring of the assignment by the consultant and the client. If necessary (e.g. in long and complex assignments), even within diagnosis, action planning and implementation, there may be a need for several evaluation exercises to review progress and interim results and, possibly, to adjust the assignment plan and the work methods used.

On the other hand, it is often impossible to complete evaluation right away at the end of the assignment. If measurable results cannot be identified immediately, or if the projected performance cannot be achieved until some time later, there is a case for follow-up evaluation.

Independent evaluation by the consultant

Clients will have their own policies and practices for evaluating the use of consulting and other professional services. A client may even choose not to evaluate a completed assignment. To a consultant, assignment evaluation is one of the basic tools for managing quality, controlling and developing staff, and building excellent relations with existing clients. Evaluation of completed assignments is a part of the consultant's knowledge management. As a matter of principle, a consultant should evaluate every assignment for his or her own benefit, even if the client has decided not to evaluate.

The questions to be asked are not very different from those mentioned above, although the focus may be slightly modified. The consultant will stress self-evaluation, looking specifically at areas where the consulting firm has experienced problems and seeks to make improvements.

It is difficult to be objective and unbiased in self-evaluation. Some consulting firms therefore seek feedback from clients, using various data-gathering and evaluation instruments. Questionnaires submitted to clients are the preferred instrument. The questions should invite the client to be frank about every aspect of the relationship and the work performed, including the competence and attitude of the consulting staff, their flexibility, behaviour, creativity, availability, helpfulness and other qualities that make the difference between mediocre and excellent assignments.[2] If the client takes the trouble to answer, the consultant should in turn provide feedback to thank the client and tell him or her what action will be taken on the answers and suggestions.

Other frequently used instruments include interviews, discussions with senior personnel in the client firm, follow-up visits, study of the client's internal evaluation reports (if made available to the consultant), and similar.

It should be noted that in quality certification according to ISO 9001 standards, assignment evaluation using feedback from clients is compulsory (see Chapter 32).

11.3 Follow-up

Often, the client and the consultant may agree to terminate a particular assignment without completely discontinuing their working relationship. Any further work done by the consultant which is related in some way to the current assignment is called follow-up. The desirability of some follow-up is often identified in the evaluation of the assignment. If the consultant is convinced that follow-up is in the client's interest and that he or she has something more to offer to the client, this may be suggested in the final report and meeting with the client.

The advantages to the consulting organization are obvious. In addition to providing income, a follow-up service is an invaluable way of learning about the real impact of operating assignments and about new problems that may have arisen in the client organization. New assignments may develop from these visits.

Many clients may also find that follow-up services are a useful form of assistance through which new problems and opportunities can be discovered and addressed before they become serious. However, no client should be forced to accept a follow-up arrangement if he or she is not interested in it.

Follow-up of implementation

For many reasons, the client may be interested in a follow-up arrangement. He or she may wish the consultant to take a fresh look at the situation created by the implementation of the proposals, because of new technical developments in the area covered by the assignment or for other reasons. When IT systems are delivered and installed by consultants, their further assistance is usually required for maintaining and upgrading the system.

The consultant may visit the client every three months over a two-year period, to review progress, to help to take any necessary corrective measures, and to find out whether or not new problems have arisen. If a new intervention is required that exceeds the scope of these periodic visits, the consultant may make a separate proposal for this, but the client will be absolutely free to accept or decline it. Outsourcing arrangements can also follow on from completed consulting assignments.

Retainer arrangements

Follow-up visits related to specific assignments are normally programmed for a limited period of time. If the client is interested in maintaining a more permanent working relationship with a consultant, a retainer arrangement may be appropriate (see section 1.4). Many retainer arrangements develop from successfully implemented consulting projects.

11.4 Final reporting

Before and during the assignment the client will have received several reports:

- the report in which the assignment was proposed, based on a preliminary diagnostic survey;
- in some instances an inception report, prepared shortly after the start of the assignment, outlining a detailed plan of work;
- progress reports, whose number and scope varies, in which modifications in problem definition and assignment plans may have been proposed;
- reports and documentation linked with the submission of proposals for the client's decision prior to implementation.

Whatever the pattern of interim reporting, there is normally a final assignment report issued at the time the consultant withdraws from the client organization. The consulting firm itself requires such reports, which will be of help, above all, to other staff members who undertake similar assignments.

Report to the client

For a short assignment, this may be the only report and so has to be comprehensive. For longer assignments, the final report may refer to previous reports and go into detail only on the events since the last report was written. In every case, as a closing report, it should tidy up all the loose ends and cover the essential end-of-assignment facts and confirmations. It should be known before it is written whether the consultant is to provide a follow-up service. If so, the report may not be quite as "final" as it otherwise would be.

In addition to a short but comprehensive review of work performed, the final report should point out the benefits obtained from implementation and make frank suggestions to the client on what should be undertaken, or avoided, in the future.

Some consultants, especially in the OD sector, regard final reports as redundant if the client has worked closely with the consultant throughout the assignment and there is obvious satisfaction with the approach taken and the results. Final reports are not compulsory. However, the fact that one has to be produced (it can be a very short one) encourages discipline and rigour and stimulates thinking on what was really achieved and what could have been done in a better way.

Evaluation of benefits

An evaluation of benefits should be included in the final report if this is practical, i.e. if the consultant is leaving the client after a period of implementation which lends itself to evaluation. In other cases, it may be submitted later, as already discussed.

Through the evaluation of real benefits the consultant demonstrates the correctness and accuracy of both the preliminary assessment and the evaluation of alternative solutions.

Clearly, implementation must have progressed far enough, and the conditions of operating the new technique or system must have become normal and stabilized, if an evaluation of benefits is to give objective information. The consultant should emphasize the direct benefits obtained as a result of the assignment and leave the consideration of indirect benefits (e.g. no increase in fixed costs) to the client.

In presenting the benefits, the report should focus on measurable economic, financial and social benefits that have been or will be drawn from superior performance. However, the report should also describe the new capabilities, systems, opportunities and behaviours created by the assignment and show their impact on performance, as discussed in section 11.2.

Most management consulting firms prefer not to point out the savings-to-fee ratio. Such analysis is left to the client, who needs to appreciate that not all benefits can be costed and that the ratio may be low in many simple, low-risk assignments, whose impact on overall and long-term business results is limited.

Evaluation of the consulting process

Whether to include the evaluation of the consulting process in the final report is a matter of judgement. There may be a strong case for doing so if the client can learn from it for the future, and if the client's behaviour during the assignment was the reason for some superior or substandard results. The consultant and the client should agree on how detailed and open this section will be, and what matters will be discussed but not included in the final report.

Suggestions to the client

Although the job is completed, the consultant can show that he or she sees the client organization in perspective by pointing out possible further improvements, opportunities, bottlenecks, risks, action that should not be delayed, and so on. In any case the consultant has to make suggestions on how the new system introduced with his or her help should be maintained, controlled and developed after his or her departure. An agreement reached on a follow-up service would also be confirmed in the final report.

A good consulting report should be capable of commanding the respect of the client, who will consider it a source of further learning and guidance. He or she should also be able to show it to business friends and associates as the record of a worthwhile achievement.

Some useful suggestions on writing and presenting consulting reports can be found in Appendix 7.

Assignment reference report

In addition to the final report to the client, consultants should compile an assignment reference and evaluation report for their own organization, as will be described in section 31.5.

The client's internal report

Some organizations using consultants prepare internal reports on completed assignments. In addition to summary information the report may include the client's assessment of the job done and of the consultant's approach and performance. Although this is most useful, it is not common. The report is not intended for the consultant, but some clients may be happy to share it with the consultant, who should not miss the opportunity to obtain a copy.

---

[1] *Consultants News* (Fitzwilliam, NH), July/Aug. 1991, p. 6.

[2] See, e.g., the client feedback questionnaire suggested by David Maister in *Managing the professional service firm* (New York, The Free Press, 1993), pp. 85–86, and also reproduced in M. Kubr: *How to select and use consultants: A client's guide*, Management Development Series, No. 31 (Geneva, ILO, 1993), p. 176.

PART III

CONSULTING IN VARIOUS AREAS OF MANAGEMENT

CONSULTING IN GENERAL AND STRATEGIC MANAGEMENT 12

Each of the next 15 chapters deals with consulting in a specific area of management. The intention is not to provide an exhaustive analysis of management techniques, practices and problems in each area but, in keeping with the spirit of the book, to show how management consultants can help clients and how they normally operate in these areas, and to mention some recent developments of which they should be aware. These chapters can serve, therefore, as an introduction to a more detailed study of consulting in various areas of management.

12.1 Nature and scope of consulting in corporate strategy and general management

A considerable amount of management consulting concerns the very existence, the basic goals or mission, the business policy and strategy, and the overall planning, structuring and control, of an organization. These problems were at one time defined as general management, but are now more commonly referred to as corporate strategy or strategic management. Consultants who concern themselves with these issues are strategy or general management consultants – as distinct from specialists who intervene in one functional area (e.g. finance), or deal with a particular technique such as computerized production control or employee incentive schemes.

But how does a company know if it requires the assistance of an all-round management consultant? In some cases this is quite obvious from the state of the business: a deteriorating overall performance, growing dissatisfaction of the staff, the generally bleak prospects of the industrial sector, and so on. The business may be in crisis, or close to it, and it is not clear how to restore prosperity. In other cases, a problem that seems at the outset to be a special or functional one (inadequate marketing methods, say) may have ramifications in other areas of management and eventually is found to be only a symptom of a much deeper general management problem affecting the whole organization.

In such organizations it is common to find that top management has no clear idea of where the company is going or what it is trying to achieve. In short, there is a lack of strategic direction. In others, top management has some sense of strategic objectives but has failed to communicate its vision to middle and lower management and to the workforce – and, in consequence, the strategies are never implemented.

A benchmark is now available which makes it much easier to recognize organizations that have lost their way in strategic terms. There is now widespread acceptance that the ultimate objective of private sector corporations – and therefore the guiding principle underlying all decisions made in those organizations – should be the creation of shareholder value.

Any sign that the organization's strategies are evolving in directions that do not maximize value – such as excessive diversification away from the core business or pursuit of a range of incoherent and conflicting business objectives – provides a signal that the Board and top management would benefit from the fresh viewpoint that a skilled strategy consultant can provide.

The issue of shareholder value will be discussed further in Chapter 14, "Consulting in financial management". Furthermore, Chapter 23 will show how social responsibility can be integrated in corporate strategy in ways that are compatible with the concept of shareholder value.

The special nature of general management

The most prominent characteristics of problems handled in general management consulting are that they are:

- *long-term:* they involve decisions about major capital investments and other resource allocations, acquisitions, divestments and corporate reorganizations that will have an impact on the organization's success or failure far into the future;
- *multifunctional:* the consultant deals with several functions of the business (production, technology, organization, marketing, etc.) and focuses on the interaction between these functions and on problems involving more than one function;
- *interdisciplinary:* the consultant must be able to view business problems from several angles; typically, a business strategy problem may have technological, economic, financial, legal, psychosociological, motivational, political and other dimensions.

General managers, too, have been chosen for their ability (real or expected) to free themselves from short-term "fire-fighting" and to deal with multifunctional and interdisciplinary problems. Experience shows that many of them find this difficult. There are general managers, previously excellent plant managers, who continue to be plant managers in their new position! This is an area where a management consultant can be of great help to the client – the general manager who has to change his or her habits, learn how to deal with new functions, look at the problems of the business from new angles, and above all free himself or herself from day-to-day operating concerns sufficiently to be able to think about longer-term strategy.

In fact, general management consultants are also a kind of specialist: their speciality lies in combining other specialities into a balanced and coherent multifunctional and interdisciplinary approach. Like the general managers, however, general management consultants turn to other specialists when appropriate. They must know how to use the specialist's skill and advice, and help the client to do the same, to prevent situations where particular specialists (e.g. market researchers or financial analysts) would dominate the business.

Diagnosing organizations

As explained in detail in Chapter 7, many consultants prefer to carry out a quick preliminary survey of the organization before proposing a specific problem-solving assignment. Thus the first technical contact between the client and the consultant is often at the general management level, before the consultant moves into specific areas identified by the survey. It is essential at this early stage that the consultant understands what the client management believe their mission and strategic objectives to be. If they are internally inconsistent – or if they are not consistent with the maximization of shareholder value – these issues will have to be resolved before any detailed diagnosis is undertaken.

There are situations where a thorough diagnostic survey (diagnosis, audit, etc.) of the whole organization is required in preparation for important decisions on the future of the business. This is particularly true where the "value" concept is being introduced for the first time, and the appropriate "value drivers" have to be determined for each operating level. A comprehensive diagnostic survey may also precede a major restructuring or reorganization, an acquisition, a merger, a privatization or a decision to close down a business. The consultant's mandate is to help the client to diagnose the organization; he or she may even be asked, as an independent expert, to provide an objective and neutral report on the status, strengths, weaknesses and development prospects of the business. The assessment of the management systems used and of senior managerial personnel may be included. The assignment may end with the consultant submitting a report on the diagnosis. Diagnostic surveys of this type may be fairly extensive and difficult assignments. While a quick survey is a matter of a few days, comprehensive and in-depth surveys may take several months, depending on the size and complexity of the organization and on the nature of its problems.

Some comprehensive diagnostic surveys intervene too late, when the company is no longer susceptible of rescue, or when rescue would require resources that are not available. In certain cases a crisis could have been prevented by undertaking a thorough diagnosis at an earlier date, and arranging for a periodic business diagnosis, or self-diagnosis, as a preventive measure. The consultant may have an opportunity to help a client to design and install a scheme for regular self-diagnosis. This opportunity should not be missed.

Organizational level of interventions

In many cases the general management consultant intervenes at the highest level in the organization: with the chief executive or the top management team. Even leaders who are keen to introduce change often do not realize what will be involved, or do not see that they ought to start by changing themselves. They frequently have a particular self-image, though the consultant may find that this image is not shared by other people in the organization. The consultant's problem then lies in persuading management of the need to change thinking and behaviour at the very top.

The possibility of working directly with the chief executive and the management team provides an excellent introduction to the organization, rapid access to key data, a true picture of the operating style of top management, and usually strong support from the top for the consultant's work. Yet it is often risky to confine intervention to top management level. The general management consultant needs to find out how top management is perceived throughout the organization, and how management policies influence the work style, performance and job satisfaction of employees. Furthermore, general management is also practised at intermediate and lower levels in the management hierarchy, and eventually affects every single worker. For example, supervisory management often constitutes one of the weakest links in the management hierarchy.

Consulting style

In general and strategic management more than in any other area, the consultant cannot avoid dealing with issues affecting management's personal interests, self-image and authority. Advice on crucial issues of a company's direction, strategy and leadership can easily be perceived as criticism aimed at particular persons. Yet the objective is to strengthen and improve management, not to undermine it. Also, the consultant does not want to see his or her proposals rejected by senior management. Experienced consultants therefore attach great importance to choosing the right consulting style.

Many entrepreneurs and senior managers are lonely and isolated people when it comes to discussing their basic goals and values and their style. The general management consultant may well be the first person able and willing to talk to them about these issues. Personal counselling (see section 3.7) may be needed, and the consultant should not hesitate to offer it tactfully to the client.

A frequently debated issue is the choice between participative and process consulting approaches, and those where the consultant acts primarily as an expert in the subject. If the client is not able or willing to participate, the consultant may decide to give the best expert advice possible, which the client may decide to use or to ignore. However, in strategy and general management consulting, the risk of rejection is extremely high, as witnessed by countless consulting reports, plans and proposals that have been ignored by the clients. Furthermore, core issues concerning the very existence, mission, strategic direction or restructuring of a client company can hardly be fully understood and properly resolved if handled by outsiders only. All the reasons that speak in favour of participative consulting in any area of management are doubly valid when dealing with strategy, organization, corporate culture, corporate governance and similar general management issues.

12.2 Corporate strategy

The concept of corporate strategy has made a significant contribution to the advancement of management practice and theory over the past 30 years. Consulting in corporate strategy (business strategy, strategic analysis, strategic planning, strategic restructuring, etc.) is a rapidly growing area of management consulting. Some consultants have made corporate strategy their main or exclusive field of intervention. Consulting in corporate strategy has been strongly influenced by changing fads and fashions. During the 1970s there was a growing use of quantitative techniques and models, and strategic studies began to be dominated by young econometricians and operational researchers, with excellent education but often without business experience, and with little knowledge of people, or of social and other problems that determine strategy in reality. The following decade saw a welcome swing back to pragmatism.

A further development of the 1960s and 1970s was that many business firms created strategic planning units, and planning was seen as a distinct staff department function. The 1980s saw a strong swing away from such departments, which in any case rarely commanded the attention or respect of top management. It is now increasingly recognized that strategic planning is far too important to be left to planning staff, and that participation in the formulation of strategies is an intrinsic part of the work of senior management.

Even though the role of the planning department has diminished, however, the need for external consultants has increased. Senior operating executives always have some difficulty in stepping back from their immediate priorities and thinking about the longer term. Their workloads make it difficult for them to track all the developments in the company's environment that need to be taken into account in the formulation of strategic plans, and it is notoriously difficult for them to make an honest evaluation of their organization's weaknesses relative to competition. The consultant brings an open mind to these issues. Many boards of directors develop long-term relationships with consultants who advise them on strategy development, and clearly find such advice invaluable.

Strategic vision

Corporate strategy is usually defined as the organization's response to environmental opportunities, challenges and threats, consistent with its resources and its competencies relative to its competitors. This latter point is so important that some writers define strategy entirely in terms of the search for competitive advantage. It is important to remember, however, that strategy is not an aim in itself but a set of paths and choices for achieving the organization's goals in the future. This is where a consultant can start helping the client. Many organizations practising strategic planning actually lack a vision of the future. Some do not even have a clear understanding of the present; they have not asked the strategist's fundamental question: "What business are we in?" Yet an understanding of this must be the starting-point of any sound strategic analysis.

A strategic vision should be as rational as possible and not a result of wishful thinking. However, total rationality is not achievable for one simple reason – the future is unknown and is being shaped by a myriad of independent actions all over the globe; the client's own actions will form only a tiny fragment of this future, however important the business is. Nor is it possible to evaluate every possible course of action. The personal values and judgement of the key decision-makers therefore play a vital role in positioning the organization for the future. Harold Leavitt has described this role as "pathfinding".[1] Other writers describe it as a "sense of mission".

It is for this reason that current thinking on corporate excellence and strategy puts so much emphasis on *organizational leadership*. A leader is an individual (or team) with a vision of the future position of the organization. Furthermore, a leader is able to express this vision in goals understandable to people in the organization, and influence and motivate people to achieve these goals. There is a unity of vision, and a unity of actions guided by this vision.

Industry and competitor analysis: determining competitive advantage

A competitive advantage is a key dimension of survival and success in environments where organizations must compete with each other. This advantage is not a trick that can last a few months (e.g. a smart advertising campaign), but an inherent capacity to sustain superior performance on a long-term basis. The search for such advantage must therefore start with a systematic analysis of the industry and sector in which the enterprise operates, and of the competitive forces at play.

Much of the most important development in strategic thinking in the past 20 years has been in concepts and models that facilitate this kind of analysis. The "five forces" model proposed by Michael Porter identifies five key areas that management needs to understand: (1) the competitive structure within the industry/segment itself; (2) the threat of new entrants; (3) the threat of substitute products or technologies; (4) the power of suppliers; and (5) the power of customers.[2] Kenichi Ohmae suggests "key success factors" on the basis of which the business unit should compare itself with its competitors.[3] Another of Michael Porter's concepts, the "value chain", assists in determining where in the enterprise's operating cycle these key factors are to be found. Products and market positions can be brought into better perspective by using product/market life-cycle models. None of these models claims to describe reality for any one particular company: rather, they are an aid to thinking about reality. They are certainly tools which any consultant working in this area needs to have.

Equipped with such tools, the consultant can be most helpful in examining whether the client business does indeed enjoy any competitive advantage, or in developing a strategy for achieving one. He or she can draw the client's attention to the ways in which organizations regarded as excellent achieved and maintained their competitive advantage. He or she can point out certain factors that tend to be characteristic of all firms that possess such an advantage (for example, priority attention paid to the clients' needs and satisfaction, and to the quality of products and services). But above all, the consultant can help the client to think honestly about the industry's characteristics, the keys to success, and just how the client's enterprise matches up to the competition in these key areas.

After the analysis comes the moment of truth: specifying the strategy to be followed. The consultant can help the client organization choose among the alternatives that are available to it, bearing in mind the real capacities of the technical and production staff, production facilities, marketing networks, business experience and the like. Once again, thinking on the subject of corporate strategy has provided insights that can clarify the decisions that have to be made. Michael Porter has highlighted the distinction between two fundamental approaches or, as he terms them, "generic strategies". One of these is to concentrate upon becoming competitive through "cost leadership", i.e. by having the lowest costs in the industry (though this does not, of course, necessarily mean having the lowest selling prices). The other is to concentrate upon "differentiation", which means offering the customer superior quality and a unique package of features. Clearly, no enterprise can afford to ignore either costs or quality completely. Porter believes, however, that no company can hope to dominate its field in both cost and differentiation, and that any attempt to do so will lead to being "stuck in the middle" with neither the most competitive costs nor superior product features.

Practical examples of the strategic choices to be made are:

- offering state-of-the-art technologically advanced products not available from other firms or available from very few (differentiation), and regularly abandoning these products and moving on when the technology becomes common and prices start to drop;
- providing service to clients with speed and reliability superior to that offered by competitors (a further form of differentiation);
- selling high-quality and particularly reliable products for relatively high prices, and/or products tailored to the particular needs of clients who find standard products unsatisfactory (differentiation again);

- selling standard products of acceptable but not particularly high quality at very competitive prices (cost leadership).

In defining a competitive advantage, emphasis is put on the notion "sustainable". The client will have to evaluate, and enhance as appropriate, his or her ability to adapt to changed conditions, and to innovate. For example, only organizations that are closely linked to technological research and where the flow of technological innovation has become a permanent internal process can choose the provision of state-of-the-art technology as their business strategy and hope to sustain differentiation on this basis.

Technology in corporate strategy

The role of technology in developing differentiation and implementing a winning corporate strategy is another area where management consultants can be extremely useful to their business clients. There are several reasons for this:

> A company that integrates technology into its strategy significantly improves its chances of reaping benefits from technological changes. Whether it decides to be a technological leader or not, the results of integrating technology into strategy can improve a company's determination of priorities among technology options, identify the technical resources needed to achieve business goals and speed up the movement of ideas into production.[4]

However, technological developments occur simultaneously in so many areas, and so rapidly, that even large companies with well-staffed R&D departments and information services find it increasingly difficult to keep abreast of developments, and think of possibilities offered by technologies and materials created in other sectors and countries.

Increased emphasis on technology strategy and its impact on manufacturing, marketing and other strategies is a new challenge to many management consultants, who often used to handle strategy simply as a factor affecting marketing and finance decisions. Some consultants have already responded by establishing research and development (R&D) departments which can both participate in consulting assignments in corporate strategy and undertake specific R&D tasks for their clients. Evaluating the potential of new technologies and providing technological information analysed from the viewpoint of its potential business applications has become a rapidly growing service. Several important consulting firms already offer such a service to their clients. Consultants advising on business development opportunities and projects in developing countries are increasingly involved in questions of technology transfer, helping to choose both the appropriate technology to be used and the terms under which such a transfer can be effectively implemented.

This trend is likely to continue, and management consultants who devise new services in response to clients' pressing needs will themselves gain a distinct competitive advantage. It is clear, however, that the technology that will be most influential in the future is information technology – with all its associated ramifications in telecommunications and the Internet. The implications of these developments are discussed in section 12.3, and in Chapters 13 and 16.

The environment of business

The environment in which organizations operate is becoming so complex, variable and even confused that managers find it more and more difficult to identify significant information and monitor changes that should be reflected in corporate strategy. Writers in the field of strategy increasingly refer to the need for systematic "PEST" analysis – a convenient shorthand for the areas that such an analysis needs to examine:

- the political environment;
- the economic environment;
- the social environment;
- the technological environment.

Here again, management consultants can be of great help. Some clients may need guidance in order to become more aware of the environment and so realize that ongoing or forecasted environmental changes can have far-reaching consequences for their businesses. Other clients may be aware of the scope and depth of environmental changes, but lacking the skills and resources needed to collect necessary information and draw the right conclusions from its analysis. They find it difficult to determine what information is relevant, or may be relevant in the future.

As a result, many consulting firms increasingly provide services to clients in matters of corporate strategy which focus on environmental information and analysis. In addition, these firms help clients to devise systems and procedures in which environmental analysis is internalized to become a standard part of the strategic management system. In some cases (e.g. in small and medium-sized firms in rapidly changing industrial and service sectors), clients may require long-term support from a competent information agency, which screens and monitors the environment, or some aspects of it, on their behalf. Some consultants are already building up a new client service for this purpose.

Environmental analysis tends to embrace new issues in addition to classic marketing, economic, demographic and financial information. Analysis of the social environment is necessary if the company is to address effectively social responsibility issues and determine their place in corporate strategies (Chapter 23). New regulations concerning product quality, safety, or the protection of the natural and living environment can determine the life or death of firms whose products or technologies are affected. Some of these regulations have a long gestation period, while others are adopted very quickly. Political and social interests, as well as organizations, are involved in the promotion of new regulations. Seen from another angle, new regulations also offer new opportunities to firms that can adapt their products faster than their competitors, or that come up with new products that specifically serve the purpose of increased safety or reduced pollution.

As regards the legal environment of business in general, many companies find it impossible to keep track of all strategically significant changes in their home country, let alone changes having an impact on foreign operations. Management consultants can help clients with this task, in collaboration with law firms if appropriate. Even so, the environment can never be completely understood, let alone predicted – a problem that is discussed in section 12.3.

Emergent strategy

Everything written above is based on the assumption that strategy formulation is a logical and rational process. An analytical structure has been developed which facilitates a structured step-wise approach: understand the environment in which the organization operates, understand the industry and the key success factors in that industry, understand the company's own strengths and weaknesses, understand its competitors, and understand what competencies the organization will need to have. All of this is valid and correct. However, consultants who give the impression that such an approach will produce the correct strategy will appear naïve. At best, it will produce the strategy that fits best with the available information, but that information can never be complete.

Virtually all business decisions are made in a state of uncertainty, and the uncertainty in strategic-level decisions is often even greater than in other areas. Changes in the social, economic and political environment are notoriously difficult to forecast and anticipate. However much time is devoted to understanding the strengths and weaknesses of competitors, it is rarely possible to have access to their strategic thinking. The rate of scientific and technological development has consistently outstripped all expectations. Developments in any or all of these areas can invalidate the most carefully planned strategies. A well-reasoned strategic plan to make a major investment in a developing country, for example, may be made redundant if the democratic government of the country is replaced in a military coup. A new product that was about to be launched may have to be cancelled if a competitor introduces a clearly superior one.

It must be clear, therefore, that the strategy that is actually implemented will never be quite the same as the one developed from the rational analysis. Strategic thinkers and writers now make a distinction between intended strategy and emergent strategy. It is of course necessary to have an intended strategy, because without one the organization will be completely reactive rather than proactive. As time passes, however, the various uncertainties will start to be resolved, and existing strategies will need to be modified accordingly. The emerging situation will reveal unforeseen problems, and possibly also emerging opportunities. The mission and strategic objectives may remain largely unchanged, but the strategies by which they are to be achieved should be subject to continual review and modification.

Implementing strategy

Strategy that remains on paper is of little use. Further, as outlined above, what is implemented is never the same as the "paper" strategy, but something emergent and dynamic. Strategy implementation is, in fact, much more difficult than strategy formulation. The consultant must help the client to develop operating systems, procedures and technical capabilities for putting these constantly evolving strategies into effect. This raises a number of issues, including that of communication. While certain strategic choices may have to be kept strictly confidential, the failure to communicate important choices to staff will mean that no one in the organization, except the planners and top managers, will adhere to the strategy chosen. Activities such as production planning and control, inventory management, quality improvement and staff development, as well as leadership and management style, are critical to the successful implementation of strategy.

The consultant can help the client, too, in developing competence for adapting strategy to new opportunities and constraints. No strategy is valid forever, and the rapid pace of change in the business world and its environment means that strategy formulation and review must be an ongoing process. There is a clear need for a monitoring, or "early warning", system to detect trends, events and ideas that may lead to a change in corporate strategy. Once again, internal management may have neither the time nor the detachment to undertake this task properly. The company's management system, including procedures for auditing and redefining strategy, should be flexible enough to make adaptation possible. This means, in particular, encouraging people in marketing, production, R&D and other departments to keep their eyes and ears constantly open for signals and ideas that may have a bearing on strategy. The consultant's role is to pull all of this information together and determine its implications.

Consistency with internal capabilities

In consulting on strategy, consistency with the internal capabilities of a company is as important in consulting on strategy as the alignment of the firm with the business environment. Every pattern of corporate strategy has its own requirements as regards the technical profile and capabilities of the staff, as well as managerial and work style and employee motivation. Clearly, an ambitious differentiation strategy intended to maintain the company at the cutting edge of technological innovation, without much concern for costs and prices, requires a different style and working climate from a strategy that is not too demanding as regards latest technology but seeks to achieve cost leadership through rigorous cost control of standardized, high-volume work operations.

Ideally, not only management but also other staff members should be associated with strategy formulation. The process of defining strategy is even more important than the content for achieving staff commitment and a shared belief that the strategy chosen is a way to success.

Company transformation strategies

Management consultants are often called in when the development pattern of a company deviates substantially from normal. These tend to be difficult assignments, with an uncertain chance of success, often carried out under severe time pressure, for example if the client organization is in serious financial difficulties, or feels that it would miss an exceptional opportunity if the consultant takes too much time over the analysis or in helping to identify candidates for a merger or an acquisition. These assignments usually involve radical and deep changes in most activity sectors of the firm and strongly affect its management. Examples are mergers and acquisitions, turnarounds, large-scale outsourcing, divestment, downsizing, changes in ownership structures, and privatization of state-owned companies, all pursuing the objective of making the company more competitive, profitable and effective. These company transformation and renewal strategies will be reviewed in more detail in Chapter 22.

12.3 Processes, systems and structures

The structuring of an organization concerns the division of tasks and responsibilities among people, the grouping of tasks and people in units, the definition of vertical and horizontal information flows and collaborative relations, and arrangements for coordination. The purpose of structuring has in the past been to provide a more or less stable framework for the effective functioning of organizational processes and the total organization, i.e. of all its members, resources and units, in achieving common goals. This is yet another area in which rapid shifts are taking place, as structures become less rigid and formal.

The products of structuring are various systems and subsystems – organization systems, management information systems, decision-making systems, control and evaluation systems, systems for handling emergencies and crises, and so on. Any complex organization is operated through and with the help of these systems. However, experience shows that structures and systems can easily become a straitjacket, for example, if they try to standardize and prescribe behaviour for situations that are very specific and where standardization does more harm than good. The design and maintenance of systems is a costly affair; some kind of cost–benefit analysis is therefore required in starting a project to design or revise a system. Many organizations need help to prevent proliferation and overlapping of systems, as well as to avoid lack of coordination and conflicting requirements of various systems for supplying and interpreting information.

The process perspective

Recent thinking has emphasized core organizational processes as the principal criteria for developing systems and structures. Traditional fragmentation of activities and tasks is tending to give way to integration which is made possible by modern technologies, in particular information technology. In describing the business process re-engineering approach, Michael Hammer and James Champy stress "focus on redesigning a fundamental business process, not on departments and other organizational units". As they put it, "the fragmented processes and specialized structures are unresponsive to large changes in the external environment – the market, ... and display appalling diseconomies of scale, quite opposite of what Adam Smith envisioned".[5]

Other current trends, however, are leading in a somewhat different direction. The focus may be on the core process, but there is increasing recognition that much of the process is likely to take place outside the organization itself. This is sometimes referred to as the development of the "virtual company", and is itself an outcome of the "information revolution". A recent article notes: "We reject a virtual organization as a distinct structure (like functional, divisional or matrix). Instead, we treat virtualness as a strategic characteristic applicable to any organization."[6]

The thrust of the concept is that developments in information and communication technology have made it possible for the organization to develop much closer links with its customers, suppliers and distributors, to the extent that key parts of the overall "process" can now take place outside the organization itself. The Internet, for example, facilitates the testing and modification of product design in conjunction with "consumer communities". Relations with such communities present both opportunities and dangers. Used properly, they can enhance the organization's image and prestige, but misused, they have the potential to do immense damage. Information technology provides other kinds of opportunity for interacting with customers: remote sensing of the performance of consumer products, and problem diagnosis and even problem solution over an Internet link.

The implications for the organization's interaction with its suppliers are even more far-reaching, and it is not surprising that it is the "B2B" (i.e. business-to-business) sector of Internet activity that has developed most rapidly. Most large organizations recognize the importance of good supplier relations. Many are now going far beyond this, and recognizing that a range of activities that were previously carried out in-house could be more efficiently performed by external specialists. Thus National Semiconductor, for example, has recently outsourced all of its logistics operations to FedEx, and Fidelity Funds Management distributes its funds through the Charles Schwab organization. Perhaps the process has been taken furthest by the Nike company, which has entrusted all of its manufacturing and much of its marketing and public relations to outside specialists.

Some critics have argued that such a process eventually leaves a company with no real reason for existence: one coined the phrase "the hollow company" to apply to such organizations. Other commentators, however, see an exciting possibility – of organizations that concentrate entirely upon creating value in the form of intangible assets – intellectual properties – and outsource all tangible assets and activities to outside specialists. This is an area that offers much for the consultant to think about, and on which many clients will need an outside opinion.

Decision-making systems and practices

In many organizations it may be the method and organization of decision-making (for both key and routine matters) that cause trouble. Excessive centralization of operational decisions may deprive the organization of the flexibility needed to react to new market opportunities. Fragmentation of processes and responsibilities makes quick decisions extremely difficult. The "virtualization" process adds a further complication, namely the need to include a variety of external agencies in the decision process.

The need to examine and reform the decision-making system may be the very reason why the consultant has been brought in. It may concern:

- the classification of decisions in groups by their nature, urgency, financial implications, degree of complexity, etc.;
- the ways in which typical decisions are taken (this may be quite difficult to find out);
- the respective decision-making roles played by staff specialists and line managers;
- the role of collective bodies in preparing and adopting decisions;
- the participation of employee representatives in decision-making;
- the decision-making and advisory roles of individuals in informal positions of influence;
- the responsibility for decisions, their implementation, and control of implementation;
- the use of decision-making techniques, models or formalized procedures.

The possibilities for improvement in this area are tremendous and general management consultants are well advised to pay close attention to them.

Management information systems

Most managers are aware that information has become a strategic asset of business and that the world is undergoing an information revolution. However, it is a long way from recognizing the new role of information to actually developing and implementing effective management information systems.

Many general management consultants focus on this area and offer services such as: analysing the existing information system; defining the information required for strategic management and operational control; harmonizing and integrating systems used in various departments; and choosing and introducing appropriate information processing technology. This work concerns both external information (on the environment and the enterprise's relations with this environment) and internal information (on resources, processes and results achieved). The purpose is to make sure that the client has the information that is essential for strategic and operational decisions, but at the same time avoids collecting and developing information that is of no direct use. To decide where the limits are is difficult, and it may be preferable to cast the "information net" more widely rather than to save money at the risk of missing some essential information.

In today's consulting, management information systems are often handled as a problem of information technology, including the choice, installation and effective use of appropriate hardware and software. Yet this is only one side of the problem. Information technology is a key factor determining what sort of information and how much of it a company will be able to collect, process and analyse. Choosing the information that is needed for preparing and making decisions is not the computer specialist's problem but the information user's (and his or her management consultant's) problem. Close collaboration between the two has to be established and maintained in developing effective information systems (see also Chapter 13).

Organizational structure

Examining and redesigning the organizational structure used to be the classical intervention of many general management consultants. When the basic structure was agreed, the consultant produced detailed diagrams and charts, as well as job descriptions for each unit and position within the client organization. The end-product was often a set of organizational charts and instructions but, in fact, the principal benefit to the client was the effort and analysis that went into this job. Forgotten and "orphan" activities were rediscovered, aotivities for which nobody seemed to be responsible were defined, and overlapping activities were reassigned or done away with.

Today's management consulting goes beyond the rather narrow approach taken by the "reorganization experts" in the past. Structure is treated as one of the factors of excellence, which is linked in many ways with strategy, organizational culture, the competence and motivation of employees, new technology and other factors. Competent and committed staff working in a loosely organized framework will produce better results than incompetent people inserted in a perfect formal structure. In any event, every consultant must realize that formal organization reflects only a small part of the very complex network of relations existing in an organization.

Reorganizations destroy existing work relations, collaboration patterns and socialization habits. Unjustified and frequent reorganizations paralyse enterprises and institutions, and generate lethargy rather than innovation and efficiency. A decision to reorganize often reflects management's failure to identify and tackle the real issue. Therefore consultants are more and more cautious, and tend to prescribe reorganization only if there are very valid reasons for it (e.g. a new division must be established because the existing structure is clearly not able to put a new product on the market in the shortest possible time). Conversely, major changes of organizational structures are often necessary in companies in transformation, as will be discussed in more detail in Chapter 22.

12.4 Corporate culture and management style

Finally we turn to the "soft" and "intangible" side of organizations. The concept of culture was explained in Chapter 5. We emphasized that, when entering a new organization, the consultant has to find out as much as possible about its specific culture. This is done in order to develop a full understanding of the values and motives underlying managerial and employee behaviour, and so assess the organization's potential for making improvements. Organizational culture may be found to be one of the causes, or even the main cause, of the difficulties experienced (e.g. due to the conservatism of senior management and the impossibility of submitting new ideas). In such a case, culture may even become the central theme on which the assignment would focus.[7]

Consulting in corporate culture became extremely popular at the beginning of the 1980s, in particular in the United States. Some consultants have not escaped the danger of regarding and prescribing cultural change as a panacea: "Corporate culture is the magic phrase that management consultants are breathing into the ears of American executives", wrote *The New York Times* in 1983.[8] Nevertheless, in warning against the corporate culture fad we must not throw out the baby with the bathwater. Interest in corporate culture and in the impact of culture on long-term organizational performance is basically a positive phenomenon, needed for a balanced approach to organizational problems. If organizational culture is ignored, a sophisticated planning or management information system is unlikely to lead to any improvements in performance.

A change in corporate culture will rarely be an explicitly stated task in a consulting assignment. Yet in some situations corporate culture requires the consultant's special attention, for example:

- when a company is in difficulties. A strong traditional and intransigent culture may prevent the company from assessing its condition realistically and proceeding with changes that have become inevitable.
- when a company has grown very rapidly. There may be various problems. The original culture of a small family company may have become a straitjacket. There may be many new managers and workers, coming from different cultures. Growth by acquisitions may lead to serious cultural clashes.
- when major technological and structural change is planned. Revolutionary changes in products, technologies, markets, and so on have strong cultural implications.
- when there seems to be a conflict between the company's culture and values that prevail in the environment, for example, if the public increasingly expects a company to behave in ways that are contrary to its culture.
- when the company's operations are internationalized and it has to adapt to foreign cultures.

Corporate culture: what to recommend

The consultant will try to ascertain the aspects of the corporate culture that stimulate and inhibit further growth and performance improvement. He or she will point to values and norms that need to be discarded or changed, and to those that should be preserved and even reinforced.

If the consultant has had previous experience with corporate culture issues, he or she may be able to be more specific in suggesting what to do (e.g. in defining corporate mission and objectives; explicitly affirming the value system; enhancing consultation and participation; modifying symbols used to obtain cultural cohesion; changing established role models; reorienting the rewards system; or providing training and information needed to support new cultural values and norms). The consultant who finds that the client organization's culture is hardly noticeable may be able to suggest how to create a stronger culture, congruent with the goals, resources and external environment of the organization.

Leadership and management style

Leadership and management style are closely related to corporate culture, and certain aspects of style can become part of the organization's culture. Managers tend to behave in accordance with the organizational culture, in ways in which the owners, other managers and employees expect them to behave. At the same time, the style of an individual manager is co-determined by his or her personality, which may be in harmony or in conflict with existing corporate culture. If there is a conflict, it is usually resolved in one of two ways: either the style of a strong personality at the top will affect corporate culture, and be accepted as a feature of a new culture, or the existing strong culture will not accommodate the person's style and he or she will have to alter it, or leave the organization.

Here again the consultant may face a wide range of rather delicate situations in which, even if he or she has no explicit mandate to make proposals in respect of leadership and management style, it may be necessary to find a tactful way of making the client aware of the problems, and help to resolve them by coming up with a feasible solution.

The following situations and problems are quite common in organizations:

- People would like to support the manager, but they do not really know what he or she wants and they do not understand his or her priorities; there is a problem of formulating ideas and goals clearly, and of communicating them to people.
- The manager uses an authoritarian style rather than consulting people, discussing problems and priorities with them, and explaining decisions.
- People are puzzled by the way in which the manager allocates his or her time: he or she speaks about priorities, but spends time in dealing with trivial issues.

- Innovation is encouraged in theory, but the manager gives it no overt support in planning and distributing work, shows no personal interest in innovative projects, and does not reward innovators for their achievements.
- The manager deals with different situations in the same way; this rigidity means that the style used may be adequate in one situation but totally inadequate in another.
- Because a top-level manager exhibits a strong style (which can have either positive or negative characteristics), and favours people who use a similar style, managers throughout the organization try to copy the style even if it does not fit their own personality.

The consultant can achieve a great deal by making a manager aware, through personal counselling, of the strong and weak sides of his or her style. Awareness of one's style is a first step towards improvement. Even if a manager does not wish or is not able to change style radically, it is useful to be aware of weaknesses, to mitigate them, and to compensate for them.

12.5 Corporate governance

General management and strategy consultants have always been interested in corporate governance since many questions for which they are brought into the company have to be examined and decided on at this highest level of strategic decision-making and control. However, until recently, corporate governance per se, i.e. its concept, scope, structure, methods, selection and competence of Board members, responsibility, quality of decisions, inefficiencies, gaps, relationships to senior management, relationships to shareholders and other stakeholders, questions of conflict of interest, and similar issues tended to receive little attention. Often these issues were regarded as a confidential province of the owners, in which external consultants should not be involved, and where the only concerns were whether the Board was established and its meetings held in conformity with law and corporate governance standards (if any).

Over the past decade, views on the role of corporate governance have changed considerably thanks to growing pressure from dissatisfied shareholder circles and the public. Corporate governance is no longer regarded as an exclusive province of the largest investors and top managers. Governments have been forced to intervene to tighten up legislation and controls; shareholder assemblies have become more active and critical; companies themselves have been looking for more effective and transparent styles of corporate governance. This has created challenging consulting opportunities at general and strategic management level.

Current issues

In earlier times the governance process was simple and automatic because the providers of the organization's risk capital – its equity – were directly involved in its management. Present-day problems in governance arise because the diversification of share ownership over thousands of individuals has produced a separation between ownership and control and has, in the process, transferred power into the hands of the organization's professional managers. The theoretical safeguard – that the common shareholders possess the ultimate power through the use of their voting rights – no longer works, because the individual shareholdings are too small and widespread to permit effective voting except in very exceptional circumstances.

The shareholders are, of course, represented by the organization's Board of Directors. In theory the Board is appointed by the shareholders, who can remove and replace its members at any time. In practice the Boards have increasingly tended to become self-perpetuating bodies. Even worse, particularly where the Chair of the Board is also chief executive officer (CEO), the Board will consist primarily of working executives who report directly to this individual and of perhaps one or two non-executive directors whose Board membership depends on the Chair's invitation. In such a situation the Board has little incentive to consider the needs or wishes of the shareholders.

It may well be asked what useful function a consultant can perform in such circumstances. The answer is that a consultant who has access to the Board has an opportunity to persuade the members of the error inherent in such a policy – not only because it is morally wrong, but because it is ultimately likely to be self-defeating. A Board that ignores the interests of its shareholders is likely to encounter opposition from a number of different directions. In some countries, particularly in Scandinavia, shareholder associations have already developed considerable power and influence. This was demonstrated a few years ago, when there was a proposal to merge the car-manufacturing activities of the Volvo Group with the Renault Company of France. The proposal had the strong support of Volvo's chief executive, but failed, partly because of opposition within Volvo's own management, but even more because of its rejection by the Swedish Shareholders' Association. Such action is not yet common in the English-speaking countries, but the formation of the ProShare organization in the United Kingdom is perhaps an indication of future developments.

The most effective restraint on Board freedom, however, comes from the institutional shareholders. The individual private shareholder, owning only a few shares, may have little or no influence at Board level, but the institutional shareholder – a pension fund, investment trust or insurance company owning millions of shares – is an altogether different player. In the past such large institutional shareholders tended not to interfere in the management of the companies in which they invested. The shares owned by such institutions were, in fact, often referred to as being "in safe hands", in that if the institutions voted they invariably did so in favour of the existing management. In recent years, however, these institutions have become less compliant. Some, if they disagree with management policies, simply "vote with their feet" by selling their shareholding in the company and reinvesting elsewhere. An increasing number, however, are taking a more active role, by making their views known to management. If management fails to listen, the institutions are increasingly willing to use their massive voting power to remove and replace the existing Board. In taking action to protect their own interests, the institutional investors are largely protecting the interests of the small shareholders as well.

New requirements on Boards also reflect the current trends towards enhanced social roles and responsibilities of business. Boards are increasingly expected to take the lead and be proactive in making socially responsible strategic decisions and seeking to increase shareholder value in ways that are socially acceptable, responsible and sustainable (see Chapter 23). For the time being, most of these requirements have been formulated mainly as broad guidelines or principles, but it can be expected that they will be gradually converted into specific standards for Boards.

Improving and applying the standards

There are considerable differences in the quality of corporate governance in different countries. The issue is not so much whether national legislation prescribes a one-tier or two-tier Board or allows both, but the quality of national corporate governance culture, which is part of the local business culture and tradition. It is now widely recognized that, despite the problems of governance existing in many corporations, on the whole corporate governance is a more developed field and its practice has attained higher standards in English-speaking business cultures. In other countries and regions the situation varies. Serious deficiencies of corporate governance are found, not only in the transforming economies, where there is little tradition and experience of corporate governance, but even in countries where a market economy has traditionally functioned smoothly and without any major political upheaval.

For example, in 2001 in Switzerland, flaws in the working of the Swissair Board were identified as major causes of damaging acquisition decisions and serious financial losses. The president of the country's national assembly was publicly criticized for being a chairman or member of 48 Boards, from all of which he subsequently resigned. In many countries, questions such as Board member competence, integrity, independence, responsibility, conflict of interest, and more efficient and transparent Board operation have yet to be given proper weight and consideration.

It is encouraging that an important and visible movement for enhancing corporate governance standards has started. A great amount of guidance and support, including training for Board members, is available from the Organisation for Economic Co-operation and Development (OECD), some national institutes of directors and other authoritative sources.[9] Many companies will appreciate the help of experienced consultants who have a thorough understanding of governance as well as of the financial, social and institutional environments. International and wider social perspectives are more and more necessary in structuring Boards and improving their work. Consultants should seize this opportunity.

---

[1] H. J. Leavitt: *Corporate pathfinders* (Chicago, IL, Irwin, 1986).

[2] See M. Porter: *Competitive strategy* (New York, The Free Press, 1980), and idem: *Competitive advantage* (New York, The Free Press, 1985).

[3] K. Ohmae: *The mind of the strategist* (New York, McGraw-Hill, 1982).

[4] A. L. Frohman: "Putting technology into strategic planning", in *California Management Review* (Berkeley, CA), Vol. XXVII, No. 2, Winter 1985, p. 48.

[5] M. Hammer and J. Champy: *Re-engineering the corporation* (New York, Harper Business, 1993), pp. 40 and 29.

[6] N. Venkateraman and J. C. Henderson: "Real strategies for virtual organizing", in *Sloan Management Review*, Fall 1998, pp. 33–48.

[7] For a more detailed discussion of corporate culture, see T. E. Deal and A. A. Kennedy: *Corporate cultures: The rites and rituals of corporate life* (Reading, MA, Addison-Wesley, 1982); E. H. Schein: *Organizational culture and leadership* (San Francisco, CA, Jossey-Bass, 1985); or F. Trompenaars and C. Hampden-Turner: *Riding the waves of culture: Understanding cultural diversity in business*, second edition (London, Nicholas Brealey, 1997).

[8] S. Salmans: "New vogue: Corporate culture", in *New York Times*, 7 Jan. 1983.

[9] See e.g. OECD: *Principles of corporate governance* and related documents of the OECD Task Force on Corporate Governance, *Standards for the Board* and other publications of the Institute of Directors in the United Kingdom; Bob Tricker: *Pocket director* (London, The Economist, 1998); studies and papers available from the Centre for Corporate Effectiveness of the Henley Management College.

13 CONSULTING IN INFORMATION TECHNOLOGY

Since the previous edition of this book was published in 1996, information technology (IT) has developed dramatically. IT consulting has also grown in scale and in sophistication. Indeed, the need for consulting support in order to realize the promise of information technology has arguably been the engine of growth for the management consulting industry as a whole.

13.1 The developing role of information technology

Walk into almost any business today and you will see a computer on every desk. The senior managers who now start the day by logging-on to their email account are the same people who once proudly declared that they could not operate a keyboard. In part, this change has come about through education and new attitudes to technology, but the main driver of change on the desktop is the increasing standardization, accessibility and power of graphical interfaces and the easy availability of applications for communications, word-processing and other common business tasks. It simply does not make sense for managers to ask a secretary to print out their email when they can read it for themselves on the screen.

Communication within organizations, by email and through the corporate Intranet, is now much richer and often more democratic than in the past. Email has become the communication medium of choice in a world of global business where managers are constantly on the move between different time zones.

Radical change has also occurred behind the scenes in the corporate data centres of large organizations and in the computer rooms of smaller ones. Again the story is one of technology power and standardization. De facto standards created by the leading proprietary technology vendors rest upon more fundamental international standards such as the hypertext transfer protocol that forms the basis for the World Wide Web. With a little encouragement from fears of the so-called "millennium bug", many organizations abandoned their old legacy systems and installed a set of interconnected packaged applications. For the first time this has enabled business to have end-to-end flow of information across their value chain and out to customers and suppliers. Consultants have played a significant role in helping to implement these large-scale information systems, such as electronic point of sale (EPOS) systems, enterprise resource planning (ERP) and customer relationship management (CRM).

All these systems provide access to an ever-increasing volume of data. It is often said that managers today are data rich and information poor. E. Goldratt[1] provided a neat definition of the word information: "Information is the answer to the question." Developments in data warehousing and data mining are helping provide answers to basic questions such as "who is buying our product?" Decision support systems are enabling managers to test their decisions on the computer before they commit themselves and their organizations.

Consultants and IT vendors have recognized that the logical successor to information management is knowledge management. IT systems can help to locate and to share knowledge but there are limitations. As Peter Drucker has said: "Information only becomes knowledge in the hands of someone who knows what to do with it."

The biggest development that did not happen in the late 1990s was artificial intelligence (AI). This technology has been studied for decades, but the goal of a truly intelligent machine seems to recede as we try to approach it. Successful applications have appeared in restricted specialist areas and a lot of development work has gone into "intelligent agents" to do searches on the Internet, but AI is still not a mainstream application. And yet the need is great: artificial intelligence offers the promise, at last, of helping us to cope with data, information and knowledge.

E-business is covered in detail elsewhere in this book (Chapter 16) but the most fundamental change of all, the commercialization and rapid development of the Internet, cannot be ignored in any discussion of information technology. Bill Gates, the chairman of Microsoft, has said that one of the reasons for his success lay in his being one of the first people to envisage a world in which computing power was so cheap as to be practically free. We are rapidly moving into a world in which international communication through the written and spoken word, and the still and moving image, is so cheap as to be practically free. It is too early to say who has the best vision for this new world.

It would be unwise to be too specific in predicting technology development but some current trends seem set to continue. The trend towards the "extended enterprise", with information systems that cross organizational boundaries, seems set to continue. Technology will also reach further into the home via the Internet and digital television, putting the majority of consumers on-line.

Another obvious trend is towards mobility. There is a clear need to be able to access the same information in an accustomed manner wherever one is in the world: at work, at home, in a client's office, in a car or in an aircraft. This can be done now but at the expense of some personal time and trouble to overcome the limitations of the technology. The need for simple transparent access to the same information from any location is likely to be satisfied within the next few years.

Increasing bandwidth on the Internet will allow much increased use of multimedia, and this trend will be limited only by the ability to find or generate multimedia content, not the ability to store or disseminate it.

It seems inevitable that the amount of information available to us will continue to increase. Data-warehousing, data-mining, decision-support and knowledge-management technologies are available but are not easy to apply and are still very expensive. Technology has in a sense created the problem of information overload: there is a great need for technology to provide a solution.

13.2 Scope and special features of IT consulting

In order to exploit the promise of information technology, a company must purchase, develop and integrate a vast range of hardware, software and trained people. A reliable and flexible network infrastructure must be built. Databases must be constructed, populated and protected from loss or malicious damage. Individual software applications must be written or purchased and installed. Information systems users must be trained. The goal today is integrated information systems that stretch end to end, from suppliers, through the company itself, and out to customers and consumers. Specialist suppliers exist for all of the components of the company information system: hardware suppliers, network specialists, software houses and application service providers (ASPs). However, few if any companies find it economical to maintain a permanent workforce with the vast range of skills needed to install, develop and integrate these complex systems. The traditional role of IT consultants has been to bridge the gap between a company's in-house IT capability and the range of IT suppliers that it must deal with.

This symbiotic relationship of consultants and hardware and software providers has led to a complex web of business relationships. For instance, the installation of an enterprise resource planning (ERP) system is a large project that can take up to three years to complete. The suppliers of the software will usually have partnerships with consultants who are skilled in helping clients through this difficult and often frustrating process. Close relationships between suppliers and consultants can be beneficial for all parties but can lead to ethical dilemmas when it comes to giving advice on selection of suppliers. Consultants are faced with a range of strategic options, from maintaining strict independence at one extreme to becoming almost an in-house consultancy for a software house or network supplier at the other extreme. Each point on this spectrum brings different costs, different market opportunities and different risks. Consultants should be clear with themselves and with their clients as to where they stand.

The role of IT consultants and the skills needed are evolving rapidly as it becomes increasingly obvious that technology cannot be left to the technologists.

The nature of the experience that customers, suppliers, employees, investors and the general public have of a company is now largely determined by technology. A company database that gives a slow response on the World Wide Web is just as annoying as a sales assistant who offers a slow response in a shop. A badly designed Web site will have the same effect on sales as a confusing store layout. There is an increasing need for a rare breed of people with hybrid technical and business skills. Consultants can help meet this need, both by making the best use of rare multitalented individuals and also by assembling effective multidisciplinary teams.

Is IT really so different?

The ever-closer relationship of IT with other aspects of business implies that IT consulting and management consulting should also be converging. This is certainly true but there are additional barriers to exploiting information technology that are not so acute in other fields of business.

Information technology is inherently complex and obscure to most non-specialists and the scope of the technology is so great that even the information technologists cannot hope to understand all of it. Selection of suppliers is not an easy process and no technology supplier today can offer a "one-stop shop" for all the software and hardware that a company needs. Consultants can help to bridge the gap between those who understand the technology and those who understand the business need.

IT projects deliver an intangible product that is difficult to envisage before it is built. When a new factory is being built, everyone can see the building rising from its foundations and the machinery being installed. Mistakes become obvious before they become irrevocable. When a new software system is being built, future users may see nothing at all for a long time until the system is implemented, when they may suddenly be faced with a dramatic change in the way they work. Experienced IT consultants can help their clients design the system to meet the business need, bridge the gap between developers and users, and anticipate problems before they become obvious when the system goes live.

Technology capabilities are changing rapidly and it can be argued without undue cynicism that technology fashions change more rapidly still. It is almost impossible for any manager to keep up to date with developments in IT. The larger consulting firms are able to draw on a wide range of specialists. Smaller consultancies either restrict the range of their work or rely on a network of consultants to increase their flexibility.

Who are the IT consultants?

It is obvious from what has been said so far that individuals with the skills to be good IT consultants are not easy to find. Consultant firms will often recruit people who have already spent some years in the IT industry. The typical career progression in the industry is from routine operating jobs, through technical development into project leadership, and then to general management. Opportunities exist to make the switch to consultancy at several stages, and IT consultants may have a great depth of technical experience gained over many years or may have relatively little. The breadth of experience will also vary greatly between consultants. Many IT specialists change jobs frequently to gain experience and advancement but they will often work with one particular technology or even one proprietary technology platform, and this will limit their range and flexibility.

So much for gaining technical skills, but what about managerial skills? Some consultants will have gained their managerial experience as an IT manager or consultant. Others will have studied for an MBA degree to help them make the transition from technical expert to consultant.

The other route into IT consulting is from general management consulting. Some IT consultants with a background in management or strategy rely on sound business skills combined with a general knowledge of what IT can do rather than the technical detail of how it is achieved.

Information technology still carries a degree of mystique and clients sometimes have a rather naive belief in the abilities of the IT guru. It would be wise for consultants, aspiring consultants and their clients to remember that nobody can be an expert at everything.

13.3 An overall model of information systems consulting

This model (figure 13.1), adapted from Michael Earl, shows that in thinking about applying information technology to a business, it is possible to gain a great deal of clarity by answering four simple questions: *why? what? which? how?* Clarity about the question being asked will help clients in choosing, briefing and managing consultants and will help the consultants to ensure they deliver what the client expects.

Why should we spend scarce resources on technology?

The answer to this question can only be given in terms of business strategy. Technology can support an existing strategy or it can permit a strategy that would otherwise be impossible. For instance, small companies can now enter international markets through the Internet. A strategic idea like this one is simple enough to grasp, but the interplay of strategic and operational implications is both far-reaching and subtle.

The intellectual tools of strategy formulation, such as "critical success factor analysis" or "value chain analysis", are equally applicable when the focus is on information technology. However, their use requires a particular kind of person: someone skilled in strategy formulation but also very familiar with the

Figure 13.1 A model of IT consulting

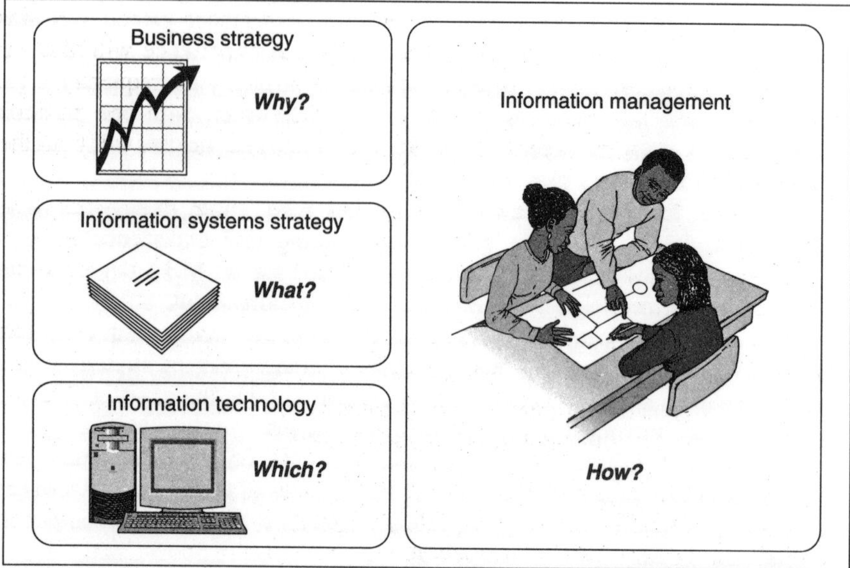

Source: Adapted from M. Earl: *Management strategies for information technology* (Englewood Cliffs, NJ, Prentice-Hall, 1989).

capabilities and constraints of current technology. Most companies will look to consultants to provide the breadth of experience that is needed.

Typical consulting assignments would be:

- investigation of competitive advantage through information technology;
- study of the need for reactive changes to the adoption of technology by competitors;
- review of business strategy in the light of recent technology developments.

What technology applications shall we build?

This is the central question of an information systems strategy. Technology is expensive and no company can afford to waste resources on developments that do not support the business objectives or on developments that are outmoded or premature. It may be an attractive idea, for instance, to experiment with e-commerce, but would it be better to delay this development until the customer database has been improved?

A sound *business* strategy is the starting-point for developing a portfolio of future or enhanced IT applications with clear priorities. However, a sound business strategy by itself does not necessarily ensure an optimum set of IT applications. John Ward's concept of an application portfolio can be used to balance present and future needs. The portfolio can be divided into "support", "mission-critical", "strategic" and "experimental" applications.

Figure 13.2 An IT systems portfolio

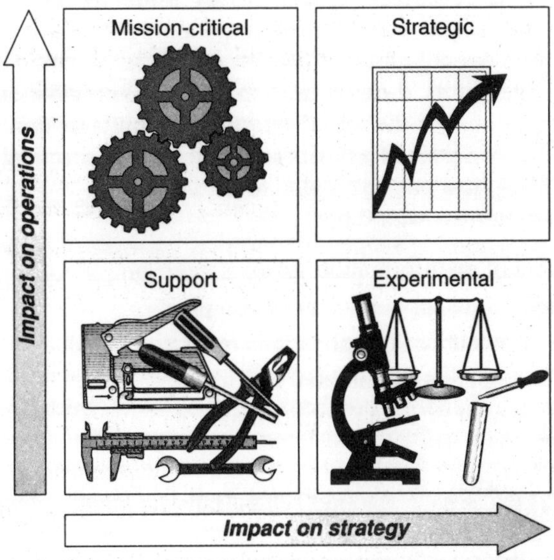

Source: J. Ward and P. Griffiths: *Strategic planning for information systems* (New York, Wiley, 1996).

Every company has a number of "support" applications that are useful but not necessarily vital to the business. Many desktop applications are in the support category. Companies will want to ensure that their support applications are user-friendly, standardized and cost-effective.

Other applications, such as call-centre support, are "mission-critical": if they cease to work, even for an hour or two, then the objectives of the business are in jeopardy. Professional management is vital for these mission-critical systems. Cost must take second place to security and availability. Mission-critical systems are often based on standard software that has been modified for the company concerned.

The company that is looking to the future cannot rely solely on support and mission-critical systems for today. There will need to be a small and manageable number of "strategic" systems in the pipeline. These are the systems that differentiate the company from its competitors or that will transform the business for tomorrow, perhaps by permitting radical new products and services or by changing the way a business connects to its suppliers, customers and business partners. Information technology for e-business is a strategic system for many companies today. Strategic systems must be justified and managed in a business-like rather than in a technical way. Cost must be weighed against risk, potential benefit or even future survival. The systems will either be custom-built or will combine a standard package with company competencies in some unique way that is difficult to copy.

The fourth element of an IT portfolio comprises the "experimental" systems. Some money and resources should be set aside for new ideas and new technologies that might come to nothing or might turn into real strategic applications. The overall cost of this element of the portfolio must be limited but, within budget limits, the emphasis should be on creativity rather than cost.

By helping to answer the *what?* question, consultants can help to turn the broadly based imperatives of a business strategy into a practical and achievable portfolio of IT applications and a plan to achieve them.

Typical assignments would be:

- development of an information systems strategy;
- development of an application portfolio plan;
- screening of potential IT applications for business value;
- financial justification of potential applications;
- risk assessment of future IT applications.

Which technology, *which* vendors, and *which* hardware and software?

There is an English-language consumer magazine that is simply entitled *Which?*. This magazine tests consumer durable products and makes recommendations as to which product to buy. Other countries have similar magazines. Unfortunately, the purchaser of commercial IT products has no such simple guide. Managers must make basic choices about such things as the standard operating system or network architecture, together with numerous decisions on items of hardware and software. This is the most technical aspect of IT application, but in choosing the technology managers must not forget the business needs that they are trying to address. Consultants have a large role to play in assembling a blend of technical and business expertise to advise on these difficult issues.

Typical assignments are:

- development of information systems architecture;
- comparison of competing software systems;
- choice of preferred vendors.

How can the technology and its implementation best be managed?

A company can have the best possible strategy, the best portfolio of IT applications, the finest hardware and software, and still fail to manage the technology or fail to complete the implementation projects before the changing environment renders the strategy or the technology obsolete.

The basic principles of technology management are little different from those in any other field of business, but there is a wealth of experience in practical ways of coping with the unique features of information technology that were listed earlier in this chapter. Consultants can review existing management practices or help develop new ones. There is a wide range of ways in which consultants can help in this field; typical assignments include:

- audit of IT management practices and processes;
- benchmarking and setting of service standards for the IT function;
- assistance with project planning and management;
- providing specialist expertise such as database design;
- providing contract managers to cope with peaks in a company's workload;
- advising on systems integration and compatibility;
- staff training and helping clients to develop and maintain functional IT literacy.

Outsourcing

Outsourcing provides one possible answer to the question of *how* to manage the technology, although it does not absolve management from the need to ask *why* the business needs technology and *what* aspects of technology are appropriate. Some managers who signed long-term outsourcing contracts have regretted that they also delegated the issue of *which* technology to use to their outsourcing suppliers. The latter are sometimes reluctant to keep the technology up to date while the contract still has some years to run.

Companies often consider outsourcing the functions where they have relatively little expertise or interest. In this case, independent consultants will be needed to supply the expertise to choose a supplier and write the outsourcing contract. The alternative of accepting a standard contract from the outsourcing supplier can lead to extra costs or restrictions on the business that are not always apparent at the time the contract is signed.[2]

Ten years ago, outsourcing was an all-or-nothing affair and contracts were for five years or longer. Now it is much more selective and contracts are typically shorter, perhaps as short as two years.[3] This is happening partly because of increasing competition among the outsourcing suppliers and partly because companies are finding it harder to look ahead and decide what may or may not be strategic IT in five years' time. This added complexity in the outsourcing decision offers further opportunities for consultants to add value by advising on what to outsource, how to do it, and for how long.

13.4 Quality of information systems

The traditional measures of success in any business project are time, cost and quality; but what does "quality" mean in the context of information systems and how can consultants help with quality assurance?

A prerequisite for quality is a strategic and business analysis, as described in the previous section; but this is not enough. C. K. Prahalad and M. S. Krishnan[4] distinguish three aspects of quality:

- Conformance to what the system was designed to do. For instance, a payroll programme that allows arithmetical errors or a banking system that is open to attack by hackers is simply not acceptable.
- Satisfaction of the needs of its users. This becomes increasingly difficult as the range of users increases from trained employees, to trusted customers to members of the general public. To quote F. F. Reichheld and W. E. Sasser:[5] "The focus of quality control in any service environment switches from zero *defects* in the product to zero *defections* of customers."
- Flexibility to meet new business needs and user needs that have not been fully foreseen. Many examples of competitive advantage through information technology have arisen because users see new ways of using existing systems.

Consultants can help ensure the conformance aspects of quality by good project management and software engineering. Satisfaction of user needs results from consultation, experiment and prototyping. Flexibility is a trade-off. It must be built into IT products at an early stage in their design and will carry a significant cost. Sometimes it is better to scrap an inflexible system and start again rather than to try to build on shaky foundations.

13.5 The providers of IT consulting services

The variety of providers tends to grow as the relationship between IT and management consulting becomes more complex and as new generations of IT systems become commercially available. A short overview is given here. For advice on selecting consultants see box 13.1.

Strategy consultancies

In the past, the international high-level strategy consultancies tended to work at the corporate rather than the functional or operational level. However, the growth and strategic importance of IT has given them no choice but to become closely involved in IT strategy. The best of these firms are leaders in understanding the impact of IT on business strategy, and the best firms will be honest about how far they regard implementation of IT strategy as being within their competence and their interests.

General management consultancies

IT consulting is the biggest and fastest-growing segment of management consulting as a whole. It follows that any large firm of general management consultants will have a large IT consulting practice and will have built up a lot of experience. One selling-point for the larger consultancy is the ability to carry a project through from strategy to actually running the hardware if necessary.

Box 13.1 Choosing an IT consultant

The following guidelines should help in the selection of an IT consultant. Although these are addressed to the client, consultants should also bear these points in mind and recognize the difficulties that clients have in buying the services that they sell. The guidelines should be read in conjunction with Appendix 1, "The client's ten commandments", which suggests general principles for selecting and using consultants.

1. If you are likely to need IT consultants (and most organizations do), then budget well ahead so that you are not forced into a time-and-materials contract that looks cheap in the short run but may be expensive in the end. You should also budget for time to manage the consultants.

2. Be very clear about what you want. What are the tangible deliverables? What are the intangibles? What will it be like when you get to the end of the project? Decide if skill transfer to your staff is an important deliverable.

3. Be very clear about the scope of the project. "Scope creep" is endemic in IT projects and can be in the interests of the consultants, at least in the short term. Consultants should note the difference between "selling-on" a follow-up project and allowing the current project to drift.

4. Develop relationships with a small number of consultancies. Competitive tendering is a time-consuming process for client and consultant and is sometimes done so badly as to be worse than useless. If you need to go out to tender, then limit the number of competitive quotes.

5. Talk to other clients of your chosen consultant before making a final decision. This is unlikely to reveal any real horror stories but it will enable you to form a view on how well the consultants will fit your organizational culture and way of working.

6. Check the breadth of skills on offer. Is the consultant essentially a specialist in technology or a strategist? Can the firm offer a broad service? Will some aspects of the service be offered through their partners or subcontractors?

7. Make sure you meet the individuals who will be working on the project, not just the senior consultants who are doing the selling.

8. Be honest about your budget and demand honesty from the consultants as to what they can deliver for that price.

Many consultants will have formed partnerships with hardware or software manufacturers. Although it can be argued that this militates against their impartiality, most clients value the increased technical capability that arises from a well-managed and open partnership.

Specialist IT consultants

The growth of the IT consulting sector has fuelled tremendous growth and diversification in consultancies that started out as IT specialists. In the same way that the general management consultants have been forced to embrace IT, the one-time specialists have recognized the need to develop general management skills. Firms that started from a technology base now rival the traditional consultants in size. Mergers, alliances and spin-offs have further blurred the boundaries so that the distinction between the large general management consultancies and the technology-based ones is largely a matter of history.

New entrants

The underlying market strength of IT consulting, and in particular the rise of the Internet, has allowed new entrants to appear and to grow rapidly. Many have started by providing a specialized service such as Web site design. Some of these are maturing into full-service companies while others continue to specialize.

Hardware and software suppliers

It has always been a feature of IT consulting that some of the largest players are the hardware and software suppliers themselves. This tendency has intensified through strategic alliances of various kinds so that few of today's consultancies could claim to be truly independent of the IT manufacturers.

"Virtual" consultancies

The great diversity of skills needed to implement IT systems has facilitated the rise of "virtual" consultancies.[6] These are formed on a project basis and teams usually come together because a leader, either a firm or an independent consultant, has an opportunity to bid for work that is too large or complex for him or her to handle alone. This method of working can be very effective but it is hard for clients to judge the capabilities of the network in advance. It is therefore safest to start by employing a virtual consultancy on a relatively small-scale, low-risk project.

Individual consultants

Individual consultants offer a valuable source of expertise and a potentially independent source of advice. The risks of using a single individual can be mitigated by looking carefully at their track record and their references and by allowing them to prove themselves first on a small project. Although individual consultants are unlikely to have a formal alliance with a hardware or software manufacturer, they are inevitably influenced and limited by their own experience. A consultant with broad experience of different systems is better able to select the right tool for the job whereas, paraphrasing a piece of homely wisdom: "to the consultant whose only tool is a hammer, every problem starts to look like a nail".

13.6 Managing an IT consulting project

Objectives and deliverables will have been discussed during the process of tendering for the consultancy work. However, before the consultant starts work in earnest, the client and the consulting team should set aside time to meet and clarify the objectives further. Investment of personal time will be amply repaid later in the project. Objectives often contain conflicts, for instance between cost and flexibility or between the demands of different users. Many ill-defined objectives have resulted from an attempt to hide these conflicts rather than facing up to them at the outset. If the objectives change as the assignment proceeds, then go back to reclarify and replan.

Plan to have an explicit time buffer between the completion of the consultancy work and the first critical deliverable such as a "go-live" date. All projects need contingency time for unexpected events but client and consultant often feel embarrassed about this "padding" and implicitly conspire to hide the safety time by accepting overestimated times on every single task in the project. Neither the client nor the consultant can manage safety time that is hidden within the tasks, and it is in the wrong place: it should be at the end of the project. Overestimating on each task gives a false illusion of safety to those whose duty it is to deliver the task – an illusion that is often rudely shattered when a critical bug is found the day before the go-live deadline. Risky projects need a longer time buffer, typically up to a third of the overall time available. This way of working requires a different approach by all concerned: more honesty in estimating task times, constant monitoring of the project buffer and immediate action if the safety time begins to be eaten away at a faster rate than the project is progressing.[7]

There should be one person who acts as the client for the project and, if it is a significant project, a top-level manager should act as a sponsor. For large multifaceted projects, the sponsor will need to assemble and chair a steering committee with the brief of ensuring that all stakeholder needs are met.

Clients should think hard about whether they have the time to manage the consultants. It is possible to employ someone – another consultant perhaps – who is not connected with the main consulting contractor to manage the consultants.

Client and consultant should also plan for the time of the specialized people within both organizations who will need to work together. If the consultants cannot deliver a key specialist such as a database designer at the right time, then the whole project will be delayed. On the other hand, if the consultants cannot gain access to the people they need to talk to, such as specialists, senior managers or end-users in the client organization, then they will have a legitimate reason for late delivery.

Client and consultant should work together to develop a stakeholder analysis and keep it up to date. Think of everyone who could be affected by the project and map them according to the degree to which they are affected. Manage all these relationships according to their importance and review the status and importance of the relationship with each stakeholder periodically as the project progresses.

For long projects, set intermediate objectives or milestones. Monitor any drift that occurs in these milestones but do not simply sacrifice quality to achieve an arbitrary milestone. A milestone is a guide to controlling a complex project; it is not a weapon for beating a consultant who is a day behind schedule.

Every project needs its own information system. This can be as complex as a networked project management system or an intranet site and it can be as simple as an agreement for client and consultant to meet for lunch once a month. Remember that "days to do" on any part of a project is a more useful figure to monitor than "days done".

Keep control of scope. Either the consultant or the client may suggest additional work and this may be justified but it is usually better to treat additional work as a separate project. "Scope creep" has been the death of many an IT project that eventually collapses under its own weight and has to be scrapped or radically truncated.

13.7 IT consulting to small businesses

The personal computer and the Internet offer unprecedented technology power to small companies but many small-company managers have neither the expertise nor the time to exploit this power. This leaves them vulnerable to unscrupulous or ineffective vendors of information technology. Small companies have a great need of IT consulting assistance but they may not have the cash flow to pay for it. One answer may be to obtain some form of government grant to support business or technology development. The alternative is for the consultant to find a way of working that is very time-effective.

Consultants who have worked with larger companies should not assume that it is much simpler to carry out an assignment with a small one (see also Chapter 24). Many business issues are common to large and small companies, but some are peculiar to the small ones. Small businesses employ fewer specialists than large ones and typically have little slack resource of any kind. In order to compensate for the lack of economy of scale, they often need to respond faster than their larger competitors. The loss of one order can change business priorities in an instant. Owner–directors may have aspirations and personal agendas that are quite different from those of managers and directors of larger companies.

However, the need to link technology to business needs is just as important for the small company as it is for the large one. Appropriate technology may take the form of one or two specialized high-technology applications or a wider application of standard packages. Company-wide application of complex technology is not an option for most small businesses, and with fewer employees to coordinate there is less need for it.

Consultants to small companies will need to help their clients think through the same IT questions as their larger brethren: *why? what? which? how?* The analysis will need to be done in a very time-effective manner, perhaps in several short stages over an extended period of time rather than by the consultant working full time and producing a comprehensive report. Many directors of small companies seem to value a long-term relationship with a trusted and experienced outsider whom they can call upon for advice or support from time to time. This mode of working can be difficult for the consultant with a busy schedule but sharing the problems and the excitement of small-company management can also be very rewarding.

13.8 Future perspectives

If we are to understand the development of the IT consulting profession and to make some predictions about its future, then we need to get back to basics. Beneath all the turbulent development of information technology, some trends have remained surprisingly constant. The underlying hardware technologies have continued to follow Moore's Law: "Processing power doubles every 18 months while cost holds constant." The explosive growth of the Internet has proven the truth of Metcalf's Law, a less well-known "law" of technology, which states that "the value of a network is proportional to the square of the number of users".

Technology, however, cannot develop solely in the laboratory: it must be applied, and the application must add enough economic value to finance further development. Michael Porter[8] has identified five stages in the application of technology. The first stage is the automation of discrete transactions, such as order entry. The second stage is the automation of whole business functions, such as human resource management or accounting. Many businesses today are in the third stage, which is the use of IT to integrate multiple business activities by using customer relationship management, supply chain management and enterprise resource planning systems. Porter discerns the beginnings of a fourth stage in which the suppliers, channels and customers of an entire industry are integrated from end to end. Finally, he foresees a fifth stage in which the whole integrated value system is optimized in real time. This would mean for example that product designs would continually adapt to the inputs from suppliers, factories and customers.

In short, the underlying growth of technology shows no signs of slackening and there is no lack of ideas to apply the technology. The experts in application of technology are the consultants, so it is natural that information technology itself and the IT consulting profession have grown symbiotically. There is every indication that this growth will continue.

---

[1] E. M. Goldratt: *The haystack syndrome: Sifting information out of the data ocean* (Great Barrington, MA, North River Press, 1991).

[2] J. Barthelemy: "The hidden costs of IT outsourcing", in *Sloan Management Review*, Spring 2001, pp. 60–69.

[3] M. C. Lacity, L. P. Willcocks and D. P. Feeny: "IT outsourcing: Maximise flexibility and control", in *Harvard Business Review*, May–June 1995, pp. 84–93.

[4] C. K. Prahalad and M. S. Krishnan: "The new meaning of quality in the information age", in *Harvard Business Review*, Sep.–Oct. 1999, pp. 109–118.

[5] F. F. Reichheld and W. E. Sasser: "Zero defections: Quality comes to services", in *Harvard Business Review*, Sep.–Oct. 1990, pp. 105–114.

[6] "The reality of virtual consulting", in *Consultants News*, Jan. 1999, p. 4.

[7] For a more detailed discussion of this topic see R. C. Newbold: *Project management in the fast lane: Applying the theory of constraints* (CRC Press–St. Lucie Press, 1998).

[8] M. E. Porter: "Strategy and the Internet", in *Harvard Business Review*, Mar. 2001, pp. 62–78. On current trends, see also J. Hagel and J. S. Brown: "Your next IT strategy", in *Harvard Business Review*, Oct. 2001, pp. 105–113.

CONSULTING IN FINANCIAL MANAGEMENT

14

All consulting projects and assignments involve the use of financial and accounting data, and all management consultants, whatever their particular field of specialization, inevitably find themselves concerned with financial issues and practices. There are two reasons for this. The first is quite simply that finance and accounting provide the working language of business, and it is virtually impossible to analyse the operations or results of any complex organization except in financial terms. The second reason is that there are close and complex linkages between finance and all other functional areas. Decisions made in any area of line operations (such as an increase in the social benefits provided to workers) will have an impact on the organization's overall financial position, and may call for a revision in existing financial plans and budgets. Equally, a decision that appears to be entirely financial in nature, such as a reduction in short-term bank borrowing, may impose a real constraint on other operating areas. Virtually all consulting assignments uncover such linkages.

The present chapter focuses on the special problems of consulting in the analysis of capital investment projects, rather than the use of financial information in general. Even here, however, the impact of financial decisions and policies on other areas of activity cannot be overlooked, and such issues will be examined as they arise in the course of the chapter.

It is pertinent to ask whether the management consultant is the person best qualified to assist clients in this complex area. After all, there are other professionals who work in the financial area: bankers and accountants. Are they not the obvious source of such advice? Both groups are specialists, however, whose competence covers only a part of the financial area.

Managers who need advice on financial matters will frequently turn first to a firm of independent accountants, and in many cases this will be the firm that audits the company's financial statements. Most accounting firms regularly provide such assistance, and are a valuable source of advice on the design of budgeting and reporting systems, and on taxation. The accounting company that has an ongoing relationship with the client has the advantage of a close working knowledge of many aspects of operations, and will have a shorter "learning curve" than other consultants.

There are, however, some serious limitations in the use of accountants as general management consultants. There is a fundamental difference between advising (where the client is the management of the company) and auditing (where the accountant's responsibility is to the shareholders, creditors and general public). The potential conflict of interest is clear. An accountant who has advised the company on key financial decisions should not be placed in the position of having to produce a critical evaluation of the results of those decisions in the audit report. Some countries, indeed, legislate to keep audit and advisory work separate, although the combination continues to be accepted in English-speaking countries.

Apart from the question of probity, there is also an issue of competence. A distinction must be made here between the major public accounting firms and the smaller firms and sole practitioners. The larger companies have developed "management services" divisions, organizationally separate from the audit function and equipped with a wide range of consulting skills. The small firms and independent accountants, however, are often far from being "full-range" financial specialists, and the specialist training of a conventional accountant may make it difficult for him or her to recognize the limitations in established accrual accounting and to think in cash-flow terms, to plan on the basis of probabilities and alternative scenarios, or to accept some of the more recent developments in costing and budgeting.

The company's commercial bank is an alternative source of financial advice. In the field of liquidity management and credit control, the advice of the local bank manager may be very useful, particularly as it will be supported by specialized knowledge about the financial situation and general credit rating of actual and potential customers. But again, it must be recognized that the training and experience of commercial bankers are biased; they may be highly skilled in credit assessment, but are likely to know little about company valuation or the workings of the securities markets.

Merchant bankers (investment bankers in United States terminology, or *banques d'affaires* in France) are much more actively involved in consulting. The traditional role of merchant banks has been to act as agents and intermediaries in the issue of securities, advising on the terms of the issue and providing underwriting services. In recent years, their role has expanded to include a wider range of advisory services, although it remains a specialized one. They are actively involved in merger and acquisition activities, and are increasingly in competition with the commercial banks in risk management and other treasury operations, but they are not much involved in day-to-day corporate financial operations such as credit and liquidity management.

The constraints and specializations of these various types of organization provide an opportunity to the general consultant who can take a wider viewpoint spanning the full range of financial decisions. Preparing for such a role involves a major investment of time, but the consultant willing to make such an investment will be in a position to offer a unique service to the client.

14.1 Creating value

It is now almost universally recognized in business literature that the ultimate objective of all financial decisions – and indeed, of all strategic management decisions – is to create value. In the English-speaking countries this is explicitly seen as value for the common shareholders. In legal terms, this was never in doubt. The shareholders are the legal owners of the company. They provide its permanent capital funds. In a liquidation they have only a residual claim on assets, and they have a claim on the company's earnings only after all other claimants have been satisfied.

Other providers of funds are lenders, who take a limited risk for a limited return. The shareholders take an unlimited risk and commit their funds without safeguards. In return they have the right to nominate a board of directors to supervise the company's operation, and to ensure that it is managed in their interest. Dissenting voices are suggesting that equal weight should be given to the claims of other stakeholders – employees, suppliers, customers, lenders, the local community and even society at large. In practice, the two approaches can be harmonized. Paying due consideration to other stakeholders' needs and interests is both a moral responsibility and good business sense and it is unlikely that value can be maximized in the long run if such considerations are ignored (see Chapter 23 for a detailed discussion of corporate social responsibility). But the shareholders are the ultimate claimants to the residual incremental value created after all the other claims have had due consideration, and maximization of shareholder value will be the underlying philosophy in this chapter.

Despite the clear ownership position of the common shareholders, it is only in recent years that shareholder value has come to be used as the basis for management decision-making. A first step in making the concept operational was to understand how value is created. In fact, three different concepts are in common use – though fortunately they lead to similar courses of action. One approach, pioneered and promoted by the consultants Stern, Stewart and Company, is market value added (MVA), which regards value as the difference between the market value and the book value of a company's equity. Another view is the "free cash flow" approach, which takes the view that value is created only when the cash produced by a company's operations exceeds the incremental investments required in fixed assets and working capital, and sees the value of a company as the present value of those future free cash flows. The simplest approach, however, and the one that will be used in this chapter, is that value is created only by making investments in which the return on invested capital (ROIC) exceeds the weighted average cost of capital (WACC).

The importance of a clear concept of value is that it provides the basis for developing a set of financial strategies and actions – value drivers – aimed at maximizing value. This is an area where finance and strategy come very close. Strategy is usually thought to be about developing a competitive advantage. The reason for a competitive advantage, though, is simply that it makes it possible

– either because of premium pricing or through a cost advantage – to maximize the positive spread between the return on capital and its cost. On the assumption that the company is already using an optimal capital structure and accessing funds in each category as cheaply as possible, the focus will tend to be on finding the drivers that are the key to maximizing return on invested capital. This in turn leads to the identification of the key “drivers” in each area of operations. These will in the first instance take the form of financial ratios. The next step is to formulate a set of targets, guidelines and instructions on how performance in these key areas is to be improved.

It is also necessary to recognize that different operational drivers will need to be identified at different levels in the organization. At divisional level, gross margin may be a key driver. In an individual plant, capacity utilization may be seen as key. For the transport function within the plant, a driver may be as specific as access time per transaction. In every case, the drivers will have to be clearly explained to the people responsible. In the application of value-based management techniques a careful communication of the objectives of the approach to everybody involved is essential.

Shareholder value and executive compensation

Finance writers, analysts and consultants are increasingly aware that the interests of working directors and senior executives do not always coincide with those of the shareholders. The problem is usually discussed under the title “agency theory”, which postulates that the people appointed to act as agents in the interest of the shareholders may have conflicting motivations. A strategy of diversification of products or markets for risk reduction reasons, for example, may result from the fact that the professional managers are risk-averse. The shareholders, however, can easily manage risk for themselves by diversifying their shareholdings, and may prefer that the individual companies in which they invest stick to their core strategies. The problem is even more evident when the company receives a take-over offer: the price offered may well be a fair one for the shareholders, but the transaction may result in many of the directors and executives losing their jobs. The board may therefore advise the shareholders to refuse an offer which is actually in their interests.

One way in which companies seek to overcome this problem is to make sure that the interests of the professional managers coincide with those of the shareholders, by giving them shares or, more commonly, stock (share) options. The practice is a sensible one, within limits, and has the further benefit of making it less likely that key executives will be seduced into leaving and perhaps going to work for competitors. But two reservations must be made. One is that if the awards are excessive the practice may lead to shareholder protests, particularly if the company has not been able to increase its dividend payments at a similar rate. It is important to ensure, therefore, that any such awards are related to performance rather than automatic. Secondly, the widespread use of such incentives has largely coincided with a lengthy period of increasing corporate profits and share prices. If the economy were to enter a period of recession and of bear markets these practices would lose their value, and might indeed lead to widespread demotivation of senior executives who believed that they had foregone salary increases in favour of such incentive payments.

14.2 The basic tools

It will be difficult for the consultant to assist a client in the finance area unless this client is financially literate, that is, possesses some basic understanding of accounting and financial terms and procedures, and is able to use them in a simple financial analysis. Bringing the client up to speed in financial appraisal is therefore a prerequisite for further consulting work in finance.

This book is not the place to set forth the basic principles of accounting or of financial analysis. We assume that a professional consultant has already mastered basic financial skills. It may still be in order, however, to offer some advice as to how he or she should go about educating clients who do not possess such skills. A wealth of instructional material on financial analysis and appraisal is now available. So much material is offered, in fact, that the consultant can play a useful role by reviewing as much of it as possible and selecting an appropriate combination for the client's needs.

Whatever medium is selected to provide instruction for the client, there are certain essential elements that need to be covered, and that the consultant will need to bear in mind in putting together a training package.

Bookkeeping

The conventional approach to the teaching of accounting invariably started with bookkeeping. For managers this is time-consuming and, we believe, unnecessary. The concepts of "credits" and "debits" can also be dispensed with. The emphasis should be not upon how financial information is collected, but upon how it is used in managerial decisions.

Accounting principles

There are some basic accounting principles that clients must understand because financial statements will otherwise be meaningless. The essential items are:

- the concept of accrual, and the resulting differences between "accounting" and "cash-flow" figures;
- conservatism, and the "lower of cost or market" rule;
- the concept of non-cash charges (depreciation and amortization);
- the distinction between the company (corporation), as a legal entity, and its owners.

Financial statements

Clearly, the client must be familiar with the basic components of a financial report. Understanding the balance sheet is important. Some trainers and consultants, however, give undue emphasis to the balance sheet and largely ignore the income statement. The consultant should seek out material that not only gives equal time to the analysis of the income statement, but that brings together information from both documents to produce an analysis of sources and uses of funds.

Ratio analysis

Virtually all financial analysis involves the calculation and use of ratios. The problem is that there are so many ratios, and so many variations on them, that the client is likely to become thoroughly confused. Fortunately, nobody needs to be familiar with scores of different ratios. It is much better to select a dozen or so, and then become completely proficient in their use. But while a few ratios will suffice, the shortlist must include representatives of four quite different areas. They are:

- *Liquidity*, or the ability of the company to pay its bills as they become due. The quick ratio, or acid test, is clearly the most important ratio in this respect. For companies making significant use of debt financing, the times interest earned or interest coverage ratio is equally important.
- *Managerial efficiency*, as expressed in turnover. The most important ratios here are accounts receivable expressed in average daily sales, and inventories expressed in average daily cost-of-goods sold.
- *Capital structure*: the relative proportions of debt and equity funds. The actual ratio used may be long-term debt to equity, total debt to equity, total debt to total capital, or one of many other possible formulations. It is important to choose one of these ratios and to use it consistently.
- *Profitability*, the most important area of all. Ratios include return on total assets, return on equity funds, and many possible variations on these. While all are acceptable, it is important to supplement them with the one ratio that removes the influence of existing financial structure on profitability: earnings before interest and taxes as a percentage return on total assets.

Equipped with these basic tools and concepts, the client will be better able to explain his or her requirements and to understand the consultant's analysis and recommendations. There are, of course, instances in which the client will prefer the consultant to do the financial appraisal, or comment on the financial appraisal done by the client. Here again, the consultant should use these opportunities to develop the client's competence in basic financial analysis.

14.3 Working capital and liquidity management

In order to survive, an organization must be able to meet all its commitments as they fall due, i.e. to pay its bills on time. The efficient management of working capital, therefore, and particularly the provision of adequate levels of liquidity at all times, are crucial.

Definitions

Accountants define working capital in accounting terms as the difference between current assets and current liabilities. This is a static approach, and not a very useful one. Liquidity – the ability to meet commitments and to pay bills – comes from the availability of cash. A company could have considerable working capital in the accounting sense (because of very large inventories) but no cash, and thus be on the point of insolvency. The approach taken here will be based on cash flows rather than on accounting concepts. One of the most useful services the consultant can perform is to educate the client to think, and to plan, in cash-flow terms.

Working capital and the operating cycle

Every manufacturing business has an intrinsic operating cycle, in which materials are purchased, stocked, converted into finished products and finally sold. Even service industries have such a cycle, though its duration is shorter. Cash flows out of the organization when purchases are made, and returns when accounts receivable are collected. Consultants can help clients to understand their organization's own unique operating cycle, and to find ways of increasing operating efficiency so that the cycle is shortened and cash is conserved. In most organizations, improvements of 25 to 40 per cent in cash utilization may often be made simply by careful analysis and the application of common sense.

One of the factors that the consultant should remember (and one of the advantages he or she has over the banker or the accountant) is that the changes leading to improvements in cash utilization are as likely to be in production or other operating areas as in purely financial ones. Improvements in inventory control leading to a reduction in average stock levels, and improvements in quality control that reduce wastage and scrap, will reduce the cash tied up in the operating cycle just as effectively as an improvement in collection of accounts receivable, or an acceleration in the transfer of funds from remote locations to a central concentration account. The very fact that most managers working in non-financial areas do not fully understand the cash-flow consequences of their activities makes this a field in which the consultant has a particularly valuable contribution to offer.

Managing cash

While the entire operating cycle has cash-flow implications, the management of cash itself should not be overlooked. Here, the banks are indeed the experts, and most major banks have actively developed and marketed cash management systems in recent years. The consultant can play a useful role, however, by assisting the client in evaluating the bewildering array of different packages, in which the banks offer combinations of concentration banking, lock-box collection systems, remote disbursement, zero-balance accounts, intra-group payments netting, and so forth, and in finding a solution appropriate to the client's needs.

14.4 Capital structure and the financial markets

Every business organization needs an adequate capital base to support its operations. It has been repeatedly demonstrated that operating a business with inadequate capital – which in British financial circles is called "overtrading" – is one of the most widespread causes of business failure. In addition to having adequate capital, the business must have an appropriate capital structure: the right mix of equity funds and debt. All of this is easily said, but difficult to achieve in practice.

Determining an effective capital structure

A major portion of current financial theory is concerned with the capital structure of companies and with the effect of long-term financing decisions on the cost of capital to the organization. Most of the theory is based upon assumptions that do not reflect reality, however. In addition, the theory is usually expressed in a highly quantitative form. Once again, a consultant who is conversant with the current financial literature can play an invaluable role in helping clients to identify the usable and useful concepts that are now beginning to emerge from this mass of theory.

The management of an organization's capital structure actually involves a two-stage decision process. The first task, when any new financing operation is proposed, is to review the organization's current capital structure in the light of management's policies, accepted debt/equity ratios, market conditions and, most important of all, expected cash generation and use over a period of some years. The consultant's help can be invaluable here. On the basis of this analysis a decision can be made whether to seek new equity funds or additional debt. Once this is complete, the second stage involves the determination of the exact type of security to be issued, the selection of underwriters, the pricing and timing of the issue, and so forth. These second-stage decision areas are the distinct professional field of the investment or merchant banker, and the general consultant should ensure that the client seeks such specialist services at the appropriate time.

Using debt funds

There are great advantages to using debt funds: judicious amounts of debt increase the earnings per common (ordinary) share through the leverage effect, and the fact that interest charges are tax-deductible makes the net cost of borrowed funds relatively low. In general, debt financing will be the first choice if the company can safely add the proposed new borrowing to its existing debt. The key task in capital structure management, then, is to determine the company's debt capacity. There are many possible approaches to this question, but few of them are fully satisfactory. Policies that allow some external standard or institution to determine the decision (for example, keeping a debt/equity ratio more or less equal to the average for the industry, or limiting borrowing to what can be done without lowering the rating of the company's debt securities by the rating agencies) are unlikely to produce optimal results.

In most cases, the consultant will face a difficult task in this area. He or she will have to re-educate clients away from rules of thumb, and convince them that nothing can replace a systematic analysis. The ability of a company to use debt depends upon its ability to service that debt, i.e. to meet all interest charges and repayments of principal as they fall due. This in turn depends upon cash flows.

The importance of debt management was brought into sharper focus by the experiences of many companies during the recession of the early 1990s. The period of rapid growth in the countries of the Organisation for Economic Co-operation and Development (OECD) during the period from 1985 to 1989 was characterized by an unprecedented increase in both corporate and consumer debt, particularly in Japan, the United Kingdom and the United States. The reasons for this were complex. Although strong growth in output (over 4 per cent in 1988) gave rise to an upsurge in capital investment, conditions in the capital markets made many companies reluctant to issue equity. A particular factor in the United Kingdom was that the large privatization issues, all of them somewhat underpriced, tended to squeeze corporate issuers out of the equity market. In consequence, the average "gearing" or leverage of the British corporate sector doubled between 1987 and 1989. The economic slowdown after 1990 therefore caught many United Kingdom companies with unprecedented levels of debt. Interest rates were kept high by the Government's exchange rate mechanism (ERM) policy. Companies quickly found that cash flow fell below their debt-servicing commitments, and a high rate of corporate failures and liquidations was the result.

Could such problems have been foreseen and avoided? Yes: but in times of high growth the attention of line management is understandably concentrated on expanding output to meet demand rather than thinking about the next downturn. Yet we know that a GDP growth rate of 4 per cent is not sustainable for long in mature economies, and by 1989 there were clear warning signals from the commodities markets as well as from the financial world. Both consultants and outside directors should have been looking ahead and advising caution.

One of the consultant's tasks, then, is to persuade the client company to undertake a long-term projection of the cash likely to be generated by its operations, not only under normal economic conditions, but also during periods of economic uncertainty and recession. This is likely to require the use of simulation techniques, and the development of a computer-based model of the company's financial dynamics. Few companies can undertake such projects without outside assistance. Effective consulting work in this area depends upon the availability of a consulting team that combines financial expertise with electronic data processing (EDP), systems analysis, and programming skills. Consulting organizations that are willing to develop such teams can expect growing needs for their services as more and more companies realize the fundamental importance of such an analytical approach to financial decisions.

Dividend policy and share repurchases

The determination of an optimal dividend policy is a particularly complicated issue, in that it has implications for management of working capital, decisions on capital structure and maximization of shareholder value. Payment of a large and stable cash dividend pleases most shareholders, and facilitates subsequent new equity financing. On the other hand, the payment of a cash dividend is an obvious drain on the company's liquidity, and management has to be careful not to establish the dividend at a level that cannot be supported. This is another reason for the careful simulation of the company's cash flows under various economic conditions. Management is usually reluctant to increase dividend payouts, even in periods of exceptionally high earnings, in case they have to reduce them again when profits decline and cash is scarce. Any decrease in a dividend once established is believed to send a very negative signal to the market.

At times, however, some companies find themselves with large amounts of cash, possibly as the result of a divestment. What should be done with it? Again, the criterion should be shareholder wealth. If the directors believe that they have adequate internal investment opportunities that promise a rate of return higher than the shareholders could achieve for themselves, the funds should be invested. If not, they should be returned to the shareholders. Rather than disrupt the established dividend policy, the distribution should be treated as a non-recurring event and accomplished by repurchasing shares. There are a number of ways in which this can be done. One is simply to buy shares in the open market, which tends to be a rather slow process. Another is to make a tender offer to all shareholders at a fixed price and for a limited time. The most popular, however, is the "Dutch auction", in which shareholders are invited to offer shares for sale and to state what price they will accept, with the company selecting the lowest price that provides the required number of shares. The one thing that all of the methods have in common is that they will increase the share price, so that all shareholders, whether they sell or retain their shares, gain value.

14.5 Mergers and acquisitions

Mergers between companies or the acquisition of one company by another provide many opportunities for consulting work. Most of these opportunities come in the post-merger phase, when work begins on the rationalization of the production and marketing activities, and the reconciliation of the different budgeting systems, personnel policies and a host of other procedures. There is, however, one key financial task that must be undertaken before the merger, and for which consultants are often needed – the determination of the fair value of one or both of the companies involved. A consultant may also be called upon to advise as to the method of payment to be used. He or she will normally have either the acquiring company or the one to be acquired as a client, but in some cases of "friendly merger" may be advising both organizations.

Valuation of a company

There are essentially four approaches to the valuation of a company. Value can be based on:

- the current market price of the company's common stock (if the stock is listed and actively traded);
- the market value of the assets;
- capitalized future earnings; and
- replacement or duplication value, which is an estimate of the cost of building up a similar organization from scratch.

The first of these, the current market price, is widely used. It does not in fact give a fair value of the company, but provides a "floor price" below which negotiations cannot go: if the common shares have recently been changing hands at, say, US$50, then any offer that values the total company at less than $50 per share is unlikely to be acceptable. The other three approaches do try to establish a fair value. A consultant may be called upon both to advise upon the method to be used and to assist in its implementation.

In recommending a *basis for valuation*, the consultant should obviously pay close attention to the client's particular situation and needs. If the client is the company which is receiving the offer, then the appropriate method will be whichever yields the highest value: the consultant will not suggest a price based on current earnings if he or she estimates that the realizable value of the physical and financial assets of the company is higher. But when the client is the acquiring company (that is, the company making the offer) the situation is more complicated. The appropriate valuation method will depend on the company's motives for making the acquisition, and these motives in turn will depend on its corporate strategy and long-term plans. If the acquisition is being made simply as part of a diversification strategy and the company that is being purchased will be allowed to continue its operations largely independently, then a figure based on capitalized earnings will be appropriate. In this case the main task of the consultant will be to scrutinize the current and forecast earnings of the company to ensure that they are credible and based on sound accounting practices, and that no special "window dressing" has taken place to increase reported earnings at the expense of long-term financial health.

The consultant is likely to be most deeply involved when the client organization is making an acquisition for operating reasons rather than pure diversification: in order to gain additional production capacity, for example, or to acquire new products that will complement its existing product range. In such a situation it will be necessary both to establish asset values and to adopt the "replacement" approach. Some consultants have developed particular expertise in asset valuation and have become known specialists in this area.

Method of payment

The selection of the method of payment to be used in making the acquisition is a highly complex question which requires both expert knowledge of the financial markets and special skills in determining the tax consequences of the different methods. Possible methods include a simple cash payment for the shares of the other company, a cash payment for assets, a "stock for stock" exchange, and the use of bonds, notes, preferred stock, convertible bonds, convertible preferred stock, or any combination of these. The transaction may be at a fixed price, or may use a sliding-scale payment contingent upon future performance. Because of the complexity of the matter the consultant should recommend to the client the use of an appropriate team of specialists, which will include investment bankers, tax specialists and legal advisers.

Methods of control

Where the client organization has been systematically growing through acquisitions and has many subsidiaries and affiliates, an important question is how to control the various activities. The optimal relationship between corporate headquarters and the operating entities will depend on the nature of the underlying growth or diversification strategy and the extent of the diversification.

In organizations that have made acquisitions only in areas and activities closely related to the original business – an approach often called the "core strategy" or, more colloquially, "sticking to the knitting" – the relationship is typically one in which all key policies are determined by the corporate headquarters. This approach is described as "strategic control". In such an organization the line executives in operating units will make major decisions on current operations only after discussion with the corporate level or within clear policy guidelines, and heads of staff activities in the subsidiaries will be similarly subject to supervision and control by their corporate counterparts.

An alternative philosophy exists, however. The completely unlimited approach to diversification – buying whatever appears to be a bargain without consideration of its strategic fit – was the hallmark of the conglomerates of the 1960s and 1970s and is now in disrepute. Organizations created in this way proved eventually to be unmanageable. But a number of large organizations – with the Hanson Group in the United Kingdom and United States markets being the best-known example – have been very successful through a policy of expansion into "manageable" activities: any product or service that can be allowed to operate largely independently with a minimum of head office involvement. For Hanson, this means activities that are concerned with "commodity" type products and services, requiring little capital investment and no sophisticated research and development.

In such an organization, the corporate headquarters directs through a system of essentially financial control. The management teams appointed to run the subsidiary activities are given performance objectives set in financial terms, particularly return on investment. Superior performance is rewarded, and under-performers are replaced. In such an organization, the setting and monitoring of financial objectives are clearly among the key activities.

Acquisitions and shareholder value

Useful though acquisitions may sometimes be in achieving a company's strategic objectives, a note of caution is appropriate here. As stated previously, the objective of all managerial decisions and actions should be the creation of value for the shareholders. The price paid in such transactions is therefore critical. If the price is too high, value is being taken away from the acquiring company's shareholders and given to the shareholders of the company being acquired.

In almost all acquisitions, the price paid is above the market value for the shares of the acquired company; if the transaction is a contested one, that premium may be as high as 40–50 per cent above market price. However, financial theory asserts that the markets are quite efficient, and fairly value companies on the basis of all known information. The payment of a price so far above the market price, then, can only be justified if it is believed that the acquisition will produce enormous synergy, and that the acquired company will be worth much more under its new management than it was before. Sometimes this is true. In many cases, however, synergy is illusory and the price paid proves to have been unjustifiably high. One of the most valuable services that any consultant can perform for the client is to persuade the chief executive not to become so involved with a potential acquisition that he or she pays a price that destroys value for his or her shareholders.

Corporate divestments and spin-offs

It is sometimes necessary to point out to clients that a company can create value for its shareholders by selling off some of its operations rather than acquiring others, particularly where those operations produce little or no synergy with the core activities but are consuming capital and executive time. The potential for creating value may be even greater if some of the existing operations can be "taken public" rather than simply sold. Many large and diversified companies have strategic business units (SBUs) operating in areas that the market capitalizes at a higher rate than it does the parent company's principal line of business. This was once particularly true of the major tobacco companies, which had diversified widely simply to reduce their dependence on tobacco sales. The result can be that some divisions, which would have a price/earnings ratio (P/E) of perhaps 20 if they were separate legal entities, are instead being included with the parent and awarded a P/E of only 12. If the directors of the company do not recognize the situation for themselves and release value for their shareholders by spinning off these divisions as separate companies, it is almost certain that a predator will do it for them.

14.6 Finance and operations: capital investment analysis

Most business organizations tend to generate more investment proposals than they can immediately finance. They therefore require a systematic method of calculating the economic attractions of such investment proposals, and of ranking them in order of preference so that the limited funds available go to the most productive investments. In most companies, the analysis of capital investment proposals is still done partly or wholly on the basis of "rules of thumb" or personal preference, which again leaves scope for useful input from a consultant.

Choosing among analytical methods

The consultant's first task in this area should be to persuade the client that outdated and simplistic methods of investment appraisal, such as a simple rate-of-return analysis or the "years to payback" principle, are unsatisfactory and yield misleading results. This is one area in which the need to maximize shareholder value appears in its sharpest perspective. Investment in projects that produce a return that exceeds the company's cost of capital will create value. Investment in any other projects will destroy value. The simple methods of the past are unable to distinguish between the two.

The consultant, therefore, should encourage the use of a technique based upon the time value of money. The general term used for this approach is discounted cash flow (DCF) analysis, and there are two methods of implementing it. Most textbooks advocate the calculation of net present value (NPV) and the use of NPV per dollar invested as the decision criterion.

It should be noted, however, that this method requires the company to calculate its overall average cost of capital, which is then used as the discounting rate, and that this figure is difficult to develop and often unstable (see the section "Calculating the cost of capital" below). The alternative approach, the internal rate of return (IRR), has some theoretical disadvantages but enjoys the practical advantage of not requiring a cost-of-capital calculation. It is much more widely used than the NPV approach and should be the consultant's first choice if the client is not financially sophisticated.

The selection of an analytical method and a decision criterion, however, by no means solves all the problems in this area. The various investment proposals facing a company are likely to be very different in nature. In particular, some of them, such as proposals to replace old machinery which is giving rise to high maintenance costs with new but similar equipment, involve neither risk nor uncertainty. Other projects, such as the replacement of a known but outdated technology with an advanced but unfamiliar one, clearly involve both uncertainty and risk. It becomes very difficult to rank one project against another unless some adjustment is made for the differing degrees of risk.

Calculating the cost of capital

In order to apply the NPV approach for project evaluation it is necessary to use the correct discounting rate, which should be the company's weighted average cost of capital. This is not easy. The cost of loans and debt capital is generally evident: because the interest on debt is tax-deductible, the cost of debt funds is the interest cost less the tax shield. Thus, if a company has an interest cost of 6 per cent and pays corporate taxes of 36 per cent, the effective cost of its debt is 6 x (1 – 0.36), which is 3.84 per cent.

The cost of equity capital, however, is not the cost of the dividends paid out (some companies pay no dividends) but the rate of return that the equity market requires the company to make. A useful benchmark is available to estimate this. The general rate of return on the equity market is known. If the particular company under study is considered more or less risky than the market, its required return will be accordingly higher or lower. This riskiness is determined by plotting the past pattern of returns that the company has produced over a number of years against the corresponding returns for the equity market as a whole. The resulting relationship (actually a covariance, but shown graphically as the slope of the regression line) is called the "beta" of the company. A company that is neither more nor less risky than the market is said to have a beta of 1.00. A company with more risk than the market – that is, more volatile returns – will have a beta of more than 1.00, and a low-risk company a beta of less than 1.00.

If the return on the equity market is known, subtracting the risk-free rate (the yield on short-dated government securities) gives the equity market risk premium. By applying the company's beta to this, the cost of equity is obtained.

For example, if:

Risk-free rate	=	5%
Equity market return	=	15%
Company beta	=	1.25
Then the cost of equity capital	=	5% + (15% – 5%) x 1.25 = 17.5%

and it now becomes straightforward to calculate the overall weighted cost of capital.

Sensitivity analysis

In order to arrive at a ranking for proposed projects, many companies will need outside assistance. The most satisfactory solution is to adopt a "sensitivity analysis" approach. Projects that are seen as important but also as involving a high degree of uncertainty should be modelled (simulated), so that the model can be run many times with different values for key variables. A project to build a plant for the production of a radically new product, for example, may involve considerable uncertainty both about the time needed to bring the new product into production and about its market acceptance. The model would therefore require numerous reruns with different assumptions about the time needed to bring the plant on stream and about the likely sales volumes; a probability distribution of expected net cash flows should be developed from the results.

Once again, this is an area in which the consulting organization will best be able to help its clients if it can offer the services of a specialist team in which financial consultants work closely with computer experts.

Follow-up of project effectiveness

There is yet another valuable service that the consultant can provide in this area. Many companies, even those that have adopted relatively sophisticated procedures for the evaluation of project proposals, overlook the need for systematic follow-up and monitoring of subsequent project performance. A project may be adopted because it appears to promise a very high discount-adjusted rate of return. If it fails to perform as well as expected, it is important to find out why. Was there an unexpected downturn in the economic environment? Did the project encounter unforeseen technical problems? Were the marketing staff unduly optimistic in predicting sales? Or were the forecasts of sales and earnings consciously inflated for political purposes by an "empire-building" divisional head? The development and installation of a follow-up system to answer such questions will rapidly pay off in improvements in project selection, and is one of the most useful tools that the consultant can provide.

14.7 Accounting systems and budgetary control

Financial consultants may be invited to assist their clients in the development of accounting systems by means of which various transactions are recorded, collected and classified, entered into the various ledgers and books of account, and finally used to prepare the organization's formal financial statements. This, however, is the work of qualified accountants, and consultants who are not also accountants should recommend that their clients obtain proper professional assistance in this area.

Budgetary versus accounting systems

Consultants participating in general management services activities are likely to be asked to assist in the design of budgetary systems rather than formal accounting systems. The emphasis here will be on management accounting – methods of collecting and analysing data to support internal decision-making rather than formal financial reporting. Both the objectives and the methods of management accounting are different from those of financial accounting, and the difference is essentially one of timeliness versus accuracy. Financial accounting emphasizes accuracy and detail, but produces reports that are historic. If decisions are made only when formal financial accounts are available, it is likely to be too late for those decisions to be effective. Clients need information quickly to support their decision-making, and in this context information that is approximate but timely is of far more value than information that is accurate but late.

The budgetary and control system will differ from company to company and should be developed for the individual organization rather than bought "off the shelf". For most manufacturing companies, the component parts will include:

- a profit plan;
- the capital investment budget;
- wage and salary budgets;
- purchasing budgets and inventory control procedures;
- manufacturing direct cost budgets;
- general overhead budgets;
- sales, marketing and promotion budgets;
- recruitment and training budgets;
- the overall cash budget.

Most of these budgets will be further broken down by division and by department, reflecting the structure of the company.

Budgetary control

The consultant needs to keep in mind the multiple objectives that underlie any system of budgetary control. They are:

- that expenditures of funds and commitments of resources resulting from decisions in the various operating areas do not reach an overall aggregate that places an unacceptable strain on the company's financial structure and resources;
- that all revenue and cost items be planned and coordinated in order to ensure a positive stream of earnings and cash flows, and to guarantee the organization's liquidity;
- that all actual revenue, cost and expense items can be monitored and compared with budgeted levels, and the variances understood and corrected.

One consequence of the recent recession and the resulting strain on corporate cash flows has been a growing temptation to depart from list prices and to accept any order that appears to cover direct costs and to make at least a contribution to overheads. This places a renewed emphasis upon the distinction between full and marginal costs as a basis for pricing and output decisions.

The issue is clearly not well understood by many managers. Enthusiasts of marginal costing point to situations in which the company will clearly maximize its cash flow by taking decisions on a contribution basis. Others point out that in the long run an organization can stay viable only by ensuring that all of its costs are safely covered by its revenues. Both are of course correct. Marginal costing should not be the basis of pricing strategy, but it may still be valid to use it in tactical decisions. The key is to understand the importance of lead times and opportunity costs. Although it has been said that in the long run no costs are fixed, on a shorter time scale most of them are in fact fixed, and any additional contribution to covering them is welcome. The consultant can be of great help in identifying appropriate time scales for the various categories of decision.

The contribution concept is not only used in making pricing decisions and in deciding whether or not to accept a particular order. It is also widely used in making decisions about product mix. These decisions lie on the borderline between finance/accounting and production/operations, and like many other borderline decisions are often made on the basis of imperfect knowledge and misconceptions. Most managers will readily accept the logic of trying to maximize the production of those product lines on which the contribution appears to be greatest. Developments in the operations area, however, increasingly raise questions about the validity of this approach in some important cases. Where scarce capacity in some particular process acts as a bottleneck, it is the contribution per product per unit of scarce resource time that should be the basis for decision-making. Consultants will find that this is yet another area in which they may have to educate clients – and should note that there are some excellent and enjoyable computer-based simulation games to assist them.

Consultants must be acutely aware that designing a budgetary control and management information system involves much more than itemizing the budgets needed and deciding how often they should be prepared. Attention will have to be given to the company's organizational structure and existing procedures. In a large company it may be necessary to create a number of profit centres or investment centres, or even to designate some divisions as near-autonomous strategic business units. In smaller organizations, a simple cost-centre approach is likely to be used.

Once the organizational structure is agreed, it will be necessary to design procedures for the collection and submission of data for the development and review of budgets by higher authorities and for the determination of corrective action. Paper forms and/or data processing programs and documentation must be selected. In this, as in most other areas, the development of the new procedures will involve a partnership between the consultants and key company people from the finance, organization development, data processing and personnel departments, while line managers must be consulted at all stages to ensure that the completed system meets all their needs. Finally, the consultant will be actively involved in training company staff to operate the new procedures and will probably remain on call until the system has been successfully implemented.

14.8 Financial management under inflation

At the time of writing (2001), inflation is not an immediate problem in any of the major industrialized countries. In the countries of Western Europe and North America, the rate of increase in both producer and consumer price levels is below 3 per cent per annum, and in Japan it is actually negative. In such conditions inflation can be ignored in business decision-making without disastrous consequences.

Companies that operate in other parts of the world, however, need to take inflation more seriously, particularly if they anticipate making capital investments in such areas. In many parts of Latin America and in the countries of the former USSR, the rate of price escalation is erratic and has often approached hyperinflation in recent years. Few managers fully understand how to take anticipated inflation into account in their planning and budgeting.

Inflation accounting

The aspect of inflation that has been most widely discussed in business circles is its impact on reported earnings. Conventional accounting permits only the original purchase value of capital goods and of inventory items to be used in calculating operating earnings. The resulting profits figure is therefore seriously overstated because the calculation of profit has not made proper provision for the replenishment of inventory or for the replacement of capital assets as they wear out. There has been widespread debate concerning the introduction of new accounting rules that would provide for inflation adjustment and thus generate a lower but more realistic earnings figure.

Much of the inflation accounting debate has hinged upon the method of adjustment to be used. All the proposed systems seek to establish the use of more realistic current values of assets rather than the historic (original) ones, but differ in their methods.

One approach, the replacement cost or current cost method, necessitates finding the current price in the market of equipment similar to that being used, and using this current market price as the basis for depreciation.

An alternative method – index adjustment or current purchasing power – retains the historic purchase price as its basis but multiplies this historic price each year by a factor obtained from an inflation index to give a new depreciation base.

The first method is clearly more accurate but administratively tedious and costly; the second method is more approximate but much easier to apply.

Up to now, the inflation accounting debate has been largely sterile for three reasons:

- Accountants have been unable to agree as to which adjustment method should be used.
- Some accountants do not accept any form of inflation adjustment, believing that any such system would turn accounting into a highly arbitrary and inexact process.
- Most serious of all, very few tax authorities will accept inflation-adjustment accounts for the determination of corporate tax liabilities. Until such accounts are acceptable for tax-reporting purposes, it is unlikely that many companies will be willing to adopt them as the primary reporting vehicle.

Financial operations under inflation

Successful management under high inflation is not simply a matter of changing accounting procedures. There are practical operating steps to be taken. Consultants can provide services to clients in many areas, primarily the following:

- the development of forecasts of inflation rate, either by primary analysis on the basis of monetary aggregates or by combining the forecasts available from official bodies and financial institutions;
- the incorporation of inflation expectations in the company's strategic planning procedures;
- the modification of capital investment analysis procedures to take explicit and systematic account of inflation expectations, particularly inflation differentials where wage costs, for example, are expected to rise more quickly than selling prices;

- the review of working capital management procedures, in recognition of the increased need to speed up the conversion of financial assets and to minimize unproductive cash balances under inflationary conditions;
- the recognition of the close relationship between inflation rates and interest rates, and the anticipation of likely interest rate changes in planning the company's capital structure;
- continuing emphasis upon the close relationship between inflation rates and changes in the value of currencies in the foreign exchange markets leading to an increase in the importance of management of foreign currency exposure.

Although inflation rates are currently below their peaks in most OECD countries, this area is likely to be one of uncertainty and concern for many years to come. Yet many executives still find it difficult to think logically about inflation or its effects, and attempt to ignore it – with grave results. The educational requirement in this area is one of the greatest challenges facing the financial consultant.

14.9 Cross-border operations and the use of external financial markets

Where the client company is engaged in any form of cross-border operation, either selling its products and services in foreign countries or purchasing some of its own materials from foreign suppliers, a number of important additional complications arise. Many of the issues involved are unfamiliar to corporate executives. The field of international finance is, then, a fruitful one for the consultant with the requisite expertise.

The most important issues arising in this area can be grouped under three subheadings, as follows:

- determining foreign exchange exposure;
- hedging techniques and decisions;
- using external money and capital markets.

Determining foreign exchange exposure

Very few companies engaged in cross-border trading are able to invoice their products and purchase their imported supplies entirely in their own domestic currency. As soon as sales are invoiced in a foreign currency, or the company contracts to purchase items priced in a foreign currency, a foreign exchange exposure exists. Many companies are unable to identify the exact extent of their exposure, and a consultant may be of considerable assistance here. The confusion that exists in many companies arises from the fact that there are three distinct kinds of foreign exchange exposure. The consultant needs to understand them all and to be able to assist the client in recognizing them, determining their relative importance and deciding what to do about them.

Many multinational companies, especially those whose headquarters are located in the United States, are much concerned with *translation exposure*: the risk of gain or loss when the assets, liabilities and earnings of a subsidiary are "translated" from the foreign currency in which the subsidiary's books are kept into the parent currency (US dollars). Such losses are real in so far as they influence the parent's overall reported profit and loss, and taxes on income. In another sense, however, they are unreal, in that they arise from a particular accounting convention, and that a change to a different accounting basis may change a translation loss into a translation gain. The consultant must be familiar with the current rules of the client's national taxation authorities and the degree of freedom permitted under those rules. Where there is no freedom of manoeuvre under the regulations, it may be necessary to advise the client to change the currency denomination of his or her liabilities to minimize the translation exposure.

Transaction exposure is simpler to understand and affects all companies that engage in international trade. Whenever a company commits itself to a transaction – whether a sale or a purchase denominated in a foreign currency – there exists the risk of gain or loss if the value of that foreign currency changes in relation to the company's own domestic currency. If a Swiss company supplies pharmaceutical drugs to a British buyer, giving 90 days' credit and invoicing in pounds sterling, then that Swiss exporter will make a loss if the value of the pound falls relative to the Swiss franc during 90 days: the number of pounds received by the seller will buy fewer francs. The exporter's home currency cash flow is reduced, and the loss in this case is clearly a real one. The consultant will probably not need to become much involved in the determination of exposures of this type: most companies are aware of their transaction exposures. They may still, however, be unsure what to do about them.

The third type of exposure, which is now increasingly referred to as *economic exposure*, is more complex. It deals with the impact of an exchange rate change upon the organization's overall long-turn profitability, rather than simply its effect upon currently outstanding transactions. Assume, for example, that a Swiss exporter sells watches to a distributor in the United States, and that the value of the dollar now falls abruptly against the Swiss franc. The immediate effect may be a transaction loss if a recent shipment of watches, invoiced in dollars, has not yet been paid for. The longer-term effect is much more serious: the Swiss manufacturer must choose between keeping the same dollar price, which will now yield fewer francs for every watch sold or, alternatively, holding the price in Swiss francs constant, which means increasing the dollar selling price, probably losing sales and market share to competitors from lower-cost countries. The need for professional advice in this area is clear.

It is surprising to recall that when early editions of this book were being prepared the size of the currency market was unknown. Best estimates suggested that total transactions in the foreign exchange markets probably amounted to something like US$200 billion per working day, a very large amount of money. The first systematic measurement of the market (by the Bank of International Settlement) was undertaken only in 1989 and published in early 1990. It revealed that transaction volume had reached US$650 billion per day. By early 1993 the market was approaching 1 trillion dollars, and by the year 2000 had reached almost US$1.5 trillion. These astonishing figures mean that total currency transactions in a year are more than ten times the total world trade in goods and services. It is therefore questionable whether the central banks of the world – even when acting together – can hope to control these markets effectively.

The importance of understanding and managing currency exposure was even more clearly underlined by the events of September 1992. During the previous 18 months there had been increasing reason to believe that, at least in Western Europe, exchange rate volatility could be discounted: the Portuguese escudo and the pound had joined the exchange rate mechanism (ERM) of the European Monetary System, and both the Swedish krona and the Finnish markka had been linked to the ECU. It appeared that both the actual and the prospective members of the then European Community were moving rapidly towards currency unification. The need for currency management was expected to diminish accordingly.

The wave of speculation that was triggered by the Danish referendum dramatically changed the nature of the currency markets. Within a very few days the lira and the pound had left the ERM, the Spanish peseta had been devalued within the mechanism, the Swedish krona and the markka had been cut loose from their ties to the ECU, and the French franc was under heavy downward pressure. Volatility, which had been unusually low for more than a year, rose to its highest level since the collapse of the dollar in 1985. The lesson is clear. The currency market is unpredictable, and its size makes it unmanageable. Companies cannot afford to ignore or be complacent about their exchange exposures.

It is important to emphasize that the problems of exchange risk exposure have not disappeared with the introduction of the single European currency, the euro. Currency transaction exposure has certainly been eliminated between two countries that are both members of the euro zone. The euro continues to float relative to other world currencies, however, and to date has been distinctly volatile. The hopes of those advocates of the single currency who expected the euro to have the strength and stability of the German mark have not been fulfilled. A proposal by the previous German foreign minister that the euro should have at least published target ranges against the dollar and yen was promptly turned down as impractical by the European Central Bank (ECB). More recently – and apparently reluctantly – the ECB has had to enter the market to prevent further falls in the value of the euro against the dollar. Foreign exchange management, in short, remains a key part of a company's overall risk management.

Hedging techniques and decisions

Once the foreign exchange exposures have been determined, the next step is to decide whether they should be hedged or covered, and if so, how. Many companies turn to their commercial banks for advice. The local bank manager, however, probably has no experience of, or special training in, foreign exchange management. Consequently, his or her advice is likely to be highly conservative. Many bankers tell their clients: "You are in the business of making and selling products, not speculating in the foreign exchange markets. You should therefore cover all outstanding exposures by buying or selling the foreign currency in the forward market."

Any consultant working in this area should realize that this advice is an oversimplified answer to a very complex problem. A policy of 100 per cent cover by using the forward market does at least lock in a known rate of exchange, but not necessarily an advantageous one. Using the forward market can in fact be considered just as much a speculation as holding an open (uncovered) foreign exchange position: both policies will ultimately provide either a gain or a loss, depending upon the relation between the forward price when the transaction was generated and the spot price on the day the transaction matures. Beware of textbooks offering formulae that claim to calculate the cost of hedging at the time the transaction is undertaken: the cost can only be calculated retrospectively when the final spot price is known.

The most important service that the consultant can provide in this area is to show the client that there are no simple golden rules or magic formulae available, and that foreign exchange operations require a systematic step-by-step analysis and decision process. The required steps are as follows:

(1) Determine overall foreign exchange exposures and distinguish between the different types of exposure as described above.

(2) Evaluate these exposure positions in the light of the best available forecasts and expectations concerning foreign exchange price movements, and decide if there are serious exposures that may produce foreign exchange losses. If so, hedging will have to be considered. For most companies, it will only be practical to cover transaction exposures on a continuing basis.

(3) Consider the possibility of hedging the exposures by operational means, rather than purely financial ones. A company that regularly exports goods to Italy and invoices those sales in lire, for example, may be able to offset this exposure by purchasing some of its own raw materials and supplies from Italian companies. Another method, particularly useful for large transnational companies with a high level of intra-group transactions, is "leading and lagging": a deliberate acceleration of some payments and delay of others in order to take advantage of expected exchange rate movements.

(4) If operational hedging is not possible and some form of financial operation is to be used, the next question is whether the risk is so serious as to require 100 per cent cover, or whether partial hedging is acceptable. The specialized services that supply foreign exchange forecasts can usually advise on this point.

(5) Obtain from the banks the best available quotation for a forward transaction, and compare this with management's expectations about what might happen to the spot rate. For example, suppose a British company has an exposure in Swiss francs, and the exposed position is expected to continue for 90 days. The spot rate is, say, £1 = 2.42 Swiss francs, but the banks quote a 90-day forward outright bid rate of £1 = 2.55 Swiss francs, a significant forward discount on the franc. The question now is not whether the Swiss franc will fall, but whether the spot price in 90 days' time will be above 2.55. If it is expected to fall further, then the transaction should be covered. If it is expected to fall, but only to, say, 2.47, then it will be cheaper *not* to cover the transaction.

The consultant will find that many client companies, including some that have been making regular use of the forward markets for hedging purposes and consider themselves quite sophisticated in this area, do not realize that it is possible to achieve the same result by using the money markets. For example, a company that is based in Switzerland, but sells regularly to the United Kingdom and invoices in sterling, will have regular "long" sterling exposure. Rather than hedge such exposures by selling the pounds forward, the company could borrow pounds in the London money market, use those pounds to buy Swiss francs, and use the francs for working capital purposes. The pound borrowing creates a sterling liability which offsets the long sterling position arising from the exports. The consultant should be able to show the client how to compare the cost of such an operation with conventional hedging and to explain that when the local currency generated (Swiss francs in this example) can be used to repay an existing overdraft or credit line, the interest saving may be enough to make this the least-cost form of cover.

The period since 1982 has seen the development of another and quite different approach to foreign exchange hedging in the form of the currency option. Active trading in such options started in the Philadelphia Stock Exchange, and has spread rapidly. Other exchanges (Chicago, London) are offering similar facilities and, even more significantly, major banks are selling such options on a custom-tailored basis. The option is essentially different from any other form of hedging in that its use is indeed optional – the option holder has the right to buy or sell currency at a stated price if he or she chooses. There is no obligation to exercise the option if it is not advantageous to do so. This approach therefore offers a degree of protection if the currency movement is adverse, coupled with the possibility of making a profit if the movement is in a favourable direction. The pricing of options is very complex, and the markets have unique procedures and jargon.

The option form is still not well understood by many treasurers, some of whom consider it to be an exotic instrument that can only be used by people with advanced degrees in mathematics. This is particularly unfortunate in that the basic option is now being supplemented by more specialized derivatives such as the "double option", the "average rate" option, the "knockout" or "exploding" option and the "compound" option. These are important developments, and can be used to solve some kinds of exposure in particularly effective ways.

Space limitations preclude the examination of all of these recent developments, but one in particular will be described to illustrate the kinds of feature they offer. Many companies export their products to foreign buyers on a regular basis. Consider, for instance, a British company that exports monthly consignments to a buyer in Germany, and invoices the sales in German marks. The exchange rate of the pound to the mark fluctuates. In months in which the mark is strong the company makes additional sterling profits, while in months in which sterling has strengthened against the mark the company loses out. However, the company's overall profit at the end of the year will not depend upon the exchange rate at any particular point in time but on the average pound/mark exchange rate over the year. The development of a form of currency option based upon the average rate enables the company to hedge its real exposure position. Compared with the alternative of hedging with options on each individual shipment, the cost saving will be about 40 per cent.

Here again there is an opportunity for the consultant to perform a valuable service. The client needs to be assured that options and other recent derivative financial instruments are both relevant (even for small companies) and readily available. But even once the client has accepted the usefulness of such techniques, the pace of development is such that he or she will have great difficulty in keeping up to date. There is a need for continuing assistance here.

Using external money and capital markets

Small companies in most countries automatically and quite logically look to commercial banks in their own country as the usual source of external funds. As companies grow in size and sophistication, however, the possibility of using external financial markets presents itself. Corporate management will initially have little knowledge about such markets, and may believe them to be exotic, perhaps dangerous or open only to the multinational giants. This is a further area, therefore, in which the management consultant's role is primarily an educational one.

The consultant can point out to the client that there are a number of international financial markets – the Eurocurrency market (sometimes called the Eurodollar market, although the dollar segment is only a part of it), the Eurobond market, and several foreign bond markets – existing in various centres, particularly New York, London, the Swiss and German financial centres, and Tokyo. The various international bond markets cater primarily to the "high-quality" borrower and a relatively small company may find access difficult. The Eurocurrency markets, however, despite their ability to accommodate single transactions of US$5 billion or more on a syndicated basis, are readily accessible to the medium-sized company, both as a source of loan funds and as a temporary investment medium for corporate cash that will later be needed as working capital.

Banks operating in the Eurocurrency market often pay a slightly higher interest rate on funds deposited than the domestic banks, and at the same time may charge a slightly lower rate on the loans they make. This is a perfectly logical outcome of the fact that the Eurobanks have cost structures that are significantly different from those of domestic banks, the most important difference being the absence of any reserve requirements against their deposits. Their lower operating costs allow them to work with a smaller spread between their borrowing and lending costs than can domestic banks, and their customers benefit accordingly.

It is important that the client understands, however, that these markets involve additional risks as well as opportunities. Virtually all lending in the Eurocurrency market, and a significant part of the issues in the Eurobond market, are made at floating interest rates. The borrowing rate is not fixed for the life of the financing, but is tied to market rates and re-set every three or six months. The rate is typically a fixed spread – a half per cent or more – above the London inter-bank offered rate (LIBOR), the wholesale cost of funds in the inter-bank market. When the LIBOR rate is around 5 per cent this may not seem threatening, but it should be remembered that during the early 1980s LIBOR went over 20 per cent. If the client does decide to use floating rate financing, it is necessary to think seriously about risk management.

The consultant should also be aware of a particularly interesting financing technique that barely existed a decade ago, but which is now extremely important: the medium-term note (MTN). These notes are in effect bonds, but are issued under an ongoing agreement with a specific bank or dealer. The total financing undertaken by a large company operating in the euro MTN market may be US$1 billion or more. At the other extreme, however, an MTN programme can be mounted in a domestic market, often by quite modestly sized companies, with individual issues of as little as US$5 million. Most of the notes are issued with a maturity of between 2 and 5 years. MTN is in fact the most flexible of all forms of financing. Each issue under the programme can be tailored to fit a perceived "window of opportunity" as it arises, using whatever coupon, maturity and currency best match the current preferences of the market. Given the flexibility, speed and low issuing costs of this vehicle, it is hardly surprising that in less than ten years it has reached a size that rivals that of the established Eurobond market itself.

Nevertheless, the area is a complex one, and the consultant will have to guide the client through a mass of new terms and procedures. There is much for the consultant to learn in this rapidly developing field of professional services.

CONSULTING IN MARKETING AND DISTRIBUTION MANAGEMENT 15

Consulting work involving the client's marketing activities differs in several ways from that dealing with other functions. It is in its marketing that the firm finds itself in contact with external entities (competitors and customers) having an independent existence. The firm's survival depends on how well it manages to adapt to the market conditions influenced by the activities of these entities.

One of the paradoxes of the marketing function is that when it is looked at closely it tends to disappear, like a stream going underground. It is first found at the very highest level of the firm, in its overall strategy formulation. It then resurfaces in the organization and management of the various market-related activities: sales, advertising, product development, market research, and so on. This leaves a definite gap in the organization chart. Matters concerning the firm's overall strategy, of which marketing strategy is an important part, can only be decided at the topmost level of the organization, while running the various activities is predominantly a middle management function. As compared with his or her counterparts in the other management functions (production, finance, and so on), this leaves the senior marketing manager in a somewhat ambiguous position, and the same necessarily applies to a management consultant working with this manager. Because marketing is integral to the success or failure of the enterprise, it affects and is interdependent with every other business discipline.

A consulting assignment that embraces the marketing function will usually develop into two quite separate tasks, one at the strategy formulation level and the other at the activities or implementation level. These two tasks are treated separately below. It is convenient here, however, to note briefly a third type of consulting activity.

The third type is market research, the study of the prospects and performance of a firm's products in the market. Market research consultants do not necessarily carry out marketing consultancy, but their findings can notably affect strategic direction. However, marketing management consulting assignments may involve some market research to verify (or invalidate) the client's assumptions about the corporate image, the nature of customers, the perception and use of existing products and needs, and the acceptability of future new products. Since this work is often very specialized and may require substantial numbers of trained interviewers, the consultant, unless he or she belongs to an organization with its own market research division, may find it more efficient and less time-consuming to subcontract the research to a specialist rather than to undertake it internally. The consultant should keep abreast of market research techniques, market research organizations, the areas in which they specialize and the quality of their work. The consultant should also keep up to date on trends and changes in the market research field.

Information technology (IT), using computers, the Internet and telephone networks, is now firmly established in marketing and distribution. Its growth has been explosive, as witnessed by developments in e-commerce and e-business (see Chapter 16). Applications, for the next few years at least, will be limited more by the ingenuity of the users than by the capabilities of the technology. Its effects have been profound and are by no means confined to e-commerce applications. The marketing consultancy that does not keep in touch with developments in this field will rapidly become obsolete.

15.1 The marketing strategy level

Strategic decisions in marketing have far-reaching implications for the enterprise as a whole and for the management of particular functions, such as production, product development or financial control. It is no wonder, therefore, that even minor proposals may meet with strong objections from senior management of other departments. Major changes, such as dropping or adding product lines, committing substantial funds to advertising or product promotion, developing new products to satisfy new market demands or changing overall pricing policies, are clearly general management decisions to be taken at top levels.

A useful starting-point is to classify the client's orientation towards the market. Three classifications are recognized: product-oriented, production-oriented, and market-oriented. In a product-oriented firm the emphasis is on the product itself while in the production-oriented firm the dominant considerations in product design or modification are those of ease, cost-efficiency or capacity of production. In both cases, market considerations are ignored or suppressed. In a market-oriented firm the decisions are based on analysis of market needs and demands. The object is to capitalize on the opportunities the market offers that fall within the production and R&D capabilities. This approach can produce all of the good effects of the other two orientations, and avoids their drawbacks. More importantly, it can identify new opportunities. Figuratively speaking, the management of the firm asks the following questions:

- What are the problems of our customers that our products (or services) can solve more efficiently or better than products of other suppliers?

- Who, in addition to our current customers, has these same needs?
- What particular circumstances of our customers, actual or potential, would suggest modifications in our products, conditions of delivery, after-sales service, etc.?
- Can we use our existing facilities and skills to design, produce, market and distribute this product, or do we need to acquire new facilities and/or skills?
- Can we offer an effective and affordable solution to the problem and still produce an acceptable profit?

The idea of thinking in terms of providing solutions to problems is a very useful one in marketing. It helps considerably in identifying new markets, finding new products for existing customers, finding new customers for existing products and, most importantly, discovering potential and possibly unsuspected competition.

As a very simple case, consider a manufacturer of nuts and bolts. This enterprise probably thinks of itself as a metalworking business, and looks for new business on this basis. But what about its customers? Their problem is joining things together. So the firm could meet competition from firms making welding equipment, rivets, cotter pins, or glue. This threat is also an opportunity, since the firm's sales force and distributors are already in touch with people who form a potential market for these items, which suggests that they could profitably be added to the firm's product line if they could be manufactured with existing facilities. The costs of marketing are high, so anything that can add to the effectiveness of the various marketing functions (i.e. reduce the unit costs of marketing activities) can be surprisingly profitable. Such help can come from selling more items per sales visit, sending out more items per shipment, and turning small, unprofitable accounts into medium-sized ones. Creatively developing products is a key to success.

Another emerging theme is that of the global market. A wide range of branded goods, from jet aircraft and cars to compact disc players, jeans and hamburgers, is being sold worldwide with little or no adaptation to local conditions. Production for a global market gives substantial economies of scale compared with production for a national market, and even compared with multinational firms that adapt their production to what they believe are local preferences. Thus national and multinational firms are vulnerable in the face of firms that adopt a global strategy.

Stated in this way, this thesis appears to advocate a product orientation rather that a market orientation, and it is ironic that the chief proponent of the global market strategy was Theodore Levitt, whose 1960 article was such a devastating attack on firms obsessed with their products.[1] It can also, however, be interpreted as an assault on the marketing excesses of the boom years when marketers became hypnotized with their own jargon, marketing departments were swollen beyond all reason, and markets were segmented for segmentation's sake.

The global market concept is still a controversial subject, but it appears to be widely accepted that the firms that most successfully weathered the hard years of the 1980s were those that had adopted and understood the marketing concept, and applied it in pursuit of clear objectives. Marketing has emerged leaner and fitter. Globalization has also expanded beyond the effects on manufacturers and service providers to embrace industrial and retail customers.

Marketing strategy analysis

Since the firm's products are the hub of its whole marketing strategy, the first step in a marketing assignment should be to analyse the client's whole product line in the way described above, checking whether the products (1) provide answers to consumers' problems, (2) are mutually supportive, and (3) can be modified to solve consumer or market problems. It is also important that the range of products offered is consistent with the firm's overall objectives. Ideally, all the products in the line should be of interest to every customer, and should fit in well with the production facilities. This ideal is unlikely to exist in practice, of course, and a certain amount of departure from it must be tolerated. Consultants should pay attention, however, to the "odd" product, which is in line because it fits the production facilities but is aimed at a different set of customers and thus requires a sales effort out of proportion to its potential sales. Such spare production capacity might be better used in producing items for other firms under contract or subcontract. Also, a check needs to be made for gaps in the product line which could be filled by buying-in, in order to make full use of the available sales efforts. Since each product maintained in inventory requires space and cash, seeking opportunities to eliminate slow-selling items (line consolidation) can be equally beneficial as a cost-cutting/profit improvement issue. Reviewing the product line and eliminating slower-selling items should be an ongoing process.

Such an analysis should provide a sound basis for the consultant's recommendations for potential product additions or deletions that need further investigation. For example, the marketing manager might insist that some sizes in a product line, although very small sellers, are necessary because the firm's distributors demand a full line from their suppliers. This should be investigated (sometimes "demand" means simply a mild preference), as should the possibility of "buying-in" the more extreme sizes. The analysis is also, of course, a prerequisite for a review of the client's new product development programme.

It is widely believed, probably correctly, that recessions bring managers back in touch with business basics that are too easily forgotten in boom times. In periods of recession, the quality of goods and reliability of delivery are generally perceived as more important than price, especially by industrial purchasers. The implications of this for marketing strategy are clear.

In many enterprises pricing is regarded as the special province of accountants, who determine the prices at which the marketing staff must sell. Yet this is an area in which both marketing considerations and cost criteria apply. If a marketing consultant finds that prices are being set by unilateral decisions of accountants, he or she should review how this affects marketing and the volume of sales. This may lead to a revision of pricing policy, including the establishment of new procedures for price setting. The ultimate objective would be to make better use of prices as a marketing tool, but without running the risk that an increased volume of sales of underpriced products would cause a financial loss. It should be noted that absorption costing and other cost accounting methods can give rise to misleading ideas about the profitability of different items in the product line. Pricing is a major tool in the marketing manager's toolbox but prices cannot be adjusted in a vacuum – the effects of a pricing action must be carefully assessed, evaluated and tested (if possible) before the action is finalized.

Another problem area for consideration by top management is the firm's public image – the opinion that customers, current and, more importantly, potential, have of the firm. This should be broadly consistent with the image the firm has of itself, and which its product line, advertising, public relations and sales staff are expected to create.

The consultant who suspects a clash between the client's internal and external images should investigate this possibility thoroughly. How to approach it is a question of consulting strategy. To change a firm's image is a difficult decision to take; the case for change must therefore be very strong. For example, the marketing consultant may call for the help of an independent market research consultant of good reputation, familiar with attitude research techniques. In any case, the relevant evidence should be collected and presented by a disinterested party, so that the client is assured of the objectivity of the recommendations.

Concentration in retailing

The trend towards concentration, apparent for many years in food retailing, is, if anything, intensifying and extending into other goods. For example, hardware is increasingly being sold through do-it-yourself outlets, themselves often subsidiaries of other retailers. Large speciality retailers have become dominant in the United States and other countries in office supplies, pet supplies, toys, computers, books and other similar categories. This trend will have increasingly profound effects on the marketing of such goods:

(1) The major firms will obviously use their purchasing power leverage to get the greatest possible discounts; this drive will be strengthened as the chains fight for market share. In order to maximize purchasing power many chains have moved to centralized purchasing, which means that all buying, for many regional divisions, is being consolidated into one central buying office. As many retailers globalize (e.g. Walmart, Safeway), there is a move to aggregate volume from multiple countries to obtain preferred pricing and promotion from manufacturers.

(2) The major retailers will try to influence and to participate in manufacturers' advertising. In recent years, power has shifted from the manufacturer to the retailer; retailers now aggressively sell advertising and merchandising support without which a manufacturer's products cannot survive.

(3) Selling techniques have changed. A large part of the role of the salesperson dealing with independent firms and small chains is to function as "order takers", and the actual selling function is relatively limited. With re-ordering being increasingly automated through the use of sophisticated computer programs and electric point-of-sale ordering, the order-taking function is being reduced, and centralized purchasing means that the salesperson now deals with buyers who are sophisticated negotiators with abundant data at their disposal. This will entail corresponding training for sales representatives if they are to hold their own in these negotiations.

(4) The spread of house brands and generics means that in many lines of goods major retailers are in effect competing directly with manufacturers on ground of their own choosing. Some brands such as Sears Craftsman or Kenmore have built brand identity and brand loyalty.

(5) New retail formats, which reflect the further specialization in merchandizing, are proliferating: in the United States, examples include club stores (Sam's, Costco) and specialty retailers such as Circuit City (appliances), Toys'Я Us (toys), Kids'Я Us (children's clothing), Home Depot (home improvements and hardware), Office Depot (office supplies), CompUSA (computers), and PetSmart (pet supplies).

At the other end of the scale, many small food retailers are being forced to become convenience stores in order to survive. The different mix of goods sold by such stores is reflected in changed stocking and purchasing patterns by their wholesalers; this may work back in due course to different assemblages of manufacturing facilities.

These trends are affecting, and will continue to affect, the overall and marketing strategies of all the firms involved, and the marketing consultant must be aware of them and of their effects if he or she is to provide sound advice to clients.

What the advice is will depend on various factors, such as the strength of the client's brand name, the technology behind the products (a new product that can be copied in a matter of months has no market strength), the legal protection of the technology, product or concept, the negotiating skills of sales staff, and so on. One practice that must be looked at with concern is that of recouping the discounts exacted by large customers by charging high prices to small customers. This hastens their demise and makes the manufacturer even more dependent on a few large customers, any one of whom could stop buying his products and bankrupt him in a matter of months.

There would seem to be good prospects for the consultant who can show groups of non-competing manufacturers how to provide low-cost support to corresponding groups of wholesalers and retailers. It must surely be safer for a manufacturer to have a hundred healthy customers than four or five overgrown ones. Whether the client has the vision to perceive this is a matter for question.

15.2 Marketing operations

Different firms have different ideas about which operations are part of the marketing function and which are not. Selling, advertising, promotion, dealing with distributors, packaging, package design, new product concept development and market research are considered by most enterprises to fall within the responsibility of the marketing manager. Responsibility for transportation and storage of finished goods (physical distribution) is usually less clear.

For over two years, a Canadian firm deferred action on a consultant's report which recommended the building of an intermediate storage and distribution warehouse, with expected savings to the firm of about Can$2 million a year. The simple reason was that no one could decide which department was to operate the proposed warehouse. While this degree of organizational futility is rare, the case nevertheless shows that top management may have difficulty in making decisions concerning the administration of activities that cross departmental boundaries.

Such situations should be detected at the diagnostic stage and the assignment formulated to include the appropriate recommendations. The marketing consultant who comes across such a case would be well advised to consult his or her supervisor, because organizational fuzziness in these areas could slow the progress of the assignment substantially or even stagnate it.

Sales management

The consulting activities in sales management are straightforward. Proper training and motivation of sales staff are key items to be checked, as is the way that sales staff divide their effective selling time between existing and potential customers, and among large, medium and small accounts. Another point to check is whether the client's advertising is being used to increase the sales staff's effectiveness by generating curiosity and interest in the minds of customers. Such interest makes it easier to obtain appointments and helps discussions to get off to a good start. This aspect of advertising is particularly important in marketing industrial goods.

Motivation of sales staff is a complex matter, given the conditions under which they work. A wide variety of incentive programmes is in use. The primary motivator, of course, is the payments system, which usually includes a base salary, a commission and a bonus component. The consultant should check that the incentive system is fair to the salesperson and is designed to obtain the results desired by the enterprise (to encourage the selling of profitable items in preference to less profitable ones).

Application of information technology can do a great deal to increase sales effectiveness. It can save much time spent in producing reports, preparing orders, and so on, and leave more time for active selling, and it can promote more effective selling by making up-to-the-minute information on stock position and other relevant matters available during the sales call.

As the marketplace becomes more diverse and complex, so must the sales management process. The vice-president of sales must manage field sales managers, sales channel specialists (i.e. club stores, convenience stores, military commissaries, etc.), sales promotion or sales merchandizing specialists, private label specialists, and so on. Many of the field sales managers must also be trained to motivate brokers and/or distributors through whom they sell.

Sales management today must continually evaluate the advantages and disadvantages of assigning sales personnel by geographical area (all the accounts in a given area), channel (convenience stores, department stores) or account (Sainsbury, Kroger, K-Mart).

Customer relationship management

Maintaining and building the customer base is the foundation for growth. Businesses grow by maintaining current customers and increasing their purchases while, at the same time, adding new customers. Obtaining new customers at the expense of established ones is likely to slow growth and drain resources.

Customer relationship management (CRM) is a concept built on the premise that, by increasing customer satisfaction, maintaining databases on customer habits, preferences, and past purchases, and building ties between the customer and the seller, loyalty can be built among current customers and new customers can be more easily attracted. CRM is simply a process with the goal of making business relationships more profitable. To achieve this, marketing, sales and customer services must work together and share available information on the customer. New CRM computer applications facilitate this effort. With the development of faster computers with larger storage capacity, the opportunity to collect, store and utilize data on customers has provided new marketing opportunities (see also Chapter 16). Currently CRM tends to be viewed and treated by many consultants as a sophisticated IT application; however, it is above all a business concept and an attitude towards customers, and is therefore equally applicable in small firms with few customers and simple IT facilities.

Advertising and promotion

Usually companies can obtain good advice on advertising and promotion from an advertising agency, but occasionally a situation may arise in which those responsible are rather uninspired and new ideas are needed. The consultant should check that the role of advertising and promotion in the client's marketing mix has been fully thought out, and is consistent with the type of product being sold: for example, "push–pull" advertising for fast-moving consumer products, producing leads for salespersons of industrial goods, or image-building for prestige goods. Next, the consultant should ensure that this role has been properly communicated to the advertising agency. Finally, the consultant should ensure that the agency has correctly interpreted the instructions in terms of the advertising message and the choice of media.

A common but undesirable practice is that of setting advertising expenditures purely as an arbitrary percentage of sales, either past sales or forecast sales. It is much sounder to plan advertising campaigns in terms of objectives and to calculate the money needed to attain these objectives. This amount may be quite out of line with the resources available, in which case the objectives should be redefined on a more modest scale. This method has the advantage of giving the client some idea of what might be expected from the advertising expenditure.

Advances in information technology, allowing the use of large demographic databases, are leading to changes in advertising practices and the way campaigns are planned and managed. Data are now collected from all types of sources (shoppers at a specific store, purchasers of a specific brand or category, frequency of using a specific service, etc.). The resulting databases (which some consider an intrusion on personal privacy) afford the opportunity specifically to target individuals or groups within a larger population.

In working with a client's advertising agency, or with issues which may be considered the agency's responsibility, the consultant must continually be aware of the sensitive nature of the client/agency relationship and should avoid becoming an adversary of the advertising agency. Such a situation is unproductive and could lead to the consultant's dismissal from that phase of the project.

Distribution channels

The trend towards concentration in the retailing of consumer goods is bringing with it corresponding changes in the distribution channel for these goods. The manufacturer is increasingly being replaced by the retailer as the "channel captain". The reduction in the number of independent retailers, and in their share of trade, is also reducing the importance of the wholesaler. This trend is reinforced by the increasing sophistication of the physical distribution process, which reduces the need for the intermediate storage function performed by wholesalers. Interest charges increase the costs of holding stock and also contribute to the weakening of the wholesaler. This reduction in available options means that marketing consultants will be less involved than previously in assignments involving channel policies. These will be replaced to some extent by assignments dealing with physical distribution.

This increase in retail concentration is also present in developing countries, although so far it is not as advanced as in the developed countries. In developing countries the wholesaler is still an important factor in the distribution channel. However, consultants should be aware that many manufacturers, particularly the larger ones, have a tendency to maintain large sales forces who visit retailers directly, bypassing the wholesalers. This may be because of a desire by marketing managers to keep tighter control, but unless the manufacturer has a wide product range it is likely to be excessively costly. The consultant should be able to evaluate the costs of this and other alternatives.

Franchising is a form of distribution channel which has been widespread in the United States for many years, and is now increasingly found elsewhere. Marketing consultants have seldom had much work with franchises, but this will probably change as an ever wider variety of goods and services is marketed through this type of structure.

New product development

New product development is very much an interdepartmental process, involving overall strategy, marketing, R&D, engineering, production, finance, sales, and so on. Information about the size of the potential market, competing products, competitors' possible reactions, prices, the way customers will use the product, even the ability of distributors to provide maintenance and repair services, should be analysed and evaluated at the very beginning, if the design work is to start off in the right direction. The marketing department's involvement should, if anything, increase as the development progresses.

The consultant's role in this function is twofold. In the first place, the consultant should verify that the marketing department can supply reliable information of the type described and, if not, advise on how to develop that capability. Secondly, he or she must ensure that accurate and usable data are provided to all functional groups involved in the process and that all parties are in agreement on the assumptions made.

New product development is a vital function, because the firm's future lies in these products or services. Yet the process of new product development is very often a hit-and-miss affair, which attracts little attention from top management.

Packaging

Package design, both structural and graphic, is an intrinsic part of new product design, and is often the major component in refurbishing existing products. Its importance, particularly in the case of fast-moving consumer goods, is often underrated. The package can enhance convenience of use (as in the case of spray containers for window-cleaning products) or can even be used for other purposes (as when honey is packaged in coffee mugs or beer mugs), thus giving otherwise indistinguishable products a distinct competitive edge.

Attractive packaging design is a way of getting customers' attention on crowded supermarket shelves, particularly in health and beauty aids. There is also an opportunity to create a coherent brand image by developing a matched set of containers for a range of products. At the same time the package must satisfy retailers' requirements for stackability (there was a case of an otherwise excellent product which failed because it was in a wedge-shaped package which could not be stacked on the shelf), and protection against pilferage, damage and tampering in transit, in storage, or at the retail store. At the wholesaler and bulk transport level the package has to meet dimensional requirements for being held on pallets or in containers without excessive waste of space.

In the industrial goods field as well, packaging must primarily take into account the requirements of product protection, and storage on pallets and in containers. Even here, the concept of value added in packaging can be used constructively. For example, diesel-generator sets could be shipped in standardized containers which could be reassembled on site to form sheds for the equipment.

Modern materials and techniques are making packaging a rapidly developing area. The consultant who expects to undertake marketing assignments should keep abreast of these developments. Subscriptions to one or two of the relevant trade journals and visits to exhibitions could be good professional investments.

15.3 Consulting in commercial enterprises

In commercial enterprises, stock turnover is one of the key issues. In a well-run firm this forms the focal point of all activities; purchasing and stock level planning are based on stock rotation objectives. The consultant's first task in such enterprises should be to check the stock (inventory) control procedures. If these are found to be unsatisfactory, suitable procedures will have to be established. Different types of goods need different stock-control systems, and seasonal sales fluctuations (e.g. Christmas, beginning of school year, etc.) must be anticipated in inventory planning.

The establishment of stock-control procedures comes first, because further work will need the data such procedures will produce. Indeed, very often the assignment aims to achieve no more than the installation of good stock-control procedures and the training of management in using stock-control data for planning and administration. In recent years the concept of just-in-time inventory management has become very popular. It allows a business to keep inventory levels at a minimum while reducing the risks of running out of stock.

Some assignments, however, will also have various general management aspects (e.g. setting up management-by-objectives (MBO) programmes in multidepartment firms), and sometimes training in specialized techniques will have to be arranged.

The above account for the bulk of what might be called corrective or remedial consulting activities in commercial enterprises. Some firms, however, get themselves into more serious trouble through unsound policies. In these cases the remedies are usually obvious, if drastic, and the consultant's main function is to provide management with the support needed to make disagreeable or unpalatable decisions.

For example, a retailer of luxury goods (watches, sports goods, and so on) might have been enticed into giving extended credit terms because it is so much easier to sell such goods in this way, only to find accounts receivable equal to six months' sales or more.

Quite often retailers will pick store locations that are unsuitable for the goods they handle, for example, trying to sell large household items in a convenience store site or vice versa. A variation of this situation is the case of the real-estate developer, with little knowledge of retailing or consumer behaviour, who builds a shopping centre and leases space to retailers who are inappropriate for that location. Problems of this kind tend to appear soon after the shopping centre "boom" starts in any area; they are quite common in many developing countries.

15.4 International marketing

There was a time when international trade consisted of developing countries exporting raw materials to, and importing manufactured goods from, developed countries. This simple dichotomy is no longer valid. A rapidly growing variation of this theme (which will probably become dominant in the not-too-distant future) is that developed countries export manufacturing technologies to developing countries, with manufactured goods flowing in the other direction. This leads to corresponding changes in marketing consulting, with developed-country consultants being asked to evaluate prospective host-country markets in connection with proposed technology-transfer activities through joint ventures or other arrangements, and developing-country consultants having to evaluate developed-country markets for manufactured goods and set up suitable marketing channels. Consultants in both developed and developing countries will need knowledge of export credit guarantee systems, preferential tariff systems, "most favoured nation" and World Trade Organization agreements, and other arrangements that influence international trading. They will also, of course, have to find out how much of their marketing experience is culture specific, and so not transferable to other countries.

In the future, international trade alliances such as the North American Free Trade Agreement (NAFTA) between the United States, Canada and Mexico, or the Maastricht Treaty in Europe could substantially change the way products are produced and marketed in these areas.

In addition to these new trends in international marketing, the consultant may be asked to advise on the more traditional form of export marketing. This differs from international marketing in degree rather than in kind, the principal differences being the complications of the required paperwork (shipping firms will usually take the responsibility for this) and the additional difficulties of working with distributors in a remote country (language, distance, product training and support, etc.). Banks, with their international contacts, can be helpful in checking references and credit ratings, and the exporter and consultant can call upon the services of the commercial attaché of the national embassy in the destination country.

The main point to keep in mind about going into exporting is that it is not a quick fix for getting rid of surplus goods or finding an outlet for spare production capacity. Developing an effective international distribution network requires time and effort, and must be taken very seriously if any success is to be achieved. There must be a definite commitment of financial and human resources to a planned programme with a specific objective.

15.5 Physical distribution

At long last physical distribution (often referred to as logistics) is coming to be regarded as a distinct and serious activity, accounting for a substantial part of the total costs of an enterprise. Consultants will find themselves increasingly being asked for advice in this area.

Complications can arise in such assignments from three sources. First, there is the problem of arriving at a clear definition of the authority and responsibilities of the distribution manager, as the physical distribution function is affected by decisions made in all departments, from purchasing through to sales, and procedures that minimize costs within each department will not necessarily result in the lowest overall cost. This can result in difficulties in reconciling conflicting objectives. Secondly, very few firms have cost-accounting systems geared to reporting physical distribution costs, so the assignment will usually have to be extended to include changes in cost accounting. Thirdly, although a substantial amount of operations research work has been done in this area and useful results obtained on some topics (for example, vehicle scheduling), there are still no algorithms that can conveniently be used in physical distribution planning for calculating how to arrive at overall lowest costs. Trial-and-error methods are too time-consuming to be practicable in a system of any complexity. Computer-based simulation programs ease this problem, and the advent of decentralized computer availability can make such programs part of the regular toolkit of physical distribution management. Specialized software, electronic data interchange (EDI) and electronic funds transfer (EFT) are all elements in the management of the supply chain into and out of the plants.

15.6 Public relations

Public relations (PR) is a component of the marketing mix, and at the same time transcends marketing in that it addresses a much wider audience than simply the firm's customers. This audience includes the general public, government regulating agencies, shareholders, and the firm's employees themselves. However, it is in the nature of PR that the corporate image it seeks to create in the minds of these various audiences will inevitably feed back into and affect the image held by the firm's customers. For instance, a presentation given to stock market analysts and reported in the financial pages of the newspapers cannot be kept secret from customers. It is therefore important for the marketing department to be involved in the design of PR campaigns to avoid creating conflicting images.

Expenditure on PR has increased dramatically in recent years, as companies have started to use it proactively rather than simply reactively. Press conferences are tending to replace (at much greater expense) press releases. PR consultants are being brought in to train executives in how to handle media interviews or manage crises (e.g. product recalls) and to advise on corporate image creation.

The consultant should check that the images which the client's advertising and PR efforts seek to create are consistent with each other, and that there is close liaison between the marketing and the PR functions. The consultant may also recommend training in dealing with media interviews for some senior managers. Statements made by named officers of the firm carry much more conviction than those made by an anonymous spokesperson, but this is a two-edged weapon, and a poorly handled interview can generate undesirable publicity even if the underlying situation is favourable to the firm.

---

[1] T. Levitt: "Marketing myopia", in *Harvard Business Review*, July–Aug. 1960, pp. 45–56. See also idem: *The marketing imagination* (New York, The Free Press, 1983).

CONSULTING IN E-BUSINESS 16

E-business consulting is a broad subject covering everything from advice on strategy to building an Internet site, to implementation interventions in business activities. It includes strategy formulation, marketing, IT infrastructure development, financial management, human resources developments – in short, every part of business activity. It also includes services provided to public administration, where the term "e-government" is increasingly used (see section 26.5).

This chapter focuses on some areas that are specific to e-business consulting. It aims to convey an appreciation of where the "e-part" within management consulting can add real value. It should be noted that the speed of development of e-business is extremely fast and the landscape is changing continuously.

16.1 The scope of e-business consulting

The key aspect of e-business is its focus on digitization of business processes. The universal connectivity permitted by the growth of the Internet and a standardized way of communicating across different computing platforms is shifting the balance of importance from the physical world to the digital world. While in the past physical assets, such as production capacity, transport capacity and labour, were strategic assets, today information, digital network channels and knowledge are considered of higher value.

Figure 16.1 illustrates the types of e-commerce relationship between buyer and seller, according to whether the relationship is a business-to-business (B2B) or business-to-consumer (B2C) interaction. The upper two quadrants are traditional business interactions; however, the lower two quadrants are worth some attention. The C2C quadrant is not new in that the second-hand goods pages in newspapers have long offered a channel for matching buyer and seller. What is different is the enormous reach and volume that trading sites, such as

Figure 16.1 Classification of the connected relationship

		Buyer: Business	Buyer: Consumer
Seller	Business	**B2B** Integration of the value chain through direct connections or online marketplaces	**B2C** Online stores and shopping sites in consumer goods, travel and information sites
	Consumer	**C2B** Online aggregation of purchasing power by consumers in consumer goods and travel	**C2C** Connecting customers with other consumers to sell goods or create online communities

eBay.com, have achieved in a relatively short time. The C2B box may not be strictly correctly labelled as consumers rarely sell to business. The quadrant is however relevant as it reflects the phenomenon of consumers creating virtual and short-term coöperatives via the Internet, turning the tables on business by inviting "tenders" for supply of goods and services. A good example of this type of cooperation is letsbuyit.com.

In this chapter we will use the now popular term "dot.com" to refer to a primarily Internet-based business which uses the Internet to transform or significantly reshape a market or business process. A good example of a dot.com is Amazon.com, which has reshaped the book retailing market. Companies such as Yahoo, which have created new markets on the Internet, are also dot.coms. The term "bricks-and-clicks" refers to businesses in existing markets that use IT technology to transform business processes and that communicate with customers and partners via the Internet. An example is ThomasCook.com, which transferred a good part of its business of selling holidays and travel to the Internet. Cisco Systems, with its end-to-end Internet-connected business processes, provides another example of how companies can achieve competitive advantage in a traditional market. In fact, the bricks-and-clicks approach is as much about organizational speed, flexibility and an ability to make things happen as it is about Internet technology.

This approach has to be compared with that of the vast majority of companies, which at best have a static Web site with no commercial transactions, and use email only for internal communication. These companies will be referred to as "bricks-and-mortar" companies; some of these aspire to move their business to a bricks-and-clicks set-up.

The focus on digitization of business processes creates a technology-based overlay on functional and interdisciplinary management consulting. The consultant working on an e-business consulting assignment therefore needs additional expertise in this area.

To give guidance on where e-business consulting is often used, we first segment the market into different types of organizations with differing consulting requirements. Figure 16.2 sets out the structure that will be used in this chapter.

Much of the e-business consulting for bricks-and-mortar and bricks-and-clicks companies builds on existing processes. In addition to business firms, this group also embraces government (public administration) organizations. The main differences between this group and the dot.coms are:

- The dot.com entrepreneur or team often lacks the skills required to get the business off the ground.
- The perceived need for fast launch and business development makes outsourcing and buy-ins by dot.coms a large part of the IT infrastructure and business processes.

This contrasts with a bricks-and-mortar company, which has an existing organizational structure and IT infrastructure structure and is generally well established in a mature and slow-moving market.

A hybrid of the two types is a bricks-and-mortar organization that sets up a separate dot.com, fully funded, in partnership with other companies or through venture-capital providers. These hybrids are often connected to traditional (legacy) systems and company cultures with the added challenge of competing in a new, fast-moving, entrepreneurial and risk-taking business environment.

It could be argued that the biggest shortfall in management expertise is in bricks-and-mortar companies, whose managers lack e-business understanding and IT knowledge. Indeed, much e-business management consulting is about filling this gap. The consultant must therefore (a) possess adequate expertise in both business and technology, and (b) ensure that the organization has internalized the new business requirements before closing the assignment.

The e-business consulting field can be viewed from either a functional perspective or a market perspective. The *functional view* would divide the field into four disciplines:

- strategy development,
- creative interface design,
- technology deployment,
- organizational implementation support.

The *market perspective*, whether it is a B2C or B2B proposition, changes the balance of importance between the four disciplines above. A B2C proposition requires first-class skills in Web site design, so that the look, feel and ease of navigation of the site encourage purchases and repeat visits. For instance, the content and design of a Web site for the travel industry needs to

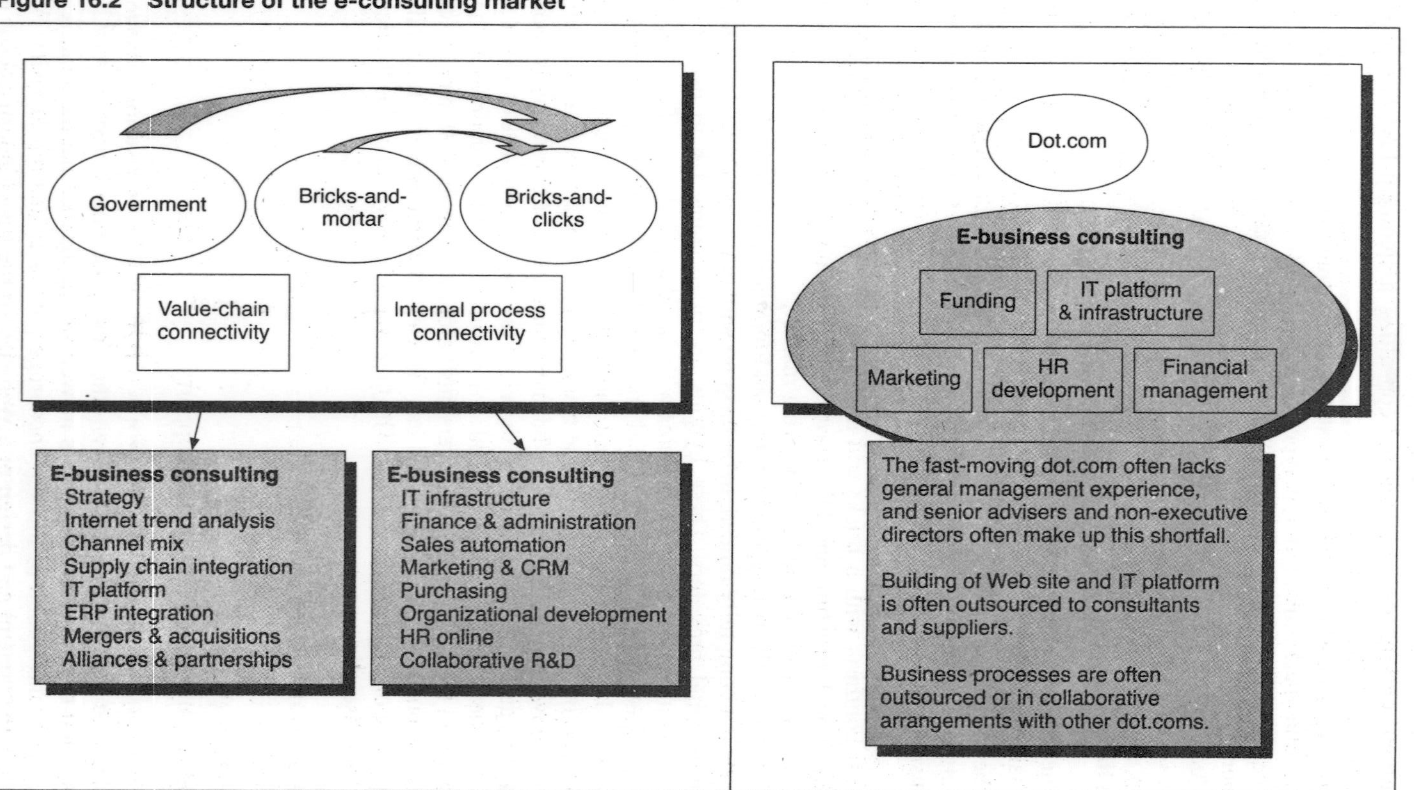

Figure 16.2 Structure of the e-consulting market

respond to the customers' holiday dreams and aspirations. In a B2B proposition, although it is important that the Web site is attractive and easy to navigate, the crucial factor is its integration with back-office systems and real-time information from various sources. The technology integration in B2B either extends directly into the customers' enterprise resource planning (ERP) systems or connects with customers via online marketplaces and portals.

In migrating to a bricks-and-clicks environment, the degree of success will depend on the strategy, the Web site design, and choice of technology, but also critically on how well the organization is able to implement the resulting organizational changes. The historical record of technology-led change should teach us this; however, it is fascinating to observe how often the organizational implications are neglected.

E-business consulting in bricks-and-mortar and bricks-and-clicks organizations, both in business and government organizations, can be divided into the *external perspective* (value-chain connectivity) and the *internal perspective* (internal processes). In some areas the issues are the same but the viewpoint is different. In particular, the internal perspective often has a strong element of organizational impact.

16.2 Bricks-and-mortar and bricks-and-clicks: value-chain connectivity

Strategy formulation

Much has been written about the demise of the traditional strategy analysis tools, such as PEST (political, economic, sociocultural, technological) analysis of the external environment, industry analysis such as Michael Porter's five forces analysis, value-chain analysis, generic strategies such as differentiation and achieving lowest-cost positions, and core competencies. The reality is that these tools and techniques are still valid for use in highly uncertain business environments such as the Internet. In fact, they provide frameworks for analysing business strategy in competitive environments (see also Chapter 12). It can therefore be concluded that the traditional strategy consulting firms, such as McKinsey and Boston Consulting Group, will continue to offer value and thrive in the Internet era.[1]

What is also clear, however, is that the strategic intent must be evaluated substantially more frequently in the new environment. The traditional 3-5 year planning horizon no longer holds and organizations must be prepared to change direction immediately in the face of new developments in the business environment. The question of potential new competitors must be taken very seriously and asked much more broadly than in the past. Analysis of the core competencies required to compete in a market is increasingly important as more and more of the organization's value is based on its intellectual capital. New competitors may find the barriers to entering a market relatively low if they

Box 16.1 British Telecom entering new markets

Deregulation and international competition in the telecommunications industry has put increased downward pressure on prices for voice and data transmission. The search for new sources of revenue by previously state-owned telecommunications companies, such as British Telecom (BT), has created new entrants in a number of market sectors. BT, for instance, is applying some of its core competencies in managed business services, and in management consulting is using what it has learnt from "e-enabling" itself.

Managed business services

Few in IBM or Accenture would have considered BT a potential new entrant in the market for managed business services in the mid-1990s. Managing complex computer networks, high network availability, strong security and software expertise are the core competencies in this sector. This is in fact BT's core expertise, and it has entered the market by offering Internet-based business services, such as supply chain management, customer relationship management, IT services etc. Sitting as a spider in the networked economy is a great vantage point and BT is working hard to capitalize on this position.

Consulting services

BT is a large organization with more than 100,000 employees. To meet the new challenging environment they have had to adjust their strategies, implement sweeping changes and move swiftly at the strategic level. The need to reduce costs has resulted in the goal to have 4000 of its employees working from home and a large part of the staff learning how to operate as a roaming workforce. To do this BT has used technology extensively and is now converting what it has learnt to a growing management consulting service, helping organizations harness technology and implement organizational change.

The BT.com web site provides an extensive list of case studies on home working, implementing communications technology and general business advice.

Source: www.BT.com (11 March 2001).

have the critical knowledge and skills that a new business environment requires. An example of new competition is British Telecom's entry into the consulting and managed business services (outsourced and new services) arena (box 16.1).

The analysis of substitute products and services is more challenging in an Internet environment due to the reliance on technology and IT systems. Rapid development means that current technology may be obsolete much sooner than expected. As a consequence, good consulting advice requires excellent knowledge of technological trends both as products and as business support infrastructure.

Where the Internet certainly imposes major challenges for advisers and consultants is in analysing new services and business models. This is the known dilemma of asking potential customers and business partners about a new product or service they have never seen before. The classic anecdotal example is of a major consulting organization advising Ericsson in the early 1980s that mobile phones, which at that time weighed one kilogram and had a battery life of a few hours, were unlikely to be important mass-market products in the future!

Despite the difficulty of predicting the future, the traditional tools of marketing consultants – focus groups, mock-ups of products and services, scenario-building processes – continue to be useful techniques for evaluating markets for new products and services.

New business models

The response to new business models may have more scope to draw on existing experiences than the current debate would indicate. All the so-called "new" market models that have been connected with the Internet "model" have in fact their equivalent in the off-line world (see box 16.2).

What is "new" is that these models are applied in new business environments, and the global connectivity of the Internet offers very fast growth and business development in new segments. The nightmare scenario of many CEOs is that someone will enter his or her market with a different business model and change the financial dynamics of the market overnight. An example of this is offering high-value content for free on a Web site that generates revenue from another source, such as e-commerce transactions and advertising.

One of the first actions in an e-business strategy consulting assignment should be to address the question of *potential new business models*. The fundamental question that must be answered is which part(s) of the organization's business environment and markets is or could be digitized, i.e. could be transferred to and stored on a computer. Let us take, as an example, retail sales of petrol. Clearly, the actual product cannot be transferred to a computer. However, the service of providing petrol has considerable information value, i.e. where the nearest petrol station is, the most convenient way to it from the current position of the car, and the current price of petrol. The mobile Internet services in development are addressing exactly these questions and therefore have the possibility of entering the value chain of petrol retailing. To ensure that the current retailers of petrol are not marginalized, with new players taking value out of the value chain, the major oil companies are investigating how this new technology is likely to affect their business and what should be their strategic response. Taking the analysis a step further, car and truck manufacturers have a prime position as the driver is likely to be in the car or truck when requiring information on the nearest petrol station. Consequently, the manufacturers are investigating what type of in-car connectivity and services they could offer, hence taking value out of the petrol retail market's value chain.

As this example suggests, there is still a traditional value chain involved, with the various players capturing value depending on their bargaining power. The barriers to entry, building of potential switching costs, competencies required to compete, and establishing the value to the user are traditional strategy questions that need to be addressed also in the Internet-enabled business environment.

Box 16.2 Pricing models

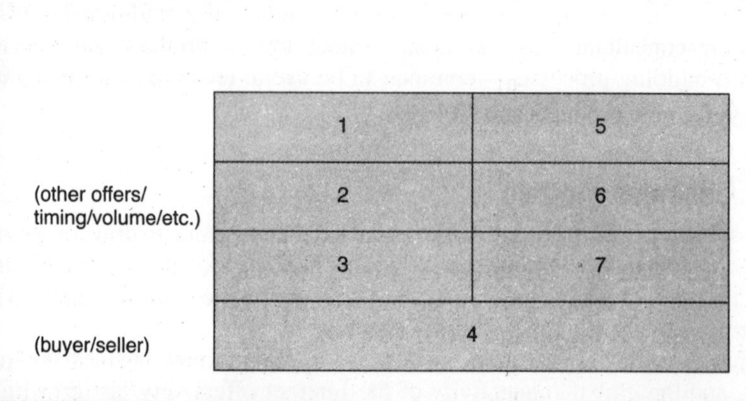

In different business models, prices are set in different ways. In the "traditional economy", there are examples of all the methods represented in the figure. Traditional retailers generally offer a fixed price (box 1), though some also use contingent prices (e.g. "5 for the price of 4") (box 2). House sales are typically in box 3, along with many consumer-to-consumer private sales ("offers in region of" or "offers in excess of"). As the indicative price becomes less firm and more of an invitation to haggle, pricing shades into box 4, as in the classic bazaar. Box 4 is also used for the letting of complex contracts, where pricing options may be explored around different detailed specifications, trying to establish where there is greatest scope for overall value creation. Box 5 is used for sealed purchase bids, for example, and box 6 is used in the traditional auction, where the buyer offers a price contingent on what other buyers may offer. The infamous "exploding" employment offers of consulting companies to MBA graduates (where the offered salary or bonus dropped with every day of delay in accepting the offer) would also fit in this box. Finally, box 7 is sometimes used in commercial invitations to tender or, more mundanely, in the "hopeless shopper" case (I'm looking for a present for about $30).

E-business models frequently use enhanced and speedier data management to move towards more buyer-driven and interactive pricing mechanisms. The "reverse auction", heralded as a major Internet innovation, is simply another example of box 5 for "e-tailers" such as Priceline.com. It is only "reverse" in that the buyer specifies what is wanted as well as a price, but it has direct parallels in some traditional media such as "classified advertisements". The impact of the general shift "down and right" is to promote more differentiated and value-based pricing. Some expect this to lead to more efficient value capture from the demand curve, others simply see it as a means of increasing buyer power. Two critical issues concern the transparency of different prices to different buyers, and the extent of justifying differences by having various versions of a product.

Source: Marcus Alexander, Ashridge Management College.

Value-chain integration

One of the biggest sources of impact on business is the potential for value-chain integration. The Internet's universal connectivity is opening up standardized and cost-effective global communication channels outside the corporation. The areas of high growth in e-business consulting are *supply-chain integration* and *collaborative working*, which both lead to outsourcing opportunities in new areas of the business process.

The extension of the supply chain is primarily a question of making available information on movements of products, forecasts of demand and just-in-time delivery. An example would be the seamless flow of information when a can of drink is purchased from the supermarket, via the drinks packager to the manufacturers of cans, suppliers of ingredients and transport providers. The goal is for every partner in the product flow to have the same information at the same time. The benefit is faster throughput and reduced material in the supply chain, i.e. increased asset turnover and reduced working capital requirements, but also reduction in "old" inventory and slow-moving goods. It is a complex process, involving numerous IT systems, software platforms and communications protocols. Few firms would (or should) have the expertise to design and implement such systems, hence there is ample scope for large e-consultancies to offer integration services and advice. The specific skills that are valued by clients are:

- integration of enterprise resource planning (ERP) systems;
- procurement expertise;
- contracts negotiations and service-level agreements (SLAs);
- logistics expertise;
- linking of payment systems via banks and payment providers.

A very specific application of value-chain integration is the development of *online market places and exchanges*. These are intermediaries in vertical or horizontal markets, which facilitate trade between buyers and sellers. The historical comparison is the market square, where local produce was sold and bartered. The logical extensions to this are markets for trading shares and financial products, such as foreign currency, government and corporate bonds, and commodities markets such as the Chicago commodities exchange, which is trading products like coffee, orange juice, and meat products.

The development of marketplaces for industrial products such as chemicals, plastic, office materials and engineering products has forced companies to learn how to interact and trade with their customers and suppliers in new and different ways. At the time of writing few organizations have the experience and knowledge required to handle the new dynamics of the online marketplace. Consulting advice on strategy is important, as is advice and implementation support when punching a channel through the internal IT system's firewall to reach the marketplace. The potential consequences for the internal organization, either in the sales department or in procurement, are substantial, and change management support should form part of the implementation of new ways of running the internal business processes.

Value-chain connectivity is relatively well established in some industry sectors, such as the automotive industry, where fixed connections through dedicated electronic data interchange (EDI) links have been around since the 1970s. The difference between EDI and the Internet as a platform is that the Internet is an open architecture in contrast to EDI's dedicated connections between two parties.

One benefit of EDI is that the two parties operate a common data standard, hence integration with their ERP systems is relatively straightforward. The HTML language used on the Internet is not well suited to integration with ERP systems, since it is a text-based description of the interface with the user and directions to a database rather than a description of the content. New languages, such as XML (extended markup language), BizTalk, etc. are required to integrate Internet-based communication with a multitude of systems and users. XML uses tagging principles to describe the type of data the information contains. In many industry sectors, such as financial services, chemicals and the semiconductor industry, discussions are taking place to define industry standards to describe commonly used descriptions and data. As a consequence, consulting advice is required for many medium-sized and small organizations to follow developments in their sectors.

Developments in mobile Internet technology are a relatively new area of connectivity between customers and organizations. With the expectation of continued growth in the use of mobile devices and investments in high-bandwidth wireless network technology, companies are developing products and services that will meet a new set of needs. Again, technology is driving commercial developments.

Providing consulting advice in the mobile Internet market is challenging. It is about predicting needs and offering benefits from products and services that do not yet exist. The most challenging aspect is to understand who is going to make money from these products and services and how. It is a classic consulting assignment, using scenario-building, learning from other similar markets, and customer-testing of new concepts and ideas to predict the right products and marketing strategy.

A considerable amount of technology consulting will be required to bring together the disparate technologies connecting the Internet with content providers, mobile network operators, billing systems, handset manufacturers and end users, ultimately on a global scale.

Mergers, acquisitions and alliances

Integration of the value chain and increased information flow raise the possibility of forward and backward integration of processes and value-adding activities. An important opportunity for consulting is advising companies on the strategic implications of potential mergers and acquisitions. The acquisition route was very attractive until early 2000 as dot.com shares were highly valued; hence there were opportunities to acquire companies and pay with shares.

An example was AOL's acquisition of Time/Warner in 2000. Time/Warner had a very large physical presence and traditional assets compared with AOL; on the other hand, being a dot.com, AOL had highly rated shares but was very small in terms of comparative turnover. Ultimately, value creation in mergers and acquisitions depends on successful integration of the organizations. AOL, as a fast-moving and flexible dot.com, is integrating a large and established organization encompassing many different businesses; commentators are following the process with great interest. Consulting companies that seek to get involved in this type of transaction need solid experience of both the dot.com culture and the more traditional culture of established large organizations.

Mergers and acquisitions are often driven by financial engineering benefits as much as by market rationale. Since dot.coms rarely have a large balance sheet to leverage debt, corporate activity more often involves alliances and partnerships rather than mergers and acquisitions. The speed of development and a need to shift direction quickly make alliances and partnerships suitable ways of acquiring skills, technology or customer access, rather than acquiring another organization outright. Strategic e-consulting advice is often used to assist in finding partners and for mediating in negotiations.

The potential for outsourcing

Value-chain integration, alliances and partnerships begin to raise questions about which parts of the organization are the absolute core assets and what could be outsourced. In addition, the pace of technological development and the need to move quickly make outsourcing an effective means of staying competitive (see also section 22.7).

Traditionally, outsourcing has been common for IT and this trend is likely to continue with increased use of application service provider (ASP) solutions. However, with the universal connectivity offered by the Internet, there are now few areas within any organization that have no potential for outsourcing. Examples of potential areas are:

- eProcurement: Outsourcing the complete procurement process to an intermediary, particularly procurement of non-production-related input.
- eHRM: Outsourcing of all administrative processes relating to personnel such as payroll, benefits, expenses, information, advice and online training. Early experiences suggest that significant savings can be realized.
- eR&D: Specialist organizations are available to carry out contract research and development projects. This is established practice in software development but the scope is increasing substantially in industries such as pharmaceuticals, technology and medicine.
- eFinance: Accounting and order processing are IT-heavy applications and there is a trend to outsource low-value administrative work and data processing.

Few organizations would claim that their finance function is a core activity. One issue holding back the outsourcing of the whole function is concern about security and confidentiality; however, there is little doubt that there will be further developments in this area over the coming years.

- eSales: Contracting out of sales activities is traditionally done through agents and distributors. The pharmaceutical industry uses this approach in particular for some of its generic products. Connections via the Internet offer new possibilities to increase the scale of sales activities by combining products and services from several suppliers in a market sector or geographical area. The traditional middleman could well rebound by bundling products and selling through electronic channels.
- eProduction: The drive for scale and focus is pushing organizations to outsource production of parts and subsystems. The industry often quoted in this regard is the automotive industry, which relies heavily on submanufacturers and acts in large part as a product development and marketing company, assembling the final product in response orders from customers and dealers. The critical Internet-related aspect is to have interconnected systems and to share data and information in an efficient and cost-effective way. The large automotive procurement hub, Covisint, suggests that one of its value-adding functions is the creation of a common platform for sharing data and information on current and future products among a large number of suppliers and manufacturers. The sensitive aspect is of course the business intelligence held by Covisint, which will have detailed information on materials flow and projections for a large part of the world's automotive industry.

Outsourcing of traditional activities on the scale indicated above is no small challenge. It requires a fundamental rethink of how organizations will be managed and led in the future. The relationships between employers, employees and partners are becoming less clear-cut and, for many organizations, this is uncharted territory.

In summary, the rapid development of the Internet is creating major changes in value chains and in the way business interacts with customers and partners. Few organizations have the experience to devise strategic responses to the developments; the role of consulting firms is to transfer learning from other organizations as well as to apply rigorous processes in challenging the existing practices and evaluating alternatives.

16.3 Bricks-and-mortar and bricks-and-clicks: internal processes

A number of areas in the internal processes of organizations have opened up with the advent of the Internet. Some of the opportunities mentioned above, such as procurement and online marketplaces, are affecting the internal organization in fundamental ways. This reflects a trend towards outsiders having a much clearer view of an organization's inner workings. This could be the supplier managing the inventory of strategic inward goods by having access to production planning data; or it could be customers having the possibility to book production capacity to suit their own scheduling. The following sections describe some of the trends in different functional parts of the value chain where e-business consulting is often required.

IT infrastructure

This is the obvious and traditional area of IT consulting (see Chapter 13). An important development is the application of *data warehousing* to make data from many sources available to the internal organization as well as to selected outside partners, suppliers, or customers. Data warehousing is one means of overcoming incompatibility between computing platforms and software packages, but it also allows cross-tabulations and assembly of differing sets of data.

One important drawback is that the data warehouse is not updated in real time, hence an understanding of the business process is critical if the system is to be of benefit. A classic example is a regional bank in Germany that was an early provider of Internet banking services. The Web site was designed and customers were logging on at an impressive rate and considered the site very good. However, after a few months customers began to complain that the system was inaccurate. It turned out that the Web site was connected to the bank's regular back-office system, which was updated once every 24 hours during the night. This meant that, if a customer entered a transaction in the morning and went back to the site in the afternoon, the receiving accounts would not have been updated to include the transaction. It sounds simple, but the team had not thought that customers would use the system so often, hence a 24-hour processing frequency was deemed sufficient. Predicting customer behaviour is one of the core skills of the e-business consultant.

Finance and administration

These are traditionally IT-heavy functions within organizations. However, the emergence of the Internet has put new demands on this part of the organization. Two of these are:

- remote access to financial information via the Internet by executives and staff who are away from the office;
- the opportunity to outsource the finance system function to an ASP.

In both cases, one of the critical aspects is security of access. Many companies are reluctant to provide access to business-critical systems, such as accounting information, because of the risk of hackers destroying data or unwelcome visitors having access. Both large consultancies and skilled individuals can charge high fees for highly specialized advice in this complex technical environment. The general question of outsourcing the accounting function was covered in the previous section.

Sales force automation

Software-based sales management tools began to be developed in the mid-1990s and are now an established market. Consulting activity in this area is around management of sales resources and implementation of effective systems, as well as on the IT aspects. The field is increasingly complex because of the proliferation of devices used, from laptop personal computers and palmtop computers to personal digital assistants (PDAs) and mobile phones. It is likely to become even more difficult to keep pace with the introduction of high-bandwidth devices from 2003 when the third-generation mobile networks become available. The sales force of the future is likely to demand connections to the organizations' ERP systems with real-time information on prices, stock availability and delivery.

A major challenge for sales management is the emergence of online trading exchanges. This new type of intermediary is changing the relationship with customers. It requires new skills from the sales organization and challenges the process and added value offered by a sales force. It can be predicted that sales organizations in many market sectors will move towards an advisory and consultative selling role, with automated systems dealing with transactions and taking orders online directly from the customers' ERP systems. The biggest risk is that the organization will lose its close relationship with and understanding of its customers in a drive to reduce costs and automate processes, and this must be guarded against.

Customer relationship management

A subject closely related to sales force automation is customer relationship management. A recent survey showed that managers thought the future development of the Internet would benefit their organizations most in improved customer relationship management.[2] Briefly, this is about technology linking together all internal and some external information about a customer and seamlessly delivering it to the customer interface, irrespective of the delivery channel, i.e. via call centre, Web site, field sales, etc. This is a complex process that requires good understanding of computing and software platforms, database design and business processes.

The trend is to offer multichannel delivery to customers. The customer may interface with the organization several times and often via different channels. The challenge is to make sure that the same data are available and to manage the cost, since the cost of delivery can vary in a ratio of 100:1 between a field visit and interaction via a Web site.

Segmentation, marketing and channel mix

In this area, the Internet excels in delivering new value to innovative and rule-breaking organizations. The low cost of delivery, scalability and potential to segment markets in a fine-grained way offer great opportunities. The example in box 16.3 illustrates the point.

Box 16.3 EasyRentaCar.com breaks the industry rules

EasyRentaCar.com was started by Stelios Haji-Iaonnou in March 2000. Using Internet technology, it fundamentally challenges the traditional business model of car rental. Rather than fixed list pricing, EasyRentaCar uses the airline model of dynamic load pricing, e.g. if you book in advance the price is low, starting at £9 per day (Feb 2001); for a next-day booking on a popular weekend the price goes up to £27. The price changes as more cars are booked. This is to be compared with fixed prices of around £30–40 from the traditional rental companies.

All bookings take place via the Internet and the paperwork is kept to a minimum. EasyRentaCar is established in regional airports in the United Kingdom and major European cities. Cars must be returned to the same rental point. Collection is further away than the normal rental car pick-up point to reduce costs and is therefore less convenient.

There is no choice of car, as EasyRentaCar offers only Mercedes A-class. This is a trade-off for the customer, but substantially reduces the maintenance and running cost for EasyRentaCar. The fact that Stelios has committed to buy 9000 A-class cars (approx. 4% of the total production) has given him good bargaining power in the price negotiation.

To maximize utilization, the car has to be returned before the agreed time and any extension of the return is heavily penalized (£50). The insurance cost is dependent on the driver's past driving record, e.g. a middle-aged driver with no points on the driving licence has a lower cost than a 20 year old with speeding tickets.

The business model uses Internet technology extensively and it forces decisions on clear trade-offs by the customer in return for very low prices.

Source: www.EasyRentaCar.com (11 March 2001).

Besides challenging the traditional rental car industry, the EasyRentaCar case demonstrates the possibility of segmenting markets in new ways:

- By offering a different level of service such as depots away from the airport, in regional rather than main airports, offering one type of car only, charging preparation fees separately and insurance based on actual driving records etc., EasyRentaCar is reducing running costs substantially.

- By using Internet bookings, administration costs are kept low.
- Because the company uses dynamic pricing to maximize utilization of vehicles, early bookers can get very low prices.

Points 2 and 3 are only practical and cost-effective through the use of the Internet. Taking all three points into account, EasyRentaCar has created a new segment of car rental customers: the cost-sensitive, time-rich and flexible customer segment, which would be unlikely to hire a car from the traditional car rental companies.

Purchasing organization

Purchasing systems are important, but traditionally paper-based, systems in organizations. Internet technology is about to transform drastically this part of the business process. Non-production resources will be purchased online via new intermediaries or through marketplaces. Decision-making for purchases will be devolved within the organization rather than centralized in the procurement department.

Online exchanges will increasingly be used to make purchases of strategic supplies through auction and bidding processes. Price transparency and higher price volatility will require new skills and internal processes to deliver effective purchasing processes.

Consulting opportunities in this area of business will continue to be plentiful in the coming years.

HRM processes online

This is another important part of business but often with a low profile in organizations. There are two important trends for the consulting professional to consider:

- A traditional paper-based process offers opportunities for automation and distribution within the organization through the intranet or Internet.
- The increasing emphasis on a knowledge-based organization makes recruiting, developing and retaining talented staff a high priority for the human resource department.

The first point is a classic automation opportunity. The second implies combined use of Internet technologies to attract applicants and to deliver training cost-effectively, and systems to provide a flexible and attractive working environment, such as occasional home working, easy and efficient communication when travelling, etc.

With the increased speed of change the HR function must be able to contribute at the strategic level, to understand the new competencies the organization requires, and to fulfil those requirements.

Box 16.4 The ThomasCook.com story

When Thomas Cook, a travel company based in the United Kingdom, launched its online travel booking site, ThomasCook.com, in 1999, it sent two strong messages to the travel market and its competitors. First, it set up a dot.com as a separate business from its existing retail and call-centre-based direct sales models, and second, it chose to use its highly valued offline brand for the online business. This contrasted with most of its competitors, which were either new start-ups or financially backed by existing travel businesses, and had fancy new dot.com names.

The decision to use the Thomas Cook brand has clearly been beneficial, as ThomasCook.com has among the strongest brand recognition of online travel sites and very high visitor ratings. ThomasCook.com offers over 2 million package holidays, a wealth of destination information, weather reports, etc. plus a very strong flight-only booking engine. One of the early lessons learned by the dot.com team was how to design a site that would offer a returning visitor a very different experience depending on the purpose of the visit. They found that they had to design the site to offer:

- Inspiration – helping you to dream up where you want to go.
- Information – all you need to make up your mind.
- Transaction – the quickest way of getting what you want.

The site design has three different pathways with clear links to other parts of the site. This is a complex process and the key skill is to be able to "walk in the customers' shoes".

The decision to set up the dot.com as a separate business was crucial for its development. Thomas Cook is a relatively large company and had been doing the same type of business for 150 years. To make the dot.com business successful, they had to move fast, break a few internal rules, and create a new culture different from that of Thomas Cook. Many discussions were held and battles fought in the early days of development, but shared learning also took place.

The next step in the development is to integrate the online business with the high-street retail shops and call-centre business. Thomas Cook, as other B2C businesses, has clearly concluded that B2C is a multichannel proposition and that customers want to interact with the travel agency in different ways.

Source: Discussions with Bill James: bill@billjames.com

Organization development

The impact in this area has yet to become visible in most organizations. New forms of organizational design and new relationships between employees, contractors, partners and customers are emerging; new leadership styles and roles are being debated and discussed. An increasing use of consulting support and advice is likely as senior executives grapple with the issues.

16.4 Dot.com organizations

In comparison with bricks-and-mortar organizations, the dot.coms are generally characterized by higher speed of development, fewer organizational resources, and more openness to outsourcing many parts of their business processes. They also have additional requirements, such as start-up funding, not normally needed by bricks-and-mortar organizations. What is similar is the need for ERP connections in B2B, and excellence in Web design and in B2C propositions.

Funding

Many dot.coms seek consulting advice in relation to creating a business plan and raising finance. Many large consultancies offer this type of service, including various types of *incubators* and *accelerators*. Incubators and accelerators help entrepreneurs who have a good idea, but lack the staff and/or expertise to take the business through the pre-operations stages. The incubators usually offer a network of contacts and sources of finance, in addition to expertise in building Web sites. The work is sometimes performed on a "no success, no fee" basis and payment in equity or equity options (see section 30.4) can sometimes be negotiated.

Independent consultants and non-executive directors are often used by dot.coms. Here the focus is on expertise in a specific market sector, a network of contacts, and experience of building entrepreneurial businesses. Many successful entrepreneurs use the money they have made and their expertise by investing in and advising new start-ups.

There are of course the traditional corporate finance advisers who provide advice on the process of raising finance and structure deals. Integral to corporate finance advice is legal and tax advice. There are many firms that specialize in funding negotiations and advice on corporate structure.

IT platform and infrastructure

The traditional providers of technology consulting are obvious players in this arena; however, much of the success of pure-play Internet consultancies comes from winning contracts to build the Web sites for dot.coms. Since a dot.com could start with a clean sheet of paper, there are no legacy ERP systems to integrate, so they use Internet-only technology from the beginning. The outsourcing of much of the deployment of IT infrastructure, running of systems, and possibly development comes quite naturally if the existing IT infrastructure does not need to be changed. Financial resources are often not sufficient to make investments in hardware and software or to build the expertise to run the systems. Another reason for outsourcing the IT infrastructure is the need to scale the business fast, hence adding capacity on a flexible basis is important. Vendor-based financing of IT equipment is relatively common, with the caveat that it is risky to finance start-ups.

Dot.coms often use a wide range of independent consultants and contractors when building their online business. Contacts and personal referrals create a tightly knit network of expertise that can be drawn on when needed. This has led to the development of a new breed of consultants, sometimes called "virtual networked consultants". There is a main contact who assembles a team for a specific project, while at the same time subcontracting part of his or her time on another project. Many of these consultants have major consulting firm experience but value personal freedom and the possibility of avoiding the administrative burden of being part of a large organization.

These virtual consultants make use of the power of the Internet with Web-based project management, discussion rooms and electronic methods of keeping track of the progress of projects. The growth of virtual consultancies is likely to continue, with diversification of the consulting market to meet the need for specialist skills and a flexible approach.

Financial management

This is a typical function where dot.coms use external resources in the early development of the business. The provider of finance is likely to request that an experienced finance director is part of the management team; however, the administrative process is often outsourced to an accounting firm or independent contractors who are used as skilled resources paid on a time basis, rather than building an in-house capability. With the development of the business it is likely that an ASP solution will be preferred more often by a dot.com than a bricks-and-mortar company. Again, this view is driven by the fact that the dot.com can build the finance function from scratch.

Marketing

In the early development of e-commerce the dot.com often relied on the Internet as the prime marketing channel. Advertising and click-through affiliate marketing were important sources of revenue. By early 2001, signs of change in the marketing mix and channel strategy among the dot.coms started to emerge. For instance, Internet banks are establishing high-street banking outlets and Amazon.com is building warehouses in new locations. As a consequence, traditional skills and expertise in multichannel marketing in a variety of media are increasingly sought after. Advertising agencies that have built up expertise in Web design are likely to be valued more for their traditional marketing skills than their Web design expertise in the future.

HR function

One of the biggest challenges for a fast-growing dot.com is recruiting, developing and retaining highly skilled staff. The early dot.coms relied heavily on the attraction of share options rather than well-thought-through HR policies and systems. With the general fall in dot.coms share prices, HR issues, recruitment and organizational design are of increasing importance in attracting talent and retaining expertise. The need for consulting advice and support in this functional area is growing.

16.5 Internet research

A consulting area that has grown very rapidly is market analysis and technological and business forecasting concerning the future of the Internet. Firms addressing these issues combine analysis of technology development, the actual usage of the Internet and the predicted future business implications. Internet research firms employ large numbers of business analysts specializing in either market sectors or technology fields, and offer off-the-shelf reports as well as tailored assignments. Typical offerings include:

- Internet usage trend analysis
- market size estimates
- technology trends
- technology assessment.

The boundaries between traditional consulting firms and market research firms are becoming blurred and many Internet research firms are hiring business consultants to sell advice using the results of their research, or to do contract research for particular clients. Consulting firms in turn are buying Internet research firms to gain access to knowledge and skilled staff.

Another sector that traditionally has a strong emphasis on market research is investment banking. The research departments of investment banks are skilled in analysing market sectors for their equity sales teams who are advising investors to sell, hold or buy a particular stock or invest in particular sectors. Although not yet competing with management consultancies, they certainly hire specialist consultants to deepen their knowledge of the e-business aspects of market sector analysis.

The addresses of selected firms, institutions and Web sites involved in Internet and e-business-related research and information services are in Appendix 3. Some Internet-based resources are free, while some require registration or subscription. The challenge for any observer or consultant in the e-business field is to keep abreast of developments. A key step is to establish a well-developed but focused set of resources that provide regular updates and prompts when new and relevant information is available. New technology, such as context-sensitive search and artificial intelligence, is emerging, but for a while yet, searching, reading and searching again will be the order of the day. In addition to the sources listed in the appendix, many large consulting and IT firms are also important providers of information.

---

[1] See also M. E. Porter: "Strategy and the Internet", in *Harvard Business Review*, Mar. 2001, pp. 63–78.

[2] The survey e-research@ashridge by Helen Wildsmith, completed in Jan. 2001.

CONSULTING IN OPERATIONS MANAGEMENT 17

The term "operations" essentially describes the process of transforming certain inputs into required outputs in the form of goods or services. As such, operations are not restricted to manufacturing but apply also to other activities, such as construction, transport, health care, public administration and all kinds of services.

This process of transformation requires decision-making on the part of operations management with a view to getting an output of the desired quantity and quality delivered by the required date and at a set (as a rule minimum) cost. The consultant's task is to advise management, whenever necessary, on the best means of achieving this objective. In most cases, operations management consultants are able, in the performance of their functions, to measure and assess the results of their work.

Operations materialize the value chain, which comprises product development, marketing, inbound logistics, production, outbound logistics, sales and after-sales services. Operations consultants therefore need to consider the effect of their propositions on the overall value chain. Increasingly a supply chain perspective is taken to coordinate and integrate the components of a value chain. Supply chain management focuses on organizational aspects of integrating separate firms as well as coordinating flows of materials and information within a production and distribution network. The term supply chain management is often used synonymously with logistics.[1]

17.1 Developing an operations strategy

How can operations consultants contribute to improving the performance of production and distribution systems having in mind an optimization of the whole value chain? Problems submitted to the consultant may have very different degrees of importance to the client organization.

At one end of the scale there are problems that belong to the group of basic choices. An operations or production consultant may have an important say in a team that is examining the client's business strategy. At the opposite end of the scale there are myriad problems whose common denominator is the need to meet certain criteria with regard to productivity, quality, cost, or job satisfaction in the performance of specific production tasks. Such problems tend to be operational in nature. But the consultant will be well advised not to lose sight of the broader needs of the client organization, as it is not unusual for assignments in very specific production fields to disclose problems that are much more profound and lie outside the production area itself.

In defining an improvement programme or project, consultants, together with their clients, should:

- establish competitive performance criteria and levels;
- develop a clear understanding of available operations choices (best practice);
- select the consulting approach.

Performance criteria and levels

Speed, quality, productivity and customer focus, as well as their continuous improvement, characterize operations:[2]

- The speed imperative is translated into criteria such as time to market for new products or services, response time to orders from internal or external customers, and manufacturing lead time for production.
- Quality and productivity are increasingly defined in terms of the customers' need and desire and translated into product specifications by using tools such as quality function deployment. In product development, productivity and quality mean achieving high leverage from critical resources, as well as an increased number of successful projects developed in a truly cross-functional development process. With tools such as total quality management (see Chapter 21), efforts are made to improve quality and productivity in operations by increasingly concentrating on processes and not only on products.
- Customer focus aims to meet the increasing expectations of ever-more segmented customers who are offered, for most products and services, a wide choice. Here, the efficient translation of these demands into products and services with distinction and integrity has to be tackled.

Consultants are used to implement all these performance criteria or competitive imperatives, as shown in box 17.1. In the drive to restructure production, consultants should, however, be careful not to generate too many projects which cannot be absorbed and sustained by existing production facilities and staff.

In defining performance criteria and setting performance standards, a client company assisted by a consultant is well advised to search for those best practices of superior companies, competitors and non-competitors, which are

Box 17.1 Performance criteria of operations

Performance criterion	Driving force	Consultants contribute to
Speed	– Intense competition – Fast-changing customer expectations – Accelerated technological change – Shrinking product life cycle – Reduced contribution margins	– Shorter development cycles – Better targeted products – Accelerated capital rotation – Reorganization of processes emphasizing speed – Instigate continuous improvement
Quality and productivity	– Exploding product variety – Sophisticated discerning customers – Increasing complexity of process technology – Environmental concerns	– Promote creativity combined with total product quality – Emphasize quality of manufacturing processes – Tap and develop knowledge of all staff – Develop cross-functional problem solutions – Focus on "value added"
Customer focus	– Customer expects to be treated as individual – Intense competition – Crowded/saturated markets	– Define quality in terms of customer – Streamline supply chains inside/outside the company

Source: Adapted from: S. G. Wheelwright and K. B. Clark: *Revolutionizing product development* (New York, The Free Press, 1992).

relevant to achieving superior performance. Benchmarking (see description in Chapter 20) has been used by many consultants to help clients establish performance levels in production and operations by comparing the client's current practices with those of sector leaders, competitors or other companies able to offer, and willing to share, useful practical experiences. In the approach developed by the Xerox Corporation, the interfirm comparison methodology, traditionally used with financial data, has been applied to product design, manufacturing and customer services by seeking to identify, evaluate and use the best approaches developed by successful competitors.

Making operations choices

In implementing performance improvement programmes according to the above criteria, the most complex aspect is perhaps the wide variety of choices a consultant faces, a summary of which is given in box 17.2. Often these choices

Box 17.2 Major types of manufacturing choice

Capacity	Amount, timing, type
Facilities	Size, location, specialization
Equipment and process technologies	Scale, flexibility, interconnectedness
Vertical integration	Direction, extent, balance
Vendors	Number, structure, relationship
New products	Hand-off, start-up, modification
Human resources	Selection and training, compensation, security
Quality	Definition, role, responsibility
Systems	Organization, schedules, control

Source: S. G. Wheelwright and R. A. Hayes: "Competing through manufacturing", in *Harvard Business Review*, Jan.–Feb. 1985, p. 101.

are sold as a complex package such as "lean production".[3] Lean production advocates a reduced vertical integration, where the original equipment manufacturer (OEM) produces only about 20–30 per cent of the product value. Parts and components are bought from a reduced number of suppliers with whom close collaboration is developed. Suppliers take up product development tasks and synchronize their production "just-in-time" with the OEM. Consultants are often called in either by the OEM or by suppliers to develop lean production practices which make such an enterprise network operate efficiently.

Another package of choices concerns the implementation of information technology (hardware and software) in operations aiming at computer-integrated manufacturing. In several cases, this is introduced or planned simply to keep up with competitors, and without the necessary preparatory work. Computer applications have found their way into production through computer-aided design (CAD) and computer-aided manufacturing (CAM). There have been several developments in CAM, as well as the introduction of flexible manufacturing systems. Advanced planning systems and efficient consumer response applications support supply chain management. Operations consultants would do well to remind their client organization that if the plant layout is poor, the product design old, production planning and control not the best, and standards loose, transferring these ills to a computerized manufacturing system is not going to help much. Therefore, business process improvement (BPI) programmes are usually an integral part of client-based solutions.

Furthermore, it is the rule rather than the exception that new technology is introduced alongside traditional technology. This may be a permanent arrangement or a transition phase, and the consultant must be able to diagnose the problems and improve the efficiency of the traditional technology, either to increase productivity and cut costs or as a prelude to the introduction of new technology.

Selecting the consulting approach

There is not only a wide variety of operations choices, but also a variety of consulting approaches that are applicable to operations.

Process or product focus. In order to improve the performance of operations, consultants have to decide together with their clients whether to focus on certain products, on certain processes, or on cutting overhead costs independently of products and processes. For a company wishing to improve speed of delivery, for example, it would be useful to look into order processing, which would generally be similar for a whole range of products. If the task is to increase the contribution margin of products that have a high share of sales, then the consultant would be well advised to analyse the production sequence for these products. An overhead reduction approach will be appropriate if there is a high percentage of overhead costs and if there are too many products and processes to achieve short-term performance improvements.

Technical expertise or change management skills. While operations consultants have traditionally acted very much as industrial engineering or technology experts, they have had to learn how to lead and assist in complex organizational and technological change processes. It is still a major challenge for an engineer to acquire process consulting skills and be sensitive to people's concerns in proposing changes in established production practices. The failure of consulting projects can often be attributed to an imbalance between technical expertise and the skills required to lead change processes (see Chapters 3 and 4).

Revitalization or incremental improvements. Increasingly, clients call in consultants in operations management in order to modernize operations and to achieve "quantum leaps" in speed and efficiency. For such cases, consultants have devised revitalization approaches to identify and radically improve processes that are essential for creating value and meeting customers' demands; other processes are not restructured, but are discontinued and dismantled. State-of-the-art production and information technologies are essential for achieving process integration and reorganization, which is the opposite to traditional process fragmentation into thousands of small tasks.

In contrast, continuous and incremental improvement, following the principles of *kaizen* (in Japanese, "gradual unending improvement"), builds on existing systems with the objective of using every opportunity and involving everyone – top and middle management, supervisors, specialist staff and workers

– to make small improvements. To achieve incremental improvements, a consultant may be given the task of installing continuous improvement processes: a total quality approach, for example.[4]

Revitalization should be followed by an incremental improvement approach to sustain overall high performance levels, as there is a well-known tendency for performance levels of production systems to erode with time. Furthermore, even if the latest production and information technologies have been applied, there is always scope for smaller improvements suggested by the customers, the company's own staff, the suppliers of the technology or the consultants.

Notwithstanding the approach taken, the consultant in most cases will have to deal with three major components of production systems:

- the products;
- the processes, including methods and organization of work;
- the people involved.

The consultant can concentrate on any of these areas in line with the agreement reached with the client. In many cases, however, this classification is somewhat artificial – problems to do with product quality, for example, may be due to poor methods of work, or poor training of workers, and so on. Nevertheless, for the purpose of structuring his or her thoughts the consultant may find this approach helpful.

Within each area, the consultant has at his or her disposal a variety of operations and management techniques ranging from the simple to the highly complex. In the planning area, for example, techniques can range from simple bar charts to network planning to advanced operations research tools and supply chain simulations. The choice depends on the situation faced and the degree of sophistication of the industry concerned. No attempt will be made in this chapter to describe these techniques, and readers are referred to the various publications dealing with operations management and operations research. Instead, we will concentrate on the systematic approach to identifying and prescribing methods for improving productivity, reducing production costs, and improving quality, speed and customer focus, so that the consultant develops an approach that is process- and problem-oriented rather than single-technique-oriented (see also Chapters 20 and 21).

17.2 The product perspective

The product range

A product may start as a single substance or as a multitude of raw materials, processed to give quality characteristics that match a predetermined standard. It is rare to find enterprises that produce only one product. Usually there is a "product line", or a number of products, produced to order, or for stock, or both. In the majority of cases, a few products will either form the bulk of items produced or represent the most expensive (and presumably yield the highest rate of return). The consultant would then be well advised to start the assignment by analysing these product lines to identify the one or more products representing the bulk of production, or the highest value, and to focus attention on certain major areas in respect of this particular product or products. At the same time, this analysis may help to bring another question to the fore: is there a need for all these product variations, or can some products be eliminated or standardized? Pruning the product range would be the first task in systematically restructuring production systems before looking more closely into the remaining products and their production.

Increasingly, environmental considerations play a role in decisions about the continuation, modification or discontinuation of products. The selection of reusable or biodegradable materials, product modifications to allow cleaner production processes, and a "cradle-to-grave" approach in defining product specifications open a whole range of new consulting tasks in production.[5]

In recent years, outsourcing has become a major strategy, allowing companies not only to concentrate on their core competencies but also to offer a wide range of complex products.

> Why do some companies move quickly and efficiently to bring to market outstanding new products, while others expend tremendous resources to develop products that are late and poorly designed? How do designers, engineers, marketers, manufacturers, and senior executives in these companies combine their skills to build competitive advantage around product and process development?... What can managers do to bring about significant improvement in the performance of their development process?[6]

These are questions that clients increasingly ask their consultants with a view to restructuring product development processes.

To render product development more efficient, consultants will have to look into four areas: strategy; translation of customer demands into products; design for manufacturing; and organization of the product development process.

Product development strategy

In assisting a client to define a product development strategy, the consultant may encounter a number of common problems (see also box 17.3):[7]

- *The moving target:* The basic product or process concept misses a shifting technology or market.
- *Mismatches between functions:* What one part of the organization expects or wants from another part may prove to be unrealistic or impossible, e.g. the engineering department may design a product that the production department cannot produce, or only with difficulty.

Box 17.3 Central themes in ineffective and effective development projects

Problematic projects		Outstanding projects
Characteristics	Consequemces	Selected themes
Multiple, ambiguous objectives; different functional agendas	Long planning stage; project becoming vehicle for achieving consensus; late conflicts	Clear objectives and shared understanding of project's intent throughout organization; early conflict resolution at low level
Focus on current customers and confusion about future target customers	Moving targets, surprises and disappointments in market tests; late redesigns; mismatch between design and market	Actively anticipating future customers' needs; providing continuity in offerings
Narrow engineering focus on intrinsic elegance of solutions; little concern with time	Slipping schedules; schedule compression in final phases	Maintaining strong focus on time to market while solving problems creatively; system view of project concept
Reliance on engineering changes and manufacturing ramp-up to catch and solve problems; "we'll put a change order on it when we get to manufacturing"	Poor, unrepresentative prototypes; many late changes; poor manufacturability; scramble in ramp-up; lower than planned yields	Testing and validating product and process designs before hard tooling or commercial production; "design it right the first time"
Narrow specialists in functional "chimneys"	Engineering "ping-pong"; miscommunication and misdirected effort; use of time to substitute for integration	Broad expertise in critical functions, team responsibility, and integrated problem solving across functions
Unclear direction; no one in charge; accountability limited	Lack of a coherent, shared vision of project concept; buck passing; many false starts and dead ends	Strong leadership and widespread accountability

Source: S. G. Wheelwright, I. Clark and R. A. Hayes: *Dynamic manufacturing* (New York, The Free Press, 1988), p. 14.

- *Lack of product distinctiveness:* New product development terminates in disappointment because the new product is not unique or as justifiable as the organization anticipated.
- *Unexpected technical problems:* Delays and cost overruns can be traced to overestimates of the company's technical capabilities or to its lack of resources.
- *Unresolved policy issues:* If major policies have not been articulated clearly and shared, short-term.decisions will have to be made during the "heat of the battle", often with negative implications for the whole organization.

Translation of customer demands into products

Here the consultant has to focus on cross-functional information flows, particularly between marketing, research and product development, and on the structural processes of translating this information into product specifications via techniques such as quality function deployment. The tendency of engineers to "over-engineer" products should be limited by introducing target costing techniques. A cost target is set for the whole product and subsequently broken down into cost targets for each component, to avoid cost and price overruns which are quite common for new products. Target costing also allows better negotiation with suppliers based on a fixed cost target.

Design for manufacturing

In many cases, a traditional or successful product will continue to be produced for years with little thought being given to its design features. In other cases, product design is considered to fall solely within the domain of the marketing staff, and it is left to them to make all decisions in this area. Development work leading to a design involves more than just producing an appealing product. It should be based on the full cooperation of several enterprise functions, particularly marketing, production and costing.

On the production side, the consultant is concerned with the fact that a design will normally predetermine the process and method of work, the type of raw materials, jigs or fixtures, or materials-handling equipment that will be used. This is true of the product as well as of its constituent parts. The most frequent questions that the consultant needs to ask are:

- How many parts is the product composed of? Can some parts be eliminated through better design? Have any unnecessary features been removed?
- Can certain component parts be standardized to match parts of other products and so enable the use of the same machines, tools, jigs and fixtures?
- Can some components be replaced by cheaper ones that would perform the same function?
- Does the design lend itself to easy handling?

- Can a change in the design eliminate one or more processes? (For example, a process of stamping a metal production may eliminate one or more processes of assembly, though it could also alter the appearance of the product.)
- Can some component parts be standardized? Can variety still be obtained in the product line by using different combinations of components?

The consultant knows that products have to be matched with the equipment on which they are manufactured (e.g. with its dimensions, precision, productivity and cost), and vice versa. In a number of cases, he or she may have to examine this relationship and make recommendations to the client concerning either the product or the equipment used, or both. As mentioned earlier, any proposed modifications in product design should be checked with the marketing specialists for their market penetration potential.

Organization of the product development process

It is not unusual for reorganization of the product development process to reduce development time and costs by two-thirds compared with traditional systems.[8] Consultants should look into the following:

- cross-functional problem-solving (including at least marketing, R&D, manufacturing, purchasing, logistics, financial control);
- early detection and solution of development problems (frontloading);
- development team structure;
- project management techniques.

Optimization of these elements should ensure that products are designed for marketing and manufacturing concurrently with the engineering process, entailing a substantial reduction in costs and time to market. Rapid prototyping and other advanced simulation techniques can also substantially reduce time and cost of development.

17.3 The process perspective

The basic units of value creation are business processes, which can be defined as a sequence of activities that takes one or more inputs and creates an output that is of value to the customer. In operations, order fulfilment, which has a client order as input and delivered goods as output, is perhaps the most important value-generating process.

Most major consultancy firms offer their own business process or performance improvement (BPI) programmes, which are usually part of an overall change management methodology. Apart from a change management methodology, process improvement involves looking into specific technical areas and applying the relevant industrial engineering techniques. In general, consultants will have to consider the following areas:

- demand forecasting and production planning;
- supply chain and materials management;
- inventory management and utilization of materials;
- flow of work and layout, and logistics;
- setting and improving performance standards (at workplace level);
- maintenance;
- cleaner production and energy saving;
- quality management.

These areas are reviewed briefly below, with the exception of quality management, which is the subject of Chapter 21.

Demand forecasting and production planning

A major challenge of demand forecasting and production planning is the integration of planning approaches and systems across networks of legally independent firms. The enterprise resource planning (ERP) systems used for transaction handling and order execution in most firms nowadays have been supplemented by advanced planning systems for coordinating flows of resources and information, avoiding bottlenecks and meeting due dates. Efficient consumer response and supply management strategies are increasingly integrated into planning systems. The implementation of planning systems has become a major business for operations consultants worldwide.

The choice of the planning method to be used depends on the nature of the operation. In process or line production operations various methods of planning can be applied, ranging from simple and traditional scheduling and charting to the use of sophisticated queuing or waiting-line models. However, special projects, such as the construction of a plant or building of a ship, necessitate the use of network planning methods such as the critical path method (CPM) or the programme evaluation and review technique (PERT), which allow a more rational allocation of resources.

In the case of production that is geared for distribution (as distinct from made-to-order goods or special projects), the starting point for a planning process is the forecast of demand, which is worked out with the marketing specialists. The consultant should check the reliability of such forecasts before going into production planning itself. A discrepancy between sales forecasting and production planning can result in either lost orders or excess inventory, and is often a subject of contention between the marketing and production departments. In addition to the forecast, which is translated into an aggregate of operations for various products in the product mix, the consultant has to calculate the machine hours required for each product component, determine the total working time, and introduce a certain flexibility in the planning system to allow for emergency situations.

One difficulty lies in the fact that there are invariably bottleneck operations, but instead of concentrating on them, many consultants gear their planning and scheduling to all operations. An effective analytical and planning exercise should indicate shortages of machine or operators' hours in certain work centres and present proposals to management to relieve these difficulties.

Supply chain and materials management

With reduced contribution margins per unit of product sold, increased capital rotation has become an important strategy to maintain the profitability of a company at an acceptable level. Supply chain management, which has become another area of consulting in operations, is the process of developing and managing a firm's total supply system, including internal and external components. It includes and expands the activities of the purchasing function and the procurement process from a strategic perspective. Materials management concentrates on the coordination and control of the various materials activities. Consulting in supply management may deal with topics such as early involvement of suppliers in product design, supplier selection and qualification methods, the development of vendor building programmes, setting up of cross-functional teams in procurement, etc.[9]

In addition to the more strategic orientation of supply chain management there is still much scope for services in the traditional area of materials management.

Inventory management

Consultants need to keep in mind three types of inventory: *raw materials*, *work-in-progress* and *finished products*. One general principle should govern all these: the need to keep them at a minimum but safe level. For raw materials and finished products, a safe level is one that allows for uncertainty of delivery or avoids opportunity costs resulting from lost sales. The notion of such a safety stock, or buffer stock, is not a justification for having a high stock level, nor should it be used indiscriminately to take advantage of quantity discounts or special modes of delivery.

For finished products, the desired level of stock needs to be determined in close consultation with the marketing and finance specialists in an effort to balance opportunity costs against carrying charges (the cost of carrying the inventory).

Great savings in carrying charges can be made if the work-in-progress inventory is kept to a minimum. To achieve this, however, the consultant may have to look at the balance of operations, remove or reduce bottlenecks, and propagate the virtues of a system in which no or very little inventory is allowed to accumulate beside each machine.

In most industries, stock levels have been reduced dramatically in recent years with the implementation of just-in-time (JIT) concepts for all three types of inventory. JIT requires close cooperation between suppliers, the producer and clients, a stable production process, and a "zero defect" quality policy. Conversely, JIT is sometimes difficult to implement for reasons such as the need for more frequent transport from suppliers to producers, congested transport networks, especially in big cities, and the tough requirements on the suppliers.

Most consultants approach the problem of the raw materials inventory by analysing the values of the various items to distinguish the "A" items (which are few in number but very costly) from "B" and "C" items (the latter being the great multitude of relatively cheap items that are carried in stock). An ordering strategy is then developed for the "A" items resting on the use of inventory models to determine the economic order quantity by balancing ordering costs against carrying charges. Quantity discounts can also be evaluated against incremental carrying charges, and a decision can then be reached as to when a quantity discount offer can be attractive. The problem, however, lies in the determination of the buffer stock level. Under normal circumstances, this is calculated by balancing opportunity costs against carrying charges. For the "B" items, ordering is carried out through regular review of stock, or whenever a minimum level is reached. For "C" items, mass orders may be placed at certain points in time.

Utilization of materials

While the focus of attention here is on the raw materials which go towards shaping the final product, the assignment can be extended to cover other materials used in the production process, such as packaging material, fuel, and even paints and lubricants. This is an area where substantial savings can be achieved without too much effort, particularly in certain industries such as manufacture of garments, furniture, metallic products and the like. It stands to reason that the higher the percentage of material cost, the more there is a need for a proper investigation of this area. There are three approaches to reducing waste material:

- changes in design, with a view to reducing waste of raw material;
- if the design cannot be changed, then efforts may be undertaken to improve the yield, by changing the method that is used in cutting garments, metal or wood so as to reduce waste to a minimum, or by changing the original size of the raw material used;
- inevitably some waste will result during the various sequences of production. Two questions should come to mind: can this waste be reworked to yield another by-product or component, or can it be sold?

These questions have gained particular relevance because of a number of environmental regulations forcing producers to recycle materials, operate closed systems or take responsibility for the reuse of wastes. Recycling and waste management have become a special area for consultants.

Flow of work and layout

The organization's production operations normally conform to one of three major types. The first is production by fixed position, in which case the product is stationary and the workers and equipment move, as in building aeroplanes, heavy generators, or ships. Layout can sometimes be improved by shortening the distances travelled by workers, materials and equipment. However, the margin of manoeuvrability is rather limited.

The second is in-line production, where the equipment and machinery are arranged according to the sequence of operations, as in bottling plants, car assembly and food canning operations. In these cases, the layout is more or less dictated by the sequence of operations, which determines how the machinery is placed. Nevertheless, two sorts of issue can be examined by the consultant: the original balance of operations; and the problems that result from the fact that, in many cases, as the enterprise develops and the product line expands, or demand for the product changes, additional lines may be added which often do not work in harmony with the original line. The operations can therefore become unbalanced, with certain stages producing at a faster rate than subsequent or preceding stages. A schematic diagram showing the sequence of operations and the time it takes to perform each one can be quite helpful. Depending on the type of problem faced and the complexity of the situation, correcting for balance can range from simple proposals, e.g. increasing the number of workstations on parts of the line, additional machines or improvement in the method of work, to more sophisticated heuristic approaches.

The third type of organization is that of functional arrangement, where all identical machinery is grouped together and the products move between these machines, depending on the sequence required for each. This is the case in many woodworking workshops and in the textile industry. This type of arrangement allows the consultant to do more to improve productivity through better layout and organization of operations. The key is to identify whether there is one or more finished products that constitute a high percentage of total volume. The machinery needed to produce such items is then detached from a functional layout and arranged along a line layout. The gains in productivity in this case can be substantial.

Logistics

The logistics function in a company can always be described and handled as a flow of information and a flow of goods. As both flows are very complex, the project frame for BPI must be carefully designed. As a checklist we recommend marking on a graph all logistics elements to be covered by the project. The example shown in fig. 17.1 is taken from a company producing and maintaining equipment, which wanted to improve the logistics for spare parts. The defined objectives for this project were: decrease stock by 30 per cent; decrease handling costs; increase delivery performance; and decrease administrative costs.

Figure 17.1 Business process improvement in the area of logistics

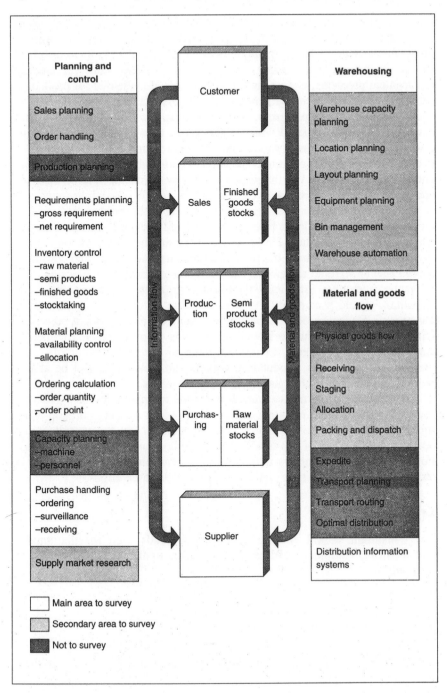

Planning and control

Sales planning

Order handling

Production planning

Requirements plannning
–gross requirement
–net requirement

Inventory control
–raw material
–semi products
–finished goods
–stocktaking

Material planning
–availability control
–allocation

Ordering calculation
–order quantity
–order point

Capacity planning
–machine
–personnel

Purchase handling
–ordering
–surveillance
–receiving

Supply market research

Customer

Sales | Finished goods stocks

Produc-tion | Semi product stocks

Purchas-ing | Raw material stocks

Supplier

Information flow

Material and goods flow

Warehousing

Warehouse capacity planning

Location planning

Layout planning

Equipment planning

Bin management

Warehouse automation

Material and goods flow

Physical goods flow

Receiving

Staging

Allocation

Packing and dispatch

Expedite

Transport planning

Transport routing

Optimal distribution

Distribution information systems

Main area to survey

Secondary area to survey

Not to survey

Setting and improving performance standards

This is probably one of the most intricate problems that faces an operations consultant. Performance standards are needed for a variety of reasons, including the determination of labour costs, and hence the ability to decide on matters of pricing and bidding, in "make or buy" decisions, in machine replacement problems, and so on. Such standards are essential for production planning, wages and incentive schemes. Invariably a certain standard exists for every piece of work performed, either a formal recorded standard, or a perceived informal standard which a supervisor or a worker estimates for a given job. The consultant is called upon either to review a formal standard or to establish one. A crucial point is the need to perform the assignment with the knowledge and approval of the persons whose performance is to be assessed, and of the workers' representatives.

Before setting standards, a consultant working in this field should examine the way a certain operation is being performed and attempt to develop an easier and more effective method. He or she utilizes a number of well-known charts such as the operation chart, the flow chart and activity charts. The consultant should also understand ergonomics and essential elements of job design.

While numerous jobs lend themselves to methods improvement, the consultant should give priority to those that are critical because they either constitute a bottleneck or are repeated by a number of operators. A consultant will find it most useful to invite suggestions from workers, foremen or supervisors, and managers, to involve them in the working out of a new method. In many cases, production workers and technicians will be able to point to improvements that may escape the consultant.

To determine performance standards for the improved systems, generally speaking, one of three methods can be used: works sampling, a stop-watch time study, or predetermined time standards. Alternatively, the consultant may opt for a combination of two or all of these methods at a given working place. For example, work sampling may be used to determine the allowances to be included in a "standard time" based on stop-watch observations.[10]

Maintenance

The consultant should enquire about the methods used for maintaining and repairing equipment and machinery. In particular, it is appropriate to find out:

- if a preventive maintenance scheme exists, whether it is justified and how it is implemented;
- whether a proper inspection schedule exists;
- if a cost estimate of repairs is made and kept for each machine;
- how normal greasing and lubrication are done and whose responsibility it is to do these jobs.

The consultant should also enquire about emergency repairs and consider whether increasing the size of the maintenance crew could reduce the length of time machines are down. In addition, a consultant can examine whether the life of certain individual components of equipment or machines could be prolonged through either redesign or change of lubricant. Finally, machine replacement problems should be studied in relation to maintenance costs.

If major equipment is to be overhauled, especially in process industries, the consultant can help the client to achieve considerable savings by introducing scheduling for such operations (applying network planning techniques if necessary).

Because disruption of production due to machine breakdowns can be very costly, there is a growing trend towards making production staff more maintenance-conscious. Seminars on proper identification of causes of breakdowns, and on the training of both production operators and maintenance crew (which may suggest assigning a certain responsibility to operators for simple oiling and lubrication), could be followed up with performance review seminars at a later stage. Approaches involving all personnel, such as the total productive maintenance (TPM) approach, can pay handsome dividends.

Cleaner production and energy saving

The discussions on sustainable development, along with tighter environmental regulations, have led many companies to review their ways and means of production in light of ecological criteria.[11] Consultants may be called in, for example:

- to audit production facilities and propose improvement programmes;
- to assist with environmental impact assessments of major investments;
- to perform life-cycle analyses of products;
- to implement "pollution prevention pays" initiatives, often integrated in total quality management (TQM) or in staff suggestion schemes.

At present, many corporations are implementing the ISO 14000 standard to achieve an integrated environmental management system. In addition, specific technical advice may be sought on topics such as energy saving and recycling.

With the rise in energy costs, there is a need in many client companies to achieve substantial savings in the use of energy. These can result from simple good housekeeping (such as checking that thermostats are functioning and properly set, steam and air leaks repaired, and so on), from minor investments in additional insulation, heat recuperators, power-factor correction and the like, or from major investment decisions about changing to low-waste, low-energy processes. Many of these issues can be highly technical and require the intervention of specialists. The operations consultant's contribution lies essentially in examining whether a potential saving in energy costs can be achieved, bringing this to the attention of the client, and assisting management in deciding how to set up and implement an energy-conservation programme.

17.4 The human aspects of operations

Companies worldwide are trying to overcome autocratic, highly hierarchical and Taylorist organization concepts which cannot cope with the competitive imperatives of customization, innovation, speed, productivity and quality. Consultants can play a major part in facilitating the transition process to high-performance work systems. A consultant in operations management will have to deal with the human and technical aspects of production in an integrated manner. Furthermore, the consultant has to help the client to choose among a wide range of practices and techniques, and to effectively combine and apply those that are appropriate in a particular client context.

It is sometimes difficult for consultants to convince their clients that the traditional approach of fine-tuning subsystems without reviewing the overall organizational structure will not yield the desired success. Therefore, optimization of the aspects of operations described below should always be carried out with a view to the overall concept of production organization.

The quality issue is perhaps the best proof that the human element is the determining factor in any operation (see also Chapter 21). It would be naive to propose, let alone implement, any recommendation without the involvement of the employees concerned and without examining its impact on people. There are two major areas in operations management consultations to be considered in this respect: physical working conditions and safety improvement; and job enrichment and group work.

Physical working conditions and safety improvement

The consultant needs to pay attention to measures at the workplace to protect workers from adverse conditions of temperature, humidity, light and noise levels, as well as air contaminants, dust and radiation, exposure to which may cause poisoning or occupational diseases.[12]

Ideally, either hazards should be eliminated altogether or the workers should be removed from direct contact with hazardous situations. If this proves not to be feasible, then either the source of hazard should be isolated or the worker provided with protective equipment and clothing. A common mistake is to concentrate on the so-called technical aspects of accident prevention – the provision of protective gloves, boots or goggles, and guards for machinery. In most plants, however, over half of the accidents are caused more through human misjudgement and negligence than through the absence of guards or protective equipment.

The consultant can discover much revealing information by analysing past accident records for the causes of accidents, the department, hour of the day, and day of the week in which they most frequently occur, and even the person injured. This information can prove invaluable for a concerted plan of action to introduce a safety scheme. Any such scheme should invariably include training. Since accidents can happen despite all precautions, it is also appropriate to check on the availability and adequacy of health care, first aid and emergency and sanitation facilities, as well as fire protection systems.

Job enrichment and group work

Many operations consultants are productivity-conscious and can underestimate both the need for job satisfaction and the impact of job satisfaction on productivity. In a production environment, the process design, the method of work, the arrangement of work assignments and the physical working conditions greatly affect the workers' satisfaction. There are several ways that job satisfaction may be increased, including job enlargement and job enrichment. Time cycles for tasks can be lengthened, particularly in the case of tedious, monotonous jobs; work can be made more varied by adding other tasks to the original one; or more authority may be delegated to workers who can then take their own decisions on certain work-related matters. In the same spirit, the authority of operators to decide on how to customize services can be increased in many service sectors.

Considerable research has been done on group work under various names: new forms of work organization, sociotechnical systems, industrial democracy and semi-autonomous groups. Whole factories (for example, the Volvo plant in Kalmar, Sweden) have been designed around these concepts, and many industries in Japan, Europe, North America, Australia, and some developing countries have introduced such systems with a reasonable degree of success. These systems rest on two fundamental concepts. First, in designing and modifying work, it is necessary to consider the technical and social issues together. Thus improved methods of work have to be reconciled with the social needs of the working group in terms of factors such as the variety and the degree of challenge the job offers, the opportunities for learning and advancement, and so on. Secondly, people performing a certain task should participate in redesigning their own job.[13]

In this respect, small-group activities in particular are well known. Quality circles have over the years extended their scope of activities to cost reduction and productivity improvement. The success of the quality circles idea prompted many companies in developed and developing countries alike to follow the Japanese model, adapting several of its features, with varying degrees of success. It is clear that the participation of production workers and supervisors in issues relating to their work is gaining wider acceptance.

Involvement and participation at the shop-floor level may seem to be at odds with a production consultant's job perceived in a traditional way. This is not the case: all depends on the consultant's and the client's attitudes. A consultant who approaches the assignment claiming to know all the answers and wanting to impose his or her views will invariably fail. There are many technical and human aspects of each job that have to be taken into consideration when designing or modifying an operation, and no one can be expected to know every detail. The consultant may be surprised to find how readily people will respond to enquiries, and offer helpful suggestions for improvements, if they feel he or she is sincere, appreciates their views and has their needs and interests at heart. A consultant who develops such an attitude will soon find that involvement and participation, far from being obstacles, are key factors in the success of any assignment in production and operations.

---

[1] For a more detailed coverage of operations and production management, see for example R. B. Chase, N. J. Aquilano and F. R. Jacobs: *Production and operations management* (Homewood, IL, Irwin, 1998). Also, many of the topics covered in this chapter are treated in more detail in G. Kanawaty (ed.): *Introduction to work study* (Geneva, ILO, 4th ed., 1993).

[2] See, for example, S. G. Wheelwright, I. Clark and R. A. Hayes: *Dynamic manufacturing* (New York, The Free Press, 1988); or R. Schonberger: *World class manufacturing* (New York, The Free Press, 1982).

[3] See J. Womack, D. Jones and D. Roos: *The machine that changed the world* (New York, Rawson Associates, 1990).

[4] Cf. M. Hammer and J. Champy: *Re-engineering the corporation* (New York, Harper Business, 1993).

[5] See, for example, K. North: *Environmental business management: An introduction,* Management Development Series, No. 30 (Geneva, ILO, 2nd ed., 1997).

[6] S. G. Wheelwright and K. B. Clark: *Revolutionizing product development* (New York, The Free Press, 1992), p. xi.

[7] Ibid., pp. 29–31.

[8] For an example from the automobile industry see K. Clarly and T. Fujimoto: *Product development performance* (Boston, MA, Harvard Business School Press, 1991).

[9] For a good overview see D. W. Dobler and D. N. Burt: *Purchasing and supply management* (New York, McGraw-Hill, 6th ed., 1996).

[10] For a detailed discussion see Kanawaty (ed.), op. cit.

[11] See North, op. cit.

[12] Extensive literature on these topics is available from ILO.

[13] See J. E. Thurman at al.: *On business and work* (Geneva, ILO, 1993).

CONSULTING IN HUMAN RESOURCE MANAGEMENT 18

18.1 The changing nature of the personnel function

Personnel management, one of the traditional areas of management consulting, has undergone many changes over the past 20 to 30 years.

When consultants started dealing with the "people" side of business organizations, most of them tended to confine their interventions to problems grouped under the term "personnel administration". In French-speaking countries personnel problems were included in the so-called *gestion administrative* (administrative management). In nearly all countries, a personnel administration specialist typically dealt mainly with personnel records, regulations and procedures, job evaluation, remuneration, and "employment" issues such as recruitment, selection, induction, promotion, discipline, termination of employment, and handling of grievances. Over the years this has broadened considerably. The main changes that currently affect the nature and role of the personnel function occur in the following areas.

First, the subjects of personnel management – people working in organizations – have changed and continue to change in many respects. People have become better educated and prepared for their jobs, more aware of their rights, better informed and more interested in many issues of national and international economics and politics. Their value systems have changed; their employment and life aspirations have increased. Human relations within organizations have become complex, diversified and difficult to handle. These changes reflect not only technological development but also the significant trends of political and social change, such as the democratization of more and more countries (most dramatically, of course, in the former communist bloc), or the emergence of new social organizations and pressure groups (e.g. environmentalists and consumerists).

Second, an increased number of personnel issues, including conditions of employment, work and remuneration, are affected by legislation (including, in regions such as the European Union, international legislation), or have become the subject of collective agreements between workers' and employers' organizations. When dealing with these questions the personnel consultant must be fully aware of issues such as the existing legal and labour-relations frameworks, the role of the trade unions and other workers' representatives, and the need to inform or consult them in conformity with local practice.

Third, organizations are increasingly recognizing the value of their human resources, in terms of both cost and contribution. For most organizations, labour is the major operating cost item. Even where it is not, the skills and abilities of individual employees are critical. Human resources are the only ones that can generate added value out of other resources. Increasingly, organizations are coming to see their employees as a source of competitive advantage. It is recognized that most inventions or new services are readily copied by competitors, but the knowledge that is held within the organization, and the effective management of that knowledge, are much less easy to replicate. The important knowledge, of course, is not that which is written down, but the knowledge that exists in the minds of the organization's people. Thus, achieving a balance between the cost and the capacity of human resources is a critical factor in organizational effectiveness and success.

One result of these changes has been the development of the concept of human resource management (HRM), as distinct from the more narrow concept of personnel administration or personnel management. Employees are viewed as the most valuable resource of an organization and from this basic premise a number of conclusions can be drawn as to ways of treating people. On the one hand, a focus on the cost side of the equation could involve a series of steps to limit spending on human resources and to link people more closely to results. It could include, for example, buying in labour capacity from outside the organization. On the other hand, a focus on capacity could lead to significant investment in motivating people for higher performance, in the role of leadership, through investment in training and development, or the choice of staff development systems.

A wide range of organizational development theories and concepts have emerged, and are being applied to the analysis of human problems in organizations, and to methods likely to increase the effectiveness of individuals and groups in achieving organizational goals.

Fourth, technological changes have had a significant impact on the way people are managed. This impact has been felt throughout the HRM environment, from the global integration of business through to the way that communication with employees is conducted. Before identifying a few key effects it is worth making the point that throughout the world there are vast numbers of employees almost untouched – at least directly – by technological change. Even within highly technical industries, international airlines for example, there are still people whose job is mainly to shift heavy materials by hand. Nevertheless, the impact of technological change operates at all levels. At the global level, technological change has "shrunk the globe", making it easy to transfer goods and services around the world, improving the position of some nations and putting others under pressure. At the national level, technological change has led to a transfer of employment from primary industry (agriculture, forestry, fishing) to manufacturing, and from manufacturing to services. In broad terms, the richest countries have the highest proportions of people in services and the lowest proportions in the primary sector. Within industrial sectors, technological change has led to the collapse of some industries or companies and the emergence of others, and to reductions in employment in some workplaces and expansion in others. More recently, we have seen the "fourth wave" (after primary industry, manufacturing and services): information technology. Inside organizations, technological change has had a major impact on the structure of jobs, on the way work is done and even on the shape of the organization. In the IT sector, for example, it is now possible for employees to work considerable distances away from their employer's offices, in their own time, linked to their superiors by the telecommunications system. At the most practical level, the new technology enables an employer to address "personal" letters to each of a large number of employees. This vast range of effects of new technology, from very significant and global to very local, has had an inevitable and extensive impact on HRM.

Fifth, the increasing internationalization of economies, the development of multinational trading blocs and the growth of international organizations (profit- or policy-based) have also had an impact on HRM. It is increasingly recognized that the management of people is more culture-bound and value-laden than any other area of management. Practices regarded as standard in one country or organization may be unthinkable in another environment (e.g. flexible working hours, open-plan offices, dining-rooms common to all staff irrespective of position and grade, direct access to top managers, or the use of confidential personnel files). Both personnel practitioners and management consultants have become more cautious and more selective in transferring personnel practices from one environment to another when dealing with people of different ethnic, social, cultural, religious and educational backgrounds. Sensitivity to this diversity has increased with the growth of international business, the advent of modern enterprises and organizations in developing countries, the expanding employment of foreign workers and managers, and improvements in management education.

We are living in an era in which the role of personnel and human resource management is being reassessed and enhanced, new demands are formulated and new approaches developed. This long-term change process creates many fresh opportunities for consultants. Both personnel specialists and general managers face increasingly complex human problems and find it difficult to keep informed about all conditions and factors to be considered in personnel decisions. In many cases they will appreciate help from an independent and objective human resource professional.

18.2 Policies, practices and the human resource audit

Consultancy in human resource management can take many forms, from the most comprehensive (the assessment of the labour force of a company that the client may be considering purchasing, or a total evaluation of the way in which the client's employment practices contribute to overall corporate strategy) to the very limited (a single management seminar or advice on dealing with a difficult employee). This section deals with the comprehensive consultancy work, while subsequent sections deal with the subjects that may either form part of that work or stand alone.

In the early stages of an assignment the consultant and the client may agree that a thorough diagnosis of the human resource management function is a desirable starting-point and should be undertaken before deciding how to focus the consultant's intervention. Often, there are existing organizational policies for dealing with the major elements of the personnel function – recruitment, staff development, promotion and transfer, salary increments, labour–management relations, and so on.

However, the consultant may find that the "policies" are often only pious hopes and good intentions. For a personnel policy to be worthy of the name, it should fulfil several criteria:

- it should be written and understandable, and should present a comprehensive coverage of the function;
- provision should be made for ensuring dissemination of important elements of policy to all the relevant sections of the organization;
- it should be soundly based, and consistent with public policy and current legislation;
- it should be internally consistent with the organization's stated general objectives and policies;
- specific personnel policies (e.g. staffing, development and administration) should be mutually supportive;
- it should be established as a result of multilevel discussion and consultation throughout the organization, including consultations with employees' representatives as appropriate.

The consultant may first attempt to appraise existing personnel policies and procedures by investigating, analysing and comparing policies with actual results obtained over a set period, by means of a systematic, in-depth audit. The major purpose of the audit is to provide information for and explanation of human resource management and development practices. To achieve this, information should be sought from all functions and levels throughout the organization.

The procedures for conducting the audit can vary considerably. Basically, they consist of obtaining information of a quantitative and qualitative nature from various records and reports, supplemented by interviews, questionnaires, surveys, informal discussions, and so on. Information may be obtained by means of a latitudinal study (e.g. a department-by-department assessment of safety records or absenteeism in which the percentage of lost time and other ratios are calculated on a comparative basis). Alternatively, a longitudinal study may be used in which a sample of individuals is examined in depth over time,

Box 18.1 The human resource audit (data for the past 12 months)

Stated policies	Regular practices	Example findings of audit
1. **Recruitment**		
To promote, where possible, from within the organization	Recruitment from external sources an ongoing and continual procedure	95% of appointments is made from external sources. High staff turnover of 40% per annum
2. **Training**		
No stated policy	Organization sends senior members on courses conducted by professional associations at request of individuals concerned	Staff claim only limited opportunities for promotion and development; feel they have to go elsewhere to "get on"
3. etc.		

in the light of the effects of the organization's policies on their performance. Hard data should be sought. If possible, data (e.g. on turnover, absenteeism, grievances, accidents, etc.) should be compared with those available from other comparable organizations.

A recommended method for setting out a human resource audit is to list the organization's policies in sequence, to write down the practices regularly employed by the organization and the results obtained from the study, and then to draw the appropriate conclusions and recommendations. An example is given in box 18.1. A list of personnel policies for audit purposes would include references to the full range of practices influencing the cost, capability and effectiveness of employees: organization; personnel planning; recruitment; selection; induction; transfers and promotions; performance assessment; training and development; communications; remuneration and allowances; job evaluation; fringe benefits; social and welfare benefits; safety and health; industrial relations; discipline; motivation; and administration.

A commonly used approach for obtaining information required by the audit, or by other interventions in human resource management and development, is the *interview*. Principles of interviewing were discussed in Chapter 8 and will not be repeated here. However, for the consultant working in HRM there is an additional, very significant element – confidentiality.

The consultant can expect to receive a good deal of information that must be held in confidence. The higher the level of trust engendered by consultants, the more they can expect to receive confidential or private data. Not all of the data may be related to the identified problem. New problems may surface that had not been anticipated during the entry phase. The consultant may have to go back to the client to renegotiate the problem and the focus of the consultation.

If the interviews are to be effective and are to produce the data needed, the consultant must work in an ethical manner. The rules must be established with the client prior to the work starting. Generally, ground rules are established that all data gathered will be merged and individual sources will not be revealed. If the client agrees, then the consultant can indicate this to the individual respondents when arranging interviews. If a respondent is still hesitant, this could indicate a low level of trust in the organization.

The results of the human resource audit should, if necessary, point out the need for definition, refinement, or rewriting of organizational policies. Similarly, a review of the organization's regular practices may suggest improvements to facilitate conversion of policies to actual procedures. Inadequate or totally absent data indicate that urgent attention is required. The principal result of an effective audit is a set of conclusions as to what needs to be improved in one or more areas of HRM. These areas are reviewed in the following sections. However, the audit may also reveal other significant problems, such as missing links between staff training and the business development strategies pursued by the company.

The client may be satisfied with the audit and convinced that enough guidance has been received to implement the conclusions without further help from the consultant. Or the consultant may be requested to assist in planning and implementing the changes that are required.

18.3 Human resource planning

The purpose of human resource planning is to make sure that the organization has the right number of people of the right profile at the right time. Many organizations do not discover the importance of this until they face a major problem – either the shortage of competent people becomes an obstacle to expansion or technological change, or the organization employs more people than it can afford and has to retrench.

In many cases a management consultant will be called in, once the problem has manifested itself, to help identify emergency measures to be taken if, for example, there is an acute shortage of competent staff, or if significant redundancies are anticipated. However, an emergency situation provides an opportunity to demonstrate the advantages of human resource planning treated as part of, and coherent with, strategic corporate planning.

The consultant will be able to help the client in combining various human resource planning techniques. If enough detailed information is available on the structure of production or other processes, it may be possible to define and describe all necessary job positions. This implies that a detailed job description is worked out for every job. This is particularly appropriate where the organization and the environment are stable. Increasingly, detailed lists of jobs cannot be established with accuracy, or units have rapidly changing functions and need to adapt readily to new conditions (this is typical, for example, in jobs with a high technology or knowledge content). In such conditions, organizations are tending to work with broader technical profiles of the kinds of people who will be needed, describing their educational background and experience; or with annual targets for individuals (output oriented), rather than defining tasks (input).

Here again, relevant interfirm comparison and benchmarking techniques may be of help, but they should not be used mechanically. The consultant must be able to show the client the numbers and profiles of staff in comparable organizations that achieve similar or better results, and the reasons for the difference. This underlines the relationship between the planning of human resources and of productivity and performance improvement.

18.4 Recruitment and selection

The consultant may be asked to provide advice on how to improve the recruitment and selection of various categories of personnel, including management personnel. Arguably, getting the right people into the organization is the most important issue in HRM: if that is done well, most other problems are easily soluble; if it is done badly, the resultant problems will multiply.

Recruitment

Recruitment is the process of attracting applicants for jobs within the organization. Here the consultant can help with advice on specifying the details of the job and the person required, and can clarify the means of advertising the vacancy. This may well include the most common and cost-effective method – using word-of-mouth channels – but might also involve the use of government or private employment agencies, or advertising in the local press or radio. Increasingly, organizations are using the Internet for recruitment. This has the advantage of getting the advertisement out cheaply to a potentially worldwide audience, though advertisements are often ethnocentric in nature, thus reducing their appeal in many countries. The downside of such methods is that they can attract considerable numbers of applications, which will need careful screening and processing.

Executive search

Executive search ("head-hunting") is a special service offered by some larger management consulting firms, or by consultants who are specialized in this function. It is used by a number of business and other organizations to fill important managerial or specialist positions. The advantage of using an executive search specialist is that such a person can develop information on potential sources of recruitment and undertake a systematic search and objective selection in a way that is usually outside the capabilities of a line or personnel manager.

Business firms turn to executive search specialists if they do not want to advertise a job publicly, or if they are seeking candidates in areas where advertising does not work. Most candidates also find executive search useful: some of them are glad to learn that they could have a more challenging career with another employer, while others appreciate a confidential discussion on alternative job opportunities, particularly if in their current position it is difficult for them to make the first contact or show interest in another job.

The executive search function involves: the building up of files and contacts needed to identify potential candidates and recruitment sources (an international search firm may have thousands of names of potential candidates in its computerized files); assistance to clients in analysing the job to be filled and defining the ideal candidate; active and methodical search for candidates (by direct approach, search through various business contacts, in some cases advertising, etc.); contacts with candidates for the purpose of interviewing them and ascertaining their interest in the job; evaluation and preliminary selection of candidates; arranging interviews for the client with preselected candidates; and follow-up contacts with the selected candidate and the client.

Executive search consultants often have their own professional associations (as in the United States) or are members of national associations of management consultants. Codes of ethics for executive search have been adopted in several countries. For example, such codes forbid charging fees to the candidates or accepting any payment from them; the cost of the search operation is charged to the client according to an agreed scheme (as a rule, 30 per cent of the annual salary of the candidate recruited).

As in other areas of recruitment, executive search is being drastically affected by the use of the Internet and a lot of these activities are likely to develop this way in the future.

Selection

Selection is the process of choosing between applicants. Some basic principles should be followed: the pool of candidates should not be restricted by irrelevant criteria such as sex or nationality; references should be checked; recruitment interviews should be properly conducted against prepared criteria by people who know about the job. In some organizations the problems faced are delicate. Political, ethnic or other criteria may prevail over technical competence, or trade union membership may be required as a condition of employment.

The consultant's professional responsibility requires him or her to advise the client on what should be changed in the best interests of the organization. But the client will be unlikely to follow advice that is deemed unrealistic because of political or other constraints that are not under his or her control.

In most instances, however, improvements in selection and recruitment will be feasible. The consultant may identify a more objective procedure and more precisely defined criteria, or may suggest and carry out a training programme for staff responsible for selection.

Some consultants assist clients with testing and assessing candidates for managerial or technical jobs. This is done through such procedures as interviews, dexterity or psychological testing, assessment centres and careful checking of references.

Retention

Given the increasing shortage of skills in some sectors and countries, an important role for the consultant is often to focus the organization on retaining staff rather than just recruiting them. An analysis of turnover rates (recruitment and terminations of employment), retention rates and employee flows through the organization is a good way of highlighting the problem. Organizations in the high-technology sector frequently find themselves in "bidding wars" for new staff, while simultaneously their employees are leaving them in considerable numbers. It is cheaper and more effective to design programmes to keep those employees within the workforce: training and development, interesting work, profit or equity sharing can all have a positive effect. The simple assumption that the problem is uncompetitive pay levels is sometimes right; but often the situation is more complex. The management consultant should get the organization to consider introducing exit interviews aimed at finding out from those who leave what is causing them to make that decision. Exit interviews are best carried out by someone other than the immediate line manager and have to be handled sensitively.

Termination and outplacement

One unfortunate consequence of the competitive situation in industrialized economies throughout the world has been a huge growth in recent decades in terminations of employment. Many consultants now provide specialist advice on this subject, ranging from policy to practical support. At the policy level, consultants can help an organization determine how many people should be retained and how many should go, how to ensure compliance with relevant laws and collective agreements, and how to announce the resultant policy. At the practical level consultants are often called in to provide outplacement services – giving psychological, career, retraining and financial planning assistance to those who will be leaving the company. The concern for the welfare of the individuals who are made redundant can ease the process considerably, and a skilful and caring consultant can do a lot to make a difficult situation more bearable.

18.5 Motivation and remuneration

Motivation

Every organization aims to achieve certain economic and social objectives, but the resources at its disposal are limited. It tries, therefore, to motivate its personnel towards the achievement of a range of goals, which may include societal, organizational, group and individual goals. An HRM consultant may be requested to assist in determining what motivational tools and strategies should be used. This may include, for example:

- The improvement of the overall *organizational climate* (the psychological and motivational environment of the organization). This climate strongly affects the motivation of people at every level in the organization to work and to achieve. It is determined primarily by the people management practices of senior managerial staff, by the employment and working conditions, and by the encouragement given to individual and group initiative, innovation, creativity and self-development.
- The enrichment of *job content*, where, by changing the structure of the work to be performed, the consultant endeavours to assist in creating intrinsic job interest and increasing job satisfaction, and developing a more flexible and efficient workforce. There is evidence that increased team working, increased autonomy for teams and employee involvement generally have a positive motivational effect.
- *Reward systems*, where the appropriate behaviour is shaped as a result of certain rewards, particularly financial and material ones. This requires a feedback system, so that the incentive used (e.g. pay) is tied as directly as possible to actual individual or group performance. However, the role of non-financial rewards or incentives is important and must not be underestimated when trying to enhance staff motivation.

These methods do not operate independently, but affect separate components of the motivational process and call for different levels of intervention on the part of the organization and of the consultant. Consultants commonly face complaints by clients about the lack of motivation of the managers or their staff for achieving higher performance in organizations where people are relatively well paid. A thorough study is needed to determine the weight of various factors affecting staff motivation. The study may reveal that the client assumes that a good salary is a stronger motivational factor than it really is. It may be that the salary level is taken for granted by the employees concerned, that the client and the employees differ in their views on what salary level is adequate, or that certain adverse factors in the working environment negate the effect of good salaries. For example, employees often regard interesting job content and real prospects for future career development as more important for job satisfaction than the level of their salary.

Wages and salaries

In some assignments, the consultant will be requested to assist in examining and reorganizing the wage and salary system. This kind of consultancy arises from the fact that increasing competition (or spending restrictions in the public sector) focuses attention on the costs of employment – a major operating cost for almost all organizations. In addition, the requirements of new technology and the consequent abolition or reorganization of tasks, or demands for flexible working practices, mean that pay systems have to be adjusted to fit a new reality. The challenge to existing and well-accepted structures is obvious and the importance of establishing acceptance of any new structures is clear.

In Europe and elsewhere this problem has been compounded by moves towards the "individualization" of pay (often in a non-union setting) and "pay for performance" (where individuals in the same job may receive different salaries depending upon managerial judgement of their performance). This has increased pay variability.

Variable pay presents major problems. First, there is the problem of establishing clear targets and monitoring performance against them so that managerial assessments are acknowledged to be fair and not arbitrary. Second, there is the issue of what percentage of pay is variable: too much and it threatens individuals' livelihoods, too little and it fails to motivate. Third, the issue of guaranteed limits has to be addressed: if the organization is successful or people perform well, they receive pay increases – but what happens in other circumstances? Do individuals take a pay cut? These are all issues that well-prepared consultants can bring to the organization's attention and help to resolve.

In the same vein, there has been a spread of financial participation in the success of an organization through stock options or profit-sharing, particularly in Europe and North America. Again, such systems can help to generate commitment and retention and are often seen as a fairer way to share the wealth that has been generated. There are often tax and other advantages that can accrue to the employees and the organization. A key question concerns whether the systems should cover just the senior employees (more usual in the United States) or all employees (more common in Europe).[1]

In most of the developing world, and still in much of the developed world, wages and salaries are fixed using a more traditional and clearly structured approach. The problem will be to develop a salary system that works efficiently and fairly from the point of view of both the organization's management and its employees (and, where appropriate, their representatives). Logically, the consultant approaches such a problem by conducting a job analysis, followed by job evaluation and the building of a job structure so as to develop an equitable salary system and a plan that can accommodate periodic reviews, supplementary remuneration and appropriate fringe benefits. Obviously, the consultant cannot see wage and salary problems as purely technical ones and has to be well informed on legislation and industrial relations practices related to wages, especially on collective bargaining. The problems most frequently met in this area include:

- distorted salary systems (e.g. the wage differentials do not reflect the relative difficulty and importance of particular categories of jobs);
- no relationship, or a very weak one, between salary and real performance at work;

- wage and salary differentials that do not motivate employees towards training and self-development or to seek promotion to more responsible and more rewarding jobs;
- obsolete salary and pay structures, which have not been adapted to the requirements of new technologies and to the changing structure of jobs;
- little or no flexibility in using individual and group bonuses and special rewards for encouraging high performance, and in demonstrating that such performance is important to the organization and is therefore properly remunerated by management;
- excessive secrecy in matters of salaries and other rewards, giving rise to various suspicions about the actual pay levels of certain individuals, and reducing confidence in the objectivity and fairness of management over questions of pay.

The sensitivity of pay issues, particularly in certain cultures, means that these problems are rarely easy to handle, although from a strictly technical viewpoint the solution may be straightforward. The consultant should be cautious in establishing, and assessing with the client, the feasibility of changes, and the way in which the necessary changes are to be announced, introduced and maintained.

Social benefits

There are other issues in the field of salaries and compensation which now attract considerable amounts of consultancy work, in particular those related to financial benefits other than pay: social benefits, tax and actuarial services, pensions and insurance. In many parts of the world there are specialized consulting firms (some quite large) whose task is to ensure that employers and employees obtain the maximum benefits from their investment of money in these areas. This often involves advising on the source and location of investment opportunities and on minimizing taxation. This type of consultancy requires a detailed knowledge of financial markets and the laws of the relevant country. It is often controlled by legislation so that only qualified individuals can offer such services. As financial and legal requirements become ever more complex, this is likely to be a growth area for consultancy.

Job analysis, evaluation and classification

Job analysis includes the collection, organization and examination of information on what people do in a particular job. Job analysis is used not only to produce job descriptions for recruitment and other purposes, as discussed above, but also for *job evaluation*, that is, determining job worth. Depending on the job in hand, the order of complexity of the job evaluation system usually moves from (1) whole job ranking schemes, through (2) job classification, to (3) points evaluation systems, and (4) factor comparison methods. Worldwide, whole job ranking is probably the most frequently used, although larger companies often prefer the points evaluation system.

Job classification involves the setting of wage and salary levels by classifying jobs within the organization and comparing the levels of pay with contribution to organizational success, and to competitive or other firms with a comparable job structure and conditions of business. The market value of individual jobs is given consideration, using various sources of information such as surveys and reports published by management associations, government departments, or independent business information services.

In practice, however, many jobs are not evaluated, or, if they are, their evaluation is only one of the factors determining the rate of pay:

> While many employers believe that employees' pay should be differentiated on the basis of current performance, many others (perhaps a majority) believe that seniority, age and past performance and loyalty should have equal or greater weight in individual pay determination. Managers may claim that they have merit or performance-based pay systems, but many studies indicate that they are more accurately based on current performance plus seniority, or seniority alone.[2]

Changes in the way work is done (e.g. as a result of new technologies and particularly developments in new forms of work organization) have changed the jobs people do in critical ways. The dramatic changes in technologies, job structures and staff competence requirements are generating new demands for advice and assistance.

18.6 Human resource development

Human resource development (HRD) is a fast-growing area of consulting in personnel and human resource management. There are consultants who specialize in this area, while many firms have established important HRD divisions and train most of their staff members in various aspects and technologies of HRD. As clients have become better informed about HRD, and hence more cautious, competent and demanding in selecting HRD programmes and consultants, the "charlatans" who previously viewed HRD as a source of easy income have become known for what they are.

The main purpose of HRD is to help people in organizations to face the challenges created by technological and other changes, to adapt to new requirements, to develop skills, and to achieve the levels of performance needed to stay competitive. A true HRD professional does not promise spectacular changes in attitudes and competence as a result of a few workshop sessions. The HRD specialist makes the client aware of the complexity of the human side of the enterprise, and of the need to consider all factors affecting motivation, behaviour, interpersonal relations and performance of people in organizations. It is important to warn the client against inconsistencies in personnel and HRD practices, as these can devalue the impact of many well-intentioned but partial and uncoordinated staff development measures.

Ideally, HRD should be allied to significant ongoing or projected changes in the organization or its policies so that the change and the development are mutually reinforcing. The specialist needs to be informed about the availability of a wide range of techniques for human resource and organization development and for productivity and performance improvement (see Chapter 20), but must also be aware of the cultural bias of certain techniques and the need to avoid a mechanistic transfer which disregards differences in local cultural values and social systems.

HRD is an area which is to a considerable extent bound by national culture. The approach to career planning, the exposure of inadequacies that require training and the informal, even humorous, training style that may work very well in the United States, for example, would be totally inappropriate in China. Consultants need to be aware of these variations. Even so, some general trends are discernible. There are moves to raise the profile of HRD within organizations, to make it more flexible and tailored to individuals and to take a broader view, so that people would develop through job rotation, through careful mentoring by a superior, and by self-study as much as through classroom-based courses. At the same time, and perhaps rather paradoxically, companies are increasingly likely to insist that HRD is tailored to the immediately foreseeable needs of the organization, so that the cost–benefit equation is more obviously positive.

HRD is a very broad topic and it is not possible here to review all the approaches and techniques used.[3] Rather we will point to certain management concerns that may call for a consultant's intervention. The reader should also refer to Chapter 4 on consulting and change, where several HRD and OD techniques are discussed in some detail.

Staff training and development

An HRD consultant can act as an adviser on how to increase the effectiveness of staff training and development, or can be directly involved in preparing and delivering in-company training. Typically, assignments in this area aim to answer such questions as:

- How can staff training and development be related to the goals and problems of the organization and make it performance-oriented?
- How can the training needs of various categories of personnel be identified?
- What should be the content and methodology of staff development programmes and how should they be organized?
- How can the impact of staff development on organizational performance be evaluated and the optimum level of investment in HRD determined?
- How can the training unit be organized and the competence of the training director and in-company trainers increased?

- What benefits can be drawn from sending managers and staff specialists to external courses at business schools, management institutes, consulting firms, productivity centres, and elsewhere? What sort of relationship should be established with external units offering training programmes, and should these units be used for mounting tailor-made in-plant programmes?
- How can employees be motivated for training and self-development and for using the results of training in their work? What obstacles need to be removed if training is to have the desired impact on both individual and organizational performance?

In some countries trade unions are heavily involved in the provision of training. In others the trade unions or employee representatives can be partners in training, helping to ensure that its importance is recognized, that its content is relevant, and that employees are enthusiastic about undertaking it.

Where the consultant is directly involved in the organization and delivery of training, it is useful to go through the same checklist of questions in relation to training policy to ensure that the programme offers maximum benefit.

One question that consultants often have to answer concerns the cost of training individuals who, in a free labour market, may leave, taking their acquired skill to another organization. Part of the answer is that few organizations can afford not to invest in the skills of their employees, whatever the risk, and part is that a clear and coherent human resources management and training policy often motivates people to stay. There are also examples of competitors working together in an attempt to reduce costs and increase cost-effectiveness of training.

Career development and succession planning

Career development is a significant aspect of human resource development, although its importance may not be the same in all cultures. The consultant should be able to explain the consequences of the absence of career planning to the client. Although in many organizations a detailed plan of the career path of every individual may be impossible or undesirable, it should be possible to establish a career development policy as guidance for staff development and for motivating individual performance. Without constituting a legal commitment to every individual, such a policy provides a clear model against which employees can compare their own expectations and gear their self-development and work improvement efforts, with obvious gains in motivation and productivity.

Linked to the concept of career development is that of succession planning: who will take over as senior managers of the organization when the current ones retire or leave? Many organizations have no plans even for such predictable events. Individuals with potential should be identified in good time and the organization should work on preparing them for promotion. Alternatively, plans need to be made for external recruitment. The consultant can play a useful role in reminding organizations' leaders of their "organizational mortality" and in sensitively arranging for smooth successions.

Performance appraisal

Performance appraisal has been one of the weakest links in HRM systems. Many small organizations do not practise any performance appraisal on a regular basis. A number of medium-sized and large organizations have introduced structured performance appraisal schemes, but the reality tends to be very different from declared objectives and policies. The consultant is likely to find that, even where regular performance appraisals do take place and performance reports are duly produced and signed, no conclusions are drawn and no use is made of the appraisals in deciding on staff development, promotions, transfers, merit increments, and so on. In some organizations annual appraisals have become formalities that must be carried out but do not reflect real performance. In other cases the appraisal reflects only the subjective views and preferences of direct supervisors.

While it is not hard to find out about the formalism and other weaknesses of performance appraisals, it is much more difficult to change a deeply rooted practice. The consultant can help the client to realize that appraisal ought to be concerned with actual performance rating, that appraisers require training in performance assessment techniques, and that sensible performance appraisal commences with well-established organizational, group and individual goals. Current thinking concentrates on these, and simple reporting forms, rather than on complex and time-consuming paperwork.

The important task, of course, is the management of performance, not the organization of a system. Good managers will always be able to motivate and assess the outputs of their staff; no system will make poor managers do it properly. A key role for consultants is to bring this message home to the organization. However good the appraisal system is, it cannot be a substitute for inadequate managers. The development of a performance appraisal system that achieves the organization's objectives will almost always require a careful look at the quality and development of the organization's management team. Whatever organization and techniques of appraisal are chosen, the improved system will require the support of employees' representatives and strong management commitment.

Organizational development

Many consulting interventions in the HRD field are of the OD type. The original definitions of OD emphasized the application of behavioural sciences for assisting organizations in identifying, planning and implementing organizational changes. Interventions focused on organizational processes such as communication, sharing of information, interpersonal relations, team building, the use of meetings or the ways of resolving conflicts, rather than on providing solutions to substantive technical issues involved in the process. More recent approaches aim to combine "classical" OD with diagnosis and resolution of specific (technological, organizational, financial) problems, and to implement organizational performance improvement programmes in which many other diagnostic, problem-solving, process re-engineering and change management techniques are used (see also Chapters 4 and 22). This requires that an OD consultant should also be versed in a particular area of management and business. Equally, consultants in various technical areas of management, as well as all-round generalists, can increase their effectiveness by mastering OD principles and some OD techniques.

Towards a learning organization

A useful concept reflecting contemporary thinking about change and organizations, as well as the recent experience of a number of dynamic companies, is the "learning organization".[4] It brings a new dimension to corporate strategy and to training and development. Instead of having a separate training and development function, the whole organization is viewed as a learning system where individuals learn from the organization's actions and from developments shaping its environment, and where the organization as a whole learns from actively participating individuals. Both individual and organizational learning are used as inseparable elements of strategic management and change.

These features have been stressed in the various definitions of learning organizations. For example, according to the Training Commission in the United Kingdom, "a learning organization is one which facilitates learning and personal development of all its employees, whilst continually transforming itself".

In learning organizations, continuous learning by individuals is regarded as necessary for organizational survival and for achieving organizational excellence in a rapidly changing business environment. It is facilitated and stimulated in accordance with the following principles:

- learning is linked both to organizational strategy and to individual goals;
- emphasis is on on-the-job development and action learning;
- specialist training courses are available across the knowledge/skills/value spectrum;
- the principal focus is on learning about developments in the company's environment, science and technology, and new management and business concepts that could and should be used to improve organizational performance and competitiveness in the future;
- training to fill existing competency gaps related to current business activities is not neglected;
- new and open forms of training activity are utilized, including distance learning, Internet-based programmes and self-development, and individuals have the main say in choosing the forms they use;
- learning is regarded as a continuous process, not as a sequence of separate and mutually unrelated courses or other events;
- the career and reward systems provide strong recognition of learning.

However, encouraging individual learning is not enough to become a learning organization. Individual learning must be turned into organizational learning. Therefore learning organizations aim to develop the following features:

- learning in teams is encouraged;
- various formulas are used to share information and results of individual and team learning throughout the organization; results of individual learning must be available to any other collaborator who may need them;
- managers act as trainers and coaches and are responsible for the transfer of information, ideas and competencies among individuals and teams within their units, and with other units in the organization;
- managers focus learning on the organization's goals, opportunities and future perspectives without neglecting training needed for achieving short-term objectives and making immediate improvements;
- management makes sure that learning is effectively used for planning and implementing organizational changes;
- the main responsibility for staff development is vested in line managers; but human resource and training managers have a prominent position in the company's power structure and participate in conceptual and strategic thinking and planning concerning the organization's future.

Learning organizations learn from their own internal environment and experience, making sure that positive experience is rapidly disseminated and replicated, while negative experience is objectively assessed and acknowledged, and measures are taken to avoid repeating it (e.g. in other parts of the organization or by new staff members). Ideas and critiques are collected through suggestion schemes and meetings, opinion and corporate climate surveys are used, open discussion and feedback are practised, innovation and experimentation are encouraged, and internal records and reports are carefully studied.

Learning from the external environment includes:

- learning from customers (satisfaction, complaints, changing needs and demands, changing tastes, ideas on new and better services, joint work on product and service improvement);
- learning from competitors and other organizations involved in comparable activities (e.g. through benchmarking);
- learning about new developments in science and technology;
- learning about market trends and changes;
- learning about economic, social, institutional and other developments.

At a minimum level, a learning organization can respond to information learned and analysed. At an optimum level, it is forward-looking and proactive, changing and improving products, services and processes without waiting for such a change to become inevitable as a result of more dynamic competitors or unhappy customers.

Both HRD and strategy consultants can render an invaluable service to their clients by helping them to understand and implement the learning organization concept. It is important to see that it is not a definitive and closed model which a company would have to adopt or reject in its totality. It is a philosophy, an approach to strategy, customers, people management and learning. It can be applied at various levels of sophistication. It is therefore fully accessible to companies that are not sector leaders, to small companies and even to organizations in difficulties. It may well prove to be a more effective way of getting out of difficulties than various restructuring schemes in which individual and organizational learning are underestimated.

The learning organization concept has much in common with knowledge management – another recent concept aiming to help companies to develop, apply, utilize and maintain the knowledge required by their business (see Chapter 19).

18.7 Labour–management relations

Consultants, in whatever area of management consulting, must always bear in mind that their recommendations can have implications for the labour–management relations of the enterprise or industry with which they are concerned. For example, a consultant developing and recommending new remuneration schemes must be aware of possible collectively bargained obligations in the pay area that cannot be avoided without further negotiations with the trade union or other workers' representatives (e.g. works councils provided for by statute and with powers in this sphere). Similarly, changes in work organization suggested by a production management consultant may have to be negotiated with the trade union because of collective agreements or, in a number of countries, under legislative requirements. In virtually every area of management, consultants must ascertain the implications for labour–management relations of various courses of action that they are considering for recommendation to their clients. Beyond that, a good case can be made, in certain circumstances, for using the existing processes and institutions of labour–management relations (e.g. consultation and negotiation), and perhaps even inciting the development of new processes and institutions, in mapping out strategies for change.

This being said, there are circumstances in which, and subjects on which, it would be inappropriate, given the labour–management relations system or traditions of the country, industry or enterprise concerned, to consult – much less negotiate – with trade unions or other workers' representatives. There are still some issues that are considered exclusively the prerogative of management. These vary from country to country and even from situation to situation. They are issues in respect of which, for various reasons, workers' representatives have no need to be involved; indeed, informing them prematurely could be deleterious to the effective functioning of the enterprise. A thoroughly professional consultant will know, or find out, how to distinguish between situations where prior consultation or provision of information on change is necessary, helpful or appropriate, and those where it is not.

The contexts of consultancies on labour–management relations

The experienced consultant on personnel management/human resource management/ labour–management relations should be aware of the various legal obligations and constraints in the country or region in which he or she is principally operating. However, given the globalization of business and of the consultancy profession, consultants may well have to become acquainted with the law and practice of industrial relations in countries other than their own. In addition, the increasingly numerous regulations and directives in the labour–management relations field issued by regional groupings, such as the European Union (EU), must be taken into account.

In all cases, regardless of the setting, the cultural context of labour–management relations must be given its due if the consultancy is to be successful. Advice on labour–management relations that would be highly pertinent in Western countries could be inappropriate in an Asian setting. For example, there is some doubt whether a North American or European style grievance procedure could be effective without substantial adaptation in certain Asian countries where interpersonal confrontation on an individual level is simply not countenanced. These cultural issues and their implications for labour–management relations may not always be easy for a non-native consultant to appreciate and incorporate into his or her recommendations, but an effort must be made to understand them and take them into account.

The remainder of this section examines various points relevant to a labour–management relations consultancy. However, it should be noted that, while technical advice in this field may be provided by those who are highly specialized in labour–management relations proper, consultants in personnel and human resource management often possess or develop the necessary expertise, and are called upon to advise in this area.

Timing and the threshold question

The consultant may be called in because problems already exist in labour–management relations, because there are internal or external forces that are likely to lead to problems, or because advice is needed on formulating or refashioning labour–management relations policies. The reform or refashioning of such policies is particularly pertinent when industries and organizations are concerned with restructuring. Whether brought about through managerial initiative or through consultation or negotiation with workers' representatives, measures associated with restructuring, such as retrenchment, flattening out of management, changes in work organization and the like, can have enormous implications for both the climate and practice of labour–management relations in the organization.

In virtually every case in which a labour–management relations consultant is called in, a key question will be the presence or absence of workers' representatives, in particular of a trade union in or for the organization. Where a trade union or other form of workers' representation exists, the nature and potential role of that representation must be clarified. Once it is determined that there should or could be a role for workers' representation in the consultant's project, the consultant must try to understand (in the case of a trade union) the representativeness of that union, the nature of the leadership of the workers' representation body, and the internal politics and power centres within it. Only then is it possible to pursue effective and constructive contacts with that body.

In many countries, especially in the developed world, collective bargaining and labour relations with trade unions are coming under pressure from an increasing individualization of the employment relationship. Not only are people less likely to join trade unions, but many organizations are now actively developing more personal and less collective ways of dealing with their employees – varying pay within a group, individual performance appraisal, personal letters to employees, and even individual negotiation of pay and conditions. This should however not be exaggerated: the evidence from Europe is that employers are likely to be developing individualization of employee contacts whilst retaining a commitment to good relations with the trade unions. Neither should individualization be overlooked. Consultants may well be asked to become involved in individualization projects either implicitly or explicitly as part of a policy aimed at weakening the union's influence.

Consultants should be able to help the client explore the advantages and disadvantages of both collective bargaining and collective relations on the one hand, and individualization on the other. A key criterion is that the organization has a well-thought-through, coherent and consistent approach to these issues: a good consultant will help the client to develop such an approach.

Principal areas of labour–management relations consulting

The essential questions in labour–management relations with which the consultant may be called upon to deal could include one or more of the following:

(1) Workers' representation. Advice on dealing with workers' representatives on a day-to-day basis is often an element of a consultancy. As mentioned, these may be (a) trade union representatives from within or outside the organization (including officers or staff of union federations with a unit within the organization), or (b) workers' representatives provided for in legislation or, infrequently, through general procedural collective agreements, and who are elected by all the employees of the organization. The latter generally have no direct or organic links with a union and are not subject to union discipline, but often have strong unofficial links with a union. Both types of workers' representation may coexist in the same organization (or branch, if the scope of the consultancy is wider than, for example, a single enterprise). In such cases the consultant must exercise great care in determining which – if any – matters are appropriate for interaction with one or the other type of workers' representation. This is not always easy, as the relative competence of the two types may not be clearly delineated and there may even be jurisdictional struggles between the two. It might also be noted at this point that, adding to the complexity of the question, workers' representatives are in one way or another becoming increasingly involved in the labour problems flowing from restructuring of organizations; and such restructuring can be a very conspicuous aspect of management consulting. Finally, in recent years there has been a diminution of trade union militancy in a number of countries (but certainly not all) and consultants may wish to consider this aspect when framing their advice.

(2) Disputes and grievances. A consultant may be requested to address the mechanics of handling workers' grievances, including advice on the setting up of grievance procedures or other conflict resolution procedures. In this area the consultant may have to consider the scope of the procedure proposed (or proposed to be negotiated with workers' representatives). Should the grievance procedure, for example, be all-encompassing or restricted to alleged treatment inconsistent with an existing agreement or with the provisions of works rules? What of the protection of certain managerial prerogatives that might be called into question by a conflict resolution procedure? And what should be the client's position with regard to the possibility of agreed arbitration procedures for unresolved grievances or in the case of impasses in collective bargaining? In this regard, increasing attention is being paid in certain countries to the possibility of using different forms of alternative dispute resolution through either agreed or unilaterally initiated procedures. These are but a few examples of issues that could be evoked – or that the consultant may wish to evoke – in this area.

(3) Collective bargaining. The significance of collective bargaining will depend to some extent on the level at which it takes place – for the industry as a whole, for the industry in a particular region or locality, for a group of enterprises, or at the enterprise or work-site level. In most cases where there is a form of workers' representation at the enterprise or workplace some bargaining will take place at that level. If this is the level at which the consultancy arises, then bargaining becomes crucial. The consultant may be called upon to carry out one or more of three functions in this regard: to develop the skills of the managers concerned with bargaining; to participate as a member of the employer's bargaining team; and to act as management's spokesperson in negotiations. In all cases, the organization's permanent management team has to take ultimate responsibility.

Given the trend towards decentralization of industrial relations and collective bargaining in many countries where the focus of bargaining has traditionally been at higher levels, this function of consultants is receiving increasing emphasis. Collective bargaining on issues such as the introduction of new technology and increased labour flexibility (particularly in terms of workforce size, remuneration and job content) normally takes place at the enterprise level. But even if, for example, collective bargaining is centred at the industry or branch level, the consultant may still have to advise the employer or the employer's bargaining team on certain matters, as an input to the formulation of bargaining positions and strategy by the employers' association.

(4) Management–worker consultation and cooperation. A consultant may be called upon to advise on machinery and procedures for management–worker consultation and cooperation on matters of common interest, such as productivity or welfare and recreational facilities (as opposed to issues of an adversarial nature, such as grievances or bargaining demands). New emphasis on this area is reflected in various individual and group employee incentive schemes, as well as in different types of quality management group programmes. Indeed, legislation or higher-level collective agreements increasingly call for or encourage the development of machinery for greater consultation and cooperation, and even mechanisms for workers' participation in managerial decision-making (co-determination) in certain areas. At the same time care should be exercised by the consultant to ensure that appropriate distinctions are made so as not to subvert the collective bargaining process (particularly where legal strictures might exist in this area).

(5) Employers' position in tripartite consultations. The position to be taken by employers' associations in tripartite (government/employers/trade unions) or bipartite (either with governments or trade unions) consultations at the national and, sometimes, branch levels can be defined with a consultant's help. Such consultative mechanisms, sometimes ad hoc but more frequently of a standing nature, exist in most countries and deal with broad economic and social questions. With national-level consultations individual employers may require guidance in fashioning their input into their association's position and strategy. In fact, consultants would do well to impress upon their clients the importance of such input, and participation, since the decisions ultimately emanating from national-level consultations almost always have at least an indirect impact, and sometimes a direct impact, on the fortunes of the enterprise.

(6) Partnership agreements. Increasingly some organizations in various countries are trying to develop a different approach to these issues through working closely with trade unions, but moving away from a confrontational and distributive approach towards one based on partnership. There is still much discussion about whether this is merely a re-labelling of collective bargaining when the union is very weak or whether it is genuinely a new development. There are certainly some cases however where the union and the management have agreed to a new way of working, with open-book management (managment accounts available to the union); commitment to decisions made with no balloting of members; and joint agreement to facilitate change. Consultants are nearly always crucial in the initial process of getting managers and unions to understand the challenge such agreements make to their established ways of conducting business and to work through the changes that will be necessary. Such agreements demand honesty from the various sides and that can make the negotiations extremely sensitive; the consultant's role is to keep everyone on track during difficult sessions and to ensure that the focus remains on the agreement. There is a more extensive role to be played after the agreement has been signed because its success will depend on the agreed changes being accepted by local line managers and union representatives: if they do not change their approaches, the formal agreement will fail.

(7) Dismissal and redundancy. Principles and procedures for dismissal and redundancy (whether within or outside the context of collective bargaining) are often subject to treatment by consultants. Here again the freedom of action of the parties involved may be restricted by legislation or agreed provisions. In most countries there are restrictions on abusive or unjustified dismissals and, perhaps less frequently, arbitrary selection of those to be let go in a redundancy situation. However, within these limitations there are normally details, procedures and criteria to be worked out and the consultant may have to make a contribution on this score.

Trade unions as clients

While typically it is enterprise management that engages the consultant, a development in more recent years has been the provision of labour–management consultancy services to trade unions. There may also be cases where the consultant is engaged jointly by management and the trade union.

An important and developing area of this work involves helping the unions to manage themselves more strategically. In general, the people who manage trade unions had not seen their careers as managing complex, multi-site organizations with, sometimes, extensive cash turnover and large investment. For senior union officers, this is exactly the position they find themselves in – invariably with little training or expertise in the task. Nevertheless, the members expect their representative organization to be as well managed as possible. There is thus a role for consultants in helping senior officials understand their managerial role within the union and in ensuring that the union is strategically well managed.

Importance of the legal framework

In providing advice, an important place must be given to the relevant legal framework of labour–management relations. This framework is different in every country and, at times, in particular industries. In certain countries, for example those in Central and Eastern Europe, legislation is only now settling down from the frequent amendments and modifications of the early and mid 1990s. For these countries, this is a time of discovery and experimentation.

Similarly, many countries in the developing world, particularly Latin America and Africa, have moved towards political democracy, and this has entailed radical change in labour–management law and practice.

The legal framework might reflect rules on:

- trade union recognition and the employer's obligation to deal with a given union;
- workers' representation at the workplace, and the protection (e.g. supplementary protection against dismissal or retrenchment) and facilities (e.g. time off, office space, access to members) that may have to be afforded to trade union and other workers' representatives;
- forms and substance of workers' participation in decision-making within the enterprise (e.g. rules concerning works councils and their role, or membership of workers' representatives on company boards);
- the formation and content of individual contracts of employment, and their relationship to any collective agreements which may be in, or later come into, force;
- legal rules (both legislated and resulting from judicial decisions) concerning termination of employment;
- the situation of public service employees and how labour legislation applies to, or excludes, them.

It is always necessary for consultants to take account of existing legal prescriptions in charting courses of action to be recommended to clients. Moreover, even company rules on conditions of employment promulgated by management (employee handbooks and the like) may have juridical or enforceable status. Whether they do or not, consultants should take them into consideration; they may even wish to suggest changes in such rules. Where particularly complex legal problems arise, or have to be resolved in the course of the consultancy, it may be necessary to have recourse to the services of a qualified lawyer specializing in labour law.

Provisions of collective agreements

The labour–management relations consultant must be fully aware of the relevant provisions of existing collective agreements that apply to the enterprise concerned (whether such agreements are for the industry, the region or the enterprise itself). He or she must also be aware, in certain cases, of possible interpretations of those provisions which may have been made by labour courts, arbitrators or other decision-making bodies. Even past interpretations of collective agreement provisions made by management (and in respect of which the trade union has raised no challenge) might be relevant. If this examination should result in a consultant finding that changes in the collective agreement are warranted or should be sought (and provided that this aspect is not clearly outside the terms of reference), then his or her advice may make due reference to this.

Custom and usage

Rules resulting from laws and regulations, and from collective agreements, are only two of the significant norms which may have to be considered by the labour–management relations consultant. In virtually all established enterprises, organizations and industries, there will be labour–management customs, usage and practices which often require the same respect and attention that is accorded to official regulations. At times these customs, usage and practices are common to a specific region or locality. Examples are ex gratia payments and bonuses, time off which has been traditionally granted to attend to certain family, personal or religious matters, and so on. It is essential that the consultant is fully aware of – and if necessary actively finds out about – such customs, usage and practices as are relevant to the consultancy. There will, of course, be occasions when certain of them should be dropped or changed. The consultant may well be in a position to influence appropriate changes in established labour–management relations practices, even those that are ingrained in the organization. Indeed, this may be a crucial aspect of the consultant's assignment. However, the consultant must realize that in embarking on such a course of action, or in making the pertinent recommendations, extreme care should be taken, and consideration given to the possible – and sometimes unforeseen – consequences and implications of breaking with traditional practice.

There might even be legal consequences since, as alluded to above, certain practices may be interpreted as having the status of acquired and enforceable rights.

Interaction with workers' representatives

It is important that the consultant becomes familiar with the position, outlook and concerns of the trade union or other workers' representatives who will be involved in any course of action that he or she might recommend, since reactions from the workers' side can have a significant influence in such recommendations. However, before entering into personal contacts with such representatives, the consultant should, in agreement with the client, consider what contacts would be appropriate before and during the framing of recommendations. Dealings with workers' representatives, and particularly trade union representatives, can be very delicate, and the consultant should discuss with management just what areas encompassed by the consultancy may be touched on in such contacts.

The consultant also needs to know the limits of his or her authority to commit management should the contacts be of a nature where even tentative commitments may be made or inferred. Among other things, the delicacy of contacts between the consultant and trade union representatives lies in their implications for inter-union and intra-union politics as well as possible leadership competition within unions. If the consultant and the management are perceived to be taking sides or demonstrating partiality towards one group or another (even if this is not the case), both the consultancy itself and labour–management relations in the organization may be compromised.

The consultant is nevertheless well advised to recommend that every opportunity for constructive consultations between management and workers' representatives be seized (whether or not there are legal requirements in this regard). This is almost always desirable, but is particularly so when new labour–management relations policies are being considered or introduced. The cooperation or acquiescence of trade union or other workers' representatives resulting from such consultations can often be a crucial factor in the success or failure of the consultant's efforts.

18.8 New areas and issues

International human resource management

One issue in human resource management that is attracting increasing attention – and is a rapidly growing area of consultancy work – concerns international HRM. The growing internationalization of business and of HRM has already been noted. Increasing numbers of people are living and working outside their home country (expatriates). Traditionally these people were government representatives (civil and armed services), members of religious groups and charities, and staff of major multinational corporations (MNCs) sent from developed to developing countries. This pattern has changed, as the large MNCs have generally reduced the number of international transferees, while smaller companies have moved into the area. This process has been facilitated by the growth of international trade blocs such as the Association of South-East Asian Nations (ASEAN), the North American Free Trade Agreement (NAFTA) and the EU. Within the EU in particular, there are now Union-wide legislation and policies aimed at easing the movement of people seeking employment across national boundaries.

This is a field that has tended to be dominated by consultants from two broad areas. Accounting firms, financial consultancies and employee benefits consultants advise on pay, taxation and pension issues. Recruitment consultancies have gradually moved into international assignments as their clients have become more international. There are now a number of organizations specializing in international recruitment, particularly for the three main groups of internationally mobile employees: senior managers, technical specialists and, somewhat paradoxically, relatively unskilled people such as hotel workers, construction industry labourers and household servants. One criticism that may be levelled here is that, for the managerial jobs in particular, too much attention is paid to previous experience and not enough to intercultural adaptability. In other words, it is assumed that a manager who is successful in one country will also be successful in another country. However, there is now considerable evidence to show that the process of managing varies from country to country.

Box 18.2 Current issues in Japanese human resource management

In Japan, consultants are finding a need for a bifocal approach to the management of human resource issues in their client organizations. For the immediate and near term, they must help the clients restructure their HR strategies, systems and practices to allow the transition from the traditional economy to the new economy. At the same time, for the longer term, they must assist clients in reorganizing their HR management to face the next generation of HR issues that is certain to be brought upon them by the accelerating demographic shift.

(1) Current and near-term issues

With the transformation of the national economy from a domestically oriented, regulated and manufacturing-based one to a globally driven, deregulated and knowledge-based one, industries and companies have found their traditional HR systems built on lifetime employment and the seniority principle increasingly rigid, costly and uncompetitive. These systems have saddled them with a constantly rising proportion of aged workers whose cost has been rising relentlessly with seniority. Their traditional revenue base, on the other hand, has been steadily eroding with the transformation of the national economy.

While companies have reduced their workforce costs through massive programmes of early retirement, layoff, plant and office closing, and business divestment, they have called upon management consultants to redesign and redevelop their HR management into merit-based systems linked more directly with performance. Consultants, playing a larger role than ever, have introduced compensation, performance management and career management systems that, in place of seniority, are based on jobs (*shokumu*), results or outcomes (*seika*), roles (*yakuwari*) or, alternatively, competency (*kompitensi*).

More importantly, their consulting level has moved up from functional management, where HR managers and specialists are their main clients, to the strategic planning level, with top management making key decisions on the consulting project. Frequently, projects arise from the decision of corporate management to change their business model. Even a project coming from HR executives more often has a strategic orientation, as they themselves respond to the challenge of business transformation and raise their sights above their conventional functional priorities.

(2) Longer-term issues

The demographic bomb, which is seen in developed societies all over the world, is ticking most loudly in Japan and promises to change the face of the national HR system possibly faster and more forcefully than in any other developed society. Already in 2000, the proportion of the population aged between 15 and 44 years fell below 40 per cent. By 2025, it is most likely to drop further to somewhere near 30 per cent. Japan will then have the highest proportion of elderly people (65 and older) and the lowest proportion of productive-age population (15–64) of all the developed countries.

This "age shock" will first tear apart the pension system of the country unless it is revised soon with the expert assistance of HR and benefits consultants, incorporating the self-help principle and the defined contribution design. The new demographics will further alter the new HR management equation formulated in 2000, by driving companies and consultants to introduce new systems that entice retired and retiring employees to stay on the job and work much longer than they are allowed to work now.

Other HR management systems and practices that companies have developed to deal with the current and near-term issues are also likely to have severely limited life-spans if the new economy, as widely expected, generates a fast-rising, insatiable demand for workers with high knowledge skills. Consultants will then be recruited to help companies remodel their HR management systems to make them more diverse, flexible, friendly and attractive to a non-traditional workforce, inevitably composed of female and foreign workers as well as male workers, young and old.

To respond to this highly complex professional demand, consultants will need to remodel themselves into professionals with broader social competence in addition to greater technical expertise.

Authors: Eiji Mizutani and Osamu Ida.

Expatriate managers are expensive and crucial people in their organization, under pressure to establish themselves and their families in the new country and having to adapt to different cultural requirements. Often they fail to make the transition successfully – at great personal and organizational cost.

A growing number of organizations specialize in the full range of expatriate HRM consultancy: recruitment, training, briefing, transfer, adaptation, pay and benefits, evaluation and return. Before addressing the technical issues of recruitment or pay and benefits, consultants in this area should press the client to answer key strategic questions: "Why send expensive expatriates when there are talented and well-educated locals?", "Why not use more (or fewer) expatriates?", "How do you know that the expatriates are adding more value than they cost?" and "What role will the expatriate undertake at the end of the assignment?"

New forms of work

New forms of work outside the standard full-time, long-term employment package (called contingent work, atypical work or flexibility) have become established in developed countries, at least, as a key aspect of the management of human resources. Flexible ways and times of working are traditionally more common in less developed economies. As economies advance they create established patterns of doing things: job descriptions, normal working hours, legal constraints on employment contracts, and so on. However, in some of the

Box 18.3 Current issues in European HR management

A major HRM research programme, the Cranet survey, now has over 25,000 responses from employers in 22 European and a dozen other countries. It provides hard evidence on the roles and functions of human resource departments, recruitment, compensation, training, industrial relations, communication with employees and flexible working practices.

The evidence from the survey confirms differences in HRM policies between different sizes of organization and different sectors of the economy (in particular between the public and the private sectors). The central finding of the research, however, is that while there are common trends throughout Europe there are also significant national differences.

Five key areas of common development can be identified:

(1) **Pay.** Pay determination is being increasingly decentralized from the national industry collective bargaining level to individual organizations or even to units within organizations. Furthermore, pay is becoming an area for increased variability, with individuals having their pay and rewards determined outside national or sector-level bargaining arrangements. Performance-related pay, however, seems to have stopped spreading as organizations are now more likely to pay for competence, leaving it to managers to ensure the best use of that competence.

(2) **Flexibility.** There has been widespread growth in "atypical" work (temporary, casual, fixed-term, part-time, etc.). This extension of different forms of employment varies by country, and countries are at different levels in their use of these new employment relationships – but growth is the norm in all countries.

(3) **Equal opportunities.** Policies for providing equal opportunities for women are widespread throughout Europe, but are frequently not translated into action. Despite recent tensions, action against discrimination on grounds of race or ethnic origin is still rare.

(4) **Training.** Training is seen as the key issue for HRM in most European countries. Spending on training continues to increase even during periods of lower economic growth. The manner in which training is assessed, organized and evaluated varies markedly between countries.

(5) **Trade unions.** Trade unions are entrenched and influential bodies throughout Europe, although membership figures vary considerably. In most, but not all, countries, unions have declining memberships.

Although the evidence shows common trends, there is also considerable variation across countries, and noticeably in the way these common issues are handled. The role and influence of human resource departments differ from country to country. Consultants need to be knowledgeable about the common trends in issues – but aware of the national variations in human resource departments and the way they manage these issues.

Author: Chris Brewster.

more developed economies these have come to seem restrictive. The increasingly difficult, and often internationally competitive, environment is leading the most sophisticated organizations to stress flexibility of human resource practices to meet the requirements of the business more exactly.

The growth in flexibility can be seen in various forms. Numerical flexibility – the ability to employ different numbers of people – is now widespread. Even the famous lifetime employment in the major Japanese companies or companies such as IBM or Daimler Benz has been overtaken by economic pressures and production requirements, and these companies have started reducing numbers. Working-time flexibility – working outside the usual morning to evening hours – is spreading as organizations find that they have to use their equipment for longer hours to cover their costs, or to be available to customers early or late in the day.

A wide variety of innovative arrangements involving part-time working, varying shift patterns, minimum/maximum hours and annual hours contracts are now common in North America and Europe. Contractual flexibility – appointing people to share jobs, or accept short-term jobs or a less-committed relationship with the organization – is now quite usual. Finally, financial flexibility – varying pay in accordance with the individual's performance or the organization's ability to pay – is also growing.

One important result of flexibility for workers is that it opens up new job possibilities for many people, both women and men, who would not otherwise be able to go to work. Work that offers flexible hours or that is limited to certain periods of the year may allow people to choose jobs that suit their personal needs and preferences regarding family responsibilities (care of children or elderly relatives), educational requirements, or lifestyle. Parents of school-age children, for example, could well be available for work on a part-time basis for a few hours in the middle of each day or in the evening, or at particular times of the year (e.g. outside school holidays). Thus, flexible working not only attempts to match the available work much more closely to the employer's work requirements, it also opens up the labour market to a wider group of employees and hence improves the employer's ability to select the best people.

In dealing with issues of work and employment flexibility, the consultant should not overlook the wider social implications. There may be a need for improved social services, changes in public transport scheduling, and so on. The HR consultant may be well placed to suggest to the client what new services could facilitate work flexibility, or what new arrangements should be proposed to local government or transport authorities.

Human asset (human capital) accounting

A growing area of consultancy, particularly for the major companies, is in measuring and controlling the costs and benefits of employment. In most organizations, the people employed account for the largest single operating cost. Consultants should be able to help organizations manage this resource in the same way as they do others – to assess its costs and show its value. Of course, this is more complicated for people than it is for, say, electricity, but an attempt should be made. Employers often do not realize the total costs of employment: not just wages, but benefits, accommodation, recruitment, administration etc. Equally, they often find it hard to identify the added value of each employee. The major consultancies now have differently titled approaches aimed at reducing the complexity of humans to financial numbers. This is still a very inexact science, but one that seems likely to be an increasing source of work for management consultants.[5]

The role of the personnel/HR department

Personnel and human resource departments have come under increasing pressure to prove their own added value to the organization: they are expensive overhead costs. So there has grown up a specialized form of consultancy aimed at assisting these departments to clarify their objectives, their ways of working and their outputs (as opposed to the obvious inputs of resources). This can involve benchmarking other organizations and can raise some hard issues if, for example, the HR department seems to be significantly larger than that of a relevant competitor. The important point for the consultants to focus on is the measurement of outputs: what is it that the department is adding to the organization? Is it worth the costs involved? It is often the case that there is a substantial gap between the administrative and system-controlling role that the department performs and the strategic, knowledge management role that the department would like to undertake. Identifying this and helping the specialists to develop action plans to bridge the gap is a growing role for HR consultancies.

Human resource information systems

A relevant aspect of the assessment of the HR function concerns the degree of sophistication of the information and communication systems used: the human resource information systems. The technology is now available for every line manager to be able to access, in real time, the complete records of every member of their staff, including all details of their competencies, skills and training. With this kind of information availability many of the other aspects of HR work (training and development, assessment systems, human resource planning, careers and succession planning, etc.) become both easier and more powerful. Few HR departments take full advantage of such systems and many are still caught in the vice of administration and paper-shifting. There is now an extensive range of consultancy work to help HR departments select the most appropriate and cost-effective system.

Unfortunately, work is often done by IT consultants, who may sell the organization a system that is, perhaps, more sophisticated, and usually more expensive, than is needed. Since it is rarely possible to spend another large sum of money to replace such a system, the organization becomes stuck with a computerized facility that may be almost unused. It is generally better to obtain advice from specialist HR consultants able to ensure that the key questions of what the organization wants to use the system for, and how much use will be made of it, are asked first, and that the system selected has maximum credibility and use rather than being the "latest thing".

Subcontracting (outsourcing) of HRM

The focus on the role of the HR department and the growth of HR information systems has led some consultancies to offer to undertake all, or key elements of, the HR task on behalf of clients. They can often provide expertise and depth of knowledge that is lacking in the organization. Some elements of HRM (compensation, insurance) have traditionally been outsourced in some countries. In many cases individual issues, such as training, have been outsourced to experienced training consultants or to the education system, but the notion of taking over the whole task, or key elements of it, is new. There have been some highly visible decisions by some well-known companies to outsource all aspects of their HR systems, but whether this will become a trend or turn out to be just a fad is still a matter of debate. There are cost and efficiency advantages, and loss of expertise and strategic control disadvantages. Consultants are already helping organizations compare the two sides of the coin so that they can reach sensible decisions.

The logic of subcontracting or outsourcing the administration of the HR system is clear, even if it goes against the modern tendency to view the implicit knowledge that resides in an organization's people as a key competitive asset. A more widespread phenomenon, and one that often has a different purpose, is the outsourcing of the human resources themselves: moving the work from people employed within the organization to others working elsewhere – sometimes even in different countries. The purpose of such outsourcing is usually cost reduction: work can be allocated to people who are paid significantly less or, where the work is undertaken in another country, where social protection is poorer.

There are arguments that such developments are inevitable, given the nature of global capitalism, and even that they have a benefit in spreading at least some kinds of work to poorer countries. There is also, however, a developing backlash whereby NGOs and other social groups are highlighting bad practices in the subcontractors and creating significant difficulties for the outsourcing organization. Consultants who are asked to advise on such matters should do so cautiously, emphasizing both the advantages and the disadvantages of various arrangements, and the long-term financial benefits of ethical behaviour.[6]

---

[1] E. Poutsma, A. Pendleton, J. van Omerren and C. Brewster: *Financial participation in Europe*, Report to the European Foundation for the Improvement of Living and Working Conditions (Dublin, January 2000).

[2] W. F. Glueck: *Personnel: A diagnostic approach* (Plano, TX, Business Publications, 1982), p. 296.

[3] See also selected guides to management and human resource development in Appendix 3.

[4] See e.g. M. Pedler, J. Burgoyne and T. Boydell: *The learning company: A strategy for sustainable development* (Maidenhead, Berkshire, UK, McGraw-Hill, 1997).

[5] See e.g. U. Johanson and H. H. Larsen: "Human resource costing and accounting", in C. J. Brewster and H. H. Larsen (eds): *Human resource management in Northern Europe* (Oxford, Blackwell, 2000).

[6] See also P. Drucker: "They're not employees, they're people", in *Harvard Business Review*, Feb. 2002, pp. 70–77.

CONSULTING IN KNOWLEDGE MANAGEMENT 19

19.1 Managing in the knowledge economy

The competitive position of economies – in particular of the highly industrialized countries – is already or will be determined by their capacity to create value through knowledge. This structural change is reflected in theories of endogenous growth, which stress that development of know-how and technological change are the driving forces behind lasting growth. Knowledge is increasingly recognized as the principal source of value generation (see figure 19.1). The most recent economic growth comes not just from general advances in knowledge and the state of technology, but also from intangible financial products, entertainment, and computer software. Quah calls this "the weightless economy", which he defines as not just more and better technology, but a reduction of distance between knowledge production and consumers, removing the intermediaries of traditional intellectual property protection and manufacturing. With fast interactions across countries, international learning processes become faster, and new competitors enter traditional businesses. The newest technologies – computers, the Internet – also allow consumers to get closer to knowledge production. The traditional trade-off between reach and richness of interactions between producer and consumer seems to be no longer valid.[1] The newest technologies produce new weightless goods – software, video entertainment, and health and financial consulting services – that can be considered as if they were knowledge. Little sits in the chain between knowledge production and final consumption. As information and communication technologies are the main drivers of this new economy, authors talk about the digital or information economy.[2]

Despite the preponderant contributions of intellect and services in creating value and growth of modern companies, current management control systems, economic models and social measurement devices focus on physical assets and physical or physically measurable outputs. It is only recently that organizations have started to become aware of their intellectual capital such as the competencies and capabilities of employees, the company's relationship with customers and

Figure 19.1 Knowledge: a key resource of the post-industrial area

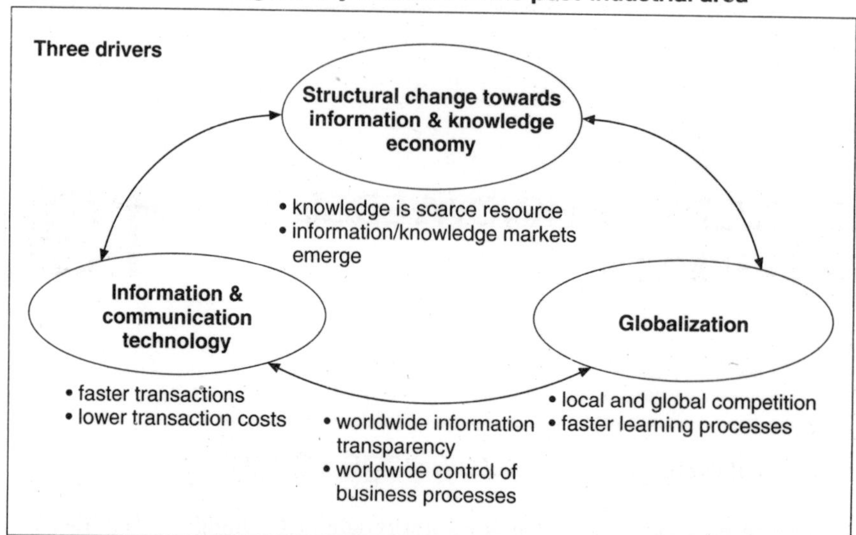

suppliers, patents, licences, systems for leveraging the company's innovative strength and ability to create value.

Traditional organizations, however, often encounter difficulties in activating their knowledge and in learning from others. Do any of the following problems sound familiar?[3]

- Your company has been asked to tender for a major project. Collating the necessary information – from the organization's relevant track record to an individual consultant's experience – becomes a project in itself. You meet the deadline but the tender document is not as good as it could or should have been. You lose the pitch.
- You are faced with a serious, but unusual, failure in your plant, threatening to bring your operations to a standstill. Somebody remembers that the same situation arose a couple of years before, but there is no record of the methodology used to solve the problem the previous time, or of who was involved.
- The internal telephone directory is out of date the moment it is printed. It gives names and formal titles, but has very little information about the people or what they are good at. In no sense does it provide an effective tool for finding people with specific expertise or experience.
- A senior professional leaves the organization to join a competitor. Soon, her whole team has left to follow her. Only untrained juniors are left behind and there are no records of the team's know-how.
- There are large discrepancies between the performance of different divisions carrying out essentially the same task. You are conscious that best practices are not captured and shared. You are frustrated by the lack of formal processes that allow such sharing.

These examples highlight knowledge problems in organizations. Readers can probably identify similar problems in their own or their client organizations. The examples also demonstrate the potential benefits of consulting in knowledge management (KM), which often concentrates on the following objectives:

1. **Enhance operational effectiveness:** avoid double work, improve quality, make better use of time by capturing and sharing knowledge.
2. **Improve responsiveness to internal and external clients:** provide high-quality services, give consistent and timely answers to queries taking into account all relevant information, speed up roll-out of new products and processes by improving access to knowledge sources.
3. **Develop competence:** develop the core competencies of the firm, align individual competence development, create the necessary enabling conditions (values, human resource policies, incentives).
4. **Foster innovation:** combine experiences, project ideas within and across sectors, and provide spaces and processes to transform ideas into new services, programmes and projects.

19.2 Knowledge-based value creation

Knowledge in organizations takes many forms. It includes the competencies and capabilities of employees, knowledge about customers and suppliers, the know-how to deliver specific processes, codified and protected knowledge in the form of patents, licences and copyrights, systems for leveraging the company's innovative strength and so on. Knowledge is the product of individual and collective learning, which is embodied in products, services and systems. Knowledge is related to the experiences of people in organizations and society.

Understanding knowledge: information – knowledge – competence

For firms, knowledge is a resource and an intangible asset and forms part of the so-called intellectual capital of an organization. In order to understand how knowledge-based value creation works, management has to understand what knowledge is and how it is related to the competitiveness of a firm. In the following the underlying terminology of value-based knowledge creation is explained by means of the so-called competence ladder (figure 19.2).

Let us start at the bottom of the competence ladder. People communicate by means of symbols – letters, numbers or signs. These symbols can only be interpreted if there are clear rules of understanding. These rules are called syntax: symbols plus syntax become data. For example, combining the digits 1, 3 and 5 and the symbols for degree Celsius plus a full stop to 13.5 °C transforms symbols into data. These data can only be interpreted if they are given an exact

Figure 19.2 The competence ladder

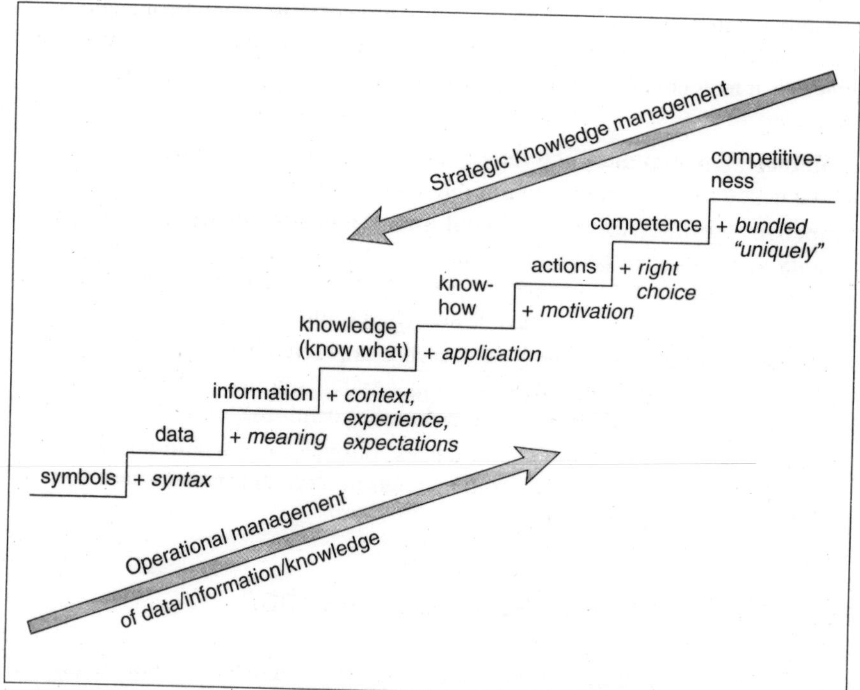

meaning. They become information if we add to the data that it refers to air temperature, and give the precise time and place of that temperature. This information will be interpreted differently according to the context, and the experience and expectations of people. While information is organized data, knowledge refers to the tacit or explicit understanding of people about relationships among phenomena. It is embodied in routines for the performance of activities, in organizational structures and processes and in embedded beliefs and behaviour. Knowledge implies an ability to relate inputs to outputs, to observe regularities in information, to codify, explain and ultimately to predict.

In the development of knowledge different levels can be distinguished. The first, "know what", is a result of internalizing information. This will create value for an organization only if a person is able to apply the information, that is to transform "know what" into "know-how" by means of application. This transfer can be difficult – consider the many people, for example, who read the operating instructions of a mobile phone and want to apply the information to program specific functions. If the mental models of those who have written the instructions are different from those of the people who need to apply them, the users may not be able to interpret the instructions correctly.

The ability to apply knowledge is based on specific motivations ("know why"). People will only act if they are motivated. Therefore, an important management task to enhance knowledge-based value creation is to ensure the right motivational set-up so that workers develop, share and apply their knowledge in line with the objectives of the enterprise. Value is created when the right knowledge is applied at the right moment to solve a specific problem or to exploit a new business opportunity. The right choice of knowledge at the right moment is *competence* or expertise. With Roos and von Krogh,[4] "we view competence as an event, rather than an asset; this simply means that competencies do not exist in the way a car does, they exist only when the knowledge (and skill) meets the task".

The interaction of an actor with an audience, the way a successful salesperson sells or the adaptation of strategies to the client's needs of the moment by an experienced consultant reflect competence. If the competencies of persons or organizations are bundled in a way that is not matched by other organizations, this gives *competitiveness*.

This description of the competence ladder shows that knowledge in organizations is only in a small part explicit. Using the metaphor of an iceberg, the small part visible above the water is *explicit knowledge* and the larger invisible part under the water is *tacit knowledge*. According to Polanyi,[5] tacit knowledge is personal, context-specific, and often unconscious, and is therefore hard to formalize and communicate. Explicit or codified knowledge refers to knowledge that is transmissible in formal, systematic language. Polanyi points out that "we can know more that we can tell". The transformation of explicit to tacit knowledge and vice versa is an important process in knowledge creation and distribution, as discussed further below.

Coming back to the competence ladder, the objective of *knowledge-based management* can be formulated as the transformation of information into knowledge and competence in order to create measurable value in a sustainable manner. This requires each step of the competence ladder to be built. As with a real staircase, it is not possible to say that the top stair is more important than the bottom one – all steps have to be built. The bottom-up view reflects the operational processes of information and knowledge management, whereas the top-down view reflects the strategic approach of defining the competencies of an organization and its members that will probably lead to competitiveness.

Transforming knowledge: processes of knowledge creation and distribution

Nonaka and Takeuchi[6] postulate that knowledge is created through the interactions between tacit and explicit knowledge in four different modes, as illustrated in figure 19.3. These four ways of converting and creating knowledge are the basis for value creation. The transfer of tacit knowledge to tacit knowledge is called *socialization*. It is a process of sharing experiences and thereby creating new tacit knowledge such as shared mental models and technical skills. Socialization takes place when an apprentice observes a master, or when a newly hired consultant is integrated into a project group and learns through observation, imitation and practice. Sharing experience is the key to socialization and value

Figure 19.3 Four modes of knowledge transformation

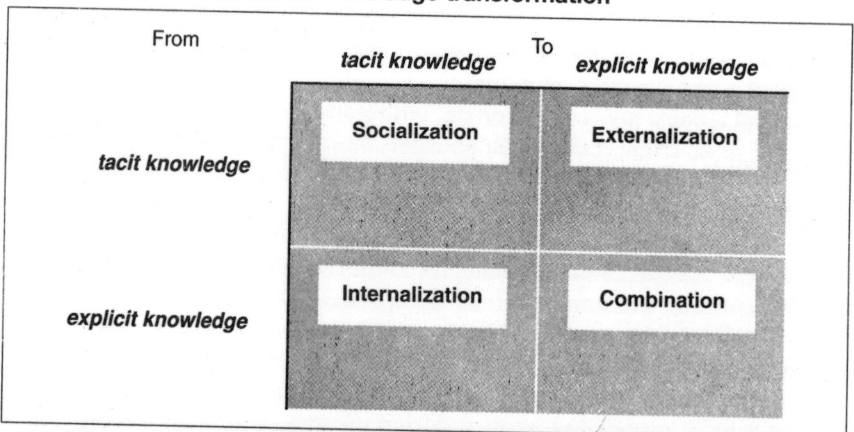

Source: I. Nonaka and H. Takeuchi: *The knowledge-creating company* (Oxford, Oxford University Press, 1995), p. 72.

creation in knowledge-based organizations. The mere transfer of information will often make little sense if it is abstracted from the associated emotions and specific contexts in which shared experiences are embedded.

Externalization is the process of articulating tacit knowledge into explicit concepts. Externalization happens when a manufacturing process is described for the purposes of an ISO 9000 certification. In management consulting, externalization takes place when the project profile is written in order to provide specific information on project development and on lessons learnt as a basis for future similar projects. Many firms have a database of lessons learnt. As externalization will reveal only part of the tacit knowledge, it is better not to rely exclusively on written statements, but to enable for example consultants who have to plan a new project to have personal contact with those who have carried out similar projects before. Similarly a real process will always differ from the formal project description. Externalization is the basis for reflecting experiences, for formalizing learning processes and ultimately for standardization and process improvement.

Combination refers to the transfer of explicit knowledge to explicit knowledge. Individuals exchange and combine knowledge through documents, meetings, and communication networks. They reconfigure existing information by sorting, adding, combining and categorizing explicit knowledge which may lead to new information. In consulting, for example, different presentations may be combined and reconfigured for a sales presentation to a new client.

Internalization is the process of embodying explicit knowledge into tacit knowledge. It is closely related to learning by doing. A great part of our formalized learning processes happens by internalization.

According to Nonaka and Takeuchi's model, knowledge creation is a continuous and dynamic interaction between tacit and explicit knowledge which happens at the level of the individual, the group, and the organization, and between organizations. It is therefore an important management task to create opportunities for interactions between these levels so that knowledge conversion can happen. Enabling conditions include:

- **Intention:** The most critical element of corporate strategy is to conceptualize a vision about what kind of knowledge should be developed and to operationalize it into a management system for implementation.
- **Autonomy:** At the individual level, all members of an organization should be allowed to act autonomously as far as circumstances permit. This may increase the chance of introducing unexpected ideas.
- **Fluctuation and creative chaos:** This means to adopt an open attitude towards environmental signals, to exploit the ambiguity of those signals, and to use fluctuation in order to break routines, habits or cognitive frameworks.
- **Redundancy:** In business organizations, redundancy refers to intentional overlapping of information about business activities, management responsibilities and the company as a whole. Sharing redundant information promotes the sharing of tacit knowledge and thus speeds up the knowledge creation process.
- **Requisite variety:** In order to deal with challenges posed by the environment, an organization's internal diversity must match the variety and complexity of that environment. Everyone in the organization should have the fastest possible access to the information and knowledge they need. When information differentials exist within the organization, individual members cannot interact on equal terms, which hinders the search for different interpretations of information.

Valuing knowledge: intellectual capital and its measurement

As knowledge has come to be seen as a valuable resource in organizations, attempts have been made to structure the knowledge base and attribute value to these assets. There are basically two types of approach to valuing intangible assets in enterprises. The first type builds on the difference between the market value and the book value of a company. This difference, traditionally called goodwill, is in this first approach declared as the value of intangible assets. While this approach may give an indication of the extent to which intangible assets influence the market value of a company, it cannot give more detailed insights into the structure of the intellectual capital. The second type of analytical approach structures intellectual capital into elements and tries to quantify these assets or evaluate them in qualitative terms. Figure 19.4 shows the different categories of intangible assets that an organization may possess or have access to.

A widely publicized approach has been developed by the Scandia Insurance Company in Sweden, which structures intellectual capital into human, organizational and customer capital. Stewart[7] proposes an *intellectual capital navigator* using similar categories. The intellectual capital index of Roos et al.[8]

Figure 19.4 Components of intellectual capital

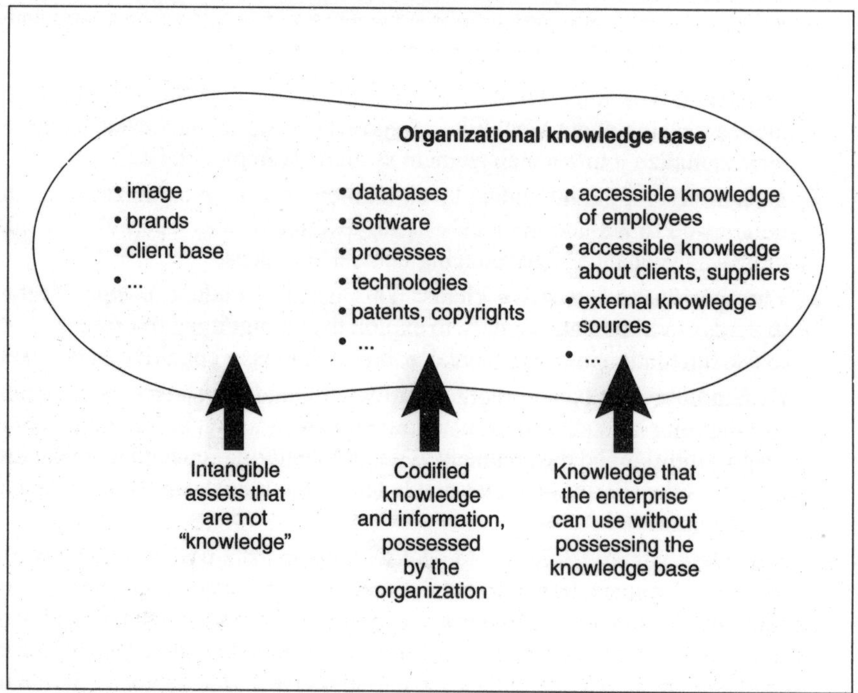

is based on relationships, innovation, human and infrastructure capital. For each of these elements indicators are developed and can be aggregated to an intellectual capital index which is then plotted against time. Sveiby,[9] together with the Swedish enterprise Celemi, has developed a so-called *intangible assets monitor*, which structures intangible assets into external structure, internal structure and competence of employees, each category being viewed under three criteria: growth/renewal, efficiency and stability.

Each of these approaches has its particular difficulties in defining clear-cut indicators for intangible assets. In addition, it is debatable whether a company should develop an evaluation procedure for its intangible assets that is not integrated into its overall strategic planning and accounting systems.

For these reasons, a number of organizations have started to use the *balanced scorecard* developed by Kaplan and Norton[10] to integrate the different assets of a company. The balanced scorecard usually considers four perspectives: a financial perspective, a customer perspective, a process perspective and a learning and growth perspective. The advantage of the balanced scorecard is that it allows different perspectives of the enterprise to be integrated and "balances the financial and tangible aspects and the intangible aspects of managing an enterprise". It also demonstrates how the knowledge base contributes to value creation, in terms of customers, finances and processes.

Managing knowledge: knowledge technology versus knowledge ecology (culture)

Can knowledge be managed like finances or other physical assets? As described above, knowledge is linked to people and based on individual experiences, beliefs and expectations. It is to a great extent implicit and unconscious. If this is the case, knowledge cannot be managed by deterministic management models. While consultants and IT vendors may attempt to sell hardware and software solutions under the heading of knowledge management, clients increasingly understand that knowledge does not equal information and usually cannot easily be measured, classified and stored in databases. The technocratic view of knowledge management, which deals mainly with capture and storage of knowledge in data systems, is increasingly giving way to a *knowledge ecology* or *knowledge culture* approach.

This approach holds that it is not possible to manage knowledge but it is possible to create enabling conditions for creating and sharing knowledge. Like a plant, which will grow in the right conditions, employees need the right ecology or organizational culture to produce knowledge and to share it with their colleagues. Managing therefore means creating an environment of trust and openness, and developing incentives that align individual interests with the interests of the company and foster boundary-free behaviour. This is, however, a much more long-term and difficult task than implementing an IT tool, which is why consultants are often tempted to sell such tools without creating the environment in which they can produce results. IT applications aimed at capturing explicit, codified information also have their place in a knowledge ecology. Furthermore, good information management is a basis for knowledge management. Consultants should therefore ensure that all the steps of the competence ladder are built, from document and information management up to building a knowledge ecology in the enterprise.

The knowledge management strategy of a company also depends on its business. Is value creation based on the reuse of codified knowledge or on channelling individual expertise to provide creative new solutions to problems? Hansen et al.[11] compare what they call a codification and a personalization strategy (see figure 19.5). A *codification strategy* is based on reuse of knowledge and relies on codification. It draws heavily on explicit knowledge and uses IT as a tool to store and share knowledge. This approach is not able to transport implicit knowledge and is rather suited for standard solutions. A *personalization strategy* capitalizes on so-called expert economics. It relies on networks of people sharing particular tacit knowledge. A consultant who has to propose a knowledge management solution for a client should therefore first look into the type of business in order to decide how much codification and how much personalization is needed.

Both codification and personalization are also means of protecting the organization against losses of knowledge. Firms should ensure that a person's knowledge is passed on before he or she leaves the organization and that there

Figure 19.5 What is your strategy to manage knowledge?

	Codification	Personalization
Competitive strategy	Provide high-quality, reliable and fast implementation of information systems by reusing codified knowledge.	Provide creative, analytically rigorous advice on high-level strategic problems by channelling individual expertise.
	Reuse economics:	**Expert economics:**
Economic model	Invest once in a knowledge asset; reuse it many times.	Charge high fees for highly customized solutions to unique problems.
	Use large teams with a high ratio of associates to partners.	Use small teams with a low ratio of associates to partners.
	Focus on generating overall revenues.	Focus on maintaining high profit margins.
	People-to-documents:	**Person-to-person:**
Knowledge management strategy	Develop an electronic document system that codifies, stores, disseminates and allows reuse of knowledge.	Develop networks for linking people so that tacit knowledge can be shared.
Information technology	Invest heavily in IT; the goal is to connect people with reusable codified knowledge.	Invest moderately in IT; the goal is to facilitate conversations and the exchange of tacit knowledge.
Human resources	Hire new college graduates who are well suited to the reuse of knowledge and the implementation of solutions.	Hire MBAs who like problem-solving and can tolerate ambiguity.
	Train people in groups and through computer-based distance learning.	Train people through one-to-one mentoring.
	Reward people for using and contributing to document databases.	Reward people for directly sharing knowledge with others.

Source: M. T. Hansen et al.: "What's your strategy for managing knowledge?", in *Harvard Business Review*, Mar.–Apr. 1999, pp. 106–116.

are several people with similar levels of competence in order to avoid dependence on single experts (personalization). The storage of information in databases and the protection of sensitive knowledge by specific rights of access and firewalls (codification) is another means of protecting knowledge. A third way of protecting against imitation is through legal measures such as patents, trade marks, copyright, licences (see Appendix 5) and non-competing agreements with employees who leave the firm.

A great number of knowledge management models and concepts have been developed by researchers, enterprises and consultants, based on either the technocratic or the ecology/culture approach. Most models cover both process and the enabling environment. Increasingly, the metaphor of *knowledge markets* – the interaction of knowledge sellers and knowledge buyers – is used as a basis.

19.3 Developing a knowledge organization

The organization as a knowledge market

In organizations, new knowledge is created continuously as people learn and gain experiences. On the other hand, people are continuously seeking information and knowledge in order to solve specific problems. Knowledge moves through organizations, is exchanged, bought, forgotten, lost, found, generated and applied to work. We can therefore describe organizations as knowledge markets, which can help us to understand the driving forces and barriers to managing knowledge, and to develop effective enabling conditions and market mechanisms for generating and exchanging knowledge.[12]

The task of consulting in knowledge management or developing knowledge management in a professional service firm is therefore to develop a knowledge market. Following this metaphor, in any organization there are knowledge sellers, knowledge buyers, intermediaries such as knowledge brokers, and media through which sellers and buyers interact. In order to create knowledge markets and make them work, enabling conditions, principles and rules have to be defined and the supporting knowledge media and infrastructure have to be developed.

Enabling conditions for knowledge markets

The knowledge ecology approach holds that knowledge cannot be managed but that conditions that enhance knowledge flows can be created in organizations. Apart from the physical and IT infrastructures, these enabling conditions include "soft" factors such as strategic vision, values, attitudes, relationships, objectives and incentives. A corporate strategic vision should formulate clearly the contribution of knowledge and people to sustained corporate competitiveness. Values that create the right spirit for knowledge creation and exchange include trust, openness to change, professionalism, a passion for excellence, and the self-confidence to empower others in a boundary-free fashion.

A corporate vision and values are easily proclaimed but it is difficult to live up to them in daily business. As values are manifest in behaviour, it is advisable to describe the desired behaviour of managers and professionals in an organization. Performance appraisal and personal development should be based on evaluation of behaviour. In many cases, changing behaviour is the major challenge in developing a knowledge-based organization. Consultants can contribute to this by proposing careful change management and organizational development support.

Vision and values are operationalized through business objectives. Organizations should formulate objectives that relate not just to market penetration and financial indicators but also to knowledge and learning. Business objectives should refer to the competencies needed for business development and the ways to acquire them. The balanced scorecard (see section 19.2) provides a good framework for developing qualitative and people-related business objectives and measures to implement them.

To reinforce the right behaviour across a company, incentive and compensation systems need to be appropriately adapted so as to align the interests of individuals, groups and the company. Compensation schemes that put total company performance before individual profit centres, subsidiaries or units, as well as non-monetary incentives, gain importance in a knowledge organization. A reputation as an expert in a specific field, opportunities to learn, efficient equipment, good relations with clients, free time or interesting work are often more esteemed rewards than mere monetary incentives.

Knowledge managers have an important role to play in this context. Some firms have created positions of "chief knowledge officers" or similar to act as market makers and knowledge brokers. These officers usually have four main roles:

- they are entrepreneurs who launch and support new and often risky initiatives for creating and sharing knowledge;
- they act as consultants and change agents to harmonize new ideas and long-term visions with the day-to-day business;
- they are technologists, familiar with the newest developments in information and communication technology and applications for enhancing information and knowledge flows;
- they are ecologists who can create enabling conditions for knowledge creation and sharing.

Principles and rules for knowledge markets

Knowledge markets will only work if some basic rules and guiding principles are respected.

- *The common interest principle:* People will cooperate in sharing knowledge only if they have a common interest. The common interest principle comes into play when a company sets up an experience exchange group, when a "community of practice" (see below) is formed, or when best practices are shared.

- *The lighthouse principle:* The lighthouse is a metaphor for leading expertise and orientation. Knowledge markets will not function without lighthouses, which may be determined by benchmarking, by friendly competition, or by peer rating (in the case of experts). For example, in an international manufacturing network, lighthouse factories are those that use the best available technology, have the most efficient process, and so on. Many organizations have created so-called centres of excellence, where they bring together their leading expertise, making them responsible for the further development of competencies. In consultancy we quite often find so-called "practice centres", which systematize expertise in a specific topic, such as organization development. The lighthouse principle can also be applied in comparing subsidiaries of a company. For example, a firm may seek to optimize processes through a "best in class" programme: in a friendly competition, subsidiaries throughout the world compare their productivity and quality data, the best subsidiaries explain what they do in a quarterly newsletter, and there is periodic interchange between subsidiaries with a view to learning from the best.
- *The push–pull principle:* Relevant information should be "pushed" out to all interested people in order to create pressure for change. At the same time, knowledge media should allow knowledge buyers to "pull" the knowledge that is relevant for the solution of their problems, and to determine with whom they want to collaborate. A study by the American Productivity and Quality Center[13] concluded that a combination of push and pull is required: push approaches are characterized by the desire to store knowledge centrally and distribute it throughout the organization whereas pull approaches expect people to look for the knowledge they need. Neither approach seems to work alone.
- *The give and take principle:* Knowledge will only flow in an organization if people adopt a philosophy of give and take. Davenport and Prusak call this reciprocity. Reciprocity may be achieved less directly than by getting knowledge back from others as payment for providing it to them. Knowledge-sharing that improves profitability will return a benefit to the sharer now and in the future. Whether or not a knowledge seller expects to be paid with equally valuable knowledge from the buyer, he/she may believe that being known for sharing knowledge will make others in the company more willing to share with him/her. To promote the give and take principle, a number of companies have established "miles for knowledge" programmes. In such programmes, staff get a number of credit points which they can distribute to colleagues who have helped them to solve problems or have provided valuable knowledge for a project, etc. These accumulated points can be used later on to ask for credits for participating in seminars, getting more sophisticated equipment, or similar. As a rule, these programmes have a limited life span and are used to sensitize people to knowledge networking.

Knowledge media

There is a great number of media through which knowledge in organizations is identified, transferred, shared and generated. Some of them are listed below. Companies tend to hire consultants to implement these media. They should not, however, implement them in an isolated manner, but should give particular attention to the necessary enabling conditions for these media to work in the knowledge market.

- *Yellow pages.* "Who knows what" can be identified by so-called yellow pages where people are listed by area of competence. Yellow pages allow people who have expertise in a specific topic to be quickly identified.
- *Knowledge maps and skill profiles* describe in more detail what people or groups of people know. This information is useful for staffing projects, for assessing current competencies as a basis for staff development, and to increase the employability of staff. Increasingly professionals are compiling their own individual competence portfolios. To establish skill profiles, the roles of people in the organization are defined and competencies described for each role.
- *The collective memory* of an organization includes databases and groupware applications, as well as the capture-and-retrieval system for relevant knowledge, codified and described in electronic handbooks, manuals, process descriptions, project profiles, sales presentations and so on. It is important to have a concise taxonomy for storage and retrieval of pieces of knowledge. Some consulting firms employ so-called knowledge stewards or journalists to write project profiles, prepare stories[14] or provide advice on preparing documents in standard formats and to act as guides through the information system. The use of collective memory depends on ease of retrieving information and high-quality content. Help functions for users are essential. Moreover, collective memory and workflow have to be integrated. In preparing an offer, for example, a consultant should be able to obtain a listing of similar projects by typing the project title into the system. The collective memory needs constant marketing to encourage people to make use of it and to provide information for it.
- *Communities of practice* are groups of people informally bound together by shared expertise and an interest in joint enterprise, such as consultants who specialize in a particular topic, e.g. strategic marketing, frontline managers in charge of cheque processing at a bank, service engineers and so on. Some communities of practice meet regularly, others are connected primarily by email networks. People in communities of practice share their experiences and knowledge in free-flowing, creative ways that foster new approaches to problems. The communities complement existing organizational structures, and are a vehicle for learning close to real problem situations. Communities of practice help drive strategy, start new lines of business, solve problems quickly, transfer best practices, develop professional skills and recruit and retrain talent.

- *Centres of excellence* are organizational units (practice centres, etc.) recognized for their leading-edge strategically valuable knowledge. They are mandated to make that knowledge available throughout the firm. Unlike communities of practice, where people participate in a personal, informal and voluntary basis and do so outside their work role, centres of excellence usually have at least some full-time staff and an official mandate. In many consultancy firms, centres of excellence or practice centres have been developed to leverage products and processes across countries and regions. Centres of excellence often run a rapid response network, guaranteeing consultants a quick answer to queries. With the emerging popularity of communities of practice the borders between centres of excellence and communities of practice tend to be blurred.

Apart from these permanent organizational features a number of *events* can be created by knowledge organizations to enhance networking and knowledge-sharing, including regular project reviews and debriefings, consultant conferences, open-space meetings or problem-solving workouts, which were pioneered and made popular by General Electric. Electronic newsletters, chat groups, topical discussions, knowledge-mapping, creativity sessions, etc. are further media and techniques to enhance knowledge creation and sharing. Consultants can act as organizers and facilitators of such activities, bringing together sometimes several thousand people.

Knowledge infrastructure

Knowledge media are often supported by, or based on, IT infrastructure and applications. Information and communication technology is used to store and exchange information and is thus an important enabler for knowledge management. Based on intranet and Web-based infrastructures, which provide the roads on which pieces of information can travel and the parking lots where they can be stored, a number of specific applications are sold by consultants as "knowledge management solutions". The most common are as follows:[15]

- **Data warehousing.** The warehouse takes transactional data, and groups information to reflect relationships between customers, products, processes, geography, time, finance, logistics, etc.
- **Intelligent agents.** These tools allow information searches to be customized. The agent learns with the type of information downloaded by the user, reviews journals and presents periodic updates on desired topics. A consultant might thus receive relevant headlines on new developments in business process improvement without having to read many journals.
- **Document management, content management, groupware and work-flow management.** There has been an evolution from solutions and technologies focused on managing scanned paper to those capable of

managing documents and parts of documents (content management) in a variety of electronic formats. In addition the document that "thinks" for itself has come of age. A document can now decide when it should make itself visible and have to be acted upon, and then automatically get itself sent to the next person in the workflow.

- **Data mining.** These tools reveal and allow the analysis of previously unknown relationships and facts within a database. They can show patterns of client behaviour and are often used in customer relationship management.

Apart from the above tools, communications software such as chat rooms, videoconferencing and other advanced technologies can assist networking of people in large organizations. The knowledge infrastructure not only comprises information and communication systems but also the physical infrastructure. The physical infrastructure of offices and spaces for social contact also influence the communication behaviour of people. Open office layouts, meeting zones or lounges help to create a collaborative environment.

Implementation paths of knowledge management

Based on the above considerations, organizations supported by consultants will have to decide how to implement knowledge management initiatives. Frequently asked questions include: should we designate a knowledge manager to encourage knowledge creation and transfer from a central position, or should we support decentralized initiatives? Should we improve information management before dealing with knowledge management? Should we follow a personalization or a codification strategy? Which measures should we consider to align behaviour and encourage knowledge-sharing?

How and with what intensity an individual company deals with the subject will depend on its specific conditions, tasks, and objectives and on its environment. A traditional chemical company will follow different paths than a new software firm. Based on a study of knowledge management initiatives, North and Papp[16] have derived four implementation paths, which are shown in figure 19.6. Paths 1 and 3 are the most common.

Path 1: From information management to knowledge management. Firms start by implementing IT systems and specific applications such as databases, yellow pages and discussion panels, and subsequently recognize the need to create a support structure to ensure consistency of content in databases. This implementation path relies heavily on a knowledge codification strategy, but often lacks adequate procedures to select relevant knowledge and ensure efficient storage and availability of information. In the second phase, those responsible for knowledge management actively promote the use of the above instruments. Networks of people such as communities of practice are supported and competence centres are created. Incentives for knowledge-sharing are

Figure 19.6 Implementation paths for knowledge management

	Phase I	Phase II	Phase III
Path 1	• Implementation of ICT systems • Installation of databases, discussion panels, Yellow Pages	• Responsible officers motivate interested persons to use the platforms • Development of informal and formal networks	• Creation and transfer of knowledge are encouraged by incentive systems and permanent management support
Path 2	• Designation of a coordinator for knowledge transfer, who encourages the exchange of experience and sets an example	• Emergence of thematic networks, supported by a suitable ICT infrastructure	• Formalization of informal cooperation • Cooperation is rewarded (incentive systems) and supported by top management
Path 3	• Pressure to change (→ internal or general benchmarking study) • Exchange of best practices	• Emergence of interest networks • Participants store specific information in databases and maintain discussion forums	• Corporate culture changes • Incentive systems are modified with regard to knowledge criteria
Path 4	• Top management initiative → creation of teams, project groups, etc. • Initiation of pilot projects	• Informal networks emerge • Adaptation of the ICT infrastructure according to requirements of the network participants • Responsible officers motivate people to join the networks	• Knowledge creation and transfer are supported by incentive systems and permanent internal marketing measures

→ Knowledge organization

developed in a third phase. The danger of the IT-centred path is that the needs of users are not adequately reflected and systems do not effectively support the workflow. Relevant knowledge resides in the heads of people and is not accessible via databases.

Path 2: Knowledge managers as change agents. This path starts with the appointment of a knowledge manager to be responsible for knowledge creation and transfer, and who coordinates and guides the evolution of networks of people. This strategy is heavily dependent on the personality of the knowledge manager and his or her ability to structure a consistent knowledge management programme.

Path 3: The problem-oriented path. Knowledge management initiatives arise from internal and external competition, which makes efficient and continuous sharing of knowledge indispensable and results in the emergence of networks of people with common interests, who face common pressures. Pilot initiatives are started to exchange best practices, improve specific processes or use synergies in projects. Project leaders of initiatives develop individual knowledge management solutions. The challenge of this path is to integrate the many knowledge management initiatives into an overall concept, deploy a common IT infrastructure and apply consistent incentive systems.

Path 4: The top-down approach. In this case, knowledge management is initiated directly by corporate management. Points of departure are visions or strategic goals. Following these strategic objectives a corporate knowledge management framework and a number of pilot projects are usually created. Projects encourage cooperation and creation of networks as well as the development of new forms of incentive systems. The IT and communication infrastructure is adapted accordingly.

Box 19.1 The Siemens Business Services knowledge management framework

Background

Siemens Business Services (SBS) was established in 1995, emerging from units of the former Siemens Nixdorf Informationssysteme AG. The merging units had already successfully pursued an extensive process of culture change, so that a receptive climate for knowledge management existed. Furthermore, there was a belief that knowledge management solutions should not just be tool-oriented. Therefore a knowledge management framework based on the knowledge market concept was developed (see figure opposite). It was based on the business strategy to manage knowledge as a corporate asset. Core competencies were described and individual knowledge management initiatives, designed to add value to the relevant business areas, were supported.

The second element in the framework was the creation of a knowledge culture and organization. Concrete measures included time allocations for employees to take part in knowledge-sharing or knowledge-creation activities. Contribution to the corporate knowledge base and personal development were evaluated in the annual staff dialogue. The networking of employees has given rise to communities of practice of various degrees of maturity. Knowledge exchange is guided by the market principle which required to make the knowledge of sellers transparent. In order to better connect knowledge buyers and sellers, knowledge brokers were instituted; they can be seen as human search engines who are accessible to anyone in the organization with a question about a specialist area. Knowledge brokers are responsible for classifying, categorizing, storing and managing the relevant information, coordinating specific research, and monitoring the results of expert forums. They also act as change agents for further cultural development and contribute to the introduction of new platforms or functions. The knowledge marketplace is built on explicit knowledge such as documents, processes, methods, and business patterns, and furthermore allows access via yellow pages to people who have knowledge in specific areas.

Key propositions

As part of its project planning, SBS determined a number of critical factors for successful knowledge management, which were then confirmed in external consulting projects:

1. Knowledge management requires problem-based trading. It should not start with a solution-based model, but with an in-depth examination of the initial situation in the unit, or the entire company, in order to develop solutions for specific problems (e.g. cultural barriers).
2. Knowledge management requires support and clear communication of the objectives by management, as well as active staff approval.
3. The kind of knowledge that is critical, and its origin, must be identified and knowledge management must be defined as an integral part of the business process. For example, the SBS unit identified project delivery as its core business process, and project experience as its most valuable knowledge.
4. Process owners must be identified and given clearly defined roles and specific responsibilities for output.
5. Best practices for capturing knowledge must be defined, as well as for achieving and retaining the required quality (filter processes).
6. The economic value of knowledge does not lie in possessing it, but in using it. When the knowledge management reaches a certain stage of maturity, actually having information is no longer the decisive factor for success, but rather how it is interpreted and applied.
7. It is necessary to look at and implement knowledge management in its entirety.
8. Knowledge management topics should not run in parallel with other projects, but should be integrated into them. In many groups within a company there are highly knowledge-intensive projects, such as e-business topics, the success of which can be increased by looking at them from a knowledge management point of view.
9. Knowledge management programmes must be aligned to corporate goals. Knowledge management cannot be run as an end in itself, but must be clearly aligned to the strategic objectives of the company. At Siemens, for example, these objectives involve supporting the paradigm shift from a product company to a solution- and service-driven company.
10. A technical platform must be provided based on existing architectures. Knowledge management must not appear simply as a "new" tool to the employees involved. Existing information and communication architectures should be part of knowledge management project planning.

continued overleaf

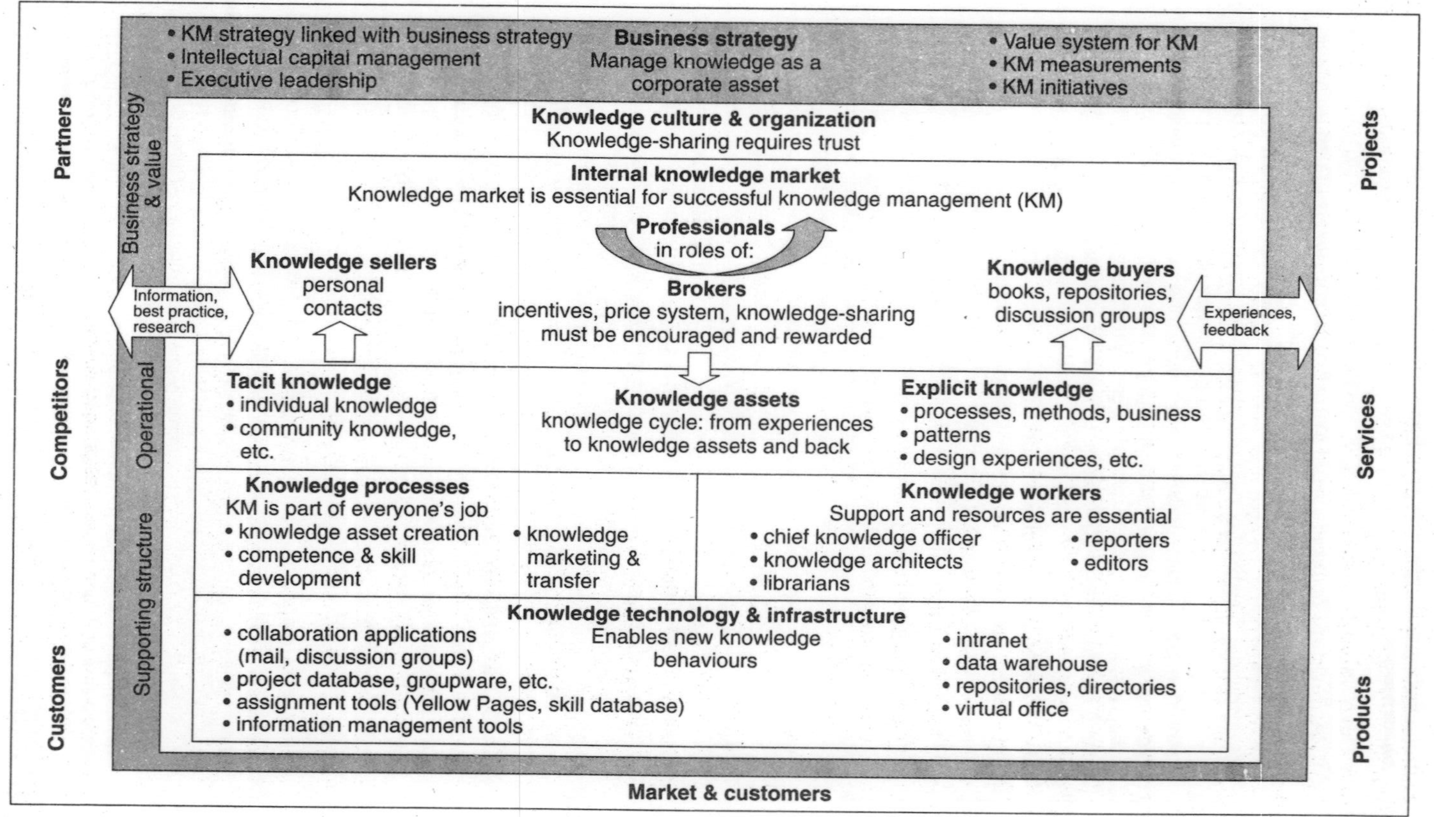
Partners
Competitors
Customers
Business strategy & value
Operational
Supporting structure
• KM strategy linked with business strategy
• Intellectual capital management
• Executive leadership
Business strategy
Manage knowledge as a corporate asset
• Value system for KM
• KM measurements
• KM initiatives
Knowledge culture & organization
Knowledge-sharing requires trust
Internal knowledge market
Knowledge market is essential for successful knowledge management (KM)
Professionals
in roles of:
Information, best practice, research
Knowledge sellers
personal contacts
Brokers
incentives, price system, knowledge-sharing must be encouraged and rewarded
Knowledge buyers
books, repositories, discussion groups
Experiences, feedback
Tacit knowledge
• individual knowledge
• community knowledge, etc.
Knowledge assets
knowledge cycle: from experiences to knowledge assets and back
Explicit knowledge
• processes, methods, business
• patterns
• design experiences, etc.
Knowledge processes
KM is part of everyone's job
• knowledge asset creation
• competence & skill development
• knowledge marketing & transfer
Knowledge workers
Support and resources are essential
• chief knowledge officer
• knowledge architects
• librarians
• reporters
• editors
Knowledge technology & infrastructure
• collaboration applications (mail, discussion groups)
• project database, groupware, etc.
• assignment tools (Yellow Pages, skill database)
• information management tools
Enables new knowledge behaviours
• intranet
• data warehouse
• repositories, directories
• virtual office
Market & customers
Projects
Services
Products

11. The pilot projects must have clearly defined, measurable objectives that can be achieved in less than six months. However, the change to a knowledge-based company involves a process that can span several years. Planning the pilot projects, in particular, is an important task for the successful implementation of knowledge management. The pilot groups must be selected in such a way that the results can be applied to other groups, or at other locations.

Source: D. Rahmhorst: "A guided tour through the Siemens business services knowledge management framework", in T. Davenport and G. Probst: *Knowledge management case book* (Munich, Publicis MCD/Wiley, 2000), pp. 126–140.

---

[1] P. Evans and T. S. Wurster: *Blown to bits* (Boston, MA, Harvard Business School Press, 2000).

[2] D. Tapscott: *The digital economy* (New York, McGraw-Hill, 1996); see also D. F. Aldrich: *Mastering the digital marketplace* (New York, Wiley, 1999).

[3] KPMG: *The knowledge journey: A business guide to knowledge systems* (London, KPMG Consulting).

[4] J. Roos and G. von Krogh: "The epistemological challenge: Managing knowledge and intellectual capital", in *European Management Journal*, Vol. 14, No. 4, 1996, pp. 333–337.

[5] M. Polanyi: *The tacit dimension* (New York, Anchor Day Books, 1966).

[6] I. Nonaka and H. Takeuchi: *The knowledge-creating company* (Oxford, Oxford University Press, 1995).

[7] T. A. Stewart: *Intellectual capital* (London, Nicholas Brealey, 1997); see also L. Edvinsson and M. S. Malone: *Intellectual capital* (New York, Harper Business, 1997).

[8] J. Roos et al.: *Intellectual capital* (New York, New York University Press, 1998).

[9] K. E. Sveiby: *The new organizational wealth* (San Francisco, CA, Berret-Koehler, 1997).

[10] R. S. Kaplan and D. P. Norton: *The balanced scorecard* (Boston, MA, Harvard Business School Press, 1996).

[11] M. T. Hansen et al.: "What's your strategy for managing knowledge?", in *Harvard Business Review*, Mar.–Apr. 1999, pp. 106–116.

[12] K. North: *Wissensorientierte Unternehmensführung* (Wiesbaden, Gabler, 2nd ed., 1999).

[13] American Productivity and Quality Center: *Knowledge management consortium benchmarking study, Final report* (Houston, TX, APQC, 1996).

[14] S. Denning: *The springboard: How storytelling ignites action in knowledge-era organizations* (Boston, MA, Butterworth Heinemann, 2001).

[15] M. Deviani: "The search for knowledge", in *International Consultants' Guide*, July 1999, pp. 18–20.

[16] K. North and A. Papp: "Erfahrungen bei der Einführung von Wissensmanagement", in *Management*, No. 4, 1999, pp. 18–22.

CONSULTING ON PRODUCTIVITY AND PERFORMANCE IMPROVEMENT 20

The role of productivity as a major contributor to company competitiveness and national welfare is universally recognized. Generally, productivity is a measure of the quantity and quality of what is produced in relation to the resources used, both human and physical. Productivity is affected by the quality of the whole human and business environment. However, the principal area where productivity growth is created is the enterprise, as it is here that the whole range of available resources and conditions come together to produce goods and services. The effectiveness of the combined functioning of these resources in a given macroeconomic, institutional, social and natural environment is reflected in productivity.

Helping clients to understand and increase productivity has always been one of the fundamental objectives of management consulting. However, concepts of productivity and approaches to improvement have undergone many changes. The "scientific management" and "rationalization" movement initiated by Frederick Taylor, with its concentration on the workplace and on the simplification and better organization of production, was in fact the start of productivity consulting. It developed numerous techniques for improving productivity and efficiency, many of which are still in use.

Productivity improvement is nowadays a key element of most management and business consulting work, although often productivity is described in terms of business efficiency, performance, total quality, or competitive edge. The productivity dimension looms large in business process re-engineering, total quality management (TQM), company performance improvement, *kaizen*, benchmarking and corporate excellence.

This chapter begins with a short review of changes in productivity concepts, factors and conditions. It then focuses on a few issues that form the core of consulting for productivity and performance improvement: productivity analysis, strategies and approaches to improve productivity, and programmes for improving company productivity and performance. At the end we provide a brief overview of the major techniques and tools for improving productivity.

20.1 Shifts in productivity concepts, factors and conditions

Problems with productivity often start with a poor understanding by management of its real meaning. In a survey by the American Management Association in the United States, 95 per cent of respondents agreed with the statements that productivity related to quality of outputs as well as quantity (but what about costs?) and 90 per cent thought that productivity referred to output per person-hour (only?).[1]

Changes in understanding productivity

Conventionally, productivity has been considered as the ratio of physical output to input. This implies that productivity is simply production-oriented and concerns manufacturing activities only. In practice, however, an organization has multiple objectives and requires resources to meet them. Furthermore, objectives are seldom met as a result of one particular resource: multiple resources produce the final result through their interaction. Besides, some objectives may be achieved at the cost of others. There is, therefore, a need to have a new – more holistic and systemic – look at productivity.

Since the modern business cycle includes processes of management, supply, marketing and sales, client service and client relationships, and many others, the concept of productivity needs to be expanded to cover all of them, not only production. Therefore, for example, the concept of labour productivity – the ratio of output to the labour input – may be misleading because the productivity of labour can be increased by using different components and parts, or by installing new capital equipment. The concept of capital productivity is equally unsatisfactory because increasing capital productivity is dependent on many factors other than capital, such as knowledge, skills, systems and technology.

Because of the evident deficiencies in single-factor productivity measurement, the concept of multifactor productivity has emerged. Multifactor productivity is a composite measure of how effective and efficient a company is in using its labour, capital, technology, management, organization, and other factors. But even this approach is internally focused and does not refer to customers, and is therefore becoming less relevant.

Companies can also achieve higher productivity by producing goods or services that are more valuable to customers. The new paradigm shifts the focus from the input side of the productivity equation to the output side or *value-added* aspects of productivity. The traditional concept of "producing more with less" is less and less relevant; many companies now seek to produce more valuable outputs that satisfy customers with the same or more resources. The "high road" to productivity improvement is characterized by actions to enhance the outputs, whereas the "low road" focuses on reducing the amount of inputs, particularly of human resources.

Major factors and conditions affecting productivity

Awareness of the main external and internal factors affecting productivity is of critical importance to both clients and consultants. External productivity factors are conditions in the business environment; management cannot control these but should be aware of them and their dynamics. Internal productivity factors are those that are under effective control of management and include factors related to resources (input), processes and output (figure 20.1). Provided that external factors have been properly taken into account in the business strategy, the main potential for productivity improvement lies in internal productivity factors.

In many cases, productivity problems have a multifactorial nature and it is more constructive to think about creating particular conditions by optimizing many different factors. For example, one key condition may be an effective *productivity management system*. Another critical condition of sustainable productivity improvement is applying *innovation and new technology* coupled with *entrepreneurship*.

To compete successfully today, companies have to be highly entrepreneurial, which means permanently innovative in business strategies, processes, products and services. Most traditional companies lack such an entrepreneurial spirit. In a survey by PricewaterhouseCoopers of more than 800 companies in seven countries, 50 per cent of managers said they would launch a new product or service only if they believed it had an 80 per cent or higher chance of success, in terms of adding market share in a set time. This indicates a lack of willingness to take risks. Many companies suffer from "analysis paralysis" prior to launching a new product. In many cases this leads to more wastage than if they were to accept a certain amount of failure in return for some breakthroughs.

More innovative companies generally grow faster. Businesses in which less than 10 per cent of annual revenue comes from products launched in the previous five years have a 30 per cent chance of seeing their sales decline, as competitors capture their market share.

Innovation requires a combination of strategy, financial commitment, operational integration, entrepreneurship and competent people. This means investing in the company's intellectual capital and the people likely to participate in the innovation learning process. Managers have to ensure the cumulative and collective character of this learning process and provide an entrepreneurial, innovation-friendly learning environment. To free the entrepreneurial spirit in a company, the first shift in strategy should be to move from resource *allocation* to resource *attraction*.

Sustainable competitiveness is also closely linked to the level of technological capability. A company that cuts its investment in research and development will often lose much more than it saves. It has been reported that a dollar spent on R&D returns eight times more than a dollar spent on new machinery. New machinery can help you do old work better, but R&D leads to innovation – new products that are of higher value than the ones they replace. Research and development are necessary but not sufficient for achieving a competitive position

Figure 20.1 An integrated model of productivity factors

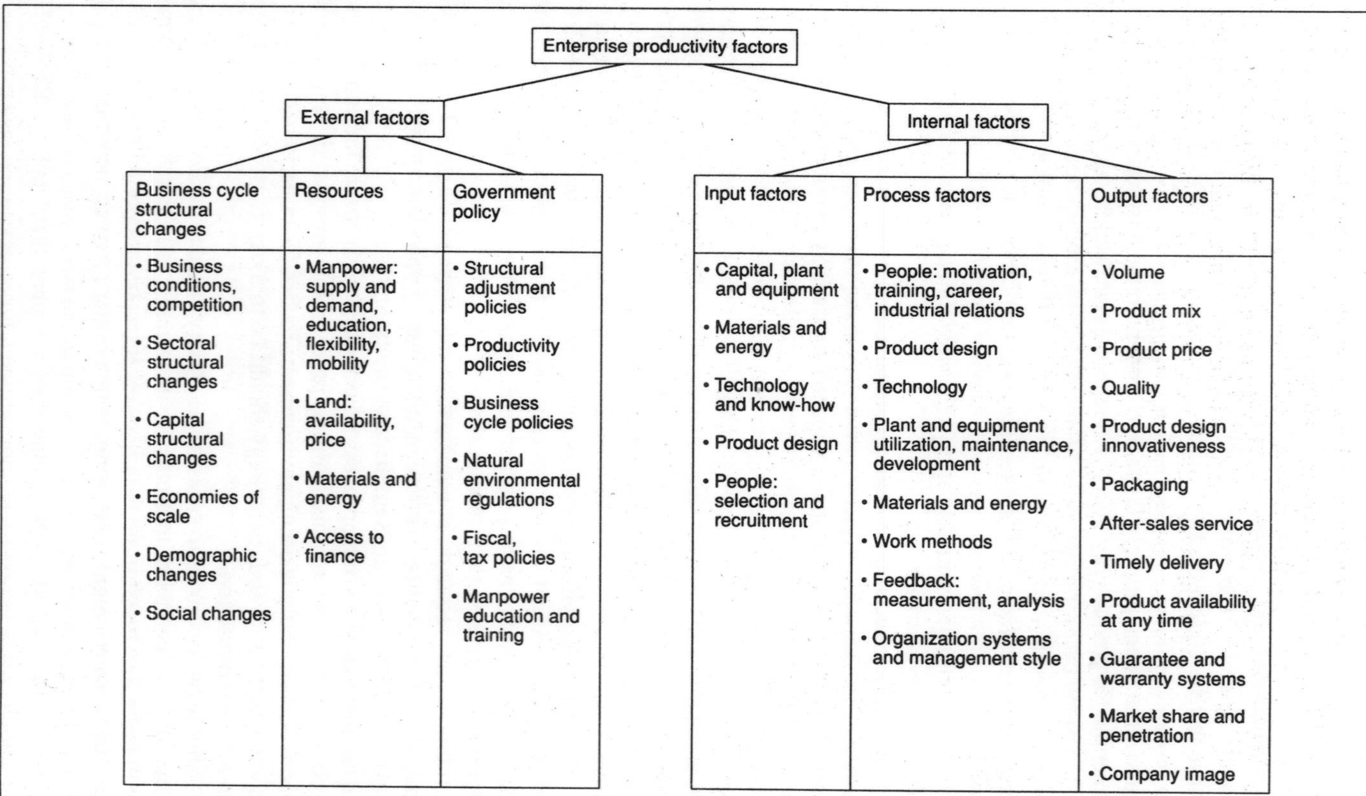

in the market. The way technology is used and managed is important as well; it is most effective when coupled with innovation.

Some of the most admired companies in traditional sectors owe their success to their masterful use of information. Toyota built powerful competitive advantages through simultaneous engineering, *kanban* ("just in time"), and quality control – all of which depend on techniques for processing and utilizing information. WalMart exploited its electronic links with suppliers and the logical technique of cross docking to achieve a dramatic increase in inventory turnover. And thousands of companies that have embraced TQM, re-engineered their operations, and focused on their core competencies have chosen to define their managerial goals in terms of information flows. IT can be used to create business value by managing risk in financial management, to reduce costs by improving business processes and transactions, and to add value for customers with information about products and services before, during and after sales.

Manufacturers are also beginning to tap the Internet's potential, transforming e-business into the engine of industry. In 1999, Ford unveiled the AutoXchange, a massive online shopping centre for all its goods and services. The company expects to save US$8 billion in a few years from lower prices and improved supplier productivity. The glassmaker Corning claims that it will be able to reduce its average procurement cost from US$140 to US$10 by using a Web-based catalogue in its science products unit. Business-to-business transactions (B2B; see Chapter 16) transform every step in the conventional business practice from order-taking to delivery. According to some experts, B2B exchanges enable many smaller companies to become part of large networks, which was previously impossible.

Knowledge management, including *knowledge-sharing* (see Chapter 19), is becoming another important condition for productivity improvement. For example, sharing knowledge is one of the three business processes for which the General Electric CEO Jack Welch takes personal responsibility (the other two are allocating resources and developing people). At Shell, employee teams meet weekly to consider ideas emailed to them by others in the company. In 1999, the teams, called game changers, collected 320 ideas. Of the company's top five new business initiatives in 1999, four came from the collaborative work of teams. Experience indicates that the best knowledge-sharing happens in the companies that create *communities of practice* – clusters of people linked by common practical interests or activities and sharing knowledge focused on their practical needs.

The most critical condition for sustainable productivity growth is the *quality of employees and managers*, and this demands good human resource management practices. This, however, is often ignored in practice. Workers who would like to be more productive are often held back by repressive management practices. The importance of "job fit" is often ignored in hiring and promotion. Research by Anderson Leadership in the United States found that 50 to 85 per cent of employees in client organizations were miscast in their jobs.[2]

Another condition related to human resource management practices is an enabling and supporting policy environment, and corporate management

Figure 20.2 A results-oriented human resource development cycle

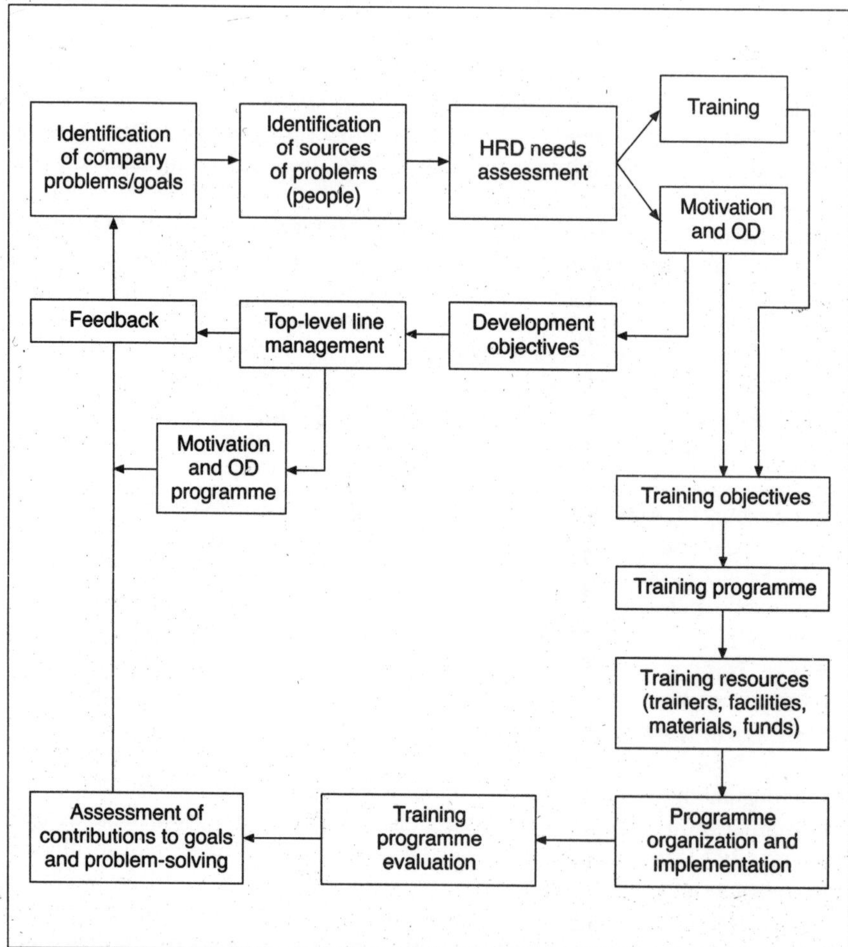

accountable for the performance achieved by its workforce – hence the importance of *corporate culture* for productivity improvement. This culture needs to support collaboration to ensure the involvement of all people making work-related decisions.

Figure 20.2 provides a general model of links between company objectives and problems, employees' specific training needs and approaches that can be combined with the envisaged productivity improvement measures in a single results-oriented and flexible human resources development consulting cycle.

The first phase of this model includes identification of company goals and problems, the sources of the problems, and personnel training and development needs. The results of this phase provide the necessary information for the second phase – identification of development and training objectives.

Development objectives provide information for designing organizational development (OD) programmes, while training objectives serve as a basis for training programmes. After both programmes have been implemented, the results are assessed and compared with the objective and/or company needs. The cycle can be repeated if necessary.

Such integration of business objectives with training and development helps to improve organizational performance by making people aware of the need to change and assisting them in solving strategic and operational problems.

An important condition for a successful productivity drive is a system for recognition and sharing of productivity gains. Gain-sharing, profit-sharing and payment by results or performance are generally positively related to corporate productivity provided the system is comprehensive, based at the appropriate level and developed with the involvement of the workforce. It is important that connections between bonuses and improvements in productivity are clearly understood by the personnel.

Partnership between employers and workers' organizations, and trust and confidence between management and employees, are also important enabling factors of productivity improvement. Measures to promote such trust include secure employment, information-sharing, productivity gain-sharing, participative management, training, and fairness in relationships.

20.2 Productivity and performance measurement

Productivity measurement and analysis form the foundation of sound productivity improvement consulting. The success of productivity measurement and analysis depends largely on a clear understanding by all stakeholders of the relationship between productivity and the effectiveness and efficiency of the organization. Productivity measurement can stimulate operational improvement: the announcement, installation and operation of a measurement system can improve labour productivity, sometimes by 5 to 10 per cent, with no other organizational change or investment. Productivity indices also help to establish realistic targets and checkpoints for diagnostic activities during an organizational development process, pointing to bottlenecks and barriers to performance. They can also indicate where to look for opportunities to improve and show how well improvements are progressing. There can be no real improvement in industrial relations or proper links between productivity and compensation policies without a sound measurement system.

Shifts in productivity measurement approaches

The traditional approach is to measure productivity as the ratio of output to input, or products to resources used. This is not always relevant. Many companies today are more interested in measuring total productivity than only labour or capital productivity. Total productivity measures reflect the relationship between the total value added and the total input of an enterprise, as well as the quality of their interrelationships. In addition, there are other performance indicators, such as profitability, return on investment, quality, customer needs satisfaction, social climate, and environmental impact, that need to be assessed.

A survey of the most admired companies by *Fortune* in October 2000 stressed that they all focus on performance measurement.[3] Though 80 per cent of them used profits as a measure of success, the best companies were much more likely to use return-based methods of measurement, such as assets, equity, capital, and shareholder value. When it came to charting their performance, these companies were more likely to focus on customer- and employee-based measurements. Almost 60 per cent relied on customer indicators like satisfaction, loyalty, and market share. And 40 per cent charted employee retention, career development, and other employee-oriented measurements – almost three times the percentage among companies that did not make the list.

Many executives from the best companies report that these measures encourage cooperation and collaboration, and help companies to focus on growth, operational excellence, customer loyalty, human capital development, and other critical issues. They use these measurements to link performance with real rewards. The top organizations create performance measures that focus on all drivers of their businesses – financial performance, shareholder value, and employee and customer satisfaction. Productivity is just one of the most important sources of profit (see figure 20.3).

The recognition of customer focus as an important part of any competitiveness strategy has led many consultants to look for measures that are closely linked to both customer satisfaction and value creation. Indeed, the purpose of any business is to create and provide products and services that are of value to customers. In the long run, a business organization can produce shareholder value only if it first produces competitive *customer value added* (CVA). CVA can be expressed as the relationship between the degree of customer satisfaction with the product or services and the satisfaction with the price paid. An organization can also be said to create CVA when it provides products and services for customers that are of greater value (or worth) than those of competitors. CVA can be measured through market surveys of customer satisfaction and calculated as the ratio of the company performance relative to its competitors as follows:

CVA = Perceived value of the company offers / Perceived value of competitive offers

If the CVA ratio is below one, then the company has no competitive advantage in its offers. The higher above one the CVA ratio, the greater the competitive advantage of the company offers.

Improvement in productivity is the result of the combined efforts of many stakeholders with different objectives and perceptions about organizational effectiveness. No part of an organization is so simple that it can be measured adequately by one indicator, and a "family of measures" should therefore be used. By drawing together a set of measurements from the perspectives of its

Figure 20.3 The contribution of productivity to profits

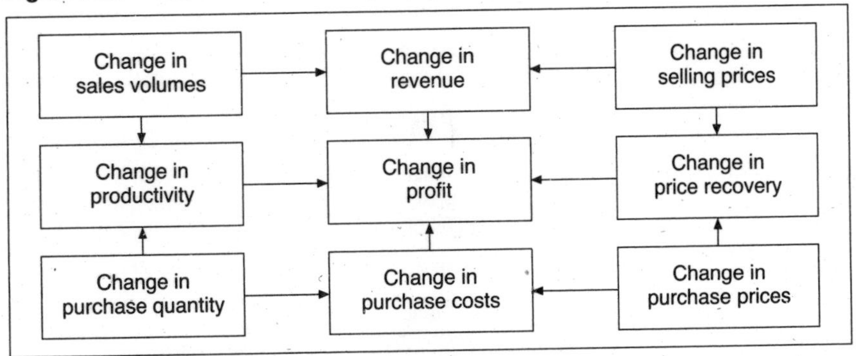

Source: Adapted from European Association of National Productivity Centres (EANPC): "Productivity, innovation, quality of working life and environment", in *Memorandum* (Brussels), Feb. 1999, p. 6.

various stakeholders – customers, employees, stockholders, owners, suppliers and communities – an organization can avoid the shortsightedness that often results from focusing on a single measure of success.

As is the case with any organizational change (see Chapter 4), consultants may meet some resistance to productivity and performance measurement. Reasons may include potential misunderstanding and misuse of measurement, fear of exposure of inadequate performance, additional time and reporting demands, reduction of autonomy, and others. Implementing a productivity measurement system is an organizational change and should be managed as a change process.

20.3 Approaches and strategies to improve productivity

There are many approaches to improving organizational productivity and performance, ranging from incremental, small-steps improvement to radical strategic changes. One of the most important tasks of the productivity consultant is to make conscious and educated judgements on the needs of the client organization. Does the organization have the potential and reserves to cope with incremental continuous improvements? Or is the client already in a situation where only radical strategic intervention can help? The two approaches will be considered separately.

Incremental continuous improvement

The essence of incremental continuous improvement is reflected in the *kaizen* approach developed in Japan and described in many publications. It involves making continuous small improvements that require little or no investment,

Figure 20.4 ***Kaizen* building-blocks**

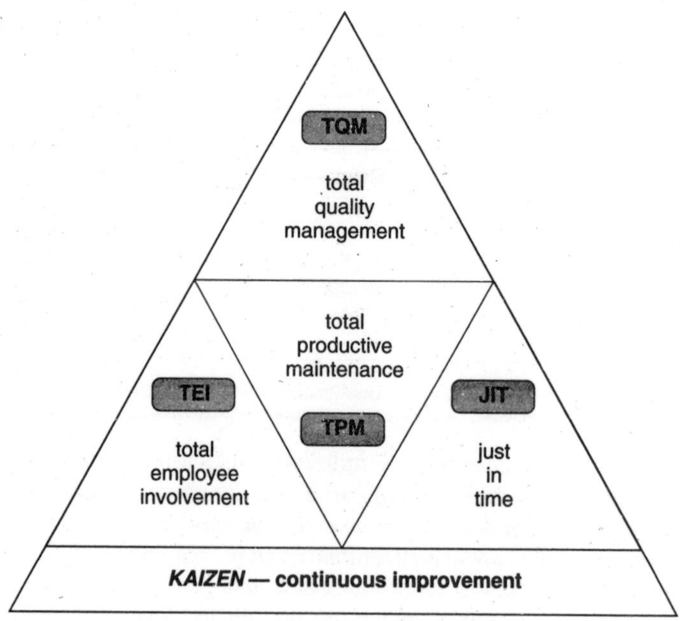

Source: J. DeWeese: "The people–machine connection at Texas Instruments", in *National Productivity Review* (New York), Summer 1999, p. 40.

involving all employees in making them, and providing structured opportunities, systems and tools for increasing productivity. Its main objectives could be, for example, eliminating waste, reducing defects, keeping the workplace tidy, improving quality, and developing good working habits. The main building-blocks of *kaizen* are *total employee involvement (TEI), just-in-time (JIT), total productive maintenance (TPM) and TQM* (figure 20.4).

For example, *kaizen* involves workers in maintenance operations by harnessing the symbiotic relationships between processes, operators and maintenance technicians through:

- taking positive actions to eliminate barriers to operator maintenance
- training operators to perform routine set-up and maintenance tasks
- supporting a steady stream of process modification projects, and
- rotating operators to interesting jobs elsewhere in the organization.

The most important task of continuous improvement is to achieve sustainable growth in productivity through elimination of all kinds of waste – of materials, energy, labour-time, machine-time – anything that does not provide value to the customer. Sources of waste could be poor design, inappropriate technology, wrong choice of materials, carelessness, improper work methods, material scrap, rejects, pollutants, movement inventories, machine breakdown, delays in obtaining repairs and other services, inefficient space utilization, employees' problems, idle money, work in process, and many others.

A preventive approach focused on reducing the generation of waste is most effective. The development of waste management indices, such as the reduction index, collection index, recovery index, and disposal index, at various stages of the process can help in monitoring and reducing waste and improving productivity. One such effective approach to reducing waste and improving the quality of environment is the *green productivity approach* developed and popularized recently by the Asian Productivity Organization (box 20.1).

Another important task of continuous improvement could be saving on *small capital expenditures*. Here we are not talking about strategic investments, but small amounts of money within the approved budget. But are they really small? Any company can create far more sustainable value by reducing its capital expenditures through rigorous evaluation of the small-ticket items that are usually rubber-stamped. Those "little" requests – which could take up to 80 per cent of the remaining budget after strategic items – often prove to be unnecessary (duplicating other requests) or very expensive. But few managers have the time, energy, or inclination to question their justification.

It may be useful to ask the following eight questions concerning small-ticket capital budget items, as suggested by T. Copeland:[4]

To operating managers:

- *Is this your investment to make?* Often a unit manager will overstep his or her boundaries and put in a request for an investment that is someone else's responsibility.
- *Does it really have to be new?* Overall costs can be 30 to 40 per cent lower if a company continues using an existing machine for five more years instead of buying a new one.
- *How are our competitors meeting compliance needs?* A good way to combat conservative and costly compliance with different regulations is to require unit managers to look into the practices of other companies.

To senior managers:

- *Is the left hand duplicating investment already made by the right?* Many organizations with complicated operations have a tendency to accumulate excess capacity, sometimes up to 70 per cent.
- *Are the trade-offs between profits and capital spending well understood?* Often managers will request new assets, neglecting future productivity and creating a culture that places earnings above all other performance measures.
- *Are there signs of budget "massage"?* It is common for unit managers to be reluctant to propose reductions in their capital spending, for fear that the head office will not be generous when they need an increase. On the other hand, asking for more money could provoke an encounter with internal auditors. So they "massage" the budget, shuffling expenditures between budgets items or spending money urgently before the end of the budget year.

Box 20.1 Green productivity practices

Steps	Tasks
I. Get started	1. Formation of green productivity team
	2. Walk-through survey of the production process
	3. Preliminary identification of waste-generating operations
II. Analyse process steps	4. Detailed process study
	5. Preparation of process and activity flow chart
	6. Preparation of materials balance
	7. Identification and characterization of sources of waste
	8. Assignment of costs to waste streams
III. Conduct energy audit	9. Causal analysis for waste generation from known sources
	10. Identification of energy usage areas
	11. Preparation of energy balance
	12. Identification of energy losses
V. Generate waste prevention options	13. Causal analysis for energy loss
	14. Process optimization studies
	15. Development of waste prevention options
V. Select waste prevention solutions	16. Preliminary selection of workable options
	17. Assessment of technical feasibility
	18. Assessment of economic impact
VI. Implement waste prevention solution	19. Evaluation of environmental aspects
	20. Preparation of implementation plan
	21. Implementation of waste prevention solution
VII. Study pollution control	22. Monitoring and evaluation of results
	23. Treatability studies of effluents
	24. Design of appropriate pollution-control systems
	25. Implementation of pollution-control system
VIII. Maintain green productivity	26. Performance evaluation of pollution-control system
	27. Sustain waste prevention and control
Go to step II	28. Identify and select next focus area

Questions to be put at the end of the process:

- *Are shared assets fully used?* Businesses in networks may use a lot of shared assets, and are thus highly sensitive to slow-moving bureaucratic procedures. If shared assets are not fully used most of the time, it means that a company has problems with coordination.
- *How fine-grained are capacity estimates?* If measurements of need for equipment are not adequately fine-grained, managers can underestimate the capacity of equipment networks.

Quantum leaps and large-scale strategic improvements

"Quantum leap" improvements are necessary to achieve dramatic breakthroughs in products and services design and delivery, competitiveness, creation of new markets and similar. The changes are drastic and require considerable investment in new technology, equipment, and product development, as well as major changes in production processes. Such changes are normally organization-wide and affect a large number of employees. The gains can be substantial and strategic in nature, but resistance and difficulties in implementation are likely to be much higher than with *kaizen.*

Approaches and programmes that produce major improvements in productivity and performance exhibit one common characteristic. They do not start by identifying and dissecting current problems, shortcomings and underutilized resources with the intention of devising a better method and so increasing productivity. Their starting-point is the client's vision of the future and a strong desire to translate this vision into reality. This vision could be to become a sector leader, achieve a significant competitive advantage, offer a completely new sort of product or service, or cut costs by 30–40 per cent.

The most important method for achieving new and ambitious goals is strategic management coupled with productivity improvement programmes or projects (PIP). Strategic management requires a *business strategy* defining the business in which the organization operates ("the right things to do") and *capability strategies* defining the organization's general capabilities and operational competencies ("to do things right"). With this approach, productivity and performance improvement can be directed to a future purpose, which serves as the main common target and driving force for the consultant and the client. It helps the client organization to develop a long-term perspective within which to determine and realize short-term goals, and to learn to work towards its purpose over time. We mention below a few choices related to performance improvement that are emerging as a result of recent shifts in the business environment.

Innovative or adaptive strategies? The most basic choice, which makes the further design of strategy easier, is between an innovative and an adaptive strategy. An innovative strategy means investing in productive capability or new combinations of inputs which generate higher-quality, lower-cost outputs. In contrast, an adaptive strategy does not attempt to upgrade and recombine the firm's assets and inputs. In its extreme form, an adaptive strategy can entail disinvestments, which reduces the ability to create value tomorrow; it extracts value today without putting new value-creating capabilities in its place, thus reducing the ability to compete. An adaptive strategy can make sense in the short or medium term. An innovative strategy is a development process that takes time and a delay in its introduction can make it more difficult to develop an effective innovative response.

Competitive advantage through strategic capabilities. Winners in the global marketplace demonstrate management capability to coordinate and redeploy competencies within the organization. These dynamic capabilities must be tuned to customer needs; they should be unique or difficult to replicate so that products and services can be priced with little regard for competition. Any assets that can be bought and sold at an established price, that can readily be assembled through markets, or that can be replicated through formal contracts with a portfolio of business units cannot be considered as strategic. A capability that is difficult to replicate or imitate can be considered a distinctive competence.

Competitive growth strategies. Companies that select the growth path as their main direction have to apply special growth-oriented strategies. Growth is hard to achieve and even harder to sustain. Three general conclusions emerged from a 1999 review of the fastest-growing companies:[5] young growing companies need to see themselves as much larger enterprises almost immediately; sustaining value-creating growth requires heavy investment in IT, R&D and capital assets; and the ability to form and manage alliances to share learning is a key strategy for companies of all sizes and in all sectors.

Moving down the value chain. Providing services is generally more lucrative than making products. The top companies are starting to create new business models to capture profits at the customer end of the value chain. They have gone "downstream", towards the customer, to tap into valuable economic activity that occurs throughout the entire production cycle. Downstream markets offer important benefits besides revenue. They tend to have higher margins and require fewer assets than manufacturing. And because they tend to provide steady service-revenue streams, they often work against business cycles and provide more economic stability. To capture value downstream, producers have to expand their definition of the value chain, shift their focus from operations to customer allegiance, and look again at their vertical integration.

Customers as partners in innovations. Businesses today consider customers as an important source of information, and as partners in R&D and product-testing. Thanks largely to the Internet, consumers increasingly engage in active dialogue with manufacturers, and create and compete for value, becoming a new source of competence for corporations. For example, more than 650,000 customers tested a beta version of Windows 2000® and reported back on their ideas for changing some of the product features. The value of this collective R&D

investment by customers was estimated at more than US$500 million.[6] Dialogue with customers dramatically improves organizational flexibility.

The following assumptions are of critical importance in designing strategies for radical improvements in productivity and performance:

- The future is more important then the past.
- Intangibles are more important than tangibles.
- Speed is intrinsic to economic value.
- Derivatives become the core events.
- Wealth comes more often from the periphery than from the centre.

Combining strategies

The two strategic approaches to productivity improvement could be combined to give a third approach. While the two ways are contradictory to each other and should not be applied simultaneously, if applied successively they could be very effective. *Kaizen* could assist in eliminating evident waste and inefficiency before an organization undertakes a project for dramatic strategic improvement.

Learning from best practices through benchmarking

One of the best ways to improve company competitiveness and productivity is through benchmarking – studying how world-class companies operate. Productivity consultants should be aware of this important and popular method, which involves not only examining performance results but also understanding what lies behind them. Companies' success may be based on optimal staffing structure, use of new technology, organizational design, ability to network, or many other things. But often the essence of their strategy is to bring all these elements together, forming combinations that change continuously, while at the same time pursuing innovation.

Benchmarking is a continuous process of assessing products and services against the toughest competitors or the companies recognized as industry leaders. It is a process of identifying and understanding outstanding practices in organizations anywhere in the world and adapting them to help in improving your company performance. It requires being humble enough to admit that others are better at something, and wise enough to try to learn how to match and even surpass them. Benchmarking can be applied in many areas, the most important of which are strategy, products, processes and competence. Benchmarking provides information needed to focus and support improvements, and develop a competitive advantage. In productivity analysis, benchmarking helps to identify specific activities and practices that ought to be changed. A good example of benchmarking is given in figure 20.5, which illustrates Nokia's corporate fitness ratings in comparison with other computer and electronics companies.

Kari Tuominen provides an interesting and practical benchmarking model,[7] which is described briefly in box 20.2.

Figure 20.5 Nokia's corporate fitness rating

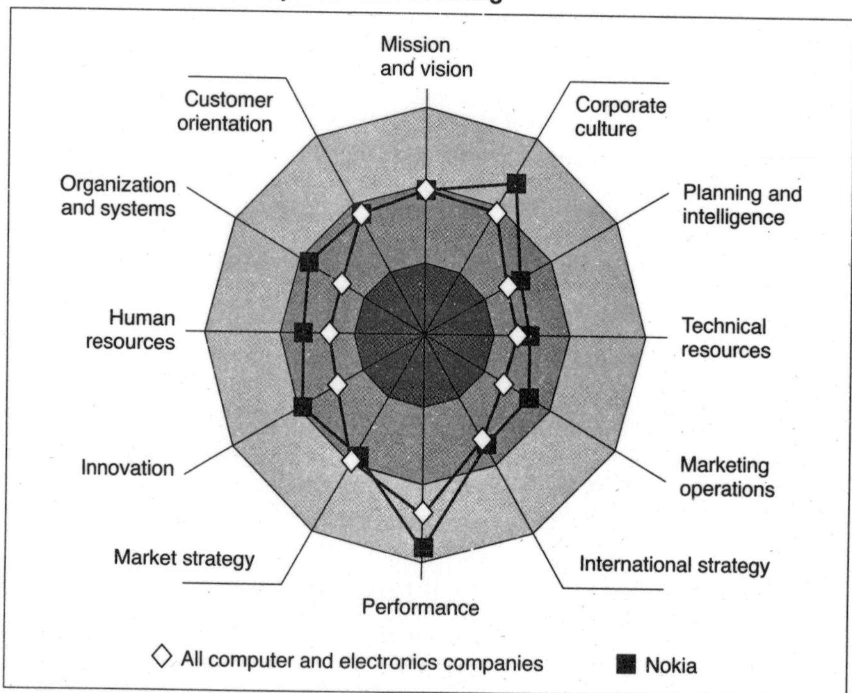

Source: R. Maruca: "Entrepreneurs versus executives at Socaba.com", in *Harvard Business Review*, July–Aug. 2000, pp. 30–38.

Benchmarking tells us what the best companies have in common and what could be useful for a consultant to be aware of in advance. Normally, the best companies are those that consistently serve customer needs better. Customer-focused practices usually result in lowest total cost, highest quality, most responsive lead-time, reliable service, and customer satisfaction and loyalty. The next most important feature of the best companies is an ability to learn and an open learning culture, which encourages managers to search for continuous improvements, and develops a corporate-wide perspective on how best to create value and reduce costs.

As mentioned earlier, the most admired companies focus on performance measurement. Their measurement systems are heavily focused on implementation success. Every activity takes time and costs money. The longer things take, the more they cost. Time is, therefore, a good neutral measure for competitive benchmarking. It separates activities into value-adding and non-value-adding. And we know that customers do not want to pay for time that is not adding value to the operation.

All world-class companies have operating strategies that include total quality commitment, simplified continuous flow, flexible responsiveness, participation and involvement, and supply-chain networking. Best-practice

Box 20.2 Benchmarking process

Steps	Tasks
1. Determine what to benchmark	Identify key performance figures with a critical impact on the company's success. This will influence the search for a benchmark company
2. Identify benchmark companies	Identify benchmark companies that are significantly better than yours in terms of the selected performance measures
3. Measure performance gap	Identify performance gaps between you and the benchmark company, and how performance areas have improved and are expected to be developed
5. Identify excellence enablers	Identify factors that account for difference in performance and that need development to achieve improvement
5. Learn how we do it	Develop an understanding of your own process. Measure performance and identify practices to achieve a satisfactory performance
6. Learn how they do it	Visit company. Develop an understanding of their process. Measure their performance, identify aspects of the process that contribute to excellence, compare performance and observe the root causes and enablers, determine gaps
7. Establish performance goals	Establish performance goals for improvements. Determine ideas to be implemented immediately after the visit, as well as long-term goals
8. Adapt and implement	Prepare plans and schedules and implement them. Adapt and implement the best methods, practices, and enablers into your own process
9. To gain superiority, continue development	The aim is to use continuous measurement to ensure that the objectives are achieved and the benchmark level exceeded
10. Start again with higher targets	Determine the long-term target, and start again from the beginning

companies pay serious attention to *changes in the workplace*, such as work organization, which includes changes in the production process, job content, work allocation and organizational structure; human resource management practices; and industrial relations practices.

Enterprises that invest effectively in intangible assets through training are also likely to report positive performance trends in terms of revenue. Investments in human capital today are generally concentrated on well-educated and skilled employees at the core rather than on less skilled workers at the periphery. Best-practice companies tend to use *lean production systems*, though not in an extreme form, which would reduce flexibility to adapt to sharp market changes and would also have adverse social implications.

The best companies are distinguished by their *high productivity*. A wide range of approaches, tools, methods and techniques have been developed for improving productivity. These include continuous improvement, learning organizations, enterprise restructuring, business process re-engineering, strategic cost management, TQM, organizational rejuvenation, Six Sigma, 5S, *kaizen*, strategic business units, green productivity, innovative organizations, value creation, knowledge management, customer orientation and many others. Implementing different combinations of these approaches enables companies to enhance management dynamism, harness employee potential, apply new technology more effectively, improve process management, reduce waste and provide higher value for less money.

20.4 Designing and implementing productivity and performance improvement programmes

A productivity consultant should be prepared to answer the typical client's question: "Why do we need a separate productivity (or performance) improvement programme? Can't we just improve our existing management and raise the discipline of employees?" It should be pointed out that productivity embraces all components, processes and activities of an organization. Depending on economic conditions and the stage in the life cycle of the organization, not only incremental, but also systemic and radical changes, may be needed. Radical changes can be introduced only through a horizontal productivity (performance) improvement programme (PIP) across the board. There is no standard PIP relevant for all situations; a PIP always has to be tailor-made to suit specific organizational objectives, conditions and business environments. We will therefore discuss here some principles to be applied in designing and implementing such a programme.

General conditions of success

A sound productivity improvement programme should start with a clear and easily communicated definition of the concept of productivity improvement. It should explain why organizational improvement is important, evaluate current operating situations and the reasons for the current status, and develop models of excellence and policies and plans for improvement. The objective of productivity improvement should always be expressed in terms of organizational improvement. The overall PIP objectives should be followed by detailed action plans.

The PIP can be successful if a number of conditions are fulfilled within an organization. The first one is that top management is commited to the programme and there is an effective organizational arrangement headed by one of the top managers. All managers and employees should be aware of and understand the programme objectives and there should be open communication between different organizational elements. The programme should be linked with strategic goals and measurement processes that are practical and easily understood. The productivity improvement techniques chosen should be appropriate to the situation and needs. Monitoring, evaluation and feedback processes to identify results and barriers should provide the basis for design improvements. Recognition of the key role played by workers is crucial and should be demonstrated through a sound productivity gain-sharing system supported by sound labour–management relations. Finally, there must be pressure for change within the organization and its external environment. Top management and consultants should provide leadership in programme design and implementation, as well as permission to experiment with new solutions.

There are many reasons to enter into a PIP, such as a negative balance sheet, new products, equipment, technologies or materials, stronger competition, demand for more flexibility in production, or need for shorter delivery time and better services. Managers and consultants should be sure that there are enough positive factors to give a reasonable chance of success, that the time is right and that conditions are generally favourable.

Structuring the process

A systematic eight-step approach to designing a planning process for performance improvement, suggested by Scott Sink,[8] is shown in figure 20.6.

To run a productivity programme in an organization, a programme manager must be able to suggest processes that can be used to identify problems, and to work out and implement solutions. The intra-enterprise productivity processes include, among others, suggestion schemes, quality circles, task forces, action teams, productivity committees and steering committees, which should be fully understood and used by the programme manager.

Deciding on a productivity improvement programme

The decision to enter into a PIP should be taken in the same way as for any other investment: the cost of the investment should be compared with the likely benefits and risks. The payback period for a PIP should normally be between 8 and 18 months. To prepare to make the decision to invest in a PIP, the first step must be the identification and assessment of potential savings. The best way is

Figure 20.6 The performance improvement planning process

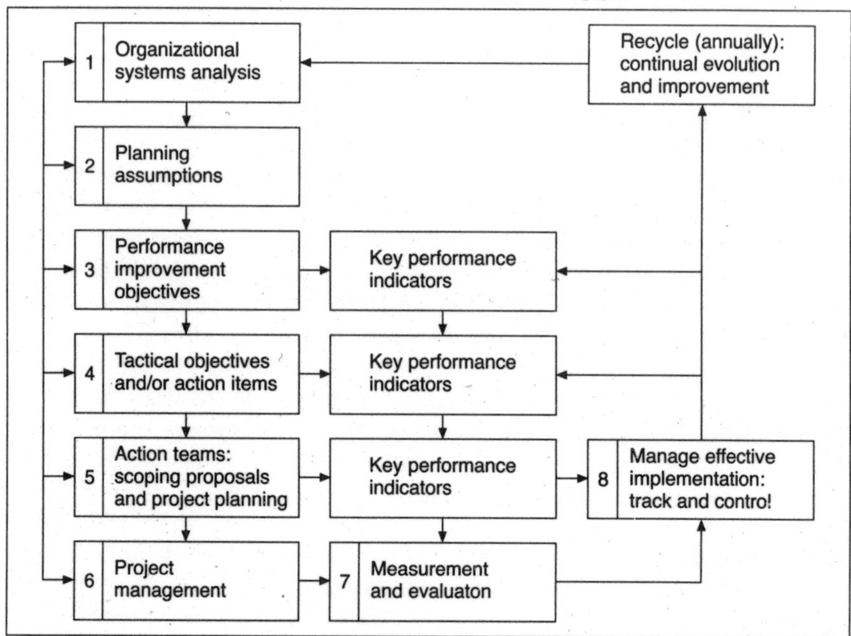

Source: S. Sink: "TQM: the next frontier or just another bandwagon to jump on?", in *QPM – Quality and Productivity Management* (Blacksburg, VA), Vol. 7, No. 2, 1989, p. 18.

to look at the big outputs and the large blocks of cost. Usually large potential areas are directly related to product costs: the consultant should take the products with highest output and look into their cost elements such as materials, value added per production area, tooling, design cost, overhead cost and distribution cost.

Once a good reason for a project and the areas for big potential savings have been identified, the framework for the PIP has to be set. This includes: specifying the reason to start a PIP, so that people commit to the programme; identifying where potential savings could come from, what is the value or the percentage of cost of the potential savings and what risks must be taken to obtain them; and ensuring that most of the areas where potential savings can be made are covered.

The "royal road"

The "royal road", used in many productivity improvement programmes, is outlined in figure 20.7. It consists of three phases:

Phase I – The Pre-Survey, or Preliminary Survey Phase, to identify aims and "sell" the programme to management.

Phase II – The Survey Phase, to set goals and obtain commitment of all responsible area managers.

Figure 20.7 The "royal road" of productivity improvement

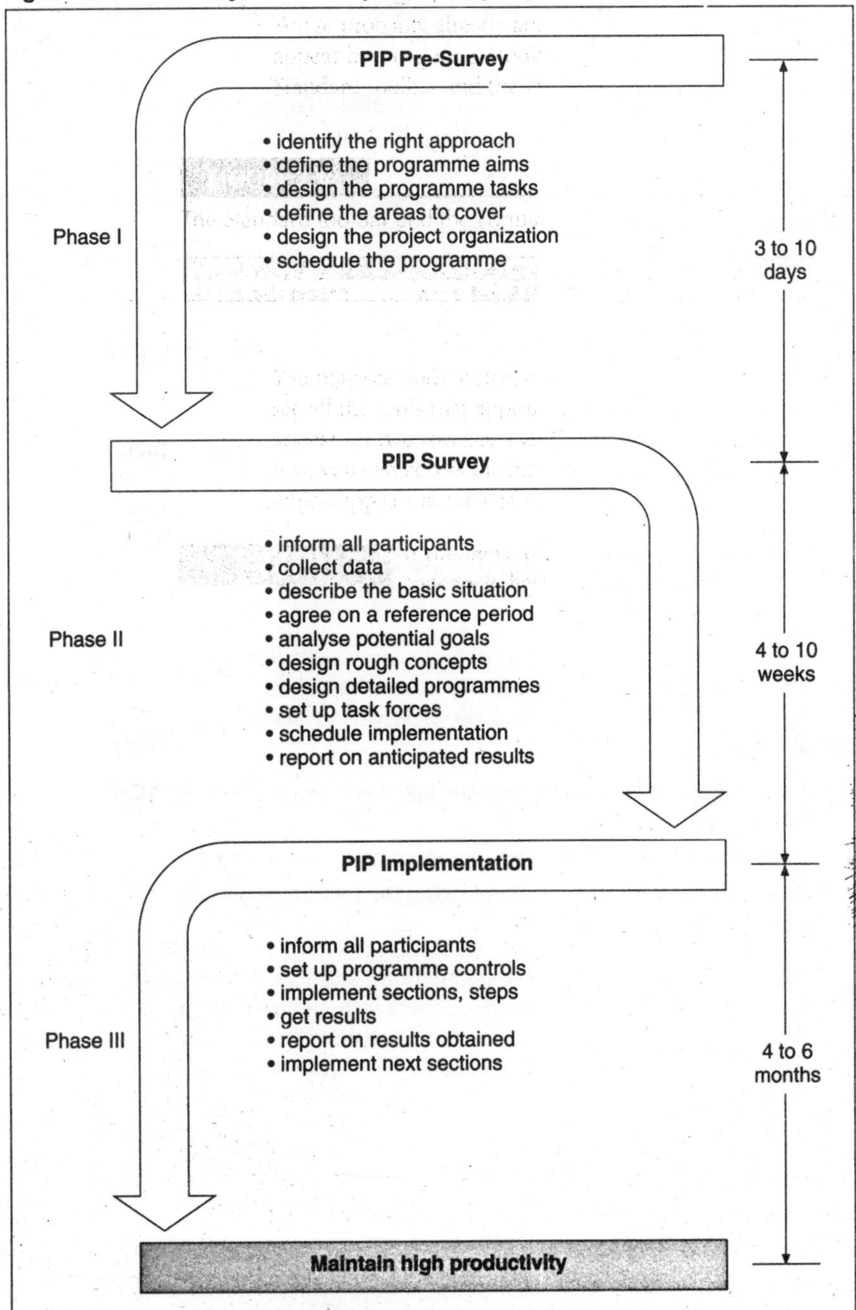

Source: J. Prokopenko and K. North: *Productivity and quality management: A modular programme* (Geneva and Tokyo, ILO/APO, 1996).

Phase III – The Implementation Phase, to design and develop the productivity improvement tasks in detail, implement the measures for improvement and control, and evaluate the results.

To run a successful PIP, it is vital to involve management in the decision-making process from the very beginning. If "stop/go" decision milestones are incorporated into the programme after each main step, management becomes very much involved in decisions on directions, aims, expected results, necessary changes and investments to be made.

All reporting by the PIP team to management should be focused on decision-making. This makes it easy to understand which data have to be collected and checked, and how measures for improvement have to be presented as clear, accurate and convincing information to the decision-makers.

For a PIP to be implemented successfully, the project team has to be well motivated to achieve the results aimed for. At the end of the implementation phase the results should always be documented by quantitative data reflecting the improvements actually achieved.

20.5 Tools and techniques for productivity improvement

It is very important for a productivity consultant to be aware of productivity techniques and tools. In deciding on productivity techniques, managers and consultants need to understand:

- how comfortable the improvement team will be with the technique in the tasks it is supposed to deal with;
- how well the team understands the technique's language;
- how much the team knows about using the techniques or how rapidly it can be trained.

If managers and consultants understand the purpose, language and relations among various improvement techniques, using them will be easier. They will be able to combine them in complementary rather than competitive ways. The following should be taken into account in selecting the productivity improvement techniques:

- The needs of the process customer (internal or external) in identifying the method.
- The technique should be as simple as possible for the task.
- Everybody must understand it; and everybody affected by it must have the opportunity to contribute to its development and implementation.
- It must empower people to perform better and have a motivating and not a punitive character; it must be non-manipulative, honest and unambiguous.

Box 20.3 Some simple productivity tools

Activity analysis	Predetermined tome standards
Brainstorming	Process flow chart
Cause and effect diagram	Quality circles
Cost control	Setup reduction analysis
Downsizing	7 quality tools
Energy conservation	Simple productivity measurement
Employee participation	Statistical process control
Force-field analysis	Suggestion schemes
5S good housekeeping	Time study
Gantt charts	Value analysis
Job enlargement	Value engineering
Job enrichment	Waste reduction
Job rotation	Work analysis
Motion study	Work organization
PERT charts	Work simplification
Poka-yoke	Work sampling
Productivity training	Work study

Productivity improvement techniques may be old or new. In most cases old tools are simpler and less sophisticated than the new ones. New developments do not necessarily imply that old productivity tools should be – or are being – discarded. For example, Taylorism is the application of well-proven techniques for working efficiently in performing well-defined operations and is still used widely today despite its shortcomings. Old productivity tools may be particularly relevant in less sophisticated operations and companies. Box 20.3 gives some examples of relatively unsophisticated productivity tools.

It is worth noting that most of the "new" tools are in fact a combination of well-tested and simple old techniques, including tools of industrial engineering. Complex objectives and problems demanding integrated across-the-board solutions call for more sophisticated and integrated multiple tools. Box 20.4 lists some sophisticated, multipurpose techniques, a number of which are broadly used in many organizations.

So far we have mentioned here more than eighty different productivity tools. Many of them overlap by purpose, or by focus (economics, technology, management, behaviour, etc.); some of them are sophisticated, others less so. It is difficult to navigate among them. Here are a few tips on choosing an appropriate tool:

- Identify techniques that have universal appeal or cross-over capability.
- Create a common organizational language for diverse professional groups.

Box 20.4 Multipurpose productivity techniques

Activity-based costing (ABC)	Multivariate analysis
Activity-based management (ABM)	Objective matrix
Balanced score cards (BSC)	Operations research
Benchmarking	Outsourcing
Business excellence awards	One-to-one marketing
Business process re-engineering (BPR)	Pay-for-performance
CAD/CAM/CIM	Plan–do–check–act (PDCA)
Conflict management	Project management
Cost–benefit analysis	Quality function deployment (QFD)
Customer satisfaction measurements	Sampling surveys
Customer segmentation	Scenario planning
Concurrent engineering	Self-managing teams
Cycle-time reduction	Six Sigma
Cross-functional teams	Statistical tests
Economic value added (EVA)	Strategic alliances
Electronic data interchange (EDI)	Strategic planning
Experiments design methods	Supply chain analysis
Gain-sharing	Supply chain integration
Growth strategies	System thinking
Group dynamics	Taguchi methods
Group performance appraisal	Theory of constraints
Just-in-time	Time compression management
Kaizen (continuous improvement)	Total employee involvement (TEI)
Knowledge management	Total productive maintenance (TPM)
Learning organization	Total quality management (TQM)
Mission and vision statements	Virtual teams

- Create cross-functional teams of members who can educate each other about various tools from their functional disciplines. Key decision-makers must understand and use the language for multiple tools.
- Assess the improvement methods that the functional groups in the organization currently use and understand their commonality.
- Integrate productivity tools to reach a solution that ensures that improvement occurs and which all groups can support.

Another good approach is to mimic the improvement efforts and techniques used by the competition. Some consulting companies systematically assess the evolution of these techniques and shifts in their popularity among business managers. A recent survey by Bain Consultants[9] indicated that over the past decade some management tools and techniques, such as one-to-one marketing,

TQM, and benchmarking, have become particularly popular. The three most popular tools were used by at least three-quarters of respondents: strategic planning (81 per cent), mission and vision statements (79 per cent), benchmarking (77 per cent) and customer satisfaction measurement (71 per cent). Worldwide, satisfaction was highest for cycle-time reduction, one-to-one marketing, strategic planning, and mission and vision statements. Firms worldwide are least satisfied with the application of knowledge management, strategic alliances, and activity-based management. The survey also found that most successful companies use more frequently the top ten improvement tools given in box 20.5.

Box 20.5 Tools used by most successful companies

1. Pay-for-performance
2. Cycle-time reduction
3. Strategic planning
4. Mission and vision statements
5. Customer satisfaction measurement
6. Growth strategies
7. Customer segmentation
8. TQM
9. One-to-one marketing
10. Scenario planning

It should be realized that only very few of the techniques and tools described here are needed for any particular productivity improvement project. The most important considerations in selecting tools are the purpose, organizational readiness, and management and productivity team awareness and skills as well as the competence of the consultant in using the tools.[10]

---

[1] P. Vrat, G. Sardana and B. Sahay: *Productivity management: A system approach* (London, Narosa Publications, 1998), p. 6.

[2] D. Anderson: "Aligned values + good job fit = optimum performance", in *National Productivity Review*, Autumn 1998, pp. 23–30.

[3] "Measuring people power", in *Fortune*, Oct. 2000, p. 66.

[4] T. Copeland: "Cutting costs without drawing blood", in *Harvard Business Review*, Sep.–Oct. 2000, pp. 155–164.

[5] N. D. Schwartz: "Secrets of Fortune's fastest-growing companies", in *Fortune*, Sep. 1999, pp. 32–49.

[6] C. Prahalad and V. Ramaswany: "Co-opting customer competence", in *Harvard Business Review*, Jan.–Feb. 2000, pp. 79–87.

[7] K. Tuominen: *Managing change: Practical strategies for competitive advantage* (Milwaukee, WI, ASQ Quality Press, 2000), p. 209.

[8] S. Sink: "TQM: The next frontier or just another bandwagon to jump on?", in *Quality and Productivity Management* (Blacksburg, VA), Vol. 7, No. 2, 1989, p. 18.

[9] D. Rigby: *Management tools and techniques: Annual survey of senior executives* (Boston, MA, Bain & Company, 1999).

[10] Most approaches and techniques discussed in this chapter are examined in more detail in other ILO publications. See J. Prokopenko and K. North (eds.): *Productivity and quality management: A modular programme* (Geneva and Tokyo, ILO/APO, 1996), and G. Kanawaty (ed.): *Introduction to work study* (Geneva, ILO, 4th ed., 1992).

CONSULTING IN TOTAL QUALITY MANAGEMENT 21

In this chapter we discuss not only improvement of the quality of products and services, but also the much broader issues of the quality of human activities, processes, decision-making systems and organizations, i.e. total quality management (TQM).

21.1 Understanding TQM

A successful business relies on making profitable sales to its consumers; it will retain its existing customers and attract new customers only if it knows their requirements, and delivers products and services that conform to them. This can be done by (1) ensuring that the design process results in outputs that meet customer requirements and that can be produced cost-effectively; (2) minimizing inefficiencies such as waste and rework; and (3) ensuring that all activities are directed at satisfying customers' needs.

The term "quality" has suffered over the years by being used to describe attributes such as beauty, goodness, expensiveness, freshness, and even luxury. So, a car may be described as a "quality car" when, in reality, it is an expensive or luxurious car. Management consultants should be aware of the modern concept of quality, which is defined as total *conformance to requirements*. These requirements include the total customer requirement, not just a product or service specification. To manage quality, management and employees should:

- recognize the existence of both external and internal customers;
- fully understand and agree on their customers' needs and expectations;
- deliver what was agreed, without any exception;
- be efficient as well as effective in meeting agreed customer requirements;
- continuously seek to improve performance in meeting customer expectations.

Thus, the most important objective of quality management is to fully satisfy agreed customer requirements at the lowest overall cost to the organization. But the best companies are those that aim even higher – to delight and excite their customers.

"Sell" quality to the client

To sell the idea of TQM, the consultant should explain to the client that it is not one more management fad or another tool for a quick fix. It is a solid overall approach to improving product and service quality, the way of doing things, and the quality of business and operational systems. It was not invented by anybody in particular, though the idea came from the United States. It has been gradually developed thanks to contributions from many specialists, consultants and companies, and has passed through both successes and failures.

TQM has grown gradually over a period of more than 40 years, starting from the quality control (QC) and quality circles movement in Japan. Around 1946, American experts introduced statistical quality control (SQC) to Japanese telecommunications industries. Visits by Deming to Japan between 1950 and 1952 established the foundation for future development. In the process of practising quality control, it became obvious that the use of statistical techniques was not enough to improve quality: there had to be total participation, from top management to workers. Also, efforts made in production departments alone were not enough: QC activities, therefore, were also applied in engineering, purchasing and sales departments. Moreover, it gradually became understood that QC techniques were useful not only for quality control but also for cost reduction and productivity improvement.

After Deming, Juran also visited Japan and suggested that quality control should be used not only for the production line, but also as an important management tool. Later in the 1950s, Feigenbaum proposed total quality control (TQC), which was brought to Japan in 1958 by the Japanese Productivity Center. Since the beginning of the 1960s, Japanese companies have been using TQC consistently, expanding it to engineering, marketing, general office staff functions, and business planning. TQM is synonymous with TQC as used in Japan.

In the 1960s in the United States, emphasis was put on the idea of "doing it right the first time" (zero defect), which led to the quality assurance (QA) concept. This involves identifying, analysing and writing down all procedures, and using this documentation to ensure that all processes are coordinated and that all employees know what is expected of them and are trained accordingly. However, QA has not contributed significantly to continuous improvement. As Deming correctly noted, just because nothing is wrong this does not mean that everything is right. TQM emerged when QA was added to approaches such as just-in-time, lean production, simultaneous development and continuous improvement (*kaizen*). As a result of this evolution, TQM was adopted by many companies throughout the world. When adopted fully and practised correctly,

TQM is a visionary cultural movement that encourages employees to share responsibility for delivering quality services and products.

The main characteristics of TQM

There is no common and universally accepted definition of TQM. The best way to understand it is to review its most common ideas and features. Some specialists describe TQM as a revolutionary philosophy that requires radical and pervasive change within the firm. Others argue that TQM is not just a philosophy, but a strategy. Although it is true that TQM requires a change in mentality, it seems to be more helpful for consultants to present TQM as a strategy for improving operations and results. Indeed, managers seem to be more willing to talk to consultants who offer help with strategy and tools than to those who tell them about TQM philosophy and culture.

In Japan, TQM tends to be viewed as systematic, scientific, company-wide activities that place importance on customers. It aims to apply business principles by which a company can increase sales and profits as a result of achieving customer satisfaction. The most important features of TQM, explaining the essence of this approach, are:

- A priority emphasis on improving quality and customer satisfaction, primarily through a systemic way of improving products and services; structural approaches to preventing, identifying and solving problems; and a lifelong process of product development through teamwork.
- Widespread and extensive involvement, supported by considerable staff training, in basic quality management and process analysis/improvement techniques, and ongoing communications about the organization and its mission, vision, goals and performance.
- Numerous continuous incremental process improvements predominantly attained through ideas generated and supported by extensive employee involvement and data-driven decision-making. The notion of "totality" is reflected in involving all levels of strategic planning, management control, process design and operations.
- Considerable ongoing involvement and support by top management, as well as long-term thinking; willingness to wait three to five years for cultural changes and substantially improved overall outcomes.

TQM advocates the development of true customer orientation, teamwork and inter-unit cooperation, structured problem-solving, a reliance on quality assurance standards and measurement, a system of rewards and recognition for excellence, and long-term commitment to the ongoing process of improving quality. It creates an environment that contributes to positive morale and recognizes that products and services embody the efforts, creativity, values and collective personality of their producers. The fundamental engines for TQM are empowering, energizing and enabling.

For management consultants, it is important to realize that TQM is not a new programme with a beginning and an end; rather it is a permanent process for achieving excellence, which is a moving target in itself. TQM is not good for fighting fires and other short-term fixing activities. It means continuously meeting agreed customer demands at the lowest cost by releasing the potential of all employees. This holistic approach includes internal and external customers, a sense of commercial reality through cost awareness, and making use of people's full potential.

Objectives and benefits of TQM

The objectives and benefits of TQM fall into two major categories – revenue enhancement and cost reduction. Significantly improved product performance – features, reliability, conformance, durability, serviceability or perceived quality – should result in increased demand. A reduction in total product cycle time improves availability and the ability to provide a tailored customer service. Such benefits translate into increased market share and usually increased revenues. Improved quality control reduces material costs, direct and indirect labour costs and working capital. Again, reduction in total product cycle time reduces inventory stock holding costs.

Thus, the use of TQM substantially improves financial and other key broad-based organizational outcomes. For example, financial investment in adopting TQM is primarily an investment in education and training for employees and management. TQM requires employees to be empowered to make decisions regarding process and product quality – to be their own troubleshooters. Therefore, successful TQM implementation results in:

- Meeting customers' requirements and ensuring their satisfaction; increasing market share, revenue and return on assets; reducing internal costs; providing higher employee satisfaction; understanding better the competition; and developing an effective competitive strategy.
- Achieving a top-quality performance in all business and operational areas, not just in product or service quality, through critical and continuous examination of all processes to remove non-productive activities and waste.
- Involvement of everyone in continuous improvement, not just people directly involved in the quality function; greater focus on work processes and improvements; identification and solution of problems at lower levels by people close to the work who are empowered to deal with the problems.
- Less fire-fighting and rework, and more data-based efforts to eliminate the root causes of problems; more up-front effort to clarify requirements and prevent defects and errors.
- More open and frequent communication horizontally among people who view and treat each other as customers and suppliers, better interdepartmental cooperation.
- Intolerance of, and action taken on, defects and errors that have previously been ignored.

All the above considerations and benefits could be used by consultants in promoting the TQM approach.

21.2 Cost of quality – quality is free

Mediocre managers are likely to ask (or at least think) first how costly a quality improvement or TQM initiative might be. Conversely, they start thinking about losses caused by poor quality only when it is too late. For management consultants, it is important to be well prepared to illustrate the cost of losses due to poor quality and the cost of preventing such losses. The balance is always positive, but you have to prove it.

The cost of quality[1] (COQ) includes two components: the costs of attaining quality and the costs of poor quality. The first component includes costs that add value to the business, while the second includes costs that add no value to the business. The activities that generate costs in the first category are planned, which means that these costs can be controlled. The costs of the second category are often due to deficiencies in the way work is carried out in the company, and represent a real loss to the company. Technically, COQ consists of the costs of conformance and of non-conformance. Figure 21.1 shows how these costs might evolve; note that for a small investment in prevention, failure and appraisal costs can be considerably reduced.

Figure 21.1 Typical quality cost reduction

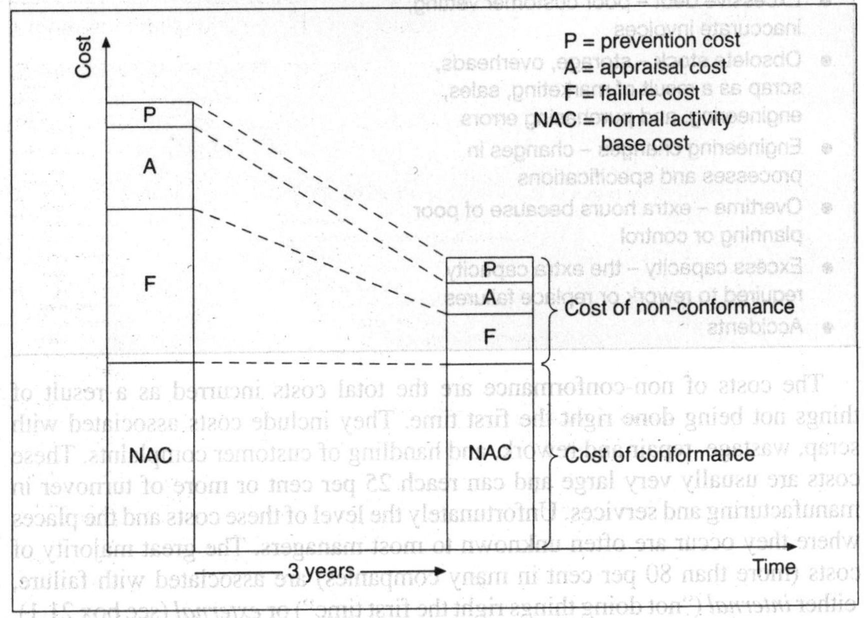

Box 21.1 Cost items of non-conformance associated with internal and external failures

Cost items of internal failures

- In warranty repairs – correcting defects after delivering products
- After-sales support – solving problems when product is in use
- Product recall – repairing, handling and investigating recalled products
- Scrap – lost material, machine time and labour
- Downgraded product – product sold at reduced prices
- Rework – labour, equipment and materials used in rework
- Lost efficiency – effective capacity diverted to corrective action
- Customer complaints – customer pacification
- Liability insurance – premium for product liability and settling claims
- Administration – meetings and paperwork associated with failures
- Excess inventory – because of errors and poor material control procedures
- Excessive debt – poor customer vetting, inaccurate invoices
- Obsolete stock – storage, overheads, scrap as a result of marketing, sales, engineering, and purchasing errors
- Engineering changes – changes in processes and specifications
- Overtime – extra hours because of poor planning or control
- Excess capacity – the extra capacity required to rework or replace failures
- Accidents

Cost items of external failures

- Lost opportunities – customers lost because product is late to market, previous non-conformance delivery, poor communication
- Customer complaints
- Bad debt
- Returned products
- Product liability
- Extended warranty product recall
- Overdue accounts receivable
- Poor morale – excessive staff turnover and reduced efficiency

The costs of non-conformance are the total costs incurred as a result of things not being done right the first time. They include costs associated with scrap, wastage, repair and rework, and handling of customer complaints. These costs are usually very large and can reach 25 per cent or more of turnover in manufacturing and services. Unfortunately the level of these costs and the places where they occur are often unknown to most managers. The great majority of costs (more than 80 per cent in many companies) are associated with failure, either *internal* ("not doing things right the first time") or *external* (see box 21.1).

The costs of conformance are the total costs incurred in ensuring that things are done right the first time. These include planned inspections and tests, and quality-related education and training. The costs are typically associated with designing procedures, defining the processes and process control, and can be classified into two groups: the cost of *prevention* and the cost of *appraisal*. Box 21.2 provides examples of the most typical costs for both groups.

Management consultants should explain to clients the major reasons for the need to have data on the cost of poor quality, other than the general one of reducing costs by improving quality. Savings in quality costs would have a significant and positive impact on the bottom line results.

It is of critical importance to advise the client to introduce a COQ system (within the TQM or separately) that will enable the financial consequences of quality problems to be quantified and areas for quality improvement and cost reduction identified. Also the COQ system should enable management to link quality improvement efforts to the bottom line by reducing costs or increasing revenue. It would also show clear links between quality improvement efforts and tangible results in terms of cost reduction, higher sales and profits, and improved productivity. Such a system would provide customers with solid evidence of what the company is doing to ensure high quality in order to differentiate it from the competition and increase customer satisfaction.

The process of setting up the COQ system could be as follows:

- The first step will be to identify quality cost items under the prevention, appraisal and failure model (see boxes 21.1 and 21.2).
- The second step is to collect and report on quality cost data. Once an organization has identified the poor-quality costs to be captured in the COQ system, it should assign them to specific activities and collect the associated data.

Box 21.2 The cost items of conformance

Prevention costs

- Planning and designing procedures and instructions on how to do the task
- Vendor assurance
- Process capability studies
- Quality training and education
- Quality improvement programmes and projects
- Collection, analysis and reporting of quality data
- Maintaining equipment
- Planning quality assurance process
- Working with suppliers

Appraisal costs

- Incoming inspection
- In-process inspection and control
- Final testing and inspection
- Production trials
- Materials consumed during inspection and testing
- Analysis and reporting of inspection results
- Field performance testing
- Calibrating test equipment
- Audit of the prevention system to ensure its continued effectiveness

- The third step is to analyse the quality costs to identify opportunities for improvements over time and highlight the magnitude of current problems. Assigning quality costs to problems that are endemic will draw attention to these costs. Various methods can be used to analyse the COQ data collected, the three most common of which are trend analysis, variance analysis and Pareto analysis.[2]
- Finally, it is necessary to institutionalize the process of quality improvement and quality cost reduction to ensure that the business objective of higher quality at lower cost continues to be met. This means that the COQ system must be implemented systematically, with the quality improvement effort being planned, coordinated and sustained.

21.3 Principles and building-blocks of TQM

While the TQM design and process will be different in different companies and circumstances, there are some common basic principles and building-blocks of the system.

Principles

Principle 1: Focus on customer satisfaction and delight.

This principle drives the entire TQM process. Every department and work unit has customers, whether internal or external. Managers and employees have to be customer-focused to meet or exceed customer expectations, creating not only customer satisfaction and loyalty, but delighting them. Emphasis should be placed on improving the practices of frontline personnel, delivery mechanisms and logistics, customer focus and processing of customer requests. Measurement of customer satisfaction through surveys, focus groups, benchmarking and market analysis provides the best evaluation of TQM results.

Principle 2: Quality improvement requires the strong commitment of top management.

The leadership must be committed to TQM and be the driving force behind it. It must create a vision that will take the organization from its current position to where it wants to be. Top management must clearly specify which actions will improve quality; they cannot delegate this responsibility. To demonstrate commitment, involvement and leadership, management must establish and communicate clear corporate values, principles and objectives relevant to quality; channel resources towards these objectives; invest time in learning about quality issues; and monitor the progress of any initiatives.

Principle 3: Quality is a strategic issue.

Quality should be a part of the company's goals and strategies and integrated in the way the organization conducts business, including product and process design, planning and budgeting. Quality must be also a part of the corporate mission. Therefore, TQM requires integrated planning systems that coordinate strategic quality planning with other strategies for products and services, logistics, distribution, customer service, manufacturing and sourcing. It also entails streamlining design processes, integrating engineering systems, forming cross-functional teams, and integrating quality design techniques into process design.

Principle 4: Employees are key to consistent quality.

Employees are natural sources of ideas for ways to improve quality and customer service. The best companies incorporate quality and customer service into performance appraisal and reward systems. They encourage full participation and involvement, employee empowerment, recognition, reward and motivation to instill a dedication to quality at every level. TQM also requires a highly skilled, knowledgeable workforce, well trained in its tools and methods. The process usually begins with awareness training for top managers, followed by training of mid-level managers and finally of non-managers. Continuing education and training are integral components of any TQM process.

Principle 5: Quality standards and measurements must be customer-driven.

Explicit quality standards for performance are essential. The company's definition of product and service quality should include the criteria that customers use when they perceive value. A customer's product preference is determined by the perceived quality/price ratio of one product in relation to other competing products. Cost of quality is also a useful measure of performance. Measurement is essential to ensure that planned improvements are implemented.

Principle 6: Many programmes and techniques can be used to improve quality.

Quality control and improvement must occur continuously in day-to-day operations. Process simplification is a low-cost, low-technology way to increase quality and effectiveness, through focused operations, smooth and continuous material and paperwork, management-by-eye, synchronization with customers and suppliers, and other techniques. More sophisticated techniques could also be used, such as statistical quality control, quality circles, suggestion systems, and quality-of-work-life projects, as well as automation, computer-based design and manufacturing, product design improvement and benchmarking.

Principle 7: All company activities have potential for improving product quality; therefore, teamwork is vital.

Quality improvement requires close cooperation between managers and employees and among departments. TQM involves preventing errors at the point where the work is performed. Under this system, every employee and department is responsible for quality and should try to provide defect-free products or services. Successful companies remove barriers between specialists and create a climate for teamwork.

Building-blocks

Components. The TQM system is composed of three major business structures or components (see figure 21.2). The first one is *strategic policy management*, which is the process that enables an organization to implement a results-oriented approach. It provides a focus on strategic and operational priorities and promotes resource alignment independent of organizational boundaries. Through strategic policy management, the organization's vision is formulated and then broken down into key components. The second component, *process management*, is instrumental in involving all employees in TQM. Every employee is linked to a superior's accountability and is a part of the process to fulfil that accountability. This is the realm of process management and a key to defect prevention and employee *involvement and empowerment* – the third component.

Policies and objectives defining the organization's aspirations. These provide a context and a focus for the quality improvement actions taken by all employees and include the business mission, operating principles and business objectives.

Processes. These include the quality delivery process, the quality improvement process, the quality management process, and cross-functional process management. The *quality delivery process* emphasizes the customer focus, ownership and self-measurement of workgroup outputs, assessment of customer satisfaction and process efficiency and identification of opportunities for improvement. The *quality improvement process* has to provide a simple

Figure 21.2 TQM business structures

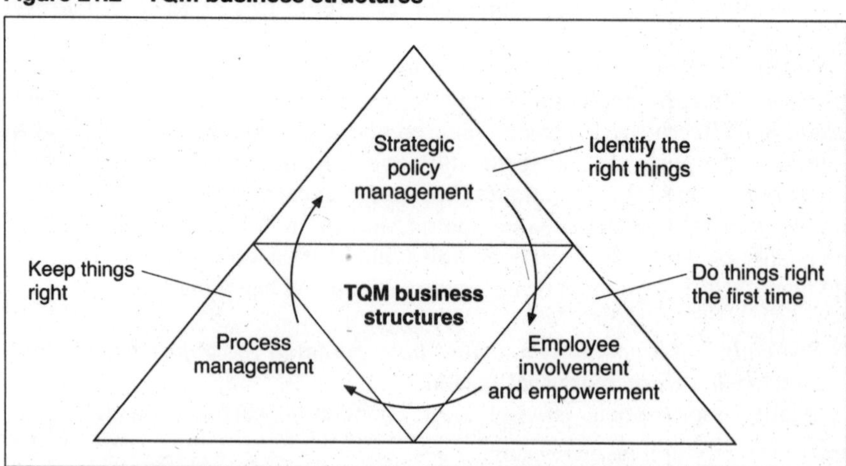

Source: R. Seemer: "Winning more than the Malcolm Baldridge National Quality Award at AT&T Transmission Systems", in *National Productivity Review* (New York), Spring 1993, p. 144.

structured process whereby every workgroup can prioritize, select and realize opportunities for improving business performance. The *quality management process* ensures that the total quality strategy is implemented throughout the organization; all workgroups identify, develop and implement improvement projects and ensure that these projects meet the criteria defined by management. *Cross-functional process management* ensures that process improvements are communicated from the originating workgroup to all other users of the process and that total processes are optimized rather than particular functions.

Organization. The TQM organization involves the business organization structure, quality support organization (quality managers in major business functions, quality facilitators, quality trainers) and quality function organization (quality office, company quality managers and assistants, and technical staff). Many companies have set up a quality council made up of 6 to 8 key managers and executives to develop the organizational strategy for TQM implementation.

Training. A total quality training strategy should involve all members of a workgroup and train them together. Training should be based on work actually performed in a format such as "concept–case study–application to own job". Managers should lead the training of their workgroup and be responsible for its effectiveness. Training should be cascaded down from the top of the company, thus enabling senior managers to provide role model leadership and example to lower levels in the application of vital quality concepts, processes and techniques.

Motivation. A system of rewards and motivation is a very important building-block of the TQM system. All employees must be motivated to commit to the concepts, apply the processes, and become involved in achieving total customer satisfaction at lower cost and reduced lead-time. To motivate employees to participate in TQM it is important to provide systematic feedback on performance and to recognize achievements.

Quality management team. The quality management team is the primary agent for TQM in an organization. It must plan, implement and advocate for change, and it must become the role model for change in the organization. Members of the team are responsible for implementing the plan in their own areas of business. The team must include the key people who lead the business units. The team should meet monthly to review progress, with problem-solving done between meetings. Each member of the team should also lead change in his or her part of the organization.

Quality assurance (QA) system. This is a management system designed to monitor activities at all stages (product design, production process, purchasing, delivery and service) to prevent quality problems and ensure that only conforming products reach the customer. The key features of an effective QA system are effective quality management and periodic audit of the system to ensure that it is effective and that it continues to meet changing requirements. Modern QA practice strives to get things right first time; it is a preventive discipline addressed to the people who produce the goods and services, virtually eliminating the need for external quality control inspection. QA really becomes effective only when the organization is totally committed to quality, which has become part of its culture.

Quality awards

Quality awards are an important part of quality improvement systems, including TQM. Management consultants can advise on the design and purpose of quality recognition by making clients aware of the world's best awards systems, such as the Deming Prize (Japan), the Malcolm Baldridge Award (the United States), and the European Quality Award. They all play a key role in the quality movement in three major markets.

The Deming Prize serves as a symbol of company-wide quality efforts, the pursuit of continuous improvement, and the extension of quality management to the suppliers of the firm. The Baldridge Award focuses on customer satisfaction, and has popularized concepts such as competitive comparisons and benchmarking. The European Quality Award incorporates a host of new ideas – impact on the community, employee satisfaction, and financial and non-financial results. European quality prizes are awarded to companies that demonstrate excellence in the management of quality as their fundamental process for continuous improvement.

21.4 Implementing TQM

One of the common reasons for failure of TQM is a lack of understanding that it is not a programme but a process. The process should integrate and optimize a number of business and operational processes, including business vision and strategy development, product and services creation and manufacturing, different support processes, suppliers' and customers' relationships, effective use and development of company capabilities and resources, and many others. This means that the approach of management consultants in advising on TQM should be evolutionary, particularly if a client organization is new to the TQM philosophy and approach. A simple and systematic road to TQM is outlined in box 21.3.

However, while this road provides a good perspective on the process of moving towards TQM, real life is more complicated. These steps cannot always be used, for example in organizations that already have some experience in quality improvement and management.

Box 21.3 The road to TQM

1. Understanding quality
2. Commitment to quality
3. Policy on quality
4. Organization for quality
5. Measurement of costs of quality
6. Planning for quality
7. Design for quality
8. System for quality
9. Capability for quality
10. Control of quality
11. Teamwork for quality
12. Training for quality
13. Implementation of TQM

Where to start

In some cases, the consultant may need to apply a more sophisticated approach. It may be useful to make a distinction between four stages:

- ***TQM I***, the simplest start, covers quality control and quality assurance. This embraces all aspects of *quality* that have to be managed throughout the organization. Quality is defined as conformity to specifications.
- ***TQM II*** applies the "total" concept to management and quality, as more attention to people and their attitudes begins to take effect. It is realized that the people-management implications of quality are all-pervasive.
- ***TQM III*** also applies the "total" approach to management, but with the spread of the paradigm towards customers, "total" takes on a broader sense when linked to quality. It no longer simply refers to ensuring quality but is expanded to mean delivering what the customer wants.
- ***TQM IV*** is a way of life in which everyone works wholeheartedly to do the best for customers, be they internal or external. *Quality means giving customers the best value possible, not just what they think they want*. Going beyond satisfaction, the total capability of the organization must be marshalled to delight customers by determining and fulfilling their latent as well as their manifest needs. This has fundamental implications for the way the entire company is organized and led. TQM IV stands for a way of managing that empowers everyone in the organization to devote their full energies and talents to being competitive in delivering value to the customer.

Recognizing the four stages of TQM evolution has practical value in:

- helping to diagnose where a company stands in the implementation process;
- ensuring that quality improvement does not end with TQM I or TQM II; it is only the beginning;
- ensuring that a company does not plunge into the full sophistication of TQM IV without putting in place the elements of TQM I and II;
- realizing that TQM IV has transcended its origin and is better understood as a shift of attention from product quality (TQM I) to delivering value to the customer.

These four stages can also be a useful tool for a consultant when deciding how an organization should make practical use of the profusion of TQM techniques. The consultant and the client can start their cooperation at any phase depending on the degree of client readiness.

Organization-wide TQM process

Before discussing the TQM process it would be useful to illustrate it through the linkages between its main process elements. Figure 21.3 shows the main elements

Figure 21.3 TQM process blocks

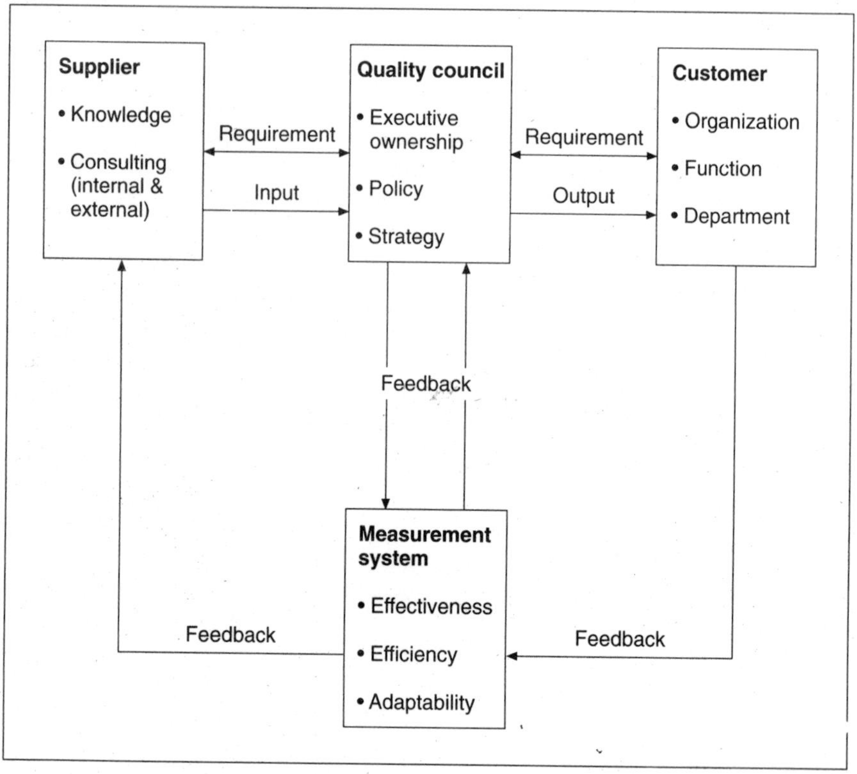

– customer, supplier, and the organization's TQM support and measurement system. The description below describes in more detail the characteristics of each phase of TQM.

Phase 1 – Diagnosis

This should start with a diagnosis of customers' perceptions of suppliers' performance, and of how much cash is lost through problems with materials and ineffective time. Having made this diagnosis, it is important to continue to ask the opinions of customers, suppliers and employees to remain in touch with the changing situation. This phase also includes the organization quality audit – the "before" situation – establishing the need for TQM, and assessing the cost of quality, market share and profitability trends. It is also important to assess the status of the quality management system and to carry out employee opinion surveys. The consultant has to define the concept of TQM and "sell" it to the senior management team.

Phase 2 – Management commitment

Obtaining the commitment of top management to TQM is essential if the process is to advance and benefit the organization. A series of workshops should be run, to give the top management an opportunity to understand the process that is about to begin, agree a vision, and decide on the first steps of the implementation plan. The agreed direction should be shared with all personnel, to ensure their participation. The sense of ownership of the TQM process really starts here.

Phase 3 – Establishing process ownership

All people in the organization need to understand which part of the process is their responsibility, and who their customers and suppliers are. Once the business and individual processes have been mapped, the departments should also be mapped. Any process without an owner should be assigned one; then people can start agreeing on process requirements. To do this, it is necessary to identify stages in the process flow where excessive communication occurs, identify bottlenecks, and eliminate processes that do not add value. The focus should be on process output requirements that are not being met.

Phase 4 – Defining the TQM introduction programme

Here it is necessary to define the content of the total quality introduction programme, to plan the training cascade and follow-up, develop the system development programme and plan the introduction of cross-functional process management. Consulting activities in these areas call on professional training and project planning skills and will involve working closely with the human resources department.

Phase 5 – Developing and delivering total quality training

Training should start with top managers, and focus on leadership, supporting and translating quality goals, identifying potential improvement opportunities, managing project teams, TQM and quality improvement principles, application theory, project team approach to quality improvement, the role of facilitators and the process for nominating them. Team members and team leaders, as well as facilitators, should be trained in project management, communication of goals, gaining commitment, and the process for submitting possible projects for quality improvement.

Phase 6 – Intensive action

Quality problems are addressed at functional and cross-functional levels and coordinated by the steering group or quality council with the aim of getting as many people as possible involved. The TQM support system should be developed, to support quality improvement projects, provide professional input, monitor the cost of quality, develop a project database, report on cost–benefit, etc. A tracking system for projects should be established. The company quality council should set quality goals, draft a statement of commitment, objectives and measures, define the quality process and the operation of quality teams, assign roles and criteria for facilitators, define the need for formal evaluation of the quality improvement process function by function, and arrange for publicity and recognition.

Phase 7 – Review and restart

As problems are solved, and more success is achieved, recognition is natural. New improvement targets are then needed to further reduce the costs associated with failure. This is also where preventing problems should become more important than solving them, if it has not already become the norm. The quality improvement process should be reviewed and evaluated regularly, and decisions taken on whether to restart, expand, disband or maintain existing efforts.

The above TQM process provides only very general guidelines and consultants should not take them as a rigid TQM process flow. It also provides a structure for a number of smaller quality improvement projects, which actually constitute the essence of the TQM process.

21.5 Principal TQM tools

Publications describing and recommending tools for quality improvement and management proliferate and a number of these tools were developed well before the emergence of TQM. We review here the most important tools without going into detail. It is useful to group these tools by two major dimensions: the first one according to the step of the quality improvement process, and the second reflecting the level of sophistication of the tool. The tools can also be broken down into analytical and management tools (see box 21.4).

The classification suggested by the Juran Institute[3] (see figure 21.4) illustrates how some quality improvement tools could best be used at different steps of the quality improvement process, providing some useful hints for consultants.

Several surveys have indicated that most Fortune 500 companies embracing TQM register less than 10 per cent quality improvement per year.[4] Among the main reasons for this poor performance is selection of relatively ineffective

Box 21.4 Tools for simple tasks in quality improvement

Analytical tools

- Pareto charts
- Cause and effect diagram (fishbone or Ishikawa diagram)
- Frequency distribution (scatter diagram)
- Stratification
- Control and line charts
- Failure and effect analysis
- Taguchi loss function
- Histogram
- Brainstorming

Management tools

- Affinity diagram
- Plan–do–check–act (PDCA)
- Interrelationship diagram
- Tree diagram
- Matrix diagram
- Matrix data analysis/star plot
- Process decision programme chart
- Arrow diagrams
- Force-field analysis
- Process capacity index
- Quality assurance system chart
- Flowcharts

Figure 21.4 Quality tools according to quality improvement steps

Tools by step	Barriers/aids	Benefit/cost	Box plot	Brainstorming	Cause-effect	Control chart	Control spread	Cost/quality	Data collection	Flow diagram	Graphs/charts	Histogram	Pareto analysis	Planning matrix	Planning network	Scatter diagram	Selection matrix	Stratification	Tree diagram
Step 1: Identify the project																			
a. Nominate projects	–	–	–	●	–	–	–	●	●	●	–	–	–	–	–	–	–	–	–
b. Evaluate projects	–	–	–	×	×	–	–	●	●	○	○	–	●	–	–	–	–	–	–
c. Select a project	–	–	–	–	–	–	–	●	●	–	–	–	●	–	–	–	●	○	–
d. Ask: Is it QI?	–	–	×	–	×	–	–	–	●	○	–	×	●	–	–	×	–	○	–
Step 2: Establish the project																			
a. Prepare mission statement	–	–	–	–	–	–	–	●	–	○	○	–	○	–	–	–	–	○	–
b. Select a team	–	–	–	–	–	–	–	–	–	○	–	–	–	–	–	–	–	–	–
c. Verify the mission	–	–	–	–	–	–	–	○	○	○	○	–	–	–	–	–	–	–	–
Step 3: Diagnose the cause																			
a. Analyse the symptoms	–	–	○	×	×	–	–	●	●	●	○	○	●	–	–	–	–	●	–
b. Confirm or modify mission	–	–	–	×	×	–	–	–	●	●	●	–	●	–	–	–	–	○	–
c. Formulate theories	–	–	–	●	●	–	–	–	–	○	–	–	–	–	–	–	–	○	–
d. Test theories	–	–	●	×	×	–	–	○	●	●	●	●	●	○	○	●	–	●	○
e. Identify root cause(s)	–	–	●	×	×	–	–	○	●	●	●	●	●	○	○	●	–	●	○
Step 4: Remedy the causes																			
a. Evaluate alternatives	–	●	–	●	○	–	–	–	●	●	–	○	○	–	–	○	●	○	–
b. Design remedy	–	–	○	×	×	–	–	–	○	●	●	○	○	●	●	○	○	○	●
c. Design controls	–	–	○	×	×	●	●	–	–	●	–	○	○	–	–	○	–	–	–
d. Design for culture	●	–	–	●	–	–	–	–	–	–	–	–	–	–	–	–	–	–	–
e. Prove effectiveness	–	–	–	–	–	●	●	–	●	●	–	○	○	–	●	○	–	–	–
f. Implement	–	–	–	–	–	–	–	–	–	●	–	–	–	●	●	–	–	–	●
Step 5: Hold the gains																			
a. Design effective quality controls	–	–	○	×	×	●	●	–	–	●	–	○	○	–	–	○	–	–	–
b. Foolproof the remedy	–	–	–	–	–	●	–	–	–	●	–	–	–	–	–	–	–	●	–
a. Audit the controls	–	–	–	–	–	●	●	–	●	–	●	–	●	–	–	–	–	–	–
Step 6: Replicate and nominate																			
a. Replicate the project results	–	–	–	–	–	●	●	–	●	●	–	○	○	●	●	○	–	–	●
b. Nominate new projects	–	–	–	–	–	–	–	–	–	●	–	–	●	–	–	–	–	–	–

Key: ● Frequently used ○ Occasionally used – Rarely used × Never used

Source: Juran Institute: *Quality improvement guide* (Wilton, CT, 1993).

Box 21.5 Powerful tools for company-wide TQM

- Six Sigma
- Design of experiments (DOE)
- Multiple environment overstress test (MEOST)
- Quality function deployment (QFD)
- Total productive maintenance (TPM)
- Benchmarking
- Poka-yoke (mistake proofing)
- Next operation as customer (NOAC)
- Team-based quality organization (TBQO)

tools. For example, some companies have used ISO 9000 over world-class quality systems (such as TQM, Deming Award, Malcolm Baldridge National Quality Award and the European Quality Awards). Other reasons are selection of poor quality measurement over meaningful metrics such as the cost of poor quality and cycle time, and using statistical process control instead of product/ process optimization.

Another common problem is ignoring powerful tools, such as "next operation as customer", which focuses on the internal customer as scorekeeper and evaluator and is particularly useful for improving white-collar quality and productivity. Using only weak tools produces confusion, frustration and disenchantment among workers. Some more powerful – though not necessarily the latest – tools are mentioned in box 21.5.[5]

Six Sigma. This quality improvement method is based on the quality philosophy developed by Motorola and adopted by many other organizations, including General Electric. It offers a set of tools that apply equally to design, production and service, and is based on setting attainable short-term goals while striving for long-range objectives. It uses customer-focused goals and measurements to drive continuous improvement at all levels in the enterprise. Six Sigma is designed to help organizations reduce costs and increase productivity and profits through statistical problem-solving tools that lead to breakthrough improvements with measurable bottom-line impact. The long-term objective is to develop and implement processes so robust that defects are measured at levels of only a few per million opportunities. Six Sigma provides a measure that applies to both product and service activities: *defects per million opportunities (DPMO)*. It focuses on defining customer satisfaction measures and using teams to continually reduce the DPMO for each measure to 3.4. This number is so small that it is perceived as "virtual perfection". The fact that it is not zero allows people to buy into Six Sigma intellectually.[6]

Design of experiments (DOE). DOE can be applied to design, product/ process features, optimization and chronic-problem-solving in manufacturing and with suppliers and customers. The objectives of DOE are to:

- separate important variables from unimportant ones and enlarge the tolerances of the latter to substantially reduce costs;
- optimize the important parameters to establish realistic specifications and tolerances;
- freeze the parameters to prevent technician and maintenance people from changing them, intentionally or unintentionally;
- control peripheral quality "leaks", such as accuracy of measuring instruments, environmental factors, and defects with process certification.

Its benefits include quality improvement of 10:1 or 100:1 with one, two, or three experiments; effective cost and cycle time reduction; heightened employee morale with higher success in chronic-problem-solving; greater customer loyalty; and enhanced overall factory effectiveness, including profits and return on investments.

Multiple environment overstress test (MEOST). Since warranties to customers are constantly escalating – from one year to three or five years or even lifetime – the design reliability must keep pace. The objectives of MEOST are to combine environmental stresses at the product design stage both to simulate actual customer use and to go beyond normal conditions to a maximum practical overstress. Only by going beyond "the horizon of design stress" can the weak links in design be detected. MEOST does for reliability what DOE does for quality: it can virtually eliminate field failures. In doing so, it removes one of the major causes of customer complaints and defections and can substantially reduce product recalls and liability lawsuits. MEOST can reduce the need for field service, which is notorious for its inefficiency and ineffectiveness, and for large inventories of spare parts.

The MEOST methodology is as follows:

1. Obtain a profile of the maximum environmental stress levels likely to be seen in the field simultaneously (thermal cycling, humidity, vibration, voltage, etc.) and design test chambers that simulate such combinations of stresses in the laboratory.
2. Test the product for a small fraction of its guaranteed lifetime in the field, gradually increasing both time and combined stress up to design stress. There should not be a single failure. If there is, institute immediate failure analysis and corrective action.
3. Continue beyond the design-stress level up to a maximum practical overstress (generally 10 to 20 per cent beyond design stress). Ignore isolated failures. If, however, there are four or more failures of the same type and the same mechanism, institute immediate failure analysis and corrective action.
4. Repeat steps 2 and 3, but for double the time. If the test is a success, the product qualifies for production and eventual shipment to the customer.
5. After six months, retrieve a few units and repeat steps 2 and 3. A plot can then be made of percentage of failures versus time and can be extrapolated to determine whether the guaranteed lifetime is met.

Quality function deployment (QFD). QFD can be used to capture the voice of the customer at the customer–marketing–design interface for new products and services. The objectives of QFD are to:

- determine the customer's requirements and expectations before conceptual design is translated into prototype design;
- let the customer rate each requirement in terms of importance and the organization's performance versus that of its best competitors;
- determine the important, difficult and new aspects of the design based on the "house of quality" matrix;
- deploy product specifications into part specifications, process specifications and production specifications, using similar "house of quality" matrices.

QFD has enabled organizations to design in half the time, with half the defects, half the costs, and half the staff of previous comparable designs. It can accurately evaluate customer complaints, effectively link customers, designers, manufacturers and suppliers, and quickly transfer knowledge to engineers. As a result, QFD greatly facilitates customer excitement and loyalty.

Total productive maintenance (TPM) is a system of maintenance covering the entire life of the equipment in every division, involving everyone from top executives to the shop-floor workers. It involves promoting productive maintenance through morale-building, management and small-group activities in an effort to maximize equipment efficiency. In simple terms, TPM uses plant capability to its fullest extent by reducing equipment stoppages, enhancing equipment capability, and improving safety, health, and environmental factors in the expectation that such improvements will contribute to better quality and higher profits.

TPM is also a tool for changing an organizational culture that tolerates maintenance costs of between 9 and 15 per cent of sales, and that adopts the mentality "if it ain't broke, don't fix it". Maintenance personnel in 50 per cent of plants in the United States still spend more than half their time fixing problems instead of preventing them. TPM aims to radically improve process and equipment quality and productivity, increase plant throughput, reduce cycle time and inventories, and establish worker maintenance teams for preventing, not correcting, equipment problems.

Benchmarking. In benchmarking, organizations learn and adapt from the best companies to improve manufacturing and services. In TQM the process of benchmarking is similar to that described in Chapter 20 among the approaches to productivity improvement.

Poka-yoke. This tool eliminates operator-controllable errors, thereby improving the performance of manufacturing line operators. The objectives of poka-yoke are to provide sensors – electrical, mechanical or visual – that warn an operator that a mistake has been made or, preferably, is about to be made and can be avoided. Its benefits include direct, fast and non-threatening feedback to the operator, virtual elimination of the need for statistical process control, higher throughput, customer satisfaction and, indirectly, better design of products that are easier to manufacture.

Next operation as customer (NOAC). NOAC helps to improve the quality, cost, and cycle time of white-collar jobs and can therefore be applied to all service organizations as well as to support services in manufacturing companies. It transforms vertical management into horizontal, breaking down departmental walls with cross-functional teams, and revolutionizing business processes. It replaces evaluation by supervisors with internal customer evaluation. The process is as follows:

1. Establish a steering committee and improvement teams, and identify the process owner.
2. Identify the process problems; quantify their impact on quality, cost, cycle time and morale.
3. Identify internal customers and their priority requirements; obtain agreement on internal suppliers' ability to meet them.
4. Determine the frequency of feedback from internal customers as scorekeepers, and the consequences of meeting or not meeting customer requirements.
5. Make a flowchart of the entire process.
6. Determine the average cycle time for each process step and the total cycle time.
7. Separate non-value-added steps from value-added ones and estimate the reduction in steps and cycle time if the non-value-added steps could be removed.
8. Eliminate or reduce the non-value-added steps using tools such as field analysis, value engineering, design of experiments, process design, and job redesign.
9. Examine the feasibility of a different approach to the business process, including elimination of processes by using value engineering and other creativity tools.
10. Conduct management reviews of internal customer scores and track progress against well-established business parameters.

21.6 ISO 9000 as a vehicle to TQM

ISO 9000 is a series of international standards for quality systems recognized and adopted worldwide.[7] In December 2000 the standards were updated and replaced by ISO 9000:2000, which any consultant advising on TQM should be aware of. About 100 countries have adopted ISO 9000 or its equivalent as national standards. Adherence to ISO 9000 has in some cases become mandatory for companies wanting to apply for public sector contracts, sell medical or telecommunications equipment, and similar.

ISO 9000 can be used for external quality assurance purposes and can be considered a foundation or "starter kit" for an organization establishing a continuous improvement process. It provides guidelines on establishing systems for managing quality products or services. ISO requires organizations to document practices that affect the quality of their products and services. Organizations are then expected to adhere to the procedures to gain and maintain certification. ISO 9000 standards focus on generating confidence in product conformance and on process management with the customer as the driving force. The December 2000 version stresses eight quality management principles on which the standards are based: customer focus, leadership, involvement of people, process approach, system approach to management, continual improvement, factual approach to decision-making, and mutually beneficial relationships with suppliers.

Among the changes made in the latest version are a reduced number of standards; explicit requirements for achieving customer satisfaction and continuous improvement; a more logical structure; an approach based on managing organizational processes; standards that are easier to use by the service sector and by small businesses; and the possibility of going beyond certification to achieve satisfaction not just of customers, but of all interested parties, such as employees, shareholders and society as a whole. However, since the new ISO standards have only recently been introduced, we will refer to earlier experience in integrating ISO with TQM, which remains relevant also under the new ISO system.

The certification process

If an organization wants to be become ISO 9000 certified, it has to be evaluated by an independent auditor, who assesses whether it is "safe to drive" its goods and services in other organizations. If the quality system is found reliable, the organization will be registered and given a certificate. The requirements an organization has to meet to be registered are what most business people would consider common-sense business practices.

There are at least *four ways* to go about documenting for ISO 9000:

- Hire a consultant to come into the organization to document the processes.
- Assign someone within the organization (possibly an internal consultant) to accomplish this task.
- Buy ISO documentation already complete (plug-and-go). Some businesses sell quality system procedures for each process required by the standard. Companies that are starting up may wish to adopt this approach, since they can change each documented procedure or work instruction to fit their environment.
- Have the process owners document their own process (this is probably the best way).

The most typical path to certification (or registration) is as follows:

1. Start by securing top management commitment and involvement, develop teams and team spirit.
2. Conduct ISO 9000 assessment. Undertake a preparation process, which entails understanding the requirements, assessing current compliance (gap analysis), establishing an internal audit system and documenting processes.
3. Get or develop a quality assurance manual. This is a good way to get all the necessary documentation together.
4. Conduct education and training. Everyone, from top to bottom, needs training in understanding the ISO 9000 vocabulary, requirements, role of the quality manual, and the benefits that will be derived from the system. They also need to be aware of the actual day-to-day process of upgrading and improving procedures.
5. Prepare document of work instructions. Processes that have been improved will need new documentation. Once completed, this manual should outline every process that affects the quality of the finished product.
6. The final step in the ISO 9000 programme is an audit by a company-chosen registrar, to verify that the system is working as described in the quality manual and that it meets ISO 9000 requirements. The audit system includes a first-party audit and a third-party audit. The first-party audit is performed internally by a trained person according to the established standards and documentation. The third-party audit involves independent reviews and registration by an external body. Second-party audits, which are performed by the customer at a supplier's location, are not necessary if the supplier is ISO 9000 registered.

Some limitations of ISO 9000

ISO 9000 certification does not guarantee success in business. The focus is often on paperwork, which may not directly benefit the firm. Registration can be expensive and has unfortunately become a vehicle to increase consulting revenue. The majority of registrations come as a result of customer demands, rather than from internal needs to improve quality. The true value of ISO 9000 registration lies in using the standard's structure to improve or re-engineer processes. The pararaph on documentation is an ideal place to start consulting in process improvement, since it contains the requirements for the structure needed to begin improvement. Up to 80 per cent of the businesses that fail to attain the standard on their first attempt flounder because of some aspects of the documentation paragraph.

Consultants should be aware of the most common limitations, problems and complaints from organizations about ISO 9000, such as:

- ISO does not focus on a company's results and performance, or the extent of market complaints, the rate of defects, or the amount of sales following the installation of a quality system. Rather it assesses what activities are managed and in what ways.
- ISO assesses not the technology content and level of the goods produced but the quality system instituted for their production. Furthermore, it does not indicate whether the product conforms to technical standards, but examines the nature of the quality systems.
- The registration process is expensive (for small companies it could cost about US$25,000 and for large ones up to $1,000,000) and requires a mountain of paperwork.
- Some experts believe that ISO 9000 has become a pursuit of a quality certificate rather than a pursuit of quality. It focuses too much on the company and not enough on its customers.
- Some people believe that ISO discourages free thinking, employee empowerment and creativity. The standards focus rather on process management, and give very little attention to the human side of quality.

There have been proposals from different quarters that there should be more industry-specific standards, and that registers should be subject to more regulations, which would streamline the process and increase the effectiveness of registration in assuring the quality of products and services. Also, there is a trend towards less emphasis on ISO 9000 registration. The newly updated ISO 9000 standards took into consideration the above concerns. However, it is not our objective to analyse ISO 9000 standards in detail; for the purpose of this chapter, we consider them as a vehicle to move towards TQM.

From ISO 9000 to TQM

The above-mentioned problems of ISO 9000 do not mean that it should be ignored as a consulting instrument in quality improvement. ISO 9000 can be regarded as a prerequisite for successful TQM. The prior existence of a successfully operating QA system can help to maintain the improvements achieved by TQM. ISO 9000 could easily be incorporated within and used for TQM, by upgrading quality assurance and incorporating the ISO elements into TQM in a "friendly" manner.[8]

Thus, after achieving ISO 9000 registration, managers and consultants should aim to move towards TQM. After registration, it should be much easier to promote significance of quality in business management, develop a long-term quality policy, upgrade goal setting through TQM, focus attention on positive results, and develop a culture and mechanisms of continuous improvement. Useful additions to the ISO processes would be to empower employees in decision-making and self-management; move faster into such TQM areas as new product development, building quality design into processes, improving cross-functional cooperation, and human resource development in the concept of and methodologies for total quality.

21.7 Pitfalls and problems of TQM

Like any management approach, TQM does not protect from failures and implementation problems. According to data provided by the Juran Institute,[9] 80 per cent of the companies that tackled TQM in the 1980s failed. One of the reasons is that the origin and dissemination patterns of TQM are quite different from those of almost every other management innovation of the past 30 years. As a result, many companies have misunderstood and misapplied it. It has not received the careful academic scrutiny that has served to give credence and authority to other innovations in organization and management.

Management may well go into a TQM process without a proper understanding of the necessary organizational conditions for its successful implementation, or of the barriers existing in the company. Some of these barriers are:

- Lack of awareness among top managers about TQM, its potential, when to use it and their own role in managing quality.
- A company culture that is not conducive; changing culture is difficult.
- Middle managers who are reluctant to change their attitudes and behaviour.
- Lack of time and funding for the training and development of teams.
- Difficulty in quantifying tangible benefits, leading to a feeling that the effort is not worth while.

However, in most cases, poor results of TQM are caused by top managers. They often have an incorrect vision disconnected from organizational values and behaviour, and their objectives are vague and short-term. They do not understand TQM and fail to set an example, believing that others have to change and perform better but not them. Very few senior managers understand statistics, and do not look at the world in terms of data and facts but rather through gut feeling. Also, employees are often not well trained in the new skills required by TQM; they may feel threatened and are not properly motivated since they do not see the potential benefits of TQM. Too much emphasis on doing things right the first time often kills creativity and initiative, and deprives employees of learning from experience.

In many organizations, CEOs and senior line managers are late in confronting issues of software quality. As a result, many companies have accumulated a lot of incompatible, customized software systems designed to handle the same applications. IT companies often face similar problems, particularly if they have grown rapidly through a series of acquisitions.[10]

Ignoring the customer is another common mistake in implementing TQM. And certainly one of the major management mistakes is selecting TQM for the wrong task. TQM cannot be used, for example, to introduce very fast and radical change. It is not a cure-all. It does not directly address such factors of success as competitive positioning, marketing, financial structure, diversification, organizational structure and corporate strategy, nor does it adequately support aggressive cost management. The TQM approach to organizational restructuring is ineffective in most situations, especially where organizations need fast and significant improvement.

21.8 Impact on management

The long road towards TQM takes companies into a new landscape where authority, decisions and innovation are much more widely shared. That is why the first priority in implementing company-wide TQM is to recognize its revolutionary character and permit it to drive system-wide changes. TQM demands that top management become agents of change, redefining management roles and structure, and accepting loss of their own power in the process. Attempting to foster quality improvement in production operations in the lower echelons of the organization while maintaining conventional top-down management inevitably creates conflict. Thus, TQM upsets traditional power structures and ways of doing business. It changes the way people work and the processes used – from design to delivery. TQM holds that change within an organization is inevitable.

Implications for management style and practices

Consultants have to make sure that management takes ownership of TQM and allows it to cascade down the entire organization. Ownership of TQM comes in the form of management making a total commitment to excellence, and it cannot be delegated since ownership rests with the top management. It is a strategic decision which signals a total organizational commitment to excellence, to be embraced by all. An organization that starts on the TQM journey should have an appropriate system in place to achieve managerial excellence.

A good summary of the features of the TQM management style has been made by Kano.[11] It includes:

- *Management by facts:* managing or following the PDCA cycle on the basis of facts rather than relying solely on experience and intuition (although they are important).
- *Process management:* paying attention to the process steps of the job, so that planned and targeted performance results are always achieved.
- *Three types of managing – maintenance, improvement and development:* maintenance is needed to hold the current level of performance steady when it is at the desirable level; improvement is the activity needed to upgrade the current level to a more desirable one; development-type management should promote innovations and creativity.
- *Standardization versus creativity and flexibility:* creating new products and services does not necessarily mean creating completely original activities from scratch. New products and services invariably include some activities and components that were in previous products and services. There is a need to be original in those areas where there is no previous experience.

Impact on organizations

Since TQM requires dramatic changes in processes and management practices, it requires a different type of organization as well. Jobs become less specialized, not only horizontally, but vertically too; employee participation in high-level management decisions increases; flows of information and communication become less vertical and more lateral and open. Because of diffusion of coordination and involvement of cross-functional teams in horizontal communication with other teams and units, managers' span of control increases and some layers of middle management and corporate staff are removed. These changes result in flatter, team-based organizational structures built around processes, not power; clusters and networks become part of corporate structure. It is difficult to implement TQM in a rigid bureaucratic organization.

Within an organization, TQM creates an environment that produces excellence and completely changes the organizational culture. Since dealing with culture may take years, TQM should normally be considered as a long-term approach that in itself facilitates the development of a culture that is consistent, committed, systematic and process-oriented. The following terms express in a telegraphic way what is involved:

- empowerment;
- team-based;
- collaborative management;
- 100 per cent involvement in quality;
- continuous learning;
- everyone trained in quality tools;
- strong human resource policies;
- respect for the individual.

If the necessary organizational culture has not been clearly identified and communicated throughout the organization, this should be the first step prior to applying the TQM approach. The simplest way is to determine what the existing culture is and then decide how the TQM approach will fit it, or to identify the gap between what exists and what is desirable from the TQM perspective. A value clarification exercise should start with a review of the elements of the TQM strategy, and then progress to an analysis of what needs to happen within the organization for that strategy to be successful. Values and guiding principles should be the central focus.

21.9 Consulting competencies for TQM

TQM is very similar in its philosophy to the continuous improvement or *kaizen* system (see Chapter 20). The approach is built on a similar set of assumptions which require a process-consulting approach rather than an expert-oriented one (see Chapter 3). The process is one of transforming the organization from within, versus top-down and often forced structural change.

Particularly important for a TQM consultant, besides a thorough knowledge of quality concepts, processes, tools and techniques, are skills in facilitation, questioning, observation and interactive behaviour analysis; patience; communication skills; and the ability to contribute ideas and opinions only when this is required for continuing the TQM process.

---

[1] S. Krishnan, A. Agus and N. Husain: "Cost of quality: The hidden costs", in *Total Quality Management* (Abingdon), July 2000.

[2] R. Yogendram: "Cost of quality. Why is it critical?", in *Productivity Digest*, Feb. 1999, pp. 37–40.

[3] Juran Institute: *Quality improvement guide* (Wilton, CT, 1993).

[4] K. Bhote: "A powerful new tool kit for 21st century", in *National Productivity Review*, Autumn 1997, pp. 29–38.

[5] Ibid.

[6] A. Gabor: "He made America think about quality", in *Fortune*, 30 Oct. 2000, pp. 119–120.

[7] See www.iso.org., visited on 2 Apr. 2002.

[8] Y. Iizuka: "Integrating ISO 9000 with Japan's TQM", in *APO Productivity Journal*, Winter 1996, pp. 3–21.

[9] H. Blackiston: "A barometer of trends in quality management", in *National Productivity Review*, Winter 1996, p. 17.

[10] C. Prahalad and M. Krishnan: "The new meaning of quality in the information age", in *Harvard Business Review*, Sep.–Oct. 1999, pp. 109–117.

[11] N. Kano (ed.): *Guide to TQM in service industries* (Tokyo, APO, 1996).

CONSULTING IN COMPANY TRANSFORMATION 22

The growing competition linked to globalization, the introduction of new technology, economic liberalization and deregulation, and changing societal expectations and values create an environment of permanent turbulence. Faced with such turbulence, few companies have escaped the need to reorganize, downsize, outsource, acquire or divest. Over the past twenty years, thousands of companies have tried to remake themselves into better competitors, including large organizations such as Ford, General Motors, BMW, British Airways and Cisco.

Whether it is a one-time action to increase shareholder value or an ongoing process aimed at improving general competitiveness, restructuring is going to stay high on the agenda of top executives, social organizations, governments and certainly management consultants. As a result of environmental pressures and changes, a new paradigm of the company has been emerging. The modern company must be flexible, highly customer-oriented, with temporary structures and fewer levels of management. Its managers should have a broader span of control with lower levels having more power and bigger roles. Project teams and self-managing teams are becoming more frequent features of the flexible and successful organization. The company owns and controls its core – the core competencies – while breaking down existing boundaries by outsourcing non-core functions to best-in-class and long-term business partners.

Such a business model requires a corresponding executive mind-set, organizational strategy, corporate culture, and operations achieving the following strategic shifts:

- from vertical integration to value acquisition;
- from seeing organizational size as an advantage to seeing flexibility as an advantage;
- from focus on cost control to focus on generating shareholder value;
- from focus on control of resources to focus on core competencies;
- from managing *how* to managing *what*.

The firm is thus viewed as a dynamic institution, which is continuously reconfiguring its structures, resources and capabilities by innovation, learning and practical experience. As a result, there is a strong movement from functional management to process management, from a focus on power to its decentralization, and from managing physical assets to managing knowledge. All these and other fundamental shifts require a proper organizational framework to facilitate and support them.

22.1 What is organizational transformation?

Company transformation takes many forms and has many banners – turnarounds, revitalization, mergers and acquisitions, outsourcing, etc. – and covers a wide variety of changes. It could be the deliberate modification of formal relationships among organizational components, or redesign of work processes, or delayering and elimination of structural elements through outsourcing, spinning off, selling off, and divesting businesses. Transformation could also include downsizing or re-engineering, but in itself it is a much broader and more inclusive concept. It can include the modification of financial structures (share repurchases, reducing debt/equity ratios, and issuing new shares), market structures (changing product/service portfolio), technological structures (automation), production structures, and organizational structure, and also delocalization (transferring production units to lower-cost locations). It could cover changing the portfolio of existing businesses (selling off unproductive divisions or activities and entering new businesses through acquisition or internal growth, rationalization or spin-offs). Restructuring even goes beyond the confines of the organization itself to embrace other elements of the value chain; it can dramatically affect the organizations of suppliers, customers and other business partners and corporate stakeholders. But in almost every case the basic goal remains the same: fundamentally to transform the ways of conducting business in order to cope with a new, more challenging and more complex environment.

Transformation may be viewed as a three-stage process following a sequence of restructuring, revitalization, and renewal.[1] *Restructuring*, also called the awakening stage, is especially relevant to underperforming firms. The transformation process in these firms often starts with a major downsizing, pruning the product or service portfolio, and overhauling structures and management processes, which help to redefine the firm's vision and redesign its strategic and core competencies. At the end of this stage, the firm reaches a minimum threshold of profitability that allows it to survive, but this is not enough to restore competitiveness. The focus in the second stage, *revitalization*, is on improving the firm's growth and profitability. The effort may include identifying new business opportunities and competencies, as well as strategic alliances to access these opportunities and competencies with the help of others. The third and final stage is *renewal*, when the firm seeks to be continuously engaged in identifying and eliminating waste, building and sharing new capabilities, and rejuvenating its strategies – thus embodying aspects of both restructuring and revitalization at the same time.

Experience with organizational transformation during the past 15 years has taught us some important lessons. First of all, transformation is not just about reducing costs, improving profitability, or re-engineering. It is also about people and their concerns; it is reinventing strategies and management processes and must involve the whole organization as a social organism. It must be driven by new ideas, new concepts and a shared perception of opportunities.

22.2 Preparing for transformation

One of the first tasks of a consultant in assisting with organizational transformation is to identify just a few important reasons why the company needs to restructure and which justify an effort that is not going to be small, and in which managers and employees alike will face many difficult decisions. The general principles and methods of change management, as discussed in Chapter 4, apply; what is particular to overall company transformation is the combined impact and requirements reflecting the importance, speed, depth, complexity, risks and future consequences of the change process.

In these situations, management consultants normally help clients to deal simultaneously with two major issues: (1) preparing the organization for transformation; and (2) identifying and overcoming the resistance to change.

Preparatory steps

The consultant should start by assessing if the organization is generally resistant or sensitive to change. *Change-resistant* organizations constantly deny the need for change despite the influence of fast-moving external factors. While inertia takes the company in the direction that has served it well in the past, its environment moves in a different direction (figure 22.1). Over time the gap between outside reality and company position widens, and increasing amounts of energy are required to resist change. At some point, the pressure for change becomes too big and a catastrophic event occurs – perhaps sales fall off dramatically or markets suddenly dry up. Whatever the event, there are two possible outcomes: the organization either dies or some radical upheavals occur as the organization takes drastic steps to realign itself with reality. *Change-sensitive* companies make continuous and incremental changes in response to the changing environment. They are keenly aware of their customers' needs and competitors' strengths and extremely receptive to new ideas. Change-sensitive organizations are also able to influence and monitor the environment rather than being controlled by it. As a result, they are poised to take new opportunities.

To cope with the transformation, it may be necessary to create certain capabilities. For example, management may be advised:[2]

Figure 22.1 The change-resistant organization

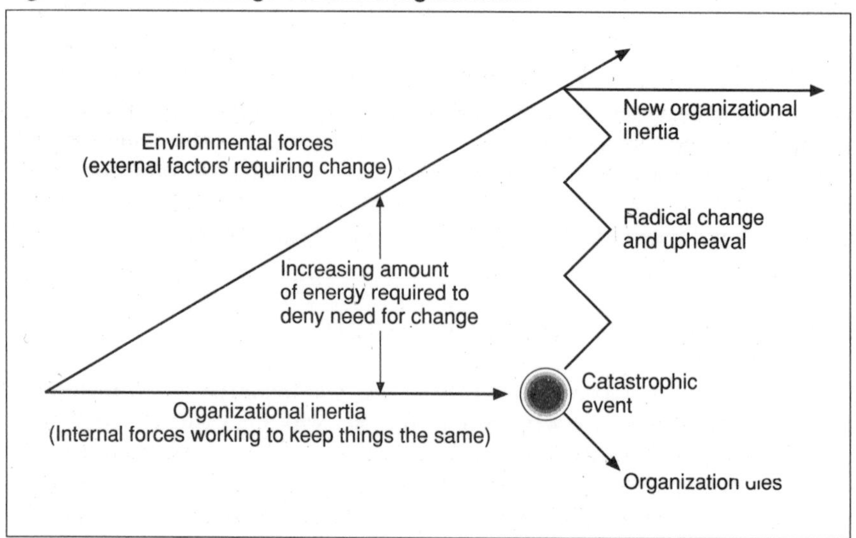

Source: M. Hennecke: "Toward the change-sensitive organization", in *Training*, May 1991, pp. 54–59.

- to create new organizational structures in which new processes can be developed;
- to establish an independent organization to develop the new processes and values required to solve the new problem;
- to acquire a different organization whose processes and values closely match the requirements of the new tasks.

In assessing organizational readiness for transformation some key questions should be answered: is this change a burden or a challenge? Is the change clear, worth while and real? Will the benefit of the change begin to appear quickly? Is the change limited to one function or a few closely related functions? What will be the impact on power and status relationships? Will the change fit the existing organizational culture? Is the change certain to happen?

To answer these questions and identify transformational needs it is necessary to do an *industry analysis* (characteristics, trends, key factors for success, opportunities and threats); a *competitor analysis* (actual and potential competitors, their strengths and weaknesses, capabilities and limitations, strategies and future moves); a *societal analysis* (important changes in government policy, consumer attitudes, employee expectations); and a *company analysis* (strengths and weaknesses; share performance; cost, quality, delivery time, reliability and service in present and potential markets; trends in market share and in profitability by product, by country, by distribution channel and by customer category).

Overcoming resistance

To cope with resistance to change, the consultant and management have to start by creating discomfort and dissatisfaction with the existing situation. Changing the mind-set of the key players in the organization generally requires a strong jolt of some kind. Pressures from inside and outside the organization can effectively promote awareness of the need for change. Creating a shared mind-set characterized by collective ambition, commitment, motivation, a sense of urgency that some form of action is needed, and an external focus is critical to start the transformation.

The next move is to create hope for something better in the form of a new vision and mission, in order to break the vicious circle of despair. It is the leaders, with help from consultants if necessary, who should identify the challenges faced by the organization, point out the source of the distress, and clearly present the negative consequences of a failure to act. Benchmarking with other organizations is a good way to illustrate performance gaps and their consequences. As a buffer against excessive stress, leaders must present a viable alternative to the existing situation. At this point drawing up an action plan is crucial so that staff can perceive the change programme as something realistic.

To create awareness and support for transformational efforts and to implant a strong message that "something is deadly wrong in this company", Gary Hamel proposes that an "insurrection" should be started in the following way.[3]

1. *Establish a point of view.* It should be powerful, credible, coherent, compelling, and based on data, speak to people's emotions and have a clear link to the bottom line.
2. *Write a manifesto.* You need it to pass on your idea to others. It must capture people's imaginations, and provide a vision and hope.
3. *Create a coalition.* Build a group of colleagues who share your vision and passion. It is easy to dismiss corporate rebels when they are fragmented and isolated.
4. *Pick your target.* Identify and target a potential champion – someone who can yank the levers of power and get the support of senior management.
5. *Coopt and neutralize.* You need to disarm and coopt opponents, not demean and humiliate them.
6. *Find a translator.* You need someone who can build a bridge between you and the people with the power.
7. *Win small, win early, and win often.* None of your transformational efforts is worth anything if you cannot demonstrate that your ideas actually work.

22.3 Strategies and processes of transformation

Organizational transformation can be slow, incremental, evolutionary and people-oriented, or rapid, revolutionary, dramatic and company-wide, with economic performance as the first priority. Different approaches require different transformation strategies and consulting approaches. The consultants' role is to facilitate the process and to be a resource.

Although consultants come with certain values and ideas about what makes an effective human organization, they should not recommend a corporate-wide programme through which top management should implement their ideas. They should rely rather on stimulating and supporting the process of discovery and learning. If beliefs and values need to change, if change emerges from employee participation in solving problems, and if the objective of change is to create a learning organization, then large consulting firms delivering elegant packaged solutions will not always succeed. Process consultants, who do not come with prefabricated solutions, can lead managers and other employees through a process of gradual analysis, redesign and change.

Some useful principles

Today there is renewed interest in organizations that are organic, flexible, agile, or "reconfigurable". Their structure consists of a stable part and a variable part. The stable part consists of "homes" for specialists in functions, which also host generalists on rotating assignments. The variable part of the structure consists of mechanisms and networks integrated across the functions, for example, cross-functional teams used in most companies today. Such organizations can be easily adjusted to incremental changes.

The larger and the more radical the transformation projects, the greater the likelihood that the client organization lacks the requisite implementation skills, managerial consensus, and motivation to change. A better alternative to these high-risk mammoth consulting undertakings is a model based on a series of rapid-cycle sharply focused projects. Each one will yield some measurable return while also expanding the client organization's capacity to learn and carry on subsequent change.

To implement such focused and modest projects, dozens of interrelated changes need to be realized in an integrated and coordinated way. While the consulting team might help to make some of the technical changes, they will be able to assist with only a small number. The rest will have to be identified and carried out by the organization itself. In this way, the company starts to learn. The first and most common way is to start the change with rationalization, by instilling more discipline and support, then moving to revitalization by spreading the action and building trust, and finally moving on to regeneration. The second way is for the company to start with more integration and then to move to regeneration. The third – and the most difficult – way is for a company to go straight to regeneration (as General Motors did) trying to balance discipline, support, stretch and trust.

When dealing with large-scale, radical changes in a turbulent environment the consultant may help to put the following key elements in place:

- *Pattern-breaking*, to free the system from structures, processes, or functions that are no longer effective or useful; to eliminate dysfunctional patterns of behaviour to allow new learning and new options.

- *Experimenting*, to generate new patterns better suited to the present environment, by providing direction, generating commitment, strengthening bonding and cultivating support.
- *"Visioning"*, to choose a new perspective around which the system can be reorganized, to generate alignments, cultivate mutual trust and encourage commitment.
- *Bonding and attunement*, to harmonize members to move the system towards new ways of doing, thinking and learning. This could yield more options and choice, provide flexibility and encourage openness.

The following conditions are the most important ones for transformation; if they are not already present, they should be created:

- **Shared vision and strategy for transformation.** These should define business requirements, outline expected results, link technology clearly to the achievement of business objectives, and provide a plan for achieving results.
- **A breakdown team to manage the transformation process.** Appoint a group of people that has the mandate, skills and vision to manage the changes, as well as the resources to drive the restructuring.
- **Empowerment of line managers and staff** to make change a bottom-up process that drives decision-making down to the lowest managerial level.
- **Partnerships between technical and business specialists.** Mechanisms must be in place to optimize overall results rather than those of individual procedures or departments.
- **Innovative procedures, institutionalization and reinforcement of results.** Employees must acquire new skills, job knowledge and procedures as well as develop new mental models.

The greatest opportunities for improvement are often found in the "white spaces" between functions. It is important to identify and concentrate on critical processes, which have a strong impact on total organizational performance. All non-value-adding activities such as the movement of materials and other physical assets should be kept to a minimum or eliminated because they add cost without adding value. *Process management*, as a major concern in improving company operations, ignores functional power, hierarchy and bureaucracy. It concentrates on horizontal integration to reduce costs and improve quality, service and speed, and focuses on the whole process, working backwards from output or sales to decide which actions and functions are required. The basic objective of process management is to take a holistic view of the process and align the whole value chain to provide a high level of customer satisfaction, achieve the best possible performance, and increase competitiveness.

Before making judgements about the transformational strategy, both consultants and managers need to understand clearly where the company is in its business life-cycle and its development sequence – in *evolution* or

Figure 22.2 Linkage between transformation types and organizational conditions

	Component	System
Radical	nonlinear innovation	business concept innovation
Incremental	continuous improvement	business process improvement

Source: J.G. Hamel: *Leading the revolution* (Boston, MA, HBS Press, 2000), p. 18.

revolution. In *Leading the revolution*, Gary Hamel[4] illustrates relationships between different types of changes starting with continuous improvement (the evolutionary approach) and going to business concept innovation (the most radical, revolutionary approach) when the whole system is to be fundamentally changed (figure 22.2).

The most difficult problems arise when large mature organizations are to be transformed. Despite the fact that many of these attempts fail, there are companies that provide good examples of transformational efforts. The experience of these companies provides some lessons that are of interest to consultants intervening in similar organizations. Here are a few hints on how mature organizations approach successful transformation:

- *They renew by instilling a customer perspective and focusing on customer demands.* Competitive advantage comes from understanding and meeting customer needs in unique ways. Hewlett Packard did this by incorporating internal and external customer satisfaction into its performance appraisal system.
- *They renew by increasing their capacity for change.* To experience renewal, business cycle lengths must be reduced and capacity for change increased.
- *They renew by altering both the hardware* (strategies, structures, and systems) *and the software* (employee behaviour and mind-set). Transformation comes only when new hardware is supported by appropriate software.
- *They renew by creating empowered employees* who act as leaders at all levels of the organization. They become leaders by having influence and control over the factors that affect their work performance and possessing the necessary competencies.

Figure 22.3 Relationships between business performance and types of transformation

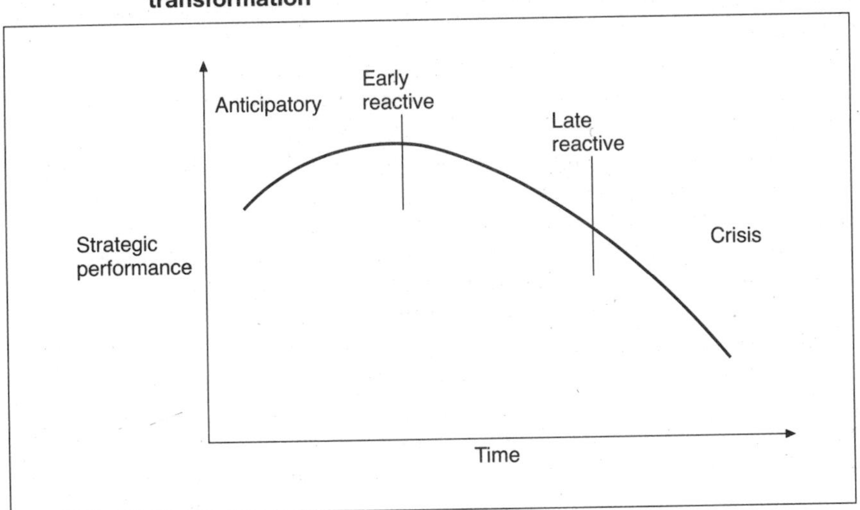

Source: J.P. Killing: "Managing change: The urgency factor", in *Perspectives for Managers* (Lausanne, IMD), Vol. 29, No. 1, Feb. 1997.

Strategies

There are many different strategies for planning and implementing transformational efforts and it is impossible to recommend one single approach. We discuss here a number of strategic approaches, mostly successful, to cover the most typical cases and transformational conditions.

One of the first strategic components for any transformation is to *create a sense of urgency*. In your situation, how urgently is restructuring required? Are you on the brink of crisis? Already in crisis? Try to place your company where you think it belongs on the "crisis curve" (figure 22.3). Initially, at the left side of the diagram, the business is performing well, but over time performance gradually flattens out and then begins to decline at an increasing rate until the business ends up in crisis.

We can consider different possible transformational strategies depending on where your business is on the crisis curve. An *anticipatory change situation* is one in which the current business performance is good, and there is a common perception that it is likely to remain that way for some time. The consultant however sees something that indicates that performance may decline in the future if preventive action is not taken. A *reactive change situation* is attained when no action has been taken in an anticipatory situation. In this case, margins may be gradually shrinking, growth rates or market share declining, or perhaps key customers are becoming dissatisfied. It is not yet a crisis situation. Some managers would think that significant change is required, but not all. A *crisis change situation* indicates that managers failed to start managing change in the anticipatory and reactive situations, and the company has slid down the curve into crisis. At this point, the need for transformation will be apparent to both management and consultants, and creating urgency for change will not be a problem.

The real challenge in creating urgency comes when the company is in a *reactive situation*. Here, you have to start on a broad front, and you do not have much time to pursue a debate. You can disrupt routine, indicating that a new one has to be started. Killing a sacred cow, such as cutting research funds for a long-standing project that is not delivering, or selling a business that does not fit with future plans, could pave the way for other, less dramatic changes. Some specialists in transformation propose also firing a key resistor or transferring him or her to a less important post. You have to identify the people who will have the greatest impact on the success of the transformational process.[5]

Some consultants prefer to develop conditions and organizational sensitivity to changes rather than focusing on strategies. Gary Hamel suggests provoking the emergence of revolutionary management rules similar to those that helped Charles Schwab, GE Capital, and Royal Dutch Shell to become revolutionaries capable of reinventing themselves again and again.[6] Some of them are outlined below.

Set unreasonable expectations. When you have objectives that are outlandish, it forces you to think very differently about your opportunities. A person with a 20 per cent target is going to do different things from someone with a 10 per cent target. Only non-linear innovation will drive long-term wealth creation.

Stretch your business definition. Get a few people together to start redefining your company in terms of what it knows and what it owns rather than what it does. Virgin spans industries as diverse as air travel, package holidays, music retailing, banking, and radio broadcasting. It will enter a business if it believes it can (a) challenge existing rules, (b) give customers a better deal, and (c) be more entertaining and competitive.

Create a cause, not a business. Schwab migrated its business to the Web, knowing that the move would force it to slash prices by 60 per cent. In most companies there would be months, perhaps years, of savage debate before such a change, as happened in Merrill Lynch.

Listen to new voices. More often then not, companies are reinvented by outsiders free of the prejudices of veterans. Yet, in most companies strategy is the preserve of the old guard, the same people talking to the same people year after year. GE Capital put together a young team – all under 30 – and asked them to tell where the opportunities were. Without new voices the chance for revolution is nil.

Design an open market for ideas, capital and talent. What makes Silicon Valley a hothouse of business innovation is the existence of three tightly interconnected markets: a market for ideas, a market for capital, and a market for talent. Radical ideas are the only way to create wealth.

Lower the risks of experimentation. Virgin has an exit plan for any business it enters, in order to minimize potential damage. Most start-ups and new ventures fail and management has to accept that. A prudent investor prefers to invest in a portfolio than in any single project.

Act like a cell – divide and divide. Division and differentiation are the essence of growth. When companies stop dividing and differentiating innovation dies and growth slows. When Virgin Records showed the first signs of lethargy, the owner Richard Branson took the deputy managing director, deputy sales director, and deputy marketing director and made them the nucleus of a new company.

Pay your innovators well. A lot of companies talk about intrapreneurship and ask people to take risks, but if those people succeed they get nothing more than a small bonus, and if they fail they get fired. You cannot reward entrepreneurs as you reward stewards. You need spectacular rewards for people who make a non-linear change in the business. Microsoft has created a compensation scheme that gives the start-up team an outsized stake in the new venture's success. It is not unusual for a young team member to end up with US$1 million in stock for helping to build a new business.

Summary view of the transformation process

The overall transformation process can be structured in stages as shown in box 22.1, based on the experience of many transformation projects. This box can be used as a checklist in designing tailor-made transformation processes for specific situations.

Box 22.1 Eight stages for transforming an organization

1. Establish a sense of urgency

- Examine markets and competitive realities.
- Identify and discuss crises, potential crises, and major opportunities.
- Mobilize commitment through joint diagnosis of problems and opportunities.
- Conduct a company-wide survey to assess organizational culture.
- Create a sense of urgency and reinforce the need for deep change.

2. Form a powerful guiding coalition

- Put together a group with enough power to lead the transformation.
- Get the group to work together like a team.

3. Develop a vision and strategy

- Assess the current situation and the desired future.
- Develop a shared vision, values and goals to direct the transformation effort.
- Develop strategies for achieving that vision.

- Identify core competencies and capabilities that differentiate the company from its competitors.
- Foster consensus for the new vision and the competence to implement it.

4. **Communicate the vision for transformation**
   - Use every vehicle possible to communicate the new vision and strategies.
   - Demonstrate effective behaviour and role model of guiding coalition itself.
   - Show clearly the objectives, their benefits and how they can be achieved.

5. **Empower broad-based actions**
   - Remove obstacles and other factors adverse to transformation.
   - Change systems, structures and work procedures that undermine the vision.
   - Encourage risk taking and non-traditional ideas, activities and actions.
   - Confront ineffective methods, devote a lot of attention to the actual work.
   - Give people the opportunity to decide how to change their behaviour.
   - Provide necessary assistance, coaching, feedback and training.

6. **Generate short-term wins**
   - Break the broad concept into bite-size projects that provide a basis for experiment and learning.
   - Fight organizational inertia, initiate actions that jolt the entire organization, send a signal that "business as usual" is over.
   - Plan and implement visible performance improvements or "wins".
   - Recognize and reward people who made wins possible.

7. **Consolidate gains and produce more change**
   - Use increased credibility to change systems, structures and policies that do not fit the transformation vision.
   - Spread revitalization to all units without pushing it too much from the top.
   - Hire, promote and train people who can implement the vision.
   - Develop new skills for implementing the new strategy, re-skill people, hire outside talent only when it is really necessary.
   - Reinvigorate the process with new projects, themes and change agents.
   - Create better performance through customer- and productivity-oriented behaviour, more and better leadership, and more effective management.

8. **Institutionalize new approaches and behaviour**
   - Articulate the connections between new behaviour and company success.
   - Provide means to ensure leadership development and succession.
   - Move to an environment of continuous improvement.
   - Institutionalize revitalization through formal policies, systems and structures.
   - Monitor and adjust strategies in response to new problems and opportunities.

Methods of transformation

Many different methods are used by companies and consultants to develop and implement transformation strategies. The most widely used methods are reviewed below. These methods are not "pure" and mutually exclusive patterns – managers and consultants often combine or switch methods or use hybrid methods reflecting their own experience and their particular approaches to transformation.

22.4 Company turnarounds

A management consultant may be asked to assist with a turnaround of a company that is in trouble. A turnaround strategy often involves total restructuring and reorganization, or constitutes a prelude to major restructuring, and usually affects all the functions and activities of a company. This is a particularly difficult strategic assignment. The consultant will probably be brought in at a very late stage, when bankruptcy may be imminent. He or she may be regarded as a potential saviour or the last hope. The management of the company is often paralysed and in panic, under extreme pressure from creditors, banks, trade unions, tax collectors and others.

Before accepting such an assignment, you should consider whether your experience is adequate for a task that carries so much risk and responsibility, and what the cost of failure will be. If you accept the assignment, you should make sure that your and the management's roles are clearly defined and understood, since there will be no time for lengthy discussions and negotiations, and some measures will need to be approved and executed immediately. If you feel that senior management itself is the cause of the trouble, or one of the major causes, you should make it clear that personnel changes may be necessary before committing yourself to the assignment.

A quick preliminary diagnosis will help to evaluate the overall situation. In particular, it is necessary to assess whether the company can still be rescued, and if so, how much this is likely to cost and whether the task is beyond the management's capabilities. If it is too late, or the cost of a turnaround operation would be prohibitive, there may be no other solution than to sell or liquidate the company.

Following the preliminary assessment, it is not advisable, and often not possible, to carry out lengthy in-depth diagnostic studies. There is a crisis situation; some creditors have to be paid today, others tomorrow, and the most competent staff may be thinking of leaving the sinking ship. Emergency measures have to be taken: a dialogue with the creditors is essential, and resources have to be found to make the payments that cannot be postponed.

The emergency measures will involve decisions that produce immediate savings, or that stop further deterioration in the company's financial condition (e.g. a recruitment freeze, restrictions on foreign travel, termination of temporary help, increased emphasis on timekeeping and work discipline, cuts in entertainment costs). Some of these measures will not produce major savings, but will rather help to create a new atmosphere in which people start to realize how serious the situation is. At this point the consultant should make sure that employees are invited to contribute to the turnaround in every possible way. This may involve establishing various means of making such participation possible, without, however, divulging information that has to be kept confidential.

Stock should be taken as quickly as possible of existing resources and of financial and other commitments, since the company will have to avoid further crises, pay interest and settle certain liabilities, while progressing with the turnaround. Step by step, the consultant will be able to complete the picture of the client company's condition. It is essential to identify the real causes of trouble. They may be external (depression in the whole sector, prices of raw materials too high, important markets lost for political reasons) or internal (incompetent management, conflict between management and trade unions). In many cases, external and internal causes are combined (external factors cause serious trouble because management did not spot them early enough, or management gradually became paralysed under the influence of adverse external conditions). Financial and other controls have to be tightened in all departments.

The external partners, in particular the creditors, must be shown that a serious turnaround exercise has started and is producing results. In some countries (e.g. in the United States under Chapter 11 of the Bankruptcy Code), a company can obtain temporary protection from creditors' claims while it is restructuring its finances and reorganizing operations in order to become solvent again.

Following the inevitable emergency measures, the turnaround programme should move to the strategic measures needed to restore financial health and viability in the long term. Time continues to be short, and every change has to be carefully programmed and the timetable controlled. The responsibilities of all managers and departments must be clearly defined, and their contribution to the total programme specified to permit evaluation and rewards corresponding to real results.

It sometimes happens that, when helping with a turnaround, the management consultant, with the client's formal or tacit agreement, steps out of his or her strictly advisory position to tell the client what to do, or even to give direct instructions to the client's employees. There is no general rule governing how far such behaviour can go, in particular if it helps avoid a crisis. There have also been cases of consultants recruited to assist in a major turnaround who have accepted managerial positions in the client company in order to bring the whole programme to a successful completion.

Turnaround or rescue consulting is one of the fastest-growing specialities within the broader field of management and business consulting. Many turnaround consultants handle only one or two stages of turnaround, mostly to stabilize the business. Once stabilized, the business is turned over to other consultants, who continue rehabilitation by tackling the debts and taking measures to make the company profitable again.

There is no single formula for success in rescue consulting but there are some common features. First, the consultant should look for the aspects of the business with real potential. Poorly performing companies are often a hotchpotch of ill-assorted businesses, the result of previous acquisitions, and what is needed is more clarity of focus and a return to core strengths. This suggests that flagging companies need an outsider's perspective, be it from non-executive directors, consultants, or company "doctors". Experienced managers who will actually run the business are of course still necessary and consultants should be prepared to recommend them. Box 22.2 suggests a sequence of useful actions in implementing a turnaround plan.

Box 22.2 Implementing a turnaround plan

1. **Visualize where your company should be: set turnaround objectives:**
   - Double sales?
   - Finance growth only from profits?
   - Increase plant utilization from 70 to 90 per cent?
   - Reduce payroll from 12 to 9 per cent of sales?
   - Go from break-even this year to 6 per cent profit next year and 8 per cent in three years?
2. **Plan the right strategies, answering these or similar questions:**
   - Terminate losing activities?
   - Cut costly programmes?
   - Undertake new marketing?
   - Develop new procedures?
   - Merge with another company?
   - Grow by acquiring new companies?
   - Shrink operations?
3. **Implement change, keeping in mind four points:**
   - What will be done?
   - Who will do it?
   - How will it be accomplished?
   - When will it be completed?
4. **Focus first on what most affects cash flow, then move on:**
   - Identify the turnaround task you must implement.
   - Determine the relative importance of the task.
   - Develop workable action plans for each task.
   - Commit everyone to completion dates on specific assignments.
5. **Monitor the plan:**
   - Set realistic benchmarks.
   - Track your recovery against crude but predetermined goals.
   - Make adjustments when your plan goes astray.

22.5 Downsizing

Downsizing is a reduction of the workforce, often as a result of financial losses, cash flow difficulties, loss of contracts, technological changes, or action taken by competition. This reduction can be achieved by attrition, early retirement, and transfers within the company, as well as by layoffs. Indeed, downsizing – if it is managed in a socially responsible way – can be and often is a good opportunity to reduce costs, improve competitiveness and reinvigorate an organization. Radical downsizing has been a popular strategy and financial markets have usually applauded these drastic efforts.

However, downsizing can also strip an organization of valuable human assets and lead to deteriorating productivity, morale and loyalty. Downsizing can be planned and systematic, but often layoffs are done as a spectacular "quick fix" to send highly visible signals to investors. The actual impact of such layoffs on profitability may then be negligible in comparison to their magnitude. In many cases, downsizing fails to increase long-term shareholder value. The hidden economic and social costs of downsizing include the loss of key talent and valuable corporate memory, higher turnover and absenteeism, loss of customers due to a decline in quality and service, decline in entrepreneurship, innovation and risk-taking, and even an erosion of external reputation and brand image, and increased legal and administrative costs. High social costs usually stem from the effects of job insecurity, increased resistance to change, decreased motivation, stress, and loss of trust and loyalty.

Nevertheless, in certain cases downsizing is difficult to avoid. It can be both economically effective and socially responsible if it is conceived and executed as a part of wider transformation efforts. A good strategy may be continuous downsizing, with no major layoffs and a lean management philosophy and culture. The best downsizing practices normally emphasize:

- corporate social responsibility reflected in the corporate ethics and code of conduct;
- business vision, mission, strategy and goals, and aligning actions around them;
- leading transformation, not just downsizing, based on continuous improvement;
- focusing on people, communication, partnership and participation.

It is important for a management consultant to be well prepared to help with *recovery measures* after downsizing. These may involve defining a new shared vision and focusing on the future rather than the past, providing support to survivors as well as those laid off, facilitating changes in organization, job design, work-shifts and responsibilities, mapping out and updating in-house skills and translating them into company competencies, revitalizing sales and improving customer relationship management.

Recently there has been a shift from downsizing to the concept of *rightsizing*, which begins with clarification of business strategy and core activities, and definition of the optimum organizational structure and staffing requirements. This contrasts sharply with the previous tendency to carry out broad and brutal staff reductions across the board, sometimes referred to as "dumb-sizing".

22.6 Business process re-engineering (BPR)

Re-engineering was developed and launched in the mid-1980s as a technique for making radical and rapid changes in operating strategy that result in immediate competitive advantage. In this concept, changes in business processes must cross old organizational barriers; job descriptions must be rewritten; reward systems must be revised to foster individuality and internal competitiveness; new information systems must be designed and tested. There is a strong focus on cutting costs – particularly on making large numbers of staff redundant.

The earlier concepts of BPR were clearly centred on information technology (IT). The key message was that IT systems should be designed around the processes of an organization rather than localized within organizational units, as was usually the case. The view was soon extended to the organization as a whole to counteract the negative impact of functions, hierarchy and command-type structures. A modernized BPR is meant to be a fundamental analysis and radical redesign of business processes to achieve dramatic improvements in performance, including costs, quality, service and speed. It also aims to eliminate all activities that are not central to process goals, to automate all activities that do not require human judgement, and, where necessary, to facilitate such judgement at reduced costs. It is a series of interrelated activities that cut across functional boundaries in the delivery of output.

The essential idea of BPR is to redesign the core processes of the enterprise so that the organizational barriers and operational impediments between processes are eliminated. Instead of a piecemeal approach – improving the efficiency of each separate business activity or operation – re-engineering starts with the premise that companies consist of processes, or combinations of activities, that, linked together, produce an output in the form of goods and services for customers. In re-engineering, therefore, the focus is on how best to organize and assemble these processes as a whole, in order to maximize benefits for customers while ensuring efficient use of company resources.

BPR consists of two main elements. *Business re-engineering* involves the development of an organizational architecture: identifying and linking business strategy with the required processes to ensure that the strategy is delivered. *Business process redesign* refers to the redesign of any organizational process, from the total supply chain process to a single process within an individual functional department. Process redesign normally includes eliminating all non-value-added activities, simplifying the process, integrating it and finally automating it where appropriate. The whole effort is usually structured in five stages as follows:

- *Stage 1. Restructuring.* Organizational renewal generally begins with a turnaround effort focused on restructuring by downsizing and/or delayering to cut "fat" and improve productivity. The main staff reductions come from retirements, closing of plants, reorganizations, consolidations, and greater span of control.
- *Stage 2. Bureaucracy bashing.* Get rid of unnecessary reports, approvals, meetings, measures, policies, procedures, and other activities that create backlogs.
- *Stage 3. Employee empowerment.* Empowering employees helps to remove barriers between employees and managers, and builds openness and dialogue. Self-directed work-teams and employee involvement should be woven into the fabric of the organization.
- *Stage 4. Continuous improvement.* Begin by focusing on actively detecting and preventing errors using available productivity and quality techniques.
- *Stage 5. Cultural change.* Employees' mind-set – the way they think about their work – needs to be shifted.

Re-engineering programmes often seek to achieve short-term results within four to six months and to complete delivery of longer-term results within one or two years. A major advantage of the BPR approach is that it avoids or bypasses the departmental rivalries and politics that can interfere with the smooth running of more organization- or process-wide projects. In designing the re-engineering processes, it is important to focus on operations – irrespective of business functions, departments, geography, authority etc. – that run across all business areas, from raw materials procurement and manufacturing, through all the internal processes to contact with customers via sales, distribution, after-sales services and customer relationship management.

Successful BPR practices indicate that the following factors should be presented or developed:

- A preoccupation with change is important for employees to feel the urgency or see the benefits of change. The key drivers for re-engineering are customer demands, regulatory changes, increasing competition, dissatisfaction with internal operations, and costs.
- The need for clear goals is paramount for implementing a successful BPR. The business objectives need to drive the technology, and not the other way around.
- Re-engineering is a top-down approach, requiring continuing top management involvement, understanding and committed leadership. Companies must focus on redesigning processes rather than functions or departments, in order to gain maximum improvements from the BPR.
- Managing the pace of BPR is critical; a pilot project approach can help the organization gain "early wins" to validate certain concepts and techniques.

- The re-engineering task does not end once the newly re-engineered process is up and running. A monitoring system should be installed and the new process further fine-tuned and improved.

22.7 Outsourcing and insourcing

Outsourcing involves contracting with outside organizations to undertake specific activities that were previously carried out by the firm itself. It is a form of restructuring since it implies fundamental changes in strategy, organization and staffing. Specialized service companies can often provide better quality services more cheaply and more reliably, particularly in activities that require a different set of skills than the mainstream business of the company. For some time, activities such as cleaning and maintenance have routinely been contracted to specialized firms. More recently many firms have outsourced data processing, accounting, and facility management, and there is an increasing trend in manufacturing to outsource production of parts and subassembly supply. Under an outsourcing agreement, one firm purchases the ongoing provision of a product and services from another without taking a direct financial stake. It is a strategic opportunity that offers benefits over and above lower costs as a result of greater economy of scale for specialized external producers.

A management consultant has to be able to explain to the client the possible advantages and problems of outsourcing. When a product or service costs less, it frees up capital for alternative uses, or accrues to investor wealth in the longer term, and improves cash flow in the short term, as well as earnings per share.

An important source of user value is access to economies of scale and the unique expertise that a large provider can deliver. Brand or reputation value can also improve when providers deliver products and services more competently than internal personnel. Firms enter into outsourcing agreements for strategic gain as well. Value may come from an outsourcing contract if it provides for good complementarity between a user's and a provider's capabilities; if it allows the user to stay abreast of fast-changing technologies that it could not develop itself. Other key potential advantages include reduced capital intensity, transformation of fixed capital to variable costs, freeing-up of management time to focus on core, high-value-added activities and customer needs, and benefits that can be gained from supplier innovations.

A large and growing subset of outsourcing is *contract manufacturing* (between 10 and 20 per cent in some new economy sectors). The advantage of this lies in higher productivity, lower overheads and better use of expensive high-technology factories and specialized equipment. This dramatic and recent development is changing the shape of the value chain and relationships with suppliers.

PricewaterhouseCoopers proposed the following sequence of steps for business outsourcing:

1. *Analyse possibilities and cost-benefits of business process outsourcing.* Review the company's current state and define core and non-core activities. Identify effective solutions for the company's non-core operations.
2. *Define roles, responsibilities and controls.* Consider relationships between the corporation and the outsource company as a strategic, integrated partnership. Analyse various outsourcing options, identifying objectives, studying the current processes, and developing solutions. The contract must clearly address the scope of services, business processes, roles and responsibilities, organization and staffing, work plans, deliverables, schedules, budgets for time and expenses, and other management matters. It must also ensure that the company retains sufficient control.
3. *Establish measurements tied to results.* Include the means to provide information concerning the objectives. The contract should include jointly agreed performance targets for outputs, services, costs, and performance reporting as well as the outsource company's effectiveness.
4. *Plan for a smooth transition.* Formulate a detailed transition plan, and apply the firm's management methods to ensure a smooth, orderly hand-over of selected business processes from the firm to the outsource company.
5. *Launch the partnership.* Once the contract has been signed, a transition plan prepared, and internal communications plans put in place, the firm and the outsource company can initiate the new strategic partnership.
6. *Monitor and benchmark for continuous improvement.* The firm and the outsource company should provide for monitoring of processes and relationships; periodic evaluation of the outsource company's performance; execution of necessary adjustments; transformation of the outsourced functions into "centres of excellence" and use of performance benchmarking against world-class companies.

Companies must also be aware of a possible downside of outsourcing – creating a bureaucracy around it that is more unwieldy than, for example, running the IT department entirely in house. As companies increasingly compete in terms of responsiveness and flexibility, and for human talent, some observers worry that outsourcing may lead to "hollowing-out". With their value-generating activities no longer under their own roof, enterprises no longer possess the cutting edge to create innovative products, develop fresh services, or find new profit zones.

A new trend is currently leading some firms to bring their processes back in house – to "*insource*". Insourcing is often realized as shared services. Companies strip out routine, transaction-based processes common to several business divisions, and group them together in a stand-alone shared service centre (SSC). The SSC then provides the service to the company's divisions, charging each a pro rata fee for the service used. Typical processes to be insourced are financial (expenses processing, payroll, etc.), human resources (updating employee records, training, etc.), and information systems (systems support, training, etc.).

The potential of insourcing is in:

- *reducing duplication:* more ground can be covered at less cost by one large central SSC than by many small units doing the same work;
- *building commercial awareness:* staff who were previously unconcerned about costs become accountable for their time and spending;
- *letting business units focus on their core business:* managers can concentrate on improving productivity rather than on paperwork;
- *making local expertise available to all:* an expert who previously worked for one unit can now be of use company-wide;
- *offering an alternative to outsourcing:* companies can keep the cost benefits of outsourcing, with increased confidentiality and control.

As with outsourcing, there are some problems with insourcing. It comes at a cost. Usually, only large firms can afford the logistics, technology and set-up costs; and, as SSCs need fewer staff, layoffs are also usual. But what is really a matter of concern is that insourcing is not really a business. Most SSCs are only allowed to cover their costs and do not have to market themselves as outsourcers do.

22.8 Joint ventures for transformation

An effective approach to restructuring and freeing idle assets could be a transitory joint venture with a partner, leading eventually to a transfer of ownership; the terms of separation can be negotiated as part of the initial deal. Such transitory joint ventures have to be structured and managed differently from traditional joint ventures. To spot the problem of imprisoned assets, the consultant has to check the following possibilities or conditions:

- The business is not core to the future of the corporation and is under-performing compared with its potential.
- It is difficult to justify major new investments for such a non-core business.
- Since the assets are largely intangible, sceptical potential buyers under-value them.

If the above conditions are met a consultant could advise the use of a transitory joint venture. Indeed, the only way to liberate the imprisoned assets is to sell them to a buyer that wishes and has the ability to nourish them with complementary capabilities. After identifying such a buyer, the next step is to work out a mutually satisfactory deal. The challenge for the seller at this step is to reassure the potential buyer that the business is indeed "as advertised" – some kind of warranty would be useful. Next, an important issue will be to minimize disruptions as the business moves from the seller to the buyer.

Joint ventures are most effective at releasing imprisoned assets when those assets are tangled with the rest of the organization. A difficult untangling process demands a gradual approach to separating out the business, and a joint venture may be the right solution. Thus, the joint venture is more advantageous that a straight sale when the assets being liberated are intangible, such as consumer franchise, distribution relationships, human skills, and systems, which are especially difficult for outsiders to evaluate.

Tensions frequently arise between joint venture partners because their different goals may lead to different expectations of lifespan. To avoid the traps in managing the life-cycle of a joint venture, it is important to recognize that longevity is not a good measure of success. The potential gain from preserving the joint venture beyond the current project should be continuously monitored. If there is no further potential for complementarity and attractiveness to both partners, they should put in motion a process of graceful disengagement.

22.9 Mergers and acquisitions

Mergers and acquisitions (M&A), already discussed from a financial perspective in section 14.5, are widely used for transforming corporations. Smaller and younger companies bought for a specific capability can transform the acquirer into a more flexible and dynamic competitor. The purchase can help the established company reposition itself in the marketplace and the aggressive, entrepreneurial culture of the acquired firm spills over to the buyer organization. For example, Medtronic's sales doubled in 18 months after a flurry of acquisitions. Cisco Systems provides another example of successful company transformation through acquisitions (box 22.3).

Box 22.3 Restructuring through acquisitions: the case of Cisco Systems

In the high-tech arena, Cisco has found a good solution: just buy. Between 1996 and 2000, it made more than 60 acquisitions, building itself into one of the world's most valuable and admired companies. To integrate so many different cultures, Cisco has turned its expertise as a networking company inwards by building the most comprehensive internal communications network of any company in the world. Cisco Systems' acquisition process has worked well because it has kept resources, processes and values in the right perspective. Between 1993 and 1997, it primarily acquired small companies that were less than two years old, early-stage organizations whose market value was built primarily on their resources, particularly their engineers and products. Cisco plugged those resources into their own development, manufacturing, logistics, and marketing processes, throwing away whatever nascent processes and values came with the acquisitions because those were not what it paid for. On a few occasions, when the company acquired a larger, more mature organization (like StrataCom in 1996), Cisco did not integrate it. Rather, it let it stand alone and infused Cisco's substantial resources into StrataCom's organization to help it grow more rapidly.

To acquire *capabilities* is crucial. High-tech acquisitions particularly need a new orientation around people, not products, since high-tech products can become obsolete in a matter of months and replacing them needs knowledge, experience and capabilities. Once developed, technical capabilities are hard to imitate, so they provide a protective barrier, even against strong rivals. Smart acquirers want to obtain real human and systemic capabilities.

The first step, therefore, is to understand what capabilities the company really needs, and to decide what business it should be in over the next few years. After assessing market demands, managers need to identify the gaps in their product line and the products to bridge them. Finally they can outline the technological capabilities they will need. Once the capability gaps are known, companies can decide whether to develop the competence internally or acquire it from outside.

Advising clients on mergers and acquisitions has become an elitist area of consulting. This is not totally unjustified, as wide business knowledge, experience and sound judgement are required in these cases. The financial side of the scheme has to be examined carefully (see Chapter 14). However, the consultant should not confine himself or herself to the financial aspects of the acquisition proposal: a good strategic fit must come first. A scheme that is perfectly feasible and looks attractive from the financial point of view may involve unrealistic strategic choices as regards marketing, production capacity, staff capabilities or compatibility of organizational cultures; in such a case the looked-for synergy will not be realized.

There is, in fact, ample evidence that the services of skilled consultants are needed in this area of corporate activity. A number of studies, conducted by both academics and professional consultants in many countries over a period of three or four decades, have produced strikingly similar conclusions – that about 50 per cent of all mergers and acquisitions fail to produce the expected results. There appear to be two principal reasons. The first is that the price paid is often unjustifiably high. The other is that top management consistently fail to recognize the problems inherent in trying to bring together two organizations, each with its own history, values and culture. The problems are particularly intense when a large and perhaps bureaucratic organization is taking control of a smaller and more entrepreneurial one. Perhaps the most important single service that the consultant can provide in an acquisition is to try to give top executives of the acquiring company some idea of how things look from the other side. It is in the merger and acquisition context that an understanding of corporate culture is most important (see Chapters 5 and 12).

Another reason for difficulties is the failure to identify accurately the type of merger the parties will be dealing with. *Transformational* mergers, especially, must be managed quite differently from conventional ones because they are inherently more risky. The conventional M&A strategy relates to capacity transfer and is based on absorption, while transformational M&A relates to creating new capabilities to cope with revolutionary change.

Successful acquirers go out of their way to retain the best people, make their transition as smooth as possible, and keep their development energies focused.

They usually try to keep these people together in a separate division, with the leader of the purchased company in charge. Acquirers need to send a message that there will be consistency and openness in the new environment, and resist the temptation to prescribe in detail how the new people must run their operations.

22.10 Networking arrangements

Networks are spreading globally as an effective tool and structure for fundamental transformation of organizations. Companies can significantly improve productivity by focusing on the things they do best. Networks usually focus on a combination of cost reduction and customer service orientation, as the foundation for improved competitiveness. At the centre of the network should be a flagship firm, which can contribute unique capabilities. These might include competence in managing the network as a whole, developing core technologies, improving distribution and supply chains, and many others.

Networks help companies adopt agile business practices, tune in to the changing and diverse needs of their customers, and rapidly transform their supply and distribution systems as well as their own production systems. By cooperating with other firms, even competitors, companies can improve their productivity and competitiveness through better access to innovations and new technology, venture capital and new markets at lower costs, while sharing risks and liabilities with network partners. They can have more efficient specialization around their core activities while learning about new management practices.

What has made networking so popular is the fact that today's corporate partners are more and more interested in long-term strategic alliances where gains are made over many years. The formation of strategic networks means that power often resides in a group of companies acting together as partners. Information technology increases the opportunity to use cooperative strategies to reduce costs, enter new markets, and improve competitiveness. The most common types of cooperation range from exchange of information and experience to more complex and formal relationships such as consortia. In between there are supply/value-chain partnerships, licensing, strategic alliances and others.

An excellent illustration of developments in networking is the rapid spread of *contract manufacturing* among electronics firms. Contract manufacturers such as Flextronic, Solectron, Celestica, Jabil and hundreds of other small firms have taken about 11 per cent of the market for electronics hardware. The amount of contract manufacturing is growing by more than 20 per cent a year, which is more than twice as fast as the electronics industry as a whole. Another form of networking, dealing with knowledge management between firms, is *network intelligence*, which can enable executives and entrepreneurs to grasp many phenomena shaping the future of technology companies. As network technologies have advanced, both the location and the mobility of network intelligence have changed dramatically.

Another form of networking is a *network incubator*, which provides mechanisms to foster partnerships among start-up teams and other successful Internet-oriented firms, thus facilitating the flow of knowledge and talent across companies and forging marketing and technology relationships between them. With the help of such an incubator, start-up companies can network to obtain resources and partner with each other quickly, allowing them to establish themselves in the marketplace ahead of competitors. These incubators provide fledging companies with preferential access to potential partners and advisers. Network incubators combine the best of two worlds – the scale and scope of large corporations and the entrepreneurial spirit of small venture-capital firms – as well as providing unique networking benefits.

Virtual teamwork also represents an excellent form of networking. Communication technology now enables the balance of work to shift from stable functions tied to physical locations to electronically connected teams irrespective of location. This increases the ability of companies to gain access to specialized knowledge. Such a virtual model can bring savings as well: saving from reduced travel time, reduced office space, and avoidance of duplication of personnel can reach upward of 50 per cent of project costs. The model is also able to exploit different time zones and reduce product development time through the creation of a 24-hour workday spread across different locations.

22.11 Transforming organizational structures

As companies around the world continue to transform their strategies and structures to become more agile, the sources of competitive advantage are increasingly shifting away from traditional economic drivers such as large size, economies of scale, and proprietary technologies. Increasingly, companies are using continuous change, virtual and self-managed teams, networks and cellular organizations to revamp their strategies and ways of doing business. The fundamental objective of these shifts is to create a new type of organizational design that facilitates the rapid creation and sharing of new sources of knowledge throughout the firm.

One of the most important tasks for management consultants in advising on organization restructuring is to balance and align innovation, initiative, competence-building, flexibility and standardization. Growing decentralization and autonomy of administrative and business units have made organizational alignment or integration a critical management tool, which stimulates company learning and innovation. Harmonizing strategy and organization design is an ongoing challenge for senior managers and management consultants in all firms, but larger companies face additional challenges, in integrating numerous internal divisions.

The organizations of the past, most of which are still in existence, were not designed to cope with constant change. They were designed for permanent employment, high fixed costs, regular work, and narrow skills and task boundaries, and offered security in exchange for loyalty and commitment. New organizations need to be designed for flexible resources, changing demands, quick reaction to market behaviour, low fixed costs, focus on core competencies and capabilities, and emphasis on talent.

The most dramatic change for those used to conventional corporate structures is the fluidity of new-style organizations. The walls around and inside corporations are collapsing and the large enterprise is already breaking down. Physical assets are no longer so advantageous: it is information and intellectual assets that matter.

Grassroots innovation in companies requires appropriate structures to provide a smooth flow, exchange and implementation. As the computing and financial service industries have shown, vertical integration breaks down when innovation speeds up. The big telecommunications firms that will win back investor confidence soonest will be those with the courage to rip apart their monopolistic structures along functional layers, to swap size for speed, and to embrace rather than fear disruptive technologies. Dell is deliberately and decisively anti-hierarchical. It has no fancy corporate offices. In fact there are only four offices, for the chairman and vice-chairmen (two of them share one office); everybody else has a cubicle.

A very important new rule is emerging: do not try to predict change precisely, but make the company structure flexible enough to respond to it. Consolidating or decreasing the number of divisions improves resource-sharing and creates sufficient critical mass to learn or build a new core competence. Divisions that benefit from such consolidation can be combined into a single larger unit. At the same time, many companies have reduced the size of their divisions to adjust to changing conditions without compromising their ability to learn and share knowledge throughout the system. By having smaller divisions or local networks, these firms can innovate faster.

In a network – a project or an alliance, for example – managers have to be everywhere. The network web is so fluid that managers cannot afford to remain in the centre: they have to move around to facilitate collaboration and energize the whole network. They need to encourage people who already know how to do their work. In a web everyone can be a manager: whoever draws things together becomes a de facto manager. For companies to thrive in today's economy, management has to be put in its place – not at the top of the chart but within it, at the centre of a hub, or throughout a web.

It should be remembered that organizational design is just a framework to create favourable conditions for implementing company vision and strategy to meet customer needs and become competitive. What matters is whether the organization structure is sufficiently flexible and permeable to allow business processes, knowledge and experience to flow throughout the organization, regardless of where they originate.

22.12 Ownership restructuring

Recently many companies have enhanced shareholder value by restructuring their capital, ownership and assets.

Spin-offs occur when the entire ownership of a subsidiary is divested and shares in the newly formed company are distributed as dividends to shareholders.

Equity carve-outs are the sale by a public company of a portion of common stock of one of its subsidiaries through an initial public offering (IPO). Each carve-out subsidiary has its own board of directors, operating CEO, and financial statements, and its shares are quoted on one of the stock exchanges. The parent company, which usually retains a majority of the shares, continues to provide strategic direction and selected central resources. Equity carve-outs have assumed a prominent place in US equity activity, with an average of almost 50 carve-outs a year. Some analysts believe that carve-outs are the best way to unlock unrecognized values in public companies.

Leveraged buy-outs are the technique of buying the shares of a company and issuing bonds, sometimes referred to as junk bonds, to finance the purchase. This makes it easier for conglomerates to shed non-core assets.

Management buy-outs are another form of ownership restructuring in which some managers within the company buy all the outstanding shares because they believe they can considerably improve performance and enhance the value of the company. In *employee buy-outs*, the employees become the owners of the business. Another variation is a *management buy-in,* in which an external management team buys all the shares, dismisses the existing management team and creates a new private company. In some cases these opportunities arise when a business, whether independent or part of a larger group, is losing money and cannot be sold to another company.

Employee ownership has been offered in an increasing number of companies in the form of stock options, share purchase plans and profit-sharing to improve the motivation and commitment of employees.

22.13 Privatization

Privatization refers to instances of ownership restructuring, leading to total business and financial restructuring, where assets are transferred from government (central or local) to private owners. Although the main privatization moves were completed in the developed free market economies in the 1980s and in the former centrally planned economies in the 1990s, in many countries privatization still represents an opportunity and challenge to consultants. In preparing for privatization of state-owned and state-controlled organizations, and implementing the privatization process, most governmental institutions have to rely to a considerable extent on external expertise. This may concern issues such as pre-privatization sector studies, privatization policies and procedures, enterprise restructuring, valuation, diagnostic and feasibility studies, management and staff training, searching for buyers, the creation of an effective market-economy infrastructure, corporate governance, legal issues, and so on.

Management consultants engaging in privatization projects should have a solid background in the sector and a track record showing that they are able to solve practical diagnostic, structural and strategic problems of companies. Management consulting firms with a good background in sector studies, business diagnosis, corporate strategy and restructuring are well placed to take the lead in advising clients on important privatization projects. They can help clients to identify and involve specialized advisers able to handle legal, financial, environmental and other aspects of particular projects.

In a typical assignment, the consultant may be called in to undertake the following tasks:

Technical and strategic assessment. These data would cover products and services; licences and technical know-how (marketability, competitive situation); technical layout and condition of business premises and facilities; productivity, management and human resources.

Evaluation of the strategic and financial situation. This will cover issues such as strengths and weaknesses of the company (markets, customer base, competitiveness, market share); threats and opportunities for the future privatized enterprise and the company's ability to cope with external influences; actions to secure the company's position in the local and/or international market; and financial performance (cash flow, profitability, financial structure, working capital, liquidity, quality of receivables and other assets, the company's ability to finance itself). Owing to their generally extensive vertical and horizontal integration, many public-sector companies have to be split up or restructured to become manageable and attractive to investors. The consultant should analyse the company and as a first step suggest a horizontal separation, which might include the sale of non-essentials via various asset deals to different investors. As a second step the company may be separated into core business units, after which individual parts of the value-adding chain can be privatized separately in different asset deals. For any consultant, the most important focus of the strategic and technical assessment must be the viability, competitive advantage and development prospects of the company after privatization.

Valuation. Valuation plays a basic and vital role in the privatization process. A consultant may encounter a broad range of problems in conducting a valuation. Assumptions about future domestic and international trends (i.e. interest rates, exchange rates and inflation) in a rapidly changing market, as well as the legal and financial environment, must be dealt with. To ensure that investors become and remain interested, the valuation of the company has to be fair and reasonable and the consultant may be asked both to advise upon the method to be used and to assist in its application.

Strategy for privatizing a company. After all the data have been collected and the company valued, the seller may ask the consultant to advise on the privatization strategy. Such strategies may involve, for example:

- privatizing the company as a whole via a public offering of shares; sale of shares by auction, either open or limited to pre-selected bidders; sale of shares through direct negotiation or private placement or in exchange for vouchers;
- splitting up the company into smaller units;
- various combinations of these approaches.

Searching for investors and marketing. This may be the most important and valuable input the consultant can make. Prospective investors may be in other countries or sectors, and may be unaware of the opportunity. The consultant should assess not only their financial potential and interest in the deal, but mainly their real potential for keeping the company alive and developing it after privatization. Errors in choosing investors have been the main cause of failures and asset-stripping of many privatized companies.

Negotiations and documentation. Once the seller has received a written offer, the consultant can assist in evaluating the offer, negotiating the purchase of the enterprise with the potential investor, and handling issues such as providing warranties, developing business plans, and defining payment schedules.

In a privatized enterprise, the transfer of ownership rights, and the related legal and organizational restructuring, is usually only the beginning of its total transformation. Privatization changes the owner and the rules of the game and creates new opportunities, but provides no guarantee that the new enterprise will be immediately prosperous. It therefore creates fertile ground for the application of the various approaches and methods of company transformation and renewal reviewed in the previous sections. This has been well understood by the many consultants who have chosen to focus on post-privatization consulting.

22.14 Pitfalls and errors to avoid in transformation

It is rare for a transformation programme to be evaluated as a total success. To begin with, managers and consultants often focus excessively on drawing up perfect plans for change and insufficiently on supporting their implementation and removing organizational and cultural obstacles to the new vision and strategic change. Also, transformation efforts tend to focus more on activities than on results. With results-driven changes, a company introduces only those innovations that can help achieve specific goals. Results-driven programmes bypass lengthy preparations and aim at quick, measurable gains within short periods.

Other problems have been the *re-engineering illusion* and *downsizing trap* (cost reduction versus added value). Restructuring is a strategy for growth, a process for adding value and enhancing an enterprise's capacity to deliver products and services. In practice, however, many companies have applied it as a methodology for downsizing and mere cost-cutting. When re-engineering focuses on eliminating people without making significant changes to reduce the amount of work, there is little likelihood that the firm is gaining long-term benefits.

Many programmes have not been keyed to specific results. This means that dramatic improvements have been made in processes that do not significantly add value or improve bottom-line results. This can happen when re-engineering is approached on too low a level, without a clear strategy and without identifying the real problems: the expectation is that activity-centred steps (training, quality control, new measurements, etc.) will lead automatically to better business performance.

Very often management ignores short-term results. When activity-centred programmes fail to produce improvements in financial and operational performance, managers seldom complain, since they are afraid of being accused of preoccupation with the short term at the expense of the long term. This leads to failure to create short-terms wins. There is also a very common phenomenon of "the tail wagging the dog", for example when technology rather than business becomes the driver for restructuring. Because of inability to link cause and effect, there is virtually no opportunity to learn useful lessons and apply them to future programmes.

A big problem in organizational transformation occurs when management fails to involve those directly affected by transformational efforts. Although planning must be top-down, implementation generally works best when it is bottom-up. Also attempts to improve business results at the expense of the quality of life of employees and other social aspects sooner or later lead to failure. As a result, management fails to create a sufficient powerful guiding coalition.

Many years of experience in transformation indicate that, in most cases, it is necessary to replace the top managers who have taken the company to the situation where radical change became necessary. These managers, as a rule, are unable to lead the transformational efforts, particularly radical ones. Proposing new candidates for top management positions, or at least advising on their competence profile, is often an important task of management consultants. These candidates should possess qualities of transformation leaders.

People who possess an internal locus of control feel that they are in charge of their own lives; they perceive their destiny as affected by their own decisions, not by outside factors. Such people are generally self-confident, relaxed, active, striving, achieving, future- and long-term oriented, proactive and innovative. Their strong belief in their own capabilities makes them resistant to influence, coercion and manipulation. People with an external locus of control, on the other hand, often see changes as a threat. Because they do not feel in control of the forces that affect their lives, they adopt a rather passive stance towards change and, as a result, they are often prone to various depressive reactions. Companies subjected to a turbulent environment – those for whom change is the norm rather than the exception – would do well to select "hardy" people who have an internal locus of control.

As a minimum to succeed in organizational transformation, corporate stakeholders and management consultants should start the process by securing the best available leaders who have a vision and can inspire, motivate, act decisively and promptly, coach and build team spirit.[7]

---

[1] See B. Chakravarthy: "The process of transformation: In search of nirvana", in *European Management Journal*, Vol.14, No. 6, Dec. 1996, pp. 529–539.

[2] See C. M. Christensen and M. Overdorf: "Meeting the challenge of disruptive change", in *Harvard Business Review*, Mar.–Apr. 2000, p. 67.

[3] G. Hamel: "Waking up IBM", in *Harvard Business Review*, July–Aug. 2000, p. 142.

[4] G. Hamel: *Leading the revolution* (Boston, MA, HBS Press, 2000).

[5] J. P. Killing: "Managing change: The urgency factor", in *Perspectives for Managers* (Lausanne, IMD), Vol. 29, No 1, Feb. 1997.

[6] G. Hamel: "Reinvent your company", in *Fortune*, 12 June 2000, pp. 105–120.

[7] See e.g. J. Kotter: *Leading change* (Boston, MA, HBS Press, 1996).

CONSULTING ON THE SOCIAL ROLE AND RESPONSIBILITY OF BUSINESS 23

This chapter provides guidance on the best approaches to consulting in the area of *corporate social responsibility, social responsibility of business*, or *corporate citizenship* (these terms will be used interchangeably in this chapter). This is a new and difficult area of consulting, which addresses fundamental business concepts and purposes and the increasingly complex relationships of business firms with their environment. It is an area that is value-laden and controversial, where businesses have to face diverse and even conflicting interests, requirements and pressures. Its importance has grown considerably over the past decades and will continue to grow in future years.

Firms that accept that the landscape for the social role of business is changing confront many challenges. They must make up for the deficiency in existing knowledge, competence and systems around corporate citizenship management and begin to develop their capabilities. They need reliable and balanced guidelines on how to act. They therefore appreciate help from consultants in facing both policy and operational issues related to their social roles, functions and relationships, especially if the consultants can demonstrate their ability to help in preventing conflicts and crises. Part of the consultants' role is to convince clients that social responsibility is becoming a more and more important part of business fundamentals. Consultants are called to help their clients define how they should relate to stakeholders, and take into account issues that are typically the province of the public and civil sectors. Both facets require consultants to persuade, and then guide their clients into unmapped territory and non-traditional roles. Clients and consultants alike have no less of an agenda than to redefine the concept of "business as usual".

23.1 The social dimension of business

Some managers and consultants view the current efforts to enhance the social responsibility of business primarily as a defensive reaction to the multiple criticisms and pressures to which companies are increasingly exposed – a kind of public relations exercise. They feel that it is more important to be *perceived* as a good corporate citizen (hence to be less exposed to criticism and pressure groups) than to actually be one. If there were no criticism and no pressure groups, business could go on as usual. Numerous businesses around the world regard the consideration of their social role and responsibility – if they pay attention at all – as an academic and not very realistic concern. These views constrain their capacity both to understand the depth and breadth of the social responsibility of business and to act with foresight.

The social dimension of business, i.e. the relationships between business and society and the impact of business activity on the life and development of society, and vice versa, is not something new that has emerged in the past 20–30 years owing to factors such as the tremendous growth of power of the multinational corporations, dissatisfaction with globalization or the increasing aggressiveness of some pressure groups. Whether one likes it or not, social responsibility is inherent in any business activity. Business activity is social activity *par excellence*.[1] Business firms are institutions of society established for producing, distributing and delivering goods and services needed to satisfy a wide range of social needs. They interact with all other social institutions and influence the lives of individuals, families and wider communities as employers, educators, organizers of joint work, sellers, buyers, taxpayers, creators and users of resources and infrastructure, investors, producers of wealth, and so on. Each of these functions has a social dimension and implications.

These truths are as old as business itself. What is relatively recent, however, is (1) the unprecedented dimension, power and role of business in global development; and (2) a new level of perception, awareness, criteria, standards and goals, and the will and capacity to take action on social responsibility issues, both on the part of business and on the part of governments and other institutions and organizations.

It should be noted that socially responsible behaviour in business is a relative concept. Its definition is influenced by geography, culture, tradition, education, political orientation, wealth, industrial dynamics, and so on. For example, countries with less developed markets and social services may expect business corporations to contribute to the creation of modern economic sectors in production and services, employment, provision of social services, education and infrastructure. In other countries, institutional and political conditions may mean that priority is given to human rights, environmental protection or ethical advertising. In countries with well-developed labour legislation and institutional mechanisms for its enforcement, companies have no choice but to comply with this legislation. Conversely, in countries with weak institutional mechanisms and public administration the demand for self-regulated corporate citizenship may be much greater.

Within countries, different businesses, social groups and societal organizations may have different expectations and apply different standards in respect of various aspects of social responsibility. Some are interested only in defending their immediate short-term interests, while others consistently adopt wider and longer-term views based on the principle of sustainable development. Some are anti-business, confrontational and suspicious of every new initiative taken by private enterprise, while others recognize common interests and the need to negotiate, compromise and seek solutions that benefit everyone. This is, after all, how societies are structured and function. It is normal that there is not a single uniform view and concept of what is economically and socially feasible, beneficial and necessary. Practical solutions have to be negotiated, developed by a democratic process, adopted by agreement, recommended to stakeholders, and revised and renegotiated when conditions change.

Thus, to move from being a noble theoretical principle to a practical operational concept, corporate responsibility needs an effective societal and institutional environment, which helps to define it, determine its specific characteristics and measures, harmonize approaches, build consensus, promote new concepts, negotiate what needs to be negotiated, enforce what needs to be enforced, and control implementation. Developing this environment, together with a public policy that encourages a greater sense of social responsibility, is as important as enhancing the recognition of the social roles of business among managers, entrepreneurs and investors.

23.2 Current concepts and trends

The driving forces

Over recent decades, the concept and practice of corporate social responsibility or citizenship have been influenced by a series of related developments, which have brought the issue to the forefront.

Government retrenchment. An extremely important driver of the current concept of corporate citizenship is government retrenchment. The fall of the communist and command-economy systems was followed by a commercial explosion, and new policies such as reduced tariffs within and between nations, putting a strain on the public purse. At the same time, mature democracies around the world face a situation in which more and more public funds are tied to non-discretionary (mandatory) support programmes (health, unemployment, etc.) leaving fewer resources to address increasingly complex social problems in education, social exclusion, digital divide, and safety. As businesses thrive, they are increasingly expected to engage in solving societal problems, and to focus their considerable resources on filling the gaps left by government retrenchment. Countries with no tradition of corporate philanthropy or volunteerism are thus beginning to embrace such concepts.

Globalization and the economic power of business. Improved technology (such as global telecommunications and inexpensive transport), opening of national economies, dynamic global capital markets, and access to low-cost labour are among the factors creating truly global enterprises. Transnational firms now produce, source and sell their goods around the world. Their operations in many cases touch literally every part of the world, and affect the well-being of a wide spectrum of stakeholders – both positively and negatively – across the globe. Owing to their economic and financial power they are very strong players, able to mobilize, invest and transfer resources in excess of the GNP of many States.

The intensifying backlash and activism against business practices connected with globalization underscore the growing dissatisfaction with corporate power and behaviour. Protesters have raised questions concerning corporate practices towards the environment, human rights, payment of livable wages, sourcing policies, and destruction of the cultural infrastructure or internationally uncompetitive local industries and agriculture, to name a few.

Crises. A number of prominent crises have focused the attention of the world on corporate behaviour. The explosion of the Union Carbide plant in Bhopal, India, in 1985 led to stringent guidelines for environmental, health and safety standards along with new efforts to promote communication and transparency, such as Responsible Care and further reporting requirements demanded by governments around the world. The Exxon Valdez oil spill heightened the call for environmental management and reporting, and led to coalitions such as the CEREs Principles.[2] Shell's experiences in Nigeria and the North Sea have demonstrated the power of activism and the "court of public opinion", leading a number of companies to take more seriously their relationships with non-governmental organizations (NGOs) and community activists. In some cases a crisis is both inevitable and necessary – as long as there is no crisis, warnings are not taken seriously and neither the businesses involved nor the regulators are willing to act.

Incentives. While the threat of the "stick" looms large, the size of the "carrot" encouraging socially responsible behaviour in the corporate world has grown as well. This new perspective sees corporate citizenship as supporting the corporate value chain. Evidence is growing that corporate citizenship may be an important differentiator in the minds of consumers and employees. "Reputational capital" appears to be gaining more and more credence in financial markets. Built on a foundation of trust rather than image, reputation is influenced significantly by the attitudes of key stakeholders towards companies. A reputation as a good corporate citizen is viewed more and more as an important asset in risk management. This is particularly relevant for companies and industries that find their "licence to operate" becoming more influenced by grassroots organizations and stakeholders. Finally, a more radical revolution is occurring as leading companies re-examine their business models. Environmental responsibility is being recast as efficient manufacturing. Traditionally excluded markets in low-income and minority communities and least developed countries are increasingly viewed as the last commercial frontier. Another facet of this revolution is the proliferation and fast growth of socially screened mutual funds, which include or exclude firms on the basis of social performance criteria.

The influence of activism and pressures for compliance. Since the 1960s, grassroots activists have achieved success in influencing industrial behaviour. In the United States, activists helped drive the introduction of landmark regulations around safety, the environment, and community reinvestment (regulating banks against discriminatory lending and investment practices). On a global level, the Sullivan Principles organized coalitions of diverse constituencies to discourage investment in South Africa under the former apartheid regime. This activism was the precursor of notable global efforts around labour standards, access to treatment for AIDS, and globalization. The exposure of sweatshop labour connected to major brands of consumer goods focused attention on corporate manufacturing, sourcing and labour practices. Improvements in telecommunications systems are playing a profound role in creating an inexpensive infrastructure to facilitate grassroots activism at the global level.

The increasing visibility and influence of civil society. Surveys from polling organizations such as MORI have found that the public trusts civil society organizations far more than corporations. The United Nations estimates that there are over 29,000 international NGOs, many of which have a significant voice in the discussion of the social role and responsibility of business.

Growing involvement of international organizations. Governmental and other official organizations, including the United Nations, the OECD, the ILO, the EU and others, have called for the active participation of business in social affairs and have led the agenda in defining socially responsible corporate behaviour (box 23.1):

- The United Nations has taken a global leadership role by championing the United Nations Global Compact, a set of voluntary corporate codes of conduct around labour, human rights and the environment, which also embodies recommendations developed by other international agencies. The United Nations Secretary-General has solicited the partnership of the private sector to solve the global HIV/AIDS crisis and to support economic and social development.
- The OECD[3] has developed comprehensive *Guidelines for multinational enterprises* and several other instruments for corporate responsibility, including *Corporate governance principles*, *Guidelines for electronic commerce* and *The bribery convention.*
- The ILO[4] has adopted the *Declaration on Fundamental Principles and Rights at Work and its Follow-up*, the *Tripartite Declaration of Principles Concerning Multinational Enterprises and Social Policy* and a number of international labour conventions and recommendations.
- The Commission of the European Communities published a green paper, *Promoting a European Framework for Corporate Social Responsibility*, which placed the debate on corporate social responsibility in the wider framework of the Commission's proposals for a European strategy for sustainable development.

Box 23.1 International guidelines on socially responsible business

United Nations: The Global Compact (www.unglobalcompact.org)

The Global Compact derives from the Universal Declaration of Human Rights, the ILO's Declaration of Fundamental Principles and Rights at Work and the Rio Principles on Environment and Development. It uses the power of transparency and dialogue to identify and disseminate good practices, and calls on world business to uphold nine universal principles:

Principle 1: Support and respect the protection of international human rights within their sphere of influence.

Principle 2: Make sure their own corporations are not complicit in human rights abuses.

Principle 3: Freedom of association and the effective recognition of the right to collective bargaining.

Principle 4: The elimination of all forms of forced and compulsory labour.

Principle 5: The effective abolition of child labour.

Principle 6: The elimination of discrimination in respect of employment and occupation.

Principle 7: Support a precautionary approach to environmental challenges.

Principle 8: Undertake initiatives to promote greater environmental responsibility.

Principle 9: Encourage the development and diffusion of environmentally friendly technologies.

OECD Guidelines for multinational enterprises (www.oecd.org/EN/document/0,,EN-document-187-5-no-27-24467-187,FF.html)

The OECD Guidelines are the only comprehensive though non-binding recommendations to enterprises on how to operate in harmony with government policies and societal expectations. They provide guidance on appropriate business conduct across the full range of enterprise activities. Although directly addressed to multinational companies, they are appropriate for all private, state-owned and mixed enterprises. They cover: general policies, disclosure, employment and industrial relations, environmental management, combating bribery, consumer interests, science and technology, competition, and taxation. Another OECD instrument, *Principles of corporate governance*, focuses on the rights and responsibilities of shareholders, and provides a number of suggestions on best practices, listing requirements and codes of conduct.

ILO Tripartite Declaration of Principles concerning Multinational Enterprises and Social Policy (www.ilo.org/public/english/employment/multi/index.htm)

The Declaration contains recommendations that are universally applicable to all enterprises, employers' and workers' organizations, and governments. The principles offer guidelines to multinational companies, governments, and employers' and workers' organizations in areas such as general policies, employment, training, conditions of work and life, and industrial relations, including freedom of association and collective bargaining. Its provisions are reinforced by a number of International Labour Conventions and Recommendations which the social partners are urged to bear in mind and apply, to the greatest extent possible.

European Union: Green Paper on Promoting a European Framework for Corporate Social Responsibility (europa.eu.int/comm/off/green/index_en.htm)

The Green Paper published in July 2001 takes up the "triple bottom-line" concept and is intended to launch a debate on how best to combine business profitability with the twin concepts of sustainability and accountability. The paper reviews a wide range of conceptual and practical issues of corporate social responsibility within firms and towards society at large. It emphasizes a holistic approach, an encouraging policy environment and the need to fully instil social responsibility in business culture.

Global Reporting Initiative (GRI) Guidelines (www.globalreporting.org)

The GRI aims to create a reporting framework that will enable reporters to respond efficiently and consistently to stakeholder demands, benchmark their performance against similar enterprises, position themselves as proactive in managing their business and external relations, and strengthen their reputations in capital, labour and customer markets. The framework is: (1) a CEO statement describing key elements of the report; (2) an overview of the reporting organization; (3) executive summary and key indicators; (4) vision and strategy that integrate economic, environmental and social performance; (5) policies, organization, and management systems including a discussion of stakeholder engagement; (6) qualitative and quantitative indicators of an organization's economic, environmental, and social performance. These should include both generally applicable indicators and organization-specific indicators for the three areas. *Economic performance* should include: profit, intangible assets, investments, wages and benefits, labour productivity, taxes, community development, suppliers, and products/services. *Environmental performance* should include: energy, materials, water, emissions/ effluents/wastes, transport, suppliers, products and services, land use/ biodiversity, and compliance. *Social performance* should include: workplace, human rights, suppliers, and products/services.

Note: All websites visited on 4 April 2002.

A key factor in favour of the codes and systems being established by the leading international agencies is that they represent the understanding, recognition, compromise and consensus reached by the key stakeholders internationally, regionally and nationally. Principles of corporate responsibility are likely to be more credible if they have been developed through a process of open consultation among leaders from business, workers, governments, civic society and academia.

Awareness and private initiatives. Many important business corporations and organizations representing business circles have a greater awareness of the social role and impact of business and recognize the need to enhance its social responsibility. New organizations have been established for this purpose. A coalition of NGOs has created the *Global Reporting Initiative* (GRI).[5] The Council on Economic Priorities has designed a Social Accountability system called SA8000. Business groups such as the Caux Roundtable have adopted their own sets of principles. Companies like Levi Strauss have designed codes of conduct that have been used as templates for their peers in industry. Codes of business or conduct focused on social issues and business ethics are used by many companies. Many private initiatives have their origin in academic institutions, business support groups and consultancies, which design tools to guide managers through the challenge of managing corporate citizenship. These include The Standards of Excellence developed by the Center for Corporate Citizenship at the Boston College in the United States, Business in the Community's "Principles", The Corporate Citizenship Company's London Benchmarking Group, AccountAbility's Social Audit, KPMG's ethical audit, PricewaterhouseCoopers' global sourcing audit, and a growing number of others.

Concepts and terminology

At its core, managing the social role and responsibility of business, or corporate citizenship, involves engaging, relating to and managing networks of stakeholders that include shareholders, customers, employees, suppliers, community/social interests and environmental interests. A stakeholder is commonly defined as any individual, group, or interest than can influence, or is influenced by, the operations of a business. Other definitions try to distinguish the relative primacy of stakeholders by identifying *the relative levels of risk* that a stakeholder creates, or bears, from corporate activity.

By (at least roughly) equating the importance of these stakeholders, businesses manifest their citizenship by producing benefits along a "triple bottom line" for shareholders, society and the environment. This is no simple task. The problem starts with the fundamentals – what term is the most appropriate? There is a fair amount of debate regarding the merits of terms such as corporate citizenship, corporate responsibility (used by OECD), corporate social responsibility (used in the Green Paper of the EU), social responsibility of business, corporate social performance, business ethics, corporate social accountability, community relations, corporate community involvement, social investment, external relations, public affairs, corporate reputation, and others. The leading terms are *corporate social responsibility*, *social responsibility of business* and *corporate citizenship*. Those who employ these terms fall into separate camps that either equate their meanings, or distinguish them broadly.

The OECD, for example, stresses that "corporate responsibility involves the search for an effective 'fit' between businesses and the societies in which they operate. The notion of 'fit' recognizes the mutual dependence of business and society – a business sector cannot prosper if the society in which it operates is failing and a failing business sector inevitably detracts from general well-being."[6] The Center for Corporate Citizenship defines corporate citizenship as "the process by which companies act as economic and social assets to the communities they impact by integrating societal interests with other core business objectives".[7] Others use the "triple bottom-line" (shareholders–society–environment) concept. In contrast, institutions such as Warwick University and Business for Social Responsibility[8] define corporate citizenship as both the performance and ethical obligations of business in a number of areas, including (but not limited to) human rights, community, labour relations, customers, shareholders, environment, suppliers, manufacturing, codes of conduct, philanthropy, marketing and ethics. Corporate citizenship is also defined by some as the manner in which a company manages complex relationships with a variety of key stakeholder groups. Others use rather narrow definitions such as involvement in community affairs.

This variety of terms and definitions for corporate citizenship creates some confusion. Constituencies advocate for their preferred terminology, while companies find themselves sorting through a variety of pitches from potential consultants that use the same language to describe different things, or different languages to describe the same thing.

In part because definitions are imprecise, the practice of corporate citizenship lacks the precision of other functions. Currently, several definitions and related advisory and other services are vying for the attention of corporate managers. Many overlap, but some are quite distinctive. Consultants generally advocate that *their* system is the most thorough, germane and measurable. With no clear base for judging what constitutes scope and excellence in corporate citizenship, it is very difficult for clients to judge competing approaches.

This diversity of approaches and denominations is likely to be with us for quite a while, and managers and consultants alike have to live with it. Anything that touches on the social role of business is value-laden, conceptually complex and difficult to translate into generally supported practical solutions. Many issues are controversial and solutions can only be found step by step, through negotiation and compromise. Recommendations and guidelines adopted by international agencies or other bodies provide a broad orientation, but in most cases there are no benchmarks or role models for particular situations.

The actual practice of many North American, Australian and British corporations tends to emphasize philanthropy and community involvement. This model leans heavily towards the concept of "mutual advantage", also known as the "win–win". The idea is that corporate involvement in social concerns should serve the greater good, while also supporting profitability.

In contrast, businesses in continental Europe are developing a broader concept of socially responsible behaviour that typically rests on the three pillars of labour relations, environmental responsibility, and human rights. In Europe, corporate citizenship concentrates on the practice and behaviour of the enterprise more than its contributions to social development. This model emphasizes transparency of corporate policies, decision-making and behaviour. It also calls for proactive initiatives to obtain the views and feedback of key stakeholders regarding the various dimensions of corporate citizenship. This model encourages businesses to design formal strategies and policies that balance profit maximization with stakeholder concerns. Developed economies in south-east Asia share a similar concept of citizenship, but emphasize in particular the firm's relationship with its employees.

Less developed countries tend to place greater emphasis on the participation of multinational enterprises in solving problems of social development and welfare. At a local level, these countries are concerned with enterprise development, including certain aspects of citizenship – such as product reliability, customer service and corporate governance – that more advanced economies may take for granted.

There is thus no single arbiter that in effect accredits the standards, objectives, benchmarks, criteria and even the basic concepts of corporate citizenship. With these differing perspectives, it is important for consultants and clients to understand how the field of practice has developed, where it may be going and what can be drawn from the various approaches. Being open to other approaches, even if they appear to be culturally strange and unpractical, and helping clients to aim at the same, is an essential quality of consultants in this field.

Problems faced by decision-makers in business

Currently, most managers are unequipped to handle the issues that corporate social responsibility encompasses. Most advanced management programmes have little or nothing in their curricula that would help managers begin to understand its dynamics. If such programmes do not address these considerations, then other business leaders with backgrounds in engineering, science, law, or other subjects can hardly be expected to have the training necessary to tackle social responsibility issues. In daily practice, managers often have to address issues of responsibility brought about by crises, external pressures, or new regulations, often outside the total business context. They act as a fire brigade to avoid further problems and the deepening of conflicts rather than being strategists and planners.

Managers generally find it difficult to keep abreast of new and revised recommendations, guidelines, codes, standards, reporting formats and other instruments aimed at promoting social responsibility of business. They are confused not only by terminology, as mentioned above, but also by overlapping initiatives, by the reluctance of some organizations to harmonize their concepts and coordinate or merge their instruments, and by the number of invitations to adopt new codes and meet new demands. They may appreciate that this reflects the state of the art, and the complexity of the issues, but a proliferation of competing codes and guidelines causes confusion, additional costs and inefficiencies, and often slows down practical action.

Also, the globalizing vision of shareholder capitalism is somewhat in opposition to the idea of higher corporate social responsibility. This model dictates that a firm's primary obligation is to satisfy the interests of its owners by maximizing the return on shareholder investments. In this regard, strict adherents of shareholder capitalism contend that corporate responsibility should encompass only activities that support shareholder wealth creation. Any activity that distracts from this aim is, by the logic of the shareholder model, unethical. Advocates of corporate citizenship therefore need to convince sceptics that there is in fact no contradiction between profit maximization and corporate responsibility, and that corporate citizenship is increasingly becoming necessary to achieve and maintain shareholder wealth. In contrast, it is argued by some that corporate citizenship is the process of maximization of *stakeholder value*. Advocates contend that by managing and building relationships with key stakeholders, everyone – including shareholders – benefits. Consultants therefore should be prepared in any engagement to demonstrate the concrete business value that corporate citizenship produces.

There will be instances in which consultants will work with sceptical managers for whom the business case is either highly intangible or essentially non-existent. Examples include situations in which the bottom line clearly argues for a company to leave a region, whatever the consequences to the local economy and the well-being of employees and their families. Companies may find that it is much cheaper to continue to use a highly polluting technology than to introduce a clean technology. Or they may feel that they need to subcontract to local suppliers with dubious ethical records in order to compete. While it may be possible for consultants to argue that such actions are ultimately unprofitable, at times the weight of evidence to the contrary may be formidable.

Managers who are aware of the social role and impact of their business may still hesitate between adopting a reactive or a proactive stance. Being reactive is often easier, especially if some issues have not been fully clarified or if the manager does not have the full understanding and support of the board of directors and shareholders on social responsibility issues. Action may thus be confined to responding to a specific requirement, pressure, threat, law, standard, inspection report or crisis. In this case, something has to be done and the Board cannot object. Conversely, a proactive approach will require vision, foresight, courage and risk-taking. It may involve thorough analysis, patient and persevering negotiation and excellent communication. It may give the company a new image and competitive edge. It may also be costly and difficult to sustain if a self-imposed standard is far ahead of the industry standard and a company could well continue without it in the given environment (typically anti-corruption initiatives and avoidance of conflicts of interest in some business cultures, or environment-sensitive behaviour in the absence of appropriate legislation and inspection).

International agencies and other leaders are unanimous in advocating a proactive approach to corporate social responsibility. By behaving proactively, a business demonstrates its independence and its understanding of the strategic dimension of corporate social responsibility, as well as its creativity in developing and applying practical approaches.

23.3 Consulting services

In their attempts to address the various demands and developments concerning corporate citizenship, firms are turning to consulting companies for assistance. In a rapidly expanding and wide-ranging field, consultants are assisting companies to develop corporate visions and strategies for their citizenship efforts, guiding them in introducing management systems to support the visions, and helping them prepare for certification under various schemes. The participants in this field and the firms involved range from global consultancies, such as PricewaterhouseCoopers and Ernst & Young, to individuals operating locally. Given its recent emergence, the field of consulting in corporate citizenship is relatively undeveloped.

The scope for consulting projects in the corporate citizenship arena is vast. It is an area in which, by definition, a consulting project focuses not on a function, initiative, product line or business unit, but the sum total of the business. To become a good corporate citizen often means a complete retooling – a comprehensive organizational change initiative – and this may be more than any consultant and client can hope to accomplish. Even the process of deciding how to approach the issue is tricky to say the least. Some look to create high-level planning systems; others believe a reporting or auditing process will drive performance; others approach the work from a communications angle; still others offer services around programming and specific initiatives. Specific programmes can range from establishing a volunteer programme, to creating procedures to ensure ethical global sourcing. Box 23.2 outlines a typology of corporate citizenship consulting which demonstrates the considerable breadth of the field.

There is an emerging consensus among business leaders around the process elements involved in corporate responsibility. There is growing agreement that it should be managed in an integrative, strategic fashion, with commitment of leadership who specify goals, assign roles, and ensure cross-functional integration, effective and efficient resource allocation, and appropriate management and communication systems. At the same time, there is a convergence of views that the corporate citizenship strategic management process should create systems for transparency, accountability, stakeholder dialogue and engagement, and measurement/verification.

Thus, while there are many directions for consulting in corporate social responsibility, in the absence of a clear definition of need, clients will do well to start with a strategic planning process that sorts through critical questions, identifies priorities, reveals critical relationships, provides concrete decisions, and specifies actions.

Box 23.2 Typology of corporate citizenship consulting

Strategy consulting. Senior executives are beginning to ask how they can design a strategy for their business that will embrace the vision and purpose of corporate citizenship, prioritize goals and objectives, specify the allocation of resources, define management roles and responsibilities, and measure outcomes. Once the strategy is defined, the firm may need consultants to support its implementation, monitor progress, and help measure results. Particular elements that support strategic "fact-based management" may require consultant support as well. These may include data collection activities, such as stakeholder surveys and internal staff interviews, and additional analyses. This arena of consulting may be the most wide open. Companies are employing the services of the "Big Five" consultants, major business strategy consultants (such as McKinsey), public relations firms, marketing research firms, NGOs, non-profit business organizations, smaller specialized consulting firms and individuals.

Community involvement. Demand for consultants to support corporate community involvement strategies and projects has increased steadily over the past decade. In part, this is because the Anglo-American approach centres its citizenship activities around community involvement. A promising trend is that more companies are looking to design holistic strategies that create trust-based relationships with, and promote the well-being of, community stakeholders as one determinant of business success. This serves as a powerful opening to broader conceptions of corporate citizenship. One exciting derivative of this work is an orientation away from corporate giving to the formation of cross-sector partnerships. These convene representatives of business, government and the voluntary sector to address problems of mutual concern, with the goal of creating mutual advantage. However, there remains plenty of work for consultants who focus on providing support for corporate giving programmes, cause-related marketing, and community-based events.

Environmental performance. This is a relatively mature consulting field. There are numerous firms and individuals that work with companies to support improved environmental management from both strategic and technical angles. A relatively new development, however, is consulting around sustainable environmental and community development. This type of consulting often engages in large-scale, holistic community and environmental planning. Consultants facilitate processes that convene representatives of key stakeholder groups who work together with corporate peers to define environmental performance plans, community involvement, and communication processes. More ambitious initiatives will expand the scope to look beyond the company's impact on sustainable development, to initiatives in which the consultant helps position the business as a leader of community-wide sustainable development initiatives.

Reputation management. The field of reputation management is growing, and while it overlaps with corporate citizenship, it is also distinct. As with corporate citizenship, there are a number of competing definitions and niche speciality areas. Some focus solely on corporate citizenship, and some not at all. The author's own preference is for a holistic approach that connects the variety of factors defining reputation (such as brand, product performance, customer satisfaction, employee satisfaction, corporate citizenship, and others). Certain of the "Big Five" firms, such as PricewaterhouseCoopers, have reputation management programmes. Several large public relations firms such as Sedgwick also provide such services, along with boutiques such as Walker Information and ProbusBNW.

Performance system consulting. As noted earlier, a variety of corporate citizenship performance systems are being developed (International Labour Standards, SA8000, GRI, ISO 14000, Standards of Excellence). As companies begin to "sign on" or endorse certain principles, they are seeking consultants who can help them to implement systems and meet reporting criteria.

Social auditing and reporting. Social auditing and reporting is another subfield of corporate citizenship with its own competing definitions and approaches. Typically, social reports communicate the range and scope of a company's citizenship activities, and provide a vehicle for an open discussion of shortcomings. Social reports require a rigorous process of development, but generally do not employ research methods to determine the consequences of corporate behaviour on stakeholders. However, social reports do require companies to conduct an accurate accounting of the full scope of resources they provide to corporate citizenship activities. Consultants in this arena also attempt to report on environmental, health and safety records in plain terms, and to discuss openly any controversies in which their client may be involved. Shell, Ford Motor, and Dow Chemical are companies that have received praise for the level of candour they have shown in their social reports. Groups like Sustainability have been leaders in consulting on social reports. Other consultancies take slightly different approaches. The Corporate Citizenship Company concentrates on accurately accounting for the total contribution a business provides to the community. In the United States, a variety of large and small communications firms support reports that are public relations vehicles to signal that their client cares for its communities. Other firms work with consultants to produce environmental, health and safety reports in compliance with government regulations.

A social audit, in contrast, is more ambitious, and tries to provide an accurate account of the positive and negative impacts a company has had on its stakeholders. Like its financial counterpart, social audits are verified by credible third parties. Social audit consultants often use strict methodologies. Some, like Simon Zadek and AccountAbility, use qualitative research methods such as stakeholder attitude surveys. Others work to design an accounting model that quantifies impact and provides a social balance sheet. Certain audits are focused on specific issues; for example, PricewaterhouseCoopers and Ernst & Young have designed processes to audit the labour practices of subcontractors operating in developing countries. However, few efforts have been successful in arenas beyond the environment.

Social auditing and reporting is done much more often in Europe, and various countries outside of the United States. However, more firms within the United States are beginning to explore these approaches.

Business ethics. Ethics consultants work with companies on a range of initiatives that may be broad or narrow in scope. Large-scale initiatives may create guidelines for ethical decision-making, and operations for line managers from a variety of departments. More specific initiatives can include training and policies around ethical contract negotiations with foreign partners, and harassment and mistreatment of workers. Ethics consultants also reach into a variety of citizenship areas, including the design of codes of conduct and performance systems.

Communication. Many companies do not have enough staff to add citizenship-related activities to their agenda. There is a growing need for consultants who can temporarily serve as contract staff to implement citizenship projects. An especially common area is internal and external communications to promote citizenship activities.

Specific consultancies around major operating lines. In many respects, each function of the business possesses its own set of social responsibility issues that may require the support and guidance of consultants. As a matter of principle, every consultant advising on specific functions, systems or aspects of a business needs to be aware of the social dimension involved and to help the client to make socially responsible choices and decisions, or to direct the client to an appropriate specialist competent in such questions (see section 23.5).

23.4 A strategic approach to corporate responsibility

To assist clients to achieve excellence in corporate responsibility, consultants should possess expertise in strategic management and organizational change processes. For an approach to be successful, it must be integrated into the overall business and operational strategy. If corporate citizenship practices are fundamental to all business operations, it is less likely that specific initiatives will be discontinued, or will be removed from the day-to-day concerns of decision-makers and managers. Consultants can serve their clients by helping them formulate and implement a corporate citizenship strategy, develop their codes, strengthen their stakeholder involvement, measure performance, and train/coach their senior executives and middle managers in leadership and management. Clients can then use consultants to provide advice and support on the more specialized and technical aspects of social responsibility, such as environmental remediation, human rights practices, supply chain management or community involvement.

The elements of a strategic management approach to corporate citizenship are captured in a framework developed by Sandra Waddock and Charles Bodwell at the ILO and called "total responsibility management" (TRM):

> TRM approaches can potentially provide a means for integrating external demands and pressures for responsible practice, calls for accountability and transparency, the proliferation of codes of conduct, managing supply chains responsibly and sustainably, and stakeholder engagement into a single approach for responsibility practices within the firm.[9]

The TRM approach builds on well-known performance management systems such as total quality management. Figure 23.1 illustrates the three main elements or levels that make up the emerging TRM approach: (1) vision-setting and leadership systems, (2) integration of responsibility into strategies and practices, and (3) assessment, improvement and learning systems. The logic of the system is similar to that of strategic management processes used for any function of the business. The difference is in the details of its implementation. To use a TRM approach, consultants must understand the social context in which their client operates. The discussion below details how consultants can support their clients through each level of the framework, and provides guidance on the particular skills and processes consultants should have ready in their toolkit.

Level 1 – Vision-setting and leadership systems

At this level, consultants typically work with top management to define a strategic agenda for corporate citizenship and to drive a change process from the top down. In particular, consultants should assist their clients in implementing the following steps:

- **Defining the integration between traditional business strategy and corporate citizenship.** This process should clarify and express a corporate citizenship business model that describes the interdependence between the company's social role and responsibility and its business success. This definition will, for example, provide the underpinnings to help decision-makers to understand the elements of the triple bottom line, and how they can reinforce one another. Defining the link between conventional business strategy and the social role of business is essential for ensuring the long-term sustainability of corporate citizenship processes.
- **Identifying priorities for corporate citizenship.** After defining the integration of business and citizenship strategies, decision-makers need to identify strategic priorities that will drive resource allocation and management systems dedicated to addressing specific issues such as labour practices, supply chain management, environment, community and others. This process may involve selecting one or more of the multilateral codes of conduct (such as those listed in box 23.1) to endorse and implement.
- **Leadership roles and commitment to strategic goals.** The consultant should work with senior executives to define specific strategic goals, corporate policies and measurable objectives for their corporate citizenship strategy. In practice, these goals should reflect an intersection of business outcomes and social/environmental outcomes. Consultants should then work with senior managers to define their specific roles in driving and communicating the strategy.
- **Committing to core citizenship processes.** As noted earlier, corporate citizenship management frameworks commonly emphasize stakeholder engagement, transparency, social reporting, and measurement. Many of these tactics are unfamiliar to corporate managers. They represent new ways

Figure 23.1 The total responsibility management system

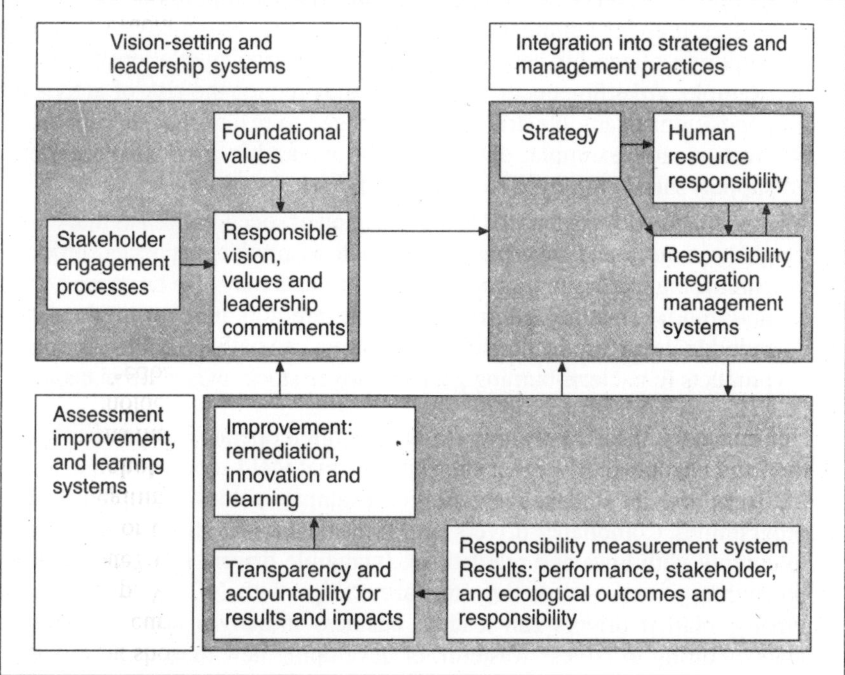

Source: S. Waddock, C. Bodwell and S. Graves: "Responsibility: the new business imperative", in *Academy of Management Executive*, May 2002 (forthcoming).

of doing business, and may conflict with conventional policies related to secrecy, financial reporting, and tightly controlled communications practices. Consultants should work to underscore that these tactics will be necessary to support strategic goals, and to secure the commitment of senior executives to support and lead the processes.

Succeeding at this first level of an intervention is not easy. It requires the consultant to mix science and art in defining an integrative corporate citizenship strategy that senior executives can comprehend, support and lead. Consultants need to come prepared with a toolkit of knowledge and methods that support strategy formulation.

Identifying key motivating drivers for corporate citizenship. It is vital for consultants to understand the factors that motivate corporate citizenship within a given organization, and to build the consciousness of key managers around these motivating drivers:[10]

- *Values:* are based on morals, and a desire to "give back" to society.
- *Compliance:* government regulations and grassroots activists create pressures for compliance. This leads to corporate policies and strategies that respond to legislation, criticism, inspection, pressure groups, etc.

- *Intangibles:* intangible factors include reputation, brand and relationships. Intangible drivers often lead to responses that attempt to minimize the risks of pressures for compliance and create savings for the business. Proactive corporate citizenship becomes a tool to create trusting relationships with, for example, governments or NGOs, and thus reduce the risk of activism and opposition. Intangible drivers can also lead to responses that support value creation. For example, developing the intangible asset of reputation can support sales and employee recruitment and retention.
- *Market:* market drivers lead to the inclusion of social, as well as market-based goals in projects and investments, such as product launches, production, purchasing, or employee training. The projects may also be carried out with non-traditional stakeholders. Examples are job training of low-income individuals, clean production technologies, socially responsible consumer products (e.g. clean-burning gas), employee stock ownership plans, etc.

Unfortunately, these motivating drivers often operate independently of one another, and encourage divergent strategies that yield suboptimal outcomes for the business and its stakeholders. For example, values may lead to charity programmes. Compliance drivers may guide the business to do the least possible to comply with laws and regulations. Intangible drivers may lead to strategic philanthropy, cause-marketing, or partnerships with NGOs and government. Finally, market drivers can lead to business initiatives such as redesigning manufacturing to be less wasteful, or developing new markets in low-income areas. Most companies keep these strategies separate, and fail to optimize the resources they invest in corporate citizenship.

Understanding and applying the business case. As discussed earlier, leading models of corporate social responsibility contend that there is no contradiction between social responsibility and profitability. In fact, the argument goes, social responsibility increasingly performs a high-value support role for the bottom line. Research supports the claim that corporate citizenship adds value to traditional business goals, such as consumer attraction and retention, employee recruitment and retention, worker productivity and overall financial performance. In addition, it supports such considerations as innovation, reputation and "licence to operate".

Consultants must first present the business case and help clients to understand how their own business and particular line functions will benefit from corporate citizenship. Consultants must also be prepared to help clients to build creative strategies that use citizenship approaches to meet societal obligations while generating returns on investments. To succeed, citizenship consultants need a broader perspective than most traditional management consultants.

Organizational diagnosis. There are two dimensions of organizational diagnosis – the marketplace and society. The marketplace is the province of traditional management consultants, but it is essential that corporate citizenship consultants possess an understanding of their client's business fundamentals. There are two reasons for this. First, consultants need to speak their client's language. Managers who are sceptical about corporate citizenship may perceive the consultant as an infiltrator representing forces that are (in the extreme) conspiring to shut down operations. Second, consultants need to be able to translate and integrate. Managers often have difficulty in conceptually linking their day-to-day responsibilities with the requirements of corporate citizenship. Consultants can provide a valuable service by helping to build this conceptual bridge between the fundamentals of business and citizenship.

The second dimension of organizational diagnosis is an understanding of the relationship between the business and society, which is where the majority of citizenship concerns are played out. Depending on the project, the consultant may need technical expertise, such as in environmental analysis. However, the consultant should also possess broader, strategic knowledge, including how to diagnose current practice and performance around key dimensions of citizenship. Where is the company's performance effective and where is it inadequate? Consultants will do well to use frameworks such as the Global Compact or the OECD Guidelines, which can help them to make judgements and to legitimize conclusions.

Stakeholder identification. The dynamics of corporate citizenship operations manifest themselves through the interplay between a company and its stakeholders. The level of stakeholder satisfaction represents the principal form of feedback on the strengths and weaknesses of corporate management. It is therefore essential for corporations to identify and engage with key stakeholders. However, transnational organizations face a vast array of stakeholders. The challenge for consultants and their clients is to identify the key stakeholder groups – and their representatives – that should be part of the corporate responsibility strategy. One pitfall to avoid is assigning the main role to stakeholders who appear to be most threatening and behave most aggressively. Consultants should possess expertise in stakeholder analysis, mapping and relationship-building.

Issues identification and environmental scanning. The social, cultural, institutional, legal, supervisory and political environment for corporate citizenship is crucial. Consultants need to help their clients assess how current corporate operations intersect with the environment to create either vulnerabilities or opportunities for the client's relationship and behaviour towards key stakeholders. Strategic information is needed that helps a company to craft policies and programmatic responses. The issues identification and scanning process should also help a company select its top strategic priorities. A company in a service industry, for example, may have few if any direct concerns regarding supply chain management and sourcing. However, it may have significant concerns regarding the quality of education systems as it struggles to find, recruit and retain adequately skilled employees.

Strategy formulation. The consultant should work with the client to take the outcomes of the above processes and formulate a strategic plan that is focused and clear. The plan should help managers demarcate a path between goals and concrete projects, owners, roles, measures and timelines. In citizenship consulting, a strategic plan serves as the client's touchstone. It not only specifies purpose and activities it helps managers answer fundamental questions regarding the relevance of corporate citizenship, its purpose, and fit within the organization.

Level 2 – Integration of responsibility into strategy and practices

At this level, consultants can work with both senior executives and mid-level line managers. It is at this point that the company begins to implement its strategy – designing processes, systems, practices and programmes based on the new goals and priorities. Consultants may assist their clients in the following steps:

- **Creating management performance systems.** To implement a corporate citizenship strategy successfully, goals and action plans have to be transformed into an operational agenda and reflected in performance contracts of business lines, departments and managers.
- **Redesigning practices and creating programmes.** The company will need to design new practices and systems to support the goals of corporate citizenship. If, for instance, a goal is to avoid suppliers that violate the human rights of their employees, then the company will need to create specific policies, strategies, management systems, monitoring mechanisms and reporting systems. Alternatively, if the company's goal is to reduce greenhouse emissions, it will need to modify its production model. Redesigning corporate practices and policies will typically require specialized expertise.
- **Process implementation.** At this level, the company will form and implement systems to engage stakeholders, monitor issues, and develop mechanisms to increase transparency. These processes should not be formed and managed in isolation, but integrated across business lines, and used as tools both to implement strategy and to create feedback mechanisms to reformulate the strategy.

At this level of intervention, the consultants' toolkit needs to expand to include content expertise for specific issues as well as knowledge of organizational behaviour, change and strategy. Toolkit elements include the following:

Organizational change. Consultants will often find that there is much within the client organization that resists the implementation of corporate citizenship strategy, structures and programmes. Resistance (see also Chapter 4) may be intentional or unintentional. In either case, the challenge it presents to consulting initiatives is formidable. Consultants need to possess skills in change management and strategic planning. It is advisable for consultants to work only with organizations in which senior executives have demonstrated their commitment, and it is often useful to solidify this commitment by making the point of contact a senior-level manager. When this is not possible, it is important to use formal engagements to involve senior executives throughout the process. If the initiative is being driven from the bottom (or middle) upwards, rather than top-down, it is important for the consultant to assess realistically what can be achieved. A consultant can provide a valuable service by coaching middle managers on leadership and change initiatives, and by guiding the client through the change process. Consultants are also advised to insist on a participatory methodology that involves a variety of managers from important departments. They should work with key client contacts to develop a map of key stakeholders within the organization who should play an active and engaged role in the project.

Management support and coaching. A significant barrier to the change process is lack of expertise, experience and knowledge among managers on the social role and responsibility of the business. Consultants can design and implement training programmes that are tied into corporate strategy, and that support the management of corporate citizenship initiatives.

Technical and policy expertise. Given the complex organizational dynamics of corporate citizenship, it is easy to overlook that consulting initiatives require at least a modest level of technical and content-specific knowledge. Corporate citizenship engages the business in an array of policy issues and concerns that it has probably previously ignored. Clients will look to consultants to provide guidance and knowledge in these areas. The challenge for consultants is to help the business understand how it can engage in social issues effectively, while preserving its core business mission and functions.

Level 3 – Assessment, improvement and learning systems

At this level, consultants will work with both senior executives and line managers, and provide the company and its stakeholders with feedback about performance, direction for improvement, and the information needed to revise and improve the corporate citizenship strategy.

Measurement systems. These include systems that measure the impact of the strategy for the business and its stakeholders, as well as systems to determine whether the operations are managed effectively and efficiently. Measurement of corporate citizenship is at an early stage of evolution. At this level, consultants will need to bring expertise, knowledge and creativity to the process of creating measurement systems.

Reporting, monitoring and verification systems. Related to measurement, these systems function as the principal vehicle for increasing corporate transparency and accountability to stakeholders. These systems are also at an early stage of development. Consultants will need expertise in designing effective reporting, monitoring and verification systems.

Improvement and innovation. By tracking and measuring impacts and performance, consultants can work with clients to learn from measurement and reporting systems, and help define plans to improve performance, drive innovative practices, and enhance the existing strategy.

Communication. Clients need help to spread information about corporate citizenship to senior executives, their peers, employees and external stakeholders. Each audience will require different messages and different communication vehicles. Understanding and implementing communication approaches is therefore a critical dimension of a consultant's skill set.

23.5 Consulting in specific functions and areas of business

In the previous two sections, we have viewed consulting in corporate responsibility in its totality, emphasizing its strategic and general management nature and the need to treat it as a core dimension of the business. We have dwelt on these questions because of their relative novelty and importance to companies and consultants that want to make a good start. Indeed, a fragmented and haphazard approach, merely reacting to external influences and requirements as they occur, is not one that we recommend. It is in the interest of every business to have an overall view of all its activities and relationships where questions concerning social responsibility may arise, a fair assessment of both its economic and social performance, a framework for dealing with these questions, and a basic policy to which decision-makers can refer in handling particular issues.

In practice, however, most questions of ethics and responsible behaviour are addressed in connection with specific decisions. For example, company policy may well adhere to the principle of ethical advertising in general terms, but applying that principle consistently requires considerable understanding of consumer psychology (including child psychology, cultural sensitivities, etc.) in addition to the knowledge of general corporate policies and ethical advertising. There are various elements and issues of ethics and social responsibility in product liability and quality, intellectual property, productivity, supplier selection, competition practice, recruitment and staffing, personnel management, staff education and training, management of employee pension funds, safety and health protection – indeed in virtually everything that a business does or chooses not to do.

There is, however, a fundamental implication for consultants. Corporate responsibility generalists will probably focus on broader, interdisciplinary and strategic issues, especially when companies start taking their social responsibilities seriously and need assistance with general orientation, concepts, assessment, relationships, strategies and policies. Conversely, in specific technical fields and functions, there is likely to be little scope for these generalist approaches. Some consultants may find a niche for themselves by specializing, for example, in advice on ethical advertising. However, all consultants intervening in special fields and areas of business should be aware of the general framework and principles of corporate responsibility, and versed in the social and ethical aspects of their special fields of intervention. The same applies to managers. This is the only way to implement corporate citizenship company-wide, beyond a simple declaration of general business principles.

23.6 Future perspectives

Currently, there is a clear trend to a continued "bull market" for corporate social responsibility and citizenship. Protests against globalization, the prominence of international economic and business forums, and the threat of global catastrophes such as HIV/AIDS or the greenhouse effect have created new expectations for the role and performance of business that are unlikely to disappear. The social performance of manufacturing and service companies will increasingly affect their brands. "The next big thing in brands is social responsibility. Brands are becoming an effective weapon for holding even the largest global corporations to account."[11]

Consultants are uniquely positioned to make an impact in this arena. Many of the most interesting developments, research and thinking come from consultants or organizations that integrate theory and practice. At the same time, the competitive landscape of consultants poses risks for managers. There is anecdotal evidence of an apparent proliferation of consultancies, some of which appear to be selling a new conception of the wheel. Corporate citizenship is an immature field, and consultants therefore have a unique opportunity to come up with new approaches and services, and to influence organizational development in profound ways, shaping strategies and structures and pointing the way ahead for the years to come. With this potential, there are no clear moorings. Managers who follow a strategy of buying well-known brand names may find a safe choice but may also find solutions that are disappointing.

At its core, the social role, impact and responsibility of business is about an expanded vision of business performance. In this respect we have the experience of other concepts and movements to draw upon. Quality, at one point, seemed alien and impossible to measure. Environmental management once seemed out of place, but has made great strides. Human resource and human capital development used to seem foreign but has become fundamental. Corporate social responsibility looms on the horizon as one of the next transformative management movements. Consultants have a unique opportunity to drive and shape the agenda.

---

[1] "The core element of corporate responsibility concerns business activity itself – the function of business in society is to yield adequate returns to owners of capital by identifying and developing promising investment opportunities and, in the process, to provide jobs and to produce goods and services that consumers want to buy. However, corporate responsibility goes beyond the core function of conducting business." (OECD Web site, www.oecd.org//daf/investment/corporate-responsibility/faq.htm, visited on 4 Apr. 2002.)

[2] Formerly the Valdez Principles (CEREs stands for "Coalition of Environmentally Responsible Economies").

[3] OECD Web site (op. cit.), and OECD: *Corporate responsibility: Private initiatives and public goals* (Paris, OECD, 2001).

[4] See www.ilo.org, visited on 4 Apr. 2002.

[5] See www.globalreporting.org, visited on 4 Apr. 2002.

[6] OECD Web site (op. cit.).

[7] See www.bc.edu/bc-org/avp/csom/ccc/index.html, visited on 4 Apr. 2002.

[8] See www.bsr.org, visited on 4 Apr. 2002.

[9] S. Waddock and C. Bodwell: *From TQM to TRM: The emerging evolution of total responsibility management approaches* (Geneva, ILO, 2001).

[10] The discussion on motivating drivers and stages of development is from: S. Rochlin and J. Boguslaw: *Integrating business and development: Winning management strategies* (Boston, MA, The Boston College, 2001).

[11] *The Economist*, 8 Sep. 2001, p. 30 (quoting a corporate identity consultant Wally Olins).

CONSULTING IN SMALL-BUSINESS MANAGEMENT AND DEVELOPMENT 24

The use of consultants by small enterprises is now an established trend in business. As activities relating to the conduct of business become more complex, the need for outside assistance usually increases. Managers of small-scale enterprises who want to remain competitive need to consider using consultants as they would use other support services, such as bankers, lawyers, accountants and trade associations.

Consultants can play an important role in economic development by assisting people to set up small enterprises. For new entrepreneurs, the start-up phase is the most difficult; consequently, more and more consultants focus on this important aspect of enterprise development. Consultants and small-business development centres often arrange training for entrepreneurs who intend to initiate new enterprises.

Existing small enterprises use consultants mainly to solve specific operational problems. The duration of the consultancy will depend on the specific problem but most consultancies can be accomplished within a few months. Longer consultancies may be required if the problem concerns expanding business operations. Expansion takes time and the consultant may be involved periodically for one or two years.

Each stage of business establishment and growth brings new challenges and opportunities for the small-scale entrepreneur. New entrepreneurs have to be prepared for the additional demands that the business will make on their time, and to balance their working time with time for their family and for social pursuits. This can be particularly difficult for women entrepreneurs, as they often have responsibility for child care and household management.

Within economic policies pursuing structural adjustment, trade liberalization and privatization, the small-enterprise sector is now recognized as the key area to supply job opportunities and to provide goods and services. As a result, there has been an upsurge in consulting assignments to meet these new demands. This, in turn, has introduced a new dimension to the economic and social development field, i.e. the development of resource personnel to advise governments and non-governmental agencies in promoting small-enterprise development. Essentially, these new forms of consulting service address the critical areas of policy formulation and implementation: developing strategies; designing, implementing and evaluating programmes; managing development projects; and catering for the needs of specific target groups, such as women entrepreneurs, young entrepreneurs, and entrepreneurs with disability.

24.1 Characteristics of small enterprises

Definition of a small enterprise

The definition of a small enterprise tends to vary according to the nature of its activities, the purpose of the definition, and the level of development where the enterprise is located. The criteria for describing an enterprise as "small" might be the number of employees, the money value of sales, capital investment, maximum energy requirements, or various combinations of these and other factors. As the ILO suggests,[1] "it is up to each country to formulate its own definitions for micro, small and medium-sized enterprises". In most discussions and writings on the subject by management consultants, a small enterprise is taken as one in which the administrative and operational management is in the hands of one or two people, who also make the important decisions in the enterprise. Such an operational definition has been found to include more than 85 per cent of all small enterprises no matter how defined.

The consultant should be aware of a number of factors that usually distinguish the small from the larger enterprise. First, the small enterprise is primarily financed from personal or family savings with limited recourse to outside finance during the formative stages. The assistance of the family, in terms of both finance and moral support, plays a vital role in most small enterprises. Second, the manager has close personal contact with the whole workplace; and, third, the enterprise usually operates in a limited geographical area. These "smallness" factors greatly influence the consultative process.

The small enterprise possesses distinct advantages, including the ability to fill limited demands in specialized markets; a propensity for labour intensity and low-to-medium-skill work; and the flexibility to adapt rapidly to changing demands and conditions. Managerially speaking, there is an advantage in having a personal involvement in dealings which goes beyond price, product and delivery dates. Owner–managers are usually more highly motivated than salaried managers – they work longer and harder, and provide greater motivation to workers by personal example.

A simple organizational structure means more direct and less complicated lines of communication inside and outside the business. The smallness of the firm assists in identifying and developing the capabilities of workers more quickly than in larger firms.

The small enterprise can also experiment with or enter new markets without attracting unwanted attention from large firms. It can cater for extremes in the market – either the right- or left-hand tails of the distribution curve – since mass marketing for the average consumer is usually taken care of by big business. Similarly, the smaller firm can more quickly exploit changing market patterns and the "floating" consumer who drifts in the marketplace.

Special problems of small enterprises

Problems of small enterprises may be general or specific. Problems of a general nature involve legal aspects of business, access to credit and raw materials, access to markets, lack of appropriate technical and managerial assistance, and weakness in identifying or grasping new business opportunities.

Management consultants should be aware of problems at the level of the enterprise, as well as at the level of the individual entrepreneur. These may appear more formidable to the manager of a small enterprise than problems in a large corporation might appear to its chairperson. The following list demonstrates the range of difficulties that may be encountered:

- Whereas large, well-organized enterprises can usually afford both good line-management and specialist staff, the person managing the small enterprise is relatively isolated, and has to deal with policy, administration and operational problems simultaneously whatever his or her personal biases and limitations.
- Small-enterprise managers often operate with inadequate or, at best, minimum quantitative data. To save on operating costs, they are likely to dispense with information systems, a weakness that can become glaringly apparent when the enterprise starts to grow.
- Some small enterprises may pay only minimum wages, have few fringe benefits, and offer low job security and few promotional opportunities, and may therefore have difficulties recruiting high-calibre employees.
- Professional investors are seldom attracted to the new small enterprise (although "business angels" are an increasingly popular source of financial partners for small firms), and managers are severely limited in their ability to raise initial capital. This problem is compounded when, as is very often the case, an enterprise runs into growth problems, or experiences operating difficulties, and the manager attempts to raise additional finance in order to cope.
- Because of the problem of limited reserves, coupled with low capacity to borrow, the small enterprise is particularly vulnerable to economic downturn and recession.
- Although ability to change and adapt rapidly is regarded as a natural strength of a small enterprise, this quality may be nullified when an opportunity requiring rapid change suddenly appears. The manager may be too occupied with ongoing operational problems to be able to think clearly about the future of the business.

- The hand-to-mouth financial existence of the enterprise does not allow many opportunities for staff training and development, with consequent loss in realizing the full potential of the human resources within the enterprise.
- High productivity is difficult to achieve since the small enterprise does not enjoy the low costs of the large firm, which can, for example, buy at a discount, achieve economies of scale, call on its sophisticated marketing and distribution system, and engage its own research and development and systems design teams.
- The small firm is usually limited to one or a few products or services, with the result that in times of trouble it cannot diversify activities as can large-scale enterprises.
- The manager is often not able to understand and interpret government regulations, actions, concessions, and so on, to best advantage.

The small enterprise is a relatively fragile structure with limited resources to overcome its problems. Even minor problems can be life-threatening to the enterprise. In one country it was estimated that the failure rate for small enterprises within the first two years of operation was as high as 50 per cent.

Reluctance to use consultants

Many small-enterprise managers are reluctant to use outside consultants for the following reasons:

- They believe that only large enterprises can afford the consulting fees charged.
- In many instances, consultants will not have practical experience in the type of business needing assistance.
- Managers are reluctant to provide outsiders with facts and figures relating to the business.
- Identification of a competent consultant is difficult and time-consuming, because most managers have little previous contact with consultants.
- In developing countries, there is often a shortage of female consultants with whom female entrepreneurs may feel more comfortable sharing their problems.
- Using a consultant may be viewed by the manager as an admission of lack of competence.

Notwithstanding these doubts and fears, many small-business managers need to talk to an attentive and helpful listener about their concerns and worries. John Harvey-Jones described his experience in the following terms:

> I had not fully realized how lonely the life of someone running a small business can be. Of course every businessman has relationships with his customers, his suppliers, his bank manager, and so on. He also knows a number of his competitors. But remarkably few people running small businesses have any

> friend or confidant on whom they can test their ideas, or with whom they can talk openly about their business, its opportunities and its threats, and their feelings about the business. It seems to me that business people badly need a business equivalent of that excellent organization, The Samaritans. In many cases just talking about the way a business is running brings a feeling of support and a strengthening of conviction, which is badly needed when you feel alone and threatened by immense external forces.[2]

To overcome the preconceptions of owner-managers, consultants need to provide information and data that will indicate the value of their services, if possible referring specifically to other small companies that have used consultants. Studies have shown that most small-business owners who have used consultants have obtained the following benefits:

- an independent professional viewpoint;
- an overall company check-up and expert evaluation;
- a fresh perspective on marketing and market development;
- ideas for coping with growth;
- training for manager and staff which otherwise would not have taken place;
- help in developing a strategic approach.

24.2 The role and profile of the consultant

In dealing with small enterprises, the consultant handles the whole spectrum of management and needs to be more of a generalist than a specialist. It can be taken for granted that consultants should be professionally trained and have considerable experience in management principles as applied to small-enterprise development. Of prime importance is knowledge of the interaction of the functions of the small enterprise, since change in one function usually has immediate repercussions on others. Furthermore, it is useful for the consultant to be at least familiar with the various entrepreneurial development approaches that provide a conceptual basis for current small-enterprise development practices.

Mastery of business fundamentals is essential for a successful career in consulting with small enterprises. When assisting the manager of a small enterprise, it is important to ensure that all managerial tasks are completed, even imperfectly, rather than having 75 per cent of the tasks completed to perfection while the remaining 25 per cent are neglected. The consultant must keep in mind the total picture of the business to ensure that functions of administration and operation are harmonized and integrated. Patience and dogged perseverance are often required in encouraging the manager to complete chores ranging from accounting to staff training, while preventing him or her from concentrating solely on preferred technical activities, such as the production of goods and services.

The consultant's role is complicated by the fact that the main consulting duties lie in developing the manager and others who contribute to managing the enterprise at the same time as being expected to provide feasible practical solutions to a wide range of specific problems, for example, in finance, sales, production and purchasing. Although the subject matter is specific, it generally exceeds the limits of a particular function or technique. The consulting technique is broad, and may include assistance with implementation, where necessary, and informal training.

Routine consulting reports, as usually submitted to larger organizations, are not needed for small enterprises. Written reports should be short, simple, and kept to a minimum; often, a report is submitted only at the end of an assignment to explain what was done and why, and what is required in the future.

The consultant should also appreciate that clients are not necessarily the most educated and skilled managers available. Moreover, there are often no training facilities at hand to help remedy obvious deficiencies. Thus, rather than adopting a professional air and emphasizing his or her expertise to influence the client, the consultant should use a simpler style. Coaxing, praising and reprimanding are likely to be more effective in obtaining the results desired.

The client–manager of a small enterprise may feel a severe sense of failure if forced to use a consultant. The consultant should, therefore, be alert to the possible need to restore a client's self-esteem in addition to providing technical assistance.

Unquestionably, lack of data is a major handicap in undertaking a consulting assignment with a small enterprise. Usually the sole source of information is the manager, who is often "too busy" to be interviewed. The consultant must use ingenuity, persistence and tenacity to extract the required information.

During the past 30 years, many governments, employers' organizations, trade associations, chambers of commerce, associations of entrepreneurs or small business clubs, private companies and similar bodies have established special services and facilities for small enterprises, including:

- supply of credit (loans and guarantees);
- reduced tax rates (to enable accumulation of the capital necessary for survival and growth);
- reserved and preferential markets for goods and services (special government set-asides, offsets and subcontracts);
- industrial estates, parks or incubators;
- product design and quality control services;
- advisory services on export possibilities;
- market research and feasibility studies;
- assistance with sales and marketing, such as trade fairs, exhibitions and buyer–seller meetings:
- reduced-cost bulk purchase of raw materials.

Although he or she is probably able to obtain advice directly from technicians in charge of particular services, a manager or owner of a small enterprise may find it difficult to decide when and how to use such services. The management consultant has to advise on the whole range of services, recommending priorities and advising on acceptable costs of such services. This includes advice on where to find relevant information. In developing countries, management consultants are increasingly involved in advising local small and medium-sized enterprises on technology transfer, joint ventures with enterprises from industrialized countries, subcontracting, or franchising.

Good health, persistence and stamina are among the consultant's chief assets, together with a sensitive and supportive attitude. Small-enterprise managers have little respect for conventional working hours and, once preliminary fears are overcome, quickly learn to ask for help whenever and however they see fit. The consultant may be viewed as being similar to the family doctor – always on call – and some clients will take advantage of this.

Responsibility is also disproportionate. In most conventional consulting assignments for large organizations, there is some room for error as reports are checked by supervisors and important reports are examined by the manager of the consulting unit. However, when dealing with small enterprises, mistakes by the consultant can be fatal to the organization requesting assistance. Since such assistance tends to be direct and immediate, the consultant has limited time to check ideas and proposals with colleagues. Paraphrasing Reinhold Niebuhr's famous prayer, the Asian Productivity Organization has set out the role of the small-enterprise consultant in the form of a "consultant's prayer":

God grant me
COURAGE to change what I can,
PATIENCE to accept what can't be changed, and
WISDOM to know the difference.

The consultant usually works under extreme pressure since assistance is often not sought until a crisis has developed and the manager is unable to resolve the problem. By employing a judicious blend of resource and process forms of consulting, the consultant is expected to do whatever is necessary to assist the manager. In the final analysis, it must be remembered that the consultant's job is to consult and not to manage. If consultancy advice is not accepted or followed by management, the consultant should be guided by the saying "you can lead a horse to water, but you can't make it drink". Similarly, the consultant should not be held responsible for the failure of a small firm, nor should the consultant claim responsibility for its success. The consultant should concentrate on the success of the assignment, and "ownership" of the enterprise and its successes and failures should reside with the owner.

24.3 Consulting assignments in the life-cycle of an enterprise

The review in previous chapters of management situations and problems dealt with by consultants includes a number of concepts and experiences relevant to consulting in a small enterprise. However, certain situations are specific to small enterprises.

Small-enterprise consultants need to change as business activity changes. They must be aware of information and how to gain access to it. It is essential for consultants to understand the uses of software packages and computers in relation to small-enterprise operations, especially how to convert computer print-outs into useful information for the small-enterprise manager. Emerging areas of concern for small enterprises lie in the fields of information and communications technologies, the impact of globalization and World Trade Organization agreements on small enterprises (and on specific sectors such as textiles), and industrial relations in countries where workers' associations and trade unions are making their claims heard and felt.

Communication skills are becoming increasingly important for consultants and may eventually overshadow even technical knowledge and other skills. Consultants need to use their communication skills to "pull out" problems and to "plug in" solutions. The consultant must have a good network of highly skilled technicians who can assist with specific problems, such as in marketing, technology or computer applications. Once a solution is determined, the consultant has to use his or her communication skills to convince the manager of the benefits of implementing the solution.

The small-enterprise owner is faced with a host of problems and the consultant should be prepared to meet the various needs. The consultant may be considered a "one-stop shop" for all necessary assistance. The stages outlined below serve to illustrate the range of problems faced by consultants when dealing with a manager whose enterprise is passing through a typical life-cycle.

Stage 1: The very beginning

Biographical evidence suggests that successful small-enterprise owners and managers commonly possess particular qualities. They are often the first-born of a family and have had to assume a more than average amount of responsibility at an early stage in life. In many cases they are the offspring of self-employed persons, but are not necessarily in the same occupational grouping, trade or service. Such people have had a sound but not necessarily extended education and, as a rule, more than five years' experience of working as employees.

As regards personality, they are inclined to be optimistic and moderate risk-takers (as opposed to gamblers or non-risk-takers); control over their own destiny rather than just making money is a key motivating factor in their life. Such people are usually married, but with minimum distractions caused by family life – there is usually an understanding spouse who appreciates the demands made on the marriage partner. Family support can count for a lot in the successful running of an enterprise; where there is family opposition, the role of the entrepreneur can be a lonely and difficult one.

A key characteristic is that successful entrepreneurs are mentally and physically very active. They are usually well organized and manage time efficiently. Success may result not so much from quality, but from the quantity of schemes prepared and developed. In short, the greater the effort, the greater the chances of success.

When dealing with a beginner, the consultant should take stock of the client's background, interests, and family situation and support, to judge whether the client is a probable or a possible entrepreneur, and develop the assignment accordingly. The project should be closely examined, taking into account the strengths and weaknesses commonly found in small enterprises, and the strengths and weaknesses of the individual entrepreneur. A checklist of items to be reviewed should be worked out.

Stage 2: Starting up

Assuming that the client wishes to launch a new enterprise, the consultant should, after reviewing and discussing the proposal, prepare for at least three possibilities and develop appropriate contingency plans:

(1) What is the best that might happen (the "blue skies" approach)?
(2) What is likely to happen (the basis for the "business plan")?
(3) What is the worst that can happen (realistically assess the "downside risk")?

The consultant should talk freely with the client about the first two possibilities, which are usually "creative" problems, whereas the third, which is a "corrective" problem, should be reserved for the consultant's own counsel, because (a) the client is unlikely to listen to, or agree with, the "worst possible" alternative, and (b) encouragement rather than discouragement should help attain the full potential of the proposal. The consultant must, however, draw up detailed contingency plans for all three alternatives if for no other reason than to make allowances for "Murphy's law" ("If anything can possibly go wrong, it will!").

A good small-enterprise manager can usually generate many ideas very rapidly. The consultant should encourage this and assist the client to obtain and record relevant quantitative data about these ideas for two reasons: first, to assist in making a logical choice between alternatives; and second, to use as supporting evidence should the manager experience uncomfortable afterthoughts about a scheme once started.

Mistakes will be made, particularly in the early stages – they are part of the general learning process. The consultant's task is to minimize the errors made by the manager in these stages. It is, however, better to ensure that an ineffective scheme never takes off than to attempt to salvage an impossible project at a later date, which gives rise to the consulting maxim: "Giving birth is a lot easier than resurrection." If necessary, allow the proposal to lapse and encourage the client to try afresh when more evidence and support are available. If it is decided to go ahead with the enterprise, full commitment should be encouraged. Effective decision-making and prompt action are vital; there is little room for compromise or error in a new enterprise.

From a functional point of view the consultant should encourage clients to use the services of some specialists from the outset if they can be afforded because, if the enterprise grows, the specialists will be familiar with its history, practice and results, and thus able to assist in a meaningful way. The specialists might include:

- a legal firm (of good repute and the best that can be afforded);
- an accountant (possessing the same qualities as the legal firm);
- a banker (a person, not an institution, so that rapport and trust are established at a personal level);
- an insurance agent (similar qualities as the banker);
- a marketing representative, adviser or market researcher (this clearly depends on the type of enterprise; where the enterprise is not intrinsically marketing-oriented, it is often sound practice to make links with experts or agents during the formative stages);
- an IT consultant (to advise on suitable applications and pitfalls to avoid, the selection of hardware, outsourcing and training).

Small-enterprise consultants require a wide range of functional expertise, with, perhaps most importantly, emphasis on financial matters. The finance field presents problems both in attracting formation capital and in controlling expenses and income; consultants not well versed in these fields are a danger to clients and cannot claim professional competence in the true sense of the term.

It is often only by thorough expert financial appraisal that the consultant is able to undertake the necessary though unpleasant task of recommending discontinuation of an enterprise rather than encouraging a holding operation, which will eventually lead to insuperable problems for all involved.

This fear of failure deserves greater emphasis in the start-up stages of the enterprise than may seem warranted. Often the savings of family and friends are used to finance the capital requirements of the new enterprise simply because no one else will lend the money. This alone may suggest that the scheme is probably not particularly sound. If no financing agency considers a proposal worth while (and they take into account an allowance for failure), why should a consultant recommend that family savings be jeopardized in a risky undertaking? There should always be proprietor equity in a venture, but not simply because no one else is prepared to support it. When preparing the third (worst-of-all) contingency plan, if project failure is likely to cause undue hardships the consultant is professionally obliged to dissuade the client from undertaking the venture.

During the start-up phase the consultant might reflect on the following checklist, which is based on a considerable number of studies designed to pinpoint potential problem areas in small enterprises. In order of importance for diagnosing trouble areas the consultant should look for deficiencies classified as the seven "M"s:

- managerial (lack of experience);
- monetary (lack of capital, poor cost control);
- material (poor location, too much stock);
- machines (excessive purchase of fixed assets);
- marketing (inappropriate products for insufficient markets);
- mental (lack of planning for expansion);
- motivation (wrong attitudes to work and responsibility).

Stage 3: Getting bigger

Having negotiated stages 1 and 2, the consultant may be faced with a brand new set of events which emerge as the enterprise matures and the consulting assignment takes on a progressive look. This is the time to examine thoroughly the weaknesses to be overcome, opportunities to develop further, and alternative resource allocations to help the enterprise benefit from the most favourable opportunities. When assisting the manager to allocate resources, the consultant may care to refer to the "four to one principle", which can be set up as a rule of thumb:

- 80 per cent of sales come from 20 per cent of customers;
- 80 per cent of movements result from 20 per cent of stocks;
- 80 per cent of disciplinary problems are caused by 20 per cent of staff;
- 80 per cent of the sales are generated by 20 per cent of salespeople; and so on.

The consultant should encourage the manager to "play percentages" and concentrate on critical areas. During this maturation phase the manager, submerged in day-to-day operational problems, is usually not able to pay attention to the long- or medium-term planning essential for continued growth and survival. Consultants can assist by encouraging the manager to look to the future. For example, they can prepare current organization charts and job descriptions and compare these with how they should look in five to ten years, showing likely changes. New developments usually require a little inspiration, considerable incubation, and a great deal of perspiration. Therefore, the consultant should make sure that the manager plans appropriate resources and allocates the time required for future growth and development.

A notable feature of successful managers is that they are exceptionally well organized. This should be encouraged as part of the management development process by introducing systems, encouraging managers to read on management subjects, and insisting on forecasts, budgets and controls. Probably during this maturation phase an accountant (financial controller) post should be established.

Marketing will also become increasingly important as the business develops and grows. The entrepreneur should be encouraged to develop a customer orientation, recognize the importance of market research, and be able to accept customer complaints as providing valuable suggestions for improvement and reducing problem areas.

The consultant will have to draw on his or her knowledge of comparable enterprises to judge the productivity of the client. Access to a range of interfirm comparisons, in the form of input/output and productivity ratios, is an invaluable asset, especially if corrective measures become necessary. The consultant must know where such information can be obtained.

This third stage can lead to a consolidation stage where an optimal level of growth has been achieved, and further expansion could be perceived as threatening to the entrepreneur. As the business continues "getting bigger", inevitably the enterprise and the entrepreneur are getting older. Consultants have a vital role to play in assisting entrepreneurs to develop succession plans, involving their interested and dynamic daughters and sons in the future development of the enterprise.

Stage 4: Exit from the enterprise

Eventually the enterprise may grow to a size where it can no longer be considered small, and issues pertaining to growth, finance, corporate structure, delegation and the like will arise. The small-enterprise consultant should then judiciously refer the manager to specialists capable of assisting in the new situation. Alternatively, the manager may decide to forego the routine running of the enterprise and start something new, revert to becoming an employee, or retire. At that point, the enterprise must be disposed of.

Assessing the monetary value of an enterprise is usually done in one of three ways:

(1) *liquidation or forced sale value*, where the enterprise is put up for auction and sold to the highest bidder (if any);

(2) *book value*, where items are assessed at cost less depreciation and sold piecemeal to selected markets;

(3) *market value*, where the entity is sold as a going concern and items such as goodwill are included in the price.

Varying conditions (such as the death of the owner) may determine which of these assessment methods will be used. Generally speaking, the market value provides the best return to the seller.

The consultant is obliged to assist the client to obtain the best possible deal. Nevertheless, the consultant should keep in mind that the best sales are those involving a willing seller and a willing buyer. To arrive at this happy situation the consultant should encourage the seller to "leave something in it" for the new owner. By doing so the chances of a sale are enhanced, time is often saved and the possibility of recrimination is reduced. Trying to obtain the greatest possible amount of money from the potential new owner may go into the realm of diminishing returns.

Another end-of-the-road situation occurs when the manager is succeeded by a family member or someone else. With small enterprises, except in areas of obvious equality and responsibility such as a partnership of doctors or lawyers, shared management seldom succeeds. For purposes of direction, control and responsibility it is usually better to have one identified manager than to split authority between, say, two siblings. If it can be arranged, family succession in an enterprise should follow only after the offspring have been exposed to working in outside situations, otherwise managerial inbreeding is likely to occur.

24.4 Areas of special concern

Counselling the start-up entrepreneur

We examined earlier (section 3.7) the relationship between counselling and consulting. The counsellor works mainly with and for individual clients, rather than for an organization. The counselling relationship is, and should be, a personal and intense one, and is likely to involve areas far beyond the particular management issues that led to the assignment.

The decision to start a new business can be one of the most important steps that any woman or man ever takes, and involves far more than straightforward business and management issues. It is extremely important that the client alone makes the final decision. Counselling should empower people to take fundamental decisions of this sort for themselves rather than simply advising them what to do.

Many people launching their own business for the first time do so because they have been jolted out of their normal career path by a shock, such as redundancy, or by a personal "determining event", such as bereavement, divorce or a forced move to an unfamiliar country. Such an experience can marginalize the person, and may encourage him or her to look beyond the ordinary and expected courses of action to new and unfamiliar fields, such as starting a new business. People in this position are often unsure, lack self-confidence and need support but, because they are marginalized, they may not have access to friends and family who would normally help on such occasions. The professional counsellor can thus fill an important gap.

Counselling usually goes beyond business issues. An entrepreneur starting a new business has to involve the whole family, since lifestyles and financial security are almost certainly going to change and some members of the family may also have to work in the business. Some marriages break up, while others are strengthened and enriched by the experience of starting a business. A counsellor has to ensure that would-be entrepreneurs think through all the implications.

The counsellor should neither encourage nor discourage clients, but should help them to look at the situation from every angle and to make their own decisions. Some people may be overconfident and blind to possible difficulties, while others may lack the confidence to think clearly about the options facing them. The counsellor must judge whether the client needs a "wet blanket" of realism, or a "firecracker" of enthusiasm. The client should not be pushed in any particular direction but should be helped to be in the proper frame of mind to make the right decision.

Potential entrepreneurs often expect counsellors not only to be sympathetic listeners but also to provide them with useful contacts, particularly with bankers and other sources of finance, or potential customers. Successful entrepreneurs are, above all, good networkers and the counsellor should be happy to play this role. However, there should be no recommendation of a particular contact or collaborator to the client. Names can be provided and introductions made, but the counsellor should not play the role of a marriage broker, since this could seriously prejudice his or her effectiveness as a counsellor. This is even more important when the counsellor is not being paid by the client but by a third party, such as a business support agency or even a bank. The counsellor must be scrupulously neutral in every respect.

Entrepreneurs often have to produce business plans, either as part of a course or in submitting an application for funding to a bank. While preparing these plans can be a somewhat barren and automatic exercise, an effective counsellor can help clients to produce plans that not only satisfy external requirements but also make a valuable contribution to the decision on whether to start at all. The various components of the business plan can be used as assignments to structure the counselling process.

Counselling people starting new businesses can be an extremely demanding task, because the whole future of the client and his or her family may be involved. It can also be most rewarding. The contribution of a genuinely effective counsellor may well be forgotten or even denied by the client, particularly if the business becomes successful, but the counsellor can take satisfaction in assisting someone through a critical stage of life.

Consulting for family enterprises

The use of consultants by small family enterprises or co-entrepreneurs is not common. Even if there is an initial contact, few formal consulting assignments are ever achieved. Because of the intimate relationships between family members, they may be reluctant to discuss business conflicts and problems. Personal and business problems become intertwined and in many cases are extremely difficult for the consultant to identify, let alone resolve.

Before attempting to solve the business problems, the consultant should meet separately with each family member in order to understand the family dynamics as they relate to the operation of the business. The consultant should attempt to gain the support and trust of each family member *before* meeting them as a group to discuss their business problems.

When family ties are strong, family pride can be a major factor in resolving the conflict. Where family ties are weak, it may be better to propose that some members leave the business and pursue other career opportunities.

A special feature in counselling the family enterprise is the question of succession. For the reasons mentioned earlier, there are likely to be emotional as well as managerial and business issues to consider. The consultant needs to maintain a professional role and to bring up topics, such as wills, possible death duties, taxation and other items, which family members may wish to avoid. The consultant might start by evaluating the enterprise's strengths and weaknesses, and recommend an orderly succession process that protects shareholders' and directors' interests. Once these items are in place the consultant might introduce the subject of the profile of a likely successor. It is recommended that fees be charged on a time basis rather than on the basis of capital participation to quieten possible anxieties among family members. Contingency plans should also be prepared to deal with events such as the premature death of the senior member.

Extension services

Private consultants are not widely used on a fee-for-service basis by small enterprises in most developing countries. Recent research has shown that a wide range of business development services (BDS), including consultancy, are provided in ways that are embedded in normal business relationships, thus reducing the risk to the acquirer of the service.[3] Consulting is often provided through government-sponsored extension services to small enterprises. There is currently widespread debate about whether this is a good use of public funds;[4] in particular, whether these funds could be used to support the provision of services by a wider range of actors within the private sector, rather than subsidising delivery for a relatively small group of recipients. In the current scenario, extension service agents take the initiative to visit small enterprises, and provide entrepreneurs with services and advice on the spot. Such assistance may include the following activities:

- advising on all aspects of management, work organization, and product design, development and adaptation; emphasis may be on price calculations, bookkeeping and financial planning;
- domestic and export marketing, including subcontracting and inventory control;
- materials procurement;
- choosing technology and solving technical problems, including those related to needs for skills, space, public utilities and equipment, and procurement methods;
- advice on potential sources of finance and help in gaining access to finance, for example by preparing loan requests;
- identifying training requirements for workers and owners/managers, and potential training sources;
- explaining government regulations and dealing with related paperwork, including taxes and legal questions such as incorporation of enterprises, registration, licensing, grants, etc.; and
- quality control and standardization, particularly where subcontracting and export promotion are important.

Only rarely is it necessary or possible for the extension service to be involved in all of these functions at the same time. Specific involvement will depend on the nature of the target group, both in terms of its technical qualifications and the subsector to which the target entrepreneurs belong, e.g. manufacturing, construction, tourism, commerce, and so on. There is general agreement, however, that an integrated approach has to be taken to assess and meet the needs of small enterprises. Such an approach would combine, for example, training, technological assistance, credit and, in some cases, physical infrastructure.

The extension service agent may be viewed as a trouble-shooter who identifies problem areas and refers the entrepreneur to specialized assistance such as a chamber of commerce, professional association, trade and artisan group, private consultant, training institution, or larger enterprise. The value of the extension service must be judged by its ability to perceive the needs of entrepreneurs, to diagnose correctly problems that occur, and to provide timely and useful advice and support.

24.5 An enabling environment

Building a positive policy, legal and regulatory environment is one of the most effective ways to assist small enterprises. The policy and regulatory frameworks have two broad functions: (1) they allow government to manage the macroeconomy coherently and predictably, to achieve sustainable social and economic objectives, and (2) they level the playing field for small enterprises, which are key elements of the microeconomy. Small enterprises require a legal framework that improves the business environment for ethical commercial transactions (e.g. protection against unfair competition) and provides incentives for more business start-ups and expansion.

In some cases, small-business consultants may be requested to assist in analysing and improving the environment for business creation and promotion. The client may be a finance ministry, a local administration or a small-business association preparing requests and proposals for improvements in the policy, legal and regulatory environment.

The consultant needs to know about institutions, policies and regulations that constitute the environment. Usually this environment reflects general economic and development policies, negotiations, assessments and compromises and is likely to change only when well-documented analyses and proposals come from the small businesses concerned. Small-business consultants are uniquely placed to help their clients, and their clients' associations, to formulate and promote such proposals for improvement.

Characteristics of an enabling environment

Generally speaking, small enterprises fare better in a diversified, innovative, flexible and vibrant environment, with a well-functioning market for inputs and outputs. In such a market, linkages can be formed between small and large enterprises and across the small-enterprise sector generally, so that joint ventures, subcontracts, supplies and marketing efforts are facilitated. A positive environment is also characterized by networks and institutions that provide business development services and access to capital, participate in social dialogue and advocate improvements in the policy, legal, procedural and regulatory environments. Regulatory, administrative, reporting and control procedures are in place, but are transparent, and in line with the capabilities of small economic operators. Finally, in a positive environment, small enterprises have a political and policy voice to make their needs heard and the achievement of social objectives is promoted without undermining competitiveness.

Whether an environment enables or constrains small enterprises depends on many factors. These are described below in terms of their influence on the development of small enterprises. Government has three distinct roles in shaping the small-enterprise environment: (1) to establish policies and laws; (2) to execute programmes, regulations and procedures; and (3) to carry out administrative tasks. While each field is important individually, the connections among them are of special interest.

Policies and laws

The policy and legal framework sets the directions and intentions of government, underpins development efforts and influences the role that the small-enterprise sector performs in the national, provincial and local economy. An enabling environment for small enterprises requires a favourable overall policy framework, both for enterprises and entrepreneurship. Such a framework needs to create confidence in the management and evolution of the economy. This requires stable, well-designed policy instruments and mechanisms. Several policy areas affect small-enterprise operations and combine to create the overall policy environment. These include monetary and credit policies, taxation, regulatory and control policies, trade and export policies, labour market policies, planning and zoning, sector policies, regional policies, education policies, and policies targeted at specific groups.

Policy generally reflects government positions. Where this not the case, differences may be ascribed to:

- **Outdated policy**, where policies in force no longer reflect the views of government. This can occur when a new government is elected or when a country has recently undergone significant political or economic change.
- **Poorly defined policy**, where policy is formulated in an unclear or ad hoc manner. This may result from inadequate understanding of the development needs and potential of small enterprises; a lack of interest in, or priority for, small-enterprise promotion; unforeseen effects of policy implementation; and/or a lack of coordination (e.g. no ministry to take overall responsibility).

- **Excessively complex policy**, where policy is formulated in a piecemeal fashion creating duplication or a confusing collection of priorities and directions.
- **No policy**, where there are gaps in the overall small-enterprise policy framework and no clear understanding of the government's intention.

An absence of clear policies creates problems for small enterprises and for any assessment of the legal and regulatory framework, since there is no benchmark against which proposals for reform and change can be considered. Understanding what constitutes good policy is crucial. A good policy is not necessarily one that gives an open door to all small enterprises – some restrictions may be required. Environmental policies, for example, may restrict the operation of enterprises that threaten the environment.

To design appropriate policies for small enterprises, the following questions should be asked:

- Do the policies recognize the role that small enterprises play in development?
- Are policies based on an accurate understanding of the dynamics of small enterprises?
- Do they promote a diverse and dynamic economy?
- Do they inhibit any legal or human right, e.g. do they prohibit certain people from starting a business?
- Do they favour large business over small enterprises?
- Do they put small enterprises in competition with government?
- Is there a continuous monitoring of policy impact and feedback to policy-makers?
- Is there coherence among policies developed by different ministries?
- Is there coordination between development and implementation of policy?

Programmes, regulations and procedures

Good policies provide a basis for an enabling environment. However, the procedural and regulatory mechanisms through which policy is implemented must also be considered. At the national level, central government provides overall policy direction and the legislative basis for development. Monetary, tax, trade, education, labour and other policies are usually implemented by central government, but in many cases other levels of government (e.g. local and provincial) also have an important role to play. There is a risk that regulatory functions at the local level will constrain growth of small enterprises. Government decentralization can mean that provincial and local governments are required to deal with many regulatory and administrative functions affecting small enterprises and may not have the capacity to do so. Small enterprises often face legal and regulatory problems caused by:

- **Excess of regulation**, preventing small enterprises from taking advantage of market opportunities and accessing inputs at competitive prices.
- **Inadequate regulations**, providing insufficient protection of the entrepreneur (e.g. ambiguous property rights and poor enforcement of contracts).
- **Poor administration of regulations**, where processes for administration are overly bureaucratic and inefficient.
- **Lack of clarity**, where regulations are complex and convoluted, and require a lot of time for compliance; too many forms, too many government agencies to deal with, too many obligations, and high reporting costs are typical.
- **Lack of transparency**, where the administrative processes are closed, and there are opportunities for corruption.
- **Duplication**, where regulations duplicate one another or are incompatible.
- **Frequent changes**, where government authorities change regulations and make it difficult for business people to keep up to date with requirements.
- **Lack of awareness**, where regulations are not properly communicated, interpreted, or promoted to the small-enterprise owners, or where there is lack of understanding by the enforcers of the regulations.
- **Regional disparities**, where the impact of the legal and regulatory environment varies between urban and rural settings.
- **Lack of small-enterprise input**, where small enterprises are unable to provide input to the policy development process.

Administrative procedures

Administrative procedures require careful attention when assessing the environment for small enterprises to ensure that they are consistent with their policy, legislative and regulatory base. They are the point of interface between government and the small-enterprise owner or manager and can greatly affect the small-enterprise environment.

Administrative burdens on small enterprises should be kept to a minimum because they hinder development and growth. An unsupportive administrative environment can be particularly damaging because small businesses do not usually have resources to fall back on, or the managerial and technical capacity to deal with changing economic and business policies, complex licensing and authorizations procedures, and fluctuating fiscal and monetary regulations. When assessing the legal, regulatory and administrative requirements, the following questions can be relevant:

- **Can it be eliminated?** Is the regulation or requirement really necessary? What are the reasons for it? Is it a side-effect of other regulations? What alternative mechanisms could be used to achieve the same outcome?

- **Can it be simplified?** If the regulation is necessary, can the requirements for meeting it be made more user-friendly? Can some steps be eliminated? Can some forms be made simpler and easier to complete?
- **Can it be combined with other requirements?** Is it possible to minimize duplication and repetition? Can several regulations be satisfied with only one submission?
- **Can it be better communicated?** If there is misunderstanding or confusion about the regulation, can it be promoted better to avoid time-consuming and costly mistakes?
- **Can it be decentralized?** Small enterprises are found everywhere. Decentralized administrative centres where entrepreneurs can fulfil their legal and regulatory responsibilities can be of great value.

A process for policy reform

It is not possible to propose universal actions for policy, legal and regulatory reform. What works in one country may not work as effectively in others. Reforms should target specific areas where changes can promote small enterprises. Alternatively, especially where a high degree of structural change is needed, they may entail a complete realignment of the policy, legal and regulatory environment. In the former Soviet Union, for example, the transition from a centrally planned to a free-market economy required the transformation of the entire legal and regulatory framework. This was also the case in South Africa with the ending of apartheid.

A four-step approach can be applied when advising policy-makers on policy reform:

1 Allow key stakeholders to identify how a country's current policy and regulatory environment affect small enterprises.
2 Provide inspiring examples of how other national, provincial and local governments have removed barriers to small-enterprise growth.
3 Support formulation of an action plan for reform and provide technical advice on its implementation.
4 Measure the effects of the reform process.

Useful guidelines for consultants and policy-makers on improving the small-business environment are available from several international agencies, including ILO and OECD.[5]

Subsidized small-business consulting schemes

In some countries the policies for promoting small-business development include subsidized consulting schemes. Variants of such schemes exist in countries as different as the Czech Republic, Germany, Singapore, the United Kingdom and the United States. These schemes tend to exhibit certain common characteristics:

- the consultant provides assistance in certain priority areas, such as business policy and planning, export development, job creation or quality improvement;
- in some schemes, the small-business client chooses from a roster of consultants who have provided extensive information on their qualifications and experience, and who have been approved by the agency responsible for the scheme;
- the client co-finances the project (say 40–60 per cent of the cost), and the total cost or the fee rate charged is within set limits;
- the sponsoring agency has the right to review the work performed before authorizing payment.

Another form of subsidizing advisory, training and other professional services to small businesses is through direct budgetary subsidies, provided by governments or development agencies to small-business development institutions, such as the extension services mentioned in section 24.4. These institutions are thus able to apply reduced fee rates and provide certain services (e.g. a quick assessment of the business and definition of the need for a consultancy) free of charge. To some extent, these schemes have benefited from substantial financial support because the underlying rationale, of generating employment for disadvantaged groups, has broad political support, and the countries concerned can readily afford such interventions. The recent introduction of impact monitoring has, however, led to a broader debate about whether this is indeed the most cost-effective use of public funds.

24.6 Innovations in small-business consulting

It has been assumed for some time that subsidized professional services to small-business clients may be helpful in certain conditions, particularly in developing countries or regions. However, they do not provide a panacea, and donors are constantly looking for more innovative methods to stimulate increased take-up of business services through a variety of channels. The small clients' needs for information and advice are tremendous and continue to grow because of the increasingly complex institutional setting and difficult business environment of most countries. Small-enterprise owners are usually unable to allocate sufficient time and resources to keep abreast of developments and to take a detached critical look at their business from time to time. Conversely, many consultants and other advisers exhibit a clear preference for larger-business clients who have more money, can afford larger assignments and higher fees, and offer technically more interesting work opportunities (and references) to the consultants. Some consultants do not mind working for small clients, but they may fail to appreciate the differences and treat them in the same way as large-business clients.

There is thus a need for innovative approaches to small-business clients. While all the principles discussed in the previous sections remain valid, consultants need to intensify their efforts to devise and apply formulas that make their services fully understandable, easily accessible and attractive to large numbers of smaller clients. In short, small-business consulting must become more user-friendly and client centred.

One-stop shop and integrated assistance

The so-called one-stop shops or counters provide small-business clients with an advisory or information service on various aspects of the business. They can provide information materials on a wide variety of topics, help with filling in forms, preparatory work for credit requests, and so on.

In other cases, generalist business consultants can provide their clients with comprehensive and complete advice, bringing together a number of relatively small and inexpensive inputs on various aspects of the business, under the coordination of an all-round generalist. The client does not have to make separate searches for different specialists, sign several contracts, provide the same basic information many times, and coordinate the work done. The consultant must ensure excellent selection of specialist inputs and a fair coverage of the issues at hand. A useful service for busy small-business clients is for their consultant–generalist to monitor developments (e.g. in taxation, export regulations, changes in social charges, new markets) likely to affect the business. The consultant can then take the initiative to call and inform the client about such developments, suggesting how his or her firm could help the client to react to these new opportunities or constraints.

Standard instruments and checklists

Cheaper and more user-friendly consultancy services can be provided by combining various standard self-diagnostic, business-planning and other instruments and checklists with personalized advice introducing and supplementing these instruments. If the procedure is simple and clearly described, a short briefing or even written instructions can enable a number of clients to prepare the same data and undertake the same diagnostic or planning exercise. The consultant's personal intervention can then be limited to reviewing the results with the client, and suggesting appropriate action. Standard instruments can be used by junior (and less costly) consultants (or even business students), who would ask a more senior colleague for advice, or suggest that the client ask for such advice, only if this is warranted by the client's specific situation and needs.

Self-development and training packages

In helping small-business people to understand fully their business and its potential, and to improve their management skills and business results, consultants can suggest various learning packages. The consultant can guide the client through the learning material and supplement it by more specific information and advice, or direct the client to training events based on the published package.

In many countries a chamber of commerce, local banks or consulting firms have published such learning materials tailored to the needs of local small businesses, and reflecting the specific problems of local legislation and commercial and banking practices. Internationally tested and widely used materials also exist – the ILO's *Start and improve your business (SIYB)* programme is available in 35 languages and has been used in 80 countries.[6]

"Hot-line" service

Either a private consulting firm or a public small-business development or extension service can establish a "hot-line" telephone service for entrepreneurs who need urgent information and advice. This may be a paying service, on a subscription or ad hoc basis, or it may be a free public service providing emergency help and suggesting how and where to ask for further assistance.

Working with groups of entrepreneurs

In group approaches to providing advice, more clients are served simultaneously and the cost per client is lower. In addition, the participants can learn from each other and develop useful contacts for the future. Various group approaches have been used by trade and employers' associations, extension services, small-business development centres, and individual private consultancies, in particular (but not only) in developing countries. Often they are used in working with women entrepreneurs.

A group approach is applicable if the clients have some common problems and interests and if they are prepared to work together; this may require sharing some business information. If small firms from the same sector get together, they are likely to be competitors, although they clearly will have many common interests. If the clients are not from the same sector, they still may have experiences to share, e.g. on common business issues or processes and activities that exist in every business. As action learning, benchmarking and other approaches have demonstrated, a great deal can be learned from entrepreneurs and managers working in seemingly completely different sectors.

Benchmarking (see also section 20.3). This technique is based on comparison of detailed and specific information on selected processes, services, and so on, followed by an analysis of the differences between firms and a study of approaches that have helped certain participants to achieve better results. In facilitating such an exercise, the consultant can provide data for comparison, ask the right questions, make the participants aware of common issues, stimulate the discussion, and help to identify best practices and introduce improvements.

Action-learning workshops (see also section 4.5). Participants in such workshops get together in order to work collectively, and to learn from other participants' experience in solving problems faced by their organizations. As a rule, in the first phase, the workshop focuses on identifying problems and designating the problems that are of interest to most participants and should be examined collectively. The problems selected are then analysed in greater depth by the whole group or by subgroups, to come up with one or more possible solutions. The groups could meet once a week and continue for some 8 to 12 weeks. If the group's knowledge and experience are not enough, the group may define information and training requirements that can be met by the consultant acting as facilitator or another expert invited for the purpose.

Business clinics. This is an arrangement whereby a group of small-enterprise owners/managers meets to get advice and exchange experience on how to deal with the problems faced by all of them. It can be a one-off exercise (e.g. a one-day session) or a set of four to eight meetings similar to those run in action learning. A business clinic can be combined with an interfirm comparison when the members of the group compare their results and exchange experiences. In other cases, a business clinic may be organized to deal collectively with problems identified by extension officers or other small-business advisers, or chosen by the small-business owners themselves.

Self-help and solidarity groups. In several developing countries, such groups have been established by small-scale entrepreneurs with the support of technical assistance agencies, including voluntary non-governmental organizations. The groups are concerned with training, sharing experience and, in some cases, obtaining small-scale credit. A great deal of this work has been done in the microenterprise sector (see Chapter 25).

IT and e-business services

Many current information technology applications are fully accessible and suitable for small firms. As mentioned in section 13.7, IT has become a strategic tool and a major factor in the competitiveness of small firms, and no consultant can afford to ignore it. Small entrepreneurs need objective information and encouragement, since many of them feel that the newer applications and Internet-based services are not really for them, or constitute an unnecessary luxury or a financial burden that can be avoided. They may not see the business and financial advantages that many applications can bring to a small business. In a sense, IT can be a greater blessing to a small firm than to a large one, helping to resolve many problems related to the small size of operations and limited resources and competencies. Conversely, entrepreneurs also need the help of trusted advisers to avoid the trap of buying unnecessary, unreliable, excessively complex and too costly applications and equipment proposed to them by some vendors.

Outsourcing (see also Chapter 13). Outsourcing can free up the entrepreneur and his or her staff, who are typically tied up in many administrative and other tasks that prevent them from devoting more energy and time to core business and technical issues. In addition to bookkeeping and accounting, which have traditionally been outsourced by many small companies, external application service providers (ASP) can handle many services more economically and at a higher level of quality than internal staff.

E-business (see also Chapter 16). Consultants can help small-business people to realize that key decisions concerning e-commerce and e-business are not about technology but about business and marketing strategies and methods. Approaches to e-business should be driven by business considerations, not by technological thinking. It is, however, necessary to be aware of the opportunities created by the latest IT developments. It may also happen that a fashionable application that is not strictly necessary may have to be acquired if competitors have already done so. The options below highlight some of the choices that entrepreneurs face:[7]

- *Minimalistic* – set up a low-end Web site, essentially a brochure on the net describing your product and service offering. Use basic email communications systems for correspondence with key suppliers and clients, or for internal use. This approach provides at least a first base for future development.
- *Inside first* – drive internal operations online, with effective knowledge management, and an intranet to support staff, designed to improve operations and cut costs. The conversion of the organization to an online way of thinking sets the platform for extending communications systems beyond the enterprise.
- *Clicks-and-mortar* – use online delivery as an additional sales and marketing channel for broadening reach, cutting costs, improving client relations, or occupying the digital space to guard against competitive activity.
- *Buy-side and sell-side cooperation* – set up interactive communications with suppliers and/or customers to cement existing relationships and enhance service delivery.
- *Collaborative partnerships* – seek online partners for increasing purchasing power or establishing sales channels. Partnerships can be entered into at lower unit cost to produce a collective effort that makes real impact. It can keep a small company relevant in online terms where it would otherwise run the risk of being marginalized by online initiatives of larger groups.
- *Pure-play spin-off* – separate the online and traditional businesses by introducing a new and independent operation that can learn from the existing business, but is not hampered by existing infrastructural overheads. The freedom and agility of pure-play companies can result in a lower cost base, allowing manoeuvrability into niche areas. A sound business model is required to ensure sustainability and prevent conflicts between the two wings of the business.
- *Online repositioning* – be the first in the digital economy space. Redesign the product and service offering from first principles, looking at cost, client servicing needs, etc. Discard outdated products and systems that do not fit within your future vision. A totally new strategy for market entry is required, which comes at a high cost and potential risk, but offers commensurate rewards from dominating the market if successful.

- *Online start-up* – define a role that adds value or satisfies a market need that is not (or cannot be) satisfied by traditional businesses. Look carefully at the cost of attracting visitors and at the revenue models. Venture capital or corporate backing may be required.

In the years to come, advice on effective approaches to e-business by small firms will be an important area of consulting. Recent research has unveiled numerous flaws and inefficiencies in the Web sites of both large and small firms, which often rushed to have one because it was thought essential, but which were unable to create and sustain one that served a clear business purpose, improved marketing and was perceived by customers as real help.[8]

Business incubators

New models of business incubators have been launched by banks, IT firms, individual investors and other sponsors, to support the creation of new businesses by the providing a range of IT and other services and facilities, including space for accommodation, Internet and communication services, administrative support, finance and technical and business advice. They tend to be selective and prefer to host new business ventures in new technologies and e-business. They can provide space and facilities for several new businesses under one roof, or operate as virtual incubators working with a number of entrepreneurs in different locations. Many consulting firms have been among the founders and principal sponsors, or have been associated with incubators by advising and coaching individual entrepreneurs. In working with start-ups in fields covered by some incubators, the consultant may also help the client to weigh the pros and cons of starting in isolation but fully independently, or accepting the facilities and advantages of an incubator, which usually also have their cost side or may impose constraints that the entrepreneur may be reluctant to accept.

---

[1] The ILO Job Creation in Small and Medium-Sized Enterprises Recommendation, 1998 (No. 189).

[2] J. Harvey-Jones: *Troubleshooter 2* (London, Penguin, 1992), p. 2.

[3] See www.ilo.org/public/english/employment/ent/sed/publ/wp5.htm. (visited on 4 Apr. 2002).

[4] See www.ilo.org/public/english/employment/ent/papers/guide.htm. (visited on 4 Apr. 2002).

[5] In 1998 the ILO's International Labour Conference adopted Recommendation No. 189 (see note 1). This promotional instrument describes a wide range of possible actions, from which the most feasible in each national context can be selected. Ideally, it can be used as a checklist of ways to promote employment growth in small enterprises. The ILO provides assistance in the implementation of the Recommendation through its InFocus Programme on Boosting Employment through Small Enterprise Development (IFPSEED). See http://ilolex.ilo.ch:1567/english/redisp1.htm; and www.ilo.org/seed. In 2000, the OECD developed *The Bologna Charter on SME Policies*. See www.oecd.org/dsti/sti/industry/smes/act/Bologna/bologna_charter.htm; and an OECD policy brief ("Small and medium-sized enterprises: Local strengths, global reach", in *OECD Observer*, June 2000). Sites visited on 4 Apr. 2002.

[6] The *SIYB* programme includes three main components (1) *Start Your Business* for business starters – the training output is a bankable business plan; (2) *Improve Your Business* for small-scale entrepreneurs with limited prior exposure to business training – the training output is an action plan for improvements of the participant's business performance; and (3) *Expand Your Business* for growth-oriented small-scale enterprises – the training output is a strategic growth plan. It provides a comprehensive set of training materials for various target groups in the small-business sector.

[7] See also www.ebusreport.com (visited on 4 Apr. 2002), and *The e-commerce handbook 2000: Your guide to the Internet revolution and the future of business*, produced for South African businesses.

[8] See, e.g. "Net profit: Corporates go back to basics to get their websites right", at www.ebusinessforum.com/index.asp?layout=rich_story&doc_id=3910 (visited on 4 Apr. 2002).

CONSULTING FOR THE INFORMAL SECTOR 25

There is a group of small businesses, which many people would not call businesses at all, but which are nevertheless in most countries a far more important source of employment and incomes, for far more people, than large or small formal businesses. These are the enterprises belonging to what is sometimes known loosely as the "informal sector", or "micro-enterprises"; that is, the vast numbers of very small-scale income-generating activities through which millions of people attempt to make their living and survive, particularly in the developing countries.

Everyone is aware of these micro-enterprises, although they may not think of them as potential clients for management consulting. They are crowded along the pavements and in the slums of big cities, as well as in the official and unofficial marketplaces. They are a major source of income in rural areas, where many people own no land at all and those who do own land have little to gain by spending more hours of labour on their tiny holdings. They include vendors, tailors, snack-food processors, roadside cycle and car mechanics, blacksmiths, cobblers and almost everything else. Although they are often perceived as a nuisance by those who can afford to purchase what they need from more formal and sophisticated sources, these micro-entrepreneurs provide essential goods and services at a place, time and price that are convenient not only for other poor people like themselves, but also for customers from other social groups and larger businesses.

25.1 What is different about micro-enterprises?

The importance of informal-sector entrepreneurs as employers and suppliers does not in itself mean that management consultants can help them in any way. It is important to recognize that they are a very different client group – if indeed they can be clients at all – from large or even small formal businesses, such as were dealt with in Chapter 24.

Heterogeneity of the group

To provide guidance that is of any practical use, it is important to acknowledge the heterogeneity of micro-enterprises and their needs for assistance. It is useful to think of them in *two major categories.*

First, there are the very small, home-based, informal enterprises, typically with one to three employees including the owner, using basic skills and technology, with small assets, supplying a limited local market, and often having a limited life expectancy. Perhaps 99 per cent of these enterprises will never be in a position to consider using the services of private consulting firms, and paying a full charge for these services – although there is some evidence that they do obtain such services from informal consultants who work on the same "financial scale" as the micro-enterprises themselves. They are businesses, however, and have to be managed. They can benefit from technical advice as can any other enterprises. Sound advice can help them to survive, adjust to changes in their environment, improve quality, product diversity and earnings, and even lay down foundations for growth.

We focus here on the specific needs of this category of the smallest and least sophisticated micro-enterprises (see box 25.1). As pointed out in section 1.1, management consulting is not only a separate professional service that can be purchased from independent firms on commercial terms, but is also a method of providing advice and assistance aimed at improving management and business. This chapter will discuss mainly the second side of consulting. It will show that the consulting method can be applied by a wide range of organizations interested in assisting the informal sector, either separately, or in conjunction with other business transactions or social services (the term "embodied consulting services" has also been used). Consultants and others seeking to render a socially useful and productive service to these entrepreneurs will have to combine technical know-how and aptitude with considerable social skills. In many cases they will have to engage in personal counselling (see sections 3.7 and 24.4) rather than strictly technical advice.

The second large category of micro-enterprises comprises those that have already reached a higher level of sophistication and size than the first group. Typically they employ up to nine workers, use some motorized equipment on permanent premises, take part in subcontracting arrangements, and so on. The owners, especially the younger ones, may have acquired a basic education in a local language and some formal technical training. They still operate as informal-sector units with all the advantages and constraints involved. In several respects, this second group is on the borderline between the traditional informal sector and the modern small enterprise (see Chapter 24). Some of them will "graduate" from the informal sector; others remain in this sector for various reasons. Consulting services for this category exhibit some characteristics of assistance to the informal sector, but most of the methods and approaches to small-business consulting described in Chapter 24 will also be applicable.

Box 25.1 Consulting in the informal sector – a mini case study

Laxmi is one of a large number of women in a village in northern India who earn their living embroidering the uppers of traditional slippers which are then sewn to the soles of the shoes, and sold in the neighbouring community, in Delhi and elsewhere.

Laxmi buys the ready-cut uppers and the thread from a supplier in the village; if she has enough cash, she can choose from a number of different suppliers and then sell the embroidered part to one of several local businesses which assemble the complete slippers. If, as is more often the case, she has to buy on credit, she is restricted to one supplier and she must also sell the embroidered upper back to him; in this case, she earns about half the amount per day she can earn when she is free to pick her own suppliers and customers.

Laxmi's two younger sisters, and her invalid mother, help in piercing the holes and other simple tasks; she does not pay them, or herself, any regular wage. Her brother drives a rickshaw in New Delhi and occasionally brings home money, and other members of the family sometimes earn a few rupees from casual work on neighbouring farms, while Laxmi makes up the necessary sums to feed and clothe the family as and when this is necessary.

A field worker from a local nongovernmental organization that was trying to assist the leather workers in this community called on Laxmi one day. Laxmi had heard about this organization, and after some brief introductions she was quite happy to tell the field worker all about her business. The field worker took careful notes on a simple form which she had been trained to use by her employers. She also looked carefully round the hut where Laxmi and her family lived, and asked a few questions about what she saw, including a fairly large pile of dusty but apparently completed embroidered uppers which were half hidden under a blanket in one corner.

After about one hour's discussion, the field worker felt able to advise Laxmi on what was clearly her main problem, namely her lack of working capital. She did not tell Laxmi what she should do, but through discussion led her to suggest that she should try to accumulate her own working capital by restricting her own drawings to a fixed amount every month. Laxmi saw that she could raise a small sum by disposing of the stock of finished components which she had unfortunately embroidered in a slightly outdated pattern; she agreed that it would not be difficult to find a shoemaker who would be willing to buy them, and that it would be better to accept a low price rather than to keep her money tied up in this way.

The field worker also told Laxmi about the savings and credit groups which her organization was helping the local people to establish; this would enable her to save more regularly, and perhaps eventually to borrow from the accumulated fund if the group so desired.

Laxmi was very happy with the discussion; when the field worker returned a month later she had disposed of the surplus stocks and had joined the savings group. She was not sure whether she could restrict and control her monthly drawings as they had agreed at their earlier meeting, but she was already making regular weekly savings of a small sum with the savings group.

Author: Malcolm Harper.

Some specific sectoral characteristics

We have seen that small businesses are usually managed by only one or two people, who have to deal with all the different functions that are entrusted to specialists in larger firms. In micro-enterprises there is no separate management function as such; the owner, who is usually the sole worker as well, is primarily a cobbler, a tailor or a vendor. She or he (and in most countries it is more likely to be "she") makes the same sort of decisions about prices, products, finance, and so on as any other manager, but management is not conceived as a separate activity and decisions are made on an ad hoc basis.

The owners of formal small businesses are often criticized for not separating their business finances from their personal affairs, and consultants often have to help them to set up systems to do this. Because most micro-enterprises are a means of economic survival for the owners and their families, it is often impossible – and it may be wrong – to try to make the separation; the time and resources devoted to the enterprise, and the earnings from it, have to be related to the economics of the whole household. It may even be appropriate for the enterprise to operate only on a seasonal basis, since there are more profitable opportunities at some times of year. This is clearly very different from the situation of formal businesses.

Small businesses generally have little written data with which a consultant can undertake an analysis, but most micro-enterprises in the informal sector have no written records at all, except perhaps some note of amounts owed to them by customers who have bought on credit. Women in particular, who dominate the smallest end of the informal sector, often have little or no education; not only do they have no records of activities and commercial and financial transactions, but they lack the basic knowledge to keep or use them.

The people who own and work in these micro-enterprises also differ in other ways from the entrepreneurs who have established more formal businesses. Very few of them are likely to have started their enterprises by choice. Most would prefer to have even a very modest job in a formal enterprise, or perhaps to work on the land; they are micro-entrepreneurs not by choice, but because there was no alternative. They are often people from the economic and possibly also the social margins of society, such as unemployed youth, refugees, migrants, widows or the disabled, for whom jobs in the formal business sector are not available. This obviously has important implications for the ways in which they view the future of their enterprises.

Many of the skills needed for survival in the informal sector are very different from those required in larger enterprises, and they are certainly not the type of skills in which most management consultants are themselves experts. Successful micro-entrepreneurs are above all "streetwise": they have the right contacts, they know when and where the hand of the law is likely to fall and how it should be avoided, and they are adept at improvisation. Those of us who are used to operating in a more structured and sheltered environment can probably learn a great deal from these people.

25.2 Management problems of informal-sector entrepreneurs

Suboptimal use of scarce resources

In spite of the many differences, as outlined above, the owners of micro-enterprises make many of the same mistakes as formal business managers, and they need similar advice. Shortage of finance is often their main constraint, and they may have to pay exorbitant rates of interest for loans, since banks and other formal financial institutions are not usually willing to lend money to people with no fixed business address, little or no formal education, and no tangible assets beyond a temporary stall, a push-cart or a few hand tools. It is therefore vital that they deploy their funds in an optimal way, but they often fail to do this, investing disproportionately in credit, in stocks, or in other assets.

Similarly, raw materials are often an important constraint. Many carpenters, tailors and others fail to calculate the profitability of each product, using their scarce materials suboptimally and producing a product mix that is less profitable than it could be. It is particularly important for an outsider to find out exactly why the business owners are behaving in this way, since there may be sociocultural reasons which mean that apparently mistaken policies are in fact the best course. Some petty traders, for instance, invest all their earnings in what appear to be excessive stocks, rather than saving money for new capital items which they admit they need; their reason, however, may be that they are all too aware that the members of their extended family will lay claim to any cash resources for personal expenses such as school fees, hospital charges or even food and clothing, and it is easier to retain money that is tied up in stock.

Poor record-keeping

It is important not to assume that somebody who is not keeping records in the normally accepted way is not keeping them at all. Even illiterate business people usually have some system for recording sales on credit, and most people who work with money have some idea of what figures mean even if they cannot read or write words. Illiterate people are often able to remember far more information than those of us who are fortunate enough to have been taught to read and write, and some illiterate business owners have ingenious systems for controlling stocks and cash. A formal education is certainly not a necessary condition for business success on any scale; after all, there are quite a few illiterate millionaires in Europe and the United States, and even more in countries where illiteracy is more common.

The owners of informal enterprises can often benefit from keeping and using better recording systems. However, they usually have not had many years of formal education and many find it very difficult to apply what they are taught in a training course to the particular situation of their own business. New recording systems, and any other changes, must be designed to take account of the particular circumstances of each business and the ability of the owner. This means that on-site individual consultancy, although it is more expensive per client than classroom training, is more suitable for the owners of micro-enterprises.

25.3 The special skills of micro-enterprise consultants

Consultants who are used to working with written records, however inadequate, may find it difficult to work with illiterate clients; the lack of any documents that even resemble formal accounts may compound the social difficulties of dealing with people who have no office and even no fixed premises. The consultant may have to meet the client in his or her shanty home in a slum, in a noisy temporary workshop or even squatting on the ground in a public marketplace, where discussions are constantly interrupted by customers, the client's children or a crowd of curious onlookers whose presence severely inhibits the client's willingness to share personal financial information.

Eliciting information

It is quite possible to elicit usable financial information, even from completely illiterate business owners, but it is not easy. The consultant must avoid any form of accounting jargon. A financial picture of the enterprise has to be put together from information which may be obtained in a quite different sequence from that to which the consultant is accustomed. It is usually necessary to cross-check information, such as daily or monthly sales figures, by asking for the same information in different ways. A village baker may have only a very approximate idea of the total figure of his monthly sales, but he is more likely to know how many bags of flour he uses each month, and how many loaves of bread he makes from each bag, or how many loaves he sells each day, and at what price.

A successful micro-enterprise consultant must be able to elicit, collate and analyse information on the spot, and then assemble the information in a way that shows where the money in the business comes from and how it is being used, as well as giving a rough idea of the income and the costs over a period, which may be a day, a week, a month or a season, depending on the nature of the business and on the way its owner runs it. This is of course an approximate balance sheet and profit and loss account. This analysis is as useful for a micro-enterprise as it is for a larger business, and the consultant may find that the owner's skill in managing his or her very small capital compares favourably with the management of resources in larger and more generously funded businesses.

The consultant must also use other senses. A roadside carpenter may state that he has no stock of partly finished goods, but a dusty pile of pieces of chairs under a workbench will show that this is not the case. Or a trader who says that she never gives credit may be observed to sell a bag of flour to a customer without any cash changing hands. Micro-business people do not usually deliberately deceive people who are trying to help them, but mistakes of this sort occur because of failure to communicate. The consultant must also use the sense of touch and even the sense of smell; a finger will show up the coating of dust on redundant inventory, and a smell can show up a fruit vendor's poor stock rotation methods. Simple cleanliness and good order can often make all the difference to the sales levels of a micro-enterprise, and the most immediate advice might be to sweep the floor and tidy up the stocks. These are humble suggestions, but are often relevant in far larger businesses as well.

Respect for existing business practices

Micro-enterprise consultants have to develop a special sense of respect and understanding for their clients. When you observe what appears to be illogical business behaviour, you must ask yourself what you would do in the same circumstances, with the same pressures and constraints. You may conclude that the business owner is actually coping well with very difficult circumstances. Some market traders, for instance, turn their stock over once or even twice a day. Vendors, such as the people who sell newspapers and other items to car drivers waiting at traffic lights, display remarkable marketing skills in their choice of potential customers and their decisions when to cut off a potential sale because the traffic is about to move and there will be no time to collect the money. Sales representatives who work in a more formal environment can learn a great deal from this form of marketing.

Providing information

The owners of micro-enterprises are often unaware of their rights and obligations under the law, and this can be particularly important when the regulatory environment is being rapidly liberalized. Local officials may not know, or may not want to know, about old rules that have been relaxed or new rights that have been extended, and consultants can provide a vital window on the world.

Technology is also changing rapidly, and this can bring new opportunities, such as new materials to be recycled, new intermediary or maintenance services to be provided, and new markets to be addressed.

Governments, at the local and national level, have traditionally been hostile to informal-sector business, but this too is changing, and new sources of finance, training opportunities, more secure locations and new market opportunities are being made available. People working in the informal sector frequently lack the time, the facilities and the skills to obtain information about favourable changes of this sort, and it is often more difficult to disseminate information about changes in regulations than it is to make the changes themselves. In some countries, commercial radio stations now focus on the informal sector as listeners and as a target market, informing micro-business about changes in an informal way. Outside advisers can also act as valuable intermediaries in communication of this sort.

25.4 Outreach to micro-enterprises in the informal sector

There are, therefore, many ways in which consultants with appropriate attitudes and skills can be of significant value to micro-businesses. It is by no means easy to acquire these attitudes and skills, and the consultant may have to "unlearn" a great deal of what he or she knows before being able to work effectively with micro-enterprises. The major problem, however, is the tiny scale of each individual enterprise and the vast numbers involved. How can a consultant possibly reach out to more than a minute fraction of the people who could benefit from his or her services, and how can the costs be kept to a level commensurate with the likely benefits? The approaches described in section 24.6 are of interest, but here are some more ideas.

Picking winners

One approach is to concentrate on the rather small number of micro-business people who are real micro-entrepreneurs, with the apparent potential to graduate soon from the informal sector and to develop their businesses into prosperous formal enterprises. It is far from easy to identify these potential winners. Furthermore, the transition to formal status may not always be in the interests either of the owner or of the employees, since it involves costs such as registration fees and taxation which may not be covered by the benefits arising from improved access to formal resources. Nevertheless, many of the world's large business corporations started in an informal way, and some of today's micro-enterprises will be tomorrow's big businesses: management consultancy *may* help a few more of them to achieve this.

There are numerous tests for measuring entrepreneurial potential, but their effectiveness is limited with people of little education. Therefore the best way to select high-potential individuals is to get them to select themselves. Many agencies offer advisory services free of charge to micro-enterprises, on the assumption that they cannot afford to pay. They may indeed be unable to cover the full cost, but the best way of ensuring that clients are serious, and that they believe they can benefit from a consultancy, is to make a charge that is significant for them. If they are not willing to make a sacrifice in order to obtain a service, the error lies not with them but with the marketing or the quality of the service; this applies as much to management consultancy as to any other product.

Lower-cost consultants

Another approach to overcoming the problem of the cost of consultancy in relation to the scale of the individual enterprise is to employ less qualified and thus less expensive consultants. Although micro-enterprise consultancy is not easy, it is possible to train people with no specialist qualifications, and no more than three or four years of secondary education, to provide an effective and useful micro-enterprise advisory service. They need regular close support and supervision, and the organization and management of such a service is more akin to an extension service than to normal management consultancy, but such services can be cost-effective. In particular, such people may be more familiar with the problems of the informal sector from their own experience, and therefore be in many ways more effective than highly educated individuals.

Micro-enterprise consulting can also provide a useful form of training for consultants. People who are learning how to provide management advice to larger formal businesses can benefit enormously from being exposed to the informal sector and trying to advise the owners of micro-enterprises. They will probably benefit far more than their clients. Indeed, as long as they are closely supervised to ensure that they do not give wrong advice, management and business administration students from colleges, universities and business schools can be effective micro-enterprise consultants. Anyone who is running management courses should seriously consider introducing such a consultancy as a component of the course.

Working through groups

Another approach is working with groups, as already discussed in Chapter 24. Not only can this reduce the costs but, more importantly, many serious problems faced by people working in the informal sector can only be solved if they get together. Consultants can help them to see the benefits of sharing experience and undertaking joint action, and can advise their elected leaders on the effective management of their joint activities. For example, municipal authorities are often reluctant to allocate space for micro-enterprises, and the police and other government services may harass micro-business people unnecessarily; an individual can do little to prevent this, but if business owners come together and present a common front they can often achieve a great deal. Consultants can help with appropriate contacts and advise on strategies and techniques.

In other cases, micro-enterprises can benefit enormously from jointly performing certain functions, such as selling their products, purchasing raw materials or arranging for specialized processing, which require special skills or are not economical for a single unit to perform on its own. Micro-entrepreneurs often find it difficult to initiate and organize such common activities, whether or not they are officially registered as cooperatives, because the activities are so much larger and more complex than the micro-enterprises themselves. Management consultants can provide valuable technical assistance in this area. They can also help to dissipate prejudices concerning cooperative organizations, which in many countries have gained a bad reputation as a result of being misused for political purposes and of incompetent management.

Groups of small entrepreneurs can be informal and ad hoc, and may exist as long as the group members perceive a need to get together to discuss and resolve common issues, or to obtain a service that no one could afford individually. More formal groupings include associations of various types and degrees of formality, as well as cooperatives.

Consulting for group activities of this sort is difficult. It is often tempting for the consultant to cease to be an adviser and to become effectively the manager of an enterprise or a grouping. The owners of the group themselves may allow or even encourage an outside adviser to do this, because their main interest is in the operation of their own micro-enterprises. The result may be that the consultant finds himself in the position of a full-time manager rather than an adviser, and the group becomes dependent on his or her continued presence. While this is a danger in any consulting relationship, it is particularly great in the case of group enterprises, where none of the members really "owns" the undertaking in a personal way. Such enterprises are like the proverbial village donkey: everybody feels that it is somebody else's responsibility to take care of it, and as a result nobody does.

Management consultants working with groups of entrepreneurs or cooperatives must be sensitive to the variety of interests involved, in addition to avoiding the creation of dependence. It is also tempting for an outsider to advise, persuade or even compel the owners of micro-enterprises to form groups because it appears to be in their interests. Many group enterprises have a short existence because they have come together not on the members' own initiative but because somebody else (whose livelihood did not depend on the group's success) thought that this would be the right approach.

An effective management consultancy for a cooperative or other group of micro-enterprises will indirectly help the individual members by improving their access to credit, their marketing, their raw material supply or whatever other function the group organization performs on their behalf. This does not in itself improve the management of the individual micro-enterprises. It is possible, however, to reach the individual members through their group: training workshops can be organized for members who wish to attend, and the group's managers can require members to maintain a certain standard of quality control or other improvements as a condition of doing business with them.

This must obviously be done very carefully, since the group's managers are ultimately responsible to the members who employ them, but group pressure can be a very effective way of motivating micro-entrepreneurs to do what is in their own interest. The more successful members of a group are often willing to act as informal management consultants to their fellow-members, in order to improve the standards and thus the earnings of the group as a whole. An effective management consultant must be able to mobilize this multiplier effect, by teaching the opinion leaders simple techniques for making diagnoses and recommendations. The messages may seem elementary to an experienced consultant, but the communication task must be very subtly managed.

Alternative channels

Full-time management consultancy for individual micro-enterprises is not usually an economic proposition (see box 25.2), but there are other routes through which they can be reached. Many organizations are in regular contact with micro-enterprises: manufacturers and distributors of fast-moving

Box 25.2 Private consulting services for micro-enterprises

A Philippine consulting group, established a number of years ago by ten professionals with various sorts of expertise, has chosen to work for the micro-enterprise sector in addition to serving formally established and registered businesses, government agencies and social organizations. Each member of the group works individually as a consultant on his or her own projects, but they also work together whenever required by the size and complexity of the assignment. Direct consulting to micro-enterprises represents only a part of the group's activities.

The group carries out consulting for enterprises employing three to nine workers, which in the Philippines are micro-enterprises according to the official government definition. These enterprises are involved in a wide range of activities, including leather products (shoe production and repair, bags), wooden furniture, food processing (e.g. fruit preservation), processing of by-products from animal hides and skins, metal-working, etc. The micro-entrepreneurs serviced by the group often include members of the local community and personal friends.

The micro-entrepreneurs are visited by members of the group and also come to the consultants' offices when they need help. The types of services provided include: management and technical training; assistance in bookkeeping; preparation of loan applications for banks' feasibility studies; assistance in establishing market linkages and in organizing participation in marketing events (e.g. exhibits, fairs); advice on types of products and quality control; advice on policies and regulations; and referral to other sources of information and assistance. These services are provided to micro-entrepreneurs either directly, or indirectly through subcontracts to government agencies and nongovernmental organizations (NGOs).

Services are provided on a short-term basis or over longer periods of time, but written contracts between the consultants and the entrepreneurs are rare. Rather, services are based on verbal agreements between people who trust each other.

The micro-entrepreneurs pay fees for these services either in cash or in kind (e.g. goods produced by the micro-enterprise). Advance payments are sometimes made, but more generally the members of the consulting group are paid after the services have been rendered. In many cases, payments are made on the basis of results achieved.

The fees applied are a function of the services rendered, actual costs incurred (e.g. travel costs, time devoted to the assignment), and the size of the enterprise. Fees range from as little as a few hundred pesos (less than US$10) to several thousand pesos (US$100 or more). This level of fees represents a fraction at the revenues of the group, which come from larger consultancy contracts from government agencies, NGOs and donors.

Author: Moïse Alal.

consumer goods such as cigarettes, sweets, contraceptives and razor blades often depend on informal vendors for a large proportion of their sales, while other manufacturers sell large quantities of supplies such as welding gas, vehicle spare parts or food ingredients to micro-enterprises. Such firms will sell more of their products if their informal outlets are better managed. Sales representatives who are in contact with micro-enterprises can help both their own employers and their customers if they are able to provide simple business and management advice in addition to selling their products.

Some banks too have started to realize that micro-enterprises can be valuable customers for financial services, both as depositors and borrowers. These banks may employ field agents to collect savings and loan repayments; these agents can also help their customers save more and repay more reliably, by providing basic management and business advice along with financial services. Municipal inspectors have traditionally harassed micro-enterprises, but local authorities are now starting to appreciate that informal-sector business activities provide both employment and important local services to the public. It is easier for inspectors to enforce health, safety or location regulations if they are able to offer management advice while carrying out their primary responsibilities.

Voluntary organizations working with the poor used primarily to provide welfare services such as elementary education and basic health care, but many of them are now starting to help people to increase their incomes through self-help and entrepreneurship. Community development staff and social workers are turning into bankers and consultants to micro-enterprises; they too offer an indirect route through which a specialist consultant can reach the owners of micro-enterprises.

Indirect management and business consulting, as described above, is clearly very different from direct selling of business advice. A consultant may be asked to advise and assist such organizations in their work with micro-enterprises, and to train their field workers in consulting and counselling skills. In other cases, it may be appropriate to suggest involvement of this kind to a larger client company as a way of increasing the effectiveness of field representatives, or possibly as part of the client's efforts to contribute to social development and enhance its image in the community. In these cases, the management consultant will have to assess the weaknesses and needs of the micro-enterprises with which his or her client is involved, and then suggest and demonstrate simple techniques for providing on-site management advice which can easily be taught to non-specialists.

In conclusion, it should be clear from the above that consulting for micro-enterprises is very different from consulting for large and even small businesses in the formal sector, both in the nature of the work itself and in the channels through which it may be necessary to reach the clients. Consultants should never fall into the trap of believing that such work is simple or beneath his or her attention, or not worth doing at all. Even though the management techniques that are needed may be very simple, the tasks of diagnosis and communication are difficult. The task is even more complex when the consultant has to reach micro-entrepreneurs indirectly, through field agents such as sales representatives or social workers who may have little or no management knowledge and perhaps misgivings about business in general.

The task is, however, well worth attempting. The number of people working in micro-enterprises is vast and their problems are often so serious as to affect the very survival of themselves and their families. For people as poor as most micro-enterprise operators, even a modest increase in income can significantly improve their whole lifestyle: there are few areas where management and business consulting can have such a significant impact on the welfare of so many people.

CONSULTING FOR THE PUBLIC SECTOR 26

The provision of consulting services to public administration and the public sector must respond to the particular challenges and problems of the sector. In turn these challenges and problems derive from the national, social and economic context and, in large measure, the present and future policies of the government. Governments turn to consultants because the challenges they face are new and complex, and the right responses are difficult to find in the absence of precedents, experience, and resources for adequate analytical and conceptual work. In addition, governments are constantly exposed to political pressures and criticism, which may or may not be justified. Comparisons with the private sector are frequently made, hence the growing interest in evaluating and using private sector experience to enhance effectiveness and efficiency in the public sector.

26.1 The evolving role of government

The role of government in modern society is pervasive.[1] Not only do governments provide or regulate a vast array of services, they also provide the legislative framework for governance. Government can achieve its objectives in many ways: by producing and delivering a service itself; by making direct payments to individuals and businesses; by setting up a government-owned commercial enterprise; by providing direct grants or low-interest financing loan guarantees; by offering tax incentives to individuals and businesses; or by regulating business and other activities of individuals and organizations.

The total outlay of government is between 30 and 50 per cent of gross domestic product (GDP) in most Western industrialized countries, while in some developing countries the public sector represents an even higher proportion of GDP. Governments also provide a relatively high percentage of total national employment. An exhaustive list of challenges facing the public administration sector in various countries would be very long indeed. Governments have sought assistance from consultants on a wide range of economic, social and administrative issues.

David Osborne and Ted Gaebler have expressed openly what many other scholars and practitioners believe – government needs to be reinvented.[2] There can be no prosperous and democratic society or flourishing market economy without a strong and effective government. Criticizing governments in general terms is of little use: what is needed are workable proposals. Osborne and Gaebler suggest ten broad principles, or directions, that underscore how public organizations can "reinvent" and structure themselves, moving from centralization to decentralization, from monopolies to competition, from bureaucratic to market mechanisms and from funding inputs to funding outcomes or results (box 26.1).

When management consulting was first introduced to public sector management, assignments tended to be general in nature. In recent years a number of factors have changed this pattern. Government programmes are becoming more complex. There is a need to improve the productivity and social impact of government services in the face of shrinking budgets and the steadily increasing demand for more diversified and higher-quality public services. Advances in information technology are both facilitating and requiring the redesign and re-engineering of major government programmes and services. As a result, the nature of consulting services required by this market is becoming more specialized and more complex. Most of these services tend to be in one or more of the following four areas.

- *Strategy and policy advice*, generally related to wide societal or administrative problems facing the public sector. Management consulting services are generally bought by the top echelon of public sector managers and politicians, who aim to clarify options and determine the optimum direction in a highly complex environment. This market is small, and is generally limited to consultants with publicly recognized experience in the policy area.
- *Designing, developing and managing programmes and operations* is an area in which there are far more frequent requests for management consulting assistance. These requests may be made by public managers, in reaction to an evaluation or audit, or may be triggered by consultant marketing.
- *Adjustment* of the machinery of public sector organizations. These adjustments usually focus on organizational structures, processes and supporting systems such as finance, procurement and human resource management. Concerns to increase productivity and use new information technology to the full have greatly intensified the pressures for public sector managers to restructure the processes and systems for which they are responsible.
- *Facilitating change processes* in public sector organizations. Whether the change is to the structure of the organization and its way of doing things, or to supporting systems, the management of the change process itself is critical to the success of the organization. Consulting support in establishing continuous learning, total quality and performance management processes can provide the framework for the change process. With the reduction of in-house

Box 26.1 Reinventing government

The ten principles:

1. Catalytic government: steering rather than rowing.
2. Community-owned government: empowering rather than serving.
3. Competitive government: injecting competition into service delivery.
4. Mission-driven government: transforming rule-driven organizations.
5. Results-oriented government: funding outcomes, not inputs.
6. Customer-driven government: meeting the needs of the customer, not the bureaucracy.
7. Enterprising government: earning rather than spending.
8. Anticipatory government: prevention rather than cure.
9. Decentralized government: from hierarchy to participation and teamwork.
10. Market-oriented government: leveraging change through the market.

Source: D. Osborne and T. Gaebler: *Reinventing government: How the entrepreneurial spirit is transforming the public sector* (New York, Plume, 1993).

services, public sector organizations are increasingly retaining consultants to provide training and counselling services to their staff. Training is frequently needed in management and communication skills for new organizational processes, as well as in standard management and technical areas.

Some governments have made considerable progress in evaluating their experiences and defining policies for working with consultants. For example, in 1994 the Government of the United Kingdom published a major review of its use of external consultants.[3] In 1999, a statement of best practice concerning the use of consultants was signed in the United Kingdom jointly by the Government, the Management Consultancies Association, and the Institute of Management Consultancy.[4] Many governments have internal guidelines for the selection and use of consultants.

26.2 Understanding the public sector environment

The worst error a consultant can make in entering the public sector is to believe that management is the same everywhere and that solid private sector experience provides all the answers. True enough, drawing on private sector management know-how is currently one of the principal ways of improving public management. However, there are significant differences in complexity, driving and impeding forces, time horizons, resource constraints, hierarchical relations, organizational cultures and traditions, individual motivations and other factors that make public sector processes and organizations different from private ones.

Most, if not all, public sector problems are embedded in larger social, economic, political or administrative issues. It is very important to understand thoroughly the nature and dimensions of the problem. The problem presented is often deceptively simple, and it is sometimes necessary to build problem definition (with the various stakeholders) into the consulting process. Inadequate problem definition, conflicting views of what the real problem is and how it should be handled, and an insensitive approach to social, political and environmental issues can lead to an unmanageable assignment, especially in its later stages.

Public sector decision-making

Public sector decision-making is the process by which a government or government agency responds to a societal or an administrative issue.

Societal issues are those social or economic problems or opportunities that require collective action by society, generally through a government programme or agency. Government programmes – be they services produced or arranged by the government, regulatory programmes or economic grants to individuals or businesses – require careful analysis, planning and organization.

Administrative issues are problems or opportunities related to the machinery of government. A government is a large administrative system, organized to provide different types of service or to deliver regulatory programmes. As with any large administrative system, it must develop organizational structure, policies and procedures. It must also operate a multitude of administrative services. These administrative services may or may not affect the public at large, but their quality and productivity strongly influence the efficiency and image of the whole public sector.

Figure 26.1 illustrates in simplified form the process by which government responds to societal and administrative issues and adopts a particular programme. The process is initiated when issues arise in society or in the machinery of government. Public sector decision-making usually comprises four major steps, in each of which there may be a demand for management consulting assistance.

To understand the nature of the issue, data collection is required (step 1). Many public issues are by their nature complex, and data collection may be extensive. Data may be collected from secondary sources or as primary data by surveys or other means. It is particularly important to understand the scope of the issue being examined and the decision elements that the data will have to illuminate, in order to decide on the extent, depth and nature of the data gathering.

The collected data are analysed (step 2) to develop different strategies for a programme. Once again this analysis may be relatively simple or very complex depending on the nature of the issue.

Consultation with major stakeholders (step 3) is not unique to public decision-making, but it is of particular importance in the government sector. Invariably societal issues and some administrative issues affect a great many people in different ways. Clearly identifying and consulting stakeholders, both within government and in society, can be essential to the weighing of strategy alternatives and the eventual success of a programme.

When the three preceding steps have been completed, an alternative is selected (step 4) from which to develop a programme. This selection will be heavily influenced by the opinions of all stakeholders, including the government of the day, the public at large, special interest groups, and the body of public servants. While good data collection, analysis and consultation can greatly facilitate decision-making, decisions themselves are strongly value-based and, unlike most private sector decisions, must respond to many conflicting interests and criteria.

Once a decision has been made, it must be translated into a carefully designed programme, which should be evaluated during and after implementation. The evaluation may lead to adjustments to the programme. A specific initiative may not involve all the steps of the process as described, but generally a significant initiative must go through the entire process. As shown in figure 26.1, the process becomes more political in the later stages of decision-making.

The consultant–client relationships in support of decision-making in the public sector are summarized in box 26.2.

Figure 26.1 The public sector decision-making process

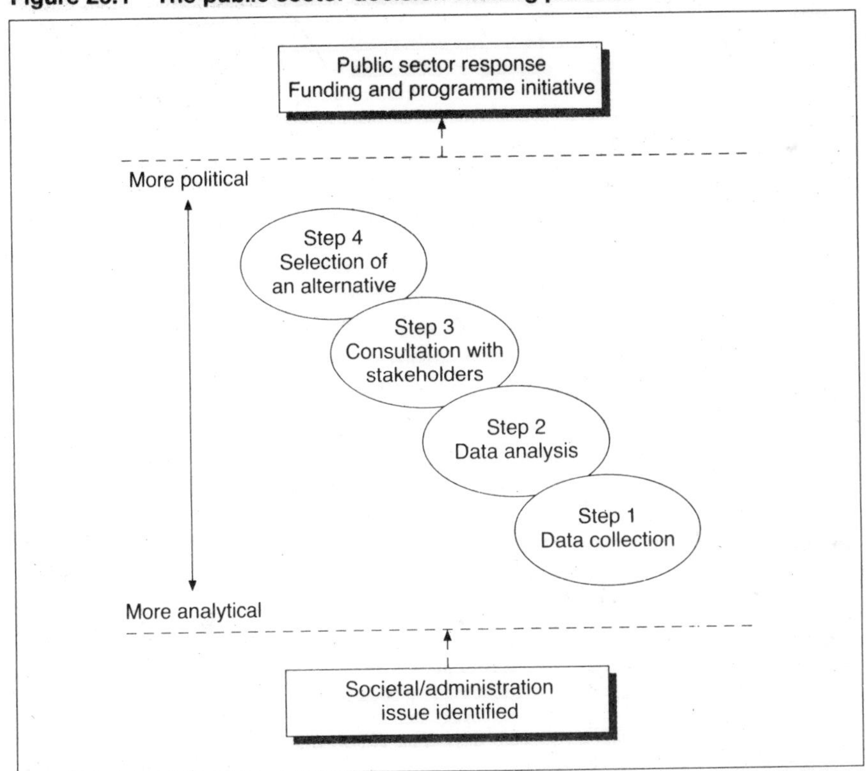

Box 26.2 The consultant–client relationship in support of decision-making

Issue	Private Sector	Public Sector
1. Identification of client	Usually clear	Difficult
2. Nature of client	Single person or small groups	Many persons or groups
3. Client objectives	Relatively clear boundaries and targets	Multidimensional and complex; irregular boundaries
4 Methodology	Important, but often less so than results	Very important, especially consultation and facilitation
5. Constraints	Relatively few, known	Many, difficult to define
6. Accountability for decision	Personal, small group	Collective, large group
7. Decision-making commercial criteria	Based on objective	Political, value-based
8. Documentation/ report	Not always important	Very important; a public document
9. Results	Generally measurable	Often not measurable
10. Evaluation	Informal	Formal and complex
11. Implementation	Almost immediate	Depends on political will, resource allocation, etc.

National and local politics

Important decision-making processes in the public sector are political processes even if the issues concerned are technical. Minor administrative decisions, seemingly without any political implication or significance, may involve political criteria and can become politicized under certain circumstances. Senior administrators may well emphasize their independence and non-political approach to decisions; but politics are omnipresent and the power of political parties and their coalitions shapes public sector decision-making through senior personnel appointments, reorganizations, budget increases and cuts, changes in legislation, decisions taken by the council of ministers, and more or less direct personal interventions and lobbying. Invariably, politicians think of the political impact of legislation, budgetary choices, resource allocations, decentralization, programme proposals, investments, changes in public services and their costs, etc.

The nature of a particular national or local political scene is extremely important to consulting. In an atmosphere of political polarization, hostility and confrontation, even the most rational and needed practical proposals may be difficult to pursue and may be considerably delayed or even discarded.

Opposition parties may attack and destroy them for purely political reasons. In less confrontational political environments, national interests may prevail over ideology and political party interests, though not without negotiation and compromise. The status, quality and independence of the civil service will also influence the quality of relationships of public administrations with consultants.

Social objectives

A key requirement of political decision-making is the balancing of social and economic objectives in developing and implementing public policies and programmes. Social objectives may include the development of specific regions, the promotion of small businesses, job creation, education and services for minority and underprivileged groups, equitable distribution of contracts and purchases, the development and improvement of public services, provision of vital but costly services to remote regions, environmental protection, and so on. A problem often faced by consultants is that social and economic objectives and criteria are vague, inaccurate or even conflicting. It is usually necessary to seek an operational (explicit and measurable) definition and categorization of social objectives, draw attention to their cost side and consider alternative ways of financing them.

Attitudes to change and to consulting

Seasoned administrators, who may have seen many unnecessary reorganizations, unfulfilled political promises and failed projects, tend to be cynical about new change proposals and consulting projects. The pressure of competition and the opportunities created by globalization, market liberalization, new technologies and other developments tend to have a smaller impact on public administrations than on private businesses. Consultants may be viewed with suspicion and distrust, as outsiders who have the easy job of writing another report and then leaving the organization, while the public manager will once more be left with a proposal that cannot be implemented, without any real support from superiors, and with insufficient resources. Consultants may be seen as privileged individuals whose remuneration is out of proportion to their experience, contribution and responsibility.

The consultant's attitudes and behaviour

Experienced consultants are aware of these apprehensions. They realize that the key issue is to develop a relationship of trust and an understanding of the client as a person. Many public managers are competent and dedicated people working in systems that do not encourage high performance, make changes difficult, and require special skills and approaches to get anything improved. The consultant must not only understand why certain things are possible and others not, but must empathize with the client and develop a true partnership in working on

Box 26.3 "Shoulds" and "should nots" in consulting to government

"Shoulds" that work

1. Show knowledge of the agency's methods, procedures and processes.
2. Demonstrate genuine interest in the public sector work environment and the difficulties faced by public servants.
3. Learn the specialized jargon.
4. Understand how the agency is measured.
5. Treat each government employee as an individual, separate from governmental stereotypes.
6. Match your own staff qualifications closely to the agency's requirements.
7. Recognize that decisions often take longer than in business.
8. Respect the fiscal year constraint.
9. Identify and meet the client's perception of a good job.

"Should nots" that don't work

1. Refrain from a hard-sell approach.
2. Avoid designing projects that require a great deal of interdepartmental cooperation.
3. Don't just finish a project but "ease into the completion", suggesting review steps and follow-up activities.
4. Don't forget to keep the client fully informed and closely involved, even if the client tries to avoid responsibility.
5. Don't underestimate the role of the written agreement, especially with deliverables.

Source: W. P. Cordeiro and S. A. Bartik, "How to consult to government", in *Journal of Management Consulting* (Milwaukee, WI), Fall 1993, pp. 20–24.

solutions that the client can accept as his or her own and defend with superiors, elected public bodies and even with the public at large. It is important to believe that quality public services are essential to the life and development of the community, including healthy development of the private sector. A negative and unduly critical attitude to public sector managers and other civil servants is counterproductive and inhibits effective problem-solving.

26.3 Working with public sector clients throughout the consulting cycle

Marketing

Most marketing to the public sector (development of leads and identification of consulting projects) is through networking and personal contacts. A good network can only be developed over the course of time and requires constant effort to maintain. In a limited number of cases, it can lead to direct selection, but more often will facilitate pre-selection and shortlisting.

Most large assignments in the public sector are awarded on the basis of competitive bids; the success ratio of firms bidding competitively varies but is not very high, and preparing proposals is both expensive and time-consuming. Consultants are therefore well advised to develop an efficient process for competitive bidding and to try to maximize their chances of repeat business, which is much less expensive to obtain than is new business. It is useful to develop some business as sole-source, directly awarded contracts: these are generally small, but are relatively inexpensive to obtain and permit consultants to build up and maintain good client contacts.

Selection through public procurement

The selection of consultants, as indeed of other goods and services, has to comply with legislation and rules applied to public procurement in general. A general description of consultant selection is given in Chapter 7 and Appendix 1. What, then, is typical of the public sector? Invariably, formal, precisely defined and structured procedures are used. Most probably there will be an official document, issued by a government agency, which describes the procedure and criteria for selecting a consultant and provides information and guidelines, contract clauses, forms and the like.

The reasons for the use of mandatory formal procedures in the public sector can be summarized as follows:

- to give all eligible candidates the same chance;
- to increase the probability of identifying and choosing the most suitable consultant;
- to make selection "transparent" and less open to criticism;
- to reduce the risks of favouritism, nepotism and corruption;
- to harmonize the approaches used and transfer good experience among various government departments and public agencies;
- to improve the overall quality of consultant selection and appointment in a complex public sector environment.

As a rule, the procedure separates project identification and the drafting of terms of reference from project implementation. A consultant who helps the client to develop a new project idea, analyse the situation and the client's needs, and produce the terms of reference is regarded as an "insider" and is not usually authorized to participate in the bidding for project execution. The consulting process is thus split into two separate phases, for which different consultants are engaged. This can create technical difficulties and discriminates against the consultants who do the creative and conceptual work of designing the project and producing terms of reference. Conversely, consultants who implement a project may not feel responsible for conceptual flaws because they follow the instructions – which may be very detailed – in the terms of reference. They can always refer to the terms that were given to them if the client is not happy with the focus of the assignment and the results produced.

Data banks. Many public sector organizations maintain a data bank of consultants. These data banks may have thousands of consultants and consulting firms, classified by skill areas. In some cases, registration with the relevant data bank is a prerequisite to receiving invitations to make a proposal or being eligible to supply services.

Competitive bids. Depending on the size of the proposed consulting assignment, competitive bids may be requested from consulting firms or individual consultants. Bid documents must generally conform to detailed specifications; failure to respect these specifications leads to the disqualification of the bidder. The evaluation procedures of these bids also depend on the size of the proposed assignment: the criteria, and often the results, are usually available to the bidder.

Budgetary constraints. There may be a strict budgetary constraint limiting the size of the assignment, or predetermining its time schedule.

Managerial discretion. Despite the predominance of formal procedures, public sector procurement of consulting is not totally inflexible. As a rule, small assignments may be arranged by direct selection or using simplified procedures. In certain cases, the appointment of consultants who have done a satisfactory job may be authorized for further services related to the previous job.

Contracting

Both consultants and public sector client agencies may have their standard contract formats. In such a situation, the consulting firm will normally be more flexible and agree to accept its client's mandatory contract format. Several aspects of contracts with public sector clients (see also Chapter 7 and Appendix 4) ought to be stressed:

- Definition of results should be clear and detailed (what results, including their quantity and quality, who will identify and endorse results, who will assess quality, who will have the final word).
- There needs to be a clear understanding of what is meant by implementation and how far the consultant should go, e.g. in implementation of a new system, what is understood by "system"? Does the consultant have to deliver a preliminary proposal, complete documentation, a system that works, a system plus trained staff to operate it, a system that has attained agreed parameters? etc.
- The participation of the client's management and staff should be specified precisely, especially for projects that cannot be completed without this participation.
- Confidentiality is a key issue.
- The consultant's right and obligation to contact directly and consult the public administration's own clients, users and stakeholders should be specified.

- The fee structure should be clear (what is reimbursable and at what rates, e.g. subsistence allowances, first-class air tickets or hospitality expenses).
- The budget and payments structure and schedule should be clear (to comply with budgetary and payment periods and procedures of clients).
- The fee levels should be specified. Requests for proposals generally ask for detailed information on pricing, including the daily rates and time allocation of individual consultants. Often maximum or set fee rates are established by regulations, and these may be below market rates in the private sector.

Implementation

Many experienced consultants consider that in the public sector, people and process problems prevail over technical problems. It is important to adopt an approach that includes full consultation and communication with all stakeholders. Consultants can be excessively idealistic or tempted to recommend the best theoretical solutions. While there is academic satisfaction in finding a "best" solution, what matters most is finding solutions that are practical, acceptable and stand a good chance of being implemented. A recommendation that leads to real change is worth any number of elegant reports that will gather dust on the shelf. Full consultation will ensure that conclusions and recommendations do not surprise and antagonize stakeholders, although it is in the nature of societal problems that not all stakeholders will be equally satisfied with a recommendation.

As with all consulting, public sector assignments must be managed for quality, scheduling and budget. Perhaps the greatest risk with public sector work lies in inadequately forecasting the amount of time necessary for working with stakeholders and for the decision process in general. There are no short cuts in the process of consultation with stakeholders, and neglecting this process can have painful consequences. Another characteristic of most public sector assignments is the need to produce well-edited reports: these documents are, or might be, made public and care and time should therefore be given to their production.

26.4 The service providers

The market for management consulting services in public administration is large and challenging. With the current changes and new challenges, the demand for public sector consulting in many countries is likely to remain stable or even increase in the future.

Private consulting firms

Many public sector assignments are large and complex enough to require the resources and experience of large consultancies that can mobilize multi-functional consultant teams and run parallel activities in a number of public agencies. Indeed, all major consultancies on the international scene have worked for governments and consider public sector contracts to be a standard and fairly stable part of their service portfolio. Some consultancies are known as specialists in certain fields, e.g. in consulting to local government or national health administrations. However, various projects provide opportunities for smaller consulting firms and also for individual consultants, especially if they become known to civil servants as specialists in their fields of activity.

Institutes and schools of administration and management

Institutes and schools of administration and management tend to regard consulting to government not only as a source of income, but as a service that is complementary to training and education and provides the institution with needed insights into the administrative and decision-making practices of the public sector. Governments, in turn, seek the advice of professional researchers and educators from both public and private institutions on a broad range of issues, especially in the fields of public policy, policy analysis, strategies of government modernization and reform, service ethics and staff development. Professors of law, political science, public administration and management are often chosen as senior advisers to government institutions and members of various expert committees. Their influence on changes in public administration can be considerable.

Internal consulting groups

In marketing services to the public sector, management consultants must also be aware of the frequent presence of internal consulting groups within public sector organizations (see also section 2.6). While the number of these groups has been decreasing, they still exist in many countries. Some of them provide free consulting services to government clients, while others charge fees (as a rule subsidized) for their services. The range of services provided varies significantly: some groups provide only limited services such as personnel and audit, while others provide a wide range of services.[5]

The procedures for public sector managers purchasing the services of internal consulting groups are generally simpler than those that apply to private sector purchases. Most internal consulting groups complement their own resources by hiring consultants on subcontract from the private sector, and can therefore be valuable clients for private sector consultants. Some internal consulting groups also manage other consultants on behalf of an agency and provide information to government on consultants' competencies and profiles and on competitive fee rates. On the rare occasion that an internal consulting group is fully dependent on revenue, i.e. self-financing, it can provide a yardstick for reasonable fee rates for consultants hired by government.

Developing a niche

Not even the largest consulting firms are capable of providing the full range of services needed by the public sector. Consultants therefore need to choose their niche and position themselves as experts in their area. There are several ways to define a niche:

- by territorial criteria;
- by level of government (federal, provincial or state, local, government agencies);
- by sector (health, education);
- by functional specialization (IT, statistics, finance);
- by methodological specialization (issue identification, facilitation of meetings, change management, training, surveys); or
- by various combinations of these criteria.

To compete within the chosen niche, consultants should develop a strategy based on product/service differentiation from other firms. A clear and communicable focus for the firm is essential for success in public sector consulting.

Building an image

It takes effort to build a successful practice in public sector management consulting. A good firm develops a team that is capable of offering quality services on demand and builds a track record of providing excellent customer service and durable solutions to problems. Through successful assignments a firm develops a reputation and builds its image in the minds of its clientele. A firm cannot serve clients well unless it allocates at least a small part of its revenues to research. This research should produce significant information on public sector issues, and the new products and ideas that are essential for the continuous development of a consulting firm. Research also ensures the involvement of staff with current issues facing target public sector organizations, keeping their learning current in the process. Publishing the results of research can be an excellent marketing vehicle for the consulting firm, as well as reinforcing its image. A firm should also aim to communicate its successful project experience through articles, Web sites and public speaking engagements.

26.5 Some current challenges

A number of innovative approaches and programme responses have emerged in the public sectors of various countries.[6] Because of their novelty, magnitude and complexity, they have generated new opportunities and demand for consulting.

Privatization

Privatization emerged in the 1980s as a radical programme response aimed at reversing trends that had literally gone out of control, such as the branching out of governments into new areas previously in the private domain, and the continuation and proliferation of state-owned enterprises and public agencies irrespective of failure to make them more performance-oriented in the highly politicized public context. The underlying rationale of privatization efforts has been: (1) that the private sector should do what it can do better, and more effectively, in the interest of the whole nation, and (2) that governments do not become stronger and more useful by running an endless number of different services and activities, but by focusing on policies, regulations, controls and services that only a government can develop and maintain on behalf of the community.

The transfer of public enterprise assets from governments to private owners has been the main form of privatization. Indeed, many people view it as synonymous with privatization. Yet there are other ways and areas of privatization. It has to be stressed, too, that privatization of ownership in the legal sense is not enough. It is more important to create a competitive environment where market forces can play their role, and where private and public initiatives complement and support each other (see also section 22.13).

To management and business consultants, privatization offers a wide range of opportunities for creative and challenging work for the government, special privatization ministries and agencies, and private companies interested in acquiring public enterprises. Assignments include a wide range of policy and operational issues, such as selecting privatization strategies and methods, business diagnosis and valuation, technical and financial restructuring, reorganization, downsizing, auctioning, etc. These assignments are multidisciplinary and require the involvement of accountants, auditors, lawyers, investment bankers and others. The management consultant may be in the position of lead agency or have a specific task under the leadership of another agent, as a rule an investment banker or an accounting or auditing firm. In addition to advising on the transfer of ownership in particular industries or utilities, consultants may take the initiative to advise governments on the pitfalls of poorly conceived privatization initiatives and on improving the regulatory and competitive environment. The negative consequences of some recent privatization initiatives, such as the California energy sector or the British railways, demonstrate amply that there are many opportunities for consultants to help governments view privatization projects from a wider and longer-term perspective.

Process re-engineering

In service tasks it is important to ask the question: Why are we performing this task and what results can be expected of it? A lot of unproductive work is done when people concentrate on tasks without looking at the entire process of which the task is a component. A good example is the task of accounts payable, which is part of the process of procurement of goods. Concentrating on the task of accounts payable makes the task cumbersome and creates several labour-intensive operations (like matching procurement orders with receipt of goods in inventory), which must be coordinated to achieve results. Progress in information technology enables organizations to develop new ways of doing things that are more efficient and less labour-intensive, and that reduce the time needed to achieve results. Using information technology and better-trained staff to re-engineer administration and other processes has become an important strategy to improve the productivity of public sector organizations.

Restructuring public agencies and organizations

In the recent past, governments in various countries have restructured their public sector organizations with the following objectives, among others:

- to clarify the accountability of ministers and departments by giving them more authority in functional areas;
- to separate policy-making from programme delivery activities;
- to promote innovation and risk-taking by relaxing some public service constraints on managers and stimulating entrepreneurial behaviour;
- to make organizations more efficient by improving human resource management;
- to undertake projects to pilot new work options, such as teleworking.

An example of restructuring has been the creation of special operating agencies for the delivery of certain government programmes. These agencies are given a stable policy environment, and full responsibility for the delivery of an operational programme. They have a clearly defined mission, mandate and budget, and are required to operate efficiently using many private sector practices. They are separate from the policy development functions of the parent department but operate within clearly defined limits through a memorandum of understanding. They are given wide exemptions from the constraints of the public service, for example in matters of budget, retaining operational surpluses from year to year, and of personnel.

Other structural changes involve reducing the number of management levels by eliminating certain middle management positions, or making adjustments to budgetary processes by eliminating distinctions between salary and operating budgets. There are also numerous initiatives to improve people management by introducing modern management thinking on quality and customer service, empowerment, training and learning, working in a task force environment, and so on.[7] In the United Kingdom, the government found it useful to apply the European "business excellence model" to stimulate performance improvement within public services.

Public–private partnerships

The concept of public–private partnership provides a useful approach to the division of roles and to cooperation between public and private sector organizations. The questions are: In what ways can public and private organizations work together to take full advantage of the possibilities of each sector in providing necessary services? How can they design and operate joint programmes and enterprises, combine resources and share responsibilities? What safeguards would help to prevent old scepticism and mistrust concerning the other sector and to resolve conflicts before they become antagonistic? What should be done to achieve synergy on a long-term basis?

In recent years, new kinds of public–private initiatives have been rapidly developing rapidly in various regions, in building and managing transportation and communication infrastructure, waste management, health services, cultural and sport facilities and institutions, public information, regional development and other activities. New formulas are being developed for service outsourcing, quality and cost control, joint enterprises, programmes and foundations, co-financing, mobilizing private capital for public purposes, risk and profit-sharing, etc.

Preparing governments for accession to the European Union (EU)

Important changes are taking place in the public administration of European countries that have applied, or are planning to apply, for membership of the EU. One of the principal prerequisites of membership is public administration that complies with European standards and is able to ensure the application of the *acquis communautaire*, i.e. the EU legislation that is binding for all EU members and superior to national law. In addition to making national law compatible with EU law, preparations for membership include major programmes of public administration reform that are country-specific, but that all include clusters of initiatives such as:

- decentralization and strengthening of regional and local administration;
- development of capacities for active participation in Community activities and programmes, including the structural funds;
- building of institutions and development of procedures for enforcing application of Community standards in a number of sectors;
- regulatory reforms;
- reforms of public budgeting and financial control;
- restructuring and modernization of the civil service;
- extensive training and development of public administration staff at various levels of the hierarchy.

These programmes put great and unprecedented pressure on the governments involved, which in many cases are turning to consulting firms to make up for the shortage of internal capacities for planning and managing change, bring in new perspectives and private sector experience, and keep the whole process moving within an extremely tight timeframe. Consultants who can show competence and commitment at this stage are likely to gain a long-term competitive advantage and get further business from these governments at later stages, e.g. in developing and implementing programmes sponsored by EU structural funds, for which a considerable amount of consulting expertise will once more be required.[8]

E-government

The impact of advances in information technologies on government services and processes is profound: it concerns processes, information bases and flows, linkages and communication among services and organizations, provision of information and other contacts with citizens, knowledge management within public administration, organizational structures, and work methods in all areas of government and administration. The opportunities for practical application of new, faster, more reliable, user-friendly and ever cheaper information technologies and systems in public administration and services are at least as significant as in business organizations (see also Chapters 13, 16 and 19).

Advanced and large-scale IT applications are already in full use in many government services. However, governments often struggle with problems of coordination, compatibility, cost-effectiveness, interlinkages, standardization, sharing of data, confidentiality, coping with new demands and pressures, and others. A common ill continues to be a lack of policies and capabilities for choosing and modernizing IT, managing and supervising large and complex IT projects, and sharing experience among various government agencies. IT-related decisions are often left to officials who are ill-prepared for the task and cannot turn to an internal government service for advice and help.

Since the late 1990s, the Internet has created new opportunities for enhancing government services and improving public administration with the support of new information and communication technologies. Shortly after e-business, the concept of "e-government" has been coined; it has even been said that e-business could never develop fully and effectively without e-government.

It is fair to say that the reaction of many governments, including their regional and local bodies and municipalities, has been surprisingly entrepeneurial and fast. The scope and quality of information provided to citizens and the business sector through public administration portals and Web pages has expanded and improved dramatically in a short time. Transparency and openness have increased. Public officials are becoming more accessible through email; consultations with the public are taking place on important new programmes and decisions. Communication, consultation and information-sharing within public administration are accelerating and improving. However, as in business, this is just the beginning of a process that will revolutionize administration in future years.

Here too, management and IT consultancies have an important mission.[9] Governments will continue to be short of internal capacities for programme design, selection, monitoring and evaluation. They will need protection from unscrupulous vendors trying to sell them costly systems that are not fully suitable or compatible. They will be looking for reliable and cost-effective service outsourcing arrangements, and will be keen to keep pace with developments in the private sector without losing sight of the specific conditions, needs and resources of public administration.

---

[1] World Bank: *The state in a changing world, World Development Report 1997* (Oxford, Oxford University Press, 1997).

[2] D. Osborne and T. Gaebler: *Reinventing government: How the entrepreneurial spirit is transforming the public sector* (New York, Plume, 1993).

[3] *The Government's use of external consultants* (London, HMSO, 1994).

[4] See: www.hm-treasury.gov.uk, visited on 4 Apr. 2002.

[5] J. Prokopenko, H. Johri and C. Cooper: *Internal management consulting: Building in-house competencies for sustainable improvement*, doc. No. EMD/20/E (Geneva, ILO, 1997).

[6] See e.g. *Modernizing government*, White Paper and action plan of the United Kingdom Government, on www.cabinet-office.gov.uk/moderngov, and Management Consultancies Association: *Business, government and the new citizen* (London, MCA, 2000) on www.mca.org.uk. Sites visited on 4 Apr. 2002.

[7] See also "Value for money, best value and measuring government performance", special issue of *International Review of Administrative Sciences*, Vol. 66, No. 3, Sep. 2000.

[8] Technical support to these changes is provided by a joint EU Phare and OECD programme SIGMA. See e.g. *Preparing public administrations for the European administrative space*, SIGMA Paper No. 23, 1998. Also on: www.oecd.org/puma/sigmaweb, visited on 4 Apr. 2002.

[9] See "Successfully marketing to the government", in P. Meyer: *Getting started in computer consulting* (New York, Wiley, 2000). Examples of services in e-government can be seen at the e-government knowledge channel www.egovt.tv (visited on 4 Apr. 2002), established by KPMG.

PART IV

MANAGING A CONSULTING FIRM

FUNDAMENTALS OF MANAGEMENT IN THE CONSULTING PROFESSION

27

The previous parts of this book have shown how management consultants operate in serving their clients. Chapters 27–35 look at the consultant's work from a different angle, showing that management consulting must be managed as a professional service and as a business if is to satisfy clients' needs and, at the same time, achieve good results in commercial and financial terms.

In practice this is often ignored. There are consulting firms, including some fairly large ones, that devote all their talent and energy to finding new assignments and dealing with the problems of their clients, while neglecting the management of their own operation. The inevitable consequences are inefficiencies, internal conflicts, and flaws in the services provided.

Clients are often aware of this. The message is often heard, "Healer, heal thyself", or "Consultant, take your own medicine". While any professional service firm requires management reflecting its nature and complexity, the case of management consultants is a particularly delicate one. Management is their daily bread and helping clients to manage better is their main activity. If clients are to take their advice seriously, consultants must be seen to practise what they preach. If this is not the case, clients will understandably doubt the consultant's ability to deal with other people's problems.

27.1 The management challenge of the professions

As a relatively young profession, management consulting should be able to draw some lessons from the management experience accumulated by older and better-established professions, such as law or accounting. Unfortunately, management is a relatively new and underdeveloped field in all professions. Professional firms historically have been managed in one of two ways – badly or not at all.

Management, as a distinct function and approach to running an organization, starts being practised systematically and consistently only when it becomes a recognized necessity. As long as professionals operate as individuals, independently or through loose groupings, sharing some physical facilities and administrative support, but each serving his or her own clients and ignoring the clients of colleagues, the management function looks superfluous, even undesirable.

The key factor leading to the management of professions was the growing size and complexity of professional firms and of the tasks they tackled. The second factor was changes in the market and in competition. With the gradual disappearance of protective regulations and traditional attitudes inhibiting competition, professional firms started to be exposed to market pressures and opportunities like businesses in any other sector of the economy. Issues such as marketing, selling, product life-cycle, profitability, innovation and efficiency became important and had to be addressed.

Conversely, certain factors have hampered the advent of modern management in the professions. First is the ambiguous attitude of many professionals to management. While they generally do not object to belonging to a well-established and financially strong firm, as individuals they cherish their freedom and dislike discipline. Many of them do not want to have anything to do with management or paperwork. This creates paradoxical if not inextricable situations. In Bruce Henderson's words, "the basic paradox is the requirement to manage the unmanageable".[1]

Another constraint has been the shortage of managers for professional service organizations. The best professionals can be the worst managers. Many professionals are prepared to devote some time to management, say by supervising a small team, if this does not take up more than a third or a half of their time. Few are prepared to give up all client work to become full-time managers of other professionals. Also, their colleagues must be willing to accept them as managers. Compromises therefore have to be adopted, mostly by combining management with direct work for clients, or rotating managerial roles. This, however, is more difficult in large firms, some of which have recruited full-time managers from outside – with mixed results.

A third constraint has been the underdeveloped body of knowledge on the management of professions. Understandably, meaningful concepts and theories could not start developing as long as there was no practical ground, accumulated experience and demand. Significant contributions are few, and these date mainly from the past decade.[2]

In summary, the case for competent and effective management of professional service organizations seems to have been made. In addition to the competence, integrity and motivation of individual professionals, the management of professional teams and organizations is increasingly recognized as a key factor of service quality and business performance. Yet many professional firms have a long way to go to become well-managed organizations.

In identifying the management requirements of consulting activities, we look first at consulting from two different perspectives. First, consulting is a professional service and some of its management requirements are determined by this characteristic. Section 27.2 will attempt to review them and to point out practical implications. Second, consulting is a business activity and must be viewed and managed as a business. This will be the theme of section 27.3. The last part of the chapter will provide a synthesis of the two perspectives.

27.2 Managing a professional service

Understanding the nature of the service

It has been pointed out many times that professional services produce intangible outputs or products. In consulting, the product is the advice given to the client. Alternatively, if implementation is included, one could say that the final product is the change that occurs and the improvements achieved in the client organization thanks to the consultant's intervention.

Such a product is difficult to define, measure and evaluate. The client's view of the product and its real value may be quite different from the consultant's. In marketing his or her services, what the consultant is selling is essentially a promise – of help that will satisfy the client's needs. To use Theodore Levitt's words, clients cannot "see, touch, smell, taste or test" the product before deciding to purchase it.[3] They have to look for surrogates in assessing whether the consultant is likely to deliver what has been promised.

This explains the crucial role of self-assessment, self-discipline and an ethical approach in marketing and delivering the consulting service. Often the consultant will be the only person able to judge what services to offer in general, and what he or she can promise and actually deliver to a particular client.

There are ways of reducing uncertainty by increasing product tangibility. The client can be given a manual describing in detail how the business will be diagnosed, what data will be examined, comparisons made, ratios produced and suggestions developed. Or the consultant may be offering a system or a procedure, which will be delivered as such, in its standard form, or with adaptations and supplements. As discussed in Chapters 1 and 2, service and product commodification has progressed in consulting. Any large consultancy has some tangible standard products to offer and some small firms have been completely built around one or two proprietary systems. Yet the basic issue remains the same. Every client organization is unique and there is no certainty that even an excellent standardized system will be effective in every client's environment. Even the largest consultancies are not in the mass production and "ready-to-wear" business but in "tailor-made" services and products.

Determining what services to standardize is a key strategic decision. There are consultants who have spoilt their reputation by selling standard packages to clients who needed an individualized approach. On the other hand, a standard system or methodology applied flexibly and with imagination, and in combination with and in support of an individualized approach where appropriate, can increase the quality of the service and reduce the costs both to the consultant and to the client.

Managing the consultant–client interface

Building and managing a clientele is a crucial issue in managing professional consulting. If there is no client, there is no consulting. The consultant does not produce for stock, getting ready for prompt delivery once a client calls. The client is a direct participant in the production of the service. As a minimum, he or she helps the consultant to define the scope of the advice, provides needed information, and then receives the advice. In process consulting, it is the client who produces, while the consultant acts mainly as a catalyst.

The link between the consultant and the client is a highly individualized one. On each side of the partnership there is one person or a small team. Whatever the size and complexity of the professional service firm, it sends individual professionals or relatively small teams to clients for specific assignments. Large consulting firms can handle larger and more complex projects (the largest projects including major inputs of IT may involve hundreds of consultants), and can support consultants on assignments with the collective know-how of the whole firm. Nevertheless, even a very large firm operates through individual client assignments and cannot think of selling services to unknown customers through networks of retailers.

Clients, and the quality of relationships with clients, constitute the consultant's "customer capital". This capital has to be created, built up, maintained, improved, expanded and rejuvenated. Situational variables determine when a consultancy needs to focus on finding new clients, entering new markets, promoting repeat business with existing clients, offering clients new value and better quality, analysing and restructuring the clientele, etc.

The intangibility and the nature of the interface with clients determine the consultants' approach to quality assurance. Within the profession, and even within one firm, it is virtually impossible to refer to independent and fully objective benchmarks for measuring and evaluating quality. Yet service quality is one of the basic characteristics inherent in a professional approach. Providing every client with a service of the best possible quality is a professional goal in its own right, not merely a condition of being able to sell an assignment and making sure that the client will pay for it.

Because consulting aims to satisfy specific client needs, the degree to which these needs are met is normally regarded as the main criterion for evaluating service quality. Quality management and quality improvement are therefore built on feedback from clients and focus on increasing client satisfaction. When appropriate, however, quality management has to reach beyond this criterion. This will be the case when working with uninformed clients, whose requirements may well be below the consultant's own conception of high service quality.

Quality also means being up to date and providing a service of appropriate technical level or modernity. The consultant–client relationship is knowledge-based: consultants provide and help to apply knowledge (theoretical and applied knowledge, experience, know-how, expertise, benchmarks, etc.), which clients purchase for use in running and developing their businesses. Often the consultant will be better placed than a particular client, or even a whole class of clients, to judge the desirable degree of novelty and sophistication of this knowledge. Being proactive in consulting therefore implies that the consultant thinks even of the needs of which a client has not been aware, and helps the client to realize all his or her possibilities. The consultant also warns the client against spending on fancy techniques and systems that are not appropriate to the client's conditions and that are beyond the client's resources. Managing knowledge transfer and assuring quality are important dimensions of firm management since clients recruit consultants with a tacit understanding that the firm will take full responsibility, not only for providing consulting time, but also for the technical level and sophistication of the inputs, the transfer of knowledge and the quality of the service.

Managing knowledge

To be able to transfer knowledge to clients, a consulting firms creates, develops and manages its own knowledge base. Knowledge management as such is nothing new and most professional firms have always used it to some extent: information systems, documentation, report libraries, client files, project debriefings, brainstorming sessions, news sheets and similar services and activities have been used for years. What is new today is a more structured and conceptual approach, the use of powerful and flexible IT systems and the Internet, and increased emphasis on tacit knowledge and its sharing within the firm, with clients and through professional networks.

The current practice of knowledge management addresses several critical issues. It defines the particular field and kind of knowledge that is unique to the consulting firm (ideally constituting the firm's competitive edge), structures and encodes this knowledge, organizes formal databases, selects and applies appropriate technologies for recording, organizing, retrieving and exchanging knowledge, provides for easy online access by all staff, and establishes procedures for continuous updating and upgrading. Special attention is paid to ways and incentives for identifying and sharing tacit knowledge and to fostering a knowledge culture, or knowledge ecology, within the firm (see Chapter 19).

Managing professional workers

Professional consultants, including the beginners in the firm, are used to dealing directly with clients and spend more time with clients than with managers and other colleagues within their firm. The firm, on the other hand, must know that it can rely on the competence and integrity of its professional staff, including not only the senior partners but also the younger colleagues.

In some established professions there is a well-defined path to the required level of competence and integrity, including university studies, attendance at a graduate school, and practical training and indoctrination over a number of years in a professional firm. Membership of a professional institution or special examinations may be required. The result of this process is a reasonably high degree of standardization of skills, permitting the definition of a range of jobs that even a relatively junior professional should normally be able to perform with no or limited supervision. Even the attitudes of professionals tend to become fairly standardized; thus it can be predicted how they will react and behave in typical situations in which they intervene.

In management consulting the situation is more complex and less stable, for several reasons. It is a young profession, and consultants employed by any one firm usually have different educational and practical backgrounds. It is almost necessary for them to come from various schools and business environments, so that the firm can handle a variety of assignments and deal with management problems that require a multidisciplinary approach. Being able to contribute different insights and perspectives is extremely valuable. Furthermore, the behavioural aspects of handling technical and human problems, and the professional's ability to work with people and help them to cope with organizational change, are probably more significant in management consulting than in other professions.

Staff turnover has always been quite high, but has recently become extremely high in some firms which recruited large number of new consultants during the e-business euphoria of the late 1990s but had to terminate them a few years later. Also, many consultants find new employment opportunities outside consulting or start their own businesses.

The ten points in box 27.1 summarize the key issues of people management in consulting firms. People management is probably the most important but most delicate management function, because it involves highly skilled, independent, ambitious and often very individualistic people who may easily be irritated by insensitive or bureaucratic treatment. Within people management, the first and the last points in box 27.1 are crucial: (i) recruit only those people who possess a talent for consulting, and (ii) realize that superior performance in the often unstructured and difficult context of consulting can only be achieved and sustained by people with strong internal motivation, which must be enhanced, not weakened, by the consulting firm.[4]

Managing the consulting firm's culture

Despite their high level of knowledge and skill – or perhaps because of it – consultants as individuals are difficult to manage. Many of them are used to getting on with the job for the client and deciding what to do without waiting for instructions from their superiors. They tend to have their own concept of management in a professional firm: managers are responsible for creating favourable conditions for professional work (which includes finding new work and securing finance), but should not intervene in individual projects and assignments. Some professionals resent any control or interference in their work with clients, while others are prepared to accept it from people they respect.

Box 27.1 Challenges in people management

In managing their professional staff, consulting firms face challenges such as:

- how to select and recruit staff with potential for high-quality, practically focused, results-oriented and independent work with clients;
- how to build up a homogeneous operating core with people possessing heterogeneous backgrounds and skills (e.g. finance and accounting, information science, behavioural science, statistics, economics, law or industrial engineering);
- how to develop a common philosophy of consulting and a team spirit while maintaining the diversity of personalities, attitudes and approaches needed for various assignments;
- how to maintain this common philosophy when staff turnover is high;
- how to find the right degree of decentralization of technical and business decisions related to client assignments (e.g. which decisions can an operating consultant on assignment take, and which need input from a manager or partner);
- how to make sure that not only the skills, but also the personalities and work styles of consultants and clients will be matched in order to establish a productive consultant–client relationship in every case;
- how to build, maintain and utilize a collective knowledge base and encourage knowledge-sharing within the firm;
- how to provide the sort of leadership that appeals to professional workers with a developed sense of independence;
- how to remunerate people fairly for their personal achievement and their contribution to the professional excellence and profitability of the firm;
- how to motivate people to superior performance, life-long learning, initiative, entrepreneurship, risk-taking, professional integrity and loyalty to the firm.

Some consultants are strong individualists and one may be tempted to ask why they actually stay with a firm. Some stay because they have chosen to work as technicians and do not want to be bothered with administrative and marketing problems. Others appreciate the advantages of teamwork and collaboration with professional colleagues. There is a third group for whom work in a professional firm is mainly a learning experience, and who do not feel committed to staying in consulting until retirement.

The attitudes that prevail depend very much on the organizational culture and management style of a particular firm. Indeed, consulting firms tend to exhibit various organizational cultures. The firm may be nothing more than a collection of individuals housed under one roof, and physically not even under the same roof, since consultants spend most of their time with clients. The management of the firm may act as an employment agency, whose main objective is to find work, keep consultants occupied and provide common support services to the employees. The firm's culture may be weak, almost non-existent. In contrast, there are firms that are known for their strong cultures. They have developed values that are widely shared within the firm. New recruits have to adopt them quickly and if they find it impossible, they usually do not stay with the firm for long.

Consulting firms' cultures are shaped by their founders and other leading personalities in addition to reflecting the common principles and values of consulting. As a rule, strong professional cultures are found in firms that are well-established and recognized sector leaders. They define how the firm views and handles various behavioural and ethical issues, such as learning and self-development, hard work, discipline, initiative, coaching by superiors, competition among staff, sharing of information and knowledge, dealing with clients, confidentiality, conflict of interest, personal responsibility for quality work, and honesty in billing.

Organizational cultures are difficult, but not impossible, to manage. Leaders can change cultures by providing role models and motivating and educating colleagues. In managing the firm it is important to have a correct picture of the firm's culture and of values that need to be either encouraged and supported, or discouraged and changed.

Providing leadership

The experience of the best consulting firms, small and large, has demonstrated the crucial role of leadership. Leadership is needed to build up a professional organization with a stimulating culture, whose individual members adhere to common values and work together as coherent teams in pursuing common professional and business goals. Leadership motivates individuals towards superior performance, service quality and loyalty to the firm. True enough, not every professional needs the same kind and amount of leadership and some consultants may even resent being exposed to it. However, without leadership, a professional firm is bound to operate as a mere collection of individuals, not as a firm, and almost certainly below its potential. It will end up by disintegrating sooner or later.

Leadership in the professions is a rare commodity. It requires a combination of superior professional achievement with the personal qualities of a leader: a genuine interest in people, organizational talent, and an ability to set an example, maintain morale and provide feedback and encouragement. Professional workers resent leaders whom they cannot respect as more knowledgeable, experienced or productive professional colleagues and as persons with a genuine interest in leading and helping others.[5]

This makes the choice for management positions difficult. If possible, managers in consulting and other professions should also be natural leaders, and should be willing to assume both leadership roles and administrative responsibilities.

27.3 Managing a professional business

Management consulting is a business, and has to be treated as such, in all cases where an independent service is provided to clients for a fee, and where the firm has to finance its existence and growth from its earnings. This applies to the vast majority of organizations that provide consulting services. Internal and subsidized consulting services constitute an exception and some principles of managing professional businesses may not apply to them. Still they can benefit greatly from being structured and managed as quasi-businesses.

Recognizing that consulting is a business

It is not always easy to call a spade a spade. For many years, professional firms resented being regarded as businesses, and even now some professionals feel uneasy about selling their services or discussing fees, which they regard as beneath their dignity. Consultants are often torn between being professional and commercial.

Yet a professional service must find a buyer or client who is willing to purchase it and to pay an adequate price for it. There is a more or less developed and structured market for professional services, and competition among professionals is increasingly regarded not only as normal and acceptable, but as necessary and beneficial to the clients. The marketing of professional services has undergone spectacular changes over the past decades, and in many countries further changes are likely in the years to come.

Like any other business, a professional consulting firm needs to be profitable. Its profits will depend on many variables, some of which are not under the firm's control (e.g. general demand for professional services), while others are (e.g. the uniqueness and the quality of the services provided, its reputation and marketing skills, and the efficiency of operations). Profit planning, and deciding on the use of the profits, are important in every consulting firm that wants to be in a healthy financial position, motivate and compensate its people correctly and have sufficient resources for further development.

Traditionally consulting businesses were highly labour-intensive and getting into consulting required relatively little initial capital. All a new entrant to the profession needed was his or her own talent and a small working capital to cover living and other expenses until fees could be collected on a regular basis. He or she could even borrow this money, and start working from home without renting expensive office space. Many sole practitioners were thus able to become consultants on their own, even if quite a few of them had to make personal sacrifices at the beginning of their consulting careers.

Management consulting is now tending to become more capital-intensive. Consultants have to spend more on information and communication technologies, computer systems, Web sites, information and databases, licences, advertising, research, publications, and so on. Consulting firms need finance for growth through mergers, acquisitions and cooperation agreements with other firms, for international expansion, and for the development of new product and service lines, including proprietary and commoditized methodologies, systems and software. In the economics of consulting, a shift is taking place to longer-term considerations, including raising capital, the cost of capital, investment and return on investment, and to an increasing weight of other than direct staff costs in the firm's cost structure and financial management.

The cost of the firm's human capital, i.e. those people "whose talent and experience create the product and services that are the reason customers come to it and not to a competitor",[6] has to be increasingly treated as an investment, despite the fact that human capital is not owned by the firm and has no financial value from an accounting point of view.

A business model for consulting firms

The basics of consulting firms' economics are reflected in the profit model developed by David Maister[7] and applied by the Association of Management Consulting Firms (AMCF) in its annual surveys. This profit model is a variant of the traditional DuPont formula for industrial companies, breaking down aggregate data into analytical ratios. "Return on equity" is replaced by "profit per partner" and the global formula is as follows:

$$\underset{\text{(Profitability)}}{\frac{\text{Profits}}{\text{Partners}}} = \underset{\text{(Margin)}}{\frac{\text{Profits}}{\text{Fees}}} \times \underset{\text{(Productivity)}}{\frac{\text{Fees}}{\text{Consultants}}} \times \underset{\text{(Leverage)}}{\frac{\text{Consultants}}{\text{Partners}}}$$

The understanding of the formula permits firm management to focus on particular factors that affect business performance, and to manage the relationships between these factors.

Leverage. Leverage ("an increased means for accomplishing some purpose", according to *Webster's Dictionary*) is one of the basic concepts underlying the structure and operation of professional firms. The general principle is simple: leverage is achieved by employing a number of (less experienced and lower-paid) junior professionals for each (more experienced and more highly paid) senior professional. In many instances, the senior professionals will be the firm's co-owners (partners), while the juniors will be the salaried employees. Leverage assumes a rational and efficient division of tasks: the seniors are mainly responsible for finding and managing work, while the juniors are mainly responsible for executing client assignments under the seniors' guidance and supervision.

In practice, the principle of leverage can be applied in different ways depending on the nature of the services provided, the clients' needs and preferences, the career planning in the firm and other factors. Very demanding, state-of-the-art and highly responsible work does not permit the use of the same number of juniors per senior professional as more routine, repetitive, standardized and technically simpler services.

Box 27.2 Leverage and profitability

The relationship between leverage and profitability can be illustrated by different examples.

1. In a consulting unit, one partner may have four operating consultants. Total earnings are $600,000, i.e. $120,000 per consultant (including the partner), while their total salaries are $450,000 – $130,000 for the partner and $80,000 for each operating consultant (ignoring the overheads and other expenses). If the partner manages to use and supervise one more operating consultant, thus increasing leverage from 4:1 to 5:1, the new total earnings will be $720,000. Earnings per consultant are unchanged, but total profit, hence profit per partner, increases from $150,000 to $190,000, i.e. by 26.6 per cent.
2. Let us assume that, to be able to guide and supervise the fifth consultant, the partner will have to alter her time allocation. Instead of doing 40 per cent billable and 60 per cent non-billable work, she will only be able to produce 30 per cent billable and 70 per cent non-billable work. Her personal billing will thus drop from $120,000 to $90,000, i.e. by 25 per cent, and the total profit will increase only by $10,000 (from $150,000 to $160,000), i.e. by 6.6 per cent. Profit per consultant will decrease from $30,000 to $26,600, i.e. by 11 per cent, although the total volume of business increased by 15 per cent.
3. In another scenario, the unit described in (1) above finds new work that is better paid, but will require different staff competence and structure. From five consultants (one partner, four operating) it passes to seven by recruiting one senior (partner) and one operating consultant. The two new consultants will be able to deliver $280,000, i.e. $140,000 per consultant, while their salaries will be the same as in (1), i.e. $130,000 for the partner and $80,000 for the operating consultant. Figures for the restructured unit as a whole will show a slightly higher profit per consultant ($31,500 instead of $30,000), but a considerably lower profit per partner ($110,000 instead of $150,000, i.e. a 26.6 per cent reduction). This has happened, despite higher fees and profits per consultant, because of the change of leverage from 4:1 to 2.5:1.

Readers can certainly think of other scenarios and their impact on profits.

Leverage has a strong impact on profitability measured as profits per partner (see box 27.2). Firms with lower fee levels and lower earnings per consultant, but higher leverage, can earn higher profits per partner than firms with higher earnings per consultant, but lower leverage.

Productivity. Increasing productivity means earning more fees per consultant employed. The first way to achieve this is to increase working-time utilization – an important target in all professional firms, but one that is limited by legislation, human limitations, and the simple but important truth that unreasonably long working hours result in lower quality and falling efficiency.

The second way is to charge higher fees per unit of time worked for clients. This cannot be an arbitrary decision if there is an accepted market rate and competition. Higher fees can be achieved by selling new, better and more sophisticated services thanks to innovation, programme development, training and self-education, and better utilization of know-how and experience within the firm.

Margin. The profit margin achieved by the consulting firm reflects above all the productivity and leverage levels. Higher consultant productivity and higher leverage generate higher margins. However, the margin can also be increased by reducing costs, such as general administration, purchase of information, and training and development costs. It is up to the firm's management to judge what is feasible and beneficial in both the short and the long term. Saving on training and administrative costs will increase the margin, but may reduce consultant time utilization (as a result of poor administration) and fee levels (if training is neglected and the consultants' competence will not increase).

Growth. As explained above, in the consulting business improvements in earnings per partner and profitability do not always require the firm to grow. There are even growth patterns that fail to increase profitability, or that reduce it, even though total profits are higher (box 27.2). On the other hand, the business may have to grow for other reasons (see also section 28.4):

- to strengthen its position on the market and capture new markets;
- to develop a more complete service portfolio and employ consulting staff able to undertake a wider range of complex assignments;
- to provide for new work opportunities, career development and staff motivation.

Other criteria and tools. The profit model described in the previous paragraphs helps to understand, and manage, the basic relationships in firms built and operating as partnerships, where the ratio of staff to partners is crucial. If a consultancy is established as a company with shares held by people or institutions who are not partners, and even publicly traded, classical ratios for measuring profitability (see section 14.2) are applicable.

Capital investment analysis (section 14.6) is becoming important in consultancies that invest heavily in research and in developing new, often commodified, products and services. These firms are also increasingly concerned with non-staff costs such as costs of equipment, software, licences, advertising and similar, and with comparing data on staff employed in direct and billable client work, and staff in research and development.

Entrepreneurship in consulting

Entrepreneurship lies at the very heart of business. In a consulting firm, the founder is the first entrepreneur. He or she is the person who has taken a chance and linked his or her personal future to the future of the new business. Although the first investment may have been modest in financial terms, it is always important in terms of human intellect and energy.

Box 27.3 Hunters and farmers

Approaches to entrepreneurship and management in the consulting business can be demonstrated by differentiating between "hunter" and "farmer" firms.

Hunter firms attempt to maximize the entrepreneurial spirit of their members by giving them maximum individual autonomy. They encourage each individual, and each small group, to respond and adapt to the local market. Marketing is a matter of individual responsibility. Firm-wide consistency (in services, markets and approach) is sacrificed in order to capture the benefits of local market opportunities.

To succeed, hunter firms must attract, motivate and reward the best entrepreneurs. Individuals rise and fall according to the results of their own entrepreneurial efforts. There is no central strategy and the focus is short term.

Entrepreneurialism, flexibility, responsiveness, and fast adaptation to shifting market needs are powerful business virtues. Any firm that can successfully maximize these will be a formidable competitor.

Farmer firms (also called "one-firm" firms) are built on a collaborative approach to professional practice and emphasize business systems such as compensation, hiring, training, organization and choice of service lines. They build their success by investing heavily in the chosen areas. What counts is not individual performance, but contribution to aggregate success. There is no way for an individual to do well unless the organization as a whole succeeds.

Farmer firms enter new markets (after thorough preparation) in a big way or not at all. Their marketing, which is approached as an organized, team-based activity, is well focused. Entrepreneurship is not a matter of individual drive and initiative, but a function of the whole firm's management.

Firms that attempt to capture the benefits of both approaches (individual entrepreneurship and collaborative strategy) must make significant compromises in management practice, which usually results in reduced performance.

Source: D. Maister: "Hunters and farmers", Ch. 28 of *Managing the professional service firm* (New York, The Free Press, 1993).

A consulting business needs entrepreneurial thinking and behaviour even when it becomes a large partnership or company employing a number of consultants. It must not turn into a bureaucracy or an academic institution. It probably needs an entrepreneurial spirit more than growing businesses in some other sectors, because of the rapidly changing needs of clients, growing competition, and the fact that consultants encounter new opportunities virtually every day. However, opportunities exist only for those who can see and are keen to take them.

It is essential to clarify the entrepreneurial role of consultants, in addition to their specific technical and managerial roles. Consultants will think and behave as entrepreneurs if they know that such behaviour is wanted and valued by the firm. They should know what is regarded as entrepreneurship: Is it getting new clients? More business from existing clients? Selling more assignments that will be easy to execute? Looking for innovative work methods? Coming up with new ways of tackling old problems? Taking the initiative to develop new fields of consulting?

Consultants need to know, too, who in the firm is supposed to think and act as an entrepreneur. Is this a guarded province of senior partners? Is every member of the firm, including the new recruits, expected to think and act as an entrepreneur?

When consulting is not a business

Not all management consulting units are independent businesses. Internal consulting units within governments and business firms (section 2.5), and consulting services of various not-for-profit organizations, cannot be categorized as businesses. Some of these units provide consulting services free, or for a nominal price, instead of charging the full market rate. Their budgets may be subsidized by their parent body, technical assistance programmes or from other sources. Some of these units may be in competition with other consultants, but their independence tends to be limited in terms of recruiting, remunerating and terminating the appointments of staff, fixing consulting fees, expanding or scaling down activities, changing the service portfolio or finding new clients.

Not all the principles involved in managing a professional business can be applied to such a unit. However, certain principles are applicable. The effectiveness of these units can be enhanced by treating them as "quasi-businesses", providing them with relative autonomy in decision-making, encouraging them to sell services, and making sure that their business results have a bearing on staff remuneration and motivation, and on the future development of the unit. Internal consulting units may compete with external consultants for work to be done within the parent organization but, at the same time, may be authorized to market and sell their services to other companies.

27.4 Achieving excellence professionally and in business

In real life, the professional and business sides of consulting are not separate. Professional decisions are business decisions and business decisions have professional implications. Key professional characteristics of the firm, such as staff competence and integrity, leadership, organizational culture, shared values, and good relations with important clients, have an economic value and are reflected in the value of the firm, fee levels, potential and real earnings, and so on. Managers of consulting firms have to address the two aspects irrespective of their personal background and preference for one or other side. The thrust of their work is sensitive, tactful and subtle balancing both of professional and business objectives and concerns, and of the interests of clients, individual consultants, partners and the whole firm. This balancing requires compromises, trade-offs, and anticipation, prevention and resolution of conflicts.

In every firm, there are pressures that can destroy the delicate profession–business equilibrium. Individuals or teams may develop services in which they are personally interested, but for which there is no market, or which are no longer profitable. Some partners will resent leverage because they prefer to do everything themselves rather than relying on junior colleagues and developing these colleagues. The firm may press consultants to increase profitability by lowering quality. Operating consultants may be asked to become more productive by saving on data-gathering and analysis. Juniors may be assigned to jobs that are beyond their competence.

A key task is the balancing of assignment and practice management. Assignments constitute the basic building-blocks in the management system of consulting organizations. Once an assignment has been identified and a contract signed, the organization appoints a consultant or an assignment team and furnishes them with needed resources. A self-contained management cell is thus created within the consulting firm. As assignments normally have a limited life-span, assignment teams cease to exist when the job is completed. Individual team members are regrouped to make up new assignment teams and new management cells, while other resources (e.g. equipment, finance) have been used up or are reallocated.

Managing and coordinating assignments are crucial activities in any consulting firm. In large firms, dozens or hundreds of parallel and overlapping operating assignments may need to be managed simultaneously, while new assignments are in preparation. However, even the best assignment management cannot ensure the functioning and development of the firm as a whole. It can even create conflicts and imbalances by favouring one assignment over others, e.g. by taking resources from one assignment just because another client speaks with a stronger voice. Assignments can also conflict with the firm's overall strategy. Future development can be jeopardized by favouring lucrative assignments from which the firm learns nothing new. Research and development may be neglected. Here again, a balanced approach is required, caring for global concerns and the needs of the firm in addition to managing specific client projects.

These global concerns and organizational needs include in particular:

- the firm's professional and business culture;
- strategy for achieving high professional standards and service quality;
- strategy for achieving profitability and growth;
- the development of new capabilities and products;
- development and promotion of the market and client base;
- management, motivation and development of the principal resource – the professional staff;
- sound financial management and control.

The terms "balancing", "trade-offs" and "compromise" used in the previous paragraphs truly define what mangers of consulting and other professional firms do for a large portion of their time, but they do not give the whole picture. First, the environment in which consultants operate, and their clients' needs, are constantly changing. The consulting firm's management must be flexible and dynamic enough to cope with and adjust to these changes. In other terms, in balancing the professional and business sides of the firm, it is not possible to return to an old equilibrium – a new one must be achieved, consistent with the changes that have taken place in the environment and in the firm itself. Coping with and managing change imply preventing discrepancies and conflicts between the professional and the business side. New markets are developed and new business models adopted, but professional standards are not sacrificed. New staff are recruited and trained but are not assigned to independent client work for which they are not competent.

Secondly, and most importantly, every consulting firm sets its own standards of performance and achievement. An equilibrium between the professional and the commercial side of consulting can be achieved and sustained at various levels of excellence. There are firms with modest ambitions, where consulting is merely a source of income to managers and staff alike; these firms aim to achieve regular income from any, even uninspired and mediocre, service. The leaders in consulting behave differently. They have high standards and pursue ambitious though not unrealistic objectives both professionally and as businesses. They are keen to have excellent business results and earn more than competitors, but never to the detriment of professional performance and quality. They aim to be leaders in every respect. This is what makes these firms attractive to talented and dynamic individuals, and to sophisticated clients seeking professional services of the highest level they can afford. This is the thrust of consulting firm management.

---

[1] Cited in H. J. Hagerdorn: "The anatomy of ideas behind a successful consulting firm", in *Journal of Management Consulting* (Milwaukee, WI), Vol. 1, No. 1, 1982, pp. 49–59.

[2] Leading publications on professional firm management are listed in Appendix 3.

[3] T. Levitt: "Marketing intangible products and product intangibles", in *Harvard Business Review* (Boston, MA), May–June 1981, p. 96.

[4] Useful ideas and learning materials on motivation and leadership in professional service firms are available from the PracticeCoach® service of David Maister and the Edge Group (see www.practicecoach.com.ai/content/what.html, visited on 4 Apr. 2002), and a handbook for managing partners and practice group leaders by P. McKenna, G. A. Riskin and M. J. Anderson: *Beyond knowing* (Edmonton, The Institute for Best Management Practices). See also P. McKenna and D. Maister: *First among equals: How to manage a group of professionals* (New York, The Free Press, 2002).

[5] Ibid.

[6] T. A. Stewart: *Intellectual capital: The new wealth of organizations* (New York, Doubleday, 1997), p. 91.

[7] This section is based on D. Maister: "Profitability: Health and hygiene", in *Managing the professional service firm* (New York, The Free Press, 1993), pp. 31–39.

THE CONSULTING FIRM'S STRATEGY

28

Many consultants are familiar with the concept of strategy and the techniques of strategic planning and management (see Chapter 12). This chapter looks at how a strategic approach can be useful to consulting firms.

28.1 The strategic approach

A strategic approach is justified if there is a need for it, not because it has become fashionable. In the past, most consultants followed no particular strategy and tried to react to any opportunity and any expression of interest from a potential client. This has changed. More and more consultants realize that they cannot be all things to all clients, and that they stand a better chance of obtaining business by offering a unique service, or by serving a market segment where they can outperform other consultants. Successful consulting firms behave increasingly as strategists even if the term "strategy" is not always used.

Purpose and goals

As in other businesses and organizations, strategy in consulting consists in choosing a path that leads from one condition (the present) to a different one (the future). The starting-point is known, or can be identified by assessing the consultant's present position, resources and capabilities. This is not difficult if there is a will to see reality as it is and not through rose-coloured spectacles.

The future is a different matter. The basic questions to answer are: What do we want to achieve? What is our basic goal and when do we want to achieve it? Such questions cannot be answered simply by extrapolating past trends. Extrapolation can be misleading if the environment and the markets are changing quickly. What is needed is a vision of the future, which is different from an assessment and projection of demand and opportunities; it is the consultant's conception of what the firm should look like and what it should achieve in the future. This is a reflection not only of ambition and imagination but also of a realistic assessment of opportunities and of the firm's strengths and weaknesses.

The two dimensions of consulting discussed in Chapter 27 have to be considered in deciding what the consulting firm should be in the future. First, the consulting firm needs to define its purpose and objectives from a *professional* point of view by seeking answers to questions such as:

- What sort of professional firm do we want to be?
- What will be our culture, our consulting philosophy and our role in solving clients' problems, in helping clients to achieve high performance levels, and in developing their learning and problem-solving capabilities?
- Do we want to become leaders in technical terms, always at the forefront of progress in technology and management methods, and the first to offer new information and new services to clients?
- Shall we confine ourselves to consulting in management, or widen the range of our service offerings? What services should we add in order to be more useful to clients?
- What new services can we afford to add to our portfolio without losing our identity and entering areas beyond our competence?

The second strategic dimension is that of a *business* activity. The key questions to ask are:

- What does our consulting firm want to achieve as a business?
- Should our strategy ensure mere survival, moderate growth or rapid expansion?
- What position in the market for consulting services do we want to achieve?
- What earnings and profits should we aim for?
- What should our firm's financial strength and independence be?

The unity of these two dimensions cannot be overstressed. Focusing only on commercial goals could kill the firm professionally. Ignoring the business side of strategy would undermine the firm's financial health and could make the proposed professional strategies unattainable.

Competitive edge in consulting

A strategic approach helps a firm to achieve a competitive edge over other providers of consulting services. A starting question is: What is our competitive advantage? Why should a client turn to us rather than to other consultants? The reason could lie in special technical expertise, a product that is unavailable elsewhere, a wide range of multidisciplinary expertise required for complex business problems, an intimate knowledge of an industrial sector, speed and reliability of service delivery, low fees, good reputation and contacts among public sector agencies, or excellent relationships with existing clients.

Not every consultant can become a guru, and in any case most clients do not need guru consulting. Clients' needs are at various levels of sophistication, complexity and novelty, and the consulting market offers a wide range of opportunities. However, the number of consultants competing for all these opportunities keeps growing. And clients themselves compete increasingly with consultants by building up internal technical, analytical and change management capabilities.

Thus, a successful consultant who is happy with his or her current achievements and chances of getting good business is probably close to losing competitive advantage. *Success can be the consultant's worst enemy.* While you are enjoying your leading position and past successes, another consultant is probably working hard on developing something new and demonstrating that he or she can perform better than you. Privileged relationships with existing clients will not save you. Clients themselves are exposed to competition and cannot afford the luxury of retaining obsolete consultants, even if they have had excellent services from them in past assignments.

In consulting, you should be absolutely honest with yourself in examining whether you have a competitive advantage. You may feel that you are good, even very good, but are you really better than your competitors? If you conclude that you possess a distinct competitive advantage today, the next questions should be: How solid is your advantage and for how long will it last? How can you maintain and enhance it? If you have no competitive advantage, maybe you can think of developing one. How? This will, of course, depend on many factors and there is no blueprint. But there are no limits to imagination and innovation. Not everybody will succeed, but everybody can try. After all, this is how management consulting has been developing – not by grand designs involving the whole profession, but by a myriad of individual efforts by both small and large firms to offer new and better services to clients.

Strategy and operations

There has been a long debate about what the concept of "strategy" means when applied to the behaviour of business organizations. Is strategic equal to long term? Is a strategic choice one that has a major impact on the nature and shape of the business? Can we talk about strategy if choice is limited and there is really only one feasible path?

In our conception, strategic decisions of consulting firms are those that will have a significant impact on the shape or profile of the firm in both professional and business terms. It is plain to see that such decisions cannot be separated from everyday operations. If a consultant who has never worked for the transport sector agrees to do a first assignment for a road transport company, this may be more than a simple operational decision. It will turn out to be a strategic decision if followed by more work from the same client and if other firms from the transport sector come with requests for advice.

If a strategic choice is made by the firm's management, it is essential to turn it into marketing and operating decisions. New clients, new services, different work for existing clients, new intervention methods, significant improvements in quality, changes in the firm's public image – these are all strategic changes requiring changes in marketing and operations. There is no strategic change without change in operations.

Flexibility in the strategic approach

Only experience can show whether the correct strategy has been chosen. Another consultant, a competitor, may have chosen to offer the same new service, and has performed better in marketing and service delivery. Both your and your competitor's choices were correct when they were made, but your competitor has been faster and more successful in implementing the strategy. As a result, you will have to revise your strategy, looking for one that takes the competitor's achievements into account.

However, the main reasons for the need for flexibility in defining and redefining strategy are not management errors, or competitors' successes, but changes in the business environment. Management consulting needs to reflect developments in technology, markets, finance, legislation, national and international politics, and any other significant factors that affect clients' businesses. Consulting strategy has to follow, or preferably anticipate, these changes. Once the financial markets have been internationalized and even small firms can think of borrowing on the international money market, a financial consultant's strategy cannot be restricted to the national financial market. Once the Internet and e-business have become a reality, no consultant can ignore them.

The need for flexibility and imagination in defining and redefining consulting strategy cannot be overemphasized. Strategy must never become a straitjacket inhibiting innovation and entrepreneurship. A consulting firm may have defined its specialization and intervention methods with great care and precision, but this should not prevent the professionals on assignments from being alert to new kinds of problem and opportunity faced by clients. Dynamic consulting firms have always encouraged their staff to think of assignment opportunities in new fields and to come up with new suggestions on how to deal with old problems. The relationship between long-term strategic choices and the need for flexibility and innovation may be delicate and difficult to monitor (remember the "hunters" and "farmers" in box 27.3), but no consulting firm can afford to ignore it.

Furthermore, taking a strategic approach does not mean that the consultant must use a heavy, time-consuming, and probably not very practical methodology for strategic assessment and planning. There is no point in trying to quantify what cannot be quantified and making detailed projections if the future is uncertain. A light and flexible approach to strategic planning and management is not only more effective, but is the only approach that has a chance of being internalized and practised systematically in a professional service firm.

28.2 The scope of client services

Some consultants are reluctant to be explicit and precise in describing the services that they are able to provide. Some think that such a description could be restrictive and that they may not be considered for work that does not exactly fit the service description. Others feel confident that their analytical and problem-solving expertise is so strong that they can handle virtually any problem. Yet service and product definition is a basic building-block of consulting strategy. It determines the firm's identity and profile, tells clients what they can ask for and expect to get, determines the expertise that the firm must build up and maintain up to date, and has considerable impact on consulting style and methodology. Increasingly, clients want to know precisely what services they can expect from their consultants. They want to be sure that, if the consulting firm includes a particular service among its offerings (e.g. organizing sales networks or assessing staff competencies), this has been a deliberate and responsible strategic choice, which is consistent with the firm's resources and experience.

The firm's core competencies

A useful perspective in choosing products and services is that of the firm's core competencies. Core competencies are defined by activity areas (these can be subjects, intervention methods, sectors, special skills or others) in which the firm has developed excellent knowledge and know-how, employs a sufficient number of well-trained professionals, keeps abreast of developments and can without any major difficulty undertake various assignments and serve a wide range of clients. The firm would normally confine its service offerings to its core competency areas, without trying to branch out into areas where it does not feel strong enough. If there is a need and demand for work outside the core competencies (e.g. in complex assignments), rather than improvising or doing second-rate work the firm would turn to subcontracting, sharing the work with an alliance partner or another convenient formula. A firm recognized as highly competent for certain sorts of services would not spoil its reputation by amateurish work in other areas.

The concept of core competencies cannot be static. Competencies change with changing experience and as a result of changes in the professional staff structure. They can be enhanced by staff development, or lost because of inertia, lack of dynamism and poor personnel policies.

Your special product

Some consultants have found it useful to develop, and offer to clients, special products, different from services or products available from other consultants. Such special products (which may be a training package, a problem-solving approach, a business diagnosis methodology, a risk assessment and management model, or other) can constitute the consultant's competitive advantage if they meet a perceived client need and if the consultant is successful in marketing them. As mentioned in Chapters 1 and 2, there has been a clear trend towards commodification, with some services offered by consultants attaining high levels of standardization.

Special products should be different from, and superior to, comparable products offered by other consultants. It is not wise to try to fool clients by using fancy brand names to market standardized consulting services that offer nothing special or different.

Product innovation

Like any other product, a professional service has its life-cycle; it passes through periods of design and development, testing, launching on the market, growth, maturity, saturation and decline. Some services become obsolete and have to be phased out sooner than others. As far as possible, in planning strategy the consultant should analyse the life-cycle of his or her particular services in order to avoid their obsolescence and be ready to change existing services or introduce new services at an appropriate moment.

A practical approach is to classify services in groups, using criteria such as the contribution of the service to the firm's income, the rate of growth of the service, expected future demand or the cost involved in developing and marketing it. Various methods of strategic analysis can be used to reveal, for example:

- services that are not growing any more, but that continue to generate a substantial part of the total income;
- services that are growing rapidly, though their relative importance in the firm's total income remains small;
- services whose volume is stagnating in certain markets, but that are in demand in other markets;
- services that could easily be redesigned and adapted for new markets (client groups, sectors, countries, etc.);
- services whose marketing and maintenance costs are excessively high;
- services that have become standardized and commodified, and can be handled by junior consultants;
- services that provide opportunities for developing new competencies and entering new markets.

To many consultants, product innovation has a narrow meaning. They confine their innovation efforts to mimicking firms that they regard as sector leaders and highly profitable professional businesses. Rather than developing their own products, they imitate or purchase products developed by others, especially if such products are in vogue and demand. It frequently happens that

Box 28.1 Could consultants live without fads?

To business journals and other observers of the consulting scene, consulting today is almost synonymous with faddishness. Consultants are regarded, and criticized, as the principal force behind the creation, use and abuse of management fads. "Consultants have always had a role in launching fads . . . but they have been working overtime to roll out new fads since the 1970s" (*Business Week*, 20 Jan. 1986). And seven years later: "Fad surfing – riding the crest of the newest panacea and then paddling out just in time to ride the crest of the next one – has been big business over the past 20 years" (*Sloan Management Review*, Summer 1993). And "there is a new-look menu over at The Consultants' Café. Good old soup of Total Quality Management and Change Management pâté are off. Perhaps you would care to try some Business Process Re-engineering instead?" (*Management Today*, Aug. 1993). The story continues: "Old consultants never die: They just go 'e'....And if you are one of the big, established strategy firms? You put out the message that you eat, drink, sleep and dream about infotech.... Everybody's poaching on everybody else's turf." (*Fortune*, 12 June 2000). What will be the next act?

A management fad can begin as one consultant's special product, and quickly turn into a popular and widely demanded and copied technique. But what is a management fad? Is it a gimmick, an irresponsible promise and a superficial approach, or can it be a new, practical and useful method whose popularity has grown beyond any expectation? It appears that the rise and fall of management fads is due as much to clients' attitudes to change as to some consultants' imagination and aggressive marketing. "A lot of American executives these days seem eager to latch on to almost any new concept that promises a quick fix for their problems" (*Business Week*, 20 Jan. 1986). Since American business sets the tone, managers in other countries quickly become infected.

If a client is looking for a fad and the consultant agrees to provide one only to avoid the real problem and please the client, it is appropriate to talk about abuse and unprofessional behaviour. If a fashionable method helps to shake up lethargic management and stimulate real improvements, it probably fulfils a useful role. Perhaps management and business practitioners need a periodic dose (not an overdose) of fads to stimulate thinking and change. Perhaps the impact of many management fads has been more psychological than technical.

large numbers of consultants simultaneously go for the same product in the belief that this is the best and easiest way of getting their share of the cake. This is how management fads emerge and their proliferation is fuelled by consultants' fear that they could be left behind (box 28.1).

Research and development strategy

There is, then, the question of what research the consulting firm should do to meet its own needs, particularly for improving its services and keeping them up to date, and for developing new competencies and services. In many consulting firms, the senior staff is busy negotiating and preparing new assignments, while the operating staff is busy serving clients. Little is done by way of research and new product development. That is why some academics have been able to compete successfully with professional consultants: basing their advice on research, they have come up with new products that have aroused the attention of the business community more than the service offerings of long-established consulting firms.

Every consultant has to decide whether or not to carry out research for product and methodology development, and if not, how to acquire the new knowledge and expertise without which product innovation is impossible. Some large and medium-sized consulting firms have chosen to do their own research, aimed mainly, but not exclusively, at developing new services. Another major benefit, which several consulting firms have already derived from research, is the demonstration of intimate knowledge of the business and management scene and of the firm's readiness to share knowledge and experience with clients and a wider management public.

Sole practitioners and small firms are in a different situation; their limited resources prevent them from engaging in extensive research and development activities. Small and focused projects, however, are within their reach. They can, furthermore, keep informed about ongoing research in universities and management institutes and participate in workshops reviewing the methods and the results of recent research. Joint research involving several consulting firms, and research organized by consultants' associations for the benefit of their members, are under-used and deserve to be explored.

In deciding to do research, a consulting firm has to face the question of relationships between research and operations. Research projects and teams separated from current client work do not seem to be the most effective solution. Better results have been obtained from research based on work for clients, using client assignments both as a source of information and for testing and applying research results. However, adequate organizational, time and financial provision must be made if research objectives are to be pursued in parallel with operational objectives. Without proper arrangements, it would be unrealistic to expect that operating consultants would also find time and energy for research and new product development.

28.3 The client base

Consulting services and products are always intended for a particular client base. Defining and developing this base are other key elements of strategy formulation. This includes considerations on serving:

- existing or new clients;
- organizations of different size (small, medium, large, very large);
- organizations in one or more sectors (e.g. energy, transport, health, banking, etc.);

- private, public or mixed-ownership organizations;
- organizations with management systems at different levels of sophistication (e.g. firms that are very advanced in applying new manufacturing and management technologies);
- firms in a limited geographical area, in a whole country, in other countries and regions, or multinational firms;
- a larger or smaller number of clients.

In consulting, as in other professional services, having a solid clientele is probably even more important than having an excellent product to offer. Clients who know and trust the consulting firm from previous experience, and are prepared to return to it with new work, are a major asset. Relationships of trust and collaboration with such clients constitute what some authors call the consultant's "relationship capital" or "customer capital", which is defined as "the value of the organization's relationships with the people with whom it does business".[1]

Invariably, the strategists of the consulting profession put great emphasis on retaining existing clients and on knowledge-sharing, marketing and other strategies aimed at these clients. In some firms, repeat business accounts for 75–85 per cent of total earnings.

This, however, has to be considered in conjunction with service specialization and the firm's overall development strategy. Growth and diversification may be impossible without finding new clients, thus increasing and diversifying the client base. Conversely, new products are needed to serve the existing client base. Clients stay with you, trust you and recruit you again, only if they see that you are developing your product line and your capabilities in accordance with their changing needs. Otherwise they have no reason to return to the same consultant.

There are, too, certain other strategy considerations. It is important to decide how many clients to serve. This may be crucial in the case of a single practitioner or a small firm. Getting large contracts from a small number of clients reduces the amount of time spent on acquisition work and ensures regular income. However, this may be a high-risk strategy, since it tends to create an excessive dependence on one or a small number of major clients, and even on individual managers in the client organizations. It may also narrow down the consultant's horizon and limit the chances to learn from new clients.

Further, the level of the clients' sophistication should be compared with the sophistication of the services that the consultant is able to provide. There are differences between clients (and countries and sectors) in terms of sophistication of their management systems, and competence of their managerial and specialist staff. Not every client requires, or can use, the latest innovations in management science and technology. Not every consultant can claim to operate at the cutting edge of management technology, and a realistic assessment of one's own level of sophistication can be one of the soundest strategic moves.

28.4 Growth and expansion

In many countries and even in international markets, large consulting organizations and single practitioners operate alongside each other. Various firms have grown in their own ways and, in many cases, no particular growth strategy has been pursued. The vision and entrepreneurial spirit of the founder or managing partner, and good performance in marketing and delivering services, have been the main factors of growth, allied with a favourable business climate.

Nevertheless, the size of the firm and the rate of growth ought to be considered when strategy is defined. These issues should be examined in connection with the range of services offered, sectoral and geographical coverage, assessment of the market, existing and newly developing competition, the consulting organization's resources, and its ability to sustain growth while maintaining or improving service quality.

Is there an ideal size of a firm?

Some consulting firms have deliberately opted for a particular size and do not try to grow beyond it. This is often justified by a combination of human and managerial factors – the desire to maintain a coherent professional team where individuals can interact with each other and a simple management structure can be used. Conversely, size can become a constraint for small firms. They may see consulting opportunities that are fully within their technical capabilities, but beyond their reach owing to the importance of the potential client, the size of the contract and the number of consultants to be assigned to the project.

It is impossible to determine an optimum size of a consultancy as a theoretical concept. Instead, it is necessary to keep in mind coherence between the firm's strategic choices and plans, and its current and projected size. Analysis may reveal that there is no reason to grow, or, conversely, that the firm must grow if it wants to capture new markets, develop new service lines, cope with competition and satisfy the ambitions of its staff.

How far can consulting firms grow?

Attitudes to firm size and growth in consulting have been strongly influenced by the behaviour of the largest service providers. In the past 10 years, these firms without exception have vigorously pursued fast growth, combining various strategies, such as new staff recruitment, mergers and acquisitions, service commodification, and service portfolio restructuring. Significant growth factors have included combination and integration of management and IT consulting and the emergence of e-business consulting. Without information technologies and systems, the growth rate would have been much smaller. The largest consultancies, such as Accenture, PricewaterhouseCoopers, Cap Gemini or Ernst & Young, now employ over 45,000 consultants each worldwide, and their annual global consulting revenues exceed US$8 billion per firm. The growth of some other large firms has been even faster, although they have not attained the dimensions of the consulting giants. Furthermore, the largest firms provide services not only in consulting, but also in audit, IT, outsourcing, venture capital and other sectors (this has started changing, however).

It appears at present that most consultancies are happy to grow, and want to grow faster than the competition if possible. The question of the limits of growth is a taboo subject in consulting circles since no firm wants to admit that it has already outgrown rational limits.

For large consultancies, their size is a precondition for being considered for large and complex projects, for actual delivery of such projects, for providing a wide range of coordinated services to important business clients in the global economy, for serving clients active in a number of different countries, and for major government projects. Clearly, large firms can also afford to spend more on research and product development, marketing and publicity. Conversely, in professional services, size inevitably leads to problems with corporate culture and identity, staff competence and quality, coordination and supervision of service delivery, quality assurance and operational efficiency. It constrains competition and increases the risk of conflicting interests. For certain tasks and clients large firms are just too heavy, inflexible and costly. Thus, although the size of consulting firms is not a hot topic at present, it is likely to become one sooner or later. There may even be a reverse trend – downsizing, spin-offs, departures of specialized teams and units, breaking up of large firms into smaller and better-focused entities, and a range of similar strategic transformations.

Growth and questions of staffing

Growth involves recruiting and developing new consulting staff. If growth is fast, it is often difficult to find new consultants, the initial training of new recruits has to be shortened, and relatively inexperienced consultants have to be assigned to jobs that may be beyond their competence. Many consulting firms that have followed a fast-growth strategy have had to struggle with considerable problems of staffing, training, indoctrination, coherence, integrity, supervision and even efficiency.

A consulting firm that does not grow, or grows too slowly, faces other problems. As members of staff age and become more experienced, they want to be promoted to senior positions and obtain corresponding increases in remuneration. The firm's leverage pattern may become distorted because it cannot maintain the normal ratio of juniors to partners. The cost of the firm's services will also grow if the higher remuneration cannot be matched by increased staff productivity.

What is to be done? The firm may try to change its product-market scope, focusing on more sophisticated services that require more experienced (and better-paid) staff. In other cases, staff turnover can help. Staff members who see no chance of promotion may leave, and can be replaced by new recruits at junior level. In one sense, such problems exist in any organization. However, they tend to be more acute, and to have a greater effect on strategy, in professional service firms, because most of these firms are limited in size and the employees are highly competent individuals with ambitious career goals. We will return to this question in Chapters 36 and 37, where consulting careers and staff development are discussed in more detail.

Mergers and acquisitions

Growth and expansion can be achieved through mergers and acquisitions. In the 1980s and 1990s, many consulting firms adopted this strategy for various reasons: to add a new service line to their portfolio (corporate strategy, information technology, marketing), to acquire access to a consulting market in another country, to become international, or just to get a larger share of the market. Some large international consultancies bought ten or more smaller firms of varying profiles. The most spectacular mergers were of course those within the Big Eight group, which reduced the group to the Big Six and later to the Big Five.

In the professions, growing through mergers and acquisitions is a courageous and risky strategy, requiring highly sensitive and open-minded management. Different corporate and national cultures have to be faced and harmonized, many structural and human problems resolved, barriers to change overcome, and clients assured that they will get the same and an even better service. It is not surprising that not all mergers and acquisitions have been unqualified successes.

Networks and alliances

As consulting projects grow larger and more complex, and clients demand the highest quality of service, fewer and fewer consultants can rely solely on their own resources. Developing new services and capabilities with the firm's own resources takes time, and may not be the right thing to do (e.g. if demand for certain services is irregular and small).

A merger or an acquisition may prove to be the solution. However, many firms do not want to lose their independence. Perhaps they have not found a suitable candidate for a merger. Or they may prefer to collaborate for some time with a partner before considering a legal merger, in order to ascertain if competency levels, consulting philosophies and organizational cultures are compatible.

Collaboration among independent professionals is nothing new. However, since the 1980s networking and strategic alliances have become an important feature of strategy in many consulting firms. They come in various forms:

- **Informal networks.** Such networks are usually formed by a group of single practitioners or smaller firms with similar or complementary profiles and interests. The network becomes a pool from which consultants choose collaborators case by case for assignments that are too large for one small firm, require special technical expertise, or extend to other countries.

- **Structured networks.** Some networks have become more regular and structured. For example, members may be listed in an information brochure and there is a moral commitment (not a binding agreement) to treat members as preferred partners in selecting collaborators for an assignment.
- **Direct interfirm agreements.** Such arrangements can concern various service lines, geographical areas or forms of cooperation. For example, a general management consultancy can have a long-standing arrangement with several partner firms (or subcontractors) for work in specialized areas such as market research, organization development, valuation or information technology. Such interfirm agreements can be more or less binding and exclusive.
- **Ad hoc project consortia.** A consortium involving two or more professional firms is established for a particular project that exceeds the possibilities of a single firm, or where the involvement of several firms is required for another reason. Technical assistance agencies often require consultants to bid for projects in partnership with one or more consulting firms from the aid-receiving country.

Cross-border alliances are particularly important for the advancement of consulting in countries where the profession is inexperienced and not well established. Many young firms in the transforming economies have drawn considerable benefits from various cooperation arrangements with Western consulting firms.

If alliances fail, this is usually due to poor selection of partners, lack of respect and trust, incompatible cultures and consulting styles, major discrepancies in competence, unrealistic expectations, poorly defined commitments or the pursuit of conflicting business objectives.

28.5 Going international

Going international is a fundamental strategic choice, with many implications for the structure, competence and operation of the firm. If the firm wants to grow, and the local market is saturated, going international may be a necessity.

By and large, consulting firms internationalize operations for the following main reasons:

- to find new markets for services;
- to respond to demands received from foreign clients;
- to satisfy multinational clients, who expect their professional advisers (consultants, lawyers, auditors and others) to provide an international service, matching the client's multinational profile;
- to tap the resources for funding of technical cooperation, provided by a wide range of national and international agencies;
- to satisfy the consultants' intellectual curiosity and quest for challenging new work opportunities.

To many consultants, becoming international is no longer a strategic choice. They made this choice 10–20 years ago, and their current problem is how to be more effective in managing and developing an international consultancy.

Different internationalization strategies have been pursued, depending on factors such as the firm's general philosophy, organizational culture, resources, creativity, and also sheer luck (e.g. in finding a good local partner firm or an exceptionally talented local manager, or winning an important international contract). Nevertheless, all consultants who have become international stress the need to understand the institutional, economic and cultural characteristics of every national market.

Internationalization has been pursued by:

- undertaking foreign assignments from the firm's headquarters;
- establishing local offices, but providing all senior and special expertise from headquarters;
- establishing local offices by recruiting and developing local consultants, and gradually phasing out managerial and special expertise provided from headquarters;
- acquiring local firms and transforming them to fit the parent firm's professional and business culture;
- acquiring local firms but leaving them almost as they are;
- using various networking and alliance building formulas, as described in section 28.4.

A key issue is finding the balance between centralization and decentralization in developing and managing the professional service side of the firm. If a centralist approach prevails, the whole firm operates more or less in the same way, following the same guidelines and using the same type and level of expertise in different countries. Ensuring uniformity and coherence is a key task of management at all levels. In contrast, fully or largely decentralized firms operate as groupings of independent national units, which may be quite different from each other in terms of technical services and consulting style. Professional guidance from the headquarters is limited, and management focuses mainly on common business development policies and issues.

28.6 Profile and image of the firm

The strategic choices discussed in the previous sections concern the principal characteristics of a consulting firm. Taken as a whole, these characteristics constitute a firm's unique identity or profile. As we have seen, many combinations are possible in choosing the firm's principal characteristics. As a result, there is an almost infinite range of different profiles among which firms can choose.

Consistency between various choices

No firm is totally free in choosing its strategies. The choices must be consistent. Decisions concerning the sort of services that will be offered, or the sort of clients to be served, require corresponding choices in other areas, such as staff recruitment and development, or the firm's own research programme. Furthermore, strategic choices cannot ignore the firm's past experience and record of achievement. The future is very much predetermined by the past. Even if the firm has the determination and the resources for major reorientation of its service portfolio and profile, it is important to analyse what can actually be changed, what the cost of the change will be, and how the clients will react.

Typology of firms' profiles

To help professional firms in better understanding their profile and developing coherent change strategies, several attempts have been made to develop typologies of professional firms (box 28.2). Any such typology has both the disadvantages and advantages of simplification. Seldom would a particular firm's profile be fully identical with one of the prototypes. Most firms are hybrids, and exhibit many other characteristics. When it comes to specific client

Box 28.2 Five prototypes of consulting firms

Danielle Nees and Larry Greiner suggest five prototypes of consulting firms, based mainly on differences in their professional and organizational culture. They emphasize that consultants from these different firm prototypes bring a pre-established style to the client. Their typology includes:

- *Natural adventurers* (consultants identified with scholarly disciplines, providing leading-edge knowledge and tackling difficult issues requiring a scientific approach).
- *Strategic navigators* (consultants applying models and analytical tools to handling complex issues of the client firms' future strategies).
- *Management physicians* (consultants focusing on the anatomy and circulatory system of client firms by analysing and improving structures, procedures, culture, leadership and other factors of efficiency and effectiveness, and on implementing the proposals).
- *System architects* (consultants dealing with systems projects requiring technical solutions, often using sets of pre-established tools and procedures; this includes installing the system and training the staff).
- *Friendly co-pilots* (advisers to senior management on business strategies and policies, and other significant issues).

Source: Adapted from D. B. Nees and L. E. Greiner: "Seeing behind the look-alike management consultants", in *Organizational Dynamics*, Winter 1985.

projects, they will also be influenced by the personalities and cultures of individual consultants and clients. Yet such simplification is conceptually useful and can help both consultants and clients to understand what is hidden behind the professional firms' names, mission statements and general service descriptions. It also helps to develop realistic strategies for the firm's future.

Image of the firm

The firm's image is the way it is perceived by client circles and even by the general public. The image concerns various aspects of the firm's profile and, in theory, should be a faithful reflection of this profile. In practice this is often not the case, owing to factors such as the firm's exceptional achievements, recent misfortunes and its treatment by the media. Also, even if there is no discrepancy between the firm's real profile and public image, this image will usually be reduced to a few characteristics and will provide a simplified (and possibly superficial) picture of the firm's resources and capabilities.

The firm's image plays an important role in developing relationships with clients and marketing the firm's services. It cannot be ignored in developing strategy. In professional services, the clients' perception of what you are is as important as what you really are. You may be the best of consultants, but if the clients perceive you differently (or if you have no image), they have no reason to turn to you. Therefore every firm needs to be aware of its image.

A self-image must not be mistaken for a real image. Professionals easily develop a self-image that is more flattering than their real image in client circles and within the profession. This can be a bad starting-point for strategic thinking.

28.7 Strategic management in practice

Strategic management is an approach, a way of thinking. Strategy is primarily synthesis, not analysis. It must not be a cumbersome procedure with a lot of paperwork and endless meetings. If it turns into bureaucracy, or if it becomes the guarded province of specialized planning units, line management and professional workers will lose interest in it. Consultants advise clients to prevent such a degeneration of strategic planning, and they must avoid this pitfall themselves. This, however, does not preclude the use of a structured strategic assessment and planning methodology, if the consultant is versed in one and has had good experience with it. There are quite a few on the market.

Self-assessment

A thorough and honest self-assessment is a necessary starting-point irrespective of the procedure and methodology chosen. It is sometimes called a "strategic audit" to emphasize the focus and purpose of the exercise. Many consultants will be able to undertake it themselves, although it is never easy to be detached and

Box 28.3 Strategic audit of a consulting firm: checklist of questions

1. What kind of professional firm are we?
2. What are our consulting philosophy and ethics?
3. What is our organizational culture?
4. What is our image in client circles?
5. How solid is our client base?
6. How do we work with clients and how do we learn from them?
7. What are our core competencies?
8. How can we assess our service portfolio?
9. What is our competitive advantage?
10. What lessons can be drawn from our growth pattern and performance record?
11. What strategies have we pursued and with what results?
12. What is our financial position?
13. How can we assess the quality and development potential of our human resources?
14. What do we know about competitors and what can we learn from them?
15. What can we learn from other professional service firms?
16. What is our potential for further growth and improvement?
17. What is our vision of the future?
18. What are our strategic options for future years?
19. What strategic and other errors must be avoided?

objective in assessing one's own performance, capabilities and perspectives. A peer audit may be helpful. In some situations, however, it will be preferable to turn to an independent adviser versed in the management of professional service firms. In any event, the audit should be based on facts and figures, not on illusions.

In self-assessment, the consultant will address the various issues reviewed in this and other chapters of our book. The checklist in box 28.3 gives an idea of the questions that need to be answered.

Learning from clients

The relationship between consultants and their clients lies at the very heart of the consulting profession. When the consulting firm is assessing and developing its strategy, clients play a special role: learning from clients is indeed a significant strategic choice. It would be arrogant, and futile, to draw conclusions on the firm's capabilities and future perspectives without asking what the clients need, want and think.

First of all, the firm must know precisely what the clients think about it. Feedback from clients concerning the services provided may be available from assignment evaluation, contacts with the managers of client organizations, industry meetings and conferences, and other sources (see Chapters 11, 29 and 32). If your firm has an active knowledge management system (Chapter 34), including client information, a lot of this information will be readily available. In addition, clients can be asked specific questions concerning their expected future needs and requirements, and can make invaluable suggestions to the consultant.

Looking at your future market

In many situations, looking at the current market and the existing client base will not be enough. For instance, a firm may have exhausted the possibilities of offering new services to its clients, or may want to be less dependent on a small number of important clients, or may feel that its products could interest potential clients in other countries or sectors.

The identification and assessment of the potential market start with a hypothesis as to what the market might be, bearing in mind the scope and level of the consultant's resources and capabilities. Fact-finding and market research might confirm this original hypothesis, suggest another definition of the market, confirm the original definition on condition that the consultant could improve his or her image, and so on.

A complete survey would cover:

- technical and economic characteristics and development tendencies of the sector(s) to be served: advanced or obsolete technology, growth prospects and difficulties ("smokestack" industries), position in respect to other sectors and national development strategies, inter-sectoral linkages, international competition;
- organizations in the sector: number, size, categories, leaders, monopolies, ownership pattern, traditions; more detailed information on organizations that are likely to be a prospective market (including names and addresses of firms, and, if possible, names of owners and senior managing staff);
- the management scene: level and sophistication of management, use of management systems and technologies, prevailing attitudes and traditions, background and competence of managers;
- practices concerning the use of consultants: demand, attitudes, experience with use, special requirements.

Assessing a potential market obviously involves much more than finding addresses of firms and some global information on them. It requires a thorough research effort; the consultant must know his or her potential market in considerable depth and detail. Various sources of information and research methods can be combined in order to develop a comprehensive picture of the market (business publications and reports, trade journals, official statistics, stock-market information, training events and management conferences, individual contacts and interviews, and so on). Information obtained directly from existing and potential clients is particularly useful.

The definition of a potential market is a delicate matter for a new consulting firm, which does not have any clientele and faces the risk of adopting either an excessively wide or an unduly narrow definition of its market. In the first case, the firm's marketing effort will be too costly and largely impractical and unproductive, embracing organizations that are unlikely to become clients. In the second case, good opportunities of finding assignments may be missed by omitting certain prospective clients.

Some consultants regard *all* organizations in the field of their specialization as a potential market, while others use a more restrictive definition and regard their market as consisting of organizations that have problems and require the consultant's help. Both approaches have their rationale. An organization that does not need a consultant today may need one tomorrow, or next year, and it will be an advantage for you if it is aware of the existence and reputation of your consulting firm. Some marketing effort may therefore be directed at creating this awareness. At the same time, every consulting firm needs assignments that will keep it occupied today, and these will be found in organizations that are experiencing problems. This includes not only organizations in difficulty, but also prosperous firms that are seeking new opportunities for developing and improving their business.

The concept of *market segmentation* is helpful in analysing the chances of a consulting firm successfully entering a new market. Segmenting the market involves subdividing potential clients and their business and management problems into smaller groups, by one or more criteria – size, geographical location, technology used, ownership pattern, financial difficulties experienced (shortage of working capital, foreign exchange problems), market served (local market, exporting, re-export), or other issues. Such segmentation is meaningful if it identifies some common characteristics of the organizations involved, reflected in their common consulting needs and in the kind of services required. It will be useful to find a market segment, or niche, which (a) is likely to need a special service or product that you are able to provide, and (b) is not fully occupied by other consultants.

Knowing your competitors

The market analysis is pursued by assessing existing and potential competitors. As a general rule, it is essential to learn as much as possible about other consultants' profiles, strategies and achievements, addressing questions such as those listed in box 28.4.

Learning from competitors does not mean aping them without imagination. Less experienced consultants can easily fall into a trap by trying to do exactly what their established and experienced competitors do, although their resources are usually inadequate for this.

Whether to compete or not is a delicate but essential strategic choice. Many consultants have decided not to compete with existing firms, but to offer a new service or special product that is not currently available from other consultants.

Box 28.4 What do we want to know about competitors?

1. Who are they (names, founders, key executives)?
2. How large and how well established are they?
3. For what markets and organizations do they work?
4. Do they enjoy a solid and stable client base?
5. What is their technical competence and range of services?
6. How do they innovate and what special products do they offer?
6. What are their consulting and marketing approaches and methods?
7. In what areas are they ahead of us?
8. What professional image do they enjoy?
9. What are their terms of business?
10. What can we learn from them and what can we do better?
11. Are we likely to win or lose if we compete with them?

However, most consulting services cannot become legally protected intellectual property (except certain proprietary systems and software packages). Sooner or later competitors will come up with the same or a similar service, and the strategy will then need to be reviewed.

Understanding the business environment and climate

Your assessment of the environment has to reach beyond the market for your particular services. Various other environmental factors affect opportunities for management consulting and the approach to take in developing and marketing new services. Some of them are listed in box 28.5. These are only examples of factors that may be important to your consulting firm. Whether a particular environmental factor is important or not, and should be examined in depth, reviewed briefly or ignored, is a matter for the consultant's judgement. A general management consulting firm that is contemplating expanding international operations will be interested in different environmental factors from a marketing consultant working with small businesses serving a limited local market.

Every consultant has an interest in the general business climate. If business is prosperous, the markets for consulting services tend to be expanding rapidly. This often stimulates consulting firms to an equally fast expansion, even if they are not always able to provide all new recruits with excellent training and maintain high professional standards.

On the other hand, economic recession and stagnation of business also affect consulting, but not necessarily all services in the same way. Services considered essential for the clients' survival, and for achieving tangible improvements in productivity and efficiency, are likely to continue to sell well. Other services

Box 28.5 Environmental factors affecting strategy

These include:

- the political climate;
- the current business climate and its expected changes;
- international political, economic and trade blocs and agreements;
- promotional or restrictive government policies;
- the dynamism of the business community;
- the availability and sources of finance for new development projects;
- local cultural values and traditions;
- local business practices and habits;
- labour legislation and industrial relations;
- legislation governing professional services, contracting, liability, and the like;
- technology trends likely to affect your clients in the future;
- environmental protection issues and policies;
- facilities offered to foreign investors.

may suffer. In many instances the recession, and falling demand, have forced management consultants to phase out training and other service packages that were relatively easy to sell in the period of general prosperity.

Following the developments in the profession

Although many consultants follow the developments in their profession virtually on a daily basis, a strategic audit provides an opportunity for a more thorough review of trends and of their possible implications for future strategy. Important changes that affect consulting services deserve particular attention. These may be changes in consulting methods, the conception of ethics, approaches to marketing and advertising, ways of combining management, technological and other types of consulting, relations between consulting and training, competition and cooperation with other professions, and similar issues.

Choosing coherent strategies

We have already mentioned that strategic choices affecting various aspects of the consulting firm are mutually related. There is a significant relationship between the basic objectives to be pursued, the services to be offered, the market segment that will be the firm's target, the image to be built up, the marketing techniques to be used, the staff to be recruited and trained, the research and product development to be undertaken, and the resources to be allocated to these activities. The aim is to develop a coherent strategy, not a set of accidental, inconsistent or even conflicting choices.

Involving staff in strategy formulation

There are valid reasons for organizing strategy formulation as an exercise involving as many members of the consulting staff as possible. This can be done through task forces, meetings, special projects, and so on. Participation in strategic thinking and planning helps to build up a team spirit, increase the firm's cohesion, and counter the centrifugal tendencies that can develop only too easily in professional firms. Both senior and junior staff members thus feel associated with the strategy that is adopted, understand the reasons for it and accept it as their own choice. They will feel like "owners" of their firm's strategy. This does not imply, however, that every strategic issue has to be discussed with all employees at every stage of the exercise. It is the task of top management to strike the right balance between adequate staff participation, confidentiality and top management responsibility.

In discussing common strategy every professional has the opportunity to compare his or her personal strategy with that of the organization to which he or she belongs. In professional services it is not uncommon for these two strategies to conflict. An individual may believe in a different mode of consulting or may just prefer to do things differently than the firm intends to do. He or she may help the firm to reconsider strategy, or decide to leave if there is no way of reconciling the two approaches.

Making strategy explicit

We have stressed that strategy should provide a framework and guiding principles for operating decisions made by all units and staff members in a consulting firm. Therefore they have to know what strategy has been chosen and understand the reasons behind it. Staff participation in formulating strategy contributes to this understanding. It is useful to inform all staff about the strategy chosen by management and about any changes. Attention must be paid to strategy in the induction training of new staff. Making staff aware of strategy is particularly important in large decentralized consulting organizations with many relatively autonomous operating units, which are exposed to a permanent danger of losing sight of common objectives and strategic choices. Also, consultant remuneration and motivation must not operate (as they often do) against strategic choices made by the firm. For example, if the firm wants to do more work for high-technology firms and phase out routine company organization work, the firm's marketers and operating consultants must be aware of this decision and be motivated towards getting new assignments that make this reorientation possible.

Some consulting firms have found it useful to have a strategic plan for three to five years rather than just a list of policies reflecting strategic choices. If such a plan has to be prepared, the firm is encouraged to make strategic choices explicit and express them in measurable and controllable terms. The plan is a tool for achieving coherence between the various choices discussed above, allocating needed resources and rejecting strategies that are not feasible. However, it may be unrealistic and unnecessary to set targets for three to five years if technology changes very rapidly, future business prospects are uncertain or the firm has not gathered and analysed meaningful information. Many consultants prefer to avoid any formalized strategic planning, and to use instead a short statement of principal strategic orientations and policies.

Strategy is an internal matter and the consulting firm may treat its strategic decisions or a statement of strategy as confidential. Yet certain aspects of strategy can be made publicly known. It may be useful to give clients, current and prospective, some information on the strategy chosen, thus helping to build up the consulting firm's image and gain clients' confidence. This is done, as a rule, through information brochures, annual reports and other publications, or in dealing with specific clients and submitting proposals to them.

Monitoring strategy implementation

In theory, operating decisions and actions should be in harmony with strategy. Often they are not. Strategy is either ignored or for some reason cannot be applied.

Usually the reason is that strategy has been treated as a staff function separated from operations. Either the real state and possibilities of operations were not considered, or the operating consultants were kept in the dark about senior management's strategic thinking. Both cases imply that the firm has been poorly managed and its strategic planning has probably been an esoteric exercise.

Monitoring the relationships between strategy and operations is an essential management function. If deviations from strategy are frequent and important, this probably indicates that the strategy chosen was inappropriate, that it has become outdated or that the firm's management has been unable to translate its own strategic choices into marketing and operational practices. Alternatively, operations may have revealed new opportunities and issues important enough to justify a revision of the firm's strategy. In any event, the firm's senior management will have to act to bring strategy in line with new realities.

When and how should this be done? A major correction of strategy (e.g. to amend an error, or seize an excellent unexpected opportunity) should be done immediately when this becomes necessary, and people in the firm should be told about it without delay. Other adjustments may be made periodically within the framework of annual performance and strategy reviews.

---

[1] T. A. Stewart: *Intellectual capital: The new wealth of organizations* (New York, Doubleday/Currency, 1997), p. 77.

MARKETING OF CONSULTING SERVICES 29

A consulting firm can exist and prosper if it gets and keeps clients. This is what marketing is about: define your market, identify clients, find out what they need, sell the consulting service to them, deliver the service to the clients' full satisfaction and make sure that once you have good clients they stay with you and do not go to a competitor.

In management consulting, as in some other professions, there has been a long debate on the appropriateness of marketing and of its various techniques. Even today, some consultants feel uneasy about "selling" their services: they regard it as unprofessional and beneath their dignity. Many consultants are poor at marketing and, if they have to market, they do so with little enthusiasm and imagination.

Yet the marketing of consulting is as old as consulting itself. James McKinsey, one of the pioneers of management consulting, spent many hours having meals with prospective clients and other useful business contacts.[1] Since McKinsey's time, the leaders of the profession have exhibited considerable dynamism in marketing their firms' services. They have systematically sought opportunities to make social contacts with potential clients, to be recommended by existing clients to new prospects, to carry out quick management surveys free of charge, and to speak at management conferences. This, in combination with the firm's reputation, used to be sufficient to attract clients to the established firms, as long as the market for consulting services was small and competition was limited.

It is not surprising then that the established firms did not favour the use of a wider range of marketing techniques, and in particular of advertising. The same attitude prevailed in consultants' associations. It was not until the late 1970s that advertising was admitted in the United States as an acceptable means of marketing professional services in a competitive environment. Stress was laid on the point that competition in professional services ought to be encouraged, as it offers the client the possibility of getting a better service for a lower price. In other countries, attitudes to the marketing of professional services have also changed.

At present, it is almost universally recognized that professional services can and have to be marketed. There are numerous publications and courses on the subject, yet many consultants have a long way to go to become proficient and effective in marketing their services.

29.1 The marketing approach in consulting

In consulting, marketing is often thought of as a distinct function, a set of activities, tools or techniques, which cost time and money and which many consultants would prefer to avoid – if only they had a sufficient number of unsolicited clients. According to this view, marketing is an unavoidable evil, something that consultants accept that they have to live with, although they do not like it.

Fortunately, more and more consultants, as indeed other professionals, regard marketing as an inherent characteristic of the service concept. Marketing is not a supplement to a professional service; it is a professional service in its own right, needed to establish and maintain an effective consultant–client relationship. It identifies clients' needs, reveals the clients' mentality, defines the best way in which the consultant can be useful and puts the whole consulting process in motion. Service marketing does not stop when a sale is made. The consultant continues to market after the contract has been signed, while the project is being executed, and even after the project has been completed.

What is to be marketed?

The marketing of consulting is strongly affected by the intangibility of consulting services. As noted in Chapter 27, clients are not able to fully examine the product they are intending to buy and compare it with products available from other consultants. Even if consultants supply structured systems and methodologies, the tangibility can never be comparable to that of industrial products, or of many other products in the service sector.

What the consultant is selling is a promise of a service that will meet the client's needs and resolve the problem. Why should a potential client buy a mere promise? Why should he or she take such a risk?

First, because the client has established, or feels, that it might be useful to get the consultant's help. Second, because the client has no alternative – buying any consulting service (even from someone who is well known personally or whose work is familiar) is always buying a promise. What has worked in one company may not work elsewhere. Even an excellent and highly standardized consulting product (methodology, package) may not work in a given situation. A client who is not prepared to take this risk and buy a promise must refrain from using a consultant.

It is fully understandable that, in buying a promise, clients will wish to reduce risk. They will be looking for ways of evaluating what they are likely to

Box 29.1 Marketing of consulting: seven fundamental principles

Successful marketing of consulting services is guided by certain general principles:

1. Regard the clients' needs and requirements as the focal point of all marketing.

There is no point in selling to potential clients something they do not need, or do not want to buy. The client may be pleased to hear that you are a brilliant and highly successful professional, but it is infinitely more important to convince the client that you care about him or her, understand the situation, are prepared to listen patiently and can help to find and implement a solution beneficial to his or her business. This is a golden rule. Your marketing efforts must be client-centred, not consultant-centred. Your client is not just another income opportunity. Your interest in the client must be genuine, and stronger than your self-interest.

2. Remember that every client is unique.

Your past experience and achievements are important assets. But they can become a trap: you may feel that you know pretty well in advance what your new client will need. Haven't you handled the same sort of situation many times before? Yet even if all other conditions appear identical (they won't be), the people involved will always be different. Acknowledge your new client's uniqueness. Show the client that you will offer an original solution, not a pale imitation of a model designed for other conditions.

3. Don't misrepresent yourself.

The temptation to offer and sell services in which you are not fully competent can be high. Often a client who trusts you will confide a job to you without requiring any evidence of your competence. To yield to this temptation is unethical; the client's interests can be seriously damaged. This is a matter of technical judgement, too. Competence in marketing involves realistically assessing your own competence, and recognizing a lack of competence and resources.

4. Don't oversell.

Marketing creates expectations and commitments. Overmarketing may create more expectations than a consulting firm is able to meet. This can be counterproductive and even unethical: some clients may need your help urgently; you promise it, but cannot deliver. Or an excessive selling effort may force you to recruit and immediately send to clients inexperienced consultants without being able to train and supervise them.

5. Refrain from denigrating other consultants.

Questions concerning your competitors' approaches and competencies come up often in discussions with clients. Nothing should prevent you from providing factual information, if you have it. However, it is unprofessional to provide distorted and biased information, or to make disparaging comments or allusions concerning competitors in order to influence your client. A sophisticated client is likely to regard such comments as an expression of your weakness, not of your strength.

> **6. Never forget that you are marketing a professional service.**
> Management consultants have to be entrepreneurial, innovative and at times even aggressive in marketing. They can learn a great deal from marketing in other sectors. Yet you are not selling biscuits or washing powder. The professional nature of the service, the clients' sensitivity and the local cultural values and norms must not be lost from sight in deciding what marketing approaches and techniques are appropriate.
>
> **7. Aim at an equally high professional performance in marketing and in execution.**
> In making efforts to find new clients, some consultants have neglected the quality of service delivery, in terms of staffing, quality control, respect of deadlines, and ensuring client satisfaction. It is useful to view marketing as a process that does not end with the signing of the contract. The execution of assignments has a significant marketing dimension. Flawless service delivery is marketing for the future.

get and deciding to whom to turn. Many clients buy without having any direct knowledge of the professional firm, because of the firm's image in business circles, or because a business friend or acquaintance has used the firm's services previously and has been satisfied.

Furthermore, the marketing of consulting services deals with both dimensions of the consulting approach described in section 1.1 – the technical dimension (the technical know-how needed to solve the client's specific management or business problems) and the human dimension (the relationship between the consultant and the client, and the consultant's ability to face human problems). The consultant has to convince the client that, from a strictly technical point of view, he or she has all the technical knowledge, know-how, access to information, and so on needed to deal with the client's technical problems and produce a solution whose technical quality is indisputable. But this is not enough. Consulting is a human relationship above all, and the consultant and the client may have to spend many hours working together. Therefore clients must be convinced that they are purchasing the services of someone with whom (at worst) they are prepared to work or (at best) they will enjoy working. This concerns the consultant's ability to work with the whole client system as described in section 3.2.

Finally, the marketing of consulting services must not ignore the fine distinction between the consulting firm and the individuals employed by that firm. True, in purchasing the services of an excellent professional firm clients normally expect a certain degree of quality, integrity and even uniformity, reflecting the firm's collective know-how and culture. Yet consultants are human beings and absolute uniformity is not only impossible, but undesirable. There will inevitably be differences between the image, know-how and standards of the firm, and the capabilities, personalities and style of individual consultants. Accordingly, the consulting firm will have to market both itself and its individual members and teams.

29.2 A client's perspective

In client-centred marketing, the consultant does not come to the client with the desire to close another sale of a ready-made product. The approach is reversed: the assessment and understanding of the client's needs come first. The consultant is asking questions such as: Can I provide a service that will meet this particular client's needs? And if I am not the only one who can provide such a service (which is usually the case), why should a client select me and not one of my competitors? What criteria will the client use? How can I be more useful to the client than other consultants? How should I market myself to get selected?

Understanding the purchasing process

As pointed out by David Maister, "the single most important talent in selling professional services is the ability to understand the purchasing process (not the sales process) from the client's perspective. The better a professional can learn to think like a client, the easier it will be to do and say the correct things to get hired."[2] We have already pointed (Chapters 3 and 7) to the role of psychological and relational factors in the selection of consultants. Since usually more than one consultant will be fully suitable from a strictly technical point of view, clients will give preference to consultants:

- with whom they are prepared to work and would like to work;
- who understand their personal worries, concerns and preferences;
- who exhibit a genuine desire to be helpful to their client;
- whom they are able and willing to trust.

Thus, it is important to keep in mind that both technical and behavioural, or psychological, criteria will be applied by clients in selecting consultants. The consultant's marketing strategy and methods used should therefore be attuned to this. It is impossible to provide a blueprint for every context.

Overemphasizing good relations (e.g. never contradicting the client during first meetings even if the client is obviously wrong) may be interpreted by the prospect as a lack of technical competence, or a tactical trick. The client may even be testing the consultant by asking awkward questions. The best approach is to be honest and sincere. It is difficult to play a role that does not suit you and pretend to be something that you are not. If you do not care about the client and are merely seeking a well-remunerated assignment, you will not be able to hide your attitude for long.

Some clients' concerns are reviewed below.

Reluctance to admit that a consultant is needed. Some managers do not want to admit to themselves that they need a consultant because this would hurt their self-esteem. Often the potential client is worried that a consultant's presence will be regarded by others – subordinates, peers, superiors, shareholders, or even competitors and customers – as an admission of incompetence and a sign of weakness.

Doubts about the consultant's competence and integrity. It is common for clients to have doubts about an external person's ability to resolve intricate problems with which management has struggled without finding any solution. Some clients feel, too, that a consultant will not really take all the trouble needed to search out a solution that is likely to work in the long term, and will simply try to place a standard package. Some organizations feel that consultants are too inquisitive and collect too much information that could somehow be misused in the future.

Fear of becoming dependent on a consultant. Sometimes the remark is heard that it is easy to recruit a consultant, but difficult to get rid of one. Consultants are said to structure and manage assignments in a way that inevitably prolongs their presence in the client organization and leads to new assignments. This can create a permanent dependence on external expertise, which could be dangerous.

Fear of excessive fees. This fear is quite widespread in small businesses. Owners and managers are sometimes not aware how the fee is calculated and justified, and with what benefits it could be compared. They may believe that most consultants try to overcharge and that using a consultant is a luxury that is beyond their means.

General feeling of uneasiness and insecurity. Asking a consultant to look into the organization's "internal cuisine" can be very disruptive. What will come out? Established practices and peaceful relations may be disturbed, but will this really be necessary? Will the result be an improvement? Is it worth while to run such a risk? Are we not opening a Pandora's box without being forced to do so?

General criteria for selecting consultants, taken from an ILO guide on the topic, are summarized in box 29.2. As not all clients use the same criteria, it will be useful if the consultant can find out what criteria will be applied to him or her as a person or a firm, and to the assignment proposals submitted to the client, and what weight the client will assign to each criterion.

29.3 Techniques for marketing the consulting firm

A wide range of techniques is available to management consultants for building up their professional reputation and image, or positioning their practice, in clients' minds. The main techniques are reviewed in this section. Their purpose is not to sell individual assignments, but to inform potential clients about the consulting firm and its products, to arouse their interest, and to create opportunities for contacts.

While certain techniques are aimed purely at public relations and image-building (e.g. advertising), other techniques aim to arouse the clients' interest by directly providing another useful technical service (e.g. information or training).

Box 29.2 Criteria for selecting consultants

In selecting their consultants, most clients would apply one or more of the following criteria:

(1) **Professional integrity** (how the consultant interprets and respects a code of ethics and conduct)

(2) **Technical competence** (knowledge and experience needed for dealing with the client's technical problem and producing results of desired level and quality)

This can be refined further by:

(a) differentiating between the competence of the firm and that of the individual (team) proposed;

(b) stressing knowledge of the client's sector of industry;

(c) in international consulting, stressing intimate knowledge of specific country conditions (economic, sociopolitical, cultural);

(d) differentiating between hard and soft skills (the knowledge and expertise concerning technical procedures, methods and systems, on the one hand, and the ability to deal with human problems and facilitate organizational change, on the other hand);

(e) stressing creativity and innovation (which may imply that past experience will be de-emphasized).

(3) **Rapport with the consultant** (mutual understanding, trust, the client's attitude to working with the consultant as a person)

(4) **Assignment design** (demonstrating the consultant's understanding of the specific problem and context of a given client organization, and the approach to take)

(5) **Capability to deliver** (structure, size, resources, location, flexibility and other features of the consulting firm, demonstrating the ability to deliver what was promised, even if conditions change)

(6) **Ability to mobilize further resources** (important in assignments that may call for expertise of other firms, new business contacts, additional capital, etc.)

(7) **Cost of services** (fee level and formula; this may not be a key criterion, but excessive fees may disqualify the consultant)

(8) **Certification of competence and/or quality** (formal competence certification of individual consultants and quality certification of consulting firms are taken into consideration by some clients, in support or as a surrogate of the criteria listed under (1)–(7))

(9) **Professional image of the consultant** (by using this criterion the client relies on the choices and assessment made and experience gained previously by other users of consulting services, or on the consultant's achievements outside consulting, e.g. as a manager or author)

Source: M. Kubr: *How to select and use consultants: A client's guide*, Management Development Series No. 31 (Geneva, ILO, 1993), pp. 77–87.

Working the referrals

Word of mouth is one of the oldest and most efficient ways in which a professional firm becomes known to new clients. Business people and managers are used to sharing information about professionals such as lawyers, accountants, engineers and management consultants. They exchange both favourable and unfavourable information, so only a firm that has rendered good service to a client can hope to have another useful referral. A manager looking for a consultant will often ask business friends for advice before turning to any other source of information.

It could appear that excellent performance in serving clients is all that is necessary to get good referrals. Experience shows that this is indeed the main factor, but not the only one. Some consultants do not leave it to chance that a satisfied client will recommend them to colleagues. They discuss their promotional needs and policies with their clients, asking them:

- to suggest who else in the business community may be interested in similar services;
- to authorize the use of the clients' names as a reference to prospective clients;
- possibly to give permission for the assignment to be described or summarized in a technical publication, in promotional material or in a management seminar;
- to speak about the consultant with other managers and business colleagues, but also with bankers, lawyers, accountants and others who may be asked for a good consultant's name by their own business contacts.

This requires an excellent mutual understanding between the consultant and the client. The client must not feel ashamed that he had to pay a consultant to deal with a problem that he should have solved by himself. Rather he should be proud that cooperation with an outstanding professional has helped him to discover new opportunities and view his problems in a wider perspective. The consultant must show the client that his concern for the client goes beyond a single contract – this is best achieved by informing past clients of the latest research and the state of the art in their sector or problem area, telling them about new services the consultant can provide, having lunch with them from time to time, and in general maintaining frequent communication. The client will then enjoy talking about his or her preferred consultant and recommend such a person or firm without hesitation. Happy clients become your best marketers, and do it free of charge!

Advertising

The purpose of advertising is to arouse the interest of a large number of potential clients by telling them that your products or services are particularly attractive to them. Advertising is making headway in management consulting and every year there is more of it. Consultants should be aware of its advantages and its pitfalls.

Those who consult in marketing and distribution tend to be familiar with advertising issues and may be able to design advertisements and advertising campaigns for their own firm. A new consultant who is not versed in advertising will be well advised to turn to a professional public relations or advertising agency before spending a lot of money on a major advertising campaign. Quite a few mass-advertising methods and media used for promoting goods and services to the wider public are less suited to the marketing of professional services.

Press advertisements have to meet two basic criteria. First, they must be placed in journals and newspapers where potential clients are likely to see them. It is therefore necessary to find out what managers and business people read. The longer the press run and the wider the circulation of a journal, the higher the cost of advertising space will be. A consultant who has helped a business or trade periodical and has developed privileged relations with the editors may be offered advertising space at a special rate.

Advertisements must meet the criteria of effective design:

- providing a small amount of essential information rather than a lot of fragmented detail;
- stressing (possibly in the heading or in another very visible way) the benefits for which the client may be looking;
- clearly indicating where and how to contact the consultant;
- appealing to the potential clients' taste and cultural values.

Advertising on radio and television has been little used by management consultants, yet it should not be completely overlooked. Some broadcasters have programmes for the local industrial and business communities on topics such as creating an enterprise, soliciting credit, saving energy or increasing productivity; an advertisement may follow such a programme.

Advertising requires considerable resources. A recent example was a worldwide advertising campaign in which Andersen Consulting announced its new name *Accenture*, and simultaneously aimed to explain to its existing and potential clients that the nature of the firm had changed and that its aspiration was "to transcend the definitions of traditional consulting, bringing innovations that dramatically improve the way the world lives and works".[3] The cost of this advertising campaign was over US$170 million.

Yet it would be wrong to assume that, owing to its huge cost, advertising is accessible only to very large consultancies. Even small firms can use it selectively and cost-effectively, choosing well the message, medium and target. Tasteless or bombastic advertising is unlikely to produce the required effect. Business people generally resent platitudes and unrealistic promises, such as have become commonplace in many advertisements for professional service providers. It is annoying to read that a consulting firm is "unique", that its approach is "totally different", that it "hands over the knowledge while others hold it", that it is "the number one", that its solutions are "always creative and innovative", and the like. It is especially annoying to read the same message again and again, from various service providers, using different words, but saying exactly the same thing.

Web pages

In the era of Internet, more and more clients seek information on consultants on the Web, consulting firms' Web pages in selecting specialists, preparing shortlists, comparing service offerings, looking for useful information on recent assignments and research completed, and similar. Clients expect that, perhaps with the exception of small firms, consultancies will have Web pages that provide meaningful, helpful and up-to-date information. Most consultancies understand and meet this requirement.

It is relatively easy to create and operate a Web site. It is, however, difficult to create a good one, give it excellent professional content, make it different from other Web sites and appealing to sophisticated clients, and ensure that it is continually kept up to date and improved. Here too targeting is important: the page is not for the general public, but for users of consulting services, who are likely to search for relevant information through the Internet. The site must be user-friendly, avoiding jargon that might be misunderstood or disliked by clients. It must be logically structured and easy to navigate. It is useful to include some technical information of interest to clients, to demonstrate that the firm is working on significant new issues and is prepared to share knowledge with clients. The site should contain something about the people in your firm and indicate how the firm can be contacted, through email or more traditional channels. It is essential that any resulting enquiries are answered, even if no new business is likely to emerge.

Branding

Some management consultants and other professional service providers have started using branding, which has amply demonstrated its power in marketing consumer goods and other products. A brand is normally defined as "a mark or label of identification" or "the kind or make of a commodity" (*Webster's Dictionary*). The idea behind branding efforts is that if the name of a consulting firm or its specific service can be turned into a well-known, respected and desired brand, clients will be attracted to the owner of the brand rather than to competitors. There has been a clear impact of two trends in professional services: growing competition (firms are constantly looking for new tools to gain a competitive advantage) and commodification (to allow a service to be sold easily to many clients). Branding, however, is a complex and somewhat controversial issue in professional services, as discussed in box 29.3.

Box 29.3 Branding – the new myth of marketing?

We seem to be inundated, from time to time, with marketing fads. These are usually fragments of some concept that, in other contexts, worked fine. But then marketers, seeking new nectars to enliven the dulled palates of accountants, lawyers, consultants, and other professionals, take these little segments and grow them to fit preconceived notions. Now the word is *branding*. Very hot. Articles. Seminars. Branding merchants. And soon, another round of broken hearts and unfulfilled promises. Lots of gold going for the cloth, but the emperor is still naked.

Yes, branding is for real – sometimes – but not as it's being touted, and not as it's being sold to unsuspecting professionals, and not as it's being used by the beclouded and otherwise duped. Despite what the branding merchants are selling, it isn't name identification, and it isn't reputation, and it isn't positioning – all of which are valid, necessary, and different elements of a successful marketing programme.

Many years ago, in the early days of marketing for generic products, marketers discovered a keen reluctance by consumers to give up the more expensive products with names they knew and were used to – names they recognized and could relate to a quality that they perceived in the product. The perception was that the familiar names – brands – were better and therefore worth more, even though the perception wasn't necessarily true. In fact, there may be no real distinction between the different brands of the same product. But if the customer *perceives* a difference in his or her own mind then the concept of branding really works. Truth told, a brand is *an attitude built on a perception.*

In brand marketing, the marketing effort is dedicated to imbuing a product – and ultimately, its producer – with those distinctions, real or imagined, that give the brand substance, validity, and acceptance. For the product, it might be said that establishing a brand is the ultimate aim of marketing. People go out and ask for the product by brand name, and will accept no substitute. Can this be done for a professional service?

- The value of the brand exists not in the product or company, but in the customer's mind. This value is measured beyond the usefulness of the product (or service) to include perceptions of "quality", consistency, reliability, and simply getting one's money's worth. It would be easy to dismiss the concept of a brand as an intangible, except that tangibility is irrelevant. To the customer with a specific brand of choice, the brand is very tangible.
- There's a difference between *reputation* – even a favorable one, with great name recognition – and a *brand*. The reputation may serve as a backdrop for receptivity for other marketing efforts, but other marketing efforts there must be. Reputation and name recognition are not the same as the array of perceptions and emotional attachments that consumers have for a brand. Subtle distinctions, perhaps, but very real ones. Everybody, including those who don't hire accounting firms, knew PricewaterhouseCoopers (then Price Waterhouse) by name, because they did the highly visible Academy Awards for years. But without a great deal of marketing activity that seems almost irrelevant to the name recognition, PricewaterhouseCoopers might not have gotten another client.

- Branding for professional service may very well be different from branding for a product. Which is not to say that there isn't some viability in branding for a professional service. But different it is, and therefore harder to do. Ultimately (and except for very large or specialized firms), people don't usually buy a firm – they buy an individual service or an individual accountant or lawyer or consultant whom they believe has the specific expertise to address their needs or problems.

But wait a minute. A major factor in successful branding for products is consistency. You can choose one brand of toothpaste over another because you know that the next tube of that brand you buy will be the same as the first one you bought. Can you say that about a service? Is the last deal you structured for a client, or the last bit of advice, going to be the same as the next one? Of course not. And in many cases, the specific service is performed only once for each client, unlike the tube of toothpaste, which is bought over and over again. The question, then, is will the service be performed for one client in the same way as it was performed for another? In view of these differences between a product and a service, how, then, can you have a brand name for an accounting or law or consulting firm?

In fact, you sometimes can, but only if some clear distinctions are made – and acted upon:

- In professional services, an entire firm is rarely capable of becoming a brand name, in which all of its services are accepted and preferred on the strength of the firm name alone. Name recognition helps, but only to serve as a backdrop.
- A firm's specific services, on the other hand, can be developed as a brand, but only if certain steps are taken. And those basic steps may just be a starter.
- The specific service must have a name that distinguishes it. Pricewaterhouse Coopers' *Change Integration*, for example. It defined its specific approach to company reengineering. The emphasis is on approach – on process. This is an important distinction in branding for a professional service.
- There must be a sense of consistency in performance of the service – a track record, a methodology, an implied or real manual of performance that suggests that, like the tube of toothpaste, the next time you hire the firm to do that job it will perform for you in the same satisfying and successful way as it did for someone else the last time it performed the service.
- The brand can be established only with the full force of marketing. That means clearly defining the service, advertising, public relations, direct mail – the full marketing arsenal. And the marketing activity must be as consistent as the service. Nothing is as fragile as a brand value. If it's not constantly sustained and polished, it quickly tarnishes, diminishes, and dies.
- It seems quite possible that a service for a firm that becomes a brand may well share an aura with other of that same firm's services – but not without strength in those other services.
- Of all the things a brand is, what it isn't is a reputation, a niche, or a position. And if you try to build a marketing programme without understanding the distinction and the realities of the differences, you might just as well burn your money. At least you'll enjoy the light of the flame.

> On the face of it, it would seem that the concept of branding may be useful for only the largest firms. Quite possibly, if for no other reason than the cost of promoting a service for brand identification. But the beauty of marketing, and the joy of it, is in finding ways to imaginatively transcend the obstacles.
>
> Reprinted by permission from *The Marcus Letter on Professional Services* (www.marcusletter.com) © Bruce W. Marcus.

Professional publications

Books for managers. Writing books to be read by managers, or as reference works, has become increasingly popular among consultants. Some recent publications based on experience and research in management consulting firms have become bestsellers, and their impact on promoting new business has been strong.

The promotional effect depends on the nature and quality of the publication. The reader must be impressed by the author's innovative approach to topical management problems, and conclude that his or her company might also benefit from such ideas and experiences. Finding the right publisher is equally important. Publications that just repeat the same old stuff using new words may bring in a few not very sophisticated clients, but will have little effect in the long run. Writing a really good book is an extremely difficult and time-consuming exercise, and those who say that every management consultant should try it are bad advisers. Yet if you feel that you have enough to say, do not hesitate!

There is a considerable need in many developing countries and in economies in transition for original management publications reflecting the real problems and experience of local business practice. There is also a need for publications providing practical and balanced advice on when and how to apply various new concepts and techniques, which may be useful in certain conditions, but tend to be oversold by their authors and vendors even to companies with different conditions. These are real and continuing challenges and opportunities for management consultants.

Articles on management and industry topics. Writing an article presents certain advantages over a book:

- The article can focus on a specific, rather narrow, topic (e.g. an interesting development in a sector served by the consultant, or an intervention technique that has helped several clients).
- The time required to write an article is relatively short.
- The readership base will be much larger if the article is published in a widely circulated newspaper or journal.
- Articles can be distributed easily and quickly through your own or other Web pages.
- Many busy managers do not read books, but do glance through articles on topics of concern.

To arouse the interest of potential clients, articles must address important topical issues. Articles based on successfully completed assignments, outlining the approach taken, the changes achieved and the benefits to the client, are particularly useful.

The choice of the medium is key. Neither the general public nor the academic community is the primary target. We therefore recommend:

- professional, business and trade journals, which are normally read by a wide management public (e.g. a consultant who wants to be recognized as an authority on road transport management should be known as an author by the readers of trade publications on transport in general, and on the road transport sector in particular);
- business and management pages and supplements of important daily and weekly newspapers;
- local newspapers, in particular those read by the local business community;
- publications of trade and employers' associations;
- the consultant's own Web page and Web pages of associations, information agencies, research firms and others, where managers would normally look for new information.

Occasional papers and pamphlets. Both existing and potential clients appreciate it if a management consultant shares with them some knowledge and experience through technical and information papers, guides, reports, briefs, pamphlets, checklists and other materials. These may deal with a relatively narrow and specialized topic, but must be of direct interest to the recipient. You should therefore choose a topic of concern to managers, providing suggestions and guidelines tested by experience. You do not have to divulge all your know-how, which constitutes your competitive advantage, but you must be prepared to say something significant if the material is not to be viewed as trivial publicity. Papers informing managers and/or specialists about the state of the art in their field, or about trends likely to affect the business, are particularly welcome.

Newsletters. A newsletter is a periodical publication whose purpose is to keep its readers abreast of developments in their field of activity on a regular basis. A management consultant can choose between a newsletter devoted entirely to news from a sector or trade, and one that also gives news from his or her consulting firm (completed projects, research done, new services started, publications, senior staff appointments, and so on). If the area covered is well chosen and the newsletter handled professionally, it can become a highly regarded reference service, used as essential information by many subscribers. Several special-focus newsletters launched by professional firms have achieved this standard. Here too, the Internet has made it easy and much cheaper to distribute newsletters. It has also increased the temptation to produce newsletters with little meaningful content.

All publications should include a reference to the consulting firm to which the author belongs, with some information on the firm and its services, and (if they agree to it) on client organizations from which the published experience was drawn.

Relations with public information media

Public information media, such as the press, television and radio, are constantly looking for information of interest to their audience. Management consultants possess, or can help to gather, organize and present, some of this information – for example, on developments in business and finance, impact of technological developments on factory and office work, new energy-saving techniques, or the likely impact of trade policies on investment decisions.

Quite a few consultants have found it beneficial to keep in touch with the media and to collaborate with them. Editors and other media people often have to meet tight deadlines, and need quick help from well-informed, trustworthy and reliable sources. They want information in a format suitable for immediate use. A consultant who understands and can respond to these requirements can expect to be quoted as a source or technical authority, or be invited to give an interview. This is likely to have a much greater promotional effect than costly advertisements in the same public medium.

Being responsive to media requirements does not mean refraining from taking any initiative. Once you understand how the media operate, the kind of information they are looking for, and how it should be presented, you can suggest topics, or directly offer a piece of news or a story, to your contacts.

News or press releases are intended for wider distribution to the media, and some consultants have had good experiences with them. A news release describing something interesting you have done in an area on which media are keen to report can be most welcome and may be used by several media; or the media may get in touch with you for further information.

Some media people have a distorted picture of management consultants and look mainly for sensational information on them (e.g. on assignments that ended up as complete failures, or on exorbitant fees charged for substandard work). Caustic articles with this kind of information appear from time to time in newspapers and business journals in various countries.

It is counterproductive to react aggressively or arrogantly. Even exposing the facts may be difficult because of issues of confidentiality or other factors. Helping the media to do their job, and demonstrating a professional approach in dealing with them, is the best way to change their attitude to management consultants.

Seminars and workshops

Management seminars, round tables, conferences, workshops, executive briefings and similar events have become popular marketing tools in management consulting. Usually a consultant invites managers to attend a session on a topic of concern to them, for example, how to handle industrial relations under new legislation, what is happening in international money markets, or how to apply new computerized information systems. The consulting firm may invite external specialists as speakers, but it is essential that its own professional staff should make a presentation to demonstrate that the firm is fully up to date and has developed interesting practical applications. If possible, work recently undertaken by the firm should be described, showing the benefits derived by clients. However, it is essential that participants perceive the seminar as a direct help to them and not merely as an exercise in selling.

There is no one best way of organizing a seminar. You have to consider whether it is better tactics to offer it as a free service to all clients, selected clients, potential new clients or a wider public; or to charge a relatively high fee; or to charge only for the meals and printed materials provided. A seminar may be arranged by the consulting firm alone, or in collaboration with a management centre or institute, a local chamber of commerce, or a trade association. It should be brief, and the time and venue must be convenient.

If the underlying purpose of a seminar is to market the consultancy, the participants should be potential clients. Ideally, you would use a selective mailing list and invite decision-makers from organizations likely to need assistance, or to be looking for opportunities in the areas that will be discussed. You will have to assess the probability of response (which may be 5–20 per cent, depending on factors such as the topic, the reputation of your firm and the speakers, the quality of the mailing list and the managers' propensity to attend seminars). It is better if invitations look personal.

In agreeing to attend, managers express interest both in the topic and in your expertise. They may be potential clients, and their names should therefore be carefully noted. Discussion with them can start at the seminar, e.g. in small groups built into the agenda or through individual contacts. While some of them may continue to talk with you after the seminar, or may ask for an appointment, you will also have a focused list for future contacts. It may be useful to call two or three weeks after the seminar, and offer to meet to discuss their specific problems in greater depth without any immediate commitment. This may open the door for new assignments.

Many consulting firms also run open training programmes, and some of them have even established special training departments or institutes. This is a direct client service whose prime purpose is skill development, not marketing. Participants do not have to come from existing or potential client companies. However, the marketing effect of these programmes can be significant. Some participants may decide to apply what they have learned and ask for the consulting firm's help. Others leave the programme with an awareness of the firm's areas of know-how and its performance in the field of training. They are likely to remember this when choosing consultants in the future.

Generally speaking, the graduates of all training programmes should be regarded in the same way as the consultant's former clients. They know your firm and if the training programme was useful to them, they will have a favourable image of you. Demonstrating that you care for them, providing them with useful information, and contacting them selectively may create opportunities for identifying and discussing new consulting assignments.

Special information services

The promotional effect of special information services can be similar to that of seminars and newsletters. A consulting firm that becomes a recognized authority in a particular area of information vital to decision-makers can use its information services to promote consulting work. A periodic information report can include references to the firm's consulting services. Responses to individual enquiries can mention and describe other services. If the information received is of value to the clients, many of them will also be interested in other technical services offered by the same firm. Conversely, if information is superficial, fragmented and haphazard, clients are unlikely to seek other services.

Management and business research

The role of research in consulting is growing and this trend has significant marketing implications. In seminars, articles, newsletters and other marketing instruments described in the previous paragraphs, the consulting firm may choose to report on its own research, or on research done elsewhere but applied in the firm's products and services. "We have researched and identified the critical factors determining the effectiveness of production systems" is probably a more convincing marketing message than: "We have long experience with improving production systems." However, potential clients may want to learn more than that you are research-minded and use research to widen and update consulting services. You should therefore be willing to share some significant findings of your research with the business community and other potential clients.

Mailing publicity materials

Probably every consultant has thought about mailing publicity materials at some point. Many consultants reject the idea, because they feel that this so-called "cold contacting" is a waste of time and money. Those who use it include both some well-established firms and newcomers to the consulting business.

It is essential to have a good mailing list. Some consultants prefer to draw up the list themselves, using information on organizations in the sector they want to serve, e.g. on small firms in a given district likely to be experiencing maintenance or cash-flow problems. Alternatively, it may be possible to purchase a focused mailing list from a trade association or a special firm.

Only well-chosen and properly designed materials should be mailed. They may include information brochures and leaflets on the consulting firm, information sheets and reports on new services, annual activity reports, reprints of articles, samples of newsletters, and similar. There is no point in flooding managers with paper; they receive too much publicity material anyhow. The materials sent should therefore be succinct and brief, and should give the potential client meaningful technical information, demonstrating the consultant's unique approach and knowledge of the business, and describing work recently undertaken. This should be supplemented by a short description of the consulting firm and profiles of its senior staff.

The manager's professional and social activities

It is in the interests of management consultants to socialize with managers and be regarded as belonging to management and business circles. This will make the consultant visible to a number of potential clients, who may well prefer to deal with a person known to them from professional and social contacts rather than with a stranger. In the same way, the consultant will also get to know bankers, lawyers and other professionals who may recommend him or her to their own clients.

Many consultants are members of management associations and similar voluntary membership bodies, local, national or international. They give talks at meetings (often for free) and serve on committees or working parties. They exhibit "relaxed initiative" – interest and availability – but should not overdo it by being so active that their behaviour becomes annoying or suspicious. A single practitioner has to consider in how many events he or she can afford to participate, while a large consulting firm can be represented by various staff members in several organizations.

Private social, cultural and sporting activities also provide opportunities for informal contacts which can generate new business. More than one consulting project has had its origin on a golf course!

Voluntary social work

Organizations involved in social work and community development are badly in need of members and advisers with administrative and management know-how. While their technical problems may not be the most sophisticated ones, helping them is often a rewarding social experience.

Voluntary social and community service gives a visible social dimension to the consultant's image, and also helps to establish contacts with managers and business people who engage in these activities.

Directories

In most countries, various directories of professional services exist and many of them include sections on management consultants. In addition to the consultant's name and address, a directory would normally also indicate areas of competence, using either standard terms and definitions chosen by the publisher of the directory, or a description provided by the consultant concerned.

It is unlikely that a potential client would select a management consultant solely from a directory listing. However, a directory may be used for establishing a shortlist of consultants, or for checking and completing information on them. If your name is not listed, a potential client may wonder why it is not. It is therefore advisable to be listed in directories that are well known and have a good reputation. This includes membership directories issued by professional consultants' associations. It is not necessary to be mentioned in every directory.

If the "yellow pages" of the area telephone directory include a section on management consultants, you should make sure that your firm is listed.

Responding to enquiries

The use of any of the marketing techniques discussed above can at some point lead to an enquiry by a prospective client. In some instances, people may be directly invited to make an enquiry (e.g. as a follow-up to a seminar they attend). These enquiries can cover a wide range of topics, including general questions on business and management, sources of information, profile of the consulting firm, work for other clients, or problems faced by the client making the enquiry.

Any such enquiry can be another effective step towards new business, or can spoil the emerging relationship and turn a potential client away. This risk is particularly high in large consulting firms, if the person contacted (who may be a telephone operator, but could equally well be a professional) is unable to put the client in touch with the right colleague, or to react properly to the enquiry.

It is useful to bear the following in mind:

- if you advertise, write articles, speak at conferences, etc., you can expect enquiries;
- resources should be made available for handling enquiries (people appointed, time reserved, answering machines installed to record enquiries in the consultant's absence);
- every enquiry should be handled with utmost courtesy and patience and at the right level (a well-informed client can be discouraged by a poor answer from a clerical assistant or an uninformed junior associate; a company manager will expect a reply from a partner or other senior consultant);
- enquiries that cannot be answered immediately should be handled in the shortest possible time;
- responding to enquiries involves marketing tactics – that is, considering how far to go: merely answering a question, showing interest in the client organization, offering a meeting, or similar;
- in certain cases the consultant will have to decide how much to reveal (it may well happen that a client could try to turn an enquiry into a free consultation);
- if you offer through your Web page to respond to enquiries, you must do so even if you feel that this will generate no new business;
- enquiries should be recorded in clients' files and suggestions for further follow-up should be made as appropriate.

Location and standing of office facilities

A happy medium needs to be struck between the prestigious image of a professional service and the economy of its operation. The right address is usually close to the sources of business. This tends to locate a firm in or near the financial or commercial quarter of the capital city or a major industrial centre. However, a good address is likely to be expensive and the consultant must be able to afford it.

The business-like appearance of the offices, the reception area and the meeting rooms where visitors are received is equally important. Consulting firms should show clients that they use up-to-date office equipment and elegant but sober and functional furniture, and have efficient internal administration. Exhibiting excessive luxury may impress a few clients, but will discourage most of them, who will quickly conclude that they will be paying for the beauty and comfort of your office facilities. Owners and managers of small firms in particular may feel uneasy in offices that are too unlike their own working environment.

Name and logo

Although many consultants are unaware of it, public relations experts consider that the firm's name and logo have a definite role in communicating an image to the public and to potential clients.

If the firm's name is well known and has become a part of its goodwill, it should not be changed, even if it no longer has a real meaning. A new firm, however, can consider alternative choices.

Names of persons. Naming a firm after the founder, owner or main partners is very popular in professional services. It is useful to know who has the key role in the firm. If a consultant is successful as an author or conference speaker, potential clients can easily see his or her association with a professional practice of the same name. On the other hand, there can be some confusion. It may be difficult to maintain a clear distinction between professional and private activity undertaken under the same name.

A quick perusal of lists of important accounting and consulting firms shows that names of persons (founders or main partners) prevail in their titles. To use a person's name is not recommended if it sounds awkward in the consultant's cultural environment, or if it can evoke bizarre associations.

Activity area. To name a firm according to its activity area (e.g. International Marketing Consultants, Road Transport Management Services) is another possibility. Such a name should be carefully chosen:

- it may become too restrictive if the consultant enters a new area (e.g. adds new fields of transport to road transport); this has happened in many consulting firms;
- it may easily lead to confusion if it is too general and if several firms in the same business community use similar names (Resource Planning Services, Resource Management Associates, Strategic Planning Services, etc.).

Acronym. It is useful to think of the firm's acronym: the original full name of many professional firms has long been forgotten and the acronym has replaced it completely.

Logo. The logo of a professional firm does not have the same importance as in mass advertising of consumer goods, but it can play a useful role in reminding clients quickly that a message is coming from a particular firm. A logo can be used on letter headings, business cards, newsletters, reports, publicity materials, and printed and visual advertisements.

29.4 Techniques for marketing consulting assignments

Every consultant prefers clients to come to him or her. Yet many consultants, in particular newcomers to the profession, would never get enough work by merely waiting for potential clients to come. They have to find clients and market assignments to them. The main techniques are reviewed in this section.

Cold contacts

Cold contacts are visits, letters or telephone calls initiated by a consultant to try to sell a service to a potential client. A lot has been said and written about these contacts. They are generally regarded as the least effective marketing technique and some consultants never use them. Yet they are still used, and newly established consulting firms may be unable to avoid them.

Cold visits (unannounced) are least suitable. Managers resent being disturbed by unknown people for unknown reasons. In some cultures, however, this is acceptable.

Cold mailing of letters is a slightly better technique. Its purpose is not to sell an assignment, but to present the consultant to the prospective client and prepare the ground for a further contact, to follow in two to three weeks.

Cold telephone calls have the sole purpose of obtaining an appointment with the client. They also allow the client to ask questions before deciding to receive or visit the consultant.

The effectiveness of cold contacts can be increased by observing certain rules. First, the prospective clients have to be properly selected. They must be target organizations, identified by research on the potential market, and the consultant must be convinced that he can do something useful for them. He should work out a list of addresses or, if he decides to buy one from an agent, he should screen it before using it.

Second, cold contacts require technical preparation. The consultant should learn as much as possible about the organization to be contacted. The worst thing that the consultant can do is to exhibit flagrant ignorance of basic facts about the client's business in the first conversation. Letters worded in general terms, or giving a lot of detailed information of no interest to the prospective client, should be avoided. Instead, individualized letters should be written, showing the client that the consultant has something specific and relevant to offer. A telephone call also needs preparation to be effective. Some consultants have checklists for preparing and constructing the conversation over the phone.

Third, the consultant should aim to get in touch with the right person. In many (but not all) organizations it should be the top executive. A cold letter should be addressed to him or her personally. In calling by telephone the consultant should try to speak with the "target person", aiming to do so at a time of day when he or she is not too occupied. Busy executives generally do not return calls unless they have a reason to do so. Therefore, if the consultant does not reach the target person, it is generally not worth while to leave a name and number, hoping that the call will be returned. Rather the consultant should call again at a moment suggested by the secretary.

A normal sequence in cold contacting would be (i) a letter, (ii) a telephone call following up on the letter and asking for an appointment, and (iii) an appointment with the client. To reach this third step does not guarantee a new assignment, but does increase the possibility of getting one.

Contacts based on referrals and leads

If a consultant "puts referrals to work" as discussed in section 29.3, there is no doubt that most contacts with new clients will take place thanks to referrals and leads. These occur in various ways:

- the prospective client asks for a meeting;
- the consultant is introduced to the prospect by a mutual business friend or acquaintance;
- the consultant gets names of potential clients from current clients.

The fact that the consultant has been recommended, or can use referrals likely to influence the prospective client's attitude, creates a favourable atmosphere for negotiating an assignment. The prospect may know a great deal from business friends and the discussion can quickly pass from generalities to specific issues. The consultant should find out how much information the client already has, to avoid repeating the obvious and omitting to provide information that the new client needs.

If the client wants no more than information, the consultant should not insist on negotiating an assignment immediately. Experience will teach the consultant how far to go in such situations. For example, he or she may suggest another contact in which the discussion could be pursued, and prior to which he or she could look at and comment on – without charging a fee – some data on the prospect's business. Or the consultant can provide detailed descriptions of assignments carried out for clients whom the prospect knows and respects. Such a contact should be followed up by a telephone call after two to four weeks. If the prospect has lost interest, the consultant should not persist.

In a similar vein, consulting firms that organize management seminars often make follow-up contacts with participants to find out whether they would be interested in a consulting assignment. An approach in several stages, as described above, should also be applied in these instances.

Responding to invitations to submit proposals

In certain cases new contacts with potential clients can be made in response to a published announcement inviting consultants to present a technical proposal for executing a project. As a rule, the client will be a public agency or, less frequently, a private organization that has chosen to apply a formal selection procedure.

In such a situation the client has not only identified himself, but probably has a fairly precise view of what has to be done. The client's own technical services, or an external consultant, will have undertaken a preliminary investigation and developed the terms of reference of the project. This description would be made available on request.

Frequently the selection procedure is in two steps:

- in the first step (preselection), consultants who are interested are invited to contact the client and provide a *technical memorandum* on their firm's profile and relevant experience; those retained are included in a shortlist;
- in the second step (selection), the shortlisted consultants submit *technical proposals* (tenders, offers), which are then examined and selected as described in section 7.4.[4]

Projects thus announced are often large and financially lucrative, and whet the appetite of many consultants. However, before a firm decides to tender, several factors ought to be considered and relevant information carefully examined:

- the prospect may already have a shortlist, or even a specific firm in mind, when starting the formal selection procedure;
- several important consulting firms may be interested in the job and competition will be tough;
- one or more firms may already have done considerable preparatory work and a great deal of marketing;
- the preparation of a technical memorandum and of a good technical proposal is time-consuming and costly (a fairly detailed diagnostic survey, including several visits to the client organization, may be needed before drawing up a proposal); this work is done at a loss by those who are not chosen and sometimes its cost is not reimbursed even to the winning firm;
- the selection procedure may be long, the consultant may be asked to submit additional information, reconsider some of the terms, rewrite proposals and pay several visits to the client; therefore he or she should not be in pressing need of securing the job and starting it quickly.

If you decide to compete for such a project you should develop a tactical plan for winning it. For example, you may feel technically fully competent for the job, but be unknown to the client. The question is: What can be done in a short time to become known to an important new prospect? Can former clients help? Is it possible to organize study visits to former clients for the prospective client's key technical staff? What else can be done without divulging confidential information? What can be done without breaking the rules governing the selection procedure?

Marketing during the entry phase

The entry phase of a consulting assignment was described in detail in Chapter 7. In many instances the client will not give a final agreement to the assignment before having seen and reviewed a technical proposal based on a preliminary problem diagnosis. The entry phase cannot be regarded as successfully completed until the contract has been signed or confirmed by a verbal agreement. The implication is clear: the marketing of a new assignment does not end at the first discussion with the prospect, but continues throughout the entry phase even if some technical work on the new assignment has already started.

The marketing dimension of the whole entry phase cannot be overemphasized. Whether there is competition or not, the consultant should think of the marketing effect of everything he or she says and does in the first meetings with the client organization, in the preliminary diagnostic survey, in formulating and presenting the proposal to the client, in giving price quotations, in formulating the contract and in suggesting how to staff the assignment.

29.5 Marketing to existing clients

There are two groups of existing clients – those for whom a consultant is currently working (current clients) and those for whom he or she has worked in the past (former clients). In all professions, firms try to keep their clients and to sell further services to them. In management consulting, this strategy results in an impressive amount of repeat business, which in some firms attains 75–80 per cent of all work. Box 29.4 shows that the cost of marketing efforts is not a negligible factor.

Marketing during assignment execution

It has been stressed many times that marketing to existing clients starts during execution of an assignment. It includes:

- being alert to any sign of the client's unhappiness or apprehension concerning the approach taken, the progress made, the costs incurred, or the behaviour of the assignment team;

Box 29.4 The cost of marketing efforts: an example

In a medium-sized German consulting firm the average size of an assignment is about US$100,000. The records show that getting an assignment from a new client requires seven to eight days of marketing effort (including a study of client conditions, making contacts, drafting proposals, negotiating, etc.). On average, the firm manages to win one of three such prospective new contracts. Hence, some 21–24 days have to be spent to generate US$100,000 of new work and one new client. In contrast, to get US$100,000 of business from an existing client requires about three to five days of focused marketing effort.

The initial marketing effort needed to obtain a new client is costly. In most instances, the first assignment will be done at a loss. This can be justified (i) if you get a good client, (ii) if you are good enough at obtaining repeat business by marketing to existing clients, or (iii) if you need a new client because you are diversifying services to new sectors, countries, etc.

Winning new clients while losing existing clients is a luxury that few professional firms can afford.

Author: Karl Scholz.

- keeping the client fully informed about the progress of the assignment and examining all potential problems and difficulties with the client as early as possible;
- keeping eyes open for further client needs and opportunities (beyond the scope of the current assignment) and mentioning these to the client in an appropriate way;
- fully demonstrating to the client that you care about him or her and will spare no efforts to provide a service that is valuable according to the client's, not the consultant's, criteria;
- resisting any temptation to extend the assignment beyond necessary limits in order to increase your current earnings.

Cross-selling

Cross-selling is a popular though controversial concept in current professional practice. It involves using established contacts and activities in one service area (audit, financial consulting) to sell other services (strategy consulting, engineering, legal advice) to the same client organization. As a rule, two or more units within a consulting firm or group are involved.

The relationship between auditing and management consulting is often mentioned as a good example of cross-selling. Some audits point directly to deficiencies or underutilized resources, and a consulting service is then offered to remedy these. Or the approach may be more subtle. If there is a good relationship with the client in audit or another area, this can be used for establishing contacts in another sector of the firm's services, hoping that the existing relationship will ease the negotiation of assignments in the new sector. In some cases it is the client who takes the initiative to avoid a time-consuming search for a new supplier of professional services.

Arguments in support of cross-selling include:

- maximizing the value of current client relationships;
- the possibility to reduce costs both to the client and the consultant since the two organizations already know each other;
- achieving synergy and enhancing benefits to the client through better coordination of different services provided to one client.

Cross-selling has also been vigorously criticized from various perspectives:

- it constrains choice, especially if, because of excellent relationships in one area, the client feels obliged to use the same firm for different services;
- the client may end up using services of a lower quality (and possibly more expensive) than if an independent selection had been made;
- in some professional firms the various service sectors collaborate poorly and are not motivated to do a good marketing job for another sector of the firm; if they cross-sell when working with current clients, they do so reluctantly.[5]

Obviously, the separation of auditing from consulting, which has gathered momentum since 2001–2002, reduces the opportunities for cross-selling in the professional service sectors considerably, but does not eliminate them completely.

Marketing to former clients

A "former" client in our conception is not a lost client, but one for whom the consultant has done some work in the past. Satisfied former clients often return to their professional advisers:

- if they have high respect for their technical competence and their continuous efforts to be up to date;
- because they enjoyed working with a particular person and/or firm;
- to avoid or simplify a selection process and have work carried out promptly.

The obvious assumption is that the client has some work in the former consultant's areas of competence. Some clients do come back by themselves, without any effort on the part of the consultant. More of them come back if the consultant includes them in his or her marketing efforts. There are no special techniques for marketing to former clients and the consultant may well be able to choose among those reviewed in the previous two sections. On the one hand, it may be unnecessary to repeatedly send basic and general information, since the firm is already known to the client. On the other hand, it is useful to send new information and ideas, demonstrating that the consulting firm is constantly developing and improving its client services, and confirming continued interest in former clients' business.

Occasional personal contacts appear to be a good form of marketing, provided that they (i) are well prepared, (ii) show the client that the consultant follows the client's business and is aware of the client's changing needs, and (iii) are made at a proper level of managerial responsibility on both the client and the consultant sides.

The last condition does not mean that junior professionals should not be doing follow-up work with former clients. It may even be very effective to involve new people in the relationship, thus showing new faces and new competencies to the client. However, junior consultants should probably talk to different people, and about different matters, than the firm's partners or principals would do.

29.6 Managing the marketing process

It is probably not an exaggeration to say that, in an increasingly competitive environment, effective marketing has become one of the key success factors in professional firms. Therefore it is not enough to state a few principles of marketing, hoping that all staff members will apply them. The marketing process has to be managed by the firm's top management, not as a separate function, but as a process and an approach that is fully integrated with everything the firm does – staff development and promotion, partner and staff compensation, organization and supervision of operations, quality improvement efforts, and so on. Marketing strategy is the central point of the firm's corporate strategy.

Marketing audit

An established consulting firm that seeks to improve its marketing should start by reviewing and assessing its current marketing practices. A marketing audit is a useful diagnostic approach for this purpose. It can be a totally self-diagnostic exercise if the firm feels capable of examining the various aspects of its own marketing, including public relations and the effect of advertising. If not, specialists in the marketing of professional services or in public relations can assist. They may be useful, for example, for interviewing clients and collecting information from other external sources in order to provide unbiased information for comparison and benchmarking.

Generally speaking, the audit would:

- examine the past and current business promotion and marketing practices (organization, information base, strategy, techniques, activities, budgets and costs) and assess their contribution to the development of the firm;

- find out how marketing is understood and practised within the firm by various units and consultant groups and what is their motivation for marketing;
- compare the findings with the marketing approach of direct competitors and other consultants;
- consider what changes in marketing will be desirable in order to meet new requirements and exploit new opportunities in the market;
- suggest how to make marketing more effective.

The benefits of a marketing audit reach beyond marketing as such. It can identify new potential areas of business, suggest new sorts of client services, reveal gaps in the firm's technical competence and staff training, and make many other practical suggestions. It can, in fact, serve as a first step to examining overall strategy and applying strategic management systematically.

Organizing for marketing

Marketing requires organization. Virtually every member of the consulting staff has some role to play in marketing, and consultants on assignments can do a lot of good marketing if they keep their eyes open and think of future business for their firm. Yet some formal organizational arrangements for the marketing function are also necessary.

Marketing manager. Whatever the size and complexity of the consulting firm, its management team should pay considerable attention to marketing. Marketing strategy will normally be discussed and decided on by senior management. If possible, one member of the senior management team should be appointed marketing manager. This can be a full-time or part-time function.

The marketing manager is concerned with the marketing function in its totality and is responsible for preparing and submitting key market analyses, strategies, programmes and budgets. Certain marketing activities will be his or her direct responsibility, e.g. training policy for marketing, advertising, press relations, mailing lists, and editing and distributing publicity information. He or she may have a small technical and administrative team for these functions. Other marketing functions and activities are not the direct responsibility of the marketing manager, but he or she has to monitor, evaluate and stimulate them in collaboration with other managers.

Roles in indirect marketing. Roles in indirect marketing (aimed at building up the professional image of the firm and creating opportunities for contacts with new clients) are normally shared throughout the consulting firm and assigned to units or individuals who can use their skills to best effect. The purpose is to optimize the use of individual capabilities: not everyone is able to write a book or article that will promote the firm. The roles have to be clearly defined, e.g. it should be determined who will be active in what management or trade association, or who will be delegated to attend a management congress.

Roles in direct marketing. Direct marketing of specific assignments is normally the function of partners or managers, who would spend 30–100 per cent of their time in contacts with individual clients, building up new relationships, trying to sell an assignment, negotiating a preliminary diagnostic survey, or following up previous work.

In some consulting firms these senior professionals are full-time marketers. They may not be the firm's top technicians, but their social, diagnostic and selling skills make them an invaluable asset. They are the firm's "rainmakers". However, many consulting firms prefer to switch the roles, e.g. by making the successful marketers also responsible for the management and supervision of assignment execution.

Direct marketing requires excellent coordination and follow-up by senior management and/or by the managers of sectors and geographical areas within the consulting firm. Uncoordinated contacting of the same client by different units of one consulting firm can damage the firm's image. Conversely, there are many opportunities to achieve synergy within consulting firms by actively sharing information on potential clients and assignments, and by keeping the interests and the possibilities of the whole firm in mind when working with particular clients.

Marketing programme and objectives

A marketing programme or plan defines the consultant's marketing objectives, strategy and measures to be taken in putting the strategy into effect. A written marketing programme makes clear what is to be done over a definite period of time, what resources are required and what contribution to the total marketing effort is expected from individuals or units within the firm.

The objectives of marketing should clearly express what is to be achieved by marketing efforts over a definite period of time in both quantitative and qualitative terms:

- *quantitative objectives* may indicate the market share to be attained and the volume of new business to be generated from existing and new clients;
- *qualitative objectives* concern, for example, the desired positioning of the consulting firm in the clients' minds, or the need to find more challenging work.

The objectives are to be achieved some time in the future – say in one, three or five years. This underlines the need to place all analytical and strategic considerations in a time perspective. For example, most of the techniques of indirect marketing used to build up a professional image take time to make any impact and have to be treated as an investment in future business.

It is not enough to define marketing objectives at the firm's level. Consulting and other professional firms often stress that every member of the firm should try to get new business, without, however, explaining what this requirement means in the case of each individual, and how he or she should go about it. Junior consultants in particular often feel perplexed, since they have generally received no training in marketing, lack information on the firm's current marketing efforts and have little or no time to think about marketing.

Mix of marketing techniques

The mix of marketing techniques has to be consistent with the firm's existing and desired professional profile, image and market penetration, on the one hand, and its personnel and financial resources, on the other hand. The optimum mix is influenced by so many factors in every consulting firm that it is impossible to give other than general guidelines. Experience tends to show that:

- It is usually preferable to combine several direct and indirect marketing techniques (reinforcing each other if possible).
- Techniques with which you feel uncomfortable or for which you lack resources should not be used, e.g. if you do not perform well in front of an audience, do not try marketing through seminars.
- Although regarded as least effective, cold contacts (personal, by mail or by telephone) are used by many consulting firms (more often by small and young firms than by large and well-established ones).
- Newcomers to the consulting business cannot afford to wait until the market comes to them and have to use techniques that put them rapidly in direct contact with potential clients.

Suggesting that you should use the techniques that give the best results (in terms of new business compared with efforts made) in your particular case sounds like a platitude. Yet this is the main criterion to apply, not what your competitors or the "stars" of the profession do.

Volume of marketing efforts

Reliable data on the volume of resources spent on marketing by various consulting firms are not available. The area of marketing is relatively new in professional services, and marketing practices are changing rapidly. Also, a great deal of indirect marketing can simultaneously be an income-generating activity (e.g. management seminars and information services for which the clients pay). Many single practitioners have to devote 20–30 per cent of their time to marketing. Some firms indicate that they spend between 5 and 25 per cent of their income on marketing. This figure is strongly influenced by the choice of marketing techniques – an advertising campaign in major business journals, for example, will be a costly undertaking.

Planning the forward workload

The very nature of their services requires consulting firms to maintain a sufficient backlog of orders for several weeks or months ahead. For any consultant there is an optimum figure that provides a reasonable safety margin and still allows new jobs to start without undue delay. Some consulting firms consider a three-month backlog of work as ideal, while six weeks are regarded as a minimum. A backlog exceeding three months implies that the order book is lengthening and some clients will be kept waiting longer for the consultant to commence an assignment. Many consultants do not attain the six-week backlog and are happy if they have work for three to four weeks ahead. This, however, is a small safety margin.

To maintain a satisfactory safety margin, the volume of new assignments, in terms of fee-earning days, negotiated in any period of time should be equal to the average volume of consulting work performed by the firm in the same period, plus a provision for required volume increase. This, of course, is theory, but it provides guidance for the firm's management. If the firm is selling at a rate below this figure, its forward load is decreasing or stagnating and there may be problems ahead.

In practice, the marketing of assignments and the planning of work have to be targeted. Ideally, the structure of the forward load should correspond as closely as possible to the relative numbers of consulting staff of different technical profiles. Clearly, it is easier to plan forward workloads for consultants who are relatively versatile and can undertake different assignments.

Pacing the marketing effort

A steady monitoring of the forward workload helps to pace the firm's marketing effort in order to avoid both under- and overselling. There must always be, in the pipeline, a number of initial meetings with prospective clients, follow-up visits to former clients, management surveys for preparing proposals to clients, assignment proposals in preparation or other marketing events. If these marketing events are not generating a normal number of new assignments, it may be necessary to allocate more of the staff's time to marketing, or to examine the effectiveness of the marketing approach used. Some firms use the ratio: accepted proposals/submitted proposals. If the ratio drops, say from 1:3 to 1:5, this is a signal that the firm's tendering policy and work quality in drafting, submitting and negotiating proposals needs to be examined.

A sole practitioner must also watch the forward workload carefully. Although she would normally allocate some 20–30 per cent of her working time to marketing, she may be tied up full time and intellectually absorbed by a longer assignment, thus risking not doing enough to prepare for future work. This must be avoided. If the consultant prefers to give all her regular working time to a current client, she must put in more hours to meet new prospects and do some marketing.

Applying the CRM approach in consulting firms

Focused and effective marketing requires systematic and consistent work with information concerning the client base. This is a key component of the consulting firm's knowledge management, or working with its "customer capital", a concept used to stress "the value of an organization's relationships with the people with whom it does business".[6] Box 29.5 gives a checklist of the kind of information that can be useful in marketing and that is worth collecting, updating and utilizing.

Box 29.5 Information about clients

Information kept in client files (card index, computer files, or similar), which are normally established for all clients, past, current and prospective, should include:

- the client's name and address; names of key owners, managers and contact persons;
- key business information on the client (or an indication of files and sources where this information is available);
- information and tips on the client's likely future development and changing needs;
- summary information on past and current assignments, including the consultant's assessment of these assignments (and a reference to assignment files, reports and other documents containing detailed information);
- information on past contacts with the client (what contact was made, by whom, with whom, and with what result, who knows the client best and can share tacit information on the client);
- information on other consultants who have worked, or tried to work, with the client, and with what results;
- suggestions concerning future contacts and future assignment opportunities (e.g. who else in the client organization might be interested, what new work might be proposed to the client).

Put in other terms, the customer relationship management (CRM) concept, recommended by many e-business and marketing consultancies to their clients, is also of interest to the consultants. A large multidisciplinary consultancy involved in a wide range of assignments, contacts, project proposals, tendering procedures, preliminary enquiries, information requests, etc. may well think of using special CRM software to monitor evolving client relationships and changing opportunities, with a view to improving client services, enhancing cross-selling, coordinating and integrating service offerings, and raising assignment profitability.

As part of their staff competency inventories, some consulting firms also record information on the marketing capabilities of staff members (including special characteristics such as languages, club membership, good and bad experience with certain types of client, and similar) and use this information in choosing who should market to particular clients.

In a small firm a simpler and less structured system would normally suffice, but before concluding that memory and tacit knowledge are all that is needed to manage client relationships, it may be useful to have a closer look at the client base (customer capital), the numbers of assignments, other client and prospective client contacts, staff turnover and client information lost with every staff departure. This may demonstrate a need for a CRM approach.

---

[1] See W. Wolf: *Management and consulting: An introduction to James McKinsey* (Ithaca, New York, New York State School of Industrial and Labor Relations, Cornell University, 1978).

[2] D. Maister: *Managing the professional service firm* (New York, The Free Press, 1993), p. 111.

[3] See *Print advertising* at www.accenture.com, visited on 4 Apr. 2002.

[4] For a detailed discussion of the procedure see M. Kubr: *How to select and use consultants: A client's guide*, Management Development Series No. 31 (Geneva, ILO, 1993), Ch. 4.

[5] See also the comments made in V. E. Millar: *On the management of professional service firms: Ten myths debunked* (Fitzwilliam, NH, Kennedy Publications, 1991), pp. 5–14.

[6] See T. A. Stewart: *Intellectual capital: The new wealth of organizations* (New York, Doubleday Currency, 1997), p. 77.

COSTS AND FEES

30

A consulting firm needs to generate adequate remuneration for the services provided and to have healthy financial relations with clients. The client should feel that the fee is commensurate with the real value contributed to the client's business by the consultant's intervention. Clients do not expect to get an excellent professional service for a low price, but they do not want to be overcharged. Consultants seek remuneration that fairly reflects the time spent and the impact achieved in working for a particular client, as well as other costs and expenses of the consultancy – the acquisition and development of the consultant's intellectual capital, service marketing, practice management and administration, etc.

However, "fair remuneration" and "value to client" in professional services are complex and intricate concepts, which are easier to discuss than to apply to a wide range of different clients and assignments. Traditionally, consultants and other professionals dealt with these issues by applying time-based fees, and using higher fee rates and various other arrangements to reflect the higher knowledge content and special contributions made in some assignments. This practice has been repeatedly challenged for various reasons. For example, Karl-Erik Sveiby asks: "What is the value of an idea that comes in the flash of a second but is based on a life of experience? It is hardly the time spent on it. Basing the value of knowledge on time spent can never be correct, still it is the most common. What other ways are there to charge for knowledge?"[1]

In this chapter, we will first review the basic considerations involved in costing the consultant's time and establishing time-based fees. We will then discuss other fee formulas and policies that aim to relate the fees charged to the particular knowledge and value imparted to the client.

30.1 Income-generating activities

A precise definition of services for which clients can be charged is essential to the costing and pricing of consulting services. If only chargeable services generate income, every other service and activity of the consulting firm will have to be financed out of this income.

Chargeable services

Generally speaking, a chargeable service is one performed directly for a particular client on a contract basis. It does not have to be carried out at the client's premises: the consultant can travel and negotiate on behalf of the client, search for information in a documentation centre, or work in his or her own office on a business plan. It should be clearly established, however, that these activities are part of a given assignment, and their results will be made available only to the client who commissioned them and who will be charged for them.

Certain activities may or may not be treated as chargeable. Travel is an example. Most consultants charge a full rate for the time spent travelling to and from the client's location and any other travel time required by the assignment. Some consultants charge at a reduced rate, while others do not charge anything (e.g. if they work for local clients and travel time is negligible).

Supervision, technical guidance and assignment control may also be charged for in various ways. Here again, some consultants prefer to give their clients precise information on the amount of supervision and similar work required by the assignment and charge a corresponding fee for it. Others consider this to be an unnecessary complication of accounting and billing procedures, for example if a senior consultant supervises several assignments during the same period of time and the cost of his or her time would have to be apportioned to these assignments.

In summary, in time-based fees the prevailing practice is to charge clients directly for all services provided to them under a specific client contract, with the exception of services for which it is impossible or impractical to charge directly.

Services that are not directly chargeable

General management and administration of a consulting firm, and marketing and promotional activities, as well as research, product development and staff training, are activities that are not directly related to a particular client assignment. The same applies to annual leave, time lost through sickness and various other time losses, including those due to a shortage of clients or to poor management of the firm.

The cost of the time spent on activities that are not directly chargeable will be spread over all clients through overhead charges. The cost of the time lost will also be spread over all clients, or it may be necessary to treat it as a loss, reducing the consultant's income.

Free client services

Strictly speaking, in a self-supporting professional practice there is no place for "free" client services: the consultant can work for free only if, for some reason, he has decided to do the work in his leisure time, if he accepts a reduction in income, or if the service is subsidized. A service that is given free to one client will normally have to be paid for by other clients. Someone will be charged for every free lunch offered to a potential client!

As regards the cost of preliminary diagnostic surveys and assignment proposals, it was mentioned in Chapter 7 that short surveys required for preparing an assignment proposal are done free of charge by some consultants and billed only if the proposal is accepted and the assignment executed. Other free services may include management seminars or information provided through the Web page; these are not charged for because they are used for general information support and marketing to existing or potential clients.

Fee-earning days

Services to clients are costed and, in many cases, charged on the basis of consultant-days (or hours or weeks). It is essential to plan for and attain the required number, which may be determined as shown in table 30.1 (assuming a five-day working week).

Table 30.1 Chargeable time

Item	Weeks	Days
Total time	52	260
– annual leave	4	20
– public holidays	2	10
– reserved against sickness	1	5
Time available	45	225
– reserved for training and meetings	2	10
– reserved for marketing and research	5	25
Chargeable time	38	190

The 190 chargeable days per consultant represent the expectation of a consulting firm for the planned period. This is a 73 per cent utilization of the total time, as determined by the ratio:

$$\frac{\text{Chargeable time}}{\text{Total time}} = \frac{190}{260} = 0.73$$

This is only a hypothetical example, and is not a standard figure. Every consulting firm has to establish its own time budget based on local conditions, and the firm's experience and strategy.

An alternative way of calculating this ratio is to compare chargeable time with days available:

$$\frac{\text{Chargeable time}}{\text{Days available}} = \frac{190}{225} = 0.84$$

Consulting firms often use this second ratio and apply differential rates to different categories of consultants. A typical time utilization rate is 80–90 per cent for operating staff, 60–80 per cent for senior staff (supervisors, team leaders) and 15–50 per cent for higher management staff (partners, senior partners, officers). Operating consultants can achieve high utilization rates thanks to the marketing, planning and coordination done by their senior colleagues. Data from various countries indicate that single practitioners who take care of their own marketing and administration achieve utilization rates of 55–65 per cent, since many of them have to spend as much as 20–25 per cent of their time on marketing (see Chapter 29).

30.2 Costing chargeable services

Fee per unit of time

The time unit used by most consultants in calculating fees is one working day, but some consultants use weekly or hourly rates. The basic consideration is simple: every fee-earning day has to earn a corresponding proportion of the total budgeted income. This, of course, is an average figure. The actual fee will be influenced by other factors, as will be shown in section 30.3.

Let us use the hypothetical example of a consulting unit described in section 35.2 and assume that the time budget of the 20 operating consultants in that unit is 190 days each and that the six senior consultants should achieve 130 chargeable days each. To keep things simple, the unit's director and the two trainees attached to the unit do not do any directly chargeable work. Let us assume, too, that the unit's target income is $3,898,000, which corresponds to the operating budget (total income) shown in table 33.1 (Chapter 33). The average daily fee rate will then be:

$$\frac{\text{Total income}}{\text{Fee-earning days}} = \frac{3{,}898{,}000}{(20 \times 190) + (6 \times 130)} = 0.84$$

Fees for various categories of consultant

Charging the same daily rate for all consultants irrespective of their experience and seniority would be a wrong policy. Many clients would insist on having only senior consultants assigned to their projects if they could get them for the same price. In contrast, some tasks that can be done by less experienced consultants would become too costly. Most consulting firms therefore apply differential fee rates for different categories of consultant. The difference in fee rates charged for various categories of consultant can be quite large (1:3 or more).

In our hypothetical case the rate for an operating consultant may be set at $800 and for a senior consultant at $1,100. This will permit the unit to achieve the same total income, assuming that the projected time utilization is attained by both categories.

Fee/salary ratio

Another ratio used by consulting organizations (the so-called "factor" or "multiple") compares the salaries paid to the fee-earning consultants with the total fees earned as follows:

$$\frac{\text{Total fees earned}}{\text{Salaries}} = \text{Factor}$$

The value of this ratio in most consulting firms is between 2.5 and 4.0, but higher ratios are not uncommon in large firms. Tables 33.1 and 33.2 (Chapter 33) show an expense structure of a hypothetical consulting firm and provide data from which the factor can be calculated.

A single practitioner can often achieve a lower ratio by operating with lower overhead expenses. For example, if he or she spends 27 per cent of the 225 days available (i.e. 60 days) on marketing, administration and other non-chargeable activities, total annual income may be $150,000 (salary $85,000, social charges $20,000, various overhead expenses $30,000 and profit $15,000), to be earned in 165 chargeable days. The per diem fee is thus $910, while the "multiple" is 1.76 (i.e. 150/85).

30.3 Marketing-policy considerations

Even if time-based fees are applied, the actual fees are not the result of a simple arithmetical operation apportioning the total income to be earned to the projected fee-earning days. Some other factors need to be taken into consideration.

Consulting fees are simultaneously an instrument of general, financial and marketing management policy. Consultants have to keep in mind not only how much the service sold costs them and what income they must earn but, at the same time, what fee is appropriate in a particular market and how much the clients will be able and willing to pay for the service provided.

Normal fee level

A "normal" fee level may be well established and generally known, and may even be recommended by a professional association (e.g. as minimum and maximum fees). Fees higher than the suggested maximum would then be acceptable only for certain special services, or might have to be justified in detail. In some countries legislation protecting free competition forbids the setting of any compulsory or recommended fee levels by professional associations or other bodies. However, statistical data and informal advice on fees may be available.

Fees charged by competitors

As in other areas, the consultant should find out how competitors calculate fees, what pricing policy they follow and what the clients think about their fees. It is equally useful to find out about the fees charged by other colleagues in the profession, who are not competitors.

Fees for different market segments

Different segments of the market served may require different fees. For instance, lower fees may be charged to small enterprises and non-profit-making social organizations than to important multinational or national business corporations. Some consultants follow this policy, while others consider it inappropriate.

Promotional fees

A promotional fee (say 10–15 per cent lower than a normal fee) is sometimes used in launching a new type of service in order to stimulate clients' interest. It is understood that it will be increased to a normal level at the end of the promotional period. This is acceptable if the clients are aware of it. It is unprofessional to interest clients in a new service and then increase the fee without warning.

Subsidized fees

Governmental consulting services may be able, or even obliged, to charge lower fees to some or all clients. This is possible thanks to government financing, whose purpose is to promote consulting and make it available to clients who would be discouraged by high fees. In some countries even private consultants may be able to work for low fees thanks to government subsidies under special schemes for assisting small enterprises, encouraging businesses to move to new geographical areas, helping underprivileged social groups to start new businesses, and similar. Alternatively, the consultant may charge a normal fee but the client may have the possibility to apply for reimbursement or a subsidy (see section 24.5).

Fees determined by clients

Government agencies or other clients may have established maximum fee levels and are unable to go beyond these in recruiting a consultant. Some consultants accept these imposed fee levels in working for clients from whom they get, or hope to get, a fair amount of business.

Congruence of fees with the consultant's image

The level of fees charged and the fee-setting technique used are elements of the consultant's professional image. Thus, a consultant who is positioned as a high-level adviser to top managers on corporate strategy issues would consistently charge higher fees than one involved in routine reorganization of office operations.

30.4 Principal fee-setting methods

Management consultants use several methods of setting fees. This reflects differences in the jobs they do and the views on appropriate ways of remunerating professional services.

Fee per unit of time

The traditional and probably still preferred method is to charge a fee according to the time spent working for a client. The unit of time used is one working day (eight hours) in most cases, but it can be one hour, one week, or one month (in long assignments).

As mentioned in the previous section, differential fee rates are normally used for different levels or ranks of consulting staff. The ratio between the fee charged for a senior expert and that for an operating consultant can be as high as 3:1. Research assistants and junior (entry-level) consultants are likely to be charged for at a lower rate than operating consultants (usually 30–50 per cent of their rate).

Easy and clear fee calculation and billing are major advantages of this technique. The clients are billed after agreed periods of time (e.g. monthly) for the time actually worked by the consulting team in the previous month. Many consultants consider this to be the only correct way of charging for professional work.

Yet objections have been raised to the notion of fees per unit of time. The client is billed for the time used and not for the intellectual input made or work accomplished. He or she might even be billed for time totally wasted, and therefore has to trust the consultant's professional integrity and competence. Or he has to control the progress of the assignment in considerable detail to be sure that he is paying not only for the time used, but also for the product as agreed in the contract.

Some clients object that this sort of fee encourages the consultant to take more time than necessary and to try to prolong every assignment. This does occur occasionally. However, it can be avoided if the client examines the consultant's proposal thoroughly, defines the maximum duration of the assignment in the contract, participates actively in the assignment together with the consultant, and monitors the progress made and results achieved.

Flat (lump-sum) fee

In this instance the consultant is paid for completing a precisely defined project or job. The advantages to the client are obvious. He or she knows how much the whole job will cost, and can also have an idea of the amount of time to be spent on the project, hence the daily rates used in costing the assignment. Finally, the client may be able to withhold payment, or the last instalment of it, if the job is not completed according to the contract.

In agreeing to these conditions, the consultant must be sure that the project will not cost more than the agreed fee. He or she cannot accept this form of fee if completion of the job depends more on the client's than on the consultant's staff. Thus, a flat fee may be charged for a market survey, a feasibility study, a new plant design or a training course, but not for a reorganization which depends much more on decisions and action taken by the client than by the consultant.

It does happen occasionally that a consultant who first agreed to do a job for a fixed price needs more time to complete it and prefers to do it for free rather than to ask for an additional payment. The reason may be that the consultant did not plan and manage the job properly. Or the assignment has taken more time for unforeseen reasons; it is vital to complete it, but the client's financial position permits no overrunning of costs. This could mean that on such an assignment the consultant will make no profit, or may even fail to recover costs.

A job can also require less time than has been quoted. This can occur if the assignment is not precisely defined and the consultant has made a generous time allowance to reduce risk. Occasionally a smart consultant may submit an excessively high quotation knowing that an uninformed or very busy client will have little insight into the project. In such cases the client will pay too much.

These and other drawbacks of a simple flat-fee arrangement have led to the development of several alternatives:

- in preparing the contract, the client and the consultant examine, in considerable detail, the consulting time and other resources required, and the risks involved;
- to protect the client, a lump sum is set as an upper limit that will not be exceeded: within this limit, if the consultant takes less time, the actual fee is paid on a time basis;
- to protect the consultant, a contingency provision is included in the contract (to be used if unforeseen conditions or events occur);
- competitive bidding is applied and the consultants are asked to justify their fees in detail; the client then analyses several bids and reviews them with the consultants before choosing one of them and approving the fee.

In current consulting practice, flat fees and their variations are becoming increasingly popular. They are the preferred formula in public sector and international technical assistance contracts, where often the direct client or the agency sponsoring the project want to have a guarantee that the allocated sum of money will not be exceeded. In addition, the client may be ill equipped for handling details and monitoring the consultant's work on a daily basis. Consultants, in turn, like these contracts because of the increased flexibility and freedom in organizing their work.

Fee plus royalty

In a growing number of cases, consultants spend time with clients to introduce, adapt and transfer an existing knowledge product (system, methodology, model, training material or similar) of the consulting firm. In these cases, various combined fee-setting formulas may be appropriate, which include separate payments for authorization to use the intellectual product provided and for the work involved in helping the client to use it. As a rule, this fee structure would apply to copyright-protected intellectual property, or patented business or consulting methods (see Appendix 5).

Fees contingent on results

Fees contingent on results – the so-called "contingency fees" – have one or both of the following characteristics: (1) the fee is paid only when specific results are achieved; and (2) the size of the fee depends on the size of the results (savings, profit) achieved.

In theory, this could be an ideal way of remunerating and motivating consultants: the consultant is not paid for spending time at the client's offices, or for writing reports, but for achieving bottom-line results. Initiative and creativity are encouraged. The client pays only if the results are real and measurable, and the payment is in proportion to the results obtained.

In practice, however, a host of problems arise:

- The consultant may be tempted to focus on easy short-term improvements, producing immediate savings, and neglect measures likely to produce benefits in the long run (such as preventive maintenance, staff development, or R&D). Excellent short-term results may even be the cause of future losses.
- It is often difficult to identify and measure real results achieved by the consultant's intervention, and separate them from other results achieved by the client.
- If results are not easily measurable, the client's and the consultant's assessment of the results may be very different (for example, they may have different quality standards), in which case disagreement and conflict are difficult to avoid.
- Sometimes the projected results are not achieved through the fault of the client, or owing to environmental forces that the client does not control, and the consultant cannot do anything about it.

- It is not easy to decide when the consultant should be paid if the results can only be measured long after the end of the assignment.
- If the client company is in difficulties, the projected results may never be attained and the consultant will get no fee whatsoever.

Contingency fees have been one of the most controversial issues in management consulting. For many years they were banned by the consultants' codes of ethics. This ban has been lifted in most countries and contingency fees are no longer regarded as unethical. This, however, does not remove the technical problems involved in their use.

Some management consultants (as well as chartered accountants) continue to reject contingency fees. Other consultants use this method of payment if they feel that they can accept the risk involved, that the client will get a substantial and measurable economic benefit, and that contingency payment is the most appropriate acknowledgement of the consultant's contribution to the improvement of the client's business.

The use of contingency fees is more common in the United States, where it has increased over the last few years, than in other countries. Most American consultants do contingency work at least some of the time. This is often explained by the more entrepreneurial attitudes of American consultants.

Equity participation

In searching for new and flexible fee arrangements convenient to certain sorts of client, some consultants have started accepting equity in payment for their services. As a rule, part of the payment would be due in cash and part in equity. This formula has been used in working for promising high-technology firms requiring substantial management and business development consulting assistance, but unable to pay the full cost of this assistance on account of a cash shortage. It became very popular during the Internet and e-business boom of 1998–2000, which saw the emergence of new formulas of consultant association with the creation of new firms and initial public offerings.

This is a sort of contingency payment since the value of equity will reflect the results actually achieved by the client firm. The consultant intervenes in a similar way to a venture capitalist. Indeed, some large consulting firms have started to provide venture capital as a line of service, in conjunction with working closely with the client during critical periods of creation and growth of the firm. Some consultants have established separate organizations for venture capital activities remunerated by equity. They undertake not to sell the equity thus earned without the agreement of the client. In these cases, the consultant is taking a considerable risk and is putting great emphasis on implementation and on results that will influence the market price of equity at a time when equity can be sold.

The use of this remuneration formula can thus act as a powerful motivator. It can fairly reflect the real value of the knowledge input made by the consultant to a young business or a restructured ailing business. Conversely, it can jeopardize consultant independence and objectivity, lead to various conflicts of interest, and tie the consultant excessively to market and stock-exchange performance of one or a few clients. In choosing this formula, consultants are making a strategic decision on what sort of professional business firm they want to be.

Percentage fee

A percentage fee is a kind of contingency fee, tied to the value of a business transaction, such as a merger, an acquisition, a property deal, a joint venture, a bond issue, or similar. Traditionally, real-estate agents and investment bankers have charged percentage or success fees for their services in these transactions. Percentage fees are common in architecture and civil engineering, where the consulting engineer's remuneration is often calculated as a percentage of the total project cost plus reimbursable direct cost.

A management or business consultant acting as an intermediary and facilitator, helping a client to negotiate a merger or an acquisition, may work for a percentage fee. Whichever side of the table the client sits, he is interested in negotiating an arrangement which is most favourable to him and acceptable to the other party.[2]

A typical example of a percentage fee is the Lehman formula, or the 5–4–3–2–1 formula, which continues to be the standard method of structuring the intermediary's (broker's or finder's) fee in mergers and acquisitions, although various modifications of the basic formula are in use. The classic Lehman formula is based on the acquisition price and uses a descending percentage scale as follows:

5 per cent of $1 to $1,000,000
4 per cent of $1,000,001 to $2,000,000
3 per cent of $2,000,001 to $3,000,000
2 per cent of $3,000,001 to $4,000,000
1 per cent of $4,000,001 and up.

Thus, the consultant's success fee for the sale of a $5 million company would be (0.05+0.04+0.03+0.02+0.01) $1 million = $150,000. An alternative formula is 5 per cent of the first 2 million dollars, 4 per cent of the next 2 million, and so on. Another variant in use is 5 per cent of the first 5 million dollars, 2.5 per cent of the next 10 million, and 0.75 per cent of any amount in excess of 15 million. A fixed percentage fee (say 1 to 3 per cent) is also practised, as well as various bonus formulas, in which a bonus is paid, in addition to the normal fee, if the selling price obtained exceeds a certain limit. The bonus can be calculated as a percentage of the whole transaction or of the part of the price in excess of the agreed amount.

Some consultants prefer different fee formulas so as to be sure to earn something even if the deal fails. For example, a retainer or per diem fee may be paid in any case, but if the deal is concluded, a percentage fee is applied and the fee already paid on a per diem basis is deducted from the amount due.

It is easy to see that the fees earned by consultants, as indeed by other intermediaries who help to identify, prepare and negotiate important business deals, can be high. However, there is a risk of failure and a lot of time will be spent on deals that never materialize. Most importantly, bringing the deal to a successful closure and obtaining a good price is a skill for which even a seasoned business person is prepared to pay a high price.

Retainer (ongoing) fee

In retainer arrangements (see section 1.4), the consultant's fee is calculated on the basis of a number of days of work in a period (say four days per month) and the consultant's normal daily fee. A retainer provides a steady income to the consultant and saves marketing time. The consultant may therefore agree to a reduced daily rate. The retainer fee is charged and paid even if the client (at his or her discretion) makes use of the consultant for less time than foreseen by the contract.

This can be a delicate issue. The client may feel that the consultant should have taken the initiative to suggest what needs to be done. This is what good consultants do – in working under a retainer, they do not take a passive stance. Instead, they closely follow the client's business and come up with their own suggestions on how they could be useful. This formula is convenient if the consultant and the client know each other well, if the relationship and the work content are quite straightforward and if there is a mutual understanding on how the consultant can be most useful.

30.5 Fair play in fee-setting and billing

None of the techniques discussed guarantees absolute precision and objectivity of remuneration for the work performed and results produced. There will always be an element of uncertainty, and of subjective judgement, which may or may not be correct and fair. Despite progress in measurement techniques, fee-setting and billing for professional consulting work continue to be matters of honesty and trust, in addition to being matters of measurement and control. Consultants and their associations are well aware of these two sides. Their concerns are expressed in the codes of conduct, which tend to pay considerable attention to billing techniques regarded as ethical, as well as to practices that are not recommended or are specifically banned by the profession.

Communicating fees to clients

Clients should be properly informed about fees and about the methods used to calculate them. They should have no reason to suspect that they are being charged an exorbitant fee and that the consultant wants to conceal an unjustifiable profit. Clients do not expect consultants to provide a high-quality service for a low price; indeed, many clients are wary of cheap consultants. Nevertheless, consulting is costly, and clients have the right to know why it is so and what they will be paying for. This is particularly important when the time actually spent with the client accounts for only a minor portion of the full cost of the knowledge provided through the assignment.

Up to a certain point, it is a matter of tactics and tact to decide when and how to communicate the fee to the client. Some clients will ask a direct question in their first meeting with the consultant (see section 7.1); they should get an equally direct answer. Others may make remarks that express their fears, or show ignorance about consulting fees and their justification. At a convenient moment the consultant should tell the client what the normal fee rate is and in what way he or she would charge for the work performed. If the client asks for more information, the consultant should explain the structure of the fee.

Such general information should be given at a relatively early stage in negotiating the assignment, to avoid disenchantment at a later date. Information on fees given in the written proposal to the client should not come as an unpleasant surprise. In particular, if the client believes that the consultant's standard fees are too high, this should become clear before a preliminary diagnostic survey and work on a detailed proposal is started. On the other hand, it may be better tactics to demonstrate professional competence, genuine interest, willingness to share knowledge and a good understanding of the client's business before starting to talk about fees.

Irrespective of the tactics chosen, there is a general rule: the client must be informed about the fees, or the basis of fees to be charged, before the work starts.

Overcharging

A universal rule concerns the appropriateness of the fee to the work actually done. As regards the time taken, the consultant may be the only person who knows how much time was really needed and spent to complete an assignment. Charging for time not worked, or spent inefficiently because of flaws within the consulting team or firm, is unprofessional, even if the client is wealthy. Charging an excessive fee for a simple job is equally unprofessional. As regards flat fees, they should not be used to blur information or to make sure that the client will pay more than if a per diem fee were used.

Double billing

Double billing must be avoided. A professional who works for two or three clients during the same trip should not charge the full travel time and cost to each client separately. A consultant who, in calculating the standard fee rates, has already made a provision for the administrative and communication charges of the firm should not charge separately for these expenses in billing individual clients.

These are straightforward issues. More delicate questions arise in connection with research, fact-finding, development and systems design work, which can serve as a basis for two or more assignments, reducing the cost of the assignments. Is it fair to charge data collection or research work performed for one client (and fully paid for by that client) once more to another client at a full rate? If not, why should the second client benefit from work financed by the first client? Why should the consultant miss the opportunity to make an extra profit if no one knows about it? These and similar questions require judgement based on both business policy and ethical considerations.

Price of exceptional expertise

In contrast to the situations described above, there are cases where any fee level can be justified and regarded as fair if the client is aware of the reasoning behind it. This may be the case when an expert is able to help with a difficult strategic decision of far-reaching importance to the client's business, to negotiate a major acquisition or to prevent a disaster. Usually such assignments will be short, and even an exceptionally high per diem or lump-sum fee will be a fair compensation for the consultant's knowledge and only a fraction of the client's possible losses or gains.

30.6 Towards value billing

The previous sections illustrate that in a professional service it is difficult, and at times impossible, to establish a clear, understandable and indisputable relationship between the cost of a service, the time required, and the results actually achieved. An ethical approach to assessing and recording time and costs, and establishing "fair" or "reasonable" fees, is essential, but it is not enough. In mature, demand-driven markets – and the consulting market in most countries is evolving in this direction – clients want to pay for value received, not for costs incurred in delivering a service. While they may be prepared to pay more than the costs if the value is high, they will resent paying a high price for a service of low value, irrespective of its real cost.

It is essential to understand the difference between cost and value. Value is not a mere reflection of costs. It is, above all, the client's perception of what has been added to the business thanks to the consultant's intervention. This perception can be very subjective. To one client, a retainer may have a high value since he can call on the consultant whenever he needs to. To another client, such easy availability has no value and she would not be prepared to pay for it.

Competition tends to ensure that a relationship between value and costs is maintained, and re-established when necessary. In a free and open market, professionals could not afford for long to sell a service of low value for a high price, claiming that this is justified by their costs. If the consultant believes that the price must be high because the cost is high, and the client fails to see a reasonable relationship between the value added to the business and the price paid, something is wrong.

These are the reasons behind the current efforts to apply what is now commonly called value billing, or value-added billing. In value billing, the price paid by the client is in proportion to the value added by the consultant. This approach does not preclude the use of any form of fee-setting and billing. A per diem fee may be perfectly correct and the daily rate may even be tripled if the issue at stake is important and the value to the client will be high. Yet in more and more cases other techniques of fee-setting are regarded as more appropriate forms of value billing.

The time when a consultant could say, "I am a professional and this is the price of my time" is gone. Increasingly, management and business consultants have to think of the value of the service rendered and of the degree of client satisfaction, aiming to judge them from the client's perspective, and discuss them frankly with the client. This will help to reduce misunderstandings and conflicts over the relationship between value and price.

A consultant's attitude to value billing was best expressed by Gerald Weinberg in his Sixth Law of Pricing: "If they don't like your work, don't take their money."[3] This view is shared by other leading professionals. Christopher Hart's firm gives the following guarantee: "If the client is not completely satisfied with the services provided by the TQM Group, the TQM Group will, at the client's option, either waive professional fees, or accept a portion of those fees that reflects the client's level of satisfaction."[4] In supporting this approach, David Maister points out that "the professional firm market-place is cluttered with claims to excellence and assertions of quality, few of which are credible to the buyer... The reality of today's market-place is that if your client is unsatisfied, you're probably going to have to adjust the fee anyway."[5]

30.7 Costing and pricing an assignment

Calculating time

The first step in costing an assignment is the calculation of the time needed to carry out the job. This calculation is based on an assignment plan (sections 7.4 and 31.1) and on estimates of the time required for each work operation. Reliable time estimates can be made only if the assignment plan is precise and detailed enough. For example, in planning the diagnostic phase of the assignment, the consultant can choose among several data-gathering techniques. The time requirements of the different techniques can vary greatly.

Considerable experience is required to assess correctly the time needed for all operations and phases of a consulting assignment. Such an assessment is normally made by senior members of the consulting firm, responsible for planning and supervising assignments. Some consultants have their own tables of indicative time data to which they can refer in assignment planning (e.g. number of interviews per working day). Such data must be applied with due regard to the specific conditions of every client and assignment.

There are cases where precise time assessment is difficult, if not impossible. Two kinds of situation are quite common.

First, either the individual who is assessing the time may be inexperienced in consulting, or the job to be carried out may be new even to an experienced practitioner. In such a case the consultant should try to obtain information on the time required in comparable situations, say from other consultants. Or, instead of making a commitment to completing the job in a fixed number of days, he or she should give only an estimate of the time and suggest a more flexible arrangement to the client.

The second case concerns assignments in which the initial phases can be planned with precision, while the subsequent phases can be estimated only roughly. Typically, the consultant may be able to make an accurate time assessment for the diagnostic phase, a rough assessment for action planning, and no more than a preliminary guess for the implementation phase. This is quite understandable owing to the number of factors likely to affect implementation. In these instances, it may be preferable to use a phased approach to assessing time and costing the assignment. Only orientation data would be given for the phases where duration and volume of work required are unclear at the beginning of the assignment. Clients who understand the nature of consulting will be receptive to such an arrangement.

Costing the consulting time

As mentioned in section 30.1, most consultants try to be as precise as possible in measuring the labour costs of an assignment. The cost of the time of operating consultants would be treated as a direct labour cost in any case. The cost of supervisory and control work, as well as various technical and administrative support operations, can be treated as either direct or indirect costs and the consulting firm will have to decide which is more appropriate.

If different categories of consultant are assigned to the project, it is customary to calculate and indicate the time and price for each category separately, so that the client knows how much he or she is to pay for the junior, intermediate, senior and very senior levels of direct services. As mentioned earlier, fee differentials can be significant and the cost of an assignment could rocket if a large part of the job is done by the most expensive tier of the consulting staff.

The total time required by an assignment, and the cost of this time, should be established even if a fee-setting method other than per-unit-of-time rate is applied. In such a case, the consultant will use it as internal management information in deciding the type and size of fee for which he or she would be able to work.

Other expenses

Expenses other than direct labour costs may be either included in the fee as overhead expenses or charged directly to the client. It is important to make this clear to the client, who should know precisely what kinds of expenses will have to be reimbursed.

Typical billable or reimbursable expenses are travel, board and lodging expenses of consultants on assignments, special services arranged by the consultant (e.g. testing, computing, printing, purchase of special equipment, drawings), long-distance communication and document delivery. In addition to listing these items it may be necessary to indicate the values, as for example, the expenses that the consultant expects to incur in travelling to and from the client's premises, and how much the client is to pay for the consultant's board and lodging, or for local transport during the assignment.

In international consulting these billable expenses may be quite high, reaching 25–30 per cent of the fees. There may even be a provision for family travel and accommodation if the consultant is to work on a long assignment abroad. Expenses defined as billable are not a part of the consultant's fees, but a separate additional item in the total assignment budget and in bills submitted to the client.

Most consultants will ask the client to reimburse these expenses without paying any additional overhead or mark-up, but some consultants add a 10–20 per cent mark-up to cover their administrative costs.

Comparing costs and benefits

Irrespective of the fee-setting method used, the client is likely to compare the price proposed by the consultant with the value gained by the client's business. The consultant, in pricing the assignment, should make his or her own calculation of this ratio, even if the client has not explicitly asked for it and has not even thought of it.

If the value to be generated cannot justify the price in the client's eyes, the assignment design may need to be completely revised. Or the client should be encouraged to think of a different approach, for example, purchasing standard record-keeping and cost-control software rather than asking the consultant to design a customized system.

Discounts and contingencies

Under normal circumstances, if the cost of the assignment has been calculated correctly there is no reason to grant any discount on a consulting fee, and the consultant cannot usually afford to do so. Nevertheless, in certain situations a reduced fee may be justified and can be offered.

A client may claim a "quantity discount" if the volume of work contracted notably exceeds the average size of assignments. For example, a consultant working for public administration may be asked to do a similar job for several agencies. Either the assignment can keep the consultant occupied for a fairly long time, or the assignment team will be larger than usual. The consultant may save on marketing time, administrative support expenses, and even on technical backstopping and supervision. A discount can also be arranged if a consulting firm already has an assignment with a client, and is offered an additional one by the same client for the same period of time.

On the other hand, in costing assignments it is difficult to ignore changes in the cost of living and price levels. A provision for necessary cost increases can be made in various ways, depending on the client's and the consultant's convenience. For example, the contract can include an "escalation clause", whereby the fees will be adjusted upwards in accordance with the officially recognized inflation rate. Or a contingency provision (say 5–10 per cent of the total cost) is made, to be used by common agreement of the consultant and the client for justified and inevitable cost increases, and for expenses that could not be foreseen before starting the job.

Schedule of payments

Both the client and the consultant are concerned not only about the amount of the fee to be paid, but also about the payment schedule. Many clients are interested in delaying payments. Consultants, in contrast, want to be paid as soon as possible after having completed the job or a part of it, and if they can get an advance payment before starting the job, they are certainly not opposed to it.

The most common arrangement is for the consultant to bill the client periodically (as a rule monthly or weekly) for work carried out in the previous period. The last bill is payable within an agreed number of days after the completion of the assignment. Payments are to be made within an agreed period of time – as a rule, 30 days after billing.

There are, then, various possible arrangements:

- In some situations (e.g. international consulting), consultants may prefer to receive an advance payment after the signature of the contract, but before starting the work; by agreeing to this, the client confirms his or her commitment to the assignment and confidence in the consultant.
- If other than per-unit-of-time fees are applied, there may still be some advance payment before the project is completed, or the consultant may propose waiting for payment until the job is finished and the projected results achieved. For example, the payment schedule may be: 30 per cent on signature, two payments of 20 per cent each during the assignment, and 30 per cent one month after the client has received the final report and bill.
- Occasionally a schedule of payments may be so important to the client that it is necessary to adjust the pace of the work to the client's financial position. For example, the client may prefer to stretch the assignment over a longer period of time. Or the consultant may be able to accept a payment schedule that differs from the actual work schedule of the assignment, but makes the processing of payments easier for the client.

In fixing their fees, consultants should find out if the payment schedule matters to the client, and whether there are any particular constraints. However, in the consulting business, it is not usual to encourage early and prompt payment by offering cash discounts to clients.

Negotiating the fee

Under what circumstances can a consultant agree to negotiate the fee with a client who wants to have a job done for a lower price? It is virtually impossible to think of universal rules. In the social and business cultures of some countries, professional fees are never challenged. In other countries everything is regarded as negotiable, and the local culture may require the consultant and the client to pass through a negotiation ritual before concluding a contract. It may even be customary to agree on a slightly lower price than originally demanded. The consultant should be aware of this and, if necessary, build in a "negotiation provision" in the first price quotation. Thus, the price agreed on after the negotiation will be the correct one, and regarded as such by both parties.

Irrespective of local habits, there may be technical reasons for negotiating consulting fees. The client may need more detailed information to become convinced that the fee is correctly set. A true professional is always prepared to give this information. Furthermore, in challenging the fee the client may actually be raising questions about the design of the assignment. As mentioned in section 7.5, the client may want to negotiate the consultant's proposal for various reasons. There may be a less costly approach. Often the client may be able to have some tasks performed by his or her own personnel instead of using consultants or their technical and administrative support services. The timetable may also have to be reconsidered for financial reasons if the client wishes to use a different schedule of payments from that proposed by the consultant.

When agreeing to negotiate the fee, the consultant should try to be well informed on the conditions under which the negotiation will take place. Will it be a formality, a ritual required by local culture? Does the client have alternative proposals (at different prices) from other consultants? Is the client happy with the design of the assignment and the competence of the staff proposed, but not with the price? Is the price proposed prohibitive to the client, or does he or she merely want to save money by pressing the consultant? Thus, the consultant should prepare for the negotiation, trying to anticipate questions and suggestions likely to be made by the client.

30.8 Billing clients and collecting fees

Professional firms bill clients and collect fees like other businesses. They may, however, face problems with clients who are not sure that they are paying the right price or that the consultant has delivered what was promised. This confirms how important it is to be clear and consistent when negotiating the assignment and informing the client about the fee rate and the billing practice.

Bills should be issued as soon as records of work performed and expenses incurred are available. This underlines the importance of a reliable and smoothly operating administration.

Information to be provided in a bill

Bills should be as detailed as necessary to avoid any misunderstanding or unnecessary query from clients. Clients must be told exactly what is being charged for and why. They should be able to refer to the contract (or the attached terms of business) in case of any doubt. They should find no unexpected charge in a bill, e.g. no separate charge for a service or supplies that they thought would be provided within the agreed fee. The information normally provided in a bill is indicated in box 30.1.

Box 30.1 Information to be provided in a bill

- Bill number
- Period covered
- Services provided (listing, dates, volume of work by each consultant)
- Fee rates and total charges
- Expenses billed separately from fees
- When payment is due
- How to make payment (currency, method of payment, account number)
- Whom to contact for queries
- Date of expedition of the bill
- Name, address, telephone and fax numbers of the consultant
- Signature and courtesy formula

Addressing and delivering the bill

Problems can arise if the consultant does not know to which department and person to address the bill. This can easily happen in large businesses and government services. The consultant should therefore find out what actually happens to the bill when it is delivered, and make sure that the right people receive copies. It may sometimes be advisable to deliver the bill personally. However, there is no reason why the consultant should harass financial or other services in organizations that are known to pay their bills correctly.

Collection period

In most countries consultants would ask for payment to be made within 30 days, and hope to receive the money within 45 days. There may be local differences, and in international consulting payments may take several months.

Payments received late result in additional charges to the consultant, and very few consultants can afford to extend interest-free credit to their clients! A late-paying client should first be reminded with courtesy – it may be enough to send another copy of the bill with a remark that perhaps the original was lost. If the consultant believes there is a problem, it may be wise to contact the client personally and find out the cause of non-payment. This can be done during a supervisor's visit if the assignment is still operational. A tactful reminder may be all that is necessary.

If a client still does not pay, the consulting team may be withdrawn. The client should then be told clearly what measures the consultant intends to take to collect the fees.

Uncollectable accounts

Whether to take a non-paying client to court or not is a delicate decision. The procedure risks being both lengthy and costly, and the result is uncertain. In many cases it is wiser to stay out of court and try to find a compromise settlement. In the consulting contract there may be a provision for a settlement through arbitration of disputes that cannot be settled amicably.

Some fees are uncollectable in any country. Consulting firms in sophisticated business environments report that they normally write off no more than 0.1–1.0 per cent of uncollectable fees. In some countries this figure can be much higher. If bad debts cannot be collected, in many countries they can be deducted from taxable income.

There are also countries where business clients consider it normal and ethical practice not to pay the last 5–10 per cent of the total fee for a project. If you intend to operate in such a country you should know about this.

---

[1] K.-E. Sveiby: *Fourteen ways to charge for knowledge* (www.sveiby.com.au, 1998).

[2] See W. M. McKoy and J. D. Roethle: "Consultants' fees for mergers and acquisitions", in *Journal of Management Consulting* (Milwaukee, WI), Vol. 5, No. 4, 1989, pp. 16–21.

[3] G. M. Weinberg: *The secrets of consulting* (New York, Dorset House, 1985), p. 188.

[4] C. Hart: *Extraordinary guarantees: Achieving breakthrough gains in quality and customer satisfaction* (New York, AMACOM, 1993).

[5] D. Maister: "The new value billing", in *American Lawyer* (New York), May 1994.

ASSIGNMENT MANAGEMENT 31

A consulting firm performs work for clients through individual operating assignments. Whatever choices are made and principles adopted as regards the firm's strategy, quality assurance, staff development or product innovation, the decisions will need to be translated into operational arrangements and intervention methods used in individual client assignments. If not, grand designs will not leave the managing partners' offices and work with clients will continue as before. Also, individual clients will judge the consulting firm on the basis of particular assignments. Clumsy and hectic assignment management is likely to be interpreted by clients as a sign of organizational incompetence and inefficiency.

This chapter focuses on the managerial and administrative aspects of assignment execution. It therefore supplements Chapters 7 to 11, which describe the stages of the consulting process. To avoid repetition, a number of references to these chapters are made in the text that follows.

31.1 Structuring and scheduling an assignment

Defining an assignment and its management requirements

The scope of an assignment (or engagement, project or case) is usually defined in the proposal to the client and in the contract (sections 7.4 to 7.6). The definition includes the start and the end of the assignment, the objectives, the proposed approach, the work programme, the consultants involved, the resources required, the degree and form of the client's involvement, the supervisory responsibility and the price to be paid. Checking the completeness and clarity of assignment definitions is an important precondition of effective assignment management. Even questions such as where the data will be processed and reports produced, or who will take care of the consultant's transport during the assignment, should be clarified. More important, however, are technical and human issues related to the client's problem and the approach to be taken by the consultants.

On the basis of this information, the consulting firm will choose how to manage each assignment. Issues on which decisions will be needed include:

- the use of a standard or special management procedure;
- the need to appoint a full-time team leader;
- the type and level of experience of senior consultants or partners charged with supervision and backstopping;
- the desirability and frequency of detailed controls;
- the need to inform and/or involve the client firm's top management;
- the opportunity to try out or test new approaches and techniques, and the desirability of doing so;
- the importance of the assignment to future business development;
- the lessons that the firm may be able to draw from this assignment.

In making these decisions, the consulting firm should be guided both by its established practices and by an assessment of the profile of the new assignment. Although there are similarities between assignments, no two assignments are exactly the same because the human context and other conditions will always be unique. If the firm has developed a typology of assignments and defined characteristic management requirements of each type, this typology needs to be used cautiously.

Assignment team leaders and supervisors

The key role in managing operating assignments is played by *team leaders* or *project managers*. As a rule, a consulting firm would have a group of senior colleagues whose experience and achievement qualify them for this critical position. The function often includes the negotiation and preparation of new assignments: the senior consultant who negotiates the assignment, does the preliminary survey of the client organization, and coordinates the drafting of the proposal submitted to the client, is then charged with managing the assignment. In doing so, the team leader must enjoy full authority and have responsibility for allocating the time of operating staff, scheduling and organizing work, and deciding on the method of work and the nature of the advice given to the client. He or she is the line manager and must be regarded as such by both the consulting firm's higher management and the members of the team. This is an important principle since the team often consists of consultants with different backgrounds and profiles. In addition, if specialist consultants have to contribute to several assignments during the same period of time, there is not only a problem of scheduling and coordination, but also one deriving from the technical approach, intellectual involvement and commitment to one or other job.

If an assignment is small and involves only one or two operating consultants, a senior consultant is usually appointed as *supervisor* of several assignments. These supervisory responsibilities include:

- periodic visits to operating consultants on assignment;
- control and assessment of progress of the assignment;
- technical guidance and support for operating consultants;
- review of important reports and proposals to be submitted to the client;
- liaison with clients over assignment progress and mutual commitments.

It is always necessary to define clearly the working relations with the client, i.e. what matters should be discussed and agreed on with the operating consultants, or with the supervisors. For example, if the assignment does not progress because the client does not spend enough time with the operating consultant, the supervisor should raise the matter with the client. When conclusions drawn from diagnosis, or action proposals, are submitted to the client, the supervisor may come to meetings and support the operating consultant with his or her authority and experience.

Staffing and scheduling assignments

Ideally, a consulting firm would like to see all its consultants moving directly from completed assignments to new ones, without losing a single working day. The starting dates and schedules of assignments are negotiated with clients in order to make this possible. An ethical approach is required, however: if the client is in a difficult situation and needs help quickly, you should never try to convince him or her to wait simply in order to make your work scheduling easier! Also, once you have promised to start, you should stick to your promise.

Before establishing detailed workplans for each assignment, the consulting firm needs to make sure that the consultants selected will be available at the necessary times and for the periods required. This may be yet another piece in the jigsaw puzzle, to be seen in the context of the total picture of operations.

First, the technical profile of the team is matched to the technical profile of the assignment. It is obvious that the choice of professional staff will vary according to the size of the consulting firm. Some large consultancies have developed computerized inventories of staff competencies and skills. Small firms either have to work in more limited fields, or employ versatile and adaptable people. In this context, the problems of a sole practitioner, or a partnership of two or three consultants, are plain to see.

Second, there is the personality factor. The correct matching of the client's and the consultant's personalities can make the difference between good and poor assignments. Guidance on the client's characteristics, in terms of likes and dislikes, habits, interests and general way of life, should have been provided confidentially by the consultant who negotiated the contract (section 7.5). The personalities of the consulting firm's staff should be known.

The client and the consultant do not necessarily have to have everything in common. There are even advantages sometimes in complementing a client of one type by a consultant of another when a modifying influence appears desirable, but the consulting firm should avoid pairing two people who are obviously incompatible. Up to a point, it can be expected that every consultant will adapt to normal and unavoidable differences, and matching people is only a matter of avoiding clashes at the extreme limits of human behaviour.

Third, it is equally important that the team leader and the team members get on well with each other. Consultants do not always see eye to eye in matters of individual preference any more than do other people.

Human relations and the atmosphere within an assignment team will affect work quality and efficiency as much as the technical competence of the operating consultants and the team leader. Professionally managed consulting firms tend to be open-minded and flexible in staffing assignments even if this can lead to inequalities in the workload of individual consultants. Team leaders are asked whom they prefer to have on their teams, or even encouraged to make their own proposals concerning the team composition. The operating consultants' preference for particular team leaders is also taken into account.

Even if all personal preferences and choices cannot be fully respected, it is important to know about them, and to draw appropriate conclusions for coaching, training and career planning. If team leaders are free to choose the members of their assignment teams, some consultants will always be in higher demand than others. The firm's managers have to face this and try to control this internal selection process, but some staff members may also have to make an effort "to be in greater demand".

Quite often the originally proposed team structure may need to be modified. Usually this is due to a time-lag of uncertain length between the submission of the proposal, its acceptance by the client, and the actual start of the assignment.

Various circumstances may affect the scheduling of the actual start and execution of the assignment. If waiting time cannot be avoided, it is necessary to decide who will wait. The consultant may have to choose between two or more clients, deciding which one will be served first (assuming that the others can wait and will agree to do so). Or a major assignment may be scheduled to start in, say, two months, but the designated team leader is available now. Will the client agree to advance the start of the assignment? Should the team leader be assigned to another job? Should he or she be kept waiting? When is this justified and when not? What will the client do if he or she has to wait?

It frequently happens that a current assignment requires more time than originally scheduled, so that there is a risk of delaying a subsequent job promised to another client. It is inconvenient to interrupt a nearly finished job, and the consulting firm would probably try to negotiate a compromise with one or both clients, for example, to start the new assignment gradually, as individual team members become available. These and similar situations require careful consideration and tactful negotiation with the clients concerned. Clients are aware of these problems, and will usually be open to a discussion of mutually convenient arrangements, especially if they are keen to get a particular consultant for their project.

Lastly, assignment and individual work scheduling should follow a golden rule: never leave any consultant unoccupied! If time-lags between assignments cannot be avoided, the consultant should attend to other activities. The consulting firm should have a backlog of jobs for this situation (training, self-development, research, visiting former clients, etc.), and should encourage individual consultants to make their own suggestions for productive use of the time that cannot be spent with clients.

Overall assignment plan

The overall assignment plan (section 7.4) covers the whole period of the assignment. It presents the operating team's main activities against a timetable (in weeks or days). It specifies the starting and finishing points of these activities, the volume of work (consultant-weeks or consultant-days) in every period in the timetable, and points of time for submission of interim and final reports and for progress control of the assignment.

Estimates of time in the overall plan can be made:

- *top down*, when the consultant knows that he or she has a certain number of work-weeks available and tries to allocate them to the different activities;
- *bottom up*, when the consultant estimates the time needed for each particular activity and compares the total time thus obtained with the established deadlines and estimates of work-weeks needed for the assignment.

Experience with the time taken for similar activities on previous assignments is useful in any case.

The length of assignments affects planning. A short assignment must obviously be planned in greater detail if it is to be completed on time. A long assignment may tempt the consultants to neglect planning since there is no immediate time-pressure. If allowed to take this line, they may suddenly become aware that half the time has been used, and only one-quarter of the programme accomplished. In long assignments, consultants also tend to lose sight of the ultimate objectives, particularly as the operating team becomes more accepted by the client. A clear plan and its regular control avoid this.

A well-calculated overall assignment plan allows for some contingencies and should have to be altered only when major events disturb normal progress. The plan can be presented as a bar chart, a table with numerical values, a network diagram (for long and complex assignments), or a combination of these.

It is useful to enter the client inputs and activities in the assignment plan in a way that permits separate control of client and consultant inputs.

If the consultancy provides quality assurance under ISO 9001 (see sections 32.2 and 32.3), a quality plan may be a separate section of the assignment plan, or may be appended to it. The plan should be available for assignment monitoring and control both to the consulting organization and to the client.

31.2 Preparing for an assignment

Liaison officer

It is usual for the client to appoint one or more staff members to provide close and continuous liaison with the consultants. The term "counterpart" is sometimes used. These people can be of great assistance to operating consultants and save their time, especially during the early investigational stages. Theirs may be full-time work. In some assignments, consultants transfer their knowledge to the liaison officers, who maintain and develop the work after the end of the assignment.

Recruitment and training of client staff

The preliminary diagnostic survey may have shown that there is a shortage of competent people in the client company, with no prospect of finding suitable candidates internally. The client may personally recruit and select additional staff, or may use the consulting unit's service. Either method will take some time. Client staff, possibly including the liaison officer, may need preliminary training in certain techniques. The consulting firm can assist in finding the most suitable courses for them to attend.

Office accommodation

A consulting team should not have to hunt for offices when it starts an assignment. Consultants need not have the best offices, but they will not be highly regarded by the client's staff if they have only a small table in a corner of a general area. Without suitable office space consultants cannot avoid wasting some of their expensive time. Also, operating consultants on assignments need privacy for interviews, discussions and meetings, keeping and studying documents, and writing. As a rule, meeting-rooms that are also used by other groups are not suitable for use as consultants' offices.

Consultant briefing

One person likely to know little about the assignment before the briefing is the operating consultant, who has probably been busy winding up his or her last assignment and has not had time to give thought to the new one. A supervisor who has been involved with the entry-phase activity is likely to know a great deal. Otherwise, the colleague who negotiated the assignment should brief them both. At the briefing meeting, the team takes over the accumulated documentation from the preliminary survey. All matters pertaining to the start of the assignment are then discussed. A checklist of points for the briefing (box 31.1) will help prevent significant omissions.

Box 31.1 Checklist of points for briefing

A. *Hand over:*

1. report to the client on preliminary problem diagnosis and proposal,
2. internal confidential notes on the client,
3. working papers borrowed from the client,
4. published or other printed matter.

B. *Convey and discuss:*

1. terms of reference and contract,
2. source of introduction to the client,
3. client's experience of consultants,
4. client organization's structure, personalities, general style of management, apparent centres of power and influence,
5. client's needs and desires, real and imagined,
6. probable attitudes of staff,
7. expected results (on what are they based?),
8. assignment strategy and plan (including quality requirements),
9. client's experience in the techniques the consultants intend to use,
10. key facts of the client's operation,
11. production processes, trade jargon and terms particular to the business and the locality,
12. contacts made with trade unions and other bodies,
13. previous work in the sector (for the same client, competitors, etc.),
14. scheduled reporting and progress controls.

C. *Inform about:*

1. commitments to the client in respect of various services of the consulting firm (training, recruitment, design, computing, etc.),
2. arrangements for invoicing and payment of fees,
3. arrangements for starting date, time and place,
4. arrangements for office accommodation, staff liaison, secretarial and other support,
5. accommodation, travel arrangements and meeting-place of consultants before going to client organization.

Briefing must never be hectic or confined to administrative arrangements. Partners and senior consultants should use this opportunity to discuss with the operating team what approach may be most appropriate and what techniques should be used in the assignment. In many firms, time and clients' money are wasted by superficial and impatient briefings provided to operating consultants by the senior staff who negotiated the assignment.

Client briefing

Many of the points that should be raised in a final check with the client are also in the list in box 31.1. The remaining precautions to be taken may depend on how much time has passed since the assignment was agreed to and what the preassignment activities were. Checks should be made to ensure:

- that the client's views and needs are still in accordance with the definition of the assignment and the terms of the contract, as mentioned above;
- that the client has adequately explained the nature and purpose of the assignment to all managers and other employees who will be in any way affected.

Introducing the consultants

The conduct of the first days of an operating assignment is of vital importance. The client has already met senior members of the consulting firm, but may be meeting the operating team for the first time. The members of the team new to the client are introduced to the managers and other employees as appropriate. These introductions should be comprehensive and include all staff who might resent being missed out. At the end, the consultants should ask tactfully if there is anyone else they should see. During introductions the consultants will sense whether the client's briefing of his or her staff was complete and understood. The team should make an effort to remember names.

Introductions may be combined with a tour of the plant or offices (which may be limited to the area covered by the consultancy). This gives an opportunity both for the consultants to begin their orientation and for the employees to get their first sight of the team. The tour could end with another tactful question: "Is there anywhere we have not been?"

During introductions the team members should talk enough to show and arouse interest, but avoid any remarks that would suggest prejudgement or overconfidence. This is the start of an exercise in patient listening.

Starting work

After the introductions the team should make time to talk among themselves and discuss impressions. They should recheck the overall assignment plan. If there is not already a short-term plan, they should draw one up to cover the next week or two. The date of their supervisor's next visit should be arranged and a copy of his or her programme in the meantime left with the operating team.

With the departure of the senior staff, the operating team is alone for the first time in the new surroundings. This can be a ticklish time, and if there is any "stage fright" this is when it occurs. It is essential for the operating team to do something immediately to establish contacts with the client's people. Making a start is more important than what precisely is done first. The longer the delay, the harder it becomes. Experience shows the consultants what initial steps would be appropriate in this new environment.

31.3 Managing assignment execution

Consulting requires considerable decentralization of operational decision-making and control. Once an assignment has started, it functions as a relatively independent project, where most matters are decided on the spot by the operating consultant or the team leader in agreement with the client. This section provides a number of ideas and practical suggestions on the short-term control of assignments. It is important, however, to consider what is applicable in each particular setting (e.g. the frequency of control visits to consultants on assignment will be influenced by distance and the cost of travel).

Self-discipline and self-control of operating consultants

The self-discipline and self-management of the operating consultants is a vital factor in assignment control. They are the full-time members of the team, and often the consulting firm's sole representatives for 90 per cent of the time of the assignment.

The consultants are in a situation where they are greatly outnumbered. They have to set an example of hard and high-quality work and intellectual integrity. It is primarily a matter of their own judgement to decide how the code of conduct and the unwritten rules of the profession should be applied in the client organization, which will have its own behavioural patterns, habits, traditions and defects. Should questions arise, the senior consultant supervising the assignment may need to help the operating team with advice and guidance.

Assignment diary. At the end of the first day of the assignment, the operating consultant should start the assignment diary. This is an essential record of activity throughout the assignment. It is written up each evening with a summary of the day's significant events (or non-events) and of progress made. It is a necessary reference for the supervisor. Every paper or note written by the operating team should be recorded in the diary and dated (sometimes the date proves to be its main value).

Time-keeping. In general, consultants on an assignment adjust to the working hours of the client organization. But the assignment programme is usually a heavy one and the consultants may need to work long hours to complete it on time. There may be both practical and tactical advantages in starting a little ahead of the rest of the staff in the morning and leaving a little later in the evening – so long as the consultants do not appear to make a virtue of it.

A consultant's home may be far from the client's premises and he or she may occasionally need to travel on a working day. If this is foreseen, it should be discussed with the client before the start of the assignment. An agreement should be reached on how the working hours and days will be counted, and whether the consultant will be authorized to take time off for travelling home if he or she has worked overtime.

When the assignment is dealing with departments working two or three shifts, the operating consultant must spend enough time on each one to find out all that is needed. The consultant's reception on a night shift is often illuminating – workers and supervisors may receive him or her warmly and appreciate that somebody is interested in their problems.

Sensitivity, anticipation and reaction. The operating consultant has to be sensitive to all the points that the supervisor would normally check. This sensitivity is allied to self-control. The consultant will encounter frustrations and must endure them with patience and good humour. Anger will only arouse opposition and the consultant may end up being baited. At times people may put forward ill-considered views or provide incorrect information. In screening and rejecting these, the consultant must use tact and show tolerance, taking care to give reasoned explanations. There may be attempts to use him or her in internal politics, or involve him or her in intrigues. If consultants keep their eyes and ears open, they may be sufficiently ahead of these games to sidestep them, and be respected the more for it. Genuine appeals must always be met with ready help: goodwill and cooperation only come if they are deserved.

Favours (perks) offered by clients. Sometimes clients arrange for their staff to be able to purchase goods in local shops at a discount, or allow the company's products to be bought at cost rather than at market price. The consultant is not a member of the client's staff, and should not expect to participate in such offers. Consultants who are invited to join such schemes should consider the privilege with care and discretion.

The same rules apply to gifts from the client. There is perhaps no danger in accepting a parting gift, made as a personal gesture at the end of a satisfactory assignment, but at any other time discretion is necessary in deciding whether and how to accept gifts.

Socializing with client's staff. It could be argued that informal contacts with members of the client organization during and after work are every consultant's private matter. This can be accepted, provided the consultant keeps in mind the existing relationships and tensions in the organization and their possible impact on the assignment. By showing a preference for certain people, the consultant may give signals on how he or she is viewing the situation in the client organization and what position he or she is likely to take. Conversely, informal relations can be extremely helpful in getting the job done. Sensitivity to the local and organizational culture will help in deciding what to do.

Control by supervising consultant and client

The supervisor should visit the assignment as frequently as its circumstances warrant. Visits are usually more frequent if the operating consultant is new, or if the assignment is going through a difficult period. Dates of visits should be known to all parties in advance so that appointments and other preparations can be made.

The supervisor should spend time with the operating consultant and client together and separately, to find out how each regards the other and the progress of the assignment. The supervisor should also consider progress in relation to the wider policies and interests of both the client company and the consulting firm.

With the operating consultants, the supervisor may check some or all of the following points:

- that frequent and satisfactory contacts are being maintained with client personnel;
- that assignment progress is up to date and under control;
- that the assignment diary is in good order;
- that the operating consultants are not under stress from any form of harassment by the client;
- that in their anxiety to reach an early balance between financial benefits and fees, the members of the operating team are not tempted to go for a quick return from some potentially dangerous scheme;
- that the opportunities for reporting to the client on progress are being used;
- that the operating consultants' morale is high, and their enthusiasm unflagging.

The supervisor should always be ready to act as a sounding-board for an operating consultant's ideas and as an audience for rehearsal of presentations. He or she should discuss the operating consultant's performance frankly and constructively with him or her, giving approval for work well done and guidance where improvement is necessary.

With the client, the supervisor should check:

- whether he or she is satisfied with the overall progress of the assignment, the contribution made by the operating team, and the relations that have developed between the consultants and the client's staff members;
- whether he or she has met all agreed obligations and inputs to the assignment.

To make control efficient, the client organization, on its side, must have its own rules for examining the progress of operating assignments. The scheduled interim reports submitted by consultants should be studied, views of staff members collaborating with consultants collected, and the consultants' working methods and behaviour observed.

There are periods, particularly in the early stages of an assignment, when the work shows no tangible results. The supervisor may notice signs of fretting, impatience, lessening interest, or simply "cold feet". The symptoms to be watched out for could be:

- people "too busy" to spend time with the consultants;
- defensive or reserved attitudes and a reluctance to talk;
- remarks like "Your man is taking up a lot of our time", "When are we going to see some results?", or "You people are costing us a lot of money".

The supervisor has to take these signs for what they are worth. They are not to be ignored, but neither are they grounds for panic. They have to be countered by whatever overt or covert means are appropriate. It could be that the client is not being sufficiently involved and does not know enough about what is going on.

From the sessions with the operating consultants, the supervisor might find that the assignment is in fact behind schedule. If so, short-term correctional measures may be agreed.

Short-term adjustments in the workplan

Sometimes, unpredictable occurrences might require a short-term plan to be superimposed on the overall plan of the assignment, in order to break an impasse or find a way round a knotty problem.

For instance, the number of operating consultants may need to be temporarily increased beyond the originally planned figures. However, the option of introducing more consultants to complete the work in a shorter time is not always available. The addition of extra consultants does not reduce the time proportionally – as a rule, four consultants require more than one-quarter of the time that one would need. There are various reasons for this, one being the necessity to coordinate and sequence activities. Also, the capacity of the client to increase the pace is limited since the consultancy is an addition to his or her normal workload. Additional consultants may even hinder rather than help in such a situation.

One way of gaining time is to allocate junior or trainee consultants to parts of an assignment that suit the particular stage of their personal development. This can save time at little or no extra cost to the client. In other cases, the client may be able to increase his or her personal involvement and thus speed up the assignment.

Major adjustment of the assignment

Supervision may reveal a need to reorient and restructure the assignment quite substantially. In long, complex assignments, such as business restructuring, reorganizations or new marketing strategies, this is quite common. In such a situation, it is unacceptable for a consultant to ignore the need and to continue along the originally agreed lines, because this is more comfortable and/or lucrative.

If the consulting contract has been properly drawn up, it will provide for a flexible and fairly quick adjustment, which may be suggested either by the consultant or the client. If such a need is revealed, the consulting firm should take the initiative and suggest to the client organization how to proceed, and how the workplan could be best adjusted.

Supervisor's report

The supervisor should keep notes and give reports to the management of the consulting firm in much the same way as the operating consultants keep the assignment diary. He or she may have five or more current assignments and cannot rely on the recollection of one control visit after making several others. These reports are for internal use only.

Liaison with the operating consultants

Whether the location of the assignment raises difficulties of communication depends on the type and size of the consulting firm and the geographical spread of its operations. Many operating consultants may be working a long way from their headquarters for extended periods.

Though the consulting firm may have a newsletter, and may hold regional staff meetings and perhaps an annual conference for everyone, an operating consultant may feel out on a limb for much of the time. The main line of live communication between him or her and the organization is through the supervisor.

The supervisor's visits are, therefore, important occasions for discussion of the consulting firm's news and for some informal talk on what is going on. The operating consultant should be made to feel that he or she still belongs to an organization. The worst feeling consultants can harbour is that so long as they are bringing in the fees nobody cares much about them. Supervisors thus have a responsibility to both their firm and their operating colleagues to keep the whole as close-knit as possible. Without this, operating consultants on a long assignment may begin to identify too much with their clients and lose their independence and objectivity.

Health and morale of operating consultants

A consultant's morale is unlikely to be high if he or she is not in good health. Consultants on assignments tend to go on working when client staff would go on sick leave. Furthermore, a hotel is not usually the most sympathetic place for someone who is ill. The supervisor should watch the operating consultants' health carefully; delaying a visit to a doctor could mean a serious illness.

A drop in morale can also occur without a loss of physical health. Isolation from one's family, frustrations of the assignment, or uninspiring surroundings all contribute. One of the tell-tale signs is that a consultant begins to hate the sight of the place he or she has to work in.

Learning by the consultants and the firm

Assignment management is a key opportunity for encouraging and assisting learning and knowledge management in the consulting firm. Normally the team leaders and supervisors are more experienced in the areas covered by operating assignments. While their more junior colleagues may have a better educational background, especially as regards recent economic, business management, information technology and other developments, they are likely to have gaps in their practical experience and broader understanding of client issues.

Experience has shown that learning must be a managed process. Team leaders and supervisors must know that they are responsible for the coaching and professional development of the junior colleagues in their teams. Time needs to be allotted for this – a quick and superficial visit by a partner, during which an operating consultant does not dare to ask any questions, is of little help. Meetings should have a technical content, not just checking if a deadline will be met and a report properly presented. Individual discussions with operating consultants can be extremely useful and encouraging for them, and can be used to touch gently on issues for which collective discussions are less suited.

The senior consultant and the whole firm also learn from operating assignments. Most innovations in consulting are the result of creative thinking, experiments and collaboration with clients during operating assignments. Team leaders and supervisors are responsible for identifying innovations, helping operating consultants to carry them through, providing additional technical inputs to perfect the approach to be taken, and making sure that the whole firm is promptly informed and can learn from every innovative project.

This, however, must be an organized process enjoying the strong support of higher management, not a mere declaration of noble intentions. The short-term pressure of client demands and billing targets is strong and there will always be a temptation to postpone indefinitely activities (which are seemingly unproductive) to build up the firm's collective know-how.

Assignment progress control by higher management

Periodic (e.g. monthly) progress reviews of all assignments should be made by higher management in the consulting firm – by top management in small organizations, and by divisional or regional management or by a senior partner in large organizations. The reviews should be based on reports submitted by supervisors and/or team leaders, information received from clients (complaints, changes implemented, additional requests), and the senior managers' own intelligence gathered through personal contacts with the clients and the consulting staff.

Assignments that are on schedule and present no technical problems do not require detailed discussion, except for those that are approaching completion; higher management should become involved in these by studying the report, planning a visit to the client to present the conclusions, and preparing for the transfer of the assignment team to another project. Problematic assignments should be reviewed in more detail, in particular if the supervisor concerned is not in a position to redress the situation by measures that are within his or her competence, and needs help from superiors.

Whenever necessary, assignment progress reviews by higher management should also discuss technical problems that have arisen. This may be the case with assignments that are particularly difficult, where new consultants or new supervisors are employed, or where new and unfamiliar methodologies are applied. It is very important for the operating teams and the supervisors to know that someone higher up is interested, not only in smooth delivery and regular income, but also in the operating consultants' efforts to apply new approaches and improve the quality of the service.

Not all technical problems can or should be referred to top management for advice or decision. Many consulting firms therefore use procedures whereby higher management would be consulted, or requested to approve the report to the client, on any assignment that exceeds a certain size (e.g. cost over $200,000), proposes an unusual solution (e.g. merging companies from different sectors), has major political and social implications (e.g. could provoke a strike), or would substantially deviate from routine practice in some other way.

Quality management, a key dimension of any assignment management and control in consulting, is discussed in Chapter 32.

31.4 Controlling costs and budgets

Both the client and the consultant are concerned about the financial side of assignment execution. The client is certainly pleased to see that the job is making progress, but since he or she is also paying the consultant's bills, it is normal to compare the progress achieved with the money that has been spent.

The consulting firm has a similar concern. If the contract stipulated a lump-sum payment, both the operating consultants and the supervisor involved must monitor carefully whether the progress made is commensurate with the time and other resources spent. It does happen that, through lack of focus and discipline, too much time is spent on fact-finding and diagnosis, and the consultants then have to complete the assignment under extreme pressure, or cannot finish it within the agreed time and budget.

However, even if a per diem fee rate is applied and no maximum budget was agreed upon, the consultant's responsibility to the client requires strict control of cumulative costs and their comparison with the progress made in the assignment. If this relationship is ignored and the client is expected to pay the fees anyhow, this can lead to a major conflict. The assignment may be phased out in an unpleasant atmosphere, or the consultant could spoil the chances of getting other work from this client.

The consulting firm needs to control assignment budgets for one more reason. It needs to know which assignments are profitable and which are not, in order to adjust its service portfolio, assignment design, work organization, staff structure and personnel management, including partner and consultant compensation. Therefore many consulting firms budget and control the complete cost and the profit made for every assignment (see also section 33.2).

31.5 Assignment records and reports

In a decentralized organizational setting, where a number of assignments are executed simultaneously and many operating decisions are taken far from the headquarters, an accurate and reliable system of records and reports is indispensable for effective assignment management, for charging clients properly, and for paying consultants their salaries and reimbursing their expenses. There are many information technology applications for professional service firms that have made this relatively easy even for smaller companies.

Notification of assignment

At the beginning of every assignment the supervisor or the team leader should prepare an *assignment notification*, which is intended to inform many sections within the consulting organization. It initiates or supplements a client file for the commercial aspects of the firm's work with that client. The notification records information as indicated in figure 31.1. If staffing is modified during the course of an assignment, a supplementary notification should be made. Rather than recording and transmitting these data manually, many consultants input them to their computerized internal control systems.

Consultants' time records

Time records, or time sheets, are the source of data for invoicing clients and for much of the control information needed by management. If recording is manual, one standard form will suffice for operating and senior consultants. It should be returned to the office either weekly or monthly depending on the requirements for invoicing and control, and should contain the following information:

- consultant's name;
- dates of period covered;
- client names (for up to, say, five assignments, surveys or visits);
- fee rates for paid work;
- number of fee-earning days per client;
- number of non-fee-earning days per consultant divided into:
  - attending public and professional events,
  - giving training,
  - leave,
  - preliminary survey,
  - promotional activity,
  - receiving training,
  - sickness,
  - supervision,
  - unassigned,
  - unpaid operating.

Figure 31.1 Notification of assignment

<table>
<tr><td colspan="3">NOTIFICATION OF ASSIGNMENT</td><td colspan="3">Assignment No.</td></tr>
<tr><td colspan="3">Client</td><td colspan="3">Industry</td></tr>
<tr><td colspan="3">Address</td><td colspan="3">Phone/fax/email</td></tr>
<tr><td colspan="6">Assigner (main contract)</td></tr>
<tr><td colspan="6">Invoices to</td></tr>
<tr><td colspan="6">Type of assignment
☐ Preliminary survey ☐ Operating ☐ Follow up
☐ Paid survey ☐ Training ☐ Other (specify below)</td></tr>
<tr><td colspan="3">Fee rate</td><td colspan="3">Special invoicing instructions</td></tr>
<tr><td colspan="6">Expenses rechargeable to client</td></tr>
<tr><td colspan="6">Operating function</td></tr>
<tr><td colspan="6">Operating consultant(s)</td></tr>
<tr><td colspan="6">Survey consultant or supervisor</td></tr>
<tr><td colspan="6">Other (trainees, etc.)</td></tr>
<tr><td colspan="2">Starting date</td><td colspan="2">Planned duration</td><td colspan="2">Finishing date</td></tr>
<tr><td colspan="3">Briefing and special conditons</td><td colspan="3">Other comments</td></tr>
<tr><td colspan="2">Date</td><td colspan="2">Issued by</td><td colspan="2">Signature</td></tr>
</table>

Operating consultants would normally enter the name of their current client, the fee-earning days to be charged and the non-chargeable days. Other consultants (supervisors, marketers, survey consultants, etc.) would enter the names of all clients dealt with personally during the period, the days spent on non-chargeable work, the days of chargeable work, fee rates, and the use made of all non-fee-earning time.

The same data can be generated and processed using a computerized time-sheet scheme. Most consultants use their personal computers, but it is important that they record the data correctly, on a daily basis, to avoid omissions and misallocations of time.

Consultants' expenses

The firm may have a standard scale of expense allowances, and rules for its application which cover an assumed normal set of conditions. This can be surprisingly difficult to draw up and administer: the "every situation is different" character of operating assignments often extends to the consultants' expenses. As a rule, consulting organizations will need to be prepared to consider any case of higher than standard expenses, at the consultant's request.

The main sources of expense are:

- accommodation and meals while away from home;
- travel;
- communication (faxes, telephone calls, etc.);
- use of special services (computing, printing, translation, information);
- entertainment of client and other business contacts.

Whether other out-of-pocket expenses are reimbursed by the client will depend on the terms of the contract. The expenses claim form should cater for any items that are to be recharged to the client.

Receipts for various expenses

Orderly administration and bookkeeping require clear rules as regards receipts for various expenses incurred both by individual consultants and by the consulting firm. The consultants must know that certain categories of expenses will be reimbursed to them only if they submit a receipt. The firm should keep receipts for all expenses that will be charged to clients for reimbursement. If an expense item is large, it may be good practice to provide the client with a copy of the receipt and add an explanation. Finally, certain receipts may be required when claiming deductions for tax purposes, or should be kept available for possible tax inspection.

If an expense item cannot be documented by a receipt, it may be necessary to establish an internal check or other document to prove that the expense was incurred and authorized, and to make sure that it is properly recorded in the books.

Reports to the client

The reports given to the client at various points of the consulting process were discussed in Chapters 7 to 11, and general principles of effective report writing are set out in Appendix 7.

Assignment reference report

This report, called the "assignment summary" by some consultants, and prepared at the end of an operating assignment, is a very useful piece of information, which makes it unnecessary to read detailed client reports for single facts on past assignments. In addition, it contains comments on the possibilities of further work with the client, and provides an input into the firm's knowledge management. The report should include information on the points listed in box 31.2.

Box 31.2 Assignment reference report – a checklist

1. Client company name and address
2. Assigner's name and title
3. Nature and size of client organization
4. Operating function of the assignment
5. Names of members of the consulting team
6. Dates of start and finish
7. Brief summary of objectives and results, what was new and creative in this assignment
8. References to all reports and documents that give details of the assignment
9. Feedback from the client on assignment quality and results (reply to a questionnaire and any other feedback)
10. Rating of the quality of the assignment by the consulting firm
    - above standard
    - standard
    - below standard
11. Rating of the value of the assignment for future reference
    - excellent
    - average
    - not to be used
12. Whether the client has agreed that the consulting firm may use him or her as a reference to prospective clients (if the rating was excellent or average)
13. Suggested future assignment opportunities that should be pursued with the same client, and what should be kept in mind in negotiating new business with him or her

31.6 Closing an assignment

It is useful to establish and announce clearly that the assignment has been terminated. This will avoid confusion in long and complex assignments involving several members of the consulting firm, a number of people in the client company, and a wide range of different activities and contacts.

The main considerations involved in closing an assignment were discussed in Chapter 11. In particular, the reader should refer to the discussions of assignment evaluation and of final reporting. But there are some further points to remember:

- In the days close to the completion date, the client should not be given the impression that the consulting firm is losing interest because the business is winding up and the payment will be forthcoming. This may happen if a new, interesting client is already lined up and the consultant is keen to start working on the new assignment.
- It is important not to leave any unfinished work, such as documentation that was promised but not produced, training that was started but not completed, or a new system that breaks down frequently. All commitments should be met by the date of termination, including seemingly unimportant ones (for example, the consultant should return all documents and equipment borrowed from the client, hand over all papers as agreed, and return the pass issued by the client organization).
- Billing will follow the established practice (section 30.8) and the specific conditions stipulated in the contract. When receiving the final bill, the client should not find an unexpected surprise or feel that there is any unfinished business. The client should have no reason to feel that the consultant is more concerned about being paid than about having done a perfect job.

Before leaving, the consultant may already be able to obtain some feedback on the client's satisfaction. He or she should inform the client about the post-assignment evaluation practised by the firm (e.g. through questionnaires or personal interviews) and ask the client tactfully if he or she would be prepared to recommend the consultant to business friends.

A successful completion of a consulting project may be a good opportunity for drinks, a dinner party or other social event, which can be hosted either by the consultant or by the client.

QUALITY MANAGEMENT IN CONSULTING

32

The concept and methods of quality management were explained in Chapter 21 and many references to quality can be found in other chapters of our book. Nevertheless, the importance and the current issues of quality management warrant a separate chapter focused on quality management in consulting.

Most management consultants claim to embody the concept of quality in their objectives, placing considerable emphasis on the quality of people, on impressive experience, and on offering clients a highly responsive professional service. Yet the image of consultants among clients is patchy; while some clients respect the consultants' service as useful and valuable, others regard them, at worst, as charlatans, or, at best, as smart alecks to be avoided.

In recent years, management consultants have begun to address the quality management of their own firms. "Physician heal thyself" is not inappropriate given that management consultants have taken the lead in devising and implementing quality management systems in their clients' organizations. There are a number of reasons for this change. When the primary emphasis was on growth during the boom years of the 1980s, high utilization and the recruitment of many new people to management consulting resulted in inadequate attention to training and process disciplines. In a much tighter marketplace, consulting practices often need to differentiate themselves more on quality of service than on skills and experience. Pressure on margins is also driving consultants to manage themselves more efficiently and to look more closely at service delivery.

32.1 What is quality management in consulting?

Professional service quality is, above all, a characteristic of organizational culture, an approach to everything a professional does with and for the client. Aiming at quality is aiming at the best possible satisfaction of clients' needs and requirements. If this concept of quality is adopted, responsibility for quality has to be vested in every professional worker. Indeed, quality is an inherent characteristic of all work that claims to be truly professional. In many instances, no one else will be able to judge whether the service actually provided is of proper quality or needs improvement. In this sense, quality management is essentially self-assessment, self-control and self-improvement.

However, the client has a contract with the consulting firm, not with its individual employee. The firm therefore needs to ensure that the same quality of service can be expected from all of its staff. Uncertainty and inconsistency as regards quality can be very damaging. Hence quality management is also a system of written and unwritten standards, policies, guidelines, controls, records, safeguards, incentives, sanctions and other tools and measures whereby quality is assessed, maintained and improved. Quality management may involve formal declarations of policies and principles. More important will be the myriad of small steps and interventions, most of them informal, in areas such as recruitment, consultant development, coaching, promotion, knowledge management, dealing with and listening to individual clients, problem analysis, helping poor performers to improve, reacting to clients' complaints, and so on.

Indeed, quality management should be omnipresent. Whatever a professional firm does (or omits to do) has a quality dimension and direct or indirect impact on the quality of services provided to clients, as well as on client satisfaction.

Furthermore, quality management must address both the strictly technical side of consulting (the knowledge base, the practical know-how, the choice of correct data and procedures, the analysis of all relevant facts, the assessment of important alternatives, etc.), and the human and behavioural side of the consultant–client relationship (caring for the clients, listening to their concerns, dispelling their worries, respecting their priorities, being helpful beyond the scope of the contract, etc.). David Maister has pointed out that while most consultants meet the quality criteria as regards the first aspect (technical quality), satisfaction levels are low, and complaints numerous, when clients are asked about the way they were dealt with by their consultants.[1]

Increasingly, clients who have themselves invested heavily in quality expect their service suppliers to think the same way. For example, some of the leading commercial banks in the United Kingdom are asking consultants to provide details of their overall policy regarding commitment to quality, to indicate independent management responsibility for ensuring that quality is promoted and implemented, and to describe quality assurance procedures for project design, service quality and support. A growing number of public and private sector clients are requesting information on progress towards ISO 9001 certification (section 32.3) and on the extent of the quality management system. Some large client organizations, particularly in the public sector, who are major purchasers of consulting services, have begun to impose quality standards. In several countries, ministries require management consultants to hold ISO 9001 certification of quality or equivalent as a precondition of tendering.

Primary stakeholders' needs

Thus, quality is above all a question of meeting clients' needs and requirements. This implies that the main focus of quality management must be on client services and satisfaction. After all, in the long run the success of the consulting firm and the consultants themselves is dependent on client satisfaction. Quality management also has an essential role in helping the firm to meet ambitious targets for utilization, profitability and consultant satisfaction, thus addressing the needs of all stakeholders (box 32.1). This concept is important: a quality management programme that does not address the needs of all stakeholders is unlikely to be successful.

Box 32.1 Primary stakeholders' needs

Clients

- services and solutions that meet their requirements and expectations
- long-term relationships
- value for money
- contractual reassurance

Owners of the consulting firm

- client satisfaction
- higher utilization
- prompt payment
- repeat business
- adequate profits
- good image of the firm

Consultants

- job satisfaction
- client satisfaction
- rewards
- career prospects

Viewing quality as important

It should be self-evident that a consulting firm that pays serious attention to improving quality can significantly improve its viability and performance. In practice, quality management and management consultants are not always easy bedfellows for a number of reasons:

- the recent history of many consultancies in both the business and public sectors is of high client demand and good rewards for owners and staff without any special effort to raise quality;
- some consultants do not value "process" highly and are often reluctant to cooperate in introducing what they may see as unnecessary and irritating "bureaucracy of quality";
- more is demanded of management, an already scarce resource, which may resist more calls on its time;
- initial costs can be substantial, particularly in investment in non-chargeable time;
- quality improvement is a slow, gradual process, in terms of both application and results, and consultants often lack the perseverance required for lasting improvements.

Responsibility for quality

In a people-centred business, it is essential that every practitioner and support team member is clear about their personal responsibility for quality. Quality service delivery depends above all on individual performance. The four basic principles in assigning responsibility for quality are:

1. *Responsibilities must be clear and clearly stated*, so everybody knows who is responsible for what.
2. *Top management must be visibly involved*, giving credibility and clout to the importance of quality.
3. *Continuity/succession needs to be assured*, thus dealing with the inevitable problems emanating from absences on assignments, changes in assignment staffing during project execution, etc.
4. *Quality assurance must be applied consistently*, to all work at all times.

The main responsibilities for quality within a consulting firm are set out in box 32.2. In a large consulting firm, key responsibilities may be delegated to a central quality management team, comprising the quality directors of the different practice areas or business units. This provides a vehicle for ensuring consistency across the practice, testing new initiatives and promoting quality awareness. Every individual director or partner needs to be aware of his or her responsibility for quality, in particular regarding the monitoring and nurturing of long-term client relationships. Regular assessment of client satisfaction through meetings and interviews is a valuable input to sustaining the delivery of quality work.

The associations of management consulting firms have an important and influential role in providing guidance on quality issue for their members and in giving clients a message that management consultants are concerned about and are taking the lead in quality management.

Box 32.2 Responsibility for quality

Role	Key responsibilities for quality
Directors/partners	Set quality policy and objectives Allocate responsibilities Review activities Establish priorities Provide role models Demonstrate commitment
Project team leaders	Ensure that quality assurance is built into all stages of an assignment Allocate project responsibilities Publish assignment plan and deliverables Produce and communicate quality plan covering quality assurance procedures, technical standards and quality criteria Coach and support operating consultants
Individual consultants	Understand quality policy Follow best practice in working with clients Document adequately
Internal auditors	Conduct systematic third-party reviews Provide balanced feedback Highlight areas for improvement

32.2 Key elements of a quality assurance programme

The definition of quality – meeting client requirements – suggests the best starting-point for any quality programme. Feedback and data from clients can provide focus and leverage to debates on quality issues and introducing measures to improve performance. It is important to use a dynamic model of quality assurance to drive a programme of continuous quality improvement. Many quality improvement initiatives have failed because they did not address real issues in a practical, sensible way, so that they become an integral part of day-to-day working and relationships. Some key dos and don'ts, based on experience, are set out in box 32.3.

The key elements of a quality assurance (QA) programme in consulting assignments can be considered under the following headings:

Box 32.3 Introducing a quality assurance programme

Do	Start from client requirements Take a long-term view Focus on a few real quality issues Obtain consultant buy-in Empower staff to participate fully Simplify processes Give feedback on the benefits
Don't	Create bureaucracy Be overprescriptive Adopt a minimalist approach (it destroys credibility) Reinvent the wheel Expect results too soon

1. Assignment management
   - assignment management procedures
   - quality plans
   - client satisfaction surveys
2. People management
   - personnel policies and procedures
   - knowledge management
   - training and development
   - coaching on the job
3. Quality programme management
   - quality policy
   - quality organization
   - focus of the programme

Assignment management

Procedures. Client feedback is a useful lead into reviewing the need for, and structure of, assignment management procedures (see also Chapter 31), if only to ensure that the focus remains firmly on matters that have the greatest influence on quality in the consultant–client relationship. It also provides a framework that consultants can more readily understand and accept.

Management consultancy is not like a factory-built standard product which can be quality-tested at the end of the line. Quality assurance, together with client involvement, needs to be built into every stage of the assignment process.

Box 32.4 Assuring quality during assignments

Assignment stage	Objectives	Activities
At the outset	To ensure that the right job is being undertaken	Defining terms of reference. Managing client expectations. Agreeing the assignment plan. Agreeing quality measures
During the work	To ensure that the job is being done correctly	Progress reports. Variation control. Documenting client contacts. Guiding and supervising operating consultants
At the end	To ensure that the job has been done properly and the client is satisfied	Formal review and acceptance. Internal review. Consultant appraisals
After the end	To ensure that the client is still satisfied and to review the work in the context of an ongoing relationship. To review consultants' performance	Client feedback through questionnaires and interviews. Update client records. Independent surveys. Feedback to consultant. Appraisals and rewards

Remedial action at the end of an assignment may be costly and too late, and may do little to repair an already damaged client relationship. Box 32.4 sets out a suggested list of main assignment activities which need to be managed and monitored to assure quality work.

Many consultants would claim that they carry out all or most of the activities listed in box 32.4. In practice, this usually involves a substantial degree of post-event rationalization and overreliance on memory rather than documentation. The client may appear to be satisfied but a better, and more profitable, job might have been done with a more rigorous approach to quality management.

It is better for the approach to assignment management procedures to be that of the zero option rather than the comprehensive compendium which ends up as a many-volume manual. Once published, such manuals are rarely consulted. The mobility, responsiveness and flexibility required of consultants are not compatible with highly documented and prescribed procedures. Useful rules are:

- make full use of checklists and "best practice" guidelines;
- define and document mandatory (minimum) work systems and procedures;
- once communicated, monitor adherence to these procedures;
- encourage consultants to comment on procedures and to suggest improvements.

There are a couple of management tools, one used at the beginning and the other at the end of an assignment, that can give excellent leverage in establishing a quality management programme. These are the quality plan and the client satisfaction survey.

The quality plan. The concept of the quality plan is open to criticism that it is bureaucratic and that it should be no different from the assignment plan, which should cover quality matters. In practice the concept is valuable in helping practitioners to focus on quality assurance, particularly in large and complex assignments.

The quality plan is an extension of the assignment or project plan (see section 31.1), and can be treated as part of it. Its contents will vary according to the nature and complexity of the assignment and the size of the assignment team. The following headings provide a skeleton framework:

(1) What are we trying to achieve: (a) assignment definition; and (b) assignment plan and deliverables?

(2) How are we going to ensure that we do a quality job: (a) organization and responsibilities; (b) quality assurance procedures; and (c) technical standards?

(3) How do we measure our success: quality criteria (time, cost, rework, etc.)?

The successful implementation of the quality plan lies in its scope and communication to all members of the team, including the client and support staff. Particular emphasis should be given to:

- initial team briefing covering the assignment plan, client expectations and quality assurance procedures;
- progress monitoring and reporting to client;
- communications and documentation of client contacts and feedback;
- control of change implemented;
- document control;
- acceptance of final report by client.

In planning for quality assurance, consideration may be given to allocating special responsibility for quality monitoring to an individual member of the team, or to appointing an independent quality auditor from outside the project team, who will carry out a peer review of the work.

An example of a quality plan is that prepared for a large international management information system project. It starts with the premises that quality must be built in from the beginning of the assignment, and that the competing interests that might compromise quality are best reconciled if they are identified and managed from the outset. The relevant quality criteria are then described both for the client (e.g. recommendations should clearly identify costs and benefits) and for the project team (e.g. no rework, clear language in presentations, meet cost targets). The next sections of the plan outline the quality assurance principles, procedures, standards and methodologies, for example, the role of the programme manager and the content and frequency of reporting.

The client satisfaction survey. The measurement of client satisfaction through surveys is an essential component of a quality programme in every consulting firm. The survey must be handled with sensitivity and confidentiality to protect clients as well as partners, directors and staff. To be equitable and acceptable, it needs to apply to all parts of a practice, and to be subject to independent management and interpretation. It is not acceptable, for example, for an individual partner to select the clients or assignments that are surveyed. It is also essential to obtain the views of the project team in analysing the client's feedback.

Postal questionnaires are relatively cost-effective if a large number of clients and projects are to be covered, and if clients are not readily accessible. Points to note are:

- the timing of sending out the questionnaire needs careful consideration;
- questionnaires should normally be returned to an independent director of quality to safeguard both clients and consultants;
- the number and complexity of questions should be limited.

Questionnaires should cover an overall scaled assessment and specific questions on areas of satisfaction and dissatisfaction and on suggestions for improvement. Open-ended questions often provide powerful feedback to project teams; on the other hand, ratings are essential to provide comparable evaluations and identify trends. The extent to which the client should be prompted in the questionnaire needs careful research and pilot studies to suit the individual firm's requirements.

Personal interviews with clients have the advantage that areas of concern can be thoroughly probed, and an opportunity is offered for strengthening the consultant–client relationship. The questions asked can be more thorough and extensive. However, the size of the firm and of the clientele may make extensive use of personal interviews prohibitively expensive. Also, some clients may feel safer in expressing their views in an anonymous postal questionnaire.

If client interviews are feasible, it is important that they are based on a standard questionnaire, so that comparisons can be made. It is also preferable that they should be conducted by a director or a partner independent of the project team.

Finally, it is important to bear in mind that:

- some clients will not cooperate, but the majority will welcome their opinions being sought;
- the value of client satisfaction surveys lies in their results being fed back to all members of project teams.

Independent market surveys. Client satisfaction surveys do not provide an assessment against competitors or benchmarking on how a firm is doing in comparison with other consultants. Many firms contribute to broad surveys of consultancy purchasers, and use their own professional associations and networks to obtain data on how they are doing competitively.

People management

Good personnel policies and people management are essential to quality management and to ensuring that continuous quality improvement is achieved. Apart from the application of high standards, appraisal and training provide the vehicles for taking corrective action and addressing client satisfaction. Quality can be enhanced by:

- the consistent application of high standards in recruiting new consulting staff and in selecting subcontractors;
- induction and training in core skills to equip consultants with the necessary competencies;
- coaching, helping and supervising people on the job;
- practising knowledge management to make sure that best practice experience is available to operating consultants and that they are encouraged to seek it and use it;
- assignment appraisals which feed into an individual's longer-term development, remuneration and promotion;
- using databases of skills and experience which enable properly structured and highly competent teams to be formed for client assignments;
- feeding back results of client satisfaction surveys into consultant appraisals and training;
- defining and publishing a code of ethics for the firm and encouraging voluntary membership in professional associations and institutes.

Within consulting firms, consideration may need to be given to "accrediting" consultants with specialist skills who have completed the required training and demonstrated competency. This protects both the firm and the clients by ensuring that certain specialist work, which may involve high risks (e.g. financial modelling), is undertaken only by accredited experts on the topic.

Quality programme management

The director or partner responsible for quality will need to provide a framework that ensures that the quality programme has direction and support, and is applied consistently throughout the firm. The starting-point is the drafting and publication of a quality policy statement. This should include:

- aims of the policy, linked to client satisfaction;
- whether there is an intention to work in conformance with an externally audited quality standard (e.g. ISO 9001:2000);

- areas in which standards will be applied (technical, client relations, cost, time, etc.);
- the name of the person or persons with overall responsibility.

The policy statement should be authorized by senior management, and communicated to all staff and subcontractors. It should be subject to regular review.

The quality programme needs to be supported by an appropriate quality organization and requires a clear focus. The steps to achieving this are:

- review all activities – preferably using client feedback;
- establish priorities for quality improvement;
- determine approaches to achieving improvement (procedures, best practice, training, etc.);
- ensure that training, appraisals and performance measures support the agreed priorities.

Small consulting firms and sole practitioners

The principles of this approach to quality management can be applied equally well to small practices and sole practitioners as to large firms. Independent review is more difficult for a small practice, and a sole practitioner will need to rely on self-generated review procedures. A questionnaire with a series of written observations against each question is a more powerful procedure than a checklist with uniform ticks. Customer review and sign-off of reports is a particularly valuable discipline for the small firm.

32.3 Quality certification

In recent years there has been considerable debate among management consultants about the relevance of externally audited quality standards to their firms. Movement towards seeking certification has been at the pace dictated by the marketplace, including in some cases direct pressure from public sector clients, who see certification as a necessary reassurance of attention to quality. As a result, many large consulting firms have started preparing for, and gaining, certification for at least some sectors of their business. The origins of this movement lie in several countries of the European Union, the Netherlands and the United Kingdom in particular.

ISO 9001:2000 quality assurance standard

The international quality standard ISO 9001:2000 was discussed in Chapter 21. These standards require the applying organization to have a quality policy and a documented quality system and supporting procedure, and to provide evidence that the procedures are being used, conformance is being monitored and there are regular reviews.

A quality audit must be undertaken by an independent certification body (such as BSI Quality Assurance, Bureau Veritas, Det Norsk Veritas). These bodies are not management consulting firms, but their function is to audit businesses and organizations in many sectors. They are accredited by government accreditation bodies.

In theory, the quality management system (QMS) should require no more than a well-run business, which takes quality seriously, should be doing already. In practice, the disciplines of a rigorously applied QMS can necessitate substantial shifts in organizational culture and work habits.

Seeking certification should not be an end in itself; there is plenty of anecdotal evidence to support this view. A superficial approach is likely to result in rejection by the consultants involved and non-conformance being readily exposed by the external auditor. It is important that the QMS reflects the needs of actual practice and, therefore, deals with real quality issues. It is also essential to involve the staff in its preparation, so that it is not seen as a bureaucratic imposition.

The assignment model (e.g. lead/enquiry, proposal preparation, assignment plan, monitoring and controlling, and completing/closing) is well suited to the application of ISO 9001:2000 standards. It has been shown to be applicable to all sizes of consultancy practice.

Clearly, ISO certification is not sufficient in itself as a guarantee of meeting client requirements. It provides independent certification that a quality management system is in place and that the practice is conforming with its requirements. But there is much more to do. Quality certification by itself is not a measure of client satisfaction, although the QMS should require that there are procedures for obtaining client feedback, and that these are in operation.

Selecting a certification body

Fees charged by certification bodies are negotiable. As there are ongoing costs of surveillance, it is worth paying particular attention to the value you will derive from the guidance of these bodies and checking out that their auditors are going to understand your business. Remember that many certification bodies are new to the auditing service and professional businesses.

Questions to be asked of certification bodies include:

- Have you been, or are you expecting to be, accredited to assess management consulting firms?
- Who recognizes your certification?
- Do you have a customer care programme?
- What are your fees?
- Can we see the curriculum vitae of your quality auditors?
- Can you provide relevant references?

The quality auditor will check the documented quality system against ISO 9001:2000 and the applicable guidelines. He or she is likely to carry out an internal audit and management review, and also needs to agree on the scope of the certificate, i.e. which parts of the practice (activity areas) are to be included. Three or four months' records based on the documented quality system are necessary before the conformance audit can be undertaken.

Problems encountered in seeking certification

It is still relatively early days to assess the real value of quality certification to management consulting firms (as indeed to other firms providing management and business services). However, there is a growing view that once the initial difficulties have been overcome, there is considerable benefit in better working methods and higher client satisfaction.

Some of the problems that have emerged are:

- resistance by partners and staff resulting in implementation being a painful process;
- overcomplicated and excessive bureaucracy;
- failure to adhere to documentation requirements;
- failure to provide feedback and use information properly, e.g. on lost tenders;
- slowness of certification bodies to receive accreditation enabling them to certify management consultants.

Some small firms and sole practitioners have expressed strong views that ISO 9001 quality standards are excessively bureaucratic, and an unnecessary burden. However, in issuing the 2000 edition of the standards, ISO has tried to simplify the procedure and the paperwork. Experience has to show whether this will benefit consultants seeking certification.

The time spent in preparing a quality manual and implementing a QMS can be considerable, and external assistance can provide expertise and resources. It is often helpful to have an external consultant examine the system before finalizing it for assessment. Points to note are:

- before employing a quality consultancy, check its track record and take up references;
- ensure that its consultants work with your staff, so ownership is in house;
- make sure that they do not overspecify your requirements.

32.4 Sustaining quality

In conclusion, client pressure and growing competition have moved quality higher up the management consultants' own agenda. Increasingly, service quality constitutes the consultants' competitive advantage. For long-term development and growth, both large and small consultancies will need to be proactive in working with clients on quality issues. As with any such development, clarification of objectives, standards, roles and responsibilities is an essential first step. ISO 9001:2000 contributes by providing standards that are externally certificated. Both clients and consulting practitioners need to share the aim of achieving continuous improvement in service delivery, and to be proactive in sustaining this.

A formalistic approach to quality must be avoided. There is a real risk that some firms will be happy to have and to exhibit an elaborate procedure, the "bureaucracy of quality", and that some clients will be unduly impressed by the formal side of quality management. No control and certification procedure can become a substitute for the quality of people in a professional firm, for their genuine concern for the clients and for their sense of professional responsibility.

The decisions concerning quality management and assurance, and the measures taken to enhance quality, depend on the firm's attitude to quality and its determination to achieve high standards. As Deming said of total quality management, "You do not have to do this: survival is not compulsory."

---

[1] See "A service quality programme", in D. H. Maister: *Managing the professional service firm* (New York, The Free Press, 1993), Ch. 8.

OPERATIONAL AND FINANCIAL CONTROL

33

This chapter deals with key aspects of short-term operational management and control, emphasizing the methods and indicators that help to monitor operations and prevent events that could reduce efficiency or lead to crises. We assume that the reader is familiar with the basics of financial and budgetary control, and the discussion therefore focuses on some specific problems of consultants and consulting organizations.

33.1 Operating workplan and budget

Operational management and control uses two basic management tools: an operating workplan and an operating financial budget. Both documents are normally prepared annually, for the next planning and budgetary year, in a monthly or quarterly breakdown. This breakdown should take into account seasonal and other variations within the 12-month period, such as a reduced workload during the holiday period, and other events, including major payments to be made or received at a foreseeable time.

Operating workplan

The operating workplan should reflect the firm's strategic choices and indicate how strategy will be implemented in the forthcoming year. It therefore determines:

- the volume of consulting and other services to be sold and delivered to clients;
- changes in the service portfolio (phasing out a service, introducing a new product, starting work in a new sector, new foreign operations);
- staff recruitment and training required;
- staff retirement and departures;
- the volume and orientation of promotional and marketing activities;

- the backlog of new assignments to be maintained;
- other measures needed to implement the work programme and to prepare for the future (research and development, organizational restructuring, investment, etc.);
- the ways in which consultants will spend their time effectively when not working directly for clients.

Extrapolation of past trends is useful for preparing an operating workplan. However, mechanistic extrapolation cannot be recommended. An analysis of business trends, and of the consulting firm's current opportunities and difficulties, will help in setting professional and business targets that are neither mere extrapolations nor unrealistic dreams.

Operating budget

The basic management tool for controlling the financial side of the firm's operation is the operating budget. In preparing the budget, the firm has to include all the expenses it expects to incur during the budget period, and to fix the projected income at a level required to cover expenses and ensure an adequate profit. If budget preparation reveals that the budget cannot be balanced, it is necessary to revise the workplan and the planned expenditure to keep them within realistic financial limits, and to re-examine the costing, pricing and other assumptions underlying the two sides of the budget.

The budgetary planning may show that the consulting firm's costs will be too high, and therefore the fees risk being excessive, or profits too low. In this case, management can look at various methods of improving efficiency and raising profits, as listed in box 33.1. The method chosen should be consistent with the firm's strategic choices. If growth in operations and income is planned, analysis should reveal how expenses will increase. The consulting firm needs to keep in mind the difference between fixed and variable expenses, and subject each expense line to detailed scrutiny before deciding whether and how it should be allowed to grow.

An example of an annual operating budget is shown in table 33.1. It corresponds to the consulting unit, employing 29 consultants, shown in figure 35.2. The salary rates and other figures in the budget are purely hypothetical and are not intended as standards for remuneration policy, or for assessing the expense structure and efficiency of any particular firm.

Structure of expenses

Nevertheless, the expense and income structure shown is within the broad limits of normal practice in a number of management consulting firms. These limits tend to be as shown in table 33.2.

Management consulting services are highly labour-intensive and professional staff salaries are therefore by far the most important single expense item in any firm. Their share in the total expense structure depends on factors such

Box 33.1 Ways of improving efficiency and raising profits

Area of intervention	Action
Efficient operations	Use staff according to competence Organize and execute assignments efficiently Increase staff utilization and efficiency Save on overhead items Bill and collect fees promptly
Fee levels	Charge more for current services Charge for services provided free hitherto
Marketing efforts	Sell and deliver more work (increase volume) Sell more profitable work Cross-sell Market more efficiently
Staff size and structure	Recruit more consultants Increase leverage Cut or replace unproductive staff Increase staff competence
Service portfolio	Cut unprofitable services Develop new and more profitable services

as the level of professional income in the particular country and firm, and the size of the consulting firm. Single practitioners and other small firms are usually able to operate with low overhead costs, reducing or completely eliminating certain items of expenditure without which a larger firm cannot operate. A single practitioner may even be able to operate without secretarial and support staff, and without renting office space.

Other expenses (grouped under lines 3–12 in table 33.1) include a wide range of different items associated with the operation of a consulting unit of a given profile, scope and level of activity. As a rule, these expenses include costs that cannot be directly related to a particular client assignment; or, if they could be, it would not be practical and efficient to do so. For example, reproduction expenses can be treated as an overhead item or a direct cost item to be charged to a particular client. Routine reproduction work (e.g. reproducing consulting reports in a standard number of copies) is normally treated as an overhead cost. Reproduction of voluminous special reports, or large numbers of additional copies ordered by the client, should be charged to the client as "billable expenses". A similar choice has to be made in the case of telephone charges and other costs.

Table 33.1 Operating budget of a consulting firm

Budget item	US$	Percentages
1. Professional salaries	1 710 000	43.9
2. Social charges and benefits on professional salaries	340 000	8.7
3. Administrative and support staff salaries	250 000	6.4
4. Social charges and benefits on administrative salaries	50 000	1.3
5. Marketing and promotion expenses (other than salaries)	160 000	4.1
6. Rentals and utilities	120 000	3.1
7. Equipment, furniture, materials, stationery	110 000	2.8
8. Communications (mail, fax, telephone)	110 000	2.8
9. Taxes (other than income taxes)	70 000	1.8
10. Library, subscriptions, membership fees	80 000	2.1
11. Staff training and development	80 000	2.1
12. Other expenses (travel, entertainment, etc.)	180 000	4.6
13. Overhead expenses (3 to 12)	1 210 000	31.0
14. Total expenses (1 to 12)	3 260 000	83.6
15. Gross profit (before tax)	638 000	16.4
16. Total income (14 + 15)	3 898 000	100.0
17. Expenses billed to clients	522 000	13.4
18. Gross billing (16 + 17)	4 420 000	113.4

Note: Item 1 ("Professional salaries") includes the following: director (1 x US$100,000 = 100,000); senior consultants (6 x US$75,000 = 450,000); operating consultants (20 x US$55,000 = 1,100,000); trainee consultants (2 x US$30,000 = 60,000); total US$1,710,000.

Table 33.2 Typical structure of expenses and income

Item	Percentage
Professional staff salaries (including social charges)	35–60
Other expenses	40–60
Gross profit (before tax)	10–25
Total income	100
Billable expenses	10–30
Gross billing to client	110–130

Expenses billed to clients (billable expenses) are often not regarded by consultants as part of their business income, even if these expenses pass through their accounts. Therefore, billable expenses are shown separately (line 17) in the operating budget.

Profit

Profit (before tax) is the difference between the total fees earned and the total costs and expenses incurred over the budget period. It provides for:

- a profit-share or bonus to the owners, partners or other employees of the consulting firm;
- establishing security reserves;
- increasing the working capital;
- financing capital expenses;
- paying a profit (income) tax.

As shown in table 33.2, in most cases the profit margin would be between 10 and 25 per cent of total income. The actual figure will depend on such factors as the possibility of charging fees that provide for an adequate profit, the ability to reduce and control expenses, and the firm's need to generate resources for further expansion of its services or for other purposes mentioned above.

33.2 Performance monitoring

The monitoring of operational and financial performance is an essential, yet often underestimated, management function in consulting firms. The purpose is not to produce statistics for their own sake, but systematically to collect and evaluate key information likely to reveal negative trends (from which will spring the need for action to redress the situation) or positive trends (which may need to be reinforced so that any opportunities disclosed are not missed).

Performance monitoring aims at immediate improvements first of all, but its strategic implications should not be overlooked. It helps to reveal changes and trends that will affect the consulting firm in the long run, such as major shifts in demand for certain kinds of service, or the increasing cost of selling services to certain markets. Adjustments to the firm's strategy can thus be based on hard data rather than guesses and estimates.

Comparing and benchmarking

It is impossible to assess performance without making comparisons: superior or substandard performance can be identified and assessed only with reference to some other performance. Consultants use comparisons and benchmarking extensively when working with clients, and they should not hesitate to apply them to their own operation.

Comparing results achieved with planned or projected targets can be revealing, provided that the targets were based on thorough analysis and realistic goal-setting, and not just on guesswork. The main documents to which this comparison refers in performance monitoring are the annual workplan and operating budget.

Comparing current and past performance can show trends in performance, as well as changes in factors affecting it.

Comparing performance with other consultants can be most instructive. This can be done in various ways:

- Consultants who are business friends can exchange and compare data informally, as colleagues who want to learn from each other.
- There can be a formal interfirm comparison scheme, run by a consultants' association or another agency. Under such a scheme, key data are collected, tabulated and distributed to participating consulting units on a regular basis, without revealing the identity of the units.
- Performance achieved by a specific consulting firm can be compared with sectoral standards. Such sectoral standards would reflect "good practice", i.e. the experience of consulting firms whose management is considered competent and performance adequate. Here again, such standards can be developed as benchmarks by an association for the benefit of its members. This book refers to a number of ratios collected from consulting firms and their associations. These operating ratios can be regarded as a form of standard.

In making comparisons, it is essential to determine the causes of superior or substandard performance: this may result from excellent or poor management of operations and assignment execution, but also from an unforeseen change in the business environment over which the consulting firm has little control.

Both data from other firms and any sector standards or averages have to be used cautiously. The situation and possibilities of your firm may be very different and so may be your objectives. While it is extremely useful to know how others perform, superficial and hasty conclusions should not be drawn from the data without comparing resources, conditions and strategies.

Key monthly controls

Operational controls have to be established and examined relatively frequently to permit action before it is too late. In practice, this will be monthly in most cases. This explains why the operating workplan and budget described above are prepared with a monthly breakdown of most data. Any deviation from the consulting unit's standards, or any undesirable trend, should be detected by management. Management will have to consider whether prompt corrective action is desirable and feasible, or whether changes in short-term indicators are signals of longer-term shifts in the market, the profession or the firm itself. Box 33.2 can be of help in establishing a list of controls that suits a particular consulting firm.

Annual controls

Not all ratios lend themselves to short-term monitoring and action, so not all need to be presented every month. A dropping backlog of work or falling income

Box 33.2 Monthly controls: a checklist

(1) **Forward workload (backlog)**

Most important; ideally it should be around three months and should not drop below one-and-a-half months; if it is too high, clients are kept waiting for too long.

(2) **Number of client visits (meetings, surveys) to number of assignments negotiated**

Indicative of the effectiveness of promotional work. An alternative ratio is volume of new business negotiated per client visit (meeting, survey), or number of marketing days required to get an assignment or to obtain a certain volume of new business (say US$100,000). This is more precise if assignments vary greatly in extent.

(3) **Actual and budgeted utilization of total time**

Can be computed for all consulting staff or by categories, e.g. for operating consultants, supervisors, partners and officers; shows not only whether the firm has enough to do, but also whether work is properly scheduled and organized for smooth delivery.

(4) **Cumulative actual fee-earning days against planned fee-earning days**

Similar use as previous ratio.

(5) **Actual and budgeted fee rate**

Can be computed for all consulting staff or by categories of consultant; helps to assess whether the firm is in a position to apply optimum fees and gives guidance in using the staff in accordance with their technical and income-generating ability.

(6) **Fees earned against fees budgeted (monthly and cumulative)**

Synthetic indicator of actual programme delivery rate in financial terms.

(7) **Fees earned against expenses (monthly and cumulative)**

Synthetic indicator of short-term performance in financial terms; can provide early warning of excessive expenses and cash shortages.

(8) **Expenses incurred against expenses budgeted (in total and by expense budget lines; monthly and cumulative)**

Permits detailed control by expense lines, providing suggestions for specific expense-cutting measures and for adjustments of budgets owing to price and other changes outside the consultant's control.

(9) **Monthly billing against monthly fees earned**

Shows whether the firm is properly organized to process work records and bill the clients as soon as records become available.

(10) **Number of months of outstanding fees**

Shows whether fees are collected within normal time limits (four to six weeks); an alternative ratio is outstanding fees as percentage of total (annual) income.

require immediate management attention, and these data are therefore needed monthly. The basic staff structure cannot be changed by short-term measures, and an analysis of relevant information once or twice a year may be enough.

An annual performance review, or audit, would examine the data collected on a monthly basis, plus other financial and non-financial data, such as:

- growth rate of business;
- gross and/or net profits compared with total income;
- profit per partner and per consultant employed;
- volume of work sold per consultant engaged in the marketing services;
- ratios indicating the structure and turnover of consulting and other staff (various categories);
- ratios showing time utilization and time allocation to various services and activities, including the structure of non-billable time;
- expense and cost structure (relative magnitude of various expense lines);
- marketing and business development costs;
- fee rates;
- partner, consultant and other staff compensation, including compensation through share options;
- non-collectable fees (bad debts) and other losses as part of total income.

It is often useful to analyse various financial ratios which can be calculated from the annual financial statements. However, before doing this, it is necessary to consider whether the ratios are as meaningful in consulting as in manufacturing industry and other sectors (owing to factors such as the relatively small volume and role of fixed assets, etc.). In addition, trends may be analysed by comparing data over five to ten years.

Here again, analysis should reveal causes and suggest a focus for future action. Increased income can be the result of better performance, but also of price adjustments to reflect inflation, while real performance in non-financial terms has not changed or has deteriorated.

A general profit model for professional firms was described in section 27.3. The model can be used for a firm's annual performance reviews, for example as recommended by the Association of Management Consulting Firms (AMCF) in its annual surveys of consulting firms.[1] The model provides both for a synthetic view of profitability (profit per partner) and for more analytical information on key factors that have affected the profit per partner ratio. The expanded model is reproduced in figure 33.1.

Organizational level of performance monitoring

The management of the consulting firm will be interested in knowing and analysing all key factors, both monthly and annual. As a rule, operating and financial performance ratios are reviewed at regular management meetings. If

Figure 33.1 Expanded profit model for consulting firms

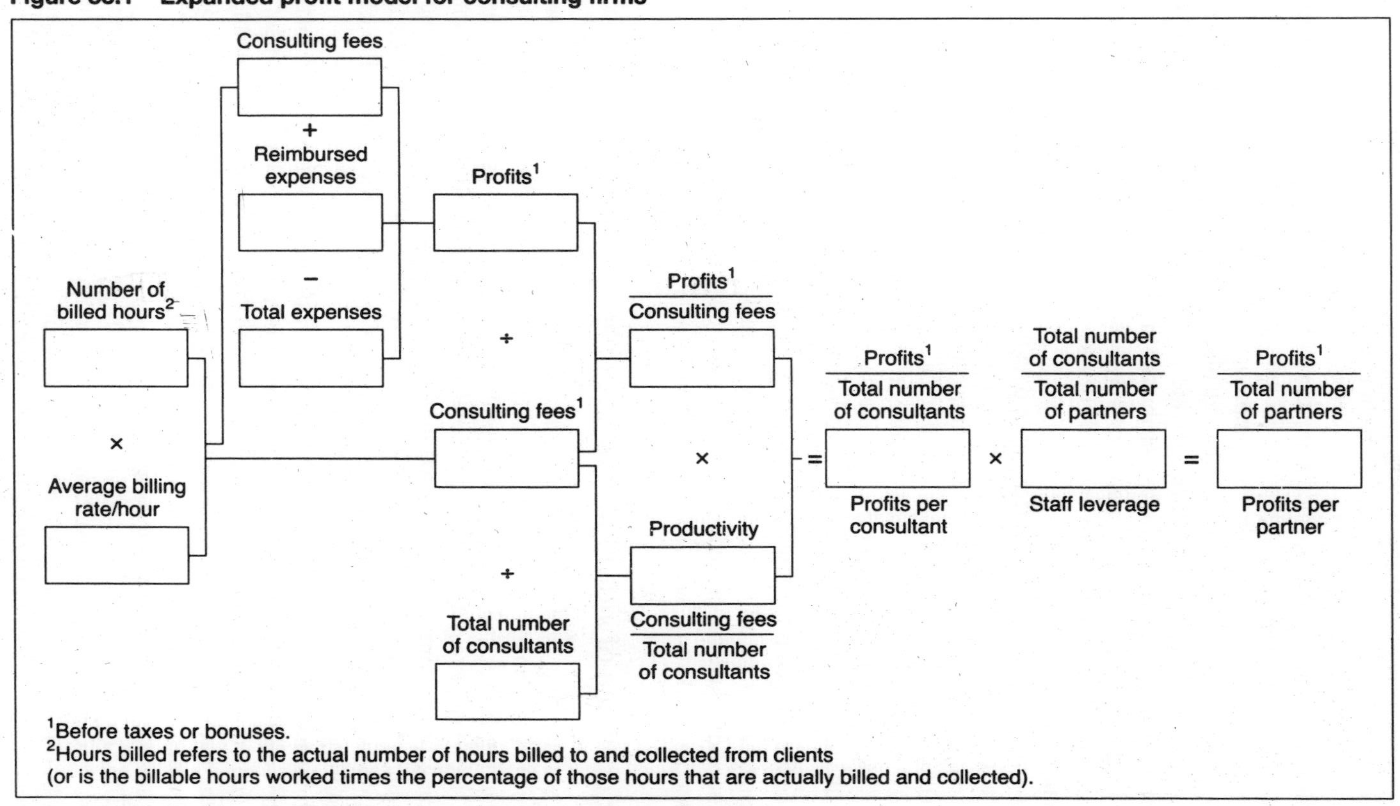

[1]Before taxes or bonuses.
[2]Hours billed refers to the actual number of hours billed to and collected from clients (or is the billable hours worked times the percentage of those hours that are actually billed and collected).

Source: ACME: *ACME 1993 survey of United States key management information* (New York, 1993).

it is decided to take corrective action, the precise target to be achieved and the responsibility for the action to be taken should be defined.

It is good practice to keep not only partners and senior members of the firm but also other consultants informed about the performance achieved by the firm, pointing out what should be improved, and how individual consultants can help and will be encouraged to make such improvements.

Selected performance ratios can be calculated and analysed by unit (team, department, service group, practice area, etc.) within the firm. Such an analysis can show which units are the main contributors to the total results achieved, and which "problem" units have become, or may become, a financial burden. This can stimulate the management and staff of these units to be more active and entrepreneurial.

It is often useful to know performance data for each consultant employed. A typical example is the ratio of volume of work sold per consultant engaged in marketing the services. Rather than calculating and examining average data per consultant, some consulting firms record and analyse the marketing performance of each individual. The same can be done in assessing programme delivery by comparing the budgeted and the real income and profitability for individual consultants. If an individual's profitability is low, the reasons can be, for example:

- the fee charged is too low in comparison with the salary paid and other costs;
- chargeable time utilization is low owing to small demand for the services of the individual concerned, or for other reasons reflecting weaknesses in service marketing, scheduling and organization.

Performance of individual assignments

In a similar vein, profitability and some other performance indicators can be calculated and analysed by assignment (project, product). For example, one consulting firm found that the profitability of its consulting assignments was low. However, most assignments generated demand for tailor-made in-plant training programmes, and also brought participants to regular open training seminars. Since these two groups of products were highly profitable, the overall result was judged as being satisfactory and the relatively low profitability of consulting assignments fully acceptable.

Information on assignment performance provides insights into issues such as the adequacy of fee formulas and fee levels for various types of assignment, assignment staffing, the use of experienced (and more expensive) consultants for the backstopping and supervision of operating assignments, the quality of assignment scheduling and administration, various expenditure (and cost) items that are not reimbursable, and so on.

The key condition is correct recording and measurement of the time spent by various categories of consultant on particular assignments. For example, it may be established that junior consultants use more time than budgeted because of poor briefing and guidance by the seniors, or that more seniors' time is used than warranted by the difficulty of the task. Furthermore, the cost of time (hour, day) of each category should be calculated (which includes a decision on whether to include and how to allocate the overhead cost).[2]

33.3 Bookkeeping and accounting

Like any business, a consulting organization needs bookkeeping and accounting to control the financial side of the operation and produce information required by law. This section gives some comments on accounting problems faced by consultants but is not meant as a complete review of accounting in professional firms. Such information is available from specialized publications.

Choosing your system

The accounting system used should be an effective management tool, fully adapted to the nature of consulting operations. It should be as simple as possible. A single practitioner who serves a few clients and has a limited range of expenditure can use a very simple system indeed. The complexity of the system will increase with the growth of the firm and the complexity of its operations, but even a large consulting firm should try to keep its accounting simple.

A consultant who is versed in accounting can decide personally what system to use. There are standardized proprietary bookkeeping systems and computer programs for small businesses and professional service firms; the consultant may be able to purchase such a system, including all forms and books, from a supplier of office equipment, software and stationery. In some countries, the associations of professional firms have issued accounting guidelines and recommendations for their member firms. An alternative is to ask an accountant to design a tailor-made system. Bookkeeping and accounting are also well suited to outsourcing and many consultants choose this solution.

The essential criteria to be considered include the following:

- What is the structure of the firm's income (volume, number of clients, frequency of payments, collection problems, different kinds of income)?
- What is the structure of the firm's expenses (different expense items, critical expense items, frequency of expenses)?
- What are the firm's material and financial resources (buildings, equipment, stocks of materials and spare parts, financial reserves, cash)?
- How is the firm's operation financed?
- What are the existing and potential problems as regards cash flow and liquidity?
- What information is critical for sound financial management and how frequently should it be provided?
- What records and reports are mandatory?

A small consulting firm may be satisfied with a simple single-entry system, using a cash book, though most consulting firms prefer a double-entry system. Every consultant, irrespective of the legal form of the business and the accounting system chosen, should separate his or her business accounts from private household accounts. This basic rule of financial management is generally recommended by management consultants to their small-business clients, and consultants will be well advised to follow the same principle in their own businesses.

Another possible choice may be between cash-basis accounting (only cash transactions are recorded) and accrual-basis accounting (accounts receivable and accounts payable are recorded). In the United States, for example, professional firms prefer cash-basis accounting since under this system only income for which cash has actually been collected is taxed.

What accounts to keep

In some countries there will be a suggested or even compulsory chart of accounts (called "accounting plan" in some countries) that both public and private companies have to use. In many cases, however, the consultant will be free to choose his or her own chart of accounts. In particular, he or she will be able to decide how detailed the chart should be.

The purpose has always to be kept in mind. Accounts from which statutory financial reports are produced will be needed. Accounts required for controlling important expenses (e.g. wages of administrative and support staff) should be kept separately in most cases. On the other hand, unimportant expense items do not require separate accounts, and a number of these items can usually be blocked in one account.

It is advisable to aim at coherence between budgeting and accounting to facilitate both the preparation and the control of budgets. If the firm decides to structure its operating budget as shown in table 33.1, its accounts for income and expenses should be structured accordingly. The accounting can be more detailed. For example, income may be recorded in several client accounts before being posted to the general ledger. However, inconsistencies should be avoided. Thus, if "marketing and promotion expenses other than salaries" are budgeted separately from salaries, they should be shown in the same way in the respective accounts. To avoid errors and confusion, it is necessary to be precise in defining what is to be recorded in what account. For example, will all telephone charges (except those chargeable to clients) be consistently charged to the communications account, or should the ones related to marketing be treated as marketing and promotion expenses? Many such decisions will have to be made.

Financial statements

In most countries, consulting firms established as corporations have to produce financial statements that include:

- the balance sheet;
- the income statement (profit and loss account);
- the statement of sources and uses of funds (funds flow statement);
- the statement of earned surplus;
- the auditor's certificate and notes on the financial statements.

The meaning and use of these statements are amply described in accounting and financial management literature.

Even if not required by law, all consulting firms, including sole practitioners, should prepare financial reports at least once a year, for self-assessment and to monitor the financial health of the firm. This can be quite a simple, though extremely useful and instructive, exercise.

---

[1] Fifteen years ago AMCF started collecting data from consulting firms of various sizes and technical profiles, on a strictly confidential basis. Using the profit model for professional firms, AMCF issues annual surveys, giving key indicators for the previous year and longer-term trends in overall performance. See AMCF: *The operating ratios for management consulting firms: A resource for benchmarking* (New York, AMCF, 2000).

[2] See also D. Maister: "Measuring engagement profitability", in *American Lawyer* (New York), July/Aug. 1994; and idem.: "Managing your clients' projects", in *True professionalism* (New York, The Free Press, 1997).

KNOWLEDGE MANAGEMENT IN CONSULTING FIRMS 34

Consulting firms were among the first organizations to have knowledge management initiatives. Generally speaking, the basic theories and principles of knowledge management outlined in Chapter 19 apply equally to consulting and other professional firms. This chapter therefore focuses on helping consultants enhance knowledge management in their own firms and activities.

34.1 Drivers for knowledge management in consulting

Knowledge as the main asset

The individual expertise, knowledge and skills of the employees, together with the collective knowledge bases of methodologies and templates, make up the main resources of a consulting firm. The maintenance and further development of these resources are essential for success. The value of the company depends largely on the capabilities and knowledge of the members of staff and the organization as a whole.

The need for efficient and effective work

Consulting firms differ with respect to their competitive strategy.[1] For example, IT consulting firms usually implement one solution for several customers, and therefore rely on reusable knowledge. On the other hand, strategy consultants offer unique solutions to individual high-level strategic problems; to succeed, the consultants need to share context-specific knowledge with each other. Both types of companies have to provide a solution, in a restricted time frame, and which meets predefined quality standards. Regardless of the strategic focus, the consultants need to have access to various pieces of information, either from documents or from other people within the organization. If appropriate solutions already exist within the company or in the market, consultants need to know about them. No consulting firm can afford to reinvent the wheel (although this is exactly what some consultants do repeatedly). Moreover, their clients expect each consultant to offer the expertise of the whole company. A failure to use all possible resources will put the consultant's professional reputation at risk.

Time is always a factor in the consulting process. The time needed to write a new proposal can be shortened by the effective use of the knowledge that exists in the company. It should be quick and easy to search for similar proposals, profiles of similar projects, and information about the customer and the respective markets. An effective knowledge management programme can simplify and support this process.

Commodification of consultancy products

Many international consulting firms now offer similar products and ways of delivering their professional services. The fees for such standardized services are under pressure. Efficient learning from projects, economies of reuse and quality assurance are essential if such low-margin projects are to be viable. Combining standard products in an overall solution presents a further challenge as different practices have to collaborate. Such projects can involve up to a hundred consultants, particularly in integrated process improvement and software implementation projects.

Globalization of clients

Another main driver of knowledge management for consulting firms is advancing globalization. As more clients become global players, consulting companies must be able to deliver the same services throughout the world in order to stay competitive. The big consulting companies need to implement global knowledge management programmes that enable their employees to access all the information available internally and externally regarding the offered services and the specific situation of the customers and their markets.

Improving competitive response

The speed of new developments, new market trends, and new ways to conduct business is driven by the speed of new technological developments. Consultants are among the first to be affected by the increased speed of developments that lead to new requirements and new possibilities. The need to learn and continuously improve one's own skills and expertise is urgent. A knowledge management programme should therefore support efforts to learn and to introduce new services, solutions and methodologies.

Preventing loss of intellectual assets

The main assets of a consulting firm are its intellectual assets, which must be cared for and cultivated. The average length of employment in consulting is considerably shorter than in other sectors. Therefore a knowledge management programme must ensure that information and knowledge remain within the company even when staff members leave. Knowledge management in this context is a means to reduce the loss of intellectual assets. It also includes legal protection of intellectual property (see Appendix 5).

34.2 Factors inherent in the consulting process

Although consulting firms differ in their organizational culture and in the sorts of services offered to clients, some factors that relate to knowledge management are common to all consulting work.

Distributed work environment

In addition to working in their own and their clients' offices, many consultants work at home, in business lounges, on aeroplanes and trains, and in libraries. Most work is done electronically, and typical technical devices include laptop computers, mobile phones and personal digital assistants (PDAs). Therefore the relevant explicit knowledge or information should be accessible remotely, and an electronic workspace that integrates all the applications is needed. Capturing new knowledge and sharing best practices must also be possible via remote access to the electronic workspace. At least some parts of the knowledge base should be portable.

Time pressure

Most work in consulting is done under time pressure. This must be kept in mind when looking at possible barriers to knowledge work. Generating, capturing, sharing and using knowledge are processes that must be neatly tied into the work processes of consulting. Treating knowledge work as something that is to be done on top of the original consulting work (and only if there is time left) will ultimately lead to a failure of the knowledge management programme.

Focus on demands of clients

All consulting work tends to be organized around the clients and their requirements. Work for the client is of the highest value; processes that directly or indirectly support the consulting process are necessary but tend to have a lower rank in the value chain. The value of a consultant's work is mainly related to the number of billable hours. This attitude naturally hinders all kinds of knowledge work, as long as the client is not willing to pay for, say, a documentation of best practices and the consultant has no separate budget for knowledge processes.

Competitive environment within firms

Most consulting firms encourage competition between their members of staff. Promotion is usually based on individual performance and consultants' ability to market themselves internally to management. Conversely, teamwork and knowledge-sharing are rarely taken into account. Part of consulting is to develop a personal success story, and many consulting firms look for individualists with a strong personality. In this respect cultural change is necessary if knowledge management in consulting is to get off the ground.

Reluctance to share knowledge

A climate of knowledge-sharing is not easily reached. In most companies the statement that "knowledge is power" is still valid. Thus many consultants are not willing to share their knowledge as they fear this will lead to a loss of status and power. They may worry that colleagues might use the knowledge without giving proper credit to its source. Also, in consulting, as in other sectors, knowledge is often tied to a specific context. When documenting best practices, for instance, it is often impossible to make explicit all the background knowledge necessary to understand the solution and use it with another client. There is a high risk that someone will use the solution in a different context and draw wrong conclusions.

Not-invented-here syndrome

Consultants are expected to deliver convincing solutions, and a consultant's credibility depends partly on how clearly he or she identifies with the solution and can demonstrate that it is really the best one. This might be one reason for reluctance to use a solution that someone else has developed.

34.3 A knowledge management programme

In consulting, as in other sectors, knowledge management should follow a holistic approach. At least the following issues need to be tackled:

- **Strategy:** What is the firm's business strategy? How does the knowledge management programme support this strategy?
- **Content:** What is the relevant content? How can this content be defined and structured?
- **Organization and processes:** Who in the organization will take care of maintaining the knowledge processes (generation, capture, transfer and use of knowledge)? How can the knowledge processes be integrated into daily work?

- **Culture and people:** What can be done to overcome barriers to knowledge processes? What does that mean for a knowledge management programme?
- **IT:** What information technology is needed for knowledge management?

Strategy

Knowledge management is a strategic issue for consulting firms, and knowledge goals are derived from the specific strategy of the firm. The business models of companies like Accenture, KPMG Consulting or Ernst & Young rely on the reuse of codified knowledge. Their success depends on the fast availability of explicit knowledge; these companies invest heavily in information technology for knowledge management. For strategy consultants such as Bain, McKinsey, or Boston Consulting Group, there is a greater need to focus on the sharing of tacit, highly context-dependent knowledge. Knowledge networks and an enabling cultural context for knowledge-sharing are essential in these companies.

At the beginning of a knowledge management project the goals must be defined, together with indicators for measuring the success of the knowledge management programme. All consulting firms operating globally need to have global knowledge management initiatives, but it might be helpful to start by identifying knowledge areas suitable for a pilot project. The success of such a pilot project can then be used to convince the whole company about the benefits of knowledge management. Knowledge must become part of the management philosophy and organizational culture. Every member of the firm must know what knowledge strategy has been adopted and what contributions to knowledge creation and sharing are expected from individual consultants.

Content

Whatever strategy is chosen, each consulting firm must also address a number of specific problems of locating, capturing and transferring knowledge. The knowledge strategy determines what types of knowledge or information are relevant for the success of the company. For consulting firms at least the following types of knowledge are important:

- knowledge about projects done for a particular client;
- knowledge about and experiences from similar projects (for other clients);
- knowledge and information about the client;
- knowledge and information about the segment (branch, sector, industry);
- knowledge and information about the environment (business, competitive, legal, social etc.);
- knowledge and know-how about the service: methodologies, templates, expertise;
- subject knowledge;
- knowledge about project management and consulting methodologies;

- knowledge of the consulting and professional service sectors (competitors, collaborators, networks, institutions, sources of expertise);
- personal skills.

Only a small portion of relevant knowledge can be codified effectively. Most of the above types of knowledge are personal, highly context-specific and hard to capture by codification. This *tacit knowledge* (see Chapter 19), which cannot easily be copied, is of the highest value to the company and constitutes its main competitive advantage. Therefore a knowledge management solution for consulting firms should have two components:

1. It should provide a database of explicit, relevant information, such as market studies, financial information about customers, daily news, case studies, packages of information concerning certain services, descriptions and courses for methodologies, project profiles, etc.
2. It should provide access to tacit knowledge through a database of experts or "yellow pages". Knowing that someone has experience in a particular field can be the key to using this expertise in solving a new problem. The principal purpose of "yellow pages" is to tell people in the organization where to go when they need expertise. The exchange of tacit knowledge can be enhanced by supporting communities of practice, organizing knowledge fairs, or introducing a mentoring model into the company.[2]

The access to explicit knowledge or information should be simplified by using a taxonomy or knowledge map to structure the relevant information. A taxonomy is highly beneficial, especially for global knowledge management, for the following reasons:

- The terms on which the structure is based build up a common language, which is a fundamental prerequisite for knowledge-sharing.
- A knowledge map enables users to navigate in the company's knowledge base. Finding knowledge or pieces of information is easier and more successful than simply using a full-text search engine.
- Browsing through the knowledge map enables new employees to get to know the company's knowledge base and knowledge management practices.

Organization and processes

The value of the knowledge base depends mainly on its being up to date and valid. Thus knowledge processes, such as capture and transfer, need to be integrated into daily working routines. In addition, it might be helpful to assign certain support functions to staff members. Many companies appoint a chief knowledge officer – a senior manager responsible for knowledge management at strategic level. On a more operational level, there are typically positions such as knowledge engineers, knowledge brokers, and knowledge managers, in charge of particular knowledge management processes.

New knowledge-related positions are usually necessary and the related roles and responsibilities need to be specified. The consultants who are both users and suppliers of knowledge need to be informed about their new tasks. As consultants work under high time pressure it is a good idea to reserve time for everybody to do knowledge work.

Hansen and von Oetinger propose a different organizational role, the *T-shaped manager*.[3] T-shaped managers are not only committed to the performance of their individual business unit but are also responsible for the sharing of knowledge across business units. Their key task is to improve cross-unit learning and collaboration. T-shaped managers aim at fostering:

- transfer of best practices,
- improvement of the quality of decision-making,
- revenue growth through shared expertise,
- development of new business opportunities.

Their main focus is not on capturing and transferring codified knowledge but on sharing knowledge and enabling the creation of new knowledge. Rather than commanding and controlling, they focus on guiding and inspiring other people. A T-shaped manager very often functions as a "human portal", i.e. he or she helps people identify others in the organization who can provide needed information, and brings them together.

As mentioned, the knowledge processes (generation, capture, transfer und use) should be integrated into the daily work routines. A requirement at the start of a new project could be the submission of a short project file describing the mission and the most relevant data. At the close of the project, a detailed documentation of best practices could be required, and could be compiled at a project closure workshop. This is one approach to managing the process of converting tacit knowledge into explicit knowledge. It is based on the fact that writing a scientific or journalistic article is a way of explicitly codifying an individual learning experience, a finding, an idea or certain thoughts. While it is not possible to train all consultants in writing such articles or notes, it is possible to use specialized staff to perform this task. These specialists might hold a project closure workshop, ask questions and try to gather useful learning points for other projects. They should be trained to ask the right questions, facilitate the process and write intelligible articles. The outcomes of a project closure workshop are not only the documentation of lessons learned but also the sharing of implicit knowledge and the possibility to reflect on the experiences.

Culture and people

The most critical factor for successful knowledge management is the people involved. They must be willing both to share their knowledge and to use the knowledge of others. Also, knowledge management can only work with the support of senior management. It must be made clear by senior management that knowledge is regarded as a highly valuable resource and that knowledge work is as valuable as direct work for clients.

Partners and senior managers have a particularly important role to play in creating a knowledge-sharing culture. Building teams, supporting cross-selling, and contributing to product development and to learning from projects demonstrate that partners and senior managers take knowledge management seriously. Factors to be considered when managers are being assessed as possible partners should be their contribution to the firm's knowledge base and their ability to foster knowledge creation.

Another way of stressing the value of knowledge is by rewarding individuals for sharing knowledge. Bonus payments for knowledge work could be a possibility. Membership in something like a best practice club could be a reward in itself. Ultimately people should realize that knowledge-sharing keeps their business going. A climate of trust is crucial to the success of knowledge management.

Information technology for knowledge management

Information technology is an enabler to the knowledge management programme. In the context of global knowledge management IT has a special role: the knowledge management initiative must be supported by a global IT strategy. A fast network and a standardized software infrastructure are prerequisites of knowledge-sharing and collaboration. Large consulting firms might consider sophisticated technologies such as data warehousing, data mining, document management and intelligent agents. An enterprise information portal can provide global access to the company's knowledge base. Fast remote access via modem and laptop computer or mobile telephone is necessary for effective work. The portal should incorporate personalization, offering a means to customize layout and content and store shortcuts and frequently used links to Web sites.

Simpler systems can also be valuable. An Intranet with a home page for each employee can help advertise the interests of individual consultants. A series of specialist discussion groups on the company email system or participation in an open discussion on the Internet can stimulate exchange of ideas. The ability to carry out a keyword search on previous reports and presentations can avoid a lot of repetition of work.

Easy and rapid access to external expertise is also vital. The World Wide Web can provide a wealth of information at a very small cost. Commercial information services are more expensive but they give instant access to company, marketing and industry reports or the full text of academic and business journals, magazines and newspapers.

For an information search, both a powerful full-text search engine and a taxonomy should be provided. Collaboration tools such as messaging and document management are also useful. Chat rooms, discussion groups, or virtual knowledge markets can allow tacit knowledge to be exchanged.

The integration of workflows has obvious advantages: a portal can not only provide access to a form for a vacation request but also allow the consultant to fill in the form and transfer it to the responsible department electronically.

34.4 Sharing knowledge with clients

Sharing knowledge with clients[4] is increasingly regarded as one of the main purposes of consulting and other professional services (see Chapters 1 and 3). However, declaring that knowledge-sharing with clients is the firm's policy is not enough for practical purposes. Knowledge-sharing is not automatic and can be hampered by inappropriate attitudes and work methods. Consultants working on client assignments will need their firms' guidance and technical support on questions such as:

- whether they are free to choose what knowledge to share during assignments;
- what knowledge is to be treated as the firm's trade secret (see Appendix 5) or as confidential and is thus not to be shared with anyone without the prior approval of the consulting firm's management;
- who in the firm will answer questions on knowledge transfer and sharing, and provide guidance;
- what knowledge-sharing will be regarded as an integral part of an assignment workplan and contract;
- how much time consultants should allocate to knowledge-sharing and what methods they should use;
- how to handle intellectual property issues when transferring knowledge to clients or creating new knowledge jointly with clients (Appendix 5).

Knowledge-sharing must not be hampered by bureacratic procedures, and experienced consultants will usually be able to decide how to proceed when working with particular clients. However, knowledge-sharing is an attitude and a skill, and some consultants – especially in small or medium-sized firms – may need encouragement and guidance to be more effective at it (box 34.1).

Furthermore, many consulting companies have started to disseminate and share knowledge with their whole clientele or with the general business public. This is sometimes done in traditional ways, through papers, articles, books, conferences, newsletters and similar. Some companies, however, offer access to certain parts of their knowledge base, either via the Internet or through specially designed extranets. A well-designed knowledge base and an authorization model are fundamental to this business model. "Pay per view" priced content is already used as an additional way to exploit internal knowledge externally. In addition to allowing knowledge to be shared, these approaches arouse interest in the firm and demonstrate the firm's continued support to existing clients.

All these initiatives have their costs and need to be monitored and coordinated. Quality and respect for users are critical. Some consultants have posted trivial,

Box 34.1 Checklist for applying knowledge management in a small or medium-sized consulting firm

1. Discuss the KM challenge with partners. Choose one partner as KM officer, manager or coordinator (not to act in directive manner, but as driving force, coordinator and adviser behind the KM effort). KM needs to be recognized and started as a meaningful activity, important to the future of the firm. Inform all colleagues.
2. Define key areas of KM interest – these should be 4–7 key strategic practice and competency areas where the firm is active and that it wants to improve and develop. Include information on clients and their needs and pursue knowledge-sharing with clients as a strategic objective.
3. Appoint 1–2 partners responsible for KM in each area in addition to doing client work and promotion.
4. Define the objectives of KM for each area (becoming market leader, offering new services, catching up with competition, improving quality, etc.) related to business and firm strategy objectives and client needs and requirements.
5. Define key terms for the KM effort in each area.
6. Define and organize a database, including: project (assignment) profiles, presentations, literature, reference works, key periodicals, Web links, directories, internal expertise, external experts, other sources, etc.).
7. Choose software adequate to coverage, objectives, volume and resources; provide facilities for internal communication and knowledge-sharing.
8. Develop a competency profile for each partner and consultant in chosen key areas, e.g. rating knowledge of each in each area as basic, good, or expert.
9. Define individual development targets by area (becoming a top expert, keeping up to date, acquiring basic knowledge, ignoring the area, etc.). Link KM with individual development efforts.
10. Define with partners and all consultants their individual roles and responsibilities for making inputs in the database and generally contributing to KM.
11. Make sure that all consultants have direct and easy access to the system wherever they are and that their time is not wasted on lengthy searches for relevant knowledge or by circulating trivial and irrelevant information to them.
12. Focus the whole effort on the future; from existing (older or recent) documents and sources include only essential know-how and sources that will remain important in the future.
13. Among completed projects (client contracts) focus on those that were important, that offer a lot of learning, that were in prospective markets, that could be easily replicated to save time, where the firm could develop its own internal standard, etc.
14. Do not produce documents and files for their own sake; be selective and rational.
15. Organize regular knowledge-sharing events offering significant learning – on important current or completed projects, outcome of conferences, new legislation and business trends, new consulting opportunities – always sticking to the key areas of business.

16. Circulate only a minimum of information to all or most consultants, but make sure that they do get the information they need.
17. Circulate and exchange some well-selected information and tips of wider professional and intellectual interest beyond the defined areas of business (on issues such as ethics, conflict of interest, new trends in business and management, new "fads" and the firm's view on them, etc.).
18. Discuss from time to time the functioning and effectiveness of your system at partner meetings and with other consultants and make corrective measures. Flexibility and adaptability are essential. Make sure that the system does not stagnate.

Authors: Klaus North and Milan Kubr.

obsolete, self-laudatory or negligently prepared information and technical papers on their Web sites, at times making promises that are never met. Clients who see this are unlikely to take the consultant's statements about knowledge-sharing seriously.

---

[1] M. T. Hansen et al.: "What's your strategy for managing knowledge?", in *Harvard Business Review*, Mar.–Apr. 1999, pp. 106–116.

[2] T. H. Davenport and L. Prusak: *Working knowledge* (Boston, MA, HBS Press, 1998).

[3] M. T. Hansen and B. von Oetinger: "Introducing T-shaped managers – knowledge management's next generation", in *Harvard Business Review*, Mar. 2001, pp.106–116.

[4] See also R. Dawson: *Developing knowledge-based client relationships: The future of professional services* (Boston, MA, Butterworth-Heinemann, 2000).

STRUCTURING A CONSULTING FIRM 35

Because there is a wide variety of consulting firms, these firms use many different structural arrangements. Structure must never become a straitjacket. Our review of structural arrangements, including the legal forms of business, will therefore refer to some typical arrangements, but without aiming to provide a blueprint for all situations. Every consulting firm is unique and its structure reflects many factors, including the nature and volume of activities, personalities, the strategy chosen, traditions, and the legal and institutional environment.

35.1 Legal forms of business

In most countries consultants can choose among several legal forms of business organization. This choice is not always completely free. Local legislation may include special regulations for organizing and operating professional services, or for firms with foreign ownership. Therefore an international consulting firm may have to use different legal forms in different countries. Unless the consultant is sufficiently knowledgeable in legal matters, he or she should seek a lawyer's advice. An accountant's or tax adviser's viewpoint is equally important because the forms of business organization differ as regards registration, taxation, record-keeping, reporting and liability.

Sole proprietorship

A sole proprietorship is a business owned and operated by a single person. The owner may be a single practitioner, or may have a number of associates. While normally and legally there is no limit to the number of staff, it is usual for a "sole owner" to employ only a few associates, and perhaps only for the duration of specific assignments. The firm's net income is taxed as the owner's personal income; the owner's liability for debts incurred by the firm is unlimited.

Sole proprietorship is a simple form, suitable for those who are starting in consulting but have some previous management experience, or who prefer to remain completely independent in their consulting career. In addition to working on assignments, the sole practitioner has to market future assignments. The risk is quite high in the case of sickness. Even if the single practitioner has health insurance and income-loss insurance, a prolonged illness may adversely affect business contacts. The firm normally ceases to exist with the death or retirement of the owner (although his or her estate remains liable for outstanding debts).

Partnership

Partnership[1] is a common form of business in management consulting and in other professional service sectors. It entails a contract between two or more people to set up a firm in which they combine their skills and resources, and share profits, losses and liabilities. Under most legal systems, the partnership does not have to be on an equal basis: a consultant may enter a partnership with a junior colleague on a 60–40 or other basis; or one or more of the partners may wish to devote less time than the others to the partnership and will accordingly accept a smaller share of both profits and losses.

The advantages of partnership include the division of labour to optimize the use of the partners' skills, the possibility of undertaking more important and complex assignments, the possibility of continuing the business in the absence of one of the partners, and a better utilization of resources such as office space, equipment and secretarial support.

The disadvantages include the unlimited liability of each partner for errors and obligations of all other partners arising from the business, the need to reach agreement on every important decision, and the difficulties involved in harmonizing the personal preferences and styles of the partners.

It is generally recommended that a clear and unambiguous partnership agreement should be drawn up, even if local legislation does not explicitly require one. Much more important, however, is the composition of the group: individuals who have difficulty working together, have different conceptions of professional service and ethics, or do not trust each other for any reason should avoid becoming partners. Even if partners respect and like each other and are generally happy with their firm model, problems may arise and grow into conflicts that can destroy the partnership. Many professional partnerships survive because the partners have developed a high degree of tolerance to different personal values and behaviours and are prepared to compromise. It is also necessary to reach agreement on the different roles that partners can best play, including a voluntary delegation of general management authority and responsibility to one of the partners.

In some legal systems it is possible to establish a *limited partnership*, which includes one or more general partners (with unlimited liability), and one or more limited partners, whose third-party liability is limited to a specific amount (which can be zero).

Partnerships are usually not limited by law as to size, but in practice are often confined to a comparatively small number of people. If a unit expands, while it may retain something of the spirit and title of partnership, it might be advisable to consider transforming the business into a corporation.

Corporation

Many consulting firms are established as corporations or limited liability companies.[2] The corporation has two fundamental characteristics: (1) it is a legal entity that exists separately from the owners (i.e. does not cease to exist after an owner's death or withdrawal from business); and (2) the owners have no personal liability for the obligations and debts of the corporation (the shareholders are protected from liability incurred by the company, except in certain cases, especially when it is established that the corporate form was abused in order to avoid personal liability). The major advantages of incorporation include:

- considerable flexibility in doing and developing business;
- the possibility of easy changes in the number of co-owners or shareholders; there can usually be a sole owner, and therefore even a sole practitioner can incorporate a business;
- the possibility of transferring ownership interests or shares;
- the possibility for individuals to be simultaneously owners and employees of the corporation;
- greater flexibility in raising finance;
- the possibility of retaining earnings for reinvestment in the firm;
- separate taxation of personal income (salary, bonuses and dividends) and the corporation's profits, and the possibility of deducting certain employee benefits and certain types of corporate expenses from taxable income (the level of taxation is often a major factor in deciding whether to incorporate or not); it should be noted that this may sometimes operate as a disadvantage due to double taxation on the corporation's income and on the dividends paid to shareholders.

On the other hand, a corporation must comply with a number of requirements stipulated in the company or other law of the country. These include, in particular:

- compulsory registration (incorporation) prior to starting business, which involves certain costs;
- a statement of corporate purposes (objects of the company); in some countries the corporation is not authorized to do business outside the scope of this statement;
- keeping of accounts and other records, with periodic reporting;
- in certain circumstances, public auditing of company reports and (in some countries) the publication of these reports;

- the organization and definition of responsibilities of corporate bodies and top management (shareholders' meeting, board of directors, officers, etc.).

Moreover, corporate directors can be personally liable both civilly and criminally for certain corporate acts of malfeasance or misfeasance.

Management consultants in various countries have adopted special arrangements in using the corporate form. With few exceptions, they do not "go public", i.e. the shares are not available on the stock market, but ownership is reserved to a group of senior consultants (officers, principals, partners, etc.). Promotion to this level in the hierarchy may include not only an entitlement, but an obligation to purchase a certain number of shares and thus invest in the firm. The maximum number of shares that can be owned by one member of the firm is often limited (often to between 1 and 5 per cent of the shares) and the owner must resell these shares to the company (thus recovering the money put in) when retiring or leaving for any other reason.

In some consulting firms there is one – or more – majority owner who actually controls the firm. Usually he or she would be the sole founder, or one of the partners who established the firm, who at some point decided to transform the firm into a corporation and widen the ownership base. In a small number of cases, consulting firms are owned by other business corporations (by banks, accounting firms, engineering firms, or others), management schools, employers' associations or other bodies.

Some consulting firms use all the profits for developing the business and creating reserves, while others distribute a part of the profit to the shareholders, or to all employees (see section 36.4).

Many consulting and other professional firms have maintained the partnership form even when they have become larger, or have continued to be managed and to behave as partnerships after having been restructured as corporations. Currently this traditional approach is being challenged. If there are hundreds of partners and consultants, the ideas on which the partnership formula is based (undivided responsibility, direct participation, full consensus for key decisions, etc.) are increasingly difficult to apply. Further difficulties are encountered in raising capital needed for expansion, product development and modernization, and in facing liability issues (see section 6.5). Some large management and IT consultancies have therefore chosen to become corporations and to sell a part of the shares to the public through an initial public offering (IPO) rather than sticking to the classical partnership formula.[3] Of course, if a significant number of shares are in the hands of outside investors, the professional firm is as exposed to the uncontrollable forces of financial markets as any other publicly quoted firm.

Legal aspects of working with other consultants

Consultants may consider working with other consultants in a number of situations, for instance when they need to draw on specific expertise or to collaborate on a larger project. When consultants (individuals or firms) cooperate with other consultants on specific projects, they usually retain their independence and legal form of business and the relationship is governed by an agreement defining the objectives and scope of cooperation. For example, if a consortium is established for a complex consulting project, one firm would normally act as the consortium leader and be in a contractual relationship on one side with the client and on the other side with firms that are consortium members but legally act as subcontractors.

In these instances, the following legal issues generally need to be considered:[4]

- Under whose name are the consulting services performed when several consultants are involved? If a consultant engages a subcontractor who has no contractual relationship with the client, the consultant will generally bear responsibility for the work of the subcontractor. In addition, the consultant may, in certain circumstances, face joint liability for malpractice or breach of contract by another member of the consortium, even if that member is not the consultant's subcontractor, to the extent that the consortium is deemed to constitute a partnership. The consultant should examine whether such risks are covered by his or her malpractice insurance.
- The need for a non-competition undertaking prohibiting the other consultant from providing services to the client during a specified period of time.
- The ability of the other consultants to make commitments on behalf of the leader or to change the terms of the assignment.
- The protection of confidential information received from the client and shared with the other consultants.
- The protection of confidential information, know-how and intellectual property of the leader provided to the other consultants for the purposes of the project.

Other forms

Not all management consulting units are independent businesses. Some units are established and operate as divisions within private corporations that have wider purposes and offer other types of service (accounting, auditing, engineering consultancy, etc.) in addition to management consulting. In such cases, the legal entity may not be the consulting unit in its own right, but the organization to which the unit belongs.

There are also consulting units established as, or within, associations, foundations, public agencies and other non-profit-making organizations. However, the corporate form tends increasingly to be used for these units in order to enhance their independence, motivation, responsibility and liability. For example, a management institute can often be organized as a corporation, or a public agency can create (and own) a professional service company that sells services to clients in both the public and private sectors.

35.2 Management and operations structure

Corporate governance and top management

The pattern of the consulting organization's top management depends very much upon its legal statute. In firms constituted as corporations (limited companies) there will be a board of directors. In a small firm the directors would generally be the general manager (managing director) and the senior consultants (partners). In a large firm there may also be external board members who, being non-executive, can play a useful role in the sense that they may preserve the same detachment in guiding the firm as the consultants have in advising their clients. They also tend to be chosen because of their range of business interests and contacts. In partnerships, decisions on key policy matters may be reserved for periodical meetings of all partners.

Consulting units that are not independent firms may have a governing body comprising a cross-section of managers from private and public enterprises, representatives of chambers of commerce and employers' associations, senior government officials, and possibly other members in addition to one or more senior managers from the unit.

The key position in the management hierarchy is that of the chief executive officer (CEO), who may be called principal, general manager, president, managing director, managing partner, director-general, or simply manager or director. In a partnership, the CEO would be elected by a partners' meeting for a fixed period.

The CEO may use a management committee in the usual way for involving other managers or designated senior partners in dealing with issues requiring collective discussion or decision. Other committees may be established for dealing with issues such as strategy, quality, business promotion and marketing, IT, or staff compensation. They may be permanent or ad hoc. As in other businesses and public organizations, there may be a tendency to create a committee each time an issue cannot be immediately resolved or needs to be examined in a collective. A proliferation of overlapping committees, and meetings of the same people under different committee denominations, are not signs of effective management.

The individual at the top will most probably be a career consultant (a senior partner) with considerable experience and managerial talent. On reaching the top, he or she may experience problems similar to those faced by managers of research and other professional services – he or she must stop thinking and operating primarily as a technician and concentrate on managing (see also Chapter 27). Some consulting organizations have recruited top managers from outside, from among individuals who have been excellent business managers but not necessarily practising consultants. There is no universal rule – the candidate's competence and personality will determine whether he or she will be able to cope with the challenge of the job, provide strategic leadership and strengthen the firm by subtle but persistent coordination and control.

Operating core

Consultants spend most of their time working for clients on specific assignments. Normally they do most of their work at clients' premises, and once an assignment is completed, they move physically to another client. In the management system of a consulting firm, individual assignments are treated as basic management cells with precisely defined terms of reference, resources and responsibilities. However, assignments are only temporary management cells and structuring by assignments would not provide for stability and continuity of internal organization. Most consulting firms therefore structure their operating core – the professional staff – in more or less permanent "home" units (called "practice groups" in some professions). Consultants are attached to these units according to some common characteristics in their background, clientele served, or areas of intervention.

Functional units. Functional units, the most common type of internal structure in the past and still quite widespread, used to be organized by the basic functions of management, such as general management, finance, marketing, production and personnel. A consulting assignment may be fully within the function area covered and the unit can therefore staff and supervise the assignment from its own resources. In other cases, the unit would "borrow" staff from other units for the duration of the assignment. This is particularly common in complex assignments dealing with various aspects of a business.

Service line units. Recently, consulting firms have started to give priority to units established by technical problem areas and new product lines, such as strategy and policy, organization development, total quality management, business restructuring, mergers and acquisitions, knowledge management or customer relationship management (CRM). As a rule (though not always), these service lines cut across functions and disciplines and focus on a particular approach or method of business improvement. Such units are regarded as more flexible and dynamic structures that can be closer to clients, enjoy more autonomy within a larger firm, change and innovate more easily and behave as entrepreneurs.

Sectoral units. Units that are sectorally specialized (e.g. for construction, banking, insurance, road transport, health) are often established if this is justified by the volume of business done in a sector and by the need to have teams that are recognized as sectoral experts. It is impossible to suggest a minimum size for such a unit. Even a smallish unit with all-round experts in a sector may play a useful role in developing and managing assignments, which can also make use of specialists from other units. If a certain sector generates a sizeable amount of work, a sectoral unit may become more or less self-contained and employ a wider range of specialists on a permanent basis in addition to its sector generalists.

Geographical units. Geographical (territorial) units are often established when a consulting firm decides to decentralize in order to get closer to the clients and increase efficiency (e.g. by reducing transport and communication expenses). They exist in two basic forms:

- offices whose main purpose is marketing and liaison with clients in a delimited geographical area; these units tend to be small, staffed by a few generalists, and equipped by certain services for supporting operating assignments; assignments can thus be staffed by consultants from the unit and from headquarters;
- fully staffed local (area) branches that can take care of most assignments using their own personnel; these units are effective if the volume and structure of business done in the area concerned are relatively stable, or if the business is expanding steadily. A major advantage for the consultants is that they do not have to be absent from their homes for long periods.

Geographically decentralized units are most common in large consulting firms. A small firm must weigh the advantages of getting close to the clientele against the cost of the operation and the firm's ability to keep technical and administrative control over geographically distant units. There are, in addition, various combinations. For example, a decentralized geographical unit may specialize in the sector or sectors featuring most prominently in the area covered by the unit.

Some examples

Figure 35.1 shows a general organizational structure used by a number of large consulting companies in various countries. In contrast, figure 35.2 shows the structure of the professional core of a consulting unit employing 29 consultants. It is a hypothetical example, which we will use to illustrate typical organizational considerations. A unit of this size can make up a whole consulting company, or constitute a division in a larger company or a management services department in an industrial concern.

The unit employs six senior consultants, of whom four work as team leaders and supervisors of operating assignments, and two concentrate on marketing and management surveys. The 20 operating consultants will, as a rule, be specialists in various management functions. Among the supervisors in the unit, three may also specialize in managing assignments in functional areas, while the fourth may be an all-round general management expert, able to manage assignments covering several functional areas. The 20 operating consultants can work in assignment teams or individually on small assignments. Thus, the supervisors will either work as team leaders on large assignments, or supervise several operating consultants working individually for different clients.

The general criteria concerning the firm's leverage (section 27.3) should be kept in mind. Significant factors determining expansion are market demand, and the availability of operating consultants with sufficient experience and knowledge to be appointed as supervisors or team leaders. At least three to five

Figure 35.1 Possible organizational structure of a consulting company

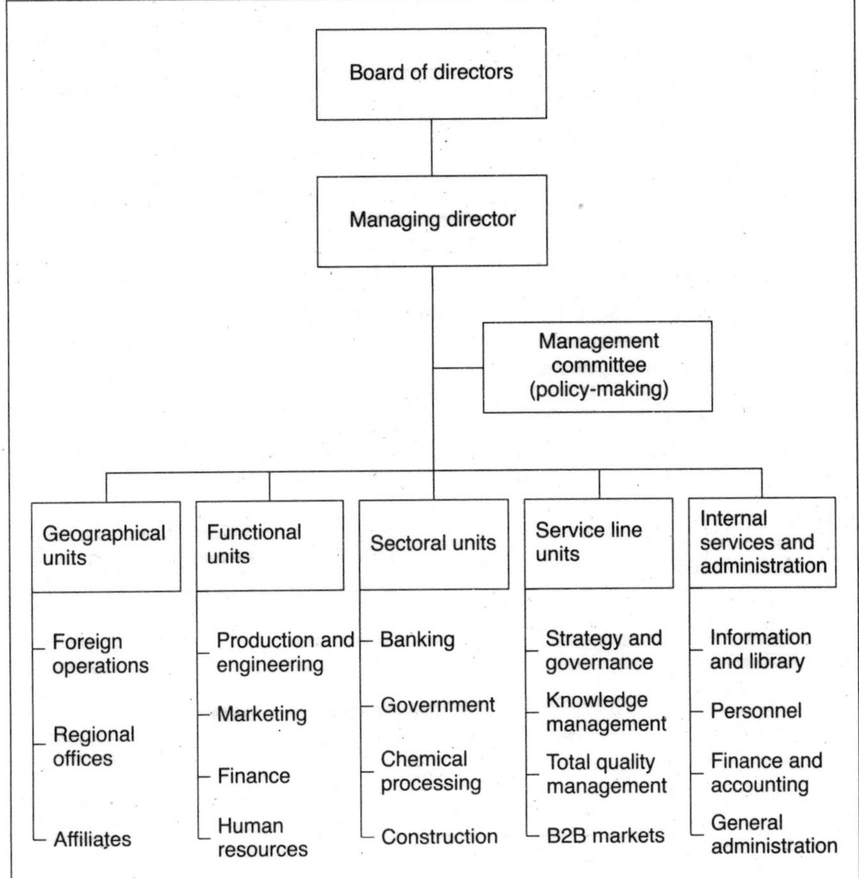

years of experience, encompassing both a range of assignments with companies and a variety of techniques, are required. To replace the operating consultants as they rise to higher levels or leave, new consultants must be already trained. For this reason a stable organization includes two or three trainee consultants in every group of 25 to 30, as shown in figure 35.2.

Another factor affecting expansion is the ratio of specialist to generalist consultants. Where an assignment calls for several disciplines, the supervising consultant may accept overall responsibility but call on a specialist to oversee special techniques as required. To meet the full range of client demands, the consulting firm may have to call on some highly specialized consultants, e.g. in productivity measurement, logistics, operations research or franchising. It is of course difficult to find a constant demand for these types of service within a smaller unit.

Figure 35.2 Professional core of a consulting unit

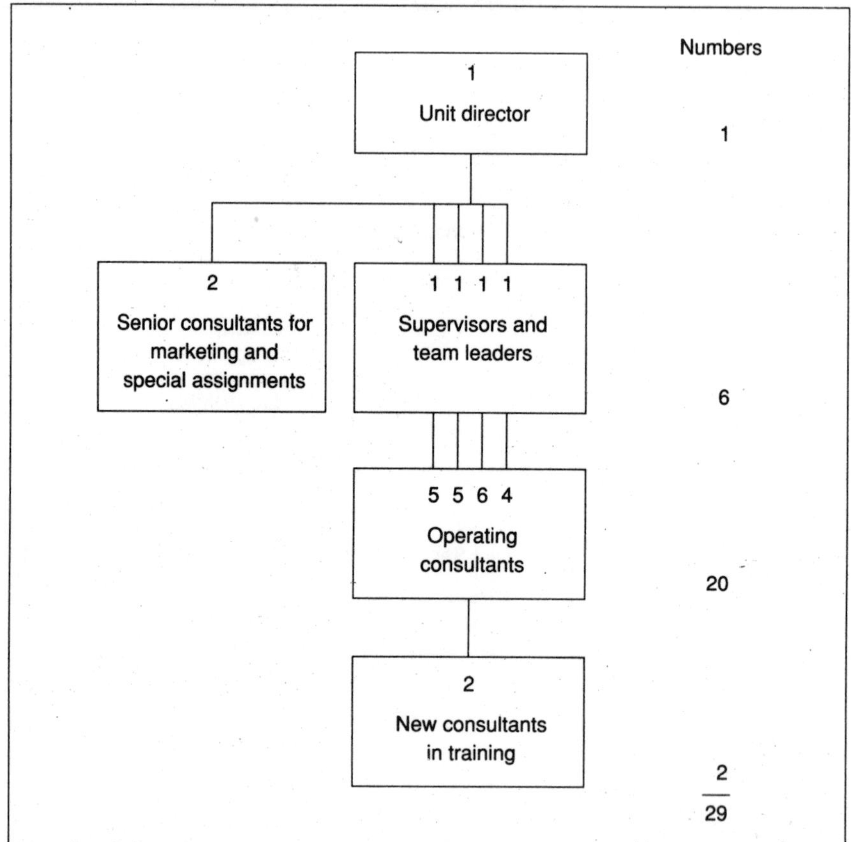

Matrix management

As suggested in the foregoing discussion, many consulting organizations practise some sort of matrix management. Both operating consultants, and their more senior colleagues who work as team leaders or supervisors, have their "home" units – functional, sectoral or geographical. However, not all assignments remain totally within the province of these home units.

The organizational culture of a consulting firm must provide for considerable flexibility to facilitate the rapid establishment of an effective collaborative relationship and a team spirit in starting new assignments. Any member of an assignment team must accept his or her role in the team, and the coordinating role of the team leader, as soon as the team is constituted and starts tackling the job. If this were not the case, the start would be slow and costly, to the detriment of the client.

However, the role of the home unit extends beyond the function of a pool of specialists from which operating consultants can be drawn. The head of a marketing consulting unit is also interested in what is happening in the assignments to which he or she has detached marketing consultants, even if these consultants work under the immediate supervision of a team leader from another unit.

The head of the unit is responsible for technical guidance, control and knowledge-sharing of operating consultants in the special field of marketing, and carries out this responsibility in various ways: by organizing technical meetings of marketing consultants, briefing consultants before assignments, reviewing consulting reports, discussing the progress of the work with the team leaders, visiting the marketing consultants on assignments, and so on. Guidance and control have to be exercised in agreement with the team leaders and supervisors, and in a way that does not undermine the operating consultants' authority in the clients' eyes.

Flat organizational structure

In addition to matrix management, most consulting firms prefer to use a relatively flat organizational structure. The number of rungs on the management ladder between an operating consultant and the firm's top manager is usually between none and three, depending on the firm's size, complexity and service diversification. Such a structure encourages collaboration, interaction with peers and knowledge-sharing within the operating core rather than referring matters upwards through the chain of command.

International operations

Organizational arrangements for international operations reflect the strategy pursued by the firm (section 28.5). They also need to take account of factors such as the frequency, relative importance and predicted future trend of these operations, the institutional and legal setting in countries where work is to be done, the possibility of repatriating earnings, language requirements, and local practice concerning business and professional services.

Consultant missions. If work abroad is irregular and small in volume, consulting firms usually prefer to send their staff on missions from headquarters. This is how foreign operations start in most consulting firms. It can be an expensive arrangement, not only because of the cost of long-distance travel and living and other expenses of operating consultants, but also because of costs incurred in negotiating, preparing and supervising assignments in foreign countries.

Offices in other countries. Having gained some experience with consulting in other countries, a consulting firm may feel that it is more effective to have a permanent presence where the market is. The establishment of a foreign (country or regional) office is often the solution. As with decentralization within the home country, this office may start as a small one, staffed mainly for marketing, liaison with local businesses and government, and as a support for operating teams coming from headquarters to work on specific projects. Legally speaking, a foreign office will often take the form of a "branch", i.e. a registered extension of an existing firm rather than a new entity with a separate legal identity.

Foreign subsidiaries. Fully staffed foreign subsidiaries have been founded by many large consulting firms that regularly undertake a substantial amount of foreign business. Such subsidiaries may be quite independent of the parent company in operational matters, but provision is always made for policy guidance, quality control and maintaining a financial relationship with the parent company. There is a growing tendency to staff foreign subsidiaries with local professionals. The number of consultants from headquarters is gradually reduced, once they have created and developed a foreign operation and recruited and trained local staff. Conversely, foreign subsidiaries are supported from headquarters in various ways (including long-term detachment and short-term missions of consultants) in new fields.

Association with local consultants. Some countries require foreign consultants to offer and provide services in association with a local consulting firm. For example, this requirement may be stipulated in an invitation to tender for an assignment. Even if there is no such regulation, consulting firms operating abroad often find it useful, for a number of reasons, to negotiate and execute assignments and to organize their foreign operations in association with local consulting firms. This association can have various forms, such as shared ownership of a foreign company (on a fifty-fifty or other basis), or an arrangement whereby the precise scope of collaboration is defined separately for every assignment. There have been cases of abuse, e.g. if the association is established with the sole intention of formally satisfying, but actually bypassing, legislation in order to get contracts, and the local consultant is a "man of straw". Another form of abuse is using local and considerably lower-paid consultants in executing contracts drawn up on the assumption that the work would be done by foreign consultants, and priced accordingly.

Administration

Many single practitioners and other small consulting units are proud of having minimal administrative expenses because they are able to handle many jobs personally, with the help of a spouse, a part-time assistant or a bookkeeper. However, as the consulting firm grows, its administrative and support services reach a volume that justifies permanent staff and solid organization. Reliability, versatility and initiative are the key qualities required in addition to technical proficiency and discretion. Consultants who are busy with clients, and often absent from their own offices for long periods, must be sure that they can rely on their administrative assistants and other collaborators to handle messages, travel arrangements, contacts by clients, report processing and transmission, search for documents, and many other administrative and housekeeping services that cannot, or should not, be directly handled by the consultants.

Office staff. Because the majority of operating consultants are able to make some use of their clients' administrative services, and to use their own personal computers, consulting firms usually need only a small office staff at the headquarters. The smaller the staff, the more its members need to be versatile and willing to help in any part of the daily work.

In a small unit the following staff may be employed:

- administrative assistant (who may also act as the manager's secretary and/or office manager);
- accounts clerk/cashier (to keep time and other records, invoice clients, pay salaries and expenses, purchase office supplies, etc.);
- receptionist/telephonist/typist (who would help in typing correspondence and reports);
- one or two more secretaries/assistants if necessary.

It is logical that larger units will require more office staff. At some point the establishment of an administrative service unit, headed by a senior administrative assistant or office manager, will be justified.

Bookkeeping and accounting. In organizing bookkeeping and accounting the consultant is faced with several alternatives. Many single practitioners do their own accounting, not only to save on administrative expenses but in order to keep control of their financial position and of the efficiency of their operation. Even a consultant whose main field of intervention is production or personnel may find it useful to do his or her own accounting.

In small consulting firms, routine bookkeeping may be done by an accounts clerk or administrative assistant as mentioned above, while financial and tax reports would be prepared by one of the consultants, or by an external accountant employed on a part-time basis. Many consultants have all bookkeeping and accounting (including tax returns) done by an external accountant.

35.3 IT support and outsourcing

Management consultants who do not use the best available technology are not likely to inspire their clients and are losing an opportunity to learn and to gain IT efficiencies for themselves. Consultants are expensive knowledge workers and investment in IT is relatively easy to justify if it saves their time or improves their effectiveness. Consultants, like the managers of any other business, should ask themselves the fundamental questions outlined in Chapter 13: *why? what? which? how?* The answers will depend on the individual business and will change as technology develops, but there are certain characteristics of all consulting firms that give some clues to IT needs.

A consulting firm needs IT applications and equipment that suit the sector of professional services in general and of its own business in particular. It should therefore not hesitate to seek the advice of an IT consultant or software supplier who is familiar with the field. The choices made should reflect the critical characteristics of a consulting business.

Consultants are mobile and communicate

The first critical characteristic is the nature of consulting work. Today's consultant stepping onto an aircraft to go to the next assignment is likely to be carrying, at a minimum: a laptop computer with peripherals, a personal digital assistant (PDA) or electronic organizer, and a mobile telephone, as well as a few metres of connecting wires and an assortment of adapters for different electricity supplies and telephone sockets. These separate pieces of equipment may be combined in the future but the need for messaging, information storage, and information presentation will remain. In the office, the consultant will probably want to plug the laptop into a docking station and connect to the office network. The goal is to have the same information and the same connectivity wherever one is in the world. Technology for mobile workers is developing rapidly and consultants should monitor it carefully and experiment to find the most appropriate. This does not necessarily mean "most powerful". It is generally better to use a reliable system, which clients and other collaborators are using, rather than to have a fancy leading-edge system that is non-standard.

Mobile consultants must keep in touch with their clients and their own firm all the time. Email and voicemail are essential. Access to some kind of teleconferencing facility is becoming increasingly important. The quality of communication can be much enhanced by the use of multimedia applications and possibly virtual reality. This is an area that is likely to develop rapidly in the next few years.

Generally speaking, consultants should have easy 24-hours-a-day access to their firm's information and knowledge base, including information on clients and assignments, skill inventories, brochures and press releases, templates for presentations, proposals, contracts, learning materials, internal manuals, guides and bulletins, reports, and so on.

Some kind of contact database is essential for every consultant. Firms will often regard these data as a corporate asset and will want to centralize them. Individual consultants may want to keep them to themselves. Disputes over who owns the data or who has access are less important than the quality of the data and the ease of retrieval. Some of the client management systems on the market seem overly complicated, while some consultants manage quite well with a simple electronic address book. A simple system that works is a lot better than a complex one that doesn't.

IT support to management and administration

The second characteristic is the nature of management and administration of consulting firms. The system chosen should allow consulting assignments or projects and other kinds of activities (such as training or research) to be planned and controlled, and should link the time records of individual consultants with overall control of operations, billing, bookkeeping, accounting, budgeting and budgetary control, cash-flow management, knowledge management, and other areas of management and administration. Such systems are on the market, but may not always suit the firm's profile despite the vendors' promises; hence cautious selection is warranted. System compatibility and integration need to be kept in mind to avoid costly and ineffective solutions that respond to partial needs rather then to the overall needs of the whole firm and its consultants.

Both hardware and software support need to be standardized throughout the firm to avoid incompatibility and conversion difficulties, and facilitate upgrading and scaling. Simplicity and user-friendliness are key, since even IT-literate consultants are not necessarily IT technicians.

Professional service automation (PSA) solutions offered by some IT providers integrate critical processes such as customer relationship management (CRM), assignment management, project management, resource management, time and expense capture, billing, support and knowledge management. The offer of integrated systems for professional service firms, covering key management functions and reflecting their mode of working with clients, is likely to continue to expand.

Outsourcing

IT solutions for consulting firms can be Internet-based and outsourced in the same ways as any other business and management services. Management and IT consultancies have been actively promoting outsourcing to their clients, and the large consulting firms are therefore well placed to identify which of their own internal services could be performed better and more economically by external providers. Deciding what to outsource may be more difficult for small firms, most of which have long outsourced their bookkeeping and accounting (not through the Internet, however), but may hesitate to outsource other functions and services using the Internet, perhaps with the exception of Web site design and maintenance. Like many small firms in other service sectors (see section 24.6), turning to a specialist for advice on Internet-based IT and business services may be the wisest solution.

35.4 Office facilities

Headquarters accommodation

In all circumstances, headquarters accommodation should reflect the fact that consulting is predominantly a field operation and not a head-office activity. While a "good address" can enhance the firm's image and has other advantages, such as the proximity of many clients, the total office space required can be relatively small.

The accommodation needed for the internal administrative and support services is self-evident. The reports library may start in a small way with a few lockable filing cabinets, but in time may need a room of its own. At the beginning it may share this room with the reference library of books and other documentation files, but with the growth of the unit more space will be needed.

As for consulting staff, the partners and other senior staff members involved in supervision and practice development need office space at headquarters. Operating consultants and associates need at least a desk each (though not individual offices). In addition, it is useful to have a meeting-room, space for training workshops, and some small rooms for receiving clients and other visitors.

A large number of consultants sitting at their desks instead of working with clients is generally considered to be a signal that something requires examination!

Sole practitioner's office

A sole practitioner may be able to operate from home without renting office space. However, this is not always desirable from the client-relations viewpoint. In some countries, an office in a town centre or business area may be essential. To avoid excessive accommodation and administrative costs, sole consultants and other professionals often share an office, and a secretary or assistant, with other independently operating colleagues.

---

[1] See, e.g., D. B. Norris: "To be or not to be – a partner", in *Journal of Management Consulting* (Milwaukee, WI), Vol. 7, No. 3, Spring 1993, pp. 46–51; and H. Ibarra: "Making partner: A mentor's guide to the psychological journey", in *Harvard Business Review*, Mar.–Apr. 2000, pp. 147–155. While a partnership is essentially a business form in English-speaking countries, other legal systems generally offer similar types of vehicles.

[2] The term "corporation", as used in this section, encompasses various types of business companies recognized by individual legal systems. For example, a number of countries recognize so-called joint-stock companies or companies limited by shares (e.g. the French "société anonyme" or "SA" and the German "Aktiengesellschaft" or "AG") as opposed to limited liability companies (e.g. the French "société à responsabilité limitée" or "SARL" and the Dutch "Besloten Venootschap" or "B.V."), which usually have a simpler structure and are subject to lighter regulation, but are not best suited to raising large amounts of finance. Tax treatment may also differ. It is recommended to seek specific advice on the types of companies permitted in the jurisdiction in which you are planning to engage in business.

[3] For a discussion of the problem see, e.g., "Partners in pain", in T*he Economist*, 9 July 1994, pp. 63–64; and V. E. Millar: *On the management of professional service firms: Ten myths debunked* (Fitzwilliam, NH, Kennedy Publications, 1991), pp. 39–44.

[4] See, e.g., E. Biech and L. Byars Swindling: *The Consultant's legal guide: A business of consulting resource guide* (San Francisco, CA, Jossey-Bass/Pfeiffer, 2000), pp. 111–124.

PART V

DEVELOPING CONSULTANTS AND THE CONSULTING PROFESSION

CAREERS AND COMPENSATION IN CONSULTING 36

Management consulting is a profession with its own objectives, methods, rules and organization. To individuals who join this profession, consulting is a career in which they may spend the main part of their working lives.

36.1 Personal characteristics of consultants

To become a career consultant is to make a major life decision. Individuals considering the career and consulting firms should therefore think very carefully about the characteristics that make someone a suitable candidate.

Management consultants have discussed these characteristics many times and useful advice can be found in several publications.[1] As for any profession, there is no one perfect model against which every entrant can be measured, but there are certain characteristics that affect the consultant's chance of success and personal job satisfaction. These characteristics differentiate the consulting profession from other occupations that also require a high level of technical knowledge and skill, but that have other objectives and use different methods (e.g. research, teaching, or management jobs with direct decision-making authority and responsibility). In management consulting, particular importance is attached to analytical and problem-solving abilities, as well as to competence in the behavioural area, in communicating and working with people, and in helping others to understand the need for change and how to implement it.

What kind of person is able to perform appropriately the multiple roles required of a management consultant? The qualities a consultant needs fall into two broad categories: *intellectual abilities* and *personal attributes*.

"Dilemma analysis" ability

Intellectually, the consultant needs to be able to make a "dilemma analysis", because an organization that uses a consultant may well be facing a situation that appears insoluble. If the difficulty could easily be solved by the operating manager, a consultant would not be needed. The consultant must recognize that a dilemma, whether real or not, exists in the minds of those within the organization. The consultant's role is to discover the nature of the dilemma and to determine the real cause of it, rather than what is thought to be the cause.

To accomplish this, the consultant must have a special type of diagnostic skill, and should approach a study of the organization's dilemma by means of an existential pragmatism that takes into account the total client setting and all situational variables. It is only through skilful examination of the organization's fabric that the structural relationships between the various subsystems that comprise the total organization can be seen, together with the interdependent nature of its individuals, groups, substructures and environmental setting.

In order to make this kind of dilemma analysis, insight or perception and intuition are necessary. Insight is vital because any dilemma requiring outside assistance will be part of a complex situation. The toughest task is to penetrate this complexity and isolate the key situational variables. Unless the important factors can be sifted from the maze of detail, and cause separated from symptoms, accurate diagnosis is impossible.

Sense of organizational climate

Intuition, or "sensing", must be coupled with insight in order to assess the nature and patterns of power and politics in the organization. Bureaucratic and managerial structures, both public and private, often do not function optimally. Underlying and intermingled with the functional operations of the organization are the dynamics of internal power and politics. Invariably, people are vying with each other for organizational influence or for some internal political reason. Very often the consultant has been brought in, not just to provide needed assistance, but also as an instrument of a strategy designed to secure an objective related to such influence.

Unless the consultant can intuitively sense the organizational climate, he or she runs the risk of being a pawn in a game of organizational politics. Conversely, the consultant who has the ability to recognize and understand the dynamics of the internal power and political relationships can use them in pursuit of whatever change objectives client and consultant conclude are appropriate.

Apart from these diagnostic abilities, the consultant needs implementation skills. Obviously, he or she must have some basic knowledge of the behavioural sciences, and the theories and methods of his or her own discipline. But more than these, the consultant needs imagination and experimental flexibility. Resolving dilemmas is essentially a creative activity. No real-life situation is going to fit perfectly into the models suggested by standard techniques or textbook methods. The consultant must have sufficient imagination to adapt and tailor concepts to meet real-life demands.

Furthermore, the consultant must be able to visualize the impact or ultimate outcome of the actions proposed or implemented. This is as much a process of experimental trial and error as of *a priori* solutions. The courage to experiment and the flexibility to try as many approaches as needed to solve the problem are important ingredients in the practitioner's make-up.

Integrity

Other important qualities required of the consultant are personal attributes. Above all, he must be a professional in attitude and behaviour. To be successful, he must be as sincerely interested in helping the client organization as any good doctor is interested in helping a patient. The consultant must not conceive of himself as, or portray the image of, a huckster of patent medicines. If a consultant is concerned primarily to make an impression or build an empire, and only secondarily to help the client organization, this will soon be recognized by the organization's leaders. People in management are generally astute individuals, and can recognize objectivity, honesty and, above all, integrity (see also Chapter 6).

When entering a client system, a strong tolerance for ambiguity is important. The consultant's first acquaintance with an organizational problem tends to be marked by a degree of bewilderment. It takes time to figure out the true situation, and during this period the consultant is going to experience a certain amount of confusion. He or she must expect this to occur and not be worried by it.

Coupled with this type of tolerance must be patience and the ability to sustain a high level of frustration. Curing a client's ills is likely to be a long and difficult process. Substantive changes, full cooperation and complete success are unlikely in the short term. Inevitably, attempts to change people's relationships and behavioural patterns are going to be met with resistance, resentment and obstructionism from those who will be, or think they may be, adversely affected. It is important for the consultant to have the maturity and sense of reality to accept that many of his or her actions and hopes for change are going to be frustrated. Such maturity is necessary to avoid experiencing the symptoms of defeat and withdrawal that commonly accompany the failure of a person's sincere efforts to help others.

Sense of timing and interpersonal skills

Finally, the consulting practitioner should have a good sense of timing, a stable personality and well-developed interpersonal skills. Timing can be crucial. The best conceived and articulated plans for change can be destroyed if introduced at the wrong time. Timing is linked to an understanding of power and of the political realities in the change situation, and to the kind of patience that overrides the enthusiasm surrounding a newly conceived idea or training intervention that one is longing to try out immediately.

Obviously, consulting involves dealing with people rather than with machines or mathematical formulae. The consultant must have good interpersonal skills and be able to communicate and deal with people in an atmosphere of tact, trust, politeness and friendliness. This is important because the impact of the consulting practitioner's personality must be minimized to keep it from becoming another variable in the existential setting and so contributing to the complexity of the situation. Beyond this, success will depend on the persuasiveness and tact of the consultant in dealing with the client.

How to interpret these requirements

Box 36.1 summarizes the key intellectual abilities and personal qualities of a management consultant in telegraphic form. It could be argued that only a very mature and exceptionally capable and versatile person can possess all the qualities mentioned. In recruiting a new consultant, it is therefore necessary to consider what qualities the person must possess on recruitment, and what qualities he or she will be able to acquire, or improve, through training and experience.

36.2 Recruitment and selection

The foundations of a successful career in consulting are laid at the moment of recruitment: only candidates who meet certain criteria will have a good chance of becoming fully competent consultants and moving up the career ladder to their own and the consulting firm's satisfaction. Hence a careful search and a thorough appraisal of candidates are extremely important.

Recruitment criteria

While consulting firms apply different criteria in recruiting new consultants, a comparison of their practices allows for some general conclusions concerning personal characteristics, education, practical experience and age.

Personal characteristics were discussed in section 36.1.

Education is carefully examined in every case. A university degree (first degree, master's degree or doctorate) is required for all management consulting positions. The relevance of the field of study to the particular field of consulting is considered, and in some cases candidates must have a specific educational background, for example, a doctorate in psychology, or a degree in computer science. The consulting firm is equally interested in the performance of the candidates during their university studies, in particular in project assignments during which the students have practised fact-finding, communication and other consulting skills.

Practical experience (a minimum of five to ten years) used to be required by all consulting firms, but this has changed in recent years. Some important firms have started recruiting up to 30 to 50 per cent of new consultants directly from university or business school, particularly in special fields where it is difficult to recruit people with required technical knowledge and experience

Box 36.1 Qualities of a consultant

(1) Intellectual ability
- ability to learn quickly and easily
- ability to observe, gather, select and evaluate facts
- good judgement
- inductive and deductive reasoning
- ability to synthesize and generalize
- creative imagination; original thinking

(2) Ability to understand people and work with them
- respect for other people; tolerance
- ability to anticipate and evaluate human reactions
- easy human contacts
- ability to gain trust and respect
- courtesy and good manners

(3) Ability to communicate, persuade and motivate
- ability to listen
- facility in oral and written communication
- ability to share knowledge, teach and train people
- ability to persuade and motivate

(4) Intellectual and emotional maturity
- stability of behaviour and action
- independence in drawing unbiased conclusions
- ability to withstand pressures, and live with frustrations and uncertainties
- ability to act with poise, in a calm and objective manner
- self-control in all situations
- flexibility and adaptability to changed conditions

(5) Personal drive and initiative
- right degree of self-confidence
- healthy ambition
- entrepreneurial spirit
- courage, initiative and perseverance in action

(6) Ethics and integrity
- genuine desire to help others
- extreme honesty
- ability to recognize the limitations of one's competence
- ability to admit mistakes and learn from failure

(7) Physical and mental health
- ability to accept the specific working and living conditions of management consultants

from business firms. The idea is that talented and dynamic individuals will quickly acquire the necessary practical experience by working in teams with more senior consultants. Executives in business and consulting firms tend to agree that recruiting young consultants without experience is not ideal, but they see no alternative.

The *age at which candidates are recruited* reflects the required education and experience. The lower age limit is usually between 25 and 30 years. In many cases there is also an upper age limit. It may be difficult for a senior manager or specialist, who has reached an interesting position in terms of responsibility and pay, to switch over to consulting unless he or she is directly offered a senior position with a consulting organization. This happens only in special cases, for example, if senior people have to be recruited from outside to start new lines of consulting or head new divisions.

As a general rule, most consulting firms try to avoid recruiting new staff at senior level. Consulting emphasizes certain work methods and behavioural patterns, and some people would find it difficult to learn and internalize these after a certain age and at a high level of seniority. Also, it is not always easy to adapt to a firm's culture and style. The upper limit for recruitment therefore tends to be between 36 and 40 years. Of course, if an individual decides to open a private consulting practice, he or she can do it at any time. There are retired business executives and government officials who start consulting at the age of 55–60. Some managers who are made redundant turn to consulting, at whatever stage of their career they are, rather than look for another management job in a saturated labour market.

Recruitment sources

There are two main sources of recruitment: business enterprises and universities. But any other source is acceptable, provided it gives the candidate the required experience and skills. Many consulting firms advertise job opportunities in business journals and management periodicals, thus opening their doors to any candidates who meet the criteria.

A good source might be client organizations, although under normal circumstances a consultant should not use this source owing to conflict of interest (see Chapter 6). But there are exceptions. A client may willingly authorize a consultant to offer a job to an employee whose personal qualities would be better utilized in consulting than in the present job.

When recruiting directly from universities and business schools,[2] consulting firms aim to get the best students. They may interview 20 or more candidates for one position. In some countries, consulting careers with leading firms enjoy such a good reputation that the best graduates are interested.

However, consulting firms compete for recruits among themselves, with other professions and with investment banks, IT service providers and other firms, including those in the most dynamic and forward-looking sectors. Therefore the relationship is often reversed: it is not the consulting firm that chooses among numerous high-quality applicants but the young graduate who can choose among several attractive job offers. Consulting firms cannot afford to recruit mediocre people, and they therefore seek to make consulting careers attractive.

Interviewing and testing

Candidates for consultants' posts are usually asked to fill in an application form (personnel questionnaire), supply a detailed curriculum vitae, and provide other evidence of professional work achievements (articles, papers, doctoral thesis, etc.). References given by the candidate and other references identified by the consulting firm are generally carefully checked for every candidate who looks interesting (by correspondence, personal visits or telephone calls).

Applicants may be subjected to multiple interviews: by the personnel officer, a manager of the consulting firm, a supervising consultant to whom the candidate might be attached after recruitment, and one or two other consultants. Emphasis is on obtaining as complete a picture as possible of the knowledge and experience of the candidate and of personal characteristics relevant to consulting.

In some consulting firms tests are used as aids in selecting new consultants. These include both cognitive tests (designed mainly to measure knowledge) and psychological tests (related to personality, attitudes, interests and motivation). If personality and attitude tests are used, the results should be evaluated by a professional psychologist. Tests can convey useful information about the candidate, but their importance in the choice of consultants should not be overrated. They sometimes provide distorted information because of the ambiance in which the test is administered, or because some tests that are widely used become well known and hence less effective. In general, mature candidates do not like these tests.

Medical examination

A medical examination will generally be required, as is usual in the case of long-term employment. This will take account of the lifestyle of consultants, which in most cases is more demanding on the individual's physical and mental fitness, resistance and endurance than many other jobs with a comparable technical content.

Selection

As any new entrant to the profession is seen as a potential career consultant who may stay with the firm for many years, the selection of those who will be offered employment requires careful evaluation of the applicants, based on all information provided by each applicant, reference checking, multiple interviews and, possibly, tests. Managers of consulting firms should avoid making final decisions on selection without consulting a number of experienced colleagues: every recruitment warrants a collective assessment.

36.3 Career development

The great diversity of career structures in consulting firms reflects their different history, size, technical areas covered, consulting modes used, and even personal preferences of the key decision-makers. But certain patterns emerge from this diversity.[3]

In large firms, the consultants progress through four or five principal grades, or ranks, during their career. Small firms use only two or three grades. In pursuing flatter and leaner structures, some large firms have also reduced the number of rungs in their consultants' career ladders.

Career progression implies that the consultant will take on more responsibility, which can be:

- supervisory (team leadership, project management, supervision of assignments);
- promotional (management surveys, marketing, negotiation and selling of new assignments);
- managerial (managing organizational units in the firm, functions in general and top management);
- technical (directly performing assignments that require particularly experienced and knowledgeable consultants, training of new consultants, development of methods and practice guides);
- various combinations of these four alternatives.

A summary description of a typical career structure is given in box 36.2.

Factors affecting careers

In a typical consulting career there is a significant relationship between progression in rank and role. A higher rank means a more difficult role and more responsibility. The relationship is not the same in all firms. Some prefer a conservative approach, whereby precisely defined functions are assigned to each rank in the consulting hierarchy. Thus, only a consultant of a high grade would negotiate with a potential client. In contrast, many firms are increasingly flexible in deciding what consultants can and should do, irrespective of rank. For example, a consulting project may be managed by an individual in any of the four principal grades (starting at the operating consultant level), depending on the scope of the project and the capabilities of the individual. These firms encourage young operating consultants to assume responsibility for more difficult jobs and for managing assignments, and thus to expand their capabilities, as soon as possible after joining the firm. Even consultants with relatively little experience are encouraged to manage projects, present results to clients, and take initiative in working with clients.

Career advancement is based above all on achievement. As seniority is difficult to ignore, individuals who cannot demonstrate high achievement are encouraged to move on. If they stayed, they would see their younger colleagues

Box 36.2 Career structure in a consulting firm

First level: junior consultant (trainee, research associate, analyst, entry-level consultant)

This level exists only in some firms, which recruit new consultants as trainees (for 6–12 months); their main task is to master the essential consulting skills as quickly as possible.

Second level: operating consultant (resident consultant, associate, associate consultant, management consultant, consultant)

The operating consultant is the front-line professional who does most of the consulting work at client organizations. Every operating consultant has a special field of competence, as a rule in one management function or in special techniques. Normally the consultant would undertake a number of operating assignments in varying situations, individually and as a team member, for a period of three to five years before being considered for promotion to the next level.

Third level: supervising consultant (team leader, project manager, senior associate, senior consultant, manager)

The main responsibilities of consultants promoted to this level include team leadership (e.g. in assignments requiring expertise in general management and involving several functional areas) and supervision of operating consultants. A consultant at this level also continues to execute directly certain assignments that require an experienced person. Further responsibilities may include training, management surveys, the marketing of new assignments, and maintaining contacts with clients.

Fourth level: junior partner or equivalent (principal, manager, survey consultant)

Consultants at this level carry out a number of marketing and management functions. Typically they spend most of their time in promotional work (visiting clients, doing management surveys, planning and negotiating new assignments). Some may be personally in charge of important client assignments, while others head organizational units within the firm, or coordinate and control a number of client projects.

Fifth level: senior partner or equivalent (officer, director, partner, managing partner, vice-president, president)

Senior and top management responsibilities prevail at this superior level, including strategy and policy direction. Consultants at this level are also concerned with practice development, do promotional work with important clients, and may be personally in charge of complex and major assignments. In most firms they are the owners, but there are firms where the junior partners or principals (the fourth level) also belong to the group that owns the firm.

advance more rapidly, which would inevitably create jealousy and lead to frustration. It is often emphasized that every young consultant should be regarded and treated as a potential partner, and that career development to partner level should not take longer than 6–12 years.

Fast career progression has a positive motivational effect on consultants and creates a dynamic and competitive working environment. However, a firm that adopts fast career progression as a policy must be prepared to cope with certain problems. If the firm's growth is fast enough, the number of senior positions grows as well and promotions can be fast also, but if growth slows down or stops, promotions become difficult. Some firms have therefore introduced special promotion schemes for technically competent and experienced individuals for whom supervising and managerial jobs are not available, or who are not interested in these jobs. An alternative is to reorient the firm to more complex assignments and thus increase the demand for senior consultants. This enables the firm to change the overall ratio of operating to senior consultants; for example, instead of employing two seniors for every five operating consultants, the new mix of projects might permit the firm to employ three seniors and change the ratio from 5:2 to 5:3. This, however, is a sensitive issue of the firm's economics and strategy (see Chapters 27 and 28).

Staff reviews

There are two reasons why systematic staff reviews (performance assessment) are probably more important in consulting and other professional firms than in other sorts of organization:

- The career patterns described above require consultants to develop rapidly and assume a widening range of responsibilities. It is difficult to find work for consultants whose growth potential is limited and who will not be able to keep pace with their more dynamic and ambitious colleagues.
- The operational environment in which a consultant works (individual role in an assignment, team leader, immediate colleagues, client staff) changes frequently, and an operating consultant may be a member of five or more different teams within one year. Performance evaluation must therefore be organized to collect and assess all the information needed for the consultants' careers and professional development in this constantly changing work environment.

Thorough evaluation of a new consultant should therefore start during his or her initial training, and several reports should be prepared (see Chapter 37).

The second element in systematic staff evaluation is formal performance review at the end of each assignment. These reports are prepared by the team leader or supervisor, discussed with the consultant, and filed in personnel records. Feedback from clients should also be sought, both informally and through client feedback questionnaires (see Chapters 11 and 32).

The third element is periodic performance appraisals. As a rule, these are more frequent in the first two or three years of the consultant's career. They are generally based on reports from all assignments and evaluate performance, competence and prospects in areas such as:

- the technical subjects covered;
- consulting methodology and style;

- teamwork;
- team leadership, supervision, coordination;
- marketing and client relations;
- training and self-development;
- special personal characteristics, manners, interests and talents.

Every periodic performance appraisal must aim to tell both the firm and the individual, openly and clearly, where to focus improvement efforts. If an individual consultant would be better advised to look for a career outside consulting, a performance appraisal should reveal this and make an unambiguous recommendation. It is unfair not to tell young consultants that their career prospects are limited, thus creating unrealistic expectations and merely delaying a painful decision.

It is useful for consultants to prepare for every performance appraisal by completing a structured self-evaluation. The consultant thus assesses and describes his or her own achievements, progress made, strengths, weak points and needs, which is a good starting-point for evaluation by the supervisor and the firm. It also reveals the consultant's personal perceptions of standards and work performed and his or her self-assessment ability.

Staff turnover

Not all consultants will stay with one firm until retirement. Staff turnover figures in consulting are quite high: an annual turnover of 10–15 per cent is considered as normal, a 5–10 per cent turnover as low. The reasons for consultants' departure include:

- different views on how to do consulting;
- different views on career advancement;
- entrepreneurship (quite a few consultants employed in consulting firms decide to start their own consulting practices);
- personal preference for other careers (business management, government administration, university teaching, politics, etc.);
- insufficient promotion prospects;
- personality clashes.

Large consulting firms tend to have a higher staff turnover than small firms. Many young professionals join these firms in order to gain diversified experience in a relatively short time, without intending to stay in consulting. This is less common in small firms. In addition, small firms usually try to be more adaptable to the needs and aspirations of individual staff members even if this means reorienting and restructuring the firm.

In a large firm, most consultants who leave do so at the operating consultant's level. Voluntary departures at the partner level are relatively rare. However, forced and negotiated departures of partners, before retirement age, have recently become more frequent. In searching for leaner structures and competitiveness in a difficult business climate, a number of consulting firms have come to the conclusion that they cannot afford to sustain large numbers of highly paid (though not always highly productive) partners without undermining the firm's financial health and staff morale.

A sole practitioner's career path

Most individuals who start their own consulting business do so after between 8 and 15 years of practical business experience, or after having worked for several years for a consulting firm. Those who go directly into independent consulting without any previous experience usually set up in IT or other special fields where technical knowledge is key and businesses are prepared to use technical experts without practical experience.

For a sole practitioner, the question of promotion to a more senior position does not arise. What normally happens, however, is that, as he or she becomes more experienced and ambitious, a sole practitioner is able to undertake more complex and difficult jobs, and to charge higher fees. Nevertheless, many sole practitioners get into situations where important career choices have to be faced. They could progress technically and take on more challenging assignments, but this may require giving up personal independence and agreeing to work in a team. One consultant may decide to expand the firm and employ other consultants. Another consultant may join a large consulting firm if a senior position is offered, while a third may establish a network and cooperate with other small firms.. A fourth will reject all these alternatives and look for assignments requiring special expertise and a great deal of experience, but small enough to be undertaken by an individual. The consulting business offers enough opportunities to satisfy a wide range of different career aspirations.

36.4 Compensation policies and practices

The compensation policies and practices of management consulting firms are based on principles similar to those in other firms in the professional service sector. Compensation reflects factors such as:

- the technical complexity and special requirements of consulting work;
- individual talent;
- the situation in the market for consulting services;
- the financial performance of the firm;
- the contribution of the individual consultant to the development and financial performance of the firm.

Financial compensation is not regarded as the only way to motivate consultants. Long-term motivation is emphasized by demonstrating to the new recruits that in due course they will be promoted to the partner level, when they will earn considerably more. The nature and the job content of consulting, as well as the exceptional learning opportunities and business contacts provided by consulting assignments, are also strong motivational factors.

Entry-level and operating consultant compensation

At entry level, consulting firms compete among themselves and with other employers for the best talent. As a result, salaries offered to new recruits tend to be higher than those offered by firms in industry and commerce. In the total remuneration package, the base salary usually accounts for more than 90 per cent and may attain the full 100 per cent. Hence, the role of bonuses and profit-sharing is relatively small, although some firms stress that consultants at all levels should be eligible for some bonus.

The bonus paid to junior and operating consultants may be discretionary and depend only on the profitability of the firm as a whole. Alternatively, the consultants may get a bonus that is related to the fees they (or their team) earn from their own clients, and to new business that they generate for the firm.

If individual fee-earning and new business generation are strongly reflected in the bonus paid, the message is clear that this is what the firm expects from you. As a result, young consultants will become less interested in helping other colleagues, engaging in teamwork or spending time on activities for which no bonus is likely to be paid.

Experience has shown that even a small discretionary bonus is valuable for consultants at any level. However, a bonus should not be paid automatically, without a review of the consultant's work performance. Also, the bonus should not send the wrong signals on what the firm values most in the consultants' behaviour and performance.

Partner compensation

Partner compensation is a complex and delicate issue of management in professional firms. The partners are in a dual position – they own the firm, and are therefore entitled to part of the profit, and they carry out specific managerial, marketing or consulting jobs, for which they are paid a salary. The prevailing formula used for partner remuneration tends to be a base salary plus profit share or bonus. For example, in 1998 senior partners in American consulting firms were awarded bonuses and profit-sharing amounting on average to some 29 per cent of their base salaries.[4] In 1999, the average annual compensation in consulting firms covered by a Kennedy Information Research Group survey was as follows: recent MBAs US$79,000; consultants US$97,000; project managers US$158,000; and partners US$388,000. Thus, remuneration of partners was four times that of operating consultants.[5]

Partners and other professionals in equivalent positions manage the firm and play key roles in promoting the business. Their roles and performance ought to be reflected both in the compensation formulas used and in the actual level of compensation. If partner compensation criteria disregard, or are in conflict with, the firm's goals and policies, even the best strategic plan will be nothing more than a piece of paper.

In small consulting firms with a few partners, simple income or profit division formulas are quite common. If there are three partners in a firm, each of them may be allocated one-third of the profits. The formula causes no difficulties if, within the small team, there is a team spirit, a clear division of responsibilities and an understanding of who does what for the development of the firm. The three partners will probably be able to speak frequently and openly about these questions and change the focus by mutual agreement (e.g. spend more time on coaching a new associate or start looking for a new line of business). It may be unnecessary and even contrary to the firm's well-established practices to formally reflect such agreements in changed partner compensation.

The matter gets more complex with the growth of the firm's business and the number of partners and consultants employed. There will be a need for a compensation plan for partners that reflects and supports the firm's strategic goals and priorities. As a rule, the plan will use a combination of a few criteria (say three to five), which may be quantitative and measurable (e.g. the partner's personal billings) or qualitative and judgemental (e.g. the partner's contribution to junior staff coaching and training, or to building up the firm's image in professional and client circles). Each criterion will be assigned a weighting. Consistency between the criteria declared and actually applied is essential (see box 36.3).

The practical impact of each criterion needs to be carefully considered. Furthermore, periodic performance evaluation ought to be applied even to partners in senior management positions, using a formula that stresses collective assessment and is acceptable to senior professionals. For example, a partner can be asked to prepare a self-assessment of performance using the main criteria chosen by the firm. This is then reviewed by a compensation or management committee and discussed with the partner in a committee meeting or individually.

Shares and share options

During the 1990s, the use of shares and share options to compensate consultants gained importance. Consultants thus followed the trend that had become widespread in business, in the IT and e-business sectors in particular. Data from 1998 provided by the Association of Management Consulting Firms (AMCF) showed that such ownership was not available in only 31.5 per cent of the 62 firms surveyed. It was available to all employees in 24.1 per cent of firms, to junior partner level and above in 16.7 per cent, and to senior partners in 24 per cent of the firms surveyed.[6]

This compensation technique strengthens the link between the performance of the firm and individual compensation. It stimulates the consultant's interest in

Box 36.3 Criteria for partners' compensation

(1) **Seniority**

Widely used. Still an exclusive criterion in some distinguished professional firms. Encourages partners to get used to a stable income level irrespective of current personal effort and achievement.

(2) **Profitability of firm**

Widely used. Encourages partners to focus on helping each other, promoting teamwork and improving the whole firm's results.

(3) **Profitability of activity supervised or managed**

Widely used. Puts a high premium on actual results of the partner's projects (assignments) or of a unit for which the partner is directly responsible.

(4) **Personal billing**

Widely used. Stimulates interest and initiative in doing individual billable work. Also remunerates for a high personal billing rate (fee rate) reflecting individual competence and image (which can be a separate criterion).

(5) **Personal selling**

Encourages finding new clients and projects, or obtaining new work from existing clients. Possible refinement: differentiating between new work of routine (repetitive) nature, and projects providing for acquiring new competencies, entering new sectors or similar.

(6) **Client satisfaction**

Encourages partners to look after clients, assure high quality and manage assignments to their clients' full satisfaction.

(7) **Training and development of consultants**

Stresses transfer of experience and know-how, and the partner's role in coaching and developing younger consultants.

(8) **Contribution to the profession**

Remunerates voluntary association and other work serving the profession.

(9) **Contribution to the success of others**

Rewards collaboration and help to other units through sharing of information, providing advice, giving leads, helping to negotiate new assignments. etc.

(10) **Contribution to knowledge management and development in the firm**

Rewards research, new method development, writing of practice guides, knowledge-sharing and other work enhancing the firm's knowledge and competence.

(11) **Building up the firm's image**

Encourages writing of articles and books, reporting at conferences, membership of government and mixed committees, etc.

(12) **Self-development**

Stimulates learning to enhance the partner's competence and contribution to the firm.

(13) **General management**

Remunerates for management positions within the firm's structure.

Box 36.4 Ideas for improving compensation policies

- Work backwards from marketplace pricing and cross-check against industry benchmarks.
- Take non-billed time into account.
- Avoid excessive fixed costs by developing a compensation plan driven by bonuses.
- Consider discrete bonus pools for different levels of seniority.
- Determine the range of compensation varations depending on the firm's culture.
- Develop a systematic process for allocating bonus pools.
- Compensate rainmakers based on sales targets.
- Try additional nontraditional elements of compensation.
- Convert the firm from a partnerhip model to a public company to provide stock-option incentives to employees.
- Create "near-partner" positions that offer earlier equity- or profit-sharing.
- Accelerate tracks to partner or equivalent status.
- Don't try to fool consultants with complex compensation plans.
- Be prepared to change the plan.

Source: Kennedy Information.

the growth of the firm's total value, which will be the value certified by the market in firms whose shares are publicly traded. If the firm is closely held, the price of the shares will be determined by valuation. As a rule, there will be established formulas for repurchasing the shares from consultants on retirement or termination of contract on terms that are fair both to the consultant and to the firm.

Obviously, to use this technique, the firm must be established as a corporation and shares or share options must be distributed and taxed in accordance with local legislation (see also section 14.1). Consultants accept the formula in the belief that the firm's market value will grow and seek to increase this value through their personal performance. The impact can be disappointing and counterproductive if the firm's value skyrockets or falls for reasons unrelated to professional performance.

Compensation policy

In conclusion, it is useful to stress that a compensation policy or plan has a strong impact on the climate in the consulting firm. Consultants at all levels should know what the policy is and how it is justified. They should have no reason to suspect that the firm's management uses a double standard in applying the policy to different staff members and different levels of the consulting hierarchy. The purpose of a compensation policy is to motivate the whole staff and stimulate achievement, not to protect privileges and create tensions between groups and categories of consultants. Salaries must be competitive at all levels to attract and retain able and competent professionals and build up the firm's human capital.

Compensation policy should be proactive, not merely reactive to observed market trends, and should aim to prevent the exodus of talent and to motivate individuals for a long-term view of their career, learning and achievement. Box 36.4 summarizes the conclusions reached by the Kennedy Information survey.[7]

---

[1] The first significant attempt to define these characteristics was made by the Association of Management Consulting Firms (AMCF, formerly ACME) in the United States. See P. W. Shay: *The common body of knowledge for management consultants* (New York, ACME, 1974). In 1989 ACME published a revised edition of this first guide under the title *Professional profile of management consultants: A body of expertise, skills and attributes*. See also Ch. 10 in G. Lippitt and R. Lippitt: *The consulting process in action* (San Diego, CA, University Associates, 2nd ed., 1986).

[2] To facilitate contacts between consulting firms and students, the Harvard Business School has established a Management Consulting Club. The School and the Club publish a periodical career guide. See *The Harvard Business School Guide to Careers in Management Consulting, 2001 Edition* (Boston, MA, HBS Press, 2000). See also www.WetFeet.com, a Web site for students interested in careers in e-business and other Internet-related consulting.

[3] There is little published information on the career patterns in various consulting firms. Information from several North American firms can be found in the consulting career guide of the Harvard Business School, op. cit.

[4] See AMCF: *Operating ratios for management consulting firms: A resource for benchmarking* (New York, 2000).

[5] See Kennedy Information: *Compensation and recruiting trends in management consulting* (Fitzwilliam, NH, Kennedy Information, 2000).

[6] AMCF, op. cit.

[7] See Kennedy Information, op. cit.

TRAINING AND DEVELOPMENT OF CONSULTANTS 37

The previous chapter noted that all entrants to the consulting profession should have an excellent educational background and that a great many will also have several years of practical experience. Yet consulting has its own special training and development requirements that are additional to whatever a new consultant may have learned at university, at business school, and in former jobs.

There are four main reasons for this. First, consulting on how to do a job is different from actually doing that job. A new consultant must develop a full understanding of this difference and acquire the technical and behavioural skills that are specific to consulting.

Second, the breadth and depth of technical knowledge required to advise clients usually exceed what a new consultant has learned during his or her studies and previous employment. A new consultant with five to ten years of business experience may have worked in two to four jobs and experienced a relatively small number of business and management contexts. This does not provide enough experience for giving the best possible advice to the client. In addition, a new consultant may have to update and upgrade the technical knowledge acquired during university or business school studies.

Third, most new recruits will join the firm without any prior education in consulting per se. University and business school courses in management consulting are rare. Those that exist are elective and attended by small numbers of students.

Fourth, the new entrant is joining a consulting firm which, it can be assumed, has a particular consulting philosophy and strategy. This will concern issues such as the objectives of consulting, the methods and techniques used, the ways in which clients should participate, and ethical considerations. There is a need to "indoctrinate" the new recruits in the consulting firm's professional approach, so that they identify themselves with its philosophy and culture.

Further, the consultant's education does not end with the completion of initial training. "Least of all can consultants afford to take the attitude that the old ways of doing things are good enough. Probably no group is more severely challenged by the information explosion than management consultants. Learning must be a life-long job for consultants", wrote Michael Shays in 1983, when he was President of the Institute of Management Consultants in the United States.[1]

How does a consultant learn? What is the most effective way of developing a competent consultant? University education can provide the future consultant with a solid fund of knowledge and some analytical tools. However, like managers, consultants learn from experience above all. This includes the consultant's own direct experience, on assignments in which the task is to deal with problems and situations that provide meaningful learning opportunities. In doing so the consultant also learns from the clients' experiences. Furthermore, the consultant learns from other consultants – his or her colleagues in a team, the team leader and other superiors, consultants who worked for the same client previously, and other members of the profession.

Learning on the job, by practising consulting, is therefore the main and generally recognized method of learning. This is how most consultants acquired their proficiency in the past, and even now some consultants advocate that on-the-job learning is the only way to become competent in consulting. However, learning on the job alone is not enough and should be supplemented (but not replaced) by other learning opportunities, including formal training in courses and workshops. This is the approach that we adopt in this chapter, and that is increasingly supported by leading firms and professional associations of consultants.

37.1 What should consultants learn?

A remarkable diversity of personalities, clients, subjects handled, intervention methods and consulting firms' philosophies is a prominent feature of the consulting profession. Because of this diversity, there are probably as many different paths to individual proficiency as there are consultants. As in other professions, some individuals will learn faster than others and achieve higher proficiency, owing to a happy concourse of a number of circumstances: talent, drive, educational background, complexity and novelty of assignments executed, and leadership and support provided by the consulting firm.

The training and development policies of consulting firms, and of the profession at large, tend to respect this diversity, offering a range of choices that permit learning to be harmonized with individual needs and possibilities. At the same time, the profession has aimed to achieve the necessary minimum level of uniformity and standardization, reflecting the common and prevailing needs of consultants at various stages of a typical professional career. Leading consulting firms and professional associations have devoted a lot of energy to these questions. As the profession is a young and rapidly evolving one, and distilling common needs and principles from constantly changing diversity is not easy, the task is far from being completed. Nevertheless, some useful guidance and support materials, outlining the consultants' professional profiles and common knowledge base, are available.[2]

Elements of consultant competence

Generally speaking, a consultant's competence can be described in terms of personality traits, aptitudes, attitudes, knowledge and skills. These elements of competence are interlinked and influence each other.[3]

Personality traits and aptitudes were mentioned in the previous chapter in the discussion on recruitment criteria. Traits determine how a person will react "to any general set of events which allow the trait to be expressed".[4] Thus, traits define a typical thought pattern and resultant behaviour characteristic of a person in a variety of situations. Examples of personality traits are propensity to take initiative, ambition, flexibility, patience, self-confidence, shyness, and the like. Examples of aptitudes are manual dexterity or linguistic ability.

Attitudes are a person's feelings for or against certain issues, and therefore they reflect values that a person holds. They concern matters of human preference and result from choices between competing interests. Examples of attitudes or values are a preference for oral rather than written communication, tolerance of other people's religious beliefs and cultural values, or preference for having people of certain nationalities or technical backgrounds as direct collaborators.

Knowledge is retained information concerning facts, concepts, relationships and processes.[5] It is useful to distinguish between general and specialized knowledge. In consulting, general knowledge concerns economic, social, political and cultural processes, institutions and environments that constitute a general background for consulting interventions in specific organizations or systems. There are then two sorts of specialized knowledge. The first concerns the object of consulting, i.e. the consultant's special sector or technical area of intervention. Examples of sectors are manufacturing, banking and insurance, while examples of technical areas are marketing, production organization, job evaluation and corporate strategy. The second area of knowledge concerns consulting per se – its principles, processes, organization, methods and techniques.

Skill is the ability to do things: to apply knowledge, aptitudes and attitudes effectively in work situations. Skills too can be broken down into several groups. Some of the consultant's skills will be generic, e.g. social and cultural skills. Other skills will be common to consultants and their clients (managers and entrepreneurs). The difference will be in the required breadth and depth of mastery of certain skills. Probably the consultant will be more skilful in interviewing and providing advice than a typical manager, but may lag behind managers in the skills of organizing, coordinating, mobilizing people and speedy decision-making. There are, then, the skills that are particular to consultants, advisers and other helpers whose job has been described as "getting things done when you are not in charge".[6] These professionals have to be competent in assessing the problems and opportunities of organizations for which they are not responsible and where they have not worked, developing and presenting proposals, providing feedback and reports to decision-makers and their collaborators, and so on.

The difference between the content and the level of competence is significant. Thus, various elements of managing consultancy projects are listed among key consultant skills and components of their body of knowledge. However, there will be a difference in the required level of this competence between an entry-level consultant and a partner supervising several major projects. This difference will have to be duly reflected in training programmes for various levels of consultants.

A body of consultant knowledge and skills

In Chapter 6 we referred to a defined "body of knowledge" – an overview of the areas of generic competence of a mature and experienced management consultant. As a rule, such a document will indicate common threshold competencies, not those required for doing a particular job or achieving superior performance.[7]

It is useful to refer to a complete text of a body of knowledge in designing a training programme for consultants. However, it is important to remember that these documents are not intended to lay down the scientific foundations of consulting as a field of learning. The reader may well conclude that, in his or her particular context, other topics should be covered in training, or the topics listed should be grouped and presented in a different way. Irrespective of differences in terminology and layout, the principal areas covered in a common body of consultant knowledge will normally be close to those outlined in box 37.1. The multidisciplinary nature of consulting is obvious, as the topics listed draw on sociology, psychology, statistics, economics, management and organization theory, and other disciplines. Some topics are confined to the description of good or best experience without aiming at scientific analysis and theoretical justification.

Substantive area of expertise and the business environment

Training and development in the substantive areas of the consultant's expertise and in the wider business, institutional, legal and social environment are becoming ever more important. There are several reasons for this. New recruits to consulting may have an excellent technical background but a rather narrow perspective and limited knowledge of the environments in which businesses operate. As they progress in their careers and accept more complex assignments, many consultants need to master new areas and widen their knowledge base to cover areas outside their original background and main area of competence.

Another reason is the extremely high speed with which management concepts and techniques emerge, gain importance and popularity, and become obsolete – to be replaced in many cases by other concepts and techniques. This race for originality and novelty forces consultants to be always fully up to date and well informed. While it is not easy to recognize the difference between essential state-of-the-art developments and passing fads, a management

Box 37.1 Areas of consultant knowledge and skills

Orientation to management consulting

- Nature and objectives of consulting; consultants and clients; consulting and change
- Basic consulting styles and approaches
- Types of consulting services and organizations

Consulting and other professions

- Management consulting as a career
- Organization of the profession
- Professional ethics and conduct
- Historical development, present position and future perspectives of consulting
- Professions close to consulting (audit, legal advice, training, etc.)

Overview of the consulting process

- Framework and stages of a consulting assignment (project)
- Entry
- Diagnosis
- Action planning
- Implementation
- Termination

Analytical and problem-solving skills

- Systematic approach to problem-solving in management and business
- Methods for diagnosing organizations and their performance
- Data collection and recording
- Data and problem analysis
- Techniques for developing action proposals
- Creative thinking
- Evaluating and selecting alternatives
- Measuring and evaluating project results

Behavioural, communication and change management skills

- Human and behavioural aspects of the consulting process and the consultant–client relationship
- The client's psychology
- Behavioural roles of the consultant and the client
- Consulting and culture
- Techniques for diagnosing attitudes, human relations, behaviour and management styles
- Techniques for generating and assisting change in people and in organizations

- Managing conflict
- Communication and persuasion techniques
- Teamwork and the conduct of meetings
- Using training in consulting; assessing client training needs; designing training programmes
- Management and staff training concepts and techniques
- Courtesy and etiquette in consultant–client relations
- Effective report writing and presentation

Marketing and managing assignments

- Principles of marketing in professional services
- Marketing approaches and techniques
- Consultant selection criteria and procedures
- Proposals to clients (planning, preparation, presentation)
- Consulting contracts and their negotiation
- Fee setting
- Structuring, planning and staffing an assignment
- Managing and controlling an assignment
- Reporting to the client and to the consulting firm

Managing and developing a consulting practice

- Considerations in establishing and structuring a consulting firm; legal forms
- Economics and strategy of a consulting firm
- Governance, organizational culture and management style in professional firms
- Knowledge management
- Recruiting, developing and remunerating consultants
- Financial management of the firm
- Operational management and control; monitoring performance
- Leading and coaching consultants
- Quality assurance and management
- Professional responsibility and liability
- Information technology in professional firms
- Internal administration and office management

consultant cannot afford to answer a client enquiring about a new technique: "I've never heard of it", "You can ignore it, it's not important to you", or "Our firm does not use this technique".

Furthermore, information and telecommunications technology is omnipresent and rapidly changing in all sectors and functions of management. Training and retraining in IT and its management applications have therefore become a standard part of any consultant development programme.

Consultants who specialize sectorally need to keep abreast of sectoral developments, including sector-specific technologies, principal products, leading producers and distributors, competition, restructuring of firms, economic trends and prospects, employment and social issues, environmental considerations and the like.

Consultant development matrix

The consultant development matrix in figure 37.1 gives a rough idea of how training needs change in the course of a typical consulting career. To simplify, three stages in the career are shown (initial, advanced, managerial). Between these stages, there is a shift in emphasis from basic, operational and methodology issues, which dominate initial training, through assignment (project) marketing and management (which includes leading teams of consultants), to practice management and development. As indicated in the matrix, owing to the rapidly changing state of the art in consulting, every area requires updating at all levels of the hierarchy.

Impact of the firm's strategic choices

In Chapter 28 we stressed the need for consistency between the consulting firm's basic strategic choices, and the training and development of its professional staff. Although some common basic training has to be given to all consultants, firms do not normally develop their staff to make them more competent in general terms, but to fit the firm's particular profile and to understand and implement its strategy. Strategies can be very different, and so will be training policies and programmes. For example, firms engaged mainly in the development and installation of management systems will provide a great deal of formal and structured staff training in the design and application of these systems. Firms practising action learning and process consulting as their principal intervention technologies will put more emphasis on behavioural, communication and human resource development approaches and techniques.

37.2 Training of new consultants

Objectives of training

The overall objective of an initial training programme for new consultants is:

> To ensure that the consultant has the ability and confidence to carry out assignments in his or her field of management.

As consulting is not easy, initial training must explain and demonstrate this, but at the same time provide enough guidance for new entrants to start their first assignment confident of their ability and enthusiastic.

Figure 37.1 Consultant development matrix

Areas covered	Level			
	Initial	Advanced (project manager)	Managerial (partner)	Updating (all levels)
1. Substantive expertise				
1.1. Main area	★★★	★★	★	★
1.2 Context, environment	★★★	★★	★★	★
1.3 Related areas	★★★	★★	★	★
2. Consulting approach				
2.1 Basics, general principles	★★★	★		★
2.2 Methods and techniques	★★★	★★		★
2.3 Managing change	★★★	★★★	★★	★
2.4 Ethics, professionalism	★★★	★★	★★	★
3. Managing the process				
3.1 Marketing assignments	★★	★★★	★★	★
3.2 Managing assignments	★	★★★	★★	★
4. Managing the firm				
4.1 Practice management		★★	★★★	★
4.2 Practice development		★★	★★★	★

The overall objective quoted above can be broken down into four sub-objectives, as follows:

> 1. To ensure that the consultant can investigate an exiting situation and design improvements.

This requires the ability to gather information and analyse it critically, to identify all aspects of the problem, and then to design practical improvements using imagination and creativity.

> 2. To ensure that the consultant can develop a collaborative relationship with the client, gain acceptance of the proposed changes, and implement change satisfactorily.

The ability to make contacts with people easily, an understanding of factors stimulating or inhibiting change, a sound knowledge of the techniques of communication and persuasion, and good interaction with people during implementation, are vital parts of a consultant's armoury. They should be stressed and practised during initial training.

> 3. To ensure proficiency in the consultant's field or discipline.

This includes knowledge of the technical aspects of the field, some of which consultants may not have encountered in their previous career, and the ability to apply them to a client's problems. At the same time, consultants must be able to see the problems of their particular functional field in the broader context of an overall management strategy, and relate them to other functional areas and to the environment in which an enterprise operates.

> 4. To satisfy the management of the consulting firm that the consultant is capable of working independently and under pressure to the required standard.

It would be unrealistic to require new consultants to be able to tackle any difficult assignment immediately after training. Nevertheless, by the end of the initial training period they must have demonstrated their ability to handle a field assignment. At the same time, a systematic evaluation of the trainees' performance should give the firm enough information about the strengths and weaknesses of new colleagues for the team leader to be able to help them with proper guidance and coaching during the first assignments.

Patterns of initial training

The design of an initial training programme depends on many variables, including the specific needs of individual trainees and the resources and policies of the consulting firm. The practices of consulting firms vary. There is a broad range of initial training programmes, from precisely planned and structured programmes to totally informal training of undetermined duration. It is not the purpose of this chapter to prescribe one particular pattern for all conditions. There are, however, certain principles that should be reflected in any programme for new consultants, and also certain patterns that have given good results in various situations.

Individualization. New entrants have different backgrounds in terms of knowledge and experience, and different personal characteristics. There should not be a uniform initial training programme, although some elements of initial training will be given to every new consultant. We show below how the training programme can be individualized without becoming too difficult and expensive for the consulting firm to organize.

Practicality. Some aspects and methods of consulting can be explained and simulated during a course, but most of the training has to take the form of practice in carrying out the various steps of a consulting assignment and in interacting with clients, under the guidance of a senior consultant. The programme must include both observation of experienced consultants in action and direct execution of practical consulting tasks.

Stretching the trainees. The programme should demonstrate that consulting is demanding in time, effort and brainpower, so that trainees are under no illusion about the responsibilities and performance standards they have accepted in their newly chosen profession.

Length of programme. Although it could be argued that new consultants will need several years of experience to become fully competent and able to operate with a minimum of guidance and supervision, it would be impractical, and psychologically unsound, to maintain them in the category of trainees for too long. Assuming normal conditions of recruitment, the period of initial training should not exceed 6 to 12 months.

Coaching. The new consultants' learning will be strongly influenced by the nature of the work assigned to them and by the behaviour of their supervisors and other senior colleagues. Therefore professional firms in consulting and other fields make their team and practice leaders, partners and other seniors personally responsible for the development of younger and less experienced associates. Most of this development is done informally and in a one-to-one relationship, by discussing technical, behavioural and other relevant issues, helping the young professionals to cope with difficulties, and suggesting improvements in a friendly manner that does not imply any negative assessment.[8]

Basic components of the training programme

An ideal programme of initial training will have three basic components:

- training courses for new consultants;
- practical field training at client organizations;
- individual study.

A training course for new consultants will cover those aspects of consulting that have to be given to all trainees, and can be dealt with in a classroom situation, using a variety of training methods, as discussed in section 37.3. As a rule, this will be a full-time residential course and its total duration may be between 2 and 12 weeks. Large consulting firms can afford longer courses, and hold them at their own headquarters or training centres. Small firms may have to send their new members to an external course for management consultants, complementing it with short workshops dealing with their specific policies, work concepts and issues.

Field (on-the-job) training is intended to develop a range of practical skills, demonstrate consulting in action, and mould the trainees' attitudes towards their new profession on the basis of personal first-hand experience. It should provide opportunities and time for improving characteristics such as judgement, analytical and problem-solving ability, interpersonal relations, and ability to communicate and persuade. The training programme will also aim at improving other qualities such as self-confidence, integrity and independence. In planning this part of the training the consulting firm enjoys great flexibility, provided that it has enough clients willing to receive newly recruited consultants, and experienced consultants who have the time, ability and motivation to train and coach new colleagues.

Whether the time spent by the trainee at a client organization should be charged to the client is a delicate matter, which should be discussed frankly with clients, without imposing arrangements that they are reluctant to accept. In examining the curricula vitae of consultants proposed for an assignment, the client will easily identify new recruits with little or no consulting experience and will wish to be informed not only about these new consultants' capabilities and usefulness, but also about financial arrangements. While it is justifiable to ask clients to pay some fee if a trainee's work produces tangible results, it is neither reasonable nor fair to expect individual clients to bear directly the cost of training new consultants. This should be a general overhead in the consulting firm's costs. A compromise solution may be found by charging a reduced fee, or a fee for a part of the trainee's time. The same applies to the trainer's time – if the trainer is an operating consultant, time spent on guiding and coaching trainees should be foreseen, and not charged to the client.

Assignments for which the client will be charged a flat fee may provide a more favourable training ground than if the fees are time-based. The client who knows that the fee will remain the same irrespective of the number of consultants used and time spent will feel more comfortable about the use of inexperienced consultants in the project team.

Individual study is another component that provides for flexibility of training. A new consultant can fill some knowledge gaps by reading books and articles, final assignment reports, operating manuals and other documentation.

In an ideal situation these three components of the initial training may be combined and scheduled as follows:

- first (introductory) part of the course for new consultants (say between two and six weeks);
- field training (length as necessary and feasible);
- second part of formal training (say one to six weeks), including one or more specialized seminars or workshops on operating methods, and familiarization with technical services, people and documentation at the consulting firm's headquarters;

- field training continues as appropriate;
- no specific period is reserved for individual study – this will be done in parallel with the course and with field training (the consultant may have to be prepared for many hours of overtime).

A consulting firm may, however, find it impossible to follow this schedule for various practical reasons: the number of trainees may not warrant an in-house course, or the firm may only be able to afford a short introductory workshop for new entrants. The training task may thus become more difficult for everybody concerned and the new entrants will have to pick up much more through individual study and by observing colleagues at work.

The trainer's role

During recruitment and selection, new consultants meet senior people in the organization only for a short time. Thus the trainer is the first member of the organization whom new consultants get to know well. He or she sets an example of how a consultant behaves, and demonstrates how to achieve results largely without the authority to impose ideas. The trainer therefore plays an important part in developing the characteristics that differentiate consultants from managers, executives, accountants, auditors or researchers. Apart from instilling knowledge, the trainer sets the tone for new consultants in their work with clients, and helps them to identify with the consulting firm's philosophy and culture.

The head-office trainer is usually a senior person with wide experience of consulting and training. He or she has overall responsibility for the training of new consultants, including the programming of field training. He or she is in charge of the central training course for new consultants and will personally give a number of sessions in the course.

In a training course for consultant induction, each trainee should be viewed as an individual who will spend much of his or her time as the sole operating consultant on an assignment. Behaviour within the group and ability to join in the common cause should also be noted, as well as reactions to the problems and ideas discussed during the course. The trainer should not take a teacher-and-pupil attitude and the atmosphere in the course room should not be that of a schoolroom. This point may seem obvious, but trainers also have to learn to do their job and some may start in a rather pedantic way. A trainee should consider the trainer a good friend and counsellor on whom he or she can rely at any time for guidance and help.

Field trainers are operating consultants or team leaders working with clients. They are already practising in the field in which the new consultant will operate, and arrange for him or her to gradually take over a part of the assignment. They too must have training and coaching capabilities, be sympathetic to the needs of the new consultant, and be able to impart enthusiasm for working with a client. The field trainer develops a very special relationship with the new consultant. As the two of them will be spending some evenings together, a bond of friendship is usually forged, which may persist for many years after training is completed.

Evaluation of training

The progress of new consultants in training should be watched carefully by those in contact with them and a series of reports issued. The purpose is to ascertain whether the training is achieving its objectives, propose corrective measures (extension of the training programme, inclusion of new subjects for individual study, and the like), and gather information on the strengths and weaknesses of the trainees (this is invaluable to those who will supervise their first assignments). Needless to say, evaluation also helps to improve the training policies and practices of the consulting firm.

Many consulting firms use a system of confidential reports in which the trainers (both at head office and in the field) give their personal appraisal of the trainee. At least two reports are required: one at the end of the induction training course and one at the end of field training. Additional reports may be required if the initial training is broken down into several assignments involving different team leaders, or if the length of field training warrants interim progress reports.

The standard against which the new consultant is measured is the standard expected by the firm of operating consultants on their first assignment. The question to be answered is: "On present showing, will he or she be ready to operate at the end of the training?" Consistency of interpretation of the standard by the central trainer, field trainers and supervisors derives from their common experience and their knowledge of current operating requirements.

The trainers should review with the trainees how they are progressing, informally during work and training sessions, and in formal discussions held when an evaluation report is prepared. New consultants must be told about their strengths, weaknesses, and any other relevant aspects of their work. In addition to these discussions, senior members of the consulting organization should meet with new consultants during training. Apart from giving all the participants an opportunity to talk about the work and progress, these meetings ensure that new consultants become fully integrated members of the firm. They show that management is interested in the new consultants, aware of their progress, and making plans for their assignment after completion of training.

The importance of open criticism and frankness need hardly be stressed. Both the future effectiveness of the consulting organization, and the long-term career prospects of new consultants, depend on the excellent professional work of each individual. Any doubts about a new consultant's ability should not be hidden, but discussed with him or her and with the supervisors. If the doubts cannot be resolved by the end of the training programme, a decision is required on whether the new consultant stays or terminates employment. On balance, termination of employment at this early moment may be the better choice, both for the new consultant and for the organization. An early termination will be an exception if the initial selection of candidates is carried out in a competent manner.

At the end of the initial training programme it is useful to draw conclusions on the further training needs of the new consultant and on the best ways of meeting them (by giving preference to certain types of assignment at the beginning, by further individual study, by attaching the consultant to team leaders chosen for their particular qualities, etc.).

The design and execution of the training programme also require evaluation. Trainees may be asked to comment on the course in the usual way. These can give general or specific comments on the content of individual exercises and the performance of each trainer. Care is necessary to preserve confidentiality – trainees may be reluctant to openly criticize their current or potential future superiors. However, feedback to individual trainers can spur them to improve their sessions.

Comments and criticism may be obtained from senior consultants responsible for the early assignments. They may find the new consultants lacking in specific skills; these deficiencies may be due to omissions, or poor coverage of certain subjects, either in the initial head-office training course or during the field training. New consultants should also be asked, both during and after field training, whether they found the practical preparation for the first assignments adequate.

37.3 Training methods

Training-course methods

New consultants are trained using a variety of methods, with emphasis on participative methods and on those where the trainee can adjust the pace of learning to individual capabilities.

Subjects that involve mainly the imparting of knowledge may require some lectures, but these should be supplemented by discussions, practical exercises, case studies and other techniques. In many cases, lectures can be replaced by individual reading (e.g. on the origin and history of consulting, on types and specialization of consulting firms), or by audiovisual learning packages (e.g. videotapes or Internet-based learning material). Subjects involving skill improvement require techniques that permit practice. This can be done to some extent in a training course by using properly chosen learning situations and exercises. Experience with methods suitable for training in process consulting skills is summarized in box 37.2.

Case studies can introduce the new consultant to various consulting situations and provide good material for discussion; the consulting firm may be in a position to prepare its own case studies, or histories, based on experience from previous assignments. Appendix 6 provides suggestions on using the case method in consultant development and suggests some sources of suitable case material.

Practical exercises can lead the new consultant through common consulting practices, such as:

Box 37.2 Training in process consulting

Internal development programmes need to draw on knowledge in such fields as industrial sociology, political science, organizational behaviour, psychology, social psychology and interpersonal communication. But such programmes need to emphasize skill more than knowledge, through discussion and role-playing sessions in which the skills are acquired through practice, reflection, and experimentation. The discussion should not be about what the trainees *should know*, or even about what they *should do*, but about what they *are doing*, here and now, and about what they have done and will be doing, in specific interactions with members of a client organization. In other words, process-skill development sessions should primarily consist of open discussion among colleagues of specific client case situations, supplemented by role-plays of actual and desired consultant–client interactions. The sessions should be led by someone expert at facilitating this kind of experiential learning, who can bring to bear, when relevant, simple but powerful behavioural concepts to assist in understanding past events and to stimulate useful experimentation with new approaches.

The three most relevant skills to develop for an effective consulting process are, in my opinion: diagnosing behaviour, listening, and behaving authentically.

Diagnostic skill is developed by examining and discussing what is taking place within client organizations. These discussions develop hypotheses that can be tested in subsequent client contacts. In such discussions and experiments with different approaches, consultants may discover, perhaps to their discomfort, that effective diagnosis of behaviour is often in part an intuitive and not just a logical process.

Listening of a very special kind is an essential consulting process skill. Good consultants learn how to listen with understanding to what is meant as well as to what is said, to feelings as well as to facts, to what is hard to admit and not just easy to say. There is no way to develop this skill except by practising it, with the benefit of feedback from a friendly audience which has heard the same words and observed the same non-verbal signals. It is easy to tell consultants how they ought to listen and have them agree that this is desirable. But to help them to learn that they do not listen as well as they think, and then to produce a worthwhile improvement in this ability in practice, requires a series of carefully designed and effectively conducted workshop sessions. It does not happen all at once.

Behaving authentically needs to be seen as an equally necessary skill. Consultants need to be able to be themselves, to behave according to their own values, and sometimes to confront clients with unwelcome facts and opinions. Again, small group discussions and role-plays of actual experiences provide the best setting in which to develop the skill of understanding oneself as well as others, and of usefully and constructively expressing one's own point of view even when the other person may not want to hear it.

Author: Arthur Turner.

- effective speaking and persuasion;
- interviewing;
- analysing company accounts and preparing ratios;
- discussion leadership and control;
- written communication;
- methods charting and work measurement;
- designing systems and procedures.

Role-playing provides an excellent way of introducing consulting practice into learning situations. It takes place in a controlled situation, i.e. in a classroom, where mistakes are used to enhance learning and have no disastrous consequences. For example, as a large part of a consultant's work on assignment consists of presenting proposals to clients and their staff, it is useful to organize role-playing exercises in:

- interviewing staff to obtain facts about an assignment problem and find out about their expectations;
- dealing with awkward situations or complaints from staff about proposed changes;
- persuading members of the client's staff to accept a new method of operation;
- explaining to the client conclusions drawn from the financial reports;
- presenting an assignment report to the client;
- dealing with embarrassing questions from the client or members of his staff.

Role-playing exercises need to be realistic, and test the participants under conditions as near as possible to those found in everyday life. Feedback after the exercise is essential. This suggests four requirements:

- a trainee playing the part of a consultant;
- other trainees playing client or other roles;
- at least two trainees acting as observers, with a brief to watch for certain features of the players' behaviour;
- the preparation of thorough briefs for all participants.

Time should be allowed for briefing the role-players and observers, and for the absorption of the material including the preparation of any figures. After the role-playing, observers can comment and a general discussion should be held to identify lessons to be learned. Aids such as tape recorders or closed-circuit television may be used.

Field-training methods

In field training, the consultant learns mainly by doing practical diagnostic, problem-solving and project work in direct collaboration and interaction with other consultants and the client. As this is carried out in a real-life situation which may be very sensitive to errors, at the beginning the trainee will be guided and controlled by the trainer in more detail than might be necessary in other situations. It may not, however, be easy to find situations in which new consultants can practise a wide range of the techniques that should eventually make up their consulting kit.

Here again, feedback on what the consultant did and how he or she did it is an essential dimension of training. The team leader or supervisor acting as field trainer must provide this feedback, creating an atmosphere in which any aspect of work and behaviour can be openly discussed without embarrassing the new colleague.

Role-playing can be used to rehearse activities before the "live" show. In this form of role-playing, the new consultant and the trainer rehearse in the office or at home in the evening, and are able to anticipate snags.

In certain cases a complete real consulting project can be used as a training experience. This has been done in several courses for consultants, as well as in various types of course for managers and students of management. Such a simulation exercise can be very close to an actual situation. Yet the differences should not be lost from sight: if the client has agreed to a consulting project, but does not pay a normal fee for it, this may affect the participation and attitudes of the client staff when working with the trainee consultant.

37.4 Further training and development of consultants

In management consulting lifelong education is a must. This idea is not new. Many consultancy firms have gained and maintained their excellent reputation precisely because of their continual efforts to upgrade staff competence.

Principal directions of consultants' development

Most staff development activities in consulting firms fall under one or more of the following five areas.

Upgrading functional proficiency. Keeping abreast of developments and becoming more knowledgeable and competent in their own field together form the basis of operating consultants' further development. Many training and development activities in consulting firms are geared to this objective.

Mastering new fields. Consultants may learn new subjects complementary to their main field in order to broaden their ability to undertake assignments touching on several management functions, perhaps with a view to becoming all-round consultants, able to lead teams of mixed functional specialists, to act as advisers on general management problems, and to undertake diagnostic surveys of business companies and other organizations. Another reason for learning new subjects may be the consulting organization's intention to become active in new technical fields. Many consulting firms prefer to transfer their more dynamic consultants, familiar with the organization's philosophy and practices, to these new activities rather than staff them with new recruits.

Upgrading behavioural and process-consulting skills. Experience has amply demonstrated that the initial training of new consultants is just a first step in developing the know-how needed to perceive, diagnose, understand and influence human behaviour in organizations. Further training of all consultants (without exception) therefore deals with the "how" of management consulting as it relates to people, including effective client–consultant relations, the consultant's role in organizational change, and the process-consulting skills required for various situations.

Upgrading knowledge-sharing skills. Sharing knowledge is both an attitude and a skill. Many consultants need more and better training in working with information; searching for relevant information; assessing relevance and filtering information overload; identifying and recognizing new patterns and trends; structuring and formulating knowledge in ways that make it suitable for sharing and transfer; sharing information, experience and knowledge with colleagues; transferring knowledge to clients and working with clients to develop new knowledge; combining and harmonizing knowledge transfer with other consulting tasks and interventions, etc.[9]

Preparing for career development. This includes personal development needed for the positions of team leader, supervisor, division head, partner and other senior positions concerned with client relations, management and business expansion. Career advancement carries with it the need to use a broader approach and develop technical competence in several fields.

Organization and methods of further development

Certain features of consulting practice make further training and development difficult to organize. Typically, consultants working with one firm in the same discipline are geographically dispersed on individual assignments. To arrange a technical discussion among specialists may require a special organizational effort. Furthermore, the highly individualized character of many consulting assignments encourages consultants to become individualists, and this creates a constant problem in sharing work experiences with other colleagues.

Nevertheless, the profession also has many features that facilitate the consultant's development. A consultant's energy and time are much less absorbed by routine matters and established procedures than those of a manager in the same technical field. The consultant can approach every new assignment as a challenging exercise where innovation is both possible and desirable, and can thus refine his or her method almost continually. Consultants are never short of opportunities to apply ideas and suggestions found in the literature or other sources. Furthermore, consultants learn a great deal from their client organizations; to reinforce that learning they must compare, evaluate, generalize, conceptualize and try to apply a new, more effective approach to successive assignments. They have to remember that every client organization and every assignment is unique, and that past solutions cannot be mechanically applied to new situations.

Clearly, most of the learning from experience, including the consultants' own and their colleagues' experience, as well as the clients' experience, takes place on the job: it is learning by doing and by observing how others do. It should, however, be enhanced by other learning opportunities and approaches.

Professional guidance and coaching by senior consultants. Partners, supervising consultants and team leaders, among others, are generally responsible for the development of consultants who report to them. They provide guidance when assigning work, examining work progress and discussing solutions to be proposed to clients. Such discussions can easily be broadened to inform the operating consultants of experience from other assignments, or techniques used by colleagues. A major feature of coaching by senior consultants should be to help operating consultants to develop their personal qualities and communication skills. Informal discussions should be arranged within the assignment teams on experience gained from joint work, and used for staff development on a regular basis.

Workshops and conferences. Short workshops and conferences for professional staff are organized in many consulting firms. There may be an annual conference which deals with technical and methodological topics useful to all consultants, as well as policy and administrative matters. Workshops and seminars may be organized in functional divisions, on a regional basis, or in other ways. There are also various external seminars on management and consulting topics from which consultants might benefit. Such services are available from consultants' associations, management institutes, and in some countries also from private consultants who train other consultants.

Knowledge management. Consultant development is one of the main purposes of knowledge management in consulting and other professional firms. Learning is facilitated by, for example, easy access to relevant information and its sources, posting of and pointers to information of particular interest, internal bulletins and intranets, regular events for exchanging information and experience, and systematic debriefing following completed projects (see Chapter 34).

Reading. Consultants have to acquire the habit of reading the main business and professional periodicals, technical papers, important new publications and internal consulting reports relevant to their field.

Research and development assignments. Special project assignments, such as developing a new line of consulting, preparing an operating manual, or evaluating the methodology and results of comparable consulting assignments, are excellent learning opportunities for senior staff members.

Training others. One of the best methods of self-development is training other people. Consultants have many opportunities to do this: for the client's personnel during assignments, at the consulting firm's training centre, as supervisors of younger consultants during operating assignments, as part-time teachers at management institutes and schools, or as speakers at professional conferences.

Preparing for supervisory and managerial functions. Promotion to the role of supervisor usually takes place after several years in an operating role. Some experience of the role is gained by seeing seniors in action, and by guiding new consultant trainees. Training on promotion is usually quite short and provided by experienced seniors who are good trainers. Training may be given partly in formal sessions at head office and partly with experienced seniors in action. Head-office training and briefing require about three weeks, while coaching by an experienced senior may extend over some months. During this time the promoted consultant works largely alone, with only occasional guidance and advice from a more experienced colleague.

Planning and budgeting

The diversity of individual consultants' career paths and training needs, as well as the desire to be flexible in meeting current clients' requirements, make it difficult to plan staff development and to stick to what has been planned. Yet some planning is useful.

Some consulting firms use indicative standards showing the amount of formal training which, on average, a staff member would undergo in one calendar year: for example, between 40 and 60 hours of formal training. A corresponding budget can then be worked out, bearing in mind whether the training will be arranged internally or externally. As a rule, the cost of training per staff member will be higher than in many other sectors.

Individual planning is even more important. It is useful to establish training objectives that reflect career objectives, against which the consultant can measure his or her progress. In particular, such training objectives should be defined for the first years of operating, based on the evaluation made at the end of the initial training programme, and the subsequent periodical performance reviews. While some flexibility in deciding on participation in specific training events will always be required, training must not constantly be put off in order to cope with the current workload.

37.5 Motivation for consultant development

In consulting, more than in many other occupations, the individual bears the main responsibility for his or her own development. The consultant's professional development is above all self-development, and the results achieved will depend mainly on the person's ambition, initiative, determination, perseverance and intellectual capabilities. This is self-evident to the sole practitioner, who knows very well that he or she takes full responsibility for his or her own future. However, a member of a consulting firm working on jobs assigned by management can also show a great deal of initiative and interest in achieving career goals and training objectives, and can find a great many opportunities for improving competence. After all, if consulting is your career choice, you want to be sure that you control your career and that you will fare well in this rapidly changing sector. Self-development is a key to achieving this goal.

Most consultants understand that stopping learning makes them vulnerable, less interesting to clients and an easy target for competitors. Invariably, personal development and learning get high marks in consulting firms' priority concerns. To many consultants, learning is a vital need, a natural part of their lifestyle. There are, however, forces and constraints that can hamper consultant development quite seriously.

A consultant's natural desire to learn tends to wane if he or she sees that the firm is more interested in, and remunerates its staff better for, achieving short-term objectives such as high personal billing and bringing in new clients. In a similar vein, if the firm is keen to get more of any business, the consultant will be discouraged from looking for assignments that provide good opportunities for learning something new, but are more risky and difficult to negotiate or execute.

If promotion and pay clearly favour other criteria (e.g. seniority or higher management's personal preferences), this policy may have a negative effect on self-development. To see senior partners occupying the same positions for years and collecting the same pay cheques without any self-development or performance-improvement effort is demotivating, not only to younger consultants but also to other partners.

A poor choice of trainers can be equally damaging. This has happened in consulting firms where the trainers' jobs were given to those seniors who were not so good at dealing with clients or managing operations.

Most importantly, all professional firms stress that training and coaching the staff members assigned to them is a crucial responsibility of all professionals, including those in the highest management functions in the firm. In practice, however, many senior professionals devote all their time and know-how to firm management, business promotion and dealing personally with important clients. This tends to be encouraged by the compensation system, which may ignore, or allocate a small weight to, the senior consultants' contribution to the development of other staff members. If this has been the prevailing practice for years, it has probably turned into a cultural value. Senior professionals who remember that they "had to make it" without any help from their superiors often think that the next generation should be treated in the same way.

In summary, to be successful in consultant development, a consulting firm has to achieve coherence between policy statements, strategic objectives, resource allocation, current assignment management, organization of training and staff motivation at all levels, starting with the newly recruited trainees and ending with the firm's managing partners. Consultants must know what the policy is and must be encouraged to comply with this policy throughout their career.

37.6 Learning options available to sole practitioners

To survive and progress in their field, sole consulting practitioners need to continuously improve their competence. Human capital is the sole practitioner's most precious resource. However, a sole practitioner lacks the knowledge base, training resources, support and interaction with colleagues available in larger consultancies. Conversely, he or she enjoys more freedom and flexibility in choosing clients, moving to new fields of intervention, choosing what and when to learn, and deciding about his or her own future.

There are forces that discourage sole practitioners from spending time and money on self-development. Paradoxically, success and high earnings from current business are the most dangerous enemies. A consultant who is in great demand will be tempted to think that he or she has no reason to worry about future earnings.

Other consultants complain that they lack time for self-development, are too tired after a heavy working week, cannot concentrate on studying in hotel rooms, or must use every free moment to look for new business. These reasons sound quite realistic and understandable. Yet they cannot justify the lack of self-development in any profession.

If you are a sole practitioner, the following principal options are available to you.

Self-assessment

From time to time, or periodically and regularly if you find it easier (but at least once a year), take a short pause, sit back and think about your career path:

- Have you defined your life and professional goals?
- Are you getting closer to your goals?
- Are clients fully satisfied with your work?
- Are you satisfied with what you have been doing for your clients?
- What have you learned and applied since the last self-assessment?
- Do you feel tired, burned out and out of date?
- Have you once more continued to do the same without any perspective and further learning?

When assessing motivation for learning and self-development, it is essential to be honest. Ambitious professional goals and a strong will to learn go hand in hand:

- Are you motivated enough to work hard for your personal development and professional future?
- Do you want to be one of the best experts in your field or are you merely looking for regular income and survival in the business?

Networking

In the absence of the professional environment and resources of a large firm, a single practitioner can draw a lot of benefit from networking with other professionals who have similar concerns.

Informal contacts with other consultants and managers are the simplest form of networking. Association work comes next. Associations are a useful source of contacts, information and learning opportunities. An active participant in an association can suggest and help to start new association activities and recommend topics as themes for meetings, committees and workshops.

Business alliances with other independent professionals can be helpful not only for finding new work and delivering projects that exceed the possibilities of one consultant, but also for exchanging experience and learning from others.

There is no networking without reciprocity: while you want to learn from others, they are keen to learn from you. They will give if you give.

Looking for technically challenging assignments

Learning is encouraged and facilitated if the consultant keeps looking for assignments that are not a mere repetition of work done many times before. This, of course, is more easily said than done if new business is scarce. Yet it is an objective that can be pursued as a matter of deliberate personal choice.

Formal training opportunities

Short seminars and workshops are useful forums where sole practitioners can update and widen their knowledge of management and business topics or consulting approaches. Careful selection is required in order to avoid losing time and money in training events that, because of their purpose and quality, are not suited for consultants. Training opportunities are available from some consulting institutes and associations, which also help consultants to select suitable courses elsewhere. For example, the United Kingdom Institute of Management Consultancy publishes a list of approved training providers and courses suitable for consultants at various points of their careers. Both providers and courses are approved and listed if they meet set criteria of relevance and quality.[10]

Preparing for certification

In a number of countries, professional institutes provide voluntary certification of management consultants (see section 6.4). Preparing oneself for certification may be a good opportunity for studying new literature on consulting and reading about topics not usually handled in everyday work, or participating in a course specially designed to prepare consultants for certification.

[1] E. M. Shays: "Learning must be a life-long job for consultants", in *Journal of Management Consulting* (Milwaukee, WI), Vol. 1, No. 2, 1983.

[2] A number of university courses addressed to consultants or graduate students in the United States and other countries have been based on this guide. It is also useful to refer to materials produced by consultants' associations and institutes. In 1989, the Association of Management Consulting Firms (AMCF) in the United States published *Professional profile of management consultants: A body of expertise, skills and attributes*, and *Management consulting: A model course*. This model course is intended for university programmes in consulting, but provides useful guidance for other consultant training courses. The International Council of Management Consulting Institutes (ICMCI) has compiled a *Common body of knowledge for management consultants* (see www.icmci.com, visited on 4 Apr. 2002).

[3] R. E. Boyatzis: *The competent manager: A model for effective performance* (New York, Wiley, 1982), and M. Kubr and J. Prokopenko: *Diagnosing management training and development needs: Concepts and techniques*, Management Development Series No. 27 (Geneva, ILO, 1989).

[4] Boyatzis, op. cit., pp. 28–29.

[5] The term "knowledge" is used here in a narrower sense than in knowledge management (cf. Chapters 1 and 19).

[6] See G. M. Bellman: *Getting things done when you are not in charge* (San Francisco, CA, Berrett-Koehler, 1992).

[7] See www.icmci.com.

[8] Useful suggestions on leading and coaching professional workers are in P. J. McKenna and G. J. Riskin: *Herding cats: A handbook for managing partners and practice group leaders* (Edmonton, The Institute for Best Management Practices, 1995).

[9] See also R. Dawson: *Developing knowledge-based client relationships: The future of professional services* (Boston, MA, Butterworth-Heinemann, 2000), Ch. 10.

[10] See www.imc.co.uk, visited on 4 Apr. 2002.

PREPARING FOR THE FUTURE 38

What can management consultants do to be prepared for the future, when we know that change is the only constant and that our predictions of the future will at best be inaccurate and at worst completely wrong? How important will e-business really be? What will be the political situation and business strength of the Far East? How will international financial markets be regulated in ten years' time? It would be useful to know the answers to these and similar questions, if not with certainty, then at least with a fair degree of probability. Consultants and other professionals alike could thus prepare for the future, with poise and without overrating passing fads, while attending to current business and doing their best to meet their clients' current needs. This, however, is a scenario of dreams. In the economic and business reality of today, there are some broad and long-term trends that are irreversible and most consultants are aware of them. But developments can be slower or faster than expected, and can take many deviations that for some time go against the long-term trends. There will be many surprises even for those who try to be forward-looking and feel that they are well informed.

The changes that have taken place during recent decades have demonstrated amply that it is not possible to prepare for the future in any simple and conventional way, by extrapolating current trends. There is always a degree of risk in choosing among probable future scenarios. There is also risk in learning and one might well spend a lot of time and resources on developing knowledge and skills for which there will be little demand in a few years. Yet we hear again and again that the future belongs to those who are best prepared for it and who can see and take the new opportunities more quickly than others. How can we cope with this dilemma? How do consultants stay fit and avoid being bypassed by events and surpassed by competitors?

In this chapter, we have chosen not to review and comment on all plausible developments that may affect consulting in future years. Many of them have been mentioned in the previous chapters, have been reviewed in literature,[1] and are regularly debated at consultants' conferences. We prefer therefore to point out attitudes and patterns of behaviour that any individual consultant or firm can adopt that will help them to cope with future events for which they will be largely unprepared. Many readers are probably aware of these principles and may already be applying them purposefully or intuitively.

38.1 Your market

The thrust of what a consulting firm can do for its clients' and its own future is to be alert to the changes occurring in the consulting market. This means the changes that have already taken place and to which many firms have probably started to react, as well as emerging changes that may be hardly perceptible, and changes that are predicted but not yet certain.

The principal long-term change, which has already generated important demand for consulting in the past decade and will continue to do so for many more years, is the shift to an information and knowledge-based economy. Firms active in all productive and non-productive sectors, including those in the IT sector themselves, are less and less capable of following all the developments that may affect their business, and maintaining up-to-date capabilities for making choices and decisions concerning their markets, strategies, alliances, customer relationships, logistics, financing, intellectual capital and its protection, effective management and control systems, outsourcing, productivity improvement, and so on. Hence they are turning to external sources of expertise, in particular to management, business and IT consultants.

A common challenge faced by firms in all sectors concerns the Internet and e-business: How important is it really to them? How deeply will firms be affected? How should the Internet and e-business be reflected in corporate strategy? How should physical and virtual processes in the value chain complement and reinforce each other? What pitfalls and inefficiencies are to be avoided? What lessons must be drawn from recent experience? Who can provide the best help? Even very large industrial and service concerns have to be selective in deciding about their core activities and strategies and need to purchase a great amount of knowledge, know-how and expertise from external sources. They need consultants and other professional service providers now and they will need them even more in the future. This is also the main reason why outsourcing has been progressing so rapidly as to become a major source of income for large consultancies in management and IT.[2]

How far can this go and where will it stop? It is difficult to say, but it is possible to visualize extreme scenarios in which the totality, or a very large portion, of the management function is outsourced to external management-cum-IT service providers, while the client provides the basic business directions, resources and corporate governance. This is already happening in contexts where consultants are used for managing turnarounds, or company management is subcontracted to them for prolonged periods by firms in difficulties. A reverse trend can also be seen, however: insourcing from consultants and other professional service

Box 38.1 Change in the consulting business

The way to change a management consulting business is to stay focused on your market. The key success factor, the only way to survive, is to stay very very close to what is in the minds of the managers you are dealing with... What I have learned over the last year is that you might have thousands of people organized to deal with the big projects but if it is not what clients want to buy, you can forget it...

Last year we were being attacked by "little animals" that hadn't existed before, with exotic names, and they did not just have exotic names but they behaved in an odd way... At first we were really shaken because these people were claiming to be the ones actually shaping the business in the United States. As a manager of a consulting firm I was pretty scared by all that and we were asking ourselves how we were going to get out of this mess, collectively and personally too. All these new jobs were not offered to us. As managers we were far too expensive for these little start-ups, so they were the ones who were going to have all the benefits of the outsider and they were going to have a lot more fun in the process.

A year later where are we? Most of the competitors who really scared us last year have practically disappeared. Most of them could not cope with classic delivery problems. The big companies, like Cap Gemini, Accenture and so on, were a bit slow to make their move but once they made it they were difficult to beat... It is amazing what new activities exist now. Personally I manage an activity I knew nothing about a year ago. The speed and agility with which these big firms have evolved in the course of last year is really something worth studying.

We have learned quite a few things. Above all, that in the Internet area strategy and technology are completely interdependent. As someone who grew up in a strategy environment, I dare say that without IT we would not go very far in our area. Basically the technology in my area defines the strategy... Business-to-business marketplaces are today the most challenging area in the field of strategy: how do you get competing firms to cooperate in this area? This is as important as outsourcing... We need to think about transition issues: how to move from one world, where these two things were completely separate, to a world where integration is much more important.

Of course, consulting companies will survive the Internet. The best consultants will have the modesty to recognize that they don't know all the answers, but they can deal with the issues that are foremost in the minds of the clients. And they can demonstrate it by results.

Author: Claude Hoffmann, Executive Director of B2B Market Place, Cap Gemini Ernst & Young, addressing a consultants' conference in Lyons, March 2001.

providers. Clients have already started to question the wisdom of overdependence on external sources of knowledge and experience in preparing strategic and operational decisions and running or restructuring important business processes. The e-business euphoria of 1999–2000 and its sudden death proved to be a useful lesson to businesses that were relying excessively on enthusiastic but inexperienced and sometimes fairly pushy "e-consultants".

In any event, major market trends and forces will continue to shape and reshape the consulting market and, in the information economy, powerful forces will fuel the growth of demand for consulting. These include globalization and the need to address seriously some of its negative consequences and unresolved problems, the impact of demographic changes, migration trends, the emergence of new markets, the interaction of different cultures, changing consumer criteria and priorities, radical changes and small shifts in global and regional geopolitics, new and more powerful communication technologies and networks, to name a few. Some consultancies have already worked with governments and large multinational businesses to research, monitor, shape or mitigate even some of these fundamental development trends. However, more and more businesses will be affected by developments that in the past looked remote and even irrelevant to them.

The consulting sector also faces trends and forces whose origin can be traced to research, entrepreneurship and strategic options of consulting or IT firms themselves. Consultants are inventors and creators of their own markets and their own future, probably more so than other professionals. The demand for many current consulting services and products exists thanks to some consultants who invented, structured, packaged, sold and delivered such services to certain clients, thus whetting other clients' appetite, and inciting other consultants to copy and try to improve these services, or present them under different labels. For example, the current trend to outsourcing is being shaped by IT and management service providers working on software for particular activities and processes and for systems integration. Integrated and more user-friendly and easy-to-apply software packages will not only become a new commodity; they will make redundant the services of many consultants who currently advise businesses on software selection, purchasing, adaptation, upgrading, compatibility, coordination and integration. Management and IT consultants have to swim with the stream, looking for new issues where clients need and appreciate help – as engineering and work study consultants had to do when production automation started to embrace and integrate whole processes rather than single operations in process and manufacturing industries.

Peter Drucker's words are as true today as they were when written 20 years ago: "The management consultant is not only a major part of the practice of management. He has been, above all, central to the development of the theory, the discipline and the profession of management."[3] Yet some consultants feel that they are not really concerned with this role of pathfinder and creator of new responses to their clients' problems and new business opportunities. They feel that only very large consultancies with huge professional and financial resources, and a small number of "management gurus", can aspire to such a role. They consider that most consultants can be followers and copiers at best, and will only be picking the leftovers anyhow. Experience points to the contrary. There is no such thing as a market divided, dominated and blocked once and for all. It is well known that even IBM's position was weakened for several years by the advent of the personal computer, the importance and impact of which were underestimated by IBM's management. Currently, even in the IT software business dominated by large players such as Microsoft, IBM, Oracle or SAP, we can see that there is great scope for smaller inventive players, not only in very specific business applications, but also in the basic and generic operating systems underlying the Internet, as demonstrated by open-source software such as Linux, and by new applications addressing issues for which even the large software developers may be short of expertise, staff and sometimes even ideas.

Advancing commodification of consulting and IT services, and of knowledge transfer more generally, is a trend that needs close monitoring. Many consultants will face strategic decisions with far-reaching implications for their firms' profiles and the development of their personal competencies. As more and more systems for planning, record-keeping, control, customer relationships, supply management, diagnosis, benchmarking and learning become standardized, structured, packaged and available for wide use as computer software, guides, manuals, checklists, or other self-help and do-it-yourself tools, clients will increasingly be in a position to purchase these products off the shelf and perform themselves many tasks for which they used to turn to consultants. The question will then be: what is left for a consultant who is not a major producer of commodified products and services? It may be futile to compete with the producers of such services unless you are in a position to create, and also to sell, better, more attractive or very special products. Recent experience tends to demonstrate that this will always be possible, though not for everyone since commodified products will increasingly require extensive research and development, upfront investment and intensive marketing.

However, commodification of consulting and IT products has limits and will never deprive consultants of all opportunities to seek creative solutions to their clients' unique problems. Management cannot be reduced to installing and operating computerized systems, however promising and user-friendly they may appear to be. In respect of standard products that will be available to managers in growing numbers, consultants will be needed to help with assessment, selection, adaptation, application, training, and so on. Sophisticated clients will not necessarily welcome products that have been sold to thousands of different businesses as "the" solution. There will continue to be a vast array of choices, problems and opportunities faced by management in running businesses and other organizations, where information technologies will be applied as a routine, but professional judgement and initiative will still be needed to make and implement decisions, to innovate, and to react better and more quickly and efficiently than competitors.

Many of the problems and opportunities will concern the human and social side of the enterprise, which will always be affected by a wide range of factors, many of them emotional, irrational, cultural and unpredictable and which do not lend themselves to standard packaged solutions. Consultants who have started seeking the remedies to all clients' problems in sophisticated systems and technologies will need to re-learn some old truths about business and people. People will make the difference even in the Internet and knowledge-economy era, but only in companies where managers and leaders care for people and understand how to motivate, inspire and develop them. Human resources and human capital will constitute a challenging consulting market in any period, even when qualified staff appear to be abundant and many companies seek to cut expenses by investing less in people.

Many challenges faced by companies will reflect changes in the external environment, to which companies have to adapt and which are mostly outside their control, but which can often be anticipated and analysed and to which an endless range of new responses can be found by innovative managers and consultants. Consultants are already helping clients to cope with many new issues requiring creative and innovative responses consistent with the clients' external and internal environments. Examples include the social role and responsibility of business, corporate governance, human capital management and development, education and learning, knowledge management and knowledge-sharing, using emotional intelligence, networking and alliances, providing management expertise to organizations of civic society and voluntary social services, coping with new roles of public administration and searching for efficiency in public services, and e-government. Some of these issues have been somewhat overlooked or viewed as less important or less pressing during the "new economy" euphoria of the late 1990s, but since then the harsh economic and social reality has returned to the forefront of attention and no business can ignore it.

Consultants will also have to cope, and help clients cope, with changes that are difficult if not impossible to anticipate, including crises and natural or manmade disasters. The events of 11 September 2001, and the subsequent deterioration of the political and business climates, caught many companies unprepared not only for a disaster of unprecedented magnitude (against which it was virtually impossible to plan adequate protective measures or get full insurance), but for any major crisis. These events showed the importance of risk and crisis management, contingency and business continuity planning, leadership, courage and responsibility in difficult times, security, insurance and reinsurance, disaster recovery management, and other fields and measures usually regarded as a luxury and a financial burden when business "goes as usual". Companies worldwide are increasingly looking for expert advice and help with these concerns, which are not entirely new, but currently require new approaches and resources.

In summary, there are signs that we may be witnessing a fairly deep polarization of two major strands of consulting:

- one concerned with the creation of increasingly standardized and commodified, and in most cases also computerized and Internet-based, systems and tools and their dissemination to large numbers of clients (which may no longer be called consulting);

- one helping managers to cope with new, changing and often hardly predictable trends, situations and challenges, that concern various dimensions of businesses and other organizations and their interface with the economic, social, institutional, political and other environments (the core of consulting).

It may well happen that the first strand will turn out to be an essentially defensive use of consulting services and products, since it will provide largely affordable services and tools that anyone can easily acquire, and indeed will have to acquire in order to stay competitive. Conversely, the second strain will be predominantly offensive, forward-looking, continuously seeking new and non-standard responses to new challenges and aiming to provide clients with a competitive advantage. In practice this polarization may not be so absolute and both strands will be needed by clients in various combinations.

Consulting firms, then, will have to choose between the two strands, or make a deliberate decision to be in both, with all the implications for strategic positioning, staff profiles, consulting style, and management of the firm. Not all consultants will be able to choose freely, since it will be impossible to ignore existing competition and market segmentation. The freedom of decision will also be constrained by the firm's own culture, competencies and other resources.

An equally important market choice concerns the sort of clients for whom the consulting firm works. Large professional service firms have always preferred large clients and large contracts, but over the past decade this inclination has become even stronger. This segment of the market cannot, however, maintain a two-digit growth rate for ever, especially when new application software, outsourcing, systems integration and commodification will take some work away from the consultants and also result in price reductions. It will be important for consulting firms of all sizes, but small and medium-sized consultancies above all, to find ways and approaches that make them more accessible and attractive to small clients. In the small-business sector in any country, but in transitional and developing economies in particular, the use of external expert services has usually been confined to accounting. At present, small firms can buy many standard software programs and outsource business processes and functions. This, however, is only a partial remedy to their problems. Many of them are disoriented and lack resources for choosing and implementing the most appropriate IT solutions. Their use of e-commerce is limited to poorly designed and inefficient Web sites and they are unable to fully understand and exploit all the opportunities created by deregulation, opening of public markets, falling trade barriers, changing consumer behaviour, networking with large firms and other small businesses, and the Internet in particular.

In the highly competitive consulting markets, small and medium-sized consultancies will also have the tremendous weight of advertising against them. To conquer the markets, large consultancies use publicity and spare no resources to put their current and potential clients in the right mood, create and solidify emotional links with clients in addition to technical links, suggest to clients that looking for their brand is equal to going for the best expertise, and make the clients feel that by not using their services the clients' businesses are being deprived of something special. Powerful advertising tools are too costly to be used by small and new consultants looking for new clients. Thus advertising serves mainly to strengthen the position of a small group of already very powerful and successful players, since they are the only ones who can afford enough of it to make an impact, when in fact they need it least. One can only hope that the growing sophistication of clients will mean that they do not believe everything in the advertising that some consultancies have been producing.

Of course, publicity and advertising are standard and perfectly correct tools for marketing and promoting professional services, including consulting. The question is how they are used. The limits of professionalism and taste have been reached, and probably crossed, in some cases, thus shifting the balance between the professional and commercial sides of consulting towards the commercial. Some consultants do not hesitate to promise the moon to potential clients. Writing about the Big Six and the changes in their attitudes since the 1980s, Mark Stevens pointed out that "for generations, members of these huge influential practices considered themselves professionals who happened to be in business. But beginning in the 1980s, this view flip-flopped: increasingly they saw themselves as businessmen who happened to be professionals. The distinction is critical."[4] The same could be written today about quite a few firms in consulting and other professions.

38.2 Your profession

The comment by Mark Stevens may be regarded as irrelevant and unfair by some professionals. They will argue that, in their firms, there has never been the slightest danger of misrepresentation, conflict of interest or sacrificing of clients' interests and service quality to earnings and profits. Yet it is useful to keep constantly in mind the delicate balance between professional and commercial objectives in operating any professional firm and planning its future.

The current international climate in business and society is most favourable to those who provide business- and management-related professional services. As mentioned elsewhere, there are more and more issues in which industrial and service firms, governments and even social and voluntary not-for-profit organizations will need advice and help from independent professionals. The trend towards treating knowledge as a commodity and an object of business is fairly pronounced, although in some fields the limits to trading in knowledge and making profit from it have yet to be negotiated, fine-tuned and codified by legal texts and ethical rules.

However, the future will belong to true professionals, not to instant experts willing to promise and sell anything to uninformed clients without worrying about the outcome. Professional culture and responsibility are not dead concepts and if in some professional firms they have given way to the get-rich-quick culture, these firms would be well advised to reconsider their long-term objectives and value systems. The professional service sector enjoys considerable clout with business and government clients, who recognize it as a source of useful knowledge and experience that they themselves lack. More and more clients realize that, to stay competitive and meet the expectations of their own stakeholders, they must buy and apply this knowledge. It would be a great disservice to the consulting profession if this advantageous position should be wasted because of some consultants who accept assignments they are not qualified for, or leave clients with costly systems that will never attain the promised parameters.

Balancing the professional and the commercial sides of consulting, or any other professional service, is an extremely delicate issue when demand for services is high, change fast, time pressure strong, competition severe but not always orthodox in its approach, markets liberal and temptation to reduce standards difficult to resist. Yet from a long-term perspective there is no alternative.

Profound and far-reaching structural changes in the professional service sectors have commenced and their end is not in sight.[5] The partition and dismantling of the largest accounting and other professional service empires is on the way. Some of these firms are facing a crisis of credibility, confidence and even identity. Simultaneously, new integrated and multiservice giants are being created through acquisitions of management consultancies by IT service firms, or vice versa. Further spectacular changes can be expected and some may be very surprising. Where there are minimal legal and regulatory barriers, anyone can acquire an established professional service firm, especially if that firm has been restructured as a joint stock company and its shares are traded on the stock markets. Some mergers and acquisitions may create new kinds of innovative providers integrated along the value chain, combing specific sector products or services with IT, business, management, and other professional systems and services. Conversely, other mergers and acquisitions may be opportunistic, creating clumsy conglomerates and having a short life.

Where is the client in this process? Serving clients' evolving interests in the best and most effective ways is the credo of all consultants. However, in referring to clients and their interests, many consultants' mission statements and advertisements contain a mix of rhetoric and reality. Professional firms that merge, split, buy other firms, or expand operations with sometimes astronomic speed will always argue that it is in their clients' interest, and point to benefits, such as better service for global clients, systems integration, caring for cultural diversity, quality assurance, or getting closer and giving a faster response to the client. And they will be right – from a certain perspective and within certain limits. Other issues may be overlooked or suppressed, such as growing conflict of interests and loss of objectivity, painful and uncertain harmonization of incompatible cultures, the danger of turning a personalized and fine professional service into an anonymous mass-market process, and the levelling – and in some instances even lowering – of individual consultant competencies.

Clients, however, are not passive observers of the consulting scene. They have become more sophisticated in selecting and using consultants. More and more of them are able to insist on getting tangible and measurable results from their consultants, and value for money. Consultant–client collaboration and transfer of knowledge are already quite intensive in many assignments and will become more intensive and versatile in the future. These relationships will increasingly influence the development of consulting and other professions alike. Clients have a role in shaping the professions. In restructuring and redesigning their services and products, and adopting new business models, consultants will have to listen more to clients, dialogue with them, give priority to client-friendly models and approaches, and scrupulously avoid behaviour that irritates and repulses clients. After all, consulting and other professional services can only exist if there are clients who believe in their value, and are willing to pay for them.

38.3 Your self-development

A consultant who wants to invest in self-develoment to prepare for the future can seek inspiration in the overall development and structural changes of the markets for professional services and of the professions themselves. He or she will need to keep abreast of developments, not only in management consulting, but in IT and other professional and business services. A broad understanding of the ongoing and expected changes in technology, business and society is necessary. An ability to view narrow and special technical issues from a wider business and societal perspective has traditionally been a major asset of consulting professionals, and remains important, not only to the generalist but also to the specialist. Without this ability, management consultants would be IT, quality or other systems technicians, probably providing a useful technical service within narrow limits, but missing the view of the total enterprise and its complex human and business fabric.

Against this background, you can assess both your current competencies and your future potential. Being a consultant, you are probably objective, critical and realistic enough in judging yourself. You are able to compare and judge, using the right benchmarks. You are aware of your strengths and weaknesses. Discussing these issues with colleagues and with management helps, but eventually every consultant has to take full responsibility for decisions on his or her future, especially if considerable time and energy are to be invested in learning, and strong personal commitment will be necessary. This is not only every consultant's right, but also a matter of a developed sense of responsibility to oneself, the clients, the firm and the whole profession. Not only organizations need to "reinvent themselves"; management and business consultants have to reinvent themselves even more courageously and more frequently than any of their clients.

An individual's vision of the future and of personal capabilities and goals may not always coincide with that of his or her firm. In some firms, there is a discrepancy between policy statements on learning and development, and current reality. The firm may realize that its future depends on the skills of its staff remaining up to date. But it may strongly prioritize current income-generating client work, even if this is routine and repetitive and offers no learning opportunities to the consultants. These issues need to be discussed, and solutions adopted and implemented. If management does not take the initiative and is reluctant to invest in human capital, individual consultants employed by the firm should not hesitate to do so. After all, an individual, not the firm, is the primary owner of his or her intellectual capital.

38.4 Conclusion

Consulting to management is a fascinating profession. While consultants may feel threatened and constrained by competition from other service sectors, new regulations and various other forces, new trends and changes keep opening new horizons for them. Currently the main business, social, technological and other trends are creating more opportunities and more demand for consulting than in the past. In professional service sectors we have witnessed a great deal of restructuring, and further structural changes are likely to be forthcoming, as indicated by the performance record, growth pattern, restructuring experience, visibility and social prestige of leading consulting firms. Consulting is in a delicate equilibrium between the professional service approach and objectives, and the commercial approach and objectives, in all respects, including strategy, firm management, individual assignment design and execution, knowledge-sharing with clients and people development. The leading consultants have always exhibited a remarkable capacity to understand and maintain this equilibrium, restore it when it is disrupted, adapt to the changing needs of their clients, and pursue excellence both professionally and as businesses. This capacity is the best safeguard of the future of consulting.

---

[1] See, e.g., F. Czerniawska: *Management consultancy in the 21st century* (Basingstoke, Hampshire, Macmillan, 1999), and R. Dawson: *Developing knowledge-based client relationships: The future of professional services* (Boston, MA, Butterworth-Heinemann, 2000). See also *E-business consulting: After the shakeout*; *The global consulting marketplace: Key data, forecasts & trends*; and other reports on the consulting industry produced by the Kennedy Information Research Group and available from Kennedy Information.

[2] It is useful to follow sources focused on recent development and trends, such as M. Porter: "Strategy and the Internet", in *Harvard Business Review*, Mar. 2001, pp. 62–78; J. Hagel and J. Seely Brown: "Your next IT strategy", ibid., Oct. 2001, pp. 105–113; "Ten smart moves – corporate IT that's worth a closer look", at www.ebusinessforum.com of the Economist Intelligence Unit, 7 Dec. 2001; or "How about now? A survey of the real-time economy", in *The Economist*, 2 Feb. 2002.

[3] P. Drucker: "Why management consultants?", in *Perspectives* No. 234 (Boston, MA, The Boston Consulting Group, 1981).

[4] M. Stevens: *The Big Six: The selling out of America's top accounting firms* (New York, Simon & Schuster, 1991), p. 22.

[5] See also "Spoilt for choice" (special report on professional service firms), in *The Economist*, 7 July 2001.

APPENDICES

APPENDIX 1

THE CLIENT'S TEN COMMANDMENTS (CHOOSING AND USING CONSULTANTS)

If you are a user of management consulting services, or a potential user, this appendix is for you. The Ten Commandments summarize, in telegraphic form, the critical points of which you need to be aware. If you are a consultant, the Ten Commandments can help you to understand better your client's approach and main concerns. Remember: consulting produces good results if consultants are competent in serving clients and clients in using consultants.

1. **Learn about consulting and consultants**
2. **Define your problem and look for opportunities**
3. **Define your purpose**
4. **Choose the right consultant**
5. **Develop a joint programme**
6. **Cooperate actively with your consultant**
7. **Involve the consultant in implementation**
8. **Monitor progress**
9. **Evaluate the results and the consultant**
10. **Beware of dependence on consultants**

Now, let us look at the meaning of each Commandment.

1. Learn about consulting and consultants

Management consulting is a young, dynamic and rapidly developing profession. It has changed considerably with the advent of the Internet and e-business. You can be sure that you will find a consultant for any business or management problem you face. But who are these consultants? How do they work? Are they really as good as one often hears? You want to get replies to these questions. Don't wait until the last moment before recruiting a consultant. Find out about consulting and consultants, and try to become a well-informed client who knows the management and business consulting scene.

- This book can give you a lot of information. It describes how consultants operate, market their services, charge for services and assure quality. Of course, there are other publications and sources of information on consulting. A great amount of relevant information is available through the Web (see Appendix 3).
- There are publications specifically on choosing and using consultants. The ILO has published a companion volume to this book under the title *How to select and use consultants: A client's guide*. Brief guides to selecting consultants are available from many consultants' associations.
- Reading a book or retrieving information from Web sites is not enough. Speak with business friends, screen management and business periodicals, attend meetings of management or consultants' associations and ask for information, be alert to news on developments in consulting and other professional services to management.
- Criticizing consultants is very fashionable. Make sure that you are informed about such criticism and the flaws that do occur in consulting (and other professional services), but don't judge the value of consulting on the basis of sensational press articles or books.
- It is essential to know who is who. Try to collect information on consultants (firms and individuals) who may interest you. What is their speciality and approach? For whom have they worked? How do they share know-how with clients? What is their reputation? Are their fees within your reach?

2. Define your problem and look for opportunities

The purpose of consulting is to help clients to solve their management and business problems. If you have no problem, you do not need a consultant. Therefore you should be convinced that your organization has a problem that warrants a consulting assignment.

- Define your problem as precisely as possible. What is or could go wrong? What do you want to improve? Why do you need a consultant? Are you sure that you and your own people cannot solve the problem?
- Look for new opportunities. Rather than correcting past shortcomings and errors, a consultant may help you to develop new business, tackle new markets, exploit new technologies, mobilize new resources and increase your competitive edge.
- If the idea of using a consultant comes from members of your staff who seek your approval, ask them to be explicit and precise in defining the problem and the reasons. Do not accept superficial and vague justification.
- Keep the definition of your problem open. The consultant will in any case make his or her own diagnosis, and may show that your original definition was biased, narrow or incomplete. The final definition of the problem must be agreed by both the client and the consultant.

3. Define your purpose

The task of the consultancy will be to help in solving your problem, but you should look at your problem from a wider perspective. What will be the purpose of resolving the problem? What do you want to achieve? What will your organization gain? Where do you want to get to and what effort are you prepared to make?

Your purposes should be formulated as specific objectives of the consultancy: action (operational) objectives and learning objectives.

- Remember that consultants can intervene in various ways. Consider what you want from the consultant in planning and implementing changes in your organization. Information that you lack? Expert advice on your decisions? A new information system? An improved organizational climate? Increased production and sales? Higher profitability? Each of these choices will require a different intervention method and a different volume of consulting services. Your action objectives will reflect your choice.
- Your learning objectives are equally if not more important. It has been said many times that effective consulting helps clients to learn from their own and the consultant's experience. Define what you want to learn and how you would like to learn during the assignment. This will be your learning objective.
- Write your objectives down, trying to be as precise as possible. Be flexible and be prepared to redefine these objectives after having spoken with your consultant or received his or her proposals, and even after the work has started. Your consultant may help to redefine your objectives in your own interest.

4. Choose the right consultant

To choose the right consultant is essential, but it is not an easy matter. It requires information, an effective selection procedure, skill in assessing consultants, and patience. Some risk is always involved, but a proper approach to selection will minimize this risk. Your aim is to get the right consultant for your organization and the kind of problem you have. You and the consultant will have to understand and trust each other, and enjoy working together. Remember: it is you who is choosing the consultant, not the consultant who is choosing you.

- Take the choice of a consultant very seriously. Never recruit "someone who just happens to be around" and is easily available, or who has just sent you a flattering letter or an elegant publicity brochure, unless you are sure that he or she is the ideal choice.
- Use shortlists of consultants, carefully screen candidates to be put on the shortlist, get information on their capabilities, clients and past assignments, check leads and references given to you by business associates, colleagues, consultants' and management associations, friends, and any other source.
- Be cautious in using consultants who claim that they can do anything and are vague and evasive when asked about their approach, clients and work performed. A true professional would never pretend to be an expert in all fields.
- Try to apply a rigorous (though not rigid and bureaucratic) selection procedure, including rating, comparing and evaluating consultants' proposals and qualifications. Make the choice as objective as possible to try to minimize the risk of errors. Improve the procedure on the basis of experience.

- Never give a major assignment to an unknown consultant. If possible, test new consultants on small and short jobs. Do not pay an unknown consultant an advance for future work.
- Be sure that you choose not only the consulting firm, but also the individual consultants employed by the firm (who may not be the people who came to propose the assignment to you). The consultants have to have personalities and technical skills that match your organization.
- Make sure that the consultant of your choice is fully up to date, versed in IT developments, aware of existing legislative frameworks and business cultures, informed about key sources of information and expertise, connected with professional networks in consulting and other business services, and able to view your specific problems and concerns from a wider economic and social perspective.
- If your consultant is to be sponsored by a technical assistance project or fund, make sure that you have a final say in selection. The consultant will work for you, not for the sponsor, and the sponsor will hold you responsible for the outcome. A free consulting service may turn out to cost you a lot if you are not in charge.
- If a consultant has deserved and earned your trust, do not hesitate to use him or her again. Not only will selection be easier and less risky, but you may get new ideas, information, inspiration, counsel and help beyond your expectations and beyond the terms of any formal contract.

5. Develop a joint programme

The consultant you have chosen may be the best one, but he or she is not your employee, and his or her presence and intervention will create an unusual situation in your organization. Careful planning and preparation of the assignment are essential.

- Review the proposals received in detail with the consultant, ask questions, suggest improvements in the approach and the workplan.
- Clarify the consultant's role and your own, the style of consulting to be used, and responsibilities for all phases of the assignment. Who will do what? How will you and your staff cooperate with the consultant? Are you sure that the consultant will not do work that your people can do (this can reduce cost and speed up execution)?
- Reach an agreement on the programme of work to be implemented, the timetable and deadlines to be observed, measurable and controllable results to be attained, reports to be submitted to you and control sessions to be held at critical points of the assignment.
- Settle the financial side clearly and unambiguously: the fee formula and level, the reimbursable expenses, the conditions, form and frequency of payments.
- Sign a contract with the consultant in a form that is customary in your business environment. Use a written contract and make sure that it complies fully with legislation. Confine the use of verbal agreements to small jobs and to consultants whom you know well and trust totally.

6. Cooperate actively with your consultant

The modern concept of management consulting emphasizes the client's active participation at all stages of the assignment. Both the consultant's and the client's best brains are needed to make the assignment a success. And you can only learn by working with the consultant, not by reading reports and reviewing the results of the consultant's work. But your involvement will not happen automatically – a real effort is required, especially since a consulting assignment is an additional job to the normal work of your organization.

- Tell your staff about the consultant's presence; introduce the consultant to everyone who should meet him or her.
- Make the right people available at the right time. You will gain nothing by assigning second-rate staff to work with a first-rate adviser.
- Provide readily all information related to the assignment and needed by the consultant (confidential information not required for the assignment does not have to be shared).
- Look for ways of improving the design of the assignment, increasing your participation and enhancing the consultant's efficiency – he or she is working for you and the ultimate benefit will be yours.
- Cooperating in the assignment does not mean irritating the consultant, holding his hand, always looking over his shoulder, delaying decisions on his proposals and not letting him proceed with the job. If this is your attitude, do not use consultants.

7. Involve the consultant in implementation

A universal problem faced by consultants and clients alike is that too many assignments end before implementation. The report looks fine – but can it be implemented? Can the new scheme work? Are you able to make it work? Will the purpose be achieved? Certain consultants are only too happy to leave the client without implementing the proposals. The true professionals do care about implementation and are sorry if they cannot participate and learn from it.

Remember that modern consulting tends to be results-oriented and consultant remuneration more and more results-based. This is not possible if the consultant does not participate in implementation.

- Make it a principle that your consultant will be involved in implementation.
- Choose a degree and form of the consultant's involvement that suit your organization. Several alternatives will be available in most cases.
- If cost is what worries you, choose a light involvement: you implement, but the consultant helps to debug the new scheme and is available if problems arise.
- In any event, avoid implementation by the consultant without the active participation of your staff.

8. Monitor progress

There are many reasons why the course of a consulting assignment may deviate from the path originally agreed. Because it is your assignment, and you are keen to get results, it is in your interest to monitor progress closely and take corrective measures before it is too late.

- Your monitoring will reveal whether the consultant:
  - understands your organization;
  - is taking the right technical direction;
  - is observing the timetable;
  - is behaving as a real professional (with integrity, tact, commitment, efficiency);
  - is providing inputs of the right quality and quantity;
  - is sharing information and facilitating learning;
  - is not facing unexpected obstacles;
  - has no friction or conflict with your staff;
  - is likely to accomplish the agreed objectives.
- Monitor your own performance:
  - are you respecting your commitments?
  - can you keep pace with the consultant?
  - are your staff helping the consultant, ignoring him or her, or making difficulties?
- Pay special attention to the collaborative spirit in which the assignment should be taking place.
- Do not underestimate the financial aspects of delivery:
  - is the consultant billing you regularly?
  - are the bills clear and correct?
  - are you paying without delay?
  - will the assignment remain within agreed financial limits?

Conclusions from monitoring should be reviewed with the consultant and decisions promptly taken on needed adjustments. If the time frame of the assignment cannot be extended, slow and superficial monitoring may lead to situations where nothing can be improved any more.

9. Evaluate the results and the consultant

Many assignments end in a bizarre way. The consultant leaves the organization, a report is submitted and accepted, bills are paid and everyone seems to be happy. Yet the client cannot really say whether the assignment was worth while, or whether the benefits obtained justified the costs. No lessons are drawn for future assignments, or for the possibility of using the same consultant again.

- It is in your interest to evaluate every assignment on the basis of facts and figures, not of superficial impressions and hearsay ("the consultant was a very nice and really helpful guy, everyone around here liked him").
- Evaluate the results obtained. What has changed? Will the changes be lasting? How much will they cost us? What problems remain unsolved? What opportunities have been missed?
- Evaluate the consultant. Has she delivered as promised? What could we learn from her? Was working with her an exciting experience? Would we use her again?
- Write your evaluation down. The consultant may contact you again and other people in your organization will want to know how he or she performed when working with you. Such information should be available to your colleagues and successors.
- Evaluate your own approach. Have you done well in this assignment? What have you and your colleagues learned? Have you become more skilful in working with consultants? Are you making effective use of them? Where do you need to improve?

10. Beware of dependence on consultants

You and your staff may have appreciated and enjoyed the presence of a professional consultant in your organization. Yet the purpose of consulting reaches beyond making professional expertise available to your organization for dealing with current problems. Every assignment should increase your abilities and your independence in dealing with future problems. Dependence on consultants would be a symptom of a very unhealthy state of affairs.

- Do not delegate to consultants any decisions that are your responsibility and that you have to take.
- Do not get used to always having a consultant around to whom you hand over every complicated matter. Conversely, it may be useful to have a long-term relationship with a consultant who could be your special adviser, sounding-board, source of new ideas and contacts, or personal counsellor.
- Do not turn to consultants with the same task again: you and your staff should have learned how to tackle it.
- Develop internal consulting capabilities for dealing with issues for which an external expert is not necessary or which require an intimate inside knowledge of your organization.
- Do not put all your eggs in one basket – diversify your sources of external expertise. But stay in touch with consultants whose performance was excellent and who have earned your trust.

* * *

The Ten Commandments are not intended to teach you how to use consultants, but they do stress critical points to bear in mind when choosing consultants and working with them. If you want to learn more about consulting, read about it and speak with people who have used consultants. Try to get objective and balanced information. And then try it out, first on a small assignment, but one dealing with a real problem.

When you and your organization become experts in working with consultants, you may find it useful to define your own policy for using management consultants and other professional services. The Ten Commandments provide some guidance on this, but you should establish a policy that reflects your unique needs and experience.

APPENDIX 2

ASSOCIATIONS OF MANAGEMENT CONSULTANTS[1]

Argentina

Consejo Asesor de Empresas Consultoras
Leando N. Alem 465, 4"g"
1003 Buenos Aires
mz@lvd.com.ar

Australia

Institute of Management Consultants (IMCA)
Level 2 The Mansion
40 George Street
Brisbane QLD 4000
imc@imc.org.au
www.management-consultants.com.au

Austria

Fachverband Unternehmensberatung und Informationstechnologie
Wirtschaftskammer Österreich
Wiedner Hauptstrasse 63
1045 Wien
office@wkubdv.wk.or.at
www.ubit.at

Bangladesh

Bangladesh Association of Management Consultants
98 Malibagh (DIT Road)
Dhaka 1219

Institute of Management Consultants Bangladesh (IMCB)
c/o Survey Research Group of Bangladesh
396 New Eskaton Road
PO Box 7092
Dhaka 1000
hgas@nsu.agni.com

Belgium

Association belge des Conseils en Organisation et Gestion (ASCOBEL)
Place des Chasseurs ardennais 20
1030 Brussels
ascobel@skynet.be
www.ascobel.be

Brazil

Associação Brasileira de Consultores de Organização (ABCO)
Rua da Lapa 180
COB 20021 Rio de Janeiro

Instituto Brasileiro dos Consultores de Organização (IBCO)
Av. Paulista 326, 7th andar - cj.77
CEP 01310 São Paulo

Bulgaria

Bulgarian Association of Management Consulting Organisations (BAMCO)
1 Macedonia Square, 17th floor
Sofia 1040
bamco@delin.org
www.delin.org/bamco

[1] All Web sites visited on 4 Apr. 2002.

Canada

Canadian Association of Management Consultants (CAMC)
BCE Place, 181 Bay Street
Galleria, Box 835
Heritage Building, Suite 2R
Toronto, Ontario M5J 2T3
camc@camc.com
www.camc.com

China

Dingdian Zi Xun You Xian Gong Si
[Institute of Management Consultants China]
PO Box 4033
JianguomenNei DaJie
Beijing 100001
imc@263.net

Institute of Management Consultants Hong Kong
c/o The Poon Kam Kai Institute of Management
University of Hong Kong Town Centre
3/F Admiralty Centre
18 Harcourt Road
Hong Kong
info@imchk.com.hk
www.imchk.com.hk

Management Consultancies Association of Hong Kong (MCAHK)
PO Box 47537, Morrison Hill Post Office
mca@hkgcc.org.hk
www.mca.org.hk

Croatia

Croatian Management Consulting Association (CROCA)
Draskoviceva 47a
10000 Zagreb

Cyprus

Cyprus Association of Business Consultants
30 Grivas Dhivenis Avenue
PO Box 1657
1511 Nicosia
oeb@dial.cylink.com.cy

Institute of Management Consultancy Cyprus
Cyprus Technology Foundation
Ionio Nison 1
1st fl., Akropoli, PO Box 20783
1663 Nicosia
techinfo@industry.cy.net
www.industry.cy.net

Czech Republic

Asociace pro poradenství v podnikání (APP)
[Association for Consulting to Business]
Veletržní 21
17001 Praha 7
asocpor@iol.cz

Denmark

Danish Institute of Certified Management Consultants
Chr. Richardts Vej 3, PO Box 782
5230 Odense M
info@dicmc.dk
www.dicmc.dk

Dansk Management Råd (DMR)
14A, 2.sal, Amaliegade
1256 Copenhagen K
info@danskmanagementraad.dk
www.danskmanagementraad.dk

Finland

Liikkeenjohdon Konsultit (LJK)
[The Finnish Management Consultants]
Eteläranta 10
00130 Helsinki
ljk@ljk.fi
www.ljk.fi

France

Syntec-Management
Chambre syndicale des Sociétés de Conseils (SYNTEC)
3 rue Léon Bonnat
75016 Paris
www.syntec-management.com

Office professionnel de Qualification des Conseils en Management
3 rue Léon Bonnat
75016 Paris

Germany

Bundesverband Deutscher Unternehmensberater e.V. (BDU)
Zitelmannstrasse 22
53113 Bonn
info@bdu.de
www.bdu.de

Greece

Hellenic Association of Management Consulting Firms (SESMA)
Elikonos 13
Chalandri
15234 Athens
sesma@hol.gr

Hungary

Association of Management Consultants in Hungary (VTMSZ)
11 Szt. István Krt.
1055 Budapest
hetyey@mail.externet.hu

India

Institute of Management Consultants of India
Centre 1, 11th fl., Unit 2
World Trade Centre
Cuffe Parade
Bombay 400 005
imci@vsnl.com

Indonesia

Ikatan Nasional Konsultan Indonesia
Jl. Bendungan Hilir Raya 29
Jakarta 10210

Ireland

Institute of Management Consultants Ireland
Confederation House
84/86 Lower Baggot Street
Dublin 2
info@imci.ie
www.imci.ie

Association of Management Consulting Organizations (AMCO)
Confederation House
84/86 Lower Baggot Street
Dublin 2

Italy

Associazione professionale dei Consulenti di Direzione e Organizzazione (APCO)
Corso Venezia 49
20121 Milan
info@apcoitalia.it
www.apcoitalia.it

Associazione delle Societe di Consulenza Direzionale e Organizzazionale
(ASSOCONSULT)
Piazza Velasca 6
20122 Milan
info@assoconsult.org
www.assoconsult.org

Japan

ZEN-NOH-REN
Kindai Building 6F 12-5
Kohimachi 3Chome
Chiyoda-Ku
Tokyo 102-0083
imcj@zen-noh-ren.or.jp
www.zen-noh-ren.or.jp

Jordan

Institute of Management Consultants of Jordan
9 Mogadishu Street - Um Uthaina
PO Box 926550
Amman 11110
imc@go.com.jo
www.imc.com.jo

Latvia

Latvian Association of Business Consultants (LBKA)
Akas Street 5-7
Riga 1011
lbka@lbka.lv
www.lbka.lv

Malaysia
Institute of Management Consultants Malaysia
Level 1, Menara Sungei Way
Jalan Lagun Timur, Bandar Sunway
Petaling Jaya 46150

Mexico
Asociación Mexicana de Empresas de Consultoría (AMEC)
calz. Legaria 252
Mexico City 17, DF

Netherlands
Orde Van Organisatiekundigen en-Adviseurs (OOA)
PO Box 302
1170 AH Badhoevedorp
ooa@wispa.nl

Raad Van Organisatie Adviesbureau (ROA)
PO Box 85515
2508 CE The Hague
roa@bikker.nl

New Zealand
Institute of Management Consultants New Zealand Inc.
PO Box 6493
Wellesley Street
Auckland
ron.evans@hawkeye.co.nz

Nigeria
Institute of Management Consultants Nigeria
PO Box 9194
8th fl., NNDC Building (Ahmed Talib House)
18/19 Ahmadu Bello Way
Kaduna
nimc@inet-global.com

Norway
Norges Bedriftsrådgiverforening (NBF)
c/o Interforum Partners AS
Askerveien 61
1384 Asker
catom@online.no

Poland
Stowarzyszenie Doradcow Gospodarczych w Polsce (SDG)
[Association of Economic Consultants in Poland]
ul. Rakowiecka 36
02 532 Warsaw
sdg@sdg.com.pl
www.sdg.com.pl

Portugal
Associação Portuguesa de Projectistas e Consultores (APPC)
Av. Antonio Augusto Aguiar 126, 7th fl.
1050 Lisbon
info@appconsultores.pt
www.appconsultores.pt

Romania
Associata Consultantilor in Management din Romania (AMCOR)
7–9 Piata Amzei, Sc. C, ap. 6
70174 Bucharest
svasta@mail.kappa.ro

Russian Federation
Association of Consultants in Economics and Management (ACEM)
12 Petrovka
103756 Moscow
acem@tsr.ru

Singapore
Institute of Management Consultants Singapore
20 Maxwell Road
09-08 Maxwell House
Singapore 069113
secretariat@imcsingapore.com
www.imcsin.org.sg

Slovakia
Slovenská asociácia pre poradenstvo v riadeniu (SAPR)
[Slovak Association for Management Consulting]
Mudroňova 47
81103 Bratislava

Slovenia
Association of Management Consultants of Slovenia (AMCOS)
Dimiceva 13
1504 Ljubljana
infolink@gzs.si
www.gzs.si

South Africa
Institute of Management Consultants South Africa
PO Box 798
Hurlingham Manor 2070
imcsa@global.co.za
www.imcsa.org.za

Spain
Asociación Española de Empresas de Consultoría (AEC)
Orfila 5, Esc.1-4C
28010 Madrid
aec@wanadoo.es
www.consultoras.com

Instituto de Consultores de Organización y Dirección
Orfila 5, Esc. 1-4D
28010 Madrid

Sweden
Sveriges Managementkonsulenter (SAMC)
Kungsgatan 48
11135 Stockholm
anders.grufman@grufman.reje.se
www.samc.se

Switzerland
Association suisse des Conseils en Organisation et Gestion (ASCO)
Forchstrasse 428
Postfach 923
8702 Züllikon
office@asco.ch
www.asco.ch

The former Yugoslav Republic of Macedonia
Management Consulting Association
Partizanski Odreni Bld. 2
Skopje 91000

Turkey
Management Consultancies Association of Turkey (MCAT)
YDD, Maslak-TEM Kavsagi
Yeni Camlik Cd. No.1,4 Levent
Istanbul 80660
myalnizoglu@arge.com

United Kingdom
Institute of Management Consultancy (IMC)
3rd Floor
17–18 Hayward's Place
London EC1R 0EQ
consult@imc.co.uk
www.imc.co.uk

Management Consultancies Association (MCA)
49 Whitehall
London SW1A 2BX
mca@mca.org.uk
www.mca.org.uk

United States
Academy of Management
Management Consulting Division
www.uwf.edu/mcd

American Institute of Certified Public Accountants (AICPA)
Membership Section for Consulting Services
1211 Avenue of the Americas
New York NY 10036-8775
ssacks@aicpa.org
www.aicpa.org

Association of Management Consulting Firms (AMCF)
308 Lexington Avenue, Suite 1700
New York NY 10168
info@amcf.org
www.amcf.org

Institute of Management Consultants USA
Suite 800
2025 M Street
Washington DC 20036-3309
office@imcusa.org
www.imcusa.org

National Bureau of Certified Consultants (NBCC)
2728 Fifth Ave.
San Diego, CA 92103
nationalbureau@att.net
www.national-bureau.com

Europe

European Federation of Management Consulting Associations (FEACO)
Avenue des Arts 3/4/5
1210 Brussels
Belgium
feaco@feaco.org
www.feaco.org

European Foundation for Management Development (EFMD)
88 rue Gachard
1050 Brussels
info@efmd.be
www.efmd.be

Interregional

International Coach Federation (ICF)
1444 I Street NW, Suite 700
Washington, DC 20005
United States
icfoffice@coachfederation.org
www.coachfederation.org

International Council of Management Consulting Institutes (ICMCI)
858 Longview Road
Burlingame, CA 94010-6974
United States
icmci@icmci.org
www.icmci.com

International Federation of Consulting Engineers (FIDIC)
BP 86, 1000 Lausanne 12
Switzerland
fidic@fidic.org
www.fidic.org
(regional and national associations of consulting engineers are listed at the FIDIC Web site)

APPENDIX 3

INFORMATION AND LEARNING SOURCES FOR CONSULTANTS

This appendix lists selected information and learning sources of particular interest to consultants.[1] It concentrates on basic and common issues of consulting, such as methodology and style, general trends, change management, the professional approach, firm management, selection and use of consultants, the consulting industry and related professions. It does not aim to cover specific business sectors or management functions and techniques.

1. Handbooks, guides and monographs

Consulting practice and methodology

Block, P.: *Flawless consulting: A guide to getting your expertise used* (San Francisco, CA, Jossey-Bass/Pfeiffer, 2nd ed., 2000).

Kawase, T.: *Human centred problem solving* (Tokyo, Asian Productivity Organization, 2001).

Nadler, G.; Hibino, S.: *Breakthrough thinking: The seven principles of creative problem solving* (Rocklin, CA, Prima Publishing, 1994).

Nadler, G.; Hibino, S.; Farrell J.: *Creative solution finding: The triumph of full-spectrum creativity over conventional thinking* (Rocklin, CA, Prima Publishing, 1995).

Sadler, P. (ed.): *Management consultancy: A handbook for best practice* (London, Kogan Page, 1998).

Schein, E.: *Process consultation revisited: Building the helping relationship* (Reading, MA, Addison-Wesley, 1999).

Weinberg, G.: *The secrets of consulting: A guide to giving and getting advice successfully* (New York, Dorset House, 1985).

Weiss, A.: *The ultimate consultant: Powerful techniques for the successful practitioner* (San Francisco, CA, Jossey-Bass, 2001).

[1] All Web sites visited on 4 Apr. 2002.

Selection and use of consultants

Kennedy Information: *A buyer's guide to management consulting services, 2000 edition* (Fitzwilliam, NH, Kennedy Information, 2000).

Kubr, M.: *How to select and use consultants: A client's guide*, Management Development Series, No. 31 (Geneva, ILO, 1993).

Professional approach

Bellman, G. M.: *Getting things done when you are not in charge* (San Francisco, CA, Berrett-Koehler, 1992).

Bellman, G. M.: *The consultant's calling: Bringing what you are to what you do* (San Francisco, CA, Jossey-Bass, 1990).

Dawson, R.: *Developing knowledge-based client relationships: The future of professional services* (Woburn, MA, Butterworth-Heinemann, 2000).

Maister, D.: *Managing the professional service firm* (New York, The Free Press, 1993).

Maister, D.: *True professionalism* (New York, The Free Press, 1997).

Maister, D.; Green, C. H.; Galford, R.: *The trusted advisor* (New York, The Free Press, 2000).

McKenna, P.; Maister, D.: *First among equals: How to manage a group of professionals* (New York, The Free Press, 2002).

Change and culture

Beckhard, R.: *Agent of change: My life, my practice* (San Francisco, CA, Jossey-Bass, 1997).

Hamel, G.: *Leading the revolution* (Boston, MA, HBS Press, 2000).

Hofstede, G.: *Culture and organizations: Software of the mind* (London, HarperCollins, 1994).

Kotter, J.: *Leading change* (Boston, MA, HBS Press, 1996).

Senge, P. et al.: *The dance of change: The challenges to sustaining momentum in learning organizations* (New York, Doubleday, 1999).

Trompenaars, F.; Hampden-Turner, C.: *Riding the waves of culture: Understanding cultural diversity in business* (London, Nicholas Brealey, 2nd ed., 1997).

Human resources, training and development

Craig, R. L.: *The ASTD training and development handbook: A guide to human resource development* (New York, McGraw-Hill, 4th ed., 1996).

Pedler, M.; Burgoyne, J.; Boydell, T.: *The learning company: A strategy for sustainable development* (London, McGraw-Hill, 2nd ed., 1997).

Prokopenko, J. (ed.): *Management development: A guide for the profession* (Geneva, ILO, 1998).

Senge, P.: *The fifth discipline: The art and practice of the learning organization* (New York, Doubleday, 1990).

Shaw, P.; Phillips, K.: *A consultancy approach for trainers and developers* (Aldershot, Gower, 1998).

2. Consulting industry surveys and critiques

Czerniawska, F.: *Management consultancy in the 21st century* (Basingstoke, Macmillan, 1999).

E-business consulting: After the shakeout (Fitzwilliam, NH, Kennedy Information, 2001).

E-business realities and their implications for consultants (Fitzwilliam, NH, Kennedy Information, 2001).

E-consulting: Winning strategies for the new economy, a sector survey report by Fiona Czierniawska (Lafferty Publications, 2000; www.lafferty.com).

The global consulting marketplace: Key data, forecasts and trends, 2002 edition, and a number of other comprehensive studies of the consulting industry and its trends (Fitzwilliam, NH, Kennedy Information).

The Harvard Business School Guide to Careers in Management Consulting, 2001 Edition (Boston, MA, HBS Press, 2000).

Micklethwait, J.; Wooldridge, A.: *The witch doctors: What the management gurus are saying, why it matters and how to make sense of it* (London, Heinemann, 1996).

O'Shea, J.; Madigan, C.: *Dangerous company: The consulting powerhouses and the businesses they save and ruin* (London, Nicholas Brealey, 1997).

Pinault, L.: *Consulting demons: Inside the unscrupulous world of global corporate consulting* (New York, Harper Business, 2000).

Regional and country reports on consulting services; reports on consulting in Europe, United States, Japan and China (ALPHA Publications).

Shapiro, E.: *Fad surfing in the boardroom: Reclaiming the courage to manage in the age of instant answers* (Reading, MA, Addison-Wesley, 1995).

Survey of the European management consultancy market, regularly updated (FEACO).

Vault guide to the top 50 consulting firms (www.vault.com).

3. Periodicals and newsletters

Consultants' Advisory (PMP Group); IT report for consultants and systems integrators.

Consultants News (Kennedy Information); monthly newsletter of the consulting industry.

Consulting Magazine (Kennedy Information); monthly magazine.

Consulting: Le mensuel international du conseil (Groupe Mm); monthly trade bulletin (in French).

Consulting to Management; quarterly journal of the profession, former *Journal of Management Consulting* (www.C2M.com).

Global IT Consulting Report (Kennedy Information).

International Consultants' Guide (PMP Group); guide for consultants, system integrators and analysts.

International Consultants' News (PMP Group); international news report.

IT Consultant (Penton Technology Media); monthly professional magazine.

Management Berater (Management Berater Verlag); consulting journal (in German).

Management Consultancy (VNU Publications); monthly trade journal with focus on IT.

Management Consultants' News (PMP Group); monthly news report with focus on IT.

Management Consultant International (Kennedy Information).

The Marcus Letter; www.marcusletter.com; focus on marketing of professional services.

Professional Consultancy; magazine of the Institute of Management Consultancy, United Kingdom.

The Rodenhauser Report (Consulting Information Services); regular electronic briefing service, includes a weekly email column "Inside Consulting".

What's Working in Consulting (Kennedy Information); monthly guide providing practical tips and suggestions.

4. Directories of consultants

Consulting 2001: Le guide professionnel des sociétés de conseil (Groupe Mm).

The Directory of Management Consultants 2002 (Kennedy Information).

The European Directory of Management Consultants 1997/98 (FEACO).

5. Information services, agencies and Web sites

ALPHA Publications
www.alpha-publications.com
(reports on major markets for management consulting services)

www.amazon.com
(booksellers and source of bibliographic information on available and forthcoming publications)

American Society for Training and Development (ASTD)
1640 King Street, Box 1443
Alexandria, VA 22313-2043,
United States
www.astd.org

Asian Productivity Organization (APO)
Hirakawacho 1 chome,
Chiyoda-ku, Tokyo, 102-0093 Japan
www.apo-tokyo.org

B2business.net
www.b2business.net
(network for e-business professionals)

Business 2.0
www.business2.com
(Internet magazine and Web site)

Chartered Institute of Personnel Development (CIPD)
CIPD House, Camp Road
London SW19 4UX, United Kingdom
www.cipd.co.uk

CIO
www.cio.com
(e-business information links and research)

Consulting Information Services, LLC
191 Washington Street
Keene, NH 0341, USA
www.consultinginfo.com

The Economist e-business forum
www.ebusinessforum.com

Fast Company
www.fastcompany.com

Forrester Research
www.forrester.com

Gartner Group
www.gartner.com

Groupe Mm
31/35 rue Gambetta
92150 Suresnes, France
groupemm@groupemm.com
www.groupemm.com

Harvard Business Review
www.hbps.harvard.edu
www.hbr.org/explore

IDC
www.idc.com, www.idg.com
(information and research on IT and e-business)

Information Central on Management Consulting Worldwide
www.mcni.com

Kennedy Information
One Kennedy Place
Route 12 South
Fitzwilliam, NH 03447, United States
www.kennedyinfo.com, and
www.ConsultingCentral.com

Lafferty Publications
The Tower, Enterprise Centre
Pearse Street, Dublin 2, Ireland
cuserv@lafferty.com
www.lafferty.com

Management Berater Verlag
Stuttgarter Strasse 18–24
60329 Frankfurt am Main, Germany

NOLO Law for All
www.nolo.com
(information on legal aspects of business services)

Planète Conseil
www.syntec-management.com

PracticeCoach
www.practicecoach.com.ai
(consultancy and training for professional firm management)

Prime Marketing Publications Ltd.
(PMP Group)
Witton House, Lower Road
Chorleywood, Herts WD3 5LB
United Kingdom
icn@pmp.co.uk

Prosavvy
www.Prosavvy.com
(advice and assistance on selection of consultants)

Society for Human Resource Management
1800 Duke Street
Alexandria VA 22314,
United States
shrm@shrm.org
www.shrm.org

US Small Business Administration
www.sbaonline.sba.gov

VNU Business Publications
32–34 Broadwick Street
London W1A 2HG
United Kingdom
marc_brenner@vnu.co.uk
www.managementconsultancy.co.uk

www.WetFeet.com
(advice on careers in Internet consulting)

Most leading management and IT consulting firms also provide useful information through their Web sites.

6. Associations of consultants

Associations and institutes of management consultants are listed in Appendix 2. Most of these membership organizations provide information not only to members, but also to other consultants and the wider public. An overview of available information services and sources can be found at their respective Web pages, some of which also provide links to other sources.

APPENDIX 4

TERMS OF A CONSULTING CONTRACT

This appendix supplements section 7.6 on consulting contracts. These contracts come in many different forms and degrees of detail. It is useful to be aware of differences in national legislation and practice concerning contracting in general, and contracts for the provision of professional services in particular. In international contracts, the client and the consultant should agree on the applicable law, which is usually the law of the client organization's home country. In exceptional and justified cases the consultant and the client may agree to apply the law of the consultant's country or the law of another jurisdiction that is considered neutral by both parties.

The consultant may be requested to accept the client's standard form and conditions of contract. This is normally the case if the assignment is part of a programme financed by a technical assistance agency or a development bank, and if the work is for public sector clients.

In other cases, the consultant will be able to use his or her own form of contract, or develop a contract in agreement with the client. To support their members, some consultants' associations have prepared standard contract clauses, or guidelines for contract terms and conditions, reflecting the profession's experience.

In any event, it is strongly recommended to consult a lawyer on the contract form to be used and on unusual contract clauses suggested either by the client or the consultant. Certain provisions that may look familiar and are sometimes referred to as "boilerplate" (e.g. indemnification and dispute resolution clauses) may prove particularly onerous for one of the parties if they are not properly drafted.

The comments that follow are structured in accordance with the checklist in box 7.6, "What to cover in a contract – checklist" (section 7.6).

1. Contracting parties

It should be made clear not only who signs the contract (and its cancellation, amendments, etc.), but also who will make operational decisions on work progress, changes in the workplan and staffing, and results. In reality, there are several categories of "client" in most organizations, as pointed out in section 3.2. Technical assistance contracts are often signed by the funding agency, but the real client is the organization receiving assistance. What will be its roles and rights in preparing and implementing the contract?

2. Scope of the assignment

This section describes the work to be performed, the objectives to be achieved, the timetable and the volume of work. Although it is the core section of the contract, its importance is often underestimated. Many consultants feel that their objective should be to sign the contract even if the scope of work has not been fully clarified and could be viewed differently by the consultant or the client. Their credo is: Why bother with detailed work descriptions and plans when we know well that eventually the client will want something else? While flexibility is the consultant's major virtue, a lack of detail and precision in outlining what should be done and achieved has made the life of many consultants and clients difficult.

3. Work products and reports

This section describes the so-called "deliverables", i.e. specific documents and reports that the consultant will be transmitting to the client during and at the end of the assignment. Here, too, a great deal of misunderstanding can be avoided by being as specific as possible in describing what the client will receive. What is "a report"? What do we mean by "complete documentation on a training programme for sales managers"?

Unnecessary written reports should not be requested. They take up both the consultant's and the client's time without changing anything in the course of the assignment. Conversely, the need for frequent and short progress review meetings is not fully appreciated in many contracts.

4. Consultant and client inputs

Consultant inputs to the assignment are those that have to be provided within the given contract framework. This may include names (and curricula vitae) of operating consultants, names of partners and other seniors responsible for managing and backstopping the assignment, management systems and other proprietary know-how to be provided, and other inputs. It should be clearly stated which inputs will be provided within the agreed fee and which will only be available against additional payment. Any such additional inputs will require the client's prior approval.

Furthermore, there should be no ambiguity as regards changes in the agreed inputs – when and under what conditions would the consulting firm be authorized to assign different staff, and when and how would the client be able to ask the consultant to replace the staff assigned to the project. If the client has selected not only a consulting firm, but also particular people within the firm, the client's view should prevail in any such changes.

Client inputs, such as time spent on the assignment by managerial and technical personnel, or administrative support, are often taken for granted and vaguely defined. In implementing assignments, many consultants do not insist on timely and full provision of inputs promised by clients. This practice increases the duration and costs of many assignments, and can cause a great deal of disenchantment. The consultant proceeds alone with the work, only to find that the client is not happy with the results and will not accept them.

5. Fees and expenses

Chapter 30 provides comments on desirable and undesirable fee-setting and billing practices. In drafting a contract, the fee formula applied, the estimated or agreed total fee, the conditions under which fees may be adjusted, and any expenses that will be charged separately should be clearly set out.

6. Billing and payment procedure

This procedure is also described in Chapter 30. The contract should set out the conditions to be met in requesting advance, interim and final payments, such as the reports that have to be submitted and accepted, the time records to be provided, and the way of presenting bills.

7. Professional responsibilities and standard of care

As a rule, the consultant will refer to the consulting association's or his or her firm's code of ethics and professional conduct (and attach such a code to the contract text). If necessary, the contract may also include special clauses on questions such as conflicts of interest to be avoided or activities from which the consultant agrees to refrain.

8. Representations

Consultants should avoid making false or inaccurate statements during the negotiations or in the contract in describing the firm's or individual consultants' capabilities and achievements. By misrepresenting or overstating their education, experience, work methods and results achieved, the consultants who fail to meet their clients' expectations may, in addition to tarnishing their reputation, expose themselves to liability for breach of contract or fraud.

Before stating, for example, that you employ only "highly qualified and proficient staff" or that your problem-solving or change-management methodology has "saved clients millions of dollars", you should consider whether you would be in a position to substantiate such statements were you required to do so in judicial proceedings brought by an unhappy client. Obviously, a distinction should be made between such self-laudatory statements which, if not a sign of good taste, are usually not susceptible of attracting liability. For example, a consultant may state that he or she is an "excellent professional", or "leading authority in his or her field". This may be untrue, but it is not a misrepresentation within the meaning defined above.

9. Confidentiality

During the assignment, the consultant may have access to confidential information of the client. Conversely, the consultant may, in certain cases, disclose confidential information to the client in performing the assignment. Each party agrees to keep confidential the information disclosed by the other party. Confidential information should be clearly identified. The parties will wish to exclude certain categories of information. Information that is publicly available is a common exclusion. Other exclusions may include information that a party is required to disclose by virtue of applicable law, court decision or government action. It is advisable to consider whether the confidentiality obligation should last indefinitely or end after a few years.

10. Protection of intellectual property

Increasingly, consultants use methodologies and training materials covered by copyright, patents or trademarks (see also Appendix 5). The contract will set the conditions under which these materials are available to the client (limited use within the client firm, no reproduction, fee to be paid for use, and similar).

Copyright in the materials produced as part of the assignment can be handled in various ways and is a matter of negotiation. Some clients insist that any copyright to works produced for their money belongs to them. Other clients want to be able to use the materials at their own discretion within the limits of their organizations, but agree that copyright should stay with the consultant (especially if the material is not a joint product of the consultant's and the client's work).

In many civil law countries, copyright is not transferable. However, the consultant may grant the client an exclusive or non-exclusive licence to use the work, namely to carry out certain acts that would otherwise infringe the copyright in the work (for example, the consultant may agree that the client will have the exclusive or non-exclusive right to publish, edit and broadcast the work).

11. Liability

As pointed out in section 6.5, legal liability is a relatively new phenomenon in consulting contracts and in many contract texts there is no reference to any liability. Yet liability questions should be given due consideration and the consultant may wish, or be obliged to, take out a liability insurance. This is especially the case if the advice to be provided will have a major impact on the client's business decisions, or if the consultant is designing and delivering systems that will strongly influence the client's operations (typically in information technology consulting).

Many clients will expect the contract to contain a clause whereby the consultant agrees to indemnify the client (and possibly the client's employees, directors and officers) with respect to any and all damages, claims, costs, expenses and losses that may be suffered or incurred by the client in connection with a breach of contract by the consultant and/or wilful misconduct or negligent acts of the consultant. Such an undertaking may cover a number of situations, including personal injuries suffered by the client's employees during a training session organized by the consultant, as well as losses caused to the client by the consultant's failure to deliver on time. The consultant should have his or her lawyer review the indemnification clause to ensure that it is fair and that it does not require the consultant to indemnify the client beyond what is usual. The consultant may sometimes also obtain a reciprocal indemnification undertaking from the client, though its scope will usually be more limited. Before agreeing to provide indemnification, the consultant should confirm that this will not negatively affect the coverage of his or her liability insurance.

The contract may attempt to limit liability and provide, for example, that the total amount of indemnification that may be owed by the consultant shall in no event exceed the total amount of fees paid by the client. However, in certain jurisdictions, a limitation of liability may not be validly agreed, or may be agreed only under certain conditions; you should therefore check whether the proposed limitation is valid under the contract's governing law.

12. Use of subcontractors

The use of subcontractors by the consulting firm may be authorized in some contracts and the client may choose to set the conditions for such use. As a rule, reliance on a subcontractor does not excuse a breach of contract since it is the consultant rather than the subcontractor who is party to the consulting contract.

13. Termination or revision

The contract should describe the steps to be taken upon completion of the assignment, including the settlement of all commitments by both parties and the submission and acceptance of all reports and documentation.

In addition, the contract may provide for the right of the client to terminate the contract without any reason or if specified external conditions occur. Such external conditions may include, for example, a change in business environment rendering the advice useless for the client. There may, however, be a mandatory notice period (say, one week in a simple management advisory assignment, or 30–60 days in a major engineering consultancy), and/or the client may have to pay the consultant an indemnity (e.g. fees for one month of work or 20 per cent of the remaining fees). If the client wishes to terminate the contract owing to poor performance of the consultant, a precise procedure should be followed (giving the reasons in writing, asking for a reply and immediate action, etc.) and the notice period may be shorter.

The consultant must also have the possibility to withdraw from the contract in certain circumstances, e.g. if the client is not paying or has suspended operations for a defined period of time. The contract would stipulate the procedure to be observed by the consultant. If the client has been declared bankrupt, the consultant can normally terminate the contract without notice.

Turning to revisions, the contract may determine the dates and conditions for periodic revisions to reflect changed circumstances and client needs, and the procedure for unplanned revisions suggested by either party.

14. Arbitration

The contract may provide for the resolution of disputes in court or through an alternative dispute resolution (ADR) mechanism, such as mediation or arbitration (a single arbitrator or board of arbitrators). As a rule, consulting contracts use arbitration for settling disputes that cannot be handled amicably. The contracting parties agree on the rules of arbitration and the body to which the case would be referred. The laws of the country in which the arbitration takes places will generally govern the possible means and grounds of appeal against the arbitration award. Therefore, the arbitration forum should be selected carefully.

15. Signatures and dates

It should be made clear which representatives of the client and consultant are authorized to sign the contract and its amendments, bills, formal correspondence, and legally binding commitments related to the approval and execution of the contract.

* * *

Further guidelines on contracting are available in:

- World Bank: *Guidelines: Selection and employment of consultants by World Bank borrowers* (www.worldbank.org/html/opr/guidetxt/, visited on 4 Apr. 2002).
- European Union: *DIS Manual* (Brussels, 1999). See europa.eu.int/comm/enlargement/pas/phare/index.html.
- International Federation of Consulting Engineers (FIDIC): *Client–consultant agreement (White Book)* (Lausanne, 3rd ed., 1998). See www.fidic.org./bookshop, visited on 4 Apr. 2002.
- E. Bleach and L. Byars Swindling: *The consultant's legal guide* (San Francisco, CA, Jossey-Bass/Pfeiffer, 1999).
- Institute of Management Consultancy (United Kingdom): *Standard terms and conditions of engagement* (www.imc.co.uk/index3.html, visited on 3 Apr. 2002).

APPENDIX 5

CONSULTING AND INTELLECTUAL PROPERTY

Intellectual property refers to creations of the mind: inventions, literary and artistic works, symbols, names, images and designs used in commerce.[1] The term "intellectual property" is used essentially to indicate those industrial, scientific, artistic and other creations that can be legally protected. As a rule, ideas themselves cannot be protected, but their description or formal documentation can be. Various legal instruments are available for the protection of intellectual property, including copyright, industrial designs, trademarks and patents. In certain cases, several types of protection are available for a particular creation.

Copyright protection arises automatically from the moment of creation of the copyright work. Protection under patents, designs and trademarks, on the other hand, is subject to registration. The registration of a patent may take several years as patents are granted only after lengthy investigations. The owner of intellectual property may generally grant a licence permitting a third party to use intellectual property on agreed terms. In return, the licensee may agree to pay a lump sum or to make royalty payments. Protection is usually awarded on a territorial basis. Therefore, a firm that wishes to obtain patent or trademark protection in several countries will, as a rule, need to apply for protection in each country. However, certain international conventions, such as the 1989 Madrid Protocol relating to the international registration of trademarks, provide for a single international registration, although protection will be granted only in the countries designated by the applicant under the conditions set forth by the national laws of these countries.[2] The cost of protecting intellectual property internationally can be substantial. For example, one company has recently spent some US$10.6 million to extend its trademark protection from North America and Western Europe to the rest of the world.[3]

Until recently, most management and business consultants had only vague notions of intellectual property issues and paid marginal attention to them. At best they tried to avoid infringing copyright when using publications and training material authored by others. Consulting contracts often included copyright-related and similar provisions that did not conform to legislation. Consultants involved in research and development, product design, technology transfer and marketing issues were of course aware of intellectual property, but they tended to refer such matters to specialized lawyers.

During the 1990s, the attitudes to protection and utilization of intellectual property changed dramatically in most of the world's leading businesses, in particular in the IT, e-business and telecommunications sectors.[4] Intellectual property started being viewed and used as a strategic business tool, to generate income, thanks to active patent-licensing policies, protect core technologies and business methods, increase the market value of companies by assigning the correct value to their intellectual property, and develop strong patent portfolios in negotiating cross-licensing agreements with important business partners and even competitors.[5] Thus, IBM managed to increase its annual income from intellectual property from US$30 million in 1990 to US$1.54 billion in 2001. Microsoft increased its patent portfolio from 5 in 1990 to some 1350 issued patents in 2000. Intel is known to have concluded a number of advantageous cross-licensing agreements since inventions of new semiconductor technologies are impossible without acquiring dozens of licences to use patented technologies. Dell secured 42 issued and pending patents on its business model. With progressing commodification of consulting services (see Chapters 1 and 2), many consultants have found it useful to secure legal protection of their own products. All these developments coincide with the advent of the knowledge-based economy, where new knowledge needs to be not only created, disseminated, shared and sold, but also legally protected. Intellectual property management and economics have become major elements and tools of knowledge management and corporate strategy.

Thus, in a relatively short time, intellectual property has become a burning issue for consultants. In a nutshell, consulting firms may face intellectual property issues in the following principal contexts:

- in advising clients on business and marketing strategies, activities and projects involving intellectual property;
- in creating and applying knowledge that can and ought to be legally protected;
- in creating new knowledge jointly with clients and subsequently jointly managing and exploiting this knowledge;
- in using legally protected knowledge created by others and in transferring this knowledge to clients.

This appendix aims to outline briefly the key current issues in intellectual property protection and management, to facilitate their general understanding and correct appreciation by consultants. These issues may concern the consulting firm itself, its client company, or both. This appendix addresses only the main forms of protection of intellectual property rights. It does not deal with areas of specialized interest such as, for example, the protection of databases or plant breeders' rights. In addition, it does not specifically deal with the protection that may be afforded by law against unfair competition, namely dishonest or fraudulent practices in trade or commerce that are susceptible of injuring competitors or customers. However, unfair competition law may be the only form of protection available against the misappropriation of intellectual property where protection may not be claimed under specific intellectual property rights.

For handling specific issues of intellectual property, it may be necessary to turn to specialist lawyers and technicians, who often specialize in only one field such as copyright, patents, trademarks or Internet-related issues (which are particularly complex).

Trade secrets

Information that is not known to the trade, and that gives the consultant or his or her client a competitive edge, is generally known as a *trade secret*. Trade secrets may include customer lists, business methods, manufacturing processes, industry data and any other information with economic value. The protection afforded by law to trade secrets is often the only type of protection available. Trade secrets are protected against further disclosure by persons to whom the information was disclosed in confidence as well as against misappropriation by third parties. Trade secrets are not subject to any form of registration. However, they enjoy protection only to the extent that adequate measures are taken to keep the information confidential. The protection ends once the information becomes publicly available. In addition, there is no protection against someone discovering the information through independent means.

It is essential for businesses to develop and implement adequate measures to keep trade secrets confidential. This concerns both the clients' and the consultant's own trade secrets, which often are not explicitly discussed or referred to in contracts and when starting assignments. Talkative consultants may then unintentionally reveal confidential information to their social contacts or other clients. When disclosing a trade secret to a client or another consultant (e.g. a subcontractor), the consultant should obtain an express undertaking to keep the information confidential (see also contract terms in Appendix 4).

A frequent and often strategically important choice faced by clients and consultants is: Shall we aim to keep a new method or technique secret (limited legal protection, but no need to reveal the secret) or shall we secure a patent (strongest protection, but precise description of the method will become publicly available, the procedure will be long and costly, and it may be easy to copy our method)? Are we fast enough in developing our technologies and business methods to be always ahead of competitors, to be sure that they will always be late in copying us?

Copyright[6]

The purpose of copyright is to prevent others from taking unfair advantage of a person's creative efforts. Copyright can usually subsist in any production in a literary, scientific or artistic domain, whatever may be the mode or form of its expression. All of these productions can usually be protected only if they are the author's own intellectual creations. In addition, copyright generally protects expression rather than ideas. Examples of copyright works that may be relevant to consultants include computer programs, sound recordings, videos, books, manuals, training course materials, and other writings such as proposals, technical reports and other materials produced by the consultant.

Copyright gives the author of the work the exclusive right to reproduce, adapt, translate, distribute and perform his or her work. However, the law permits certain acts that would otherwise infringe copyright in order to provide a fair balance between the rights of the copyright owner and public interest. These exceptions are usually permitted in certain special cases that do not conflict with normal exploitation of the work and do not unreasonably prejudice the copyright owner's legitimate interests. Commercial use of a work is usually not a permitted act.

Consultants frequently incorporate portions of sound recordings, videos, photographs, written materials and other works protected by copyright into their own presentations and materials. As regards publications, the use of limited passages from the publication of another author is usually authorized under certain conditions so long as the consultant gives credit by clearly identifying the publication and its author. If the use of another author's publication exceeds the bounds of what is permitted, the consultant must, in addition to giving credit, obtain the copyright-holder's permission (usually this will be the author or the publisher). Such permission must always be secured to use other types of works such as sound recordings, photographs, cartoons, animations and videos. The permission may usually be obtained from the copyright-holder or from a collecting society entrusted with the administration of copyrights and collection of fees on behalf of authors.[7] The permission is sometimes subject to the payment of a lump sum or royalties. As noted above, copyright protects expression rather than ideas. Thus, it is usually lawful to use (unprotected) ideas if the presentation is changed. However, while it may be legal, it is unethical to use someone else's unprotected ideas without giving credit (unless independently arrived at).

A particular issue is raised by works created by employees or by consultants for clients. The latter are usually known as *works-for-hire*. In certain legal systems, copyright in a work created by an employee is owned or controlled to a large extent by the employer if the work was created by the employee in the course of his or her employment. As regards works-for-hire, the client will usually be permitted to use the work only for the purposes resulting from the agreement between the consultant and the client, unless agreed otherwise by the parties (see also contract terms in Appendix 4).

In most countries, copyright protection generally exists from the moment of creation of the work. The term of protection of copyright varies depending on the country and on the type of copyright work, but will generally not be less than the life of the author plus 25, 50 or even 70 years after his or her death. Copyright protection is generally free of charge.

The Bern Copyright Convention administered by the World Intellectual Property Organization, and the Universal Copyright Convention lay down minimum standards for protection and provide for reciprocity of protection between the countries that have ratified the conventions. Both conventions have a significant number of members. While the Bern Copyright Convention provides that protection of copyright shall not be subject to any formality in the contracting states, the Universal Copyright Convention permits contracting states to require compliance with formalities, including registration and payment of fees. As a prerequisite to obtaining protection in a country with formalities, works must bear the *copyright symbol* © accompanied by the name of the copyright owner and the year of first publication placed in a visible location on the material.[8] In any event, it is advisable for the consultant to place such a notice on his or her materials since it reminds third parties that the work is protected and informs them of the owner of the copyright.

Registered industrial designs

The law of registered designs protects drawings and shapes that can be used to produce an article industrially. An industrial design is the ornamental or aesthetic aspect of an article. This implies that it must appeal to the eye. The law does not protect any technical features of the article to which the design is applied. A design may usually be protected only if it has not been previously published or registered. The protection of designs is subject to registration[9] and is awarded on a territorial basis.

Trademarks

The main function of trademarks is to identify the goods or services of an enterprise and to distinguish them from the goods or services of others. The goodwill associated with a trademark can be very important. Any sign that has a distinctive character and is not deceptive can usually be registered as a *trademark.*[10] Signs that are devoid of any distinctive character because they are too simple, or that contain a direct reference to a product or service, usually may not constitute trademarks. In addition, if there is a likelihood of confusion with an earlier trademark registered with respect to identical or similar goods or services, the trademark will not be registrable. Examples of signs that can constitute trademarks include words, letters, numbers, graphical representations, three-dimensional marks, and combinations thereof.

Protection must be applied for, and is subject to the payment of registration and renewal fees, though unregistered signs may sometimes benefit from limited protection under trademark or unfair competition legislation.[11] A trademark can be registered with respect to specific classes of goods and services.[12] The owner of a trademark has the exclusive right to use the trademark in relation to the classes of goods or services for which it is registered. Protection may be jeopardized if the trademark is not used or asserted against infringers. Generally, the trademark is infringed if an identical or similar sign is used with respect to identical or similar services. In certain legal systems, the law prevents others from taking unfair advantage of trademarks enjoying widespread recognition, known as *trademarks of repute* or *well-known trademarks*, by providing that the trademark is also infringed by its use with respect to non-similar goods or services.

Trademark protection is territorial, and priority in a trademark is generally determined according to the date of filing or (less frequently) first use in the relevant territory. Thus, an applicant may be prevented from securing registration in certain jurisdictions of interest because others may have acquired rights in those jurisdictions thanks to earlier filing.

The use of the *trademark* ™ symbol or *service mark* ℠ symbol means that the owner is claiming trademark rights. Service marks perform the same function as trademarks, but they are used with respect to services rather than with respect to goods. In most legal systems, trademarks may also be registered with respect to services and service marks do not exist as a separate category. The *registered symbol* ® is used with respect to *registered trademarks*. Although not mandatory, the use of these symbols is recommended to inform third parties that trademark protection is claimed.

Some consultants have started using trademarks to protect the denominations of their diagnostic, assessment, problem-solving, training, self-development and other materials and instruments. For example, the Web page of Andersen (www.andersen.com) in 2001 contained KnowledgeSpace®, Global Best Practices®, Value Dynamics®, Human Capital Appraisal™, Fit-Cost-Value™ and Market Integration℠. In some cases even common words and their combinations have been used by consultants as registered marks or trademarks. For example, one consulting firm has put a trademark symbol ™ on "Managing Organizational Change", thus trying to protect its exclusive right to use this "original and unusual" denomination of one of its instruments.

Patents

Patent law relates to inventions and is the strongest instrument of protection. It confers a monopoly of generally 20 years to exploit the invention in return for disclosure of details with respect to the invention. After expiry of the term of protection, anyone may use the invention. Thus, patent law protection is incompatible with trade secrets protection, which requires the information to be kept confidential.

The invention must be capable of industrial application. This requirement is usually met if the application of the invention produces technical effect, namely if the use or working of the invention produces certain tangible and physical consequences. In certain countries, software leading to technical change may be patented under certain conditions. In addition, the invention must be new. An invention is new if it does not form part of the state of the art, which includes all technical knowledge available to the public at the time of application for protection, whether through publications, writings, other patents or even oral descriptions, irrespective of the part of the world where the information becomes available. Therefore, before demonstrating or describing his or her invention to others, the consultant or the client should ensure that this will not jeopardize the application by compromising its novelty. Finally, the invention must involve an inventive step. This requirement is generally met if the invention is not obvious to a person skilled in the art.

The owner of the patent has the exclusive right to make, use, sell, distribute and import the invention. The law usually provides for a system of compulsory licences to prevent abuse of the monopoly by the patent owner. For instance, such a licence may be applied for under certain conditions if the invention is not used to a sufficient extent.

Licensing rates vary from industry to industry, but are usually between 1 per cent and 5 per cent of the gross sales of products or services that employ a patented technology. Another approach, the "25 per cent rule", sets royalties as a percentage of net profits.[13]

Patent protection must be applied for, and is granted on a territorial basis, though international registration is provided for under certain international conventions, such as the Patent Cooperation Treaty of 1970 and the European Patent Convention of 1973. The registration process usually takes several years due to the lengthy investigations needed to establish whether the prerequisites for protection are met. The cost of protection may be very substantial, especially if protection is sought in a number of countries.

Historically, the breadth of patent protection has been tempered by a number of exclusions, including so-called mental steps, mathematical algorithms, abstract ideas, laws of nature, mere chemical formulas, fundamental truths, original causes, principles, motives, systems of bookkeeping and others, because they do not satisfy the requirement of industrial application or technical effect. *Business methods* were part of this list. Also computer software "unassociated with physical elements or process steps fell outside the scope of the patent statute because it was considered either the implementation of a mathematical algorithm, or a business method".[14] However, in a now famous ground-breaking 1998 decision in *State Street Bank v. Signature Financial Group*, the US Court of Appeals for the Federal Circuit ruled that a data-processing system configured for management of a "hub-and-spoke" mutual fund system, which apparently amounted to a "method of doing business", was patentable. Since the State Street decision, numerous business method patents have been registered in the USA. Examples of such patents include electronic payment processes, incentive and reward models, Web advertising and user interface arrangements. While business methods are generally still not eligible for patenting in Europe, it cannot be excluded that the position will change in the future.

The inclusion of business methods among patentable intellectual property following the *State Street* decision can be viewed either as a courageous innovation that will boost new developments in IT and the knowledge-based economy, or as a decision that opens a Pandora's box. A rush to get business and Internet methods patented has started. It is therefore no surprise that this move has provoked an animated debate in professional and business circles.[15] There are fears that trivial and obvious methods may be granted legal protection, that patenting of business methods is a wrong policy which will hamper progress especially in e-business and new fields more generally, that patents may be granted on methods that have already been in use but have never been patented, that business methods and software patents should in any case have a much shorter life span than other patents (Jeff Bezos mentions 3–5 instead of 20 years) and that a public comment period before the patent is issued should allow for the business and Internet community to provide "prior art" references to the patent examiners and help to avoid the proliferation of bad patents.[16]

This is a matter of direct interest to management consultants involved in the development of new business approaches, methods and programmes and systems – to be followed closely.

Intellectual property rights and the Internet

The Internet is an open, borderless medium, which permits communications and transactions between a potentially unlimited number of parties located anywhere in the world. These transactions increasingly involve intangible materials that form the subject matter of intellectual property rights. Thus the Internet represents a new challenge for the protection of these rights. There are frequent tensions between the global nature of the Internet and the system of intellectual property rights, which essentially involves protection on a country-by-country basis. In addition, it is often difficult to determine the applicable law and the court having jurisdiction in case of infringement of intellectual property rights.

Since the Internet allows for an unlimited number of copies of a protected work to be made and distributed virtually instantaneously, it is an environment particularly propitious to the infringement of intellectual property rights. Copyright may be infringed by simple actions such as appending protected materials available on the Internet to an email sent to your clients or incorporating protected images or photographs into your Web site. Users may infringe trademark rights by including in their pages a logo or icon that is registered as a trademark in certain jurisdictions. The practice of posting hypertext links on your Web site, enabling the user to access another site at the click of a button, may also infringe intellectual property rights in certain cases. Technological protection devices are being developed. Currently, encryption and watermarking are the most commonly used techniques. Encryption consists of providing information in a scrambled form so as to control the access to it by (for example) charging a fee for the decryption key. Watermarking is a way to include in a work information concerning the rights-holders, with the aim of dissuading others from appropriating someone else's work.

The Internet enables the transmission and use in digital form of text, computer programs, sound, images and audiovisual works, all of which are protected by copyright. Copyright may also subsist, for example, in the structure and layout of a Web page. Intellectual property legislation generally lags behind technological change, and is therefore difficult to apply to the new issues raised by the Internet. For example, under the traditional conception of copyright, copyright can be theoretically infringed by each temporary copy of a copyright work as it is transmitted over the Internet.[17]

Many of the above-mentioned business method patents issued recently relate to the Internet. They provide protection for various techniques used by companies to promote and sell products and services over the Internet, such as techniques for sales and purchasing, online auctions and advertising.[18]

An increasing number of transactions are realized entirely over the Internet, with no other contact occurring between the supplier and the customer, either through personal visit, mail, telephone or other means. Accordingly, trademarks enabling suppliers to distinguish their products or services from those of other suppliers on the Internet are a key instrument of electronic commerce. However, the use of trademarks on the Internet upsets all traditional conceptions and definitions of rights. For instance, in countries where trademark protection is subject to prior use, can Internet use constitute prior use? While the answer appears to be positive, proving prior use may represent a challenge if the trademark was used exclusively on the Internet.

In addition, it is unclear how a trademark may be infringed by its use over the Internet. Should there be a link between the user of a sign and the country in which the trademark enjoys protection, or is it sufficient that the sign can be visible on a computer screen in the country? The latter interpretation could potentially lead to trademark infringements in countries where the owner of the sign was not even considering doing business. While it has been suggested that users could place disclaimers on their sites to avoid creating a link with particular countries, there would be practical difficulties in identifying the relevant countries. In the bricks-and-mortar world, the territoriality of trademark rights sorts out the problem of conflicting rights: two different people in two different countries can hold rights over the same sign with the same legitimacy. On the Internet, borders are abolished and the rights become conflicting.[19]

A frequent type of potential infringement is the unauthorized use of trademarks as *metatags*. A metatag is a keyword embedded in a Web site's HTML code, which enables Internet search engines to categorize the contents of the site. In this case, the trademark is not used to distinguish particular goods or services. It is used to make a search engine list a particular Web site in response to search instructions, and the user may see the contents of the Web site by clicking on the search results. The trademark is not readily apparent to the human eye. Courts in some jurisdictions have found use of trademarks as metatags to constitute a trademark infringement. Under another practice, known as the "sale" of trademarks as keywords, a search engine "sells" a keyword to an advertiser. Whenever the keyword is entered into the search engine, an advertisement automatically appears along with the search results. While trademark owners have challenged this practice in court, it is still unclear whether it will be treated as a trademark infringement.

Another issue is raised by the bad faith registration of domain names identical or similar to well-known marks, known as "*cybersquatting*". Domain names on the Internet are generally issued on a first-come first-served basis and, therefore, it is possible to apply for an Internet domain name even if you are not a company with that name. The cybersquatter's intent is generally to resell the domain name to the trademark owner for a profit. Various remedies have been suggested, notably giving the exclusive right to use a trademark as a domain name to the trademark owner.

Harmonization of national legislations is essential to achieve adequate protection of intellectual property rights on the Internet. Examples of harmonization efforts at the international level include two treaties concluded in 1996 under the auspices of WIPO to deal with some of the challenges posed by the Internet, namely the WIPO Copyright Treaty and the WIPO Performances and Phonograms Treaty. In addition, in 1999, the Internet Corporation for Assigned Names and Numbers (ICANN)[20] created a mandatory administrative dispute-resolution system with respect to top-level domains such as .com, .net. and .org. Disputes arising from abusive registrations of domain names (for example, cybersquatting) may be resolved by administrative proceedings brought by the holder of a trademark before an approved dispute-resolution provider.

Products of joint consultant and client work

Increasingly, the results of consulting projects are the products of joint work by the consultant and the client. If new knowledge suitable for legal protection is created, the key questions are with whom should the intellectual property rights be vested and who should benefit from them. Whenever such questions can be anticipated, a sufficiently precise and detailed reference should be made in the contract, to avoid later conflict or feelings of bitterness.

The issues to address include the following:

- Applicable legislation may determine the copyright-holder, but since the client will finance the work it may be agreed that the client will be licensed to use it and draw the financial benefits from this use. The use may be limited to the client's field of activities and/or to a geographical area. Conversely, the consulting firm may want to retain the right to use the products of its work in other projects, which may be restricted to clients who are not the current client's competitors.
- Consideration should be given to the importance of actual intellectual inputs to the project; for example, the product may be based on an already existing method or programme owned by the consultant and constitute only an adaptation to the client's particular conditions.
- It should be made clear who will be responsible for soliciting legal protection and who will bear the costs, which are modest for copyright but may be much greater if patents or trademarks are involved.
- The agreed arrangement should be fair and reflect the sound principles of knowledge-sharing between consultants and clients, thus paving the way for creative and mutually beneficial future collaboration.

Finally, it is worth recalling that intellectual property, as any other issue in business, is not only a matter of law and business, but of ethics. A definition of "fair knowledge protection practice" may not always be available from the legislator and will depend on the consultant's or his or her client's value judgement, especially in new fields where law tends to lag behind technology, the market and social expectations.

---

[1] See www.wipo.org (visited on 4 Apr. 2002) and *WIPO intellectual property handbook* (Geneva, WIPO, 2001).

[2] There are, however, exceptions to this rule, one example of which is the Community Trade Mark (CTM). CTMs have effect throughout the European Union and may be registered with the Office for the Harmonisation of the Internal Market established in Alicante, Spain.

[3] FT Director, *Financial Times*, 21 June 2001.

[4] See, e.g., WIPO: *Primer on electronic commerce and intellectual property issues* at ecommerce.wipo.int/primer/index.html. (visited on 4 Apr. 2002).

[5] For a recent overview of the trends see K. G. Rivette and D. Kline: "Discovering new value in intellectual property", in *Harvard Business Review*, Jan.–Feb. 2000, pp. 54–66.

[6] A distinction must be drawn between the common law concept of copyright, based on economic rights, and the civil law concept of *droit d'auteur*, which stresses the importance of the "moral rights" of the author. For instance, copyright to a work is not transferable as such in civil law countries, although a similar result may usually be reached thanks to the grant of an exclusive licence to use the work.

[7] Examples of such collecting societies include the Performing Right Society (PRS) and Phonographic Performance Ltd (PPL) in the United Kingdom.

[8] In the United States, copyright protection exists from the moment of creation of the work. However, registration of the work with the US Copyright Office in the Library of Congress provides the owner of the work with a number of advantages and is a prerequisite to the exercise of certain rights, such as the right to sue for infringement. Therefore, registration is considered as good practice.

[9] It is worth noting that, in certain systems, for instance the United Kingdom, unregistered designs are also protected if certain conditions are met. In the United States, designs are protected as a special category of patent.

[10] The other types of marks that can be protected are certification marks and collective marks. *Certification marks* are signs used by several undertakings under the control of the owner of the sign. They indicate that the services or products meet certain quality standards, share the same geographical origin, manufacturing process or other common characteristics. *Collective marks* are intended to distinguish the products or services of the members of an association from the products or services of others.

[11] It is worth noting that, in certain countries, one may acquire the right to use a sign with respect to specific goods or services through continued use for a certain period of time without registration being required. However, while such prior use of a sign is opposable even to the owner of the same trademark or a similar trademark, it usually does not mean that others can be prevented from using the sign in relation to the same goods or services. Limited protection for unregistered signs may also be available under unfair competition law. For example, passing off, or attempting to pass off, the goods or services of one person as the goods or services of a competitor by using a sign similar or identical to that of such competitor, may be prohibited under unfair competition legislation if certain conditions are met.

[12] There are 34 classes for goods and 8 classes for services.

[13] Rivette and Kline, op. cit., p. 62.

[14] For detailed information see *Business methods patents: Navigating the sea of controversy*, and W. J. Marsden and J. A. Huffman: *EBoom or EBust? "Business methods" patents and the future of Dotcommerce*, at the Web site of Fish & Richardson (www.fr.com, visited on 4 Apr. 2002).

[15] See, e.g., *An open letter from Jeff Bezos on the subject of patents* (www.amazon.com/exec/obidos/subst/misc/patents.html, visisted on 4 Apr. 2002).

[16] A number of important issues are raised in "Patently absurd?", in *The Economist Technology Quarterly*, 23 June 2001, pp. 42–44.

[17] The EU Copyright Directive adopted in 2001 provides, however, that temporary copies that are necessary for the transmission of digital data do not lead to an infringement of copyright.

[18] For example, one such patent was awarded in 1999 to protect Amazon's "one-click" technology, which allows a customer to place an order by clicking only one button.

[19] The question of territoriality of trademark protection also arises in relation to judicial injunctions. By ordering that an infringing use of a sign be ceased on the Internet, a court would in fact extend trademark protection provided by one country to the entire world, giving a "global effect" to its injunction. It is to be hoped that the courts will find a way to impose a localized prohibition through their injunctions, for example by prescribing the use of disclaimers or adequate technical means.

[20] The ICAAN is a technical coordination body for the Internet created by a broad coalition of its business, technical, academic and user communities.

APPENDIX 6

USING CASE STUDIES OF MANAGEMENT CONSULTING

1. Approach to using case studies

In teaching and learning consulting approaches and methods, the case method offers many advantages. It permits trainees to learn from experience and introduces consultants to various real-life situations that they could not experience or observe directly in their professional practice. It provides illustrations of consulting principles and methods, many of which are difficult to understand fully without having seen how they are applied in practical work with clients. Trainee consultants can work through the situations described in case studies and discuss how they themselves would act, work with the clients as well as with fellow consultants, and seek solutions. Both hard and soft methods of management and consulting can be taught and learned through the case method.

Consistent with the principles of the case method, *case studies* do not describe the complete case, including the final solutions and their consequences, thus leaving space for analysis, discussion and the search for solutions. Following the discussion of a case, the actual solution adopted in practice can then be made available and compared with the conclusions reached by course participants.

There are, then, *case histories* that describe consulting projects from A to Z. Some of them have been developed by consulting firms as learning materials from their own projects. This, however, is often difficult and rather delicate, since a true case history would in most cases have to reveal some facts about the client or the consultant (personalities, behaviour, competencies, relationships, flaws) that organizations often prefer to treat as confidential, or simply want to conceal because they are not proud of them. Indeed, in consulting it is not always easy to write a case history that everybody who knows the project is happy with.

A limited number of case histories of consulting are publicly available from the literature or on the Internet. A number of publications (some of them are listed in Appendix 3) have scrutinized the successes and failures of consulting in the past decade. These publications include material that not only provides entertaining reading but can also be used to study consulting. For example, the history of consulting to Figgie International, published by O'Shea and Madigan in *Dangerous company*, is full of lessons and can serve either for self-study or as a basis for discussing consulting approaches, strategies, methods, communication with management, roles and responsibilities, project monitoring, consultant selection and evaluation, control of costs, etc. In recommending case histories to learners the trainer or training adviser should keep the purpose in mind and also make provision for discussing the key issues arising. Inexperienced learners might draw wrong conclusions and develop a distorted picture of the consulting profession from sensational histories of extraordinary successes or failures.

2. Where to look for case material[1]

- Your personal or your firm's experience is the best source of case material, provided that there are no barriers to translating this experience into meaningful learning material (confidentiality, the client's agreement, willingness to reveal delicate issues, ability to conceptualize and see issues of wider importance to learning behind particular events and facts).
- Case clearing houses; for example, Harvard Business School Press (see www.hbsp.harvard.edu) distributes case materials on consulting to the Hewlett-Packard's Santa Rosa Systems Division written by Michael Beer and Gregory C. Rogers, and other relevant cases. A selection of consulting cases can be found in the case database of the Management Consulting Association attached to the Leonard N. Stern School of Business of the New York University (www.stern.nyu.edu).
- Books on the consulting industry (see Appendix 3).
- Business and professional journals, books and Web sites provide from time to time case histories that represent good material for the study of consulting. A few recent examples:
  - A case study of "e-consulting" (Vanessa Richardson and Julia Lawlor: "Resolving the consultant clash") appeared in the 13 Feb. 2001 issue of the *Red Herring Magazine* (www.redherring.com).
  - Consulting to small business is the subject of a case history "When consultants attack: A client's story", in *Consultants News*, Apr. 2001 (www.KennedyInfo.com).
  - Consulting to a family business is the subject of "The ghost in the family business" by Warren D. Miller, in *Harvard Business Review*, May–June 2000, pp. 34–51.
  - Learning from failure is the purpose of W. Czander's case history "A failed consultation", in *Consulting to Management*, June 2001, pp. 26–31.
  - "Waking up IBM: How a gang of unlikely rebels transformed Big Blue" by Gary Hamel, in *Harvard Business Review*, July–Aug. 2000, pp. 137–146, describes how IBM caught the Internet wave and what roles internal change agents/consultants played in this major transformation process.

- Case histories demonstrating the impact of people management on financial performance of offices of professional service firms in different countries can be found in D. Maister: *Practice what you preach: What managers must do to create a high-achievement culture* (New York, The Free Press, 2001).

3. Guidance on the case method

Concise guidance on the case method itself is provided in Chapter 14 ("Case method") by John Reynolds, in J. Prokopenko (ed.): *Management development: A guide to the profession* (Geneva, ILO, 1998). See also C. R. Christensen: *Teaching and the case method* (Boston, MA, HBS Press, 1987).

4. Case history of process consulting

Process consulting is particularly difficult to explain and understand if the description is reduced to general concepts and principles. Therefore in the remaining part of this appendix we give the full text of a case history of process consulting, the Apex Manufacturing Company case, written by Edgar H. Schein and taken from the first edition of *Process consultation: Its role in organization development* (Reading, MA, Addison-Wesley, 1969).

Apex Manufacturing Company

1. Initial contact with the client and defining relationships

The contact client from the Apex Manufacturing Company was a divisional manager one level below the president. The company is a large manufacturing concern, organized into several divisions. The contact client indicated that there were communication problems in the top management group resulting from a recent reorganization. Because the company expected to grow rapidly in the next several years, they felt they should work on this kind of problem now.

He spoke openly about his concern that the president needed help in handling certain key people, shared his worries that the president and his key subordinates were not in good communication, and indicated that recent company history suggested the need for some stabilizing force in the organization. I asked him whether the president knew he had come to me and what the president's feelings were about bringing in a consultant. The contact client indicated that the president as well as other key executives were all in favour of bringing someone in to work with them. All saw the need for some outside help.

Eventually, after many months of working with the president and his six key subordinates, I arrived at a point where all of them saw me as a potentially useful communication link. They asked me quite sincerely to report to each one the feelings or reactions of others whenever I learned anything I felt should be passed on. At the same time they were quite open with me about each other, knowing that I might well pass on any opinions or reactions they voiced to me. They did not want me to treat everything as confidential because they trusted me and each other enough.

This case was of great interest because of my own feeling that my having to serve as carrier of this type of information was not an ideal role for me, and reflected an insufficient ability on their part to tell each other things directly. Hence I took two courses of action. First, I tried as much as possible to train each man to tell others in the group directly what he thought about an issue. At the same time I intervened directly in their process by passing on information and opinions if I felt this would aid the working situation.

A simple yet critical event will illustrate what I mean. Two members, Pete and Joe, did not always communicate freely with each other, partly because they felt some rivalry. Pete had completed a study and written a report which was to be discussed by the whole group. Three days before the report was due, I visited the company and stopped in at Pete's office to discuss the report with him and ask how things were going. He said they were fine, but frankly he was puzzled about why Joe hadn't come to him to look at some of the back-up data pertaining to Joe's function. Pete felt this was just another bit of evidence that Joe did not really respect Pete very much.

An hour or so later I was working with Joe, and raised the issue of the report. Joe and his staff were very busy preparing for the meeting but nothing was said about looking at the back-up data. When I asked why they had not done anything about the data, Joe said that he was sure it was private and would not be released by Pete. Joe wanted badly to see it, but felt sure that Pete had deliberately not offered it. I decided there was no harm in intervening at this point by reporting to Joe how Pete was feeling. Joe expressed considerable surprise; and later in the day, he went to Pete, who gave him a warm welcome and turned over to him three volumes of the data which Joe had been wanting to see and which Pete had wanted very much to share with him. I had to judge carefully whether I would hurt either Pete or Joe by revealing Pete's feelings. In this case I decided the potential gains outweighed the risks.

Getting back to setting the proper expectations on the part of the company, I have to make it very plain that I will not function as an expert resource on human-relations problems, but that I will try to help the group solve those problems by providing alternatives and by helping them to think through the consequences of various alternatives. I also need to stress my expectation that I will gather data primarily by observing people in action, not by interviewing and other survey methods (though these methods would be used whenever appropriate). Finally, I have to point out that I will not be very active, but will comment on what is happening or give feedback on observations only as I feel it will be helpful to the group.

The fact that I will be relatively inactive is often a problem for the group because of their expectation that once they have hired a consultant they are entitled to sit back and just listen to him tell them things. To have the consultant then spend hours sitting in the group and saying very little not only violates this expectation but also creates some anxiety about what he is observing. The more I can reassure the group early in the game that I am not gathering personal data of a potentially damaging nature, the smoother the subsequent observations will go.

In summary, part of the early exploration with the contact client and any associates whom he involves is intended to establish the formal and psychological contract which will govern the consultation. I feel there should be no formal contract beyond an agreement on a per diem fee and a potential number of days to be devoted to working with the client system. Each party should be free to terminate or change the level of involvement at any time. At the psychological contract level, it is important to get out into the open as many misconceptions as possible, and to try to be as clear as possible about my own style of work, aims, methods, and so on.

2. Method of work

The method of work chosen should be *as congruent as possible with the values* underlying *process consultation.* Thus, observation, informal interviewing, and group discussions would be congruent with:

(1) the idea that the consultant does not already have pat answers or standard "expert" solutions; and
(2) the idea that the consultant should be maximally available for questioning and two-way communication.

If the consultant uses methods like questionnaires or surveys, he himself remains an unknown quantity to the respondent. As long as he remains unknown, the respondent cannot really trust him, and hence cannot really answer questions completely honestly. The method of work chosen, therefore, should make the consultant maximally visible and maximally available for interaction.

Often I choose to start a consultation project with some interviewing, but the purpose of the interview is not so much to gather data as to establish a relationship with each of the people who will later be observed. The interview is designed to *reveal myself* as much as it is designed to *learn something about the other person.* I will consider the use of questionnaires only after I am well enough known by the organization to be reasonably sure that people would trust me enough to give direct and frank answers to questions.

In the Apex Company, the exploratory meeting led to the decision to attend one of the regular meetings of the executive committee. At this time I was to meet the president and the other key executives to discuss further what could and should be done. At this meeting, I found a lively interest in the idea of having an outsider help the group and the organization to become more effective. I also found that the group was willing to enter an open-ended relationship. I explained as much as I could my philosophy of process consultation and suggested that a good way of getting further acquainted would be to set up a series of individual interviews with each member of the group. At the same time, I suggested that I sit in on the weekly half-day meetings of the executive committee. The interviews would then occur after several of these meetings.

At the initial meeting of the group, I was able to observe a number of key events. For example, the president, Alex, was very informal but very powerful. I got the impression initially (and confirmed it subsequently) that the relationship of all the group members to the president would be the key issue, with relationships to each other being relatively less important. I also got the impression that Alex was a very confident individual who would tolerate my presence only as long as he saw some value in it; he would have little difficulty in confronting me and terminating the relationship if my presence ceased to have value.

It was also impressive, and turned out to be indicative of a managerial style, that Alex did not feel the need to see me alone. He was satisfied from the outset to deal with me inside the group. Near the end of the initial meeting, I requested a private talk with him to satisfy myself that we understood the psychological contract we were entering into. He was surprisingly uncomfortable in this one-to-one relationship, had little that he wished to impart to me, and did not show much interest in my view of the relationship. I wanted the private conversation in order to test his reaction to taking some personal feedback on his own behaviour as the consultation progressed. He said he would welcome this and indicated little or no concern over it. As I was to learn later, this reflected a very strong sense of his own power and identity. He felt he knew himself very well and was not a bit threatened by feedback.

Part of the initial mandate was to help the group to relate to the president. In the interviews which I conducted with group members, I concentrated quite heavily on what kind of things went well in the relationship; what kind of things went poorly; how relationship problems with the president were related to job performance; in what way the group members would like to see the relationship change, and so on. I did not have a formal interview schedule, but rather, held an informal discussion with each member around issues of the sort I have just mentioned.

Intervention by the consultant

In the Apex Company, I found that the treasurer consistently made the operating managers uncomfortable by presenting financial information in an unintentionally threatening way. He wanted to be helpful, and he felt everyone needed the information he had to offer, but it often had the appearance of an indictment of one of the other managers; his costs were too high, his inventory control had slipped, he was too high over budget, etc. Furthermore, this information was often revealed for the first time in the meeting, so that the operating manager concerned had no forewarning and no opportunity to find out why things had gone out of line. The result was often a fruitless argument about the validity of the figures, a great deal of defensiveness on the part of the operating manager, and irritation on the part of the president because the managers could not deal more effectively with the treasurer.

As I observed this process occurring repeatedly over several weeks, I decided that merely drawing attention to the pattern would not really solve the problem because everyone appeared to be operating with constructive intent. What the group needed was an alternative way to think about the use of financial control information. I therefore wrote a memo on control systems and circulated it to the group.

When this came up for discussion at a later meeting I was in a better position to make my observations about the group, since a clear alternative had been presented. My feeling was that I could not have successfully presented this theory orally because of the amount of heat the issue always generated, and because the group members were highly active individuals who would have wanted to discuss each point separately, making it difficult to get the whole message across.

In working with the Apex group I found the written "theory memo" a convenient and effective means of communication. With other groups I have found different patterns to be workable. For example, if the group gets away for a half-day of work on group process, I may insert a half-hour in the middle (or at the end) of the session to present whatever theory elements I consider to be relevant. The topics are usually not selected until I observe the particular "hang-ups" which exist in the group. I therefore have to be prepared to give, on short notice, an input on any of a variety of issues.

A final method of theory input is to make reprints of relevant articles available to the group at selected times. Often I know of some good piece of theory which pertains to what the group is working on. If I suggest that such an article should be circulated, I also try to persuade the group to commit some of its agenda time to a discussion of the article.

The key criterion for the choice of theory input is that the theory must be relevant to what the group already senses is a problem. There is little to be gained by giving "important" theory if the group has no data of its own to link to the theory. On the other hand, once the group has confronted an issue in its own process, I am always amazed at how ready the members are to look at and learn from general theory.

Agenda-setting interventions may strike the reader as a rather low-key, low-potency kind of intervention. Yet it is surprising to me how often working groups arrive at an impasse on simple agenda-setting issues. In a way, their inability to select the right agenda for their meetings, and their inability to discuss the agenda in a constructive way, is symbolic of other difficulties which are harder to pinpoint. If the group can begin to work on its agenda, the door is often opened to other process discussions. Let me provide some examples of how this approach works.

In the Apex Company I sat in for several months on the weekly executive-committee meeting, which included the president and his key subordinates. I quickly became aware that the group was very loose in its manner of operation: people spoke when they felt like it, issues were explored fully, conflict was fairly openly confronted, and members felt free to contribute. This kind of climate seemed constructive, but it created a major difficulty for the group. No matter how few items were put on the agenda, the group was never able to finish its work. The list of backlog items grew longer and the frustration of group members intensified in proportion to this backlog. The group responded by trying to work harder. They scheduled more meetings and attempted to get more done at each meeting, but with little success. Remarks about the ineffectiveness of groups, too many meetings, and so on, became more and more frequent.

My diagnosis was that the group was overloaded. Their agenda was too large, they tried to process too many items at any given meeting, and the agenda was a mixture of operational and policy issues without recognition by the group that such items required different allocations of time. I suggested to the group that they seemed overloaded and should discuss how to develop their agenda for their meetings. The suggestion was adopted after a half-hour or so of sharing feelings. It was then decided, with my help, to sort the agenda items into several categories, and to devote some meetings entirely to operational issues while others would be exclusively policy meetings. The operations meetings would be run more tightly in order to process these items efficiently. The policy questions would be dealt with in depth.

Once the group had made this separation and realized that it could function differently at different meetings, it then decided to meet once a month for an entire day. During this day they would take up one or two large questions and explore them in depth. The group accepted my suggestion to hold such discussions away from the office in a pleasant, less hectic environment.

By rearranging the agenda, the group succeeded in rearranging its whole pattern of operations. This rearrangement also resulted in a redefinition of my role. The president decided that I should phase out my attendance at the operational meetings, but should plan to take a more active role in the monthly one-day meetings. He would set time aside for presentation of any theory I might wish to make, and for process analysis of the meetings. He had previously been reluctant to take time for process work in the earlier meeting pattern, but now welcomed it.

The full-day meetings changed the climate of the group dramatically. For one thing, it was easier to establish close informal relationships with other members during breaks and meals. Because there was enough time, people felt they could really work through their conflicts instead of having to leave them hanging. It was my impression that as acquaintance level rose, so did the level of trust in the group. Members began to feel free to share more personal reactions with each other. This sense of freedom made everyone more relaxed and readier to let down personal barriers and report accurate information. There was less need for defensive distortion or withholding.

After about one year the group decided quite spontaneously to try some direct confrontive feedback. We were at one of the typical monthly all-day meetings. The president announced that he thought each group member should tell the others what he felt to be the strengths and weaknesses of the several individuals. He asked me to help in designing a format for this discussion. I first asked the group members whether they did in fact want to attempt this type of confrontation. The response was sincerely positive, so we decided to go ahead.

The format I suggested was based upon my prior observation of group members. I had noticed that whenever anyone commented on anyone else, there was a strong tendency to answer back and to lock in on the first comment made. Hence, further feedback tended to be cut off. To deal with this problem I suggested that the group discuss one person at a time, and that a ground rule be established that the person being described was not to comment or respond until all the members had had a chance to give all of their feedback. This way he would be forced to continue to listen. The ground rule was accepted, and I was given the role of monitoring the group to ensure that the process operated as the group intended it to.

For the next several hours the group then went into a very detailed and searching analysis of each member's managerial and interpersonal style, including that of the president. I encouraged members to discuss both the positives and the negatives they saw in the person. I also played a key role in forcing people to make their comments specific and concrete. I demanded examples, insisted on clarification, and generally asked the kind of question which I thought might be on the listener's mind as he tried to understand the feedback. I also added my own feedback on points I had observed in that member's behaviour. At first it was not easy for the group either to give or receive feedback, but as the day wore on, the group learned to be more effective.

The total exercise of confrontation was considered highly successful, both at the time and some months later. It deepened relationships, exposed some chronic problems which now could be worked on, and gave each member much food for thought in terms of his own self-development. It should be noted that the group chose to do this spontaneously after many months of meetings organized around work topics. I am not sure they could have handled the feedback task effectively had they been urged to try sooner, even though I could see the need for this type of meeting some time before the initiative came from the group.

In this case, my intervention tended to help the group move from chaotic meetings toward a differentiated, organized pattern. In the end, the group spent more time in meetings than before, but they minded it less because the meetings were more productive. The group also learned how to manage its own agenda and how to guide its own processes.

Feedback systems to groups and individuals

After getting to know the top-management group through several group meetings, I suggested that it might be useful to interview and give feedback to the next level below the vice-president. There was some concern on the part of the senior group that there might be a morale problem at this level. Initially I was asked merely to do an interview survey and report back to the top group. I declined this approach for reasons already mentioned: gathering data to report to a higher group would violate process-consulting assumptions because it would not involve the sources of the data in analysing their own process. I suggested instead that I conduct the interviews with the ground rule that all my conclusions would first be reported back to the interviewee group, and that I would tell top management only those items which the group felt should be reported. The group would first have to sort the items and decide which things they could handle by themselves and which should be reported up the line of authority because they were under higher management control. The real value of the feedback should accrue to the group which initially provided the data; they should become involved in examining the issues they had brought up, and consider what they themselves might do about them.

The above-mentioned procedure was agreed upon by the top management. One vice-president sent a memorandum to all members who would be involved in the interview programme, informing them of the procedure, his commitment to it, and his hope that they would participate. I then followed up with individual appointments with each person concerned. At this initial appointment I recounted the origin of the idea, assured the interviewee that his individual responses would be entirely confidential, told him that I would summarize the data by department, and told him that he would see the group report and discuss it before any feedback went to his boss or higher management.

In the interview I asked each person to describe his job, tell what he found to be the major pluses and minuses in the job, describe what relationships he had to other groups, and how he felt about a series of specific job factors such as challenge, autonomy, supervision, facilities, salary and benefits, and so on. I later summarized the interviews in a report in which I tried to highlight what I saw to be common problem areas.

All the respondents were then invited to a group meeting at which I passed out the summaries, and explained that the purpose of the meeting was to examine the data, deleting or elaborating where necessary, and to determine which problem areas might be worked on by the group itself. We then went over the summary item by item, permitting as much discussion as any given item warranted.

The group meeting had its greatest utility in exposing the interviewees, in a systematic way, to interpersonal and group issues. For many of them, what they had thought to be private gripes turned out to be organizational problems which they could do something about. The attitude "let top management solve all our problems" tended to be replaced with a viewpoint which differentiated between intra-group problems, inter-group problems, and those which were higher management's responsibility. The interviewees not only gained more insight into organizational psychology, but also responded positively to being involved in the process of data gathering itself. It symbolized to them top management's interest in them and concern for solving organizational problems. Reactions such as these are typical of other groups with whom I have tried the same approach.

Following the group meeting, the revised summary was then given to top management, in some cases individually, in others, in a group. My own preference is to give it first individually, to provide for maximum opportunity to explain all the points, and then to follow up with a group discussion of the implications of the data revealed in the interviews. Where the direct supervisor of the group is involved, I have often supplemented the group report with an individual report, which extracts all the comments made by interviewees concerning the strengths and weaknesses of the supervisor's style of management. These focused feedback items have usually proved of great value to the manager, but they should be provided only if the manager initially *asked for this type of feedback.*

In giving either individual or group feedback from the interview summary, my role is to ensure understanding of the data and to stimulate acceptance of it, so that remedial action of some sort can be effectively undertaken. Once the expectation has been built that top management will do something, there is great risk of lowering morale if the report is merely read, without being acted upon in some manner. Incidentally, it is the process consultant's job to ensure that top management *makes this commitment initially* and that high-level officials understand that when the interviews are completed there will be some demands for action. If management merely wants information (without willingness to do something about the information), the process consultant should not do the interviews in the first place. The danger is too great that management will not like what it hears and will suppress the whole effort; such a course will only lead to a deterioration of morale.

The results of interviews (or questionnaires) do not necessarily have to go beyond the group which is interested in them. One of the simplest and most helpful things a group can do to enhance its own functioning is to have the consultant interview the members individually and report back to the group as a whole a summary of its own members' feelings. It is a way of hauling crucial data out into the open without the risk of personal exposure of any individual if he feels the data collected about him are damaging or that the analysis of such data will result in conclusions that are overcritical of his performance.

The giving of individual feedback can be illustrated from several cases. In the Apex Company I met with each of the vice-presidents whose groups had been interviewed and gave them a list of comments which had been made about their respective managerial styles. I knew each man well and felt that he would be able to accept the kind of comments which were made. In each case we scheduled at least a one-hour session, so we could talk in detail about any items which were unclear and/or threatening.

These discussions usually become counselling sessions to help the individual overcome some of the negative effects which were implied in the feedback data. Since I knew that I would be having sessions such as these, I urged each interviewee to talk at length about the style of his boss and what he did or did not like about it. In cases where the boss was an effective manager, I found a tendency for subordinates to make only a few vague generalizations which I knew would be useless as helpful feedback. By probing for specific incidents or descriptions, it was possible to identify just what the boss did which subordinates liked or did not like.

Making suggestions

The consultant must make it quite clear that he does not propose any particular solution as the best one. However frustrating it might be to the client, the process consultant must work to create a situation where *the client's ability to generate his own solutions is enhanced*. The consultant wants to increase problem-solving ability, not to solve any particular problem.

In my experience there has been only one class of exceptions to the above "rule". If the client wants to set up some meetings specifically for the purpose of working on organizational or interpersonal problems, or wants to design a data-gathering method, then the consultant indeed does have some relevant expertise which he should bring to bear. From his own experience he knows better than the client the pros and cons of interviews or questionnaires: he knows better what questions to ask, how to organize the data, and how to organize feedback meetings; he knows better the right sequence of events leading up to a good discussion of interpersonal process in a committee. In such matters, therefore, I am quite direct and positive in suggesting procedures, who should be involved in them, who should be told what, and how the whole project should be handled.

For example, I recall that in the Apex Company the president decided at one of their all-day meetings to try to give feedback to all the members. He asked me to suggest a procedure for doing this. In this instance I was not at all reluctant to suggest, with as much force and logic as I could command, a particular procedure which I thought would work well. Similarly, when it was proposed to interview all the members of a department, I suggested exactly how this procedure should be set up; I explained that all the members had to be briefed by the department manager, that a group feedback meeting would have to be held, and so on. I have not been at all hesitant in refusing to design a questionnaire study if I thought it was inappropriate, or to schedule a meeting on interpersonal process if I thought the group was not ready.

In conclusion, the process consultant should not withhold his expertise on matters of the learning process itself; but he should be very careful not to confuse being an expert *on how to help an organization to learn* with being an expert *on the actual management problems* which the organization is trying to solve. The same logic applies to the evaluation of individuals; I will under no circumstances evaluate an individual's ability to manage or solve work-related problems; but I will evaluate an individual's readiness to participate in an interview survey of his group or a feedback meeting. If I feel that his presence might undermine some other goals which the organization is trying to accomplish, I will seek a solution which will bypass this individual. These are often difficult judgements to make, but the process consultant cannot evade them if he defines *the overall health of the organization* as his basic target. However, he must always attempt to be fair both to the individual and the organization. If no course of action can be found without hurting either, then the whole project should probably be postponed.

3. Evaluation of results

Considerable value change and skill growth occurred over the course of the first year. During this time I spent a great deal of time in two major activities: (1) sitting in on various meetings of the top-management group; and (2) conducting interview and feedback surveys of various key groups, as managers decided they wanted such interviews done. In addition, there were periods of individual counselling, usually resulting from data revealed in the interviews.

I have already given examples of the kind of specific activities which occurred in the group meetings, interviews and feedback sessions. It was clear that with increasing experience, the group was learning to tune in on its own internal processes (skill), was beginning to pay more attention to these and to give over more meeting time to analysis of interpersonal feelings and events (value change), and was able to manage its own agenda and do its diagnosis without my presence (skill). The group first discovered this from having to conduct some of its all-day meetings in my absence. Where such meetings used to be devoted entirely to work content, the group found that even in my absence they could discuss interpersonal process with profit. The members themselves described this change as one of "climate". The group felt more open and effective; members felt they could trust each other more; information was flowing more freely; less time was being wasted on oblique communications or political infighting.

During the second year, my involvement was considerably reduced, though I worked on some specific projects. The company had set up a committee to develop a management development programme. I was asked to sit in with this committee and help in the development of a programme. After a number of meetings, it became clear to me that the kind of programme the group needed was one in which the content was not too heavily predetermined. The problems of different managers were sufficiently different to require that a formula should be found for discussing the whole range of problems. One of the reflections of the value change which had taken place in the managers was their recognition that they should be prime participants in any programme which they might invent. If a programme was not exciting or beneficial enough to warrant the committee's time, it could hardly be imposed on the rest of the organization.

We developed a model which involved a series of small-group meetings at each of which the group would set its own agenda. After every third meeting or so, a larger management group would be convened for a lecture and discussion period on some highly relevant topic. Once the first group (the committee plus others at the vice-president level) had completed six to eight meetings, each member of the original group would become the chairman for a group at the next lower level of the organization. These ten or so next-level groups would then meet for six to eight sessions around agenda items developed by themselves. In the meantime the lecture series would continue: After each series of meetings at a given organizational level, the model would be reassessed and either changed or continued at the next lower level with the previous members again becoming group chairmen.

My role in this whole enterprise was, first, to help the group to invent the idea; second, to meet with the original group as a facilitator of the group's efforts to become productive; third, to serve as a resource on topics to be covered and lecturers to be used in the lecture series; and, fourth, to appear as an occasional lecturer in the lecture series or as a source of input at a small-group meeting. As this procedure took form, my involvement was gradually reduced, though I still met with the original committee to review the overall concept.

In recent months I have met occasionally with individual members of the original group and with the group as a whole. My function during these meetings is to be a sounding-board, to contribute points of view which might not be represented among the members, and to help the group to assess its own level of functioning. I have been able to provide the group with some perspective on its own growth as a group because I could more easily see changes in values and skills. It has also been possible for the group to enlist my help with specific interpersonal problems. A measure of the growth of the group has been its ability to decide when and how to use my help, and to make those decisions validly from my point of view in terms of where I felt I could constructively help.

4. Disengagement: reducing involvement with the client system

The process of disengagement has, in most of my experiences, been characterized by the following features where:

(1) reduced involvement is a mutually agreed upon decision rather than a unilateral decision by consultant or client;

(2) involvement does not generally drop to zero but may continue at a very low level;
(3) the door is always open from my point of view for further work with the client if the client desires it.

In most of my consulting relationships there has come a time when either I felt that nothing more could be accomplished and/or some members of the client system felt the need to continue on their own. To facilitate a reduction of involvement, I usually check at intervals of several months to see whether the client feels that the pattern should remain as is or should be altered. In some cases where I have felt that a sufficient amount has been accomplished, I have found that the client did not feel the same way and wanted the relationship to continue on a day-a-week basis. In other cases, I have been confronted by the client, as with the Apex Company, with the statement that my continued attendance in the operational group meetings was no longer desirable from his point of view. As the president put it, I was beginning to sound too much like a regular member to be of much use. I concurred in the decision and reduced my involvement to periodic all-day meetings of the group, though the initiative for inviting me remained entirely with the group. Had I not concurred, we would have negotiated until a mutually satisfactory arrangement had been agreed upon. I have sometimes been in the situation of arguing that I should remain fully involved even when the client has wanted to reduce involvement, and in many cases I have been able to obtain the client's concurrence.

The negotiation which surrounds a reduction of involvement is in fact a good opportunity for the consultant to diagnose the state of the client system. The kind of arguments which are brought up in support of continuing (or terminating) provide a solid basis for determining how much value and skill change has occurred. The reader may feel that since the client is paying for services, he certainly has the right to make unilateral decisions about whether or not to continue these services. My point would be that if the consultation process has even partially achieved its goals, there should arise sufficient trust between consultant and client to enable both to make the decision on rational grounds. Here again, it is important that the consultant should not be economically dependent upon any one client, or his own diagnostic ability may become biased by his need to continue to earn fees.

---

[1] All Web sites visited on 9 Apr. 2002.

APPENDIX 7

WRITING REPORTS

The different reports written by consultants are mentioned in various chapters of the book according to the occasions and purposes that call for them. This appendix reviews the essential principles of writing and producing reports in consulting.

1. Reports in perspective

In most consulting work, written communication complements oral communication, but in some cases the written report will become the main or the only communication channel. In addition to summarizing and conveying information and stimulating the client to act, reports to clients have other important functions. They contribute by their quality and presentation to the impact the consultant makes during the assignment. They also affect the consultant's general reputation. When the personal contacts between consultant and client are limited (for example, if the client obtains written proposals from several consultants and will select one on the basis of these proposals), persuasion may be a vital feature of a report.

An excellent consulting report meets three basic criteria:

- First, it is reader-friendly. Its structure, style, terminology, arguments used and any other features are selected with regard to the client's background, needs and preferences. The basic question is: "What sort of report will render the best service to the client and will be easily read and understood by the client?" and not: "What sort of report do we like to produce in our firm?" Obviously, in many cases the client will have no particular preference and will leave the choice to the consultant. Yet the question must be asked, and discussing it directly with the client may be helpful.
- Second, the report should be easy for the consultant to write. Ease of writing leads to ease of reading. In addition, it saves time and money for the client, who is going to pay for the time spent by the consultant on writing, and use his or her own time studying the report. In an extreme case, a poorly drafted report may put off the client and achieve the opposite of what was intended.

- Third, and most importantly, the aim of every report is to convey a particular message. This message (or purpose) needs to be clarified before the report is drafted. This course of action will help the consultant to structure the report, choose a convenient style, and organize facts and information in support of the message to the client.

As a check, you should ask yourself about the necessity and purpose of any report you intend to produce:

- Why is the report necessary?
- What is its message?
- What will it achieve?
- Is there a better way of achieving this purpose?
- Is now the time for it?
- Who is likely to read it and make use of it?

As a matter of principle, consulting reports should not repeat information obtained from the client or well known to him or her, and general information on the background situation, with the exception of information that directly justifies conclusions or documents the work performed. The essence of information is *news*. Thus, the information content of reports should consist of:

- facts discovered for the first time by the consultant;
- newly discovered significance of known facts;
- newly found connections between known effects and hitherto unknown causes;
- solutions to the client's problems, and their justification;
- results achieved and changes made or proposed;
- facts showing to the client that he or she needs to take action, and any other facts commanding the client's attention.

2. Structuring the report

The contents need to be arranged in the best sequence for the nature and purpose of the report and for the desired reaction to it. This may be difficult. The author may be tempted to describe the whole assignment and the whole analytical and thinking process of the consulting team, but the client is looking for results and proposals that will be tangible improvements to the business. Although the author may hope the reader will start at the beginning and read through to the end, there is no guarantee of this. This is one of the hazards of written communication. Persuasion requires careful build-up through a reasoned sequence which the reader may choose not to follow.

A *table of contents* is essential (except in very short reports); it is regrettable that many reports do not have one. The best place for the table of contents is at the very beginning of the report, i.e. preceding any introduction, preface, or summary. In some countries (e.g. France) it has been customary to give a table of contents at the very end.

The whole report should he carefully planned. It will contain certain main ideas and topics, some of which will have subdivisions. It may help to start by producing an outline listing the main points and ideas.

Marshalling the body of a report into a logical structure is aided by having a formal system of numbers and/or letters for main headings, subheadings and so on. The wording after each number may be printed in a different style. A decimal system may be used, as in the example on the left, or numbers and letters, as in the example on the right:

1. *Main heading*	I. *Main heading*
1.1. Subheading	1. Subheading
1.1.1. Sub-subheading	A. Sub-subheading
	(i) Listed item
	(ii) Listed item

The advantage of such a scheme is that it makes the writer think about priorities and helps him or her determine which topics are genuine subdivisions of others. It promotes the orderly organization of the structure and points the way to economy of layout and avoidance of repetition.

For example, a report covering three subject areas, Buying, Stores and Production, deals with three statements about them: Findings, Conclusions and Recommendations. Which of the three layouts below may be the best?

1. *Findings*	1. *Buying*	1. *Buying*
1.1 Buying	1.1 Findings	1.1 Findings
1.2 Stores	1.2 Conclusions	1.2 Conclusions
1.3 Production	1.3 Recommendations	
2. *Conclusions*	2. *Stores*	2. *Stores*
2.1 Buying	2.1 Findings	2.1 Findings
2.2 Stores	2.2 Conclusions	2.2 Conclusions
2.3 Production	2.3 Recommendations	
3. *Recommendations*	3. *Production*	3. *Production*
3.1 Buying	3.1 Findings	3.1 Findings
3.2 Stores	3.2 Conclusions	3.2 Conclusions
3.3 Production	3.3 Recommendations	
		4. *Recommendations*
		4.1 Buying
		4.2 Stores
		4.3 Production

For any particular report one of these may prove easiest, but if "Findings" tell the client nothing new, there is no point in belabouring them. "Conclusions" usually lead straight into "Recommendations". It could even be that the whole report can be written as for section 4 in the third column, the recommendations themselves being written so as to make the findings and conclusions quite clear. A consulting report is not a research paper, but carries a practical message that should stimulate and orient action.

Everything depends on priorities, weights, balance and purposes; a scheme of marshalling helps to sort these out.

Appendices are useful for taking out of the body of a report detailed descriptions, listings, tables, charts, diagrams, etc. that would break up the continuity of reading and would be difficult to fit in. The body of the report is essentially for reading and quick examination of summary data. Appendices can include items which, though they make a contribution, require more lengthy examination. It does not help to make a case if the reader is suddenly confronted with several pages of closely tabulated figures. Small tables or diagrams, however, are not disturbing. They break the text monotony, convey selected or summarized information, and should be maintained in the main text.

Acknowledgements have to be made, especially in final assignment reports. This will require tact. If names are mentioned there must be no omissions: every genuine helper likes to see his or her name on the list. At the same time, to include someone who has been more of a hindrance than a help – and knows it – may cause mixed feelings all round. If the list would be too long, it is better to leave it out and settle for general thanks and the remark that "it would be an impossible task to mention everyone who ...".

3. Drafting the report

Executives are flooded with reports, and hate long and badly written ones. It is useful, therefore, to observe certain principles, which have been summarized in box A1.

If there is enough time, the first complete draft should be put aside for a day or two, after which anything wrong is more easily seen and revised. When it looks right to the author, someone else should read it. An operating consultant's draft will normally be read by the project manager or supervisor, who will often see things that a less experienced consultant would miss. There are, however, some dangers at this point: any report can always be improved, and the temptation to work on it until it is "perfect" may be hard to resist. As with most things, there is a point of diminishing returns.

When drafting the report, the consultant may find that the outline chosen originally is not the best one. There is no point in sticking to an inconvenient outline. However, if the client agreed to that outline beforehand, he or she should also be asked to agree to a modified outline to avoid a possible misunderstanding.

If the report is a collective piece of work and the co-authors are known to have different personal styles, final editing should be foreseen. Consistency and homogeneity (of style, layout, terminology, length of sections, etc.) are key characteristics of excellent reports.

Box A1 Principles of clear writing

1. Keep the report as short as possible.
2. Consider your reader, his or her outlook and experience.
3. Write to express, not to impress.
4. Write naturally: style that flows smoothly and does not draw attention to itself is the most effective.
5. Try to keep sentences short; vary their length but keep the average around 20 words.
6. Avoid clumsy sentences and carefully blend short and long words.
7. Use familiar words, avoiding rare or far-fetched ones.
8. Avoid jargon unless it is sure to be familiar to the reader and you know what it means.
9. Avoid unnecessary words that give an impression of padding.
10. Use terms the reader can picture: call a crane a crane, not "a lifting facility".
11. Put action into your verbs; use the force of the active voice; use the passive voice to vary the style.
12. Keep every item of a report relevant to the purpose.
13. Ensure that the contents include all the points necessary to the purpose.
14. Keep a proper balance, giving space and emphasis to each item according to its importance.
15. Keep a serious "tone" as befits a serious purpose; do not tempt the reader to read between the lines; if you do you are at the mercy of his or her imagination.
16. Be careful in the use of numbers: figures tend to draw attention to themselves; decide when absolute values have more significance than percentages and ratios, and vice versa; when quoting figures from other sources, be exact; when estimating, consider the order of accuracy and round off.
17. If you quote from other sources give precise and complete references.

Source: Some of the principles are adapted from R. Gunning; *The technique of clear writing* (New York, McGraw-Hill, 1952).

4. Typing and printing the report

The report should look professional in every respect. Its cover and binding should give an excellent impression without looking luxurious. Inside, the layout of the text should allow a generous margin for binding and notes made by the reader, be impeccably printed on a laser printer or similar, and free from extraneous marks and alterations. Any graphs, charts and diagrams should be well drawn and in every respect up to the standard of the typescript.

The consulting firm may have its own standard format that not only distinguishes its reports but responds to requirements for filing and control in its reports library. Within the covers, the body of the report may also have a standard layout for division and subdivision of the contents, which can be used if it is not in conflict with the purpose and spirit of a particular report.

The final draft prepared for reproduction should leave the secretary in no doubt as to precisely what is required. The author should take the trouble to lay out the text as it should appear in the final version. The author is also completely responsible for reading the report once more before transmission to the client and ensuring that no mistakes remain.

The production of reports has been greatly improved by judicious use of word processing. At present, most consultants prepare their reports, or their inputs to collective reports, on their personal computers, often directly at clients' premises. All contributors must then strictly adhere to a common format set by the firm. Corrections and amendments can be made easily by the report author or editor.

A client may wish to receive an electronic version of the report in addition to, or instead of, printed copies. Systems compatibility should be kept in mind because conversions of documents are not always flawless.

* * *

Useful guidance on report-writing and editing in English is provided in B. Minto: *The Minto pyramid principle: Logic in writing, thinking and problem solving* (London, Minto International, 3rd ed., 1996), excerpts of which are in the *Journal of Management Consulting* (Milwaukee, WI), May 1998, Nov. 1998 and May 1999. See also: *The Economist Style Guide* (London, The Economist Books, 2001).

SUBJECT INDEX